Dictionary of Literary Biography

1 *The American Renaissance in New England,* edited by Joel Myerson (1978)

2 *American Novelists Since World War II,* edited by Jeffrey Helterman and Richard Layman (1978)

3 *Antebellum Writers in New York and the South,* edited by Joel Myerson (1979)

4 *American Writers in Paris, 1920–1939,* edited by Karen Lane Rood (1980)

5 *American Poets Since World War II,* 2 parts, edited by Donald J. Greiner (1980)

6 *American Novelists Since World War II, Second Series,* edited by James E. Kibler Jr. (1980)

7 *Twentieth-Century American Dramatists,* 2 parts, edited by John MacNicholas (1981)

8 *Twentieth-Century American Science-Fiction Writers,* 2 parts, edited by David Cowart and Thomas L. Wymer (1981)

9 *American Novelists, 1910–1945,* 3 parts, edited by James J. Martine (1981)

10 *Modern British Dramatists, 1900–1945,* 2 parts, edited by Stanley Weintraub (1982)

11 *American Humorists, 1800–1950,* 2 parts, edited by Stanley Trachtenberg (1982)

12 *American Realists and Naturalists,* edited by Donald Pizer and Earl N. Harbert (1982)

13 *British Dramatists Since World War II,* 2 parts, edited by Stanley Weintraub (1982)

14 *British Novelists Since 1960,* 2 parts, edited by Jay L. Halio (1983)

15 *British Novelists, 1930–1959,* 2 parts, edited by Bernard Oldsey (1983)

16 *The Beats: Literary Bohemians in Postwar America,* 2 parts, edited by Ann Charters (1983)

17 *Twentieth-Century American Historians,* edited by Clyde N. Wilson (1983)

18 *Victorian Novelists After 1885,* edited by Ira B. Nadel and William E. Fredeman (1983)

19 *British Poets, 1880–1914,* edited by Donald E. Stanford (1983)

20 *British Poets, 1914–1945,* edited by Donald E. Stanford (1983)

21 *Victorian Novelists Before 1885,* edited by Ira B. Nadel and William E. Fredeman (1983)

22 *American Writers for Children, 1900–1960,* edited by John Cech (1983)

23 *American Newspaper Journalists, 1873–1900,* edited by Perry J. Ashley (1983)

24 *American Colonial Writers, 1606–1734,* edited by Emory Elliott (1984)

25 *American Newspaper Journalists, 1901–1925,* edited by Perry J. Ashley (1984)

26 *American Screenwriters,* edited by Robert E. Morsberger, Stephen O. Lesser, and Randall Clark (1984)

27 *Poets of Great Britain and Ireland, 1945–1960,* edited by Vincent B. Sherry Jr. (1984)

28 *Twentieth-Century American-Jewish Fiction Writers,* edited by Daniel Walden (1984)

29 *American Newspaper Journalists, 1926–1950,* edited by Perry J. Ashley (1984)

30 *American Historians, 1607–1865,* edited by Clyde N. Wilson (1984)

31 *American Colonial Writers, 1735–1781,* edited by Emory Elliott (1984)

32 *Victorian Poets Before 1850,* edited by William E. Fredeman and Ira B. Nadel (1984)

33 *Afro-American Fiction Writers After 1955,* edited by Thadious M. Davis and Trudier Harris (1984)

34 *British Novelists, 1890–1929: Traditionalists,* edited by Thomas F. Staley (1985)

35 *Victorian Poets After 1850,* edited by William E. Fredeman and Ira B. Nadel (1985)

36 *British Novelists, 1890–1929: Modernists,* edited by Thomas F. Staley (1985)

37 *American Writers of the Early Republic,* edited by Emory Elliott (1985)

38 *Afro-American Writers After 1955: Dramatists and Prose Writers,* edited by Thadious M. Davis and Trudier Harris (1985)

39 *British Novelists, 1660–1800,* 2 parts, edited by Martin C. Battestin (1985)

40 *Poets of Great Britain and Ireland Since 1960,* 2 parts, edited by Vincent B. Sherry Jr. (1985)

41 *Afro-American Poets Since 1955,* edited by Trudier Harris and Thadious M. Davis (1985)

42 *American Writers for Children Before 1900,* edited by Glenn E. Estes (1985)

43 *American Newspaper Journalists, 1690–1872,* edited by Perry J. Ashley (1986)

44 *American Screenwriters, Second Series,* edited by Randall Clark, Robert E. Morsberger, and Stephen O. Lesser (1986)

45 *American Poets, 1880–1945, First Series,* edited by Peter Quartermain (1986)

46 *American Literary Publishing Houses, 1900–1980: Trade and Paperback,* edited by Peter Dzwonkoski (1986)

47 *American Historians, 1866–1912,* edited by Clyde N. Wilson (1986)

48 *American Poets, 1880–1945, Second Series,* edited by Peter Quartermain (1986)

49 *American Literary Publishing Houses, 1638–1899,* 2 parts, edited by Peter Dzwonkoski (1986)

50 *Afro-American Writers Before the Harlem Renaissance,* edited by Trudier Harris (1986)

51 *Afro-American Writers from the Harlem Renaissance to 1940,* edited by Trudier Harris (1987)

52 *American Writers for Children Since 1960: Fiction,* edited by Glenn E. Estes (1986)

53 *Canadian Writers Since 1960, First Series,* edited by W. H. New (1986)

54 *American Poets, 1880–1945, Third Series,* 2 parts, edited by Peter Quartermain (1987)

55 *Victorian Prose Writers Before 1867,* edited by William B. Thesing (1987)

56 *German Fiction Writers, 1914–1945,* edited by James Hardin (1987)

57 *Victorian Prose Writers After 1867,* edited by William B. Thesing (1987)

58 *Jacobean and Caroline Dramatists,* edited by Fredson Bowers (1987)

59 *American Literary Critics and Scholars, 1800–1850,* edited by John W. Rathbun and Monica M. Grecu (1987)

60 *Canadian Writers Since 1960, Second Series,* edited by W. H. New (1987)

61 *American Writers for Children Since 1960: Poets, Illustrators, and Nonfiction Authors,* edited by Glenn E. Estes (1987)

62 *Elizabethan Dramatists,* edited by Fredson Bowers (1987)

63 *Modern American Critics, 1920–1955,* edited by Gregory S. Jay (1988)

64 *American Literary Critics and Scholars, 1850–1880,* edited by John W. Rathbun and Monica M. Grecu (1988)

65 *French Novelists, 1900–1930,* edited by Catharine Savage Brosman (1988)

66 *German Fiction Writers, 1885–1913,* 2 parts, edited by James Hardin (1988)

67 *Modern American Critics Since 1955,* edited by Gregory S. Jay (1988)

68 *Canadian Writers, 1920–1959, First Series,* edited by W. H. New (1988)

69 *Contemporary German Fiction Writers, First Series,* edited by Wolfgang D. Elfe and James Hardin (1988)

70 *British Mystery Writers, 1860–1919,* edited by Bernard Benstock and Thomas F. Staley (1988)

71 *American Literary Critics and Scholars, 1880–1900,* edited by John W. Rathbun and Monica M. Grecu (1988)

72 *French Novelists, 1930–1960,* edited by Catharine Savage Brosman (1988)

73 *American Magazine Journalists, 1741–1850,* edited by Sam G. Riley (1988)

74 *American Short-Story Writers Before 1880,* edited by Bobby Ellen Kimbel, with the assistance of William E. Grant (1988)

75 *Contemporary German Fiction Writers, Second Series,* edited by Wolfgang D. Elfe and James Hardin (1988)

76 *Afro-American Writers, 1940–1955,* edited by Trudier Harris (1988)

77 *British Mystery Writers, 1920–1939,* edited by Bernard Benstock and Thomas F. Staley (1988)

78 *American Short-Story Writers, 1880–1910,* edited by Bobby Ellen Kimbel, with the assistance of William E. Grant (1988)

79 *American Magazine Journalists, 1850–1900,* edited by Sam G. Riley (1988)

80 *Restoration and Eighteenth-Century Dramatists, First Series,* edited by Paula R. Backscheider (1989)

81 *Austrian Fiction Writers, 1875–1913,* edited by James Hardin and Donald G. Daviau (1989)

82 *Chicano Writers, First Series,* edited by Francisco A. Lomelí and Carl R. Shirley (1989)

83 *French Novelists Since 1960,* edited by Catharine Savage Brosman (1989)

84 *Restoration and Eighteenth-Century Dramatists, Second Series,* edited by Paula R. Backscheider (1989)

85 *Austrian Fiction Writers After 1914,* edited by James Hardin and Donald G. Daviau (1989)

86 *American Short-Story Writers, 1910–1945, First Series,* edited by Bobby Ellen Kimbel (1989)

87 *British Mystery and Thriller Writers Since 1940, First Series,* edited by Bernard Benstock and Thomas F. Staley (1989)

88 *Canadian Writers, 1920–1959, Second Series,* edited by W. H. New (1989)

89 *Restoration and Eighteenth-Century Dramatists, Third Series,* edited by Paula R. Backscheider (1989)

90 *German Writers in the Age of Goethe, 1789–1832,* edited by James Hardin and Christoph E. Schweitzer (1989)

91 *American Magazine Journalists, 1900–1960, First Series,* edited by Sam G. Riley (1990)

92 *Canadian Writers, 1890–1920,* edited by W. H. New (1990)

93 *British Romantic Poets, 1789–1832, First Series,* edited by John R. Greenfield (1990)

94 *German Writers in the Age of Goethe: Sturm und Drang to Classicism,* edited by James Hardin and Christoph E. Schweitzer (1990)

95 *Eighteenth-Century British Poets, First Series,* edited by John Sitter (1990)

96 *British Romantic Poets, 1789–1832, Second Series,* edited by John R. Greenfield (1990)

97 *German Writers from the Enlightenment to Sturm und Drang, 1720–1764,* edited by James Hardin and Christoph E. Schweitzer (1990)

98 *Modern British Essayists, First Series,* edited by Robert Beum (1990)

99 *Canadian Writers Before 1890,* edited by W. H. New (1990)

100 *Modern British Essayists, Second Series,* edited by Robert Beum (1990)

101 *British Prose Writers, 1660–1800, First Series,* edited by Donald T. Siebert (1991)

102 *American Short-Story Writers, 1910–1945, Second Series,* edited by Bobby Ellen Kimbel (1991)

103 *American Literary Biographers, First Series,* edited by Steven Serafin (1991)

104 *British Prose Writers, 1660–1800, Second Series,* edited by Donald T. Siebert (1991)

105 *American Poets Since World War II, Second Series,* edited by R. S. Gwynn (1991)

106 *British Literary Publishing Houses, 1820–1880,* edited by Patricia J. Anderson and Jonathan Rose (1991)

107 *British Romantic Prose Writers, 1789–1832, First Series,* edited by John R. Greenfield (1991)

108 *Twentieth-Century Spanish Poets, First Series,* edited by Michael L. Perna (1991)

109 *Eighteenth-Century British Poets, Second Series,* edited by John Sitter (1991)

110 *British Romantic Prose Writers, 1789–1832, Second Series,* edited by John R. Greenfield (1991)

111 *American Literary Biographers, Second Series,* edited by Steven Serafin (1991)

112 *British Literary Publishing Houses, 1881–1965,* edited by Jonathan Rose and Patricia J. Anderson (1991)

113 *Modern Latin-American Fiction Writers, First Series,* edited by William Luis (1992)

114 *Twentieth-Century Italian Poets, First Series,* edited by Giovanna Wedel De Stasio, Glauco Cambon, and Antonio Illiano (1992)

115 *Medieval Philosophers,* edited by Jeremiah Hackett (1992)

116 *British Romantic Novelists, 1789–1832,* edited by Bradford K. Mudge (1992)

117 *Twentieth-Century Caribbean and Black African Writers, First Series,* edited by Bernth Lindfors and Reinhard Sander (1992)

118 *Twentieth-Century German Dramatists, 1889–1918,* edited by Wolfgang D. Elfe and James Hardin (1992)

119 *Nineteenth-Century French Fiction Writers: Romanticism and Realism, 1800–1860,* edited by Catharine Savage Brosman (1992)

120 *American Poets Since World War II, Third Series,* edited by R. S. Gwynn (1992)

121 *Seventeenth-Century British Nondramatic Poets, First Series,* edited by M. Thomas Hester (1992)

122 *Chicano Writers, Second Series,* edited by Francisco A. Lomelí and Carl R. Shirley (1992)

123 *Nineteenth-Century French Fiction Writers: Naturalism and Beyond, 1860–1900,* edited by Catharine Savage Brosman (1992)

124 *Twentieth-Century German Dramatists, 1919–1992,* edited by Wolfgang D. Elfe and James Hardin (1992)

125 *Twentieth-Century Caribbean and Black African Writers, Second Series,* edited by Bernth Lindfors and Reinhard Sander (1993)

126 *Seventeenth-Century British Nondramatic Poets, Second Series,* edited by M. Thomas Hester (1993)

127 *American Newspaper Publishers, 1950–1990,* edited by Perry J. Ashley (1993)

128 *Twentieth-Century Italian Poets, Second Series,* edited by Giovanna Wedel De Stasio, Glauco Cambon, and Antonio Illiano (1993)

129 *Nineteenth-Century German Writers, 1841–1900,* edited by James Hardin and Siegfried Mews (1993)

130 *American Short-Story Writers Since World War II,* edited by Patrick Meanor (1993)

131 *Seventeenth-Century British Nondramatic Poets, Third Series,* edited by M. Thomas Hester (1993)

132 *Sixteenth-Century British Nondramatic Writers, First Series,* edited by David A. Richardson (1993)

133 *Nineteenth-Century German Writers to 1840,* edited by James Hardin and Siegfried Mews (1993)

134 *Twentieth-Century Spanish Poets, Second Series,* edited by Jerry Phillips Winfield (1994)

135 *British Short-Fiction Writers, 1880–1914: The Realist Tradition,* edited by William B. Thesing (1994)

136 *Sixteenth-Century British Nondramatic Writers, Second Series,* edited by David A. Richardson (1994)

137 *American Magazine Journalists, 1900–1960, Second Series,* edited by Sam G. Riley (1994)

138 *German Writers and Works of the High Middle Ages: 1170–1280,* edited by James Hardin and Will Hasty (1994)

139 *British Short-Fiction Writers, 1945–1980,* edited by Dean Baldwin (1994)

140 *American Book-Collectors and Bibliographers, First Series,* edited by Joseph Rosenblum (1994)

141 *British Children's Writers, 1880–1914,* edited by Laura M. Zaidman (1994)

142 *Eighteenth-Century British Literary Biographers,* edited by Steven Serafin (1994)

143 *American Novelists Since World War II, Third Series,* edited by James R. Giles and Wanda H. Giles (1994)

144 *Nineteenth-Century British Literary Biographers,* edited by Steven Serafin (1994)

145 *Modern Latin-American Fiction Writers, Second Series,* edited by William Luis and Ann González (1994)

146 *Old and Middle English Literature,* edited by Jeffrey Helterman and Jerome Mitchell (1994)

147 *South Slavic Writers Before World War II,* edited by Vasa D. Mihailovich (1994)

148 *German Writers and Works of the Early Middle Ages: 800–1170,* edited by Will Hasty and James Hardin (1994)

149 *Late Nineteenth- and Early Twentieth-Century British Literary Biographers,* edited by Steven Serafin (1995)

150 *Early Modern Russian Writers, Late Seventeenth and Eighteenth Centuries,* edited by Marcus C. Levitt (1995)

151 *British Prose Writers of the Early Seventeenth Century,* edited by Clayton D. Lein (1995)

152 *American Novelists Since World War II, Fourth Series,* edited by James R. Giles and Wanda H. Giles (1995)

153 *Late-Victorian and Edwardian British Novelists, First Series,* edited by George M. Johnson (1995)

154 *The British Literary Book Trade, 1700–1820,* edited by James K. Bracken and Joel Silver (1995)

155 *Twentieth-Century British Literary Biographers,* edited by Steven Serafin (1995)

156 *British Short-Fiction Writers, 1880–1914: The Romantic Tradition,* edited by William F. Naufftus (1995)

157 *Twentieth-Century Caribbean and Black African Writers, Third Series,* edited by Bernth Lindfors and Reinhard Sander (1995)

158 *British Reform Writers, 1789–1832,* edited by Gary Kelly and Edd Applegate (1995)

159 *British Short-Fiction Writers, 1800–1880,* edited by John R. Greenfield (1996)

160 *British Children's Writers, 1914–1960,* edited by Donald R. Hettinga and Gary D. Schmidt (1996)

161 *British Children's Writers Since 1960, First Series,* edited by Caroline Hunt (1996)

162 *British Short-Fiction Writers, 1915–1945,* edited by John H. Rogers (1996)

163 *British Children's Writers, 1800–1880,* edited by Meena Khorana (1996)

164 *German Baroque Writers, 1580–1660,* edited by James Hardin (1996)

165 *American Poets Since World War II, Fourth Series,* edited by Joseph Conte (1996)

166 *British Travel Writers, 1837–1875,* edited by Barbara Brothers and Julia Gergits (1996)

167 *Sixteenth-Century British Nondramatic Writers, Third Series,* edited by David A. Richardson (1996)

168 *German Baroque Writers, 1661–1730,* edited by James Hardin (1996)

169 *American Poets Since World War II, Fifth Series,* edited by Joseph Conte (1996)

170 *The British Literary Book Trade, 1475–1700,* edited by James K. Bracken and Joel Silver (1996)

171 *Twentieth-Century American Sportswriters,* edited by Richard Orodenker (1996)

172 *Sixteenth-Century British Nondramatic Writers, Fourth Series,* edited by David A. Richardson (1996)

173 *American Novelists Since World War II, Fifth Series,* edited by James R. Giles and Wanda H. Giles (1996)

174 *British Travel Writers, 1876–1909,* edited by Barbara Brothers and Julia Gergits (1997)

175 *Native American Writers of the United States,* edited by Kenneth M. Roemer (1997)

176 *Ancient Greek Authors,* edited by Ward W. Briggs (1997)

177 *Italian Novelists Since World War II, 1945–1965,* edited by Augustus Pallotta (1997)

178 *British Fantasy and Science-Fiction Writers Before World War I,* edited by Darren Harris-Fain (1997)

179 *German Writers of the Renaissance and Reformation, 1280–1580,* edited by James Hardin and Max Reinhart (1997)

180 *Japanese Fiction Writers, 1868–1945,* edited by Van C. Gessel (1997)

181 *South Slavic Writers Since World War II,* edited by Vasa D. Mihailovich (1997)

182 *Japanese Fiction Writers Since World War II,* edited by Van C. Gessel (1997)

183 *American Travel Writers, 1776–1864,* edited by James J. Schramer and Donald Ross (1997)

184 *Nineteenth-Century British Book-Collectors and Bibliographers,* edited by William Baker and Kenneth Womack (1997)

185 *American Literary Journalists, 1945–1995, First Series,* edited by Arthur J. Kaul (1998)

186 *Nineteenth-Century American Western Writers,* edited by Robert L. Gale (1998)

187 *American Book Collectors and Bibliographers, Second Series,* edited by Joseph Rosenblum (1998)

188 *American Book and Magazine Illustrators to 1920,* edited by Steven E. Smith, Catherine A. Hastedt, and Donald H. Dyal (1998)

189 *American Travel Writers, 1850–1915,* edited by Donald Ross and James J. Schramer (1998)

190 *British Reform Writers, 1832–1914,* edited by Gary Kelly and Edd Applegate (1998)

191 *British Novelists Between the Wars,* edited by George M. Johnson (1998)

192 *French Dramatists, 1789–1914,* edited by Barbara T. Cooper (1998)

193 *American Poets Since World War II, Sixth Series,* edited by Joseph Conte (1998)

194 *British Novelists Since 1960, Second Series,* edited by Merritt Moseley (1998)

195 *British Travel Writers, 1910–1939,* edited by Barbara Brothers and Julia Gergits (1998)

196 *Italian Novelists Since World War II, 1965–1995,* edited by Augustus Pallotta (1999)

197 *Late-Victorian and Edwardian British Novelists, Second Series,* edited by George M. Johnson (1999)

198 *Russian Literature in the Age of Pushkin and Gogol: Prose,* edited by Christine A. Rydel (1999)

199 *Victorian Women Poets,* edited by William B. Thesing (1999)

200 *American Women Prose Writers to 1820,* edited by Carla J. Mulford, with Angela Vietto and Amy E. Winans (1999)

201 *Twentieth-Century British Book Collectors and Bibliographers,* edited by William Baker and Kenneth Womack (1999)

202 *Nineteenth-Century American Fiction Writers,* edited by Kent P. Ljungquist (1999)

203 *Medieval Japanese Writers,* edited by Steven D. Carter (1999)

204 *British Travel Writers, 1940–1997,* edited by Barbara Brothers and Julia M. Gergits (1999)

205 *Russian Literature in the Age of Pushkin and Gogol: Poetry and Drama,* edited by Christine A. Rydel (1999)

206 *Twentieth-Century American Western Writers, First Series,* edited by Richard H. Cracroft (1999)

207 *British Novelists Since 1960, Third Series,* edited by Merritt Moseley (1999)

208 *Literature of the French and Occitan Middle Ages: Eleventh to Fifteenth Centuries,* edited by Deborah Sinnreich-Levi and Ian S. Laurie (1999)

209 *Chicano Writers, Third Series,* edited by Francisco A. Lomelí and Carl R. Shirley (1999)

210 *Ernest Hemingway: A Documentary Volume,* edited by Robert W. Trogdon (1999)

211 *Ancient Roman Writers,* edited by Ward W. Briggs (1999)

212 *Twentieth-Century American Western Writers, Second Series,* edited by Richard H. Cracroft (1999)

213 *Pre-Nineteenth-Century British Book Collectors and Bibliographers,* edited by William Baker and Kenneth Womack (1999)

214 *Twentieth-Century Danish Writers,* edited by Marianne Stecher-Hansen (1999)

215 *Twentieth-Century Eastern European Writers, First Series,* edited by Steven Serafin (1999)

216 *British Poets of the Great War: Brooke, Rosenberg, Thomas. A Documentary Volume,* edited by Patrick Quinn (2000)

217 *Nineteenth-Century French Poets,* edited by Robert Beum (2000)

218 *American Short-Story Writers Since World War II, Second Series,* edited by Patrick Meanor and Gwen Crane (2000)

219 *F. Scott Fitzgerald's* The Great Gatsby: *A Documentary Volume,* edited by Matthew J. Bruccoli (2000)

220 *Twentieth-Century Eastern European Writers, Second Series,* edited by Steven Serafin (2000)

221 *American Women Prose Writers, 1870–1920,* edited by Sharon M. Harris, with the assistance of Heidi L. M. Jacobs and Jennifer Putzi (2000)

222 *H. L. Mencken: A Documentary Volume,* edited by Richard J. Schrader (2000)

223 *The American Renaissance in New England, Second Series,* edited by Wesley T. Mott (2000)

224 *Walt Whitman: A Documentary Volume,* edited by Joel Myerson (2000)

225 *South African Writers,* edited by Paul A. Scanlon (2000)

226 *American Hard-Boiled Crime Writers,* edited by George Parker Anderson and Julie B. Anderson (2000)

227 *American Novelists Since World War II, Sixth Series,* edited by James R. Giles and Wanda H. Giles (2000)

228 *Twentieth-Century American Dramatists, Second Series,* edited by Christopher J. Wheatley (2000)

229 *Thomas Wolfe: A Documentary Volume,* edited by Ted Mitchell (2001)

230 *Australian Literature, 1788–1914,* edited by Selina Samuels (2001)

231 *British Novelists Since 1960, Fourth Series,* edited by Merritt Moseley (2001)

232 *Twentieth-Century Eastern European Writers, Third Series,* edited by Steven Serafin (2001)

233 *British and Irish Dramatists Since World War II, Second Series,* edited by John Bull (2001)

234 *American Short-Story Writers Since World War II, Third Series,* edited by Patrick Meanor and Richard E. Lee (2001)

235 *The American Renaissance in New England, Third Series,* edited by Wesley T. Mott (2001)

236 *British Rhetoricians and Logicians, 1500–1660,* edited by Edward A. Malone (2001)

237 *The Beats: A Documentary Volume,* edited by Matt Theado (2001)

238 *Russian Novelists in the Age of Tolstoy and Dostoevsky,* edited by J. Alexander Ogden and Judith E. Kalb (2001)

239 *American Women Prose Writers: 1820–1870,* edited by Amy E. Hudock and Katharine Rodier (2001)

240 *Late Nineteenth- and Early Twentieth-Century British Women Poets,* edited by William B. Thesing (2001)

241 *American Sportswriters and Writers on Sport,* edited by Richard Orodenker (2001)

242 *Twentieth-Century European Cultural Theorists, First Series,* edited by Paul Hansom (2001)

243 *The American Renaissance in New England, Fourth Series,* edited by Wesley T. Mott (2001)

244 *American Short-Story Writers Since World War II, Fourth Series,* edited by Patrick Meanor and Joseph McNicholas (2001)

245 *British and Irish Dramatists Since World War II, Third Series,* edited by John Bull (2001)

246 *Twentieth-Century American Cultural Theorists,* edited by Paul Hansom (2001)

247 *James Joyce: A Documentary Volume,* edited by A. Nicholas Fargnoli (2001)

248 *Antebellum Writers in the South, Second Series,* edited by Kent Ljungquist (2001)

249 *Twentieth-Century American Dramatists, Third Series,* edited by Christopher Wheatley (2002)

250 *Antebellum Writers in New York, Second Series,* edited by Kent Ljungquist (2002)

251 *Canadian Fantasy and Science-Fiction Writers,* edited by Douglas Ivison (2002)

252 *British Philosophers, 1500–1799,* edited by Philip B. Dematteis and Peter S. Fosl (2002)

253 *Raymond Chandler: A Documentary Volume,* edited by Robert Moss (2002)

254 *The House of Putnam, 1837–1872: A Documentary Volume,* edited by Ezra Greenspan (2002)

255 *British Fantasy and Science-Fiction Writers, 1918–1960,* edited by Darren Harris-Fain (2002)

256 *Twentieth-Century American Western Writers, Third Series,* edited by Richard H. Cracroft (2002)

257 *Twentieth-Century Swedish Writers After World War II,* edited by Ann-Charlotte Gavel Adams (2002)

Dictionary of Literary Biography Documentary Series

1 *Sherwood Anderson, Willa Cather, John Dos Passos, Theodore Dreiser, F. Scott Fitzgerald, Ernest Hemingway, Sinclair Lewis,* edited by Margaret A. Van Antwerp (1982)

2 *James Gould Cozzens, James T. Farrell, William Faulkner, John O'Hara, John Steinbeck, Thomas Wolfe, Richard Wright,* edited by Margaret A. Van Antwerp (1982)

3 *Saul Bellow, Jack Kerouac, Norman Mailer, Vladimir Nabokov, John Updike, Kurt Vonnegut,* edited by Mary Bruccoli (1983)

4 *Tennessee Williams,* edited by Margaret A. Van Antwerp and Sally Johns (1984)

5 *American Transcendentalists,* edited by Joel Myerson (1988)

6 *Hardboiled Mystery Writers: Raymond Chandler, Dashiell Hammett, Ross Macdonald,* edited by Matthew J. Bruccoli and Richard Layman (1989)

7 *Modern American Poets: James Dickey, Robert Frost, Marianne Moore,* edited by Karen L. Rood (1989)

8 *The Black Aesthetic Movement,* edited by Jeffrey Louis Decker (1991)

9 *American Writers of the Vietnam War: W. D. Ehrhart, Larry Heinemann, Tim O'Brien, Walter McDonald, John M. Del Vecchio,* edited by Ronald Baughman (1991)

10 *The Bloomsbury Group,* edited by Edward L. Bishop (1992)

11 *American Proletarian Culture: The Twenties and The Thirties,* edited by Jon Christian Suggs (1993)

12 *Southern Women Writers: Flannery O'Connor, Katherine Anne Porter, Eudora Welty,* edited by Mary Ann Wimsatt and Karen L. Rood (1994)

13 *The House of Scribner, 1846–1904,* edited by John Delaney (1996)

14 *Four Women Writers for Children, 1868–1918,* edited by Caroline C. Hunt (1996)

15 *American Expatriate Writers: Paris in the Twenties,* edited by Matthew J. Bruccoli and Robert W. Trogdon (1997)

16 *The House of Scribner, 1905–1930,* edited by John Delaney (1997)

17 *The House of Scribner, 1931–1984,* edited by John Delaney (1998)

18 *British Poets of The Great War: Sassoon, Graves, Owen,* edited by Patrick Quinn (1999)

19 *James Dickey,* edited by Judith S. Baughman (1999)

See also DLB 210, 216, 219, 222, 224, 229, 237, 247, 253, 254

Dictionary of Literary Biography Yearbooks

1980 edited by Karen L. Rood, Jean W. Ross, and Richard Ziegfeld (1981)

1981 edited by Karen L. Rood, Jean W. Ross, and Richard Ziegfeld (1982)

1982 edited by Richard Ziegfeld; associate editors: Jean W. Ross and Lynne C. Zeigler (1983)

1983 edited by Mary Bruccoli and Jean W. Ross; associate editor Richard Ziegfeld (1984)

1984 edited by Jean W. Ross (1985)

1985 edited by Jean W. Ross (1986)

1986 edited by J. M. Brook (1987)

1987 edited by J. M. Brook (1988)

1988 edited by J. M. Brook (1989)

1989 edited by J. M. Brook (1990)

1990 edited by James W. Hipp (1991)

1991 edited by James W. Hipp (1992)

1992 edited by James W. Hipp (1993)

1993 edited by James W. Hipp, contributing editor George Garrett (1994)

1994 edited by James W. Hipp, contributing editor George Garrett (1995)

1995 edited by James W. Hipp, contributing editor George Garrett (1996)

1996 edited by Samuel W. Bruce and L. Kay Webster, contributing editor George Garrett (1997)

1997 edited by Matthew J. Bruccoli and George Garrett, with the assistance of L. Kay Webster (1998)

1998 edited by Matthew J. Bruccoli, contributing editor George Garrett, with the assistance of D. W. Thomas (1999)

1999 edited by Matthew J. Bruccoli, contributing editor George Garrett, with the assistance of D. W. Thomas (2000)

2000 edited by Matthew J. Bruccoli, contributing editor George Garrett, with the assistance of George Parker Anderson (2001)

Concise Series

Concise Dictionary of American Literary Biography, 7 volumes (1988–1999): *The New Consciousness, 1941–1968; Colonization to the American Renaissance, 1640–1865; Realism, Naturalism, and Local Color, 1865–1917; The Twenties, 1917–1929; The Age of Maturity, 1929–1941; Broadening Views, 1968–1988; Supplement: Modern Writers, 1900–1998.*

Concise Dictionary of British Literary Biography, 8 volumes (1991–1992): *Writers of the Middle Ages and Renaissance Before 1660; Writers of the Restoration and Eighteenth Century, 1660–1789; Writers of the Romantic Period, 1789–1832; Victorian Writers, 1832–1890; Late-Victorian and Edwardian Writers, 1890–1914; Modern Writers, 1914–1945; Writers After World War II, 1945–1960; Contemporary Writers, 1960 to Present.*

Concise Dictionary of World Literary Biography, 10 volumes projected (1999–): *Ancient Greek and Roman Writers; German Writers; African, Caribbean, and Latin American Writers; South Slavic and Eastern European Writers.*

Dictionary of Literary Biography® • Volume Two Hundred Fifty-Seven

Twentieth-Century Swedish Writers After World War II

Dictionary of Literary Biography® • Volume Two Hundred Fifty-Seven

Twentieth-Century Swedish Writers After World War II

Edited by
Ann-Charlotte Gavel Adams
University of Washington

A Bruccoli Clark Layman Book
The Gale Group
Detroit • San Francisco • London • Boston • Woodbridge, Conn.
ST. PHILIP'S COLLEGE LIBRARY

Advisory Board for
DICTIONARY OF LITERARY BIOGRAPHY

John Baker
William Cagle
Patrick O'Connor
George Garrett
Trudier Harris
Alvin Kernan
Kenny J. Williams

Matthew J. Bruccoli and Richard Layman, Editorial Directors
Karen L. Rood, Senior Editor

Printed in the United States of America

The paper used in this publication meets the minimum requirements of American National Standard for Information Sciences–Permanence Paper for Printed Library Materials, ANSI Z39.48-1984. ∞™

This publication is a creative work fully protected by all applicable copyright laws, as well as by misappropriation, trade secret, unfair competition, and other applicable laws. The authors and editors of this work have added value to the underlying factual material herein through one or more of the following: unique and original selection, coordination, expression, arrangement, and classification of the information.

All rights to this publication will be vigorously defended.

Copyright © 2002 by The Gale Group
27500 Drake Road
Farmington Hills, MI 48331

All rights reserved including the right of reproduction in
whole or in part in any form.

ISBN 0-7876-5251-2

To Birney, Kristina, and Victor,
and to the memory of
Ann-Marie and Gunnar Gavel

Contents

Plan of the Series xv
Introduction xvii

Lars Ahlin (1915–1997) 3
Torborg Lundell

Ingmar Bergman (1918–) .13
Birgitta Steene

Carina Burman (1960–) .35
Barbro Ståhle Sjönell

Sven Delblanc (1931–1992) 44
Rochelle Wright

Inger Edelfeldt (1956–) .57
Sarah Death

Kerstin Ekman (1933–) .66
Rochelle Wright

Per Olov Enquist (1934–) 82
Ross Shideler

Katarina Frostenson (1953–) 90
Ia Dübois

Jonas Gardell (1963–) 98
Matthew M. Roy

Maria (Kristina) Gripe (1923–) 106
Birgitta Steene

Lars Gustafsson (1936–) 115
Ia Dübois

Lars Gyllensten (1921–) 131
Barbara Lide

Ulla Isaksson (1916–2000) 145
Rose-Marie G. Oster

Tove Jansson (1914–2001) 151
Boel Westin

Per Christian Jersild (1935–) 167
Ross Shideler

Willy Kyrklund (1921–) 176
Paul Norlén

Sara Lidman (1923–) 185
Birgitta Holm and Paul Norlén

Astrid Lindgren (1907–2002) 199
Eva-Maria Metcalf

Torgny Lindgren (1938–) 213
Elizabeth deNoma

Kristina Lugn (1948–) 219
Tanya Thresher

Jan Myrdal (1927–) 227
Cecilia Cervin

Lars Norén (1944–) 236
Lars Nylander

Agneta Pleijel (1940–) 246
Ebba Segerberg

Göran Sonnevi (1939–) 252
Kevin Karlin

Per Olof Sundman (1922–1992) 260
Rick McGregor

Märta Tikkanen (1935–) 270
Kathy Saranpa

Tomas Tranströmer (1931–) 277
Joanna Bankier

Birgitta Trotzig (1929–) 291
Steven P. Sondrup

Göran Tunström (1937–2000) 297
Kathy Saranpa

Books for Further Reading 305
Contributors 307
Cumulative Index 311

Plan of the Series

... Almost the most prodigious asset of a country, and perhaps its most precious possession, is its native literary product—when that product is fine and noble and enduring.

Mark Twain*

The advisory board, the editors, and the publisher of the *Dictionary of Literary Biography* are joined in endorsing Mark Twain's declaration. The literature of a nation provides an inexhaustible resource of permanent worth. Our purpose is to make literature and its creators better understood and more accessible to students and the reading public, while satisfying the needs of teachers and researchers.

To meet these requirements, *literary biography* has been construed in terms of the author's achievement. The most important thing about a writer is his writing. Accordingly, the entries in *DLB* are career biographies, tracing the development of the author's canon and the evolution of his reputation.

The purpose of *DLB* is not only to provide reliable information in a usable format but also to place the figures in the larger perspective of literary history and to offer appraisals of their accomplishments by qualified scholars.

The publication plan for *DLB* resulted from two years of preparation. The project was proposed to Bruccoli Clark by Frederick G. Ruffner, president of the Gale Research Company, in November 1975. After specimen entries were prepared and typeset, an advisory board was formed to refine the entry format and develop the series rationale. In meetings held during 1976, the publisher, series editors, and advisory board approved the scheme for a comprehensive biographical dictionary of persons who contributed to literature. Editorial work on the first volume began in January 1977, and it was published in 1978. In order to make *DLB* more than a dictionary and to compile volumes that individually have claim to status as literary history, it was decided to organize volumes by topic, period, or genre. Each of these freestanding volumes provides a biographical-bibliographical guide and overview for a particular area of literature. We are convinced that this organization—as opposed to a single alphabet method—constitutes a valuable innovation in the presentation of reference material. The volume plan necessarily requires many decisions for the placement and treatment of authors. Certain figures will be included in separate volumes, but with different entries emphasizing the aspect of his career appropriate to each volume. Ernest Hemingway, for example, is represented in *American Writers in Paris, 1920–1939* by an entry focusing on his expatriate apprenticeship; he is also in *American Novelists, 1910–1945* with an entry surveying his entire career, as well as in *American Short-Story Writers, 1910–1945, Second Series* with an entry concentrating on his short fiction. Each volume includes a cumulative index of the subject authors and articles.

Since 1981 the series has been further augmented by the *DLB Yearbooks,* which update published entries, add new entries to keep the *DLB* current with contemporary activity, and provide articles on literary history. There have also been nineteen *DLB Documentary Series* volumes which provide illustrations, facsimiles, and biographical and critical source materials for figures, works, or groups judged to have particular interest for students. In 1999 the *Documentary Series* was incorporated into the *DLB* volume numbering system beginning with *DLB 210: Ernest Hemingway*.

We define literature as the *intellectual commerce of a nation:* not merely as belles lettres but as that ample and complex process by which ideas are generated, shaped, and transmitted. *DLB* entries are not limited to "creative writers" but extend to other figures who in their time and in their way influenced the mind of a people. Thus the series encompasses historians, journalists, publishers, book collectors, and screenwriters. By this means readers of *DLB* may be aided to perceive literature not as cult scripture in the keeping of intellectual high priests but firmly positioned at the center of a nation's life.

DLB includes the major writers appropriate to each volume and those standing in the ranks behind them. Scholarly and critical counsel has been sought in

---

*From an unpublished section of Mark Twain's autobiography, copyright by the Mark Twain Company

deciding which minor figures to include and how full their entries should be. Wherever possible, useful references are made to figures who do not warrant separate entries.

Each *DLB* volume has an expert volume editor responsible for planning the volume, selecting the figures for inclusion, and assigning the entries. Volume editors are also responsible for preparing, where appropriate, appendices surveying the major periodicals and literary and intellectual movements for their volumes, as well as lists of further readings. Work on the series as a whole is coordinated at the Bruccoli Clark Layman editorial center in Columbia, South Carolina, where the editorial staff is responsible for accuracy and utility of the published volumes.

One feature that distinguishes *DLB* is the illustration policy—its concern with the iconography of literature. Just as an author is influenced by his surroundings, so is the reader's understanding of the author enhanced by a knowledge of his environment. Therefore *DLB* volumes include not only drawings, paintings, and photographs of authors, often depicting them at various stages in their careers, but also illustrations of their families and places where they lived. Title pages are regularly reproduced in facsimile along with dust jackets for modern authors. The dust jackets are a special feature of *DLB* because they often document better than anything else the way in which an author's work was perceived in its own time. Specimens of the writers' manuscripts and letters are included when feasible.

Samuel Johnson rightly decreed that "The chief glory of every people arises from its authors." The purpose of the *Dictionary of Literary Biography* is to compile literary history in the surest way available to us—by accurate and comprehensive treatment of the lives and work of those who contributed to it.

The *DLB* Advisory Board

Introduction

The writers included in this volume represent a cross section of the most important Swedish authors of the twentieth century. The ambition has been to achieve a balanced selection of prominent Swedish writers from different decades, movements, genres, and gender, with preference given to authors published in English translation. Representative Fenno-Swedish writers have also been included, since they write in Swedish and are part of Swedish cultural history.

This introduction is intended to place the writers in their context and to sketch an outline of major events and movements that have influenced the writers of twentieth-century Swedish literature. This outline is based in the theory that literature reflects and is itself a reflection of the surrounding social and political world. There have been many attempts to group writers and literary works into periods in order to get a better grasp of shared ideas and trends of the century. One early tradition divided the writers by decades. A division of the writers into *tiotalister* (writers of the 1910s) and *fyrtiotalister* (writers of the 1940s) was common until the midpoint of the century. Such a division may have been justified around 1950, when decades seemed convenient to define the dominant trends, but this way of surveying the literature has not worked well for the latter part of the century. Another tradition allows the two world wars to split the century into the pre–World War I period, the interwar period, and the post–World War II period. This division may be more applicable for the literatures of the neighboring Scandinavian countries of Denmark, Norway, and Finland, who experienced the wars firsthand. It has also been less useful for surveying the works of Swedish women writers, who have had other battles to pursue, in addition to the human concerns and fears of war, and have focused on more immediate and practical issues, such as getting a voice in society. Recent attempts to view literary works as modernist or postmodernist have also proved less than satisfactory because of the difficulty in coming up with a clear definition of the terms. The period from 1950 to 1985 is referred to in *Svenska Litteraturens Historia,* a Swedish literary history edited by Lars Lönnroth and Sven Delblanc, as "Medieålderns litteratur" (The Literature of the Media Age). In the introduction to volume five, Lönnroth focuses on the entry of the television sets into Swedish living rooms as a decisive factor for Swedish literature entering into the "media age" and thus the global arena. The barrage of information, through all kinds of print and electronic media, that began to flood writers and readers makes a strong case for the 1960s being the decade that changed the fundamentals of reading and writing fiction in Sweden.

At the turn of the century Sweden was just entering the industrial era, emerging from being a predominantly poor and agrarian society. Industrialization had come late to the Scandinavian countries. The changing society is reflected in the literature of the time.

The decades just preceding the twentieth century, from 1870 to 1900, have traditionally been referred to as "det Moderna Genombrottet" (the Modern Breakthrough) in Scandinavian literature. The term was coined by Danish critic Georg Brandes in a series of influential lectures at the University of Copenhagen in the 1870s. Brandes challenged Scandinavian writers to abandon their provincial preoccupation with national history and folklore and enter into the European literary arena and debate contemporary social problems. The first to respond to the challenge in Sweden was August Strindberg. Issues such as a more just society for the working class, equality between men and women, sexuality, and prostitution were hotly addressed in his early works. After his spiritual reorientation in the mid 1890s, his so-called *Inferno* crisis, Strindberg turned away from social and political issues and became more introspective in focus and more experimental in form. With these works he set the stage for movements such as Expressionism and modernism in Swedish and European literature.

The other internationally most prominent name at the turn of the century is Selma Lagerlöf, called "drottningen i vår litteratur" (the queen of our literature) by poet Hjalmar Gullberg, who saw her as the most important Swedish woman since Saint Birgitta in the fourteenth century. Lagerlöf's first novel, *Gösta Berlings saga* (1891; translated as *The Story of Gösta Berling,* 1898), with its exaltation of beauty, wild adventures, nature mysticism, and the power of love, broke in every respect with the socially engaged literature of realism and naturalism of the Modern Breakthrough. Her stories and novels, which continue to be loved and read today, are among the most frequently translated works in Swedish literature. Motion-picture directors from Mauritz Stiller in the 1920s to Billie August in the 1990s have been inspired to turn her stories into movies. She was awarded the Nobel Prize for literature in 1909.

The World Exhibition of Art and Industry in Stockholm in 1897 can be said to have ushered in a new era of modernity in Sweden. The event introduced the cinematic medium to Sweden with the filming of the arrival of King Oscar II to the exhibition. New industrial discoveries, such as Alfred Nobel's invention of dynamite, Sven Winquist's self-regulating ball bearings, and L. M. Ericsson's table telephone all held great promise. They led to the founding of companies such as Bofors (armament), SKF (ball bearings), and L. M. Ericsson (telecommunications) and opened possibilities for easier communication between people and places. The industrialization brought people to the big cities, and publishing houses and newspapers located their offices in the metropolitan areas. Writers and journalists flocked to the cities to get their works published and to take part in the cultural debate. Thus, culture became centralized in the cities.

In his last will and testament Nobel donated his entire estate to the establishment of a fund that was to be invested and distributed in yearly prizes "to those who during the preceding year had conferred the greatest benefit on mankind" in the fields of physics, chemistry, medicine, literature, and peace. The first Nobel Prizes were awarded in 1901. The task of selecting the literature recipient of the Nobel Prize was assigned to the Swedish Academy, a venerable institution founded by King Gustav III in 1786. Every year this institution chooses the author who has produced "the most outstanding work of an idealistic tendency." In the early years there was some confusion as to what Nobel really meant by "idealistic tendency," and many prominent and worthy authors of the time were passed by, among them Strindberg, Henrik Ibsen, and Leo Tolstoy. Lagerlöf was the first Swedish recipient and the first woman to receive the prize for literature.

The first decade of the new century brought political unrest. The Union with Norway, in force since 1814, caused tension and bitter conflicts between Sweden and Norway. The Union was officially dissolved in 1905. The Social Democratic Party, founded in 1889, pursued its fight to extend suffrage during the first decade. In August 1909 a general strike, the so-called *Storstrejken,* paralyzed Sweden, a sign of the increasing power and voice of the working classes.

In literature two trends seem to dominate the first decades: the fin-de-siècle flaneurs, influenced by the French symbolists, and the bourgeois realists, who viewed the new industrialized society from a middle-class perspective. The flaneurs were disillusioned city dwellers who strolled around Stockholm, observing people and events and describing them with melancholic and ironic distance. At a time when Stockholm was changing into a modern city, Hjalmar Söderberg observed the transformation wrought by new fashionable buildings, parks, and avenues, and described it in a finely tuned prose. The so-called bourgeois realists were of a more practical disposition in their focus on everyday life and contemporary societal issues. Several of these writers started their careers as newspaper journalists, among them Elin Wägner. In her novel *Norrtullsligan* (The Nortull Gang, 1908) she provides an important piece of women's history in her quick-witted portrayal of the life of women office workers in Stockholm, struggling to survive on minimal salaries while fending off sexual harassment. In *Pennskaftet* (The Pen Holder, 1910), a term she coined for a woman journalist, Wägner portrays the fight for the right to vote and the new sexual freedom of single women in the city. The greatest psychologist of the bourgeois realists, Hjalmar Bergman, achieved his breakthrough in 1910 with *Hans nåds testamente* (1910; translated as *The Baron's Will,* 1968). In masterpieces such as *Markurells i Wadköping* (1919; translated as *God's Orchid,* 1924, and as *Markurell's in Wadkoping,* 1964) and *Farmor och Vår Herre* (1921; translated as *Thy Rod and Thy Staff,* 1937), he portrayed the changes in bourgeois life in a provincial town with its growing industrialism.

In 1919 Swedish women got the right to vote. Finland had extended the same right to women in 1906, the first country in Europe to do so, in connection with a constitutional reform. Four women were voted into the Swedish parliament: Kerstin Hesselgren, a teacher of home economics and an excellent public speaker with a solid Swedish and international education; Agda Östlund, from a socialist, working-class home; Elisabeth Tamm, from an upper-class, noble family; and Bertha Wellin, a registered nurse. Although of different backgrounds and talents, they immediately started to work on legislation to extend legal rights for women: for occupational safety and health, better salaries and working conditions, contraception, and children's health issues. In 1920 a new marriage law was instituted that gave women rights equal to men's within marriage. A married woman now had legal rights to manage her own affairs and to enter into legally binding agreements, something that Nora Helmer had not been allowed to do in Ibsen's play *A Doll's House* (1879). "Kvinnliga Medborgarskolan vid Fogelstad" (The

Women's Citizen School at Fogelstad) was founded at the estate of Elizabeth Tamm in 1925. Several twentieth-century women writers without funds or access to higher education attended the school, among them Moa Martinson.

Lyrical modernism is said to have its sources in political and social conflicts and specifically in World War I. Since Sweden did not participate in World War I, it is not surprising that the first modernistic poetry in the Swedish language was written and published in Finland, since people in Finland experienced the war firsthand. The first and most influential poet of lyrical modernism is Edith Södergran, whose free-form poems in *Dikter* (1916; translated in *Complete Poems*, 1992) caused consternation and shocked the literary establishment. When Södergran died from tuberculosis at the age of thirty-one, another of the important Fenno-Swedish modernists, Elmer Diktonius, arranged for her last collection of poems, *Landet som icke är* (1925; translated in *Complete Poems*) to be published.

In Sweden, Pär Lagerkvist introduced modernistic poetry with his expressionistic poem "Ångest" (Anguish, 1916). Ten years later Birger Sjöberg, known for his sweet and idyllic *Fridas visor* (Frida's Songs, 1922), startled the literary establishment by the expressionistic form of his poems in *Kriser och Kransar* (Crises and Wreaths, 1926). Another important early modernist is Karin Boye, author of the poetry collections *Moln* (1922; translated as *Clouds*, 1994), *Gömda land* (1924; translated as *Hidden Lands*, 1994), and *Härdarna* (1927; translated as *The Hearths*, 1994). As one of the founders and editors of the modernist journal *Spektrum*, she helped introduce T. S. Eliot's "The Waste Land" (1922) to Sweden in 1932, which had a great influence on the Swedish poets of the 1930s and 1940s.

In 1930 the Stockholm Exhibition–a proud display of the expansion and capacity of Swedish industry–introduced *Funktionalism* (Functionalism) as the coming and dominant trend in architecture and interior design: the purpose should decide the form. It was viewed with suspicion and disapproval by conservative cultural forces in Sweden but with hope and enthusiasm by a new generation of writers, such as Ivar Lo-Johansson, who remembers his impressions in the autobiographical novel *Författaren* (The Author, 1957).

Swedish industry had prospered in the years after World War I. In the 1930s, however, Sweden was struck by the worldwide economic crisis, which had broken out in the aftermath of the stock-market crash in the United States in 1929. Falling wages and rising unemployment caused political unrest among the working class. It culminated in a strike and demonstration in Ådalen in northern Sweden in 1931. The military, called in to keep order, ended up shooting at the demonstrators, killing five people. In the spring of 1932 Swedish financier Ivan Kreuger, called the "Swedish Match King," committed suicide in a hotel room in Paris. The so-called Kreuger crash caused many bankruptcies and collapses of companies, with devastating results for many individuals, among them poet Gunnar Ekelöf, who lost his entire paternal inheritance and economic base. The election of 1932 brought the Social Democrats to power and, with them, an agenda of social reform. This agenda was the start of the gradual implementation of the Swedish welfare state, with an eight-hour workday and economic security for all.

Two trends dominate the literature of the 1930s: the proletarian realists, often referred to in Swedish as *autodidakterna* (the "autodidacts," or "self-taught"), and the modernists. The proletarian realists came from poor, often rural backgrounds and had little or no formal schooling. Their thirst for knowledge drove them to read voraciously, however, and educate themselves through lending libraries, folk high schools, newspapers, and travels. Their novels depict the oppressive social and economic reality of the life of factory and farmworkers. This school of writers is rather generously represented in this volume, since their works have met with scholarly interest in the United States and many of their works have been translated into English. The important names associated with the proletarian realists are Moa Martinson, Jan Fridegård, and Ivar Lo-Johansson. Martinson is distinctive among the proletarian realists with her feisty yet compassionate portrayal of the lives of working-class women in early industrialized Sweden. Her novels have remained popular and continue to be read and reprinted.

Like several others among the autodidacts, Harry Martinson moved on to make his most important contributions in other genres and movements. He became one of Sweden's finest nature poets–modernistic yet accessible. His epic poem *Aniara* (1956; translated, 1963 and 1991), set in space, is a dystopian portrayal of the post–World War II arms race. It has become one of the classics of twentieth-century Swedish literature. Eyvind Johnson–after a series of four autobiographical novels later published in one volume as *Romanen om Olof* (The Novel about Olof, 1945)–wrote highly acclaimed historical novels. His trilogy about Johannes Krilon, comprising *Grupp Krilon* (Group Krilon, 1941), *Krilons resa* (Krilon's Journey, 1942), and *Krilon själv* (Krilon Himself, 1943), is a protest in allegorical form against the Nazi terror in Europe. Vilhelm Moberg has become best known for his four-part epic *Utvandrarromanen* (1949-1959; translated as *The Emigrants*, 1951; *Unto a Good Land*, 1957; and *The Last Letter Home*, 1961), about Swedish pioneers emigrating from Småland, Sweden, and settling in nineteenth-century Minnesota, a series that brought him fame and popularity both at home and abroad. This series can certainly be viewed as a precursor of the documentary novels of the 1960s.

The year 1931 is considered to be the real breakthrough for Swedish modernism. In an article in *Dagens Nyheter,* Artur Lundkvist proclaimed "Frihet åt poesin!" (Freedom to poetry!). A new generation of poets with contacts on the international scene brought new forms and ideas to Swedish poetry. Lundkvist, another of the autodidacts, became one of the most prolific poets and prose writers of the century, with a production that includes poetry, fiction, travel narratives, essays, and reviews. He made his debut in the anthology *Fem Unga* (Five Young Men, 1929) together with Harry Martinson, Gustav Sandgren, Erik Asklund, and Josef Kjellgren. In a free, modernistic form these five young poets glorified life and sexual freedom in their poems. In an oft-quoted characterization they were referred to as "the primitivist school of phallic worshippers" in the *Anglo-Swedish Review* (December 1934). Lundkvist came to play a key role in introducing international poets and novelists to Swedish readers. As a member of the Swedish Academy he was also a knowledgeable and influential member of the Nobel Prize Committee.

The most important of the modernistic poets of the 1930s through the 1950s was Gunnar Ekelöf. His first collection of poetry, *Sent på jorden* (1932; translated as *Late Arrival on Earth,* 1967) is the first important surrealist and modernist work of the 1930s. In later decades Ekelöf wrote a series of absurdist, antipoetic poetry collections, starting with *Strountes* (Nonsense, 1955). His *En Mölna-Elegi* (1960; translated as *A Mölna Elegy,* 1984) has been called the most advanced experiment with the quotation-allusion technique in Swedish literature.

When World War II broke out in September 1939, all the Nordic countries declared themselves neutral. Sweden succeeded in staying out of the war when the Nazis occupied Denmark and Norway. The occupation of the neighboring Scandinavian countries, however, did cut off Sweden's trade with the Western world, which, in addition to the poor harvests in 1940–1941, caused severe shortages of food and other commodities.

The so-called *fyrtiotalismen* (fortyism) is the traditional designation for the anxiety-filled and guilt-ridden modernism of the decade, centered around the literary journal *40-tal,* published from 1944 to 1947. Characteristic of the works of the 1940s is the feeling of powerlessness and pessimism resulting from the brutal reality of World War II. Important impulses also came from Jean Paul Sartre's existentialism and Franz Kafka's nightmarish realism. The genius of the 1940s generation was Stig Dagerman, who wrote both novels and drama in his short life, before ending it himself at the age of thirty-one. Other important novelists making their debut in the 1940s are Lars Ahlin and Ulla Isaksson. Both have written works with a clear religious orientation. Isaksson has also written screenplays for Ingmar Bergman, including *Jungfrukällan* (1960; also distributed as *The Virgin Spring*). Among the important poets of the 1940s are Erik Lindegren, whose "shattered sonnets" in *mannen utan väg* (man without road, 1942) were little understood by the critics of the time; Karl Vennberg; and Werner Aspenström.

The Communist takeover of Czechoslovakia in 1948 fueled a fear of communism, which provoked strong editorial responses in the Swedish daily newspapers, particularly that of Herbert Tingsten of *Dagens Nyheter,* to argue that Sweden should abandon its official policy of neutrality and join the North Atlantic Treaty Organization. A group of authors and intellectuals, Lundkvist and Vennberg among them, advocated a "tredje ståndpunkten" (third point of view), an individualistic independence of both blocs. Although Sweden's official policy was one of neutrality, the writers embracing the third point of view were viewed as more sympathetic to the ideology of the Eastern bloc, or "cryptocommunists" in the words of Tingsten.

The 1950s produced such a variety of literary styles and genres that no unified trend can be clearly distinguished and identified. *Fyrtiotalisterna,* such as Ahlin, continued to publish. In his introduction to volume five of *Den Svenska Litteraturen,* Lönnrot points to 1954 as a year of some significance. That year Dagerman committed suicide, and the poet Lindegren published his last collection. The same year, Tomas Tranströmer, probably Sweden's greatest living poet, made his debut with *17 dikter* (17 Poems, 1954).

Writers who became known during the 1950s are individualists, sometimes academics, who often explore philosophical and religious questions. Most of them have continued to publish and remain active. Lars Gyllensten, a professor of medicine, explores in his novels a humanistic and moral philosophy in an absurd world that seems to lack a system of absolute values. Willy Kyrklund, very much an individualist and difficult to pin to any decade or movement, elegantly blends philosophy, humor, and irony in his short prose texts and dramas. Birgitta Trotzig focuses on existential issues, often of a religious character, particularly after her conversion to Roman Catholicism in the 1960s.

In the 1950s moviemaker and novelist Ingmar Bergman established himself as the world's foremost *auteur du cinéma,* meaning an artist with both the literary and visual talents to transpose the art of storytelling to the motion-picture medium. Bergman has written almost all of the screenplays to his more than fifty features, creating a new hybrid genre between script and novel in which the screenplays become self-contained literary works, companion pieces to his movies. Few other authors have been able to portray their religious and metaphysical questioning in such stunning form, both literary and cinematic.

In the 1960s television became a major cultural force in Sweden. It had a deep influence on writers and readers of Swedish literature. The Swedes have always been avid readers of daily newspapers, often subscribing to several, but the news clips on television succeeded in making the catastrophes of the world more real and visual and bringing them into the comfortable living rooms of the welfare state. Sweden was at this time one of the wealthiest countries of the world, with both a welfare state and a prosperous economy, which seemed to allow for the coexistence of socialism and capitalism. Göran Sonnevi's poem "Om kriget i Vietnam" (On the War in Vietnam, 1965) captured the startling contrast of world catastrophes and the Swedish welfare state. It became impossible for writers of the 1960s and 1970s to avoid addressing what was happening in the "real" world and to take a stand. Readers started gradually to lose interest in the fictional worlds of literature. In the 1960s *faktaböcker* ("fact books," or nonfiction) became so popular that they for a while overtook the sales of literary fiction. The readers wanted to be informed of the here and now, not be transported into fictional worlds. The mass-market pocket book had been introduced in Sweden in 1957. Reprints of best-selling nonfictional works were published in inexpensive pocket book series such as Aldus, PAN, Tema, and Prisma.

In the latter part of the 1960s and the beginning of the 1970s, the political sympathies of the intellectuals shifted to the left. Student revolts at the universities in Paris and at Berkeley made headlines in the newspapers and filled television news broadcasts in 1968. In May of the same year the students of Stockholm University occupied their union building in protest against university reforms. Olof Palme, who took office as prime minister of Sweden in 1969, openly opposed the American intervention in Vietnam.

The literature of the 1960s and 1970s became intensely involved with political and global issues. Jan Myrdal created a new genre, the report genre, starting with *Rapport från kinesisk by* (1963; translated as *Report from a Chinese Village*, 1965). The son of Nobel Prize winners Gunnar and Alva Myrdal, whom he has publicly criticized, Myrdal has also reflected on his role as an individual author and the responsibility of the intellectuals in a series of autobiographical works, beginning with *Confessions of a Disloyal European* (1968), first published in English. Sara Lidman also has spent much of her career addressing the important global, social, political, and environmental issues of the time. When the first American bombings of North Vietnam took place in the fall of 1964, she started her ten-year-long involvement with the antiwar movement and with the people of Vietnam. A report from her visit to North Vietnam in 1965 was published as *Samtal i Hanoi* (Conversations in Hanoi, 1966). In 1968 she published *Gruva* (The Mine, 1968), a collection of interviews with the miners of the state-owned mine fields LKAB, in the north of Sweden. The book caused a greater uproar in Sweden and started a literary trend of documentary books from all sectors of contemporary life. A year after the publication of *Gruva* the general strike at LKAB broke out. Per Olov Enquist got much publicity for his documentary novel *Legionärerna* (1968; translated as *The Legionnaires*, 1973), about the extradition of Baltic war refugees from Sweden to the Soviet Union at the end of World War II. In search of the truth of this historical event, he combined documentary and fictional elements into a more "real" portrayal of the events.

During the 1970s and 1980s, environmental issues were brought to the forefront of public consciousness, particularly the question of nuclear power. The accident at the nuclear power station in Chernobyl in the Soviet Union in 1986 brought home the dangers of this once promising source of power. In February 1986 Prime Minister Olof Palme was assassinated on a street in Stockholm. It was a wake-up call to the Swedes that their safe and secure welfare state was crumbling.

From the 1970s and onward, there is a renewed interest in broad epic novels and a return to the countryside, often in an historical setting, perhaps as a reaction to the politically engaged 1960s. Sven Delblanc is a supreme stylist and a broad epic storyteller. He was also a professor of comparative literature at Uppsala University and coeditor of *Svenska Literaturens Histoira*, a multivolume history of Swedish literature published shortly before his death in 1992. He is best known for his two tetralogies: the first, the so-called Hedeby series, published in the 1970s, comprises historical novels depicting the time of his own childhood and youth. The second tetralogy, published in the early 1980s, portrays the experiences of his maternal grandfather, in the novels about Samuel and his descendants. Kerstin Ekman started her career writing crime novels. In the 1970s she shifted to broad and realistic historical narratives focusing on working-class women in the small town of Katrineholm. Since the 1980s, her novels have become increasingly more complex, with lyrical elements and fantastic, mythical substructures, while emphasizing social and environmental concerns. Her *Händelser vid vatten* (1993; translated as *Blackwater*, 1997), an ecofeminist crime novel, won several major literary prizes for

1993 and has become one of the most critically acclaimed novels of the 1990s. P. C. Jersild is profoundly interested in the most important social, political, and ontological questions of the time. He was a practicing physician for twenty years of his literary career, specializing in social and preventive medicine. He retired from medicine one year before the publication of *Babels hus* (1978; translated as *House of Babel*, 1987), a realistic and controversial novel about the Swedish health-care system that is regarded as a classic in Sweden. Lars Gustafson has gained international recognition as a philosophical poet and novelist. He has received several international literary honors. Göran Tunström is a storyteller of warmth and magical realism. In his best-known novel, *Juloratoriet* (1983; translated as *The Christmas Oratorio*, 1995), he pays tribute to his literary foremother, Lagerlöf. Torgny Lindgren, a member of the Swedish Academy, writes broad biblical novels such as *Bat Seba* (1984; translated as *Bathsheba*, 1989) and legend-like, disturbing novels such as *Hummelhonung* (1995; translated as *Sweetness*, 2000).

Clas Zilliacus notices "en generöst företrädd och med generös bredd berättad kvinnling prosa" (a generously represented female prose, narrated with generous breadth) in the last decades of the twentieth century in his introduction to volume two of *Finlands Svenska Litteraturhistoria* (The Swedish Literary History of Finland, 2000). Two Fenno-Swedish women writers are represented in this volume: Solveig von Schoulz and Märta Tikkanen. Schoulz was until her death considered the grand old lady of Fenno-Swedish prose and poetry. Her subject matter often deals with psychological tension of everyday situations and events. Her protagonists are usually women, whose lives are portrayed with compassion and in a masterly, precisely crafted prose. Schoulz was an important mentor for Tikkanen. Tikkanen calls herself a feminist and a writer, but not a feminist writer. Many of her works have received prominent attention and been widely translated, among them *Män kan inte våldtas* (1975; translated as *Manrape*, 1978) and *Århundradets kärlekssaga* (1978; translated as *The Love Story of the Century*, 1984).

On the contemporary literary scene there are serious concerns that reading and writing literary fiction is losing its prestige in Swedish cultural life. Author Lennart Hagefors complained, at a Conference for Swedish Teachers in the United States in 1998, that television and movies have sapped the energy out of literature and suggested that *Likgilitighet* (Indifference) was the trend of the 1990s. Best-sellers, particularly thrillers and crime novels, now dominate the book market. At the Bok- och Biblioteksmässa (Book and Library Fair) in Göteborg in 1997, one of the seminars, organized by the Bonnier-owned *Månadsjournalen*, centered on the question "Har svenska män slutet läsa?" (Have Swedish men stopped reading?) Statistics and surveys indicate that men prefer factual accounts over fiction, while women read more books than ever before, but women want to "känna igen sig" (recognize themselves)–be confirmed–in the novels they read. Publisher Svante Weyler of Norstedt concluded that literature has indeed lost its status in society.

Nevertheless, there are new and interesting writers, both male and female, in Swedish literature today, and the well-known authors of the 1950s to the 1980s continue to write and publish for a seemingly more narrow field of readers of literature. Among the contemporary poets are Tomas Tranströmer, whose poetry is extremely direct and accessible and who have gained a broad following both in Europe and the United States, and Katarina Frostenson, the youngest member of the Swedish Academy, whose poetry resembles musical compositions and is considered more difficult. Two outstanding names among contemporary dramatists are Lars Norén and Kristina Lugn, both of whom started as poets and are provocative and violent in their dramas. Norén continues to prove himself as the most important dramatist since Strindberg. His drama about psychopathic criminals, *7:3* (1998), was staged by the same criminals on whom it was based, causing an uproar in Sweden. Lugn is more provocative in tone than in subject matter; her plays are usually about the ways in which female identity is constructed. Since taking over the directorship of the theater Brunnsgatan Fyra in Stockholm, she has become an important force in the theatrical world in the Swedish capital. Notable among the prose writers are Agneta Pleijel, who writes philosophical novels, most recently *Lord Nevermore* (2000), and who was awarded the prestigious Selma Lagerlöf Litteraturpris in 2001; Inger Edelfeldt, who writes novels with sensitive portraits of protagonists with frail egos and difficulties living in the real world; Carina Burman, a literary scholar focusing on the eighteenth and nineteenth centuries, whose first novel, *Min salig bror Jean Hendrich* (My Dear Departed Brother Jean Hendrich, 1993), an intimate portrait of the life of eighteenth-century poet Johan Henric Kjellgren, was an instant success and was reprinted several times the same year it was published; and Jonas Gardell, who writes humorous novels of frustrated men and women who hesitate to break out of their middle-class reality and pursue their dream or love.

Literature for children and young adults

In 1983 a Chair in *Barnlitteratur* (Children's Literature) was instituted at Department of Comparative Literature at Stockholm University. Literature for children and young adults had finally gained sufficient recognition and respect to be considered an artistic pursuit in its own right and thus worthy of research and documentation. Some of the reasons behind this new professorship were the international recognition and obvious literary merits of the works by authors such as Astrid Lindgren, Tove Jansson, and Maria Gripe. All three have received the prestigious H. C. Andersen Medal–considered to be a "Nobel Prize" for children's literature–by the International Board on Books for Young People (IBBY), founded in 1953.

In 1900 Ellen Key, influential essayist, pedagogue, and feminist, predicted in a manifesto, aptly titled *Barnets århundrade* (1900; translated as *The Century of the Child,* 1909), that the new century would focus on the rights of the children. Up until this time children's literature was primarily geared toward instruction and instilling good morals and manners. Little attention was given to the aesthetics of the books or the needs of the children.

Picture books became popular at the turn of the century. The most important name in this genre is Elsa Beskow, who was both an artist and a writer. Her first picture book, *Sagan om den lilla lilla gumman* (1897; translated as *The Tale of the Wee Little Old Woman,* 1982) continues to be read and reprinted more than one hundred years after it was first published. Her interest in botany and nature is evident in *Tomtebobarnen* (1910; translated as *The Little Elves of Elf Nook,* 1966), which depicts the life of an elf family in the forest throughout the seasons of the year, with detailed, accurate drawings of flowers, animals, and mushrooms.

Another classic from the early part of the century is Lagerlöf's *Nils Holgersons underbara resa genom Sverige* (two volumes, 1906–1907; translated as *The Wonderful Adventures of Nils,* 1907, and *The Further Adventures of Nils,* 1911). The book was originally commissioned as a textbook on Swedish geography and history by the Swedish school authorities. Since then it has taken on a life of its own and continues to be read and enjoyed today by both children and adults.

Up until the early part of the twentieth century, children's books were exclusively written for and read by the upper, educated classes. A working-class environment or poverty was rarely depicted in a socially realistic sense. Laura Fitinghoff's naturalistic but sentimental *Barnen från Frostmofjället* (1907; translated as *The Children of Frostmoor,* 1914) was innovative in that it describes the struggle of seven children, whose mother had died of tuberculosis and father of alcoholism, to find a new life and home together.

For young adults few books of international or lasting merit were written in the original Swedish during the first part of the twentieth century. Teenagers read translated classic works by Mark Twain, Jules Verne, Robert Louis Stevenson, Arthur Conan Doyle, Rudyard Kipling, Louisa May Alcott, Frances Eliza Hodgson Burnett, Walter Scott, and James Fenimore Cooper. One interesting story in Swedish for young adults, circulated in a small edition, was the autobiographical *En prärieunges funderingar* (Thoughts of a Prairie Child, 1917; published in Sweden in 1919) by Anna Olsson, who was born in Sweden but had immigrated to the United States with her family.

In 1945 Swedish children got their first heroine on their own terms in *Pippi Långstrump* (1945; translated as *Pippi Longstocking,* 1968) by Astrid Lindgren, the most influential writer of Swedish children's literature. Her works have been translated into fifty-five languages. Her protagonist Pippi Longstocking is a most subversive character, whose every action served to counteract the good manners instilled in earlier children's books. Consequently, she became an ideal and an inspiration for a whole new generation of boys and girls. Pippi is the strongest and richest girl in the world, and she has no parents or teachers to tell her what to do. She has been called the personification of Key's "child of the century" and the inspiration of the entire Swedish baby-boom generation.

Tove Jansson is the other beloved giant of children's literature in the Swedish language. She is the creator, both the artist and the author, of the Moomin world, a utopian society where life is threatened by chaos and catastrophes but always seems to emerge triumphant. The Moomintroll, a cuddly teenaged hippopotamus-like figure, lives in the happy and peaceful Moomin Valley with his nurturing, tender, and responsible Moominmama and his endearing but self-centered and vainglorious Moominpapa. The Moomin books have been translated into more than thirty languages.

Maria Gripe had a decade of fame and glory in the United States in the 1970s, when no less than twelve of her books were translated into English. Her breakthrough in Sweden came with *Glasblåsarns barn* (1964; *The Glassblower's Children,* 1976), a story inspired by Andersen's tale *Snedronningen* (The Snow Queen, 1845). Gripe writes from the child's perspective. Many protagonists in her books are lonely children with self-absorbed, materialistic parents who do not have time for them. While her books sometimes seem frightening to adults, children can easily identify with the feelings and societies in her stories. Another widely translated and highly original voice in Fenno-Swedish children's literature is Irmelin Sandman Lillius. Influenced by Anglo-Saxon fantasy literature, she has created a world of magical realism in the series about Tulavall.

Acknowledgments

This book was produced by Bruccoli Clark Layman, Inc. Karen L. Rood is senior editor. Charles Brower was the in-house editor.

Production manager is Philip B. Dematteis.

Administrative support was provided by Ann M. Cheschi, Amber L. Coker, Linda Dalton Mullinax, and Angi Pleasant.

Accountant is Ann-Marie Holland.

Copyediting supervisor is Sally R. Evans. The copyediting staff includes Phyllis A. Avant, Brenda Carol Blanton, Melissa D. Hinton, Charles Loughlin, Rebecca Mayo, Nancy E. Smith, and Elizabeth Jo Ann Sumner.

Editorial associates are Michael S. Allen, Michael S. Martin, and Pamela A. Warren.

Permissions editor is Jason Paddock.

Database manager is José A. Juarez.

Layout and graphics supervisor is Janet E. Hill. The graphics staff includes Karla Corley Brown and Zoe R. Cook.

Office manager is Kathy Lawler Merlette.

Photography supervisor is Paul Talbot. Photography editor is Scott Nemzek.

Digital photographic copy work was performed by Joseph M. Bruccoli.

Systems manager is Marie L. Parker.

Typesetting supervisor is Kathleen M. Flanagan. The typesetting staff includes Patricia Marie Flanagan, Mark J. McEwan, and Pamela D. Norton. Freelance typesetter is Wanda Adams.

Walter W. Ross did library research. He was assisted by Pamela A. Warren and the following librarians at the Thomas Cooper Library of the University of South Carolina: circulation department head Tucker Taylor; reference department head Virginia W. Weathers; Brette Barclay, Marilee Birchfield, Paul Cammarata, Gary Geer, Michael Macan, Tom Marcil, Rose Marshall, and Sharon Verba; interlibrary loan department head John Brunswick; and interlibrary loan staff Robert Arndt, Hayden Battle, Barry Bull, Jo Cottingham, Marna Hostetler, Marieum McClary, Erika Peake, and Nelson Rivera.

The editor would like to offer special thanks to the Swedish Institute in Stockholm and Helen Sigeland, who generously granted funds for linguistic revision of ten entries originally written in Swedish, and to Paul Norlen and Birgitta Steene, who helped revise the articles. Thanks also go to Brian Hodges and Wade Hollingshaus, who have served as research assistants at different stages of the work on this volume.

Dictionary of Literary Biography® • Volume Two Hundred Fifty-Seven

Twentieth-Century Swedish Writers After World War II

Dictionary of Literary Biography

Lars Ahlin
(4 April 1915 – 11 March 1997)

Torborg Lundell
University of California, Santa Barbara

BOOKS: *Tåbb med Manifestet: Historien om hur Tåbbs livsstil växte fram* (Stockholm: Tiden, 1943); translated in part by Naomi Walford as "Tåbb Knocks at the Door," in *Sweden Writes: Contemporary Swedish Poetry and Prose, Views on Art, Literature and Society,* edited by Göran Palm and Lars Bäckström (Stockholm: Prisma/Swedish Institute, 1965), pp. 68–79;

Inga ögon väntar mig (Stockholm: Tiden, 1944)–includes "Skändat rum," translated by Walter Johnson as "Polluted Room," in *Literary Review,* 9 (Winter 1965–1966);

Min död är min (Stockholm: Tiden, 1945);

Om (Stockholm: Tiden, 1946);

Jungfrun i det gröna (Stockholm: Tiden, 1947);

Fångnas glädje (Stockholm: Tiden, 1947)–includes "Effer år av tystnad," translated by Frederic Fleister as "After Years of Silence," in *Arts, Drama, Architecture, Music International Review,* 31 (1966), pp. 30–37;

Egen spis (Stockholm: Tiden, 1948);

Huset har ingen filial (Stockholm: Tiden, 1949);

Fromma Mord (Stockholm: Tiden, 1952);

Kanelbiten (Stockholm: Tiden, 1953); translated by Hanna Kalter Weiss as *Cinnamoncandy* (New York & London: Garland, 1990);

Stora Glömskan: Zackarias' första bok (Stockholm: Tiden, 1954);

Kvinna Kvinna (Stockholm: Bonnier, 1955);

Natt i Marknadstältet (Stockholm: Bonnier, 1957); translated in part by Walford as "How to Win a Lay-About for Science," in *Sweden Writes,* pp. 80–85;

Gilla gång (Stockholm: Bonnier, 1958);

Nattens ögonsten: En berättelse (Stockholm: Bonnier, 1958);

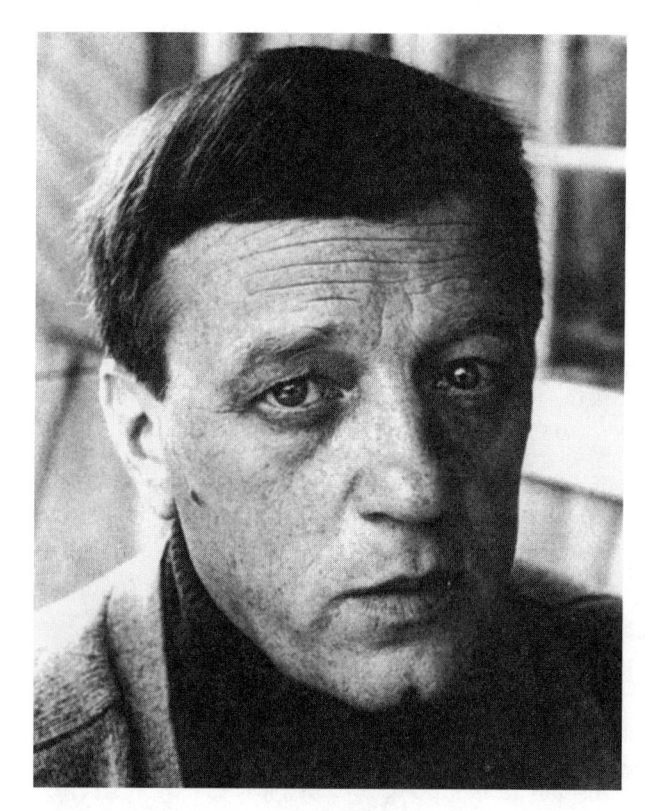

Lars Ahlin

Bark och löv (Stockholm: Bonnier, 1961);

Hannibal segraren, by Ahlin and Gunnel Ahlin (Stockholm: Bonnier, 1982);

Sjätte munnen (Stockholm: Bonnier, 1985);

Vaktpojkens eld: Berättelser (Stockholm: Bonnier, 1986);

Din livsfrukt (Stockholm: Bonnier, 1987);

De sotarna! De sotarna! Zackarias' andra bok (Stockholm: Bonnier, 1990);

Det florentinska vildsvinet (Stockholm: Bonnier, 1991);
Sjung för de dömda!: Sjung för dem som lever mellan tiderna! (Stockholm: Bonnier, 1995);
Breviarium (Stockholm: Bonnier, 1996).

Editions: *4 pjäser* (Stockholm: Bonnier, 1990);
Estetika essayer: Variationer och konsekvens (Stockholm: Bonnier, 1994).

PLAY PRODUCTION: *Lekpaus,* Royal Dramatic Theatre, Stockholm, 1948.

PRODUCED SCRIPTS: *Eld av eld,* radio, Sveriges Radio, 9 October 1949 and 19 October 1949;
"Öppen mot läsaren," radio talk, Sveriges Radio, 28 December 1961;
Väntande vatten, motion picture, by Ahlin from his short story "Kvinnan och döden," 1965;
"Världen är en övergående historia," radio talks, Sveriges Radio—comprises "Denna världen vår," 25 May 1966; "Fakta och fikta," 1 June 1966; "Sex punkter om Paulus," 28 June 1966;
Kommer hem och är snäll, television, by Ahlin from his short story, Sveriges Television, 11 January 1992.

OTHER: "Om ordkonstens kris," "Reflexioner och utkast," "Konstnärliga arbetsmetoder," reprinted in *Kritiskt 40-tal,* edited by Karl Vennberg and Werner Aspenström (Stockholm: Bonnier, 1948), pp. 9–57;
Eld av eld, in *Svenska Radiopjäser 1949* (Stockholm: Bonnier, 1950), pp. 95–139.

SELECTED PERIODICAL PUBLICATIONS—UNCOLLECTED: "Estetik och pragmatism," *Lundagård,* no. 11 (1947): 261–262;
"Ett brev," *Bonniers Litterära Magasin,* 30 (1961): 476–477.

Lars Ahlin belongs to the generation of great writers that blossomed in the 1940s and 1950s. He is among the first to indicate a change in artistic consciousness among Swedish writers by his rejection of the mechanisms of illusions of the traditional novel. The inspiration for his theories that the reader should be emotionally detached from characters and plot came from the French and German novels of the 1920s, though also the novels of Eyvind Johnson may have served as a model. He belongs to a school of writers that may be labeled "Christian realists," evoking a concept developed by Erich Auerbach in *Mimesis* (1946). Its foremost representative is Fyodor Dostoevsky. Ahlin sees the writer as a "förbedjare" (intercessor) or "identificator" (identifier) speaking on behalf of the poor, the miserable, and those without a voice of their own.

Lars Gustav Ahlin was born 4 April 1915 in Sundsvall in northern Sweden, the setting for most of his novels. He died 11 March 1997 in Stockholm, where he lived most of his life. His mother left her seven children when Ahlin was five years old, and the parents divorced in 1920. His father, a traveling salesman, was charming and full of stories but failed to provide for his family, which sank from middle-class to working-class status. For a while the children lived alone, taking care of themselves in a sibling community in Stockholm, but in 1922 they moved back to Sundsvall.

At the age of thirteen Ahlin had to leave school to support himself, which he did by selling odds and ends. After a short membership in the local YMCA and the International Order of Good Templar, he joined a Communist pioneer group because it gave him access to books and companionship. In 1933 he left this organization and Sundsvall and enrolled in Ålsta Folkhögskola (folk high school), where he met Arne Jones, an aspiring sculptor, who became a lifelong friend. Ahlin's novels often feature an artist as an important character. In 1936 he moved to Stockholm with Jones to become a writer and survived on odd jobs and a loan from a sympathetic teacher couple. In between writing novels that were rejected, he continued his education at various folk high schools, where he survived the winters thanks to the room and board they provided. He studied languages, literature, and philosophy, especially Karl Marx and Søren Kierkegaard. His main interest was theology. He read primarily Martin Luther, Anders Nygren, St. Paul, and Karl Barth. Though searching for a religious answer to the question of man's identity and worth, Ahlin also embraced the ideas of social democracy, although he rejected any labeling of his philosophy. His first novel, *Tåbb med Manifestet: Historien om hur Tåbbs livsstil växte fram* (Tåbb and the Manifesto: The Story About How Tåbb's Lifestyle Develops, 1943), was accepted by the Tiden publishing company. A productive period followed, during which novels or collections of short stories and theoretical essays appeared every year, in addition to hundreds of short stories published in newspapers and magazines. His last novel, *Det florentinska vildsvinet* (The Florentine Boar), was published in 1991. In 1946 he married Gunnel Hammar with whom he has a son, Per, born in 1948.

Ahlin's major theme concerns equality. He combines a social democratic view with the Lutheran rejection of social value based on positions in a social hierarchy. Man should, Ahlin believes, get his sense of value not from comparing himself or the status of his work to others but from seeing the value of his work as important in itself. Furthermore, since all people are interdependent, no one can be seen as more important than the other. Equality is attained in love, especially when it takes the form of agape love, making it analogous to God's unconditional love, which is indifferent to other notions of worth than love itself. In Ahlin's novels, love, like death, is a force that creates its own value through its disregard of and indifference to social worth.

The concept of death is another recurrent theme in Ahlin's work. He seems to have been inspired by Luther's lectures on St. Paul's letter to the Romans, especially with respect to the notion of eternal spiritual death that liberates man from worldly concerns. Karl Barth has also contributed to Ahlin's view on man. He shares Barth's condemnation of man's inclination to depend on institutions and systems for his sense of identity and meaning. There must be a profound change of heart, a leap of faith in a Kierkegaardian sense, and all demands for temporal, rational, and personal reassurance of worthiness must be abandoned, before man can truly "die" to the inescapable inequalities of the world. Christian and Marxist notions of death are similar in their notion of the paradox that only through death is it possible to find life or true identity. Death is thus to be understood as change. Ahlin often represents the distorted self-image of his characters through grotesque incidents and feeble and decrepit people. These characters initially base their self-image on distorted ideals, and they change when they experience the figurative death of their former distorted selves.

Ahlin's first two novels, finished in 1936 and 1939, were rejected, but his third, *Tåbb med Manifestet,* was published by the Tiden publishing company. In this novel the question of human value is discussed in terms of Tåbb's unemployment, which gives him no social value or identity, not even from the point of view of *The Communist Manifesto* (1848), his guideline in life. It deals only with the proletarian workers, and Tåbb is a lumpen proletarian, according to Marx a potential traitor to the socialist cause, because, being unemployed, he will see to his own fortune before he considers what is good for society.

During a May Day demonstration Tåbb realizes that he cannot emotionally share the sentiment of the Communist anthem, the Internationale, since he lacks proper proletarian status. This realization enables him to become aware that capitalist ideals destroy individual dignity by providing a model beyond the reach of most people. Tåbb concludes that only in death will people be free from values and subsequent feelings of degradation and worthlessness. He does not literally die, however. Eventually he ends up in his home village, where he works with his hands, fishes, hunts, and tends a garden. He has in a sense died to the *Manifesto* and reached an adulthood where he can accept opposing and yet coexisting qualities in life as well as in himself. He finds meaning in everyday work as such, a Lutheran attitude to life rather than Marxist.

The narrative flow is constantly interrupted by philosophical discussions and comments by one of the characters or the narrator. Some critics failed to see his structure as an expression of a new aesthetic and criticized him for his failure to conform to conventional "realism." Others hailed his novel as a new turn in Swedish literature. The critical reservations changed to enthusiasm over Ahlin's collection of short stories, *Inga ögon väntar mig* (No Eyes Are Waiting for Me), published in 1944.

This collection includes the one of Ahlin's finest stories, "Kommer hem och är snäll," (Coming Home and Being Nice), in which a worker coming home drunk on a Saturday evening tries to appease his wife with a bag of fruit but is unable to tell her he is sorry. She is unhappy because she cannot love him unconditionally, and instead of greeting him with a hug she sits down to peel potatoes. She is seized by existential despair, however, and throws her arms around him; they lie down together, knowing that though they may now make love, this scene will be repeated again and again. "Kommer hem och är snäll" was turned into a television drama in 1969. In the title story an unloved man is emotionally isolated from his family, who never looks into his eyes. "Inga ögon väntar mig" illustrates St. Paul's notion (1 Cor. 13:12) that seeing is an aspect of love. On the whole, the stories in this volume illustrate the Pauline saying: "I do not understand what I am doing, for I do not do what I want to do; I do things that I hate" (Rom. 7:15–19). In 1944 Ahlin received a grant from the Bonnier publishing house and the Svenska Dagbladet prize for literature, the first of many literary awards.

His next novel, *Min död är min* (My Death Is My Own, 1945), is based on Lutheran theology, as was convincingly demonstrated by Hans-Göran Ekman in *Humor, Grotesk och Pikaresk. Studier i Lars Ahlins Realism* (Humor, Grotesque and Picaresque: Studies in Lars Ahlin's Realism, 1975). The novel is divided into three parts. In the first, Georg Sylvan,

Ahlin in 1957 in front of the Villa Vingarna in Stockholm. The Swedish government had just given him the house as an award for his literary achievements (photograph by Pressens Bild).

a traveling salesman, meets Engla Käll, who takes in renters and does ironing. Sylvan's estranged wife, Olga, has suggested that he visit Engla, whom she sees as a suitable replacement; but Sylvan finds her physically repulsive and hates her trivial dreams of middle-class respectability. In their ensuing relationship he humiliates her sexually. In the second part, Sylvan and Engla celebrate midsummer in the country with a group of odd friends, reminiscent of characters from a Federico Fellini film. Frustrated by Sylvan's indifference to her, Engla hits him, her anger turning her into a raging fury. The incident changes their relationship: Sylvan is now able to face his humiliating failure as Olga's husband, and he begins to love Engla. In the third part Sylvan carries on lengthy discussions with Gösta, who feels inferior because he could not become a great artist but ended up as a tombstone cutter. Gösta seeks comfort in his philosophy of reversed values; he sees himself as standing above the common man, just because he stands below in conventional terms. Seeking to reach the extremes of defilement, he makes love to a decrepit and imbecile prostitute in a scene that shocked Ahlin's contemporaries. Gösta's act is an attempt to accept the ugly and the beautiful as equally important for the total person. Simultaneously, Sylvan finds that he can accept himself as a failure, and his degrading dependence on Olga for his definition of self-worth is gone. He and Engla can now truly relate to each other, in Buber's sense: they are separate people, she has been internalized by him and has become part of him. Similarly, her feelings are transformed, and she now sees them as two human beings united in suffering, a more intimate token of togetherness than any social ceremony.

In 1945 Ahlin also published two theoretical essays, "Om ordkonstens kris" (About the Crisis of the Art of Words) and "Reflexioner och utkast" (Reflexions and Sketches), in the journal *40-tal*. A third, "Konstnärliga arbetsmetoder" (Artistic Working Methods), was published in the same journal in 1947. These three pieces were reprinted in the anthology *Kritiskt 40-tal* (1948), edited by Karl Vennberg and Werner Aspenström.

Om (If/About/Around, 1946) is Ahlin's most daring and innovative experiment with narrative structure and his most thorough account of the destructiveness of social standards. Sixteen-year-old Bengt and his father, Peter, have been thrown out by Matilda. Peter's only ambition is to find a woman who will provide him with security for the rest of his life. Bengt, however, wants them to become self-supporting and independent. They go down to the river, hoping to find shelter in an old boat, and run into a drunken man, Oscar, waiting for his sister Sophia to take him home. Bengt begins to suspect that Sophia is his real mother, but she turns her back to him, symbolically rejecting him and motherhood. Peter wheels Oscar home in a wheelbarrow while he rambles on about the myth of motherhood, Western culture, and the father figure as a symbol of social order and structure.

Bengt finds a substitute father in Peter Sjökvist, but when he dies Bengt feels abandoned again. In the end he is free from commitments to past values and principles. His liberation is, however, passive, not a result of his conscious effort to stand on his own. The novel ends with an epilogue in which Ahlin outlines various scenarios for Bengt's future.

Om constitutes Ahlin's most consistently constructed alternative to and reaction against the "novel of illusion." He plays with point of view, which shifts constantly between an omniscient narrator, a first-person narrator, and Bengt introduces multiparts objects, thereby paradoxically creating distance to the characters through the analytical demand of this structure and at the same time involving the reader in the story. "Men nånting har hänt Bengt-mig-dig-honom-henne och vår obekante" (But something has happened Bengt-me-you-him-her and our unknown person). At times Ahlin uses three verbs to describe the same action in a sentence, inviting readers to choose which one might be most appropriate to the situation. "Min allra ömnaste 'Fru Moder,' hadahan . . . vishat-enyttajublat . . . " (My most tender "Lady Mother," he had . . . whispered-sobbed-rejoiced . . .). The reader is thus made into a collaborator in the novel and is frequently called upon to analyze its narrative structure or drawn into its many philosophical and aesthetic discussions.

After this experimental novel, Ahlin returned to a more conventional narrative structure in the novel *Jungfrun i det gröna* (Virgin in the Grass, 1947). He continues in this novel to explore the dichotomy between the ideal and reality, however. It is through his loving wife's caresses and belief in the right to live with dignity, even though one is not a successful man, that the protagonist accepts himself as the average man he is.

In 1947 he also published a collection of short stories, *Fångnas glädje* (The Joy of the Prisoners), where his central theme is loneliness and the ever-unsatisfied need for togetherness. The crippled woman in "Kvinnan och döden" (The Woman and Death) is used by men in her pathetic search for love and finally drowns herself. This story was made into a short film in 1965 titled "Väntande vatten" (Waiting Waters). The divorced father in the title story is used by his child, who exploits his father's need for love.

Ahlin's most amusing novel, *Egen spis* (A Stove of One's Own), was published in 1948. Here he sets a couple of go-getters, Herbert Lager and Evelyn Kull, against the happily asocial Harry and Sara Lustig and their family. The corrupt ambitions and selfishness of the go-getters prove to be less viable values than the love and compassion for all living things that characterize the Lustig family, however asocial they seem from a narrowly moralistic point of view. Harry Lustig's social inferiority is balanced by his spiritual superiority, and in the end, paradoxically, his world emerges as the one of order and purpose.

Ahlin has also written plays for the stage and radio. *Lekpaus* (Pause in the Game), was presented in 1948 at the Royal Dramatic Theatre in Stockholm, and *Eld av eld* (Fire from fire) was performed on the radio in 1950. Both plays were collected in *4 pjäser* (4 plays, 1990) along with the unproduced plays *Var angel är förfämde* (Every Angel is terrible) and *Gossarnade Små* (The Little boys).

Ahlin's impressive creative output of the 1940s ended with a collection of short stories, *Huset har ingen filial* (The House Has No Annex, 1949). The basic theme of the stories is that human love is not sufficient to save man from despair. Only faith in God and, as in the case of the woman artist in the title story, acceptance of one's loneliness will, paradoxically, fill man with a sense of togetherness and creativity.

Three years later Ahlin published another novel, *Fromma Mord* (Pious Murders, 1952). Here he explores the destructive impact of piety and idealism, illustrating the negative aspect of the human need to cling to some kind of belief in an unambiguous world instead of accepting the inexplicable dualism of the real world. A "pious" person in Ahlin's work is someone who thinks his commitment to a cause liberates him from his duties to his fellow man. *Fromma Mord* is another of Ahlin's intricately structured novels. Erik A. Nielsen, in *Lars Ahlin. Studier i sex romaner* (Lars Ahlin: Studies of Six Novels, 1968), sees in its fragmented form an illustration of the protagonist's isolation and his inability to communicate. Arne Melberg's discussion in *På väg från realismen: En studie i Lars Ahlins Författarskap, dess sociala och litterära forutsattnin-gar* of the dialectical pattern of the structure is especially illuminating.

This complicated and intricately structured novel was followed by *Kanelbiten* (1953; translated as *Cinnamoncandy*, 1990) about the relationship between a thirteen-year-old girl, Britt-Marie, and her mother, Sylvia, who is involved in an affair with a married man, Stellan. Sylvia is using her daughter to get her lover to leave his wife. Britt-Marie lies to Stellan's wife about being molested by him. Then she walks to the top of a hill, followed by Sylvia and her lover, who unite spiritually as they look into each other's eyes. Meanwhile, Britt-Marie performs an awkward dance and leaps off the cliff.

Her death is a result of her failure to accomplish total perfection. She cannot guide Sylvia's life in the right direction and make her live up to an ideal image of adulthood. Furthermore, Britt-Marie has not remained above unworthy acts herself in her lies to Stellan's wife. At the end she is redeemed by her death, which gives Sylvia the life with Stellan she was longing for.

In subsequent novels Ahlin focuses less on failure and more on love. This transition takes place in *Stora Glömskan: Zacharias' första bok* (The Great Amnesia: Zackarias' first book, 1954) set in the 1920s. The thirteen-year-old protagonist, Zacharias, is an idealized character who accepts life with all its flaws, pain, and joy. He first befriends a decrepit washerwoman, one of Ahlin's many old and often feeble women who represent a Lutheran-inspired notion of work as a form of love. Throughout the novel Zacharias searches for his father, who stands for spiritual freedom gained by rejecting social conventions and standards. His father does not return home until Zacharias has learned to accept death as the beginning of creation and understands that spiritual harmony comes when a man is free from restrictions of social conditioning in his view of self.

A key word in the novel is *glädje* (joy), a feeling that transports Zacharias from one reality to another without limitations of time, space, and reason. "Joy" describes a feeling of rebirth, a change of consciousness. Such change was in earlier novels defined as death. Through Zacharias's various experiences of joy his consciousness of self grows. His original wish to be without form or identity is in the end replaced with a need for a relationship with a woman. With this wish he has gained substance and identity, which, according to Ahlin, people acquire only in relating to others, especially in a male-female relationship.

Ahlin's next four novels continue to explore the many facets of love. His concept of love was especially inspired by Anders Nygren's *Eros and Agape* (1930), which Ahlin read during his formative years. In its ideal form, the novels suggest, love does not seek value but gives it.

In *Kvinna Kvinna* (Woman Woman, 1955), Torgny Larsson, a construction worker, lives apart from his wife, who tends the farm that she owns. He feels inferior to her because he, by contrast, has only his body and his working skills to call his own. He struggles with the conflict between his need for her and his need to feel independent and equal in their relationship. Gradually he realizes that his physical strength and her property are different but equal forms of power. He can reunite with Ester and is thus capable of loving and receiving love.

Natt i Marknadstältet (Night in the Market Tent, 1957) is Ahlin's most magnificent work on love. It is built around flashbacks, digressive episodes, and philosophical discussions involving Leopold, who left his wife, Paulina, because he felt humiliated and rejected. He returns during the hectic days of the market, on the same night the German consul's villa burns down. He left to seek money and social status because he believes he must earn Paulina's love with material success, although she already loves him unconditionally. Another important character is thirteen-year-old Zackarias, mature beyond his years, who is one of the author's alter egos in the novel. Afraid to fall in love with Klara, a slightly older woman whose warmth and sensuation both attracts and frightens him, he guides her around the marketplace and introduces her to the colorful assembly of people enjoying the market life. They run into Zackarias's father and Alexis Bring, the author's other alter ego, who lectures them on the nature of art and literature. Then Klara meets Jan-Alf, Paulina's illegitimate son, with whom she soon falls in love. Foreshadowing this development is a story about the eternal novelty of love, as preached by a sect of people who believed that just as each day is new, never to return, each person's past was of no concern in the present, therefore virginity was unimportant in love. Each relationship is new, that is, virginal.

When the market is almost over, Leopold returns to Paulina and tells her that he helped the German consul commit insurance fraud by setting his villa on fire. He now has money and feels worthy of Paulina's love. She is horrified, however, and when Leopold refuses to admit to any guilt she decides that she must kill him because he has turned love into a commodity that can be bought with tainted money. His value system is perverted by what Barth calls "social lusts." He sees his crime to obtain money as less shameful than accepting Paulina's love when he is poor. In the end Zacharias helps Paulina lift Leopold's dead body onto a cart, puts on a doll costume, and falls asleep with a smile between his tears. He has realized that even if he is an outsider, observing and recording the events of life, he is not free from despair and suffering, but his smile indicates that he is capable of accepting the paradoxes of life, love, and death.

In 1957 Ahlin was awarded a house to live in for the rest of his life. The following year he published a structurally less complicated novel than *Natt i Marknadstältet,* though it also has experimental qualities. In *Gilla gång* (Just As Usual, 1958) he utilizes neologisms and unconventional word formations to symbolize the distinctive qualities of love. The novel deals with an elderly couple, the school janitors Lage and Berta, and a crisis in their relationship. Lage's attitudes toward life are free of social prejudices, as is especially evident in his relationship to Gösta, who feels he must reject love because he accidentally killed a classmate when he was a boy. Lage wants to match Gösta with his daughter, Maria, who has been hurt in love and has returned home pregnant. When Berta wants her to have an abortion, Lage hits her; his belief in the absolute dignity of life leads him paradoxically to violate his wife's dignity and his love for her. Crushed by guilt for this act, he believes he must reject Berta, but she argues that the notion of unworthiness is irrelevant in a relationship based on love. In the end Lage realizes that love is a gift from God and not based on merit. He returns to Berta, and Maria and Gösta also plan to marry.

In 1960 Ahlin received two prestigious awards, the grand prize for fiction presented by the Samfundet De Nio (Society for the Nine) and the Boklotteriets Prize. The next year he published *Bark och löv* (Bark and Leaves), a novel about art and love. A writer, Erik, is in love with a painter, Aino. He wishes she would commit herself to him totally, but when his demands become too threatening to her as

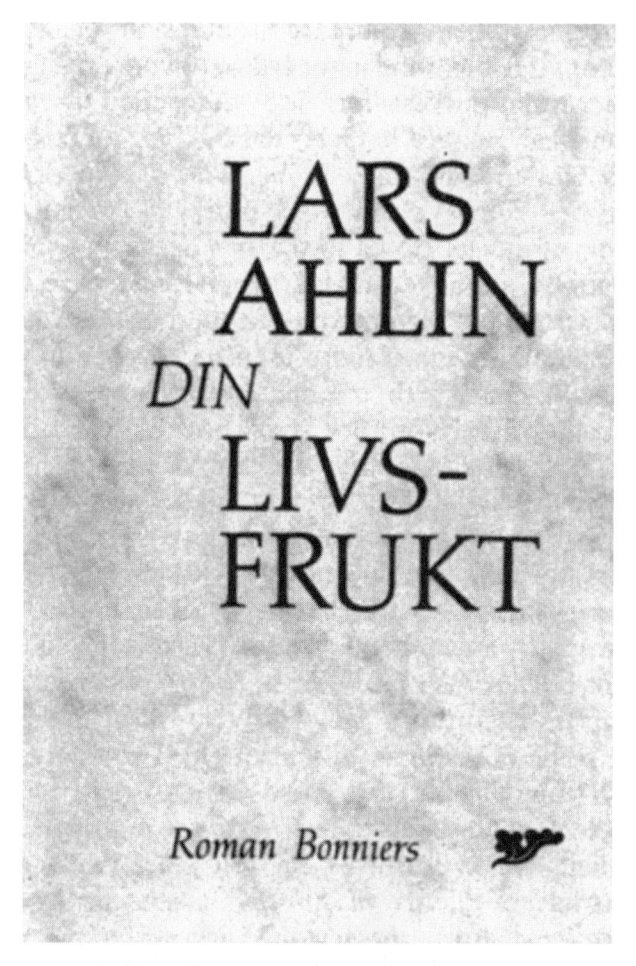

Dust jacket for Ahlin's 1987 novel, about an idealist who becomes a ruthless capitalist because of a deathbed promise to his mother (from Swedish Book Review, *1988)*

an artist, and an individual she leaves him and moves in with Georg, another writer. This development leads Erik to think back to his youth when Lee, now named Mats, was a boy working with eighty-year-old Lotten, who provided food and coffee for the dockworkers, that love is not about loving one person but is a way to relate to everybody. Erik's reflections are followed by a long monologue by Aino, who is experiencing a lack of communication between her and her audience that has made both art and life lose its meaning. In the last chapter Erik resumes his discussion with Aino about their relationship. She is now living with Georg because she is afraid of loving Erik. She keeps calling him, however. One day Georg leaves Aino and she returns to Erik, who seems to reject her at first. She caresses him and whispers "You . . . . ," thus indicating that she is ready to let him come close. The ending is reminiscent of Sylvan's relating to Engla as "Thou" in the Buberian sense in *Min död är min.*

Aino and Erik's new love signals a way to combine life, love, and art into a new language.

Though Ahlin did not publish a new novel for twenty-two years, he was not forgotten, nor was he totally silent. The government awarded him a guaranteed income for life in 1964, and in 1966 he developed a series of three radio lectures on his theories and philosophy under the general heading "Världen är en övergående historia" (The World Is a Transitory Affair). An interview with him, "Därför skriver jag" (Therefore I Write), was broadcast on Sveriges Radio in 1968, and in 1969 he was awarded an honorary doctorate by the University of Umeå. In *Bonniers Litterära Magasin* in 1970, later collected in *Estetiska essayer: Variatoner och Konsekvens* (Aesthetic Essays: Variations and Consequences, 1994), he published "In på benet" (To the Bone), in which he talks for the first time about a mystical experience in 1933 that became crucial to his concept of self and society. Sick and hallucinating, he experienced a profound revelation of the essence of existence. He realized intuitively that there exists a paradoxical kind of equality in our world, composed of extreme inequalities. In a sense the inequalities do not exist per se because they are based on interdependence between superior and inferior people whose status only exists in comparison with each other.

Ahlin's first novel in more than twenty years was co-authored with his wife, Gunnel. *Hannibal segraren* (Hannibal the Victor, 1982) explores the psychology of the wish for power and the relationship between a man of action and the one who records his actions and thus creates his image. They were awarded the Övralid Prize in 1982.

In 1985 Ahlin published *Sjätte munnen* (The Sixth Mouth), a straightforward novel about a father-son relationship without the philosophical discourses that characterize most of his earlier novels. It takes place in Sundsvall in the 1920s and has many autobiographical features. Jerker, a failure both as a husband and as a salesman, is trying to merge his family with that of Beda's. Eleven-year-old Hans is the sixth member of the family, which does not last long. Hans is more mature than his father, whom he loves boundlessly, regardless of his failure to secure a stable home for him.

In 1986 Ahlin was awarded the Fackförbundspress (Labor Union Press) Prize for literature. The same year he published *Vaktpojkens eld: Berättelser* (The Watch Boy's Fire: Stories), a collection of his stories from the 1940s and 1950s. Most of these stories deal with loneliness, at times interrupted by touches of love and feelings of togetherness. In the title story, as in the others, a teenager, not yet corrupted by the value system of adults, stands for Ahlin's belief in the interdependence and equality of all things. The teenager rebels against his parents' striving for a materially better life and skips school to nourish his fantasies at "vid randen avde vuxnae öken" (the edge of the adult's desert).

Ahlin's next novel, *Din livsfrukt* (The Fruit of Your Life, 1987), is an exciting and difficult work in the tradition of his earlier great novels. Unlike the characters from his earlier works, who tend to come from the lower social strata of society, those in this novel are wealthy capitalists. Yet, they are plagued by the same problem as his other characters: the difficulty of acquiring a feeling of self-worth in the context of the superficial ideals of modern society and culture. Again, love or its failure is one of the most important features in a character's view of self and life. The main character, Johannes, stands to inherit a fortune from his mother and follows his guardian's advice to become a business lawyer. He intends to donate his wealth to the Social Democratic Party, but his mother, on her deathbed, makes him promise to change his plans. Instead, he becomes a ruthless capitalist and tax cheat, thus increasing his wealth immensely. To lull his conscience he regularly donates to an African hospital.

Johannes's unrequited love for his mother keeps him from maturing. He is a loner except for his friendship with an artist, Östen, who talks to him about altruism. Eventually he finds the joy of love and being loved when he meets Lisbet, a successful businesswoman. They have a child who is mentally retarded, and Lisbet subsequently kills herself. Johannes's health is not stable, and rather than risk that his daughter will be taken to an institution where she will not be cared for properly, he decides to kill both of them. Material wealth and worldly success are thus shown to be no protection against personal misery and failure in love. Östen, despite his success as an artist, dies from alcoholism.

The novel is, from one point of view, deeply pessimistic. It is also deeply religious and can be read as a warning to contemporary man, who is heading the wrong way in his pursuit of external values. Only religious faith will save man from despair, as Julitta, the old housekeeper who embodies Christian unconditional love, demonstrates. As often in Ahlin's novels, a woman of low social status who spends her life nurturing and nourishing her family is a living example of love.

Johannes's story is interspersed with long discussions about contemporary events and politics and Ahlin's ever-present ideas about equality and man's interdependence, which he argues should entitle everyone to equal status and comfort in life. Ahlin comments on the philosophers that Johannes reads, Kierkegaard, Friedrich Nietzsche, and Jean-Paul Sartre, and uses Johannes's discussions with Östen to share his views on aesthetics, especially regarding the social responsibility of art and semiotics.

In 1988 Ahlin was awarded the prestigious Selma Lagerlöf Prize. In 1990 he published *De sotarna! De sotarna! Zackarias' andra bok* (The Chimney Sweeps! The Chimney Sweeps! Zackarias' Second Book), which received the August Prize distributed by Svenska Forläggareföreningen. In 1991 the cultural committee in Sundsvall, his birth town, endowed a Lars Ahlin Fellowship. The same year he published his novel *Det florentinska vildsvinet,* in which he, through the life of Ivo, an artist, discusses the role of love and sex in relationships. In this book and the previous book he also displays his fondness for playing with the language by introducing jargon and phrases from foreign languages. A collection of essays and talks from the 1940s, 1950s, and 1960s was published in 1994 under the title *Estetika essayer*. This book was followed by *Sjung för de dömda!: Sjung för dem som lever mellan tiderna!* (Sing for the doomed ones!: Sing for those live between the times, 1995). In 1996, the year before his death, he published *Breviarium* (Breviary), a collection of his letters to fellow writers and pieces on such diverse figures as Henrik Ibsen, Aristophanes, Catullus, and Susan B. Anthony.

Lars Ahlin's death, on 11 March 1997, marked the end of an era of great writers from the 1940s and 1950s. He was praised for his innovative approach to the novel, though some found that reading his novels required much intellectual work. He viewed equality as a human right defiled by the society-wide focus on hierarchies of merit. In love and death, Ahlin argues, people are equal, because neither discriminates between the upper and lower classes. Still, the complexity and erudition of his novels at times seem to contradict his egalitarian philosophy; he seems to speak for the economically disadvantaged and uneducated rather than to them. Ahlin is the writer of his generation who most consistently developed in his novels a philosophy of man that reflects the ideals of the contemporary Swedish welfare society. He had a vivid imagination and a talent for creating unforgettable characters and events, often bordering on the grotesque. His mixture of the vulgar and the sublime interrupted by his lectures on the philosophical problems facing modern man resulted in novels that entertain as well as teach.

Interview:

Carl Magnus von Seth, "Därför skriver jag," Sveriges Radio, 7 September 1968.

References:

Lars Åke Augustsson, "Lars Ahlin: A Swedish Writer of European Stature," *Cambridge Quarterly,* 9 (1979): 1–17;

Staffan Bergsten, "Lars Ahlins mystiska grundupplevelse," in *Från Snoilsky till Sonnevi: Litteraturvetenskapliga studier tillägnade Gunnar Brandell,* edited by Jan Stenkvist (Stockholm: Natur och Kultur, 1976), pp. 154–172;

Anna Boëthius, "Ensamhet och gemenskap i 'Natt i Marknadstältet,'" in *Synpunkter på Lars Ahlin,* pp. 91–121;

Hans-Göran Ekman, "En bok i boken—om Lars Ahlins majevtiska metod," *Komma,* 2 (1967): 16–18;

Ekman, "Humor och ironi i 'Natt i Marknadstältet,'" in *Synpunkter på Lars Ahlin,* pp. 122–151;

Ekman, *Humor, Grotesk och Pikaresk. Studier i Lars Ahlins realism* (Staffanstorp: Cavefors, 1975);

Furuland, "Lars Ahlin—ursprungsmiljö och bildningsväg," in *Synpunkter på Lars Ahlin,* pp. 9–42;

Furuland, ed., *Synpunkter på Lars Ahlin* (Stockholm: Aldus/Bonnier, 1971);

Lennart Göthberg, "På väg mot en ny klassicism," in *Kritiskt 40-tal,* edited by Karl Vennberg and Werner Aspenström (Stockholm: Bonnier, 1948), pp. 179–188;

Lars Gustafsson, Sven Linner, and Victor Svanberg, "Tre kring Lars Ahlin," *Ord och Bild,* 71 (1962): 155–162;

Gunnar D. Hansson, "Den dubbla tillhörigheten: En tolkning av Lars Ahlins humoruppfattning,'" *Tidskrift för litteraturvetenskap,* 1 (1971–1972): 97–109, 234–247;

Olov Hartman, "Den ringastes like," in his *Jordbävningen i Lissabon* (Stockholm: Rabén & Sjögren, 1968), pp. 112–123;

Kai Henmark, "Det levande namnet," in his *En fågel av eld: Essäer om dikt och engagemang* (Stockholm: Rabén & Sjögren, 1962), pp. 147–188;

Henmark, "Jämlikheten," "Lars Ahlins estetik-håller den?" "Sabotage mot autoritära former," in his *Jämlikheten och samtalet: Ett 60-tal artiklar och essäer* (Stockholm: Rabén & Sjögren, 1970), pp. 27–30, 65–70, 70–73;

Karl-Erik Lagerlöf, "Lars Ahlin och maskerna," in his *Samtal med 60-talister* (Stockholm: Bonnier, 1962);

Sven-Erik Liedman, "Den religionsbefriade världen: En studie om Bonhoeffer och Lars Ahlin," *Bonniers Litterära Magasin,* 31 (1962): 555–561;

Ulf Linde, "Det Ahlinska alternativet," *Bonniers Litterära Magasin,* 29 (1960): 464–475;

Linde, "Mun mot öra," *Bonniers Litterära Magasin,* 34 (1965): 249–250;

Erik Hjalmar Linder, "Lars Ahlin och 'Fromma Mord'" in *Guds Pennfäktare och andra essayer* (Stockholm: Natur och Kultur, 1955), pp. 185–195;

Torborg Lundell, *Lars Ahlin* (Boston: Twayne, 1977);

Lundell, "Lars Ahlin's Concept of Equality," *Scandinavian Studies,* 47 (1975): 339–351;

Lundell, "Lars Ahlin's Concept of the Writer as *Identificator* and *Förbedjare*," *Scandinavica,* 14 (1975): 27–35;

Arne Melberg, "Försoningens ideologi," *Bonniers Litterära Magasin,* 42 (1972): 30–38;

Melberg, *På väg från realismen: En studie i Lars Ahlins författarskap, dess sociala och litterära förutsättningar* (Stockholm: Gidlund, 1973);

Erik A. Nielsen, *Lars Ahlin: Studier i sex romaner,* translated by Jan Gehlin (Stockholm: Bonnier, 1968);

Ragnar Oldberg, "Lars Ahlin," in his *Nutidsförfattare: Prosaister och lyriker i ung svensk litteratur* (Stockholm: LT:s, 1950), pp. 115–127;

Saga Oscarsson, "Jämlikhetstemat in 'Natt i Marknadstältet,'" in *Synpunkter på Lars Ahlin,* pp. 43–90;

Göran Palm, "Jämlikhet i konflikt," *Bonniers Litterära Magasin,* 30 (1961): 808–812;

Palm, "Lars Ahlin and the New Swedish Novel," in *Sweden Writes: Contemporary Swedish Poetry and Prose, Views on Art, Literature and Society,* edited by Palm and Lars Bäckström (Stockholm: Prisma/Swedish Institute, 1965), pp. 86–95;

Palm, "Luther i Äppelviken," *Bonniers Litterära Magasin,* 35 (1965): 247–250;

Marc van den Steen, "Lars Ahlins jämlikhetsestetik: En nyckel till 'Bark och Löv,'" dissertation, Rijksuniversiteit Gent, 1979–1980;

Birgitta Trotzig, "Till de levandes lov," *Bonniers Litterära Magasin,* 34 (1964): 237–246.

Ingmar Bergman
(14 July 1918 -)

Birgitta Steene
University of Washington

BOOKS: *Jack hos skådespelarna* (Stockholm: Bonnier, 1946);

Moraliteter: Tre pjäser av Ingmar Bergman (Stockholm: Bonnier, 1948)–comprises *Rakel och biograf vakt mästaren, Dagen slutar tidigt,* and *Mig till skräck;*

En filmtrilogi: Såsom i en spegel, Nattvardsgästerna, Tystnaden (Stockholm: Norstedt, 1963); republished as *Filmberättelser 1* (Stockholm: PAN/Norstedt, 1973); translated by Paul Britten Austin as *A Film Trilogy* (London: Calder & Boyars, 1967; New York: Orion, 1967);

Persona (Stockholm: Norstedt, 1966);

Filmberättelser 2: Ingmar Bergman: Persona; Vargtimmen; Skammen; En passion: Persona and Skammen (Stockholm: Norstedt, 1968); includes "Persona" and "Skammem," translated by Keith Bradfield and others as *Persona and Shame: The Screenplays of Ingmar Bergman* (New York: Grossman, 1972; London: Calder & Boyars, 1972); and "En passion," by Alan Blair as "The Passion of Anna," in *Four Stories* (New York: Doubleday, 1976), pp. 95–129, 131–168;

Filmberättelser 3: Ingmar Bergman: Riten; Reservatet; Beröringen; Viskningar och rop (Stockholm: Norstedt/Pan, 1973); includes "Beröringen" and "Viskningar och rop," translated by Blair as "The Touch" and "Cries and Whispers" in *Four Stories by Ingmar Bergman,* pp. 7–56; 57–94;

Scener ur ett äktenskap (Stockholm: Norstedt, 1973); translated by Blair as *Scenes from a Marriage* (New York: Pantheon, 1974; London: Calder & Boyars, 1974);

Ansikte mot ansikte (Stockholm: PAN/Norstedt, 1976); translated by Blair as *Face to Face* (New York: Pantheon, 1976; London: Boyars, 1976);

Ormens ägg (Stockholm: PAN/Norstedt, 1977); translated by Blair as *The Serpent's Egg* (New York: Pantheon, 1977; London: Boyars, 1978);

Höstsonaten (Stockholm: PAN/Norstedt, 1978); translated by Blair as *Autumn Sonata* (New York: Pantheon, 1978);

Ingmar Bergman (Svensk Filmindustri)

Ur marionetternas liv (Stockholm: Norstedt, 1980); translated by Blair as *From the Life of the Marionettes* (New York: Pantheon, 1980);

Fanny och Alexander (Stockholm: Norstedt, 1982); translated by Blair as *Fanny and Alexander* (New York: Pantheon, 1983);

Laterna magica (Stockholm: Norstedt, 1987); translated by Joan Tate as *The Magic Lantern* (New York: Viking, 1988; London: Hamilton, 1988);

Bilder (Stockholm: Norstedt, 1990); translated by Marianne Ruuth as *Images: My Life in Film* (New York: Arcade, 1994; London: Bloomsbury, 1994);

Den goda viljan (Stockholm: Norstedt, 1991); translated by Tate as *The Best Intentions* (New York: Arcade, 1993; London: Harvill, 1993);

Söndagsbarn (Stockholm: Norstedt, 1993); translated by Tate as *Sunday's Children* (New York: Arcade, 1994); translation republished as *Sunday's Child* (London: Harvill, 1994);

Femte akten: Monolog, Efter repetitionen, Sista skriket, Larmar och gör sig till (Stockholm: Norstedt, 1994); translated by Tate and Linda Haverty Rugg as *The Fifth Act* (New York: New Press, 2001);

Enskilda samtal (Stockholm: Norstedt, 1996); translated by Tate as *Private Conversations* (London: Harvill, 1996);

3 för 1: Den godd viljan, Söndagbarn, Enskilda samtal (Stockholm: Norstedt, 1998);

Föreställningar: Trolösa, En själslig angelägenhet, Kärlek utan älskare (Stockholm: Norstedt, 2000)–includes *En sjalslig angelägenhet*, translated by Eivor Martinez as *A Matter of The Soul* in *New Swedish Plays* (Norwich: Norvik Press, 1992), pp. 33–64.

Edition in English: *Four Screenplays of Ingmar Bergman*, translated by David Kushncr and Lars Malmström, with a foreword by Carl Anders Dymling (New York: Simon & Schuster, 1960)–comprises *Smiles of a Summer Night, The Seventh Seal, Wild Strawberries,* and *The Magician.*

PLAY PRODUCTIONS: "Kaspers död," Stockholm, Student Theatre, 24 September 1942;

"Tivolit," Stockholm, Student Theatre, 19 October 1943;

Rakel och biografvakmästaren, Malmö, Intiman Theatre, 12 September 1946;

Dagen slutar tidigt, Gothenburg, City Theatre, Studio Stage, 12 January 1947;

Mig till skräck, Gothenburg, City Theatre, Studio Stage, 26 October 1947;

"Kamma noll," Helsingborg, City Theatre, 8 December 1948;

Rakel och biografvakmästaren, Stockholm, Boulevard Theatre, 9 November 1949;

"Mordet i Barjärna, Ett passionsspel," Malmö, City Theatre, Intiman Stage, 14 February 1952;

Jack hos skådespelarna, Lund, Lilla teatern, 21 January 1953;

Trämålning, Malmö, City Theatre, Intiman Stage, 18 March 1955.

PRODUCED SCRIPTS: *Hets,* motion picture, Svensk Filmindustri, 1944; released as *Torment,* 1944;

Kris, motion picture, based on Leck Fischer's play *Moderhjeret,* Svensk Filmindustri, 1946;

Det regnar på vår kärlek, motion picture, adapted from Oskar Braaten's play *Bra mennesker,* by Bergman and Herbert Grenevius, Sveriges Folkbiografer, 1946;

Kvinna utan ansikte, motion picture, by Bergman and Gustaf Molander, Svensk Filmindustri, 1947;

Skepp till Indialand, motion picture, adapted from Martin Söderhjelm's play, Sverige Folkbiografer, 1947; released in United States as *Frustration,* 1949;

Hamnstad, motion picture, by Bergman and Olle Länsberg, adapted from Länsberg's novel *Guldet och murarna,* Svensk Filmindustri, 1948; released in United States as *Port of Call,* 1959;

Eva, motion picture, by Bergman and Gustaf Molander, Svensk Filmindustri, 1948;

Musik i mörker, motion picture, adapted from Dagmar Edqvist's novel by Bergnam and Edqvist, Terrafilm, 1948; released as *Night is My Future,* 1963;

Fängelse, motion picture, Terrafilm, 1949; released as *The Devil's Wanton,* 1952;

Till glädje, motion picture, Svensk Filmindustri, 1950; released as *To Joy,* 1950;

Medan staden sover, motion picture, adapted from Per Anders Fogelström's novel by Bergman and Lars-Eric Kjellgren, Svensk Filmindustri, 1950;

Sommarlek, motion picture, adapted from Bergman's short story by Bergman and Herbert Grenevius, Svensk Filmindustri, 1951; released in United States as *Illicit Interlude,* 1954;

Frånskild, motion picture, by Bergman and Herbert Grenevius, Svensk Filmindustri, 1951;

Kvinnors väntan, motion picture, Svensk Filmindustri, 1952; released in United States as *Secrets of Women,* 1952;

Sommaren med Monika, motion picture, adapted from Fogelström's novel, Svensk Filmindustri, 1953; released in United States as *Summer with Monika,* 1956;

Gycklarnas afton, motion picture, uncredited, Sandrews, 1953; released in United States as *The Naked Night,* 1956;

En lektion i kärlek, motion picture, Svensk Filmindustri, 1954; released as *A Lesson in Love,* 1960;

Kvinnodröm, motion picture, Sandrews, 1955; released in United States as *Dreams,* 1960;

Sommarnattens leende, motion picture, Svensk Filmindustri, 1955; released as *Smiles of a Summer Night,* 1955;

Sista paret ut, motion picture, adapted from Bergnam's story, by Bergman and Alf Sjöberg, Svensk Filmindustri, 1956; released as *Last Couple Out,* 1956;

Det sjunde inseglet, motion picture, Svensk Filmindustri, 1957; released as *The Seventh Seal,* 1958;

Smultronstället, motion picture, Svensk Filmindustri, 1957; distributed as *Wild Strawberries,* 1959;

Nära livet, motion picture, adapted from Ulla Isaksson's short story "Det vänliga, det värdiga," by Bergman and Isaksson, Nordisk Tonefilm, 1958; released as *Brink of Life,* 1959;

Ansiktet, motion picture, Svensk Filmindustri, 1958; released as *The Magician,* 1959;

Djävulens öga, motion picture, Svensk Filmindustri, 1960; released as *The Devil's Eye,* 1961;

Jungfrukällan, motion picture, adapted from a medieval Swedish ballad titled "Töres dotteri Vänge," Svensk Filmindustri, 1960; released as *The Virgin Spring,* 1960;

Såsom i en spegel, motion picture, Svensk Filmindustri, 1961; released as *Through a Glass Darkly,* 1962;

Lustgården, as Buntel Eriksson, by Bergman and Erland Josephson, motion picture, Svensk Filmindustri, 1961;

Nattvardsgästerna, motion picture, Svensk Filmindustri, 1962; released as *Winter Light,* 1963 ;

Tystnaden, motion picture, Svensk Filmindustri, 1963; released as *The Silence,* 1964;

För att inte tala om alla dessa kvinnor, motion picture, by Bergman and Erland Josephson, Svensk Filmindustri, 1964; released as *All These Women,* 1964;

Persona, motion picture, Svensk Filmindustri, 1966; released in English, 1967;

"Daniel" in *Stimulantia,* motion picture, by Bergman and others, Svensk Filmindustri, 1967;

Vargtimmen, motion picture, Svensk Filmindustri, 1968; released as *The Hour of the Wolf,* 1968;

Skammen, motion picture, Svensk Filmindustri/Cinematograph AB, 1968; released as *Shame,* 1968;

Riten, motion picture made for television, Cinematograph/SVT, 25 March 1969; released in United States as motion picture *The Ritual,* 1969;

En passion, motion picture, Svensk Filmindustri/Cinematograph AB, 1969; released as *The Passion of Anna,* 1969;

Fårö-dokument 69, television, documentary, Cinematograph AB/SVT 2, 1 January 1970;

Reservatet, television, SVT, channel 2, 1970; released in United States as *The Sanctuary,* CBS, 24 April 1973;

The Lie, television, BBC, 1970;

Beröringen, motion picture, Cinematograph AB/ABC, 1971; released as *The Touch,* 1971;

Viskningar och rop, motion picture, Svenska Filminstitutet/ Cinematograph AB, 1972; released in United States as *Cries and Whispers,* 1972;

Scener ur ett äktenskap, television, miniseries, SVT, 1973; released as motion picture in United States *Scenes from a Marriage,* 1974;

Bergman circa 1941

Trollflöjten, television, SVT, Channel 1, 1 January 1975; released as motion picture *The Magic Flute,* 1975;

Ansikte mot ansikte, motion picture, Sveriges Radio/Cinematograph AB, 1976; released in United States as *Face to Face,* 1976;

Das Schlangenei, motion picture, Rialto Film, 1977; released in United States as *The Serpent's Egg,* 1977;

Herbstsonate/Höstsonaten, motion picture, ITC/Personafilm, 1978; released as *Autumn Sonata,* 1978;

Fårö-dokument 79, television, documentary, Cinematograph/SVT 2, 25 December 1979; also released in United States as motion picture, 1980;

Aus dem Leben der Marionetten, motion picture, ITC/Personafilm, 1980; released as *From the Life of the Marionettes,* 1980;

Fanny och Alexander, television, SVT 2, 1982; released as *Fanny and Alexander,* 1983;

Efter repetitionen, television, Swedish TV, 1984; released as *After the Rehearsal,* 1984;

Karins ansikte, motion picture, Svenska Filminstitutet, 1986; released as *Karin's Face,* 1986;

Dokument Fanny och Alexander, motion picture, Svenska Filminstitutet/Cinematograph AB, 1986; released as *Document Fanny and Alexander,* 1986;

Den, Goda viljan, television, Swedish TV, 1991;

Markisinnan de Sade, television, Swedish TV, 1992;

Goda viljan, Den, motion picture, SVT Drama, 1992;

Söndagsbarn, motion picture, Svenska Filminstitutet, 1992; released as *Sunday's Children,* 1992;

Sista skriket, television, SVT, 1995; released as *The Last Gasp,* 1995;

Enskilda samtal, television and motion picture, by Bergman and Liv Ullmann, SVT 2, 25, 26 December, 1996; released as *Private Conversations/Private Confessions,* 1996;

Larmar och gör sig till, television, SVT 1, 1 November 1997; released as *In the Presence of a Clown,* 1998;

Trolösa, motion picture, by Bergman and Ullmann, Svensk Filmindustri, 2000; released as *Faithless,* 2001.

OTHER: "I mormors hus," in program for Göteborg City Theatre production of *Mig till skräck* (1947);

Staden, in *Svenska radiopjäser* (Stockholm: Sveriges Radio, 1951), pp. 41–95;

"Spöksonaten," in program for Malmö City Theatre production of August Strindberg's play (1954);

Trämålning, in *Svenska radiopjäser* (Stockholm: Sveriges Radio, 1954), pp. 9–61; translated by Randolph Goodman and Leif Sjöberg as "Painting on Wood," *Tulane Drama Review,* 6, no. 2 (November 1961): 140–152;

"Why I Make Movies," translated by P. E. Burke and Britt Halvorson, in *The Emergence of Film Art,* edited by Lewis Jacobs (New York: Hopkinson & Blake, 1969);

"Program Note," translated by Birgitta Steene, in *Focus on the Seventh Seal,* edited by Steene (Englewood Cliffs, N.J.: Prentice-Hall, 1973), pp. 70–71;

A Matter of the Soul, translated by Gunilla M. Anderman in *New Swedish Plays* (Norwich, U.K.: Norvik, 1992).

SELECTED PERIODICAL PUBLICATIONS—
UNCOLLECTED:

FICTION

"En kortare berättelse om en av Jack Uppskärarens tidigaste barndomsminnen," *40-tal,* no. 3 (1944): 5–9;

"Sagan om Eiffeltornet," *Bonniers Litterära Magasin,* 22, no. 9 (November 1953): 498–500.

NONFICTION

"Det förtrollade marknadsnöjet," *Biografbladet,* 28, no. 3 (Fall 1947): 1;

"Ruth," *Filmnyheter,* 2, no. 11 (1947): 1–4;

"Tre tusenfotingfötter," *Filmjournalen,* 29, no. 51–52 (December 1947): 8–9, 54;

"Kinematograf," *Biografbladet,* 29, no. 4 (Winter 1948): 240–241;

"Filmen om Birgitta-Carolina," *Stockholms-Tidningen,* 18 March 1949, p. 1;

"Fisken: Fars för film," *Biografbladet,* 31, no. 4 (Winter 1950): 200–225; 32, no. 1 (Spring 1952): 18–21; no. 2 (Summer 1952): 85–88; no. 3 (Fall 1952): 110–115;

"Vi är cirkus!" *Filmjournalen,* 35, no. 4 (1953): 7, 31;

"Aforistiskt av Ingmar Bergman," *Vi på SF* (April 1957), n.p.;

"Dialog," *Filmnyheter,* 13, no. 11 (1958): 1–3;

"Varje film är min sista film," *Filmnyheter,* 14, no. 9–10 (1959): 1–8; translated by P. E. Burke and Lennart Svahn as "Each Film Is My Last," *Films and Filming,* 5, no. 10 (1959): 8, 28;

"Extract in Memory of Victor Sjöström," *Sight and Sound,* 29, no. 2 (Spring 1960): 98–100;

"Förbön," *Chaplin,* 2, no. 8 (1960): 187;

"Away with Improvisation—This Is Creation," *Film and Filming,* 7, no. 12 (September 1961): 13;

"Jag tvivlar på Filmhögskolan," *Chaplin,* 5, no. 12 (December 1963): 304–305;

"Fantastic Is the Word," *Film World,* no. 3 (1968): 4–5;

"Nu lämnar jag Sverige," *Expressen,* 22 April 1976, pp. 4–5;

"Jeder Mensch hat Träume, Wünsche, Bedürfnisse," in *Verleihung des Goethepreises der Stadt Frankfurt am Main an Ingmar Bergman am 28. August 1976 in der Paulskirche* (Frankfurt am Main: Dezernat Kultur und Freizeit); republished as "Der wahre Künstler spricht mit seinem Herzen," *Filmkunst,* 74 (1976): 1–3.

Ingmar Bergman, Swedish author and movie and theater director, is one of the foremost contributors to postwar European cinema and a leading stage interpreter of such playwrights as William Shakespeare, Molière, Henrik Ibsen, and August Strindberg. Making his published debut as a writer in 1944 in the magazine *40-tal* with the short story "En kortare berättelse om en av Jack Uppskärarens tidigaste barndomsminnen," and as a playwright in 1948 with his *Moraliteter,* Bergman has written virtually all of the screenplays to his more than fifty feature movies, creating a new hybrid genre between script, stage play, and novel, in which he avoids the technical format of regular movie scripts and presents texts that are self-contained literary companion pieces to his works. This practice garnered him in the 1950s the reputation of being the world's foremost *auteur du cinéma,* a term coined by French movie critics to designate an artist who combined a literary and visual talent to transmit the art of storytelling to the screen,

Still from Bergman's motion picture Det sjunde inseglet *(The Seventh Seal, 1957), in which Death (Bengt Ekerot) and the knight Antonius Block (Max von Sydow) play a game of chess (photograph © AB Svensk Filmindustri)*

while relying on a personal vision and style that in earlier times might have been expressed through the pen.

Recognized all over the world, Bergman has received many awards for his artistic achievements, including several Swedish Golden Beetle movie awards, Academy of Motion Picture Arts and Science awards, and other movie and theater prizes. He has also been given the David O. Selznick Award from the Producers Guild of America in 1961; the European Erasmus Prize in 1966; the Italian di Donatelli Award in 1974; an honorary doctorate in 1975 and honorary professorship in 1980 at Stockholm University; the Goethe Prize in 1976; the Alger H. Meadows Award for Excellence in the Arts in 1981; the French Legion of Honor in 1985; and an honorary doctorate from the Sorbonne in 1986.

Born at the Academic Hospital in Uppsala on Sunday, 14 July 1918, as the middle offspring of three children in a bourgeois clerical family, Ernst Ingmar Bergman was a sickly child whose arrival coincided with a crisis in his parents' marriage. His mother, Karin, had fallen in love with a young theology student, while his father, Lutheran pastor Erik Bergman, showed signs of a nervous condition that affected family life for the duration of Bergman's childhood. The marriage, though founded on love, was a mismatch. Karin Bergman, née Akerblom, came from a university milieu of prominent educators and engineers. Erik Bergman's origins were more humble: his father, an apothecary, died relatively young, and his mother supported herself and her son with the help of relatives and a seamstress job. Karin was determined to marry Erik, despite her parents' disapproval, which was not based solely on Erik's social background; they were also worried about the fact that she and Erik Bergman were distant cousins.

At the time of Bergman's birth, the family lived in the Östermalm section of Stockholm, where his father held a position in the Lutheran state church. The appointment was socially enhanced by the fact that he was at times called upon to serve as chaplain at the Swedish Court and as spiritual adviser to the queen. Maintaining a proper facade became part of the family's lifestyle. Years later, in his *Laterna magica* (1987; translated as *The Magic Lantern*, 1988), Bergman likened the situation to that of a stage performance where he and his parents and siblings were assigned certain roles: "En prästfamilj lever som på en bricka, oskyddad för insyn. Huset måste alltid stå öppet. Församlingens kritik och kommentar är konstant" (A parson's family lives as if on a platter, unprotected from public view. The home must always be open. The congregation's critique and commentary are constant).

When Bergman grew up, Sweden was still a fairly remote and provincial corner of northern Europe, a society rooted in a homogenous Lutheran culture. The social structure was hierarchic and class-divided. To the Bergman children—Ingmar; an older brother, Dag; and a younger sister, Margaretha—it seemed that life was regulated by a whole set of authorities: parents, teachers, government officials, God himself. In their world children were taught self-castigation and learned to look upon themselves as guilt-ridden sinners, as Bergman later recalled: "Mina tidigaste minnen är förknippade med förödmjukelser.... Hela samhället var byggt så att människor hade möjllghet att förödmjuka varandra, uppifrån och ner. Se på Syndabekännelsen i Luthers katekes: 'Jag stackars syndig människa, i synd född' ... Det är bara en hemsk form av förödmjukande" (My earliest memories are connected with humiliations.... All of society was so structured that people had an opportunity to humiliate each other, from above and down. Look at the Confession of Sins in Luther's Catechism: 'I poor sinful creature, born in sin.' ... It is nothing but a terrible form of humiliation). Such statements reveal the dark and self-denigrating undertones of Bergman's upbringing. They surface in some of his early stage plays, most specifically in *Mig till skräck* (Unto My Fear, 1948) and *Staden* (The City, 1951), dramatic pieces filled with young weltschmerz.

Throughout his career Bergman has reiterated the importance of his childhood memories to his creative works. Deep-rooted early experiences have continued to emerge in adulthood as fleeting images and vignettes and have often been the incentive behind a script or other literary text. Bergman also made an early acquaintance with the technical rudiments of staging and moviemaking, however, for as a child and teenager he engaged in puppetry and motion-picture projection as two hobbies at home. On festive occasions his mother arranged large family gatherings that included magic lantern shows and marionette displays. These early activities soon developed into a passion in young Bergman and determined his life's role at a relatively early age, much to the chagrin of his parents, who expected him to pursue academic studies, as would be proper for the offspring of an upper-middle-class family. Bergman did enroll as a student of literature at Stockholm University in 1938 but never completed a degree.

Bergman's early experience as an amateur puppeteer came to serve as a metaphor for a deterministic view of life. In his early plays for the theater he often cast his characters as doomed creatures governed by forces beyond their control. *Dagen slutar tidigt* (The Day Ends Early, 1948) is structured as a morality play in which all the dramatis personae are predestined to die shortly. In *Jack hos skådespelarna* (Jack among the Actors, 1946), which Bergman unsuccessfully submitted as a radio play, the characters are in the hands of a satanic director who tells them: "Se jag tickte inte att det skulle vara så dumt att ... skapa ett litet världsallt för några människor. Och jag gjorde det.... Så har jag setat där och ryckt i mina trådar. Ryck, ryck. Och människorna har lytt mig" (I thought it would be a good idea to ... create a cosmos for a few people. And so I did. Now I sit here and pull my strings. Pull, pull, jerk, jerk! The figures have obeyed me).

The puppeteer concept, which had been explored earlier by one of Bergman's admired authors, Hjalmar Bergman (no relation), survives in different forms in many of Bergman's works. It has operated as a psychological metaphor throughout his career, providing the title of his German-produced motion picture from 1980, *Aus dem Leben der Marionetten* (also released as *From the Life of the Marionettes*), in which "the medical protocol" of a murderer, Peter Egerman, suggests his mental collapse as the inevitable result of a lifelong series of human betrayals. In that motion picture, friends and family provide a more psychologically motivated form of determinism than Bergman's conceptually rather abstracted demonic director in *Jack hos skådespelarna*. In varying transformations, however, the diabolic puppeteer figure keeps returning in Bergman's oeuvre as a force of evil that forms an essential part of his vision of life, as he explains in *Berman om Bergman* (1970): "Vad jag har trott på, och trodde på länge, var att det existerar en virulent ondska som inte på något sätt är beroende av miljö eller arvsfaktorer. Vi kan kalla det arvsynden eller vad som helst—en aktiv ondska, som människan till skillnad från djuren är allideles ensam om.... Som materialisation av denna virulenta, ständigt existerande och obegripliga, för oss ofattbara,

Motion-picture director Victor Sjöström as Professor Isak Borg in a still from Bergman's Smultronstället *(1957), released in the United States as* Wild Strawberries *(photograph © AB Svensk Filmindustri)*

oförklarliga ondsko till-verkade jag en person som hade den medeltida moralitetens djävulsdrag. . . . Hans ondska var en fjäder i urverket" (What I have believed in . . . is the existence of a virulent evil that is not connected in any way to a specific milieu or to hereditary factors. We can call it original sin or anything—an active evil that man alone, unlike the animals, possesses. . . . In order to materialize such a virulent, constantly present and unfathomable evil—incomprehensible and inexplicable to us—I made up a person who had the diabolic features of a medieval morality play figure. . . . His evil was a spring in the clockwork).

Moved to a metaphysical level, the representation of an omnipotent puppeteer director finds its analogy in the silent god figure who gains a hold on many of Bergman's characters. Such an invisible and distant god turns the knight Antonius Block in *Det sjunde inseglet* (also released as *The Seventh Seal,* 1957) into a fanatic quester, compelling him to leave his newlywed wife to participate in a futile ten-year crusade. A similar power, imagined as a rapist god, separates Karin, the schizophrenic young woman in *Såsom i en spegel* (1961; also released as *Through a Glass Darkly*), from her husband and emerges as "the spider god" in the mind of pastor Tomas in *Nattvardsgästerna* (1963; released as *Winter Garden*), leading him to fail his congregation.

The different ramifications of the puppeteer/marionette concept in Bergman's works might be juxtaposed to the significance of the magic lantern, the other important object in his childhood activities. Bergman became the excited owner of a kerosene-lit projector when he was ten or eleven years old. He placed the rickety machine in a dark nursery closet, quite possibly the same one in which he had been locked up as a form of punishment and told that nasty goblins lived there who chewed off the toes of naughty children. The closet trauma appears as a psychological reference in several Bergman movies, including *Fängelse* (1949; also released as *The Devil's Wanton,* 1952), *Vargtimmen* (1968; also released as *The Hour of the Wolf*), and *Ansikte mot ansikte* (1976; also released as *Face to Face*).

The magic lantern motif reaches its fullest expression in *Fanny och Alexander* (1982, also released as *Fanny and Alexander,* 1983), which might be called Bergman's resurrection of childhood. It is a story set about ten years before his own birth and using the thirteen-year-old male title figure as his vulnerable and defiant alter ego. Alexander's life oscillates between two families, the histrionic and fun-loving Ekdahls and the stern Vergeruses, headed by his stepfather, a Lutheran bishop. These are two contrasting milieus that represent much of the social contours and mindscape of Bergman's own background.

The Vergeruses' world, with its rigid moralism and old-fashioned child rearing, bears a certain resemblance to the Bergman home on Storgatan in Stockholm, facing the imposing Hedvig Eleonora church. The family dwelt literally in the shadow of its high cupola. Bergman only lived there during his mid teens, but he turned the address into a metaphor for his own troubled adolescence, perhaps contrasting the high-ceilinged Storgatan apartment to the yellow wooden vicarage in the Lilljans Forest where he had spent most of his early childhood, in a house next to the Sofia Hospital, a private dispensary situated in a park-like setting, beyond which was the open countryside: "Even on the ground floor," Bergman told Marianne Höök, author of *Ingmar Bergman* (1962): "Även på markplanet var gardinerna aldrig fördragna på de mörka vinterkvällarna; i mors fönster stod en lampa med skär skärm som tjänade som fyr när vi sprang hem på kvällarna genom den blåsiga svarta parken" (the blinds never had to be drawn in the dark winter evenings; in Mother's window there was a lamp with a pink lampshade, which served as a beacon when we ran home in the evenings through the windy, black park).

The past gives narrative and visual shape to many of Bergman's movies through plot, costume, and setting. Selective childhood recollections find their artistic counterpart in his frequent use of flashbacks, most specifically in such movies as *Sommarlek* (1951; also released as *Illicit Interlude,* 1954), *Smultronstället* (1957; also released as *Wild Strawberries,* 1959), and *Viskningar och rop* (1972; also released as *Cries and Whispers*) in which repressed memories and subconscious fantasies are unveiled with both painful and healing consequences. By reliving her youth, the ballet dancer Mari in *Sommarlek* can finally come to terms with the loss of her lover many years earlier; and in *Smultronstället,* the aging professor Isak Borg finds both peace of mind and self-recognition through visualized traumatic recollections of his youth and unhappy marriage. In *Viskningar och rop* glimpses of the past lives of four women—three sisters and a housekeeper—are revealed in flashbacks that are signaled by red fade-outs, a shade that Bergman associates as the color of the soul. The journeys back in time are always Proustean journeys into the inner mental world of his characters.

Bergman's childhood world is also a source of sensuous joy that can give him renewed strength and comfort. Such pleasant recollections of the past are often associated with his maternal grandmother and her huge apartment in Uppsala, where young Bergman spent a good deal of time as a sickly child. Anna Åkerblom, a widow at age forty, lived alone in fourteen rooms together with her old housekeeper and surrounded by the same furniture as when she moved into these quarters as a young bride. Hers was an obsolete world, but to Bergman it seemed not faded so much as suspended in time, a place where people and objects had never been young and yet never aged. About this milieu and his relationship to it, Bergman wrote in the program notes for the premiere production of *Mig till skräck:* "Det är en värld som . . . bara existerar i minnet men som alltid är närvarande. Den är visserligen sluten och hemlighetsfullt vänd bort ifrån oss men den innebär alltid något stimulerande" (It is a world that . . . only exists in memory; but it is always present. True, it is hermetic and secretively turned away from us, but it always implies something stimulating). In *Laterna magica* he calls it ". . . en sjunken värld av ljus, dofter, ljud . . . I stillheten hos mormor öppnade sig mina sinnen och de beslöt sig att bevara allt detta för alltid" (a sunken world of light, smells, sounds . . . In the stillness at Grandma's my senses opened up and they decided to keep all this forever).

His grandmother's turn-of-the-century home, which he recalls as cluttered with various objets d'art and resounding with the ticking of clocks and the scratching of ink pens composing letters and diary notes, is recaptured in such movies as *Viskningar och rop* and *Fanny och Alexander.* To young Bergman his aging grandmother and her housekeeper took on mythic proportions. As such they were to lend their features to many clever and wise old crones in his works, pointing most obviously to the granny in the two plays *Staden* and *Mig till skräck,* as well as to the partly allegorical figure of Mrs. Åström in *Dagen slutar tidigt.* But they also inspired such portraits as the witty old Mrs. Armfeldt in *Sommarnattens leende* (1955; also released as *Smiles of a Summer Night*), Isak Borg's old mother in *Smultronstället,* who refuses to die; and the herb-collecting granny in the Vogler entourage in *Ansiktet* (1958; also released as *The Magician,* 1959) whose rapport with the innocent young Sanna takes on a fairy-tale quality; and finally as the wise and sensitive grandmother Helena Ekdahl and her grumpy old cook and housekeeper in *Fanny och Alexander.*

Bergman's professional debut took place in 1939 when he was invited to assume charge of an amateur theater group at Master Olofsgården, a Christian set-

Bergman in 1959 on the island of Fårö, the location for several of his movies and his home since the mid 1960s

tlement house in Stockholm's Old City, at that time a poor section of town. Bergman had just left his parents in a rage after a fight and moved in temporarily with the head of the settlement center, Sven Hansson, and his wife, Karin. Hansson served as a mediator between parents and son and received monetary compensation from the Bergman household for young Bergman's room and board. Hansson also solved conflicts that soon arose at the settlement center as Bergman shocked the board members with his foul language, his rehearsals on Sundays during morning service, and his rigorous and long training sessions. Productions took place on makeshift stages in an assembly hall ordinarily used for religious services or in school auditoriums. For his first production, Sutton Vane's play *Outward Bound* (1923), Bergman transformed the pulpit in the assembly hall into a bar on board a ship. Soon voices were heard demanding his dismissal.

Nevertheless, a little more than a year later Bergman was chosen the most valuable volunteer in the settlement's youth work. All the traits of his later creative activity were already clearly visible: a formidable work pace, with a dozen productions in a little more than a year; a great ingenuity in solving sceno-graphic problems; a ruthless directorial discipline combined with joyful enthusiasm; a focus on plays with moral and existential problems but also an ambition to provide a varied repertory that would appeal to a large variety of spectators; and an ability to make his productions visible. Even though Bergman's stagings were nonprofessional, the daily newspapers in Stockholm began to carry brief notices about them, and professional actors and other theater people occasionally came to a performance, among them the German playwright in exile at the time, Bertolt Brecht.

By the early 1940s Bergman was enrolled at Stockholm University but never pursued any academic degree. He attended the lectures of Professor Martin Lamm, a prominent Strindberg scholar, and wrote a seminar paper on Strindberg's fairy play *Himmelrikets nycklar* (1892; translated as *The Keys of Heaven*, 1945), which he had staged in his puppet theater at home. The paper reads like a prompt copy for a production; clearly, the live theater and the performance on stage attracted Bergman more than any academic pursuits. Soon he devoted most of his time to the Student Theatre, directing works by Strindberg and writing plays of his own, which were never published and are now apparently lost. One of them, "Kaspers död" (Death of Punch, 1942), attracted the attention of Stina Bergman, wife of author Hjalmar Bergman and head of the manuscript department at Svensk Filmindustri (SF). Under Stina's robust tutelage, Bergman made his entry into the movie world as a script reader. He was encouraged to submit synopses of his own. One of these was filmed in 1944, the year SF celebrated its twenty-fifth anniversary as a production company by launching a series of ambitious projects. Bergman's script *Hets* (also released as *Torment,* 1944) was directed by Alf Sjöberg, an established moviemaker and prominent director at the Royal Dramatic Theatre. Upon its release *Hets* caused one of the most intense public debates in the history of the Swedish cinema. Introduced by Bergman in a program for *Hets* as "kniv på en varböld" (a knife on a pus-infected boil), the movie depicts a case of bullying at a boys' school in Stockholm and was seen as Bergman's personal attack on the entire Swedish school system. As the author of the script he received more media attention than the director of the work and became notorious almost overnight.

During his formative years as an artist, in the 1940s, Bergman's ambitions were not only to forge a spot for himself in Swedish moviemaking but to gain national recognition as a stage director. Between 1946 and 1950, having left his apprentice years in amateur stage groups behind, he came to play a decisive role in theaters outside the capital. Assuming the directorship of the small City Theatre of Hälsingborg in southern Sweden, Bergman turned a stage threatened by financial collapse into a modestly lucrative and artistically noteworthy theater. After two years he moved on to the City Theatre in Göteborg on the Swedish west coast, which during the preceding ten years had been one of the most respected stages in the country. Under the tutelage of its artistic director, Torsten Hammarén, Bergman learned the simple yet difficult basics of working with actors: some are to be encouraged to stay, others are to be dismissed. But it was also in Göteburg that he met with a severe critique of his own playwriting; soon he shifted his authorship focus to screenplays while continuing to explore his lifelong fascination for the stage by producing the works of other playwrights. The world of moviemaking would always seem a precarious balancing act to him, whereas the theater was like a familiar home, providing security and vital contact. He himself once likened his dual commitment to stage and screen as the cinema being his mistress and theater his faithful wife. Returning to Stockholm in 1950, Bergman hoped in vain for an engagement at the Royal Dramatic Theatre. At the same time, Swedish movie companies had closed their studios in a lockout action to protest the high entertainment tax. Bergman was in professional limbo. To survive he wrote and produced a series of commercials for a deodorant soap, manufactured by the Sunlight Corporation. Though full of clever humor and wit, and characterized by Bergman's sense of timing, the commercials signify what must be considered a low point in his career.

Bergman's precarious economic situation as a moviemaker in 1950–1951 came as no surprise to him. Between 1945 and 1950 he had made ten feature movies for three different Swedish production companies. Some of these early works were reasonably successful, such as *Hamnstad* (1948; also released as *Port of Call,* 1959) and *Törst* (Thirst, 1949), but others were financial disasters, among them *Fängelse* (1949; also released as *The Devil's Wanton,* 1952) and threatened his future chances as a director. After *Fängelse* a well-known newspaper commentator in Stockholm, Kardemumma, gave Ingmar Bergman the epithet "Ordförande i svenska ång estunionen" (Head of the Swedish Angst Union).

By then Bergman had gained an inside look at what he termed a "brutal" commercial industry. He entered the Swedish movie market long before it became a state-supported and subsidized enterprise in 1963. In the 1940s and 1950s studio competition was often hard, production schedules were hectic, and the director was viewed as a market investment. Times were still booming in the 1940s, but many movie companies were fly-by-night operations and the moviemaking profession offered little security. Because he was fully aware of the complex economic nature of the industry, Bergman found it necessary to formulate his own work ethics in order to maintain his sense of integrity and to survive in the movie production world. In an essay titled "Det att göra film" (1954; translated as "Why I Make Movies," 1969), which was first presented as a talk at Lund University and later published in the SF-sponsored movie journal *Filmnyheter,* Bergman likened his role in the cinema to that of an acrobat performing a rope dance, balancing between popular demand and his own artistic needs. He issues what he calls his "tre kraftig verkande budord" (three most powerful commandments): to always be entertaining, to never prostitute one's art, and to look upon each new movie project as the last, that is, to focus on the motion picture in the making while keeping in mind the fickle nature of a money-making industry. In "Det att göra film" Bergman not only voices his artistic codex, but he also riles the production companies

Bergman circa 1960 (from Ingmar Bergman, The Magic Lantern, *1988)*

that curtail his creative freedom with their emphasis on box-office success.

In 1952 Bergman left Stockholm again, this time to assume the artistic directorship at the Malmö City Theatre in southern Sweden. The six years that followed are remarkable years both in terms of innovative stage productions and a steady stream of movies that eventually established Bergman on the international scene. Some of his stage productions traveled to Paris and London, and during his Malmö period he also wrote and directed such screen works as *Gycklarnas afton* (1953; also released as *The Naked Night,* 1956), *En lektion i kärlek* (1954; also released as *A Lesson in Love,* 1960), *Sommarnattens leende, Det sjunde inseglet, Smultronstället, Nära livet* (1958; also released as *Brink of Life,* 1959), and *Ansiktet.*

The various geographic areas where Bergman lived prior to the 1960s left their mark on his screenplays. In the movies before 1960 one can distinguish two specific visual styles and subject matters related to Bergman's domicile at the time. The first is a Stockholm period in which he capitalizes on a cultural dichotomy already present in the Swedish cinema since the 1930s: the juxtaposition of a problematic life in the big city versus the innocence and purity of country living. Among early Bergman movies from the Stockholm period are *Sommarlek* and *Sommaren med Monika* (1953; also released as *Summer with Monika,* 1956). Both capture the pastoral beauty of the archipelago outside the Swedish capital, with glittering waterways and the ambience of early mornings suffused with a pale, lyrical sunlight and of northern nights never quite conquered by darkness. It is a landscape of privacy and retreat, and with a particular Bergmanesque tone of ephemeral joy.

The second period is the Skåne period, stemming from the time when Bergman lived in Malmö. The flat terrain of the Skåne province may have helped create the silhouetted visual style of a movie such as *Gycklarnas afton* (1953; also released as *The Naked Night,* 1956) or the opening vignette of *Ansiktet* with Vogler's traveling troupe projected against a wide expanse of horizon. A starker world, amid marital problems and midlife artistic crises, emerges in these works.

Gycklarnas afton, generally considered one of Bergman's first masterpieces, was not well received at its initial opening. Many of his preceding movies had been shot by Gunnar Fischer, whose forte was capturing the romantic moods of a Swedish summer landscape. *Gycklarnas afton* was photographed by Hilding Bladh and Sven Nykvist, and included an expressionistic, overexposed opening sequence, depicting the humiliation of Frost, the circus clown, and his bedraggled wife, Alma, who—undressed and swimming in the nude—is cheered and taunted by soldiers on a cannon practice. The sequence has no audible speech but features Swedish composer Karl Birger Blomdahl's modernistic atonal music, especially composed for the motion picture. This form of moviemaking was totally different from the idyllic and youthful eroticism exposed in some of Bergman's earlier movies. *Gycklarnas afton* was also Bergman's first costume movie, set around the turn of the last century, and constituted a break with his previous contemporary motion-picture stories.

By the time Bergman left the Malmö City Theatre in 1958, he had behind him a stage career where his once dubious reception as a playwright had turned into an enthusiastic recognition of him as Sweden's most remarkable theater director. Critics now flocked to his productions of such plays as Goethe's *Urfaust,* Strindberg's *Spöksonaten,* Molière's *Don Juan* and *The Misanthrope,* and Ibsen's *Peer Gynt,* and he had formed, at Malmö, his own stable of actors who would follow him in his moviemaking: Max von Sydow, Ingrid Thulin, Harriet Andersson, and Bibi Andersson, to mention a few. At the same time Bergman had established himself as a box-office success in the cinema, both in Sweden and abroad. On the home front he had gained reputation as a women's director with such screen works as *Kvinnors vantan* (1952; also released as *Secrets of Women*), *En lektion i kärlek, Kvinnodröm* (1955; also released as *Dreams,* 1960), and *Sommarnattens leende*—all of them focusing on mature and independent women who learn to cope with the self-centeredness and betrayal of lovers and husbands. With the exception of *Kvinnodröm,* these motion pictures belong to Bergman's "rose period," as termed by Marianne Höök; they project a tone of sophisticated humor and erotic badinage in the tradition of such directors as Mauritz Stiller and Ernst Lubitsch.

Bergman's reputation in the comic genre pleased his major producer, Svensk Filmindustri, but his suggestion to make a movie based on a religious theme did not. However, after the international recognition of *Sommarnattens leende* at the 1956 Cannes Film Festival, it became difficult for SF to deny Bergman's repeated request to realize his idea of a movie set in the Middle Ages that tells the story of a crusader in search of God. The script was based on a stage play, *Trämålning* (1954; translated as *Painting on Wood,* in the *Tulane Drama Review,* 1961), which Bergman had written as a practice piece for his acting students in Malmö. As a concession, SF gave Bergman the modest sum of 75,000 kronor (at the time about $15,000) and thirty-five shooting days to make *Det sjunde inseglet*. True to form, he disciplined himself to complete the shooting in thirty-four days and within the allotted budget. The motion picture cemented his moviemaking reputation abroad; American critic Andrew Sarris, writing in *Film Culture* (April 1959), hailed *Det sjunde inseglet* as "the first truly existential work for the cinema." It paved the way for such major Bergman works of the 1950s as *Smultronstället, Ansiktet,* and *Jungfrukällan.*

In 1958 Bergman turned forty years old and was now at the peak of his career both as a movie and theater director. *Det sjunde inseglet* also signaled an oncoming crisis, however, in which Bergman dramatized his attempts to free himself from his religious heritage. The existential and metaphysical questioning, reflected in Bergman's major screen works from *Det sjunde inseglet* to *Tystnaden* (1963; also released as *The Silence,* 1964), was similar, in an inverted fashion, to Strindberg's midlife "psychosis," known as his "*Inferno* crisis." While Strindberg emerged from his mental upheaval with a newborn religious faith, Bergman liberated himself from his Christian background and became an agnostic, though still recognizing the presence of spiritual realities.

Inspired in part by Strindberg's medieval historical drama *Folkungasagan* (1899; translated as *The Saga of the Folkungs,* 1931), *Det sjunde inseglet* is structured like a medieval morality play in which an Everyman figure, the knight Antonius Block, returning from the Crusades to his native Sweden, encounters a series of allegorized figures, such as Death and representatives of the Holy Family. Traveling with his skeptical squire, the knight's quest seems more modern than medieval, however, and the central idea is closer to postwar existentialist thinking than to a fourteenth-century religious crusade.

Block's strong, desperate, and defiant figure reemerges in *Jungfrukällan* as the medieval farmer Töre, whose young and beautiful daughter is raped and murdered on her journey to church to offer candles to the Virgin Mary. Unlike *Det sjunde inseglet*—which seems to end in futile prayer as Block speaks for his entourage while facing Death, who has come to claim them all—Töre in *Jungfrukällan* expresses a *quia absurdum est,* telling God that he cannot understand his cruelty, yet vowing to build a church on the spot of his daughter's murder in order to honor him. In both *Det sjunde inseglet* and *Jungfrukällan,* God is taunting, distant, and silent. In the subsequent tril-

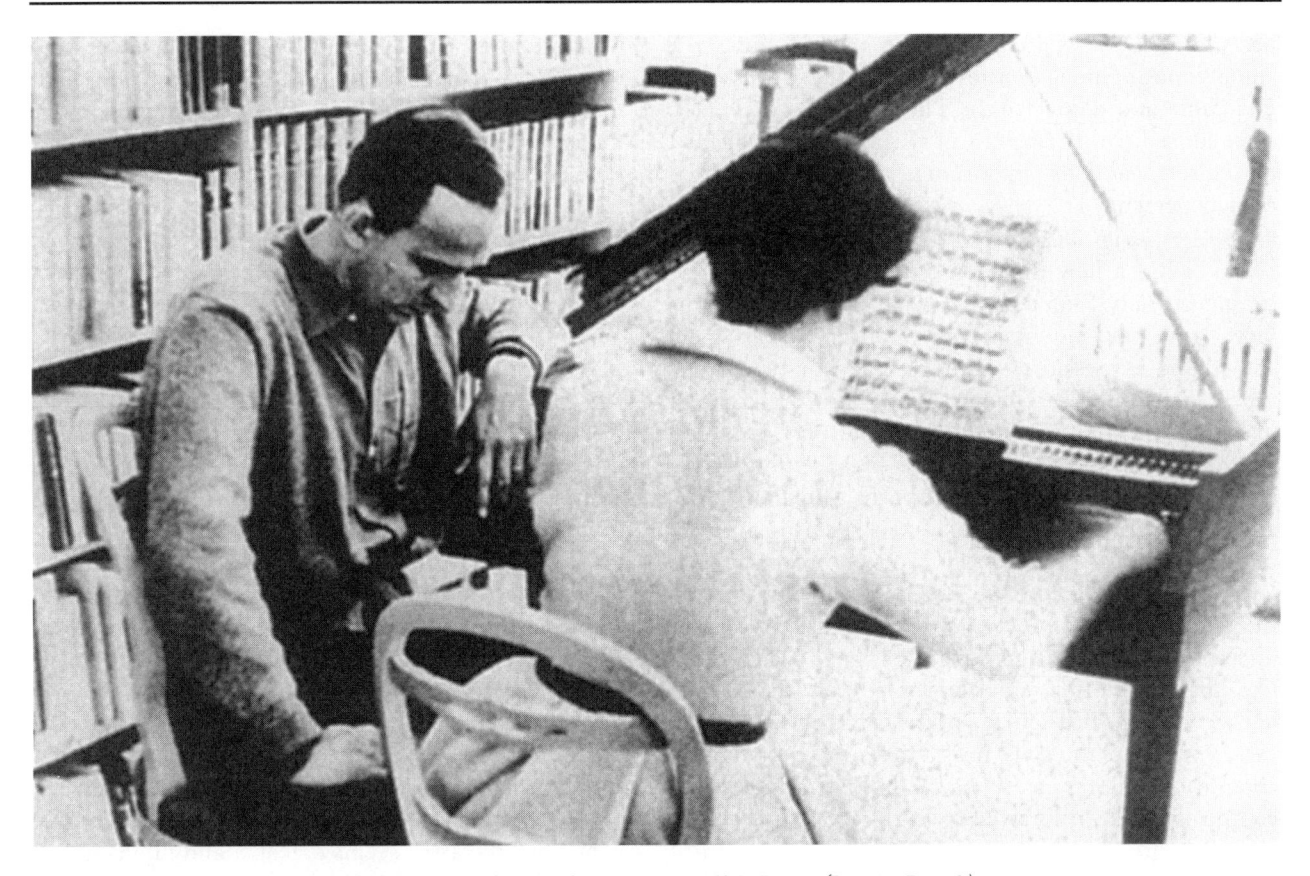

Bergman and his fourth wife, concert pianist Käbi Laretei (Proprius Records)

ogy of *Såsom i en spegel, Nattvardsgästerna,* and *Tystnaden* this godhead emerges as a usurping "spider god" who spreads anguish in those who seek him and leaves behind a psychological and metaphysical void.

These three movies constituting Bergman's trilogy tell their separate stories. What they have in common is the progression of a theme that pertains to what might be called God's silence. In a motto, printed in the 1963 edition of the screenplays, Bergman suggests that "Dessa tre filmer handlar om en reducering. *Såsom i en spegel*–erövrad visshet, *Nattvardsgästerna*–genomskådad visshet. *Tystnaden*–Guds tystnad–det negativa avtrycket." (These three films deal with a reduction. *Through a Glass Darkly*–conquered certainty. *Winter Light*–disclosed certainty. *The Silence*–God's Silence–the negative imprint.) The setting of each motion picture reflects this movement toward nihilism. *Såsom i en spegel* takes place in an isolated summer retreat on an island; *Nattvardsgästerna* (1963; also released as *Winter Garden*) is set in two almost empty country churches during the dark season of the year; *Tystnaden* is confined to a decadent hotel in a world at war. Parallel with a growing mood of negative certainty and increasing sense of entrapment, the trilogy displays a failure in human communication and a gradual distrust of the spoken word.

In *Det sjunde inseglet* the knight challenges God to speak to him. God remains silent, however, and the knight's words turn against him when he unwittingly reveals his chess strategy to his opponent, Death. In *Såsom i en spegel* the father, David, who is an author, discloses his curiosity about his daughter's illness in a diary; his words, discovered by the sick Karin, destroy her trust in him and help push her into madness. In *Nattvardsgästerna* the sound of the words spoken by Tomas, the Lutheran minister, to the schoolteacher Märta about his choice of calling drown in the noise of a passing freight train. In *Tystnaden* words are either unintelligible or are used as missiles by the two sisters, Anna and Ester, to hurt each other. In a world without God, a new language will have to be born. Ester, a translator by profession, begins to decipher the foreign language in the strange city of Timoka and gives a list of words to her young nephew, Johan, to take along as he and Anna continue their journey. Among the words are *kasi* (face) and *naigo* (hand). They suggest two honored concepts in Bergman's moviemaking approach: the close-up and the importance of touch, physical rapprochement.

In making *Såsom i en spegel* Bergman claimed to have "found a new direction for myself by concentrating on only four people," as he said in an interview from the movie journal *Chaplin* (1961). He coined the expression "chamber film" for this new type of screen work. The term was a direct reference to Strindberg's concept of the chamber play, formulated in 1907 and referring to a presentation of a small group of characters confined to a single locale and with their dramatic situation structured like a musical chamber piece, that is, with variations on a leitmotif for a few instruments. In similar fashion, Bergman now abandoned the larger orchestration of his earlier movies and no longer designed his stories like journeys in time and place. Gone are the flashbacks and historical settings of the motion pictures of the 1950s, and the only music heard in Bergman's chamber movies are a few bars of a Bach or Brahms composition, always played on a single instrument.

A crucial event occurred in Bergman's life while he was scouting for a location to film *Såsom i en spegel:* through cinematographer Sven Nykvist he discovered the island of Fårö–in part a military reserve characterized by moorlands and strangely formed limestone rocks called *raukar*. To Bergman, Fårö quickly became significant as both a real and a symbolic place. He made it his permanent home; at the edge of the Baltic Sea on an isolated part of the island he built a compound, including a private screening room and some technical facilities. After settling there in the mid 1960s he only returned to Stockholm for professional reasons.

Fårö is a sparsely populated outpost in a modern welfare state. In 1969 Bergman felt called upon to draw political attention to the island with a realistic television movie, *Fårödokument* (Fårö Document). Fårö functions also as the metaphorical setting for the screen narratives that could be called Bergman's "island movies": besides *Såsom i en spegel,* they include *Persona* (1966), *Vargtimmen, Skammen* (1968; also released as *Shame*), *En passion* (1969; also released as *The Passion of Anna*) and *Beröringen* (1971; also released as *The Touch*). These motion pictures depict characters–often artists–trapped in various dead-end crises. The road is no longer the spatial metaphor of the motion pictures, as was the case in *Det sjunde inseglet* and *Smultronstället,* but is replaced by the island landscape, as bleak and confining as a sickroom, yet absolute in its envelopment by the sea. *Skammen* can serve as a representative example. Two musicians who have both played in the same orchestra are forced to leave the mainland because of a vaguely defined civil war. Taking refuge on an island, they fail to remain outside the conflict; they are demoralized and destroyed by the events until finding themselves, at the end, with a few other refugees in a rowboat, drifting out into the endless sea, yet hemmed in by floating bodies of dead soldiers.

Bergman's island movies are starker and visually more ascetic than his earlier, richly orchestrated works. They possess a cohesiveness in mood and theme, however, that the more eclectic series of motion pictures of the 1950s lack. Bergman's portrayal of the artist reaches its culmination at this point, but the artist is without creative spark and without an audience. The difference is significant between, on one hand, Jof, the juggling actor in *Det sjunde inseglet,* or Albert Emanuel Vogler, the magic healer in *Ansiktet,* and, on the other hand, the paranoid, unproductive painter Johan Borg in *Vargtimmen* or the demoralized musician Jan Rosenberg in *Skammen*. Earlier representations of the artist oscillated between martyrdom and healing magic, while in later depictions the artist seems defeatist and nihilistic.

This development of the artist can be traced by juxtaposing two of Bergman's best-known essays: "Det att göra film" and "Ormskinnet" (The Snakeskin, 1965–1966). In the former piece Bergman formulates a metaphor of the artist as an anonymous worker rebuilding a great cathedral. When the medieval dome at Chartres burned down, all the artisans in the neighborhood came together to restore it to its former glory. They did so motivated by a common desire to honor God; they worked taking great pride in their craftsmanship. In the island movies the artist is no longer a builder of a cathedral; rather, like the obnoxious architect Vergerus in *En passion,* he is a constructor of "ett kulturellt mausoleum" (a cultural mausoleum) for people whom he despises.

The title and central metaphor of the essay "Ormskinnet" refers to a similar sort of artistic activity, represented by the frantic activity of thousands of little ants moving about inside the skin of a dead snake. No more church spires are being built in a collective act motivated by a common faith; life is a hollow snakeskin and the ants moving about inside it do so in order to amuse or occupy themselves, rather than work for a common good or the glory of God.

The 1960s was in many ways a critical decade in Bergman's life and career. In 1961, after three marriages, six children, and several common-law relationships, he wed concert pianist Käbi Laretei,

Bibi Andersson (front) and Liv Ullmann in a still from Bergman's 1966 motion picture Persona *(photograph © AB Svensk Filmindustri)*

with whom he had one child, a son named Daniel (born in 1962). Attempting a change in lifestyle, he moved with Käbi to an old villa in the prestigious Stockholm suburb of Djursholm. He was out of his element, however, and, although he admired and respected Laretei greatly as an artist, he nevertheless felt that she was totally committed to a field—musical performance—in which Bergman felt inferior. Bergman divorced Laretei in 1965, whereupon he returned to Fårö, settling into a common-law relationship with Norwegian actress Liv Ullmann. A daughter, Linn, was born in 1967. Ullmann became Bergman's leading actress in such motion pictures as *Persona, Vargtimmen, Skammen, En passion, Viskningar och rop, Scener ur ett äktenskap* (1973; also released as *Scenes from a Marriage*), *Ansikte mot ansikte, Das Schlangenel* (1977, also released as *The Serpent's Egg,* 1974) and *Höstsonaten* (1978; also released as *Autumn Sonata*). In the 1990s, having turned from acting to moviemaking, she directed Bergman's television plays *Enskilda samtal* (1996; also released as *Private Conversations/Private Confessions*) and *Trolösa* (2000; also released as *Faithless,* 2001).

In 1963 Bergman was invited to become head of the Royal Dramatic Theatre. It was a triumph for him to be asked to administer the same stage that some twelve years earlier had turned him down as a resident director. Sweden in 1963 was at the beginning of a cultural revolution that questioned various forms of elitist art, however, among them the role of the prestigious national stage. Bergman—a basically apolitical artist—soon found himself embroiled with government officials, who refused to meet his demands for increased subsidies, and with a new radical cadre of actors and other coworkers, as well as with long-term traditionalists, some of whom were forced to retire, among them the directorial icon Olof Molander.

Bergman's tenure as head of the Royal Dramatic was brief—only three years, which he, in *Bergman om Bergman,* referred to upon his resignation as "mitt livs värsta eklut" (the worst brine bath in my life). It coincided with a growing native critique of his moviemaking, initiated in 1962 by Swedish director Bo Widerberg's pamphlet *Visionen i svensk film* (Vision in the Swedish Cinema). Influenced by the

French New Wave of directors and by increasingly politicized Swedish intellectuals, Widerberg advocated a socially conscious "horizontal" cinema, as opposed to Bergman's inner-directed and "vertical" moviemaking. That is, Widerberg favored a realistic depiction of the current social scene rather than a probing into the dark recesses of the mind.

None in the new generation of Swedish directors from the 1960s followed in Bergman's footsteps. As he related in *Laterna magica,* when he came to lecture at the new Filmmaking/Drama School, Statens skenskola, in Stockholm in 1968, he was booed by the students. At the Department of Cinema Arts at Stockholm University, founded in 1968, Bergman remained a persona non grata for more than twenty years. In 1967 his movie *Vargtimmen* was bypassed as best motion picture of the year by a Swedish jury in favor of Stefan Jarl's depiction of youthful rebels, *De kallar oss mods.* The situation repeated itself when *Skammen* premiered in August 1968. Pointing to current political events—the Vietnam War and the Soviet suppression of the Prague insurrection—reviewers dismissed the portrayal of guerrilla warfare in *Skammen* as ideologically noncommittal and too abstract.

In 1964–1965 Bergman fell ill with pneumonia and an ear infection that affected his sense of balance. While hospitalized, as he related in *Bergman om Bergman,* he began to fantasize that he was a small boy "som var död och som inte riktigt fick vara död ändå därför att han hela tiden väcktes av telefonsignaler från Dramaten" (who was dead and yet was not permitted to be dead, for he was awakened the whole time by telephone signals from the Royal Dramatic). Out of this fantasy grew what Bergman has called "en filmdikt" (a film poem), *Persona,* which begins with a boy waking up in what seems to be a hospital morgue to set the narrative in motion. The theme of the narrative about two women, the hospitalized actress Elisabet Vogler and her nurse, Alma, was implied in "Ormskinnet," in which Bergman likens his own role as an artist to that of an insect who captures food from his surroundings, a parasite who feeds on others for his own amusement. This vision of an artist is transformed into the mute role of Elisabet Vogler in *Persona,* who withdraws from her stage engagement but is revitalized by her "prey," the unsuspecting and flattered Alma, who feeds Elisabet her own life story. What develops is an ambiguous and interdependent relationship, mirroring Bergman's own recognition of his role as a creative artist and director, while also revealing his longtime need of sustenance from both performers and audiences, which he earlier described in the essay "Kära skrämmande public" (1960): "Jag hatar publiken, jag fruktar den och älskar den . . . I allt jag gör, är dessa tusen ögon, hjärnor och kroppar närvarande, I förbittrad ömhet ger lag vad jag har" (I hate the public, I fear it and I love it. . . . In everything I do, these thousands of eyes, brains and bodies are present. In embittered tenderness I give what I have). The critics, if not the general public, responded well to *Persona,* and it is recognized as a modernist milestone in the cinema.

In his works from the mid 1960s onward, Bergman's characters have left their religious baggage behind, but they seldom, if ever, seem able to free themselves from the traumas of their past or from some mysterious force of the mind that takes possession of them. Johan Borg in *Vargtimmen* is driven insane by inner demons, projected as aggressive birds; Anna in *En passion* wreaks havoc on her lover, Andreas Winkelman, and herself by her fixation on a marriage and an accident in the past; the psychiatrist Jenny in *Ansikte mot ansikte* attempts to commit suicide when the ghosts of her childhood begin to haunt her; the sisters in *Viskningar och rop* all have their lives shaped by circumstances beyond their control, including illness, rigid conventions and role playing, and unhappy but insoluble marriages. Even young Alexander in *Fanny och Alexander* is pursued to the bitter end by his stepfather's evil ghost, who threatens to never let go of him. In Bergman's world no one escapes his or her destiny. The puppeteer director of his youth continues to pull the strings of his human marionettes, but now the manipulator dwells inside them like an internalized psychological demon.

Parallel to Bergman's exploration of the failing god and the failing father figure in the trilogy from the early 1960s and to the emergence of the neurotic and demoralized artist in the movies made toward the end of the decade, women begin once more to occupy a central role in his works. Women are placed in strong "survival" positions: the schoolmistress, Märta Lundblad, in *Nattvardsgästerna* supports the disintegrating, doubting priest, Tomas; the pregnant wife, Alma, in *Vargtimmen* lives through the abusive nightmares of her husband, Johan, to the point of psychological identification with his fate, yet survives to tell his story; Eva Rosenberg in *Skammen* protests her husband's murder of a young defector but stays with him to the bitter end, and it is her dream of a destroyed paradise of roses that concludes the movie; the lawyer Marianne in *Scener ur ett äktenskap* gains in insight and self-confidence after her divorce, so that the roles between self-assured husband and insecure wife become reversed. Yet, from a feminist perspective these women often appear victimized. In the con-

Bergman with his and Liv Ullmann's daughter, Linn, in 1977 (photograph by Bo-Erik Gyberg)

text of Bergman's art, however, their strong and resilient life force can bring solace, even a form of redemption.

This theme is visualized emblematically in the many pieta-like vignettes in Bergman's motion pictures from the 1960s on. Such vignettes may also involve the meeting of two women or of woman and child. In *Viskningar och rop* Anna, the faithful housekeeper, takes the dying Agnes into her bosom in a visually explicit reference to pieta paintings. Also Alexander Ekdahl finds comfort from a redemptive maternal force as his mother rocks him in the Vergerus attic or when his grandmother, Helena Ekdahl, completes his rescue from the evil impact of the Vergerus world by reading to him, like a mantra, Strindberg's famous dictum of art transcending the limitations of the human world: "Allt kan ske, allt är möjligt och sannolikt. Tid och rum existera icke; på en obetydlig verklighetsgrund spinner inbillningen ut och väver nya mönster. . ." (All can happen, all is possible and probable. Time and space do not exist; on a narrow realistic basis the imagination spins and weaves new patterns. . .). Women in Bergman's universe are both physical and spiritual foundations.

The image of the strong female in Bergman's fictional universe has a biographical analogy. His mother, Karin, had a strong "directorial" personality and was a rather complex individual to whom Bergman paid homage in his short documentary *Karins ansikte* (1986; also released as *Karin's Face*), and in the composite portrait of womanhood in *Viskningar och rop,* a movie that Bergman referred to in a 1973 television interview as an attempt to depict his mother's life and psyche, split into the three sisters: the patient and humble Agnes, the coquettish and beautiful Maria, and the stern and repressed Karin.

As Bergman shifted his focus once more to women in his motion pictures in the 1960s, he began to use color. His first color movie was the woman-dominated comedy *För att inte tala om alla dessa kvinnor* (1964; also released as *All These Women*). The shift from black-and-white film to color was not only a technical matter—the result of laboratory experiments to achieve an acceptable range of muted colors—but was also in keeping with Bergman's visual memories of the male and female worlds of his childhood. There the father figure wore the stark black frock of a man of the cloth, while the women dressed more colorfully in long rustling skirts and moved about in the prismatic world of flickering light. The father figure spoke the rhetorical words of the Bible from his pulpit; the women surrounded themselves with more muted voices.

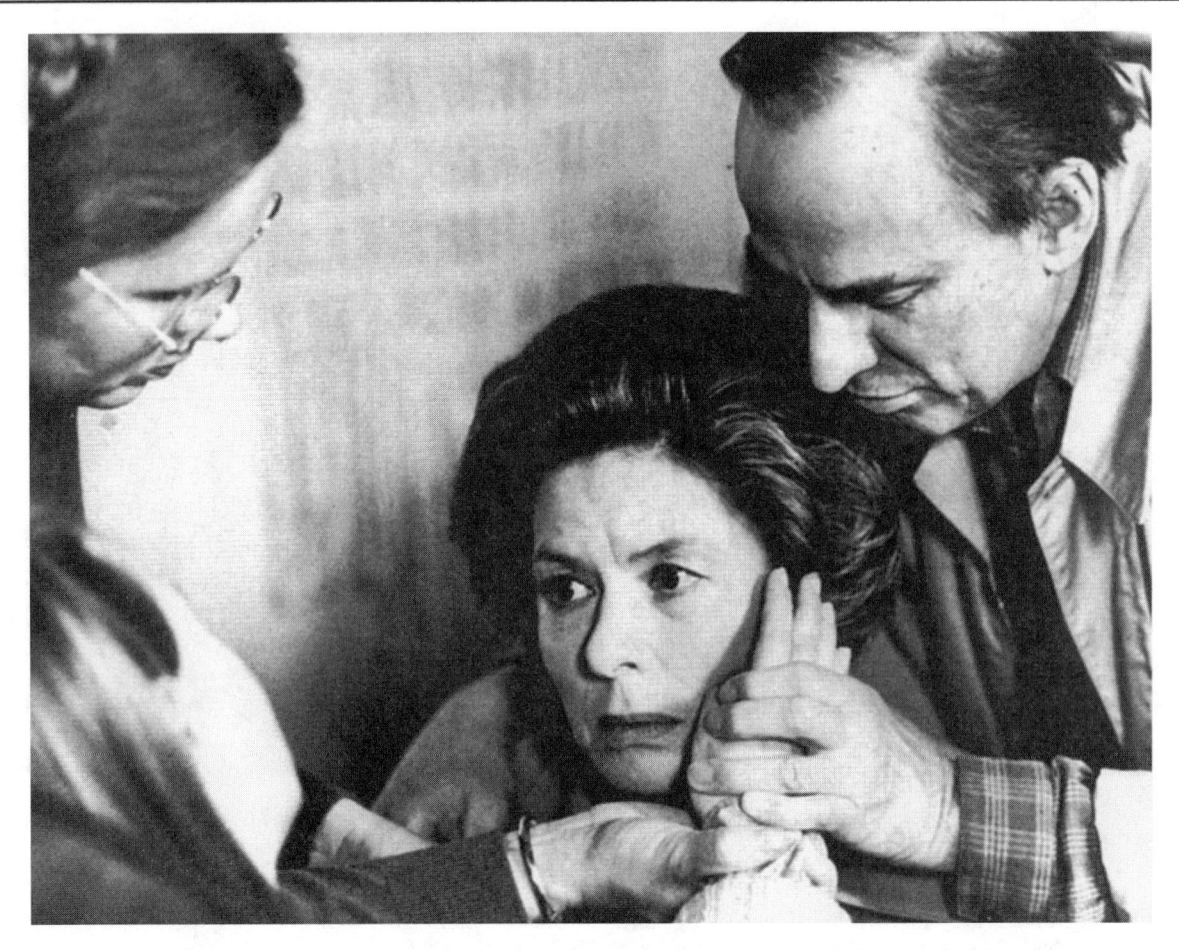

Bergman directing actress Ingrid Bergman in his 1978 motion picture, Höstsonaten *(Svenska Filminstitutet)*

Bergman has often stated that he communicates better with women than with men. In the workplace he has striven to maintain at least 50 percent women on his staff. His five official marriages and many nonlegalized relationships, resulting in a total of eight children, have involved women with artistic careers of their own, with whom he has stayed in touch professionally even after their private life together ended. His first two wives, Else Fisher and Ellen Lundberg, were choreographers; his third wife, Gun Grut, was a journalist who later got a doctorate and became a university lecturer in Slavic Languages; his fourth wife was the world-renowned concert pianist Käbi Laretel; his common-law wife Liv Ullmann was an actress who became a moviemaker. His last marriage—to Ingrid von Rosen, his mother's look-alike and a competent manager—lasted for more than twenty-five years until his wife's death in 1995. More than any other woman in his life, Ingrid came to embody the positive qualities of his strong mother and gave him the loving support without which his life might have collapsed. In an interview for Swedish television three years later, on his eightieth birthday (14 July 1998), Bergman talks about his great sense of loss after Ingrid's death from cancer.

Bergman's own marital experiences and his observations of other people's relationships provided material for the work that led to his popular breakthrough in Sweden, which did not really come until 1973 when he made *Scener ur ett äktenskap*. This drama of a contemporary couple, Johan and Marianne, whose marriage ends in a divorce, was serialized in six episodes on Swedish television. The viewer ratio increased as the series continued, as did, according to media reporting, the number of visits to family counseling by Swedish couples. In holding up a mirror to reality and bringing a real-life situation into Swedish living rooms, Bergman had served as a catalyst in prompting people to reexamine their lives.

Bergman's movies from the mid 1960s focusing on women tend to proceed more directly from the visual. Even in a talky work such as *Scener ur ett äktenskap,* Bergman is careful about defining a problem or a tense moment by pictorial rather than strictly verbal

Bergman (at camera) and his frequent collaborator, cinematographer Sven Nykvist, during the filming of Bergman's 1982 motion picture, Fanny och Alexander *(Svensk Filmindustri)*

means. When Marianne reads to her separated husband from her diary, the camera registers her face in such an intense close-up that the spectator is drawn to it rather than to her words. The television medium encouraged Bergman to use the close-up and helped liberate his moviemaking from some of its earlier staginess.

At the end of *Scener ur ett äktenskap* Marianne wakes up from a nightmare that has thrown her into a state of existential fright. The scene seems to anticipate the exploration of the troubled mind of Jenny, the psychiatrist in the 1975 television drama *Ansikte mot ansikte*. Jenny seems at first well established and secure in her life's role but must undertake a troubling quest into her past and her subconscious. In that respect she follows the harrowing explorations undertaken by the central male figures in Bergman's earlier movies but also continues the psychological drama of self portrayed with such intensity in the double female role of *Persona*.

The idealization of maternal support that is a strong factor in Bergman's fictional universe appears also in *Ansikte mot ansikte* in the figure of Jenny's caring grandmother. It is an image counterbalanced by the critical portrait of the distant mother in *Höstsonaten* and by the withdrawn mother in *Viskningar och rop*. Charlotte, the professional pianist in *Höstsonaten*, neglects her two daughters, one of whom is mentally retarded. During a rare return visit to her married daughter, Eva, the mother's total absorption in her own career becomes the basis for Eva's violent accusations of parental egotism. In that role Charlotte joins the league of self-absorbed parents in such earlier Bergman works as *Till glädje* (1950; also released as *To Joy*), *Smultronstället*, *Såsom i en spegel*, *Tystnaden*, and *Persona*, but the confrontation between parent and child is far more scathing in *Höstsonaten*, which made the work a target for feminist critique for its portrayal of a professional woman. The character of Charlotte was also seen as Bergman's exposure of his former wife, Käbi Laretei. To such an interpretation one might add that Bergman himself had remained rather distant to most of his own children. In view of his strong awareness of the female anima in his own psyche, it is quite possible to see both Elisabeth Vogler in *Persona* and Charlotte in *Höstsonaten* as veiled self-portraits.

One of Bergman's lifelong friends and coworkers, the actor Erland Josephson, once stated that Bergman could go through obstacles like a bulldozer. In January 1976 he experienced an almost crushing blow, however. He was arrested during rehearsals of Strindberg's *Dödsdansen* (1901; translated as *The Dance of Death,* 1912) at the Royal Dramatic Theatre. Taken to the police station, Bergman was charged with tax evasion, his passport was confiscated, and he was virtually placed under house arrest. The incident, which seems to reenact the humiliating exposure suffered by many of the characters in Bergman's movies, led to his mental collapse and subsequent hospitalization. Though the charges by the tax authorities were eventually dropped, he left Sweden in April 1976 to go into voluntary exile. During the next several years his domicile was Munich in West Germany, where he worked as a director at the city's Residenz Theatre. He also made three features during his German stay: *Ormens ägg* (1977), *Höstsonaten,* and *Aus dem Leben der Marionetten.* The first of these movies, set in Germany just before Adolf Hitler's takeover, was already written and planned before Bergman's exile. The second one seems to have been dictated in part by an earlier promise to Swedish actress Ingrid Bergman, who plays the leading role as the pianist mother in the movie. *Aus dem Leben der Marionetten* grew out of an idea that began to take shape in an earlier work—the story of the unhappily married couple Peter and Katarina was embedded in *Scener ur ett äktenskap.*

Bergman's years of exile are certainly more than a parenthesis in his professional career. Still, his stage productions in Munich never approached his innovative work at the Royal Dramatic Theatre after his return from exile. The Munich years crystallized the relatively narrow scope of Bergman's choice of stage repertory: working almost entirely within the classical theater, he kept returning to the same playwrights, even the same plays: Strindberg's *Ett drömspel* (1902; translated as *The Dreamplay,* 1912) and *Fröken Julie* (1888; translated as *Countess Julie,* 1912), Ibsen's *Et dukkehjem* (1879; translated as *A Doll's House*) and *Hedda Gabler* (1890), and Molière's *Dom Juan* (1665; translated as *Don Juan,* 1739). It is as if in exile Bergman gained control over his admitted homesickness by staging plays he had a previous, in some cases lifelong, relationship to.

All his life Bergman has felt secure only in familiar surroundings. He hates to travel, and it is said that during one of his rare visits abroad, to Southern Methodist University in Dallas in 1977, he spent his entire time outside the seminar room cooped up in his hotel, watching television. He is oversensitive to sharp sunlight and prefers the misty climate of Fårö. Even during his exile, he arranged to return there in the summer time.

His homecoming in 1981–1982, after various apologies and pleadings by Swedish officials, including the prime minister, was low-key but resulted in an upsurge of artistic activity for Bergman. He now made his greatest television movie, the five-and-a-half-hour-long *Fanny och Alexander;* he directed a new opera based on Euripides' *The Bacchae;* and he launched upon a remarkable series of theater productions of Shakespeare's *King Lear, Hamlet,* and *A Winter's Tale.* He also wrote the memoirs *Laterna magica* and *Bilder* (1990; translated as *Images: My Life in Film,* 1994), the novels *Den goda viljan* (1991; translated as *The Best Intentions,* 1993) and *Söndagsbarn* (1993; translated as *Sunday's Children,* 1994), television plays such as that for *Enskilda samtal,* and *Larmar och gör sig till* (1997; also released as *In the Presence of a Clown,* 1998). Much of his focus in these works was on his own background, his parents and their family—so much so that he made a special point of announcing his script for *Trolösa* as a piece with no connection to his parental background. Nevertheless, *Trolösa* is a form of personal reckoning as the narrator, named Ingmar Bergman and played by his lifelong friend Erland Josephson, conjures forth a painful memory from his past. Like much of Bergman's creative work after his homecoming, *Trolösa* forms a kind of closure: a final coming to terms with the ghosts of his childhood. In the novel *Söndagsbarn,* which was made into a movie by his son Daniel, Bergman states: "Jag började se på mina föräldrars tidiga liv, min fars barndom och uppväxt och jag såg ett återkommande mönster av patetiska ansträngningar och förödmjukande motgång. Jag såg också omsorg, bekymmer och djup förvirring." (I began to look into my parents' early life, my father's childhood and upbringing and I saw a recurring pattern of pathetic efforts and humiliating adversity. I also saw care, concern, and deep confusion.)

In a talk in 1946, later published as "Det förtrollade marknadsnöjet," Bergman defended the cinema as a magical art to be taken seriously. What he voiced was an early sign of a cultural paradigm in Swedish society. The rise of popular art, with a strong focus on the motion pictures, coincided with Sweden's emergence as a twentieth-century democracy or *folkhem.* In the bourgeois circles of Stockholm's Östermalm section, however, where Ingmar Bergman grew up, there were still clear demarcation lines between masters and servants, traditional art and popular culture. The theater continued to represent bourgeois taste, while the cinema, with its cult surrounding glamorous movie stars, was viewed, in many upper-middle-class circles, as vulgar entertainment. This cultural dichotomy is presented as a major theme in Bergman's *Gycklarnas afton,* in which the confrontation scenes take place between visiting circus performers and snobbish representatives of a small-town residential theater. Thus, Bergman's own dual commitment to the stage and the screen is transcribed and fictionalized. In reality, however, he managed to straddle the cultural chasm between traditional and popular culture by making no evaluative distinction between his work for the stage and his work in the cinema. In this way his different forms of artistic expression (including opera, radio, and television) came to anticipate a cultural leveling that is still ongoing in Swedish society.

Bergman must be considered one of the major creative minds in twentieth-century Swedish culture, an artist who also gained an extensive international recognition for his distinctive ability to present a moral and psychological vision in intense dramatic narratives, using the popular medium of the cinema as his primary vehicle. From *Det sjunde inseglet* to *Tystnaden, Persona, Viskningar och rop,* and *Fanny och Alexander,* Bergman's moviemaking has dramatized an important impasse in contemporary Western culture: how to live in a world where God no longer appears to provide psychological security and ethical guidelines. In that sense Bergman's art has been what the German movie historian Siegfried Krakauer once called "gleichzeitig"–in keeping with the times. Yet, Bergman is at the same time somewhat of a lone artist who, though making one comeback after another throughout a sixty-year career, has formed no school and has had no followers, with the possible exception of the short-lived admiration in the 1950s of the French director-critics such as Francois Truffaut and Eric Rohmer, and the accolade worship of American director Woody Allen.

Despite his international reputation Bergman has never aimed his work at foreign audiences but has defined his audience as springing from his own culture. Likewise, he has seen himself as part of a modernist Swedish tradition, represented by Strindberg in the theater and Victor Sjöström in the movies. Like these artists, his work includes a strong element of the stark Lutheran ethos, a moral view of art, and a juxtaposition of an inner world where the individual is alone with his existential pondering with an outer world defined more by the contours of a natural and rather isolated landscape and less by social conventions and political ideology.

Ingmar Bergman also shares some of the volatility and creative expansiveness of his predecessor Strindberg, and like him has helped widen traditional

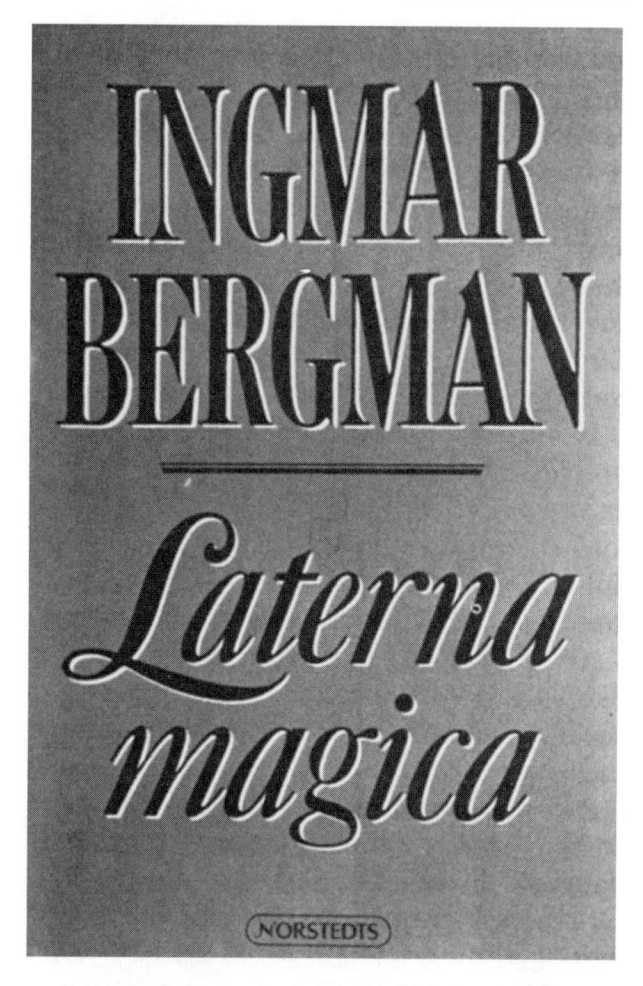

Dust jacket for Bergman's 1987 memoir (from Swedish Book Review, *1987)*

genre definitions. As a young director Bergman proudly announced in "Det att göra film" that "film har ingenting med litteratur att göra" (film has nothing to do with literature). As an aging artist, however, he has become well aware of his own fleeting literary bounderies. In *Femte akten: Monolog, Efter repetitionen, Sista skriket, Larmar och gör sig till* (1994; translated as *The Fifth Act,* 2001) he states: "The texts in this book are written without a particular medium in mind. . . . I have written as I have been used to writing for more than fifty years–it looks like theater but it could just as well be film, television or simply reading."

Interviews:

"Ingmar Bergman ser på film," *Chaplin,* 3, no. 18 (1961): 60–61;

Stig Björkman, Torsten Manns, and Jonas Sima, *Bergman om Bergman* (Stockholm: Norstedt, 1970); translated by Paul Britten Austin as *Bergman on Bergman: Interviews with Ingmar Bergman* (New York:

Simon & Schuster, 1973; London: Secker & Warburg, 1973).

Biography:

Peter Cowie, *Ingmar Bergman: A Critical Biography* (New York: Scribners, 1982).

References:

Lars Ånlander, ed., *Chaplin,* special Bergman issue, 30, new series 2/3 (1988);

Maria Bergom-Larsson, *Ingmar Bergman and Society,* translated by Barrie Selman (London: Tantavy, 1978);

N. T. Binh, *Ingmar Bergman: Le magicien du Nord* (Paris: Gallimard, 1993);

Marilyn Blackwell, *Gender and Representation in the Films of Ingmar Bergman* (Columbia, S.C.: Camden House, 1997);

Francesco Bono, ed., *Il giovane Bergman: 1944–1951* (Rome: Officina Edizione, 1992);

Hubert I. Cohen, *Ingmar Bergman: The Art of Confession* (New York: Twayne, 1993);

Jean Miguel Company, *Ingmar Bergman* (Madrid: Cátedra, 1993);

Jörn Donner, *The Personal Vision of Ingmar Bergman,* translated by Holger Lundbergh (Bloomington: Indiana University Press, 1964);

Frank Gado, *The Passion of Ingmar Bergman* (Durham, N.C.: Duke University Press, 1986);

Marc Gervais, *Ingmar Bergman: Magician and Prophet* (Montreal: McGill-Queen's University Press, 1999);

Marianne Höök, *Ingmar Bergman* (Stockholm: Wahlström & Widstrand, 1962);

"Ingmar Bergman and the Arts," special Bergman issue, *Nordic Theatre Studies,* 11 (1998);

Stuart Kaminsky and Joseph F. Hill, eds., *Ingmar Bergman: Essays in Criticism* (London: Oxford University Press, 1975);

Maaret Koskinen, "Spel och speglingar: En studie i Ingmar Bergmans filmiska estetik," dissertation, Stockholm University, 1993;

Robert E. Lauder, *God, Death, Art and Love: The Philosophical Vision of Ingmar Bergman* (New York: Paulist Press, 1989);

Paisley Livingston, *Ingmar Bergman and the Rituals of Art* (Ithaca, N.Y.: Cornell University Press, 1982);

Frederic Marker and Lise-Lone Marker, *Ingmar Bergman: Four Decades in the Theater* (Cambridge: Cambridge University Press, 1982);

Joseph Marty, *Ingmar Bergman: Une poétique du désir* (Paris: Editions du Cerf, 1991);

Philip Mosley, *Ingmar Bergman: The Cinema as Mistress* (London: Calder & Boyars, 1981);

Guido Oldrini, *La solitudine di Ingmar Bergman: In appendice interviste e scritti di Ingmar Bergman, filmografia, bibliografia* (Parma: Guanda, 1965);

Roger Oliver, ed., *Ingmar Bergman: An Artist's Journey: On Stage, On Screen, In Print* (New York: Arcade, 1995);

Willem T. O'Reilly, "Ingmar Bergman's Theatre Direction 1952–1974," dissertation, University of Santa Barbara, 1980;

Gérard Pangon and Thierry Jousse, *Ingmar Bergman* (Paris: Arte éditions, 1997);

Vlada Petric, ed., *Film and Dreams: An Approach to Ingmar Bergman* (South Salem, N.Y.: Redgrave, 1981);

Henrik Sjögren, *Ingmar Bergman på teatern* (Stockholm: Almqvist & Wiksell, 1968);

Vilgot Sjöman, *L-136: Diary with Ingmar Bergman,* translated by Alan Blair (Ann Arbor, Mich.: Karoma, 1978);

Birgitta Steene, *Ingmar Bergman* (New York: Twayne, 1968);

Steene, *Ingmar Bergman: A Guide to References and Resources* (Boston: Hall, 1987); revised as *Ingmar Bergman: A Reference Guide* (Amsterdam: Amsterdam University Press, 2002);

Steene, *Måndagar med Bergman: En svensk publik möter Ingmar Bergmans filmer* (Eslöv, Sweden: Symposion, 1998);

Egil Törnqvist, *Between Stage and Screen: Ingmar Bergman Directs* (Amsterdam: Amsterdam University Press, 1995);

Törnqvist, *Filmdiktaren Ingmar Bergman* (Stockholm: Arena, 1993);

Jerry Vermilye, *Ingmar Bergman: His Films and His Career* (Secaucus, N.J.: Carol, 1997);

Eckhard Weise, *Ingmar Bergman* (Reinbek bei Hamburg: Rowohlt, 1987);

Margareta Wirmark, ed., *Ingmar Bergman: Film och teater i växelverkan* (Stockholm: Carlsson, 1996);

Robin Wood, *Ingmar Bergman* (New York: Praeger, 1969);

Vernon Young, *Cinema Borealis: Ingmar Bergman and the Swedish Ethos* (New York: Avon, 1971);

Leif Zern, *Se Bergman* (Stockholm: Norstedt, 1993).

Carina Burman
(22 October 1960 –   )

Barbro Ståhle Sjönell
University of Stockholm

BOOKS: *Västgöten Johan Henric Kellgren,* Skrifter från Skaraborgs länsmuseum, no. 8 (Skara: Skaraborgs länsmuseum, 1987);

Vältalaren Johan Henric Kellgren, Skrifter utgivna av Avdelningen för litteratursociologi vid Litteraturvetenskapliga institutionen, no. 23 (Uppsala: Avdelningen för litteratursociologi vid Litteraturvetenskapliga institutionen, 1988);

Min salig bror Jean Hendrich (Stockholm: Bonnier, 1993); selection translated by Irene Scobbie as "From My Dear Departed Brother Jean Henric," in "Stockholm in Literature," *Swedish Book Review* supplement (1998): 90–91;

Mamsellen och förläggarna: Fredrika Bremers förlagskontakter 1828–1865, Litteratur och samhälle, volume 30, no. 1 (Uppsala: Avdelningen för litteratursociologi, Uppsala universitet, 1995);

Den tionde sånggudinnan (Stockholm: Bonnier, 1996)– introduction, "Förspel i himlen," translated by Sarah Death as "Prologue in Heaven: Uppsala 1909," *Swedish Book Review,* 1 (1998);

Cromwells huvud: Antropologisk komedi (Stockholm: Bonnier, 1998);

Hammaren (Stockholm: Bonnier, 1999);

Islandet (Stockholm: Bonnier, 2001);

Bremer: En biografi (Stockholm: Bonnier, 2001).

OTHER: "Teaterkungen, Dramen och Dramatikerna," in *Gripsholm 450 år: Jubileums Magasin,* edited by Ulla Trenter and Bie Seipel (Mariefred: Affärsinfo, 1987), pp. 12–17;

"'Qvinnans ädla och stilla kallelse': En retorisk analys," in *Johan Olof Wallin: En minnesskrift 1989,* edited by Håkan Möller (Uppsala: Erene, 1989), pp. 33–44;

"'denna förträffeliga konsten': Henrik Gabriel Porthan och retoriken," in *Historiska och litteraturhistoriska studier,* volume 66, edited by Helena Solstrand-Pipping (Helsingfors: Svenska litteratursällskapet i Finland, 1991), pp. 97–126;

Carina Burman (photograph by Cato Lein; from the dust jacket for Cromwells huvud: Antropologisk komedi, *1998)*

Poetiskt och prosaiskt: Texter från svenskt 1600- och 1700-tal, selected, with an introduction, by Burman and Lars Burman, Helikonbiblioteket, 6 (Lund: Studentlitteratur, 1992);

"Tecknerska av vardagslivet? Fredrika Bremer som ord- och bildkonstnär," in *Språket och bilderna,* edited by Birgitta Garme, Svensklärarserien, no. 212 (Stockholm: Svensklärarföreningens årsskrift, 1993), pp. 25–44;

Gustaf Wasa och andra pjäser från svenskt 1700-tal, edited by Marie-Christine Skuncke, Burman, and Lars Burman (Lund: Studentlitteratur, 1994);

"Indianen," in *Sju spådomar: 7 Svenska författare spekulerar,* edited by Magnus Brohult (Stockholm: Bromberg, 1994), pp. 37–51;

Johan Henric Kellgren, *Skrifter,* edited by Burman and Lars Burman, 2 volumes (Stockholm: Atlantis, 1995);

Fredrika Bremer, *Livet i gamla världen: Palestina,* edited by Burman and Lars Burman (Stockholm: Atlantis, 1995);

Bremer, *Brev: Ny följd, tidigare ej samlade och tryckta brev,* 2 volumes, edited by Burman (Stockholm: Gidlund, 1996);

"Sommarsol och ruskdagar i Frihetstidens litteratur," in *Rokokoo,* edited by Sirpa Juuti and Kari-Paavo Kokki, Heinolan kaupunginmuseon julkaisuja, no. 5 (Heinola: Heinolan kaupunginmuseon, 1996), pp. 19–24;

"Biografisk litteraturforskning," in *Litteraturvetenskap: En inledning,* edited by Staffan Bergsten (Lund: Studentlitteratur, 1998), pp. 67–76;

"I kyrkans och akademins hägn," "Ståndssamhällets litteratur," "Upplysningens tidevarv," "Stockholm–Paris. Gustaf Philip Creutz," and "Musikaliska sällskapet i Åbo," in *Finlands svenska litteratur historia,* edited by Johan Wrede, volume 1 (Helsinki: Svenska litteratursällskapet i Finland/Stockholm: Atlantis, 1999), pp. 100–170, 187–188;

Bremer, *Grannarne,* edited, with introduction and commentary, by Burman and Lars Burman (Stockholm: Svenska vitterhetssamfundet, 2000);

Potterism," in *Nationalencyklopedin 2000,* volume 25 (Höganäs: Bra böcker, 2001), pp. 246–249.

SELECTED PERIODICAL PUBLICATIONS–UNCOLLECTED: "Ordensvurmen J. H. Kellgren," *Samlaren,* 1988, no. 109 (1989): 101–105;

"Johan Henric Kellgrens ansikten," *Svenska Dagbladet,* 20 April 1995, pp. 29–30; translated by Peter Graves, with an introduction by Burman, as "The K & k Letter: A Dialogue with Himself by J. H. Kellgren," in *Comparative Criticism: A Yearbook,* volume 20: *Philosophical Dialogues* (Cambridge: Cambridge University Press, 1998), pp. 161–168;

"From barockdiktare och femtonbarnsmor: hyllades av samtiden men var för borgerlig och sansad för eftervärlden," *Svenska Dagbladet,* 9 July 1996, p. 14;

"Dikt och sanning: Om författarskap och forskning," *TijdSchrift voor skandinavistiek,* 1 (1997): 63–70;

"Faking the 18th Century," *Swedish Book Review,* 1 (1998): 17–24;

"En svensk Maecenas," *Biblis,* 3, no. 3/4 (2000): 11–13.

Carina Burman's first novel, *Min salig bror Jean Hendrich* (My Dear Departed Brother Jean Hendrich, 1993), was a success with both critics and the public. Enthusiastic reviewers praised the ingenious narrative technique, style, and solid grasp of history, particularly literary history, displayed in the novel. *Min salig bror Jean Hendrich* was reprinted twice in the autumn of 1993, and the paperback edition, which appeared the following year, also ran to three reprints.

Critics have compared Burman with the Swedish historian Peter Englund, whose first book, *Poltava* (1988), succeeded in awakening an interest in history by means of an initiated and accessible historical depiction of the Great Northern War conducted by Charles XII. Like Englund, Burman combines a solid academic training with a narrative talent that has brought her a large readership. Unlike *Poltava,* which is subtitled "Berättelse" (a story), in Burman's books historical fact is mixed with a fair degree of fiction.

Annie Carina Persson was born in Norrköping on 22 October 1960 as the only child of parents with cultural interests. Her mother, Ulla-Britt Persson, was an accountant and her father, Hans Persson, a manager. On leaving school in 1979, she entered Uppsala University, where she studied comparative literature, classical culture and society, Scandinavian languages, and English. She married Lars Burman, then a fellow student, in 1983, and they have three children: Annie, Alice, and August (born in 1988, 1990, and 1994, respectively).

In her essay "Dikt och sanning: Om författarskap och forskning" (Fiction and Truth: On Authorship and Research), published in *TijdSchrift voor skandinavistiek* in 1997, Burman related that she first encountered the eighteenth-century Swedish poet Johan Henric Kellgren while studying literature at the university in 1980 and writing a paper on his poem "Man äger ej snille för det man är galen" (One is not a genius because one is mad, 1787). She read his letters written from Turku, Finland, when he, like Burman, was nineteen years old and studying literature at university.

Burman was also attracted to the study of classical rhetoric, a subject that had been revived in Uppsala during the 1980s. She combined her interest in rhetoric and in the writings of Kellgren in her dissertation, *Vältalaren Johan Henric Kellgren* (The Orator Johan Henric Kellgren), which she defended at Uppsala University in the spring of 1988. Burman analyzed fifteen speeches by Kellgren dating from two decades, linking her analysis to some of his positions in society: as a tutor, as a member of various literary societies, and as a member of the Swedish Academy.

Since research into rhetoric requires fundamental insights into the different roles acted out by the orator,

Dust jacket for Burman's first novel (1993), a fictionalized account of the life of seventeenth-century Swedish poet Johan Henric Kellgren (Collection of Barbro Ståhle Sjönell)

Burman also worked hard at collecting biographical information about Kellgren, including a study of his letters and contemporary testimony. Before submitting her thesis she had published some of her biographical information in a paper on the poet's roots in his native district, *Västgöten Johan Henric Kellgren* (Johan Henric Kellgren from Västergötland, 1987), in which she provides information about his family and his education. In the same year she published "Teaterkungen, Dramen och Dramatikerna" (The King of Drama, the Dramas and the Dramatists), an article on Kellgren's collaboration with King Gustavus III concerning the writing of Swedish historical dramas, in *Gripsholm 450 år: Jubileums Magasin* (Gripsholm 450 Years: Anniversary Review).

Following her doctorate, Burman complemented her academic education by studying Latin. In 1988 she published a brief essay in *Samlaren* with material not included in her thesis, "Ordensvurmen J. H. Kellgren" (J. H. Kellgren's Passion for Secret Societies), which gives a picture of Kellgren's participation in secret societies, particularly the so-called Franciscan Society, in which he held various high offices, with its ideas influenced by the Enlightenment. Burman's interest in rhetoric led to two more extended studies: "'Qvinnans ädla och stilla kallelse': En retorisk analys" ("Woman's Noble and Quiet Vocation": A Rhetorical Analysis), on a sermon by Johan Olof Wallin, published in *Johan Olof Wallin: En minnesskrift 1989* (Johan Olof Wallin: A Memorial Publication 1989); and "'denna förträffeliga konsten': Henrik Gabriel Porthan och retoriken" ("this Splendid Art": Henrik Gabriel Porthan and Rhetoric), published in volume 66 of *Historiska och litteraturhistoriska studier* (1991). Since completing her doctorate she has divided her time between teaching comparative literature at Uppsala University and doing research on external grants. She has also lectured widely and is on the board of the Bellman Society. She has been a visiting scholar at Åbo Akademi (January through March 1985), Cambridge (April through June 1987), and the Herzog August Bibliothek in Wolfenbüttel (September through December 1992). From 1986 to 1991 she also served as a reader for Bibliotekstjänst (Swedish Library Service Agency), writing some sixty reviews. On four occasions she has received financial awards: the Gustavian Prize from the Swedish Academy in February 1989, the Municipality of Uppsala Jan-Fridegård Scholarship in March 1994, Torgny Segerstedt's Culture Scholarship in June 1997, and the Örjan Lindberger award in October 1998. When in 1992 Lars Burman received a grant for a year of research in Pisa and Wolfenbüttel, the family accompanied him. There Burman was able to devote herself to writing fiction.

Burman's research into Kellgren's use of rhetoric proved useful when she began to write *Min salig bror Jean Hendrich* in January 1992. She polished and completed the novel during her stay in Wolfenbüttel in autumn of that year. Freed from the normal academic constraints, she was at liberty to speculate about various aspects of the poet's life that the existing research could not satisfactorily resolve. Certain sections, such as Kellgren's education and the founding of the Swedish Academy, on the other hand, follow her thesis quite closely.

Writing about one of the leading Swedish poets of the eighteenth century, Burman makes use of various narrative techniques that were common among European novelists of the period. She employs narrative chapter headings with roots in the medieval fable *Roman de Renard* (1176) and Miguel de Cervantes's *Don Quixote* (2 parts, 1605, 1615). The novel begins with a remark by the secretary of the Swedish Academy, Nils von Rosenstein, from the year of Kellgren's death. Rosenstein says that he has asked two people who were close to Kellgren—his brother, the cleric Jonas Kiellgren, and Kellgren's mistress, the merchant's wife Hedda Falk—each to write an obituary of the poet. The novel concludes with "Utgivarens epilog" (the Editor's Epilogue) written by "CB," which reinforces the fiction with an account of how she happened upon the two obituaries in the course of her research and discusses the authenticity and appearance of the manuscript. The epilogue concludes with CB saying that she has been torn between publishing the manuscript in a scholarly or popular edition. The use of a fictitious editor is a well-known technique from classics such as Jonathan Swift's *Gulliver's Travels* (1726), Voltaire's *Candide* (1759), and Johann Wolfgang von Goethe's *Die Leiden des jungen Werthers* (1774; translated as *The Sorrows of Werther*, 1779), but it is also to be found in the works of nineteenth-century Swedish writer Carl Jonas Love Almqvist and in Umberto Eco's *Il nome della rosa* (1980; translated as *The Name of the Rose*, 1983). As Burman notes in "Dikt och sanning," some reviewers were taken in by the epilogue to the extent that they recommended the book as a readable Kellgren biography.

The novel alternates between the portrayals of Kellgren by his brother and his mistress. This narrative technique views the poet from two aspects while the two narrators also play prominent parts in the novel. Jonas Kiellgren is his brother's opposite: skeptical to the Enlightenment, somewhat prolix and naive and unattractive, he stayed in the countryside rather than make a career in the city, as Kellgren did. Hedda Falk's perspective is that of an intelligent and educated city dweller who takes part in literary society among Kellgren's friends, as well as that of a woman in love.

A sense of period is created in the novel in various ways. The cast of characters comprises almost exclusively authentic people, many of them from the circle of Gustavus III. There is comment on contemporary historical events such as the war with Russia, the assassination of Gustavus, and the French Revolution. The ideas of the period are represented by Pehr Falk's Swedenborgianism and discussions between Hedda and Kellgren about the Baron de Montesquieu's deterministic notions regarding the influence of climate. Various settings are faithfully described, such as the brothers' home, a country vicarage; their lodgings in Turku; the Stockholm Exchange during a masked ball; and the Falks' mercantile home in Stockholm. Texts from the work of contemporary authors are implied in various places. Some of the central scenes are based on Carl Michael Bellman's *Fredmans epistlar* (Fredman's Epistles, 1790), with its motifs from Djurgården, the green open space in Stockholm. The author skillfully indicates the personal language of the two writers. Jonas Kiellgren's language is characterized by the use of dialect words and Latin phrases, while Hedda Falk makes greater use of French vocabulary and epithets.

In collaboration with her husband, Burman was responsible for producing a series of critical editions during the 1990s. These editions include texts by Swedish authors of the seventeenth, eighteenth, and nineteenth centuries: *Poetiskt och prosaiskt: Texter från svenskt 1600- och 1700-tal* (Poetry and Prose: Texts from Seventeenth- and Eighteenth-Century Sweden, 1992) and *Gustaf Wasa och andra pjäser från svenskt 1700-tal* (Gustav Wasa and Other Plays of Eighteenth-century Sweden, 1994). In the prestigious series of Svenska klassiker (Swedish Classic Writings) published by the Swedish Academy they edited an edition of Kellgren's *Skrifter* (Writings) and *Livet i gamla världen: Palestina* (Life in the Old World: Palestine, 1860–1862) by Fredrika Bremer, both published in 1995. Burman has also, since 1994, been a contributor to *Svenska Dagbladet*, one of the most respected newspapers in Sweden.

After her work on Kellgren, Burman focused her scholarly attention on Fredrika Bremer, a writer of international reputation. She received a major research grant for the project of producing an edition of Bremer's unpublished letters. With *Brev: Ny följd, tidigare ej samlade och tryckta brev* (Further Letters: New Edition of Previously Uncollected and Unpublished Letters, 1996) Burman added two volumes comprising eight hundred letters to the previous editions of Bremer's correspondence.

For the anthology of short stories *Sju spådomar: 7 Svenska författare spekulerar* (Seven Predictions: Speculations by Seven Swedish Authors, 1994), proposed by the Swedish Academy of Engineers as part of their project "Technology and the Work of the Future," Burman borrows from Bremer. Her story "Indianen" (The Indian) is set in the 2020s, portrayed primarily through the technological developments that have changed everyday life. "Indianen" is introduced by a motto found in a letter from Bremer to Andrew Jackson Downing written in Philadelphia in the summer of 1850 during the author's journey to the United States. The principal character, ten-year-old Siv, identifies herself with Mochpedaga Wen, the Cirrus Woman, a young Indian from Fredrika Bremer's travel book *Hemmen i den nya världen* (Homes in the New World, 1853–1854). Like Astrid Lindgren's Pippi Longstocking, Siv does not want to grow up and leave her fictional world. The story suggests that the dimension that literature brings people will survive even though their conditions of life change in the future.

Her work in editing Bremer's letters provided material and inspiration for further academic works: the article "Tecknerska av vardagslivet? Fredrika Bremer som ord- och bildkonstnär" (Portrayer of Everyday Life? Fredrika Bremer as Writer and Artist), published in the yearbook *Språket och bilderna* (1993), and the extended 1995 study, *Mamsellen och förläggarna: Fredrika Bremers förlagskontakter 1828–1865* (The Spinster and Her Publishers: Fredrika Bremer's Contacts with Her Publishing Companies 1828–1865).

As with Kellgren, Burman's research on Bremer bore fruit in the form of a novel, *Den tionde sånggudinnan* (The Tenth Muse, 1996). In the introduction–which, like Goethe's *Faust* (1808), has a "Forspel i himlen" (Prologue in Heaven)–the main character, Elisabet Gran, an associate professor of literature, makes a bet with an older professor, Georg Schlippenbach, at the annual meeting of the Swedish Literary Society in Uppsala in 1909. Gran believes that it is still possible to make discoveries in archives that will throw new light on an author's work. Schlippenbach, on the other hand, maintains that everything of value has already been found and that it is now a matter of devoting oneself to problems of literary theory. He promises Gran an academic career if she succeeds, however. Gran chooses to search for letters from the first major Swedish woman poet, Sophia Elisabet Brenner, who devoted her efforts to various sorts of occasional verse, often with a feminist tendency. Much admired by her contemporaries–she was both educated and an excellent linguist–she was known as "the tenth muse." She bore fifteen children in the course of her marriage to a man who warmly encouraged her literary work. If Gran should fail in her endeavor, however, she is prepared to accept her sentence: a position as a teacher in a girls' school or marriage.

Dust jacket for Burman's 1996 novel, about an early-twentieth-century scholar who discovers the letters of the first major Swedish woman poet, Sophia Elisabet Brenner (Collection of Barbro Ståhle Sjönell)

After making this Faustian pact, she commences her hunt for the letters in the company of two emancipated female friends, a journalist and a Latin teacher. Their search takes them to the libraries of Swedish country houses, the Royal Library in Berlin, the Vatican Library, and the Herzog August Bibliothek in Wolfenbüttel, all places that Burman describes based on her experience of collecting Bremer's letters. The search is closely tied with the narrative structure of the novel, since events are either reported in letters exchanged between Gran and her friends and colleagues or in the diary that she keeps throughout the period of research. Brenner's letters are also reproduced as they are discovered in various archives and libraries. Only the prologue and the epilogue, "Nachspiel på Sju helvetes gluggar" (Follow-up Party at the Windows of the Seventh Hell) are written in the third person.

These framing chapters are set in academic circles in Uppsala, which are depicted with faithfulness to the period. In the structure of the work the author also alludes to Dante Alighieri's *Divina Comedia* (1307–1321): the nine chapters are called circles. The title of the novel also refers to the Muses of Greek mythology, who play a central part in creating suspense. The fictitious letters by Brenner that are retrieved from the depths of archives turn out to have been written to several leading women authors who were active at the end of the seventeenth and the beginning of the eighteenth centuries. In due course a secret association of women in different countries is disclosed, who, in the name of the goddess Diana, worked for international peace. Members included Aurora Königsmark, mistress to King Augustus II of Poland; the Mexican nun Sor Juana Inés de la Cruz; and Queen Kristina of Sweden. Brenner, it is revealed, trusted the Swedish warrior king Charles XII to support the goals of the association. The letters, which include messages about meetings and the election of new sisters to the association, use anagrams and codes in the style of Edgar Allan Poe.

The moon as a symbol of Diana is a leitmotiv throughout the novel–minor characters include the student Månson (Moon's son) and Miss Moon–and in the epilogue the moon acts as a counterpart to the sun in August Strindberg's introduction to his first novel, *Röda rummet* (The Red Room, 1879). In *Den tionde sånggudinnan* it is a nocturnal light that sweeps across the buildings beneath the rise on which, in the introduction, Gran enters into the pact with the Mephistophelian Schlippenbach. The novel is filled with other literary references. A magnificent account of the smorgasbord prepared for the members of the literary society in the introduction evokes earlier gastronomical descriptions in Swedish literature such as the anonymous fifteenth-century prose work *Skämtan om abbotar* (A Jest upon Abbots), and chapter 9 is interleaved with verses from the biblical book of Revelation.

In the final circle Gran is in St. Petersburg in 1917, where she discovers a stack of Brenner's letters to a Russian princess at the same time as workers are revolting in the city. Gran also has a series of erotic escapades with the Russian prince Felix Jusupov, one of Grigory Rasputin's assassins. During the riot in the city the entire collection of Brenner's letters are burned in a fire. She has now lost her wager and is prepared to accept the consequences of the defeat. In the epilogue she is subject to further temptation in the form of a visiting lecturer, Schleppfuß, who wants to persuade her to become a visiting scholar in war-torn Europe.

The search for the letters is as excitingly portrayed as in a detective novel, against the backdrop of the major world events of the 1910s, including the sinking of the *Titanic* and the outbreak of World War I. A sense of period is also created through details such as brand names of soap and cigarettes and descriptions of fashions and current books, as well as debates of the time, for example on women's suffrage, on spelling reform, and on the degenerate popular literature. The action takes place in two separate centuries, and parallels are also implied among many of the historical events and contemporary catastrophes such as the war in the former Yugoslavia and the sinking of the Baltic ferry *Estonia* in 1994, in which many Swedes died, and also to the ongoing struggle for equality of the sexes.

The novel includes a bibliography offering details of authentic letters and poems by Brenner, as well as references to newspaper articles and handbooks on history and religion that Burman used as sources. The bibliography is valuable to the reader who wishes to separate fact from fiction, since the author, as in her first novel, mixes them liberally. In composing fictitious poems and letters by Brenner, Burman displays a fine sense of the author's style.

In 1997 and 1998 Burman devoted herself to scholarly projects. She contributed a chapter on biographical literary research to a textbook, *Litteraturvetenskap: En inledning* (Literary Theory: An Introduction, 1998), and she participated in the important project *Finlands svenska litteraturhistoria* (Finland's Swedish-language Literature), contributing a section covering the period from 1730 to 1809.

At the same time, she was working on her third novel, *Cromwells huvud: Antropologisk komedi* (Cromwell's Head: An Anthropological Comedy), which was published in the autumn of 1998. Burman finished the novel during another period spent abroad, this time as a visiting fellow of Clare Hall at Cambridge University, from September 1996 to May 1997, which provided the time and the theme for her literary endeavor. The subtitle distinguishes *Cromwells huvud* from its predecessors, which had been called simply *romaner* (novels). The novel also represents a new phase in Burman's writing in other ways: the action takes place in the present day, and it is not centered on a Swedish author–rather, fiction itself is at the center.

Cromwells huvud is reminiscent of a bildungsroman. The heroine is a Swedish au pair, Malin, who finds herself in the family of a dean with four children in Cambridge. She meets and falls in love with a young student, Clive, and accompanies him to various events at the college, Lady Elizabeth Hall; she studies English and has literary ambitions. She is also courted, with some success, by a middle-aged anthropologist and museum curator, G. G. Bondeson, who arrives on the same plane from Sweden. When an academic year has passed, she is wiser and more mature and has found her way to happiness with the master of the college, an Egyptologist specializing in mummies.

Dust jacket for Burman's novel in which a Swedish au pair becomes entangled with an alcoholic anthropologist at a fictional Cambridge college (Collection of Barbro Ståhle Sjönell)

Running parallel to Malin's story is Bondeson's, who received a scholarship as a visiting researcher but who loses everything he cares for. His attempts to conquer women are unsuccessful, and he becomes increasingly alcoholic. His relationship with his wife in Sweden becomes estranged to the point that she sues for divorce, as is dramatically portrayed in their correspondence via e-mail. He loses his job at the museum, and after he fails in the spying mission given him by the master of the college, he is finally dismissed from Cambridge with a one-way ticket to Greenland, where a research post awaits him.

The environment of the college, its history and rituals, are described in great detail, and the academic year determines the structure of the novel. It is divided into three parts: Mickelsmässterminen 1996 (Michaelmas Term 1996), Fasteterminen 1997 (Lent Term 1997), and Påskterminen 1997 (Easter Term 1997). Each chapter is introduced by a heading and a subheading taken from the text of the chapter, a method of creating tension that was common in nineteenth-century novels.

The action is related by an intrusive narrator of the sort used by Henry Fielding and William Makepeace Thackeray. In metafictional fashion the narrator offers a running account of her efforts to produce *Cromwells huvud* itself. Burman also includes examples of Malin's writing in several genres, particularly her novel with its strongly autobiographical elements, as well as the beginnings of Bondeson's research project describing college life from an anthropological perspective.

Cromwells huvud is filled with literary allusions, as is underlined by the introductory mottos from the English seventeenth-century poet George Herbert, Lewis Carroll, Virginia Woolf, Hans Christian Andersen, Geoffrey Chaucer, and Evelyn Waugh. The novel also includes elements from a variety of genres, such as the fairy tale, the courtly romance, fantasy, the epistolary novel, and detective and spy fiction. In the first part of the novel Malin is described as an Alice in Wonderland, and it concludes among the tea cups of the "Mad Hatter's Tea Party" ride at Disneyland, where Bondeson is ejected from Peter Pan's Never-Never Land. Ingredients from spy stories recur in the form of murders, coded messages, secret societies, and exciting fights. E. C. Bentley, Dorothy L. Sayers, Colin Dexter, Graham Greene, Ian Fleming, and the Swedish spy-story writer Jan Guillou are among those who are referenced in the form of allusions and parodies.

The short story *Hammaren* (The Hammer) was published just before Christmas of 1999 by the Bonnier publishing house in a noncommercial edition and sent out as a Christmas gift to associates and Bonnier authors. The story takes place during three days of Christmas 1799, when two young men meet and celebrate the holidays together. The two men are Erik Gustaf Geijer and Esaias Tegnér, who later became pioneering figures of Swedish Romanticism. The meeting occurs at the home of Gustaf's family at the Ransäter estate in Värmland, a province that has been the birthplace of several important authors, Selma Lagerlöf among them. With *Hammaren* Burman returns to historical fiction riddled with literary allusions. The descriptions of nature and the strong presence of supernatural powers in the story can be read as a pastiche of Lagerlöf's works, particularly her first novel *Gösta Berlings saga* (1891; translated as *The Story of Gösta Berling*, 1917), which like *Hammaren* takes place at an estate in Värmland. Dramatic high points in Burman's short story are an attack by a pack of wolves, a sleigh race home from church, and a dangerous swim in a frozen lake by Gustaf. Both young men are attracted to an older woman, Elisabeth Liljebjörn, a magical storyteller with aspects of a wood nymph.

The events in *Hammaren* are included in the novel *Islandet* (The Ice Land), published in 2001. The novel consists of letters exchanged between Louise von Kloch and Fransiska B*** discussing the love affair between Geijer and Louise's sister Amalia von Helvig, an important German poet who kept company with both Goethe and Friedrich von Schiller. The historical point of departure is the meeting between Gustaf and Amalia during her visit to Uppsala in 1816. They are both the guests of Malla Silfverstolpe, at whose literary salon other romantic poets such as Per Daniel Amadeus Atterbom used to meet, give readings, and play music. The life at her salon is portrayed in Silfverstolpe's diaries, of which selected sections have been published.

The love story takes the form of a triangle: Gustaf must choose between duty, in the form of marriage to Anna Liljebjörn, his fiancée from Värmland, and passion, represented by his love for Amalia, a married woman with two children. In the end, the fiancée–who, like her mother, Elisabeth Liljebjörn, has magical powers–wins. Meanwhile readers witness the tentative flirtations between Gustaf and Amalia. The Ice Land becomes the symbol for the passion that is never consummated, a frozen area around the river Fyris in Uppsala, which in turn represents Sweden, a country where the freedom of women was still restricted at the time.

Among the historical figures in the novel appears a fictitious character, Fransiska B***, borrowed from Fredrika Bremer's most widely known novel, *Grannarne* (1837; translated as *The Neighbours*, 1842), where she is both the main character and the narrator. In 2000 Burman and her husband edited a scholarly edition of *Grannarne* in a series published by Svenska Vitterhetssamfundet (The Society for Belles-Lettres). In *Islandet* Burman continues the story of Fransiska: she has become a widow and been employed by the Geijer family as a piano teacher. Eventually she starts writing Gothic novels to support herself.

Islandet starts with a letter from Louise on 1 January 1832, in which she tells that her beloved sister Amalia has passed away and that it has fallen upon her to go through Amalia's papers. Among the papers she finds a story–*Hammaren*–now titled "Landskap i olja, 1799" (Landscape in Oil, 1799), which, according to Amalia, was written by Gustaf. The rest of the novel is divided into sections with similarly pictorial or painterly titles: "Interior i akvarell, 1816" (Interior in Watercolor, 1816) and "Porträtt. En daguerrotyp, 1847" (Portrait. A Daguerreotype, 1847). As indicated by the titles, the milieus of each section are painted with great care and attention. One of several leitmotivs in the novel is the legend of Vineta, previously alluded to in a short story and a novel by Lagerlöf, which conveys the idea that the past can only be kept alive by being retold.

For the two-hundredth anniversary of Bremer's birth, Burman published a six-hundred-page biography of the internationally celebrated author and champion of women's rights, a project financed by Stiftelsen Riksbankens Jubileumfond (The Bank of Sweden Tercenary Foundation). Burman displays great psychological insights in her portrayal of Bremer's development from a young girl with an insatiable thirst for knowledge to a globetrotter with a strong political agenda. The biography also describes the social and political structures of Bremer's time and documents the development of the publishing business.

With her thorough knowledge of literary history, her mastery of the pastiche, and her play on old narrative techniques, Carina Burman has created novels that are particularly appreciated by readers with broad literary backgrounds. Her novels entertain with their quotations from and allusions to earlier literature, but they also delight the average reader with their wit, suspense, and clever plots. As a novelist as well as researcher, Burman has contributed to the renewal of the interest in earlier Swedish literature.

Interviews:

Marianne Holm, "Levandegör litteraturhistorien: Carina Burman liknas vid Peter Englund," *Hallandsposten*, 12 November 1993, p. 28;

MarieLouise Samuelsson, "Avhandlingen blev en roman," *Svenska Dagbladet,* 27 November 1993, p. 33;

Annica Grenholm, "Hon ger nytt liv åt Kellgren,"*Uppsala Demokraten,* 2 December 1993, p. 26;

Anders Franck, "Carina kan sin Kellgren och berätttar *hela* historien," *Göteborgs-Posten,* 5 December 1993, p. 4;

Erik Peurell, "Från retorik till erotik," *Ergo,* 2 (1994): 16;

Björn Andersson, "Firad debutant tillbaka i historien," *Södermanlands Nyheter,* 26 June 1996, p. 4;

Anna Nordlund, "Brenners brev i Burmans bok: 1600-talsfeministen Sophia Brenners liv och verk redovisas i delvis fiktiv brevväxling," *Dagens Nyheter,* 3 July 1996, p. B7;

Anna Hellberg Lann, "Romansuccé för Uppsalaförfattare," *Uppsala Nya Tidning,* 10 August 1996, p. 3;

Magdalena Nordenson, "Flicka med flyt och skarp blick," *Nya Wermlands-Tidningen,* 17 August 1996, p. 6;

Ylva Bergman, "Forskning är sexigt," *Aftonbladet,* 21 August 1996, p. 3;

Tuva Korsström, "En sensuell lärdomsdam," *Hufvudstadsbladet,* 28 August 1996, p. 8;

Bibi Friedrichsen, "Visst är hon lik sin romanhjältinna: Forskaren Carina Burman samlar idéer i Anteckningsboken," *Norrköpings Tidningar,* 7 November 1996, p. 18;

Crister Enander, "En självklar ledamot av Svenska Akademien," *Tidningen Boken,* 7 (1996): 16–20;

Ingalill Hellman, "Det är roligt att gräva i gamla arkiv," *Nerikes Allehanda,* 24 October 1998, p. 32;

Sarah Death, "An interview with Carina Burman, March 1998," *Swedish Book Review,* 1 (1998): 4–6;

Leena Valtonen, "Cambridge var ingen vanlig stad," *Femina,* no. 10 (1998): 126–128;

Lena Karlsson, "Lekfullt om engelskt collegeliv," *impuls,* no. 12 (1998): 22–24;

Cecilia Gustavsson, "Jag sitter aldrig på Café Opera," *Aftonbladet,* 28 April 2001, pp. 34–35;

Ylva Herholz, "Carina Väcker Fredrika till liv," *ICA-kuriren,* no. 39 (2001): 8–10;

Carina Burman, "20 x 6: Förffattare om den svenska prosan," *Allt om Böcker,* no. 3 (2001): 21;

Maria Tellander, "Burman om Bremer," *Biblioteket i fokus,* no. 3 (2001): 21.

References:

Sarah Death, "Carina Burman," *Swedish Book Review,* 1 (1998): 2–3;

Peter Olsson, "Mer läsvärd än ett lexikon," *Moderna Tider* (April 2001): 66–67;

Margareta Strömstedt, "Docent Gran i frisk och fräck jakt på 'den svenska Sapho [sic],'" *Bok Journalen,* 7 (1996): 3–4;

Per Arne Tjäder, "Berättelser om 1900-talets infernaliska dynamik," *Bonniers Litterära Magasin,* 6 (1996): 49–51.

Sven Delblanc
(26 May 1931 – 15 December 1992)

Rochelle Wright
University of Illinois

BOOKS: *Eremitkräftan* (Stockholm: Bonnier, 1962);

Prästkappan: En heroisk berättelse (Stockholm: Bonnier, 1963);

Homunculus: En magisk berättelse (Stockholm: Bonnier, 1965); translated by Verne Moberg as *Homunculus: A Magic Tale* (Englewood Cliffs, N.J.: Prentice-Hall, 1969);

Ära och minne: Studier kring ett motivkomplex i 1700-talets litteratur (Stockholm: Bonnier, 1965);

Nattresa (Stockholm: Bonnier, 1967);

Åsnebrygga: Dagboksroman (Stockholm: Bonnier, 1969);

Åminne: En berättelse från Sörmland (Stockholm: Bonnier, 1970);

Zahak: Persiska brev (Stockholm: Bonnier, 1971);

Trampa vatten: Prosaprodukter (Göteborg: Författarförlaget, 1972);

Stenfågel: En berättelse från Sörmland (Stockholm: Bonnier, 1973);

Primavera: En konstnärlig berättelse (Stockholm: Bonnier, 1973);

Vinteride: En berättelse från Sörmland (Stockholm: Bonnier, 1974);

Kastrater: En romantisk berättelse (Stockholm: Bonnier, 1975); translated by C. W. Williams as *The Castrati: A Romantic Tale* (Ann Arbor, Mich.: Karoma, 1979);

Stadsporten: En berättelse från Sörmland (Stockholm: Bonnier, 1976);

Grottmannen (Stockholm: Bonnier, 1977);

Morgonstjärnan (Stockholm: Bonnier Alba, 1977);

Gunnar Emmanuel: En tidlös berättelse (Stockholm: Bonnier, 1978);

Gröna vintern (Stockholm: Bonnier Alba, 1978);

Den arme Richard: En melodram i två akter (Stockholm: Bonnier, 1978);

Kära farmor (Stockholm: Bonnier, 1979);

Ung man på havet (Stockholm: Bonnier, 1979);

Stormhatten: Tre Strindbergsstudier (Stockholm: Bonnier Alba, 1979);

Speranza: En samtide berättelse (Stockholm: Bonnier, 1980); translated by Paul Britten Austin as *Speranza* (New York: Viking, 1983);

Treklöver: Hjalmar Bergman, Birger Sjöberg, Vilhelm Moberg (Stockholm: Bonnier Alba, 1980);

Samuels bok (Stockholm: Bonnier, 1981);

Samuels döttrar (Stockholm: Bonnier, 1982);

Senecas död: Sorgespel (Stockholm: Bonnier, 1982);

Jerusalems natt: En berättelse (Stockholm: Bonnier, 1983);

Kanaans land (Stockholm: Bonnier, 1984);

Minnen från Kanada (Stockholm: Månadens bok, 1984);

Maria ensam (Stockholm: Bonnier, 1985);

Tal på Övralid 1985 (Motala: Stiftelsen Övralid/Heidenstamsällskapet, 1986);

Selma Lagerlöf (Stockholm: Svenska institutet, 1986);

Fågelfrö: Närande och giftigt från tre decennier (Stockholm: Bonnier, 1986);

Moria land (Stockholm: Bonnier, 1987);

Änkan (Stockholm: Bonnier, 1988);

Damiens: Ett sorgespel (Stockholm: Bonnier, 1989);

Ifigenia: Berättelse i två upptåg (Stockholm: Bonnier, 1990);

Livets ax: Barndomsminnen (Stockholm: Bonnier, 1991);

Slutord (Stockholm: Bonnier, 1991);

Homerisk hemkomst: Två essäer om Iliaden och Odysséen (Stockholm: Bonnier fakta, 1992);

Agnar (Stockholm: Bonnier, 1993).

Edition: *Hedebyborna: En berättelse från Sörmland* (Stockholm: Bonnier, 1993).

PLAY PRODUCTIONS: *Robotbas*, Göteborg, Ateljeteatern, 12 November 1966;

Fångvaktare, Göteborg, Göteborgs Stadsteater, 29 March 1969;

Kastrater, Stockholm, Dramaten, 22 March 1977;

Den arme Richard, Dramaten, Stockholm, 1 December 1978;

Senecas död, Stockholm, Dramaten, 19 September 1982;

Damiens, Göteborg, Göteborgs Stadsteater, 19 September 1991.

PRODUCED SCRIPTS: *Ariadne och påfågeln*, radio, Sveriges Radio, 13 December 1964;

Sven Delblanc (photograph by Harald Borgström)

Göm dig i livets träd, radio, Sveriges Radio, 16 May 1965;
Vingar, radio, Sveriges Radio, 7 January 1967;
Lekar i kvinnohagen, television, Sveriges Television, 11 March 1968;
Telefonservice, radio, Sveriges Radio, 4 October 1970;
Disputationen, television, Sveriges Television, 2 October 1972;
Gettysburg, radio, Sveriges Radio, 29 April 1973;
Stark, radio, Sveriges Radio, 8 and 12 September 1974;
Stadsresan, television, Sveriges Television, 12 April 1976;
Hedebyborna, television, Sveriges Television, 23 October–27 November 1978 (six parts);
Väntrummet, radio, Sveriges Radio, 1 April 1979;
Hedebyborna, television, Sveriges Television, 11 September–16 October 1980 (six parts);
Hedebyborna, television, Sveriges Television, 1 April–9 May 1982 (six parts);
Prästkappan, television, Sveriges Television, 29 September–13 October 1986 (three parts);
Kära farmor, television, Sveriges Television, 8 October–12 November 1990 (six parts);
Maskeraden, television, Sveriges Television, 16 March 1992;
Hemresa, television, Sveriges Television, 2 November 1993.

OTHER: *Ariadne och påfågeln,* in *Svenska Radiopjäser 1964* (Stockholm: Sveriges Radio, 1964), pp. 53–71;
Göm dig i livets träd, in *Svenska Radiopjäser 1965* (Stockholm: Sveriges Radio, 1965), pp. 73–104;
Vingar, in *Svenska Radiopjäser 1967* (Stockholm: Sveriges Radio, 1967), pp. 13–30;
Fångvaktare, in *Refuserat: Fyra pjäser,* by Delblanc, Lars Ardelius, P. C. Jersild, and Björn Runeborg (Stockholm: Bonnier, 1969), pp. 71–104;
Gettysburg, in *Svenska Radiopjäser 1973* (Stockholm: Sveriges Radio, 1973), pp. 11–36;
Stark, in *Svenska Radiopjäser 1974* (Stockholm: Sveriges Radio, 1974), pp. 21–42;
August Strindberg, *Stormar, vågor–: Dikter och prosalyrik,* selected, with a foreword, by Delblanc (Stockholm: Bonnier, 1974);
Ivar Lo-Johansson, *Passionsnoveller,* 2 volumes, selected, with an introduction, by Delblanc (Stockholm: Aldus/Bonnier, 1974);

"Hjalmar Bergman," in *Författarnas litteraturhistoria,* book 2, edited by Lars Ardelius and Gunnar Rydström (Stockholm: Författarförlaget, 1978), pp. 347–353;

"Frans G. Bengtsson," in *Författarnas litteraturhistoria,* book 3, edited by Ardelius and Rydström (Stockholm: Författarförlaget, 1978), pp. 118–125;

Väntrummet: Ett hörspel om Gustaf III, in *Svenska Radiopjäser 1979* (Stockholm: Sveriges Radio, 1979), pp. 77–96;

"Dostojevskij," in *Författarnas litteraturhistoria: De utländska författarna,* book 2, edited by Björn Håkanson (Stockholm: Författarförlaget, 1980), pp. 254–266;

"Stjernhielm–fader och föredöme," in *Att välja sin samtid: Essäer om levande svensk litteratur från Birgitta till Karlfeldt,* edited by Bengt Landgren (Stockholm: Norstedt, 1986), pp. 21–27;

Den svenska litteraturen, volumes 1–5, edited by Delblanc and Lars Lönnroth (Stockholm: Bonnier, 1987–1989)–includes sections by Delblanc.

SELECTED PERIODICAL PUBLICATIONS–UNCOLLECTED: "Ekarna och den styva leran: En studie över Ivar Lo-Johanssons 'berikade realism,'" *Tiden,* 6 (1961): 492–498;

"Sade och frihetens tragedi," *Bonniers Litterära Magasin,* 35, no. 6 (1966): 406–413;

"Bibliskt, klassiskt, sant," *Bonniers Litterära Magasin,* 50, no. 3 (1981): 151–152.

Though Sven Delblanc's reputation rests primarily on his novels, he also wrote radio plays, stage dramas, television scripts, memoirs, and many essays of literary criticism. This enormous productivity in various genres and media contributed to his overall impact; Delblanc's work reached wide sections of the Swedish population. He is, nevertheless, anything but a "popular" writer in the pejorative sense of the term. Many of his novels and plays explore complex, unsettling moral and philosophical issues, sometimes in an historical context–he was especially drawn to the eighteenth century–and sometimes in an allegorical or futuristic setting. A consummate stylist who often cultivated a rhetorical flair, Delblanc employed a prodigiously large vocabulary. Best known among the prose works are two interlocking novel series, each comprising four volumes, the first depicting the environment of his childhood and youth and the second the experiences of his maternal grandfather and his descendants. Concurrent with his creative activities, Delblanc earned a doctorate in comparative literature at the University of Uppsala and taught literature and writing there for many years. He also co-edited and contributed essays to *Den svenska litteraturen* (Swedish Literature, 1987–1989), a multivolume history published shortly before his death.

Sven Axel Herman Delblanc's paternal grandfather and grandmother were immigrants to Sweden from Germany and Denmark respectively; his maternal grandmother was Norwegian. Delblanc himself was born on 26 May 1931 on a homestead in Manitoba, Canada, where his parents, Siegfrid and Anna Delblanc, had settled with their two young daughters in 1928. Their economic circumstances, precarious from the start, worsened because of a series of bad harvests and the worldwide depression, and in 1934 the family returned to Sweden. Most of Delblanc's childhood was spent in Vagnhärad in the province of Sörmland. His parents' marriage, never harmonious, ended in divorce in 1942. His father later returned alone to Canada, where young Sven joined him during the summer of 1947. Relentless physical labor, semistarvation, and psychological abuse nearly broke him, but he managed to escape by secretly persuading his grandmother to send him a ticket home.

In 1952, after military service, Delblanc enrolled at the University of Uppsala to study literature and history. He received his licentiate degree in comparative literature in 1959 and began teaching the same year. Between 1958 and 1964 he also published articles on literary topics in the newspaper *Arbetarbladet.* His dissertation, published as *Ära och minne: Studier kring ett motivkomplex i 1700-talets litteratur* (Honor and Remembrance: A Motif Complex in Eighteenth-Century Literature, 1965), earned him a position as docent. In 1955 he married Christina Ekegård; their children, Anna and Fredrik, were born in 1960 and 1967.

Delblanc made his literary debut with *Eremitkräftan* (The Hermit Crab, 1962), an allegorical narrative, composed in lean, spare prose, that encapsulates what became a unifying theme in his entire oeuvre: the impossible, yet necessary, search for freedom and fulfillment. The protagonist of the novel, Axel, initially inhabits an enclosed, rigidly hierarchical and authoritarian society called the Prison, from which he escapes to the White City, which seems to offer a positive, unfettered alternative: everyone lives in the present, following their impulses and desires. He discovers, however, that this carefree hedonism disguises an insidious form of mind control and that a terrifying brutality lurks just beneath the surface. Fleeing once again, Axel is taken in by a fisherman and his daughter, Judith, who profess asceticism, resignation, and belief in a higher power. Their conviction that God alone determines one's fate conflicts with Axel's insistence on his own autonomy. Eventually, acknowledging the illusory nature of all external freedom, he returns to the Prison and begs to be readmitted. Vulnerable like a hermit crab, he feels safe to continue his search for another alternative only within the protection of an authoritarian shell. This apparent paradox should not be read as a defense of totalitarian systems but rather as an expression of Delblanc's deep-seated pessimism, tempered nevertheless by the insistence that human beings must behave as if meaningful action is possible.

Prästkappan: En heroisk berättelse (The Cassock: An Heroic Tale, 1963), a picaresque bildungsroman, provides a striking contrast with regard to setting and style. Events take place in 1784 in the Prussia of Frederick the Great. The characters Hermann Anderz and his sidekick, Lång-Hans, like Don Quixote and Sancho Panza, represent opposite existential stances; Hermann seeks adventure, casting himself in heroic roles, while his servant remains firmly anchored in reality. Delblanc's narrative is structured around an inversion of the myth of Hercules; rather than overcoming a series of obstacles, Hermann succumbs to them. His idealism defeated, he ends, like Frederick, as an oppressor. Despite its burlesque tone, *Prästkappan* is thus, like *Eremitkräftan*, an allegory of absolute power, doomed resistance, and capitulation.

Homunculus: En magisk berättelse (1965; translated as *Homunculus: A Magic Tale*, 1969) encompasses elements of science fiction and the spy novel as well as political satire and allegory. The protagonist, Sebastian Verdén, a modern-day alchemist, brings to life a human-like creature in his bathtub in a Stockholm suburb. International forces, both American and Soviet, want to exploit Sebastian's ability, and a wild chase ensues. In defending his creation Sebastian becomes increasingly ruthless, until his behavior is ethically indistinguishable from that of his pursuers. Preternaturally sensitive, the homunculus recoils and withers away. Finally Sebastian commits suicide, a last act of protest against total degradation. Delblanc's dark, despairing narrative illuminates the impossibility of either "pure" science or free will in the contemporary world.

A more positive alternative is suggested in *Nattresa* (Night Journey, 1967). This novel introduces the character Axel Weber, Delblanc's fictional alter ego, and explores, in allegorical guise, the author's own artistic dilemma: how to merge individual and collective interests, incorporate innovation within the framework of tradition, and reconcile potentially conflicting aesthetic and political goals. Though no definitive answers are provided, the narrative concludes on a note of hope. Critics objected that the message was unclear. Uncomfortable with programmatic demands and disavowing the claim that the sole function and purpose of literature is utilitarian, Delblanc temporarily ceased writing fiction.

Delblanc in the navy in 1951

In keeping, however, with the documentary orientation that dominated literature of the late 1960s and early 1970s, he published several books of nonfiction that blurred genre boundaries while addressing contemporary social and political issues. *Åsnebrygga: Dagboksroman* (Asses' Bridge: Diary-Novel, 1969), based on a diary he kept in 1968–1969 while a visiting associate professor at the University of California, Berkeley, comments on topical events—police brutality at the 1968 Democratic National Convention in Chicago and in the People's Park debacle in 1969, race relations, the American political system—as well as his own efforts to overcome writer's block and construct "en bro tillbaka till romanen" (a bridge back to the novel). *Zahak: Persiska brev* (Zahak: Letters from Persia, 1971) reports on a trip to Iran, undertaken on a government fellowship, and reflects on totalitarian systems past and present. *Trampa vatten: Prosaprodukter* (Treading Water: Prose Pieces, 1972), a collection of short essays ranging in tone from contemplative to polemical and satirical, makes salient observations about personal matters, Swedish politics, literature, and the academic world.

Cover for Delblanc's 1973 novel, about a race of people known as the Sibbessons (Collection of Rochelle Wright)

When he took up belles lettres again, Delblanc turned to the past, producing four historical novels set in his hometown, called "Hedeby" in his fictional world: *Åminne* (River Memory, 1970), *Stenfågel* (Stone Bird, 1973), *Vinteride* (Winter Lair, 1974), and *Stadsporten* (The City Gate, 1976), each with the subtitle *En berättelse från Sörmland* (A Tale from Sörmland). All were univerally praised by critics and attracted a large audience. In contrast to several earlier novels that focus on a single protagonist in conflict with the world around him, the Hedeby tetralogy presents a collective, an entire community. The time frame is from 1937 to 1945, but a more sweeping chronological scope is introduced through stories from the past, presented as local oral tradition, and the perspective of the narrator, Axel Weber, who looks back and comments on events that occurred when he was a child. The years included in the narrative proper represent a crucial turning point in the evolution of Sweden from a tradition-bound, patriarchal rural society to the home of social democracy, a change that Delblanc views with ambivalence.

In *Åminne* the yearly tradition of clearing the river of undergrowth has long served as a male rite of passage and is a mark of self-governance and local autonomy; assignment to the task by consensus among farmers and smallholders signals respect. When Baron Urse, facing bankruptcy and desperate for validation, insinuates himself into the cooperative venture, it fails, and thenceforward the municipality hires outsiders to do the job. The status quo is forever altered. The baron asserts a last vestige of his feudal rights by seducing young Märta, daughter of the ne'er-do-well Svensson and his long-suffering wife, Signe, but his ultimate response to economic ruin is to drown himself in the river. The illness and death of Märta's maternal grandfather, Abraham Styf, who resembles an Old Testament prophet in appearance and demeanor and whose authority among his peers was unquestioned, also represents the end of an era.

In *Stenfågel* and *Vinteride* economic hardship, bitterly cold winters followed by bad harvests, and the war in Europe bring about further change. As the aristocracy is decimated, estates are divided; many farmers, too, must leave the land. Even those who prosper, such as Lille-Lars in Näsby, encounter obstacles: the death of his only son leaves no one to take over the farm, legislation protects agricultural laborers from working overtime on demand, and the younger generation wants to move to town. Märta is the first to leave; in *Stadsporten* her mother, Signe, and younger sisters, as well as many others, have joined her.

Beginning in *Stenfågel* various characters illustrate differing political and personal responses to this period of transition and participate in an ongoing philosophical debate–with each other or in the form of internal monologue–that highlights their respective existential situations. In *Åminne* Nikodemus Johansson, an ordinary worker and a cuckold regarded with contempt in the community, is nevertheless assigned a position of responsibility in the river-clearing ritual. His integrity restored, in later volumes Nikodemus gradually rises to a position of local power through the Social Democratic Party, where he becomes a voice of moderation and compromise who consistently helps the less fortunate behind the scenes. In *Stadsporten* Kurt Karlsson, a Hedeby native transplanted to town, is among the party faithfully working to improve the common lot; he and his wife,

Nilla, display solidarity by opening their home to anyone who needs encouragement and support. Kurt is uncomfortable with the demands of radicals such as Moritz who promote strikes as a weapon of class warfare without considering the cost in human suffering. Oscar Hesekiel Ahlenius, son of the Hedeby pastor, preaches socialism to the unwashed masses in *Stenfågel* and finds a convert in Signe Svensson, but he retreats when his own privileged position seems endangered, eventually transmuting into a promising career politician with the revisionist Social Democrats. This younger generation of leaders with no personal experience of poverty and deprivation has become, Delblanc implies, a new elite, nearly as remote from the masses as the aristocracy of old.

Not everyone takes comfort in the belief that conditions are improving and progress is inevitable. Signe, prematurely aged by economic want and family responsibilities, refuses to resign herself but finds it increasingly difficult to maintain optimism and hope. Märta cannot see past her own personal situation: she wants to be a pampered, middle-class wife and grows frustrated and bitter when her youth and beauty do not help her rise socially. Her husband, Erik, in turn, is cowed by Märta's demands and depressed by his own perceived failure, so much so that an ill-suppressed death wish leads to his actual demise. Among Erik's contemporaries, Elon, a farmhand in Hedeby, gives up completely, withdrawing into passivity and isolation, while Pärsy, operating outside the law, tries to find a shortcut to riches and ends up behind bars.

In *Vinteride* and *Stadsporten* the young Axel, a peripheral figure in the earlier volumes, assumes a larger role, together with his childhood friend Agnes Karolina, Signe's daughter and Märta's younger sister. Axel, in response to an oppressive home life, becomes a pessimist and nihilist who wonders why human beings must go on living at all. Agnes, in contrast, has faith—less in God or in social democracy than in her concept of the life force itself. For years her loyal devotion and her mere presence comfort Axel, but at the end of *Stadsporten,* recognizing that they have irrevocably grown apart, he bids her farewell. In the series as a whole, however, unconditional love, symbolized by the blossoming of the wild cherry tree, functions as a kind of secular redemption, a positive counterbalance to the physical and emotional deprivation that many of the characters must endure.

Throughout the series, two groups of drinkers also illustrate changes within social groups and the gradual, if partial, leveling of class distinctions. The working-class (though unemployed) outcasts called the Arskummet (Dregs) include Svensson and three boon companions who gather daily at a local watering hole. Their so-called betters, the doctor Lundewall, the bank director Müntzing, and the herring merchant Zetterlind, congregate at a nearby town restaurant. The main activity of both groups is gossip, though Svensson's stories tend to be less malicious than the gibes of Müntzing and Lundewall. By 1945, when *Stadsporten* ends, the Dregs have disbanded: Svensson is dead of liver disease, and the others have found jobs and are more or less productive members of society. The bourgeois alcoholics continue unabated, but Müntzing and Lundewall find that their authority does not go unchallenged: they no longer can tyrannize the staff and are shunted aside, forced to share a table with "ordinary workers" such as Erik, while the solid Social Democrat Nikodemus celebrates his fiftieth birthday upstairs. When the old guard complain, they are summarily thrown out.

Especially in *Åminne,* Delblanc frequently calls attention to the role of the narrator by stressing that he chooses what material to include, by having him enter into his own fictional creation, and by explicitly denying that he is omniscient. The narrator also playfully manipulates his characters to offer alternative points of view, in particular by periodically calling forth from the shadows Baron Urse's illegitimate relative, called Mon Cousin, to provide his own commentary. Mon Cousin, in turn, refers to the narrator's coercion and to his own status as a fictional character. Delblanc thus deconstructs his own authorial role while simultaneously emphasizing that there is no single, definitive version of any story.

In the Hedeby series, Axel's family remains in the periphery. In *Kära farmor* (Dear Grandma, 1979), Delblanc turned more directly to his own family history, though the portrayal of his paternal grandmother and other relatives is less concerned with verisimilitude than with personality types. During the first half of the 1980s he published a second tetralogy, this time basing the characters on his maternal grandfather and his descendants, that again drew both critical acclaim and a wide readership: *Samuels bok* (Samuel's Book, 1981), *Samuels döttrar* (Samuel's Daughters, 1982), *Kanaans land* (The Land of Canaan, 1984), and *Maria ensam* (Maria Alone, 1985). Delblanc incorporates extant documentary material, such as his grandfather's diary, as well as the oral accounts of family members and, in the final volume, his own recollections.

Samuels bok, awarded the Nordic Council Literature Prize, traces a trajectory from hope and faith to tragic defeat, encapsulated in titles of the three sec-

Covers for the last two volumes in Delblanc's historical tetralogy set in a fictionalized version of his hometown, published in 1974 and 1976, respectively (Collection of Rochelle Wright)

tions of the novel, "Pastor Eriksson," "Mäster Samuel," and "Tok-Sams Ungar" (Crazy Sam's Children), which characterize the protagonist first as Pastor Eriksson, then as Master Samuel, and finally as Crazy Sam. Educated and ordained in the United States, Samuel discovers after returning to Sweden that the Lutheran State Church considers his training inadequate. With no help from wealthy relatives and a wife and children to support, he cannot afford an additional year of study at Uppsala. Repeated appeals for a dispensation are turned down. Samuel is forced to accept a poorly paid position as an assistant pastor on Gotland that separates him from his family. Eventually he gives up, joining them in Värmland, where he becomes a schoolmaster, a less prestigious post for which he furthermore is temperamentally unsuited. Unable to cope, Samuel gradually loses his grip on reality and dies in an asylum. The tragedy of potential unfulfilled is repeated in the next generation with Samuel's son Abel, a talented poet. Without intellectual peers and denied advanced schooling, he nevertheless refuses to become a manual laborer. This assertion of will causes him to be committed; treated as mad, he retreats into his own world, ruled by a bizarre interpretation of Gnostic philosophy, and dies young.

Samuels döttrar focuses on the women of the family. Cecilia, Samuel's wife, represents an unquestioning tradition of female compliance and servitude grounded in biblical teaching. Elin, the oldest daughter, manages to maintain an attitude of hope and high spirits in the face of adversity and eventually marries a man who, though uneducated, provides security and love. The youngest, Rebecca, is less fortunate, having inherited the family strain of mental instability. Maria, the middle daughter, at first carries on Samuel's intellectual heritage: she finds satisfaction, fulfillment, and economic independence as a teacher but then, following her mother's example of self-sacrifice, gives up her autonomy when Fredrik Weber proposes and asks her to immigrate with him to Canada.

Kanaans land concerns the Weber family in Manitoba. Fredrik embraces life on the frontier as a challenge that offers scope for his strength and energy. Maria, in contrast, suffers deeply, separated from her family, isolated from meaningful human contact, and increasingly alienated from her husband, whose violent rages are a negative contrast to the gentle, loving temperament of her deceased father. Maria's longing for home is intertwined with her longing for the comfort of religious faith, but the last vestige of that consolation vanishes when, desperately ill herself, she listens helplessly while her newborn daughter cries herself to death. Crop failure and a decline in the international agricultural market create another kind of crisis, and Maria impels the reluctant Fredrik to return to Sweden.

The final volume, *Maria ensam*, overlaps chronologically and geographically with the Hedeby series, and various characters from the earlier novels reappear. The Webers now have settled in Hedeby. Fredrik, frustrated that his dream of independence has floundered, becomes increasingly brutal toward his family and acquires a new woman. Divorce follows, and Maria resumes teaching. She finds that repatriation to her homeland, which in Canada she had regarded as the lost paradise, does not bring the happiness she had anticipated. Cecilia has withdrawn into frozen piety; Rebecca, like father and brother before her, has died mad; only Elin offers true companionship. Maria discovers as well that she cannot regain her lost faith. Bitter and broken, she eventually commits suicide.

A note of hope is nevertheless introduced through Maria and Fredrik's son Axel, again serving as the author's fictional stand-in. As a child he takes refuge from an overwhelmingly terrifying present, personified by his unpredictable, violent father, by retreating to what he calls the "land bortom land" (land beyond land), a mystical state of rapture. Given the family pattern, it seems possible, even likely, that he will forgo reality permanently. Axel's intellectual and creative gifts are reinforced through schooling, however, and as an adolescent he begins to acquire friends. Samuel's heritage can ultimately be positive and life affirming.

In the series about Samuel and his descendants, Delblanc eschews the playful manipulation of characters and sometimes rollicking style of the Hedeby novels. Instead, in keeping with the religious orientation of the pastor and his family, he incorporates biblical quotations and cadences, creating patterns of thematic and rhythmic repetition. Despite this biblical grounding, the Samuel tetralogy in its entirety can be read as a parable of the gradual secularization of Swedish society, and Western society in general, during the decades portrayed.

Between the two series, Delblanc produced—in addition to the television script of *Hedebyborna* (The People of Hedeby, 1978, 1980, 1982), broadcast in three installments of six episodes apiece—*Gröna vintern* (Green Winter, 1978), an eclectic collection of short pieces that includes imagined conversations with various fictional characters, including his own, and two volumes of literary criticism: *Stormhatten: Tre Strindbergsstudier* (Storm Hat: Three Strindberg Studies, 1979), consisting of long essays on August Strindberg, and *Treklöver: Hjalmar Bergman, Birger Sjöberg, Vilhelm Moberg* (Three-Leaf Clover: Hjalmar Bergman, Birger Sjöberg, and Vilhelm Moberg, 1980), with thoughtful assessments of the titular authors. Overlapping with the two tetralogies, he also published plays and novels that, while not linked through setting and characters, address related philosophical and existential questions.

A recurring topic, explored in various historical contexts as well as in present-day settings, is the problematic relationship of art and the artist to the dominant power structure. *Primavera: En konstnärlig berättelse* (Primavera: An Artistic Tale, 1973), though loosely connected to the fictional world of the Hedeby novels, serves primarily an autonomous allegorical commentary on the role of artistic creation in contemporary society. Delblanc posits the existence of a separate, clandestine race called the Sibbessons, survivors of a past utopian paradise that affirmed the creative and procreative impulse, who also embody hope for the future. The cast of characters includes the narrator, Erik Jerobeam Ahlenius (brother of Oscar Ahlenius from *Stenfågel*), an artist who specializes in counterfeiting modernist masters; Count Kettil Kyhle, obsessed with heraldry and his family's illustrious past; an alcoholic Finn, Penti; and the eponymous Primavera, in actuality named Vera Johansson, who performs in a pornographic live show. Though Ahlenius eventually achieves fame and fortune with portraits of prominent politicians engaged in group sex, his production is controlled by commercial interests and the patronage of the public, which is as fickle as any patron of old. The loss of Primavera, his inspiration and muse, and the mass suicide of the Sibbessons suggest the impotence of the creative life force in the face of such pressures.

Toivo Pawlo and Ulla Sjoblom in Delblanc's play Kastrater *(The Castrati, 1977), based on his 1975 novel of the same title*

Written while Delblanc was a guest at Rungstedlund, the estate of Karen Blixen (known as Isak Dinesen), *Kastrater: En romantisk berättelse* (1975; translated as *The Castrati: A Romantic Tale,* 1979) is dedicated to the memory of Babette, the great culinary artist of Blixen's "Babette's Feast" (1958). Like that story, *The Castrati* is a reflection on the significance and impact of art and the artist's dependence on an audience, thus also addressing many of the same core issues as *Primavera* but at a temporal and geographic remove: the setting is Florence on a single night in 1783, when a group that includes the Swedish king Gustaf III; the Stuart pretender to the English throne, Charles Edward; and the supremely gifted castrato singer Farinelli assembles for a séance. Farinelli, looking back on long years in service to his art and to those in political power, questions the validity of his sacrifice. The operation that made his career possible also cut him off permanently from a normal life; moreover, composers of the present reject the highly ornamented style he perfected in favor of a neoclassical ideal of simplicity. His younger colleague Marchesi, who embraces the new style, maintains that art can inspire human beings in socially beneficial ways. To King Gustaf, art serves the powerful, and Marchesi's idealism is easier to manipulate than the radical pessimism of Farinelli. Delblanc's deliberately artful and florid wordplay in *Kastrater* may be intended as an allusion both to opera seria and to Blixen. Delblanc's stage version of the novel premiered in 1977.

Grottmannen (The Cave Man, 1977), set in contemporary Sweden, focuses on a writer rather than a visual artist or performer, but the narrative once again illustrates the impossibility of complete artistic freedom and the consequent alienation of the artist in a materialistic society. The title character in *Gunnar Emmanuel: En tidlös berättelse* (Gunnar Emmanuel: A Timeless Tale, 1978), an idealistic, somewhat naive creative-writing student, is contrasted with his teacher, the pedantic, cynical, disillusioned narrator "Sven Delblanc," perhaps revealing two aspects of the author himself. That Gunnar vanishes without trace may be another indication of the futility or inadequacy of virtue and commitment. The drama *Den arme Richard: En melodram i två akter* (Poor Richard: A Melodrama in Two Acts, 1978), like *Kastrater,* uses a particular historical context to examine the relationship between the artist and those in political power. Here, Richard Strauss is portrayed as an opportunist who kowtows to the Nazis while professing to serve only music. Yet, the play concludes with the third-act trio of *Der Rosenkavalier* (1911), perhaps the most ravishing ensemble ever composed for the female voice.

Whatever the personal flaws of Strauss, the music endures. Whereas Strauss claims to remain apolitical, the philosopher Seneca, in the drama *Senecas död: Sorgespel* (The Death of Seneca: A Tragedy, 1982), enters the political arena to no avail: his involvement in a plot against Nero is discovered, and he is forced to commit suicide. Once again, the power structure and the status quo are upheld.

Kastrater is the first volume of what Delblanc subsequently referred to as "svartsynens trigoli" (the trilogy of pessimism), which also encompasses *Speranza: En samtida berättelse* (Speranza: A Contemporary Tale, 1980; translated, 1983) and *Jerusalems natt: En berättelse* (Jerusalem's Night: A Tale, 1983), historical novels concerned with the powerlessness of idealism, faith, and innocence in a world where might makes right. *Speranza*, like *Kastrater*, is set in the eighteenth century, specifically the 1790s, when the growth of rationalism was accompanied by the loss of traditional religious faith, and idealistic, egalitarian principles provided a striking contrast to unshackled autocratic despotism. The ironically named *Speranza* ("hope" in Italian) is a slave ship carrying the narrator, the young nobleman Malte Moritz, to the New World. Moritz is initially a parlor radical who parrots the slogans of the French Revolution while remaining spoiled, arrogant, and utterly ignorant of political reality. Confronted with a slave uprising, he ultimately sides with the oppressors. *Speranza* offers a scathing condemnation of naïfs and hypocrites who espouse political liberty and profess to support egalitarian principles but collapse at the first show of strength from those in power, a phenomenon not restricted to the 1790s. The final sentence reads "Speranza seglar alltjämt" (Speranza still sails).

Jerusalems natt, localized to the siege of Jerusalem in A.D. 70, is a protracted religious-philosophical debate contrasting the Hellenistic and Judeo-Christian views of life with their respective emphasis on reason and faith. Participants include Flavius Josephus, the Jewish historian who tries to serve two masters, the Romans and the Jews, and is rejected by both; Titus, the representative of earthly power and the "great idea" of Rome; and the narrator, the Greek philosopher Philemon, yet another intellectual who obeys whatever force is strongest, in this instance Titus. History, Delblanc reminds readers, is written by the victors. According to the old Jew Eleasar, the last surviving member of Jesus' inner circle, the Gospels, codified by the men who seized power when Christianity was institutionalized, have distorted Jesus' female-directed teachings, which centered on the merging of masculine and feminine characteristics.

Cover for Delblanc's 1982 novel, the second volume in his tetralogy based on the lives of his mother's family (Collection of Rochelle Wright)

Two novels of the late 1980s, *Moria land* (Moria Land, 1987) and *Änkan* (The Widow, 1988), hark back thematically to *Eremitkräftan*. *Moria land*, in keeping with a long tradition of dystopian literature, takes place several decades in the future, when Sweden has become a totalitarian state reminiscent of the Prison in the earlier novel. The title alludes to Abraham's intended sacrifice of Isaac, but in Delblanc's narrative, the father, once a writer, is a liberal and rationalist who has actually betrayed his son to the authorities. Only gradually does his guilt become apparent, since he projects it onto the world around him. The hedonistic contemporary world of *Änkan*, in contrast, resembles the White City of *Eremitkräftan*. In this fantastic tale of a woman who inherits millions, acquires a mysterious white powder that makes her young again, and assumes a new identity in order to

Cover for the second volume of Delblanc's memoirs, published posthumously in 1993, with a self-portrait of the author (Collection of Rochelle Wright)

take revenge on those who have done her wrong, Delblanc deliberately combines popular entertainment with serious social commentary. Taken together, *Moria land* and *Änkan* demonstrate, as does *Eremitkräftan*, that absolute order and unhampered freedom are equally destructive.

For decades Delblanc was preoccupied with the historical figure Damiens, would-be assassin of King Louis XV of France, and there are scattered references to him throughout his oeuvre. In the drama *Damiens: Ett sorgespel* (Damiens: A Tragedy, 1989), however, the true protagonist is not the title character, who is immediately captured and brutally tortured and executed, but his polar opposite, Cardinal Richelieu, whose triumph is a foregone conclusion in the uneven struggle of idealism versus self-serving, unscrupulous pragmatism. The other characters are either innocent victims—girls forced by poverty or the greed of others into whoredom and lackeys representing the oppressed masses—or opportunists who would

like nothing better than to follow Richelieu's example but lack his skill and single-mindedness of purpose. In a brief afterword Delblanc notes that, thematically, the play is the logical extension and conclusion of the earlier "trilogy of pessimism."

The novel *Ifigenia: Berättelse i två upptåg* (Iphigenia: Tale in Two Diversions, 1990) once again considers the role of art and the artist, providing a bitter but savagely funny reassessment of the most famous events of classical antiquity. According to this account, the poet of the *Iliad* and the *Odyssey* is not Homer but Demodokus, whose source of inspiration is frequently Dionysus rather than Apollo. The sacrifice of Iphigenia, supposedly to placate Artemis, in actuality was to satisfy power-hungry rivals of Agamemnon. Afterward Odysseus cynically manipulates Demodokus into creating a more stirring and uplifting version of what has transpired, and the myth of Iphigenia on Tauris is born. The Trojan War itself is exposed as an excuse for murder and plunder, its ostensible cause—the kidnapping of Helen—a fabrication. Delblanc strips away the supposed heroism of familiar figures to reveal Agamemnon as a vacillating weakling, Odysseus as a scheming egotist, and Achilles as a brutal, bombastic, punch-drunk pederast, while Demodokus is the unwilling but cowed servant of the powers-that-be whose function is to glorify the meaningless slaughter. Throughout, he and his friend Tersites, a Cassandra-like figure who tells the truth even when it is unpopular, carry on a dialogue about historical veracity, the distortions and outright falsifications demanded by patrons of literature, and the powerlessness of both the soothsayer and the poet. Demodokus's final humiliation comes when Odysseus throws him into a pit to force him to compose a poem in honor of his tormentor. Both the *Iliad* and the *Odyssey* become enormously popular—but Demodokus does not get credit for them.

For much of the 1980s Delblanc was engaged in a collaborative scholarly project, serving as co-editor, with Lars Lönnroth, of all but the final volume of *Den svenska litteraturen* and writing many sections of the text. He also continued to publish his own critical essays. *Fågelfrö: Närande och giftigt från tre decennier* (Birdseed: Nourishment and Poison from Three Decades, 1986) is a collection of newspaper articles on literary, political, and personal topics; the first category features a bitingly amusing satire of the method employed by the Swedish Academy in selecting Nobel Prize winners. In a more serious vein, *Homerisk hemkomst: Två essäer om Iliaden och Odysséen* (Return to Homer: Two Essays on the *Iliad* and the *Odyssey*, 1992), an outgrowth of *Ifigenia*, offers deeply insightful essays on the Homeric texts, which Delblanc had read and reread for decades. During these years he was repeatedly recognized for his creative and scholarly achievements, receiving the Öuralid Prize in 1985, the Pilot Prize in 1986, the Swedish Academy's Kellgren Prize in 1989, and the August Prize in 1991, when he also was awarded the title of professor by the Swedish government.

Both *Åsnebrygga* and *Trampa vatten* include vignettes from Delblanc's traumatic childhood; early memories and experiences also figure in many works of fiction, with Axel Weber functioning as the author's alter ego. In all these accounts, Delblanc's father, called Fredrik Weber in the novels, appears as a volatile, violent-tempered tyrant. The memoir *Livets ax: Barndomsminnen* (The Staff of Life: Memories of Childhood, 1991) retells much of this material, stripped of any fictional artifice. The author traces his fundamental pessimism and insecurity to the impact of this all-powerful, yet unpredictable and inscrutable figure, a symbol of blind oppression and might whose abuse left him emotionally crippled for life. A recurring refrain in *Livets ax* is the futility of combating a force that by definition cannot be overcome and the urge to flee either by running away or by becoming petrified, sealed off from pain. A counterbalancing positive image, the blossoming cherry tree, functions as a symbol of life, love, and hope. The autobiographical roots of significant themes and motifs in Delblanc's fiction are here made explicit.

In 1990, after completing the memoir, Delblanc was diagnosed with terminal bone cancer. *Slutord* (Final Words, 1991), a personal reflection on his response to physical pain and to the knowledge that he was dying, though subjectively true, proved premature; when the disease went into remission, Delblanc was able to complete a second volume of memoirs, *Agnar* (Chaff, 1993), published posthumously. Though written with the inescapable consciousness of mortality, this account, too, grapples with the past rather than the present. As the title suggests, *Agnar* does not represent a sustained analytical effort, but once again, the relationship to his father is of central importance. When he was sixteen years old, Delblanc, in a vain search for the benevolent, loving parent he had never had, joined his father in Manitoba. His eventual defiance of paternal authority gave him the inner strength to move on, to establish meaningful contact with others, and to pursue an education and an academic and literary career. The scars nevertheless remained. Looking back, Delblanc distances himself from his pain through gallows humor and by searching for archetypal patterns; repetitive phrases, rhetorical stylistic devices, and allusions to other works of literature and to myth lend cohesiveness to the narrative. His final creative work, the television drama *Hemresa* (Journey Home, 1993)–about an aging, mortally ill writer confronting and becoming reconciled with the past–similarly lays personal ghosts to rest. Delblanc died on 15 December 1992.

The final sentence of *Agnar* proclaims, "Med ett pekfinger kan man skapa en värld" (An index finger can create a world). Though the author is referring to his physical frailty and the sheer effort of will necessary to complete the manuscript, the line may also be regarded as an artistic credo. In thirty extraordinarily productive years, Sven Delblanc created many fictional universes. Whether historical pastiche, philosophical allegory, contemporary satire, or autobiographical narrative, they are notable for their stylistic brilliance, psychological acuity, and philosophical depth.

Letters:
Lars Helander, ed., *Kära Alice! Sven Delblancs brev till sin syster i Canada kommenterade av henne själv* (Kristianstad: Sveriges Radio, 1995).

Interviews:
Karl Erik Lagerlöf, "Frihetens villkor," in his *Samtal med 60-talister* (Stockholm: Bonnier, 1965), pp. 127–135;

Mats Johansson, "Sven Delblanc: Jag efterlyser den pragmatiska socialdemokratin," in his *Kulturen och friheten* (Stockholm: Timbro, 1982), pp. 11–19.

References:
Eva Adolfsson, "De farliga kvinnorna: Nyläsning av Sven Delblancs roman Nattresa," *Ord och Bild,* 82, no. 8 (1973): 501–512;

Adolfsson and others, "Den Axel kring vilken världen rör sig," *Bonniers Litterära Magasin,* 39 (1970): 391–400;

Beata Agrell, *Frihet och fakticitet: Om oordning, ordning, lydnad och frihet i Sven Delblancs roman Prästkappan,* 2 volumes (Göteborg: Korpen, 1982);

Agrell, "Ska man underkasta sig och tåla? Om dysterheten i Sven Delblancs romaner," in *Linjer i nordisk prosa: Sverige 1965–1975,* edited by Kjerstin Norén (Lund: Cavefors, 1977), pp. 53–105;

Lars Ahlbom, *Frihetens tragedi: Livssyn, estetik och hjälteroller i Sven Delblancs författarskap* (Stockholm: Bonnier, 1989);

Ahlbom, "Hedeby och Sven Delblancs människosyn," *Bonniers Litterära Magasin,* 44, no. 3 (1975): 139–155;

Ahlbom, *Sven Delblanc* (Stockholm: Natur och kultur, 1996);

Ahlbom, "Sven Delblancs Ifigenia: Om människooffer, dikt och sanning," *Artes,* 22, no. 1 (1996): 60–74;

Thomas Anderberg, "Gud och ondskan: Teodicéproblemet speglat i Sven Delblancs böcker om Samuel och hans familj," *Fenix*, 7, no. 4 (1989): 99–142;

Lars Bäckström, "Sven Delblanc och Hitlers barndom," *Horisont*, 44, no. 1 (1997): 38–45;

Helene Blomqvist, *"Bara kärlekens blommande träd": Delblancs Samuelssvit som struktural* (Göteborg: Litteraturvetenskapliga institutionen, 1993);

Britta Fritzdorf, *Symbolstudier i Sven Delblancs Hedebysvit* (Stockholm: Institutionen för nordiska språk, Stockholms Universitet, 1980);

Göran Hägg, "Samuels bok," in his *Tjugoen moderna klassiker* (Stockholm: Wahlström & Widstrand, 1995), pp. 70–75;

Nils Håkanson, "Sven Delblancs 'Samuel' i dokumentens belysning," *Vermlandica*, 13 (1989): 35–78;

Sten Hidal, "Samuel, Strindbergssguden och körsbärsträdet," *Signum*, 19 (1993): 217–221;

Bo Larsson, "Ett fördolt ljus," in his *Närvarande frånvaro: Frågor kring liv och tro i modern svensk skönlitteratur* (Stockholm: Verbum, 1987), pp. 53–96;

Åke Lundkvist, "Det mörka landets lockelse," in *Från sextital till åttital: Färdvägar i svensk prosa* (Stockholm: Bonnier Alba, 1981), pp. 102–146;

Péter Mádl, *Wohltäter der Menschheit: Eine Undersuchung der Kurzprosa Sven Delblancs nach 1975* (Leverkusen: Literaturverlag Norden Mark Reinhardt, 1989);

Björn Nilsson, "Delblancs presens historicum," *Bonniers Litterära Magasin*, 55, no. 2 (1986): 88–93;

Karin Petherick, "'Att dikta in en mening i vårt kaos': Some thoughts on the fiction of Sven Delblanc," in *Proceedings of the Eighth Biennial Conference of Teachers of Scandinavian Studies in Great Britain and Northern Ireland Held at Edinburgh University April 2–7 1989* (Edinburgh: Department of Scandinavian Studies, University of Edinburgh, 1989), pp. 249–260;

Petherick, "Diktverket enbart ska tala! Kring några brev från Sven Delblanc," *Artes*, 19, no. 4 (1993): 87–97;

Petherick, "Ohelgade medel eller Den nya skapelsens bankrutt i Sven Delblancs Homunculus," *Samlaren*, 112 (1991): 5–12;

Petherick, "Skuldbördans land: Sven Delblancs Moria land," *Samlaren*, 110 (1989): 77–84;

Michael Robinson, *Sven Delblanc: Åminne*, Studies in Swedish Literature, no. 12 (Hull, U.K.: Department of Scandinavian Studies, University of Hull, 1981);

Leif Sjöberg, "Delblanc's *Homunculus*: Some Magical Elements," *Germanic Review*, 49 (1974): 105–124;

Johan Svedjedal, "Gurun och grottmannen: Bruno K. Öijer, Sven Delblanc och sjuttiotalets bokmarknad," in his *Gurun och grottmannen och andra litteratursociologiska studier* (Stockholm: Gedin, 1996), pp. 69–104;

Richard B. Vowles, "Myth in Sweden: Sven Delblanc's *Homunculus*," *World Literature Today*, 48, no. 1 (1977): 20–25;

Per Wästberg, "Sven Delblancs land," in his *Lovtal* (Stockholm: Wahlström & Widstrand, 1996), pp. 29–44;

Charlotte Whittingham, "Expressing the Inexpressible: Sven Delblanc and the Role of the Artist," *Scandinavica*, 36 (1997): 59–75;

Margareta Wirmark, "Sörmland i minnet: Sven Delblanc and His Portrayal of a Province," in *A Century of Swedish Narrative: Essays in Honour of Karin Petherick*, edited by Sarah Death and Helena Forsås-Scott (Norwich, U.K.: Norvik Press, 1994), pp. 239–252;

Rochelle Wright, "Delblanc's *Kanaans land* and Moberg's Emigrant Tetralogy: Intertextuality and Transformation," *Scandinavian-Canadian Studies*, 5 (1992): 81–93.

Papers:

Material relating to Sven Delblanc is housed at the University of Uppsala Library (Carolina Rediviva). Some correspondence may be found at the private archive of his publisher, Albert Bonniers Förlag, Stockholm.

Inger Edelfeldt
(14 June 1956 -)

Sarah Death

BOOKS: *Duktig pojke* (Stockholm: Bokád, 1977); revised as *Duktig pojke!* (Stockholm: AWE/Geber, 1983);

Hustru (Stockholm: Lindfors, 1978);

Missne och Robin: En berättelse om skogen (Stockholm: AWE/Geber, 1980);

Kärlekens kirurgi: En invecklingsroman (Stockholm: AWE/Geber, 1981);

Juliane och jag (Stockholm: AWE/Geber, 1982); republished as *Nattens barn* (Stockholm: Norstedt, 1995);

Drakvinden (Stockholm: Rabén & Sjögren, 1984);

I fiskens mage (Stockholm: AWE/Geber, 1984);

Breven till nattens drottning (Stockholm: AWE/Geber, 1985);

Kamalas bok (Stockholm: AWE/Geber, 1986); excerpt translated by Sarah Death as "Rub, Rub It Out," *Swedish Book Review*, 2 (1991): 18–21;

Den täta elden (Stockholm: AWE/Geber, 1987);

Den kvinnliga mystiken: En kortfattad guide (Stockholm: Alfabeta, 1988);

Den förskräckliga lilla mamsellens stol (Stockholm: Bonniers Junior, 1989);

Hondjuret (Stockholm: Alfabeta, 1989);

Rit (Stockholm: AWE/Geber, 1991);

Genom den röda dörren, eller Sagan om den lilla flickan, Gråtkungen och Lejonpojken (Stockholm: Bonniers Junior, 1992);

Nattbarn (Stockholm: Alfabeta, 1994);

Den förunderliga kameleonten (Stockholm: Norstedt, 1995)–includes "Utflykt" and "Rovdjursvinden," translated by Death as "Getting Out" and "The Preying Wind," *Swedish Book Review*, supplement (1996): 26–39; and "Uppe på hygget," translated by Death as "Up in the Clearing," *Comparative Criticism*, volume 19 (Cambridge: Cambridge University Press, 1997), pp. 393–401;

Stackars lilla Bubben (Stockholm: Alfabeta, 1996);

Ensamrummet; En midsommarnattsdröm; När jag hatade Elaine: tre berättelser (Stockholm: Bonnier Carlsen, 1997);

Betraktandet av hundar (Stockholm: Norstedt, 1997);

Salt (Stockholm: Norstedt, 1999);

Det hemliga namnet (Stockholm: Norstedt, 1999);

Riktig kärlek (Stockholm: Norstedt, 2001).

OTHER: "Gravitation," in *Gravitation: Berättelser om att bli stor*, edited by Leyla Assaf-Tengroth (Stockholm: Alfabeta, 1994);

"Ett magiskt rum," in *Hur jag blev författare* (Stockholm: Norstedt, 1996), pp. 55–61;

"Ibland går jag över till Bosse," in *Stockholmsnoveller: Från Radions P1*, selected by Gun Ekroth (Stockholm: Sveriges radio, 1998), pp. 31–41.

PLAY PRODUCTION: *Ur askan*, Teater Giljotin, Stockholm, 1994.

PRODUCED SCRIPTS: *Nattens barn*, Sveriges Television, 1995;

Den täta elden, Sveriges Television, 1995.

Inger Edelfeldt was aptly described by the Swedish writer and critic Göran Hägg in 1990 as "denna märkliga korsning mellan Astrid Lindgren och Franz Kafka" (that remarkable cross between Astrid Lindgren and Franz Kafka). Like the renowned Swedish children's author Lindgren, she writes with deceptive simplicity and assured style and identifies with the young and vulnerable in society. Like Kafka, she is attracted to the macabre and fantastic and often employs cheerless, eerie settings where confused and unappealing characters are drawn to their seemingly inevitable fate. She is a student of human relationships and human weakness and explores the forces that mold people in childhood and adolescence. Her writing displays a wicked sense of humor and skillful mimicry of the banality of everyday language. Her prose is taut, precise, and enormously adaptable to a wide variety of styles; it was described by one prize jury as "ett språk där varje kommatecken är laddat" (language in which every comma is highly charged). She does not court the mass market, but her

Inger Edelfeldt (photograph by Jeanette Landmark)

books sell consistently, and she won critical acclaim in Sweden throughout the 1980s and 1990s for the quality of her work. She is also an accomplished artist and has provided cover illustrations for many of her books.

Ingrid Margareta Edelfeldt, known as Inger, was born in Stockholm on 14 June 1956 and brought up in a home full of stories and storytelling, herself beginning to write and draw at an early age. She was educated in Stockholm at Loviselund School in Hässelby and Nya Elementar in Åkeshov, but was the victim of bullying at school. Escaping into the world of the imagination with a few like-minded friends, she devoured legends, gothic horror stories, and fantasy literature and wrote her first book at the age of sixteen. It was eventually published some years later, in reworked form, as *Missne och Robin: En berättelse om skogen* (Missne and Robin: A Story from the Forest, 1980). Since leaving school she has devoted herself full-time to writing and illustration. She is a private person, living a hardworking and relatively anonymous life in an ordinary Stockholm suburb.

Edelfeldt's first published book, *Duktig pojke* (Clever Boy, 1977), reworked for a younger audience in 1983, is the story of how Jim Lundgren, a "clever boy" constantly teased at school, copes with the confusion of adolescence, his awakening sexuality, and his growing awareness that he is attracted to boys rather than girls. By the end of the novel, he has begun to conquer his low self-esteem by accepting and even liking what he is, coping with the reaction of his conservative parents, and moving in with his lover, Mats. This work is the first of several in which Edelfeldt chooses a male first-person narrator and signals one of her central themes: young people paralyzed and isolated by the fear of being different. The text includes some passages of commentary by Jim's mother, and this dual perspective on the child-parent relationship is important in Edelfeldt's work. The novel was well received, went into several editions, and was also successful as a radio play, which Edelfeldt adapted.

Missne och Robin is a book for children, a gripping fable of good and evil, played out in a forest setting and within a framework that again deals with the feelings of adolescence. Torun, aged twelve, is on holiday with her parents in their remote forest cabin and bored with all her childhood activities. Acting out her Robin Hood fantasies, she finds herself magically transported to another world, where she meets the teasing and elusive Missne, an androgynous, Puck-like being. Missne and an eccentric, unreliable band of good spirits and half-humans are involved in a struggle with evil forces that threaten to destroy them. In helping them to victory, Torun learns enough about adult relationships and betrayals to enable her to return to her own life with new experiences and expectations. The novel is notable for its sympathetic depiction of adolescent ennui; its varied, psychologically complex set of characters; and its characteristic blurring of gender divisions.

Juliane och jag (Juliane and I, 1982), republished as *Nattens barn* (Children of the Night) in 1995 to tie in with a television adaptation, is perhaps Edelfeldt's most directly autobiographical text to date. Employing the form and language of teenage confessions, it is narrated by Kim, a Stockholm schoolgirl, and opens with the arrival of Juliane, who has moved to the capital from a smaller town. Juliane is ostracized and bullied by a gang of other class members. Kim is drawn to Juliane, and eventually the two become friends, their alliance giving them the strength to ignore their classmates' taunts. They spend their time together writing melodramatic vampire stories, inventing new identities for themselves, and acting out their fantasies. A theme that emerges here and recurs in Edelfeldt's later books is the importance of rite and ritual to young people. They play at adult rituals or react against them, invent their own variants, and glory in all the attendant paraphernalia: Juliane and Kim, for example, indulge their taste for gothic fantasy with improvised altars, candles, and long robes.

The younger girls in *Drakvinden* (Kitewind, 1984) spend their summers engrossed in a different fantasy world; the book is dedicated to British author Captain W. E. Johns, and Johns's aviator protagonist, Biggles, is the hero whose adventures they emulate. Their holiday paradise is invaded by a newcomer, however: a boy joins their group and causes a jealous rift between them, signaling that childhood is coming to an end.

Edelfeldt has shown herself to be a master of the short story, and the collection *I fiskens mage* (In the Belly of the Fish, 1984) is her confident debut in this genre. All the stories are written from the perspective of a child or adolescent, giving powerful voice to the raw susceptibility and insecurity of childhood. Edelfeldt anatomizes the child-adult relationship and the use and casual abuse of parental power. Lonely little girls in stories such as "I fiskens mage," "Vargen" (The Wolf), and "Bollo Sé" are alternately ignored and hectored by harassed mothers irritated by their own inadequacy. They seek solace in their own fantasies and dreams, whereas the young women in "Snälla snälla Jenny" (Please Now Jenny), "Juan Carlos moustache" (Juan Carlos's Moustache) and "En fri själ" (A Free Spirit) seek to gain some power over their lives by asserting control over their own changing bodies, which thrill and frighten them. They are struggling to come to terms with all the conflicting expectations of women in the modern world. They soon face disillusion, and the girl in "En fri själ" even finds herself the object of sexual advances from her own pathetic, drunken father. Among the most memorable of the stories is "Snälla snälla Jenny," an arresting first-person account of a girl in the grip of anorexia, which has been reprinted in anthologies for schools.

Jenny's story ends with the bleak prospect of future suffering for the girl and her family, but elsewhere Edelfeldt lets the tragic and the comic go hand in hand, as for example when Elin in "Vargen" describes how it feels to be an only child trapped with a neurotic mother:

> Om Elin kom hem från skolan och lägenheten var tom, kunde hon ändå avgöra vilket humor modern hade varit på innan hon gick. Elin antog att det berodde på moderns Nerver.
>
> När hon var liten hade hon tänkt sig Nerverna som vita, krusiga saker, och den föreställningen satt fortfarande kvar. Ibland var nerverna stilla och hoprullade små nudelnystan i hörnen, och ibland kröp de fram som maskar efter ett regn och låg blanka och blottade på korkmattan. Några andra husdjur hade de aldrig haft.
>
> (If Elin came home from school and the flat was empty, she could still tell what mood her mother had been in when she left. Elin assumed it was because of her mother's Nerves.
>
> When she was little, she had thought of the Nerves as curly, white things, and that image had never left her. Sometimes the Nerves were bunched-up little nests of noodles, keeping still in the corner, and sometimes they crept out like worms after the rain and lay shiny and exposed on the cork floor. They were the only pets they had ever had.)

Rebellious little Heidi in "Bollo Sé," who is fond of imagining she is a creature living in an excrement-encrusted well, has been dressed up and taken to visit relatives, in whose home she fears she will break something by her mere presence and disgrace herself as she did once before. The strain of enduring her cousin's frilly femininity and the dinner-party etiquette is too much; she spits out her food and involuntarily lets out a primordial scream. The conflict between so-called civilized behavior and the wild side of the personality often surfaces in Edelfeldt's work; wolves and lions, sinister forests and tropical jungles lurk in a parallel world just a step away from everyday life in many of the stories in this collection. The author is aware that children

Dust jacket for Edelfeldt's 1986 novel, about a woman who breaks free of her humdrum existence by developing a wild, animal-like alternate personality (from Scandinavian Newsletter, *no. 8, 1994/1995)*

need some danger and magic in their lives, and her characters of all ages often feel the urge to escape into other personae and nonhuman forms.

The central character of Edelfeldt's next book, *Breven till nattens drottning* (Letters to the Queen of the Night, 1985), escapes from dull reality into the world of literature and art. Georg is an isolated, introverted teenager with unorthodox tastes. He writes, paints, and has a fondness for dramatic gestures, hoping all the while for the admiration of his peers but feeling that they are unworthy of his friendship. His story is told in diary form, together with the letters he addresses to his muse, Claudia, a beautiful girl whom he worships from afar. He is sadly disillusioned when he finally makes contact with her and finds her to be shallow and conventional.

This kind of blinkered, dogmatic male narrator, aesthetically supersensitive but with no social skills, appears in Edelfeldt's work on several occasions, and she acknowledges inspiration from Hjalmar Söderberg's classic first-person novel, *Doktor Glas* (1905; translated as *Doctor Glas,* 1963). Georg is in many respects a younger version of Ragnar, the narrator of *Betraktandet av hundar* (Contemplating Dogs, 1997). Georg and Ragnar are each mirrored in their style of writing: the naiveté of the self-dramatizing adolescent and the intellectual posing of the self-repressed middle-aged man. In both these books, as elsewhere, Edelfeldt shows the interesting ability to identify with strange, unappealing characters for whom the reader finds it hard to feel any warmth. Georg is depicted with great humor, and his superstitious premonitions of his own impending death are comically interrupted in the closing pages, when he breaks his leg in an absurd drama he is staging with a few fellow eccentrics in the school hall. He lies in his hospital bed trying to rationalize events for his diary, and the novel ends on a positive note as he wonders if he dares ring the night sister to ask for more paper so he can continue writing.

On the cover of her next work, *Kamalas bok* (Kamala's Book, 1986), Edelfeldt portrays her unnamed narrator with a paper bag over her head, literally and metaphorically unable to see where she is going. The novel deals with questions of female identity and self-image, its central character an immature and suggestible young woman dogged by the feeling that she could be happy, if only she were someone else. She is drifting through life, working without enthusiasm in her aunt's gift shop, where she often feels a violent urge to smash things. She is in a dull, long-term relationship with the superficial Stefan, but when he goes off on a vacation without her, what little order there has been in her life dissolves into chaos. The wild, animal-like Kamala, her alter ego, takes the upper hand; she binges on junk food and lets her apartment descend into squalor. Her irritating, energetic mother comes to reimpose order, and life seems to revert to normal. Now, however, the Kamala side of her personality is in the ascendant, mechanical sexual encounters with Stefan no longer satisfy her, and her nameless longings in the closing episode may be about to energize her.

Breaking out of some form of paralysis is a theme to which Edelfeldt often returns, and her usual technique for gaining insight into petrified lives is to allow their cowed owners to speak for themselves. Critics noted the stylistic finesse of her re-creation of the girl's cliché-ridden language and thoughts in *Kamalas bok*.

Petra, the central character of *Den täta elden* (Dense Fire, 1987), is another young woman living an aimless Stockholm life, and she is initially glad to have some structure imposed on her by the pseudoreligious, forest-dwelling sect into whose hands she falls. She takes part in strange rites and ceremonies with the three other women and their reclusive male leader, the self-proclaimed seer Alex, who exploits his position of power. Petra feels increasingly uneasy about sinister events in the sect's past but is too nervous and disorientated to leave. Finally, thinking herself pregnant by Alex and frightened by apparent preparations for a suicide pact, she runs away. Not pregnant after all but haunted by nightmare memories and fears of being hunted down, she melts back into the urban crowds. The novel is written in the third person, but from Petra's point of view. Conceived as a study of group dynamics and the psychological roots of victimhood, it was later adapted by Edelfeldt and dramatized for Swedish television.

Oppressed by conflicting messages from society and even from feminists about expectations of modern women, Edelfeldt says she was, at this time, on the verge of writing a nonfiction book discussing the subject of female identity, but she chose instead to tackle the same issues using comic-strip form, in the collection *Den kvinnliga mystiken: En kortfattad guide* (Feminine Mystique: A Brief Guide, 1988). In this work she revels in depicting a wide variety of confused, self-assertive, and self-deluding women and girls, employing an abrasive drawing style verging on the grotesque. *Den kvinnliga mystiken* was soon followed in a similar vein by the even more surreal *Hondjuret* (The Female of the Species, 1989).

Returning from the visual to the textual, Edelfeldt produced two outstanding short-story collections, *Rit* (Rite, 1991) and *Den förunderliga kameleonten* (The Wonderful Chameleon, 1995), richly varied in style but developing many of her earlier themes. The stories are generally more extended than those in *I fiskens mage*, some of which are only a few pages in length. The author has said that the starting point for almost all her fiction is a character portrait; she prefers to conceptualize one or two figures at a time rather than crowd her literary landscapes with characters.

Many of the stories in *Rit* have first-person narrators or various forms of interior monologue, and most have at their center young people, predominantly girls, experimenting with different versions of themselves, socially or sexually, in an attempt to find a foothold in the adult world. The narrators reveal themselves through their language, from the sensitive, articulate young man in "För Marie Claire" (For Marie Claire), trying to find a way to tell his closest friends he is a transvestite, to the materialism and hackneyed phrases of the pathetic teenage mother in "Bibbedi Babbedi" (Bibbly Babbly).

Many of the stories have a contemporary, urban, often specifically Stockholm setting, but some take place in the countryside of the past, notably "Som man lär sig sånger" (Like the Way You Learn Songs) and the disturbing "Uppe på hygget" (translated as "Up in the Clearing," 1997), which is set in a deliberately vague and preindustrial past, fitting for the strict, Spartan, God-fearing upbringing the child narrator experiences. The story touches on issues of childhood fear, sibling rivalry, father-child relationships, and the blurred distinction between discipline and cruelty, but the abiding image is of the petrified girl seeing her self-disciplined and overworked mother go into the forest to vent her frustrations in a wild, screaming dance.

In the contemporary setting of "Natur" (Nature), a divorced father hopes that an autumn walk in the woods by the sea near their holiday home will help him break the news to his sullen, hostile teenage daughter that his new girlfriend is expecting a baby. The outcome is disastrous: they lose their way as night falls and it turns cold, and they have to stumble on interminably, miserable and hardly speaking to each other. The narrative moves in and out of the consciousness of both characters, forcing the reader into an almost unbearably close identification with both points of view.

Edelfeldt's favorite theme, of the human need to create alternatives to the greyness and powerlessness of everyday existence, is much to the fore in *Rit*, particularly in "Mr. Strangelove" and "Den Fantastiska Lilla Flickan och Riddaren av Diamanthjärtat" (The Fantastic Little Girl and the Knight of the Diamond Heart), the seductively romantic titles of which are in deliberate contrast to the unglamorous fates of the protagonists. The reality of life is that men always wield superior physical force, and Anna-Karin, the "fantastic little girl," finds herself briefly in real danger, locked in a cupboard and threatened by her apparently mentally unstable admirer. Cissi, too, is exploited in "Mr Strangelove," losing her virginity to an aging English hippie who picks her up in a Stockholm café for what she naively assumes to be the start of a beautiful relationship. Her fruitless efforts to contact him again lead only to disillusion and unhappiness. Cissi's role as victim in this episode contrasts vividly with the dominant alter ego she creates in the science-fiction fantasy she is writing: her heroine, Cikoria de Grenadier, is a bisexual immortal in thigh boots, who can fell a man with a flick of her finger and enjoys killing her lovers after she has used them.

Stereotypes are turned on their heads in the title story. Its central character, Fredrika, is a rather shallow, image-conscious student, infatuated with her boyfriend, Robin, a fellow student and rock musician. They see themselves as rebels and are always looking for the next outrageous thing to do, so Fredrika is caught unawares when Robin suddenly decides that getting married might be fun. She initially plans a provocative anti-wedding, but begins to think again when she tries on a frothy, white wedding dress and finds herself unexpectedly excited by all the ritual preparations for a traditional ceremony. She senses herself turning into a bridal archetype, in alliance with all the women who went before her, drowning in the scent of honeysuckle and feeling "som en stor vit drake av siden, som flyger i stark sol" (like a great white kite of silk, flying in strong sunlight). Her solemn but exhilarated mood is almost shattered by the predictable awfulness of the family party, but in the closing pages the overly romantic setting of the bridal bed works some strange alchemy and the young people find their passion genuinely aroused. Edelfeldt once again reminds readers that rituals should not be despised: they are important props for those times of life when most people feel insecure.

Rit was followed in 1995 by *Den förunderliga kameleonten*. If there is any discernible development between the two collections, it is perhaps that mature characters and their interaction with the young play a more central role in the later book. The author still has much to say about the pitfalls of adolescence, though; for example, "Skönheten och odjuret" (Beauty and the Beast) is about an inquisitive group of schoolgirls at large in Stockholm one night.

As in some of her earlier work, Edelfeldt is able to keep an ironic distance and yet identify with self-obsessed, antisocial characters, who are fascinating yet repellent to the average reader. Probably least likeable is the girl in "Kras" (Crack), an immoral but pathetically inadequate creature who is a compulsive liar with equally unpleasant friends. Unemployed and out of money, she gains entry to her neighbors' flat and steals from them. She despises their comfortable lifestyle and home, but in her drunken stupor at the end actually longs to curl up in its warmth and security. This piece of writing is one of Edelfeldt's bleakest and most uncompromisingly brutal.

Quite a different mood is created in "Helena Petréns lediga dag" (Helena Petrén's Day Off), a funny account of a neurotic forty-one-year-old's futile attempt to go on the perfect picnic. In her obsessive way, she has seen a woman picnicking in a Stockholm park and decided to be like her. She makes meticulous plans, and everything seems under control, but it all begins to disintegrate as she mislays some vital makeup, struggles with her unwieldy props on public transport, and gives way to panic and claustrophobia. She senses that her carefully crafted identity is dissolving and hurries home utterly unnerved.

The artificiality of Helena's "art" of image creation is in sharp contrast to the all-consuming artistic temperament of Greta in the story "Skapelsen" (The Creation), as seen in the mind's eye of a passing stranger, a professor of art history. She happens on Greta's garden of clumsy sculptures and imagines how Greta might have become obsessed with making cement models of animals, then abandoned her husband to live in the attic and devote her life to building the figure of a dream woman. Equally destructive in her obsession with art is the central character in "Silver," a high-strung adolescent in search of truth and beauty, who finds a can of silver spray-paint in the garden shed where she has isolated herself and realizes it is aesthetically pleasurable to transform trees and other objects into art by coloring them silver. Finally, calling herself Silver, she takes off her clothes and sprays her face and body all over; she faces probable death from asphyxiation but at last perceives herself as free and beautiful.

Some of the most memorable stories in this collection have as their central characters sympathetic, ordinary people facing more universal problems of human existence. The wife and mother in "Utflykt" (translated

Cover for Edelfeldt's 1988 comic-strip collection dealing with issues of female identity (Collection of Sarah Death)

as "Getting Out," 1996) leads a normal life at home and work but keeps returning in secret to observe her old school playground and relive her painful experience of being bullied. Edelfeldt captures perfectly the cruelty of children and the paralyzing fear felt by those on whom they prey.

The theme of mother-daughter relations is perceptively handled in "Rovdjursvinden" (translated as "The Preying Wind," 1996) and in the title story, in which Elisabet, wounded by a recent divorce, finally feels confident enough to embark on social life again but abruptly abandons her plans to go to a party when she sees that her teenage daughter Elin's hurtful personal remarks conceal great underlying anxieties. Elisabet's tender description of her daughter, pale and vulnerable but full of unforeseen potential, encapsulates much of Edelfeldt's view of individual psychological development, on which many of her characters are founded.

Elisabet and Elin can discuss their problems and resolve them, but bereavement has abruptly cut off communication between mother and daughter in "Kaninernas himmel" (Rabbits' Heaven) and "Rovdjursvinden," leaving the survivor filled with self-reproach. The mother in "Rovdjursvinden" receives a visit early one morning from the police, who bring news that her adolescent daughter has been run over and killed, after an argument with her boyfriend, on a road where the howling of the wind drowned out the sound of approaching traffic. She is plunged into a grief so overwhelming that her relationships with her husband and son threaten to disintegrate, and she alienates them still further by the strategy she adopts to cope with mourning: shutting herself away to work on a fabulous, brightly colored patchwork quilt, made from scraps of her daughter's clothes. Finally, she vents her existential rage by making a flag of the quilt, taking it to a rocky coastline and setting it up to be shredded by the malevolent wind. As she does so she gives a wild scream, the primitive, involuntary scream typical of Edelfeldt's characters when anger and frustration break through self-control.

Betraktandet av hundar begins with such a scream and takes the form of diary notes written for a psychiatrist by middle-aged, prematurely retired schoolmaster Ragnar Kalmén after he is found one day standing at the open window of his flat, screaming, singing, and making wild animal noises. He is profoundly shocked by his breakdown and seeks to intellectualize it, as he does everything else in his life. Ragnar is an aesthete who virtually worships civilization and beauty: the Italian language, its great writers, classical composers from around the world, physically fit bodies, even the grace of pedigree dogs. He learned these attitudes in childhood from his ironic, pedantically academic father. People and things that do not come up to his own aesthetic standards—even his own mother and brother—are despised, and when obliged in his notes to use items of vocabulary he considers debased by the masses, he puts them in disdainful quote marks. Yet, the underlying tone of his diary is anxious and self-justifying. He is a textbook case of schizophrenia, a repressed individual who has lost all contact with his own emotions and is still little more than a father-fixated child.

Events conspire to force Ragnar into cohabiting with Ella, a woman he meets in a park. He is alternately attracted to and repelled by her, for her lifestyle represents everything he despises. The claustrophobia he feels in her company makes it inevitable that his frustrations will boil over. Events come to a head when Ella announces that she is pregnant; Ragnar has a pathological fear of babies, probably rooted in his own jealousy of his younger brother and fear of displacement. Still in the habit of indulging himself like a child (he even buys and wraps birthday presents for himself), he sees the baby as a threat to his own egocentric self. "The dead baby" functions as a leitmotiv in the book, and Ella's news that her baby (real or imagined) has died in the womb triggers Ragnar's involuntary outburst.

Another leitmotiv is that of the title: the contemplation of dogs. Ragnar admires purebred dogs and wishes he were one, no doubt an indication of a desire to regain contact with his natural feelings, his instinctive self. As in other Edelfeldt stories, the untamed side of the psyche is represented in animal form, but Ragnar typically rationalizes this symbolism by claiming that dogs' instincts are purer than the distasteful ways of humans.

Inger Edelfeldt's humanity and humor are seen to better effect in *Det hemliga namnet* (The Secret Name, 1999). It is the funny but moving story of middle-aged Helena, a somewhat ridiculous but profoundly sympathetic character driven on by fierce artistic and emotional ambitions. Her life changes dramatically when she at last meets a man who loves and respects her and who forces her to confront repressed memories of her childhood in Hungary.

In 1999 Edelfeldt also published her first volume of poetry, *Salt,* an unsentimental yet moving account of a love affair and its painful end. In language that is tactile and concentrated, the poems run the full gamut of emotions: at first ecstatic, then increasingly ambivalent, reproachful, deeply unhappy, and finally resigned.

Riktig kärlek (Real Love), the short story collection Edelfeldt published in 2001, is a set of minutely-observed tales of relationships between the sexes. Some stories are bleak, like the pedophile's story, while others are boldly and humorously life-affirming, like the fantasy of two fat ladies, "I drömmarnas land där allt är möjligt" (In the Land of Dreams Where Anything Can Happen).

As an artist Edelfeldt is much concerned with visual impact, and indeed many of the most memorable episodes in her stories do have a cinematic quality. It is perhaps not surprising that she has also done work for the theater, collaborating in particular with a small, independent group in Stockholm, Teater Giljotin. Work with its director, Kia Berglund, has resulted in scripts and improvisations, and in the production of *Ur askan* (Out of the Ashes, 1994). She has also collaborated in writing the television versions of several of her books.

In designing dust jackets for her own books, Edelfeldt appears to enjoy giving pictorial expression to her texts, and this enthusiasm is also seen in her picture books for children. The themes of these books are similar to those of her other work: childhood loneliness and vulnerability, adult indifference or betrayal, and escape into fantasy worlds. She identifies explicitly with the child's point of view. *Den förskräckliga lilla mamsellens stol* (The Horrid Little Maiden's Chair, 1989), for example, is dedicated to "dig som inte gillar att bli sutten på" (anyone who doesn't like being sat on), and is the story of a chair that comes to life and learns to loathe the weight of its self-indulgent mistress. The plump, sly-looking maiden with her ridiculous hairstyles and frilly, crinoline dresses is an unusual but successful choice for a threatening figure. Her chair longs to return to the forest from which it was made; but, like a complacent parent, she does not notice its evolving needs, and it runs away to hide in the wood and take root.

Edelfeldt's pictures have a mysterious, almost sinister quality to them, and her people often look sad. The choice of colors helps to set the mood, and the technique, particularly for backgrounds, is a sometimes visually disturbing form of pointillism. Although largely self-taught, she has developed a high level of technical skill. She includes Leonardo da Vinci, Arthur Rackham, and Maurice Sendak among the artists she admires, and elements of da Vinci's anatomic precision, Rackham's romantic, nightmarish forests, and Sendak's grotesque figures can be recognized in her pictures. Her drawing style seems to lend itself particularly well to fantasy, and she has indeed illustrated fantasy books by other authors, including Ursula K. Le Guin, one of whose works she translated into Swedish. She has also translated and illustrated Hungarian fairytales by Ervin Lázár.

Inger Edelfeldt has won several distinguished prizes, including the Nils Holgersson Plaque for the story "Gravitation"; the Svenska Dagbladet Literary Prize for *Rit;* and the Ivar Lo-Johansson Prize, Göteborgs-Posten Literary Prize, and Karl Vennberg Prize for *Den förunderliga kameleonten.* She enjoys a growing reputation beyond Sweden, and her books have been translated into many other European languages including German and French, but only a few short stories have appeared in English.

Interview:

Sofia Broomé, "En skriftlig bikt: Intervju med Inger Edelfeldt," *Bonniers Litterära Magasin,* 66 (1997): 37–40.

References:

Berit Åberg, "Inger Edelfeldt, författare, illustratör, översättare; Jag var en inställsam liten jävel," *Vi,* 33/34 (1989): 10–12, 57;

Mikaela Kindblom, "Det gör ont att bearbeta kvinnliga myter," *Hertha,* 2 (1989): 34–36;

Gunilla Noreen, "Inger Edelfeldt," in *Författare och illustratörer för barn och ungdom,* 2 (Lund: Bibliotekstjänst, 1998), pp. 165–178;

Cristine Sarrimo, "De tömda berättelserna blir till på nytt: 1980-talets svenska prosa," in *Nordisk Kvinnolitteraturhistoria,* volume 4, edited by Elisabeth Møller Jensen and others (Höganäs: Bra Böcker, 1997), pp. 523–525;

Marianne Steinsaphir, "Inger Edelfeldt," in *Femton författare* (Lund: Bibliotekstjänst, 1994), pp. 27–36;

Jonas Thente, "Flockar av narcissister/Herds of egotists," *Nordisk Litteratur* (1998): 69.

Kerstin Ekman

(27 August 1933 -   )

Rochelle Wright
University of Illinois

BOOKS: *30 meter mord* (Stockholm: Bonnier, 1959);
Han rör på sig (Stockholm: Bonnier, 1960);
Kalla famnen (Stockholm: Bonnier, 1960);
De tre små mästarna (Stockholm: Bonnier, 1961); translated by Joan Tate as *Under the Snow* (London: Vintage, 1997; New York: Doubleday, 1998);
Den brinnande ugnen (Stockholm: Bonnier, 1962);
Dödsklockan (Stockholm: Bonnier, 1963);
Pukehornet (Stockholm: Bonnier, 1967);
Menedarna (Stockholm: Bonnier, 1970);
Mörker och blåbärsris (Stockholm: Bonnier, 1972);
Häxringarna (Stockholm: Bonnier, 1974); translated by Linda Schenck as *Witches' Rings* (Norwich, U.K.: Norvik Press, 1997);
Springkällan (Stockholm: Bonnier, 1976); translated by Schenck as *The Spring* (Norwich, U.K.: Norvik Press, 2001);
Vykort från Katrineholm (Stockholm: Bonnier, 1977);
Harry Martinson: Inträdestal i Svenska Akademien (Stockholm: Nordstedt, 1978);
Änglahuset (Stockholm: Bonnier, 1979);
En stad av ljus (Stockholm: Bonnier, 1983);
Hunden (Stockholm: Bonnier, 1986);
Mine herrar. . . : Om inträdestalen i Svenska Akademien (Stockholm: Norstedt, 1986);
Rövarna i Skuleskogen (Stockholm: Bonnier, 1988); translated by Anna Paterson as *The Forest of Hours* (London: Chatto & Windus, 1998);
Knivkastarens kvinna (Stockholm: Bonnier, 1990);
Tal på Övralid 1991 (Motala: Stiftelsen Övralid/ Heidenstamsällskapet, 1991);
Händelser vid vatten (Stockholm: Bonnier, 1993); translated by Tate as *Blackwater* (New York: Doubleday, 1997);
Rätten att häda (Stockholm: Svenska Rushdiekommittén, 1994);
Gör mig levande igen (Stockholm: Bonnier, 1996);
Vargskinnet: Guds barmhärtighet (Stockholm: Bonnier, 1999);
Urminnes tecken (Stockholm: Bonnier, 2000).

Kerstin Ekman (photograph by Weine Lexius)

Edition: *Kvinnorna och Staden,* 2 volumes (Stockholm: Bonnier, 1994)—comprises volume 1, *Häxringarna* and *Springkällan,* and volume 2, *Änglahuset* and *En stad av ljus.*

OTHER: "Victoria Benedictssons arbete," in *Författarnas litteraturhistoria,* volume 2, edited by Lars Ardelius and Gunnar Rydström (Stockholm: Författarförlaget, 1978), pp. 101–108;
"Undret på Malmskillnadsgatan: Om Selma Lagerlöf," in *Kvinnornas Litteraturhistoria,* edited by Marie Louise Ramnefalk and Anna Westberg (Stockholm: Författarförlaget, 1981), pp. 228–243;

"Människans anlete," in *Mänskligt och omänskligt,* edited by Hans Andersson and Ulla-Britta Lagerroth (Lund: Lund University Press, 1992), pp. 7–20;

"Barndom," with English translation, "Childhood," by Rochelle Wright, *Swedish Book Review Supplement: Kerstin Ekman* (1995): 7–21;

"Selma Lagerlöfs mörker," in *Landet mellan strandäng och mörka skogar,* edited by Maria Lagerwall (Varberg: Utsikten, 1996), pp. 20–25.

SELECTED PERIODICAL PUBLICATIONS– UNCOLLECTED: "Ansiktet i spegeln," *Artes,* 15 (1989): 7–13;

"Att tolka en källa," *Artes,* 19 (1993): 35–47;

"Eyvind Johnson, Krilon och vikten av att samtala," *Moderna tider,* 8 (September 1997): 44–48.

The literary career of Kerstin Ekman, widely recognized as one of the most significant novelists of the postwar period, reveals an unusual trajectory and a pronounced capacity for reorientation and renewal. Ekman first garnered attention in the early 1960s as a skilled practitioner of a popular genre, crime fiction. During the 1970s her primary focus shifted to realistic narratives foregrounding working-class women, both in the preindustrial society of the not-so-distant past and in the present. Since the 1980s her novels, several of them set in remote rural locations, have become increasingly complex and demanding while continuing to attract a large readership. Lyricism, elements of fable and fantasy, mythical substructures, and intertextual references are among the formal aspects of her recent work, while thematic emphasis has often been on social and environmental issues as well as timeless existential concerns. Two novels of the 1990s reintroduce a mystery component. Elected to the Swedish Academy in 1978, Ekman has played an ongoing and prominent role in cultural debate, notably in 1989, when she resigned her chair in protest against the academy's lukewarm defense of novelist Salman Rushdie.

The daughter of Ernst Hjorth and Anna Dahlgren Hjorth, Kerstin Lillemor Hjorth was born on 27 August 1933 in Risinge, in the province of Östergötland, but grew up in Katrineholm, a small town south of Stockholm. Her autobiographical poem "Barndom" (Childhood, 1994) shares some vignettes about her parents, her paternal grandmother, and her own early years. After secondary school she attended the University of Uppsala, specializing in languages and literature and receiving an advanced degree (*filosfie magister,* roughly equivalent to an M.A.) in 1957. Subsequently, until 1959, she was employed by Artfilm as a documentary filmmaker; from 1965 to 1970 she taught at Wiks Folkhögskola. Her first husband was historian Stig Ekman. Since 1970 she and her second husband, Börje Frelin, a musician, have lived in northern Sweden, currently in the village Valsjöbyn in Jämtland.

Ekman's first three mystery novels, *30 meter mord* (Thirty-Meter Murder, 1959), *Han rör på sig* (He's Alive, 1960), and *Kalla famnen* (Cold Embrace, 1960), evolved from her experience in media and entertainment circles. Engaging and briskly paced, their literary value is slight. In contrast, the next three narratives, *De tre små mästarna* (The Three Small Masters, 1961, translated as *Under the Snow,* 1997), *Den brinnande ugnen* (The Burning Oven, 1962), and *Dödsklockan* (Death Knell, 1963), are considered part of Ekman's mature production. Though they may be classified as crime fiction, the resolution of the mystery or crime serves primarily as a framework for exploring the thoughts and motivations of individual characters and the intricacies of group interaction. Ekman employs a shifting narrative perspective that offers great flexibility, and her nature descriptions, especially of the sparsely populated northern part of the country, reveal a finely tuned attention to nuance and detail.

De tre små mästarna is set above the Arctic Circle in a remote Sami village. While investigating the death of a resident who apparently has frozen to death one winter night after a drunken fight, the plodding police inspector, Torsson, and his ebullient sidekick, David Malm, an artist and friend of the deceased, uncover a compact conspiracy of silence about circumstances surrounding the suicide of a young Sami girl with whom the dead villager ostensibly had been involved. Though the plot provides many twists, and the various interlocking mysteries are eventually resolved, the strength of the narrative lies primarily in the evocation of the landscape–desolate expanses of mountains, forest, and marshland hidden in months-long darkness or bathed in continual light–and in the insightful portrayal of collective village mentality.

In *Den brinnande ugnen* Malm is restoring the medieval murals in a small rural church in Uppland (the province just north of Stockholm) when a series of unexplained fires, clearly acts of arson, create fear and suspicion among the locals; once again he is instrumental in identifying the perpetrator. With a deft, ironic touch Ekman provides sharply etched portraits of individuals in the community while simultaneously revealing the workings of group psychology. Tension and suspense build to a satisfactory climax, not least through gripping accounts of the various conflagrations.

Dödsklockan dispenses with several commonplaces of the crime-fiction genre. The initial death is an accident, not a deliberate murder. An attempted cover-up brings unanticipated complications, but police detec-

Cover for Ekman's 1962 novel, in which an artist investigates a series of arsons in a rural community (Collection of Rochelle Wright)

tives play only a minor role in their resolution, and one intentional act of violence remains undiscovered and unpunished. These events take place during an annual moose hunt, which ordinarily promotes camaraderie among members of the hunting party. This time, however, rifts and shifting allegiances develop as several of the men struggle to reconcile their personal ethical standards with their loyalty to the collective. Right and wrong, innocence and guilt are not moral absolutes; justice is ambiguous and uncertain.

Pukehornet (Devil's Horn, 1967), Ekman's first novel after a silence of four years, signals a new direction in the author's production by deliberately confounding reader expectations. The narrative opens as Pär Lindblad and his landlady, Agda Wallin, having paid a visit to Agda's sister in an isolated rural area, are walking through the woods. When Agda keels over from a stroke and dies, Pär panics. Rather than reporting her death to the authorities, he simply takes the bus back home to Pukehornet, a tenement district of Uppsala. Initially Pär intends no deception, but as time passes he gradually begins enacting a charade, claiming that Agda is bedridden and unwilling to see anyone but him. Despite various close calls, only a little girl, Ann-Marie, actually discovers that Agda is missing, but as Pär's situation becomes increasingly problematic an unmasking seems inevitable.

In part 2 of the novel the third-person narrative perspective is exchanged for a first-person account that partially overlaps chronologically with the first part. The narrator of part 2, a woman writer who is also a tenant in Pär's building, becomes suspicious when she notices changes in Pär's demeanor. Worried that Agda needs medical attention and that Pär is taking advantage of her, she makes a series of attempts to see the landlady but is never admitted. She has more or less decided to drop the matter when a chance remark by Ann-Marie prompts her to renew her efforts. Borrowing Pär's keys while he is in a drunken stupor, she finds that Agda's room is empty.

Until this juncture, the woman tenant has functioned to some degree as a detective, if a rather desultory and unmethodical one. Now, however, rather than contacting the police or continuing the investigation on her own, she chooses to write about what she imagines might have occurred, a narrative that is revealed to be identical with part 1 of the novel. Even after discovering that there is, in actuality, no path through the woods at the spot she envisions Agda to have died, she makes no changes in her version of events and purposefully continues writing. The fictional account has taken on its own validity. When a social worker arrives in Pukehornet, demanding to see Agda, the narrator allies herself with Pär to defend their joint fictional world. The novel ends with the mystery of Agda's disappearance unresolved.

Ekman's refusal to provide a neat solution may be interpreted as a declaration that she no longer wished to be bound by the conventions and limitations of the crime-fiction genre. Instead *Pukehornet* focuses on the process of narration itself. One of Pär's coping mechanisms is to imagine himself telling a sympathetic listener what has occurred, a strategy that promotes self-deception, since it hampers him from taking action of any kind. Pär is also a failed writer, reduced to stealing another's material and publishing it under a pseudonym. For the woman tenant, producing a fictional version of events serves a more positive function by giving her a goal and helping her overcome writer's block, but it also allows her to avoid facing her personal problems. *Pukehornet* thus demonstrates that writing is both suspect and necessary: suspect because it may be a retreat from reality, but necessary because only by constructing narratives can people make sense of seemingly random events. In the novel that tacitly declares her desire to be taken seriously as a writer, Ekman explores the creative process and the problematic relationship of "real" and fictional worlds, issues to which she returns in several subsequent works.

Radical labor organizer and songwriter Joe Hill, who contributed many texts to *The Little Red Song Book*, was rediscovered both in the United States and in his homeland, Sweden, during the late 1960s and early 1970s, when a leftist political stance was common among writers and intellectuals. The miscarriage of justice that led to his execution in 1915 in Salt Lake City would seem to be suitable subject matter for political analysis and a documentary approach, the preferred technique of the period. In *Menedarna* (The Foresworn, 1970), however, Ekman takes a different approach, as indicated by her choice of a fictional first-person narrator, the peddler Solomon Purdy. Though sensitive to social and economic injustice, Purdy is a pragmatist and individualist, inclinations that are reinforced by his choice of profession. He considers Joe a friend but knows little about his organizing activities and involvement with the syndicalist International Workers of the World (IWW), also known as "the Wobblies." When Joe is arrested on trumped-up charges of double murder, Purdy expends considerable time and effort trying to help him, motivated not by commitment to the workers' cause but simply by his conviction that Joe is innocent.

Purdy's efforts are thwarted not only by a biased and corrupt criminal justice system but also by the attitude and actions of Joe and his fellow Wobblies. Joe steadfastly refuses to establish an alibi by revealing where he was on the evening of the murders. Perhaps, as some believe, he is protecting the reputation of a married woman; Joe and his supporters merely insist that his whereabouts are irrelevant, since the prosecution cannot prove he was at the scene of the crime. Purdy, recognizing that the presumption of innocence is a legal fiction and that Joe has already been tried and convicted by the press and public opinion, focuses on practical assistance: recruiting a skillful lawyer, trying to trace Joe's gun (a Luger, whereas the murder weapon was a Colt), and tracking down the mysterious Busky, who is said to have been with Joe that fateful evening. Purdy gradually realizes that for the radical labor movement Joe has become a symbol rather than a human being, and Joe himself apparently concludes that he is more valuable to the movement dead, a victim of injustice and a rallying point for further political action, than alive. Though at first he had welcomed and encouraged Purdy's help, when Busky finally is located, Joe denies ever having known him. His appeals exhausted, he is executed by a firing squad.

In Ekman's narrative Joe's actions remain unaccounted for and his motives inscrutable; the "truth" is opaque. Neither Purdy nor the reader discovers the man behind the myth. *Menedarna* is less about Joe Hill than about what he represents to his friends and followers. The legend of Hill as martyr to a cause begins taking shape even before he dies. Purdy, who writes a song about Joe (Ekman borrows the well-known ballad that begins "I dreamed I saw Joe Hill last night / Alive as you and me"), is partially responsible for its creation. Others add and subtract verses, distorting Purdy's original first-person account and including information that he knows is untrue, but audiences protest if he performs anything but the version established by consensus as authentic. This version is the interpretation of Joe's life and character that survives. Ekman seems to be suggesting not only that stories, songs, and legends assume a life of their own but also

Cover for Ekman's 1979 novel, narrated in part from the perspective of the deteriorating apartment building in which the characters live (Collection of Rochelle Wright)

that these accounts are the only ones accessible to people, since the reality they claim to represent remains impenetrable. This realization partially recapitulates the premise of *Pukehornet,* but the ramifications are greater in *Menedarna.* Since many of the characters and much of the subject matter are based on actual people and historical events, Ekman's novel about Joe Hill exposes the pretense that documentary fiction is objective or that objectivity is possible.

The evocative title of Ekman's next novel, *Mörker och blåbärsris* (Darkness and Blueberry Sprigs, 1972), alludes to the setting in the interior of northern Sweden. The area is economically depressed. Sawmill companies have bought up the land and cleared the forest, thereby undercutting the economy and destroying the beauty of the landscape. Except for a slaughterhouse that pollutes the water and air, most employment opportunities lie far away, forcing many natives to leave. The few who remain in the tiny village rely on government pensions, supplemented by the occasional odd job. Especially during the long, dark winter months, time seems to stand still; the future is at best uncertain.

Helga Wedin, twenty years earlier the beautiful young bride of a wealthy man, is now a widow strapped for cash, her deceased husband having squandered a fortune gambling on horses. She is involved in a relationship with their former hired hand, Edvard, who continues to live with her when not working in a factory farther south. At the death of her uncle, the local shopkeeper, Helga inherits his supplies, which include the ingredients for distilling *brännvin,* a potent alcoholic beverage. In part from sheer boredom, in part because the legal product sold by the state liquor store is both foul-tasting and expensive, Edvard, Helga, and

Åsa, her adult stepdaughter, recently returned from Stockholm with a baby in tow, decide to construct a still and try their luck at making moonshine.

With a little assistance from neighbors, they eventually produce a delicious, potent liquor. One midsummer weekend, this small group heads off to the mountain pastures for an uninhibited celebration. While intoxicated, Helga, Edvard, and Åsa become involved in a three-way sexual encounter, an experience that both excites and terrifies Helga. Afterward none of the participants mentions what has occurred, but at the approach of the August crayfish season–another traditional occasion for overindulgence–Helga becomes increasingly agitated. When Edvard admits that he had previously slept with Åsa while on a brief foray to Stockholm, Helga has a complete breakdown.

On one level Helga wants to be bold and liberated, but her fundamental insecurities prevent her from following through on her desires. She loves Edvard and wants to marry him but is uncertain of his feelings for her, in part because he is seven or eight years younger than she. After his confession she becomes obsessed with the notion that she seems ridiculous to Edvard and Åsa and that they have been mocking her appearance and behavior. Only after several months of reassurance and tender care from Edvard does Helga begin to believe that he is truly committed to her and has no plans to leave. Eventually she recovers enough equilibrium to offer to care for Åsa's baby, who has temporarily been placed in an orphanage, and to encourage Edvard to salvage his self-respect by refusing to work at the slaughterhouse.

Mörker och blåbärsris focuses on ordinary people for whom sexual experimentation, though initially exhilarating, ultimately exacts a heavy price, jeopardizing emotional stability and trust. Ekman's narrative provides a corrective to the notion, relatively common in the late 1960s and early 1970s, that sex without commitment or emotional involvement is healthy and affirming. Through Helga's grasping sister, her nouveau riche husband, and Simon Norén, would-be tycoon and owner of the slaughterhouse, the novel also criticizes the lifestyle of superficial materialism that characterizes much of the modern world. Though Ekman is not a cultural conservative, she shows that human beings ignore their interconnectedness with each other and with the natural world at their own peril.

Between 1974 and 1983 Ekman published four novels about the growth and development of her hometown, Katrineholm, after the arrival of the railroad: *Häxringarna* (Magic Circles, 1974; translated as *Witches' Rings*, 1997); *Springkällan* (1976, translated as *The Spring*, 2001); *Änglahuset* (Angel House, 1979); and *En stad av ljus* (A City of Light, 1983). Ekman brings a gender and class perspective to the series by focusing, especially in the earlier volumes, on impoverished working-class women and children.

Häxringarna covers a period of about thirty years, from the 1870s into the new century. Sara Sabina Lans; her daughter, Edla; and Edla's daughter, Tora, are the successive protagonists. Ekman establishes her point of view in the masterful opening paragraphs about Sara Sabina, which juxtapose her endless toil with an anonymity that extends even to the grave: the tombstone of her husband subsumes her identity with the phrase "och hans maka" (and his wife). Both Sara Sabina's grim determination and the depths to which she is forced to humiliate herself are illustrated in the following chapter when local farmers, as a lark, challenge her to a tug-of-war over a piece of shoe leather: if she can hold onto it between her clenched teeth, she may keep it. Significantly, Sara Sabina wins the contest.

Because she is bright and finishes school early, Edla is sent to work for the town innkeeper at the age of thirteen, before being confirmed. Her vulnerability is concretely illustrated by her assigned sleeping place on the table in a huge, empty upstairs room, where she is virtually a sacrificial victim waiting to be raped. Edla becomes pregnant–she herself may not know how or by whom–and dies in childbirth. For Tora, raised by her grandmother, Edla is not even a memory. Only a fading picture and a few stories about her remain.

Tora initially repeats her mother's fate by becoming pregnant out of wedlock shortly after leaving home, but Tora survives, gives up the baby to a childless couple, and finds employment as a waitress at the railroad restaurant owned by Mamsell Winlöf. She is subsequently promoted to cashier and establishes a degree of autonomy and economic independence, only to jeopardize this status by falling in love with F. A. Otter, a would-be engineer from a middle-class background. Though Otter is fond of her, he is reluctant to acknowledge the relationship publicly; more ominously, his health becomes increasingly precarious. When she becomes pregnant with their second child, Tora prevails on him to marry her but is soon left penniless when he dies. As the narrative concludes, Tora must rely on her own skills to support her two small sons.

Häxringarna emphasizes continuity and the repeated generational patterns in women's lives, patterns that have both positive and negative implications. The magic rings, or circles, of the title allude to biological destiny, especially as it pertains to women. In this regard the life and death of Sara Sabina function as a frame. The final chapter refers to and expands on the opening of the novel by describing the drawn-out, yet peaceful, process of her dying while simultaneously confirming the important life-affirming values she represents and the heritage she has, despite her anonymity, passed on to her granddaughter, Tora. Like Sara Sabina, Tora has had to humiliate herself, most notably by forcing herself on Otter, but like her grandmother she is a good, hard worker who takes pride in a job well-done. After Otter's death, when Tora begins baking bread to sell at the square, she uses Sara Sabina's recipe, and she bolsters her spirits by imagining her grandmother's voice issuing instructions. Part of Sara Sabina's heritage is the instinct never to give up. In old age she had convinced her husband to teach her to read and write, skills that serve no obvious useful purpose but that increase her sense of empowerment and self-worth. Sara Sabina attended Tora's own birth and delivered her children. When Tora returns home to ease her grandmother's passing, a circle is complete, in this instance the cycle of birth and death.

One woman in the novel prospers independently in a male-dominated society: Mamsell Winlöf. Significantly, the coming of the railroad, an emblem of technological progress and modernity, makes possible her success. A local girl from a humble background, Mamsell Winlöf breaks with convention in many ways: by living alone after returning from Stockholm (where according to malicious—and false—gossip she was a prostitute, an indication of the assumptions made about an independent woman who cannot easily be categorized), by changing her name, and by establishing her own business. Unbeknownst to many, her earnings are eventually higher than those of any of the prominent men of the town.

Though she has risen socially and economically, Mamsell Winlöf demonstrates solidarity with women of all classes, supporting them both directly and indirectly. She personally delivers baskets of food to poor families and worries about how women and children will manage when breadwinners drink up their earnings. She treats her staff well and trains them to be clean and well behaved. She tries to intervene when she realizes that Edla, though still a child, is doing the work of an adult. At the end of the novel it is Mamsell Winlöf, now retired, to whom Tora turns for advice and a monetary loan, which she receives unquestioningly and without interest.

Mamsell Winlöf also asserts herself in defense of the right of women to be treated with respect and not condescension. When her lover, the entrepreneur Alexander Lindh, refuses to invite the female teachers to a celebratory dinner after the inauguration of the new schoolhouse, she provides a special dinner in her private quarters and serves them first, before the men. As a pioneer, however, Mamsell Winlöf is lonely; her only real companions are a series of small dogs. She does have a sexual and, to some degree, romantic relationship with Lindh that apparently supplies some emotional gratification, but he is married, and furthermore is fundamentally uninterested in her thoughts and feelings. Mamsell Winlöf illustrates the degree of autonomy that an exceptional woman could achieve, but her experience and her fate are neither typical nor unilaterally enviable.

In *Springkällan,* set during the 1910s and 1920s, the focus of the narrative expands to include not only Tora and her family but also her friend Frida and several of Frida's children. Tora, ever the hard worker and frugal to a fault, has managed to purchase a café, which she hopes will provide economic security and a step up on the social scale. Food shortages, rationing, and unemployment during and after the war years thwart her goals, and she finds instead that her welfare depends on income from homemade candy, now sold instead of loaves of bread at the square. Tora continues to rely on her own competence and only reluctantly turns to friends and acquaintances for help, though she frequently extends herself to assist others. Her autonomy gives her strength, but she also develops a hard shell that masks an underlying loneliness and vulnerability.

If Tora nonetheless is moderately successful, Frida, a washerwoman, labors ceaselessly but still cannot make ends meet. The opening chapter of the novel describes, in stomach-churning detail, the specific tasks performed while doing the laundry for an upper-class household, a twice-yearly activity that takes an entire week and is physically exhausting but poorly paid. Frida has many children and an incompetent husband who first disappears and later dies in an accident. Shortly after he leaves, Frida, in her mid forties, discovers she is pregnant again and in desperation plans a self-induced abortion. Tora intervenes, promising to help her with the baby. Even so, poverty eventually forces Frida to relinquish her daughter, Ingrid, to foster parents, a circumstance that creates a rupture not only between biological mother and child but also between Ingrid and her older brother, Konrad, who has helped rear her. In some measure Tora functions as a surrogate mother to Ingrid, but the family constellation remains forever damaged.

Springkällan portrays a society in transition as traditional ways of living and modes of thought gradually give way to occupations and outlooks associated with industrialization, urbanization, and modernity. Though Ekman's narrative emphasizes the impact of these profound changes on working-class women and children, representatives of the bourgeoisie and the aristocracy also figure more peripherally, as they did in the previous volume. The paternalism of an older generation of town leaders and the social pretensions of their wives and daughters continue but are becoming outdated and ineffective. Lilibeth Iversen-Lindh, Alexander Lindh's daughter, exploits her servants while talking continually about the joy of working, but Ingrid, the youngest maid in the household, is not intimidated. When her queries about wages and time off draw only ire, she leaves with no regrets before she can be fired. The last surviving member of the old aristocracy, an ancient woman known only as Hennes Nåd (Her Grace), is a less demanding employer, but her manor house and its inhabitants are literally moldering, and Ingrid quits this position as maid voluntarily, from sheer boredom. She tells a shocked and worried Tora, who had helped her find the job—just as Sara Sabina, many years before, had arranged employment for Tora—that she does not want to serve others. Even to the independent-minded Tora, this aspiration seems incomprehensible and foolish, but to the younger generation it is self-evident.

An interest in social and political issues outside the personal or domestic sphere nevertheless remains rare. When the enlightened, progressive teacher Magnhild Lundberg campaigns for women's suffrage, she finds that working-class wives are unresponsive to her message. Ingrid's foster mother, Ingeborg Ek, the wife of a skilled laborer, views it as a mark of social and economic advancement that her husband supports her, but she finds no outlet for her prodigious energy other than repetitive, time-consuming household tasks. Intellectual curiosity among the poor seems to be a male prerogative; the sole individual in the novel who sets out to educate himself about the world and who reads for pleasure is Frida's son, Konrad. Economically, however, matters gradually improve for the younger generation, men and women alike. Another of Frida's daughters, Dagmar, incapable of hard physical labor because of a curved spine (itself a mark of poverty, since it was caused by rickets), is able to learn tailoring and set herself up as a seamstress. At the end of *Springkällan* she sews a dress for her mother, an act that gives her satisfaction and pleasure and lends Frida dignity, even beauty. The work Dagmar performs is a mute gift of love that strengthens family bonds, a marked contrast to the backbreaking toil in service of the wealthy that has dominated Frida's life.

The title of the novel alludes to its central unifying metaphor of interconnectedness. Just as groundwater forms an unseen, subterranean landscape that, in Konrad's view, mirrors the one above, human beings derive emotional sustenance from each other and reflect one another's needs. Though Himmelsö spring has been filled in and its refreshing, pure water no longer reaches the surface, the faint burbling under-

Cover for the 1998 English translation of Ekman's novel Rövarna i Skuleskogan *(1988), which recounts the adventures of a troll through five hundred years of Swedish history (Collection of Rochelle Wright)*

ground may still be heard. Similarly, individual capability and talent may be hindered or repressed, but the hidden potentiality remains.

A lyrical and allusive subtext also plays a significant role in *Änglahuset*. In a startling shift of perspective, the opening chapter presents an old apartment building, the Angel House of the title, as a sentient being. Once considered elegant, the building now is gradually crumbling; since it is made of wood, it feels kinship with a nearby linden tree and longs to merge with the forest as it molders and disintegrates. A modern town is growing up around the old building, however, and the forest is far away. For the building, and for present-day Sweden, there is no turning back.

Though many of the characters in *Änglahuset* are familiar from earlier volumes in the series, the narrative strands are less tightly woven together. Instead, significant episodes in the lives of several individuals form separate stories; the reader may, nevertheless, deduce parallels and connections among them. The time frame of the novel is the 1930s and 1940s. Despite a worldwide economic crisis and the outbreak of war in Europe, the older generation enjoys a gradual improvement in their standard of living because the newly established pension system offers security and a small financial cushion. Frida, after experiencing a vision of the forest bathed in light, finds additional comfort in religious faith. Tora, aging and worn, continues to sell candy at the square. Though she enjoys periodic get-togethers with a small circle of female friends, including Frida and Ebba, whom she has known since her years as a waitress, she is increasingly isolated from meaningful human contact. Accustomed to depending on her own strength and determination, she is deeply shaken when her body betrays her: discovering a lump in her breast, she is unable or unwilling to confide in anyone and seeks medical attention in Stockholm on her own.

While she is gone, a sudden storm destroys her booth at the square and ruins the supply of candy, leading to an angry confrontation with those she holds responsible. For days Tora shuts the door and refuses to see anyone. Only after Ebba forces her way in and Tora makes herself utter the dreaded word *kräfta* (cancer) does she slowly resume her usual activities, but surgery and radium treatments further exhaust and debilitate her. Toward the end of the narrative Tora is entering the hospital again; others suspect that she will never return.

Jenny, married to Tora's older son, Fredrik, is childless, though not by choice, and does not work outside the home. The couple have become comfortable members of the middle class, largely satisfied with the status quo; their success is confirmed in their own eyes when they are able to buy a lot on the outskirts of town and build a house. Still, Jenny experiences a vague sense of dissatisfaction. The marriage is harmonious on the surface, but something is missing, and she struggles to justify and find meaning in her life without ever achieving a sense of fulfillment.

As a young woman Ingrid feels a similar lack of direction. Her factory job is boring and repetitious, though she enjoys the camaraderie among coworkers, and she is in no hurry to get married. Then she unexpectedly falls in love with Arne, star of the local bandy team, and becomes pregnant. Indignant that her options now are limited, Ingrid nevertheless settles into marriage and motherhood while also continuing in her paying job. Prompted by her brother Konrad, a devoted communist who is dismayed that so many of his former comrades have sold out to the Social Democrats, she eventually channels her considerable intensity and frustration into labor-union activities.

The political climate of the period and the ramifications of the war in neutral Sweden are apparent through formative events in the lives of the characters. In 1938, with Fredrik on a bicycle trip through Värmland, Jenny arises early one morning to discover a group of young brownshirts performing quasi-military exercises. During the war Arne is drafted and stationed in the far north; separation and an unannounced reunion cause strain between Ingrid and her husband. Troop transports through the country necessitate a concerted effort to feed hundreds of soldiers at a time during brief stops at the local station; many women direct their dynamism and organizational talents into this activity. Some realize, however, that the secrecy surrounding train schedules disguises more sinister transports to Germany. Local aid to the embattled Finnish people when their land is attacked by the Soviet Union leads to an agony of conscience for Konrad, who feels he cannot support anticommunist forces. Jenny has a brief and ultimately unsatisfying affair with the Hungarian Jewish refugee quartered in their house. When the Bernadotte white buses arrive in town with concentration-camp survivors, the horror of the war is brought home to all.

As the title and opening chapter suggest, imagery connected with houses and rooms is central to *Änglahuset* and functions as a metaphor for individual identity. A complex and evocative association of physical with internal space occurs when Tora, trying to come to grips with her illness, has a detailed and vivid nightmare in which her living-room floor collapses. Her alienation from her own body makes even her heartbeats seem unfamiliar, like steps echoing in a strange house. Terror in the face of mortality becomes transposed into fear of being home alone. Similarly, when Frida, in her eighties, becomes senile, the dissolution of her sense of self is described as the thinning out and caving in of the walls separating memory, dream, and waking. Metaphors associated with interior space also underscore an evolution illustrated through several central characters: as social and economic conditions improve, people do not necessarily lead more fulfilling or contented lives. The challenge is no longer merely to survive, but to discover a sense of purpose from within.

The interiority of *Änglahuset,* its emphasis on state of mind rather than exterior events, as well as its central architectural metaphor, are further developed in the final novel of the series, *En stad av ljus*. Rather than the flexible third-person perspective of earlier volumes, *En stad av ljus* employs a first-person narrator, Ann-Marie Johannesson, in *Änglahuset* a foster child of Jenny's and Fredrik's who sometimes helped Tora sell candy at the square. In 1977 Ann-Marie is in her forties and has returned to her hometown from Portugal, where she lives with her husband, Hasse, to sell the house at Kapellgatan 13 where she grew up. To facilitate the task she has sent her adopted daughter, Elisabeth, off on a vacation with Jenny, but Elisabeth manages to run away. Ann-Marie, anxiously awaiting her return, is gradually overcome by a sense of inertia and paralysis and experiences a psychological breakdown.

The body of the novel is a long section called "Berättelserna" (The Stories) in which Ann-Marie recalls formative experiences from the past, experiences that in turn shed light on the present. As a young child her time was divided between the conventional, bourgeois home of Jenny and Fredrik and the apartment she shared with her father, Henning, an inventor, intellectually gifted and creative but unreliable and increasingly dependent on alcohol. In Ann-Marie's eyes the rules governing these two worlds were completely separate, and the internal conflict of trying to function successfully in both led to psychotic episodes in which she fled to another realm, a dimension she calls Choryn, where the goddess figure Ishnol and her attendant spirits instructed her in the principles of wisdom. In the real world Ann-Marie's psyche remained divided, leaving her unable to formulate goals or make meaningful decisions and choices. Her beloved father failed her repeatedly, and that parental betrayal was compounded when she discovered, as an adult, that the mother she had believed dead had abandoned the family to live with another man in a neighboring town. With no adequate role models, torn between opposing worldviews, Ann-Marie has drifted through life with no clear sense of her own identity.

The search for internal coherence, for psychic unity, that is central to *En stad av ljus* is expressed through metaphors connected with light, with water, and with houses and rooms, imagery that often refers to earlier volumes in the series. Light and transformed vision are associated with Choryn and a transcendental realm that eludes grasp, but also with the ability to perceive essence rather than surface. Similarly, water imagery alludes to invisible, subterranean truths, to memory, and to hidden, often inaccessible aspects of the psyche that sometimes break through to conscious awareness; water links Choryn and everyday reality, the transcendent and the prosaic, the unconscious and the conscious. Ann-Marie's sense of self is intimately bound up with the house at Kapellgatan 13, which represents a universe separate from the world around her, a place where she can take refuge. Simply being there physically often serves as a catalyst, allowing her to enter Choryn; when cut off from the meaning and coherence she experiences in this realm, she feels like an abandoned room.

The empty, abandoned room of the psyche has a direct physical counterpart: the former bedroom of her parents, which has been closed off since her mother went away, and the chamber hidden behind it. Near the end of the narrative Ann-Marie enters the bedroom for the first time since returning to the house and opens the door to the sealed room, thus symbolically confronting her childhood memories. The decision to piece together stories is a product of the need to fill the emptiness within her by examining and interpreting the past.

Ann-Marie discovers that the process of shaping her memories into coherent narratives helps her construct a persona. The past itself, she realizes, does not exist; instead, what people have are stories about what has happened, stories that may be fragmentary and incomplete, only partially overlapping with other accounts of the same event, but that nevertheless are necessary, both for self-understanding and for making sense of the surrounding world. In this regard *En stad av ljus* recapitulates and expands on a central theme of the earlier novel *Pukehornet,* which likewise focuses on the narrative process and its function.

Ann-Marie's alienation in the present time of the narrative is determined primarily by psychological factors, but after more than two decades in Portugal she also perceives herself to be a stranger in present-day Sweden. Passing comments and observations about others and about the town reveal how society has changed in her absence. The clothing factory owned by Ann-Marie's father-in-law, which once employed Ingrid and many other seamstresses, has been forced out of business by competition from cheap foreign labor. The family-run local newspaper has been taken over by a business consortium. As the city has grown, personal ties have become more tenuous, concern and respect for others have diminished, and old people, including Jenny, Arne, Ingrid, and Konrad, are increasingly marginalized. One sign of Ann-Marie's eventual emergence from her psychological crisis is that gradually she becomes interested in the world around her. She begins working for the newspaper, embarking on a series of articles about the history of the town's water supply. As was the case with her personal stories, constructing a coherent narrative of the past helps illuminate the present, but Ann-Marie also realizes that the history of the town is not merely the history of its institutions. In this context the title of the novel takes on its full significance, referring not only to Ann-Marie's articles but also to the entire Katrineholm series: "För varje värld jag reser står en annan opp, en lika möjlig eller omöjlig. . . . Och när jag gjorde staden ar jägrn och grus och sopor reste sig en annan stad–av ljus" (Every time I build a world another arises, just as plausible or implausible. . . . And when I made the city of iron and gravel and garbage another one arose–a city of light).

The psychological breakdown, convalescence, and recovery that is the core narrative of *En stad av ljus* is recapitulated from a more overtly personal perspec-

Cover for Ekman's 1996 novel, about the members of a women's discussion group (Collection of Rochelle Wright)

tive in *Knivkastarens kvinna* (The Knife-Thrower's Woman, 1990), Ekman's first venture into poetic idiom. Written in 1984 but published six years later, the text is primarily in free verse, with occasional passages of prose. Mirroring the disintegration experienced by the female protagonist, the narrative voice is fluid, shifting from third to second person, to a collective "vi" (we) and finally to a revealing "jag" (I) as she achieves healing and psychic unity.

The protagonist's crisis is triggered by an ectopic pregnancy that necessitates a complete hysterectomy. She experiences the operation as an invasion of her body that ruptures not only her membranes but also her sense of self, leading to a psychotic depression and a stay in a mental hospital. The medical emergency exacerbates her alienation from her husband, and after being declared cured she moves alone to a drab suburb. Her ego is fragile, however, and the recovery transitory; a suicide attempt follows. Now, however, she gradually puts back together the pieces of her shattered psyche and begins to reach out to the world around her again.

As in *En stad av ljus,* the downward spiral into psychosis and subsequent revival reveals parallels to the myth of descent into and emergence from the underworld. Ekman's poem is also interwoven with many intertextual references, in particular to the common religious heritage of the Bible and traditional hymns, but also to a pantheon of Swedish-language writers, including Selma Lagerlöf, Edith Södergran, Hjalmar Gullberg, and Karin Boye. These echoes, often disguised or inverted, lend great density to *Knivkastarens kvinna* and place the intense, intimately revealing account in a much wider literary and existential context.

At the death of Harry Martinson in 1978, Ekman was elected to the Swedish Academy, only the third woman in its two-hundred-year history to be so honored. The choice surprised some; at the time Ekman had not published many works of "serious fiction"—the

Katrineholm tetralogy was only half complete—and was still known largely as a mystery writer. She quickly established herself as a vigorous and hardworking member of the academy, serving on several important internal committees, including, from 1983, the Nobel Committee, where her training in languages and literature was put to good use. Her learned and witty analysis of inaugural addresses, *Mine herrar . . . : Om inträdestalen i Svenska Akademien* (Gentlemen . . . : Swedish Academy Inaugural Addresses), appeared in 1986. In 1978 she was also selected for lifetime membership in Samfundet De Nio (the Society of Nine), which promotes Swedish literature by awarding prizes and publishing a journal, *Svensk litteraturtidskrift*. Her resignation from the Swedish Academy in 1989 was unprecedented, a declaration of principle in defense of freedom of expression that she further articulated in the essay *Rätten att häda* (The Right to Blaspheme, 1994). Though she remains active in Samfundet De Nio, her chair in the academy's august assembly of eighteen stands empty.

Throughout her years in the academy Ekman continued to publish belles lettres. The novella *Hunden* (The Dog, 1986) provides a contrast to the primarily historical subject matter and epic scope of the Katrineholm series while simultaneously serving as a smooth transition to her next major novel, *Rövarna i Skuleskogen* (The Outlaws of Skule Forest, 1988; translated as *The Forest of Hours*, 1998). The story is simple: one cold March night in rural northern Sweden, a small puppy becomes separated from his mother and cannot find his way home again. Through a combination of instinct and good luck he manages to survive until fall, when his owner gradually tames him again. Ekman tries to convey how the world appears through the puppy's sensory perceptions while simultaneously remaining aware that such an attempt cannot fully succeed, since dogs do not translate experience into words. She avoids cloying anthropomorphic interpretations, focusing instead on detailed descriptions of nature and the seasonal cycle and only occasionally interpolating an explanation from the human perspective.

Though *Rövarna i Skuleskogen* encompasses a chronological period of half a millennium rather than half a year, like *Hunden* it has a nonhuman protagonist: the troll Skord. Parallels to the Katrineholm series are also evident. The tetralogy offers a century-long alternative history of one town after the 1870s, when the arrival of the railroad brings the modern industrial era; *Rövarna i Skuleskogen* provides an unusual perspective on selected events and periods in Swedish and European history from medieval times to the early nineteenth century, when travel on iron rails seems a scarcely imaginable future development. *Rövarna i Skuleskogen* is not, however, a conventional historical novel, but rather an extended reflection on historical development in general, on the process through which both personal and historical narratives come into being, and on what it means to be fully human.

The novel opens in a fairy-tale forest, populated by giants and trolls, where Skord simply appears, with no memories and no past. Though initially fearful, he soon gravitates toward human beings, begins following groups of children who roam the countryside begging, and develops a relationship of mutual support and trust with the orphans Bodel and Erker. As Skord gradually learns to mimic human speech and behavior and evolves an understanding of chronology and causality, historical time and place also emerge: the setting is northern Sweden in the fourteenth century. From Bodel and subsequent companions, including a priest, Ragvaldus Ovidi, and an outlaw, Baldejour, Skord hears stories—about them, about the past, and about the cosmos. Through these various accounts he begins to piece together an awareness, though necessarily incomplete, of how human beings function in and view the world. He deduces a connection between personal and historical narrative: in both, disparate events attain significance only when placed into an ordered sequence.

The next stage in Skord's maturation process is the search for a more universal truth that will explain the cosmos through metaphor and analogy. He becomes the apprentice of an alchemist who seeks to make gold from baser metals, but these attempts to master the elements fail. Overcome by ennui, he loses faith in the power of the intellect to find an underlying purpose and order in existence.

Since Skord ages at a much slower rate than human beings, he outlives those around him and periodically must move on so that his true identity does not become apparent. The fictional account, too, on several occasions abruptly skips forward in time or shifts venue with no explanation. After his gold-making efforts, Skord emerges as a barber-surgeon in the Thirty Years' War, endures imprisonment in Finland, and still later, back in northern Sweden, is captured once again by outlaws. Eventually he settles in Stockholm, where, as Dr. Kristiern Scordenius, he practices medicine according to the principles of mesmerism.

Though Skord's life is spent among human beings, he remains fundamentally Other, his true nature evident in his ability to take on the shape of an animal at will. His intermediate position is suggested by his name, a conflation of *skog* (forest) and *ord* (word). Skord's development culminates when he learns both to value the part of him that is nonhuman and intuitive rather than intellectual and verbal and to integrate the troll and human aspects of his being. In the context of selfless love he reveals the secret of his identity to Xenia Linderskjöld, who shares his affinity with the Other World as well as his shape-changing ability. Fittingly, as death approaches, he returns to the forest from which he came.

In *Rövarna i Skuleskogen,* as in *En stad av ljus,* the central importance of narration becomes both subject matter and theme. The endeavor to grasp the truth is elusive, but by describing what one perceives, by producing a coherent account, one may assign meaning to disconnected pieces of memory, visual images, or scraps of fact. Just as storytelling shapes individual identity, people construct a collective narrative of their shared past. At the same time, psychic wholeness encompasses remaining attuned to another mode of apprehending the world that is intuitive and nonverbal.

Händelser vid vatten (Events by Water, 1993; translated as *Blackwater,* 1997) represents a closing of the circle for Ekman by recapitulating many features of her earlier works. Most significantly, it incorporates some characteristics of the mystery genre while focusing on character and setting. Events take place in an isolated area near the Norwegian border in two time frames separated by eighteen years. Since Ekman alternates between several narrative strands that are of approximately equal importance, using interior monologue to convey the thoughts of major characters, no single protagonist or point of view dominates. The richness of the novel is indicated by the range of prizes it has won, including best Swedish crime novel of 1993, awarded by the Swedish Crime Academy; the August Prize; and the Nordic Council's Literary Prize for the year's best work of Scandinavian fiction.

On Midsummer Eve of 1973, a brutal double murder is committed far off in the forest. By coincidence many individuals find themselves in the immediate vicinity. Annie Raft and her six-year-old daughter, Mia, have just arrived from Stockholm to join her boyfriend, Dan, and his commune of back-to-nature romantics, who have rejected civilization and chosen a subsistence lifestyle high up on a mountainside. When he does not appear to meet their bus, they set off to find him but soon become lost in the maze of forest paths.

Meanwhile, sixteen-year-old Johan Brandberg, who lives in the nearby village, has witnessed his father attack and beat a neighbor; when the police find out, his older half brothers assume he has tattled. The brothers retaliate by lowering Johan into an unused well, and, after laboriously making his way out, he flees rather than returning home. He hitches a ride across the border into Norway with a woman who, noting that Johan is famished, ironically identifies herself as Ylajali Happolati—a reference to Knut Hamsun's novel *Sult* (Hunger, 1890) that her passenger does not recognize.

Ylja, as he calls her, takes Johan to a remote hideaway and keeps him a virtual sexual prisoner for several days, telling him he has fulfilled a prophecy and will become the new Wanderer, leader of a mysterious pre-Christian cult. Before Johan can find out more, however, she loses interest and sends him packing. Back in Sweden he learns about the murders and returns immediately to Norway, where he remains with his mother's Sami relatives. Only many years later does he revisit his home.

Also in the forest that Midsummer Eve are the district doctor, Birger Torbjörnsson, and Åke Vemdal, the chief of police, who had planned a weekend fishing trip but are forced to interrupt it when the murders are discovered. Furthermore, unbeknownst to him, Torbjörnsson's wife is nearby with Annie's boyfriend, ostensibly to join up with a group of environmentalists planning a protest action against the deforestation policy of lumber companies.

Despite an exhaustive investigation during which both Annie and Torbjörnsson briefly come under suspicion, the case is not solved. The interpersonal repercussions in the aftermath of the crime are nevertheless far-reaching. Torbjörnsson's wife leaves him, and Annie becomes increasingly distrustful of Dan and other members of the commune after discovering they have lied to police about their whereabouts.

Nearly two decades later, Annie, who has long since left the commune but remains in the area as a teacher, recognizes the man driving her daughter home one night as the boy she had glimpsed running through the forest the night of the murders. Terrified, she telephones Torbjörnsson, who has become her friend and lover. Shortly thereafter Annie is found lifeless, lying facedown in a stream by the spot where the earlier killings took place; it is soon apparent that her death is no accident. Johan is quickly absolved of blame for any of the fatalities, and Torbjörnsson's tenacity eventually leads to startling revelations about Annie's death as well as the actual events of that Midsummer Eve. While assisting Torbjörnsson, Johan also uncovers an explanation for the mysterious episode with Ylja, now a professor of folklore at the University of Helsinki.

The complex, interlocking plot is partially structured around familiar narratives and mythical patterns. Most obviously, Johan's entrapment in the well recapitulates the story in the Book of Genesis in which the brothers of Joseph place him in a pit. Ylja, the folklorist, grafts her encounter with Johan onto a preexisting mythical structure in much the same way Ekman incorporates mythical and folklore motifs into her story, and perhaps with the same motivation: to provide resonance and add another dimension that superimposes onto a mundane reality certain universal aspects of human experience.

Händelser vid vatten is also notable for its sensitivity to environmental concerns. The lumber industry policy of strip-clearing the forest is shortsighted, disrupting organic patterns of growth and renewal and destroying natural beauty, but lumbering also provides much-needed employment in an economically depressed area. Ekman offers no simple solution to the dilemma. Returning to a subsistence lifestyle is intrinsically untenable, and members of the commune encounter deep suspicion and scorn from fundamentally conservative local residents. Other attempts to resurrect the past are also tinged by nostalgia and false romanticism. Gudrun, Johan's fiercely protective mother, tells Johan that rescuing the Sami language is a lost cause and that contemporary focus on colorful emblems of traditional Sami culture ignores the actual experience of most Sami, past or present. What she and others like her most longed for in their youth was electricity.

In *Gör mig levande igen* (Revive Me, 1996) the primary setting is contemporary Stockholm. Even more than in the Katrineholm tetralogy, emphasis is on female characters, in particular seven women of varying ages who have established a discussion group. Its leader is Oda Arpman, in her eighties, indomitable and somewhat domineering, a Finno-Swedish widow with searing memories of World War II. The youngest member is Sigge Falk, a part-time doctoral student struggling to complete a dissertation on the novels of Eyvind Johnson, a seminal figure in Swedish modernism. Others in the group have varying backgrounds and professions, but they share a growing anxiety about the violence and alienation of contemporary society.

An analogous discussion group, though composed only of men, is found in Eyvind Johnson's trilogy of novels about Johannes Krilon, written during World War II. Johnson's protagonist passionately defends humanistic and democratic values in the face of rising totalitarianism; Johnson himself defied restrictions on freedom of expression during the war years by urging this course of action. Ekman has often stated her admiration for Johnson, and in *Gör mig levande igen* she provides a complex, multivalenced intertextual response to the Krilon trilogy, borrowing the polyphonic structure of the earlier work and addressing many of the same thematic concerns. Among these themes are the power of memory, of bearing witness; the necessity of taking a stand, not only through discussion but also in deed; and the importance of the literary text in stimulating debate, offering testimony, and promoting ethical behavior.

Though familiarity with Johnson's work enriches an understanding of *Gör mig levande igen*, Ekman's novel also functions independently, not only as a critique of Swedish society but also as a cross section of present-day female experience. Each woman faces a separate crisis of identity that she is unable to share with others. Oda struggles with personal failures and betrayals of the past and with the knowledge that her ability to influence others is waning; Sigge elicits disdain from the scholarly establishment when her Johnson research uncovers surprising new information, and she must simultaneously confront her boyfriend's infidelity. Most shattering is the realization of Kajan Tidström. Unbeknownst to the others, she is a Polish Jew, a Holocaust survivor. Unable to brush off the vicious anti-Semitism she encounters among Swedish youth and failing in her attempt to communicate her experience to them, she commits suicide.

Other hidden aspects of Swedish society only occasionally intersect with the everyday world of those in a position of relative privilege. Immigrant subcultures impenetrable to outsiders lead parallel but separate existences. A dark undercurrent of violence runs just below the surface. The narrative periodically returns to the girl Mariella's search for her missing older sister, Rosemarie, whose father is black. The mystery is eventually resolved when her corpse is discovered in a freezer in the cellar of an abandoned house. Since several other characters might, if they had been paying attention, have been able to intervene, the course of events is a commentary on alienation and self-involvement as well as sexually or racially motivated violence. Overall, Ekman is less hopeful than her predecessor, Johnson, about the efficacy of dialogue, whether fictional or actual, in changing the world, but she nevertheless asserts its necessity.

In *Vargskinnet: Guds barmhärtighet* (The Wolf Skin: God's Mercy, 1999), Ekman returns to the setting of *Händelser vid vatten*. Like the earlier novel, *Vargskinnet* alternates between two time frames and several points of view; there is also some overlap among the characters. In historical scope *Guds barmhärtighet* calls to mind the earlier volumes of the Katrineholm series, where progress and change are measured in the lives of individual characters. In addition, *Guds barmhärtighet* contrasts different lifestyles and value systems, of the urban middle class and destitute farmers and lumberjacks, of ethnic Swedes and Sami.

The novel opens in the late winter of 1916, when Hillevi Klarin, a midwife trained in Uppsala, arrives in Jämtland to begin her practice. Only a few days later she assists a malnourished thirteen-year-old girl who has been in labor for four days without medical attention. The girl and her extended family live in unspeakable poverty and deprivation; the baby may be the product of incest and dies shortly after birth under suspicious circumstances. Cowed into silence, Hillevi never tells anyone what has happened, but her knowledge incurs the enmity of the girl's family, with far-reaching repercussions.

Hillevi is secretly engaged to the new vice pastor of the parish, like her an outsider from Uppsala. Frustrated that he refuses to acknowledge the relationship openly and that he seems essentially uninterested in the native population, Hillevi acts on her sexual attraction for the local shopkeeper Trond Halvorsen, becomes pregnant, and marries him. Thereafter her primary concern is her family: husband, two biological children, and a foster daughter, Kristin, called Risten in her native Sami dialect. The main narrative concludes with Risten's traditional Lapp wedding some twenty-five years later.

As an old woman Risten looks back on the events of her childhood, providing another, broader perspective. Her first-person recollections link past and present, Sami and Swedes, oral culture and the written word. Though raised by Hillevi from the age of three, Risten maintained contact with her Sami roots through her uncle, a composer and performer of songs in the traditional style. Unlike many locals, Hillevi is relatively free of overt prejudice against the Sami, but her education and her enlightened, progressive attitudes make her unsympathetic to many aspects of Sami culture that attract her foster daughter. That Risten remembers only scattered phrases in her native language is emblematic of the sense of loss that dominates her account.

Another interwoven story concerns the boy Elis, cousin of the abused girl, who tries to save the baby, is beaten by his father and grandfather, and disappears across the border. Claiming amnesia, Elis leaves his true identity behind, re-creating himself as a Norwegian. While under treatment for tuberculosis, he is able to develop his natural artistic talent, and later he studies art in Kristiania. In Berlin he achieves recognition and economic security, but fascist rule makes him increasingly uncomfortable and he resolves to leave for Paris.

As far back as 1961, in the mystery *De tre små mästarna,* Ekman demonstrated her familiarity with and sensitivity to the landscape and people of the rural north. *Guds barmhärtighet* reveals a deepened perspective, one that embraces and celebrates the vanishing traditions of an oral culture without mitigating the desirability of a decent standard of living and better sanitation and hygiene. Progress, Ekman suggests, is neither linear nor unilateral. With change, something is gained, but something irreplaceable may also be lost.

Though her literary career is still evolving—*Guds barmhärtighet* is the first volume of a planned trilogy with the collective rubric *Vargskinnet,* and the short novel *Urminnes tecken* (Signs of Yore, 2000) builds on the folkloristic aspects of *Rövarna i Skuleskogen*—Kerstin Ekman's stature as one of the most influential, highly regarded, and widely read writers of the late twentieth century is secure. Her overall achievement was recognized when she received the Pilot Prize in 1995, the Ivar Lo Prize in 2000, and an honorary doctorate from the University of Umeå in 1998. The popularity of her long, complex novels belies the commonplace that readers want only to be entertained, not challenged. One of Ekman's primary contributions is that she has given voice to the female experience in both historical and contemporary contexts. Several of her works, in particular the first three volumes of the Katrineholm series, place her in the long Swedish tradition of epic realism, but her imaginative and thematic concerns encompass a far wider range. Ekman has repeatedly used regional and rural settings to address universal existential issues: the interplay of self-realization and social interaction and the interdependence of the human and the natural world. In several pivotal novels she also articulates the central, indeed essential, role of memory, dialogue, and storytelling in creating personal identity, establishing meaningful relationships with others, and constructing a broader understanding of the collective human past. By focusing on the process of narration itself, Ekman also examines how fictional worlds are created and asserts their necessity in the actual world people inhabit.

Interview:

Lars Åke Augustsson, "Även kvinnor har rätt att ta det stora greppet på tillvaron," in *Att skriva romaner och noveller* (Stockholm: Ordfronts förlag, 1993), pp. 101–113.

References:

Lars Andersson, "Den som står bakom: En figur i Kerstin Ekmans rövarroman," in *Skuggbilderna* (Stockholm: Nordstedt, 1995), pp. 9–19;

Sarah Death, "'They Can't Do This to Time': Women's and Men's Time in Kerstin Ekman's *Änglahuset,*" in *A Century of Swedish Narrative: Essays in Honour of Karin Petherick,* edited by Death and Helena Forsås-Scott (Norwich, U.K.: Norvik, 1994), pp. 267–280;

Lars Grahn, "Kerstin Ekmans komedi: Anteckningar om *Häxringarna, Springkällan* och *Änglahuset,*" *Bonniers Literära Magasin,* 48 (1979): 200–203;

Röster om Kerstin Ekman: Från ABF Stockholms litteraturseminarium i oktober 1992 (Stockholm: ABF, 1993);

Linda Haverty Rugg, "Revenge of the Rats: The Cartesian Body in Kerstin Ekman's *Rövarna i Skuleskogen,*" *Scandinavian Studies,* 70 (1998): 425–439;

Maria Schottenius, *Den kvinnliga hemligheten: En studie i Kerstin Ekmans romankonst* (Stockholm: Bonnier, 1992);

Schottenius, "Mellan kattens ögon–om *En stad av ljus*," *Bonniers Literära Magasin*, 53 (1984): 202–208;

Schottenius, "Skogen, ordet och tystnaden–om Kerstin Ekmans *Rövarna i Skuleskogen*," *Bonniers Literära Magasin*, 57 (1988): 425–428;

Schottenius, "Tvånget att bejaka–om Kerstin Ekmans *Häxringarna*," *Bonniers Literära Magasin*, 52 (1983): 235–247;

Schottenius, "De underjordiska källorna," in *På jorden: 1960–1990*, volume 4 of *Nordisk kvinnolitteraturhistoria*, edited by Unni Langås (Höganäs: Wiken, 1997), pp. 412–419;

Swedish Book Review Supplement: Kerstin Ekman (1995);

Per Wästberg, "Kerstin Ekman i de gåtfulla tecknens rike," in his *Lovtal* (Stockholm: Wahlström & Widstrand, 1996), pp. 227–251;

Anna Williams, "'Men ni är inte kärlet': Om Kerstin Ekmans *Knivkastarens kvinna*," *Bonniers Literära Magasin*, 59 (1990): 366–368;

Rochelle Wright, "Androgyny in Kerstin Ekman's *Rövarna i Skuleskogen* and Virginia Woolf's *Orlando*," in *Litteratur og kjønn i Norden*, edited by Helga Kress (Reykjavik: International Association of Scandinavian Study, 1996), pp. 87–92;

Wright, "Approaches to History in the Works of Kerstin Ekman," *Scandinavian Studies*, 63 (1991): 293–304;

Wright, "Kerstin Ekman: Voice of the Vulnerable," *World Literature Today*, 55 (1981): 204–209;

Wright, "Kerstin Ekman's Crime Fiction and the 'Crime' of Fiction: *The Devil's Horn*," *Swedish Book Review*, 2 (1984): 13–21;

Wright, "Textual Dialogue and the Humanistic Tradition: Kerstin Ekman's *Gör mig levande igen*," *Scandinavian Studies*, 72 (2000): 279–300;

Wright, "Theme, Imagery, and Narrative Perspective in Kerstin Ekman's *En stad av ljus*," *Scandinavian Studies*, 59 (1987): 1–27.

Per Olov Enquist
(23 September 1934 -   )

Ross Shideler
University of California, Los Angeles

BOOKS: *Kristallögat* (Stockholm: Norstedt, 1961);

Färdvägen (Stockholm: Prisma/Norstedt, 1963);

Magnetisörens femte vinter (Stockholm: Norstedt, 1964); translated by Paul Britten Austin as *The Magnetist's Fifth Winter* (London: Quartet, 1989);

Sextiotalskritik: En antologi redigerad av Per Olov Enquist (Stockholm: Norstedt, 1966);

Hess (Stockholm: Norstedt, 1966);

Legionärerna: En roman om baltutlämningen (Stockholm: Norstedt, 1968); translated by Alan Blair as *The Legionnaires: A Documentary Novel* (New York: Delacorte, 1973);

Sekonden (Stockholm: Norstedt, 1971; revised edition, Stockholm: Pan/Norstedt, 1972);

Katedralen i München och andra berättelser (Stockholm: Norstedt, 1972);

Berättelser från de inställda upprorens tid (Stockholm: Norstedt, 1974); includes "De trofasta Själarnas oro," translated by Jan Ring as "The Anxiety of the Loyal Souls" in *Box 749: A Magazine of the Printable Arts*, 2 (1975): 57–72; and "Spåren in stillhetens hav," translated by Ross Shideler as "The Tracks in the Sea of Tranquillity" in *Scandinavian Studies*, 49 (1975): 58–72;

Tribadernas natt: Ett skådespel från 1889 (Stockholm: Norstedt, 1975); translated by Shideler as *The Night of the Tribades: A Play from 1889* (New York: Hill & Wang, 1977; revised edition, New York: Dramatists Play Service, 1978);

Chez-Nous: Bilder från svenskt församlings liv, by Enquist and Anders Ehnmark (Stockholm: Norstedt, 1976);

Musikanternas uttåg (Stockholm: Norstedt, 1978); translated by Joan Tate as *The March of the Musicians* (London: Collins, 1985);

Mannen på trottoaren, by Enquist and Ehnmark (Stockholm: Norstedt, 1979);

Till Fedra (Stockholm: Norstedt, 1980);

En triptyk: Tribadernas natt, Till Fedra, Från regnormarnas liv (Stockholm: Norstedt, 1981);

Per Olov Enquist

Doktor Mabuses nya testamente: En detekivroman från seklets slut, by Enquist and Ehnmark (Stockholm: Norstedt, 1982);

Strindberg: Ett liv (Stockholm: Norstedt, 1984);

Nedstörtad ängel (Stockholm: Norstedt, 1985); translated by Anna Paterson as *Downfall: A Love Story* (London: Quartet, 1986);

Två reportage om idrott (Stockholm: Norstedt, 1986);

Protagoras sats: På spaning efter det politiska förnuftet, by Enquist and Ehnmark (Stockholm: Norstedt, 1987);

I lodjurets timma (Stockholm: Norstedt, 1988); translated by Shideler as *The Hour of the Lynx* (London: Forest Books, 1990);

Kapten Nemos bibliotek (Stockholm: Norstedt, 1991); translated by Paterson as *Captain Nemo's Library* (London: Quartet, 1992);

Dramatik: Tribadernas natt. Till Fedra. Från regnormarnas liv. I lodjurets timma (Stockholm: Norstedt, 1992);

Kartritarna (Stockholm: Norstedt, 1992);

Tre Pjäser: Magisk cirkel, Tupilak, Maria Stuart (Stockholm: Norstedt, 1994);

Hamsun: En film berättelse av Per Olov Enquist (Stockholm: Norstedt, 1996);

Bildmakarna (Stockholm: Norstedt, 1998);

Livläkarens besök (Stockholm: Norstedt, 1999); translated as *The Royal Physician's Visit* (New York: Overlook, 2001);

Lewis Resa (Stockholm: Norstedt, 2001).

PLAY PRODUCTIONS: *Tribaderna,* Stockholm, Kungliga Dramatiska Teatern, Fall 1975;

Till Fedra, Copenhagen, Det Kongelige, 1980;

Regnormarna, Copenhagen, Det Kongelige, 1981;

Maria Stuart, Copenhagen, Det Kongelige, 1985;

I Lodjurets timma, Stockholm, Sibyllan, 1988;

Tupilak, Stockholm, Kungliga Dramatiska Teatern, 1993;

Magisk Cirkel, Copenhagen, Betty Nansen Theater, Fall 1994;

Bildmarkarna, Stokholm, Kungliga Dramatiska Teatern, 13 February 1998.

As a novelist, playwright, essayist, and newspaper columnist Per Olov Enquist is one of the dominant Swedish authors of the second half of the twentieth century. He published his first novel in 1961 and has written prolifically since then. In contemporary Sweden, Enquist is recognized for his multifaceted talent: he is a leading dramatist whose plays have been performed throughout Europe and the United States, a major novelist whose works have been translated and admired worldwide, and one of the central figures in Swedish literary and cultural life.

Intellectually rooted in Scandinavian history, culture, and politics, Enquist first established himself as a novelist and columnist, but he gained unusual renown in Scandinavia and Europe with his documentary novel *Legionärerna: En roman om baltutlämningen* (1968; translated as *The Legionnaires: A Documentary Novel,* 1973). He continued combining his prose fiction with his public role as a literary and cultural critic and commentator until the 1970s, when he began to write plays using documentary techniques and socially conscious themes similar to those in his novels. Since then he has produced a succession of persuasive and often profound dramas and novels, and he is recognized as one of the major voices in Swedish literary, theatrical, and social life.

The central themes of Enquist's work may be traced to his childhood in Northern Sweden. Born on 23 September 1934 in the coastal region of Västerbotten, in a small village named Hjoggböle on the edge of a forest, Enquist was raised by his mother. Although his mother, Maria Lindgren Enquist, was a schoolteacher, she and her husband, Elof Enquist, came from families of pious peasants who had lived and worked in Northern Sweden for generations. Enquist's father, a laborer who sometimes worked in the nearby sawmills and sometimes as a stevedore in the local shipyards, died when Enquist was six months old. He and his mother moved to a nearby village when he was twelve years old, and they remained there, while his mother continued as a schoolteacher, until he finished high school.

Enquist moved to the university town of Uppsala in 1955 and began studies in literature, which he pursued until he completed his *filosfie magister* degree in 1960 and his *filosfie licentiat* degree, almost the equivalent of an American doctorate, in 1966. While a student in Uppsala, Enquist participated as a high jumper in track and field events until 1963; this love of sports appears later in his essays and novels. He also married and began a family during those years and earned money as a literary critic for the Swedish morning newspaper *Svenska Dagbladet*. He published his first novel, *Kristallögat* (The Crystal Eye), in 1961 and his second, *Färdvägen* (The Route), in 1963. He continued his newspaper career by becoming a columnist in 1963 for the evening newspaper *Expressen,* a position to which he has intermittently returned throughout his life.

Enquist's early novels reflect the French *nouveau roman* of the 1950s and 1960s, which, with its psychological complexity and narrative sophistication, helped the author to shape the aesthetic and critical perspectives that define his later work. Characteristic of these early novels is a self-conscious narrator's complicated and often conflicted search for identity and for insight into the nature of truth and/or reality; these overlapping themes continue throughout his writing. One could argue that Enquist's first two novels ultimately present a single theme: a withdrawal from life, which results in isolation, versus an active participation in it, which leads to self-acceptance and personal responsibility. This theme of self-acceptance, the ability to believe in or discover one's own emotional and intellectual identity, is one of Enquist's lifelong preoccupations.

In *Kristallögat* the young female narrator, Jenni, undergoes a transformation as she narrates, in almost

Cover for the published version (1980) of Enquist's play based on the Greek myth of Phaedra and Theseus (University of Washington Libraries)

psychoanalytic fashion, memories from her childhood and adolescence to Jens, a young man who becomes her lover. When Jens feels he can do no more for her, he leaves Jenni so that she can take her own final step into maturity. *Färdvägen* describes a similar process of maturation and self-acceptance. Written as a metanovel—a novel about a novelist writing a novel—it begins as an unidentified narrator stares out a train window and recollects events from his past, especially an automobile accident that changed his life. The narrator retells the story of the accident several times; each time the reader learns more about a journey through Europe in which he meets a cook who teaches him how to become involved in life, and then a young woman, Ilene, who teaches him how to forget himself and to love. In the car crash that focuses the novel, Ilene and the cook die while the narrator survives. By the end of the novel he has learned to accept his responsibility in the accident as well as to accept life rather than withdraw from it. He has apparently come to this conclusion through the process of writing the novel, though he remains skeptical of the capacity of language to convey the subtle experiences of life.

Writing performs a fundamental role throughout Enquist's authorship. In his narrators' various searches for answers to specific social or personal problems he probes the relation of the author to the text and the mediating factor of language. Even in the most documentary of his texts, the act of writing or communicating often troubles his narrators.

Part of this preoccupation with the act of writing becomes visible in the symbols and narrative structures Enquist crafts and manipulates in his novels and plays. Over the years he has gradually developed a series of images and motifs, such as birds, outcast or alienated individuals, hot and cold temperatures, embryos, and journeys, which he continually uses. These themes and images appear throughout his writing, and many of them, layered as they are with deep psychological and archetypal associations, occur within a plot based on some historical event.

This use of history and its relation to truth, reality, and art appears clearly in *Magnetisörens femte vinter* (1964; translated as *The Magnetist's Fifth Winter,* 1989), Enquist's breakthrough novel. The novel, with its fascinating narrative and complex study of scientific logic and artistic fantasy, of rationalism and emotionalism, was awarded the *Bonniers Litterära Magasin* prize, one of the most prestigious Swedish literary awards. Friedrich Meisner, the protagonist, is similar to Franz Anton Mesmer, the eighteenth-century creator of the healing method called "mesmerism." The novel uses Meisner's character and the problems of faith and power raised by mesmerism to connect allegorically with the twentieth century; for instance, the novel may be an indirect commentary on the rise and fall of Adolf Hitler and other charismatic dictators.

Reflecting actual, but conflicting, historical documents, the novel combines fact and fiction to present the story of a traveling doctor who rises to success in a small town on the basis of his seemingly miraculous healings and his personal charisma. Meisner falls into dishonor when some of his healings are proved to be fraudulent. A curious but essentially rational Dr. Selinger narrates the novel. Because he has a teenage daughter who is blind and is healed by Meisner, Selinger reluctantly participates first in Meisner's social ascent and later, by exposing him as a fraud, contributes to his descent. Exploring issues of mass hypnosis and the human need to believe in something beyond one's own physicality, *Magnetisörens femte vinter* also examines the relation between art and politics, a theme that Enquist has continued to develop throughout his career.

For Enquist, who was active in the Swedish Social Democratic Party as a young man, politics and economics constitute fundamental forces in the shaping of human existence, and these forces are located within specific personal and historical events. His next novel, *Hess* (1966), reflects this belief. A complicated, difficult, and sometimes confusing novel, *Hess* is based on Rudolf Hess, a deputy of Hitler's who was imprisoned during World War II. Almost a series of novels within a novel—one written by Hess's adjutant, Karl-Heinz Pintsch, another written by a researcher of three manuscripts Hess supposedly wrote in prison—this "open novel" (in other words, one without an obvious beginning, middle, and ending) offers an intense analysis of the relationship between an author, his text, and the reader and society at large. Because of its dense structure and its verbal representation of the conflict between the human desire for wholeness and the fragmentary nature of a reality often impossible to understand, the novel was less well received by the public. The actions, real and imagined, of the mysterious figure of Hess, who inexplicably parachuted into England during the war, and Pintsch, who was tortured by the Russians to tell what he knew about Hess, were ideally suited for Enquist's stylistic and philosophical experiment. *Hess* laid the groundwork for much of Enquist's later writing, and two years later he published the novel that established him as one of the foremost documentary novelists in Europe.

Legionärerna formulates some of Enquist's most enduring imagery and narrative techniques: a self-conscious narrator in search of the truth about an historical event; an awareness of the parallels between the past and the present; and the narrator's desire to be like a conscious embryo, at one with his environment yet able to stand apart and observe it. The novel, a representation of the dominant intellectual currents of the 1960s and 1970s, describes an ugly and tragic moment in Swedish history, the deportation of Lithuanian, Latvian, and Estonian citizens who had been drafted into the German army. The motivation for the investigation derives from the narrator's trip to the United States to observe civil rights demonstrations in Jackson, Mississippi. When the narrator returns to Sweden he begins his own investigation into the "legionnaires," for him a comparable civil rights protest in Swedish history.

Legionärerna is based on the true story of 167 soldiers from the Baltic States, most of whom had been drafted into combat by the Germans; these men surrendered to the Swedish military at the end of World War II. In accordance with treaties signed at the end of the war, all such troops were to be repatriated. These imprisoned Baltic troops believed that they would be executed by the Soviets who now occupied their countries, however, and, indeed, a few of these soldiers might have committed war crimes for which they would be tried and sentenced. After much debate and public outcry against the repatriation, the Swedish government finally returned the so-called legionnaires, some of whom killed or maimed themselves in protest, to their homelands. Enquist's novel, though it raised painful issues from the past, investigates this story through interviews and public documents and traces the lives of some of the soldiers and officers sent back to the Soviet Union. Somewhat sympathetic to the Russians, the novel demonstrates that the returned soldiers were treated fairly. The narrator's long research ultimately proves unsatisfactory for him personally, however, since no one can ever be objective

Enquist in 2001, the year his novel Lewis Resa *was published (photograph © Ulla Montan)*

enough to understand and present the truth. The novel appeared shortly after the Soviet Union invaded Czechoslovakia in 1968, and this apparent bias toward Russia within the context of the Cold War and Sweden's longstanding neutrality added to the debate surrounding the appearance of the novel.

Sekonden (The Second, 1971), Enquist's next novel, derives from his passionate love of sports as well as his intense political interests. The success of *Sekonden* affirmed Enquist, who was also working as a columnist for *Expressen* during the late 1960s and early 1970s, as one of the major authors of his generation. Reflecting his experiences during a visit to Berlin in 1970, this profound psychological novel, written as a puzzle that the narrator gradually pieces together, builds from the case of a Swedish hammer-thrower who was banned from sports for using an underweight hammer to set new records. The narrator, the hammer-thrower's son, examines not only his disgraced father's life, but also amateur and professional sports as they mirror the values of society, from the 1936 Olympics in Berlin to American professional boxing. Beginning his investigation in 1968, the same day the Russians invaded Czechoslovakia, the narrator analyzes his own flawed identity while trying to understand how and why his father could betray the track and field sports he loved. Finally, he realizes that his father's desire to give the people the new records they wanted led him to cheat. The conclusion of the novel blends socialist and Christian imagery in the term *agape,* or brotherly love, as the narrator's love and forgiveness of his father allow him to experience love in his own life and, apparently, to accept the sins of the political system in which he believes.

After *Sekonden* Enquist published *Katedralen i München och andra berättelser* (The Cathedral in Munich and Other Stories, 1972), a collection of essays, based on his newspaper articles, about the Olympics held in Munich in 1972. These essays examine not only the murder of Israeli athletes by terrorists near the end of the games, but the commercialization and class consciousness, the illusion and falseness underlying the publicity and fame of the Olympics in general. Enquist's next book, *Berättelser från de inställda upprorens tid* (Stories from the Age of Canceled Revolutions, 1974), is for the most part a collection of short stories that he wrote while a guest professor at the University of California, Los Angeles, in 1973. Narrated by a Swedish journalist who designates himself as E., these stories continue to develop Enquist's themes of alienation and social displacement. For instance, one story tells of a few meetings between the socialist narrator and a homeless American Vietnam veteran who hates Communists and loves the United States, even though he cannot find work and is planning to immigrate to Australia. Another story focuses on the manager of the narrator's apartment building, a man who abuses his wife and tenants but is himself demeaned and denigrated by the owner of the building. Each story in this collection presents an outcast or displaced person whose alienation apparently directly reflects the American social and economic system, which itself resembles a win-or-lose, all-or-nothing television game show.

Out of his stay in Los Angeles grew the play that catapulted Enquist to the forefront of Scandinavian dramatists. *Tribadernas natt: Ett skådespel från 1889* (1975; translated as *The Night of the Tribades: A Play from 1889,* 1977) is a four-character drama that depicts August Strindberg visiting a rehearsal of his play *Den Starkare* (The Stronger) in Copenhagen in 1889. *Den Starkare* is a one-act, two-character play in which only one person speaks, and Enquist's play begins with Strindberg's former wife, Siri von Essen, producing and playing the lead. Opposite Siri in the mute role is a young Danish woman, Marie Caroline David, thought by Strindberg to be his wife's lover. A Danish actor assists the two women in the production. The opening scene reveals the marital conflicts between Strindberg and Siri, then a confrontation between Strindberg and Marie unfolds during which his breakup with his wife is recounted from Strindberg's and Marie's different perspectives. The power of the play derives from its incisive dialogue about sex and sex roles. Its comic commentary on male vanity both presents and undermines Strindberg's misogyny and obsession with masculinity. In blunt language the play enacts the struggle for power between a tradition-bound, dominance-seeking male and two women who reject his authority. In this play, Enquist ultimately argues that Strindberg wrote *Den Starkare*, in which two women fight over an absent man, as a wish, a fantasy that Siri and Marie were fighting over him instead of he and Marie fighting for Siri. Enquist followed this work with the first of several works, including a play and a detective novel, that he cowrote over the next two decades with his fellow journalist Anders Ehnmark; these sometimes rich and amusing works usually reflect the two authors' strong sociopolitical commitment. These publications have added to the reputation of both authors.

In 1978 Enquist published his powerful historical novel, *Musikanternas uttåg* (translated as *The March of the Musicians*, 1985). Although the novel takes place in Northern Sweden between 1903 and 1910 and describes events related to the rise of unions and the general strike of 1909, *Musikanternas uttåg* builds on Enquist's family history. Gradually uncovering multiple narrative threads, the primary narrator, a Swedish writer named Enquist, seeks to discover why Swedish working-class families immigrated to Brazil just after the turn of the century. The story itself begins in 1903 with a young boy, Nicanor Markström, helping to capture a union organizer whom the sawmill workers consider a threat. Six years later the young Nicanor and his pious, originally conservative, but now almost starving and desperate fellow workers try without success to form a union of their own. The title of the novel alludes to the fairy tale by Jacob and Wilhelm Grimm, "The Town Musicians of Bremen," and refers to a group of workers who, like the old animals in the story, decide to leave their homes rather than stay and die. The protagonist Nicanor, who did not immigrate, lost his tongue in a fight during the workers' unsuccessful struggle to improve their wages and working conditions, but his story has been told by the narrator Enquist.

In the following years Enquist continued his role in Sweden and Denmark as author, playwright, journalist, social commentator, and, at times, public gadfly. In 1980 he wrote *Till Fedra* (To Phaedra), a play about the wife of King Theseus of Athens from Greek mythology. Enquist's drama, based on Jean Racine's *Phèdre* (1677) and Euripides' *Hippolytus* (428 B.C.) is written in a series of eight stylized, free-verse songs. The play, perhaps related to Enquist's divorce from his first wife and his concurrent move to Copenhagen, explores the relation between love and destructiveness via the character of Phaedra, the wife who falls in love with her stepson. With its intense portrait of the desire of human beings to be useful and have a purpose in life, this play sustains Enquist's concern with the theme on which he focused in *Musikanternas uttåg*.

In 1981 Enquist published *En triptyk* (A Triptych), which includes another highly successful play, *Från regnormarnas liv: En familjetavla från 1856* (The main title literally means "From the lives of earthworms," but the play was translated in an unpublished version by Harry Carlsson as "Rain Snakes: A Family Portrait from 1856.") This drama tells the story of Hans Christian Andersen's involvement with the prominent Danish couple, Johan Ludwig Andersen, a literary critic and dramatist, and Johanne Luise Heiberg, a leading actress. The play continues Enquist's technique of telling stories within stories, of intermixing fact and fiction to reveal the complexity of human sexuality and the fears related to identity and social interactions. It concludes, however, by using Andersen's story of the Snow Queen to suggest how people must join together, must communicate, to survive and help each other.

In 1984 Enquist published *Strindberg: Ett liv,* a work he called a "television novel," which constituted the highly successful book-length manuscript of a six-part television program about August Strindberg. Enquist followed this television production with a short lyrical novel, *Nedstörtad ängel* (Downfall: A Love Story, 1985), which through a series of overlapping narratives describes the bizarre yet touching story of a freak with two heads. Here Enquist's preoccupation with the nature of love and the complexity of human identity takes one of its most unique forms.

His next major stage play, *I lodjurets timma* (1988, translated as *The Hour of the Lynx*, 1990) continues his focus on love but places it in relation to faith. Set in a mental institution, the characters of the play, a young male murderer, a female therapist, and a female pastor, try to solve why the young man killed a couple living in his grandfather's house. As the youth's psychological problems unfold, the pastor discovers and accepts the boy's strange faith and his suicidal search for transcendence. This intense psychological drama explores issues of isolation, apparent madness, and the question of religious belief and the incarnations such beliefs can take; in this case, for the disturbed protagonist, a red cat represents a messenger from God.

Enquist's next novel, *Kapten Nemos bibliotek* (1991, translated as *Captain Nemo's Library*, 1992) returns to his own Norrland childhood and to his other fiction with characters who appeared in *Musikanternas uttåg* and *I lodjurets timma*. The novel presents one of Enquist's most complicated narrative structures with a narrator who often speaks from the perspective of himself as a child. The title refers to Jules Verne's mysterious and symbolic Captain Nemo, who in this novel seems to represent an almost omniscient source of knowledge. The plot tells the story of a young boy who was switched at birth with another child, then returned to his family when he was six. This reversal opens the door to a complex reconstruction of the past and of the narrator's identity. The novel seems to have allowed Enquist to bring together some of the themes that were crucial to his creative life. One senses a degree of closure in this novel as Enquist, in the imaginary world that he summons up through the imagery of a library, assembles a psychological and conceptual world that sinks beneath the sea, like Captain Nemo's submarine in the famous novel by Verne.

Enquist continues looking back at his life in a volume of personal essays, *Kartritarna* (The Map Drawers, 1992). These essays range from explanations and commentaries related to some of his own works, such as *Hess, Legionärerna, Musikanternas uttåg,* and *Strindberg,* to a description of Sweden at the time of the murder of Prime Minister Olof Palme. Two years later, Enquist published three new plays that continue his preoccupation with the relation between love and death, art and reality, history and the present. *Magisk Cirkel* (Magic Circle) takes place in 1958 with a cast of three and is based on an essay in *Kartritarna.* The plot relates to a World War II Gestapo interrogation of the leader of the Danish Communist Party, Aksel Larsen, who informed against his party, then went on to become a major Danish political leader. Another play is an historical drama based on Schiller's *Maria Stuart* and a third, *Tupilak,* is a Kafkaesque, highly stylized portrait centered around a dysfunctional family. One of Enquist's major contributions to Swedish culture in the past few years has been his remarkable screenplay for the Swedish motion picture *Hamsun* (1996), directed by Jan Troell and starring Max von Sydow, a brilliant and powerful study of the Nobel prize winner Knut Hamsun's final years.

Enquist's play *Bildmakarna* (The Image Makers), directed by Sweden's best-known director, Ingmar Bergman, opened in Stockholm in the spring of 1998. In this play Enquist again blends actual historical figures and events into a probing and symbol-laden psychological drama. Based on Selma Lagerlöf, one of Sweden's most famous authors of the early 1900s, and Victor Sjöström, the renowned silent-movie director, the play takes place in 1920 when Lagerlöf arrives to see scenes from a film adaptation of her novel. Primarily through dialogue between Lagerlöf and a highly sexual and intense young actress named Tora, the drama unfolds the hidden degradation and pain of Lagerlöf's relationship with her alcoholic father, whom she both loves and hates, and her ability to tranform that secret agony into great art.

Livläkarens besök (1999, translated as *The Royal Physician's Visit,* 2001) builds from an actual historical incident in which Johann Friedrich Struensee, the German court physician to the Danish king Charles VII, served as de facto ruler of Denmark from 1770 to 1772 until a tutor, Ove Hoegh-Guldberg, managed to overthrow him. Enquist combines history and fiction in order to probe the collision between philosophical or religious ideals and the confused complexity and ambiguity of reality. The novel succeeds in bringing out all of Enquist's formidable intellectual and creative talents; he uses history to tell a fascinating story of love and court intrigue in order to explore the minds of his eighteenth-century characters.

Lewis Resa (Lewis's Voyage, 2001) has been hailed as yet another major novel, perhaps definitively establishing Enquist as one of Sweden's foremost living authors. Employing once again his technique of combining history and fiction, Enquist turns to the region of northern Sweden where he grew up (and which he describes with such power in *Musikanternas uttåg*) to portray the history and some of the specific figures, Lewis Pethrus and Sven Lidman, who were deeply involved in the Pentecostal movement that played a major role in nineteenth-century Sweden.

References:

Eva Adolfsson and others, "Det liberala medvetandets gränser–Text om P. O. Enquists författarskap," *Bonniers Litterära Magasin,* 4 (1971): 273–287;

Beata Agrell, *Romanen som forsknings resa. Forskningsresan som roman. Om litterära återbruk och konventionskritik i 1960-talets prosa* (Göteborg: Daidalos, 1993);

Gunilla Anderman, "The Night of the Tribades: Fact and Fiction in Grez-sur-Loing," in *Documentarism in Scandinavian Literature,* edited by Paul Houe and Sven Rossel, Internationale Forschungen zur Allgemeinen und Vergleichenden Literaturwissenschaft, volume 18 (Amsterdam & Atlanta: Rodopi, 1997), pp. 148–154;

Marilyn Johns Blackwell, "Ideology and Specularity in Per Olov Enquist's *Tribadernas natt,*" *Scandinavian Studies,* 67 (1995): 196–215;

Thomas Bredsdorff, *De sorte huller: Om tillblivelsen af et sprog i P. O. Enquists forfatterskab* (Copenhagen: Gyldendal, 1991);

Bredsdorff, *The Rhetoric of the Documentary: Per Olov Enquist and Scandinavian Documentary Literature* (Minneapolis: Center for Nordic Studies, University of Minnesota, 1993);

Jean Marie Bretagne, "The Lost Balance in Per Olov Enquist's Documentary Narratives," in *Documentarism in Scandinavian Literature,* edited by Poul Houe and Sven Rossel (Amsterdam & Atlanta: Rodopi, 1997), pp. 135–138;

Eva Ekselius, *Andas fram mitt ansikte: Om den mytiska och djuppsykologiska strukturen hos Per Olov Enquist* (Stockholm: Symposion, 1996);

Ekselius, "Isen, munnen och maskarna: Om den tematiska strukturen hos Per Olov Enquist," *Bonniers Litterära Magasin,* 3 (1987): 147–160;

Peter Hallberg, "Dokumentarisk berättarkonst: Om dokumentarism och 'fiktiv dokumentarism' i Amerikansk, Tysk och Nordisk Litteratur," in *Romanteori och romananalyse,* edited by M. Gerlach-Nielsen and others (Odense: Odense Universitets förlag, 1968);

Erik H. Henningsen, *Per Olov Enquist: En undersígelse af en venstreintellektuel forfatters forsíg på at omfunktionere den litteraere institution* (Copenhagen: Samleren, 1975);

Henrik Jansson, *Per Olov Enquist och det inställda upproret: Ett författarskap i relation till svensk debatt 1961–1968* (Åbo: Åbo Akademis förlag, 1987);

Sven Linnér, "Per Olov Enquists Legionärerna," in his *Den Moderne Roman og Romanforskning i Norden* (Bergen: Bergens Universitet, 1971), pp. 68–88;

Ross Shideler, *Per Olov Enquist: A Critical Study* (Westport, Conn.: Greenwood Press, 1984);

Shideler, "Per Olov Enquist's *Hess,*" *Scandinavica,* 22 (1983): 5–14;

Shideler, "Putting Together the Puzzle in Per Olov Enquist's Sekonden," *Scandinavian Studies,* 49 (1977): 311–329;

Shideler, "The Swedish Short Story: Per Olov Enquist," *Scandinavian Studies,* 49 (1977): 241–262;

Shideler, "Zola and the Problem of the Objective Narrator in Per Olov Enquist and Per Christian Jersild," in *Documentarism in Scandinavian Literature,* pp. 120–134;

Jan Stenkvist, *Flykt och motstånd: Fyra studier i politisk dikt* (Stockholm: Norstedt, 1978);

Gunnar Syréhn, *Mellan sanningen och lögnen: Studier i Per Olov Enquists dramatick* (Stockholm: Almqvist & Wiksell, 2000);

Egil Törnqvist, "Playwright on Playwright: Per Olov Enquist's Strindberg and Lars Noren's O'Neill," in *Documentarism in Scandinavian Literature,* pp. 155–164;

Törnqvist, "Scenens Strindberg och verklighetens: Per Olov Enquists 'Tribadernas natt' (1975) som Dokumentärt Drama," in *Literature and Reality: Creatio versus Mimesis, Problems of Realism in Modern Nordic Literature,* edited by Alex Bolckmans (Ghent: University of Ghent, 1977), pp. 195–211;

Pascale Voilley, "An Evening with Per Olov Enquist: September 3, 1994," in *Documentarism in Scandinavian Literature,* pp. 107–119;

Margareta Zetterström, "Det finns ingen helgonlik objektivitet," *Bonniers Litterära Magasin,* 39 (1970): 524–532.

Katarina Frostenson
(5 March 1953 -)

Ia Dübois
University of Washington

BOOKS: *I mellan: Dikter* (Göteborg: Korpen, 1978);
Raymond Chandler och filmen (Göteborg: Korpen, 1978);
Rena land: Dikter (Stockholm: Wahlström & Widstrand, 1980);
Den andra: Dikter (Stockholm: Wahlström & Widstrand, 1982);
I det gula: Tavlor, resor, ras (Stockholm: Wahlström & Widstrand, 1985);
Samtalet: Dikter (Stockholm: Wahlström & Widstrand, 1987);
Stränderna (Stockholm: Wahlström & Widstrand, 1989);
Överblivet, photographs by Jean-Claude Arnault (Stockholm: Katten, 1989);
4 monodramer (Stockholm: Wahlström & Widstrand, 1990);
Joner: Tre sviter (Stockholm: Wahlström & Widstrand, 1991);
Artur Lundkvist: Inträdestal i Svenska akademien (Stockholm: Norstedt, 1992);
Berättelser från dom (Stockholm: Wahlström & Widstrand, 1992);
Tankarna (Stockholm: Wahlström & Widstrand, 1994);
Jan Håfström: En diktsvit till Jan Håfström och till verk av honom, bilingual edition, translated by Joan Tate as *Jan Håfström: A Suite of Poems to Jan Håfström and to Works by Him* (Malmö: Rooseum, 1994);
Vägen till öarna, photographs by Arnault (Stockholm: Wahlström & Widstrand, 1996);
Traum; Sal P (Stockholm: Wahlström & Widstrand, 1996);
Staden—en opera: Libretto (Stockholm: Wahlström & Widstrand, 1998);
Korallen (Stockholm: Wahlström & Widstrand, 1999);
Kristallvägen; Safirgränd: Skådespel (Stockholm: Wahlström & Widstrand, 2000);
Skallarna, by Frostenson and Aris Fiorentos (Stockholm: Wahlström & Widstrand, 2000).
Editions: *Samtalet; Stränderna; Joner* (Stockholm: Wahlström & Widstrand, 1992);
Från Rena land till Korallen: Dikter i urval (Stockholm: Wahlström & Widstrand, 2000).

PLAY PRODUCTIONS: *Nilen,* Stockholm, Royal Dramatic Theatre, 10 November 1989;

Katarina Frostenson (photograph by Jean-Claude Arnault; from the cover of Rena land, *1980)*

Sebastopol, Galleri Forum, December 1989;
Traum, Stockholm, Royal Dramatic Theatre, 13 February 1993;
3 monodramer, Oslo, Det Norske Teatret, 18 February 1995—comprises *Nilen, Bro, Sebastopol;*
Sal P, Stockholm, Royal Dramatic Theatre, 23 March 1996;
Staden, music by Sven-David Sandström, libretto by Frostenson, Stockholm, Royal Swedish Opera House, 12 September 1998.

PRODUCED SCRIPTS: *Sebastopol,* radio, monodrama adapted by Frostenson, Swedish Radio, 8 November 1991;

Mannen på sluttningen, composed by Carl Unander-Scharin, radio, libretto adapted by Frostenson from her "För sluttningen," Swedish Broadcasting Corporation, 13 December 1991.

OTHER: Emmanuel Bove, *Mina vänner,* translated by Frostenson (Stockholm: Tiden, 1986);

Henri Michaux, *Bräsch: Texter i urval,* interpretations by Frostenson and Ulla Bruncrona (Stockholm: Bonnier, 1987);

Marguerite Duras, *Lol V. Steins hänförelse,* translated by Frostenson (Stockholm: Schultz, 1988);

Vardagens ting: Marguerite Duras talar med Jérôme Beaujour, translated by Frostenson (Stockholm: Interculture, 1989);

Georges Bataille, *Himlens blå,* translated by Frostenson (Stockholm: Wahlström & Widstrand, 1990);

Håkan Rehnberg, *Moira: En målning i 29 delar 1988,* text by Frostenson (Stockholm: Sandler-Mergel, 1990);

Douglas Feuk and Sören Engblom, *Johan Scott* (Stockholm: Gedin, 1991)–includes poem by Frostenson;

"Några ögonblick och platser i Anders Frostensons lyrik," by Frostenson and Esbjörn Belfrage, in *Guds kärlek är som stranden och som gräset: En bok om och av psalmdiktaren Anders Frostenson* (Stockholm: Verbum, 1996), pp. 65–69.

SELECTED PERIODICAL PUBLICATIONS–UNCOLLECTED: "I framtiden måste vi lyssna: några ord om Maurice Maeterlicks dramer," *Halifax,* 9 (1995): 67–81;

"Rösten–vad är den för djur?" *Halifax,* 9 (1995): 121–124.

Katarina Frostenson rose to fame in 1992 when she was elected into the Swedish Academy. Lauded as the youngest, and most beautiful, member of the academy, she had also gained the respect and recognition few women writers have. Since her debut in 1978 with the poetry collection *I mellan: Dikter* (In Between: Poems), she had published seven collections of poetry, a drama collection, several translations, and critical essays. Her combined achievements in introducing international literature to Sweden and in creating "new" poetry and experimental drama won her the vote of the academy. Like her peers Ann Jäderlund and Birgitta Lillpers in Sweden and Pia Tafdrup in Denmark, Frostenson creates poetry that is known for being difficult and obscure. In response to questions about the unintelligible aspect of her poems, she compared them to the work of traditional Swedish poet Nils Ferlin: "nyskapande poesi har alltid varit smal.... Alla kan ju inte skriva som Ferlin. Språket är så oändligt mycket större" (Avant-garde poetry has always been narrow.... Everyone cannot write like [Nils] Ferlin. Language is infinitely greater). She claims, in fact, that she does not write to create meaning, but rather to express rhythm and tone. She wants to build texts that are beautiful, that exist in the intersection of the sensual and the intellectual.

Alma Katarina Frostenson was born on 5 March 1953 in Stockholm. She grew up in a middle-class family in Hägersten, a suburb southwest of Stockholm. Her father, Georg Frostenson, was an agronomist and her mother, Britta Frostenson, a social worker. Frostenson is as enigmatic and mystical as her poetry: she is protective of her private life.

Frostenson's style can be characterized by her affinity for tone and rhythm and by the juxtaposition of grotesque and beautiful images. Her musicality originates in her childhood, when she played the violin and loved to sing. In an interview with Kajsa Lundgren, Frostenson remarked: "Den där jävla fiolen! Jag skulle ju ha haft ett piano att hamra på i stället! Skrivandet är som en lust att slå på ett piano, att upplösa språket i rytmer och klanger" (That damned violin! I should of course have had a piano to pound on instead! Writing is like a desire to pound away on a piano, to dissolve language into rhythms and tones). Musicality also runs in her family; her uncle Anders Frostenson is a Swedish hymn writer and poet about whom she wrote the 1996 article "Några ögonblick och platser i Anders Frostensons lyrik" (Some Moments and Places in the Poetry of Anders Frostenson).

The stark combination of grotesque and beautiful images is a stylistic element that creates tension in the poem and surprises the reader. She has revealed that she loved playing with different word combinations and expressions in school, repeating beautiful ones to herself and shocking others by blurting out grotesque ones. For example, while she liked "tasting" the sound of "Andrea Doria," the name of an Italian ship, she could also cry out "Hugg dem i strupen och ät!" (Stab them in the throat and eat!) during class. The same exclamation appears in slightly different form in the poem "res dig stelna rasa in" (stand up freeze cave in) from *Den andra: Dikter* (The Other One: Poems, 1982):

Hugga in i världen, som en strupe
Suga, äta ut

Mumla viska—Skria—
dröja
Skrika till

(Cut into the world, like a throat
Suck, eat
Mumble whisper—Screech—
wait
Cry out)

Frostenson's high-school years were spent at the prestigious Adolf Fredrik School of Music in Stockholm. She continued her studies at the Stockholm University, where she received a B.A. in comparative literature, film, and drama. In 1978 she published the first book in Sweden on Raymond Chandler and the filming of his mystery novels, *Raymond Chandler och filmen* (Raymond Chandler and Film). The interest in comparative literature and foreign authors' treatment of language is apparent also in Frostenson's postgraduate work on the French author Jean-Marie Gustave Le Clézio. In fact, she started to write a dissertation on Le Clézio but left it unfinished as other projects took priority. Marguerite Duras, Henri Michaux, and Georges Bataille are other French writers whose texts Frostenson has interpreted and translated.

I mellan is Frostenson's first publication. The title itself is interesting as it is symptomatic of postmodern poetics. Exploring the in-between stage, the gap between the "I" and the word, between the fantastic and the trivial, is the force motivating postmodern poets. In the title poem Frostenson describes this phenomena as

Ingenting mer osynligt
än ordens ledljus
I dig, i mig
i mellan
Möt mig i tystnad
I mellan

(Nothing more invisible
than the guiding light of the words
In you, in me
in between
Meet me in silence
In between)

The collection is emblematic of Frostenson's youth. She was twenty-five years old at the time of its publication, and she told Lennart Lindskog in a 1993 interview that "Det är en bok som inte är förlöst riktigt" (It's a book that was not delivered as it should have been).

The similarities between the poetry of Frostenson and Tafdrup are noticeable in their early works. Poul Borum has compared Frostenson's poem "Huset är kvinnligt" (The House Is Female) from *Rena land: Dikter* (Clean Lands: Poems, 1980) with "Mit hus" (My House) in Tafdrup's debut collection, *Når det går hul på en engel* (When an Angel Breaks Her Silence, 1981). While he finds their mutual motif of the female body as a house to be typical for their generation and gender, he suggests that Frostenson's poem exhibits more fragmentation and neurosis, like a film by Ingmar Bergman, while Tafdrup's is more about ethics. These qualities affect both the images of the poem and its presentation, with the words spread out on the page. Many of the poems in *Rena land* are about a child's world. Death and hysteria are ominous in some, while others, such as "Midsommarfest" (Midsummer Party), express freedom and sensual images of food and events.

In 1981 Frostenson moved to Paris with Jean-Claude Arnault, a French photographer and opera director. They remained in Paris for four years. This sojourn proved to be fertile ground for Frostenson's later works. In Paris she walked the streets, discovering the landscape and soul of the city. Boulevard de Sebastopol, Gare d'Austerlitz, and Hôpital de la Salpêtrière are places she particularly returns to in her writings. For example, in the collection *I det gula: Tavlor, resor, ras* (In the Color Yellow: Images, Voyages, Impact, 1985), the poem "Paris Austerlitz—Salpêtrière" opens with the words

Vägg

vägg   kala talmur
svala order   kastrop
ekon samlas
till en väv   Sov
stig   Mot väggen
svälj ner frågan   Res Till tysta
tunga frågorna

(Wall

wall   bare speech-wall
cool orders   hurl-shouts
echoes gather
in a weaving   Sleep
step   Toward the wall
swallow the question   Go To the silent
heavy questions)

The hospital, the street, and the city come alive in Frostenson's fragmented text, filled with thought-provoking images that are typical of her poetry. The poem communicates her complex relation to language. Keenly aware of the pregnant silence of the

Cover for Frostenson's 1980 collection of poems about childhood joys and fears (Widener Library, Harvard University)

hospital walls, she encourages silence. Her trust in the human senses seems stronger than in language itself. In her 1997 article, "Den herrelösa dikten: 1980-talets svenska lyrik" (Poems without a Master: Swedish Poetry in the 1980s), Åsa Beckman writes that the act of bringing the invisible out into the open is connected to violence in Frostenson's works. The drama of her texts lies in the conflict between a destructive obsession to define and verbalize and a simultaneous need to speak and write to avoid silent darkness. Beckman's interpretation reflects that of Borum: "Denna ambivalens till språket är ett grundtrauma i Katarina Frostensons författarskap. Det framstår inte som en kokett estetisk hållning, utan som ett djupt personligt drama" (This ambivalence to language is a basic trauma in Katarina Frostenson's writings. It does not appear as a coquettish aesthetic point of view, but as a deeply personal drama).

The end of the 1980s were productive and eventful years for Frostenson: she completed two poetry collections, published translations, and in 1989 married Arnault and started collaborating with him at his gallery, Forum. The collections *Samtalet: Dikter* (The Conversation: Poems, 1987) and *Stränderna* (The Seashores, 1989) were published. The tension between masculine and feminine elements dominates Frostenson's poetry in these collections. In *Stränderna* the word itself is phallic, as in the sentence "Ordet stod upp, som en pelare, stelnade allt som låg omkring" (The word rose up, like a column, petrifying everything around it). The book consists of a single poetic text, titled "en våg" (a wave), which evolves with a combination of lyrical prose and poetry that evokes one individual's complex relationship to another, to nature, and to the past. Frostenson's desire to reach a new level of clarity and distinction in her writings is evident in her statement from the 1993 interview with Lindskog: "När jag skrev *Stränderna* var jag trött på en melankolisk ton som fanns i många av mina tidigare dikter. I *Stränderna* försökte jag beskriva platser så rent och tydligt som möjligt och revoltera mot ett melankoliskt betraktande av det tysta och överblivna" (When writing *Stränderna* I was tired of the melancholy tone of many of my previous poems. In *Stränderna* I tried to describe places as distinctly and clearly as possible and to revolt against a melancholy way of looking at the silent and deserted). That same year, in 1989, she was awarded a distinguished literary prize, De Nios Stora Pris.

Also in 1989, Arnault opened Forum, a gallery and multimedia stage, in Stockholm. It became instrumental for Frostenson's development of interdisciplinary projects—intertwining visual arts, music, and lyrical texts—and experimental drama. In 1990 she wrote the text for a book presenting a series of paintings by Håkan Rehnberg, *Moira: En målning i 29 delar 1988* (Moira: A Painting in 29 Parts 1988), which was exhibited in Germany and in Sweden. Four years later she wrote *Jan Håfström: En diktsvit till Jan Håfström och till verk av honom* (1994; translated by Joan Tate as *Jan Håfström: A Suite of Poems to Jan Håfström and to Works by Him*). Frostenson also collaborated with her husband in works such as *Överblivet* (Remains, 1989) and *Vägen till öarna* (The Road to the Islands, 1996). These books combine Arnault's photographs with Frostenson's texts on such themes as city landscapes, nature, mythology, music, and folklore. Importantly, the stage Forum provided was instrumental to Frostenson's development as a dramatist. The first one-act play she wrote, *Sebastopol* (1989), was written specifically for this stage.

Frostenson's monodramas established her as a dramatist in Sweden and abroad. Four of them were published as *4 monodramer* (4 Monodramas, 1990), including *Nilen* (The Nile), *Bro* (Bridge), *Sebastopol*, and *För sluttningen* (For the Descent). *Nilen* and *Sebastopol* were performed in Sweden in 1989, and *Nilen*, *Bro*, and *Sebastopol* have been translated into Norwegian and performed in Oslo as *3 monodramaer* in 1995. There is also a translation of the dramas into Serbo-Croatian. If Frostenson's interest in theater was kindled by Arnault, her own poetics and asceticism brought new dimensions to the genre. Her melodic and fragmented approach to poetry are two characteristics of her style; intertextuality is another aspect that brings richness to her texts. A host of references to Swedish and foreign authors, to songs and hymns, and to common Swedish clichés creates an intriguing maze for the initiated reader while leaving others perplexed, caught among contrasting and exclusive images. As many critics have noted, Frostenson does not use metaphors but communicates through the sensations that the sounds and images of her texts present.

Frostenson's exploration of urban streets and places in her poetry continues in the monodramas. *Nilen* takes place in a park at night, where a middle-aged woman is reminiscing about a child; *Bro* describes a bridge and a man's efforts to find his place in the city and the universe; *Sebastopol* is about the relationship between the individual and the anonymity of the street; and *För sluttningen* depicts a man lying on a hillside, singing as if trying to become one with music and ascend to heaven as a musical tone. The latter was later adapted into a libretto, *Mannen på sluttningen,* and on 13 December 1991 it was performed as an opera on the Swedish Radio. Critics have not always responded favorably to Frostenson's plays as some have found it difficult to accept her minimalist approach to stage settings and character presentations (only one character appears in each play). Others appreciated the lyrical dimension and her efforts to break down the boundaries between poetry and drama. Per Arne Tjäder, for example, suggests that "Platserna–en park, en bro, en sliten gata–är ekogrottor av allt som hänt där, nyss eller för länge sedan. Monodramerna blir därmed stämningsbilder, där rösten, talet, språket möter platsen på ett eget sätt" (The places–a park, a bridge, a worn street–are echo-caves of everything that has happened there, recently or a long time ago. The monodramas become images of moods, where voice, speech, language meet the place in their own ways).

The experimental plays brought Frostenson to the attention of a larger audience, but the poetry collection *Joner: Tre sviter* (Ions: Three Suites, 1991) brought her fame. Martin Hägglund, in "Den främmande logikens landskap: Platsen, minnet, dikten i Katarina Frostensons *Tankarna*" (1997), perceives the collection as a "vattendelare för nittio-talet" (a watershed for the 1990s)–in other words, emblematic of Swedish poetry of the time–while others have interpreted its thematic and stylistic elements. The main theme of *Joner* is a medieval Scandinavian ballad, "Jungfrun i hindhamn" (The Maiden in Hind Skin), which describes a knight who during a hunt kills his beloved, whom his mother had bewitched into a hind. Here Frostenson's complex poetics excel, replete with references to an actual murder in 1984, when two doctors murdered a prostitute and cut her body into pieces, as well as to mythology, Swedish folklore, and songs. In *Joner* the desire to see and be seen becomes a bestial need to dissect and observe. The book was lauded for the provocative images and the rhythm of the poems; it also cemented Frostenson's position as a difficult poet.

While Frostenson underscores the musical aspect of her poetry, scholars have focused on dominating images of violence and bodily mutilation in her works. Staffan Bergsten, for example, compares her repeated descriptions of mutilation with *sparagmós,* the ritualistic massacres of human bodies in Greek mythology. The fragmented text that previously characterized Frostenson's poetry is here expanded to include the human body–particularly the female body. Feminist critics interpret acts of violence on the female body as acts of gender creation. Leigh Gilmore, for example, suggests that after being mutilated "Only then may the body be interpreted as possessing a female mark of identification and identity." Furthermore, she suggests that women's self-representation is enmeshed in the rhetoric of violence.

Although Frostenson's works are difficult to understand, readers have found it impossible to remain indifferent to them. Karl Vennberg, a distinguished Swedish poet, wrote in his review of *Joner:* "Det är aldrig synd om den som skrivit en diktsamling som *Joner.* . . . Det är inte sig själv och ännu mindre sina idéer hon torgför. Det verkligt dystra med henne är istället att hon hotar förvandla de allra flesta av oss andra till triviala propagandister" (The one who has written a poetry collection like *Joner* is never to be pitied. . . . It is not herself and even less her ideas that she is peddling. The sad thing is instead that she threatens to turn most of the rest of us into trivial propagandists). The following year, in 1992, Frostenson was elected into the Swedish Academy and hailed by the Swedish media for her intellect, her integrity, and her beauty.

Frostenson's inclination to explore the soul of a city or street, to break apart language and, as she writes in her poem "Jungfrun talas," "driva meningen ur meningen" (drive the meaning out of sentences), reaches its heights in *Berättelser från dom* (Stories from Them, 1992). Frostenson calls it a fairy tale that portrays *dom* (them) as elves or gnomes that flow from the ground and the walls of buildings. Words and things are transformed into an anonymous flow of *dom,* moving with one consciousness like a lemming migration.

The book, written in lyrical prose, is characteristic of literature of the 1990s, which often describes a sense of homelessness and lack of identity. Maria Wennerström has pointed out that the book underscores Frostenson's view of language as a suffocating membrane between human beings and the world. The creatures called *dom* make words and things come alive, but when a man enters the story toward the end, harmony is destroyed as he grinds the language apart with his constant verbalizing. Again, the conflict between language and silence becomes the pivot point, which the author affirms in the foreword: "Ja, allt som går att säga om dom måste liksom motsjungas, i en och samma gest" (Yes, everything that can be said about them must, so to speak, be counter-sung, in one and the same gesture). *Berättelser från dom* is one of Frostenson's few works in prose. Yet, like her experimental drama, it is imbued with her poetry.

In 1993 Frostenson returned to the Royal Theater in Stockholm with the production of her play *Traum.* The surrealism of the play is accentuated by the title, which means "dream" in German and alludes internationally to the English "trauma." In fact, Frostenson seems to look to dreams as a place where concrete, constructive language exists. In this play a young couple is redecorating their bedroom in an effort to revitalize their lives. The absurdity of everyday life is underscored by the constant moving of things and by their dialogue, which evolves through lyrical associations interwoven with allusions to well-known songs, nursery rhymes, and fairy tales. Critics again questioned the format of her play, to which Frostenson responded in the 1993 interview with Lindskog by explaining her approach as building a story from different moments that reflect on each other rather than from a traditional storyline. Betty Skawonius, on the other hand, quotes Pia Forsgren, the director of the play, in her review in *Dagens Nyheter* on 12 February 1993. Forsgren rejoiced in having a woman express complex sides of her personality on stage when tradition still demands that "det ska vara en Nora eller en Medea som vi delvis får förstå. Men detta att få göra ett brett kvinnoporträtt om en kvinnas inre världar, där en kvinna också är *demonisk* . . ." (it must be a Nora or a Medea whom we may partly understand. But this, to develop a broad female portrait of a woman's inner worlds, where a woman is also *demonic* . . ."). Frostenson's ability to express a complex female psyche by combining fragmented, incoherent images is remarkable. Many critics have postulated that Frostenson's writing is masculine because of its intellectual content and stark imagery. Nonetheless, her influence within the cultural establishment as a female writer and artist is steadily growing.

Frostenson's break with the traditionally provincial and autobiographical style of women writers, as their works generally have been presented in literary histories, is obvious in the collection *Tankarna* (The Thoughts, 1994). While the content still defines itself by a complex plethora of mythology, city landscapes, and allusions to well-known songs and folklore, a new clarity and coherence is noticeable. Beckman suggests that Frostenson's fictional "I" no longer is fragmented, that her body is complete, and that she is in harmony with the world around her. The poem "Hägerstenen" is interesting in this context: it refers to the suburb, Hägersten, where Frostenson grew up. As she plays with the name by evoking images of stones and birds and alluding to Personne ("häger" means "heron," "sten" is "stone," and the Personne Road is a main artery in the area), the poem describes the suburb for the initiated reader and gain a biographical tone. In contrast, these insights and allusions are lost to the uninitiated reader who does not know the significance of the title "Hägerstenen." While earlier women writers often expressed their background in concrete terms, there is little in this poem that defines Hägersten and Frostenson's childhood for the uninitiated reader. She writes,

> . . . Stenen vid vägen—Personne, namnet
> på en väg slår ut och är allt—"oavtagbart"
> Det susar tall över. Endast en liten fågel
>
> flickan var grå, modern sorgsen
> Det var en sådan saknad att känna
> Av en sten som var varm och kall
> . . . .
> Med järnsmak i munnen. Med tungan mot ledstången
> med slitsåret och rotsaften
> Det var en sådan stränghet att lära
>
> (. . . The stone by the road—Personne, the name
> of a road strikes out and is everything—"No Exit"
> A murmur of pines above. Only a little bird
>
> the girl was gray, the mother sad
> Feeling was such a yearning
> for a stone which was warm and cold
> . . . .
> Taste of iron in my mouth. Tongue against the handrail
> Tear-sore and the juice of the root
> To learn was such severity)

Sorrow and loneliness imbue the poem, and many images are characteristic of Frostenson's poetic language. Although aspects of the poem are impenetrable, it is possible to perceive a new identity emerging. In 1994 Frostenson was awarded the prestigious Bellman Prize, granted by the Swedish Academy. Her growing importance abroad has also become evident as her works have been translated into more languages. In 1998 a French collection of selected poems was published, and in 1999 a German translation of *Tankarna* appeared.

At the end of the 1990s Frostenson's affinity for experimental drama and her visionary approach to dramatization intensified in the play *Sal P* (Ward P, 1996) and culminated in her libretto to the opera *Staden* (The City, 1998). In *Sal P* Frostenson returns to the hospital La Salpêtrière in Paris, where about five thousand mentally ill women were treated at the end of the nineteenth century. The hospital became renowned particularly for Jean-Martin Charcot's efforts to treat "female hysteria" with hypnotism. Frostenson states, in the introduction to her play, that La Salpêtrière was known as "smärtans Versaille" (the Versailles of suffering) and that her husband encouraged her to write *Sal P* as they discussed Charcot's research and methods during travels in Italy in 1988.

In the play, three women, Zora, Ann, and Henrika, play out their trauma and anxieties for each other, often as a rehearsal, before the Tuesday séance with Charcot and his colleagues. Frostenson's interest in language and how it relates to one's perception of reality is underscored as the three women respectively try to express their inner lives. She has revealed in interviews that she writes plays in order to know how voices sound alone, in dialogue, and in a group. In *Sal P* the interjection of well-known songs, rhymes, and sayings into the text creates signals that highlight specific moments of truth in each voice and character.

The critical response to *Sal P* was split, like the response to her earlier plays. Feminist critics, who had perceived it as an historical feminist play, wished for more information about the women and for Charcot's presence on stage. Clearly, Frostenson's aesthetics is still problematic for critics who wish for more historicity. Other critics interpreted *Sal P* from a literary perspective and found the play closely linked to French postmodern thinkers of the 1990s, particularly Julia Kristeva, who has written about the relationship between body and language. This interpretation reflects Frostenson's own statement in the introduction to the published edition of the play, where she clarifies that *Sal P* is not an historical play of the 1880s but a source of inspiration to explore the problems in giving inner life physical expression.

On 12 September 1998 Frostenson's career reached a new level with the opening of *Staden,* acclaimed as the cultural event of the year when Stockholm was celebrated as the cultural capital of Europe. Frostenson wrote the libretto to the opera, which had been commissioned from the composer Sven-David Sandström. He chose Frostenson as the writer, as he envisioned a complex lyrical text rather than an historical story line. Indeed, there is no story line in *Staden,* which is rather a symbol of intensified urbanization during the twentieth century. Sorl (Murmur) is the main character, a male personification that is mutilated in the second act and resurrected as a woman. Sorl's appearance as a male and a female character underscores Frostenson's inclination to write androgynous texts. In a 1992 interview with Per Svensson she stated that "riktigt bra författare är androgyna, tvåkönade, det är därför de kan återskapa andra människors upplevelser" (really good authors are androgynous, both male and female, that is why they can re-create other people's experiences). Her rhythmic poetry lends itself perfectly to the libretto, intensifying the visual aspects of what has been called a grandiose performance. One critic stated that Frostenson's language, her symbolic themes and intuitive repetitions, has a musical quality that is unintelligible but must be listened to. What she communicates is a complex murmur of sorrow and suffering as well as desire and courage.

The extraordinary dimensions of *Staden* were reported also in Sweden's neighboring countries by reviews in *Die Welt* (Germany) and *Hufvudstadsbladet* (Finland), for example. The music was lauded, and Frostenson's poetics and personifications of city life, human and material, impressed all but bewildered some. When discussing the libretto before the production opened, Frostenson acknowledged that her works demand a great effort and advised "Jag tror inte mina texter går att följa, man måste möta dem" (I don't think one can follow my texts, one has to encounter them).

Katarina Frostenson continues to explore the relation between the individual and the world, and the transformation of inner life and impressions into physical expressions and sounds. In *Korallen* (The Coral, 1999) she highlights the connection between nature, history, and sound through recurring references in various poems to "korall–koral–klockklang" (Coral–choral–chime) and to the goddess Echo. The poem "Brunnsgatan, januari" (Brunnsgatan, January) is reminiscent of her craft as a poet and a dramatist. Its first lines reinforce the active role her art plays in relation to human reality and existence:

> Du sa det: inte en kopia, inte
> en spegling av men ett svar på verkligheten
> skall konsten vara
> Inte skall vara–*vara*– . . .
>
> (You said it: not
> a reflection of but a response to reality
> should art be
> Not be–*be*– . . .)

Interviews:

Kajsa Lundgren, "Jag är ute efter det röriga och det grova," *Läs-Tidningen,* 2 (1983) <http://hem.passagen.sc/ingebjor/ungpoet.htm>;

Lundgren, "Berättelser om ett okänt folr," *Läs-Femina* (August 1992) <http://www.framtidendirekt.se/cgi/red/index>;

Per Svensson, "Mellan två stolar: Är Katarina Frostenson för svår för Akademin?" *MånadsJournalen,* 7 (1992): 18–25;

Lennart Lindskog, "Jag vill bygga texter som är vackra," *Sundsvalls Tidning,* 20 June 1993;

Calle Pauli, "Katarina Frostenson, Librettist," *Dagens Nyheter,* 11 September 1998.

References:

Åsa Beckman, "Den herrelösa dikten: 1980-talets svenska lyrik," in *Nordisk kvinnolitteraturhistoria,* volume 4, edited by Elisabeth Møller Jensen and others (Malmö: Bra Böcker, 1997), pp. 478–484;

Staffan Bergsten, *Klang och åter: Tre röster i samtida svensk kvinnolyrik* (Stockholm: FIB:s lyrikklubb, 1997), pp. 13–106;

Poul Borum, "PO-e-(RO)-tik: Om Pia Tafdrup og tre andre nye kvindelige lyrikere," *Kritik,* 66 (1984): 125–141;

Carin Franzén, "Ur det negativa: Om ett motdrag i Katarina Frostensons poesi," *Tidskrift för litteraturvetenskap,* 2 (1997): 41–59;

Leigh Gilmore, *Autobiographics: A Feminist Theory of Women's Self-Representation* (Ithaca: Cornell University Press, 1994), p. 164;

Martin Hägglund, "Den främmande logikens landskap: Platsen, minnet, dikten i Katarina Frostensons *Tankarna,*" *Artes,* 1 (1997): 79–91;

Stefan Jonsson, "De rubbade kritcirklarna: En betraktelse över det hemlösa nuet," *Bonniers Litterära Magasin,* 2 (1995): 4–7;

Per Arne Tjäder, "Dramats återkomst," *Allt om böcker,* 2 (1996): 13–15;

Maria Wennerström, "Stilistisk Åderlåtning: Språkliga teorier och strategier i Katarina Frostensons *Berättelser från dom,*" *Horisont,* 6 (1994): 59–67.

Jonas Gardell
(2 November 1963 -)

Matthew M. Roy
Cascadia Community College

BOOKS: *Den tigande talar/4937* (Stockholm: Författarförlaget, 1981);

Passionsspelet (Stockholm: Författarförlaget, 1985);

Odjurets tid (Stockholm: Norstedt, 1986);

Präriehundarna (Stockholm: Norstedt, 1987);

Vill gå hem (Stockholm: Norstedt, 1988);

Fru Björks öden och äventyr (Stockholm: Norstedt, 1990);

En komikers uppväxt (Stockholm: Norstedt, 1992);

Mormor gråter och andra texter (Stockholm: Norstedt, 1993);

Frestelsernas berg (Stockholm: Norstedt, 1995);

Isbjörnarna; Cheek to cheek; Människor i solen (tre pjäser) (Stockholm: Norstedt, 1997);

Så går en dag ifrån vårt liv och kommer aldrig åter (Stockholm: Norstedt, 1998);

Oskuld och andra texter (Stockholm: Norstedt, 2000);

Ett ufo gör entré (Stockholm: Norstedt, 2001).

PLAY PRODUCTIONS: *Good Night, Mr. Moon,* Moderna museet (Bion), Stockholm, 17 January 1987;

Kim å Jonas jubelkavalkad, 1988;

Kim å Jonas går igen, 1989;

Lena och Percy, Präriehund, Stadsteatern (Studion), Göteborg, 15 April 1989;

En fulings bekännelser, Stadsteatern (Stora Scenen), Göteborg, 18 November 1989;

Isbjörnarna, Stadsteatern (Lilla Klara), Stockholm, 9 March 1990;

En pall, en mikrofon och Jonas Gardell, Konserthuset, Stockholm, 15 October 1991;

Cheek to Cheek, Stadsteatern (Lilla Scenen), Stockholm, 6 March 1992;

En finstämd kväll med Jonas Gardell, Stockholm, Intiman Theater, 17 September 1993;

En annan sorts föreställning, Kosmos, Katrineholm, 1995;

På besök i Mellanmjölkens land, Lisebergshallen, Göteborg, 27 September 1996;

Människor i solen, Dramaten (Lilla Scenen), Stockholm, 20 September 1997;

Komma tillbaka, Konserthuset, Stockholm, 26 September 1998;

Jonas Gardell (from the dust jacket for Frestelsernas Berg, *1995)*

Scheherzad, Dramaten (Stora Scenen), Stockholm, 19 September 1999;

Livet, Lisebergshallen, Göteborg, 5 October 2000.

PRODUCED SCRIPTS: *Ömheten,* television, TV-Teatern, 30 October 1989;

En komikers uppväxt, television, three parts, beginning 21 September 1992;

Pensionat Oskar, motion picture, SVT Kanal 1 Drama, 1995;

Irma och Gerd, television, six parts, beginning 9 January 1997;

Cheek to Cheek, television, directed by Gardell, TV-Teatern, 3 December 1997;

Livet är en schlager, SVT Drama, 2000.

RECORDINGS: *Kim å Jonas: Klang och jubelkavalkad,* by Gardell and Kim Hedås, Göteborg, Nonstop 033-07, 1989;

Christer Sandelin, *till månen runt solen,* some lyrics by Gardell, Kista, Metronome, 9031-77637-2, 1992;

En finstämd kväll med Jonas Gardell: Live på Intiman, Bromma, Sony 476645 2, 1994.

OTHER: "Taggtråd," in *Mellan handslag och samlag: Unga svenska berättare om AIDS: En HIV antologi,* edited by Stig Nordlund (Stockholm: Brevskolan, 1987), pp. 19–30;

"Har jag bara tid så slukar jag allt," in *"Ordning, redbarhet och snabb expedition": Svenska bokhandlareföreningen 1893–1993,* edited by Thomas Rönström (Stockholm: Informationsförlaget, 1995), pp. 147–149;

Elizabeth Ohlsson, *Ecce homo,* introduction by Gardell (Malmö: Föreningen Ecce Homo, 1998).

SELECTED PERIODICAL PUBLICATIONS–UNCOLLECTED:

FICTION

"Dagen före–en julberättelse av Jonas Gardell," *Aftonbladet,* 23 December 1987, p. 4;

"Med hälsning från Ralf," *Vår bostad,* September 1988, pp. 28–31;

"En dag var du där," *Aftonbladet,* 6 August 1989, p. 5;

"Hon spottade, en tjock loska, vispad med nikotin," chapter in serial novel *Svarta måsar,* by Gardell and others, *Aftonbladet,* 19 July 1990, p. 4;

"På gränsen till kärlek," *Vår bostad,* 12 (1991), pp. 66–69.

NONFICTION

"Jag känner utanförskapet," *Aftonbladet,* 8 July 1986, p. 4;

"Jag längtar mig sjuk efter ett hem," *Expressen,* 6 August 1987, p. 21;

"Präriehundarna på äventyr i öststaterna," *Aftonbladet,* 8 September 1987, p. 4;

"Förök förstå, det är inte så konstigt att vara homosexuell!" *Expressen,* 25 October 1987, pp. 8–10;

"60-talets debatt i 80-talets perspektiv: Varför tiger Sveriges radikaler?" *Dagens Nyheter,* 15 May 1988, p. 4;

"Sveket mot de svaga," *Aftonbladet,* 10 January 1989, p. 4;

"Jean Genets livshållning: Förnedringen blir ett mirakel," *Dagens Nyheter,* 26 July 1989, p. 4;

"Gardell rätt upp & ner," *Aftonbladet,* 3 September 1989, p. 25;

"Jonas Gardell om anarkisterna, polisvåldet och massmedia," *Aftonbladet,* 24 May 1990, p. 4;

"Brännboll och brandövning," *SACO-tidningen,* 1 (1990), pp. 38–40;

"Käringen har ju inga hämningar," *Expressen,* 21 September 1991, p. 5;

"Jag kissar mitt ståtliga namn," *Aftonbladet,* 25 June 1995, p. 4;

"Som om du hade ett liv . . . ," *Aftonbladet,* 16 February 1997, pp. 4–5;

"Skeppet i kometens svans," *Aftonbladet,* 18 May 1997, pp. 4–5;

"Och ni ska minnas mitt namn," *Aftonbladet,* 26 July 1997, pp. 4–5;

"En gång för en evighet sen," *Aftonbladet,* 12 October 1997, pp. 4–5.

Stand-up comedy and serious literature rarely stem from the same source, yet Jonas Gardell has successfully established himself as one of the most prominent contributors to each of these cultural arenas in Sweden. The shift in public perception of his work, from lighthearted comedy to poignant social irony and criticism, has resulted in an equally dramatic shift in Gardell's performance venues, from restaurants and clubs to the main stage of the Royal Dramatic Theater. Gardell's award-winning novel and greatest critical success, *En komikers uppväxt* (Growing up a Comedian, 1992), has already earned him a place in the contemporary canon of Swedish literature. The Swedish Publishers' Association recognized Gardell's literary contributions when they chose to send *En komikers uppväxt* to Swedish schoolchildren on World Book Day, 13 April 2000. As a journalist, dramatist, novelist, moviemaker, songwriter, comedian, and media personality, Gardell is one of Sweden's most prolific contemporary writers.

Lars Jonas Holger Gardell was born on 2 November 1963, in Täby, Sweden, and grew up in Enebyberg, a quiet suburb north of Stockholm. His parents, Ingegärd and Bertil Gardell, had four children, of which Jonas was the third. Both of his parents worked as psychologists, and his father achieved international acclaim for his pioneering theories on social epidemiology in the work environment. While Jonas was still young, Bertil Gardell left his wife and children to marry his secretary. As a youth, the struggles that Jonas fought in dealing with abandonment and with his own homosexuality brought him intense emotional pain, which he tried to alleviate through drug abuse and attempted suicide.

Despite the personal adversity that he had to overcome, Gardell was able to build his career from humble beginnings. He supported himself as a janitor, a warehouse worker, an elderly care assistant, and an art gallery attendant before finally making

Cover for the 1992 paperback publication of Gardell's 1988 novel about the strained relationship between two dissimilar sisters

his authorial debut. In his teenage years he published his first collection of poetry, *Den tigande talar/ 4937* (The Silent One Speaks/4937, 1981). Although the collection is difficult to acquire, Gardell has reused poems from it in his later fiction. The last chapter of *En komikers uppväxt,* for example, includes the opening, untitled poem from *Den tigande talar/ 4937*:

> Allt ska vi glömma och allt ska vi förlora.
> Och någon annan dag, men inte nu, ska jag visa dig
> den hemliga grottan, den porlande bäcken
> jag aldrig fann som barn.
> (We will forget everything, and we will lose everything.
> And some day, but not now, I will show you
> the secret cave, the babbling brook
> I never found as a child.)

In an unpublished letter he sent to schoolchildren, Gardell jokingly reflects on the creative process he used in order to write fiction by describing how poems became prose pieces and prose pieces became short stories; "till slut var det en novell som svällde och blev större och till slut insåg jag med viss förskräckelse att det jag höll på med faktiskt var en roman" (finally it was a short story that swelled and became larger, and at long last I realized with a certain amount of horror that what I was actually doing was writing a novel). At age eighteen his first novel began to take shape under the title "Hjälten och Förrädaren" (The Hero and the Traitor), written in part on the back of job listings while working in an art gallery named Vita Katten (The White Cat). He eventually gave the book a new title, *Passionsspelet* (The Passion Play, 1985), and completed his first novel at age twenty.

Passionsspelet comprises two interwoven tales. It tells the story of Hampus and Johan, whose love for one another parallels the story of Jesus and Judas Iscariot in the passion play adapted, written, and directed by Hampus's father, a minister. To bind the two tales even further, there are small elements and characters that function equally well in both story lines. Hampus's mother, Maria, whose name in Swedish is the same as Jesus' mother, Mary, provides but one example of the multidimensional characters in the book. She is a loving and understanding mother who calms her husband, at times blinded by his own passions, while quietly acknowledging her son's new love interest. Johan falls in love with Hampus at first sight; they star opposite each other in the passion play and succumb to their desires already at the first rehearsal, where they engage in a kiss. In the end the fate of Johan and Hampus painfully echoes Judas's betrayal of Jesus.

Throughout many of his works Gardell refers to the Bible, angels, and different images of God. He claims that one must differentiate between using the Bible as a literary or cultural reference, as he does, and using it to discuss questions of faith. His stories mythologize contemporary times by turning familiar tales in the Old Testament, for instance, into modern tragedies. The religious aspects of his texts can be similar, such as in *Frestelsernas berg* (Mount of Temptations, 1995), which is reminiscent of the religious elements in *Passionsspelet*. His texts can also express a varying, open view of spirituality, as evidenced by the different depictions of God in *Vill gå hem* (Want to Go Home, 1988) as a polar bear and in *Mormor gråter och andra texter* (Grandma Is Crying and Other Texts, 1993) as a black lesbian "med jättelika tuttar, som vaggar omkring i Himmelen och kokar makaroner åt alla som vill ha!" (with giant tits, who swings around in Heaven and cooks macaroni for everyone who wants some!). In a personal interview in 1998 Gardell, a self-described Christian humanist, expresses his spirituality in a distinct manner while he "oavbrutet försvarar den lilla människan" (incessantly defends the little person).

In Gardell's second novel, *Odjurets tid* (The Time of the Beast, 1986), everyone creates the lies, myths, and illusions that they need in order to endure living. This premise is exemplified in the lives of four individuals: Karin, a lonely widow dying of cancer; Maria, a young woman who chooses her memories and hides the secrets of her family's past to protect herself; David, a caring young man whose life becomes easily twisted with the fates of others; and Fredrik, David's partner, who attempts to correct the mistakes he has made in the past. When working on *Passionsspelet* and *Odjurets tid*, Gardell had a self-described anxious desire to write important literature. As he told Jan Åman in *Författare i 80-talet* (Authors in the 1980s, 1988), "Jag var tidigare inte riktigt säker på att man fick ha humor i sådan här litteratur. Plötsligt tänkte jag att va fan kan inte jag få ha det för–vilket gjorde att all den här humorn plötsligt kom framsprutande" (I was not sure earlier whether or not one could have a sense of humor in this kind of literature. Suddenly, I thought, why the hell not–which made all kinds of humor suddenly come spurting forth).

Around the same time, Gardell found the ability to express humor in his writing at the same time that he met his future spouse, Swedish television personality Mark Levengood. They met in a bathhouse in Stockholm in 1986, became engaged two months later, and eventually married each other twice. Their first wedding was a private ceremony, which actress Claire Wikholm conducted in their kitchen in 1988. After the legalization of gay partnership in Sweden in 1995, they made their commitment to each other official.

Gardell's newfound ability to combine humor and social satire resulted in the first book that he succeeded in writing exactly as he wanted, *Präriehundarna* (The Prairie Dogs, 1987), about a married couple, Lena and Percy, and their son, Reine. They live in a Stockholm suburb in which people creep in and out of their residences without speaking to one another, while keeping a watchful eye on the windows across the courtyard. Lena and Percy make an unlikely couple. She smokes, drinks, has a passion for raspberry candy, and dreams of a love affair with an actor named Redde. Her husband, on the other hand, is a hypocrite and a moralizer, a civil servant in his early fifties who dreams of becoming a composer. Instead of pursuing his dreams he expends his efforts on writing angry notes to neighbors for doing things that he should not have been watching them do in the first place. Critics and reviewers have often claimed that Gardell is present in the book as the prosecutor, a character who occasionally breaks into the narrative to proclaim his own moral premises.

In the interview with Åman, Gardell takes issue with this interpretation, asserting the importance of understanding the prosecutor as Percy rather than a first-person intrusion by Gardell into the narrative. Only Percy's character can add the right dimension to the moral pronouncements in the book: hiding himself and his lies in the closet and despised by all, he still casts judgment. Reine, unlike his father with his unfulfilled fantasies, chooses to live out his homosexual desires. Much like Percy was unable to express himself adequately in *Präriehundarna*, Gardell's own father was unable to communicate at the end of his life because of a neurological disease. In 1987 Bertil Gardell died before Gardell could ever mend his relationship with his father.

Gardell has suggested that there is much to gain from rereading his books, a statement that would seem to refer to their intricate, layered structure, which only reveals itself when the reader has gained full knowledge of the complexity of the story. An indication of the complexity of his writing is the extent to which his novels refer to each other and connect to the works of other Swedish writers. The small woman dressed in black scurrying across Mariatorget in *Präriehundarna*, for instance, is a reference to Maria in *Odjurets tid*. Lena and Percy in *Präriehundarna* were named after Lena Brogren and Percy Brandt, the actors in the Göteborg City Theater production of Lars Norén's *Natten är dagens mor* (Night Is the Mother of Day, 1982). Gardell's books abound with puzzling references that reward the reader who takes the time to uncover them. The misleading simplicity in his works spurs some critics to claim that they provide no challenge because everything is clear and comprehensible. Gardell has countered that the critics have probably only understood a tenth of the depth in his books.

Misunderstanding is part of the basis of the relationship between sisters Rut and Rakel, the main characters in Gardell's fourth novel, *Vill gå hem*. Rut is the outward picture of order and success. Married with children, she functions as the polar opposite of her sister, Rakel, who gives up everything in order

Dust jacket for Gardell's 1995 novel, based on the author's painful childhood (Bruccoli Clark Layman Archives)

to live in the country, which she hates, with a man who does not love her. When Rakel finally leaves the man, she returns to take over her sister's living room and turn Rut's world upside down, connecting with Rut's son, Daniel, in the process. Just as in *Präriehundarna,* an unknown presence appears in *Vill gå hem* under the guise of the author's remarks, which break up the narrative and comment upon the action in the novel. The comments of this unknown character are often bitterly funny–a satirical retort to both the story at hand and life itself.

Fru Björks öden och äventyr (translated as "The Wonderful Adventures of Mrs. Björk," 1990), which has also been performed as an opera, brings to life a woman who is normal on the surface but filled with a need for revenge underneath. After eighteen years Mrs. Björk's first husband abandons her for a younger woman, leaving his wife with nothing. When she remarries, she finds that she is little more than a replacement for her new husband's dead wife. Finally, she decides to divorce her husband, travel to Italy to gather her thoughts, and gain revenge on her first husband. Her transformation is remarkable, and the end is literally explosive.

Gardell often bases the settings in his works on his personal experiences, as in *En komikers uppväxt,* which tells the story of a comedian, Juha, who looks back upon his youth in the fictive suburb of Sävbyholm. In Sävbyholm the adults look away from, or simply do not see, the children, who are required to make their own rules for survival. Juha's best friends are outsiders like himself: Jenny, whose clothes do not fit in, and Thomas, whose German mother tries too hard to help him make friends without realizing that he is constantly teased and afraid. Occasionally, the time line in the novel shifts to the present, when Juha writes letters to Thomas that he will never receive. Much like the narrator uses comedy to protect himself, both in his youth and in his adult life, the humor in the story makes Gardell's depiction of a difficult and painful childhood more palatable.

While writing *En komikers uppväxt,* Gardell also wrote a script for a television miniseries with the same title. The filming of the television series was finished prior to the completion of the novel, and Gardell chose to end the novel differently. The following year, in 1993, he published *Mormor gråter och andra texter,* a collection of pieces originally written for newspapers, magazines, television, radio, and stage shows. He includes essays about Robert Mapplethorpe and Bette Midler, memories of a time when sexually inquisitive children tried to catch a glimpse of what was under Tarzan's loincloth, and intimate poetry. By collecting these works into one book, he has made some of his best shorter texts available to a larger audience.

After the successful adaptation of *En komikers uppväxt* for television, Gardell was ready to attempt his first motion-picture production, *Pensionat Oskar* (1995), which was also distributed under the title *Like It Never Was Before.* Gardell's screenplay received praise at international movie festivals and was awarded a Guldbagge, the Swedish version of an Academy Award. The movie also earned Guldbagge awards for best actor (Loa Falkman) and best supporting actress (Sif Ruud). *Pensionat Oskar* tells the story of Rune Runeberg, an outwardly content individual who lives with his wife, Gunnel, and their two children in the suburbs. Their stable existence begins to be undermined when the family goes on vacation to the fictional Oskar Resort. There Rune meets Petrus, a magician who swiftly steals his heart before Rune even realizes it himself. Rune's attempts to deal with his homosexuality (apparently for the first time in his life) send him on a trip away from his family, back to Petrus, and on the road to discovering himself. Through Rune Runeberg, Gardell has succeeded in creating perhaps his first strong male character.

In *Frestelsernas berg* the dissolution of familial harmony also plays a central role. As Johan tries to reclaim some portion of Svarttjärn, the family estate, the reader learns of his tumultuous family past. The characters in the novel can be hard to like; yet, they all demand a certain amount of respect. Pain circulates throughout most of the family—from Johan's father, who abandoned the family to live with a younger woman after twenty-five years of marriage, to the older brother who terrorizes their home life because of his drug use, to Johan himself, forced to deal with his homosexuality on the night streets of Stockholm. The reference to the biblical Temptation on the Mount, however, is most evident in Johan's mother, Maria. She lives among her mementos, which are kept carefully boxed, and grasps for a life that she will never regain. Somehow she knows that her life would be as easy to end as those of the monks who have carved their monastery out of the Mount of Temptation.

> Bortom Jeriko ligger det berg uppå vilket Kristus blev förd av djävulen för att frestas.
> Frestelsernas berg.
> I berget finns ett kloster, och i klostret bor ännu några munkar, i några smutsiga små rum, mittemellan himmel och jord.
> I varje ögonblick av sitt liv måste de välja.
> Inget vore enklare för dem att göra slut på än lidandet–luta sig ut över räcket, lite för långt, och allt vore över.
> Ändå försätter de.
> Lever kvar.
> Trots allt.
>
> (Beyond Jericho lies the mountain up to which Christ was led by the devil in order to be tempted.
> The Mount of Temptations.
> In the mountain there is a cloister, and in the cloister a few monks still live in a few dirty, small rooms between heaven and earth.
> During each moment of their lives they must make a choice.
> Nothing would be simpler for them than to put an end to their suffering–to lean out over the railing, a little too far–and everything would be over.
> Still they carry on.
> Continue living.
> Despite everything.)

All she has to do to end her suffering is lean over the metaphorical edge and end her life, but she chooses nonetheless to endure. This book is closer to Gardell's own past than any other that he has written, which has led readers to also find it his saddest.

An important aspect of Gardell's career is the role his live shows have played, both in marketing himself as a cultural personality and in establishing close contact with his audience. In his live show *På besök i Mellanmjölkens land* (Visiting the Land of Two-Percent Milk, 1996), Gardell attempted to connect with his audience by providing a "terapilektion för en plågad nation" (therapy session for a tormented nation). During a trial run he decided to remove the dirty jokes, which had been known as one of the staples in his earlier live productions. Gardell still included a great deal of humor, however, in the form of impressions of Swedish skier Gunde Svan, mockery of the elegance of Ingmar Bergman and the Royal Dramatic Theater, and an account of fumbling with color-coded coupons at the grocery store. At the same time he sustained a serious discussion of murder, social passivity, homosexuality, and Nazism.

While Gardell may have begun his climb to national fame through stand-up comedy, he has also earned a rightful place among rising contemporary Swedish dramatists. The decision of the publishing company Norstedt to collect three of Gardell's most appreciated dramatic productions in a single volume in 1997 can be seen both as important recognition of his success in the field of drama and as a meaningful step forward in his career, since he considers himself to be a better dramatist than novelist. The volume includes the title play, *Isbjörnarna* (The Polar Bears, 1997), *Cheek to Cheek,* and *Människor i solen* (People in the Sun). Gardell has had to fight personal battles in order to produce works in a genre in which Sweden has produced world-renowned playwrights, such as Norén and Bergman. For Gardell, the most important part of a play is engaging the audience, which he believes he can accomplish better than his predecessors. They should laugh and cry with the characters—an emotional shift that is not too difficult to realize if the audience is caught unawares in each character's blissful folly.

Gardell has observed that when developing the characters in *Isbjörnarna* and *Cheek to Cheek,* he began with an image of a particular person. In the case of *Isbjörnarna* he began with a woman rubbing her hands together. The woman is Ilse, a mother of three children, who has come to celebrate her birthday at the apartment of one of her daughters. When her second daughter arrives, the competition begins in order to win their mother's love. The only person their mother seems to care about, however, is her son, a writer, who is unable to attend her birthday party. Ilse's bitterness increases throughout the play, and neither of her daughters wins. It is both a sad and hilarious look at feelings that lie hidden beneath the surface in an everyday home—a way of depicting life that Gardell has made his specialty.

The image that gave rise to *Cheek to Cheek* was a tap-dancing woman. Gardell explained the play to Henric Tiselius in 1993: "Pjäsen handlar om hur man beskriver en människa. Vad kan man säga om en människa. Hur beskriver man sig själv? På tre rader i en kontaktannons? Vad finns att säga om mig på begravningen?" (The play is about how one describes a person. What can one say about a person? How does one describe oneself? In three lines in the personals? What can be said about me at my funeral?). All of these worries are explored in Gardell's depiction of a transvestite, Ragnar Rönn, who meets a successful funeral home operator named Margareta through the personals. Even though Ragnar thinks that she is too old and ugly, he agrees to see Margareta, once she decides to become his "hund" (dog). Ragnar is cold and calculating, but his anguish is genuine while he searches for a way to write himself into the annals of immortality. Gardell made his directing debut with the TV-Teatern performance of this production in 1997.

Människor i solen ran at the Royal Dramatic Theater and received almost exclusively positive reviews. It depicts two couples who are vacationing during midsummer in a group of tiny cottages by the sea. They meet and decide to celebrate together, only to have their celebration interrupted by a new arrival, an old Jewish widow named Mrs. Sörensson, who is locked out of her cabin. One of the couples, Stig and Ingrid, also appears in *Pensionat Oskar,* in which Stig's unmotivated anger and Ingrid's constant apologies provide a glimpse into how each character will develop in *Människor i solen*. Siv and Svante's son, Simon, has one line, and yet, according to Swedish author Per Olov Enquist's description in the performance program for the Royal Dramatic Theater production, he is extremely communicative. When Mrs. Sörensson's biblical premonitions become a reality, she turns to Simon to save him, while the other characters fade into the distance. In an interview in 1995 with Marielouise Samuelsson, Gardell revealed that God would appear as a character named Mrs. Sörensson in his new play, which at that time was called "Två pjäser om Gud, djävulen och alldeles vanliga människor" (Two Plays about God, Satan, and Completely Normal People).

Gardell's critical acclaim for his portrayals of the so-called little people in Swedish society suggests that he has succeeded in creating characters that speak to his audience on many levels. His nationally embraced characters have indeed captured the Swedish psyche. The philosophy that Gardell employed for his second motion picture, *Livet är en schlager* (2000; also distributed under the title *Once in a Lifetime*), expressed to Frida Lindqvist in a 2000 interview, can just as aptly describe the functioning ideology for his entire career: "Jag ville skriva om helt vanliga människor och helt vanliga människor är ovanliga. Det är bara på avstånd en människa synes normal" (I wanted to write about completely common people, and completely common people are uncommon. A human being only appears normal at a distance).

Interviews:

Anna Lena Stålnacke, "Dödssynd att avstå kärleken," *Dagens Nyheter–DN på stan,* 8 August 1987, p. 3;

Gudrun Råssjö, "Jonas Gardell, författare: Man måste våga göra det man tror på. Sommarsamtal om detta livets viktiga," *Svenska Kyrkans Tidning,* 29/30 (1987): 32;

Jan Åman, "Jag ser mig som en politisk författare," in *Författare i 80-talet,* edited by Björn Gunnarson (Stockholm & Lund: Symposion, 1988), pp. 214–226;

Lina Joakimsson, "JAG gör bara det jag tycker är roligt," *Ordets makt,* 2 (1988): 46–47;

Monica Stjernström, "Konsten att hitta hem," *Arbetaren,* 47 (1988): 17–18;

Ylva Herholz, "Jonas Gardell: Fräck, uppstudsig, men också alldeles vanlig," *ICA-kuriren,* 11 (1989): 46–47;

Erik Janson, "Gardells öden och äventyr," *Land,* 36 (1990): 1;

Carl-Eric Johansson, "Jonas Gardell: Hellre komiker på snuskiga krogar än kulturdebattör," *Folket i Bild: Kulturfront,* 14/15 (1990): 36–37;

Maria Arnedotter, "Jag vill DUGA!" *Vår bostad,* 7/8 (1990): 66–67;

Magnus Jacobson, "Läsarna är också hans publik," *Östgöta Correspondenten,* 12 November 1990, special insert;

Ebba Carlsson, "Ebba pratar med Jonas Gardell," *ETC,* 1 (1991): 36–41, 82;

Tomas Andersson, "Jag är fullkomligt ute i det här landet," *Svenska Dagbladet,* 11 October 1991, p. 7;

Håkan Lahger, "Jonas Gardell: Min barndom var värre än i TV-serien," *Röster i radio TV,* 38 (1992): 4–5, 64;

Heidi Avellan, "F.d. fjant vågar skratta," *Hufvudstadsbladet,* 11 May 1992, p. 8;

Catarina Gisby, "Han är alltid på gång," *Sydsvenska Dagbladet,* 20 September 1992, pp. B1, 5;

Torbjörn Ivarsson, "Gardell superstjärna som börjar bli accepterad," *Upsala Nya Tidning,* 13 September 1993, p. 13;

MarieLouise Samuelsson, "Gardell–ett ufo i folkhemmet," *Svenska Dagbladet,* 17 September 1993, p. 17;

Lena Katarina Swanberg, "Jonas Gardell–mammas pojke," *Månadsjournalen,* 9 (1993): 21–27;

Henric Tiselius, "Gardell tar livet av sin pappa Lars Norén," *Teatertidningen,* 1 (1993): 8–12;

Helena Utte, "Gardell och hans tanter," *Norrköpings Tidningar Östergötlands Dagblad C,* 21 October 1994, pp. C10–C11;

Anna Nordlund, "Jonas Gardell erövrar sitt liv," *Dagens Nyheter–DN på stan,* 11 August 1995, p. B1;

Ola Liljedahl, "Gardells svarta bakgrund," *Expressen,* 13 August 1995, pp. 18–23;

Samuelsson, "Arbette bot mot sorg," *Svenska Dagbladet,* 16 August 1995, p. 25;

Viggo Cavling, "Grundfilosofin är att jag brinner," *Arbetet,* 9 September 1995;

Jasim Mohamed, "Jonas Gardell lapar näring i mellanmjölkens land," *Svenska kyrkans tidning,* 46 (1996): 20–21;

Dan-Erik Sahlberg, "Böckernas bok–mer än bara kulturarv?" *Trots allt,* 2 (1996): 10–15;

Jonas Klint, "Gardell låter publiken styra," *Nya Wermlands-Tidningen,* 1 March 1996, p. 23;

Par Jonasson, "Stolt och ironisk," *Smålandsposten,* 16 August 1996, p. 16;

Lasse Franck, "Jonas Gardell älskar mjölk och småstäder," *Dagens Nyheter–DN på stan* (20–26 September 1996): middle section;

Kristina Torell, "Med Jonas Gardell genom the milky way," *Göteborgs-Posten-Avenyn,* 27 September 1996, pp. 17–20;

Frida Lindqvist, "Gardell visar de osynliga," *Aftonbladet,* 5 February 2000, entertainment section.

References:

Ulla Lundqvist, "Pojkarne," in her *Läsäventyr från när och fjärran: Tolv bokpresentationer för unga vuxna* (Lund: Bibliotekstjänst, 1994), pp. 25–54, 151–153;

Marianne Steinsaphir, "Jonas Gardell," in *15 författare: Porträtt av svenska samtidsförfattare* (Lund: Bibliotekstjänst, 1994), pp. 57–65.

Maria (Kristina) Gripe

(23 July 1923 -   )

Birgitta Steene
University of Washington

BOOKS: *I vår lilla stad* (Stockholm: Bonnier, 1954);
När det snöade (Stockholm: Bonnier, 1955);
Kung Laban kommer (Stockholm: Bonnier, 1956);
Kvarteret Labyrinten (Stockholm: Bonnier, 1956);
Sebastian och skuggan: Tre sagor (Stockholm: Bonnier, 1957);
Stackars lilla Q (Stockholm: Bonnier, 1957);
Tappa inte masken! (Stockholm: Bonnier, 1959);
De små röda (Stockholm: Bonnier, 1960);
Josefin (Stockholm: Bonnier, 1961); translated by Paul Britten Austin as *Josephine* (New York: Dell, 1969; London: Chatto & Windus, 1970);
Hugo och Josefin (Stockholm: Bonnier, 1962); translated by Austin as *Hugo and Josephine* (New York: Delacorte, 1969; London: Chatto & Windus, 1971);
Pappa Pellerins dotter (Stockholm: Bonnier, 1963); translated by Kersti French as *Pappa Pellerin's Daughter* (New York: John Day, 1966; London: Chatto & Windus, 1966);
Glasblåsarns barn (Stockholm: Bonnier, 1964); translated by Sheila La Farge as *The Glassblower's Children* (New York: Delacorte/Seymour Lawrence, 1973; London: Target, 1976);
I klockornas tid (Stockholm: Bonnier, 1965); translated by La Farge as *In the Time of the Bells* (New York: Delacorte/Seymour Lawrence, 1976; London: Chatto & Windus, 1978);
Hugo (Stockholm: Bonnier, 1966); translated by Austin as *Hugo* (New York: Delacorte, 1969; London: Chatto & Windus, 1971);
Landet utanför (Stockholm: Bonnier, 1967); translated by La Farge as *The Land Beyond* (New York: Dell, 1974; London: Abelard, 1975);
Nattpappan (Stockholm: Bonnier, 1968); translated by Gerry Bothmer as *The Night Daddy* (New York: Delacorte, 1971; London: Chatto & Windus, 1973);
Glastunneln (Stockholm: Bonnier, 1969);
Tanten (Stockholm: Bonnier, 1970);
Nattpappan, Julias hus och Henri Dunant (Stockholm: Ungdomens Röda Kors, 1970);

Maria Gripe (Bonnier Carlsen)

Julias hus och Nattpappan (Stockholm: Bonnier, 1971); translated by Bothmer as *Julia's House* (New York: Delacorte/Seymour Lawrence, 1975; London: Chatto & Windus, 1975);
Elvis Karlsson (Stockholm: Bonnier, 1972); translated by La Farge as *Elvis and His Secret* (New York: Delacorte/Seymour Lawrence, 1976; London: Chatto & Windus, 1976);
Elvis! Elvis! (Stockholm: Bonnier, 1973); translated by La Farge as *Elvis and His Friends* (New York: Dela-

corte/Seymour Lawrence, 1976; London: Chatto & Windus, 1976);
. . . ellen dellen . . . (Stockholm: Bonnier, 1974); translated by La Farge as *The Green Coat* (New York: Delacorte/Seymour Lawrence, 1977);
Den "riktiga" Elvis (Stockholm: Bonnier, 1976);
Att vara Elvis (Stockholm: Bonnier, 1977);
Tordyveln flyger i skymningen . . . : En beskrivning av vissa händelser i Ringaryd i Småland, by Gripe and Kay Pollak (Stockholm: Bonnier, 1978);
Bara Elvis (Stockholm: Bonnier Junior, 1979);
Agnes Cecilia: En sällsam historia (Stockholm: Bonnier Junior, 1981); translated by Rika Lesser as *Agnes Cecilia* (New York: Harper & Row, 1990);
Skuggan över stenbänken (Stockholm: Bonnier Junior, 1982);
. . . och de vita skuggorna i skogen (Stockholm: Bonnier Junior, 1984);
Godispåsen: "Trolltider" (Stockholm: Carlsen/if, 1985);
Skuggornas barn (Stockholm: Bonnier Junior, 1986);
Skugg-gömman (Stockholm: Bonnier Junior, 1988);
Hjärtat som ingen ville ha (Stockholm: Bonnier, 1989);
Tre trappor upp med hiss (Stockholm: Bonnier Junior, 1991);
Eget rum (Stockholm: Bonnier Junior, 1992);
Egna världar (Stockholm: Bonnier Carlsen, 1994);
Boken om Hugo och Josefin (Stockholm: Bonnier Carlsen, 1996);
Annas blomma: En berättelse (Stockholm: Bonnier Carlsen, 1997).

PRODUCED SCRIPTS: *Pappa Pellerins dotter*, radio, Sveriges Radio, 1965 (seven parts);
Hugo and Josefin, motion picture, by Gripe and Kjell Grede, Sandrews, 1967;
Nattpappan, radio, Sveriges Radio, 1968 (six parts);
Tanten, radio, Sveriges Radio, 1968 (six parts);
De små röda, radio, by Gripe and Camilla Gripe, Sveriges Radio, 1970 (nine parts);
Julia och Nattpappan, television, Sveriges Television, Channel 1, 1971 (eight parts);
Elvis Karlsson, radio, Sveriges Radio, 1973 (seven parts);
Elvis! Elvis! radio, Sveriges Radio, 1974 (seven parts);
Pappa Pellerins dotter, television, Sveriges Television, Channel 1, 1974 (six parts);
Tordyveln flyger i skymningen, radio, Sveriges Radio, 1976 (twenty-four parts);
Elvis! Elvis! motion picture, by Gripe and Kay Pollack; MovieMakers/Sandrews/Svenska Filminstitutet, 1976;
Öppet brev till Gud, television, Sveriges Television, Channel 2, 1977;
Den riktige Elvis, radio, Sveriges Radio, 1977;
Det röda nystanet, television, Sveriges Televison, Channel 1, 1977;
Att vara Elvis, radio, Sveriges Radio, 1978 (nine parts);
Hjärtat som ingen ville ha, television, Sveriges Television, Channel 1, 1978;
Trolltider, television, by Gripe and Camilla Gripe, Sveriges Television, Channel 1, 1979 (twenty-four parts);
Det som sker det sker, radio, Sveriges Radio, 1982 (thirteen parts);
Agnes Cecilia, radio, Sveriges Radio, 1984 (ten parts);
Flickan vid stenbänken, television, Sveriges Television, Channel 2, 1989 (nine parts);
Agnes Cecilia, motion picture, by Gripe and Anders Grönros, Svensk Filmindustri/Sveriges Television/Svenska Filminstitutet, 1991;
Dockorna i spegeln, television, by Gripe and Camille Gripe, Sveriges Television, Channel 1, 1991 (nine parts).

SELECTED PERIODICAL PUBLICATION–UNCOLLECTED: "A Word and a Shadow," *Bookworld*, 2 (1974): 4–9.

Maria (Kristina) Gripe, who published her first work in 1954, established herself in the 1960s and 1970s as a leading Swedish writer in the field of children's and young-adult literature. At the end of the twentieth century she had more than thirty titles in print, many of which have been translated into some twenty different languages. Gripe has been the recipient of many prestigious literary prizes, such as the Scandinavian Nils Holgersson Plaque (1966), the American Lewis Carroll Shelf Award (1967), and the Hans Christian Andersen Medal (1974), issued by the International Board of Books for Young People and often referred to as the Nobel Prize of children's literature.

Maria Kristina Walter was born on 23 July 1923 in the Swedish town of Waxholm in the Stockholm archipelago. She was the eldest of two children in a bourgeois family and received a strict but loving upbringing. Her father, Karl Hugo Walter, was an army captain and her mother, Maria, a homemaker. Maria Gripe was a sensitive child, at times puzzled by the rituals and customs of adult social life. She had a close rapport with her father, who introduced her to literature and nature.

After passing her baccalaureate in 1943, Gripe enrolled as a philosophy student at Stockholm University. In 1946 she married the artist Harald Gripe, who later illustrated many of her books. The couple had one child, Camilla, who is also an author. Harald Gripe died in 1992.

The years after the end of World War II constituted a paradigmatic shift in Swedish culture, when

Dust jacket for the English translation (1976) of Gripe's 1965 novel, I klockornas tid *(Collection of Birgitta Steene)*

the traditional authoritarian lifestyle, dominated by a Lutheran work ethic, was challenged on several fronts, among them the field of children's literature. Lennart Hellsing's modernist nonsense verse for young children broke with traditional poetic syntax, and the appearance of the carnivalesque and anarchic figure of Pippi Longstocking, created by Astrid Lindgren, was evidence of a quiet revolution in the Swedish nursery—and by extension, in society. For Gripe, herself a product of a child-rearing philosophy that emphasized structure, discipline, and obedience, the new cultural climate served as a catalyst rather than a direct influence. She arrived upon the scene at a time of intense interest in child psychology and child education and felt encouraged to publish in the field of children's literature. Eventually she produced works that, in the tradition of such Scandinavian writers as Hans Christian Andersen and Lindgren, helped to upgrade writing for children to a form of literary art.

Like the somewhat older and better-known Lindgren, Gripe's production comprises two major categories of children's literature: realistic works and fantasy books. Unlike Lindgren, however, Gripe has never been drawn to the rambunctious tales of the likes of Pippi Longstocking or Emil in *Emil i Lönneberga* (Emil in the Soup Tureen, 1963), pranksters of strength, undaunted spirit, and deeply anchored self-confidence. Instead, her stories tend to be psychodramas revolving around difficult mental situations for the main characters and describing their search for personal enlightenment and self-discovery. In her trilogy about Josefin and Hugo and in her five books about Elvis Karlsson, sensitive and imaginative children take center stage. Their increased sense of self often comes about despite the failure of their parents to be supportive or to understand the vulnerability of their offspring.

According to Gripe in her 1974 article for *Bookworld*, "A Word and a Shadow," "children know so little, but believe so much." One central thought in almost all of her books is that parents and children inevitably live in different worlds, yet are closely knit together—morally, socially, and existentially. Problems arise because adult reality is something to be understood through knowledge and information, whereas a child's perception goes beyond this rational level and responds to matters in an imaginative way, seeing the facts of reality in metaphorical terms. Conversely, a child will often fail to grasp the symbolic level of adult language and interpret similes and other poetic sayings in literal ways. As a writer of children's books, Gripe herself has retained, as a guiding authorial principle, a conception of reality that is part adult, part child, which means that her characters live in a world that consists of both fragmented facts and imaginative constructions.

The key to Gripe's books lies in her use of her own childhood as an inspirational source. Believing that "childhood is in one way perhaps the only place where people can meet openly," as she wrote in "A Word and a Shadow," she shows in her stories the importance of not losing track of one's childhood, lest a vital aspect of human reality is also lost. Gripe portrays children's lives in order to uncover an adult's repressed recollection of being small and vulnerable. She accomplishes this goal by deliberately designating the child as an authorial voice. At the same time, however, Gripe always incorporates her adult persona in her narrative approach and never attempts to use a childish or childlike language. She may articulate a child's feelings, but she writes in a style that makes the child appear both unselfconscious and precocious. Few average children would possess the intellectual vocabulary that Gripe's child narrators display. A good many children would recognize the apprehensions and fears that she explores through her young narrators, however. Gripe has referred to the fictional persona that takes shape in her imagination as her "shadow" and claims in "A Word and a Shadow" that she cannot remember a time when she was not conscious of it: "A sort of friendship developed between my shadow and me. . . . and it was through my shadow that I came into relationship with the world of fantasy."

Gripe began writing short tales while still a child. She had been given the stories of Hans Christian Andersen to read, a body of work that has inspired many Scandinavian authors, including Lindgren and Selma Lagerlöf. When she showed her first attempts at storytelling to her father, however, he told her not to divulge her writing to anyone until she knew how to write like Andersen. Since her father was in many ways her adored mentor, she followed his advice and kept her writing to herself until she felt it was good enough to submit to a publisher.

Together with her books about Josefin and Hugo from the early 1960s, Maria Gripe's breakthrough came with *Glasblåsarns barn* (1964; translated as *The Glassblower's Children,* 1973), reminiscent of Andersen's story "The Snow Queen," in which two children are taken to a faraway land, which is both a fantasy world and the realm of death. In Gripe's novel two siblings, Klas and Klara, are lured away from their parents by the Lord of All Wishes Town on the other side of the River of Oblivion, a crossing to another world similar to Lethe in Greek mythology. While Andersen's lovely and beautiful Snow Queen entices the children to follow her as they press their noses against the frosty windows in their room, Klas and Klara are whisked away from their life in the poor village of Nöda (Needy) by the rich and gift-showering Lord. Totally possessed by his need to fulfill his Lady's every wish, the Lord carries away the children as a present to his childless wife. Donned in fine and precious clothes, the children become but token emblems to the Lord and the Lady, however, like the reflections that Klas and Klara see of themselves in the palace mirrors and name the "Mirror-children." Rejected by the Lady and ignored by the Lord, they are placed under the supervision of a monstrous ogre of a nurse, Nana, at which point they also lose their mirrored identity. They have ceased to be real not only to the self-preoccupied Lord and his Lady but also to themselves. Without positive confirmation from adults, the children can no longer exist.

In the meantime, back in the home of their parents, Albert the glassblower and his wife, Sophia, the children live on in anguished memories. Through a magic ring given to Sophia at the market and with the help of a wise old woman named Flutter Mildweather, Klas and Klara are rescued, at which point the story takes on more of an archetypal pattern, with Flutter and her one-eyed companion, the raven Wise Wit, representing the good forces that challenge the evil Nana and her miserable pet, the songbird Mimi. The denouement implies not only a fairy-tale reunion of parents and children but also a degree of self-recognition on the part of all the adults.

Glasblåsarns barn is both a moral fantasy tale, with the children as central figures, and a psychological story about adult self-absorption, misdirected love, and problematic relationships between husband and wife. Neither marriage in the story is free of tension: Albert neglects Sophia for his glassblowing art, and the Lord tries to control the Lady with his generosity. The conflict is not resolved until Sophia and the Lady, each in her own way, respond actively to their misery, Sophia by seeking out Flutter Mildweather and the Lady by suggesting a gift that the Lord cannot provide.

Dust jacket for the English translation (1971) of Gripe's 1968 novel, Nattpappan *(Collection of Birgitta Steene)*

As in the case of Andersen's storytelling, Gripe can claim that she writes for two kinds of readers: the children listening to the story and the adults eavesdropping in a corner of the room. And just as many of Andersen's tales seem too complex for young children, a study of Gripe's readership shows that *Glasblåsarns barn*, as well as her other fantasy tales, such as *I klockornas tid* (1965; translated as *In the Time of the Bells*, 1976), *Landet utanför* (1967; translated as *The Land Beyond*, 1974), and *Glastunneln* (The Glass Tunnel, 1969) have been most successful among young adults of junior-high-school age.

In her fantasy books Gripe tends to set up abstract binary concepts and juxtapose characters as though they were symbolic figures in an allegory or fairy tale. Such stories gain their particular strength from a simultaneous development of plot and symbolic theme. Gripe's continued pursuit of the children's genre has come to focus increasingly on character studies, however, in which the symbolic level of the fairy-tale pattern becomes internalized and transformed into a more realistically conceived psychological self-quest.

In 1900 the Swedish feminist Ellen Key published the book *Barnets århundrande* (1900; translated as *The Century of the Child,* 1909), in which the author predicted that the coming century would become especially noteworthy for its new approach to child rearing based on a more insightful understanding of childhood and of a child's mentality. Gripe's books can be seen as answers to Key's prediction in their sensitive unraveling of a child's psyche, but they paint a rather bleak picture of parenting. Her young characters are often left to fend for themselves, having parents who are either too preoccupied with their adult tasks or indifferent to the child's needs. In depicting a child's inner turmoil and his or her groping for an existential footing in life, Gripe's realistic stories project a narrative that usually revolves around one or more of the following issues: the importance of a name, the search for a role in life, and the need for ontological security. These themes form the core of the Hugo and Josefin series and the books about Elvis Karlsson. In both series readers first encounter the title figures as preschoolers.

The daughter of aging parents, Josefin does not like her given name, Anna Grå (Gray). Hence, she invents a new name for herself, Josefin Joandersson. Josefin has an exotic, non-Swedish ring to it, while Joandersson combines the two most common family names in the village: Johansson and Andersson. In this way Josefin can mark both her uniqueness as a person and her wish to have friends and be part of the community. For Elvis Karlsson, his given name would seem to fulfill the same purpose, since Elvis is a rare name in Sweden while Karlsson is an extremely common one. In Elvis's case, however, the given name has dire implications, for it has been foisted on him by his parents. Elvis's mother is an ardent fan of his American singing namesake; this young Swedish Elvis is bound to be a disappointment to his mother, however, for he can hardly carry a tune and demonstrates no signs of becoming a future pop star. His father, from whom he inherits his family name, is an ardent soccer fan, and assumes that his son will become a real "Karlsson" player (*karl* denoting the Swedish word for a tough guy). While Josefin invents a new name identity for herself, Elvis receives help from an older girl, Julia, who sends him a written message that confirms the right of each individual to his own identity–"Detta Ha är nu. Jag är jag. Peter är Peter" (This is now. I am me. Peter is Peter)–to which Elvis adds the line: "Elvis är Elvis" (Elvis is Elvis).

What is typical of all of Gripe's parent figures is their self-absorption, be it in their art (Albert in *Glasblåsarns barn*), their daily tasks (Josefin's parents), or their own often drab lives, governed by social norms and status symbols (Elvis's parents). As a result, children such as Elvis and Josefin are lonely, if not literally abandoned, and have to explore life outside their immediate family in order to discover what their future role in life might be. Such exploration is not easy since they lack what Gripe, referring to the psychologist Andrew Laing, calls ontological security, a sense of a firm footing in life and a feeling of inner comfort with themselves. Elvis's and Josefin's stories center on how they arrive at such a sense of security and self-confidence. Julia in *Nattpappan* (1968; translated as *The Night Daddy*, 1971) and Elvis achieve it through Peter, a young male babysitter who embraces other values than materialistic acquisition and bourgeois conformity. When Peter becomes Elvis's friend, he shows him respect and challenges him to learn to ride a bike. Since the prospect of balancing on a two-wheeler has become a real trauma for the physically timid Elvis, his accomplishment takes on great symbolic significance.

For Josefin, the parents' gardener, Gudmansson, whom she mistakes at first for God himself, comes to her rescue. Her attachment to him grows so strong, however, that sooner or later Gudmansson must depart out of her life in order for her to become independent. In the meantime Josefin makes friends with young Hugo, the epitome of self-confidence, who is her opposite. While she is picked on by her classmates, Hugo, who lives by himself out in the woods (his father being in prison as a draft dodger), faces up to everybody, including the teacher, and becomes Josefin's role model. Their beautiful friendship is captured in lyrical tones, and has been faithfully rendered in Kjell Grede's 1967 film *Hugo och Josephine*, based on the first two volumes of Gripe's trilogy.

After several realistic tales, which she claims were harder for her to write than her fantasy books, Gripe brought together her two areas of expertise–her adroitness at psychological realism and her skillful ability to evoke otherworldliness, a metaphysical realm of the imagination. The result was *Agnes Cecilia* (1981), subtitled "en sällsam historia" (a strange tale). It is a book for young adults and possibly the most complex of her works to that date. *Agnes Cecilia* is a coming-of-age story but told by incorporating into the psychological process of a troubled teenager a mystical presence of the past. The main character of the book, seventeen-year-old Nora, is an orphan whose parents were killed in an accident when she was little. The book has a motto, a quotation from Arthur Schopenhauer: "Therefore, everyone has to conceive of himself as a necessary being. . . ." It is a statement that reconfirms Gripe's focus on young people's need to realize their self-worth as human beings. Nora is a Sunday's child; in other words, she is a clairvoyant person who "kan höre gräset växa" (can hear the grass grow). Her name has important literary connotations both to Henrik Ibsen's *Et dukkehjem* (1879, translated as *A Doll's House*, 1889) in which Nora's namesake keeps waiting for the "miraculous" to happen, and, even more importantly, to Eleonora in August Strindberg's *Påsk* (1901, translated as *Easter*, 1912), a young girl with a mind full of premonitions and second sight. *Påsk* was written after Strindberg had embraced a Swedenborgian form of mysticism. Gripe's *Agnes Cecilia* follows in Strindberg's footsteps in that it too depicts a world in which spirits of warning and blessing inhabit an otherwise ordinary reality. A third literary intertext in *Agnes Cecilia* is a Russian folktale, which provides the rationale for Gripe's Nora to set out on her quest for selfhood:

Dust jacket for the 1976 English translation of Gripe's Elvis Karlsson *(1972), the first of five books featuring the title character (Collection of Birgitta Steene)*

Hör på vad jag har att säga dig! Du har varit mig en trogen tjänave, och nu vill jag att du skall unföra detta uppdrag:
Bege dig jag vet inte vart
för att söka
jag vet inte vad!

(Listen to what I have to tell you! You have been a faithful servant, and now I want you to perform this task:
Go, I know not where;
to seek,
I know not what!)

Through a series of mystical circumstances, including strange telephone calls and instructions to pick up a package with an old doll, Nora establishes a contact with her past that is part real, part telepathic. The doll provides a bridge between her own reality and a mysterious world but also represents her longing for a link with her dead family. When the doll disappears at the end of the story, Nora is free to live in the present and pursue a friendship with a girl her own age, whose name is Agnes Cecilia. As always in Gripe's stories, the name carries important implications suggesting religious-savior roles and alluding to literary predecessors: Agnes, God's lamb, a female Christ figure, is also the earthly name of Indra's daughter in Strindberg's *Ett drömspel* (1901; translated as *The Dreamplay,* 1912), a creature from another world who descends on earth to absorb the woes of mankind; while Cecilia, a Roman saint and martyr and the patroness of sacred music, evokes an analogy to the many strange sounds and invisible voices that Gripe's Nora encounters during her mysterious quest. Cecilia is also the name given to the main character in T. S. Eliot's religious living-room drama, *The Cocktail Party* (1950). Such intertextual allusions are in keeping with Gripe's literary sophistication and with her ambition to give children's literature the same status as adult fiction and to demand that it receive the same critical attention as mainstream literature.

Gripe's so-called Skuggan, or Shadow, books, *Skuggan över stenbänken* (The Shadow above the

Dust jacket for Gripe's 1981 novel, in which an orphan girl uses a doll to connect with a mystical otherworld (from Scandinavian Newsletter, *no. 8 [1994/1995])*

Stone Bench, 1982), . . . *och de vita skuggorna i skogen* (. . . And the Shadows in the Forest, 1984), *Skuggornas barn* (Children of the Shadows, 1986), *and Skugggömman* (The Shadow Hide-out, 1988), explore the same kind of dualistic reality as *Agnes Cecilia* and maintain the same precarious balance between psychodrama and mysticism. In a way, such a dichotomy between the real and the fantastic, between an inner world of turmoil and an outer everyday world that harbors invisible patterns of telepathy, forms the essence of much of Gripe's authorship. In a work such as *Glasblåsarns barn* the unreal is presented as a fantasy land that takes on some of the contours of many fairy tales. In the books about Elvis the psychodrama finds its own concrete emblem in a box in which Elvis keeps his innermost secret. In *Agnes Cecilia* and the Skuggan books transcendental "spirits" visit the living with strange but ultimately healing messages from the past. In the course of events the past is exorcised but is also accepted and is transformed into present reality. The process forms an analogy to Gripe's own rapport with her childhood shadow, which came to function as both a therapeutic companion and a metaphor for the author's imaginative explorations of unseen worlds.

References:

Charlotte Anckarsvärd, "Livsåskådning och symbolik i Maria Gripes ungdomsroman *Agnes Cecilia: en sällsam historia*," undergraduate thesis, University of Uppsala, 1996;

Stina Andersson, "Livet är fullt av mystiska händelser: Intervju med Maria Gripe," *Kamratposten*, 107 (1998): 8–9;

Birgitta Eklund, "Samspråk mellan text och bild: En studie av Maria och Harald Gripes böcker om Elvis," undergraduate thesis, Göteborg University, 1981;

Stefan Eliasson, "Individ, grupp och samhälle i Maria Gripes författarskap från 1960-1973," undergraduate thesis, Umeå University, 1974;

Ulf Eriksson, "Flykt eller frigörelse; civilisationskritik i Maria Gripes böcker om Hugo och Josefin," *Abrakadabra,* 4 (1991): 7-11;

Gudrun Fagerström, "Maria Gripe," in *Författare & illustratörer för barn och ungdom: Porträtt på svenska och utländska nutida författare och illustratörer,* volume 3 (Lund: Bibliotekstjänst, 1998), pp. 110-127;

Fagerström, *Maria Gripe, hennes verk och hennes läsare* (Stockholm: Bonnier, 1977);

Lars Haglund, "Några huvudlinjer i Maria Gripes författarskap från 1960 och framåt," undergraduate thesis, University of Uppsala, 1974;

Stefanie Hlubeck, "Androggynie in Jugendromanen: Anmerkungen zu einer Romantetralogi Maria Gripes," *Mitteilungen des Instituts für Jugendbuchforschung,* 1 (1992): 17-18;

Lisa Källström, *Spegelbarnen: Tankar kring Maria Gripes Glasblåsarns barn* (Stockholm: Litteraturvetenskapliga institutionen, 1992);

Maria Koren, "En beskrivning av familje relationer i Maria Gripes realistika produktion–en jämförelse med R. D. Laings idéer," dissertation, Amsterdam University, 1977;

Carina Lidström, "Mellan klockklang och tystnad: en läsövning i Maria Gripes medeltidsroman *I klockornas tid,*" in *Läsebok: En festskrift till Ulf Boëthius 2/12 1993,* edited by Lidström (Stockholm & Stehag: Symposion, 1993);

Lidström, *Sökande, spegling, metamorfos: Tre vägar genom Maria Gripes skuggserie* (Stockholm & Stehag: Symposion, 1994);

Kerstin Lindholm, *Elvis förhållande till de vuxna i "Elvis Karlsson" av Maria Gripe* (Åbo: Litteraturvetenskapliga institutionen, 1977);

Carin Mannheimer, "Maria Gripe," *Bookbird,* 2 (1973): 24-34;

Margaretha Pollak, "Maria Gripe," video (Stockholm: Utbildningsradion, 1986);

Birgitta Steene, "*Agnes Cecilia* as an Adult Children's Book," *Scandinavian Newsletter,* 8 (1994/1995): 2-4;

Boel Westin, "The Androgynous Female–(Or Orlando Inverted)," in *Female/Male: Gender in Children's Literature* (Visby: Baltic Centre for Writers and Translators, 1999), pp. 91-101.

Lars Gustafsson
(17 May 1936 –)

Ia Dübois
University of Washington

BOOKS: *Vägvila: Ett mysteriespel på prosa: Till det förflutna och minnet av vindar* (Uppsala: Siesta, 1957);

Poeten Brumbergs sista dagar och död: En romantisk berättelse (Stockholm: Norstedt, 1959);

Bröderna: En allegorisk berättelse (Stockholm: Norstedt, 1960);

Nio brev om romanen, by Gustafsson and Lars Bäckström (Stockholm: Norstedt, 1961);

Följeslagarna: En äventyrsberättelse (Stockholm: Norstedt, 1962);

Ballongfararna (Stockholm: Norstedt, 1962);

En förmiddag i Sverige (Stockholm: Norstedt, 1963);

En resa till jordens medelpunkt och andra dikter (Stockholm: Norstedt, 1966);

Den egentliga berättelsen om Herr Arenander: Anteckningar (Stockholm: Norstedt, 1966);

Förberedelser till flykt och andra berättelser (Stockholm: Norstedt, 1967); republished, with postscript by Gustafsson (Stockholm: Norstedt, 1976);

Bröderna Wright uppsöker Kitty Hawk och andra dikter (Stockholm: Norstedt, 1968);

Utopier och andra essäer om "dikt" och "liv" (Stockholm: PAN/Norstedt, 1969);

Konsten att segla med drakar och andra scener ur privatlivet: Kåserier (Stockholm: Norstedt, 1969);

Kärleksförklaring till en sefardisk dam (Stockholm: Bonnier, 1970);

Två maktspel: Hyresgästerna eller Tebjudningen som inte ville ta slut, Den nattliga hyllningen (Stockholm: Bonnier, 1970);

Herr Gustafsson själv (Stockholm: Bonnier, 1971);

Kommentarer (Stockholm: Gidlund, 1972);

Varma rum och kalla (Stockholm: Bonnier, 1972); translated by Yvonne L. Sandström as *Warm Rooms and Cold* (Providence, R.I.: Copper Beech Press, 1975);

Yllet (Stockholm: Bonnier, 1973);

Den onödiga samtiden, by Gustafsson and Jan Myrdal (Stockholm: PAN/Norstedt, 1974); second edition, with epilogue "Tankar i trappan" (Stockholm: PAN/Norstedt, 1974);

Lars Gustafsson (photograph by Hasse Persson)

Världsdelar: Reseskildringar (Stockholm: Norstedt, 1975);

Familjefesten (Stockholm: Bonnier, 1975);

Solidaritet med Tjeckoslovakiens folk: (åtta år efter ockupationen), by Gustafsson and Jan Myrdal (Stockholm: Oktoberförlaget, 1975);

Strandhugg i svensk poesi: Femton diktanalyser (Stockholm: FIB:s lyrikklubb: Tiden, 1976); translated by Robert T. Rovinsky as *Forays into Swedish Poetry* (Austin: University of Texas Press, 1978);

Sigismund: Ur en polsk barockfurstes minnen (Stockholm: Norstedt, 1976); translated by John Weinstock as *Sigismund: From the Memories of a Baroque Polish Prince* (New York: New Directions, 1985);

Tennisspelarna: En berättelse (Stockholm: Norstedt, 1977); translated by Sandström as *The Tennis Players* (New York: New Directions, 1983);

Sonetter (Stockholm: Norstedt, 1977);

Den lilla världen: Om märkvärdigheter uti människorna (Stockholm: Alba, 1977);

Kinesisk höst, with illustrations by Sven Ljungberg (Stockholm: Norstedt, 1978);

En biodlares död (Stockholm: Norstedt, 1978); translated by Janet K. Swaffar and Guntram H. Weber as *The Death of a Beekeeper* (New York: New Directions, 1981);

Språk och lögn: En essä om språkfilosofisk extremism i nittonde århundradet (Stockholm: Norstedt, 1978);

Konfrontationer: Stycken om konst, litteratur och politik (Stockholm: PAN/Norstedt, 1979);

Filosofier: Essäer (Stockholm: Norstedt, 1979);

I mikroskopet: Banaliteter och brottstycken (Stockholm: Alba, 1979);

Afrikanskt försök: En essä om villkoren (Stockholm: Norstedt, 1980);

Artesiska brunnar cartesianska drömmar: Tjugotvå lärodikter (Stockholm: Norstedt, 1980);

För liberalismen: En stridsskrift (Stockholm: Norstedt, 1981);

Berättelser om lyckliga människor (Stockholm: Norstedt, 1981); translated by Sandström and Weinstock as *Stories of Happy People* (New York: New Directions, 1986);

Världens tystnad före Bach (Stockholm: Norstedt, 1982);

Sorgemusik för frimurare (Stockholm: Norstedt, 1983); translated by Sandström as *Funeral Music for Freemasons* (New York: New Directions, 1987);

Litteraturhistorikern Schück: Vetenskapssyn och historieuppfattning i Henrik Schücks tidigare produktion (Stockholm: Almqvist & Wiksell International, 1983);

Stunder vid ett trädgårdsbord: Stycken om konst och litteratur (Stockholm: Alba, 1984);

Fåglarna och andra dikter (Stockholm: Norstedt, 1984);

Frihet och fruktan: 22 brev, by Gustafsson and Per Ahlmark (Stockholm: Bonnier, 1985);

Bilderna på Solstadens murar: Essäer om ont och gott (Stockholm: Norstedt, 1985);

Bernard Foys tredje rockad (Stockholm: Norstedt, 1986); translated by Sandström as *Bernard Foy's Third Castling* (New York: New Directions, 1988);

Spegelskärvor (Stockholm: Norstedt, 1987);

Samlade berättelser (Stockholm: Norstedt, 1987);

Fyra poeter: Gustaf Adolf Fredenlund, Bernard Foy, Ehrmine Wikström, Jan Bohman (Stockholm: Norstedt, 1988);

Frukt efter årstiden: Tankar om framsteg och utveckling (Stockholm: Ekonomifakta, 1988);

Det sällsamma djuret från norr och andra science-fiction-berättelser (Stockholm: Norstedt, 1989);

Problemformuleringsprivilegiet: Samhällsfilosofiska studier (Stockholm: Norstedt, 1989);

Förberedelser för vintersäsongen: Elegier och andra dikter (Stockholm: Natur och kultur, 1990)–includes "Elegi över den gamla mexikanska kvinnan och hennes döda barn," translated by Sandström as "Elegy for the Old Mexican Woman and Her Dead Child," *New Yorker* (8 October 1990): 42; "För alla dem som väntar på att tid skall gå," translated by Sandström as "For All Those Who Wait for Time to Pass," *New Yorker* (6 May 1991): 38; "Omkostnader i rörelse," translated by Sandström as "Itemized Expenses," *New Yorker* (6 April 1992): 30; "Austin, Texas," translated by Sandström, *New Yorker* (24 August 1992): 36;

En kakelsättares eftermiddag (Stockholm: Natur och kultur, 1991); translated by Tom Geddes as *A Tiler's Afternoon* (London: Harvill, 1993);

Landskapets långsamma förändringar: Essäer om människor och idéer (Stockholm: Natur och kultur, 1992);

Historien med hunden: Ur en texansk konkursdomares dagböcker och brev (Stockholm: Natur och kultur, 1993); translated by Geddes as *The Tale of a Dog: From the Diaries and Letters of a Texan Bankruptcy Judge* (London: Harvill, 1998; New York: New Directions, 1999);

Stenkista (Stockholm: Natur och kultur, 1994)–includes "Aristoteles och kräftan," translated by Sandström as "Aristotle and the Crayfish," *New Yorker* (7 June 1993): 84;

Ett minnespalats: Vertikala memoarer (Stockholm: Natur och kultur, 1994);

De andras närvaro: Essäer om konsten som kunskapskälla (Stockholm: Natur och kultur, 1995);

Variationer över ett tema av Silfverstolpe (Stockholm: Natur och kultur, 1996);

Tjänarinnan: En kärleksroman (Stockholm: Natur och kultur, 1996);

Vänner bland de döda: Essäer om litteratur (Stockholm: Natur och kultur, 1997);

Windy Berättar: Om sitt liv, om de försvunna och om dem som ännu finns kvar (Stockholm: Natur och kultur, 1999);

Strövtåg i hembygden (Stockholm: Natur och kultur, 1999);

Meditationer: En filosofisk bilderbok (Stockholm: Natur och kultur, 2000);

Blom och den andra magentan (Stockholm: Natur och kultur, 2001).

Editions and Collections: *Ur bild i bild: Samlade dikter 1950–1980,* includes foreword by Gustafsson (Stockholm: Norstedt, 1982);

Sprickorna i muren, with an afterword by Gustafsson (Stockholm: Norstedt, 1984)–includes *Herr Gustafsson själv; Yllet; Familjefesten; Sigismund;* and *En biodlares död;*

Där alfabetet har tvåhundra bokstäver: Samlade dikter 1981–1991 (Stockholm: Natur och kultur, 1992)–includes *Världens tystnad före Bach; Fåglarna och andra dikter; Fyra poeter;* and *Förberedelser för vintersångsen;*

Valda skrifter, 4 volumes (Stockholm: Natur och kultur, 1998–1999).

Editions in English: *The Public Dialogue in Sweden: Current Issues of Social, Esthetic and Moral Debate,* translated by Claude Stephenson (Stockholm: Norstedt, 1964);

Lars Gustafsson: Selected Poems, translated by Robin Fulton (New York: New River, 1972);

The Stillness of the World before Bach: New Selected Poems, edited by Christopher Middleton, translated by Fulton, Philip Martin, Sandström, Harriett Watts, and Middleton (New York: New Directions, 1988).

OTHER: *Svensk dikt: Från trollformler till Björn Håkansson: En antologi,* edited by Gustafsson (Stockholm: Wahlström & Widstrand, 1968); republished as *Svensk dikt: Från trollformler till Lars Norén: En antologi* (Stockholm: Wahlström & Widstrand, 1978); republished as *Svensk dikt: Från trollformler till Frostenson: En antologi* (Stockholm: Wahlström & Widstrand, 1995);

Dikterna från 60-talet, edited by Gustafsson and Torkel Rasmusson (Stockholm: Bonnier, 1970);

Nittitalsförfattare, edited by Gustafsson (Stockholm: Wahlström & Widstrand, 1971);

Michael Krüger, *I förnuftets dagsljus,* translated by Gustafsson (Stockholm: Norstedt, 1985);

Eugène Guillevic, *Bröd och stenar: Dikter 1942–1978,* translated by Gustafsson (Stockholm: Norstedt, 1985);

Rainer Maria Rilke, *Sonetterna till Orfeus: Skrivna som ett gravmonument över Wera Ouckama Knoop,* translated by Gustafsson (Stockholm: Norstedt, 1987);

Christopher Middleton, *I det dolda huset,* translated by Gustafsson (Stockholm: Norstedt, 1988);

Seamus Heaney, *I syner,* translated by Gustafsson (Stockholm: Natur och kultur, 1996).

SELECTED PERIODICAL PUBLICATIONS–UNCOLLECTED: "Mediavänstern: Nya klassens vakthund," *Svenska Dagbladet* (Stockholm), 6 June 1980;

"Vilka är årets bästa böcker," *Svenska Dagbladet* (Stockholm), 17 December 1989.

Lars Gustafsson is one of the most prolific Swedish writers since August Strindberg. Since the late 1950s he has produced a voluminous flow of poetry, novels, short stories, critical essays, and editorials. He is also one of the few Swedish writers who has gained international recognition with literary awards such as the Prix International Charles Veillon des Essais in 1983, the Heinrich Steffens Preis in 1986, Una Vita per la Litteratura in 1989, a John Simon Guggenheim Memorial Foundation Fellowship for poetry in 1994, and several others. His major works have been translated into fifteen languages, and Harold Bloom includes Gustafsson in *The Western Canon: The Books and School of the Ages* (1994). While the problem of identity has been the defining theme of Gustafsson's writings, his social criticism has often vexed the Swedish cultural elite. As a result he is seen as a controversial writer in Sweden rather than as one embraced by the establishment. Recurring references to his native province of Västmanland in his works have led Swedish critics to characterize Gustafsson as a "lokalpoet" (provincial poet). In contrast, international critics view him as a philosopher and even a "universalgenie" (universal genius), as one reviewer wrote in the German newspaper *Kieler Nachtrichten* on 28 October 1993. In 1996, when Gustafsson received the Pilot Prize in Sweden for his writings, the jury defined him eloquently as a "diktarfilosof, fantast, encyklopedist, hemmastadd främling på varje breddgrad från Västmanlands slussar till Texas vidder" (a poet philosopher, a dreamer, an encyclopedist, a stranger familiar with every latitude from the locks of Västmanland to the Texas plains).

In *The Public Dialogue in Sweden: Current Issues of Social, Esthetic and Moral Debate* (1964), Gustafsson writes: "People have spoken of the vacuum which Christianity has left behind, how a language which was meant to express the drama of the inner life ceased to be public property when the corresponding articles of faith also ceased to be. . . . They have said that it is a job for the modern author to supply us with such a language." Acutely aware of what he saw as a profound spiritual crisis in society–a crisis paralleled within the individual–he set out to find that lost language. His writings describe this search, which he conducts on two fronts: outwardly, in the form of social criticism, and inwardly, in the form of a probing quest for individual self-awareness. Gustafsson's discussions of philosophical and existential questions, with frequent mention of such authorities as Heraclitus, René Descartes, Søren Kierkegaard, Friedrich Nietzsche, and Ludwig Wittgenstein, especially displays his analytical-philosophical

Gustafsson at the University of Texas at Austin, where he was Thord Gray Professor of Literature and Philosophy in 1974 (photograph by Hasse Persson)

erudition. He shares the desire of these philosophers to identify and define human reality further and to explore the "tillstånd mellan tillstånden" (in-between stage), the dimension between the soul and the world, for answers to the enigma of human existence.

Lars Erik Einar Gustafsson was born on 17 May 1936 in Västerås, Sweden, to Einar H. Gustafsson, a merchant, and Lotten M. Carlsson Gustafsson. In *Ett minnespalats: Vertikala memoarer* (A Palace of Memories: Vertical Memoirs, 1994) he reminisces about walks to a park with his father, recalling how the smoke from his father's cigarette and the smell of his wet wartime uniform conveyed a sense of comfort and security to the young Gustafsson. On the other hand, he mentions his mother in the memoir only in relation to parental arguments, a fact that is interesting because of the elusive role that women play later in his works. His personal notebooks, donated to the University of Uppsala, reveal the author as an outsider who, as a teenager, was already thinking as an adult. The pain of isolation during these early school years–combined with his memories of yellow light reflected on his grandmother's kitchen floor, of the smell of wet wool, of the images of murky river water in his native city, and of the nature of the surrounding province–imbue Gustafsson's novels of the 1960s and 1970s.

In 1955 Gustafsson left Västerås to study philosophy, aesthetics, sociology, and the history of literature at the University of Uppsala. During the Uppsala years he often debated about the function of metapoetry in Swedish literature of the 1950s with Göran Printz-Påhlson, a contemporary Swedish poet and literary critic. He also helped establish the literary journal *Siesta* in 1956, where he debuted as a poet in the same year with "Gestaltlös sångare" (Singer without a Figure). In 1957 Gustafsson received a scholarship to study with Gilbert Ryle at Magdalene College of Oxford University, where the analytic and linguistic philosophy of Ryle and Wittgenstein became an integral part of Gustafsson's literary pursuit and the focal point of his continued academic research. He received his Filosofie Licentiat degree–a predoctoral degree–from the University of Uppsala in 1960. In 1978 he received a Ph.D.

in theoretical philosophy, also from the University of Uppsala. His dissertation, *Språk och lögn: En essä om språkfilosofisk extremism i nittonde århundradet* (Language and Lie: An Essay on Extreme Linguistic Philosophy in the Nineteenth Century), was published that same year.

Vägvila: Ett mysteriespel på prosa: Till det förflutna och minnet av vindar (Rest at the Roadside: A Mystery Play in Prose: To the Past and the Memory of Winds, 1957) was Gustafsson's first published work of prose. Yet, he considers *Poeten Brumbergs sista dagar och död: En romantisk berättelse* (The Poet Brumberg's Final Days and Death: A Romatic Story, 1959) his first novel—a romantic novel-within-a-novel, in which the narrator finds Jacob Brumberg's diary and a draft to a novel called "The Prince." This work exemplifies the romantic trend in Swedish literature of the 1950s; in *Tre Romantiska Berättelser: Studier i Eyvind Johnsons* Romantisk berättelse *och* Tidens gång, Lars Gustafssons Poeten Brumbergs sista dagar och död *och Svens Delbrancs* Kastrater (1999), Leif Dahlberg underscores certain intertextual references in Gustafsson's book, such as Friedrich von Schlegel's *Lucinde* (1799), Rainer Maria Rilke's *Duineser Elegien* (1923; translated as *Duino Elegies,* 1939), and James Joyce's *Ulysses* (1922). The erudition and affinity for philosophy, mythology, and metaphysics that characterized Gustafsson's works for the next three decades already appear in *Poeten Brumbergs sista dagar och död*. Increasingly known in literary circles at this time, he also began developing a reputation as a novice who challenges established authors.

Gustafsson's career solidified during the 1960s with the publication of four poetry volumes, three novels, and five collections of critical essays. In the novel *Bröderna: En allegorisk berättelse* (The Brothers: An Allegorical Story, 1960) identity conflicts and a childhood trauma appear for the first time. Here they are presented through the mythological motif of twins. In the three novels that he wrote during the 1960s, including *Bröderna, Följeslagarna: En äventyrsberättelse* (The Companions: An Adventure Story, 1962), and *Den egentliga berättelsen om Herr Arenander: Anteckningar* (The Real Story about Mr. Arenander: Notes, 1966), loneliness is a common theme. Gustafsson's memories from childhood, such as the reflection of yellow light on his grandmother's kitchen floor and the red schoolhouse where he was the student of an abusive teacher, permeate all three works. The autobiographical aspect of the novels are further underscored through their various depictions of a young boy growing up in Västmanland; of a college student and his adventurous journey through Europe to find out who he really is; and, finally, of Mr. Arenander, who—sharing the memories of the young boy and the college student—personifies the culmination of identity conflicts and of existential loneliness.

Since Gustafsson was involved in debates about poetics in the 1950s and published his first poem in 1956, his verse reflects the traditional style and motifs that critics have defined as emblematic of this time. His first poetry collection came out in 1962. *Ballongfararna* (The Balloonists) was followed by *En förmiddag i Sverige* (A Morning in Sweden, 1963), *En resa till jordens medelpunkt och andra dikter* (Journey to the Center of the Earth and Other Poems, 1966), and by *Bröderna Wright uppsöker Kitty Hawk och andra dikter* (The Wright Brothers Look for Kitty Hawk and Other Poems, 1968). Selections from these three volumes appeared in translation in *The Stillness of the World before Bach: New Selected Poems* (1988). In accordance with the realist trend of "nyenkelhet" (new simplicity), as practiced by Swedish writers in the 1960s, Gustafsson's verse style is direct and to the point. On the other hand, realism embraces his poetry as much as the enigmatic is omnipresent in it. His desire to make visible what is invisible motivates recurring existential questions also in these verse collections; his use of Jules Verne's science-fiction classic *Voyages au centre de la Terre* (1864; translated as *Journey to the Center of the Earth,* 1872); and their references to explorations of the North Pole—whether by balloonists or by seafarers or through alchemy and mysticism. In his foreword to *Ur bild i bild: Samlade dikter 1950–1980* (1982), Gustafsson describes the calling he felt to be a poet, at the age of fourteen: "Poesins demon eller ängel måste ha gripit mig om strupen sommaren 1950" (The demon or angel of poetry must have grabbed me by the throat in the summer of 1950). Thus, he is foremost a poet whose lyricism also informs his prose.

The 1960s were eventful and productive years for Gustafsson. In 1962 he married Madeleine Lagerberg, with whom he has two children, Joen and Lotten. Hired in the early 1960s by *Bonniers Litterära Magasin*—a journal put out by Albert Bonniers Publishers in Stockholm—he worked by day as an editor and wrote his poetry and novels at night. Gustafsson served as editor in chief of the magazine from 1966 to 1972. Through his work at Bonnier he became friendly with prominent Scandinavian and international authors and literary organizations—such as Gruppe 47 (Group 47), an association of German-speaking writers that presented his poems in translation at a reading in Sweden in 1964. Ultimately enhancing his international career, this event catalyzed Gustafsson to immerse himself in German cultural life. Since that presentation he has returned to Germany frequently to read from his own works, to write, and to lecture. Gustafsson's years at *Bonniers Litterära Magasin* were also controversial—largely because of certain social upheavals, both in Sweden and abroad. In 1965 he published Göran Sonnevi's poem "Om kriget i Vietnam" (On the War in Vietnam), which in effect demarcated a new period of political and "factional" writing in the country; "factional" is a term, prevalent in Sweden in the 1960s, that reflects a combination of the words "facts" and "fictional." Gustafsson's efforts to transform the traditional and conservative journal into a progressive and liberal medium in line with its time reaped much criticism, from both within and without the house of Bonnier.

While Gustafsson's novels and poetry evince existential and psychological questions in the personal sphere, his essay collections verify his public position as a European intellectual with a particular focus on the political and the philosophical. He takes his responsibility as an intellectual seriously, asserting in the 7 July 1980 issue of *Svenska Dagbladet* that "De intellektuellas uppgift i ett samhälle är att bidra till dess självkännedom" (The intellectuals' task in society is to contribute to its self-awareness). In *The Public Dialogue in Sweden* he suggests that the "nihilism of values" in contemporary Swedish society reflected the ongoing philosophical debates of the 1940s and 1950s. Gustafsson's interest in exploring diverse events and personae in the arts and sciences is quite evident in *Förberedelser till flykt och andra berättelser* (Preparations for Flight and Other Stories, 1967), a work that he calls a turning point in his career as a writer.

In a postscript to the 1976 edition of *Förberedelser till flykt och andra berättelser,* Gustafsson remarks that although the book was largely forgotten soon after it was first published, stories from it were later translated and received acclaim in other countries. For Gustafsson this book captures the emptiness and coldness he was experiencing at the time of its writing—conditions that he tried to depict by experimenting with different literary techniques. "Besökaren" (The Visitor), a story from the collection, describes an angel who, on a cold winter night, sees a lonely man on a country road. The angel tries to reach into the man to undo the enigma his life embodies but finds only coldness and emptiness—then leaves in horror while the man struggles toward the warmth of a yellow light shining from his house. *Förberedelser till flykt och andra berättelser* especially foreshadows Gustafsson's works of the 1970s. The juxtaposition of warmth with coldness seen in "Besökaren" reappears as a theme in the poetry collection *Varma rum och kalla* (1972; translated as *Warm Rooms and Cold,* 1975). The idea of a void sensed within an individual—a feeling that, as Gustafsson describes, results from an oppressive power system and its public lies—also recurs in his verse. These motifs dominate the five novels he wrote in the 1970s.

While Gustafsson and some critics view *Förberedelser till flykt och andra berättelser* as a transitional work, others rather see the epic poem *Kärleksförklaring till en sefardisk dam* (Declaration of Love to a Sephardic Lady, 1970; selections translated in *The Stillness of the World before Bach*) as a turning point in his writings. The poem starts with reminiscences of cold winter days in early childhood and, typical of a Gustafsson text, progresses to reflections on world literature and history. Yet, the verse is foremost an affectionate declaration to a "dam, krinna, flicka" (lady, woman, girl) who has the power to turn the speaker's coldness and bitterness into mourning and fatigue. She is his true inner self, his "anima," a metaphysical motif that Gustafsson employs in his verses of the 1970s and 1980s. Most strikingly, at the time of composing *Kärleksförklaring till en sefardisk dam* Gustafsson began to compare his writings to "ett sorgearbete" (a grief work).

The female characters in Gustafsson's works are rarely women of flesh and blood. Instead, they are creatures from mythology—such as Circe, Eurydice, and Medusa—or the persona's anima or a seductive, redheaded woman who appears in his life for a fleeting moment. In *Kärleksförklaring till en sefardisk dam* the object of the speaker's love relates to memories of women who have offered him a sense of warmth and security: "Först i tui-eller tre års åldern, / förväxlade jag dig med en mormor Emma, / . . . Nästa gång jag åter såg dig var du en sefardisk dam" / (First, two or three years old, / I confused you with a grandmother Emma, / . . . Next time I saw you, you were a Sephardic lady). The Sephardic lady does not stay a muse in this poem yet personifies the speaker's anima, which Carl Gustav Jung defined as the archetype of the human soul: "Du är min anima, och jag känner dig inte" (You are my Anima, and I don't know you). A metaphysical symbol, she also represents Gustafsson's inner quest. While the poem calls up incidents from the speaker's past—and displays images from Gustafsson's novels and poems of the 1960s—it also signals a more direct link to Gustafsson's life through the mention of certain persons, places, and

Dust jacket for the 1984 omnibus edition of five of Gustafsson's novels from the 1970s and early 1980s, each of which features a protagonist named Lars (from Swedish Book Review, 1984)

events. At the same time Gustafsson portrays the persona as a European intellectual and thus contrasts it with himself, a poet from provincial Västmanland.

On 16 September 1970, around the time that Gustafsson wrote *Kärleksförklaring till en sefardisk dam*, Jerome Hollander–then the American ambassador to Sweden–gave a talk about the Vietnam War at the cathedral in Västerås. The event drew protest and resulted in an incident of police brutality. This politicization of the religious sphere of the cathedral outraged Gustafsson, who five days later requested, in a letter to the Bishop of Västerås, that his membership in the Lutheran State Church be withdrawn. (Until recently in Sweden, citizens were Lutherans automatically at birth; in 1996 the Swedish government began the process of separating itself from the Church and made the separation official in 2000.) In 1981 Gustafsson converted to Judaism, eleven years after the Sephardic lady in *Kärleksförklaring till en sefardisk dam* occasioned the first reference to Judaism in his work.

Gustafsson spent most of the 1970s writing a "pentalogy," the five works of fiction that cemented his reputation as one of the most important Swedish novelists: *Herr Gustafsson själv* (Mr. Gustafsson Himself, 1971), *Yllet* (The Wool, 1973), *Familjefesten* (The Family Reunion, 1975), *Sigismund: Ur en polsk barockfurstes minnen* (1976; translated as *Sigismund: From the Memories of a Baroque Polish Prince,* 1985), and *En biodlares död* (1978; translated as *The Death of a Beekeeper,* 1981). All of these works were later collected and republished as *Sprickorna i muren* (The Cracks in the Wall, 1984) with a postscript by the author. The novels share a protagonist named Lars–whose life echoes Gustafsson's own–and feature the recurring phrase "Vi börjar om från början. Vi ger oss inte." (We'll start all over. We won't give in.) The first novel, *Herr Gustafsson själv,* opens with familiar images of a lonely childhood and of disturbances at school. On an airplane to Berlin the protagonist, Lars, meets redheaded Hanna von Wallenstein, a philosophy professor. With Wallenstein's help, Lars embarks on a quest into his past and his soul, commencing his "grief work." In *Herr Gustafsson själv* Gustafsson also makes repeated references to Hector Berlioz's *Symphonie Fantastique* (1830), instilling in the novel a sense of the fantastic in both its form and content.

Herr Gustafsson själv represented the author's attempt to establish his authenticity as a writer, which he did by presenting the protagonist with his own name and biographical facts, thus confusing the boundaries between autobiography and fiction. Many critics viewed his experimentation as self-sublimation. The polemic aspect of the novel—Gustafsson's criticism of the "public lie" that infiltrates society and further separates the individual from the government—was seen as a sign of the writer's own search for power. In contrast Gustafsson has asserted more than once that the novel is not about himself but rather about the 1960s. Understandably, his autobiographical style and prominent position as editor in chief of *Bonniers Litterära Magasin* made him an easy target for criticism. For example, Lars Bäckström, his former friend and colleague, wrote that

> "Herr G" i romanen visade sig ha för mycket gemensamt med den LG som är en etablerad maktfigur, kritiker i *Expressen,* förlagsman och multinationell författarföretagare inom Bonnierkonglomeratet. Från en sådan position kan man väl uträtta åtskilligt av värde men man saknar motivation, ja, det är emot ens intresse att skärskåda sig själv.
>
> ("Mr. G" in the novel turned out to have too much in common with the LG who is an established power figure, critic at the daily *Expressen,* editor and multinational author–entrepreneur within the Bonnier publishing conglomerate. In such a position one could do a great deal, but one lacks motivation, yes, it counters one's own interests, to scrutinize oneself.)

During his years with *Bonniers Litterära Magasin,* Gustafsson endured many attacks for giving the journal a new liberal slant and responded publicly to diatribes from the press. In 1972, having received a one-year fellowship from the Deutscher Akademischer Austausch Dienst in Germany, he resigned from his position and left with his family to write in Berlin, where he worked on most of his next three novels—*Yllet, Familjefesten,* and *Sigismund.*

If *Herr Gustafsson själv* is Gustafsson's most controversial novel, *Yllet* is his most emblematic because of his use of the smell of wet wool to describe the stagnation of Swedish society. Wool has an ambiguous role in the novel, as the protagonist of *Yllet* suggests: "Ylle har två egenskaper förstår ni. Det skyddar mot kyla, mot vinter och blåst. Men det sluter inne också" (You see, wool has two characteristics. It protects against cold, against winter and wind. But it also confines). Unlike Gustafsson's previous works of the 1970s, *Yllet* focuses much more on descriptions of nature in Västmanland and of life in the small town of Trummelsberg. The main character, Lars Hedin–born, like Gustafsson, in 1936– has left his career as a university academic to become a math teacher in a junior high school. He becomes increasingly frustrated and disappointed by the petty politics of the school and the community that supports it. Hedin finds relief from his suffocating existence in his efforts to rescue a brilliant student from being expelled because of misbehavior. In the course of helping the teenager, Hedin becomes romantically involved with his girlfriend. The novel is thus both a fierce criticism of the alienating bureaucracy in Sweden and a sensual yet doomed love story.

Gustafsson continued his social criticism in *Familjefesten,* in which social power is no longer merely symbolic but woven into the actual plot of the novel. In the context of a family reunion in the Västmanland countryside, the bureaucrat Lars Troäng reminisces about the government power games that he tried to stop by leaking information to the news media. Surprisingly, instead of the expected scandal, his leaks are suppressed by the media and he is viewed as paranoid. *Familjefesten* constitutes an "action novel" based on certain Swedish political scandals of the 1960s, such as the so-called IB-Affair–an incident of espionage that the secret police in Stockholm mishandled in the early 1960s. The novel both emphasizes Gustafsson's efforts to make visible the infiltration of public lies in society and reflects the topic of the dissertation–language and lies–that he was also writing at the time.

Although *Yllet* and *En biodlares död* have been more popular in Sweden and other countries, Gustafsson writes in the postscript to *Sprickorna i muren* that *Familjefesten* is the darkest of the five novels, while *Sigismund* is the best. *Sigismund* was written during years in Germany, where much of the plot is also set. Although *En resa till jordens medelpunkt och andra dikter,* his poetry volume of ten years earlier, had already evidenced his affinity for Verne, the novel occasioned Gustafsson's first attempt to introduce an element of science fiction into his prose. He makes science fiction thematic in two of the four individual stories in *Sigismund:* in one story about an intergalactic war and in another story about Sigismund, the king of Poland and Sweden in the seventeenth century. King Sigismund role-plays with someone called Mr. Gustafsson, an author writing in Berlin, and a third character, the woman painter Laura G., enhances the complexity of one of the stories as the female version of Mr. Gustafsson. The encouraging outlook "You can, if you want to" emanates from the interaction of these personages. Lies and secrets are conquered as the king awakes in his sarcophagus and Laura G. is allowed to descend into and explore Hell.

Gustafsson introduces psychological and philosophical aspects into the novel to create a light and hopeful conclusion to his exploration of the public lie. The interaction between King Sigismund and Mr. Gustafsson is played out as a philosophical Heraclitean concept of sleep and dream to emphasize the possibility of change and departure. Gustafsson invokes Heraclitus in the postscript to *Sprickorna i muren* to explain his intentions:

> En man tänder om natten ett ljus, har hans ögonljus utsläckts. Levande berör han den döde i römnen; vaken berör han den sovande.
>
> (A man lights a lamp for himself in the night, when the light of his own eyes is extinguished. The living man touches the dead in his sleep; the waking man touches the sleeper.)

This interrelation between sleep and dream recurs in Gustafsson's later poetry and prose, particularly in the novel *Bernard Foys tredje rockad* (1986; translated as *Bernard Foy's Third Castling,* 1988). Furthermore, the presence of Laura G. as a female counterpart to the author continues the idea of the anima that Gustafsson introduced in *Kärleksförklaring till en sefardisk dam.*

En biodlares död, the fifth and final novel of the *Sprickorna i muren* series, is one of Gustafsson's greatest works. Written while Gustafsson was Thord Gray Professor of Literature and Philosophy at the University of Texas at Austin in 1974, the novel is his best received work and has been translated into thirteen languages, including Japanese and Hebrew. Set once again in Västmanland, *En biodlares död* is told in the form of entries from a diary belonging to Lars Westin, a reclusive retired teacher who has died of cancer; before his death he supported himself by raising bees in seclusion. Pain–specifically, the euphoric feeling of freedom from pain–is the

Gustafsson and his second wife, Alexandra Chasnoff Gustafsson (photograph by Hasse Persson)

theme of the novel, which also focuses in part on existential questions and on Jewish mysticism. Moreover, as he once asserted, Gustafsson based *En biodlares död* both on the story of his own decisions regarding religion in Sweden and on the biblical story of Job.

While in Gustafsson's previous works, the narrative voice has been closely linked to the author himself, in *En biodlares död* the narrative "I" dissolves in extreme pain, concluding, "Jag. jag. jag. jag, . . . efter bara fyra gånger ett meningslöst ord" (I, I, I, I, . . . after only four times already a senseless word). Critics who had previously expressed irritation at the self-referential tendencies in Gustafsson's earlier writings received *En biodlares död* with respect and admiration. Åke Janzon wrote in his review in *Svenska Daglbladet* (27 January 1978) that "Lars Gustafsson undervisar inte längre, han lyssnar. Jag tror inte han någonsin nått närmare människan själv än i denna fina och sinnrika bok" (Lars Gustafsson does not teach anymore, he listens. I don't think he has ever come closer to the human self than in this fine, ingenious book).

What was regarded as fantastic and egocentric in Gustafsson's prior works of fiction are transformed in *En biodlares död* into aspects of metaphysical and religious thought. Gustafsson has compared the progression of the novels—and their increasing awareness of the self in society—to the stages of Hell, Purgatory, and Paradise in Dante's *La Commedia* (The Divine Comedy, 1306–1321). The protagonists' discovery of their frailties and fears in the first two novels corresponds to the descent into Hell, while the next two novels reflect Purgatory through the alienation of the main characters from the government and through the influence of dreams and the unconscious on them. Finally, Gustafsson renders Paradise in the fifth novel when Lars Westin, the protagonist of *En biodlares död,* finds comfort and release through spirituality.

While Gustafsson was working on *Sprickorna i muren,* he published a lighthearted novel, *Tennisspelarna: En berättelse* (1977; translated as *The Tennis Players,* 1983). The book is derived from his experiences as a visiting professor at the University of Texas and includes a variety of entertaining stories. In a scene describing an early morning tennis match, for example, the movement of the ball arouses philosophical-mathematical speculations between the players. In another of the narrative strands Gustafsson creates an intriguing mystery based on August Strindberg and his writing of *Inferno* (1897). *Tennisspelarna* was also the first of Gustafsson's novels to be translated into English. Reviewing the book for *The New Yorker* (2 January 1984), John Updike concluded that "It is farce, but underplayed, and swiftly over, leaving a certain resonance of the personal; the conjunction of sunstruck Texas realities with the intellectual murk of fin-de-siècle Northern Europe . . . is of course one the author lived through." Indeed, the intermingling of Strindberg's *Inferno,* Kurt Gödel's mathematical theories, and Nietzsche's philosophical constructs in the novel displays an erudition characteristic of Gustafsson.

Toward the end of the 1970s Gustafsson was at his peak as a poet, novelist, essayist, and intellectual. By then he had established a reputation as a brilliant cultural commentator in Sweden and Germany as well as in France and Italy, countries in which translations of *Den egentliga berättelsen om Herr Arenander* and *Familjefesten* had recently appeared. Although the Västmanland province remained his point of departure, his worldview became more global through travel experiences. His extensive travels in Africa, Asia, Europe, and the United States during this decade resulted in more prose works: *Världsdelar: Reseskildringar* (Continents: Travel Accounts, 1975), *Kinesisk höst* (Chinese Autumn, 1978), and *Afrikanskt försök: En essä om villkoren* (African Effort: An Essay about the Conditions, 1980). In 1977 Gustafsson also published a new collection of poetry, *Sonetter* (Sonnets), embodying thirty sonnets and three sestinas. While critics admired the didactic quality of the verses, they also questioned his skill as a writer of sonnets.

Nonetheless, also during this time, critics often castigated him for displays of carelessness and arrogance in his works of nonfiction. Critics especially received his postdoctorate essay collections such as *Språk och lögn, Konfrontationer: Stycken om konst, litteratur och politik* (Confrontations: Texts About Art, Literature, and Politics, 1979), and *Filosofier: Essäer* (Philosophies: Essays, 1979) with much ambivalence, casting into question his reputation for keen cultural commentary. Thus, although they lauded him for his creative use of fantasy and erudition, they simultaneously found fault with his cavalier attitude toward facts and with his continued tendency to view himself and his opinions as pivotal in social and cultural matters. As Åke Lundquist wrote in *Dagens Nyheter* (18 January 1985) in his review of *Frihet och fruktan: 22 brev* (Freedom and Fear: 22 Letters, 1985)—which Gustafsson cowrote with Per Ahlmark—"Lars Gustafssons debattmetod är auktoritär. I sina åsikter tycks han mig ofta ta miste. Han uttrycker sig arrogant och hånfullt, det är lätt att tycka illa om honom" (Lars Gustafsson's method of debate is authoritarian. His opinions are often based on misinformation. He expresses himself with arrogance and disdain, it is easy to dislike him). On the other hand, while critics questioned Gustafsson's reputation as an intellectual and a social critic, they continued to laud his poetry, particularly *Artesiska brunnar cartesianska drömmar: Tjugotvå lärodikter* (Artesian Wells Cartesian Dreams: Twenty-two Didactic Poems, 1980), excerpts from which were translated in *The Stillness of the World before Bach.* The collection harks back to his earlier poetry and incorporates themes and metaphors such as the natural life of Västmanland, the idea of the anima, the image of turbots frozen with open eyes in the ice, and the philosopher Heraclitus.

In the 1980s Gustafsson went through significant changes in his personal life. In 1981 he converted to Orthodox Judaism. Then in 1982, after divorcing Madeleine Gustafsson, he married Dena Alexandra Chasnoff, a native of Texas. Raised in the Orthodox Judaic tradition, Chasnoff was a main reason behind Gustafsson's decision to convert. In 1983 the couple settled in Austin, where Gustafsson became an adjunct professor at the University of Texas, teaching philosophy, the history of ideas, and literature on a part-time basis. He and his wife have two children, Benjamin and Karin Julia, whom he has mentioned intermittently in recent writings.

Gustafsson's style of writing was also changing at this time. Two novels that appeared in the 1980s, *Sorgemusik för frimurare* (1983; translated as *Funeral Music for Freemasons*, 1987) and *Bernard Foys tredje rockad,* especially signal this development. The linear narrative prevalent in most of his novels of the 1960s and 1970s grows fragmented in the 1980s and assumes postmodern contours. He employed this fragmented technique previously in *Sprickorna i muren,* which follows five distinct protagonists who have the same name, Lars; through the novels in that series Gustafsson suggests that these main characters represent different aspects of one person and could thus be fused into a single character. Furthermore, in both *Sorgemusik för frimurare* and *Bernard Foys tredje rockad* the action is spread over various continents–Europe, Africa, and the United States–and thus emphasizes Gustafsson's new global outlook.

Sorgemusik för frimurare relates the story of three different people–Jan, Ann-Marie, and Hasse–who have known each other since they were students at the University of Uppsala in the 1950s. Jan was an aspiring poet in college but later gave up his literary career when he left Sweden to work as a tour guide in Senegal, Africa. Ann-Marie, Jan's girlfriend at the University of Uppsala, aspired toward a career as an opera singer; her world was the music of Wolfgang Amadeus Mozart, whose *Masonic Funeral March* (1785) is reflected in the title of the novel. After university Ann-Marie leads a lonely life, however, and she never quite succeeds on stage. Hasse, in contrast, becomes a successful nuclear physicist at Harvard and travels the globe to present his research and negotiate business enterprises. He is married and lives in Austin, Texas. Both of the characters who were once aspiring artists face endings: Jan dies from cancer shortly after his return to Sweden after a long period in Africa, while Ann-Marie resigns from her position in the theater to exist merely as a receptionist at a business concern. Hasse, the entrepreneur scientist living in the United States, is the only successful person.

Sorgemusik för frimurare combines elements from Gustafsson's previous works yet hints at his new life in the United States. The character of Jan, who has Gustafsson's birth date, also has much in common with earlier protagonists. For example, like Lars Herdin in *Yllet,* Jan is unable to resist the cancer of bureaucracy and of society and the figurative death that they bring. Like Lars Westin in *En biodlares död,* Jan is also an outsider keen on exploring the existence of a metaphysical presence. Linked romanti-

Dust jacket for Gustafsson's 1986 novel, which combines the memoirs of an elderly poet and passages from a detective novel the poet is writing (from the Swedish Book Review, *1987)*

cally to both Jan and Hasse, Ann-Marie recalls the elusive woman who signifies anima in Gustafsson's works. Furthermore, she is often associated with yellow light, the metaphor that Gustafsson uses to describe moments of harmony and peace in his poetry and prose. The novel ends with a scene in which Hasse is playing tennis in the United States. Although he appears as a peripheral character in the novel, there are hints throughout that he is indeed the main protagonist. Hasse voices the same loss of self as the earlier characters, yet handles the loss in a more constructive way than the others. In spite of his strength he is a transitional figure: he still has one foot in his bourgeois past in Sweden, and he admits that his shadow–his past in Sweden–is stronger than his new self in the United States. Critics have postulated that Hasse, the successful individual, is Gustafsson's idea of a happy person. More accurately, he is a confused and resigned individual who misses his shadow and his playful games with symbols in his youth. In this context *Sorgemusik för frimurare* can be seen as a precursor to the individuation that occurs in *Bernard Foys tredje rockad*.

Bernard Foys tredje rockad is Gustafsson's most postmodern work. The development of three different plots within the novel creates fragmented situations, which–like symbols–are imbued with meaning. The French critic Roland Barthes defined such fragmentation as the ludic technique, the literary game that, according to him, is necessary to break the mirror effect of literature based on reality. For Barthes, the ludic technique makes language visible as a character in the room: the situations become scenes that give the reader more than conventional psychological analysis. This approach matches perfectly both Gustafsson's literary style and his affinity for games, an inclination he probably inherited from Einar, his game-loving father.

Bernard Foys tredje rockad is divided into three sections: "Oktobers månads tak är lågt" (October's Roof Hangs Low), "När blomblad ännu föll om våren" (When Petals Still Fell in the Spring), and "Den mogna åldern" (The Age of Maturity). The first part is a detective story, in which an American rabbi, Bernard Foy, becomes involuntarily drawn into an international espionage ring. In the second section an aging poet named Bernard Foy confesses that he wrote the previous detective story. The old poet has composed the heroic adventure to amuse himself and to avoid writing the promised sequel to his autobiography, which should have been completed a couple of decades earlier. When the poet declares that the successful publication of the first volume of his autobiography, "När blomblad ännu föll om våren," should have been followed by "Den mogna åldern" and "Oktobers månads tak är lågt," Gustafsson is actually combining the poet's reality with the simulated reality and topography of the novel at hand.

Gustafsson alerts the reader to the existence of a metanovel yet negates such an existence by frustrating the reader's expectations: the chronology of the section titles in the novel do not parallel that of Foy's proposed autobiographical work. A separate reality emerges from the titles of the poet's autobiographical project and those of the sections in the actual novel. A third, in-between stage of reality appears, underscoring the close relationship between the novel and Gustafsson's own body of work as a whole and to its autobiographical components. The title "Oktobers månads tak är lågt" and its narrative about the American rabbi points symbolically to the author's own situation as a Jew residing in Texas. The title "När blomblad ännu föll om våren" evokes childhood metaphorically: as Foy the poet spends most of his time reminiscing about his past, he regresses to a stage of infantile dependency. This situation–a Swedish poet or artist dying, whether literally or metaphorically, in his native land–also recalls Jan and Ann-Marie in *Sorgemusik för frimurare*. Finally, although the title of the final section of the novel, "Den mogna åldern," implies a narrative about an individual at a mature age, Gustafsson depicts a teenaged Foy. The teenager behaves with the insights, intellect, and perspective of a mature adult, however, rather than with the emotional despair of a youth who has just lost both of his parents. In many ways Foy as a youth exemplifies the typical Gustafsson protagonist, who suffers in isolation: the teenager hides in the dark heating ducts underneath his town in order to compose the opus that will help him overcome the pain of losing his father–a scenario familiar from *Herr Gustafsson själv*, in which the narrator states that his writing is a "grief work." The unfolding story of *Bernard Foys tredje rockad* conveys how such pain and grief are overcome.

If the three sections of *Bernard Foys tredje rockad* are read in reverse order, they reflect indeed on Gustafsson's literary career as a whole: in the beginning the teenager withdraws into himself and into an underworld to create; then, as a member of the Swedish cultural establishment, the poet–who had been regarded previously as godly by idolizing admirers–withdraws from society after suffering a stroke; and finally, the rabbi, whose courage and intellect help prevent an international nuclear disaster, represents a new culture and genealogy. Withdrawal and isolation, emotional as well as social, has characterized his main characters since Gustafsson's first literary work appeared in 1957. Expressions of anxiety and coldness are present in each work: there are examples of autism and images of Greenland ice in *Bröderna* that reappear in the first two sections of *Bernard Foys tredje rockad*. In *Herr Gustafsson själv* coldness surrounds and exists within the protagonist, and he finds solace only in memories of yellow light and in the act of speaking: ". . . talandet är moderlighet och skydd. Det är min värme, min enda form. Min vagga" (. . . the act of speaking is maternal and protective. It is my warmth, my only form. My cradle). In reverse order, the closure that Rabbi Bernard Foy represents can then be seen as a result of a long discourse that was initiated as a grief work by someone who found solace in the Jewish faith.

William Fovet, in an article for *Horisont* (1987), has emphasized the multidimensional aspect of *Bernard Foys tredje rockad*, defining the text as "ett *öppet*

Cover for Gustafsson's 1989 collection of science-fiction stories (from Swedish Book Review, *1987)*

kenst verk" (an *open* piece of art), a cosmos in itself. This perspective seems natural to an author who admires the complexity of works such as Douglas Hofstadter's *Gödel Escher Bach* (1979), in which the worlds of mathematics, visual art, and music are tied together. Gustafsson has claimed that *Bernard Foys tredje rockad* was written as an effort to transfer mathematical-musical compositions into the structure of a novel. The work also represents his attempt to create a fiction within a fiction. These innovations helped the novel attain a significant place in literary criticism and in literary history. Important as a milestone in Gustafsson's writings, *Bernard Foys tredje rockad* was also published the year that the writer celebrated his fiftieth birthday. At this juncture his life was peaceful and harmonious, as opposed to the identity conflicts and alienation that ruled before, and the novel can therefore be viewed as ending a significant period of Gustafsson's voluminous productivity. When asked whether or not *Bernard Foys tredje rockad* indeed symbolize a kind of closure, Gustafsson affirmed that he had to find "ett nytt språk" (a new language) for his future works.

In 1988 Gustafsson published *Fyra poeter: Gustaf Adolf Fredenlund, Bernard Foy, Ehrmine Wikström, Jan Bohman* (Four poets: Gustaf Adolf Fredenlund, Bernard Foy, Ehrmine Wikström, Jan Bohman), a collection of poetry in which he continues the plays on identity featured in his previous two novels. The four fictive poets personify different age groups and different styles of writing; Foy and Bohman are obviously the poet-protagonists from the two previous novels. Yet, although the reader perceives Gustafsson's influence in *Fyra poeter* through certain references to topics raised in earlier works, an additional understanding of aging and of the passage of time also emerges. Such understanding is heightened in his next collection, *Förberedelser för vintersä- songen: Elegier och andra dikter* (Preparations for the Winter Season: Elegies and Other Poems, 1990). The first part of the volume exhibits thoughtful and nostalgic memories of the past as well as reflections on the present. The juxtaposition of past and present is particularly evident in "Austin, Texas," in which the poet compares his own childhood to that of his young son, Benjamin. The poem makes Gustafsson's situation as an expatriate poignantly clear: that which is natural to the son will always be foreign to the man who grew up in a different culture and climate. Another memorable lyric is "Elegi över den gamla mexikanska kvinnan och hennes döda barn" (translated as "Elegy for the Old Mexican Woman and Her Dead Child" in the 8 October 1990 issue of *The New Yorker*), which Gustafsson wrote in memory of a Mexican woman who had been carrying a dead fetus in her womb for sixty years. The image of this woman still connected to her dead child is analogous to the grief work that the poet expressed in his writings. *Förberedelser för vintersäsongen* brought him two distinguished awards in Sweden: the Bellman Prize of the Royal Swedish Academy in 1990 and the Poetry Prize of the Swedish Broadcasting Corporation in 1993.

Gustafsson's new understanding manifests itself further in the novel *En kakelsättares eftermiddag* (1991; translated as *A Tiler's Afternoon*, 1993), which he refers to as a supplement to *En biodlares död*. Like the earlier narrative, *En kakelsättares eftermiddag* deals with loneliness and human misfortune. The life of the main character, however, has little in common with Gustaffson's own biography. In *En kakelsättares eftermiddag* Torsten Bergman is a retired tiler who lives alone in a decrepit house in which the basement, with all his tools and piles of saved tiles, is flooded with murky water. He receives a call to help a former colleague set tiles in a house under construction. When he arrives, no one is there to confirm his job or offer information, and a mystery begins to emerge as Bergman searches the building. The nameplate of a tenant, Sophie Karlsson, intrigues him; he imagines her both as a woman painter, Sophie K., who is a seductive, redheaded woman dressed in black velvet, and as his former teacher from elementary school. Elusive and absent, Sophie nevertheless has a presence in the text that is reminiscent of how Gustafsson characterizes women in his earlier works. The mysteries of the plot and his conversations with Stig, a colleague, provide the backdrop for Torsten's soliloquies about his past and his misfortunes, which—as in the myth of Sisyphus—impel Torsten to start anew repeatedly. Published simultaneously in Sweden and in Germany, *En kakelsättares eftermiddag* was soon translated into seven languages. While Swedish critics focused on the relation of the novel to Gustafsson's previous works and on its elements of social criticism, critics in France and Italy applauded its philosophical theme.

In 1993, the same year Gustafsson was awarded a John Simon Guggenheim Memorial Foundation Fellowship for poetry, his fifteenth novel was published. *Historien med hunden: Ur en texansk konkursdomares dagböcker och brev* (translated as *The Tale of a Dog: From the Diaries and Letters of a Texan Bankruptcy Judge,* 1998) has been called a *roman noir*– French for "dark novel"–because of its dominant existential theme. Gustafsson considers *Historien med hunden* the third part of a trilogy that began with *En biodlares död*, also recounted in the form of diary entries, and *En kakelsättares eftermiddag*. Apart from the character of Jan van der Rouwers, a Dutch philosopher-semanticist, *Historien med hunden* consists of distinctly Texan personalities. Gustafsson's familiarity with the city of Austin and with life in Texas is evident; he describes places and incidents with the same ease and sensitivity as he did in the earlier narratives that were set in Västerås. Good versus evil constitutes the central theme of *Historien med hunden*, in which two murders set the plot in motion. Erwin Caldwell, a judge, commits the first crime when he kills a stray dog that has been irritating him for some time; Caldwell also empties his trash on his neighbor's well-manicured lawn. The other murder is of van der Rouwers, a professor whose body is found floating in the Texas Colorado River at the Tom Miller Dam. The judge's crime and the subsequent discovery of the professor's anti-Semitic views from pieces he wrote in Belgium during World War II are reminiscent of Gustafsson's affinity for games and for philosophical explorations of identity and ethics.

By the time of the appearance of *Historien med hunden*, Gustafsson had been living in Texas for ten years. For reviewers of *Historien med hunden*, the passage of time and the impressive number of Gustafsson's publications cast his career in a new light. The novel drew quite positive responses, suggesting that critics had abandoned their diatribes against the writer. Magnus Eriksson, for example, writes in his review in *Svenska Dagbladet* on 26 August 1993: "Som vanligt präglas det hela av en oemotståndlig blanding av förströddhet, skarpsinne och infallsrikedom. . . . Som läsare kan man endast tacka för en utsökt roman och önska Herr Gustafsson välkommen hem" (The whole thing is as usual an irresistible mixture of distraction, acumen, and ingenuity. . . . As a reader, one can only express gratitude for an excellent novel and wish Mr. Gustafsson welcome home). The cynicism of past reviewers receded once Gustafsson stopped reflecting on his own life in his writing. Critics also appreciated the novelty of an American setting.

In the 1990s Gustafsson's works largely concern aging and death, perhaps because of personal tragedies and losses involving people close to him. Tomas Tranströmer, an internationally acclaimed poet and Gustafsson's friend, suffered a stroke in 1990; another friend, the esteemed writer Sven Delblanc, died from cancer in 1992; and Yvonne Sandström, Gustafsson's old schoolmate and frequent translator of his works, died in 1994. Most significantly, Gustafsson lost his father Einar, who died at age eighty-six in 1993. These losses inevitably reminded him of human frailty, and thoughts of the past and people from his past pervaded his poetry and prose at this time. One work of nonfiction, *Ett minnespalats,* consists of stories about people and events that have had a significant impact on his life and writings. *Ett minnespalats* features a sensitive and humorous eulogy that he composed for his father in the form of a chapter, "Agenten" (The Agent). In the poetry collection *Stenkista* (Caisson, 1994), Gustafsson compares the burdens of his life to the heaviness and sturdiness of a caisson. The stones that weigh the caisson down symbolize the experiences of his life:

När jag var mycket ung
fanns jag egentligen inte någonstans.

Nu med alla dessa tunga stenar ombord,
och flera kommer varje år, döda vänner,

döda anförvanter, döda förhoppningar,
för att inte tala om de stora blocken av oavslutat,

som snart börjar skymta över ytan
ligger allting ganska fast.

(*Lägga stenkista. Det är tungt.*)

(When I was very young
I didn't really exist anywhere.

Now, with all these stones aboard,
and there are more every year, dead friends,

dead relatives, dead expectations,
not to mention the great weights of unfinished business,

which soon will be visible over the surface
everything rests rather firmly.

[*To plant a caisson. That is heavy.*])

The perspective of an aging man prevails throughout the book, which also includes a poem that divides the narrator's life into decades, "Mina Decennier" (My Decades), as well as another that pays tribute to Delblanc, "Sven Delblanc 1931–1992." In addition, two rhymed poems, "Skåpets sånges" (Songs of the Cupboard) and "Envei," remind the reader of Gustafsson's stylistic playfulness and the origins of his style in the traditional poetry of the 1950s.

Gustafsson's sixteenth novel, *Tjänarinnan: En kärleksroman* (The Maid: A Love Story, 1996), features a prodigal son's return to Sweden. Dick Olsson, a bachelor living in Austin, Texas, and working as a successful consultant of computer images, learns of his mother's death in Stockholm. He has Eleonore, a Colombian and the maid of the title, take care of his house while he is away attending to his loss. Receiving a less than favorable response from critics, the novel lacks the complexity that distinguishes most of the author's earlier works. *Tjänarinnan* is still important, however, for Gustafsson's portrayal of an aging man who tries to come to terms with his loneliness and his past. The descriptions of Olsson's existential loneliness, of his thoughts about his dead mother, and of how to fit his attendance at her funeral in Stockholm into his already busy calendar make this book emblematic of Gustafsson's position at that time as an aging, successful, and busy author.

In the novel *Windy berättar: om sitt liv, om de försvunna och om dem som ännu finns kvar* (1999; Windy Tells: About Her Life, about Those Who Are Gone and Those Who Remain), Gustafsson introduces a young female narrator for the first time. Through a soliloquy delivered by Windy, a hairdresser, the plot develops in the time it takes for her to cut the hair of a University of Texas professor. She tells him about her life and her customers, most of whom are professors or students at the university. The novel recalls Gustafsson's previous book, *Historien med hunden,* in that Windy refers to its major events, such as a certain murder and the boat house fire, and to a main character, Judge Caldwell. Like *En kakelsättares eftermiddag, Windy berättar* is also an existential and philosophical work. While Torsten Bergmann, the protagonist of the earlier novel, struggled fruitlessly to complete a job or to succeed at something, Windy's life story follows her endless struggle to overcome hardships and to support her two daughters as a single mother. Furthermore, Gustafsson's increasing familiarity with the landscape of Texas is evident through his detailed descriptions of nature–which, as passages from his previous books display, also resembles his native Västmanland.

He returns to Västmanland in the short mystery novel, *Blom och den andra magentan* (Blom and the Second Magenta, 2001). The plot concerns a rare stamp: a one-cent British Guiana stamp was colored magenta by mistake in the mid nineteenth century. In 1856 a Swedish captain affixed the stamp to a postcard that he sent to his brother, who was living in the small community of Väster Våla. Someone has now learned about the stamp—the only one like it left in the world—and thinks it might still be hidden in an old nearby estate that remains largely intact. This entertaining thriller, in which an eccentric Stockholm police detective—who is a former theologian—arrives on the scene to solve the mystery, reaffirms Lars Gustafsson's affinity for intellectual games. Despite the general characterization of his writings as "grief work," *Blom och den andra magentan* attests to, if not also underscores, his pleasure in the act of creating.

Interviews:

Disa Håstad, "Lars Gustafsson vågar stå utanför," *Dagens Nyheter* (Stockholm), 3 June 1984;

Mats Gellerfelt, "Lars Gustafsson: En 50-årig pojke som gärna vill ha beröm," *Månads Journalen,* 8 (1986): 54–59;

Margareth Wijk, *Om poesi och vetande,* videotaped interview with Gustafsson, DIA Series, 1987.

References:

Lars Andersson, "Sorgemusik för frimurare," in *Att läsa Gustafsson,* edited by Ruprecht Volz (Stockholm: Norstedt, 1986), pp. 271–282;

Lars Bäckström, *Kulturarbete: Kritik 67–77* (Stockholm: Rabén & Sjögren, 1978), p. 131;

Harold Bloom, *The Western Canon: The Books and School of the Ages* (New York: Harcourt Brace, 1994), p. 557;

Nina Burton, *Den hundrade poeten: tendenser i fem decenniers poesi* (Stockholm: FIB:s Lyrikerklubb, 1988);

Leif Dahlberg, *Tre Romantiska Berättelser: Studier i Eyvind Johnsons* Romantisk berättelse *och* Tidens gång, *Lars Gustafssons* Poeten Brumbergs sista dagar och död *och Svens Delbrancs* Kastrater (Stockholm: Symposion, 1999), pp. 140, 142;

Ia Dübois, "A Subject in Becoming: The Individuation Process in Lars Gustafsson's Fiction," dissertation, University of Washington, 1991;

William Fovet, "Det ljuvt oändliga i verkets inskränkthet semiologiska anmärkningar kring Lars Gustafssons roman *Bernard Foys tredje rockad,*" *Horisont,* 4 (1987): 56–59;

Ruprecht Volz, ed., *Att läsa Gustafsson: En bok om Lars Gustafsson* (Stockholm: Norstedt, 1986).

Papers:

The personal notebooks of Lars Gustafsson are collected in the library at the University of Uppsala in Uppsala, Sweden.

Lars Gyllensten
(12 November 1921 -   )

Barbara Lide
Michigan Technological University

BOOKS: *Camera obscura,* by Gyllensten and Torgny Greitz, as Jan Wictor (Stockholm: Bonnier, 1946);

Moderna myter: Dialektist fantastik (Stockholm: Bonnier, 1949);

Det blå skeppet (Stockholm: Bonnier, 1950);

Barnabok: Romantiska artefakter (Stockholm: Bonnier, 1952)–includes "Leksöndag," translated by Richard B. Vowles as "Sunday Outing" in *Literary Review,* 9 (1965/1966): 267-271;

Carnivora: Konversationsövningar i mänskligt röstläge (Stockholm: Bonnier, 1953);

Senilia: Mimisk essay (Lund: Alba, 1956);

Senatorn: En melodram, en bildningsroman, en bildningsmelodram (Stockholm: Bonnier, 1958);

Sokrates död (Stockholm: Bonnier, 1960);

Desperados (Stockholm: Bonnier, 1962)–includes "Havets frukter," translated by Paul Britten Austin as "Fruits of the Sea" in *Sweden Writes: Contemporary Swedish Poetry and Prose,* selected, with an introduction, by Lars Bäckström and Göran Palm (Stockholm: Prisma, 1965), pp. 96-100;

Kains memoarer (Stockholm: Bonnier, 1963); translated by Keith Bradfield as *The Testament of Cain* (London: Calder & Boyars, 1967);

Nihilistiskt credo: Estetiskt, moraliskt, politiskt m.m. (Stockholm: Bonnier, 1964);

Juvenilia: Inkarnationer och exorcismer (Stockholm: Bonnier, 1965);

Lotus i Hades (Stockholm: Bonnier, 1966)–excerpt translated by Karin Petherick as "From a Writer's Notebooks," *Adam International Review,* 31 (1966): 78-79; excerpt translated by Thomas Teal as "Excerpt from *Lotus in Hades,*" in *Modern Swedish Prose in Translation,* edited by Karl Erik Lagerlöf (Minneapolis: University of Minnesota Press, 1979), pp. 15-22;

Diarium spirituale: Roman om en röst (Stockholm: Bonnier, 1968);

Palatset i parken: Retoriskt porträtt i Giuseppe Arcimboldos manér (Stockholm: Bonnier, 1970);

Lars Gyllensten

Ur min offentliga sektor (Stockholm: Aldus/Bonnier, 1971);

Mänskan djuren all naturen: Läsefrukter och kompotter (Stockholm: Bonnier, 1971);

Grottan i öknen (Stockholm: Bonnier, 1973)–untitled excerpt translated by Barry Jacobs and Leif Sjöberg as "The Witness" in *Fiction,* 11 (1992): 69-71;

I skuggan av Don Juan (Stockholm: Bonnier, 1975);

Lapptäcken-Livstecken: Ur arbetsanteckningarna (Stockholm: Författarförlaget, 1976);

Baklängesminnen (Stockholm: Bonnier, 1978);

Klipp i 70-talet (Stockholm: Alba, 1979);

Huvudskallebok: Roman i tre turer: Vindmannen, Kurri Kulum, Huvudskallebok (Stockholm: Bonnier, 1981);

Provdockan (Stockholm: Bonnier, 1983);
Rätt och slätt: Anteckningar från det där pensionatet som jag bodde på när jag skulle lära upp mig till en bättre människa (Stockholm: Bonnier, 1983);
Skuggans återkomst eller Don Juan går igen (Stockholm: Bonnier, 1985);
Sju vise mästare om kärlek (Stockholm: Bonnier, 1986);
Hjärnfilspån: Vittra vederstyggligheter och annat smått och gott, as Pär Silje (Stockholm: Atlantis, 1989);
Just så eller kanske det: Ur arbetsanteckningarna (Stockholm: Bonnier, 1989);
Det himmelska gästabudet (Stockholm: Bonnier, 1991);
Så var det sagt: Essäer, artiklar, inlägg (Stockholm: Bonnier, 1992);
Hack i häl på Minerva: Ett brevsamtal om vetenskap, dikt och moral, by Gyllensten and Georg Klein (Stockholm: Bonnier, 1993);
Anteckningar från en vindskupa (Stockholm: Bonnier, 1993);
Augustin och Celestine: Om nåra små loppors liv och leverne (Stockholm: Bonnier, 1995);
Ljuset ur skuggornas värld (Stockholm: Bonnier, 1995);
Kistbrev (Stockholm: Bonnier, 1998);
Minnen, bara minnen (Stockholm: Bonnier, 2000).

OTHER: "Information–skeninformation och brus," in *Människan i framtidens kommunikationssamhälle: föredrag och diskussioner från ett symposium arrangerat av Sekretariatet för framtidsstudier, Statsrådsberedningen, den 29-30 november på Rönneberga kursgård, Lidingö* (Stockholm: Justitiedepartementet, 1973); translated as "Information, Pseudo-information and Noise" in *Man in the Communications System of the Future,* edited by the Secretariat for Future Studies (Stockholm, 1974), pp. 39-46;
"Carl von Linné: Blomsterkung och diktare," in *Författarnas litteraturhistoria,* book 1, edited by Lars Ardelius and Gunnar Rydström (Stockholm: Författarförlag, 1977), pp. 118-132;
"François Rabelais," in *Författarnas litteraturhistoria: De utländska författarna,* book 1, edited by Ardelius, Björn Håkansson, and Lars Forssell (Stockholm: Författarförlag, 1980), pp. 181-196;
"Varför inte Kristendom?" in *Varför inte Kristendom?* by Gyllensten and others (Älvsjö: Skeab, 1981), pp. 9-26;
"Intelligens och kreativitet," in *Om kreativitet och flow,* edited by Maj Ödman and Georg Klein (Stockholm: Bromberg, 1990), pp. 181-189; translated by Keith Bradfield as "Intelligence and creativity" in *Dialogue and Technology: Art and Knowledge,* edited by Bo Göranzon and Magnus Florin (London: Springer-Verlag 1991), pp. 131-136;

"Opening Address," in *Strindberg, O'Neill and the Modern Theatre: Address and Discussions at Nobel symposium at the Royal Dramatic Theatre, Stockholm,* edited by Claes Englund and Gunnel Bergström (Stockholm: Entré/Riksteatern, 1990), pp. 9-14.

SELECTED PERIODICAL PUBLICATIONS–UNCOLLECTED: "Senilia: Tankar kring berättande och kring Thomas Mann," *Bonniers Litterära Magasin,* 24 (1955): 618-622;
"Angelägen teologi–teologi om viktiga ting. Samtal mellan Krister Stendahl och Lars Gyllensten," *Vår lösen,* 67 (1976): 349-354;
"Om litteraturens kommunikationskris," *Biblioteksbladet,* 61 (1976): 101-104.

Lars Gyllensten–novelist, essayist, satirist, and critic–is one of the foremost contemporary Swedish writers; indeed, he has been described as the only contemporary author that Sweden could present to the world as one meriting comparison with Thomas Mann and Samuel Beckett. Highly prolific and winner of several literary awards, Gyllensten still is not as well known beyond Sweden as he might be, for few of his works have been translated into widely read languages. Even in Sweden, his popular appeal is limited, for his texts–intellectually stimulating, aesthetically pleasing, and often rife with irony and playful humor–place demands on readers that not all readers of more popular literature are willing to meet. A highly cerebral wordsmith of considerable intellectual range and erudition, Gyllensten challenges readers to examine critically the various philosophical and moral ideas that he discusses. Those who accept the challenge are well rewarded.

Lars Johan Wictor Gyllensten was born in Stockholm on 12 November 1921 to Carl Gyllensten, director of a Swedish branch of a German machinery firm, and Ingrid, née Rangström, sister of the Swedish composer Ture Rangström. Except for long summers spent in the Stockholm archipelago or on a farm in southern Sweden, Gyllensten grew up in Stockholm, where he still lives and works. In his late teens, while attracted to scientific studies, he also exhibited a strong interest in literature and philosophy, reading Immanuel Kant and Friedrich Nietzsche and also becoming acquainted with Arthur Schopenhauer and Søren Kierkegaard, whose influence on his own thought he readily acknowledges. Like many young people confronting existential questions, Gyllensten was concerned with the question of how to live in a meaningful way, a concern that caused him to waver between choosing to study philosophy and literature or to study medicine. In 1940 he entered the Karolinska Institutet (Caroline Institute–Stockholm's medical university), where in 1953 he defended his doctoral dissertation and became an associate professor, advancing in 1955 to professor. In 1975 he was elected a member of the Royal Swedish Academy of Sciences.

In his years as a medical student, during which he published many papers in medical journals, Gyllensten continued to cultivate his interest in literature and philosophy, as well as his skills as a writer. By the time he received his doctoral degree, he already had published three books, including two novels, as well as many book reviews and essays on questions regarding medicine, psychology, society, politics, and literature.

In 1966 he was elected to the Swedish Academy, and in 1968 he was appointed to the Academy's Nobel Committee. In 1973, though having achieved international recognition for his scientific work, he inclined more toward his literary interests and left the Karolinska Institutet to devote himself to writing. In 1977 he was appointed permanent secretary of the Swedish Academy, a position he held until 1989. In that year, when his colleagues in the Academy refused to protest against the Iranian death order for Salman Rushdie, Gyllensten withdrew from active participation in the Academy.

Gyllensten's literary debut, in 1946, was, interestingly, a hoax. With a fellow medical student, Torgny Greitz, he composed, in one evening, a book of parodic poems, *Camera obscura,* imitating the obscure poetry popular in Sweden in the 1940s. Under the pseudonym Jan Wictor, he and Greitz submitted the book to publishing house Bonnier, where it was accepted and published. The two men acknowledged their spoof in an article in Stockholm's newspaper *Dagens nyheter* (30 December 1946).

Gyllensten's playful entry onto the literary scene exhibited his satirical bent, his sense of the ludic, and his gift for parody—elements evident in his subsequent work. His serious literary debut came in 1949 with *Moderna myter: Dialektist fantastik* (Modern Myths), subtitled "Dialectic Fantasia" and bearing the motto "Creo [sic] quia absurdum" (a collection of aphorisms, poems, vignettes, and short stories), which he described in this same book as "Boken försöker demonstrera möjligheten av att leva utan omedelbarhet, naivitet, engagement eller tro men a stället med en alltid verkande, illusionslös vilja, gör sin egen plikt" (an attempt to demonstrate the possibility of living without involvement, naiveté, or faith, but instead with a constantly active, illusionless will, which fulfills its obligation to itself). *Moderna myter* begins a series of dialectical works that exhibit a method akin to that employed by Gyllensten's acknowledged "master," Kierkegaard. As Gyllensten explains in his afterword, this technique is rooted in a crisis similar to that of Kierkegaard, who suffered "the misfortune of experiencing the collapse of the naive and self-evident engagement in the Christian faith." Gyllensten's loss of faith, which he calls "the bankruptcy of naïveté," resulted from observing a world plagued by sickness, suffering, death, unhappiness, ruthlessness, and misuse of power. His pessimistic views were confirmed by the shattering experience of World War II, with atrocities perpetrated first on the victims of the Nazi holocaust and, subsequently, on hundreds of thousands of Japanese civilians by those whom Gyllensten had regarded as "the fighters for democracy and human rights." Gyllensten further defines the bankruptcy of naiveté as the death of ideology, the collapse of political, philosophical, religious, moral, and scientific worldviews. Paradoxically, while this collapse renders people helpless and insecure, it frees them from former limitations of thought and action, enabling them to experiment with new philosophies and moral systems. The task, after World War II, was to search for a humanistic and moral philosophy in an absurd world that lacked a system of absolute values. Gyllensten once described his search as an "oavslutbar" (neverending) process or, borrowing a term from Charles Sanders Peirce, an "infinite inquiry," related, though not identical to, scientific research in a laboratory. Gyllensten's "laboratory" is the printed page.

The bankruptcy of naiveté, a theme prominent in Swedish literature of the 1940s, compares with the form of existentialism presented by Jean-Paul Sartre and Albert Camus. A striking similarity exists, for example, between Gyllensten's examination of the idea of living without involvement, as expressed in *Moderna myter,* and Camus's portrayal, in *L'Etranger* (1942; translated as *The Stranger,* 1946), of Meurseult, who does indeed live without involvement. Also noteworthy is the similarity between one of Gyllensten's aphorisms in *Moderna myter* and the ending of Camus's *Le Mythe de Sisyphe* (1942; translated as *The Myth of Sisyphus,* 1955); Camus asserts that Sisyphus, who must conduct his struggle without hope, is indeed a happy man. Gyllensten playfully echoes Camus's idea in his aphorism "Tillvaron är en dödsdans. Men det står oss i alla fall fritt att göra den till en rumba" (Existence is a dance of death. But we are, in any case, free to make it into a rumba).

Marked by its dialectic and parodic character, *Moderna myter* sets the tone for Gyllensten's literary production. All his books, for the most part, examine existential alternatives and attitudes toward life. Although they certainly can be read and appreciated individually, together they form a continuum. As Gyllensten himself stated in an essay included in the collection *Ur min offentliga sektor* (From My Public Sector, 1971), "Jag skriver egentligen inte böcker–jag försöker bygga upp ett författarskap. De enskilda böckerna skall kunna stå var och en för sig–men de ingår också i en helhet. De samtalar med varandra och polemiserar mot varandra, de kompletterar varandra och belyser varandra. Jag vill at mina böcker skall alstra ett gemensamt spänningsfält, som uppkommer just genom deras inbördes samstämmigheter och motsatser" (I actually do not write books–I am attempting to build up an authorship. The individual books ought to be able to stand for themselves–but they also form a single entity. They converse with each other, they complement each other, and they illuminate each other. I want my books to produce a common field of tension that arises precisely out of the reciprocal concord and discord of their content).

Gyllensten followed *Moderna myter* with the novel *Det blå skeppet* (The Blue Ship, 1950). Opposing the idea of living without involvement and maintaining an ironic, often cynical, distance from life, *Det blå skeppet* advocates a romantic affirmation of life. In contrast to the "modern" myths of the first book, this book harks back to the Middle Ages. Its setting, the steamboat "Framåt gunga" (Forward Roll), has been linked to the medieval worldview: its captain, enthroned on the bridge, represents God, the crew are the people on Earth, and the stokers in the engine room are the inhabitants of Hell.

The novel begins with a quotation from Sebastian Brant's *Das Narrenschiff* (The Ship of Fools, 1393), and in many ways, the ship is indeed a ship of fools. The protagonist is Abraham, the son of the ship's cook, Emma, who protects him from the fools, especially from a "Professor" Cherubini, a grotesque "Master of Black Magic." Cherubini has developed his lack of involvement with the world to the extent that he has no feelings at all, and he wants to buy Abraham and train him to be his successor. Emma gets rid of Cherubini (she manages to cast him overboard), for she wants to teach Abraham to be involved in life, to accept life, with its joys as well as its sorrows. In the final chapter, "Abraham's Sacrifice"–a title alluding both to the Bible and to Kierkegaard's Abraham in *Frygt og Baevan* (Fear and Trembling, 1843)–Emma illustrates the theme of the book, to "bet on the miracle," as she and Abraham row off in a lifeboat and she steps off the boat onto the water, walking over the waves until she disappears on the horizon. Her courage and her action to save her son from an empty existence by "betting on the miracle" is a strong invocation to embrace life, with whatever it has to offer.

Gyllensten's third book, the novel *Barnabok* (Infantilia, 1952), juxtaposes the opposing attitudes toward life examined in *Moderna myter* and *Det blå skeppet*–detachment and almost unconditional affirmation and acceptance. The protagonist, Karl-Erik, vacillates between them, primarily as they are represented by two women–Klem, whom he marries because he believes it is reasonable to do so, and Lucy, for whom he feels a passion so strong that he abandons Klem for her. At the age of approximately thirty, Karl-Erik exhibits the naiveté of a child, as well as a child's potential for violent and irrational behavior. His actions are infantile, unconscionable, and violent. Unlike Abraham, the young boy in *Det blå skeppet* who surrenders to life, Karl-Erik inclines toward death. In an attempt to create a bond that would make him and Lucy inseparable, he kills Lucy's baby girl, whom he sees as a barrier to their relationship, by drowning her in the bathtub. Metaphorically, he also kills the terrible child that he feels within himself. There is no resolution. He simply is taken away by the police, thus ending Gyllensten's third book of what has been called by Bertil Palmqvist a "dialectic trilogy" on a violent and grim note.

The somber tone continues in Gyllensten's next work, *Carnivora: Konversationsövningar i mänskligt röstläge* (Carnivores: Conversation Exercises on a Human Voice Level, 1953). The carnivores of the title are primarily humans living in a "dog-eat-dog" world. They visit upon each other outrageous grotesqueries, both individually, as illustrated by the rape of an eleven-year-old girl, and collectively–exemplified by Herod's Slaughter of the Innocents, the brutalities of the Franco-Spanish War, and the ravages of Nazism, with its brutal treatment of Jews. *Carnivora* also criticizes Christianity, with its tendency to "divide people into lambs and goats through the whole of its history." Finally, Gyllensten targets Germans and World War II, including in his text the German drinking song "Wer soll das bezahlen?"(Who is supposed to pay for this?) and making clear the impossibility of compensating for the losses of life and limb.

Before publishing his next novel, *Senilia: Mimisk essay* (Senilia: Mimic Essay, 1956), Gyllensten, pondering questions regarding narration, wrote the essay "Senilia: Tankar kring berättande och kring Thomas Mann" (Senilia: Reflections on Narration and on Thomas Mann), published in *Bonniers Litterära Magasin* in 1955. He compares Mann, whose works char-

Dust jacket for Gyllensten's 1989 collection of essays, anecdotes, and observations from his notebooks (from Swedish Book Review, *1990)*

acteristically include an immanent ironic narrator, with James Joyce, whose narrative technique is that of the absent author. Associating himself with Mann, Gyllensten switched, for a time, from using a first-person narrator (albeit with many ironic chapter titles generated by a detached narrator) to telling his stories from the perspective of an immanent third-person narrator.

Senilia is also Proustian in that, while the surface action is limited (the protagonist, Torsten Leer, lies awake on a Sunday morning, gets up, eats breakfast, and walks the dog), much action occurs in Leer's reflections. One of Leer's goals, like that of Karl-Erik in *Barnabok,* is to destroy the child within himself. To achieve this goal, he applies "förtrogenhetens färla" (the rod of familiarity) to his life, as a father might apply the rod to a child as a disciplinary measure. The technique he uses is recollection—recognizing himself in all the painful situations he can recall and eventually seeing himself objectively, as a creature he can observe with indifference. In keeping with his dialectic technique, Gyllensten not only presents Leer as a counterpart to Karl-Erik; he also creates within *Senilia* a foil character, Gunnar Gren—self-destructive and strongly reminiscent of Karl-Erik—to further examine opposing attitudes toward life.

The subtitle to Gyllensten's novel *Senatorn: En melodram, en bildningsroman, en bildningsmelodram* (The Senator, 1958) describes it as "a melodrama, a Bildungsroman, a Bildungsmelodrama." It is the tale of Antonin Bhör, whose name is a variation of the Swedish verb *bör* (ought to), a prominent Marxist politician in an authoritarian socialist state. Through experience, Bhör has come to regard his government, his situation, and life in general as a confusing Tower of Babel. Questioning his beliefs, he acts erratically and is called to account by the governor—a man named, interestingly, Treblinka. On the final page Treblinka dismisses Bhör, ordering him, in a blaring voice, not to exit through the main door to his office, for which Bhör was heading, but through a narrow side door next to the servant's door. The reader is left to guess Bhör's fate. Is his folly enough to prompt his eradication, or is he so insignificant that he simply is dismissed?

Gyllensten presents in *Senatorn* echoes of Mann's *Der Tod in Venedig* (1912; translated as *Death in Venice*, 1925), as well as three themes that he develops in subsequent works. Like Mann's protagonist, Gustav von Aschenbach, Bhör is fascinated by a young boy whom he meets at a resort hotel. Unlike Aschenbach, Bhör does not appear to have a fatal obsession with sexual love for the boy; he does, however, appear to be similarly doomed. Aschenbach, who has lived a controlled, systematic life, is suddenly confronted with irrational elements and experiences that upset his well-ordered existence and finally lead to his death. Bhör, too, becomes alienated from the philosophy and the rigid system that he had espoused, and he is left with an emptiness that he cannot fill.

Bhör meets Elisabeth, a forward, sarcastic, self-defined nymphomaniac, with whom he spends two nights at a country inn. They discuss briefly the idea of living "det lilla livet," the simple, everyday, unreflected life that they observe around them, as opposed to Senator Bhör's "important" official life. The theme of the "little life," related somewhat to that of the acceptance of life illustrated in *Det blå skeppet*, is carried out extensively in Gyllensten's next novel, *Sokrates död* (The Death of Socrates, 1960), as well as in several other works.

Gyllensten introduces two other ideas that he developed in subsequent works. The first, which became prominent in *Kains memoarer* (1963; translated as *The Testament of Cain*, 1967), is the necessity of iconoclasm, of destroying the old forms and images that surround everyone, so that they might live free to develop, to act, and to be productive.

Elisabeth introduces the last theme when she calls herself "Pasaphae." The narrator suggests that Pasiphae, the wife of King Minos, who mated with a bull and gave birth to the Minotaur, was not primarily attracted to the bestial but instead was seeking something stronger than and beyond humanity. More significantly, the narrator reminds the reader that all that is known about Pasiphae has come through the stories of others, primarily of those who came after her, and that these stories keep her alive. Such comments, typical of narrators in reflexive novels, constitute a leitmotiv in *Sokrates död* and *Kains memoarer*.

On the first page of *Sokrates död* the narrator states that his story is about a famous and frequently described death, and, like those who have told about it earlier, he cannot present a firsthand account. Gyllensten borrows material from Plato, Xenophon, Diagones Laërtius, and Kierkegaard; he also alludes to Mann's *Joseph und seine Bruder* (Joseph and His Brothers, 1933-1943) and to the Bible. Still, he presents his own fascinating and original version. Socrates does not appear in the novel, except as a corpse–and yet, he is the focus of the story. Gyllensten provides him with two wives–Myrto (mentioned by Diogenes Laërtius) as well as Xanthippe. He includes a daughter, Aspasia, possibly inspired by a clever young girl in Kierkegaard's *Afsluttende uvidenskabelig efterskrift* (Concluding Unscientific Postscript, 1846), who appears to know at sixteen years of age what it has taken Socrates seventy years to learn. In keeping with Gyllensten's dialectic mode, Aspasia, though resembling her father in some ways, represents opposing viewpoints. She joins the other female characters, whom Gyllensten presents in a sympathetic light, as they criticize the egotistic, stubborn ambition of the philosopher and extol the virtues of "the little life," described by Gyllensten in an interview as "det som försiggår i Kåltäppan som Voltaire talade om" (that which goes on in the cabbage patch that Voltaire spoke about).

In 1962 Gyllensten published *Desperados*, a collection of "expressionistic novellas," many of which are preliminary sketches for later novels about people who have taken a wrong path in life because the idols and ideologies they have followed have led them astray. In an introductory essay, which, not unusual for Gyllensten, is in the form of an interview, he refers to the novellas as "spiritual exercises," through which he examines ways of regarding ideas, individual lives, and earthly existence in general. His method of examining ideas by means of creating short fiction, or a blend of fiction and literary nonfiction, has its roots in *Moderna myter* and *Carnivora* and continues in *Mänskan djuren all naturen: Läsefrukter och kompotter* (Humans, Animals, All of Nature: Fruits of Reading and Compotes, 1971), *Lapptäcken–Livstecken: Ur arbetsanteckningarna* (Patchwork Quilts–Signs of Life: From My Notebooks, 1976), and *Just så eller kanske det: Ur arbetsanteckningarna* (Just Right or Perhaps This Way: From My Notebooks, 1989). With these collections of short essays, stories, anecdotes, and observations, Gyllensten enables readers to follow his reflections on a myriad of topics, including thoughts on what he himself has been reading, contemplating, and writing.

Also contributing to an understanding of Gyllensten's works and viewpoints on various topics and issues are the books *Nihilistiskt credo: Estetiskt, moraliskt, politiskt m.m.* (Nihilistic Creed: Aesthetic, Moral, and Political etc., 1964), *Ur min offentliga sektor, Klipp i 70-talet* (Clippings from the 1970s, 1979), and *Så var det sagt: Essäer, artiklar, inlägg* (Thus It Was Spoken: Essays, Articles, Contributions, 1992)—collections of essays and notes, many of them previously published, on aesthetic, literary, moral, political, and other topics. To these books can be added Gyllensten's thought-provoking correspondence with Georg Klein, cancer research specialist and fellow doctor-turned-writer, published under the title *Hack i häl på Minerva: Ett brevsamtal om vetenskap, dikt och moral* (On the Heels of Minerva: An Epistolary Discussion of Science, Literature, and Morals, 1993). Gyllensten is on record, however, for having cautioned readers, as quoted by Thure Stenström, "not to take him too seriously" when he writes about his own work, for, as he argues, writers "are seldom able to give a fair account of their own intentions" and that "the final artistic outcome is often far from their intentions or what they remember as having been their original intentions." Also, Gyllensten wrote to Barbara Lide in a letter dated 29 July 1992, stating "Det är ju inte sakert att en författare är den som bäst analyserar sina verk" (It is, of course, not certain that a writer is the one who best analyzes his work).

Gyllensten followed *Desperados* with *Kains memoarer*, a work that originally was a part of the novel *Juvenilia: Inkarnationer och exorcismer* (Juvenilia: Incarnations and Exorcisms, 1965) but developed into a separate novel. In 1962 *Bonniers Literära Magasin* printed two chapters of *Kains memoarer* with an introductory note, in which Gyllensten explained that his purpose was to enlarge upon the argument, introduced in *Senatorn* and *Sokrates död,* that, if people are to develop and live meaningful lives, they must first destroy their firmly established images of reality, discard rigid ways of thinking, and adopt an iconoclastic approach to life. The iconoclasm that he advocates, initially presented as a theme, led to new developments in form and narrative technique as well. Adopting the collage method similar to that used in the visual arts, Gyllensten composed *Kains memoarer* as a collection of tales, novellas, aphorisms, and observations, all pieced together by an anonymous historicist whose task is to chronicle the history of the Cainites, a sect of heretics who lived in upper Egypt in the years following the birth of Christ. The Cainites suffered, both at the hands of Roman soldiers and of Christians who persecuted those whose thinking differed from their own. Realizing that their sect was dying out, they wrote down their tales to preserve their history. The collage that Gyllensten's narrator creates is made up of both his own writings and of the fragments left behind by Cain, including his account of killing Abel and smashing Abel's stone image. After the fratricide Cain is compelled to break out of his agricultural life and begin anew.

The figure of Cain also plays a role in *Juvenilia,* the novel in which he originally appeared. *Juvenilia* has been compared with August Strindberg's *Ett drömspel* (1901; translated as *The Dreamplay,* 1912) in that, like the characters in that play, its characters too seem to split, double, and multiply, with one consciousness holding sway over them all. Gyllensten himself alludes both to *Ett drömspel* as well as to "Strindberg-pastiches" in the novel. The characters in *Juvenila* do indeed seem occasionally to drift in and out of one another, so that readers might find themselves uncertain as to who is narrating what they are reading. This effect is all in keeping with Gyllensten's collage technique, which in this novel includes a partly metafictional third-person account by a narrator who assumes the pseudonym "Cain"; conversations; letters written by the characters (including one addressed to Lars Gyllensten that is never sent); and first-person narratives by the main characters. The author provides short, "factual" curricula vitae of the three main characters: Torsten Mannelin, a doctor and supervisor of a home for retarded children; Evert von Pierow, a sculptor; and Erik Vickler (who also appears in *Senilia*), an epileptic engineer who lives off the assets from a plastics factory he once owned. The fictional letter from Mannelin, presumably to Gyllensten, includes an allusion to *Kains memoarer:* the correspondent refers to a literary project involving a "found manuscript," consisting of twenty pages, written in Greek, supposedly in the second and third centuries after the birth of Christ by members of a gnostic sect in northern Egypt, and purchased by the correspondent's former wife from a dealer of antiquities in Paris.

Through all these pieces of the patchwork collage, however, run common themes and ideas, some of which form a dialectical counterpart to *Senilia*. As Gyllensten points out in his essay "Röster om hösten" (Voices on Autumn), published in *Ur min offentliga sektor,* the characters in each novel are men between thirty and forty years old who have a strong sense of the Schopenhauerian view that life swings like a pendulum between pain and ennui, that pain and suffering can only be overcome by emptiness, and that ennui can only be destroyed by pain. In *Juvenilia,* Mannelin, von Pierow, and Vickler are men who live alone; they are either divorced, separated, or have never married. They have, to a certain extent, reached what Torsten Leer in *Senilia* was striving for: they have overcome pain. They have paid a terrible price, however, for the overcoming of pain has led to "en Obotlig leda, en dödande och förlamande steril egocentricitet" (an incurable ennui, a killing, paralyzing, and sterile egocentricity). Again, Gyllensten is illustrating the problems of a way of life carried too far. The men long to break out of their empty lives, even if it means a return to suffering. Part of what constitutes their suffering is their feeling of helplessness vis-à-vis the suffering of others, especially of children. Mannelin can do little for his incurably spastic son, and the other two are impotent in their efforts to help a retarded and sadly mistreated girl. The idea of sympathy and helplessness in the face of other people's suffering recurs in Gyllensten's subsequent works—prominently, for example, in *Grottan i öknen* (The Cave in the Desert, 1973), an illustrative excerpt of which has been translated into English under the title "The Witness" in the journal *Fiction* in 1992.

In *Lotus i Hades* (Lotus in Hades, 1966), Gyllensten opposes the feelings of frustration arising from being helpless in the face of human suffering by positing an attitude of indifference. He already had introduced this opposite stance in *Juvenilia* by having the character von Pierow refer to "the bestial and paradisiacal freedom that exists beyond human sympathy." Gyllensten prefaces *Lotus i Hades* with the refrain from Charles Baudelaire's "L'Invitation au voyage" (Invitation to a Voyage): "Là, tout n'est qu'ordre et beauté, / Luxe, calme et volupté" (There, there is nothing but order and beauty, / Luxury, calm and sensuous pleasure). Baudelaire, in other poems, wrote of the Lotus Eaters depicted in book 10 of Homer's *Odyssey* that Gyllensten alludes to in his title, as well as of Cain and Abel and "Don Juan aux Enfers" (Don Juan in Hell), whom Gyllensten includes among his shades in the netherworld. *Lotus i Hades* also bears characteristics of the French Nouveau Roman. A short lyrical work, it consists of vignettes—some of which resemble prose poems—about the characters who inhabit Hades, including Don Juan, Cain, Romeo, Odysseus, Tiresias, Jocasta, and Astyanax. Gyllensten has his characters describe themselves as wandering aimlessly in a borderland between life and death. They have forgotten almost everything of their lives on earth, and when they do come to remember anything painful, they save themselves with their "Elysian drink," which causes them to have "a brief feeling of intoxication, a quick *frenesi*–voluptuousness and oblivion." Expressing moral indignation, Gyllensten relates the escapist nature of the characters in *Lotus i Hades* to attitudes of the people of Western Europe, which he describes in the novel as "the glass veranda of Asia, with a view of the sunset," filled with only "housebroken" people who know how to behave in a house of glass. There one can live well, like the lotus eaters in Hades, and ignore the problems and sufferings of others.

With his next novel, *Diarium spirituale: Roman om en röst* (Spiritual Diary: A Novel about a Voice, 1968), Gyllensten came, in his own words, "as close to a genuine experiment as one can get." A work exemplifying Gyllensten's collage technique, *Diarium spirituale* is a reflexive novel, displaying, with its blend of fiction, metafiction, and nonfiction, a high degree of romantic irony. It is also a self-begetting novel that demonstrates the active creative process of the novelist at work. Gyllensten includes in it reflections from a personal diary and from his working notebooks that might be factual but become part of the fiction; the retelling of myths; and discussions of literature and of his literary predecessors, including, primarily, Strindberg and Emanuel Swedenborg. He also introduces the idea of what he calls "en svensk galenskapslinje" (a line of Swedish madmen): Swedenborg, with his "correspondences," his *Drömboken* (Dream Books, 1859), and his *Diarium Spirituale* (1883–1902); Carl von Linné, with his *Nemesis divina* (est. 1748); and Strindberg, with his "blå böcker" (blue books), his *Drömspel,* and his visions of Inferno. This concept is perhaps a foreshadowing of Gyllensten's fascination of the figure of the "Holy Fool" that appears in later works, such as *Grottan i öknen* and *I skuggan av Don Juan* (In the Shadow of Don Juan, 1975).

In contrast to the figures in *Lotus i Hades,* who remain in a state of semioblivion, Gyllensten presents in *Diarium spirituale* a creative writer as one who experiences a state of lethargy and descends, symbolically, into the underworld, into the hell of sterility and nonproductivity, and then returns to life, renewed and seeking to know what life might demand of him and what meaning it might have for him. Gyllensten retells the myth of the Babylonian goddess Ishtar, whose death, descent into the underworld, and triumphant resurrection parallel his own situation and the situation of many creative artists. In his painful and lethargic state Gyllensten compares himself to Cain, who, after his iconoclasm and fratricide, lived like an animal in the wilderness. What Gyllensten seeks now, however, is not the iconoclast but the inspirational voice of his novel's subtitle, the voice of Orpheus, who returned from the underworld to resume singing his enchanting song. *Diarium spirituale* concludes with Gyllensten's observation that, in writing the novel, he cast off the role of Cain and assumed that of Orpheus–a figure who returns to life and will continue to seek meaning in it.

Palatset i parken: Retoriskt porträtt i Giuseppe Arcimboldos manér (The Palace in the Park: Rhetorical Portrait in the Manner of Giuseppe Arcimboldo, 1970) has been described as "a dreamplay in the form of a novel." A man returns to his past, to a rooming house he lived in as a schoolboy, when the house belonged to a Russian named Lew Elfberg (a name that appears in *Diarium spirituale* and again in *Grottan i öknen*). Like Torsten Leer in *Senilia,* the man relives his life through his memories, many of which spring vividly to life in the old house. Some of his recollections, however, seem to come back in different versions, which is in keeping with the dream-like character of the novel. Still, as Gyllensten's protagonist sifts through his memories, he presents for the reader information about the forces that shaped his existence. His marriage, for example, resembles that of his parents. In both marriages the husband cares as best he can for an invalid wife, and communication between them dwindles to few words—and, in the protagonist's case, some violent arguments. The husband has extramarital affairs, and eventually the wife dies. Both men are ridden with feelings of inadequacy and guilt. The question arises whether the protagonist has been so affected by his parents' marriage that he patterns his own unhappy marriage after theirs. In any case, both men are plagued with the feeling of inadequacy in the face of suffering—a topic poignantly introduced in *Juvenilia* and further illustrated in *Palatset i parken* and later novels.

Palatset i parken concludes with the man going to sleep in the old house, perhaps even to his death. Interestingly, the otherwise pessimistic novel ends on a more positive note. The last words of the novel appear to be from the character's stream of consciousness, words that stress the importance of participating in life, which leads to freedom and reconciliation. These words are followed by the narrator's simple conclusion, "Och så var det ingenting mer. Dagen har upphört" (And then there was nothing more. The day had ended.)

One of the leitmotivs of *Palatset i parken* is the idea that only the gods can create something out of nothing. Humans, the offspring and journeymen of the Demiurge, cannot create; they can only re-create. They are not made in the image of God, but are servants of the Demiurge, serving among epigones, plagiarists, and bunglers. While there are external forces that create who people are, they also create themselves by what they do. This idea is associated with the subtitle of the novel: Gyllensten explains, on the dust jacket, that Giuseppe Arcimboldo is a kind of model for the novel. The observant Arcimboldo noticed that the face of a librarian is made up of books, for example, and that of a gardener is made up of turnips, rutabagas, cucumbers, and lettuce leaves. Similarly, the man in Gyllensten's novel is presented as being made up of his ideas and the memories of his own experiences; he is, however, also a slave to that which he believes himself to rule over.

While working on *Palatset i parken,* Gyllensten already was formulating his next novel, *Grottan i öknen,* described as a kind of Gyllensten anthology. *Grottan i öknen* is a triptych that spans time from 200 A.D. to the late twentieth century. The first part, "Eremiten" (The Hermit), is a novella that treats mainly St. Anthony, who turns his back on the world and goes into the desert to lead an ascetic life as a hermit, escaping the dilemma that arises when one tries to reconcile the *vita activa* with the *vita contemplativa*. Part 2, "Andarna" (The Spirits), is a kaleidoscopic series of short prose pieces that focus mainly on Athanius of Alexandria, the fourth-century bishop who, among his many writings, composed the *Vita Antonii* (Life of Anthony). Interspersed are depictions of scenes from contemporary life. Most of the pieces describe situations in which the characters experience feelings of powerlessness and despair in the face of the destructive forces of life. Part 3 of the novel is set in twentieth-century Sweden in a small town in Värmland, also the setting of *Palatset i parken,* where the name "Elfberg" from *Diarium spirituale* and *Palatset i parken* appears again. In this case it belongs to Johannes Elfberg, a financial executive who died in 1938. The idea perhaps most prominent in this section is taken from 1 Corinthians 7:29-31, in which St. Paul admonishes people to live in this world but to act as if one is not of this world. As opposed to rejecting the world entirely and living as a hermit, Elfberg establishes a kind of rest home for the mentally ill. In contrast to Anthony and Athanasius, Elfberg is a colorless character—and yet there is something saintly about him. As if he were establishing a Hegelian synthesis in the third part, Gyllensten combines in Elfberg the asceticism and *via contemplativa* of Anthony with the *via activa* of Athanasius. Elfberg, however, is more humble and more altruistic than his predecessors in the novel. He also represents, in a sense, the holy fool—especially as he is reflected through his nephew, described as a "little old man," "a gnome," a "foolish copy" of Elfberg—in keeping with the character type introduced in *Diarium spirituale* and revisited in *I skuggan av Don Juan*.

Like many before him, Gyllensten was fascinated by the Don Juan legend, as related in Tirso de Molina's *El burlador de Sevilla* (1630; translated as *The Love Rogue,* 1924). Written in the Spanish Golden Age, the drama of Don Juan parallels that of Spain. Powerful and proud, Don Juan defies God, humanity, and all that is respectable, knowing that his actions will ultimately lead to his downfall. Gyllensten regards de Molina's work as a warning to the Spain of his day, a country at its peak of power, yet headed down the path of destruction. Likewise, Gyllensten too writes in his novel of the often dire consequences of an exaggerated will to power.

The protagonist of *I skuggan av Don Juan* is not, however, Don Juan Tenorio, the arrogant nobleman who ruthlessly defies the order of his society; it is, rather, his servant, the character called "Juanito" and "Lille Johan," among other things, illustrating the Swedish proverb "Kärt barn har många namn" (Beloved children have many names). Master and servant, the two romp through a series of exciting and roguish adventures. Juanito, who stands in the shadow of Don Juan, also stands in direct contrast to him. Sensitive, capricious, and somewhat unruly, Juanito sees himself as a weak person. He strives to acquire some of the strength of his master. At the end, however, when Don Juan has gone too far with his ruthless and destructive way of life and is banished by his father to the West Indies, Juanito realizes that his master is an empty man and that, in fact, his power was not power at all; it consisted of impotence, fantasy, and a good measure of braggadocio. Juanito no longer has a desire to follow him.

It could be said that Gyllensten is presenting here a plea for the "little life" that he wrote about in *Sokrates död*. More strongly, however, through his often merry tale of the adventures of Don Juan and Juanito, he argues against the use of human power that leads to destruction.

Baklängesminnen (Memoirs in Reverse, 1978) has been described as one of Gyllensten's most open, remarkable, and accessible novels. It is filled with humor, thought-provoking observations, and comments on life and the human condition that readers can readily identify with. In a preface, the narrator asks the question, "How many of us have been present at our own lives?" He proceeds then to piece together the "fragments" of his "synthetic memoirs," arranging them so that in the first chapter, "Först föddes jag" (First, I was born), he presents an unconventional eulogy at his own funeral, while in the last chapter, "Sist dog jag" (Finally, I died), he describes his birth. The book concludes with a title page for what would seem to be the last chapter, "Sedan börjar det roliga" (Then the fun begins). Only some blank pages follow, however.

Gyllensten's next novel, *Huvudskallebok: Roman i tre turer* (Book of Skulls: A Novel in Three Rounds, 1981), consists of three narrations, or "tre böcker len" (three books in one), told by an unnamed, contradictory first-person narrator and reflecting three moods so different that it is almost difficult to believe that the narrator for each is the same character. The sections are titled "Vindmannen" (The Man in the Attic), "Kurri Kulum" (Curriculum), and "Huvudskallebok," labeled on the dust jacket as, respectively, "Andante," "Scherzo," and "Allegro."

In the first section a man relates his strange experience of being fetched from his attic by a little girl who leads him downstairs to the dwelling of an elderly man and woman who have died. His tale has a dream-like quality, and, though he wonders if he is dreaming, he says that it is not a dream but a recollection. Again, as in *Diarium spirituale,* the narrator questions what the world wants of him, and again the idea is presented, as in *Palatset i parken,* that humans do not create their own world but must learn to live in the confused—and confusing—world into which they were placed. Indeed, one of the leitmotivs that runs throughout many of Gyllensten's works is the idea that the world exists in a state of permanent confusion (often called a "Babylonisk förbistring" [Babylonian confusion]).

As its title, "Kurri Kulum," suggests, the "Scherzo" section is a satirical romp through the narrator's memories of school days. The "Allegro" section, subtitled "Färdknäppar på livets mödosamma stråt" (Stirrup Cups on Life's Arduous Journey), forms a synthesis of the somber first round and the jocose nature of the second. While the narrator still is seeking answers to how to live his life, as he was in the "Andante," the tone and style of the "Allegro" are considerably more varied. Short, anecdotal discussions are interspersed with imaginary conversations in heaven, excerpts from such works as Blaise Pascal's *Pensées sur la religion et sur quelques autres sujets* (Thoughts on Religion and Some Other Subjects, 1660) and *Der cherubinische Wandersmann* (The Cherubic Pilgrim, 1657) by the German mystic Angelus Silesius. The text frequently assumes the nature of notes that Gyllensten wrote while reading. Yet, as in *Diarium spirituale,* these notes combine with the tales and anecdotes from the other two parts to make up the novel, which, also like *Diarium spirituale,* grapples with the problem of attempting to lead a meaningful life in the confused world.

The full title of Gyllensten's next novel is *Rätt och slätt: Anteckningar från det där pensionatet som jag bodde på när jag skulle lära upp mig till en bättre människa* (Pure and Simple: Notes from the Hotel-Pensionat Where I Lived When I Was Supposed to Educate Myself to Be a Better Person, 1983). The narrator and protagonist, a painter and graphic artist who displays some similarity to Gyllensten himself, has been

Gyllensten and his fellow doctor-turned-writer Georg Klein. Their correspondence on science, literature, and morality was published in 1993 as Hack i häl på Minerva *(photograph by Ulla Montan; from the dust jacket).*

sent there by his companion Elisabeth, a practical woman who selected what she describes in a letter as a cozy little Swedish family hotel where he could meet and socialize with ordinary people. The narrator, however, who "has always stood on the sidelines of life," indulges more in observing than in interacting with the other guests at the idyllic vacation spot—a place that turns out to be a microcosm as confused and confusing, as amoral, as brutal, as comical, and as melodramatic as the world it represents.

The narrator's reports to Elisabeth are answered by requests to spare her his morbid dreams and infantile nonsense. There is much more to *Rätt och slätt,* however, than morbid dreams and infantile nonsense. The narration reads, at times, like a philosophical treatise that includes references to the Bible, Kierkegaard, Linné, Kant, Franz Kafka, Schopenhauer, Ralph Waldo Emerson, and Strindberg. It also includes comments on subjects that range from theodicy to transistor radios. Still, the main question pondered is basically the existential question that Gyllensten continues to ask: how can people live meaningful lives in the strange, confused, and often brutal world into which they have been placed?

In *Rätt och slätt* Gyllensten introduces the figure of Helene Formark, a woman who fascinates the narrator to the extent that he even fancies for a short time that he is in love with her. The contrast between the exciting Helena and the rational Elisabeth not only recalls the two women in *Barnabok,* but it also foreshadows the trio of narrator, Elisabeth, and Helene Formark that appears in the opening chapters of Gyllensten's next two works, *Skuggans återkomst eller Don Juan går igen* (The Return of the Shadow, or Don Juan Comes Back, 1985) and *Sju vise mästare om kärlek* (Seven Wise Masters on Love, 1986), as well as in his 1998 novel, *Kistbrev* (Letters in a Trunk, 1998).

In *Skuggans återkomst eller Don Juan går igen,* the narrator—the artist from *Rätt och slätt*—and Elisabeth have taken a trip to Spain to visit the land of Francisco Goya, Miguel de Cervantes, Tirso de Molina, Don Juan, St. John of the Cross, and Teresa of Avila. One afternoon in Seville the narrator enters an antique bookstore, where he buys a folder of old woodcuts that he believes illustrate the stories of Don Juan and his servant Juanito. With the pictures before him, he creates a sequel to *I skuggan av Don Juan*. The story includes Doña Isabel, whom Don

Juan seduced, abandoned, and was forced to marry before her brothers took her back home to live out her life, married to a man she never saw again. Many pages are devoted to Doña Ana, who spent most of her life as a nun. Don Juan himself becomes a penitent before he dies, and his old servant, Juanito, spends his last days in the service of Doña Isabel, who through the years has developed into a strong, self-sufficient woman. Juanito speaks the last lines of the novel, lines that praise life, as they echo, with a positive twist, Strindberg's words from *Ett drömspel* (A Dream Play) "Nothing is as we expect it to be."

Gyllensten's next work, *Sju vise mästare om kärlek,* has been described by critic Kay Glans as a "en samling fina miniatyrer" (collection of fine miniatures). The first chapter is set in Seville, where, as in *Skuggans återkomst,* the narrator and Elisabeth are vacationing. Unlike in *Skuggans återkomst,* in which the narrator thinks he catches a glimpse of Helene Formark, the attractive woman from the *pensionat* in *Rätt och slätt,* this time he actually does meet her. The *Wahlverwandtschaft* (natural affinity) that he suspected might exist between them in *Rätt och slätt* is confirmed. Lying to Elisabeth about needing to conduct some research for his work in Seville, he extends their visit for one more week, during which he enjoys a highly erotic relationship with Helene. Before they must part, he tells Helene a story–a *jataka,* an edifying fable of the Buddha in the form of an animal. He realizes later, when he is back home in Stockholm, that the story he told Helene was meant also to teach him something. From that point on, *Sju vise mästare om kärlek* is composed of a series of *jatakas,* little lessons of life and love related in the form of animal fables.

Like Plato's *Symposium,* Gyllensten's *Det himmelska gästabudet* (The Heavenly Banquet, 1991) is set at a festive dinner and consists of narrations and comments by a variety of voices, ranging from the burlesque and the bawdy to the lyrical, the tragic, and the profound. The main theme of this novel, however, is not love, as in the *Symposium,* but life, and the discussion at the banquet, a feast hosted in heaven by St. Peter, centers on "the absurd paradox that contradicts all that we know and understand," namely, that "God regarded all that he had created and found it good." Among the figures in the novel are God, St. Peter, Jesus, Ahasverus, and a chorus similar to choruses in ancient Greek drama, as well as people identified only by profession–a florist, a doctor, a captain, and an actress, for example. Despite the pessimism expressed by those who tell their stories, the novel ends on a positive note, expressed back on Earth by the chorus and a "wanderer" who finds contentment in his simple life. The optimistic message, which smacks of a certain romantic pantheism–if, indeed, one can attribute pantheism to Gyllensten–is similar to that expressed in Joseph Freiherr von Eichendorff's line from his poem "Wünschelrute" (Divining Rod, 1835): "Schläft ein Lied in allen Dingen" (A song is dormant in everything). According to Gyllensten, the world does, indeed, have a message for people. As the chorus sings at the conclusion all of creation is "ett underverk är skapelsen" (a work of creation), and all creatures are related in this dizzying world, in which life, despite its sorrows, is worth living.

Gyllensten's next three novels, *Anteckningar från en vindskupa* (Notes from a Garret, 1993), *Ljuset ur skuggornas värld* (The Light from the World of Shadows, 1995), and *Kistbrev,* form a kind of Kierkegaardian triptych. Indeed, the name "Johannes the seducer" is evoked in *Anteckningar från en vindskupa,* a reference to the "Diary of a Seducer" from Kierkegaard's *Enten/Eller* (Either/Or, 1843). Gyllensten's protagonist in this novel, also called Johannes, is a man who lives an isolated life in an attic apartment in his family's well-situated and well-appointed house. While he recalls Fyodor Dostoevsky's *Zapiski iz podpol'ia* (Notes from Underground, 1864), he also harks back, somewhat ironically, to Gyllensten's earlier novel *Rätt och slätt,* in which the narrator states that he is "en man i mina bästa år. Det har jag alltid varit" (a man in my best years. I always have been). In *Anteckningar från en vindskupa,* however, the narrator reverses the situation, stating that he is "en man i mina sämsta år. Det har jag alltid varit" (a man in my worst years. I always have been). According to Gyllensten's introduction, the writer of these "notes" is sick, disgusting, and repulsive–a man who lives his life between despair and indifference, between sensitivity and cynicism. Professionally, like the narrators in *Rätt och slätt, Skuggans återkomst eller Don Juan går igen,* and *Sju vise mästare om kärlek,* Johannes W. is a graphic artist. His most recent exhibition, a collection of satirical drawings that he describes as "simultaneously precious, brutal, and obscene," evokes comments from reviewers that read like satires of art and literary critics. While Johannes W. calls his collection "Bestiarum mysticum," a book publisher plans to print the pictures in book form, changing the title to "Eritocon" because it will "sell better."

Gyllensten includes much social criticism in the novel, once again presenting an image that he used in *Lotus i Hades*–that of the Western world as a glass veranda, comfortably closed off from the sufferings of those less fortunate. Also, the narrator regards himself as a man living in Hades and being visited by Swedenborgian "tuktoandar" (chastising spirits).

The final words of the novel are apparently those of the "Lars Gyllensten" who introduces the "notes" at the beginning, and, while they seem to complete the frame of the novel, they do not end Johannes's story, for, as the narrator of the frame states, the fictional narrator, Johannes, does indeed have more to say but has reached an appropriate stopping point. This conclusion leads the reader to believe that *Ljuset ur skuggornas värld,* described on the dustjacket as "a pendant to *Anteckningar från en vindskupa,*" might be a continuation of Johannes W.'s story. It is, however, as the introductory quotation from Jeremiah 18:3-4 suggests, a remaking of a new artifact from the same clay. The narrator in *Ljuset ur skuggornas värld* is also named Johannes W.–more specifically, Johannes Wictorsson, calling to the reader's mind both Victor Eremita, the "editor" in Kierkegaard's *Enten/Eller,* and Gyllensten's full name, Lars Johan Wictor Gyllensten. The narrator does not appear to be the same character as Johannes W., however, and although his father, like the father of Johannes W., is named Hemming, he is not identical to the Hemming that appears in the earlier novel. Other characters from both novels share names but play different roles. And yet, the two novels seem to merge somewhat, as they conclude with similar thoughts on darkness and death.

Ljuset ur skuggornas värld can also be regarded, like Mann's *Buddenbrooks* (1901), as a story of the "verfall einer familie" (decay of a family). The narrator is the only person still alive to tell the story of his rich bourgeois family–his strong and strong-willed grandparents, who built up a lucrative family business; his weak father, who was written out of the family will; and, finally, himself, a widower with no offspring to carry on the family name. The "Epitafium" at the end of the novel is even followed by pages that inform the reader of the Wictorsson family lineage.

Kistbrev appears to bring the narrators from the two preceding novels together. An old man resembling the Johannes from the previous novel discovers in the attic of a house that he owns a box containing the posthumous papers of a man who used to live there. In sifting through notes, pictures, and letters–fragments of the man's life–the narrator attempts to piece together a mental picture of that man. The writer of the notes turns out to have been Johannes Wictorsson, who describes how he depicted his parents in both *Anteckningar från en vindskupa* and *Ljuset ur skuggornas värld.* Names, traits, and experiences of the characters in many of Gyllensten's previous novels recur and are embodied in or interact with the two narrators–both the finder of the box and the dead man to whom the box belonged. Again, Gyllensten employs the Strindbergian "dream play" technique that characterizes several of his other novels: the characters do indeed seem to split, double, and multiply, while governed by one overriding consciousness.

Like so many of Gyllensten's fictional characters, the man in the attic appears to be a spokesman for Gyllensten himself. He declares, for example, "De alternativa jagen är mina ställföreträdare. Emellanåt rycker de in för att byta skepnad med den som nyss var jag . . . I inbillningen kan jag framkalla obegränsade metamorfoser och inkarnationer–gå skilda vägar–mot utopier eller dystopier, som förverkligas genom mig. De väntar i okända och bottenlösa förrådskammare på att jag skall komma och befria dem–för att släppa ut dem här i denna världens ljus och skuggor (The alternative egos are my representatives. Sometimes they step in to assume the guise of one who just now was myself. . . . In my imagination I can call forth unlimited metamorphoses and incarnations. I can take different paths–toward utopias or dystopias, which, through me, become realities. They wait in unknown and bottomless storage chambers for me to come and liberate them–to release them into the lights and shadows of this world). These lines describe, to some extent, Gyllensten's literary method. Before he releases his "alternative egos," however, he fills them with varying–and frequently opposing–viewpoints on, among other matters, the power of words, creativity, and Johan Wolfgang von Goethe's idea of *Wahlverwandtschaft* (natural affinity), all the while considering the question of how humans ought to conduct their lives in this often absurd world into which they have been placed.

In addition to his many fictional and nonfictional writings, Gyllensten has published two children's stories, *Provdockan* (The Tailor's Mannequin, 1983) and *Augustin och Celestine: Om nåra små loppors liv och leverne* (Augustin and Celestine: On the Life and Ways of Some Small Fleas, 1993), as well as an illustrated satirical story that he published under the pseudonym Pär Silje (Parsley), *Hjärnfilspån: Vittra vederstyggligheter och annat smått och gott* (Brain Filings: Learned Abominations and Other Tidbits, 1989). In 2000, he published his memoirs in a book that bears the playfully ambiguous title *Minnen, bara minnen,* which could be understood as "Memories, Only Memories" or "Memories, Bare Memories."

Bibliography:

Åke Lilliestam, *Lars Gyllenstens Bibliografi: 1946–1992*, Acta Bibliothecae Regiae Stockholmiensis, no. 54 (Stockholm: Kungliga biblioteket, 1993).

References:

Ingemar Algulin, *A History of Swedish Literature*, translated by John Weinstock, revised by Judith Black (Stockholm: Swedish Institute, 1989), pp. 210–213;

Benkt-Erik Benktson, *Samtidighetens mirakel: Kring tidsproblematiken i Lars Gyllenstens romaner* (Stockholm: Bonnier, 1989);

Kjell Espmark, "Gyllenstens Gjentagelser," and "Gyllenstens uppenbarelser," in *Samlaren* (1974): 112–118;

Gunnel Elsbeth Haack, "The Literary Unconscious: A Reading of Alain Robbe Grillet's, John Barth's, and Lars Gyllensten's Texts," dissertation, University of California, Los Angeles, 1981;

Hans Isaksson, *Hängivenhet och distans: En studie i Lars Gyllenstens romankonst* (Stockholm: Aldus/Bonnier, 1974);

Isaksson, *Lars Gyllensten*, translated by Katy Lissbrant (Boston: Twayne, 1978);

Birgitta Jansson, "Trolösheten: En studie i svensk kulturdebatt och skönlitteratur under tidigt 1960-tal," dissertation, University of Uppsala, 1990;

Hans-Erik Johannesson, *Studier i Lars Gyllenstens estetik* (Göteborg: Skrifter utgivna av Litteraturvetenskapliga Institutionen vid Göteborgs universitet, 1977);

Inge Jonsson, "Ett författarskap av förtvivlan och förtröstan," in *Humanistiskt credo: Studier och artiklar*, compiled by Barbro Ståhle Sjönell and Cecilia Wijnbladh Bergin (Stockholm: Norstedt, 1988), pp. 180–188;

Bo Larsson, *Gud som provisorium: En linje i Lars Gyllenstens författarskap* (Stockholm: Verbum, 1990);

Barbara Lide, "Lars Gyllensten's *Sokrates död:* Intertextuality and the Ludic Spirit," *Scandinavian Studies*, 66 (1994): 204–230;

Sven-Eric Liedman, "Gyllensten utan roller," in *Sverige 1965–1975: En antologi*, volume of *Linjer i nordisk prosa 1965–1975*, edited by Kjerstin Norén (Lund: Cavefors, 1977);

Liedman, "Mänskligt och omänskligt: Operationalism och existentialism i Lars Gyllenstens författarskap," *Svensk Litteraturtidskrift*, 1 (1966): 24–39;

Kerstin Munck, *Gyllenstens roller: En studie över tematik och gestaltning i Lars Gyllenstens författarskap* (Lund: Gleerup, 1974);

Gavin Orton, "A Swedenborgian Dream Book: Lars Gyllensten's *Palatset i parken*," *Scandinavica*, 23 (1984): 5–22;

Saga Oscarson, *Gyllensten som Orpheus: En studie i Lars Gyllenstens mytiska diktning* (Stockholm: Bonnier, 1992);

Bertil Palmqvist, "Satsa på undret: Lars Gyllenstens dialektiska trilogi," *Bonniers Litterära Magasin*, 32 (April 1963): 282–288;

Thure Stenström, "Fiction and Metafiction in Lars Gyllensten's Literary Work," in *A Century of Swedish Narrative: Essays in Honour of Karin Petherick*, edited by Sara Death and Helena Forsås-Scott (Norwich, U.K.: Norvik, 1994), pp. 209–221;

Stenström, *Gyllensten i hjärtats öken: Strövtåg i Lars Gyllenstens författarskap, särskilt Grottan i öknen*, Acta Universitatis Upsaliensis: Historia litterarum, no. 19 (Stockholm: Almqvist & Wiksell, 1996);

Stenström, "Lars Gyllenstens Senilia—en roman om tiden" and "Lars Gyllenstens Hans och Greta—modern parafras över klassiskt tema," in *Berättartekniska studier i Pär Lagerkvists, Lars Gyllenstens och Cora Sandels prosa* (Stockholm: Bonnier, 1964);

Lars Warme, "Lars Gyllensten's *Diarium Spirituale:* The Creative Process as a Novel," *Scandinavica*, 19 (1980): 165–180.

Ulla Isaksson
(12 June 1916 – 24 April 2000)

Rose-Marie G. Oster
University of Maryland

BOOKS: *Trädet* (Stockholm: Evangeliska Fosterlandsstiftelsens, 1940);
I denna natt (Stockholm: Missionsförbundets, 1942);
Av krukmakarens hand (Stockholm: Missionsförbundets, 1945);
Ytterst i havet (Stockholm: Norlin, 1950);
Kvinnohuset (Stockholm: Raben & Sjögren, 1952);
"Dödens faster" (Stockholm: Raben & Sjögren, 1954);
Dit du icke vill (Stockholm: Raben & Sjögren, 1956);
Nära livet; Det vänliga, värdiga (Stockholm: Rabén & Sjören, 1958);
Klänningen (Stockholm: Bonnier, 1959);
De två saliga (Stockholm: Bonnier, 1962); translated as *The Blessed Ones* (Washington & New York: Robert Luce, 1970);
Klockan (Stockholm: Bonnier, 1966);
Amanda eller den blå spårvagnen: En roman om dröm och verklighet (Stockholm: Bonnier, 1969);
Paradistorg (Stockholm: Bonnier, 1973);
Kvinnor: Valda Berättelser (Stockholm: Bonnier, 1975);
Elin Wägner 1882–1922: Amazon med tva bröst, by Isaksson and Erik Hjalmar Linder (Stockholm: Bonnier, 1977);
Elin Wägner 1922–1949: Dotter av Moder Jord, by Isaksson and Linder (Stockholm: Bonnier, 1980);
Återfunnet, Bonniers Julbok 1982 (Stockholm: Bonnier, 1982);
FödelseDagen (Stockholm: Bonnier, 1988);
Boken om E (Stockholm: Bonnier, 1994).

PLAY PRODUCTION: *Våra torsdagar,* Stockholm, 1964.

PRODUCED SCRIPTS: *Nära livet,* motion picture, Nordisk Tonefilm, 1958;
Jungfrukällan, motion picture, Svensk Filmindustri, 1960;
Siska-en Kvinnobild, motion picture, Svensk Filmindustri, 1962;
Klänningen, motion picture, Svensk Filmindustri, 1964;
De två saliga, television, TV2, 1983;

Ulla Isaksson (from the dust jacket for The Blessed Ones, *1970)*

Begriper du inte att jagälskar dig? En dikt för TV om Stina och Hjalmar Bergman, television, 1988;
Chefen fru Ingeborg, television, adapted from the novel by Hjalmar Bergman, 1993.

Ulla Isaksson's work spans almost six decades of Swedish literary history. Her debut took place in 1940, and she has strong ties to some of the writers of that generation, especially Lars Ahlin and Sivar Arner, but she is difficult to categorize as a representative of any literary decade. A writer with clear religious orientation, she is closer to Pär Lagerkvist, Selma Lagerlöf, and, among Scandinavian writers, Sigrid Undset (although Undset wrote from a Catholic perspective) than to her

1940s cohorts; questions about God's existence and nature are central to her work. Hailed by critics for her psychological sensitivity, her in-depth character analysis, and her daring choice of topics, Isaksson is by no means a popular writer in the pejorative sense. Her books have always required a commitment from the reader to enter a fictional world where much is alien and disturbing. In almost all her works, from *Ytterst i havet* (At the Outer Edge of the Sea, 1950) to *Boken om E* (The Book about E, 1994), Isaksson poses uncomfortable questions. Her protagonists live lives in extremis, in profound spiritual crises, in mental institutions, abandoned by love, or involved in fatal relationships. The author confronts them with the question *Quid est veritas?*—"What is truth?"—and suggests that the mad often give better answers than the sane.

There is at times an almost clinical aspect to Isaksson's efforts to dissect and expose the innermost secrets of her protagonists' souls. "Jag ser aldrig nagonting. . . . Allt kommer inifrån och går ut, inte tvärtom" (I never see anything. . . . Everything comes from inside and goes out, not the other way around), she told an interviewer for the *Dagens Nyheter* (12 October 1952). One might quarrel with that statement, for Isaksson is an unusually acute observer of her surroundings, but first and foremost she follows her own internal compass, independent of prevailing literary and social debates.

While Isaksson's realistic style and her attention to language is reminiscent of the works by Ahlin and her milieu most often is that of *vardagsmänniskor*—everyday people—and while she shares with Lagerkvist a religious background and recurrent Christian themes, Isaksson is different from both authors in that she writes from a woman's perspective. The lives she explores are almost always those of women. She is no one-sided apologist for all women, however: in Swedish literature it is hard to find a more devastating depiction of woman than that of "the aunt of death" in the short story that gives the collection *"Dödens faster"* (The Aunt of Death, 1954) its name, a hyena of a woman who jubilantly exploits the vulnerability of grieving people. On the other hand, the same collection includes the aunt's absolute counterpoint: a mother in a mental institution desperately longing for her children, a Christ-like figure drawn with tender compassion.

Isaksson's statement that "everything comes from the inside" explains much of the author's approach to writing and her choice of topics. A Christian existentialist with the passion of a medieval mystic, she is not moved by fashionable literary and political trends. At times she has seemed caught by surprise at attacks against her such as those that happened in the 1970s, when she published *Paradistorg* (Paradise Place, 1973) and caused a great stir among some radical feminists for her presumed lack of commitment to feminist ideals.

Many of her critics have failed to understand what Isaksson sees as her crucial role as a writer: to question moral values in society—what one critic, Bo Strömstedt, for the Swedish newspaper *Expressien* (9 August 1973) called her "missionsuppdrag" (missionary task)—and to point to the enormous consequences resulting from personal choice. As she wrote in an article for the *Dagens Nyheter* (31 December 1975), she sees it as her responsibility to ask why we act as we do, to examine the forces, conscious and unconscious, that drive those actions, and to explore the complexity hidden underneath every surface rather than presenting solutions: "De fiesta berättelser ger inga lösningar—det är inte deros uppgift" (Most tales do not give solutions—it is not their task. . . . They describe where anxiety dwells).

Not much in her background predisposed Isaksson to become a leading figure on the Swedish literary scene. Born Ulla Margareta Lundberg on 12 June 1916, Isaksson was the second of three children in a middle-class Stockholm family in which adherence to social and religious norms was de rigueur. She enjoyed a protected childhood as a popular, outgoing girl until a bout with an illness that affected her heart left her as a spectator to the many activities that she and her circle of friends so enjoyed. At that time she decided to become a writer. The tension between her serious, perfectionist mother, Greta Barsch Isaksson, and her happy-go-lucky, flirtatious father, Knut Isaksson, who nevertheless ruled the family with an iron hand, left traces in Isaksson's life and works. So did the strong sense of abandonment that she felt when she was sent to stay with her grandparents for a prolonged period of time during her mother's pregnancy and the birth of her younger brother; the distant mother figure and the struggle between mother and daughter is a recurrent theme in Isaksson's writings. Issues regarding sexuality, particularly in its most destructive forms, are also recurrent themes in her works, including *Kvinnohuset* (House of Women, 1952), *"Dödens faster," Dit du icke vill* (Whither Thou Would'st Not, 1956), and *De två saliga* (1962; translated as *The Blessed Ones*, 1970). In the annual *Bonniers Julbok* (Bonnier Christmas Book) for 1982, Isaksson published *Återfunnet* (Recaptured), a series of musings in which she reveals, in part through the retelling of dreams, many of the childhood experiences that left scars on her personality and recur in her writings.

Isaksson's family belonged to the Swedish Missionary Society, and the impact of the free church movement can be clearly perceived in her earliest works; the titles of many of her books are taken directly from the Bible. Her first novel, *Trädet* (The Tree,

1940), was submitted to the literary competition sponsored by the Evangelical National Foundation, in which it won first prize.

Isaksson passed her matriculation exam in 1937 and married David Isaksson the following year. For almost a decade she lived a fairly conventional life as a middle-class wife and mother. During this period she wrote another book, *I denna natt* (In this Night, 1942), for which she received second prize in the Evangelical National Foundation's literary competition. When her marriage ended after eight years, however, she was left alone with two sons; writing became her lifesaver. Of great importance for her development as a writer was her stay in 1947 at the Sigtuna Foundation, a Christian gathering place for intellectuals and writers. This stay came after a battle with clinical depression brought on by the dissolution of her marriage. Among a group of writers that included the leading figures in Swedish literary life of the 1940s, Ahlin and Karl Vennberg (with whom she forged lifelong friendships), Isaksson felt accepted and valued as a writer. In the evening round-table discussions at Sigtuna she strove to understand her increasing doubts about traditional Christian values in a world where God seemed largely absent.

In quick succession Isaksson wrote *Ytterst i havet* and *Kvinnohuset*. *Ytterst i havet,* with its protagonist, minister Erik Fasth (the author stated that, given the autobiographical elements in the novel, she felt safer to hide behind a male character), is a mirror of the author's own agonized feelings at that time, a naked description of her crisis of faith. The question of God's manifestation in the world is a recurring theme in Isaksson's works. Her protagonists' "awful rowing towards God" (to use a term of American poet May Sarton) often ends not in a revelation but in a confrontation with an image of God that is cruelly distorted and revolting—represented by a deformed baby in *Paradistorg* or the mentally retarded Tina in *Ytterst i havet*. A meeting with God in Isaksson's works resembles more the horrendous encounter of the priestess with the goat god in the cave at Delphi in Lagerkvist's *Sibyllan* (The Sibyl, 1956). Often God is totally silent. Isaksson's exploration of God's silence and her protagonists' efforts to find meaning in a godless world resembles the spiritual quest of movie director Ingmar Bergman, and Isaksson wrote the screenplays for two of Bergman's motion pictures, *Nära livet* (1958; released in the United States as *Brink of Life*) and *Jungfrukällan* (1960; released in the United States as *The Virgin Spring*). *Jungfrukällan,* based on a medieval ballad, explores a familiar Isaksson theme, that pride goes before a fall. The punishment for a young maiden's pride is rape and death. Even here, however, there is a sign of grace: a spring at the place where the girl was killed.

The novel *Kvinnohuset,* with its portrayal of a community of women, was Isaksson's breakthrough with the general public and was awarded the *Svenska Dagbladet* literary prize in 1952. Acclaimed by reviewers, the novel nevertheless met with some criticism for Isaksson's choice of setting. Although most of the women in the house are presumably independent career women, Isaksson chose to place them in a sphere where their working lives play a minor role, namely, that of private love relationships. There are several well-drawn portraits of women in the book, from the ultrafeminine Eva, who has found her own Adam, to Isa, for whom no man can suffice. The most successful characters are the most complex, however: the eternally deceived Anna, who ends up murdering her husband at the moment he returns to her, and Rosa, a young girl whose gift for love leads her mercilessly to her death. In the case of Anna and Rosa, Isaksson concentrates on the "awakening," the point in a relationship when doubt and truth intrude and destroy.

Kvinnohuset was followed in 1954 by *"Dödens faster,"* a collection of short stories that picks up themes from Isaksson's earlier works. It spans an emotional register of astonishing breadth and depth, swinging from the tragic and banal, as in "Tre brev" (Three Letters), the story of the jilted Bessan, to the terrifying portrait of the "dödens faster." *"Dödens faster,"* too, is a book about women and love, but it shows a darker side of women's lives than *Kvinnohuset;* odes to suffering and pain but also to the ability of human beings to survive against all odds, the stories probe the shadow sides of love—incest, adultery, madness, and violence. Hope is held out, however, in the concluding sentence of the title story: "Det finns barmhärtighet också" (There is grace, too)—the last word underlined thrice.

Dit du icke vill can be compared to Eyvind Johnson's novel *Drömmar om rosor och eld* (1949; translated as *Dreams of Roses and Fire,* 1984) and Arthur Miller's play *The Crucible* (1953) in its choice of topic. Its protagonist, Hanna, a rich farmer's beautiful wife, does not behave according to social norms, in Isaksson's works almost always an invitation to punishment by people or God. The seemingly blameless Hanna gets caught in the frenzy of the witch trials in the 1600s and almost loses her life. Characteristically for Isaksson, however, innocence and rectitude turn out to be mostly facades. Few people are truly innocent in the author's fictional world: the seven deadly sins are committed repeatedly, and the seemingly virtuous are found to have broken one or more of the Ten Commandments and—for Isaksson one of the deadliest of sins—to suffer from a hardening of the heart.

In *Dit du icke vill* Hanna has committed adultery, and her deadly sin is pride. To reach self-knowledge

Dust jacket for the 1970 English translation of Isaksson's 1962 novel De två saliga, *about a married couple who are institutionalized because of their obsessive love for each other (University of Washington Library)*

and forgiveness she must enter the netherworld of jail and its "collective" of women. The author's description of the torture of women suspected as witches takes the reader back to a time when superstition and fear of the devil permeated life. For Isaksson, as for Lagerkvist, there is no doubt about the immortality of Evil in the world. Even though in the end Hanna is released through an act of love, what stays in the reader's mind are the horrifying jail scenes. Their impact is made even stronger by the juxtaposition of fleeting moments of grace, such as the scene in which Hanna, close to death, has a vision of herself at God's breast as a suckling babe. As in Lagerkvist's work, humanity becomes the creator of God; the feminization of God by the author was considered daring in the 1950s, when feminist theology had not yet gained a foothold.

In *Klänningen* (The Dress, 1959), one of her most interesting and complex novels, Isaksson looks at the sensitive issues of motherhood and love. The novel deals with the relationship between mother and daughter and plays out against a background of aging and death. The motto in *Klänningen* is from Eccles. 12:6 and its reference to "the evil days" when "the cord be loosed or the golden bowl be broken."

As do many of Isaksson's novels, *Klänningen* centers around the longing to break away permanently. The protagonist, the middle-aged Helen, is in her "golden" years, but she senses that they will soon be over and that the stage will be taken over by her daughter Edit, who on the one hand threatens to demolish Helen's most prized possessions after her death but on the other hand longs to be embraced by motherly love.

In Isaksson's work love is blind, unpredictable, and often unforgiving; it restores and destroys. In *De två saliga* Isaksson stretches the concept of love to its extremes; as she said in a radio program on 21 January 1963, the novel includes "en undersökning av kärlekens alla beståndsdelar" (all elements of love). The novel deals with a so-called folie à deux, a mental illness in which one person is so tied to the other that they think of themselves as totally one. Here the all-consuming love between two married people turns into madness and ends in death. Their lives are recounted from hospital journals and their writings by Doctor Dettow, a physician in the mental hospital where the two were patients. In exploring the complex relationship of the protagonists in this story within a story, the author examines the gray zone between sanity and insanity, between power given and power taken. In part *De två saliga* is a Strindbergian *Dödsdansen* (Dance of Death, 1900), where love is both negated and affirmed. It also illustrates another important theme in the author's work, the importance of the Ibsenesque "livslögnen"—the "life lie"—for her protagonists, and the necessity to face the lies and illusions for any growth to take place. As in Henrik Ibsen's play *Wildanden* (The Wild Duck, 1884), clinging to life lies leads inevitably to suicide and catastrophe, as Doctor Dettow discovers.

Amanda eller den blå spårvagnen: En roman om dröm och verklighet (Amanda or the Blue Street Car: A Novel about Dream and Reality, 1969) is an example of Isaksson's expertise in exposing the life lie. In this novel she takes the Swedes to task for their tendency to see themselves as the conscience of the world rather than facing up to problems at home. The protagonist is a Swedish everyman, Nagel Nilsson, home on sick leave from his work in a developing country as he tries to come to terms with his life and the angst that has made him unable to work. Nilsson has shirked his responsibility to his ailing mother, his sister, and her retarded son, who desperately need his help. During his time on a deserted island in the Stockholm archipelago he finally understands that his whole life has been a lie. His entire family's life, in fact, has been a flight from reality into a dream symbolized by the blue-and-golden streetcar. In the end, as the masks have been torn away and greed, egotism, and irresponsibility exposed, Nilsson is redeemed by the words of his sister, Nusen: "vi får vara hur misslyckade och vidriga som helst men vi har ända rätt till kärleken. . . . Att kärleken finns—det är nåden" (however despicable and nasty we are, we still have a right to love. . . . That love exists—that's grace).

When the feminist debate was at its height in the 1970s, Isaksson was a mature writer acclaimed for her books dealing with women, motherhood, and love relationships. At the time her novel *Paradistorg* was published in 1973, she found herself the target of attacks from some of the more radical feminists for her defense of "moderlighetens princip" (the principle of motherliness, the ability to nurture). A family story played out in an old summerhouse in the Stockholm archipelago, *Paradistorg* depicts a seemingly perfect grouping of a loving family in the most beautiful of Swedish summers. The idyll is hollow, however: the family is held together by a sense of duty, and its members are emotionally fragile, lonely, or—as in the case of one of the visitors, the child King—full of rage and aggression. Isaksson's impetus for the book was a Swedish dissertation that traced children's increasing aggressiveness and isolation in an evermore fast-moving world. Some of Isaksson's critics saw Emma, a social worker who rages against the modern working mother for neglecting her child, as the author's spokesperson. In the heat of the argument it was often overlooked that "moderlighet" in this book is represented by a young man, and that the author in reality uses the three main women characters, Katha, Emma, and Saga, to express her own ambivalence about womanhood and motherhood. Isaksson herself felt that she did not take a firm stand for or against traditional motherhood but rather challenged the ideals of both social conservatives and radicals by creating a set of characters who were flawed and uncertain about their commitment and ambivalent in their actions.

Isaksson later confessed to changes in the way she came to look upon her role as a woman and as a woman writer. As she states on the cover of the short-story collection *Kvinnor: Valda Berättelser* (Women: Selected Stories, 1975): "Jag har skrivit om kvinnor hela mitt liv. Till en början motvilligt och med ganska stora mindrevärdeskänslor: det måste väl finnas annat och viktigare att skriva om! Men med åren växte en allt starkare insikt om hur bokstavligen livsviktigt det har blivit att kvinnor skriver om kvinnor" (I have written about women all my life. At the beginning against my will and with rather strong feelings of inferiority: there must be other more important things to write about. But with the years came an even stronger insight into how important it is that women write about women). This change is clear in *Kvinnor,* published during the International Year of the Woman, in which she collects older short stories together with newer ones. Many of the newer stories deal with women from past generations, and several of the old stories have been changed to reflect new insights. In *Kvinnor,* as in all of Isaksson's work, love has many facets, but so does motherhood. Motherhood is almost always synonymous with ambivalence and ambiguity. Many of her protagonists feel revulsion toward pregnancy, and some murder their children, like Laura in the novel *Klockan* (The Bell, 1966), who bakes poisoned cakes for her retarded son when the authorities threaten to take him away from her; others smother their children with love and care.

Fear, hate, and love are intricately interwoven in *FödelseDagen* (The Birth Day, 1988), a novel about an aging mother and her three daughters on the last day of the mother's life. In an interview on the publication of the book in *Dagens Nyheter* (20 August 1988), Isaksson discusses her relationship with her own mother—she calls the relationship "knölig" (lumpy) and confesses that it took twenty years for them to become close, when both she and her mother were pregnant. It is hard not to see parallels here in the relationship of the three daughters in *FödelseDagen* to their mother. They are grouped around their mother in different configurations: Birrebi, the child-like idealist; Klara, the practical one, who reconstructs a semblance of their idyllic past the night her mother dies; and Blenda, also known as Cri, the mirror of her mother, particularly her destructive, wrathful side. The novel is written from the perspective of the mother, Olga. As in *Paradistorg* the milieu seems idyllic, with a beautiful landscape and a mother devoted to nurturing her three daughters. As the novel progresses, however, truths are exposed as lies, and the characters alternately express hatred and love for each other. Isaksson superimposes the unreliable memories of her individual characters in such a way that the overall picture becomes smudged and fuzzy. As in real life, truth is elusive: "Alla som har älskat vet att jorden under dem är full av rötter: multnande rotstockar . . . sega tågor . . ." (Anyone who has loved knows that the earth beneath them is full of roots, rotting root stumps . . . tough tendons . . .). *FödelseDagen* depicts the struggle to sever the bond between mother and daughter that tethers them as if still connected by an umbilical cord, but as in *Paradistorg* there is no protagonist who evokes undivided sympathy from the reader.

In 1977 and 1980 the two volumes of Ulla Isaksson's and Erik Hjalmar Linder's biography of writer Elin Wägner were published to critical acclaim. Isaksson and Linder, a well-known critic and the famous biographer of Hjalmar Bergman, had worked and lived together since their marriage in 1963. Less than ten years after the publication of the Wägner biography Linder became ill with Alzheimer's disease. In *Boken om E,* a moving, confessional diary about Linder's last years, Isaksson describes, often through the recounting of numinous dreams, her struggles to come to terms with the slow loss of her mate, her rage against their fate, and the changes she herself goes through. Like one of the characters in *De två saliga,* of which there are many echoes in this book, she asks repeatedly "Hur kan vi leva utan kärlek, doktorn?" (Doctor, how can we live without love?). Isaksson wrestles with that question in an open and moving account, journeying through all the stages of grief—denial, anger, bargaining, depression, and finally acceptance with the simple statement at the end of the book: "Förlorad och återfunnen" (Lost and found again).

In 1995 Ulla Isaksson received the Selma Lagerlöf Prize for her literary work. She died on 24 April 2000 following a long illness.

She is remembered for her many portrayals of women's reality—both past and present—and as a writer of strong convictions and courage. She dared to tackle unpopular and taboo topics: religious hypocrisy; the destructive force of love, be it a mother's or a mate's; the dilemmas of child rearing in a changing world; and the ravages of dementia in a loved one. She has vividly described her struggle toward a feminist viewpoint and her growing conviction that women must write about women.

Interview:

Maud Adelcreu, "Kvinnohuset är ett enda stort vredesutbrott," *Dagens Nyheter* (12 October 1952).

References:

Inger Littberger, *Ulla Isakssons romankonst* (Stockholm: Bonnier, 1996);

Berit Wilson, "Contemporary Issues and Narrative Technique in Ulla Isaksson's *Paradistorg*," in *A Century of Swedish Narrative: Essays in Honor of Karin Petherick* (Norwich, U.K.: Norvik, 1994).

Tove Jansson
(9 August 1914 – 27 June 2001)

Boel Westin
University of Stockholm

BOOKS: *Sara och Pelle och Neckens bläckfiskar,* as Vera Haij (Helsinki: Förlaget Bildkonst, 1933);
Småtrollen och den stora översvämningen (Helsinki: Söderström, 1945; Stockholm: Hasselgren, 1945);
Kometjakten (Helsinki: Söderström, 1946; Norrköping: Sörlin, 1947); translated by Elizabeth Portch as *Comet in Moominland* (London: Benn, 1951; New York: Walck, 1959); revised as *Mumintrollet på kometjakt* (Norrköping: Sörlin, 1956); revised again as *Kometen kommer* (Helsinki: Schildt, 1968; Stockholm: Geber, 1968);
Trollkarlens hatt (Helsinki: Schildt, 1948; Stockholm: Geber, 1949); translated by Portch as *Finn Family Moomintroll* (London: Benn, 1950); translated edition republished as *The Happy Moomins* (Indianapolis & New York: Bobbs-Merrill, 1951);
Muminpappans Bravader: Skrivna av Honom Själv (Helsinki: Schildt, 1950; Stockholm: Geber, 1950); translated by Thomas Warburton as *The Exploits of Moominpappa, Described by Himself* (London: Benn, 1952; New York: Walck, 1966); revised as *Muminpappans memoarer* (Helsinki: Schildt, 1968; Stockholm: Geber, 1968);
Hur gick det sen? Boken om Mymlan, Mumintrollet och Lilla My (Helsinki: Schildt, 1952; Stockholm: Geber, 1952); translated by Kingsley Hart as *The Book about Moomin, Mymble and Little My* (London: Benn, 1953); translated edition republished as *Moomin, Mymble and Little My* (Seattle: Blue Lantern, 1996);
Farlig midsommar (Helsinki: Schildt, 1954; Stockholm: Geber, 1954); translated by Warburton as *Moominsummer Madness* (London: Benn / New York: Walck, 1955);
Trollvinter (Helsinki: Schildt, 1957; Stockholm: Geber, 1957); translated by Warburton as *Moominland Midwinter* (London: Benn / New York: Walck, 1958);
Vem ska trösta Knyttet? (Helsinki: Schildt, 1960; Stockholm: Geber, 1960); translated by Hart as *Who Will Comfort Toffle?* (London: Benn / New York: Walck, 1960);

Tove Jansson (photograph by Per Olov Jansson)

Det osynliga barnet och andra berättelser (Helsinki: Schildt, 1962; Stockholm: Geber, 1962); translated by Warburton as *Tales from Moominvalley* (London: Benn / New York: Walck, 1963);
Pappan och havet (Helsinki: Schildt, 1965; Stockholm: Geber, 1965); translated by Hart as *Moominpappa at Sea* (London: Benn / New York: Walck, 1966);
Vi: En romantisk bok för älskande, by Jansson and Signe Hammarsten Jansson (Helsinki: Schildt, 1965);

Bildhuggarens dotter (Helsinki: Schildt, 1968; Stockholm: Almqvist & Wiksell/Geber, 1968); translated by Hart as *Sculptor's Daughter* (London: Benn, 1969; New York: Avon, 1976);

Mumintrollen, by Jansson and Lars Jansson (Stockholm: Sveriges Radio, 1969);

Sent i november (Helsinki: Schildt, 1970; Stockholm: Almqvist & Wiksell/Geber, 1970); translated by Hart as *Moominvalley in November* (London: Benn / New York: Walck, 1971);

Lyssnerskan (Helsinki: Schildt, 1971; Stockholm: Bonnier, 1971);

Sommarboken (Helsinki: Schildt, 1972; Stockholm: Bonnier, 1972); translated by Thomas Teal as *The Summer Book* (London: Hutchinson, 1974; New York: Pantheon, 1975);

Solstaden (Helsinki: Schildt, 1974; Stockholm: Bonnier, 1974); translated by Teal as *Sun City* (New York: Pantheon, 1976; London: Hutchinson, 1976);

Den farliga resan (Helsinki: Schildt, 1977; Stockholm: Bonnier Junior, 1977); translated by Hart as *The Dangerous Journey* (London: Benn, 1978);

Dockskåpet och andra berättelser (Helsinki: Schildt, 1978; Stockholm: Bonnier, 1978)–includes "Apan" and "Lokomotiv," translated by W. Glyn Jones as "Studies in Obsession: The New Art of Tove Jansson," *Books from Finland,* 2 (1981): 60-71;

Skurken i muminhuset, by Jansson and Per Olov Jansson (Helsinki: Schildt, 1980; Stockholm: Bonnier Junior, 1980);

Den ärliga bedragaren (Helsinki: Schildt, 1982; Stockholm: Bonnier, 1982);

Stenåkern (Helsinki: Schildt, 1984; Stockholm: Bonnier, 1984);

Två berättelser från havet (Stockholm: Bonnier, 1984);

Karin, min vän (Stockholm: Bonnier, 1987);

Resa med lätt bagage (Helsinki: Schildt, 1987; Stockholm: Bonnier, 1987);

Rent spel (Helsinki: Schildt, 1989; Stockholm: Bonnier, 1989);

Brev från Klara (Helsinki: Schildt, 1991; Stockholm: Bonnier, 1991);

Visor från Mumindalen, by Jansson, Lars Jansson, and Erna Tauro (Stockholm: Bonnier Junior, 1993; Esbo: Schildt, 1993);

Anteckningar från en ö, by Jansson and Tuulikki Pietilä (Helsinki: Schildt, 1996; Stockholm: Bonnier, 1996);

Meddelande: Noveller i urval 1971-1997 (Helsinki: Schildt, 1998; Stockholm: Bonnier, 1998).

PLAY PRODUCTIONS: *Mumintrollet och kometen,* Helsinki, Svenska Teatern, 29 December 1949;

Troll i kulisserna, Helsinki, Lilla Teatern, 1958;

Muminoperan, Helsinki, Nationaloperan, 7 December 1974;

Mumintroll i kulisserna, Stockholm, Dramaten, 1 April 1982.

PRODUCED SCRIPT: *Mumintrollet,* television, by Jansson and Lars Jansson, Sveriges Radio Television, TV2, 1969.

OTHER: Solveig von Schoultz, *Nalleresan,* illustrated by Jansson (Helsinki: Schildt, 1944);

Mumintrollet, nos. 1-4, 6, by Jansson, nos. 5, 7, and 8, by Jansson and Lars Jansson (Helsinki: Schildt / Stockholm: Geber, 1957-1964);

Lewis Carroll, *Snarkjakten,* translated by Lars Forssell and Åke Runnquist, illustrated by Jansson (Stockholm: Bonnier, 1959);

J. R. R. Tolkien, *Bilbo, En hobbits äventyr,* translated by Britt G. Hallqvist, illustrated by Jansson (Stockholm: Rabén & Sjögren, 1962);

Carroll, *Alice i underlandet,* illustrated by Jansson, translated by Runnquist (Stockholm: Bonnier Junior, 1966);

Carroll, *Alice's Adventures in Wonderland,* illustrated by Jansson (New York: Delacorte/Seymour Lawrence, 1977);

Carroll, *The Hunting of the Snark,* illustrated by Jansson (Essex: Basildon, 1984);

"Tarzan den Oförliknelige," in *Barndomens böcker: Barnboksförfattarnas litteraturhistoria,* edited by Annika Holm and Siv Widerberg (Hedemora: Gidlund, 1984), pp. 209-217.

SELECTED PERIODICAL PUBLICATIONS–
UNCOLLECTED: "Prickinas och Fabians äventyr," comic strip, *Lunkentus,* 10-16 (1929);

"Mumintrollet och jordens undergång," comic strip, *Ny Tid* (3 October 1947 - 2 April 1948);

"Sagan inom verkligheten: Den ärliga Elsa Beskow," *Bonniers Litterära Magasin,* no. 5 (1959): 419-420;

"Den lömska barnboksförfattaren," *Horisont,* 2 (1961): 8-11;

"Några ord i Ljubljana," *Nya Argus,* 18 (1966): 259-261;

"Barnets värld," *Samtiden,* 3 (1984): 67-70.

Tove Jansson is known as the creator of the Moomin World, presented in a series of profoundly original books for children that have appeared in more than thirty languages. All the books are illustrated by Jansson, and her dual artistic identity as author and visual artist is clearly reflected in her extensive work, which spans from painting and illustration to novels and short stories for both adults

Jansson with her mother, Signe, the model for Moominmamma in her Moomin family stories

and children. Jansson belonged to the Swedish-speaking minority in Finland, and traces of isolation—the theme of the "narrow room" that is said to characterize Finno-Swedish novels—may also be found in her work. Catastrophes and dramatic events emanating from the larger world outside constantly threaten the free and happy spirit of the Moomin family, living in a beautiful valley of their own, surrounded by mountains. Although sometimes viewed as a paradise for escapists, the utopian character of the Moomin universe is based on resistance. It emerged in the shadow of World War II as a vision of a happy society and a peaceful world.

Tove Marika Jansson was born on 9 August 1914 in Helsinki, where she was raised as the eldest of three children. The family spent their summers in the Finnish archipelago, a tradition that Jansson and her two brothers continued as adults, although on different islands. She lived in Helsinki. Her parents were both visual artists, and the children grew up in a studio home filled with the father's sculptures. Art was sacred, Jansson writes in her autobiographical novel about her childhood, *Bildhuggarens dotter* (1968; translated as *Sculptor's Daughter*, 1969). Her father, the sculptor Viktor Jansson from Helsinki, known mainly for a series of war monuments, was a rebel at heart with a disposition for the dramatic. While studying in Paris, he met Signe Hammarsten, an art student from Stockholm, and they married in 1913. She made a name for herself as an illustrator and became one of the foremost graphic designers of books and postage stamps in Finland.

Both parents were important for Jansson's extremely early concentration on an artistic career. She is certainly the daughter of an adventurous sculptor, but just as much the daughter of a graphic artist and true storyteller. Her father loved thunderstorms and, whenever the weather was bad enough, took his family sailing to wild islands where they spent stormy nights under the sail and salvaged smuggled canisters and driftwood from the bays. Hammarsten, who came from a clergyman's family, loved to tell stories, turning narratives from the Old Testament into thrilling fairy tales. For Jansson as a child, the act of telling a story was just as sacred as the act of artistic creation. Most important, the tears of the tales created a sense of security, as she recalls in *Bildhuggarens dotter*: "Vi slächer i ateljén och sitter fram for elden och hon sager: det var en gång . . . Allt annat ar utanter och kan inte komma in. Varken nu eller någonsin" (We turn out the lights in the studio and sit in front of the fire and she says: once upon a time.... Everything else is outside and can't get in. Not now or at any time). Telling stories was a way to shut out danger.

The balanced tension between outside danger and inside security, of fundamental importance for the Moomin books, is also because of the political situation in Finland during Jansson's childhood. She was just a small child when the country was shaken by the bloody and painful civil war between the "Reds" (the communists) and the "Whites" (the conservative forces) in 1918; Finland had declared its independence from Russia in 1917. Viktor Jansson participated on the side of the Whites, like many of his compatriots in the Finland-Swedish community, and the horrible experiences of the war never left him. It affected the whole family, and a glimpse of his trauma is shown in a dramatic scene in *Bildhuggarens dotter* when "Pappa" attacks a chair with his bayonet during a late-night party, watched by the daughter who is supposed to be asleep.

Jansson's childhood and youth, seen in retrospect, was a time of training in the artist's profession, but she also had an early start in writing, training herself as a serious, working author in her diaries. She made magazines (which she sold to her classmates) and a series of small books with illustrations. When she was fifteen years old, Jansson's first illustrated story, "Prickinas och Fabians äventyr" (Prickina and Fabian's Adventure, 1929), a cartoon presenting the fantastic adventures of two caterpillars in love, was published in the children's magazine *Lunkentus*. Four years later, under the pseudonym Vera Haij, she managed to get a picture book published, *Sara och Pelle och Neckens bläckfiskar* (Sara and Pelle and the Water-Sprite's Octopuses, 1933), a fairy tale story in the spirit of Hans Christian Andersen. That she published at such an early age was to a large degree because of her mother, a hardworking illustrator of books, magazines, and journals, who introduced her daughter into the network of publishers and editors. To a certain degree, it was Hammarsten who supported the family; her father's income as a sculptor was insecure, although associated with glorious moments.

In 1930 Jansson began to study graphic design and industrial art at Tekniska skolan (The School of Applied Arts) in Stockholm, where her mother had once been a pupil. This period of "a new life" is recalled in one of the short stories in *Meddelande: Noveller i urval 1971–1997* (Message: Selected Stories 1971–1997, 1998). That she should become an artist like her parents was taken for granted, and it seems as if she had no choice. "I want to be a savage," she wrote, as quoted by Boel Westin, in her diary in 1931, "Jag ville vara en vilde! Inte en konstnär–men jag måste. For familjens skull." (not an artist–but I must, for the sake of family.) This sign of opposition, however, was only expressed in her diary. It was probably caused by the harsh economic situation of the family, but it nevertheless reveals an early awareness of the hard facts of life. Jansson continued her studies for two more years, working with book covers, decorative art, advertising, and different forms of printed matter. She finished art school in 1933. Back in Helsinki she joined the painting class at the Finnish Art Society (Ateneum) but sometimes felt restricted by its conservative ideals and the male dominance of the school. She left Ateneum in 1937 and attended various art academies in Paris the following year. Her first solo exhibition took place in 1943, but her definitive breakthrough came with her second exhibition in 1946. Still lifes, landscapes, and interiors are the main motifs of her painting from this period, often done in a French style, focusing on lights and colors.

Although the 1930s and the first years of the 1940s were mainly devoted to the visual arts, Jansson never really abandoned her ambition to write. Several short stories were published in journals and newspapers, beginning in 1934. Mainly written as travel accounts and based on experiences from some study trips abroad, they nevertheless outline some later themes in her books: the search for identity, the problems of self-deception, the dream of freedom, and a complex attitude toward loneliness. The income of an artist was insecure, however, and Jansson established herself as an illustrator, working in a variety of genres. She had good use for her early training in industrial arts and illustrated all sorts of texts, ranging from poems to advertising in newspapers, journals, and magazines.

Of special interest is her impressive production in the satirical magazine *Garm,* to which she contributed regularly for more than twenty years, beginning in 1929; she drew approximately five hundred illustrations and hundreds of covers. *Garm* was a political forum for Finno-Swedish authors, artists, and scholars, and during the war it played quite an important role for critics of the alliance between Finland and Germany, serving as a mouthpiece for antifascist and anti-Nazi opinions. Jansson's drawings and her sharp satirical portraits of Adolf Hitler (as well as of Joseph Stalin) contributed to the tough profile of the magazine and were on some occasions censored by the authorities. Her career as a political cartoonist must be seen as an act of subversion, and the experience of ideological oppression has certainly left its traces in the Moomin World. The work in *Garm* also formed an arena for the development of the characters in the forthcoming books. The moomintroll figure, in the beginning long and thin in shape, emerged as an additional signature in the *Garm* drawings. The idea of a "moomintroll" had, however, occupied her imagination rather early, but in different ways. Some diary entries from the beginning of the 1930s describe moomintrolls as terrifying figures of the subconscious, ghostly creatures of darkness, and when depicted in some later watercolors they appear in black, within an atmosphere filled with agony. These versions, made before the war, may be seen as early depictions of the dark mood that from the beginning is hidden behind the vision of the happy Moomin family.

The Moomin World took form in the shadow of the war, and the first two books are clearly marked by the apocalyptic mood of the era. The Russian bomb raids had brutally crushed any hope of peace in the winter and spring of 1944, and the sight of the burning town of Helsinki was atrocious: Jansson wrote in her diary that she "längtade bort så jag kunde gå sönder" (longed to get away so much that she could go to pieces). To counteract her despair she began to create, together with a few friends, a happy society and a peaceful, if fictional, world. One of these friends was Atos Wirtanen, politician and philosopher, to whom Jansson was engaged for a period in the 1940s. In the Moomin books the Muskrat, a gloomy philosopher who predicts catastrophes while lying on his hammock and whose favorite reading is Oswald Spengler's *Der Untergang des Abendlandes* (The Decline of the West, 1918-1922), bears some resemblance to Wirtanen. This allusion for the adult, intellectual reader is typical for Jansson, who works on different levels in her texts. The various characters stand for different drives, emotions, and dreams, revealing the imbalance between what people are and what they want to be. Jansson writes for two audiences in a literal sense.

In her Moomin books Jansson retells the old myths of creation, using them in order to construct a utopian society where life is threatened but emerges triumphant. The first book, *Småtrollen och den stora översvämningen* (The Little Trolls and the Great Flood), written during the first years of the war, remained unpublished until 1945. That same year Jansson started on the second book, *Kometjakten* (1946; translated as *Comet in Moominland*, 1951). In the first book a paradise is born literally after a deluge, and the family is established in the valley; the second book continues the story from a perspective of paradise lost and then regained. Throughout nine

Jansson's map of the Moomin Valley, the setting for her series of children's fantasy novels (from Tove Jansson, Trollkarlens hatt, *1948)*

books altogether, each playing on a basic theme of order and chaos, the concept of the family is subjected to dangers and catastrophes, threats, splits, and disruptions of various kinds. The most fantastic and exotic features in the earlier books fade in the later ones, but the split between fantasy and realism is never really clear. The central figure in the growing gallery of characters–big and small creatures of different kinds and appearances all adopted by the nuclear family–is Moominmamma. She represents the basic concept of motherhood: responsible, considerate, and tender, she takes care of the family in all possible (and impossible) ways. She is a portrait of Jansson's mother and one of the few characters in the series that is modeled after persons in real life.

Småtrollen och den stora översvämningen, a forty-eight-page book with remarkable illustrations, has been considered a simple fairy tale by some critics but is in fact quite original. The impact of classic authors such as Andersen, Carlo Collodi, and Jules Verne should not be denied, but the narrative is not

Illustration by Jansson for Trollkarlens hatt, *in which the Moomin family discovers a magician's hat with supernatural properties*

dependent on them. The opening scene is that of mother and child, Moominmamma and her son Moomintroll, who are out in the woods looking for a place to stay during the winter. The father, Moominpappa, has abandoned the family. During their search they experience dangers and threats, adventures and wonders, culminating in the great flood; the dimensions are biblical. The flood is the turning point of the story. The father is found and rescued heroically by the wife and son. This way of crossing the limits of gender, turning conventional roles upside down, is characteristic of Jansson. The reunited family find their way to the wonderful valley and the blue Moomin house (which turns out to have been built earlier by the father). While superficially resembling a fairy tale, the story describes a mother's struggle for home and family, just as many women did during the war. She possesses all of a mother's resources and strength, looking after Moomintroll, willingly taking care of the little creature Sniff, and dramatically saving a cat (a lonely mother like herself) and her kittens from drowning. She represents the life force itself, and however adventurous Moominpappa may seem, his escapades end in Moominmamma's loving arms.

Some recurrent themes of the Moomin World are established with this story, including the disruption and reunification of the family, the polarization between chaotic and idyllic forces, and the dynamic tension between catastrophes and a peaceful life. The mother is in charge of the family, overlooking her husband's unrestrained longings for a globe-trotting life. Besides Sniff, some other characters are introduced, including the hattifnatters, restless wanderers of mysterious extraction, and the hemulens. The Moomin habit of hibernation, normally from November to April, is referred to, and some glimpses of ancestral history are provided; Moomintrolls used to live behind tiled stoves in people's houses. In 1945 *Småtrollen och den stora översvämningen* was published with little notice, and the book has never been translated. Jansson refused all efforts to reprint the story, mainly because of its resemblance to a fairy tale, until 1991, when a facsimile edition was published.

The second book, *Kometjakten,* starts where the first one ends, in the valley. A terrifying comet, predicted by the sinister Muskrat, threatens life on Earth. The comet is an ancient symbol of doom in myths and tales, but as the central motif in a book for children in the 1940s, the symbol is quite unusual. The fear of final annihilation in the book can be read as an allegory of the atomic bomb or the horrors of wartime destruction in general, persistent motifs in Jansson's drawings during the war. The mission of rescue this time relies on the children, Moomintroll and Sniff, turning the story into a sort of quest. They leave the valley in search of knowledge about the comet, their goal being the scientist's observatory located in the Lonely Mountains. On the way there and back again a wide range of dramatic events occur, while the comet consistently comes closer and gets bigger, coloring the sky and the earth in an appalling red light.

The comet is the narrative center of the story; it rules the action, changes the landscape and the order of nature, sets the stage for adventure, and widens the gallery of characters. Several new characters are presented, such as the independent wanderer of the world, Snufkin; the feminine and practical Snork Maiden (who becomes the object of Moomintroll's affections); and her bureaucratic brother the Snork; the philatelist Hemulen, all of whom move in with the family in the valley in the end. *Kometjakten* mirrors Jansson's passion for adventure stories and exotic settings. Moomintroll saves the Snork Maiden from a carnivorous bush, a per-

Manuscript page for Jansson's 1950 novel Muminpappans Bravader: Skrivna av Honom Själv *(University Library, Åbo Akademi)* formance in the style of Edgar Rice Burroughs's *Tarzan* (one of Jansson's favorites), but typically enough, the heroic pattern is contradicted; the Snork Maiden in return later saves Moomintroll from a hideous octopus. However evident the construction of gender may seem, it is in fact rather blurred. *Kometjakten* ends with a rescue and the triumph of life, but the vision of doom presented during the minutes before the arrival of the comet is nevertheless implacable. The seabed lies dead and exposed, the sky is dark red, and the trees stand anxiously with trembling leaves. Life waits in agony. When the roar of the comet has ceased, Moominmamma sings her lullaby, which brings sleep and oblivion as well as the awareness of the uncertainty of human existence. This fragile balance characterizes all the Moomin books.

Writing *Kometjakten* was obviously of great importance for Jansson, a way of dealing with the fears of war, or, as in *Bildhuggarens dotter*, a way to shut out danger. She has revised the story twice, with versions published as *Mumintrollet på kometjakt* (Moomintroll Goes Comet-Hunting, 1956) and *Kometen kommer* (The Comet Is Coming, 1968). Also, the comet story is retold in the first Moomin strip cartoon, "Mumintrollet och jordens undergång" (Moomintroll and the Destruction of Earth), published in the Finland-Swedish newspaper *Ny Tid* during the winter of 1947–1948. It was made as a present to Wirtanen, editor of the paper at the time. The story was later adapted into a play, *Mumintrollet och kometen* (Moomintroll and the Comet), staged at the Swedish-language Svenska Teatern in Helsinki in 1949. Jansson wrote the script and outlined additional settings as well. The director of the play was the young Vivica Bandler, a new and upcoming name in cultural circles at that time. Jansson had met her in 1946, and the interest she developed in theater and dramatic discourse is to some extent because of Bandler. Their close friendship is reflected in the book that followed the comet story, *Trollkarlens hatt* (The Magician's Hat, 1948; translated as *Finn Family Moomintroll*, 1950).

Trollkarlens hatt is the lightest in spirit among the Moomin books, featuring the magic, excitement, and pleasure of seemingly endless childhood summers, while at the same time reflecting the basic insecurity of life, of which the Moomins are always aware. Praised by the critics, the novel was Jansson's literary breakthrough. Colorful, bright images of nature and descriptions in metaphoric language clearly reveal traces of Jansson the painter. *Trollkarlens hatt* was the first of the Moomin books to be published in English, which may explain why the English title is not a direct translation of the original. In contrast, the Swedish title immediately focuses on the main object in the story, the hat, rather than the family. This episodic narrative takes place in the valley, with the exception of a sailing trip to the lonely island of the hattifnatters. The plot centers around a magician's hat found in the valley in early spring and used as a wastepaper basket by the Moomins, who are unaware at first of its magic powers. The hat transforms everything into its opposite, and thus the excitement of the commonplace, the home and the family, becomes central. Eggshells come out as clouds and the Moomin house changes into an exotic jungle, suitable for playing Tarzan; but most frightening is Moomintroll's physical transformation into a thin and ugly creature with a big, bushy tail, a stranger to his friends and family. Only Moominmamma is able to break the spell, once again demonstrating the powers of maternal love.

The ground-freezing Groke, a lonely, apparently fearful female creature, can be viewed as the mother's dark opposite in this book. Her complex character is developed in later books, which focus on her search for warmth and companionship. The magnificent King's Ruby that is desired by both the Groke and the magician himself represents a problematic obsession with belongings in the Moomin stories, but it is also the symbol of beauty and love. It is brought to the valley by two small and "foreign" creatures, always together, almost identical in looks and with a language of their own. Here the Jansson-Bandler friendship is reflected, as these near-twins are named Tofslan (Tove) and Vifslan (Vivica), although in the English translation they are called Thingumy and Bob. The book ends with a splendid garden party under the stars one night in late August, culminating with the arrival of the magician, looking for the King's Ruby, who grants everyone a wish. *Trollkarlens hatt* is an aesthetic manifesto for life itself, and an open-minded attitude to the unexpected, the unknown, and the unusual rules the story from beginning to end. To be bored is the worst thing that can happen.

After *Trollkarlens hatt* Jansson radically shifted her narrative perspective and explored a new genre. The fictional memoir *Muminpappans Bravader: Skrivna av Honom Själv* (1950; translated as *The Exploits of Moominpappa, Described by Himself*, 1952), is narrated in the first person. It displays a sense of parody and comic irony developed earlier in her political drawings. The narrator, Moominpappa, describes his life from an unhappy childhood as a gifted but lonesome foundling, through a Sturm und Drang period up to the dramatic encounter with Moominmamma by the

Jansson with her brother, Lars, her collaborator on some of her works (photograph © Per Olov Jansson)

sea one stormy night in late autumn. The parody in this amusing story applies not only to the memoir genre itself but also just as much to the male author of memoirs and his vainglory, self-centeredness, and single-minded tendency to polish his own image. Male culture is thus the main target of the parody, but the book nevertheless demonstrates a great deal of sympathy for the hero's adventures and hardships, whether or not he is telling the truth about his turbulent life. The pattern is borrowed from the classic autobiography of Benvenuto Cellini, whose words Moominpappa recalls in his preface, although without mentioning Cellini's name. The memoirs tell of the severe and free friendship between men, and at the same time recount a story of fathers and sons. Two of Moominpappa's youthful companions turn out to be the fathers of Sniff and Snufkin. The mothers are, interestingly enough, depicted as powerful figures in their own right, although the male narrator's perspective emphasizes virtues like fertility and beauty. The magnificent Mymble is the mother of "aderton, nitton ungar" (eighteen, nineteen kiddies), among them Little My, while the young Moominmamma reaches for her powder case immediately after being rescued from drowning. Everything ends happily, with disrupted families united and sons, fathers, and mothers all looking forward to a future of possibilities. Most interesting is the fact that Moominpappa turns out to be a great storyteller, like Jansson herself. In him she projects her role as author and hides behind his writings; to be an author is obviously a male sphere of activity. The literary ambitions of Moominpappa return in later books, and, significantly, his date of birth turns out to be the same as Jansson's. The writing of Moominpappa's memoirs was obviously a project of great importance for Jansson, just as *Kometjakten* had been. *Muminpappans Bravader* was also later revised, published as *Muminpappans memoarer* (The Memoirs of Moominpappa, 1968), in which Jansson eliminates some of Moominpappa's worst exaggerations. The English edition, however, follows the original text.

The English translations of *Trollkarlens hatt* and *Muminpappans Bravader* opened the way into the international market, and the success of the Moomins in some ways made the 1950s a turbulent decade for Jansson. The first picture book set in the Moomin World was published in 1952, a few years later the Moomin cartoon strip started; and in 1958 the second Moomin play was staged in Helsinki, later performed in special appearances in Stockholm and Oslo. The picture book *Hur gick det sen? Boken om Mymlan, Mumintrollet och Lilla My* (1952; translated as *The Book about Moomin, Mymble and Little My*, 1953) displays the author's interest in dramatic discourse. In this theatrically composed unity of text and picture, settings and events constantly change through shifting perspectives, colors, and light. Illusion and reality are intertwined, as seen through the eyes of Moomintroll, who is on his way home to his mother through dark woods and desert landscapes. Different characters act as helpers or adversaries. The story deals with the horrors and happiness of the child, the principal theme being separation from the mother or, rather, the fear of losing maternal love. The theme of conquering fear and loneliness, ending in love and warm community, reappears in Jansson's second picture book, *Vem ska trösta knyttet?* (1960; translated as *Who Will Comfort Toffle?* 1960).

In the 1950s Tove Jansson also made a series of murals and frescoes and had her third solo exhibition, which was a success among the critics. At the same time two new Moomin books of different characters came out: *Farlig midsommar* (1954; translated as *Moominsummer Madness*, 1955) and *Trollvinter* (1957; translated as *Moominland Midwinter*, 1958). Verbal and visual activities were crossed and united, resulting in a multiple and progressive body of artwork. The definite confirmation of the attraction of the Moomins in the international market was an offer from Associated Newspapers in 1953, and the following autumn the Moomin cartoon started in the *Evening News* (London). It was soon syndicated in many countries around the world. The success of the cartoon series, however, had its price. Jansson had signed a contract to produce one strip a day, six days a week, for seven years. She was sent to London for a month to learn the job from professionals on Fleet Street. This apparently frightening period is reflected in her short story "Serietecknaren" (The Cartoonist), published in the collection *Dockskåpet och andra berättelser* (The Doll's House and Other Tales, 1978). Although the cartoon opened a new medium of expression, the search for new ideas and stories soon overshadowed other activities; as stated in the short story, the constant hunt for subjects is the curse of all comic-strip writers. Jansson left the business as soon as the contracted time had passed at the end of 1959. Her brother, Lars, had already collaborated with her for several years, and from that point on he took over the cartoon and continued it for another fifteen years.

The 1950s also brought decisive changes in Jansson's personal life. In 1954 she met the graphic artist Tuulikki Pietilä, who became her life companion, an encounter of importance for both her writing and painting as well. They had met as young art students in the late 1930s, and when their paths later crossed again, it did not take long to establish their relationship. Pietilä is portrayed as the philosophical rationalist Too-ticky in *Trollvinter* and, along with Jansson's mother, is one of the two main characters in the Moomin books that are drawn from real life. The year that *Trollvinter* was published was also a year of grief for Jansson, however: Viktor Jansson died in 1958, and the loss of family that Moomintroll experiences in this book may be seen in this light.

The disruption of the family is, however, already a structuring force in *Farlig Midsommar*. To some extent this novel recalls the first Moomin book in its focus on family split and reunion, but the perpetual theme of catastrophe is presented here in a new context. A volcanic eruption causes a flood in Moominvalley, and in order to save themselves, the family lands on a floating theater. They take up residence on the stage, a sophisticated setting that radically changes their perspectives on reality—the point being that the Moomins do not have the faintest idea of what a theater really is. Life is thus literally performed on the stage, like a dream. The narrative discourse is likewise dramatic, structured as a comedy of errors—William Shakespeare's *A Midsummer Night's Dream* (circa 1595–1596) is one intertext—with entanglement and deception, superstition and retribution. The characters suddenly find themselves set in new, albeit temporary, roles: the vagabond Snufkin acts as the tender father of a group of orphans, and Moomintroll and the Snork Maiden are held prisoner by a rigorous hemul. New characters such as the gloomy Misabel, the lonely Fillyjonk, and the curious Whomper are also introduced. Moominpappa returns to his role of author, composing a tragic family drama in hexameters. In the grand finale this tragedy in one act is transformed into a play of reunion and love, a grandiose feast of creation in which everyone participates, the actors on the stage as well as the audience. In the end the family returns to the valley once again, but their perception of reality is colored from then on by the theater's world of illusions and dreams.

In *Farlig Midsommar* summer still rules life in the valley, but the perspective radically shifts in the

Illustrations by Jansson for her novel Farlig midsommar *(1954), in which the Moomin family is flooded out of their home and take refuge in a theater*

next book. The winter tale *Trollvinter* represents a definite change of course in Jansson's authorship. The smell of winter is "more serious," the novel asserts in the beginning, a statement of psychological importance for the events depicted in this book. Viewed from the perspective of Jansson's career and personal life at the end of the 1950s, this new direction was quite logical. Her work on the comic strip had no doubt improved her international reputation, but the constant search for motifs and stories became an artistic prison toward the end. With her growing popularity also followed a vast range of assignments that confined her; the Moomin World had turned into a myth of its own. Writing *Trollvinter* was a way of dealing with this myth. When Moomintroll awakens from hibernation, he is confronted with a new and quite terrifying world. The sunny and adventurous summers of childhood have faded, replaced by a silent, petrified, and somewhat fearful landscape of coldness inhabited by mysterious creatures of the dark. Moomintroll has to live through his first winter on his own, until he discovers that even this frightening world can be fascinating; "now I own the whole year," he concludes in the end. His passage through the secretive essence and frozen landscape of winter turns out to be a quest, during which he has to face his darker, subconscious sides. "One has to discover everything for oneself, and get over it all alone," declares the wise Too-ticky, throughout the novel acting as a guide for the new independence that Moomintroll gradually gains. To some extent she replaces the role taken by Moominmamma in the earlier books, being both nurturing and practical, but her message is different. "Nothing is certain," she states, and this device of hers may be said to be the key to the story. Although it all ends in the lightness of spring and the reunion of the family, the urge to make a clean sweep with demands and expectations is quite clear in this novel. It is in many ways devoted to the author's encounter with Pietilä a few years earlier, and the character of Too-ticky returns in the next book, *Det osynliga barnet och andra berättelser* (1962; translated as *Tales from Moominvalley*, 1963).

Trollkarlens hatt and *Muminpappans Bravader* also rely on this literary technique: events are linked together by characters and settings. Her writing for adults includes several short-story collections, beginning with *Lyssnerskan* (The Listener, 1971), which clearly shows a disposition for short fiction. Her first published collection of stories, however, was *Det osynliga barnet och andra berättelser*. Different characters from the Moomin books are studied here in new lights, and the collection can be seen as a series of psychological portraits. Several stories deal with problems of identity, focalized through feelings of anxiety or fear. The little girl in "Det osynliga barnet" (The Invisible Child), literally frightened into invisibility, has to regain her lost self-esteem in order to become visible. In "Vårvisan" (The Spring Tune), a tiny creature finds an identity when he is given a name of his own. The last story in the collection, "Granen" (The Fir Tree), develops a kind of subversive cultural critique. Here the whole Moomin family awakens from hibernation (thus expanding the motif from *Trollvinter*) and is confronted with Christmas. Neither the word nor the feast as such have any significance for them, however. Viewed by the Moomins, Christmas turns into a strange event when "ingenting är ordnat och nån hargått förlorade, och alla springer om, Kring som tokiga" (nothing seems to be ready, and something's got lost, and everyone is running about like mad.)

"Livet är inte fridfullt" (Life is not peaceful), Jansson wrote in one of her early novels, *Trollharlens hatt,* and the consistently changing illusion of reality must be said to be a basic principle throughout the whole construction of the Moomin World. The two novels that end the Moomin suite, *Pappan och havet* (1965; translated as *Moominpappa at Sea,* 1966) and *Sent i november* (1970; translated as *Moominvalley in November,* 1970), also depend on this principle, although in a different manner. The first portrays the various personal crises experienced by a severely decimated Moomin family, who have left the valley for a barren lighthouse island. The latter double-exposes that narrative from the perspective of the autumnal, empty valley, where a group of different characters gather in search of the lost family. The psychological probing begun in *Trollvinter* continues here, concentrating on dreams and longings, emotional crises and feelings of insufficiency. The adventures take place on the inside, formed as existential questions and strongly attached to problems of identity. The settings are naturalistic, although some events and phenomena, especially in *Pappan och havet,* have a quality of magical realism. More clearly than before, Jansson places the Moomin parents at opposite poles. The novel starts with the father feeling at a loss because there is nothing left for him to do in the valley. His masculine principle impels him toward the island, away from the vegetative realm of the valley, where Moominmamma rules. Yet, this portrayal is not a case of "seductive conservatism," as the radical Swedish critics termed this symbolic book in the 1970s, with a message that mothers should stay at home while fathers are allowed to devote themselves to adventures. On the contrary, the novel shows rules and boundaries in motion, exposing a father in a vain search of the secret of the sea (symbolic of life) and a mother forced to reconstruct her earlier means of existence. While Pappa experiments, writes, and cogitates in order to find a theory of the mysteries of nature, Mamma, where she plants and paints, collects bits of wood and saws them. Finally, when Moominpappa chops up Moominmamma's blocks of wood, the key is provided for the symbolic picture in the end of the book, where a saw and an ax are laid crosswise. Mother or father, artist or author, everyone follows their destinies, but in one and the same woodshed. Between the parents is Moomintroll, struggling with problems of adolescence and left alone to explore new surroundings. Like his parents, he constructs a secret life of his own, and, like them, he strives to incorporate the unknown with the known, as in his nightly encounters with the Groke. An important part is played by the matter-of-fact Little My, an adopted child. Principles of masculinity and femininity are counterpoised in a complex pattern, set against the background of the barren and windswept island. Nature reflects the soul in the true sense of the word. Convincing children's books are full of symbols, identification, and self-obsession, Jansson states in her 1961 essay "Den lömska barnboksförfattaren" (The Sly Children's Author, 1961). In *Pappan och havet* her artistic identities are projected through Moominpappa, the author, and Moominmamma, the painter, thus demonstrating the self-possession in her work. Writing is connected with male creativity and painting with female, and the split in these two art forms mirrors one way of dealing with artistic duality. Creative ambitions are not restricted to the Moomin parents, however. Poets and artists of all kinds appear throughout the expanding world of the Moomins. Snufkin, great wanderer of the world, presents himself as a visionary poet in *Kometjakten,* while the wise Too-ticky introduces herself through lyric poems in *Trollvinter*. Results and motifs may differ, but the act of creation is never really questioned until the last book, *Sent i november*.

Self-portrait of Jansson surrounded by some of her characters (from Tordis Ørjasæter, Møte med Tove Jansson, *1985)*

In this dream-like finale of the Moomin epic, set after the family has abandoned their valley, Jansson dismounts her fictional world, leaving room for something new. Dream is more important than reality, she writes in the notes to the book, thus indicating that the picture of the happy family in the beautiful valley was indeed a vision. *Sent i november* is a book of grief, an allegory of a story that its author finds impossible to recall. The autumnal valley is filled with rain and dusk, and the atmosphere is colored by grayness and twilight. It is a novel of transformation, but a novel about the power of imagination as well. The visitors who are gathered in the empty house are all forced to reshape their stories of the family in the valley with more realistic ones; dreams and memories are necessary in life. Seen in this light, all the characters are poets or artists in one way or another, but the foremost is nevertheless the little whomper called Toft. In him, the creator of the Moomin World pictures herself (Tove-Toft) struggling with a fictional world that threatens to devour her. During his search for the lost Moominmamma, Toft must work his way through pictures and stories, dreams and illusions, a painful process metaphorically reflected through his reading about a prehistoric animal called the Nummulite, close to an anagram for the name *Mumin* (Moomin). Behind this narrative a different story is concealed, in which happiness is not taken for granted, childhood must be abandoned, and, most important, the intimate relationship between mother and child is broken. Jansson's mother died in 1970, the year during which *Sent i november* was written.

Between the last two Moomin novels the autobiographical novel *Bildhuggarens dotter* was published in 1968. Jansson said that she had reached a point at which she became convinced she could no longer write books for children; at the same time, however, she was unable to imagine writing books exclusively for adults. She resolved this dilemma by writing about her own childhood. The title chosen indicates the influence of her father, but her mother turns out to be even more important for the imaginative child in these episodes, drawn from her upbringing in an unconventional home. In Jansson's family, life is about art and work, and she describes the balance between the excitement of the commonplace and the safety of the fantastic as a natural part of the child's world. *Bildhuggarens dotter* establishes the picture of the adventurous male sculptor and the nurturing, hardworking mother, which became the standard description of the Jansson family.

This first novel explicitly addressed to an adult readership was well received, but comparison with the Moomin series was inevitable. Although the spirit of the family seems quite similar, the atmosphere created in the narrative discourse is different. The closeness between mother and daughter, shown in *Bildhuggarens dotter,* was clear from the beginning. "You understand me better than anyone," Jansson wrote in one of her early diaries. Hammarsten's impact on her life and art is obvious, as the model for Moominmamma and as a female mentor, adviser, and critic; but the maternal picture has further dimensions in Jansson's work. "Somliga drottningar regerar mycket länge" (Some queens reign for a long time), she writes in "Denstora resan" in *Dockskåpet och andra berättelser,* depicting an adult woman who is unable to set herself free from her domineering mother and devote herself to her lesbian lover instead. The disruption of the archetypal picture of the good mother had, however, already begun in *Pappan och havet* and was purposely continued in *Sent i november.*

Sommarboken (1972; translated as *The Summer Book,* 1974) offers still other perspectives, once again setting the role of the mother in a new light. This episodic novel of summer, set on an island in the Finnish archipelago, intertwines three human lives and three generations: represented by a six-year-old girl, a father, and a grandmother. The characters portrayed are all based on Jansson's family: the father on one of her two brother, Lars; the little girl, Sophia, on her niece; and the grandmother on Hammarsten. The father is in the background in the novel, constantly working at his drawing table, and the focus of the novel is on the child and the grandmother, both egocentric in one way or another. Forced to be together, they explore the small island, play games, and share experiences, but above all they intermittently discuss the conditions of life and death from their different perspectives. Some of these debates end up in almost aphoristic sentences, describing the presuppositions for the fragile balance between loneliness and friendship, young and old, love and hatred, as in one of the observations made by the child: the more you love someone, the less he likes you back. The sharp and subtle philosophy of *Sommarboken* is one of the reasons for the success of the book; its sensitive way of confronting aging with childishness is another.

This process of transcending boundaries is characteristic of Jansson's production, in which borders between words and pictures, between books for children and for adults, and between imagination and reality are erased and rendered meaningless. The constant testing of limits that developed throughout the twenty-five years of writing the Moomin books expanded the author's modes of expression. The adult books have not attracted the same attention as the Moomin books, but interest in them is increasing. The fact that Jansson started out her literary career as a writer of children's books and was soon established as one of the foremost in that field accounts in part for the lack of attention to her writing for adults. Thus, critics confronted this new direction in Jansson's career with a mixture of appreciation and uncertainty. Most disturbing seemed to be the fact that a sense of harmony was no longer the main focus of the narratives.

In painting Jansson devoted herself to nonfigurative work in the 1960s, and her purposeful orientation toward books for adults may be viewed in this light. Her writing for adults displays the same tendency toward simplification and reduction. Jansson's economical and careful way with words is clear from her first short-story collection for adults, *Lyssnerskan,* through her last, *Meddelande.* In the final story of this collection, "Meddelande"—a mixture of earlier publications and new stories—the author transforms herself into a sender of short notations and memoranda, messages that are all different from one another and united only by their function as different means of communication.

Apart from *Bildhuggarens dotter* and *Sommarboken,* only one of Jansson's later books has appeared in English: *Solstaden* (1974), a novel that was translated as *Sun City* in 1976. It was conceived during Jansson's travels around the world, together with Pietilä, in 1971. In Florida they discovered quiet communities of elderly people where all arrangements are made for rest and imminent death, and rocking chairs are lined up on verandas under perpetual sunshine. This community of frightening calmness and commercialization of death is disclosed through a series of sharp-eyed studies of characters, which examine the effects when the old people are confronted with a young and loving couple. Although the limits of communication seem hard to cross and the process of aging is ruthless, the city of the sun becomes a symbol for the faith of a last resort, a last hope for something else to come. This new turn of writing, with its pronounced focus on the unpredictable behavior of old people, was disturbing for some critics, who obviously longed for the subtle tenderness of the earlier texts, and the reception of the novel was mixed. *Solstaden* is not unique in Jansson's production, however; rather, the desire to unveil human nature is rather characteristic of her art. The problem of aging is likewise a major theme in the short-story collections, often interwoven with problems of communication and loneliness.

Problems of artistic conception, such as the compulsive search for true expression, are also constantly investigated, as in the title story in *Lyssnerskan*. A later variation of this theme is developed in the short story "Bilderna" (The Pictures) in the collection *Brev från Klara* (Letters from Klara, 1991). The conditions for creating art—the artist's problems, difficulties, demands, and expectations—are viewed from different perspectives in her whole production. The stories collected in *Dockskåpet och andra berättelser* center around different kinds of obsessions and receptivity to an idea or a project. The title story is symbolic, revealing the artist's desire to construct a closed, defined, and protected world. The characters studied in *Dockskåpet och andra berättelser* are on the verge of developing borderline personality disorders; when, one might ask, does an intense interest or a persistent preoccupation with a project become abnormal? Recurrently analyzed throughout the later work is the author's (or artist's) need for privacy and distance and the reader's consistent claim for a dialogue. The point at which contact with readers turns into an obligation is evidently a matter of great complexity for Jansson. An early example of a story with this theme is "Brev till en idol" (Letters to an Idol) in *Lyssnerskan,* but the most openhearted examination of the subject is "Korrespondens" (Correspondence) in *Resa med lätt bagage* (Traveling Light, 1987). This story consists of a collection of letters from a young Japanese girl, who is anxious to meet the author that she so much admires. The real meeting has, as the girl finally discovers, already taken place, however; in fact, the reader can only meet the author in the text.

Respect for the power of words is typical of the Jansson's literary art. The three novels that were written during the 1980s might all be seen in this light, as underscored by the title of one of them, *Den ärliga bedragaren* (The Honest Impostor, 1982). The plot centers on two women, a middle-aged, lonely children's-book writer and a young salesclerk, and explores their dangerous interplay with deceptions and lies, truth and honesty. Both women seem to fit the paradox of the honest impostor, thus underlining the main topic of the novel: self-deception. The painful search for the ultimate words is the theme of the short novel *Stenåkern* (The Stone Field, 1984), seen through the eyes of an old journalist trying to write a biography on a man he despises. In the episodic novel *Rent spel* (Fair Play, 1989) the difficulty of finding the most persuasive words reaches its final point in the episode "Killing George"; one has to kill in order to give true life to a story. To play fair is the most important thing. This novel—about two women, a writer and an artist who have shared life and work for many years—is above all a story of how to be blessed by love. As a portrayal of the long-lived relationship of Jansson and Pietilä, it is remarkable in its straightforward frankness, depicting both the habits and dramas of daily life. Although the two have lived together since the 1950s, the first artistic product of their relationship was *Anteckningar från en ö* (Notations from an Island, 1996), which describes their summer stays on the lonely island Klovharun in the Finnish archipelago. The text is by Jansson and the pictures are by Pietilä. It starts with the building of the cabin on the island in the 1960s and ends on a day in autumn more than twenty-five years later, when the time had come to leave the island. However painful this leave-taking must have been, the book ends in a hopeful mood. When cleaning the cellar, Pietilä finds a dragon: "den flög högt, nakt upp och forsätta långt ut över Finska viken" (it flew high, right up in the air and continued its flight far out over the Gulf of Finland).

Tove Jansson died on 27 June 2001. She has said that she loves borders because they imply expectations to be on one's way, representing the important movement forward. Throughout her books there are borders between security and danger, old and young, seas and islands, but they are constantly crossed and erased. Here, if anywhere, lies the key to her changing forms of art.

Interviews:

Bo Carpelan, " . . . om mina berättelser vänder sej till någon särskild slags läsare så är det väl till ett skrutt," in *Min väg till barnboken: 21 barnboksförfattare berättar,* edited by Bo Strömstedt (Stockholm: Bonnier, 1964), pp. 97–103;

W. Glyn Jones, "Tove Jansson: My Books and My Characters," *Books from Finland,* 3 (1978): 91–97.

Biography:

Tordis Ørjasæter, *Møte med Tove Jansson* (Oslo: Gyldendal, 1985).

References:

Salme Aejmelaeus, *Kun lyhdyt syttyvät: Tove Jansson ja muumimaailma* (Tampere, Finland: Suomen Nuorisokirjallisuuden Instituutti, 1984);

Birgit Antonsson, *Det slutna och det öppna rummet: Om Tove Janssons senare författarskap* (Stockholm: Carlsson, 1999);

Barbro K. Gustafsson, *Stenåker och ängsmark: Erotiska motiv och homosexuella skildringar i Tove Janssons senare litteratur* (Uppsala & Stockholm: Almqvist & Wiksell, 1992);

Sonja Hagemann, *Mummitrollbøkene: En litteraer karakteristikk* (Oslo: Aschehoug, 1967);

Tove Holländer, *Från idyll till avidyll: Tove Janssons illustrationer till Muminböckerna* (Tampere, Finland: Suomen Nuorisokirjallisuuden Instituutti, 1983);

Glyn W. Jones, *Tove Jansson* (Boston: Twayne, 1984);

Lena Kåreland and Barbro Werkmäster, *Livsvandring i tre akter: En analys av Tove Janssons bilderböcker Hur gick det sen? Vem ska trösta knyttet? Den farliga resan* (Uppsala: Hjelm, 1994);

Mirja Kivi, ed., *Moominvalley: From Stories to a Museum Collection* (Tampere, Finland: Tampere Art Museum, 1998);

Erik Kruskopf, *Bildkonstnären Tove Jansson* (Esbo, Finland: Schildt, 1992);

Virpi Kurhela, ed., *Muumien Taikaa: Tutkimusretkiä Tove Janssonin maailmaan* (Tampere, Finland: Suomen Nuorisokirjallisuuden Instituutti, 1996);

Irma Müller-Nienstedt, *Die Mumins für Erwachsene. Bilder zur Selbstwerdung* (Zürich and Düsseldorf: Walter-Verlag, 1994);

Juhani Tolvanen, *Vid min svans! Tove och Lars Janssons tecknade muminserie* (Helsinki: Schildt, 2000);

Boel Westin, "Creating a Zest for Life: Feminine, Masculine and Human in Tove Jansson's Moomin World," *Swedish Book Review* (Supplement 1990): 30–35;

Westin, *Familjen i dalen: Tove Janssons muminvärld* (Stockholm: Bonnier, 1988);

Westin, "Konsten som äventyr. Tove Jansson och bilderboken," *Vår moderna bilderbok*, ed. Vivi Edström (Stockholm: Rabén & Sjögren, 1991), pp. 51–70.

Papers:

The major collection of Tove Jansson's manuscripts and notes is at the University Library at Åbo Akademi, Åbo, Finland. "The Moominvalley Collections," a large collection of original illustrations, paintings, and three-dimensional tableaux related to the Moomin books, is at the Tampere Art Museum, Tampere, Finland. It comprises more than one thousand Moomin illustrations, more than two hundred illustrations for other children's books, and almost five hundred additional magazine illustrations and covers, mostly for the magazine *Garm*. Diary entries are found in Boel Westin's *Familjen i dalen: Tove Jansson's muminvärld* (Stockholm: Bonnier, 1988).

Per Christian Jersild
(14 March 1935 –   )

Ross Shideler
University of California, Los Angeles

BOOKS: *Räknelära* (Stockholm: Bonnier, 1960);

Till varmare länder (Stockholm: Bonnier, 1961);

Ledig Lördag (Stockholm: Bonnier, 1963);

Calvinols resa genom världen: rövarroman (Stockholm: Bonnier, 1965)–excerpt translated by David Mel Paul and Margareta Paul as "The Great Man," in *Modern Swedish Prose in Translation,* edited by Karl Erik Lagerlöf (Minneapolis: University of Minneapolis Press, 1979), pp. 155–165;

Prins Valiant och Konsum: Fickroman (Stockholm: Bonnier, 1966);

Grisjakten (Stockholm: Bonnier, 1968);

Refuserat: Fyra Pjäser, by Jersild, Ardelius, Sven Delblanc, and Björn Runeborg (Stockholm: Bonnier, 1969);

Vi ses i Song My (Stockholm: Författarförlaget, 1970);

Drömpojken: En paranoid historia (Stockholm: Bonnier, 1970);

Uppror bland marsvinen (Stockholm: Författarförlaget, 1972);

Höll Röven ren och blicken klar: En Militärfars frön det glada 1900-talet (Stockholm: Folmer Hansen, 1973);

Stumpen: En följetongsroman (Stockholm: FIB/Kulturfront, 1973);

Djurdoktorn: Roman i femtiotre tablåer (Stockholm: Bonnier, 1973); translated by Paul and Paul as *The Animal Doctor* (New York: Pantheon, 1975);

Den elektriska kaninen: En midsommar saga (Uddevalla: Författarförlaget, 1974);

Barnens ö (Stockholm: Bonnier, 1976); translated by Joan Tate as *Children's Island* (Lincoln: University of Nebraska Press, 1986);

Moskvafeber, by Jersild and Frej Lindqvist (Stockholm: Folmer Hansen, 1977);

Babels hus (Stockholm: Bonnier, 1978); translated by Tate as *House of Babel* (Lincoln: University of Nebraska Press, 1987);

En levande själ (Stockholm: Bonnier, 1980); translated by Rika Lesser as *A Living Soul* (Norwich, U.K.: Norvik, 1988);

Gycklarnas Hamlet och monologerna Balans och En rolig halvtimme (Stockholm: Norstedt, 1980);

Per Christian Jersild (photograph by Tommy Penderson)

Professionella bekännelser (Stockholm: Författarförlaget, 1981);

Efter floden (Stockholm: Bonnier, 1982); translated by Löne Thygesen Blecher and George Blecher as *After the Flood* (New York: Morrow, 1986);

Anarken: Ett lösaktigt stycke i två delar (Stockholm: Folmer Hansen, 1983);

Lit de Parade: Svart komdedi (Stockholm: Bonnier, 1983);

Den femtionde frälsaren (Stockholm: Bonnier, 1984);

Geniernas återkomst: Krönika (Stockholm: Bonnier, 1987);

Fem hjärtan i en tändsticksask: Sedeskildring (Stockholm: Bonnier, 1989);

Humpty Dumptys fall: Livsåskådningsbok (Stockholm: Bonnier, 1990);

Holgerssons (Stockholm: Bonnier, 1991);

En lysande marknad (Stockholm: Bonnier, 1992);

En gammal kärlek (Stockholm: Bonnier, 1995);

Darwins ofullbordade: Om människans biologiska natur (Stockholm: Bonnier, 1997);

Sena sagor (Stockholm: Bonnier, 1998);

Ljusets drottning (Stockholm: Bonnier, 2000).

PRODUCED SCRIPTS: *OBS! Sammanträde pågår,* television, Sveriges Television, Channel 1, 1966;

Grisjakten, motion picture, by Jersild, Jonas Cornell, and Lars Swanberg, Sandrews / Svenksa Filminstitutet, 1970;

Gamen, television, TV1, 9 April 1973;

Babels hus, television, by Jersild and Bengt Ahlfors, Sveriges Television, 1981.

Through a remarkably varied and productive authorship of novels, plays, and essays, Per Christian Jersild, who debuted in 1960 with a collection of short stories, became one of the major Swedish authors of the last half of the twentieth century. Several of his books, enthusiastically read by a large percentage of the Scandinavian reading public, became major commercial successes, an experience unusual in any country for authors of Jersild's intellectual depth and complexity. This combination of critical and popular recognition has made Jersild one of the few modern Swedish authors to be genuinely admired as both a popular and a serious writer. Remarkably, for the first twenty years of his literary career he was also a full-time physician who specialized in social and preventive medicine.

Jersild's writing reflects elements of both his creative imagination and his scientific interests and skills. Over the decades his novels have oscillated from highly imaginative and at times fantastic or futuristic works to narratives that probe and analyze characters who find themselves almost invisibly imprisoned in labyrinthian bureaucratic and social institutions. Jersild's literary career has been marked by his deep, humorous, and yet often pessimistic preoccupation with the most crucial social, political, and ontological questions of his age. Profoundly empathetic with all forms of life, Jersild uses animals—either realistic or fanciful—as well as humans as characters in his writing. His sensitivity to the pain and suffering of living beings may derive, at least partially, from his childhood.

Born on 14 March 1935 to Svea and Christian Jersild, Per grew up the youngest of three children in a family torn by opposing literary and religious interests. His father, a deeply religious man, was secretary of the Swedish Evangelical movement, while his mother, frustrated by the demands of her life as mother and housewife, regretted her inability to pursue her literary and creative inclinations. Raised to some extent by his older sister, yet close to his mother, the young Jersild realized that his intellectual predisposition toward science and technology was leading him into a career in medicine, while his fertile imagination drew him toward creative writing. As he has written in his memoir *Professionella bekännelser* (Professional Confessions, 1981), by the time he was eighteen Jersild knew that he was destined to follow both careers. As a medical student he wrote before breakfast and sometimes even rushed home to write during lunch; such intense commitment resulted in the publication of two works of fiction before the completion of his medical degree.

Jersild's first collection of short stories, *Räknelära* (Algebra, 1960), grew out of a writing class that he took with the Swedish poet Reidar Ekner, and the stories in that collection inspired many of his later novels. Jersild's first two novels, *Till varmare länder* (To Warmer Lands, 1961) and *Ledig Lördag* (Saturday Free, 1963), received little critical attention, although *Till varmare länder* has become more popular through the years and was even adapted as a libretto for an opera. *Till varmare länder* is an epistolary novel, consisting of love letters between a young suburban housewife, Barbro, and her childhood friend, Bo-Erik. Bo-Erik goes to an underdeveloped country as an ambulance driver on an expedition to alleviate the suffering of people who have burn wounds. The reader eventually realizes that the decaying health spa where Bo-Erik is stationed befits hell, and the country is run as a subtly disguised and supposedly rational police state where citizens are regulated on the basis of their intelligence. The everyday yet absurd events of Bo-Erik's nobly intentioned, if fantastic, travels contrast with the humdrum activities of Barbro's lonely suburban life. The novel, influenced by the Swedish Nobel laureate Pär Lagerkvist, questions the belief of humanity in rationality and materialism and established Jersild as a satirist in the tradition of Jonathan Swift and Voltaire. *Ledig lördag* has similar allegorical connotations in its depiction of an office party and a journey home on a subway train that takes the protagonist and a young female secretary into a seemingly endless tunnel.

Jersild's third novel, *Calvinols resa genom världen: rövarroman* (Calvinol's Voyage around the World: A Tall Tale, 1965), for which he won the Bonnier Literary Prize, brought him critical and public success and marks his literary breakthrough. Influenced by Italo Calvino and James Joyce, this picaresque novel tells the story of a Rabelaisian doctor who travels through time and space; the bizarre tale reflects Jersild's love of language and narrative experimentation. With its paradoxical and comic questioning of authority, the novel moves in blithe fashion through different periods of history, ridiculing war and satirizing social institutions—particularly medical insti-

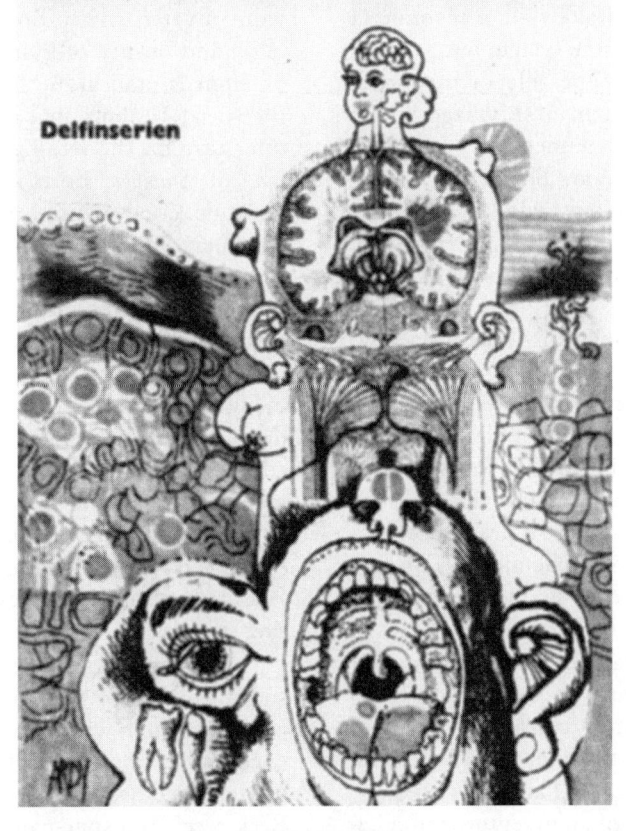

Dust jacket for Jersild's 1965 novel, a satirical fantasy that follows a doctor's travels through time and space (from Swedish Book Review *supplement, 1983)*

tutes and the doctors who work in them. The different, often contradictory, identities of the hero and the suggested alternative versions of his exotic adventures make *Calvinols resa genom världen* a parody of traditional literary narrative forms and thus reminiscent of Swift.

This use of the fantastic continues in several of Jersild's later novels. Indeed, his fiction glides back and forth between the fantastic and the realistic, as depicted in *Prins Valiant och Konsum: Fickroman* (Prince Valiant and Konsum, 1966). The novel describes three periods in the life of an alienated girl whose narrative perspective—at the ages of ten, sixteen, and then as a woman of thirty-two—blends fantasy and reality. Behind the young girl's story stands the romantic ideal of a fairy prince, who appears in shining armor at the beginning of the novel but has become an old alcoholic at its conclusion.

Jersild's next novel, *Grisjakten* (The Pig Hunt, 1968), was a major success; Jersild adapted the novel as a screenplay, and it was made into a motion picture in 1970. Drawing upon the author's own experiences with the Swedish bureaucracy, *Grisjakten* narrates in diary form the story of Lennart Siljeberg, a civil servant who accepts without question an assignment to eradicate the pig population on the Swedish island of Gotland. Siljeberg's bureaucratic language and efficiency in creating the procedures and methods for slaughtering the pigs seem absurdly comic; yet, the narrator's mindless, perfunctory approach to his duty hints at the way unthinking and dehumanizing bureaucracies sometimes lead to genocide—such as the Holocaust in Nazi Germany during World War II. The novel progresses from Siljeberg's creation of the systematic pursuit and extermination of the pigs to the point when he gets lost and finds himself hunted by his own forces with his own deadly weaponry and devotedly caring for one of the pigs. With its emphasis on the power of language to disguise or manipulate human behavior, *Grisjakten* establishes a theme that Jersild continues to develop in later novels.

Vi ses i Song My (See You in Song My, 1970) probes further into the psychology of a technocrat who, by definition, is a part of the system but believes he can fight it from within. The title of the novel evokes My Lai, the small Vietnamese village where American soldiers massacred innocent women and children during the Vietnam War. The narrator, Rolf Nylander, is a military psychologist who tries to bring democratic methods into the Swedish military. Although supposedly conscious of the power of language, Nylander is finally absorbed into the military structure and mentality; his politically liberal vocabulary and pseudodemocratic techniques for dealing with soldiers simply become new tools for controlling military personnel. Through the manipulation of language, a process of which he himself is a victim, Nylander succeeds in convincing reluctant soldiers that they should return to work in an area known to be contaminated with dangerous chemicals. The title of the novel implies that the next step will be to train soldiers to murder innocent civilians.

During the next few years, in several major and minor novels, Jersild continued to explore the relation between language and consciousness and between society and the individual. *Drömpojken: En paranoid historia* (Dreamboy: A Paranoid History, 1970) follows the adventures of an inventor from California. By rapidly propelling the narrator from one identity and experience to the next, the novel demonstrates not only how language and society manipulate the protagonist but also how they influence the reader as well. *Uppror bland marsvinen* (Revolt among the Guinea Pigs, 1972) is a collection of autobiographical short stories, charming in tone, that reflect Jersild's ongoing belief in the need to pay more attention to the conditions of workers at all levels of society.

In 1973 Jersild published two exceptional novels, *Stumpen: En följetongsroman* (The Stump: A Serial Novel) and *Djurdoktorn: Roman i femtiotre tablåer* (1973; translated as *The Animal Doctor,* 1975), both of which engage in the public debate about the social welfare system in Sweden. Although both novels make apparent that Jersild strongly supports the general principles of the Social Democratic Party, which had governed Sweden for most of the century, his works question the anonymity and bureaucracy that arose during those years. His concurrent experiences as a doctor in the public sector gave him insight into public institutions that played a fundamental role in the well-being of Sweden, a country that had one of the highest standards of living in the world.

Stumpen, first published in serial form in the magazine *Folket i bild / Kutturfront,* offers a powerful and at times almost comic portrait of a Swedish alcoholic, while *Djurdoktorn* is a futuristic novel about a woman veterinarian. Both narratives lay bare the fragility and beauty of living beings—whether alcoholics or animals—and argue for the value of life itself and for social systems that preserve human dignity and offer care for the weak and defenseless. The protagonist of *Stumpen,* Sture "Stumpen" Lindström, is a patriotic, good-natured man who accepts himself as a worthless human being and who wishes to be as little trouble to society as possible. Trying to uphold the rituals of hospital and social welfare bureaucracy, no matter how ridiculous they are, Stumpen begins to speak in the vernacular of bureaucrats and modern medical practitioners, people whose language is devoid of emotion and discourages individual human contact. A young hospital intern rescues Stumpen and takes him back to his commune, where Stumpen briefly finds a home, but—fearing that he will be imprisoned for the death of another alcoholic, who in fact died of natural causes—Stumpen ends up committing suicide.

If *Stumpen* makes readers aware of the failure of society to help a well-meaning alcoholic, *Djurdoktorn* confronts them with the relation between modern science and animal experimentation. Because she is an unemployed woman over the age of fifty, Dr. Evy Beck receives a state-paid position as a veterinarian at a futuristic medical research institution that is funded by commercial organizations. Hired to protect the health of the research animals that are ailing or dying at a financially unacceptable rate, Evy must find her way around the huge anonymous institution, assisting at first some of the researchers and the animals they use for experiments. Evy eventually comes into conflict with the commercial premises of medical research, however, by suggesting reforms that are either bureaucratically unfeasible or financially too costly. In this often humorous and always involving narrative, Jersild creates a modern world in which fundamental questions about the value of life, human and animal, are ignored by a society preoccupied with market-economy management and cost-effectiveness. The parallel stories of Evy's sick father and her care of the animals at the institution render the relationship between animal and human unavoidable. Evy herself eventually undergoes group therapy and accepts the notion that the values of the institution are more important than her own.

The 1974 novel *Den elektriska kaninen: En midsommar saga* (The Electric Rabbit: A Midsummer Saga) fancifully depicts a midsummer eve when animals—ranging from an electric rabbit who is chased by greyhounds in dog races to a dove raised in a stress laboratory—gather at their annual congress to discuss the problems they face in their daily lives. One of Jersild's most powerful novels, *Barnens ö* (1976; translated as *Children's Island,* 1986), also has comic elements and was later adapted for a movie. The novel offers a sensitive portrait of an eleven-year-old boy whose mother, an unmarried nurse, intends for him to go to summer camp while she is on vacation. Yet, the boy, Reine Larson, manages to stay at home alone in his mother's suburban apartment instead of going to the camp called Children's Island and sends postcards, supposedly written by him at camp, to his mother. Reine stays at home to contemplate and resolve what are, for him, the most serious questions of life before he passes through puberty and becomes, in his opinion, obsessed with sex the way adults are. The imaginative young narrator is gradually dragged into a series of sometimes dangerous misadventures. The novel is firmly rooted in child psychology—the title may be read either in terms of the summer camp or the isolation of children—and reflects Reine's attempt to break free of the mother who, he feels, abandoned him. While Reine does not resolve the questions of life, he seems ready at the end of the novel for puberty and maturity, stages of existence that he initially feared.

Barnens ö reflects Jersild's increasing immersion in the key social and political issues of his age. In 1978 he published *Babels hus* (translated as *House of Babel,* 1987), a work so popular that it was adapted for serial television in Sweden. Jersild based the realistic and controversial story about a large Swedish hospital on his experiences as a doctor, employing the format of the novel to engage in an ongoing worldwide discussion about the quality and nature of medical care in Western industrialized nations. Although the fictitious medical institution, Enskede Hospital, is arguably the leading character of the novel, the plot centers on Primus Svensson, an old man who suffers a heart attack, and on the people who associate with him—such as his alcoholic son and a helpful young female intern. In portraying the medical care that Svensson receives at the giant research hospital, Jersild not only creates a series of overlapping stories among the hospital staff but also has the doctors, nurses, and various other employees serve, in effect, as a model of a dehumanized Swedish society. The patients in this institution are often isolated, lonely people who receive impersonal treatment from the medical staff. The title of the novel, *Babels hus,* points out the lack of communication—largely because of the different languages and intentions—that persists at the core of such a gigantic medical-industrial complex. An intense public debate in Sweden followed the publication of the novel, and Jersild became a well-known public figure as he visited various parts of the country to participate in panels and discussions.

Dust jacket for Jersild's 1968 novel, about a civil servant assigned to eradicate wild pigs on a Swedish island (from Swedish Book Review *supplement, 1983)*

Less than a year before the publication of *Babels hus,* Jersild officially retired from his duties as a doctor in order to devote himself full time to writing. In 1980 he published *En levande själ* (translated as *A Living Soul,* 1988), another novel that examines the nature, function, and dangers of commercial industrial technology in people's lives. In this futuristic, science-fiction novel Jersild returns to his literary roots in the fantastic, relating the story of Ypsilon, a one-eyed, bodiless brain whose memory has been erased but whom researchers keep alive in an aquarium of nutritious liquid. Yet, the novel seems quite realistic as Ypsilon, in search of his identity, develops into a fascinating and involving character who fights to retain his thoughts, emotions, and independence. Ypsilon falls in love with a female attendant; makes friends, using mental telepathy, with a lab chimpanzee who knows sign language; strives to discover the purpose for which the researchers intend to use him; and, finally, tries to escape. Through this unusual protagonist Jersild explores some of the most fundamental questions about the nature of life, consciousness, and identity within the context of monopolistic global corporations and market-based economies.

In the next couple of years Jersild wrote two widely different novels. The first, *Professionella bekännelser,* was—as its title suggests—a narrative based on his own life as an author. The book focuses almost exclusively on the background of his novels and plays as well as on some of the techniques that he used and learned in writing these works. In the next novel, *Efter floden* (1982; translated as *After the Flood,* 1986), Jersild essentially picks up where he left off with *En levande själ* and writes of the dangers of technology and of its ultimate forms. *Efter floden* takes as its point of departure the intense European and American debates at the time concerning the threat of nuclear war. The novel offers a powerful warning about the future of humanity in light of nearly perpetual hostility and warfare in the world. With a small band of survivors on a Baltic island some thirty years after a nuclear war as his subject and time frame, Jersild writes the story from the point of view of Edvin, a young man who served as a slave and cabin boy for various ship captains before becoming an embittered physician's apprentice. Within this cruel and ruthless society, issues of love, friendship, and humanity itself are confronted in the starkest of terms before the last remnants of humanity are wiped out by a virus.

In his next few novels Jersild resumes his practice of employing fantasy as a means of illuminating reality. *Den femtionde frälsaren* (The Fiftieth Savior, 1984), although narrated in realistic detail, can only be described in terms of a fantasy or allegory. The novel takes place during the 1790s in a Venice threatened by the encroaching sea and by war from the French and the Austrians. The plot pivots on a man found sitting on top of one of the highest towers in the city. He calls himself Magdalenus and claims to be the fiftieth in a direct line of descendants from Jesus. Imprisoned by the Church, accused of heresy, and then tortured, Magdalenus says that he has come from the future and claims to have seen God, who is shrinking to an embryo because of the lack of good deeds in the world. Narrated by Ciacco, a stenographer and writer who records Magdalenus's tale during the weeks of his torture, a rich narrative tapestry of humorous Venetian scenes and characters starts to unfold. Ciacco and an abbot succeed in helping Magdalenus escape to a palazzo where, before being recaptured, he impregnates a marchessa. To protect the future of this fifty-first descendant of Jesus, Ciacco hides the child on a row of ships that house the fools and outcasts of the city. Part of the narrative consists of letters from Ciacco to the child, whom he considers his godson and who, by the end of the novel, has grown up among outcasts and is almost ready to face the larger madhouse of humanity. Jersild's next novel continues this exploration of the past and the present.

Geniernas återkomst: Krönika (Return of the Geniuses: A Chronicle, 1987) chronicles human progress from hominids to the future and focuses on the geniuses around the world that transformed civilization. The novel begins at the dawn of mankind and captures events in the Stone Age, in King Herod's time, and in China in the Middle Ages, going on to examine the lives of Leonardo da Vinci, Charles Darwin, Sigmund Freud, and modern military officers. With its focus on language as an intrinsically deceptive instrument in the development of humankind, the "chronicle" seems to be a text about the inability of humanity to escape its own passions and weaknesses; history in the novel culminates in a fundamentalist society that denies all the scientific knowledge and reason of the past. At the conclusion of the chronicle, all that remains outside the authoritarian state are the great geniuses of the past, who have been re-created genetically through cloning and who live as misfits in exile on an island. In its concern with what constitutes the essence of human beings, *Geniernas återkomst* anticipates Jersild's later collections of essays about the nature of life and humanity.

Fem hjärtan i en tändsticksask: Sedeskildring (Five Hearts in a Matchbox: A Slice of Life, 1989) is a memoir recounting Jersild's family life and upbringing in a lower-middle-class Stockholm neighborhood. His next book, *Humpty Dumptys fall: Livsåskådningsbok* (Humpty Dumpty's Fall: An Outlook on Life, 1990), collects essays that encompass a personal yet philosophically oriented discussion of current scientific research. Believing that, after Darwin, the traditional worldview of Western civilization has gradually become fragmented, Jersild looks at specific issues and ethics of contemporary science—such as gene research, cloning, and transplants—and their relationship to modern humanity.

Jersild's next two books differed radically from each other in theme. He based *Holgerssons* (1991) on Selma Lagerlöf's well-known children's book *Nils Holgersson's underbara resa genom Sverige* (Nils Holgersson's Wonderful Trip through Sweden, 1906). Told in the voice of a woman who interviews Nils Holgersson as an old man, the novel continues Lagerlöf's fantastic and tragicomic story. With *En lysande marknad* (A Splendid Market, 1992), however, Jersild shifts gears yet again, writing a detective story set in a private sanatorium. The novel reflects his concerns about the dismantling of social welfare in Sweden and the development of a survival-of-the-fittest market economy.

En lysande marknad takes place in the near future and is narrated by a patient held in an insane asylum for reasons the reader discovers only at the end of the novel. The patient appears sane but cannot be released because he refuses to agree that he ever was mentally unstable. As the story moves back and forth in time, between the narration inside the asylum and the events that preceded and caused the incarceration, the reader realizes that the protagonist simply carried out the premises of private enterprise and the modern market economy to their logical and deadly conclusion. Before his commitment he was a leader of a small entrepreneurial group of people who privatize the underfinanced and bureaucratically flawed justice system by discreetly becoming private investigators, judges, and occasionally even executioners. Although they sometimes succeed in imprisoning the guilty and saving the innocent, the group finances itself by blackmail or by payments from insurance companies and other corporations that save money through this perverted legal system. At the narrator's instigation the group finally plans to organize major criminal gangs by making them more efficient and less lethal; when the plan to export killers by paying them off and deporting them goes awry, this secret society of semicriminal entrepreneurs becomes a public embarrassment, and the protagonist is declared to be insane and sent to the asylum.

In 1995 Jersild published *En gammal kärlek* (An Old Love), a work related to his medical training and his concern with contemporary ethical and moral issues. The novel focuses on the life of a doctor, Agneta Sjödin-Åhslund. Once divorced, then widowed after a second marriage, this middle-aged general practitioner tries to care for her senile mother and stay involved in her grown children's lives. Agneta's life takes a new turn when she begins a relationship with an old lover, only to discover that he is dying of liver cancer. In an unbiased yet intense and personal manner, Jersild uses the novel to confront

Dust jacket for Jersild's 1973 futuristic novel, about corporate-sponsored scientific research on animals (from Swedish Book Review *supplement, 1983)*

fundamental questions about euthanasia and the right to die.

Jersild continues to balance his creative and intellectual identities in his next volume of essays, *Darwins ofullbordade: Om människans biologiska natur* (Darwin Unfinished: On Humanity's Biological Nature, 1997). Based on a series of lectures he gave at Uppsala University, the essays cast Darwin's theory of evolution by natural selection in the context of the 1990s, disclosing Jersild's own moral and philosophical perspectives on life. The book–with its emphasis on human genetic makeup and the animal within the human species–reflects Jersild's ongoing imaginative and creative exploration of the relationship between humans and nature and between consciousness and biology. By exposing the general reader to complex

Dust jacket for Jersild's 1976 novel, in which a boy fools his mother into believing that he is at summer camp by sending her false postcards (from Swedish Book Review *supplement, 1983)*

theories of science, Jersild describes the way in which human genetic history shapes current behavior, the better "att se med storre realism på oss själva" (to see ourselves with greater realism).

Sena sagor (Late Tales, 1998) brings together themes from Jersild's earlier novels and essays by telling the story of an academic researcher who writes a doctoral dissertation about nine unrelated people who have become color blind. Narrated in short, concise three- to six-page chapters, the novel starts with an almost scientific description of each individual case. The researcher, however, eventually reaches an impasse when the scientific need for a clear, narrowly focused, and preferably inexpensive solution conflicts with his desire to understand the experience of the individuals—to identify the relation between the personal and the biological. The researcher finally finds himself cut off from the clinic and from research funds, ending up a semiobjective observer who has ruined his scientific career by involving himself in the lives of his patients. Only at this point does Jersild give the researcher's name, Ulf Henry Björklund. The novel raises fundamental social and scientific issues, indeed touching on profound metaphysical questions, as its diverse characters must cope with their sudden, unexplainable color blindness.

Ljusets drottning (Light's Queen, 2000) tells the droll and often satirical story of a young man, Alex Eriksson, who returns to Sweden after a year of traveling abroad only to learn that his mother, a single parent who had supposedly adopted him, has died. The shock of her death leads to his search to find out the truth about the mysterious years of his mother's youth and his parents' identities. The journey not only leads Alex to the discovery that his mother actually gave birth to him but also takes him on a surprising exploration of the social and political trends and events of the 1970s and 1980s. He finds that his beautiful mother was first a young revolutionary and later worked as an unusual feminist who collected the sperm of anonymous male donors so that women could have children whose genes came from famous athletes, intellectuals, or financiers. With his satirical and perhaps pessimistic wit, Jersild depicts in this fanciful novel a constantly changing Swedish society and the sometimes eccentric individuals who compose it.

Per Christian Jersild's original—sometimes fantastic, sometimes realistic—novels have brought to a large reading public sophisticated and often comic insights into questions of how humans relate to each other and to the animals and life around them. For more than four decades, Jersild's novels, essays, plays, and newspaper columns have analyzed complex social problems and synthesized scientific theories to provide new insight for his readers into the history, the fragility, and the dark, humorous richness of humanity.

References:

Jonas Anshelm, *Förnuftets brytpunkt: Om teknikkritiken i P C Jersilds författarskap* (Stockholm: Bonnier, 1990);

George Blecher, "Nedför Mississippi tillsammans med Jersilds Edvin: En läsning av Efter flodenö," *Bonnier Litterära Magasin*, 55 (1986): 172–174;

Susan Brantly, "P. C. Jersild's *Geniernas återkomst* and the Conventions of Historical Writing," in *Studies in German and Scandinavian Literature after 1500: A Festschrift for George C. Schoolfield,* edited by James Parente Jr. and Richard Erich Schade (Columbia, S.C.: Camden House, 1993);

John Hewish, "P. C. Jersild's Polychronicon," *Swedish Book Review*, 1 (1988): 2–5;

Ola Larsmo, "Nedför spiralen: Om P. C. Jersilds berättarteknik," *Bonnier Litterära Magasin*, 55 (1986): 175–182;

Rut Nordwall-Ehrlow, "Frälsargestalter i P. C. Jersilds författarskap," *Horisont*, 34 (1987): 70–77;

Nordwall-Ehrlow, *Människan som djur: En studie i P C Jersilds författarskap* (Lund: LiberFörlag, 1983);

Ross Shideler, Afterword to Jersild's *Children's Island*, translated by Joan Tate (Lincoln: University of Nebraska Press, 1986), pp. 277–286;

Shideler, "The Battle for the Self in P. C. Jersild's *En Levande själ*," *Scandinavian Studies*, 56 (1984): 256–271;

Shideler, "Dehumanization and the Bureaucracy in Novels by P. C. Jersild," *Scandinavica*, 23 (1984): 25–38;

Shideler, "P. C. Jersild's *Efter floden* and Human Value(s)," *Scandinavica*, 27 (1988): 31–43;

Shideler, "Zola and the Problem of the Objective Narrator in Per Olov Enquist and Per Christian Jersild," in *Documentarism in Scandinavian Literature,* edited by Poul Houe and Sven Håkon Rossel (Amsterdam & Atlanta: Rodopi, 1997), pp. 120–134;

Swedish Book Review, special Jersild issue, 2 (1983).

Willy Kyrklund

(27 February 1921-)

Paul Norlén
University of Washington

BOOKS: *Ångvälten och andra noveller* (Stockholm: Bonnier, 1948);

Tvåsam (Stockholm: Bonnier, 1949);

Solange (Stockholm: Bonnier, 1951);

Mästaren Ma (Stockholm: Bonnier, 1952)–excerpts translated by George Simpson as "The Master Ma," in *Sweden Writes: Contemporary Swedish Poetry and Prose, Views on Art, Literature and Society,* edited by Lars Bäckström and Göran Palm (Stockholm: Prisma, 1965), pp. 143-149; and by George C. Schoolfield as "The Master Ma," in *Literary Review,* 9 (1965-1966): 295-299;

Hermelinens död (Stockholm: Bonnier, 1954)–includes "Hanseli och Greteli," translated by Paul Norlén as "Hansel and Gretel," and "Charkuteribiträdet som talade persiska," translated by Norlén as "The Butcher's Clerk Who Spoke Persian," in *Swedish Book Review,* 1 (1987): 1, 3-9;

Den överdrivne älskaren (Stockholm: Bonnier, 1957);

Aigaion (Stockholm: Bonnier, 1957);

Till Tabbas (Stockholm: Bonnier, 1959);

Polyfem förvandlad (Stockholm: Bonnier, 1964);

Från Bröllopet till Medea (Stockholm: Bonnier, 1967);

Den rätta känslan (Stockholm: Bonnier, 1974);

Gudar och människor: En myt; Zéb-un-nisá: En anekdot (Stockholm: Alba, 1978);

8 variationer (Stockholm: Alba, 1982);

Elpënor (Stockholm: Alba, 1986);

Om godheten (Stockholm: Alba, 1988);

Språket som artefakt (Lund: Tegnérsamfundet, 1992).

Editions and Collections: *Tre berättelser* (Stockholm: Bonnier, 1959);

Berättelser (Stockholm: Alba, 1979);

Prosa (Stockholm: Bonnier Alba, 1995);

Berättelser, dramatik, anföranden, artiklar (Stockholm: Bonnier Alba, 1996).

PLAY PRODUCTIONS: *Medea från Mbongo,* Stockholm, Royal Dramatic Theater, 4 November 1967;

Willy Kyrklund (photograph by Harald Borgström)

Gudar och människor, Stockholm, Royal Dramatic Theater, 19 March 1977.

Willy Kyrklund's short prose texts and dramas blend philosophy, humor, and irony with a stylistic elegance that critics have lauded frequently over the years. His short fiction often parodies traditional genres such as the fable or is based on existing stories from mythology. Indeed, he has described his prose not as literary fiction but, rather, as "tankemodeller" (conceptual models), an approach that makes categorizing his works difficult. Often viewed as an outsider–Olle Hedberg, a Swedish critic, even called him "ett primtal" (prime number)–Kyrklund does not belong to any of the various literary or artistic movements that have come and gone in Sweden in the years following World War II. Yet, although for decades his work defied easy categorization, he is now recognized in Sweden as one of the most important writers of the postwar period, as well as one of the great masters of Swedish prose.

Paul Wilhelm Kyrklund was born on 27 February 1921 in Helsinki, Finland, part of the Swedish-speaking minority in that country. His father was an engineer employed at a pulp mill in the northeastern province of Karelia–once an annex of the Soviet Union and now a part of Russia. At an early age Kyrklund began attending boarding school in Helsinki, away from home, and thereafter visited his family on holidays; in an autobiographical passage–rare for the writer–he depicts a train ride home to Karelia for the holidays in *Om godheten* (On Goodness, 1988). His university studies were interrupted by the Finnish-Russian War of 1939-1940 and World War II, but after the war he moved to Sweden and continued pursuing mathematics and languages–including Chinese, Greek, Persian, and Sanskrit–at the University of Uppsala.

Kyrklund's first book, *Ångvälten och andra noveller* (The Steamroller and Other Stories, 1948), came out while he was still a student in Uppsala. The nine stories of the collection alternate between contemporary, realistic settings and settings steeped in myth or fairy tales. The first story, "Prognos: negativ" (Prognosis: Negative), which is presumably about his own experiences in the military, took Kyrklund four years to write–a duration of time that is typical for him. Just as characteristic, however, is the relatively short length of his books, none of them running beyond a hundred pages or so. "Prognos: negativ" won a literary prize in 1945; in its depictions of military life and of the absurdities of war, it is on a par with Joseph Heller's *Catch-22* (1961). The title story of the collection, "Ångvälten," incorporates both realistic and mythological elements. Focusing on a family that lives in a contemporary suburban housing development, the story gradually resembles a Greek myth, as the father tries to stop an out-of-control steamroller yet finds himself trapped in an endless pursuit throughout a seemingly idyllic neighborhood. Arne Florin writes in an unpublished thesis that in *Ångvälten och andra noveller* "som helhet är en strävan bort från en realistisk och psykologiserande litteratur tydlig" (as a whole a tendency away from realistic and psychologizing literature is apparent), an observation that applies equally well to Kyrklund's short novels and prose collections published in the 1950s. His early work also shows strong affinities with Swedish writers of the 1940s, the supposed "fyrtiotalister" (1940s generation)–particularly, as Florin writes, in terms of "inriktningen på det existentiella och universella, den stilistiska experimentlustan, strävan efter mångtydighet" (his preoccupation with the existential and the universal, the enjoyment of stylistic experimentation, the striving for ambiguity). Critical acceptance of literary modernism in Sweden in the early 1940s paved the way for the serious, experimental literature of the late 1940s and 1950s.

While much of Kyrklund's output as a published writer consists of short stories, at least three of his early works can be called short novels. Even with these works, however, his indifference toward conventional literary fiction–an attitude he has expressed repeatedly in interviews over the years–renders the designation "novel" somewhat problematic. He experiments with narrative form in *Tvåsam* (Twosome, 1949), which, as the opening sentence states, "avser att beskriva ett själstillstånd" (intends to describe the state of a soul). The novella comprises three parts: "Övervaktmästaren" (The Über-Doorman), "Vaktmästaren" (The Doorman), and "Övervaktmästaren och vaktmästaren" (The Über-Doorman and the Doorman); Kyrklund eventually implies that Övervaktmästaren and Vaktmästaren represent two aspects of a single person. Besides making the identity of the protagonist problematic, Kyrklund also casts into question in *Tvåsam* the conventions of the novel form and of literary narration. When, for example, Övervaktmästaren goes out to deliver an official document, he passes

över en asfalterad (stenlagd) gård; ett blåmålat (brunmålat, vitkalkat) trapphus vindade sig uppåt, tre (två, fyra, fem) trappor: Mathilda (Matilda) Syrén. Han ringde (bultade) på dörren: det fanns (fanns icke) ringklocka. Antalet kombinationer är 2 ° 2 ° 3 ° 4 ° 2 ° 2 ° 2 = 384, alla lika (lik)-giltiga, det här börjar bra.

(over an asphalt [cobbled] courtyard; a blue-painted [brown-painted, whitewashed] staircase wound its way upwards, three [two, four, five] floors: Mathilda [Matilda] Syrén. He rang the door bell [knocked on the door]: there was a [no] doorbell. The number of combinations is 2 x 2 x 3 x 4 x 2 x 2 x 2 = 384, all equally [in-] different, this is starting out well).

Övervaktmästaren prefers the linear–"ordning för dess egen skull" (order for its own sake)–and dreams of an "endimensionell värld" (one-dimensional world)

Title page for Kyrklund's 1974 collection of short stories on the theme of "felaktiga känslor," or "faulty emotions" (University of Washington Libraries)

of pure, mathematical order. The problem of choice is also important throughout *Tvåsam*. In contrast, Vaktmästaren is paralyzed by guilt and by a sense of isolation from the surrounding world. The image of a membrane that surrounds an individual, cutting him off from others, recurs in the novella: "Och detta mitt tvivel blir till en tunn membran mellan mig och omgivningen, en membran vars permeabilitet just är föremålet för mitt tvivel" (And this my doubt turns into a thin membrane between me and my surroundings, a membrane whose permeability is precisely the object of my doubt). In a passage reminiscent of Franz Kafka, Vaktmästaren dreams that he is trapped inside a boiled egg. Taking a job as vaktmästaren constitutes a move away from isolation—and out of an undefined mental crisis. In the final section, however, the inner conflict between Övervaktmästaren and Vaktmästaren is played out in a series of dialogues and fantasy situations reminiscent of Miguel de Cervantes' *Don Quixote* (1605) and then resolved, at Vaktmästaren's expense, by the treachery of his alter ego.

Kyrklund's next book, *Solange* (1951), displays a similar conflict—though between two souls instead of within a single individual. Despite its fragmentary, elliptical narrative structure, *Solange* is undoubtedly Kyrklund's most popular, as well as his most lyrical, work. It established his reputation as a champion of the "little person"—a designation Kyrklund often disputed—and as a male writer with a sensitivity to female experience and psychology. The first part of the book follows the life of Solange from early childhood to her acquaintance, in the office where she is employed, with a man named Hugo, whom she marries. In simple terms Solange is a dreamer with an artistic temperament but lacks the talent to pursue her dreams. As her mother says pointedly, "Du kan inte dansa som är så omusikalisk" (You can't dance, you're so unmusical). Hugo, on the other hand, is reasonable to a self-destructive extent, a quality that Solange describes as "självstympning i förnuftets namn" (self-mutilation in the name of reason).

The second half of *Solange* concerns "det som icke hände och om den kamp som utspelades i det som icke hände" (that which didn't happen and the battle that was played out within that which didn't happen). Now married, Solange and Hugo have a son, and she has quit her job at the office. In the evening Hugo withdraws to the living room to drink strong tea and fantasize about unrealized projects. The son grows up, while life with the ever-reasonable Hugo has crushed Solange's spirit. She engages in a brief, unsatisfying affair with a writer and, in the end, commits suicide. No synopsis of the plot can convey either the intense lyricism of the book or the way the author captures in poetic language the course of a life and a marriage, told through an elliptical series of episodes and evocative passages. While critics have often focused on the sympathetic portrayal of Solange at the expense of virtually ignoring Hugo, the pathos of both characters deserves attention.

Mästaren Ma (Master Ma, 1952) is a distinctive work that draws heavily on Kyrklund's readings at that time in ancient Chinese philosophy. Often described as a pastiche, the work closely parallels—through both form and diction—an ancient Chinese text. Per Erik Ljung points out in an essay published in *Skeptikerns dilemma* that, rather than mimic a particular Chinese work, Kyrklund has labored "like the Chinese, with allusions to the Book of Odes, the Book of Rites, Mencius and Confucius" interlaced in the text. In *Mästaren Ma* three voices speak in succession: statements by Ma, "the master," are preceded by statements attributed to his wife, Yao, and, in turn, by the comments of a critic named Li. No context or other explanation for the existence of this document exists; instead, Ma's statements, which are often elaborated upon or contradicted by Yao and Li in their commentaries, directly confront the reader. *Mästaren Ma* opens with the words "Jag söker den fråga på vilken människolivet är ett svar" (I scck thc question to which human life is an answer). Swedish critics have often referred to this book when discussing Kyrklund's writing, equating the author with Ma, or at least with Ma's view of human life. Critics often cite Ma's declaration that "Jag intresserar mig icke för människorna. Jag intresserar mig för människans villkor" (I am not interested in human beings. I am interested in the human condition) as Kyrklund's own, a vicwpoint supported by the author's comments in interviews. Long considered a minor classic in Sweden, *Mästaren Ma* may well be Kyrklund's single most important work.

During the 1950s Kyrklund had a job for part of the time as a computer programmer, working on the Swedish BESK project, which was a large, UNIVAC-style computer. At this time Kyrklund also published two volumes of stories—*Hermelinens död* (The Death of the Ermine, 1954) and *Den överdrivne älskaren* (The Exaggerated Lover, 1957). These short prose texts typically reflect an economy of narrative; besides a minimum of characterization and description, they display abrupt changes in style and a frequent exploitation of conventional short prose genres such as fables. Florin writes in his unpublished thesis that "Texterna uppvisar ofta en spänning mellan generella utsagor och konkreta exemplifieringar" (These texts often show a tension between general statements and concrete exemplifications). A sense of determinism and a resulting pessimism also characterize these stories.

As in *Ångvälten och andra noveller,* many of the stories in *Hermelinens död* invoke, either explicitly or implicitly, story lines from mythology. Examples include "Sovaren" (The Sleeper) and "Fred i Bulgarien" (Peace in Bulgaria), both of which are set in distant times, while in stories such as "Hanseli och Greteli" (translated as "Hansel and Gretel," 1987) a contemporary setting belies the fairy tale or mythological references imbedded in the text. *Den överdrivne älskaren,* on the other hand, collects stories that share a common theme, the element of "dårskap" (folly) in romantic relationships. The title story, in which an archaeologist runs off with a doctor's wife from the remote Middle Eastern outpost where they are living into the surrounding desert, serves as an excellent example. Here, Kyrklund addresses a paradoxical problem explicitly: while "för lite dårskap är dårskap" (too little folly is folly), "för mycket dårskap är också dårskap" (too much folly is also folly). In "Den överdrivne älskaren" the contrast between fragile human life and an alien nature—reduced to essentials—is acute: "här är bergen nakna och deras nakenhet är fullständig, häpnadsväckande, obotlig" (here the mountains are naked and their nakedness is total, astounding, irremediable). While the doctor's wife quickly senses that things might have been arranged more reasonably, the die is cast as the jeep speeds further into the desert. The final story in the collection, the frequently anthologized "Katten" (The Cat), is one of Kyrklund's most perfectly executed pieces. Themes of manliness, gender roles, and marital relations emerge in a statistician's nighttime battle with a cat—a crisis spurred by a certain Captain Engman's stories of tiger hunting at a dinner party. The story discloses how, for Kyrklund, the erotic element of human existence is not trivialized but nevertheless often has an uncomfortably comic aspect.

During the 1950s and 1960s Kyrklund made many trips abroad to countries in the Middle East and in Central Asia and even lived for a time in a Greek island village with his wife and small children. Once, during their stay in Greece, a policeman came to Kyrklund's home in search of him, for villagers had noticed that he was seldom seen in any of the local cafés. In an interview Kyrklund described his reaction: "Jag insåg att jag icke hade levt upp till min mansroll och lovade polisen att gå oftare på krogen i fortsättningen" (I realized that I had not lived up to my masculine role and promised the policeman that I would go to the café more often in the future). Kyrklund recounts some of his experiences abroad in two travel books, *Aigaion* (Aegean, 1957), which addresses his life in Greece, and *Till Tabbas* (To Tabbas, 1959), in which he tells about a journey to Iran. In the tradition of the Swedish "reseskildring" or travel account, *Aigaion* is a mixture of observations about the various places in Greece—both well known and unknown—where the author has traveled, and speculations about Greek culture and history, often harking back to Sweden. In some respects, *Aigaion* is the most personal, as well as most topical, of Kyrklund's books. One touching section, for example, describes his five-year-old daughter's experiences with a new country and a strange language.

Kyrklund's travels in Iran in the mid 1950s resulted in a different sort of travel account. While *Till Tabbas* is full of episodes and observations as experienced and seen by a traveling narrator—such as the involved process of entering Iran from the seldom-crossed border with the Soviet Union–the book discusses in larger measure Persian language and literature and, in particular, the pervasive nature and role of religion. *Till Tabbas* offers some of Kyrklund's most direct statements on literature and evolved largely out of an early interest in non-Western languages, a fascination that he once perceived as a deliberate rejection of Western norms–a move "bortom Thermopylae" (beyond Thermopylae), as he has said in interviews. Jonas Ellerström, in an essay published in *Skeptikerns dilemma,* has also pointed out the intensity of Kyrklund's interest in Sufism because of its search for the essential conditions of human life.

In addition to works of short fiction, Kyrklund has also written plays, several of which have been produced in Sweden. In general his plays feature a rhetorical element that shows a greater kinship with classical drama–both tragedy and comedy–than with the naturalist drama of, for example, Henrik Ibsen. With their characteristic mixture of high and low theater, of irony and burlesque, Kyrklund's plays also parallel his narrative works. That he writes many of his stories in dialogue form also makes their adaption into radio plays a logical next step. One early play, *Platanhårs dialog på en ö i Aigaion* (Plane Tree Leaf Dialogue on an Island in the Aegean)–published in *Från Bröllopet till Medea* (From "The Wedding" to "Medea," 1967)–consists of dialogues between three characters named G, previously a resident of Athens and apparently an author; K, an old friend and colleague of G; and A, the wife of K. Like many of Kyrklund's narratives, the play also incorporates a story, taken from the ancient Greek historian Herodotus, about a certain Kandaules of Lydia, his wife, and his friend Gyges; the characters in Herodotus's narrative parallel the triangle existing among the three characters in *Platanhårs dialog på en ö i Aigaion.* Although Kyrklund conceived *Bröllopet* (The Wedding), which was collected in *Från Bröllopet till Medea,* from the start as a piece for the theater, it actually appeared first as a story in *Den överdrivne älskaren.* The play takes up a theme–the problem of choice–that is familiar from Kyrklund's earlier works and personified in the play by Karl, a hesitant bridegroom. Other characters are identified generically as "bride's mother" or "Oneman." As is often the case with Kyrklund, the dialogue alternates between a satirical use of social conventions and a more high-flown rhetoric that has both serious intention and comic effect.

Kyrklund's next book, *Polyfem förvandlad* (Polyphemus Transformed, 1964), is a collage of prose texts that have the theme of transformation in common and, in many respects, is the most challenging of Kyrklund's fiction works. At the time the book appeared, Swedish critics seemed not to know what to make of it, but in retrospect one can link its playful seriousness to other contemporary European avant-garde experiments with the novel form, such as the Nouveau Roman in France. Many of the texts, or segments, of *Polyfem förvandlad* are based on, or make reference to, Greek mythology as Ovid wrote about it in *Metamorphoses* (1 A.D.–8 A.D.), a work that is obviously about transformations. The opening section, for example, retells Odysseus's famous encounter with the one-eyed Cyclops Polyphemus–but from the Cyclops's point of view. *Polyfem förvandlad* is both an experimental work and an example of Kyrklund's ongoing dialogue with a wide range of cultural traditions, including Greek and Persian. The idea that traditions are passed on in fragments, like shards of pottery, recurs throughout the book, and Kyrklund leaves the task of construing meaning from his fragmentary and elliptical text up to the reader.

Kyrklund returned to playwriting with *Medea från Mbongo* (Medea from Mbongo), which was also collected in *Från Bröllopet till Medea.* This play essentially reduces Euripides' version of the Greek myth to the characters of Jason, Medea, and a chorus of three members. As the chorus points out: "Alla känner hennes dåd. Hennes namn är genomträngt av hennes gärning" (Everyone knows of her crimes. Her name is permeated with her actions). The play begins at a point of crisis in the turbulent relationship between Jason and Medea: he is on the verge of divorcing Medea and marrying the young Glauke. Kyrklund injects prosaic yet anachronistic contemporary elements–such as references to refrigerators and telephones, for instance–into the play to bring the mythical couple closer to a world his audience can understand. Jason represents common sense and smug authority; Medea describes him as flat as he hides behind his newspaper. Medea, on the other hand, is the outsider–from the unknown land of Mbongo–who has left everything behind, committing horrible crimes in her past, for love: "Det är ju offret som gör oss till människor. Den oerhörda handlingen" (It is after all sacrifice which makes us human. The unparalleled action). In the central section of the play, Medea recalls "den gången" (that time) in Mbongo, when the foreign Jason arrived to plunder the sacred tree. Her memories are vivid and sensual, while Jason's version is vague and general. Throughout the play, images of snakes are connected with Medea: "små sändebud från mörkret, mörkret som vi trampas på" (small messengers from the darkness, the darkness which we trample on). By the end, after Medea has committed the awful murders that the audience knows will take place–but that do not occur on stage–she appears as a snake-goddess, saying to Jason, "Du kan icke nå mig.–Gå, Jason. Gå och sörj!" (You cannot reach me.–Go, Jason. Go and grieve!).

Kyrklund's next published work was *Den rätta känslan* (The Right Feeling, 1974). Similar in format to *Den överdrivne älskaren*, *Den rätta känslan* groups together works of short fiction that embrace a common theme–that of "felaktiga känslor" (faulty emotions), which is introduced in the pseudoscientific prologue to the book. Typical for a work by Kyrklund, the narratives in *Den rätta känslan* range from fables and revisions of Greek myths to contemporary character studies set in Italy and Lebanon. In his dissertation on the writer, "Jaget, friheten och tystnaden hos Willy Kyrklund" (The Ego, Freedom, and Silence in Willy Kyrklund), Gunnar Arrias identifies the "diabolisk" (diabolical) element that runs through much of Kyrklund's work and is characterized by a combination of "inlevelse och illvilja" (empathy and ill will). Earlier publications, such as *Mästaren Ma*, also feature this ambivalent attitude toward the human race, but *Den rätta känslan* exhibits ambivalence in a far more pronounced way. The theme of longing for purity, often portrayed through images of light, also appears repeatedly throughout the work.

The sixth section of the book, which first appeared in a 1966 issue of the journal *Ord och Bild* (1966) under the title "Den heliga texten" (The Sacred Text), begins with a line of Sanskrit and precedes a series of commentaries–presumably on this Sanskrit text–that often contradict each other or dwell on grammatical points. In each of these brief commentaries Kyrklund imbeds a "Betraktelse (tillskriven Cucimanah)" (Observation [attributed to Cucimanah]) that describes one person's decades-long experience with this text: "Den heliga texten är numera tämligen svårläst. Detta kommer sig av att den är så smutsig" (Nowadays the sacred text is rather difficult to read. This is due to the fact that it is so filthy). While Cucimanah has not, after thirty years, read the entire text, he does occasionally scrape away "någon intressant bokstav med nageln" (an interesting letter with his fingernail). In his contribution on Kyrklund for *Den svenska litteraturen: Medieålderns litteratur 1950-1985* (1990), Ulf Olsson points out that this section, like many of the writer's texts, goes "till gränsen för textens förmåga att representera och betyda" (to the limit of the text's ability to represent and signify). The limit in the sixth section of *Den rätta känslan* is marked by the encounter between "textens bokstavlighet och dess frånvarande mening" (the literalness of the text and its absent meaning).

In 1978 two of Kyrklund's plays were published in a single volume, *Gudar och människor: En myt; Zéb-un-nisá: En anekdot* (Gods and Humans: A Myth; Zéb-un-nisá: An Anecdote). The first, *Gudar och människor*, not only alludes to Greek mythology–like *Medea från Mbongo*–but is also his most explicitly political work. As the title suggests, the play is divided into two parts. In the first, the gods of Olympus–with Zeus as the chief executive officer of a multinational corporation–hastily assemble, as in a corporate meeting, to discuss the problem of humankind. Not only have humans become superfluous, thanks to advances in technology, but they are also starving, damaging the environment, and increasing in population. The gods confess their many prior connections with humans, and Hera–quoting from August Strindberg's *Ett drömspel* (1901; translated as *A Dreamplay*, 1912)–admits, "Det är synd om människorna" (It's a shame about human beings). In the end, however, the gods agree upon a program of gradual extermination in order to clear the way for their offspring to take the place of humans on earth. They then return to what they were doing before the meeting–watching Athena demonstrate a mathematical proof. The first act in particular has an element of farce, such as when the lame god Hephaestus drags his wife, Aphrodite, and her lover, Ares, onto the stage in a bed that is engulfed in a net. In the second act, a small group of humans also assemble, for the "dagen utan morgondag" (day without a tomorrow), which they have long awaited, has arrived. Their hope for survival lies in a laser cannon that "Medes"–short for "Archimedes"–has invented. When Hermes enters the scene, however, he shows that although Medes has an innate talent for mathematics, his inadequate education has led to calculation errors and thus a faulty invention. The play ends as the "crop duster" of the gods, an airplane, arrives. *Gudar och människor* was not entirely well received upon its performance at the Royal Dramatic Theater in Stockholm but was viewed as part of a general debate in Sweden about the effects of technology and its impact on, especially, Third World countries.

The other play, *Zéb-un-nisá: En anekdot,* perhaps best exemplifies a Kyrklund work that builds on his extensive studies in Persian literature. The play harks back to an incident in the court of Aurangzéb, "född 1618, mogulfurste, Indiens kejsare" (born in 1618, Mongol prince, emperor of India). The implied narrator of this anecdote is Manucci, an Italian-born soldier and physician who is composing his memoirs

Cover for the 1978 edition of two of Kyrklund's plays, based, respectively, on Greek mythology and a Persian anecdote (University of Washington Libraries)

when the play commences. In his memoirs, Manucci relates all that he has heard about Aurangzéb's Court. In the first scene Aurangzéb, always accompanied by his shadow, confronts the newly severed head of his old teacher, who—despite being dead—begins to interrogate him on the various forms of Persian poetry. Aurangzéb's daughter, Zéb-un-nisá, is a master of the *ghazal,* the lyrical form preferred by Sufi mystics and defined in the play as a form that "utgör i sig ett slutet system, som lyder endast konstens lagar" (comprises within itself a closed system, which only obeys the laws of art). Despite being a prisoner in her father's palace, closely watched by female bodyguards and servants, Zéb-un-nisá "vet allt om kärleken" (knows everything about love)—although she has never touched, or been touched by, a man. She has, however, glimpsed a man—Áqil, through the window grate—and, with the help of her servant, grants him an audience. However, the meeting between Zéb-un-nisá and Áqil ends with dire consequences for the young man when Aurangzéb makes an unannounced visit to his daughter's quarters to discuss poetry.

Zéb-un-nisá is one of Kyrklund's most extensive explorations of the role of art and of the tension between form and content and between art and experience. Zéb-un-nisá quotes the philosopher Ibn Khaldún, who once asserted that "ordkonsten handlar om ord, icke om idéer" (literary art deals with words, not with ideas)—a point of view that may or may not be shared by the author as well. On the other hand, Kyrkland hints that Zéb-un-nisá's confinement, like the form of the *ghazal,* models "existentiell frustrering" (existential frustration), a parallel that recalls his perception of literature as a conceptual model or "tankemodell." He employs such a point of view increasingly in later plays.

Although there are relatively long intervals between Kyrklund's publications, especially by Swedish standards, no fewer than three new works came out in the 1980s. *8 variationer* (Eight Variations, 1982), like his other volumes of short fiction, groups stories according to a common theme. While this collection lacks a prologue or frame story, the theme for these variations originates in the motto of the book, a saying from the pre-Socratic Greek philosopher Heraclitus: "Tiden är ett barn som spelar leker bräde. Härskarmakten tillhör ett barn" (Time is a child moving pieces in a game. The power to rule is a child's). The word *variation* is of course a musical term, and Kyrklund invokes music further through the other titles in the collection, such as "Scherzo" and "Fuga." In "Fuga," which is Italian for "flight" but also defines a musical composition in which a melody is repeated in altered forms, an unnamed man finds himself in flight from a place whose significance he cannot recall: "Jag vet icke vart jag flyr och icke varifrån. Alla mina personliga minnen är utplånande" (I don't know to where, or from where, I am fleeing). As he makes his way through a forest, the man's only clue to his past, or his future, is a scrap of paper which he finds in his shoe and on which a street address is written; the importance of the paper is sensed yet not completely known, approaching a "sacred text" by Kyrklund's standards. When the amnesiac man comes to a road, he decides to toss a matchbook in the air to help him decide which direction to take. Eventually he arrives at a house, where he asks an old woman for food. While everything is new to the man because of his lost memory, the woman lets him know that he has visited her many times before; that she will shortly take him back where he came from; and that the whole episode will be repeated again.

The life of William Tell inspires another story in the collection, "Återtaget drag" (Retracted Move), which begins at Tell's moment of triumph, then regresses to his birth, and then moves forward again with a completely different outcome; in Kyrklund's version a childhood illness leaves Tell blind and, eventually, a poor cobbler instead of a national hero. In many of these texts blindness is associated with the element of chance or choice: "Valet är fritt, eftersom du icke vet följderna. Om du visste följderna, så vore du överhuvudtaget icke i en valsituation. Din blindhet är förutsättningen för din frihet" (You are free to choose, because you don't know the consequences. If you knew the consequences, then you wouldn't be in a situation of choice at all. Your blindness is the precondition of your freedom). As Johan Dahlbäck has observed in an essay published in *Skeptikerns dilemma,* "Utan tvivel är kärleken det mest radikala exemplet på mänsklig förblindelse i *8 variationer*" (Without a doubt, love is the most radical example of human blindness in *8 Variations*). Such is the case in "Själens åtrå" (Heart's Desire), a love story—between a divorced man and a psychiatric computer named Eliza—as well as an early example of cyberfiction.

Although *Elpënor* (1986) reflects Kyrklund's longstanding fascination with the Homeric tradition, as seen in earlier works such as *Polyfem förvandlad,* it remains a distinctive book. Kyrklund has often complained in interviews that the present-day ignorance of the works of Homer and other ancient writers makes a dialogue with that tradition much more difficult to continue. *Elpënor* focuses on a minor figure from the *Odyssey,* a crew member who dies in a drunken fall from a ladder in the rush to escape the island of Circe. While many of the events in the *Odyssey* are narrated by Odysseus himself and thus from his point of view, in Kyrklund's play the same events are presented from the perspective of the hapless Elpënor. A crucial difference is that in Kyrklund's version Elpënor, who—according to Homer—is "neither brave or intelligent," remains silent, even when Odysseus encounters him in the underworld, "oavsett Odysséen 11:83" (the Odyssey 11:83 notwithstanding). Another unusual feature of this book, as the author explains in an afterword, is that much of *Elpënor* is written in "elegiskt distikon" (elegiac diction), rather than in the hexameter used by Homer. As Magnus Florin observes in an essay published in *Skeptikerns dilemma,* "hjältar sjunger på hexameter, medan elegiskt distikon bär offrens inskrifter" (heroes sing in hexameter, while elegiac diction bears the epitaphs of the victims). In the same afterword Kyrklund also points out the impossibility of transferring ancient meters to Swedish. There has always been a lyrical element in much of Kyrklund's prose, a movement, as Magnus Florin writes, "från fiktionens logik till ordens fysik" (from the logic of fiction to the physique of words). *Elpënor* is unusual among Kyrklund's works because of the extent to which he makes use of lyric devices in a narrative context.

In the third book that came out during the 1980s, *Om godheten,* Kyrklund takes up a familiar subject in the history of Western philosophy—that of goodness. The first of the sixteen numbered sections in *Om godheten* starts with a consideration of the quality of goodness in certain animals, especially the wolf. While many of these texts are more explicitly essays or more philosophical than in earlier books, there are a few lyric examples. Goodness is often equated with light, and section 11, a poem in blank verse, concerns the desire—constantly thwarted by the conditions of human life—for light and clarity: "Så sträcker jag mig häftigt längtande / förgäves upp ur dyn mot ljus och klarhet" (So I reach out intensely longingly / in vain up out of the mud toward light and clarity). In the final sections of *Om godheten* the author speaks much more openly than before. He urges in section 13: "Vänd dig icke till ljuset med dina bekymmer. Ljuset bekymrar sig icke om dina bekymmer" (Don't turn to the light with your troubles. The light doesn't trouble itself about your troubles).

Over the years Kyrklund has evolved into a literary cult figure whose works are eagerly read and reread by a relatively small number of readers—a writer admired and increasingly emulated by younger writers but relatively unrecognized by the literary establishment. His peripheral position resulted in part from the distinctively untrendy nature of his work; indeed, one of the many challenges and attractions of his books is that, as Olsson wrote, they tend to "att undfly den slutgiltiga betydelsen" (avoid a final meaning). Although Kyrklund had received some awards in the past, the Pilot Prize—also known as the "Little Nobel"—that he received in 1990 sparked renewed interest and wider recognition from readers. His collected works appeared in two volumes in the mid 1990s, and in 1995 he received an honorary doctorate from the University of Uppsala, where he had been a student several decades before. The normally reclusive author began to make public appearances, even appearing on television. Scholarship on Kyrklund has also increased since the publication in 1981 of Gunnar Arrias's dissertation on the author. These scholarly contributions include a 1992 critical study by Gunnar Bäck on a production of *Medea från Mbongo;* a monograph on Kyrklund by Paul Norlén in 1998; and *Skeptikerns dilemma* (The Skeptic's Dilemma, 1997), a collection of essays by several Swedish scholars and critics, edited by Vasilis Papageorgiou.

Interviews:

Ulf Olsson and Magnus Florin, "Intervju med Willy Kyrklund," *Bonniers Litterära Magasin,* 55 (November 1986): 309–311;

Arne Florin and Claes Wahlin, "Intervju med Willy Kyrklund," *90tal: Tidskrift om litteratur & konst,* 1 (1990): 10–14.

References:

Gerda Antti, "Willy Kyrklund i två våningar," *Ord och Bild,* 75 (1966): 149–56;

Gunnar Arrias, "Jaget, friheten och tystnaden hos Willy Kyrklund," dissertation, Göteborg University, 1981;

Gunnar Bäck, *Ord och kött: Till teaterns fenomenologi med larssons och Kyrklunds Medea* (Göteborg: Daidalos, 1992);

Arne Florin and Sören Häggkvist, "Jag intresserar mig icke för människorna: Jag intresserar mig för människans villkor," *Bonniers Litterära Magasin,* 64 (December 1995): 42–45;

Florin, "Om godhet och annan ondska," *90tal: Tidskrift om litteratur & konst,* 1 (1990): 24–31;

Florin, "Om Willy Kyrklunds genrer och genreblandningar," thesis, University of Stockholm, 1982;

Per-Arne Henricson, "Willy Kyrklunds Medea från Mbongo," *Edda,* 75 (1975): 245–255;

Paul Norlén, *"Textens villkor": A Study of Willy Kyrklund's Prose Fiction* (Stockholm: Almqvist & Wiksell, 1998);

Ulf Olsson, "Willy Kyrklunds ironi," in *Den svenska litteraturen: Medieålderns litteratur 1950–1985,* edited by Lars Lönnroth and Sverker Göransson (Stockholm: Bonnier, 1990), pp. 36–40;

Vasilis Papageorgiou, ed., *Skeptikerns dilemma: Texter om Willy Kyrklunds författarskap* (Eslöv: Östling, 1997);

Nils Åke Sjöstedt, "Willy Kyrklunds Katten," in *Novellanalyser,* edited by Vivi Edström and Henricson (Stockholm: Prisma, 1970), pp. 168–180;

Claes Wahlin, "Högre matematik," *90tal: Tidskrift om litteratur & konst,* 1 (1990): 19–23.

Sara Lidman
(30 December 1923 -)

Birgitta Holm
Uppsala University

and

Paul Norlén
University of Washington

BOOKS: *Tjärdalen* (Stockholm: Bonnier, 1953);

Hjortronlandet (Stockholm: Bonnier, 1955)–excerpt translated by Verne Moberg as "Cloudberry Land," in *Modern Swedish Prose in Translation,* edited by Karl Erik Lagerlöf (Minneapolis: University of Minnesota Press, 1979), pp. 59–78;

Regnspiran (Stockholm: Bonnier, 1958); translated by Elspeth Harley Schubert as *The Rain Bird* (New York: Braziller, 1962);

Bära mistel (Stockholm: Bonnier, 1960);

Jag och min son (Stockholm: Bonnier, 1961; revised, 1963);

Med fem diamanter (Stockholm: Bonnier, 1964);

Samtal i Hanoi (Stockholm: Bonnier, 1966; revised, 1967);

Gruva (Stockholm: Bonnier, 1968; revised, 1969);

Vänner och u-vänner (Stockholm: Bonnier, 1969)–includes "Den ohörsamme," translated by Gunilla Anderman as "He Would Not Listen," in *An Anthology of Modern Swedish Literature,* edited by Per Wästberg (Merrick, N.Y.: Cross-Cultural Communications, 1979), pp. 125–129;

Marta, Marta: En folksaga (Stockholm: Bonnier, 1970);

Fåglarna i Nam Dinh–Artiklar om Vietnam (Eneryda, Sweden: Ordfront, 1972);

Din tjänare hör (Stockholm: Bonnier, 1977)–includes "Söndagsflickan," translated by Diana W. Wormuth as "Sunday's Child," *Swedish Book Review,* 2 (1984): 24–25;

Vredens barn (Stockholm: Bonnier, 1979)–includes "Björnflickan och övriga barn," translated by Leif Sjöberg and Stephen Klass as "The Bear Girl and Other Children," *Metamorphoses: The Journal of the Five College Seminar on Literary Translation,* 8 (Spring 1999): 49–62;

Varje löv är ett öga (Stockholm: Bonnier, 1980);

Sara Lidman

Nabots sten (Stockholm: Bonnier, 1981); translated by Joan Tate as *Nabot's Stone* (Norwich, U.K.: Norvik, 1989);

Den underbare mannen (Stockholm: Bonnier, 1983)–includes "Goliath," translated by Tate, *Swedish*

Book Review, 2 (1984): 25–27; and "Queijna under isen," translated by Susan Brantly as "The Woman under the Ice," Dimension (1994): 476–479;

Bröd men också rosor, by Lidman, Henry Cöster, and Per Frostin (Stockholm: Rabén & Sjongren, 1985);

Järnkronan (Stockholm: Bonnier, 1985)–includes "Fosterlandet," translated by Linda Schenck as "Fatherland," Swedish Book Review, 1 (1990): 37–44;

Och trädet svarade (Stockholm: Bonnier, 1988)–includes "Före ordet," translated by Eva Claeson as "Before Words," Two Lines: A Journal of Translation (Spring 1997): 52–59; "On Deforestation" and "Drought in the Third World and Our Imagination," translated by Tate in Swedish Book Review Supplement (1997): 57, 63–66;

The Village on Earth (New York: Swedish Information Service, 1991);

Lifsens rot (Stockholm: Bonnier, 1996)–excerpt translated by Tate as "Cash Crop" in Swedish Book Review Supplement (1997): 58–62;

Oskuldens minut (Stockholm: Bonnier, 1999).

PLAY PRODUCTIONS: *Job Klockmakares dotter*, Göteborg, The Studio, 26 December 1954;

Aina, Göteborg, The Studio, 25 August 1956;

Marta, Marta, by Lidman and the Västerbotten Ensemble, Göteborg, The Studio, 1970.

OTHER: "Fabel och argument," by Lidman and Elisabet Tykesson, in *Vänkritik: 22 samtal om dikt tillägnade Olle Holmberg* (Stockholm: Bonnier, 1959), pp. 140–155;

"Samtal över en avgrunn," foreword in *Fra kolonialisme til sosialisme: Et essay om økonomisk utvikling*, by Bo Gustaffson, edited by T. J. Bielenberg (Stockholm: Tidskriften Clarté, 1966), pp. 3–9;

"På väg till mamma," in *Pappa–en kärlekshistoria*, edited by Gunila Ambjörnsson (Stockholm: Legenda, 1986);

"Sara Lidman," in *Författaren själv: ett biografiskt lexikon av och om 1189 samtida svenska författare*, edited by Bo Heurling (Höganäs: Bra böcker, 1993), pp. 204–205;

"Woyzeck i Svappavaara," translated by Eva Claeson as "Woyzeck in Svappavaara," *Metamorphoses: The Journal of the Five College Seminar on Literary Translation*, 5, no. 2 (December 1997): 19–25;

"De gamla älskande i Svappavaara," translated by Claeson as "The Lovers of Svappavaara," *Metamorphoses: The Journal of the Five College Seminar on Literary Translation*, 6, no. 1 (April 1998): 53–57.

Sara Lidman is a writer with a dual reputation. On the one hand, she is a distinguished novelist and best-selling author, acknowledged by critics as stylistically innovative and as one of the most significant Swedish writers of the latter half of the twentieth century. On the other hand, Lidman's many years of political activism, beginning in Africa in the early 1960s but especially during the Vietnam War, have earned her a reputation as an articulate and always independent public voice addressing the crucial social, political, and environmental issues of her time. In her writing Lidman employs a distinctive blend of poetry and prose, deeply anchored in the oral tradition of her native northern Sweden. Her first novel, *Tjärdalen* (The Tar Mine, 1953), was an unparalleled success both with critics and the public, but she later abandoned the writing of fiction altogether for more than a decade, only to return to the novel to write a masterly five-volume series on the modernization of northern Sweden, the so-called Jernbaneepos (Railway Epic).

Sara Adela Lidman was born on 30 December 1923 in Missenträsk, a small village on the border between the provinces of Västerbotten and Norrbotten in the north of Sweden. Her father, Andreas Lidman, was a farmer on the small scale such as was formerly prevalent in that part of Sweden, while her mother, Jenny Lundman, came from the coastal village of Antnäs in Norrbotten. Sara was the third of five children and grew up in a traditional extended household, including her beloved paternal grandmother, Sara Helena, and two uncles on her father's side, Arvid and Anund Lidman.

After six years in the village school, Lidman and her elder sister Lisbeth were diagnosed with tuberculosis and sent to a sanatorium in Västerbotten. Although the illness as such was a serious matter, the sanatorium, in contrast to the village, offered books, radio, intellectual stimulation, and the companionship of young people of the same age. Several visits to sanatoriums followed, the last one in the French Alps in 1947. Lidman continued her studies (the only one in her family to do so), first by correspondence, then at a boarding school in the southern Swedish province of Småland, where students from around the country gathered to prepare for university studies. In January 1945, after temporary jobs as a waitress and at the post office as well as a brief sojourn at a drama school in Stockholm, Lidman enrolled at Uppsala University, where she studied French and English.

Becoming a writer was always Lidman's main goal. A collection of short stories written in Uppsala was accepted by Bonnier publishing house in 1947 but was later withdrawn at the author's request. Her debut publication, *Tjärdalen*, is based on an anecdote told by her father and set in the fictional village of Ecksträsk in the 1930s. The novel is a moral tale narrated in an innovative blend of local dialect, high modernism, and the religious and biblical idioms characteristic of the isolated villages of northern Sweden. Influences can be traced from northern Swedish writers such as Thorsten Jonsson and Stina Aronson. The novel was a best-seller and earned Lidman the prestigious literary prize awarded by the newspaper *Svenska Dagbladet* in 1953.

The moral question that underlies the story, which takes place over a five-day period in late June in the 1930s, is a recurring theme in Lidman's later novels: how do people treat the lowest and most vulnerable members of their communities? The *tjärdal* of the title refers to an excavation in a hillside in which tar is distilled. At the time of the story a tar mine was a potential, though difficult, source of income, requiring an entire year of effort and expectation. When the farmer Nils comes to his tar mine he finds that it has been sabotaged. The local scoundrel, nicknamed "the Fox," gets caught under the rubble while trying to sabotage it. The men of the village bring him back to his cottage but leave him to die rather than going for medical help in the nearest town; he is nursed only by the mentally retarded Vela. When Petrus, the conscience of the community, becomes aware of this crime he is deeply shocked, but he too becomes implicated when he fails to stand up to Albert, the wealthiest man in the village, who has manipulated the situation to his own financial benefit. The novel emphasizes not the social sense of shame but an individually experienced sense of guilt.

Tjärdalen was followed by another novel, *Hjortronlandet* (Cloudberry Land, 1955), set in the same province and time period. Like its predecessor, it also became a best-seller in Sweden. Eva Adolfsson, in "I Sara Lidmans gränsvärldar" (1991), describes this novel as "en rörelse mellan kvinnovärlden och fadersvärlden–där den kvinnliga polen denna gång får dominera" (a movement between the world of women and the world of the father–where on this occasion the female pole dominates). *Hjortronlandet* is a collective novel focusing on an isolated community near the village of Ecksträsk known simply as "The Island," a grouping of four small holdings on marshy land owned by the state, granted to homesteaders under certain conditions. The novel begins with the birth of Claudette (whose unusual name is mispronounced in various ways by everyone, including her mother, who got it from a French novel she had once read) to two older parents, the law-abiding but unhappy Franz and the colorless Frida.

Central to the episodic narrative are two contrasting matriarchal figures. Claudette's grandmother Anna, known as "Mother Anna" but nicknamed "The Troll,"

Lidman as a student at Uppsala University in the mid 1940s

is feared but respected for her abilities as a midwife. Stina is an earthy, even vulgar, figure, the mother of ten children, known for her unrestrained laughter. Cloudberries (which ripen suddenly and profusely every few years) are a symbol of a sudden outburst of vitality in an otherwise desolate landscape. Stina's daughter Märit is a similar phenomenon, who is considered a genius by her schoolteacher but chooses to neglect her talents, bearing a child out of wedlock before her sudden death from tuberculosis. The final sentence of the novel, coinciding with Claudette's departure from the village, may suggest the author's own relationship to her home village. "Men Ön Susade Och viskade; bakhuvudet: jag skall alltid vara med dig" (But The Island sighed and whispered at the back of her mind: I will always be with you). *Hjortronlandet* is even more strongly anchored in the oral culture of the province than *Tjärdalen,* full of its humor, inventiveness, and linguistic exuberance. Literary forerunners may be seen in Harry Martinson's *Nässlorna blomma* (1935; translated as *Flowering Nettle,* 1936) and *Vägen till Klockrike* (1948; translated as *The Road,* 1955) and Moa Martinson's *Kvinnor och äppelträd* (1933; translated as *Women and Apple Trees,* 1985)–especially for her depictions of strong, defiant, rural women—as well as in Selma Lagerlöf's *Kejsaren av Portugallien* (1914; translated as *The Emperor of Portugallia*, 1916). Lidman's own voice is unmistakable, however.

The director of the Stadsteatern of Göteborg, struck by the dramatic qualities of *Tjärdalen,* asked Lidman to write a play for the theater. Lidman's first play, *Job Klockmakares dotter* (Job the Clockmaker's Daughter), premiered at the Studio Theater in Göteborg on 26 December 1954. With 122 performances in Göteborg, the play was yet another success for the young author. It was later staged both in Stockholm and Oslo as well as nationwide by Riksteatern and as a radio performance. *Job Klockmakares dotter* was followed by a sanatorium play, *Aina,* staged both in Göteborg and Stockholm in 1956. That year, Lidman became the first Swedish dramatist since Strindberg to have two plays produced simultaneously on Stockholm stages.

In contrast to her first two novels, both *Regnspiran* (1958; translated as *The Rain Bird,* 1962) and *Bära mistel* (Bearing Mistletoe, 1960) have a single protagonist, Linda Ståhl, a powerful but complicated female character. *Regnspiran* follows her life from her birth in Eckströsk at the end of the nineteenth century (a generation before the events in *Tjärdalen* and *Hjortronlandet*) to about age twenty. Linda is an outsider who uses her verbal gifts to mimic other villagers with deadly accuracy. Even as a child she is obsessed with what she calls "byanden" (the spirit of the village), representing order and tradition, while Linda herself seems inescapably drawn to the negative aspects of her personality. An important theme of both novels is betrayal, with subsequent guilt and atonement, as well as the psychology of a Judas figure and the complex relations of father, mother, and child. *Bära mistel* continues her story as an adult woman in her mid thirties, who has left the village and runs a boardinghouse in a nearby town; she becomes involved in a hopeless attachment to Björn Ceder, an itinerant musician and, as it turns out, a homosexual. The title of the novel refers to the myth of Baldur, the beloved Norse god who was treacherously murdered by the trickery of Loki; a sprig of mistletoe was the murder weapon. In the novel Björn's ambition is to compose a ballet based on this myth, but his deteriorating mental condition prevents him from completing the work.

By this time Lidman was regarded as the leading novelist of her generation. She also became actively involved in the campaign against Swedish nuclear weapons, her first major political involvement and her first training as a speaker and debater. Lidman was one of the few Swedish writers to become actively involved in this campaign, which succeeded over the period of a few years in turning Swedish public opinion strongly against plans to make Sweden a nuclear power.

A new period in Lidman's life and work begins at about this time, characterized by active interest and involvement in people and places far from her home region. Late in 1960 she left for South Africa, which was beginning to attract attention around the world. In Sweden the writer and journalist Per Wästberg had introduced the problem of apartheid in a series of articles in *Dagens Nyheter,* and Lidman's friend, the painter Berta Hansson, had spent two years in Natal. Lidman traveled to Africa, staying briefly in Natal but soon continuing to Johannesburg. Through the writer Nadine Gordimer, she became acquainted with people in the African National Congress (ANC). In February 1961 she was arrested and charged under the notorious Immorality Act, which banned any sort of interracial relationships, when her friendship with a black activist was discovered. The charge was later withdrawn, but Lidman felt compelled to leave the country, in the process enduring a barrage of media coverage both in Sweden and in South Africa.

During and just after her sojourn in South Africa, Lidman wrote in a short time the novel *Jag och min son* (My Son and I, 1961), expanding the novel for a new edition in 1963. *Jag och min son* is Lidman's only novel written in the first person, and the unnamed narrator is a middle-aged Swedish man working in South Africa, trying to save enough money to return to the family farm in northern Sweden and support his four-year-old son. The novel is in part a psychological study of a father's idealized and often hysterical love for his young son. While not a supporter of apartheid, he nonetheless profits from it; although he works with blacks in his jobs as laborer and factory worker, he earns ten times what they do. The narrator insists that his personal goals have nothing to do with "the natives," that he is neutral, not "political." The novel demonstrates that apartheid is not only a question of race but a question of economics as well. Like the Swede working in Johannesburg, people around the world profited from the suppression of blacks. As an alternate title for the book suggested, in relation to Africa much of the rest of the world is a "en tjuv" (thief). This novel moves beyond the much-debated "racial question" of the 1950s to the kind of economic analysis of oppression that became prevalent in the 1960s.

By the time *Jag och min son* was published, Lidman had already settled in Kenya, a country then on the threshold of *uhuru,* or independence. While in Denmark in 1962 she had met Wambûi Njonjo, a young Kenyan woman who was to become the first female school inspector of the newly independent Kenya. Lidman became a cook and driver for Wambûi, traveling the countryside with her and visiting the most remote village schools. A novel written during this period, *Med*

Lidman with fellow activist writers Per Wästberg and Per Radström in 1955 (Pressens Bild)

fem diamanter (With Five Diamonds, 1964), bears witness to the profound knowledge she acquired during her stay in Kenya, influenced as well by her reading of Franz Fanon's *Les damnés de la terre* (1961; translated as *The Wretched of the Earth*, 1963). A country in transition from colonialism to a new form of colonialism is pictured in all its aspects: economic, ethnic, racial, religious, geographical, and political. This novel has, as Helena Forsås-Scott writes in her piece from *Swedish Women's Writing 1850–1995* (1997), a "stylistic sophistication that surpasses anything to be found in Sara Lidman's earlier novels."

Med fem diamanter is a love story with economic complications that frustrate the lovers' desires to be together. As in *Jag och min son*, *Med fem diamanter* has a male protagonist, Wachira, a young man caught between tribal traditions and the urban world of Nairobi. In order to marry he must pay a bride price, in this case six goats, to the woman's brothers. Wachira is forced to seek employment in Nairobi, where he is drawn into the colonial system, moving from *memsab* to *memsab*, from one misfortune to another, from one cement hut to another. The cement walls of the cramped living space provided for the native "boys," or household workers, resemble a prison. After five years (and without coming one goat closer to his goal), Wachira decides to commit the crime of which he was once accused (and which was the original impetus for his flight to Nairobi)–stealing a ring from his employer. When he attempts to sell the ring, its "diamonds" prove to be made of glass. In the wake of this total fiasco, Wachira completely loses his sense of identity. In contrast to Wachira, his older brother Thiongo has received an education and is involved in an apparently homosexual relationship with a married Indian doctor. Thiongo's attempt to help his family by loaning them the money to begin cultivating coffee is thwarted by external forces, however, when Kenya's international coffee quota is reduced. A final confrontation between the two brothers results in tragedy.

Lidman's two Africa novels are both more political than her previous novels, but despite the high artistic achievement of *Med fem diamanter* and her general success as a novelist, for more than a decade Lidman abandoned the writing of fiction altogether. In the autumn of 1964, the first American bombings of North

Vietnam took place. Lidman was one of the first to react in Sweden. In December she gave her first Vietnam speech, the beginning of a ten-year involvement with not only the antiwar movement but also with the land and people of Vietnam. As was her experience in Africa, Lidman recognized the common humanity of the villagers of her native northern Sweden and the people she came to know in Vietnam. Her output during this period was enormous: between 1965 and 1975 she wrote four articles and gave two speeches in an average month. Both then and now readers have been struck by the richness, precision, and vitality of her political writings, a polemic prose with few comparisons. Many of these articles are collected in *Fåglarna i Nam Dinh–Artiklar om Vietnam* (The Birds in Nam Dinh–Articles on Vietnam, 1972). A report from a visit to North Vietnam in 1965 was published as *Samtal i Hanoi* (Conversations in Hanoi, 1966). Lidman's account is characterized by a deep respect and personal affection for the people of Vietnam. When she first arrived in Hanoi by train from China via the Trans-Siberian Railway in 1965, she greeted her hosts in French: "Le Vietnam est le cœur du monde" (Vietnam is the heart of the world). This book shows her (as does her book of interviews with Swedish mine workers, *Gruva*, 1968) to be an exceptional listener as well as writer. Lidman made three other trips to Vietnam, in 1972, 1974, and 1979.

Other collections of her political articles include *Vänner och u-vänner* (Friends and Developing Friends, 1969) and *Varje löv är ett öga* (Every Leaf Is an Eye, 1980). The latter collection, as Försås-Scott points out in "Sara Lidman, Colonialism and the Environment," "foregrounds the interdependence between humankind and the environment that has become fundamental to her commitment," an emphasis that becomes even more pronounced in her later fiction. In line with the politically charged atmosphere of the 1960s and 1970s, not least in Sweden, Lidman's political writings were mainly judged on the basis of the critic's own political orientation, while their literary qualities–such as her mastery of polemic and satire and her ability to weave various perspectives into a single piece–were often neglected.

Lidman's *Gruva* (Mine)–a collection of interviews with the miners of LKAB, the state-owned mine fields in the north of Sweden, Svappavaara, Kiruna, and Malmberget–was published in the watershed year of 1968. Few books have caused a greater uproar in Sweden. *Gruva* introduced to many Swedish readers the conditions of modern working life in their country: the ever-present noise and fumes, as well as the hardships both physical and psychological, including the inhumanity of the management. In the wake of *Gruva* followed not only the mine strike at LKAB in 1969–1970, but also a literary trend in the form of documentary books from all sectors of contemporary life.

A play based on *Gruva* was planned but abandoned in the light of subsequent events, and instead Lidman wrote a play in collaboration with the theater troupe the Västerbotten Ensemble. *Marta, Marta* (1970), subtitled "en folksaga" (a folktale), creates a dramatic triangle between the people, capital, and the labor movement, set against the background of the general strike in Sundsvall in 1879.

The fact that Lidman had stopped writing fiction was often commented upon during this period, but the author herself has reacted strongly to what is in her view an artificial distinction between belles lettres (*skönlitteratur* in Swedish) and "rapportböcker" (documentary writing). In an interview in 1973 quoted by Birgitta Holm in *Sara Lidman–I liv och text* (1998) she pointed out that this division has meant that "man i förra fallet underlåter att ta upp den samhällssyn som finns inbyggd. I det andra fallet gör man ingen som helst språklig analys: det anses inte längre motiverat, eftersom upphovsmannen inte längre är . . . författare!" (in the former case one fails to pay attention to the view of society which is built into the work. In the latter case no literary analysis whatsoever is made: it is seen as being no longer justified, since the originator is no longer . . . an author!). *Gruva,* a classic in the genre of documentary prose, has, as Erik Zillén writes in "Motstånd som litteratur: Om Sara Lidmans dokumentär-prosa" (Resistance in Literature: On Sara Lidman's Documentary Prose, 1993), a mimetic component, where independent "estetiska komplex" (esthetic patterns) develop "direkt ur det dokumentära materialet" (directly out of the documentary material). Political and esthetic elements come together in "ett motstånd som med tiden alltmer förvandlas till litteratur" (a resistance that, in time, is more and more transformed into literature).

After the end of the war in Vietnam in April 1975, Lidman returned to Missenträsk, where she has continued to live. Her uncles had stopped operating the family farm a few years earlier, with her uncle Arvid dying soon afterward. Her parents, by now in their late eighties, were in failing health, and they both died in 1976. Her uncle Anund, who continued living at the farm, died two years later. While tending to her parents, Lidman began the background research on her planned series of novels about her home region. Most of this research involved turning to primary sources such as law books, bankruptcy proceedings, correspondence, and other archival materials, as well as interviews with local residents. Between 1977 and 1985 she published the five volumes of her Jernbaneepos (Railway Epic), a novel about the modernization of Norrland at the end of the nineteenth century. In this investigation of the

Lidman at an anti–Vietnam War demonstration in 1966 (photograph by Lars-Ake Palen)

transition from traditional rural life to modernity, Lidman's artistry achieves mastery.

At one point the protagonist of the series, Didrik Mårtensson, expresses a desire for "snön brinna" (the snow to burn). This intensely imagined work often seems to fulfill that intention, melding historical narrative and subtle psychology, local idiom and biblical elevation, universal poetry and intense sense of place. The setting of the series is the parish of Lillvattnet (Little Water) in Västerbotten in the late nineteenth century, in most respects a traditional rural society situated one thousand kilometers north of Stockholm and relatively isolated from the rest of the country. Unlike the southern provinces of Sweden, this area was cultivated, or colonized, comparatively recently, often by the younger sons of land-owning farmers who moved "oppåt marka" (a dialect expression meaning roughly "up Lappmark way," or further north) in search of land to cultivate. Historically, this region is where the indigenous Sami people and Swedish settlers first came into contact with each other. Geographically, the area is a borderland between the relatively fertile coast and the imposing mountains of the inland, possessing neither the grandeur of the mountains nor the richness of the coast.

The ways in which this area was populated is the more or less explicit background of the narrative. Ecksträsk in the novel is the fictional name for Missenträsk, Lidman's home village, as it was in her early novels. Settlers worked continuously to expand and improve the scarce arable land by "ditching," that is, digging canals to drain wetlands, an enterprise constantly referred to in the novels.

The driving force of the novel is the coming of a railroad to northern Sweden, and the events described are based on the involvement of the author's grandfather, Erik Lidman, in this enterprise, and the resulting consequences both for the family and the district. Throughout the five novels of the series there are many interconnections and a continuous chronology that in retrospect reveals the series to be a single, complex narrative.

The title of the first book in the series, *Din tjänare hör* (Thy Servant Obeys, 1977), conveys a biblical tone that recurs throughout the novel, from a brief, introductory parable titled "Lammet och Hästen" (The Lamb

Dust jacket for Lidman's 1968 nonfiction account of the harsh conditions faced by Swedish mine workers (from Birgitta Holm, Sara Lidman–I liv och text, *1998)*

and the Horse) to the reference to a well-known Swedish hymn on the last page. In a narrative prologue Abdon, one of the more prosperous men in his northern Swedish village and known by the nickname "Spadar-Abdon" (Digger-Abdon) for his zeal for manual labor, makes the long journey to Stockholm on foot to plead his case against a land surveyor who had exchanged a plot of land that Abdon had cleared for another, larger (but uncleared) parcel. The upshot is that the farmer, although capable in his own arena, hands over all his money to a "underbar man" (marvelous man) in the capital, who promises to plead his case. Abdon's folly seems emblematic of the relationship of this isolated region to the rest of the nation and the outside world in general, while the figure of the "marvelous man" (in various guises) recurs throughout the series.

The protagonist of the novel, however, is Didrik Mårtensson, who is about twenty-one years old in the spring of 1878, when the narrative begins. The events of the novel take place over roughly a three-month period. Didrik owns the most notable horse in the parish and also wears an uncommon red "busaron" (blouse or shirt), calling to mind a heathen chieftain rather than a pious farmer. His father, Mårten, is a hardworking farmer striving to overcome his alcoholic father's loss of the family farm. Mårten's polar opposite is Nicke, who lives with his wife and many children on the farm, "Månliden" (Moon Hill); Nicke does occasional day labor but is best known for his skill at hunting and carving. He represents an ongoing challenge, both to his farmer neighbors and to law and authority in general.

At the beginning of *Din tjänare hör,* Pappa Mårten observes to his wife that Didrik "Han får göra nästan vad som helst, 'n Didrik, bara han int kommer sig i superi" (can do almost anything he likes . . . as long as he doesn't fall into drunkenness). Didrik becomes known for his abstinence. There are forms of addiction, however, that his father did not prepare him for, such as the intoxication of words or the modern vice of consumerism, compulsive buying, both of which eventually contribute to Didrik's downfall.

A defining incident for Didrik is his discovery, in a borrowed newspaper, of plans to construct a railroad to northern Sweden. His potential as a leader becomes apparent at a parish meeting (in a chapter significantly titled "Gossen i templet"—The Boy in the Temple—another biblical reference), where he makes an impromptu but eloquent talk about the advantages of bringing a railroad to the district. The description of the first speech underscores the intoxicating power of words over Didrik and his listeners: "Da steg blodet åt huvudet på Didrik och han svävade upp från sin plats. Och han horde sig själv tala med en röst som han inte visste att han hade" (Then the blood rushed up to Didrik's head and he floated up from his seat. And he heard himself speak in a voice he didn't know he had). The speech attracts the attention of a local official, Holmgren, who invites Didrik to his home, loans him books, and becomes a mentor.

Just as significantly, Didrik has fallen in love with Anna-Stava, a gentle and pious "Söndagsflickan" (Sunday's child). Anna-Stava dreams that she witnesses the death of Hård, notorious both as the father of many illegitimate children and as the last person in the district to undergo a public flogging. In her dream, Hård tries to rescue Didrik's horse from the dangerous "Häst-äter-flarken" (Horse-eater Bog); while the horse escapes, he tramples Hård into the bog in the process. Anna-Stava becomes seriously ill as a result but recovers and represses the memory of what she believes she has witnessed. Much of what unfolds in the rest of the series can be found in this opening volume, although this fact only becomes apparent to the reader in retrospect.

The following book, *Vredens barn* (The Children of Wrath, 1979), demonstrates how traditional ways of life in the parish begin to fall apart. The title refers to the personal characteristics needed to thrive, or even survive, in such a desolate landscape: "Men de som överlevde konfirmationen! De hade något att komma med i fråga om livslust. De hade en livs hunger så våldsam att snö, köld, mörker och fettbrist inte förslogo som motståndare. Tusen förbud behövdes dessutom för att dessa livsdyrkare skulle finna det värt besväret" (What madness to want to be born in such a region. And ten thousand died within a year of being born, and a thousand still after having gone to school for half the winter, hundreds in the terror of puberty). The ones left after this weeding out are described in *Din tjänare hör:* "But those who survived confirmation! They had something to show when it came to lust for life. They had a hunger for life so violent that snow, cold, darkness and starvation weren't worthy enough opponents. A thousand prohibitions were needed, on top of the rest, for these worshippers of life to find it worth their while." This harrowing process also explains the pietism and religious puritanism characteristic of the region.

The episodic narrative of *Nabots sten* (1981; translated as *Naboth's Stone*, 1989) covers the period from the winter of 1879 to March 1881. The carnivalesque, anti-authoritarian mood of the narrative recalls Lidman's second novel, *Hjortronlandet*. While Didrik has found Anna-Stava, he delays actually proposing to her. Nicke is accused of illegally shooting a moose and must travel to the coastal town of Skjellet for a hearing. Holmgren hires Didrik to drive him there as well, but the two have both parallel and contrary purposes for the trip to town. Didrik has decided to purchase a "fästmansgåva" (engagement present) for Anna-Stava, a crystal carafe (an object totally out of place in any household in Lillvattnet). Didrik also meets businessman and consul Lidstedt, like Holmgren a representative of authority who sees opportunity in the young Didrik's rhetorical talents. Nicke's trial goes badly for the authorities, and on the journey home the wagon-driver's (Abdon) beloved horse, Stina, dies from overexertion. Holmgren's plans for Didrik to set up a store in his village and recruit timber cutters are set into motion. The novel ends both with Didrik and Anna-Stava's wedding and the death of Anna-Stava's grandmother, the cantankerous "a'Catarina-mor." Future complications are intimated at the wedding party as Didrik takes notice of the mysterious serving girl, Hagar.

The pace of events quickens in *Nabots sten,* the only book in the series to be published in English so far; the action leaps ahead to May 1888 and continues through April of the following year. Two elements necessary to the railroad—the store and the post of *ordförande* (chairman)—have been established. Didrik's new house has been built, Anna-Stava has given birth to three girls, and their "Storsonen" (Eldest Son) is on the way. The large house, manufactured furniture, and Didrik's use of foreign words all mark his growing distance from the traditional, self-sufficient values of his father. Through Didrik's efforts on behalf of outside corporate interests, timber felling and transport have now become a major source of income in the area, and Didrik's store provides "kolonialvaror" (colonial wares) sold mainly on credit. He has also begun to purchase logging rights himself, usually paying more than the coastal companies. In addition, Didrik performs many functions at the same time, as the company messenger, depot master, trader, supplier of railway sleepers, trustee, and chairman of the local committee.

The birth of their son during Didrik's absence at an auction in Skjellet is difficult, and Anna-Stava nearly dies. The eldest son is saved, however, by the mysterious appearance of Hagar, who for the rest of the book remains at Månliden with her ten-year-old son, Isak Otto. *Nabots sten* ends with the death of "Isänkan" (the Ice Widow), Hagar's mother and a former parish prostitute. While nursing Isänkan, Anna-Stava contracts tuberculosis. Hagar's milk runs out, and in the final scene she moves further north with her son.

In *Den underbare mannen* (The Marvelous Man, 1983) the long-awaited railway comes closer to Lillvattnet, while Didrik and Anna-Stava drift apart, each preoccupied with long-standing problems. For Didrik, accustomed to seeing things in the glow of vision and rhetoric, reality has become ordinary. He continues to be obsessed with Hagar, the woman who served as wet nurse for his son, IsakMårten. (Didrik's exaggerated love for his son at times recalls Lidman's earlier novel *Jag och min son*.) A sign of a growing sense of anxiety is his desperate journey to Avaviken, where Hagar has settled, and where he hears from her that his erstwhile allies are out to get him. Didrik fails to heed the advice that Hagar offers, however. Anna-Stava, on the other hand, must confront the vision she had as a young woman of the outlaw Hård being trampled into the bog by Didrik's horse, recalled when excavation related to the railway uncovers not only horse skeletons but also a human skull, which she believes to be Hård's. Her thoughts and feelings are narrated in an intermittent series of short passages similar to prose poems. Didrik's role in serving as spokesperson for the economic interests building the railroad also becomes precarious as the many loans and other transactions on credit that he has arranged begin to come due, without the cash to back them up.

Järnkronan (The Iron Crown, 1985) shows Didrik's fall, as the railway is completed and his complicated financial arrangements begin to collapse. The severe winter of 1892–1893 results in a shortage of seed for planting in the spring. An advertisement for "Fällmos Dunderkorn" (Fällmo's Thunder Grain) catches Didrik's eye, but the grain, transported from Sundsvall via the new railway, does not survive the first frost of the autumn of 1893. The following year the company takes legal action against him, resulting in his bankruptcy. For an irregularity involving eight hundred crowns intended for the poorest members of the parish, he is sentenced to nine months imprisonment in Stockholm—ironically recalling Spadar-Abdon's journey to the capital in search of Justice.

One of the tragic ironies of the railroad epic is that Didrik is convicted for embezzlement of public funds. The man who became chairman on the strength of his demand for a railroad instead of emergency food supplies is sentenced to hard labor on the ground of unsatisfactory accounting of the distribution of emergency aid. On top of that, the primary advocate for the railroad is to be taken by train to the Central Prison in Stockholm.

The perspective of the narrative in *Järnkronan* shifts between three distinct points of view: Didrik in his prison cell; the collective viewpoint in the parish; and Anna-Stava and her son, IsakMårten, at home at the auctioned farm. As in a court proceeding, Didrik functions as the accused, the local community as the accusers, and Anna-Stava as his defender. The truth value of the various perspectives can only be tested by means of the reader's knowledge of events and relationships acquired in the previous novels. As the novel ends Didrik returns to the parish, though not to the farm Månliden, but instead to Spadar-Abdon's farm in Ecksträsk, purchased at auction by Anna-Stava's older brother.

The actual construction of the railroad has only a marginal role in Lidman's "railway epic." The series is a distinctive blend of historical novel, bildungsroman, psychological study of the rise and fall of a local hero, love story, and family saga, providing throughout a detailed representation (and re-creation) of life in a particular place at a particular point in time. While focusing on the residents of a parish in northern Sweden, the series implicitly says much as well about the transition, anywhere, from rural self-sufficiency to a modern consumer economy.

Lidman's narrative technique in the railway series resembles a spiral, where the periodic return of events and characters vests them with renewed significance. To some degree this technique resembles the oral nature of local history: stories are repeated over and over within a village, acquiring over time the referential force of a proverb or exemplary tale. Thus, in the railroad series, the significance of an anecdote or statement may only become apparent in retrospect.

An example of a delayed association is the first time the word "konkurs" (bankruptcy) is mentioned in the work. Bankruptcy, on a gigantic scale, eventually brings Didrik to his fall. At the beginning of the epic the phenomenon is brought up by the bailiff Holmgren, in a friendly exchange over the tea set they are using. The tea service, Holmgren says, used to belong to a "En bonde som fått högsfärdsgriller i huvudet och skaffat sig allt möjligt som han inte behövde och inte hade råd med" (peasant who got delusions of grandeur and acquired all sorts of things he didn't need. And couldn't afford). Didrik, with the seed of acquisitiveness in him, asks: "Hur vet man att han inte *behövde* redskapen?" (How do you know he didn't *need* those things?). (The inexperienced Didrik also asks, "Vad betyder *konkurs*?" [What does 'bankruptcy' mean?].) Particularly significant is the way Holmgren explains the meaning of

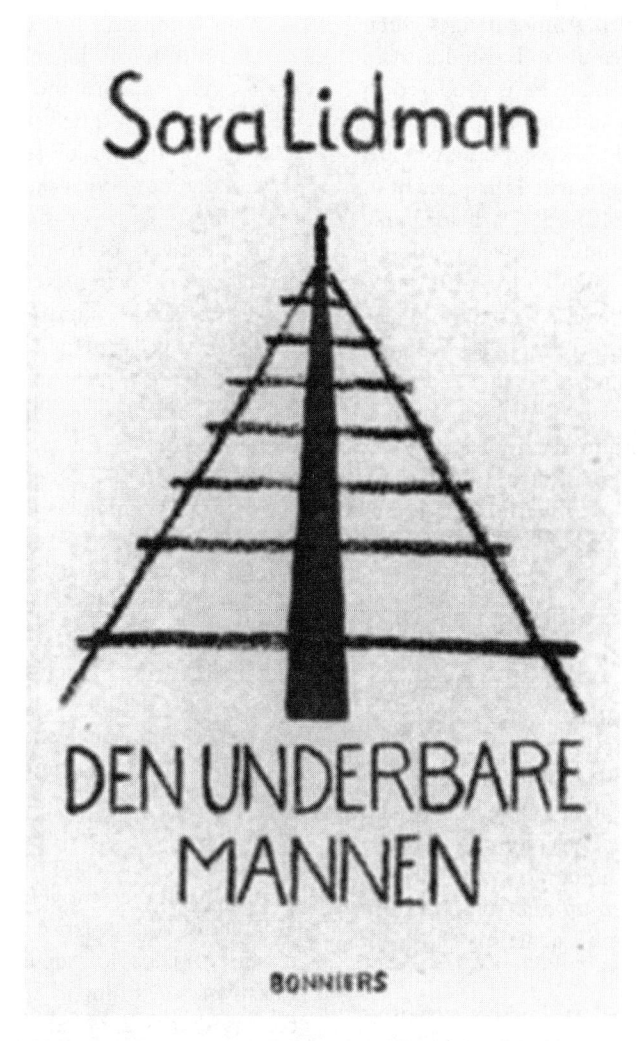

Dust jacket for Lidman's 1983 novel, the fourth of the five volumes of her Jernbaneepos (Railway Epic) series about the modernization of northern Sweden (from Swedish Book Review, May 1984)

bankruptcy a few pages further on: "Och karlen står på bar backe. Det kan bli fängelse för honom. Och det kan också bli en förhudssprängning. Smärtsamt för ögonblicket—men möjlighet för stackarn att äntligen bli karl" (And the fellow is destitute. It can mean prison for him. And it can also be a bursting of the foreskin. Painful for the moment—but a chance for the wretch to finally become a man). The threat, and shame, of bankruptcy, which Didrik's father labored his entire adult life to escape, is minimized in Holmgren's explanation, even granted the status of an initiation into manhood.

Much later, Holmgren's graphic image is alluded to on the last page of the last book of the series, *Järnkronan*. Didrik is on his way back from prison. His family, and many more along with them, have been made destitute when the bank and corporate interests recalled their loans. From the train window Didrik sees the bursting of skin, the membrane around a newborn foal. The image suggests, as Holmgren implied, that a man has been born.

Two types of movement predominate in the series and create tension in the narrative. On the one hand, there is a "progressive" movement, the trend toward modernization, communication, and civilization, represented by the approaching railroad with Didrik as its spokesman. A contrary movement both precedes and reacts to the first, retreating further north, away from the settled areas, where a fresh opportunity to eke out an independent existence always beckons. In contrast to (and often in resistance to) both of these tendencies is a stationary element, what Lidman calls the "being-in-place" of the narrative, here represented by the lamb of the opening parable and by, for example, the incessant ditching activities of Moses, Didrik's predecessor as local chairman.

The language employed by the author includes both poetic compression and dynamic progression, a mixture captured in one of Didrik's inner images when he is overwhelmed by a crystal carafe in Lidstedt's store in Skjellet and reflects on the money he is prepared to pay for it: "Det var Häst'n som sprungit ihop dess pris. Karaffinen var gjord av förtätad, förklarad hästsvett" (It was the Horse's running that had earned the price of it. The carafe was made of condensed, clarified horse sweat). Another image for the conflict between progressive and stationary elements is when Didrik observes a crane on the marsh. Besides being in its natural element, the crane, with its slow stride, embodies being-in-place. At the same time, Didrik imagines that the crane is marking out the future location of the railroad station. The construction of the railroad station, however, which requires filling in the marsh, destroys the crane's natural habitat. The movement of modernization erases the conditions for being-in-place.

Didrik comes to signify a break with his ancestors' respect for ditching and farming. The historical forces that intersect here can be summed up in a greater conflict, however: the forestry industry versus self-management, or capitalist enterprise against crofters, the settlers who came to these barren regions intent on becoming self-sufficient farmers. This endeavor coincided right from the start with the ambition of capitalists to gain access to the riches of the forest. The colonization of the inland was a prerequisite for gaining access to a workforce. Crown lands were broken up and shared out in the form of homesteads, each with a generous allotment of forest land.

Didrik's father, Mårten, is a representative crofter, a eulogist and servant of ditching, fertilizing, and growing potatoes. This enterprise is, for Mårten, a religious act, and the phrase "Your Servant obeys" means, to him, listening to "He Who Provides Growth." To Didrik, however, "Your Servant obeys" means that the "appeal" of His Majesty the King of Sweden shall get a proper answer, in other words, a railroad instead of emergency food and ditching subsidies. But Didrik is unwittingly a tool of outside forces. Whereas he believes himself a spokesman for values such as participation and communication, it is fundamentally other values that he serves: those of capital, the future exploitation of the forest.

The agent of capital is Holmgren, who first mentions the dormant riches of the forest. He connects Didrik's "discovery" of the railroad with the forest, thus giving a direction to his mission, and affirms Didrik's wish to get in touch with the King. Yes, he can write a letter. "But not as a private person. Not as a village fool with delusions of grandeur. You must be able to write on behalf of the parish"—that is to say, become chairman of the local committee.

In addition, for the purpose of transforming crofters into hardy loggers, Månliden becomes a depot with a general store and annual support from the provincial assembly. The relationship between the logging company and Didrik's store means that everyone gets an advance on goods purchased, to be paid back after the winter's work in the forest. (That Didrik is completely unaware of the long-term consequences of these arrangements, being fixed on his vision of the railroad, makes him an even more suitable participant.)

For this calculation to hold the crofters must earn money in the forest, at least enough to pay off their debts in Didrik's store. In northern Sweden the means of enticing the inhabitants to fell timber and get the logs to the river (that is, engage in wage labor rather than subsistence farming) could not be beads and trinkets but rather imported goods such as horse bells, oats for the horse, coffee, and wheat. Didrik's rhetorical skills also served to oil the machinery of trade.

In the wake of the bankruptcy of the newly indebted crofters, the generously apportioned forest regions are handed over to the companies. The crofters, even more destitute than before, are obliged to become day workers and loggers in winter. The forests in the region's interior have finally become profitable, but the changes brought about by the railroad and the attendant logging enterprises (that is, modernization) result in another movement, a dislocation, for many inhabitants of the parish. For Didrik, after bankruptcy, prison, and loss of reputation, the final destination is Ecksträsk, the home of Spadar-Abdon, a place that Didrik has always dreaded and detested. Spadar-Abdon, in his turn, ends up—after his own bankruptcy and imprisonment for forgery—on a solitary farm south of Lappträskvattnet, replacing a family who had gone still further "oppåt marka."

Lidman's two novels of the late 1990s, *Lifsens rot* (The Root of Life, 1996) and *Oskuldens minut* (A Minute of Innocence, 1999), take up the fate of Didrik Mårtensson's family after they are forced to leave the farm Månliden and take over Spadar-Abdon's farm in the village of Ecksträsk, also the setting of *Tjärdalen*. *Lifsens rot* has a female protagonist, Rönnog, who marries Didrik's son IsakMårten and comes to live on the debt-laden farm. Rönnog is in several respects an outsider in the community and in the family, with an outsider's perspective on the aging Didrik, who is still an advocate of the accoutrements of modernization (such as electricity and the telephone), though no more practical than he was as a young man. Rönnog's attempt to understand Didrik's dealings with the railroad and the source and extent of the debts that he has in effect willed to his son seems to parallel the author's own project in the railway epic. This project may also be foreseen in a statement attributed to Didrik: "Befolkandet av Inlandet har icke gått mera smärtfritt till än Avfolkandet av detsamma—om detta borde skrifvas en bok som icke skulle väja för pinsamma moment" (The populating of the inland has not come about less painfully than the depopulation of the same—a book ought to be written about this which would not flinch from painful moments). The conflict between Didrik and Rönnog is rooted in temperament; they are similar in that Rönnog, trained as a "mejerinna" (dairy manageress), is also a proponent of modernization and the adoption of progressive notions of child rearing and dairy production.

Oskuldens minut continues this exploration of Rönnog's fundamental dissatisfaction. Throughout the railway series, horses and men have been closely identified, notable examples being Didrik's horse and Spadar-Abdon's beloved Stina. Here, an elemental feminine anger is represented by an ill-tempered cow on the farm, feared by the elderly Anna-Stava but favored by Rönnog for its milk-producing capacity. This anger, normally concealed, boils to the surface when the cow, named Sabina, encounters one of IsakMårten's younger brothers in a field and wounds him badly.

At one point in *Oskuldens minut* the author makes an unusually direct statement to the reader on the difficulty of representing rural village life as she has so intensively and vigorously done: "Om att skaffa maten för dagen tar hela dagen / och om man skulle beskriva de omständigheter under vilka skaffandet besdrivs / så skulle man behöva en dag till och den skulle löpa jämsides med skaffardagen" (If procuring food for the day takes the whole day / and if one were to describe the circumstances under which the procurement is carried on / then yet another day would be required which would run side by side with the day of procurement). The process of getting the necessary water for cooking, bathing, and drinking was at that time labor intensive, and the reader accustomed to "diskbänk och kranvatten" (kitchen sink and tap water) may simply dismiss the effort to describe it as "diskbänksrealism" (kitchen-sink realism).

These last two books close a circle in Lidman's body of work that began with her early novels, all set in her home village, and continued with the novels in the railway epic. *Tjärdalen,* her first novel, was based on an anecdote told by her father, Andreas. Paternal love is an ongoing theme in Lidman's work, as well as the ray of light that runs through her language. As seen more explicitly in her most recent books, however, there is also a current of "modersvrede" (maternal wrath) that seems to have served as well as a driving force for this author's work.

Lidman has continued to write articles and engage in debates about issues such as the environment, the depopulation of rural areas, and pornography. Over the years she has been awarded many literary prizes, including the annual award of the Nordic Cultural Council and the Pilot Prize. In 1978 she was awarded an honorary doctorate by Umeå University, and in 1999 she was honored by the king of Sweden with an honorary professorship, granted each year to an individual for distinguished cultural, scientific, or scholarly accomplishments.

Since her debut in the early 1950s, Sara Lidman has been a champion of justice, both an important participant in the events of her time and an unparalleled chronicler of a previously neglected part of the past of her country. Her art has for the most part focused on her home village but with an intensity and mastery of language that have earned her a place not only in Swedish but in world literature.

Interview:
Carina Källestål and Sverker Sörlin, "Vreden som 'lifsens rot,'" *Bonniers Litterära Magasin,* 52 (1983): 322–329.

Biography:
Birgitta Holm, *Sara Lidman—I liv och text* (Stockholm: Bonnier, 1998).

References:
Eva Adolfsson, "Det oerhördas anrop," in *Nordisk kvinnolitteraturhistoria,* volume 4: *På jorden: 1960–1990,* edited by Unni Langås and Lisbeth Larsson (Höganäs: Wiken, 1997), pp. 20–27;

Adolfsson, "I Sara Lidmans gränsvärldar," in her *I gränsland: Essäer om kvinnliga författarskap* (Stockholm: Bonnier, 1991), pp. 205–241;

Maria Bergom-Larsson, "Sara Lidman—Leendet och svärdet," in her *Kvinnomedvetande: Om kvinnobild, familj och klass i litteraturen* (Stockholm: Rabén & Sjögren, 1976), pp. 123–144;

Susan C. Brantly, "History as Resistance: The Swedish Historical Novel and Regional Identity," in *Literature as Resistance and Counter-Culture: Papers of the Nineteenth Study Conference of the International Association for Scandinavian Studies,* edited by András Masát and Péter Mádl (Budapest: Hungarian Association for Scandinavian Studies, 1993), pp. 457–460;

Karl-Hampus Dahlstedt, "Folkmål i rikssvensk prosadiktning: Några synpunkter med utgångspunkt från Sara Lidmans Västerbottensromaner," in *Nysvenska studier,* 39 (Uppsala, 1959), pp. 106–168;

Helena Forsås-Scott, "In Defense of People and Forests: Sara Lidman's Recent Novels," *World Literature Today*, 58 (1984): 5-9;

Forsås-Scott, "Sara Lidman," in her *Swedish Women's Writing 1850-1995* (London: Athlone, 1997), pp. 197-215;

Forsås-Scott, "Sara Lidman, Colonialism and the Environment," *Swedish Book Review Supplement* (1997): 53-57;

Forsås-Scott, "Sara Lidman's *Järnkronan*—An introduction," *Swedish Book Review*, 1 (1990): 34-36;

Rolf Gravé, *Biblicismer och liknande inslag i Sara Lidmans Tjärdalen*, Lundastudier i nordisk språkvetenskap: Serie B, no. 4 (Lund: Studentlitteratur, 1969);

Frederick Hale, "The South African Immorality Act and Sara Lidman's *Jag och min son?*" *Tijdschrift voor Skandinavistiek*, 12 (2000): 55-80;

Birgitta Holm, "Det stoff som jernvägar göres av," *Bonniers Litterära Magasin*, 51 (1982): 51-58;

Holm, "Fästen lagda över gungfly," *Bonniers Litterära Magasin*, 63 (1994): 8-18;

Jutta Kerber, *Sara Lidmans frühe Norrlandsromane* (Münster: Kleinheinrich, 1989);

Inga Lindsjö, "Judasproblemet i 'Regnspiran,'" *Bonniers Litterära Magasin*, 29 (1960): 33-41;

Lindsjö, "Linda Ståhl och kärlekens lejon," *Rondo*, 31 (1962): 3-11;

Immi Lundin, "Sara Lidmans kvinnor: Drömda möten och dolda samband," in *Kvinnornas litteraturhistoria*, volume 2: *1900-talet* (Stockholm: Författarförlag, 1983), pp. 397-406;

Röster om Sara Lidman: Från ABF Stockholms litteraturseminarium i mars 1991, Stockholm (Stockholm: Arbetarnas Bildningsförbund, 1991);

Birger Vikström, "Om Sara Lidmans dialekt," *Bonniers Litterära Magasin*, 25 (1956): 213-217;

Gun Widmark, "Språksociologi i romanform: Om Sara Lidmans *Tjärdalen*," in *Stilistik och finlandssvenska: En samling artiklar tillägnade Birger Liljestrand den 25 juni 1991* (Umeå: Institutionen för nordiska språk vid Umeå universitet, 1991), pp. 100-111;

Gustaf Wingren and Greta Hofsten, "Adam i Lillvattnet: Sara Lidmans Norrlandsepos som skapelseberättelse," in *Årsbok för kristen humanism* (Uppsala: Förbundet för kristen humanism och samhällsyn, 1987), pp. 65-107;

Erik Zillén, "Motstånd som litteratur: Om Sara Lidmans dokumentärprosa," in *Literature as Resistance and Counter-Culture: Papers of the Nineteenth Study Conference of the International Association for Scandinavian Studies*, edited by Masát and Mádl (Budapest: Hungarian Association for Scandinavian Studies, 1993), pp. 346-350.

Papers:

Sara Lidman's papers have been left to Forskningsarkivet i Umeå, Umeå universitet, 1998. Papers owned by Leif Sjöberg have been left to Handskriftsavdelningen at Uppsala universitetsbibliotek.

Astrid Lindgren
(14 November 1907 – 28 January 2002)

Eva-Maria Metcalf
University of Mississippi

BOOKS: *5 automobilturer i Sverige* (Karlshamn, Sweden: Lagerblad, 1939); translated as *25 Automobile Tours of Sweden* (Karlshamn, Sweden: Lagerblad, 1939);

Britt-Mari lättar sitt hjärta (Stockholm: Rabén & Sjögren, 1944);

Huvudsaken är att man är frisk: Kriminalkomedi (Stockholm: Lindfors, 1945);

Kerstin och jag (Stockholm: Rabén & Sjögren, 1945);

Pippi Långstrump (Stockholm: Rabén & Sjögren, 1945); translated by Florence Lamborn as *Pippi Longstocking* (London: Oxford University Press, 1945);

Mästerdetektiven Blomkvist (Stockholm: Rabén & Sjögren, 1946); translated by Herbert Antoine as *Bill Bergson, Master Detective* (New York: Viking, 1952);

Pippi Långstrump går ombord (Stockholm: Rabén & Sjögren, 1946); translated by Marianne Turner as *Pippi Goes Aboard* (London: Oxford University Press, 1956);

Pippi Långstrumps liv och leverne (Stockholm: Rabén & Sjögren, 1946; revised, 1950);

Alla vi barn i Bullerbyn (Stockholm: Rabén & Sjögren, 1947); translated by Evelyn Ramsden as *The Six Bullerby Children* (London: Methuen, 1962);

Jag vill inte gå och lägga mig (Stockholm: Rabén & Sjögren, 1947); translated by Barbara Lucas as *I Don't Want to Go to Bed* (Stockholm & New York: Rabén & Sjögren, 1988);

Känner du Pippi Långstrump? (Stockholm: Rabén & Sjögren, 1947); translated by Elisabeth Kallick Dyssegard as *Do You Know Pippi Longstocking?* (Stockholm & New York: Rabén & Sjögren, 1999);

Pippi Långstrump i Söderhavet (Stockholm: Rabén & Sjögren, 1948); translated by Turner as *Pippi in the South Seas* (London: Oxford University Press, 1957);

Mera om oss barn i Bullerbyn (Stockholm: Rabén & Sjögren, 1949);

Nils Karlsson-Pyssling (Stockholm: Rabén & Sjögren, 1949; revised, 1982);

Pippi Långstrump i Humlegården (Stockholm: Nord. rotogravyr, 1949); translated as *Pippi Longstocking in the Park* (London: Rabén & Sjögren, 2001);

Sjung med Pippi Långstrump (Stockholm: Rabén & Sjögren, 1949);

Kajsa Kavat och andra barn (Stockholm: Rabén & Sjögren, 1950);

Sex pjäser för barn och ungdom (Stockholm: Rabén & Sjögren, 1950);

Kati i Amerika (Stockholm: Bonnier, 1950); translated by Turner as *Kati in America* (Leicester, U.K.: Brockhampton, 1964);

Jag vill också gå i skolan (Stockholm & New York: Rabén & Sjögren, 1951; revised, 1959); translated by Lucas as *I Want to Go to School, Too* (London: Eyre Methuen, 1980);

Mästerdetektiven Blomkvist lever farligt (Stockholm: Rabén & Sjögren, 1951); translated by Antoine as *Bill Bergson Lives Dangerously* (New York: Viking, 1954);

Bara roligt i Bullerbyn (Stockholm: Rabén & Sjögren, 1952);

Boken om Pippi Långstrump (Stockholm: Rabén & Sjögren, 1952);

Kalle Blomkvist och Rasmus (Stockholm: Rabén & Sjögren, 1953); translated by Lamborn as *Bill Bergson and the White Rose Rescue* (New York: Viking, 1965);

Kati i Paris (Stockholm: Bonnier, 1953); translated as *Kati in Paris* (New York: Grosset & Dunlap, 1961; Leicester, U.K.: Brockhampton, 1965);

Kati på Kaptensgatan (Stockholm: Bonnier, 1953); translated as *Kati in Italy* (New York: Grosset & Dunlap, 1961; Leicester, U.K.: Brockhampton, 1962);

Jag vill också ha ett syskon (Stockholm: Rabén & Sjögren, 1954); translated as *That's My Baby* (London: Eyre Methuen, 1979);

Mio min Mio (Stockholm: Rabén & Sjögren, 1954); translated by Turner as *Mio, My Son* (New York: Viking, 1956);

Lillebror och Karlsson på taket (Stockholm: Rabén & Sjögren, 1955); translated by Turner as *Eric and Karlsson on the Roof* (London: Oxford University Press, 1958);

Eva möter Noriko-San (Stockholm: Rabén & Sjögren, 1956); translated by Leila Berg as *Noriko-San, Girl of Japan* (London: Methuen, 1958);

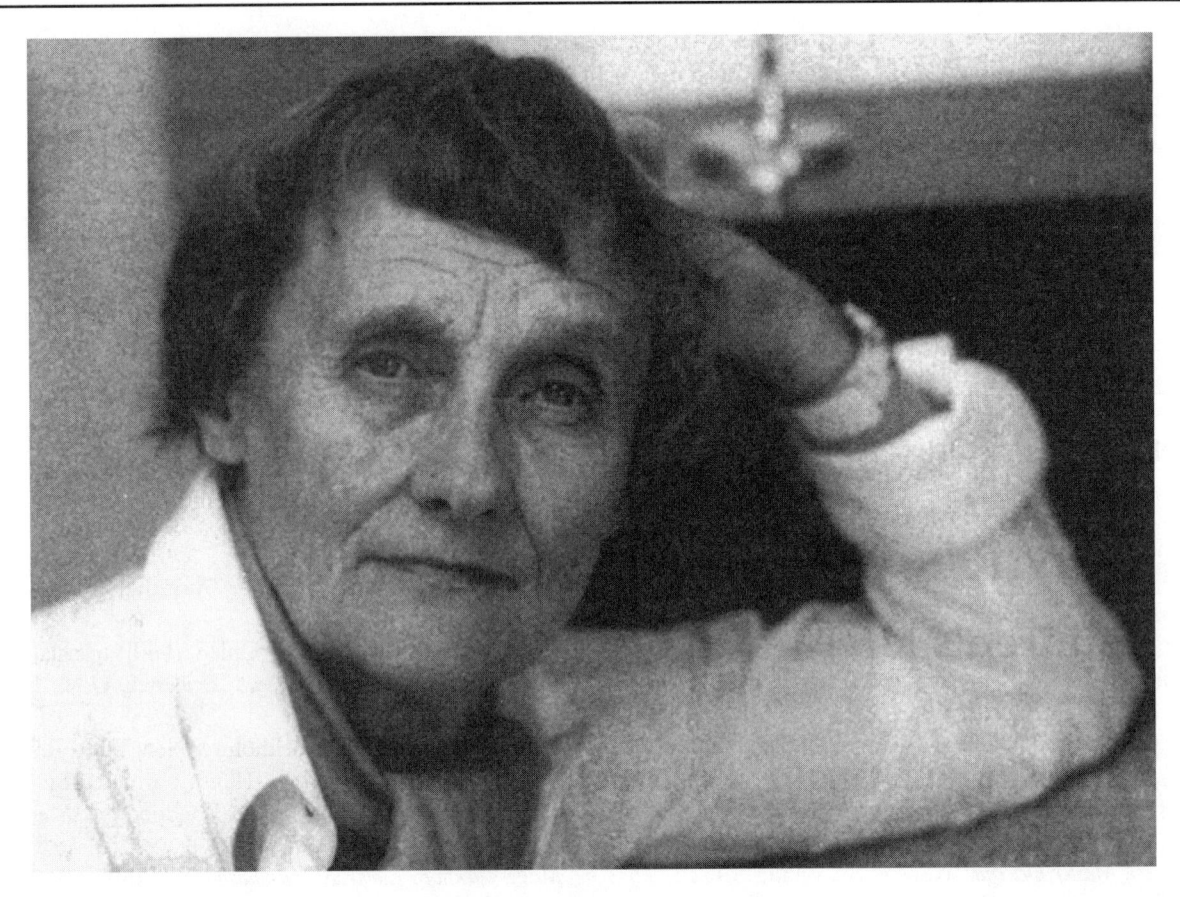

Astrid Lindgren (photograph © Pressens Bild)

Nils Karlsson-Pyssling flyttar in (Stockholm: Rabén & Sjögren, 1956); translated by Turner as *Simon Small Moves In* (London: Burke, 1965);

Rasmus på luffen (Stockholm: Rabén & Sjögren, 1956); translated by Gerry Bothmer as *Rasmus and the Vagabond* (New York: Viking, 1960); translation republished as *Rasmus and the Tramp* (London: Methuen, 1961);

Här Kommer Pippi Långstrump (Stockholm: Rabén & Sjögren, 1957);

Rasmus, Pontus och Toker (Stockholm: Rabén & Sjögren, 1957);

Kajsa Kavat hjälper mormor (Stockholm: Rabén & Sjögren, 1958); translated by Kaye Ware and Lucille Sutherland as *Brenda Brave Helps Grandmother* (St. Louis: Webster, 1961);

Sia bor på Kilimandjaro (Stockholm: Rabén & Sjögren, 1958); translated as *Sia Lives on Kilimanjaro* (New York: Macmillan, 1959);

Mina svenska kusiner (Stockholm: Rabén & Sjögren, 1959); translated as *My Swedish Cousins* (Stockholm: Rabén & Sjögren, 1959);

Pjäser för barn och ungdom: Samling 1 (Stockholm: Rabén & Sjögren, 1959; revised, 1971);

Sunnanäng (Stockholm: Rabén & Sjögren, 1959);

Lilibet, cirkusbarn (Stockholm: Rabén & Sjögren, 1960); translated as *Circus Child* (London: Methuen, 1960); translation republished as *Lilibet, Circus Child* (New York: Macmillan, 1961);

Madicken (Stockholm: Rabén & Sjögren, 1960); translated by Bothmer as *Mischievous Meg* (New York: Viking, 1960);

Bullerbyboken (Stockholm: Rabén & Sjögren, 1961); translated by Lamborn as *The Children of Noisy Village* (New York: Viking, 1962);

Jul i stallet (Stockholm: Rabén & Sjögren, 1961; revised, 1978); translated by Anthea Bell as *Christmas in the Stable* (New York: Coward-McCann, 1962);

Lotta på Bråkmakargatan (Stockholm: Rabén & Sjögren, 1961); translated by Bothmer as *Lotta on Troublemaker Street* (New York: Macmillan, 1963); translation republished as *Lotta Leaves Home* (London: Methuen, 1969);

Karlsson på taket flyger igen (Stockholm: Rabén & Sjögren, 1962); translated by Crampton as *Karlson Flies Again* (London: Methuen, 1977);

Marko bor i Jugoslavien (Stockholm: Rabén & Sjögren, 1962); translated as *Marko Lives in Yugoslavia* (New York: Macmillan, 1962);

Emil i Lönneberga (Stockholm: Rabén & Sjögren, 1963); translated by Seaton as *Emil in the Soup Tureen* (Chicago: Follett / Leicester, U.K.: Brockhampton, 1970);

Jackie bor i Holland (Stockholm: Rabén & Sjögren, 1963); translated as *Dirk Lives in Holland* (New York: Macmillan, 1963);

Jul i Bullerbyn (Stockholm: Rabén & Sjögren, 1963; revised, 1980); translated by Lamborn as *Christmas in Noisy Village* (New York: Viking, 1964); translation republished as *Christmas at Bullerby* (London: Methuen, 1964);

Vi på Saltkråkan (Stockholm: Rabén & Sjögren, 1964); translated by Ramsden as *Seacrow Island* (Edinburgh: Oliver & Boyd, 1968; New York: Viking, 1969);

Randi bor i Norge (Stockholm: Rabén & Sjögren, 1965; translated as *Randi Lives in Norway* (New York: Macmillan, 1965); translation republished as *Gerda Lives in Norway* (London: Methuen, 1965);

Vår i Bullerbyn, illustrations by Wikland (Stockholm: Rabén & Sjögren, 1965); translated as *Springtime in Noisy Village* (New York: Viking, 1966); translation republished as *Springtime in Bullerby* (London: Eyre Methuen, 1980);

Barnens dag i Bullerbyn (Stockholm: Rabén & Sjögren, 1966); translated as *A Day at Bullerby* (London: Methuen, 1967);

Noy bor i Thailand (Stockholm: Rabén & Sjögren, 1966); translated as *Noy Lives in Thailand* (London: Methuen, 1967; New York: Macmillan, 1967);

Nya hyss av Emil i Lönneberga (Stockholm: Rabén & Sjögren, 1966); translated as *Emil's Pranks* (Chicago: Follett, 1971);

Skrållan och sjörövarna (Stockholm: Rabén & Sjögren, 1967); translated by Gunvor Edwards as *Scrap and the Pirates* (Edinburgh: Oliver & Boyd, 1968);

Matti bor i Finland (Stockholm: Rabén & Sjögren, 1968); translated as *Matti Lives in Finland* (New York: Macmillan, 1969);

Pjåser för barn och ungdom: Samling 2 (Stockholm: Rabén & Sjögren, 1968);

Karlsson på taket smyger igen (Stockholm: Rabén & Sjögren, 1968); translated by Crampton as *The World's Best Karlson* (London: Eyre Methuen, 1980);

Än lever Emil i Lönneberga (Stockholm: Rabén & Sjögren, 1970); translated by Michael Heron as *Emil and Piggy Beast* (Chicago: Follett, 1973); translation republished as *Emil and His Clever Pig* (Leicester, U.K.: Brockhampton, 1974);

Mina påhitt: Ett urval från Pippi till Emil (Stockholm: Rabén & Sjögren, 1971);

På rymmen med Pippi Långstrump (Stockholm: Rabén & Sjögren, 1971); translated as *Pippi on the Run* (New York: Viking, 1971);

Bröderna Lejonhjärta (Stockholm: Rabén & Sjögren, 1973); translated by Joan Tate as *The Brothers Lionheart* (New York: Viking / Leicester, U.K.: Brockhampton, 1975);

Samuel August från Sevedstorp och Hanna i Hult (Stockholm: Rabén & Sjögren, 1975);

Madicken och Junibackens Pims (Stockholm: Rabén & Sjögren, 1976); translated by Crampton as *Mardie to the Rescue* (London: Eyre Methuen, 1981);

Visst kan Lotta nästan allting (Stockholm: Rabén & Sjögren, 1977); translated as *Of Course Polly Can Do Almost Everything* (Chicago: Follett, 1978); translation republished as *Lotta's Christmas Surprise* (London: Eyre Methuen, 1978);

Pippi Långstrump har julgransplundring (Stockholm: Rabén & Sjögren, 1979); translated by Stephen Keeler as *Pippi Longstocking's After-Christmas Party* (London: Viking, 1995);

Ronja rövardotter (Stockholm: Rabén & Sjögren, 1981); translated by Crampton as *The Robber's Daughter* (London: Methuen, 1983); translation republished as *Ronia, the Robber's Daughter* (New York: Viking, 1983);

Titta, Madicken, det snöar! (Stockholm: Rabén & Sjögren, 1983); translated as *The Runaway Sleigh Ride* (New York: Viking / London: Methuen Children's, 1984);

När lilla Ida skulle göra hyss (Stockholm: Rabén & Sjögren, 1984); translated by David Scott as *Emil's Little Sister* (London: Hodder & Stoughton, 1985);

Spelar min lind sjunger min näktergal (Stockholm: Rabén & Sjögren, 1984); translated by Crampton as *My Nightingale Is Singing* (London: Methuen, 1985; New York: Viking, 1986);

Draken med de röda ögonen (Stockholm: Rabén & Sjögren, 1985); translated by Crampton as *The Dragon with Red Eyes* (London: Methuen, 1986);

Emils hyss nr 325 (Stockholm: Rabén & Sjögren, 1985); translated by David and Judy Scott as *Emil's Sticky Problem* (London: Hodder & Stoughton, 1986);

Skinn Skerping hemskast av alla spöken i Småland (Stockholm: Rabén & Sjögren, 1986); translated by Yvonne Hooker as *The Ghost of Skinny Jack* (New York: Viking, 1988);

Assar Bubbla (Stockholm: Rabén & Sjögren, 1987);

När Bäckhultarn for till stan (Stockholm: Rabén & Sjögren, 1989); translated by Lucas as *A Calf for Christmas* (Stockholm & New York: Rabén & Sjögren, 1991);

Visst är Lotta en glad unge (Stockholm: Rabén & Sjögren, 1990); translated by Lucas as *Lotta's Easter Surprise* (Stockholm & New York: Rabén & Sjögren, 1991);

Min ko vill ha roligt (Stockholm: Rabén & Sjögren, 1990);

Hujedamej och andra visor (Stockholm: Rabén & Sjögren, 1991);

När Adam Engelbrekt blev tvararg (Stockholm: Rabén & Sjögren, 1991); translated by Lucas as *The Day Adam Got Angry* (Stockholm & New York: Rabén & Sjögren, 1993);

Astrids klokbok (Stockholm: Eriksson & Lindgren, 1997);

Den där Emil (Stockholm: Rabén & Sjögren, 1997);

Hujedamej sån't barn han var! (Danderyd: Warner/Chappell, 1997).

Collection: *Salikons rosor: Sagor* (Stockholm: Rabén & Sjögren, 1967)–includes *Mio, min Mio*, *Nils Karlsson-Pyssling*, and *Sunnanäng*.

Editions in English: *Pippi Longstocking*, translated by Edna Hurup (London: Methuen, 1956);

Pippi Goes on Board, translated by Florence Lamborn (New York: Viking, 1957);

Pippi in the South Seas, translated by Gerry Bothmer (New York: Viking, 1959);

The Tomten, adapted from Viktor Rydberg's poem (Stockholm: Rabén & Sjögren, 1961; New York: Coward-McCann, 1961);

Madicken, translated by Turner (London: Oxford University Press, 1963);

All about the Bullerby Children, translated by Evelyn Ramsden (London: Methuen, 1964);

The Tomten and the Fox, adapted from Karl-Erik Forsslun's poem (New York: Coward-McCann, 1965);

Brenda Helps Grandmother, translated by Marianne Helweg (London: Burke, 1966);

Skrållan and the Pirates, translated by Albert Read and Christine Sapieha (Garden City, N.Y.: Doubleday, 1969);

All about the Bullerby Children, translated by Lamborn and Ramsden (London: Methuen, 1970);

Karlsson-on-the-Roof, translated by Marianne Turner (New York: Viking, 1971);

Emil Gets into Mischief, translated by Michael Heron (Leicester, U.K.: Brockhampton, 1973);

Mardie's Adventures, translated by Patricia Crampton (London: Eyre Methuen, 1979);

I Want a Brother or Sister, translated by Eric Bibb (New York: Harcourt Brace Jovanovich, 1981);

The Adventures of Pippi Longstocking, translated by Bothmer and Lamborn (New York: Viking, 1997)–includes *Pippi Långstrump i Söderhavet* and *Pippi Långstrump går ombord*.

PLAY PRODUCTIONS: *Pippi Långstrump*, Stockholm, Oscarsteatern, 1948; revised, Stockholm, Folkan Theatre, 1980;

Mästerdetektiven Blomkvist, Stockholm, Oscarsteatern, 1950;

Karlsson på taket, Stockholm, Dramaten Theatre, 1969;

Mio, min Mio, Stockholm, Folkan Theatre, 1980.

PRODUCED SCRIPTS: *Luffaren och Rasmus*, by Lindgren and Rolf Husberg, motion picture, Artfilm, 1955;

Rasmus, Pontus och Toker, motion picture, Artfilm, 1956;

Mästerdetektiven Blomkvist lever farligt, motion picture, Artfilm, 1957;

Alla vi barn i Bullerbyn, motion picture, Artfilm, 1960;

Bara roligt i Bullerbyn, motion picture, Artfilm, 1961;

Nina, Nora, Nalle, television, 1961;

Tjorven, Båtsman och Moses, motion picture, Svensk Filmindustri, 1964;

Vi på Saltkråkan, television, 1964;

Tjorven och Skrållan, motion picture, Artfilm, 1965;

Mästerdetektiven Blomkvist på nya äventyr, television, 1966;

Tjorven och Mysak, motion picture, Svensk Filmindustri, 1966;

Skrållan, Ruskprick och Knornhane, motion picture, Artfilm, 1967;

Vi på Saltkråkan, motion picture, Artfilm, 1968;

På rymmen med Pippi Långstrump, motion picture, Nord Art and Svensk Filmindustri, 1970;

Pippi Långstrump på de sju haven, motion picture, Nord Art and Svensk Filmindustri, 1970;

Emil i Lönneberga, motion picture, Stella Film and Svensk Filmindustri, 1971;

Nya hyss av Emil i Lönneberga, motion picture, SF-Produktion, 1972;

Emil och Grisknoen, motion picture, SF-Artfilm, 1973;

Här kommer Pippi Långstrump, motion picture, Nord Art, 1973;

Världens bästa Karlsson/Karlsson på taket, motion picture, SF-Produktion, 1974;

Bröderna Lejonhjärta, motion picture, Artfilm and Svensk Filmindustri, 1977;

Så går det till på Saltkråkan, television, 1977;

Du är inte klok Madicken, motion picture, Artfilm and Svensk Filmindustri, 1979;

Madicken på Junibacken, motion picture, Artfilm and Svensk Filmindustri, 1980;

Rasmus på luffen, motion picture, Svensk Filmindustri, 1981;

Ronja rövardotter, motion picture, Film Teknik, Norsk Film, SVT Drama, Svensk Filmindustri, and Svenska Ord, 1984;

Alla vi barn in Bullerbyn, motion picture, Svensk Filmindustri, 1986;

Mer om oss barn i Bullerbyn, motion picture, Svensk Filmindustri, 1987.

OTHER: *Mitt Småland,* edited by Lindgren and Margareta Strömstedt (Stockholm: Rabén & Sjögren, 1987).

Astrid Lindgren is without doubt the most famous and influential Swedish children's author in the world. A rare combination of great popular appeal and high literary quality have led her fellow countrymen to call her their premier export product, and with sales of her books ranging in the millions, this designation is not unmerited. Her first book, *Pippi Långstrump* (1945; translated as *Pippi Longstocking,* 1945), brought Lindgren instant fame; long a touchstone of children's literature, it has been translated into more than sixty languages—from Arabic to Zulu. During her long career Lindgren has received many prestigious Scandinavian and international awards, especially for her fiction. In 1958 she received the Hans Christian Andersen Medal—known widely as the children's literature version of the Nobel Prize. Because of the quality of her work and the fact that many of her later books transcend age-specific audiences, Lindgren has received awards normally reserved for authors of adult fiction—such as the Karen Blixen Medal in Denmark, the Leo Tolstoy Medal in Russia, the Gabriela Mistral Prize in Chile, and the Selma Lagerlöf Award in Sweden. Lindgren has also been recognized for her moral authority and her humanitarian efforts. Both in her life and in her fiction she has consistently sided with the powerless and abused—children, adults, animals, or even trees. Her accomplishments in the humanitarian field were recognized when she received the German Booksellers' Peace Award in 1978 and the Albert Schweitzer Medal from the U.S. Animal Welfare Institute in 1989.

Astrid Anna Emilia Ericsson was born on 14 November 1907 in the small town of Vimmerby, in Småland, a province in southern Sweden. She was the second child of Samuel August Ericsson and his wife, Hanna Ericsson (née Jonsson). Her father was a tenant farmer at Näs, the vicarage situated at the edge of town. The couple had four children: Gunnar, a son and the oldest child, and three daughters—Astrid, Stina, and Ingegerd. According to all accounts by the author, her childhood was a happy one, filled with play and adventure that was interspersed with work on and around the farm. Once, in answer to the question of why her childhood was exceedingly happy, Lindgren responded that she and her siblings at Näs experienced the right combination of freedom and security during their early years. When they played, they were free to roam about, to explore, and to play make-believe, but they always felt secure in the love of their parents and adhered to their strict guidelines. Although Lindgren's siblings corroborated her assertions, the difficult periods in her adult life may also have contributed to her view of her childhood as a period of unencumbered happiness. Her young-adult years were dark, for she had mood swings and often felt out of place.

Her childhood experiences undoubtedly played a fundamental part in her stories, the overwhelming majority of which are set in small towns that closely resemble her hometown, Vimmerby, and its surroundings. Her most famous character, Pippi Långstrump, lives at the edge of a small Swedish town, and the places roamed by Pippi and other characters from Lindgren's books—characters such as the Noisy Village Children, Master Detective Blomkvist's gang, Madicken, Emil, and Rasmus—can still be visited in Vimmerby and its surroundings. Lindgren grew up in the horse-and-buggy days, as she herself has pointed out in *Mina påhitt: Ett urval från Pippi till Emil* (My Inventions: A Selection from Pippi to Emil, 1971), a collection of self-reflective essays that has not been translated into English. Vimmerby was a provincial town, where the principal means of transportation for a family was its horse and carriage. In preindustrial Vimmerby the pace of life was slower, the entertainment simpler, and the relationship to natural surroundings was more intimate. In such a setting Lindgren developed an affinity to nature that stands out in all of her writings, from her first major success, *Pippi Långstrump,* to her last novel, *Ronja rövardotter* (1981; translated as *The Robber's Daughter,* 1983).

When she wrote, Lindgren said repeatedly, she wrote for the child within—an approach to the art of writing that many children's authors share. Yet, her ability to remember vividly and in great detail what childhood was like and what her preferences and desires were at various ages make her books especially engaging. Her books show that she never lost touch with the smells, sights, sounds, and feelings she experienced as a girl. Indeed, her writing reflects the intensity and freshness with which only a child can perceive the world. Lindgren combined her ability for vivid detail with a talent for storytelling that she likely inherited from her father. The Protestant work ethic she imbibed at home harnassed her boundless curiosity and desire for experimentation and enabled her later to try many different genres

Illustration by Ingrid Vang-Nyman for Pippi Långstrump *(1945), the novel that introduced Lindgren's best-known character*

and to develop her own style. Her compassion for those in need, coupled with the courage to speak up for them, also marks a basic element in her writing. Lindgren wrote not what fashion or fad dictated–nor what publishers demanded–but what her inner sense of urgency compelled her to express.

Although Lindgren became a published author fairly late in life–she was thirty-eight when *Pippi Långstrump* appeared–literature was her great gift and passion from the time she learned to write in grade school. As a student her talent became so well known that she was called the "Selma Lagerlöf of Vimmerby," a designation she felt was undeserved. At the age of sixteen Lindgren began serving as an apprentice for the local newspaper and thus embarked on a career in journalism–a pursuit that was cut short a little more than two years later when she was forced to leave her home and family because of an unwanted pregnancy. The morally conservative climate of Vimmerby made living and working there as an unwed mother impossible, and she left for Stockholm–where she trained as, and later became, a secretary. The ensuing years were difficult for her; she had little money and was forced to leave her son, Lars, with foster parents who lived in Denmark. When she married Sture Lindgren, her boss at Kungliga Automobil Klubben, in May 1931 and finally had the means to take Lars back, she decided to forgo a career outside the home and devote herself full-time to her family, which soon included a daughter, Karin, born to the Lindgrens in 1934. Occasionally she did secretarial work on the side and even wrote travelogues and rather conventional fairy tales that were published in family magazines and in Christmas almanacs. In 1941 the Lindgren family moved into an apartment overlooking the Vasa Park in Stockholm, where Lindgren remained for the next sixty years.

Lindgren's daughter, Karin, was the source and inspiration for *Pippi Långstrump*. In 1941 she became ill with pneumonia, and every evening Lindgren sat at her bedside to tell her bedtime stories. One evening Karin asked her mother to make up a story about Pippi Långstrump, a name the little girl invented in a moment of whimsy. Since "Pippi" was an odd and unusual name, Lindgren thought the character should also be out of the ordinary and thus created a girl who defied convention. Karin loved the first story so much that she asked to hear more about Pippi every night, and over the years the spunky redheaded girl became a staple of the bedtime stories that were told in the Lindgren household. When an accident–Lindgren slipped on some ice and sprained her ankle so badly she had to stay in bed–kept her from preparations for Karin's tenth birthday, she wrote down some of the Pippi stories in shorthand and put together a homemade book as a birthday gift for her daughter.

Lindgren sent the manuscript of *Pippi Långstrump* to Albert Bonniers Förlag, a major publishing house in Stockholm. After some deliberation Bonniers refused the manuscript. Lindgren was not discouraged by this rejection, however, for the experience of writing *Pippi Långstrump* had whet her appetite for writing, and in 1944 she entered a writing competition. Sponsored by Rabén and Sjögren, a relatively new and unknown publisher in Stockholm, the contest was for book-length compositions aimed at an audience of young female readers. Much to the chagrin of the cofounder of the publishing house, Hans Rabén–who had wanted to award an established author instead of, in his view, "en vanlig hemmafru" (a common housewife)–Lindgren won second prize and a publishing contract for her novel called *Britt-Mari lättar sitt hjärta* (The Confidences of Britt-Mari).

As was true for the early, conventionally written fairy tales that Lindgren occasionally sold to magazines and to Christmas almanacs, she felt compelled to write according to accepted conventions when she drafted *Britt-Mari lättar sitt hjärta,* which was published in 1944. In writing this book and then

Kerstin och jag (Kerstin and I, 1945)—works by Lindgren that have been all but forgotten—she essentially confined herself to the expectations and limitations of the genre of girls' fiction at the time. This self-censorship in part squelched the voice that had blossomed in writing the manuscript for *Pippi Långstrump,* a narrative with roots in the oral tradition.

Pippi Långstrump was published by Rabén & Sjögren in 1945. Before submitting the manuscript, Lindgren had revised it, making it less radical in the process. In *Århundradets barn: Fenomenet Pippi Långstrump och dess förutsättningar* (The Child of the Century: The Pippi Longstocking Phenomenon and Its Preconditions, 1979), Ulla Lundqvist compares both the original manuscript and the published version in detail and shows that the early manuscript displayed a Pippi who was far less respectful of adults and of authority figures than in the published version. When *Pippi Långstrump* appeared in print one year after Lindgren had placed second in her first writing contest, the book immediately became popular with the reading public and caused quite a stir among critics and educators alike, though for different reasons. Parent organizations and educators in particular were quick to condemn *Pippi Långstrump*. According to Margareta Strömstedt's biography, *Astrid Lindgren: En levnadsteckning* (1999), John Landquist, a noted professor of education in Sweden, called the book mediocre and uncultured, while reviewers relished how it spurred certain conventions of children's literature and celebrated its spirit of revolt.

Although the setting for *Pippi Långstrump* is Vimmerby, Lindgren's hometown, and Lindgren as a girl behaved like Pippi—full of energy, wildness, and curiosity—none of the freedom Pippi takes for granted would have been tolerated by Lindgren's parents or the Vimmerby community. Moreover, the character of Pippi as a construct is actually rooted in the innovative ideas about child psychology and education that arose in Sweden in the 1930s and 1940s. Lindgren followed in those years the lively public debates about a more child-centered education and was a proponent of the kind of education that affirms children by taking their thoughts and feelings into account. This new attitude toward children had consequences for her writing, resulting in the creation of a new narrator who writes consistently from the viewpoint of a child.

Pippi Långstrump, the wild redhead who lives alone with a monkey and a horse in a ramshackle old house, responded to readers' fantasies of omnipotence and their desire for power and independence. Pippi brings adventure, excitement, and a hint of rebellion into the rather mundane and boring life of Tommy and Annika—model children who have just moved next door to Pippi at the beginning of the book. Tommy and Annika could not wish for a better playmate, since Pippi defends and protects her friends when they are in danger. She takes them on scary yet wonderful adventures and keeps them amused and entertained all the time. Pippi is also the strongest, richest, and smartest person in the world. She can lift her horse with one hand and wrestle down a circus strongman, various bullies, police officers, wild bulls, and boa constrictors. She owns a trunk full of gold pieces and can thus afford to buy thirty-six pounds of candy to distribute to the children of the town. She has had almost no schooling, yet can outwit any adult who deals with her.

Pippi's most envied quality—and thus a characterization that departs from the norm of children's literature—is her fierce independence: Pippi can do, and indeed does, whatever comes to her mind at any time. No one tells her when to go to bed or gives her a scolding. She mocks convention and authority and is able to get away with anything. Unkempt and wearing clothes that neither match nor fit, she is also loud and outspoken—a child who refuses not to be both seen and heard and who knows what she wants. Many feminists around the world who grew up with translations of *Pippi Långstrump* on their bookshelves have recalled how their discovery of this spunky heroine opened their eyes to new possibilities about themselves. For these readers, Pippi, who lightheartedly questions roles and conventions, emerged a new role model and a fount of female assertiveness. "Lever vi inte i ett fritt land kanske?" (Isn't it a free world?) Pippi asks, as she walks backward—one foot on the sidewalk, the other in the gutter of the street outside of her dilapidated house.

For most readers, however, the primary experience in reading the books about Pippi was—and continues to be—one of vicarious participation in the fun and games and in the crazy and exciting adventures that she stages and invents. Moreover, Pippi is full of fantastic stories that combine tall tales and nonsense, such as her claims about people in Egypt who walk backward and about people in India who walk on their hands. Lindgren also evokes the absurd world of nursery rhymes when Pippi tells a tale about a cow that comes flying through the window of a train car, only to sit down beside her and begin eating some of her smoked herring sandwiches. Pippi's anarchy and absurd logic render her a somewhat enigmatic figure, however, whom neither Tommy, Annika, nor the reader can ever quite figure out. These traits in Pippi challenge the otherwise near perfect harmony of the playmates.

Despite the serendipity and playfulness of her actions, Pippi is nonetheless on a mission. She never abuses her own powers and makes certain that nobody else, including figures of authority, does either. Probably not coincidentally, Lindgren created the invincible and caring Pippi in the shadow of World War II, when the writer was also working secretly to ease the plight of persecuted Jewish families and children. Pippi's role as a savior becomes quite pronounced when she saves children in danger—from a fire, a bully, a bull, a tiger, and sharks—and speaks up for the powerless and the oppressed, especially in two sequels to the first book: *Pippi Långstrump går ombord* (1946; translated as *Pippi Goes Aboard*, 1956) and *Pippi Långstrump i Söderhavet* (1948; translated as *Pippi in the South Seas*, 1957). In 1949 the first of four movies based on the *Pippi Långstrump* books was released.

In 1945 Lindgren was offered a job as an editor of children's books for Rabén and Sjögren. She accepted and worked for the company, which published most of her books, until 1970, when she officially retired. During these years her days were lengthy, split between her writing, editing, and family duties. In her childhood, long workdays had been a way of life on the farm, and Lindgren, accustomed to such a life, continued that tradition as a professional and as a mother. She wrote most of her stories in the early morning hours—often in bed and always in shorthand—before the real chores of the day began. In spite of her workload, Lindgren was a prolific author—she wrote approximately seventy books. Her productivity was especially astounding in the 1940s and 1950s: between 1944 and 1950 she wrote *Pippi Långstrump* and its two sequels, two books about the Noisy Village children, three girls' fiction books, a detective story, two collections of fairy tales, a collection of songs, four plays, and two picture books.

In 1946 Lindgren wrote her first detective novel, *Mästerdetektiven Blomkvist* (translated as *Bill Bergson, Master Detective*, 1952), a work that also earned her first prize in the last writing competition she entered. She followed *Mästerdetektiven Blomkvist* in 1951 with *Mästerdetektiven Blomkvist lever farligt* (translated as *Bill Bergson Lives Dangerously*, 1954) and in 1953 with *Kalle Blomkvist och Rasmus* (translated as *Bill Bergson and the White Rose Rescue*, 1965). In writing *Mästerdetektiven Blomkvist*, Lindgren wanted to give young readers a book to replace the cheap, gory serials that glorified murder but that they devoured. The opening line of *Mästerdetektiven Blomkvist* is "Blod!" (translated by Herbert Antoine as "Blood, no doubt!") and thus attracts readers who normally veer toward the serials. While Lindgren has in store for her audience plenty of drama and suspense—gang fights, old ruins, and subterranean passages reminiscent of Enid Blyton's fictional adventure world—she does not glorify violence in the detective story. The setting for *Mästerdetektiven Blomkvist* is a small Swedish town modeled on Vimmerby, in which a gang of three teenagers are drawn into life-threatening adventures when their skirmishes take a sudden serious turn and become deadly. Everything turns out well in the end, however, for Bill and his two teenage friends are instrumental in hunting down a gang of jewel thieves. *Mästerdetektiven Blomkvist* was made into a motion picture in 1947.

Lindgren's next book, *Alla vi barn i Bullerbyn* (1947; translated as *The Six Bullerby Children*, 1962), and its sequels—*Mera om oss barn i Bullerbyn* (More about Us Children in Noisy Village, 1949) and *Bara roligt i Bullerbyn* (Only Fun in Noisy Village, 1952)—tell stories about the Noisy Village children and reflect Lindgren's early childhood at Näs most directly and most realistically; these works have been collected and translated in the United States as *The Children of Noisy Village* (1962). Set at the beginning of the twentieth century, the Noisy Village episodes depict the fun-filled hours of play and excitement of a group of six farmer's children from Småland. In a landscape reminiscent of Sevedstorp, a small settlement not far from Vimmerby and where Lindgren's father grew up, Lisa, Karl, Bill, Olaf, Britta, and Anna live on three farms that are built next to each other. The natural leaders—as was the norm at the time—are the boys. Gunnar, Lindgren's brother, had been the natural leader of her siblings and their playmates, and many of the games the Noisy Village children play are based on Lindgren's personal experiences. The fun, games, frights, and adventures may seem quite ordinary, seen with the eyes of an adult, but they appeal to the intended audience, namely young children. Lindgren skillfully relates the intensity of the child's experience in an emotive yet simple language, evocative of the excitement that the protagonists feel in their fictional play-world. There are episodes about birthdays, about Christmas and Easter celebrations, about crayfishing in August, about going shopping without a list and forgetting several items, about candy-eating competitions, about playing "shipwreck" on the mean shoemaker's flooded meadow, and an episode about Bill tricking owls to hatch a chicken.

Lindgren's fiction for girls, *Kati i Amerika* (1950; translated as *Kati in America*, 1964), *Kati på*

Kaptensgatan (1953; translated as *Kati in Italy,* 1961), and *Kati i Paris* (1953; translated as *Kati in Paris,* 1961), in addition to the *Mästerdetektiven Blomkvist* books, are aimed at a somewhat older audience and have not aged as well as her books for a younger audience. Lindgren is truly a children's writer, and one reason is perhaps her understanding of childhood as a special period in life when pretend play and imagination dominate. She perceived the process of growing up as an experience of loss—an outlook derived from her own personal experiences of adolescence, when the ability to pretend and be engrossed in such play disappeared for her virtually overnight. Nonetheless, Lindgren claims that the joys and fresh, intense experiences of her childhood years superseded any dark or unpleasant experiences she went through later in life.

In 1954 Lindgren wrote *Mio min Mio* (translated as *Mio, My Son,* 1956), the first of three fairy tale and fantasy novels. *Mio min Mio* tells the story of Karl Anders Nilsson, an unloved and neglected foster child. One evening, as he sits alone and dejected on a park bench in Stockholm, he finds an empty beer bottle with a genie inside. The genie grants the boy a wish and takes him to Farawayland, where all of Karl's most ardent wishes and desires are fulfilled. There he is known as Mio; reunited with his real father, the King of Farawayland, he encounters warmth, love, beauty, and friendship within the kingdom. Darkness, however, threatens from the Outer Land, where Sir Kato reigns with a heart of stone, and it is Mio's task to defeat him and to break the magic spell Sir Kato has cast over the land. Mio rides through enchanted forests and kills Sir Kato with his magic sword, whereupon Sir Kato's palace crumbles and the evil enchantment is lifted. His task fulfilled, Mio decides to remain in Farawayland with his father, the King. Told in a lyrical, almost archaic prose that suffered considerably in the English translation, Lindgren uses traditional tropes of heroic and fairy tales and transposes them onto the modern world. The ending offers no other solution for Karl but escape into the world of the imaginary.

Lindgren wrote many tales and stories that touch on the plight of lonely and neglected children and was thus accused sometimes of sentimentality in her fiction. All of her fantastic tales can be read as narratives of consolation and escape. Even in the *Pippi Långstrump* books, the excursions that Tommy and Annika take with Pippi constitute an escape from the reality of their boring, conventional lives into an exciting playland. Lindgren explored further the idea of a fantasy playmate in *Lillebror och Karlsson på taket* (1955; translated as *Eric and Karlsson-on-the-Roof,* 1958) and its sequels, *Karlsson på taket flyger igen* (1962; translated as *Karlson Flies Again,* 1977) and *Karlsson på taket smyger igen* (1968; translated as *The World's Best Karlson,* 1980). In 1969 the renowned Royal Dramatic Theater in Stockholm staged *Karlsson på taket,* which was the first of Lindgren's works to be produced on a main stage.

Karlsson, a chubby, infantile, greedy, bragging, sulky, self-pitying, and self-absorbed yet seductive little man, lives in a shed on top of an apartment building. Symbolizing a less glorified image of childhood, Karlsson can fly—thanks to a propeller strapped to his back—and flying marks his only claim to fame. He visits Eric, the youngest of three children in a perfectly ordinary, upper-middle-class Stockholm family, by flying through the boy's window, usually at times when Eric feels left out, pushed aside, or belittled—in other words, at times when Eric feels sorry for himself. On these occasions Karlsson, who is "the world's best" at everything, serves as Eric's alter ego and enables the boy to forget his disappointments and flaws. Together with Karlsson, Eric acts on his mischievous impulses. They sneak up on people, tease Eric's siblings and housekeeper, dress up as ghosts, and chase dim-witted robbers.

Because of the protagonist's ability to fly, *Lillebror och Karlsson på taket* invites comparison with other works of children's literature, such as *Mary Poppins* (1934) by P. L. Travers and *Peter Pan; or, The Boy Who Wouldn't Grow Up* (1905) by J. M. Barrie. Yet, buzzing around like a bumblebee or, more precisely, like a mini-helicopter, Karlsson is too childish in nature to resemble Mary Poppins and seems more a parody than a parallel of Peter Pan. Whereas Pippi and Peter Pan roam the globe, Karlsson's sphere of influence is limited to Eric's apartment and Stockholm neighborhood, where he takes Eric on short airborne excursions. Karlsson is a lighter, more humorous version of a character Lindgren created previously in her fairy tale "I Skymmningslandet" (In the Land of Twilight), collected in *Nils Karlsson-Pyssling* (1949). Mr. Liljonkvast can also fly, but his appearance and demeanor evoke thoughts of death as well as of magic. He takes Göran, a little boy who is ill and has lost the ability to walk, on a flight to the Land of Twilight, where nothing matters anymore. They fly across Stockholm, which becomes enchanted in the twilight, and end up back in Göran's room. Whereas Karlsson's favorite saying, referring to all the damage inflicted on the furniture and toys when he and Eric play, is "Det är en vårldslig sak!" (It's a small matter!), Mr. Liljonkvast is fond of uttering "Spelar ingen i Skymmningslandet"

Emil and Alfred, the farmhand, in an illustration by Björn Berg for Lindgren's 1966 novel, Nya hyss av Emil i Lönneberga

(It doesn't matter in the Land of Twilight), words that clearly refer to death.

Besides fiction, Lindgren also wrote plays and scripts for motion pictures, television movies, and miniseries, as well as adaptations of her books for stage, screen, and television. Her first play featured Pippi Långstrump as the main character and was performed at a small children's theater in southern Stockholm only three months after the book *Pippi Långstrump* was published. From the 1950s to the 1980s the Swedish film director Olle Hellbom directed seventeen movies based on Lindgren's stories–movies that have become classics of Swedish cinema for children because of their sensitivity to the original texts and their timeless beauty. In the 1960s Lindgren began writing scripts directly for Swedish television. Her first television series for which she wrote the scripts was broadcast in 1964 and was an immediate success. Five years later she adapted the scripts for a series based on the novel *Vi på Saltkråkan* (1964; translated as *Seacrow Island,* 1968). The only one of her narratives that does not take place in a town like Vimmerby or have some connection to Småland, *Vi på Saltkråkan* tracks the adventures of the Melkerson family. They are summer guests on an island in the Stockholm archipelago, a setting quite familiar to Lindgren, who herself had a summer home there.

Lindgren also wrote original scripts for the movies, beginning in 1955 with the screenplay for *Luffaren och Rasmus.* As with the teleplay for *Vi på Saltkråkan,* Lindgren wrote the screenplay for the 1981 movie adaptation of her novel *Rasmus på luffen* (1956; translated as *Rasmus and the Vagabond,* 1960). In this cross between an orphan's tale and a journey novel, Rasmus runs away from his orphanage to find a home for himself and soon encounters Paradise-Oscar, a hobo. The two become close friends while roaming through picturesque Småland in the summer. In the end Rasmus finally finds a home when Paradise-Oscar himself, a subsistence farmer with a hankering for the life of a vagabond, and his wife take the orphan in for good. Although Rasmus has the chance earlier to be adopted by a wealthy farmer, he chooses to live with Paradise-Oscar and his wife because of the combination of freedom and security that he experiences with them.

Rasmus's choice comes as no surprise from an author such as Lindgren, not only because his preference recalls her own childhood of freedom and security but also because she famously shunned materialism. She profited in the millions from the rights to all her books, films, and television series, as well as audio tapes, videotapes, and compact discs—featuring songs she wrote and her own recordings of her stories—yet lived modestly throughout her life. Living in the same apartment in Stockholm since the 1940s, she preferred to give her money away instead of enhancing her own monetary and material wealth.

Lindgren returned to writing original novels set in preindustrial Småland with *Madicken* (1960; translated as *Mischievous Meg,* 1960), *Emil i Lönneberga* (1963; translated as *Emil in the Soup Tureen,* 1970), *Nya hyss av Emil i Lönneberga* (1966; translated as *Emil's Pranks,* 1971), and, finally, *Än lever Emil i Lönneberga* (1970; translated as *Emil and Piggy Beast,* 1973). In *Madicken* the title character is a girl who finds herself in mischief once in a while but who is warmhearted, imaginative, and enterprising. Seven-year-old Madicken lives with her middle-class parents and her little sister, Betsy, in a small Swedish town whose comfortable and idyllic environment is reminiscent of Vimmerby. Madicken's father is a journalist with social democratic, sometimes radical, ideas—a man whom the townspeople call a "gentleman socialist." Her mother is more conservative and prone to headaches. Yet, as in almost all of Lindgren's books, the parents are marginal characters. At the center of the narrative is the sisters' imaginary play world, which Lindgren portrays with both warmth and realism. For example, unlike in *Pippi Långstrump,* where Pippi leaps from a high cliff and gets up off the ground below unscathed, in *Madicken* a rooftop picnic results in a dangerous flight experiment. Madicken jumps off the roof, using an umbrella as a parachute, and ends up in bed with a concussion. Nonetheless, most of the episodes from Madicken's life are lighthearted and lack in large measure the social criticism that characterizes the second book about her, *Madicken och Junibackens Pims* (1976; translated as *Mardie to the Rescue,* 1981).

In *Emil i Lönneberga* the title protagonist is, like Madicken, a well-intentioned genius at inventing pranks. Narrated in a rather slapstick yet stylized manner, the stories about Emil also reflect psychological depth and include passages that border on poetry. The books about Emil are some of Lindgren's most loved books in Sweden. While their humor and their adaptation into television series and motion pictures have no doubt contributed to their popularity, they also offer—in the form of a diary written by Emil's mother—a vivid tapestry of life in preindustrial Småland. Emil's enterprising spirit gets him into trouble almost every day, according to his mother's record keeping. He sticks his head into the soup tureen and pours blood pudding batter and blueberry soup over his father—who also gets his toe stuck in a rat trap that Emil placed under the table. Emil hoists his younger sister, Ida, up the flagpole and gets drunk on fermented cherries. Yet, Emil escapes beatings, thanks to his mother, who rushes her son to the toolshed every time he has done something wrong. There he entertains himself by carving little wooden men, amassing quite a collection of them by the end of the third book. Despite his mischief Emil is generous and strong-minded. He shows genuine concern and determination when he rescues his friend Alfred the farmhand, who is close to death, by taking him to the doctor in a raging blizzard and thereby risking his own life.

Without question, Lindgren's books capture the emotional intensity of children and the worlds of their imagination, and her works are nourished by the rich tradition of oral storytelling that she encountered as a child. In *Mina påhitt,* a memoir of her childhood, Lindgren talks about the formative experiences of hearing her first fairy tales and of becoming, later, a voracious reader. The voice of the oral storyteller stands out in most of her stories, but it is nowhere more evident than in her own fairy tales. Moreover, Lindgren as a writer depended on inspiration and intuition; rather than an idea, a feeling or an image more likely made a story well up in her. A name such as Pippi Långstrump or Mr. Liljonkvast—also invented by her daughter Karin—by itself unlocks a world of images and stories. For example, a lonely little boy sitting alone on a bench in the park close to her house turned into the opening scene and inspiration for *Mio min Mio. Bröderna Lejonhjärta* (1973; translated as *The Brothers Lionheart,* 1975) grew out of an unearthly experience of beauty on a clear winter morning in northern Sweden and a visit to the Vimmerby cemetery, where Lindgren saw a gravestone with the inscription, "Här vila späda bröderna Fahlén" (Here lie the two young brothers Fahlén).

Illustration by Ilon Wikland for Lindgren's Karlsson på taket smyger igen *(1968), the third in her series of novels about an obnoxious but seductive little man who lives in a shed on a roof and can fly because he has a propeller strapped to his back*

Lindgren repeatedly addresses the motifs of death and dying in her stories—especially in her fairy tales. In her long life she lost many close friends and relatives rather early on: her husband died in 1952, her mother in 1961, her father in 1969, and her brother, Gunnar, and some of her closest friends died in the 1970s. As an agnostic, she did not believe in an afterlife or the hereafter—as did her devout Lutheran parents, whom she depicted in the memoir *Samuel August från Sevedstorp och Hanna i Hult* (1975). For her, however, agnosticism and skepticism belonged to the adult world, while children needed stories they could cling to when confronting death—stories to alleviate their fears. Lindgren indeed suggests that Göran, who flies through the Land of Twilight with Mr. Liljonkvast in "I Skymmningslandet," and Karl Anders Nilsson, who decides to stay in Farawayland as Mio in *Mio min Mio,* both experience death in the fulfillment of their dreams and desires. In many of her stories Lindgren creates a true children's paradise. Farawayland and the Land of Twilight may differ in details of topography, but pastoral scenes abound in these places and are infused with love, warmth, friendship, beauty, and adventure.

In *Bröderna Lejonhjärta,* Karl Lion is sickly and close to death—yet, like Mio and like Eric in *Lillebror och Karlsson på taket,* he is transformed into a strong, healthy, and good-looking boy when he enters Nangiyala, which, as a kind of paradise for children, is the equivalent of Farawayland and the Land of Twilight. In constructions of plot *Bröderna Lejonhjärta* resembles in particular *Mio min Mio.* Karl has lost his brother, Jonathan; when their apartment caught on fire, Jonathan tried to save Karl by jumping from a second-floor window with his brother on his back. The dying Karl is now confined to the kitchen sofabed, and his fantasies carry him off to Nangiyala, a place already familiar to him from the stories Jonathan used to invent and tell him. In Nangiyala the two brothers unite and eventually free Wild

Rose Valley from the cruel reins of Lord Tengil. When Tengil's fire-spewing dragon, Katla, paralyzes Jonathan in battle, Karl must then save his crippled brother by jumping into the abyss with Jonathan on his back in order to reach the new paradise, Nangilima. The double suicide that concludes *Bröderna Lejonhjärta* stirred much controversy when the novel appeared in Sweden in 1973. Critics overlooked, however, the wonderfully redemptive quality of Karl's final jump and life-affirming qualities evident in the novel through its prominent themes of nonviolence and love. Jonathan's adage and ethical guideline for Karl—and for readers—is that one must care and rally the courage to fight evil. Through *Bröderna Lejonhjärta* Lindgren was promoting the ideas of peaceful coexistence, of dignity in life for all creatures on earth, and of the need to raise children without violence and corporal punishment. Five years after the publication of the novel, she received the German Bookseller's Peace Award for both *Bröderna Lejonhjärta* and her efforts on behalf of pacifism.

In 1976, an election year, the Swedish government levied on Lindgren's income a tax that amounted to 102%, compelling her to write an open letter to the Stockholm daily *Expressen*. Her letter included a fairy tale, "Pomperipossa i Monismanien" (Pomperipossa in Monismanien), that was a barely veiled, scathing attack against the Social Democratic party, which Lindgren perceived as excessively bureaucratized, conceited, and self-serving. Although her letter and fairy tale elicited ridicule from the minister of finance, Gunnar Sträng, several fervent public debates ensued, and the tax laws were eventually reconsidered and changed. Many Swedes believed that the Social Democrats lost in the November elections of that year because of Lindgren's protest. Although she believed the party had strayed too far from its original ideals, she nonetheless remained a Social Democrat even after the events of 1976. The humanitarian tenets of the party suited her activist desires.

Lindgren believed that everything that happens in real life must have happened in someone's imagination first. She hoped that through her fiction nonviolence as a concept would enter the readers' imagination and, eventually, the imagination and cultures of the world's peoples. This message of nonviolence was the driving force of her forty-five-year writing career. In *Ronja rövardotter* the theme of peaceful cooperation—of a life independent of the exploitation of others and of nature—again predominates. *Ronja rövardotter* combines Lindgren's wisdom of maturity with modern feminist ideas in a blend of various genres, including the folktale, the robber's tale, the heroic quest, the bildungsroman—from a feminine point of view—and the romance. The struggle between good and evil that characterizes her previous fairy-tale novels also appears in *Ronja rövardotter* but is played out through the construct of negotiation, which reflects an ongoing process, rather than through a final confrontation or battle, where compromise has no currency. Fundamental existential concerns about life and death, war and peace, and nature and civilization emerge in a dramatic, suspenseful, and yet largely lyrical narrative laced with wit and humor. True to form, Lindgren writes simply—in a melodic, emphatic, and metaphoric language—while adhering to a tight plot structure, all of which make the novel truly enjoyable and exhilarating to read.

Born during a raging thunderstorm into a strong-willed family of robbers, Ronia—a Pippi Långstrump stripped of her superhuman powers—is by birthright destined for strength and a fierce sense of independence. One of the most important lessons Ronia must learn is conquering her fears as she grows up in a part of the robber's fort, deep in the forest. During her explorations of the forest she meets Birk, the only son of the enemy clan of robbers that has moved into the other half of the fort. A close friendship and then romance develop between Ronia and Birk, who save each other's lives and decide to move away from home together. Their escape is their first step toward a life together, as they refute the values of their respective parents—elders who are at constant war with each other and with society beyond the forest. Ronia and Birk vow not to perpetuate the violence inherent in a robber's way of life, a message that can be inferred from most of Lindgren's writings but that had not been stated as forcefully prior to the publication of *Ronja rövardotter*. Characteristically, however, Lindgren leaves room for some doubt in her grand vision at the end of the book. The new life that Ronia and Birk envision is, as of yet, only a promising possibility; their life together may or may not turn out to be the fairy tale that Noddle Pete, the oldest and wisest robber—and Lindgren's true mouthpiece in the novel—whispered into Ronia's ears before he died.

During the last twenty years of her life, Lindgren worked hard on behalf of animal rights. Her egalitarian attitude and humanitarian values, born of her commitment to the Social Democratic movement of her youth, led her to speak out in the 1980s against the widespread abuse of domestic animals on large animal farms in Sweden. At the age of seventy-eight, Lindgren, the farmer's daughter from

Småland, wrote yet another open letter–this time to all the major Stockholm newspapers–protesting the mistreatment of farm animals and started a campaign for improvements in animal husbandry that lasted for three years. In June 1988 the Swedish government passed "Lex Lindgren," an animal protection act that surpassed previous tough standards and that was named after the writer. The letters Lindgren wrote during her animal rights campaign were collected in *Min ko vill ha roligt* (My Cow Wants to Have Fun, 1990).

Throughout her long life Astrid Lindgren displayed the agility, energy, curiosity, wit, courage, and caring attitude that imbued her fictional heroes and heroines. She remained physically active until her death on 28 January 2002, at the age of ninety-four. In life and in art Lindgren entertained, inspired, and consoled generations of readers, influenced changes in Swedish laws, and–not least of all–hastened a reexamination of the purpose of literature in children's lives.

Bibliography:
Kerstin Kvint, *Astrid i vida världen* (Stockholm: Kvint, 1997).

Biographies:
Sybil Gräfin Schönfeldt, *Astrid Lindgren: Mit Selbstzeugnissen und Bilddokumenten* (Reinbek: Rowohlt, 1988);

Johanna Hurwitz, *Astrid Lindgren: Storyteller to the World* (New York: Viking, 1989);

Lena Törnqvist, *Astrid från Vimmerby* (Vimmerby: Eriksson & Lindgren, 1998); translated by Patrick O'Malley as *Astrid from Vimmerby* (Vimmerby: Stift. Bevarandet av Astrid Lindgrens gärning, 1999);

Margareta Strömstedt, *Astrid Lindgren: En levnadsteckning*, third edition (Stockholm: Rabén & Sjögren, 1999).

References:
Patricia Crampton, "Translating Astrid Lindgren," *Swedish Book Review Supplement* (1990): 83–86;

Vivi Edström, *Astrid Lindgren: A Critical Study*, translated by Eivor Cormack (Stockholm & New York: Raben & Sjögren, 2000);

Edström and Per Gustavsson, eds., *Astrid Lindgren och folkdikten* (Stockholm: Carlsson, 1996);

Edström, *Astrid Lindgren och sagans makt* (Stockholm: Rabén & Sjögren, 1997);

Ulla Lundqvist, *Århundradets barn: Fenomenet Pippi Långstrump och dess förutsättningar* (Stockholm: Rabén & Sjögren, 1979);

Eva-Maria Metcalf, *Astrid Lindgren* (New York: Twayne, 1995);

Metcalf, *Astrid Lingren* (Stockholm: Svenska Institutet, 2000);

Metcalf, "Astrid Lindgren–Rebel for Peace," *Scandinavian Review*, 78 (1990): 34–41;

Metcalf, "Astrid Lindgren's *Ronia, the Robber's Daughter*: A Twentieth Century Fairy Tale," *Lion and the Unicorn*, 12 (1988): 151–164;

Metcalf, "Tall Tale and Spectacle in Pippi Longstocking," *Children's Literature Association Quarterly*, 15 (1990): 130–135;

Mary Ørvig, Marianne Eriksson, and Birgitta Sjöquist, eds., *Duvdrottningen: En bok till Astrid Lindgren* (Stockholm: Rabén & Sjögren, 1987).

Papers:
Astrid Lindgren's papers are housed at the Royal Library in Stockholm.

Torgny Lindgren
(16 June 1938 -   )

Elizabeth deNoma
University of Washington

BOOKS: *Plåtsax, hjärtats instrument* (Stockholm: Norstedt, 1965);

Riksbankens sedelhistoria, 1668–1968 (Stockholm: Rabén & Sjögren, 1968);

Dikter från Vimmerby (Stockholm: Norstedt, 1970);

Hur skulle det vore om man vore Olof Palme? Fragment ur en anarkists dagbok (Göteborg: Författarförlaget, 1971);

Skolbagateller medan jag försökte skriva till mina överordnade (Stockholm: Norstedt & Söner, 1972);

Övriga frågor (Stockholm: Norstedt, 1973);

Hallen (Stockholm: Norstedt, 1975);

Brännvinsfursten (Stockholm: Norstedt, 1979);

Markus (Stockholm: Rabén & Sjögren, 1981);

Skrämmer dig minuten (Stockholm: Norstedt, 1981);

Ormens väg på hälleberget (Stockholm: Norstedt, 1982); translated by Tom Geddes as *The Way of the Serpent* (London: Harvill, 1990);

Merabs skönhet: Berättelser (Stockholm: Norstedt, 1983); translated by Mary Sandbach as *Merab's Beauty and Other Stories* (London: Collins Harvill, 1989); revised edition, translated by Sandbach and Geddes (New York: Harper & Row, 1990);

Bat Seba (Stockholm: Norstedt, 1984); translated by Geddes as *Bathsheba* (London: Faber & Faber, 1987; New York: Harper & Row, 1989);

Legender (Stockholm: Norstedt, 1986);

Ljuset (Stockholm: Norstedt, 1987); translated by Geddes as *Light* (London: Harvill, 1992);

Kärleksguden Frö: En levnadsteckning, by Lindgren and Peter Dahl (Stockholm: Norstedt, 1988);

Till sanningens lov: Rammakaren Theodor Marklunds egen redogörelse (Stockholm: Norstedt, 1991); translated by Geddes as *In Praise of Truth: The Personal Account of Theodore Marklund, Picture-framer* (London: Harvill, 1994);

Hummelhonung (Stockholm: Norstedt, 1995); translated by Geddes as *Sweetness* (London: Harvill, 2000);

I Brokiga Blads vatten: Figurer (Stockholm: Norstedt, 1999).

Torgny Lindgren

PRODUCED SCRIPTS: *Legenden om Achille Pagninis besök i Vimmerby 1869,* radio, Svenska radiopjäser / Sveriges Radio, 1977;

Släktningar vid Sju ekars kulle, radio, Svenska radiopjäs / Sveriges Radio, 1982.

OTHER: *I svenska provinsen Småland: Lyrikantologi,* edited by Lindgren and Ulla Olin-Nilson (Göteborg: Zinderman, 1973);

"Intervjun," in *Fem pjäser för amatörteaterbruk* (Stockholm: Författarförlaget i samarbete med ABF och Brevskolan, 1977), pp. 11–79;

"Fadershanden," in *Fadershanden och Giga: Två skådespel,* by Lindgren and Eric Åkerlund (Stockholm: Författarförlaget, 1986);

"Albert Engström: Ur minnesteckning," in *Årsbok: Albert Engström sällskapet* (1996), pp. 89–92;

"Från det ena till det andra," in *Hur jag blev författare,* by Marianne Ahrne (Stockholm: Norstedt, 1996), pp. 123–125.

Torgny Lindgren often credits his hometown of Norsjö in the northern Swedish region of Västerbotten and the dialect spoken there as the inspiration for the subject matter of his work and the manner of its telling. Lindgren has achieved international status as a writer by relaying these oral, regional tales into universal investigations into the human condition. His work examines such fundamental and pervasive aspects of life as the nature of power and exploitation and the dimensions and limitations of love and the body. In the last decades of the twentieth century Lindgren emerged as a forceful and prominent writer, becoming in 1991 a member of the prestigious Swedish Academy, which determines the recipient of the Nobel Prize for literature. Possessing elements of both Franz Kafka and Harold Pinter, Lindgren's style is distinctly suited to depict the ambiguities and absurdities of the present day.

Lindgren was born on 16 June 1938 in the village of Raggsjö in the Norsjö region of Västerbotten, the son of Andreas and Helga Lindgren, a farming couple. After completing his primary and secondary education Lindgren attended "folkskoleseminariet" (a tertiary-level seminar) in the town of Umeå. He thereafter earned his living as a teacher in various subjects, including geography, history, and politics. Lindgren and his wife, Stina—the couple married on 19 June 1959—lived in several different towns and regions throughout the 1960s and 1970s. They had three children: Aina, Ylva, and Torgils. After turning his attention to writing full-time in 1974 and receiving an additional degree from Uppsala University in *religionskunskap* (comparative religion), Lindgren converted to Catholicism. In 1988 the family relocated to Lindgren's home region of Vimmerby. An intensely private person, Lindgren has kept the tone of his interviews largely in the abstract, focusing on the subject of writing rather than connecting his craft with his life and history, with the exception of occasional general statements. Unlike with other literary figures such as August Strindberg or Ingmar Bergman, critics and scholars have shown little interest in relating Lindgren's work with his biography.

In reference to his earliest published works, the poetry collections *Plåtsax, hjärtats instrument* (Plate Shears, Instrument of the Heart, 1965), *Dikter från Vimmerby* (Poems from Vimmerby, 1970), and *Hur skulle det vore om man vore Olof Palme? Fragment ur en anarkists dagbok* (What Would It Be Like to Olof Palme? Fragments from an Anarchist's Diary, 1971), Lindgren has been somewhat dismissive, claiming that they were largely rehearsals for future, better work. While it is true that Lindgren's fiction was the vehicle that established his reputation, many of his consistent themes and some aspects of his style are present as well in these early verse efforts. In *Plåtsax, hjärtats instrument* Lindgren addresses the theme of the fallibility and impermanence of human beings and their efforts in love. Also present is Lindgren's ironic tone, extending as usual to himself and his subject matter:

> Om någonsin någon kommer
> eller bara en skugga
> finns jag här förenklad
> Torgny Lindgren
> en relikt
> eller kanske hellre rudiment
> Förstockat inkrökt i mig själv
> född i Tvillingarna
> rädd för resor
> bålens organ bräckliga
> Inskränkt trygg
> i knuttimrad bofasthet
> Husfriden är den enda friden
> husfrid är mitt enda arv
> husfrid och tystnad
> L'ideal et le reel
>
> (If ever anyone comes
> or only a shadow
> I am here simplified
> Torgny Lindgren
> a relic
> or maybe instead a rudiment
> Stagnated bent into myself
> born in Gemini
> afraid of trips
> the body's organs fragile
> narrowly safe
> in clenched dwelling
> domestic peace is the only peace
> domestic peace is my only legacy
> peace and quiet
> L'ideal et le reel)

These poetic works provide a preliminary outline for the major themes in Lindgren's work. In the collection *Hur skulle det vore om man vore Olof Palme? Fragment ur en anarkists dagbok* Lindgren compares the concepts of power and myth in the realms with which much of his later fiction is concerned—the civil, or political, and the theological—as the following lines from an untitled poem indicate: "Det politiska tvivlet är värre än det religiösa. De politiska avgrunderna är djupare än de teologiska. Politikens

Dust jacket for Lindgren's 1983 collection of magic-realism stories set in northern Sweden (from Swedish Book Review *[May 1984])*

helvete är gräsligare än den själsliga fördömelsens. Det politiska helvetet tillhör inte substrukturerna, det är helt enkelt närvarande, i samma storleksordning, med samma fasthet, samma konsistens som köttet och benen i min egen kropp" (Political confusion is worse than religious. The political abysses are deeper than the theological. Political hell is more hideous than spiritual condemnation. Political hell does not belong to the substructures, it is simply present, in the same degree, with the same solidity as the flesh and blood of my own body). As the subtitle of the collection suggests, the poems are a chaotic and critical look at the absurdities encountered in political discussion and debate.

In the early 1970s Lindgren turned his attention to fiction, and he completed his first novel, *Skolbagateller medan jag försökte skriva till mina överordnade* (School Trivia, While Attempting to Write to My Superiors, 1972). In this novel the educational system in Sweden of the time is skewered, portrayed as a semicompetent, monolithic bureaucracy deaf to the needs of the students. The students, for their part, demonstrate their lack of appreciation of the institution by literally rejecting the lessons of their theology classes and the principles of the capitalist means of production. Society becomes the field upon which the spirit encounters the psychic stumbling blocks of bureaucracy.

Övriga frågor (Any Other Business?) was published in 1973 and continues to examine the play between structure and the inherent chaos of life. The title itself suggests a space for unforeseen, unscheduled discussion within the forum of an administrative meeting. In this case the chaos stems from the conflict between individuals and the state, the plight of illegal immigrants and their impending expulsion from Sweden. The incident is played out in the midst of an election campaign and the protagonist, Evan,

Dust jacket for Lindgren's 1987 novel, in which a plague ravages northern Sweden (from Swedish Book Review *[1987])*

becomes an unwitting embodiment of propaganda for the status quo. Once again Lindgren lampoons, with devastating accuracy, an insidious pattern of political corruption and personal culpability.

Lindgren's several subsequent novels and radio plays, including *Brännvinsfursten* (The Sovereign of Spirits, 1979) and *Skrämmer dig minuten* (Does This Moment Frighten You, 1981), begin to investigate historical figures. In the former case liquor baron L. O. Smith appears as the flawed protagonist, and in the latter, also a novel, Swedish canonical poet Verner von Heidenstam is referenced through a character who emulates him. A self-made man extraordinaire, Smith creates a liquor empire capitalizing on the new markets and opportunities of the late 1890s.

In contrast *Skrämmer dig minuten* is set in contemporary late 1970s Sweden and features a married couple in constant masquerade. The protagonist, Folke, adopts the persona and vocabulary of von Heidenstam to address the world. His wife, Viveka, changes her assumed role to fit the occasion. Lindgren's reputation as an ironist was greatly enhanced by *Skrämmer dig minuten*. At this point in his career, however, his narrative voice and theme take a dramatic shift. Whereas he had previously depicted the relative banality of human foibles, Lindgren now ventures into a near mythic realm of good and evil, bringing to mind such writers as Pär Lagerkvist and Søren Kierkegaard.

Ormens väg på hälleberget (1982; translated as *The Way of the Serpent,* 1990) is a dark tale of brutality, lust, and avarice set in the Swedish North of the 1800s. The novel depicts the relationship of one family trying to repay a debt through two generations. Money is owed on a yearly basis to an opportunistic landlord, and subsequently to his son, both embodiments of evil. The protagonist, Jani, is the son of the woman called upon to pay the landlord with sexual service. In the course of this debt-settling, Tea bears the serpent/landlord a child called Eva. The situation eases a bit when Tea, Jani's mother, marries a local man, but worsens again when the landlord conspires to have the man imprisoned. The landlord's son, now landlord himself, claims his usual payment from his own half sister. Bringing to mind the book of Job, Jani's situation becomes increasingly unbearable as he is paralyzed in an accident and Eva dies attempting to birth a freakishly large, misshapen, stillborn baby. It is subsequently Jani wife's turn to pay the debt. Ultimately, all the characters save Jani are wiped out in an apocalyptic avalanche.

Ormens väg på halleberget earned an immense amount of critical acclaim and established the author as one of the finest in Sweden. The novel represents a more significant stylistic development than Lindgren's switch from verse to prose. Here he begins an existential investigation with many striking stylistic features, including a terseness that invites the reader to examine the implications of what is not said along with what is articulated.

Merabs skönhet: Berättelser (1983; translated as *Merab's Beauty and Other Stories,* 1989) followed the success of *Ormens väg på hälleberget* in a similar style. A selection of eleven stories, *Merabs skönhet* explores the interplay of the natural and supernatural realms. Unlike magical realism, however, with its dream-like ambiance and lush prose evidenced in Isabel Allende's work, Lindgren retains the clipped cadences of the Swedish North. If his work is to be considered magical realism, it is most akin to the stories of Jorge Louis Borges. In *Merhabs skönhet* the protagonists encounter the supernatural as one of many external forces they cannot control and, as such, must accept.

Lindgren examines explicitly religious narrative in his subsequent novel *Bat Seba* (1984; translated as *Bathsheba,* 1987), which investigates the question "Hurudan är Herren?" (What is the nature of the Lord?). This question, put into the mouths of several of the central characters, is an inquiry into the nature of power. Using the biblical story of David from the book of Samuel as a point of departure, Lindgren begins his tale the moment David sees Bat Seba from a rooftop and commands her presence and, eventually, her constant companionship after castrating and sacrificing her husband in battle.

Bat Seba demonstrates a familiar theme in Lindgren's literature, that power is absolute, unyielding, and brutal, able to construct any rationale in its service. This portrayal is exemplified in the confrontation between Uria, Bat Seba's husband, and King David, who intends to marry her as soon as Uria has been disposed of. When Uria exclaims "Så är det: jag ska offras!" (That is the way it is: I am to be sacrificed!), David arrogantly replies that "Herren har utvalt dig" (The Lord has chosen you) and rationalizes: "Ingen utom Herren kan skilja nellan offer och utkorelse" (No one but the Lord can distinguish between being sacrificed and being chosen).

Bat Seba learns quickly the political rhetoric and excels in acquiring power through whatever means she can. Indeed, the book charts the flow of power from David to his wife, a power shift mirrored by the structure of the book, which also begins from David's perspective and closes with Bat Seba's. Thematically, the novel seems to echo Lindgren's early poetic commentary on the dangers of the political versus the religious abyss and hellish torments. While many of the concerns are similar, Lindgren has matured as an artist to the point where he no longer lectures readers but rather depicts political abuses cloaked in religious righteousness.

Bat Seba was well received, winning the Esselte's literary prize, and further enhanced Lindgren's reputation as an accessible author who nonetheless chose to work on substantive issues and themes. He began also to be recognized for a particular style, an eternal, almost mythical manner of depicting his fictional worlds.

Ljuset (1987; translated as *Light,* 1992) continued to garner accolades from critics and audiences alike. Once again the setting is the Swedish North, in this incarnation ravaged by plague. The tone is bleak and existential, though not without Lindgren's trademark grim humor. The death of a child, gobbled up by a prize, mammoth pig, is just such a moment of dark comedy. The book ends with an uncharacteristic sense of renewal and continuation as the narrative comes full circle to its beginning and affirms the importance of the search for human connection. This novel, too, added to Lindgren's reputation and helped contribute to the sense of shock his next novel elicited.

Till sanningens lov: Rammakaren Theodor Marklunds egen redogörelse (1991; translated as *In Praise of Truth: The Personal Account of Theodore Marklund, Picture-framer,* 1994) defied expectations about the author and his oeuvre. Set against a background of contemporary pop culture, *Till sanningens lov* is an ironic farce about authenticity and falseness of values and individuals. Frame-maker Marklund, accustomed to a quiet life in Lindgren's native town of

Raggsjö in Västerbotten, discovers an art treasure and finds himself at the center of intrigue. The book is as thought-provoking as Lindgren's work from the 1980s but returns to the direct social commentary of his novels from the 1970s, although less discernibly political in tone. Many critics reacted strongly to the stylistic variation by reviewing the novel coolly and calling for a return to what they consider to be Lindgren's strong suit, the mythical realism of *Ormens väg på hälleberget* and *Ljuset*.

In Lindgren's most recent work, *Hummelhonung* (1995; translated as *Sweetness*, 2000), however, the author once again combines a contemporary setting with an age-old theme. In this novel a young author on the lecture circuit throughout Sweden finds herself caught in a fratricidal conflict between two neighboring brothers. Occasionally grotesque, this novel manages to combine Lindgren's saga-like style with satirical insights. *Hummelhonung* was a critical success and was awarded the prestigious August Prize in 1995.

Throughout his multifaceted career, Torgny Lindgren has forged an impressive and captivating body of work. His distinctive style continues to develop and expand in the face of new narrative tasks. His works are routinely included in lists of the best examples of Swedish fiction. With his unerring sense of irony, his ability to create and populate entire mythical worlds, as well as his astute rendering of eternal human foibles, Lindgren is assured a continued position on such lists in the twenty-first century.

Reference:

Ingela Pehrson, *Livsmodet i skrönans värld: En studie i Torgny Lindgrens romaner Ormens väg på hälleberget, Bat Seba och Ljuset* (Stockholm: Almqvist & Wiksell, 1993).

Kristina Lugn
(14 November 1948 –   )

Tanya Thresher
University of Wisconsin–Madison

BOOKS: *Om jag inte* (Stockholm: Bonnier Alba, 1972);
Till min man, om han kunde läsa (Stockholm: Bonnier Alba, 1976);
Döda honom! (Stockholm: Bonnier Alba, 1978);
Om ni hör ett skott . . . (Stockholm: Bonnier Alba, 1979);
Percy Wennerfors (Stockholm: Bonnier Alba, 1982);
Bekantskap önskas med äldre bildad herre (Stockholm: Bonnier Alba, 1983);
Lugn bara Lugn–Samlade dikter (Högnäs: Bra Böcker / Stockholm: Bonnier Alba, 1984);
Hundstunden: Kvinnlig bekännelseslyrik (Stockholm: Bonnier Alba, 1989)—excerpts translated by Ingrid Claréus as "The Dog Hour: Female Confession Poetry" in *Dimension Special Issue* (1994): 480–485;
Lugn bara lugn; Samlade dikter med efterord av Karl Venneberg. Hundstunden; Kvinnlig bekännelseslyrik (Stockholm: Månpocket, 1990);
Tant Blomma (Stockholm: Dramatens Förlag, 1993); translated by Verne Moberg as *Aunt Blossom* in *Modern Women Playwrights of Europe*, edited by Alan P. Barr (New York: Oxford University Press, 2001), pp. 511–524;
Idlaflickorna (Stockholm: Dramatens Förlag, 1993);
Samlat Lugn: Dikter och dramatik (Stockholm: Bonnier Alba, 1997);
Nattorienterarna (Lund: Bakhåll, 1999);
Bekantskap önskas med äldre bildad herre; Hundstunden; Stulna juveler (Stockholm: Bonnier, 2001).

PLAY PRODUCTIONS: *När det utbröt panik i det kollektiva omedvetna,* Stockholm, Royal Dramatic Theater, 12 December 1986;
Titta det blöder, Stockholm, Royal Dramatic Theater, 12 December 1987;
Det vackra blir liksom över, Stockholm, Royal Dramatic Theater, 4 November 1989;
Tant Blomma, Stockholm, Royal Dramatic Theater, 27 February 1993; translated by Verne Moberg as *Aunt Blossom,* Nordic Theater Festival, Barnard College, New York, 7–10 September 1995;

Kristina Lugn

Idlaflickorna, Stockholm, Royal Dramatic Theater, 15 October 1993; translated by Moberg as *The Old Girls,* Nordic Theater Festival, Barnard College, New York, 7–10 September 1995;
Detrostlösa, Stockholm, Pastateater, 18 April 1995;
Silver Star, Stockholm, Royal Dramatic Theater, 10 November 1995;
Rött, by Anna Reynolds, translated and directed by Lugn, Stockholm, Royal Dramatic Theater, 28 September 1996;
Terrence McNally, *Masterclass med Maria Callas,* translated by Lugn, Stockholm, Royal Dramatic Theater, 11 January 1997;
Rut og Ragnar, Stockholm, Teater Brunnsgatan Fyra, January 1997;

Mio min Mio, adapted from Astrid Lindgren's novel by Lugn who also wrote the lyrics. Stockholm, Royal Dramatic Theater, 11 July 1997;

Markusevangeliet, adapted from Bible by Lugn, Stockholm, Riksteatern, 14 September 1997;

Nattorienterarna, Stockholm, Teater Brunnsgatan Fyra, 26 February 1998;

Titta en älg, Stockholm, Teater Brunnsgatan Fyra, 10 February 1999;

Stulna juveler, Stockholm, Royal Dramatic Theater, 14 October 2000.

PRODUCED SCRIPT: *Gud vad jag är lycklig,* radio Sveriges radio, 1979.

RECORDING: *Om ni hör ett Skott,* read by Lugn, Stockholm, Bokbandet, 1988.

OTHER: "Människan föds skyldig: Sonja Åkesson," in *Kvinnornas Litterature Historie: Del 2 1900-tallet.* Ed. Ingrid Holmquist & Ebba Witt-Brattström (Malmö: Författarförlaget, 1983) pp. 330–344;

"Om jag inte jade tyckt så mycket om henne" in *I klänningens veck–femministiska diktanalyser.* Ed. Ulla Evers & Eva Lilja. (Gothenburg: Anamma, 1984), pp. 228–230;

I dödsskuggans dal in *Svenska Radiopjäser 1985* (Stockholm: Sveriges Radio, 1985).

"Att välja en poet for livet. Kristina Lugn om Karl Vennberg." *Boniers litterära magasin* 62; no. 4 (1993): 37–39;

"De två saliga" in *Röster om Ulla Isaksson.* (Stockholm: Arbetarnas bildningsförbund, 1997), pp. 55–60;

Terry Johnson, *Hysteria,* translated by Lugn. (Malmö, Musik & kultur, 1997);

"Gunnar Ekelöf i mitt liv" in *Röster om Gunnar Ekelöf* (Stockholm: Arbetarnas bildungsförbund, 2001), pp. 7–13.

A respected literary critic, poet, and dramatist, Kristina Lugn is a prominent figure in contemporary Swedish culture who attracts an unusually large reading audience. This popularity is partly because of the accessibility of her work with its emphasis on everyday language, easily recognizable characters, and frequent references to popular culture, and also owing to the humor Lugn uses to describe the tragic lives of her protagonists. Focusing on the alienation of the individual in a bourgeois consumer society often controlled by the media, Lugn is an astute critic of contemporary Swedish, and consequently European, culture. In both theme and style, her writing reflects the absurdity of Swedish family life in the 1990s and the psychological chaos it may cause within the individual. In particular Lugn concentrates on the alienation of women who are wrestling with the restrictions of a culturally coded femininity and simultaneously struggling to remain within the norms of acceptable social behavior. While she avoids any actual alliance to the feminist movement, Lugn's concentration on the marginalization and representation of women nevertheless makes her a favorite of Swedish feminists.

In addition to being a shrewd social commentator, Lugn is highly regarded for the lyrical poetry in her writing. Her experimentation with language, use of irony and pastiche, and blending of high and low art forms makes her an exemplary postmodern author. In her poetry the juxtaposition of precise descriptions of quotidian life in contemporary Sweden with highly emotive first-person narration brings to light the absurdity of modern existence and makes the everyday seem bizarre. Her poetic method is refined both thematically and stylistically in her dramatic pieces, which are generally short, one-act plays for a small cast built up of monologues rich in association. Often written for specific actors, her plays are characterized both by their poetic lyricism and their lack of traditional plotline and character development. All the action is found in the dialogue as the emphasis is on the psychology of the individual. Her dramas are thus often highly experimental, and yet they are filled with a comedy that makes Lugn a beloved dramatist both of critics and Swedish audiences alike.

Born in Skövde on 14 November 1948, Gundhild Bricken Kristina Lugn grew up in a middle-class environment. Her father, Robert Lo Lugn, was a major general in the Swedish army, and her mother, Brita-Stina Alinder, was a lecturer and a Swedish sling-ball champion, which caused some childhood conflict because Lugn was never athletic, in spite of her mother's encouragements to be so. Lugn claims that since the age of twelve she has been actively working on her artistic talents, something she believed was a gift from God. As a seventeen-year-old she submitted the poem "Trumpeten–emedan allt får sig en blåsning" (The Trumpet–Since Everything Is Hornswoggled) to a publisher, but it was rejected. In high school in Örnsköldsvik she recalls hearing the Swedish modernist poet Sonja Åkesson give a reading and was so inspired that she wanted to make her acquaintance. Thus she began corresponding with Åkesson's husband, Jarl Hammarberg, and–after completing a degree at the University of Stockholm in 1972 in literary history with an emphasis on poetics, aesthetics, pedagogy,

Cover for a 1990 collection of Lugn's verse that includes Hundstunden: Kvinnlig bekännelselyrik *(The Dog Hour: Female Confessional Poetry), the work for which she received the* Svenska Dagbladet *Prize in 1989 (Knight Library, University of Oregon)*

and drama—she eventually moved into the Hammarberg-Åkesson artists' collective in Bromma. Here she was not only surrounded by up-and-coming artists and writers, but she also became firm friends with Åkesson, about whom Lugn published an important and insightful essay in *Kvinnornas litteraturhistorie* (Women's Literary History) in 1983. Before launching her artistic career Lugn had various jobs, from school librarian to caregiver for the handicapped to literary critic for Swedish radio and for the national newspapers *Expressen* and *Dagens Nyheter*.

When Lugn was twenty-four years old, she made a modest literary debut with the poetry collection *Om jag inte* (If I Didn't, 1972), a collection that only sold thirty-three copies, according to Lugn. Embryonic with regard to her later style and investigations into the nature of woman's existence in contemporary capitalistic society, this collection consists of a series of narrative inner monologues by the protagonist Gun, a typical thirty-six-year-old Swede, who dies of loneliness. Unable to find a meaningful context for her life and fit into the social regulations of her community, and in spite of her desperate, masochistic efforts to fulfill her male partner's demands, she is unable to make the transition from female adolescence into womanhood. Thus, she remains in a kind of purgatory in which she is forced constantly to change, until she no longer recognizes herself and ceases to exist. Her need for security in an insecure world is ironically scrutinized, and the only liberation from her banal existence is death.

The first poem in the collection sets up a clear "I" versus "they" dichotomy, in which the protagonist rarely says anything but merely listens, laughs, and dreams. She is already alienated, both from society and from her own body, a body that only promotes self-disgust because of its associations with excreta. Throughout the collection there are subtle references to Åkesson, who was a precursor to the feminist new wave that was an important aspect of the literature of the 1970s in Sweden. Lugn makes particular use of Åkesson's poem "Självbiografi" (Autobiography, 1962), which is in itself a distinctly female pastiche of American beat poet Lawrence Ferlinghetti's 1958 poem of the same title.

Lugn's next poetry collection was more unified in theme and style than *Om jag inte* and increasingly moved toward the first-person confessional poetry Lugn later mastered. *Till min man, om han kunde läsa* (To My Husband, If He Could Read, 1976) takes the battle between the sexes to a violent conclusion, where a seemingly idyllic suburban marriage is destroyed as the wife shoots her husband in an unguarded moment described as being full of clarity. The multiple meaning of the title, which refers either to the illiteracy of the husband or the fact that, having been murdered, he can no longer read, alludes to the ironic nature of the collection and is a particular reference to Anna Maria Lenngren's satirical poem. "Några ord till min kära Dotter, i fall jag hade någon" (Some words to my dear daughter if I had one). The matter-of-fact murder confession, increasing in intensity, becomes an expression of the unconscious will to survive and the realization that survival can only happen at the expense of the Other. Whether the murder is actual or merely part of an elaborate liberation fantasy remains unclear, and the collection ends with an oblique warning that bourgeois existence is, in fact, shrouded in danger.

Violence both against oneself and, in particular, against the opposite sex is a recurring theme in Lugn's work. An ever-present reminder both of the implicit dangers of a society based on differences and the vulnerability of the members of that society, violence is used to estrange the reader from the idyllic bourgeois stage upon which Lugn's characters play out their lives. The titles of Lugn's next two poetry collections refer directly to violence: *Döda honom!* (Kill Him! 1978) and *Om ni hör ett skott . . .* (If You Should Hear a Shot . . . , 1979). *Döda honom!* anticipates subsequent collections, aiming its irony squarely at the nuclear family and consumerism. Again with an anonymous female protagonist as the primary focus, this fragmented collection of poems interweaves the first-person narrator's childhood memories with everyday scenes of a broken marriage with Kurt. A seemingly idyllic suburban life is shattered when Kurt leaves his wife for another woman but is ultimately forced to return after the wife's attempted suicide. Lugn highlights the static nature of suburban life in Sweden by emphasizing the immobility of her characters, who can do nothing but sit on a sofa. Her protagonist is confined to the domestic sphere, which Lugn describes in all its ordinary, modern perfection. Nevertheless, the woman is not happy, and in spite of trying to impose order on her life, she fails because she bases her identity on those around her. She cannot find a place in the public sphere and often sits in a no-man's-land, usually the balcony of her home, from which she watches her perfect neighbors pass by. A marginal space in this suburban landscape, the balcony becomes an extended representation both of the peripheral status accorded women and their alienation from society.

The suburbs play a fundamental role in the lyrical collection *Om ni hör ett skott . . .* , although the menacing nature of the locale is here taken to extremes. From the ominous title to the initial suggestions that in this quiet middle-class society nobody has been murdered for a long time, and that Camilla, the protagonist, has not even been threatened with a knife, or that her youngest son has not been strangled, the possibility of murder is evident, and the reader suspects that it will eventually occur. Death is the inevitable result in a society founded on oppositional differences and oppression, and Lugn depicts death both concretely and violently. The terrifying details of the possible crimes are shocking, but they are tempered and rendered ironic by the light conversational tone and direct access to the reader. Violence is shown here without any moral overtones, and fear seeps into the mundane existence of the protagonist. The facade of marital bliss, which Lugn characterizes by an overly detailed inventory of household objects and activities, becomes a futile dance of death. The astute reader notices clues in the colorless descriptions of the household, such as a bunch of dead tulips left on the hat-stand, which point not only to the intrinsically destructive relationship but also to the inherent misplacement of trust in consumer society.

One of the most striking sources of cultural images of women in this collection is advertising. Confronted by a never-ending barrage of products, Camilla believes she is inadequate if she fails to consume even the most banal of objects, and she forces her body to succumb to the ideal image of womanhood, an image characterized by a stream of cosmetics, toiletries, and clothing. The alienation of the suburban mother is here taken beyond the extremes of her geographical location and the sharp juxtaposition with her husband's centralized place in the labor force of Sweden in the late 1970s, for the text literally divides its subject. Referring to herself both with the third and first person, Camilla is able to view herself from the outside in her varying roles as child, housewife, mother, and lover. This distancing multiple perspective common in women's writing clearly reflects how the protagonist sees herself only through others' eyes and tries to conform to their opinions. She even forces her own language into the models of linguistic correctness in the world around her, but, realizing how inappropriate this language is for her, she often turns to silence.

Om ni hör ett skott . . . was published the same year Lugn made her theatrical debut with the unpublished *Gud vad jag är lycklig* (God, How Happy I Am). Since that time Lugn has been an active participant in Sweden's theater world, often writing for specific actors plays that have been performed on radio and television and in theater. She has also adapted and translated many texts for the stage. *När det utbröt panik i det kollektiva omedvetna* (When Panic Broke Out in the Collective Unconscious), which premiered on the Fyran stage at the Royal Dramatic Theater on 12 December 1986, concerns the psychological breakdown and ultimate suicide of a woman married to a genius husband, who runs a convalescent home filled with lonely female clients. That something is fundamentally awry between this woman and her husband is revealed in the first scene at the breakfast table when she refuses to pass him the liver pâté, saying that something is not right about it. The pâté is a symbol of her crumbling identity, a disintegration further indicated when she refers to herself as two separate individuals. This play—along with *Titta det blöder* (Look, It's Bleeding) and *Det vackra blir liksom över* (Beauty Is Kinda Left Out), which premiered at the Royal Dramatic Theater in Stockholm in 1987 and 1989, respectively—has not been published.

While developing her dramatic voice, Lugn continued writing poetry. In her next poetry collection, *Percy Wennerfors* (1982), a parody of epic fairy tales, Lugn's protagonist, Deborah, uses silence as her only recourse in a strange world. As all words mean the wrong things for this little girl, she resorts to quacking, crying, shrieking, and howling. Even when she does speak, she does so in the persona of the mysterious Percy Wennerfors, a male demon who calmly explains to her that a violent murder would be the result should the girl refuse to quietly submit to her feminine role. While the little girl does as she is told and dutifully conforms to her socialization by asking for a toy iron, sewing machine, dolls, and even a baby brother, she is haunted by the dev-

Cover for the published version of Lugn's 1993 play, about an encounter between two former gymnasts who may actually be two sides of the same woman (University of Chicago Library)

ilish Percy. Percy is the personification of the little girl's evil side, the threatening aspect of her nature that promises an eventual outburst of violence. This nonconforming side of her personality creates order out of her inner chaos, which is reflected in her inability to solve a simple puzzle. The alienation she feels from her parents is only enhanced by the death of her newborn brother. Believing that even touching her causes a foul smell, the little girl's self-loathing places her in direct contrast with the fairy-tale princess the poem suggests in its parodic mimicry of the traditional genre. In spite of the generic beginning, the little girl does not live happily ever after, finding only oppression and alienation, themes Lugn revisits in her next collection, *Bekantskap önskas med äldre bildad herre* (Seeking Older, Educated Man, 1983).

As the title of the collection implies, its protagonist is desperately searching for a male companion who is gifted and well dressed and who can rescue her from her mundane existence. Again Lugn suggests an absent father and inattentive mother as possible causes for the anonymous woman's longing for company, and she shrouds her existence with fears of going against social convention and thoughts of death, a personification of which she imagines sitting on her IKEA sofa. To sustain the appearance of normalcy the protagonist does as any middle-class housewife would do: she visits a furniture store. The possibility of buying new furniture, along with the kind reassurance she receives from the salesman, become symbols of the security she is searching for and underscore her need to erase the suicidal thoughts that torment her. In spite of realizing the futility of wandering about in an expanding community and having thoughts only of herself, the woman is unable to sustain any sense of belonging and resorts to death as her only possibility of escape.

The poems in this collection are less unified thematically than in previous collections, and Lugn experiments freely with different styles, from traditional rhythmic, rhyming verse poems to long, prose-like narratives. Setting an everyday conversational tone against an almost bureaucratic scientific language, Lugn is able to twist language out of its usual context and shift perspectives on it by placing it in ironic contrasts. Lugn's irony reaches its most striking point in the next poetry collection, *Hundstunden: Kvinnlig bekännelseslyrik* (The Dog Hour: Female Confessional Poetry, 1989), for which she was awarded the annual literary prize of the national newspaper *Svenska Dagbladet* in 1989. The seriousness underlying the irony and the protagonist's paralyzing realization of her alienation from society are more overt in this collection than in any other Lugn has written. In spite of finding difficulties in linguistic expression, the protagonist here rejects any typically feminine language, all of which she considers too unmanly for her use.

Confined to the home after futile attempts to enter the public sphere, the nameless housewife tries to transcend everyday reality and find a room of her own but ends up cowering beneath her kitchen counter, feeling alienated even from her own clothing. Likening herself to a wilting potted plant, a mutant kept out of its natural environment, she is panic-stricken to find out that there is something strange in the house and desperately insists that there has to be some kind of an emergency exit to life. Unable to find that emergency escape and incapable of living up to the expectations of a mother, lover, or housewife, she claims to have been robbed of her life and her female strength. As the relationship between her and her husband, who is given the generic name of Herrman, grows and intensifies, so the woman's power dwindles until she ceases to exist. The use of the third-person singular pronoun to describe the woman implies not only that her mate was the culprit, but also that the reader, and hence Western society, is complicit in this crime against female humanity.

Lugn reuses the generic Herrman in one of her most frequently performed pieces, *Idlaflickorna* (The Idla Girls; translated as *The Old Girls,* 1995), which premiered on the Lejonkulan stage at the Royal Dramatic Theater in October 1993 under the direction of Hans Klinga. *Idlaflickorna* is one of the most consistently successful productions of the Royal Dramatic Theater, always attracting a large audience of women in particular. Typical of Lugn's dramatic pieces, this intimate one-act play, with its small cast, minimal set, and brief time span for the action, is reminiscent of August Strindberg's chamber plays. The play, which explores the stormy emotional lives of two women, centers on a Beckettian meeting at Lake Garda of Barbro and Lillemor, two former Idla girls—women gymnasts under the direction of the Estonian gymnastics pedagogue Ernst Idla, who performed in Sweden to great acclaim. Men are absent in the play, although a fantasy sailor figure and Herrman, to whom both women are apparently married, are recurring elements in the dialogue. As both women share a strikingly similar background, they may represent two sides of one character, Barbro interrogates Lillemor about her life and claims to be her "Inre Skönhet" (Inner Beauty), which has been murdered by the husband. They may also be two separate women, one an emancipated intellectual psychologist and the other a faithful wife and worried mother. Regardless of how one interprets the two women, their identities are clearly highly unstable and, in fact, are only created from fragmented snippets of conversation.

Barbro adopts the role of Lillemor's daughter and eventually claims to be Lillemor, while Lillemor separately tries to retain her identity by repeatedly introducing herself. Barbro, who purports to be on a break from herself, is always trying not to be herself and is most ambitious in those attempts. She has a great dread of being alone and refuses to let Lillemor leave her, claiming that she exists only when the other woman is present. She believes that by talking they will save themselves from oblivion, but the women eventually revert to childhood fantasies told in nursery rhymes, their language finally breaking down into meaningless babble. The difficulty of communication is a theme revisited in the play as the two characters fail to converse and absurdly repeat each other's statements, literally taking the words out of each other's mouth. Wordplay and song add further alienating effects with respect to the language of the play.

Tant Blomma (1993; translated as *Aunt Blossom*, 1995), a tragicomedy for children, was commissioned by the Royal Dramatic Theater and premiered there on the Fyran stage under the direction of Richard Looft. While composing the script, Lugn had collaborated extensively with the well-known actor Thorsten Flinck, who was to play the role of the spinster day-care provider. Flinck, who had risen to fame playing overtly masculine roles both on stage and screen, found it liberating to play a lonely, middle-aged woman. His performance, in particular, embodied one of Lugn's favorite themes, namely the constructedness of female identity and the aspects of gendered experience such as motherhood that can become falsely naturalized. Like the many geraniums that adorn the stage, Tant Blomma is constricted and denaturalized by a false environment.

In the tradition of vaudeville, the dialogues and monologues in the piece are interspersed with songs that the audience is encouraged to participate in singing. The songs are taken from a wide variety of musical genres and different historical and cultural contexts, but Lugn undermines their original associations with an idyllic existence by subtly and ironically altering the lyrics. The pastiche effect is further enhanced by the intertextual nature of the dialogue, in which Lugn borrows freely both from the mass media, the Bible, the Brothers Grimm, and, not least of all, from Strindberg and his play *Pelikanen* (The Pelican, 1907) with its grotesque mother figure.

Taking place in the course of a few hours early one evening, this highly lyrical play shows how an infant and a day-care provider are waiting for the child's mother. As in Samuel Beckett's *Waiting for Godot* (1953), the endless waiting of these two characters and the real absence of the mother begs the question as to whether she really exists or, like the conventional view of motherhood, she is merely a figment of the collective imagination. Although Blomma attempts to appropriate the role of mother, she is cruelly reminded by the baby that she cannot, as mothering is for her a profession, one to which she is alarmingly unsuited. Becoming increasingly irritated at having to work overtime, she makes it

Cover for the published version (1999) of Lugn's 1998 play, about a chance meeting between two lonely middle-aged schoolteachers (University of California, Berkeley)

clear to the child that her planned evening of dancing, with its attendant dreams of finding a husband and living happily ever after, are uppermost in her thoughts. She threatens to desert the child and eventually does so, leaping out of the window to her death after her evening's entertainment is canceled. More a play about communication and companionship than a social commentary on the state of childcare in Sweden, *Tant Blomma* again exhibits Lugn's preoccupation with death. In particular it reveals the intrinsic connection of death to the mother, who, having been responsible for the creation of a life, must also accept responsibility for the ending of that life. As Vera, one of the characters from Lugn's one-act play *Nattorienterarna* (Night Orienteers, 1998) claims, death is perhaps only a normal mother calling her child home.

Nattorienterarna, which premiered at the Teater Brunnsgatan Fyra on 26 February 1998 under the direction of Åsa Kalmér, is a direct result of Lugn's mourning of her friend and mentor Allan Edwall. Lugn had known the distinguished Swedish actor since the end of the 1970s and had collaborated with him on several projects, including a cabaret tour, *De tröstlösa* (The Inconsolables), for which Lugn rewrote songs from Richard Rodgers and Oscar Hammerstein II's *The Sound of Music* (1963). Lugn cites Edwall as the person who helped her understand the intricacies of good drama. He was also influential in expanding Lugn's theatrical experience beyond script writing to directing and acting. In 1997 Lugn played Rut opposite Edwall's Ragnar in her piece *Rut og Ragnar* (Ruth and Ragnar), which premiered at Edwall's own small Teater Brunnsgatan Fyra in Stockholm. A depiction of a thirty-three-year marriage in crisis, the production only played for four shows because of Edwall's death. Since then Lugn has sought to maintain his theatrical tradition and has worked as the artistic manager of Teater Brunnsgatan Fyra.

Loss and bereavement and the necessity of coming to terms with the unalterable aspects of contemporary existence are central themes in *Nattorienterarna*. The one-act play depicts the meeting of two middle-aged, female schoolteachers, Bricken and Vera, while each is out walking one night. The play explores the faltering attempts of these lonely characters to orient themselves and find meaning in a seemingly absurd life as they stumble through a cement-gray environment in the dead of night. The play was received favorably by critics and opened to full houses, a further testament to Lugn's popularity.

Heralded by critics as the dramatist who best reflected the fragmented 1990s on the stage and who reveals a clear contemporary consciousness, Kristina Lugn was awarded the Swedish Theater Critics' Prize for innovation in Swedish theater in 1999 for *Titta en älg* (Look, a Moose), which premiered at the Teater Brunnsgatan Fyra on 10 February of that year. Mentioning the many lyrical theatrical pieces Lugn wrote in the 1990s, the committee honored her rejuvenation of the genre of poetic drama and her humorous, yet serious, investigation of the blind, existential musings of the individual. Although Lugn has exclusively worked on drama during the last decade, she has also claimed to want to return to poetry. She has maintained her position as a staff playwright at the Royal Dramatic Theater, and, perhaps in response to critics who claim her plays lack action and conflict, she has indicated a desire to write a more clearly defined narrative drama with several acts and more roles. Such dramas might mean that this loved, decorated, and often cited author will finally earn a place in academic discussion.

References:

Lars Elleström, "Tryggare kan ingen vara: Om Kristina Lugn," in *Samtida: Essäer om svenska författerskap,* edited by Ellerström and Cecilia Hansson (Stockholm: Alba, 1990), pp. 82–106;

Anne Heith, "Schamanen Lugn," *Horisont,* 39 (1992): 13–17;

Maria Österlund, "Det måste finnas en reservutgång: Om rumsligheten i Kristina Lugns lyrik," in *Hemmet, rummet och revolten: Studier i litterärt gränsöverskridande,* edited by Österlund, Pia Ingström, and Kristina Malmio (Åbo: Litteraturvetenskapliga institutionen, Åbo akademi, 1996), pp. 101–177;

Isabell Vilhelmsen, "Kristina Lugn–De udsattes talerør," in *På jorden: 1960–1990,* edited by Unni Langås and others, volume 4 of *Nordisk kvidnelitteraturhistorie,* edited by Elisabeth Møller Jensen (Höganäs, Sweden: Wiken, 1997), pp. 340–345;

Margareta Wirmark, "Det banala, det skräckfylda och det euforiska: Om Kristina Lugns Tant Blomma," *Kvinnovetenskapelig tidskrift,* 18 (1997): 122–129.

Jan Myrdal
(19 July 1927 -   )

Cecilia Cervin
University of Lund

BOOKS: *Folkets hus: Samtal vid en invigning* (Stockholm: Seelig, 1953);

Hemkomst (Stockholm: Tiden, 1954);

Jubelvår (Stockholm: Tiden, 1955);

Att bli och vara (Stockholm: Tiden, 1956);

Badrumskranen (Stockholm: Norstedt, 1957);

Kulturers korsväg: En bok om Afghanistan (Stockholm: Norstedt, 1960); republished as *Resa i Afghanistan*, photographs by Gun Kessle (Stockholm: Norstedt, 1966);

Bortom berg och öknar: Afghanistan, ett framtidsland (Stockholm: Bonnier, 1962);

Rescontra: Utdrag ur avräkningsbok för personliga conti (Stockholm: Norstedt, 1962); revised as *Samtida bekännelser av en europeisk intellektuell* (Stockholm: Norstedt, 1964); revised and translated by Myrdal as *Confessions of a Disloyal European* (London: Chatto & Windus, 1968; New York: Pantheon, 1968); revised edition translated into Swedish by Sven Stolpe as *En illojal europés bekännelser* (Stockholm: Norstedt, 1983);

Rapport från kinesisk by (Stockholm: Norstedt, 1963); translated by M. Michael as *Report from a Chinese Village* (London: Heinemann, 1965; New York: Pantheon, 1965);

Söndagsmorgon (Stockholm: Norstedt, 1965);

Chinese Journey (New York: Pantheon, 1965); translated as *Kinesisk resa* (Stockholm: Norstedt, 1966);

Turkmenistan: En revolutions övergångsår (Stockholm: Norstedt, 1966);

Moraliteter (Stockholm: Norstedt, 1967)–includes *Är Inga Eriksson människa*, translated by Claude Stephenson as *Is Inga Eriksson a Human Being*, in *Radio Plays from Denmark, Finland, Norway, Sweden Awarded Prizes in the Scandinavian Radio Play Contest Held in 1969* (Stockholm: Sveriges Radio, 1971);

Fallet Myglaren (Stockholm: PAN/Norstedt, 1967);

Ansikte av sten: Staden Angkor i Kambodja: Uppgång, storhet och fall: En berättelse om vår tid, by Myrdal and Kessle (Stockholm: PAN/Norstedt, 1968); translated by Paul Britten Austin as *Angkor: An Essay on Art and Imperialism* (New York: Pantheon, 1970);

Skriftställning, 18 volumes (1968–1998)–comprises volume 1 (Stockholm: PAN/Norstedt, 1968); volume 2 (Stockholm: PAN/Norstedt, 1969); volume 3 (Stockholm: PAN/Norstedt, 1971); volume 4 (Stockholm: PAN/Norstedt, 1973); volume 5 (Stockholm: PAN/Norstedt, 1975); volume 6,

Jan Myrdal

Lag utan ordning (Stockholm: Gidlunds, 1976); volume 7, *Tyska frågor* (Stockholm: Oktober, 1976); volume 8, *Avgörande år: Svenska frågor 1975-77* (Stockholm: Oktober, 1977); volume 9, *Klartexter* (Stockholm: PAN/Norstedt, 1978); volume 10 (Stockholm: PAN/Norstedt, 1978); volume 11, *Kampuchea och kriget: Inlägg och polemiker* (Stockholm: Oktober, 1978); volume 12, *Dussinet fullt* (Stockholm: Norstedt, 1982); volume 13, *Den trettonde* (Stockholm: Akelin & Hägglund, 1983); volume 14, *14!: Med personregister över Jan Myrdals 14 skriftställningar och sju fristående böcker inom samma ram* (Stockholm: Nya tidskrifts AB Folket i bild, 1987); volume 15, *En annan ordning: Litterärt och personligt* (1988); volume 16, *Tidens ålder* (Stockholm: Hägglund, 1992); volume 17, *Det nya Stor-Tyckland* (Stockholm: Hägglund, 1992); volume 18, *I de svartare fanornas tid: texter om litteratur, lögn och förbannad dikt* (Stockholm: Hägglund, 1998);

Garderingar (Stockholm: Norstedt, 1969);

Albansk utmaning (Stockholm: PAN/Norstedt, 1970); translated by Austin as *Albania Defiant* (London & New York: Monthly Review Press, 1976);

Kina: Revolutionen går vidare (Stockholm: PAN/Norstedt, 1970); translated by Austin as *China: The Revolution Continued* (New York: Pantheon, 1970);

Tal om hjälp: Anteckningar om hjälp och hjälpare 1959-1971 på förekommen anledning publicerade (Stockholm: PAN/Norstedt, 1971);

B. Olsen löper livet ut: Ett svenskt tvärgrepp i 13 bilder (Stockholm: Norstedt, 1972);

Ett femtiotal (Stockholm: Gidlund, 1972);

Den onödiga samtiden, by Myrdal and Lars Gustafsson (Stockholm: PAN/Norstedt, 1974);

Karriär (Stockholm: Norstedt, 1975);

Lag utan ordning (Stockholm: Gidlund, 1975);

Kinesiska frågor från Liu Ling (Stockholm: PAN/Norstedt, 1976);

När Västerlandet trädde fram: skulptur i franska och norska 1100-talskyrkor: Nationalmuseum 29 jan.-29 febr. 1976, by Myrdal and Elias Cornell, photographs by Kessle (Stockholm: Nationalmus, 1976);

Ondskan tar form (Stockholm: PAN/Norstedt, 1976);

Tyska frågor (Stockholm: Oktober, 1976);

Kina efter Mao Tsetung: Anteckningar kring uppgörelsen med "De fyra" (Stockholm: Ordfront, 1977);

Sidenvägen: En resa från höga Pamir och Ili genom Sinkiang och Kansu (Stockholm: Norstedt, 1977); translated by Ann Henning as *The Silk Road: A Journey from the High Pamirs and Ili through Sinkiang and Kansu* (New York: Pantheon, 1979; London: Gollancz, 1980);

Kampuchea hösten 1979 (Stockholm: PAN/Norstedt, 1979);

Kampuchea invaderat: Två tal och två artiklar (Stockholm: Oktober, 1979);

Indien väntar (Stockholm: Norstedt, 1980); translated by Alan Bernstein as *India Waits* (London: Heretic Books, 1984); revised edition, with new foreword by Myrdal (Chicago: Lake View Press, 1986);

Strindberg och Balzac: Essayer kring realismens problem (Stockholm: Norstedt, 1981);

Barndom (Stockholm: Norstedt, 1982); translated by Christine Swanson as *Childhood* (Chicago: Lake View Press, 1991);

Bortom bergen: Bilder från Binglingsi, Maijishan, Dunhuang och andra helgedomar längs den gamla vägen: Med ett inledande resonemang kring resandet, seendet och konsten, by Myrdal and Kessle (Stockholm: Norstedt, 1983);

Kinesisk by 20 år senare: Rapport med frågetecken (Stockholm: Norstedt, 1983); translated by Bernstein as *Return to a Chinese Village* (New York: Pantheon, 1984);

En annan värld (Stockholm: Norstedt, 1984); translated by Bernstein as *Another World* (Chicago: Ravenswood, 1994);

Ord och avsikt: Ett resonemang (Stockholm: Norstedt, 1986);

Brev från en turist (Stockholm: Norstedt, 1987);

Pubertet: En samling utskriven hösten 1946: Refuserad i februari 1947: Nu publicerad med en kommenterande inledning fyrtiotvå år senare (Stockholm: Norstedt, 1988);

En Meccanopojke berättar eller Anteckningar om ett borgerligt förnuft (Höganäs, Sweden: Wiken, 1988);

3 x Sovjet: Kommenterade resor från åren 1960, 1965 och 1988 (Stockholm: Askelin & Hägglund, 1988);

Tolv på det trettonde (Stockholm: Norstedt, 1989); translated by Bernstein and Christine Swanson as *12 Going on 13* (Chicago: Ravenswood, 1995);

På resa: Anteckningar och bilder (Stockholm: Norstedt, 1991);

När västerlandet trädde fram: Ondskan tar form, photographs by Kessle (Stockholm: Norstedt, 1992);

Inför nedräkningen: Inlagt i privata registret sommaren 1992 (Stockholm: Norstedt, 1993);

När morgondagarna sjöng: Från glömda år: En berättelse (Stockholm: Norstedt, 1994);

Mexico: Dröm och längtan (Stockholm: Fisher, 1996);

Maj: En kärlek (Stockholm: Norstedt, 1998);

Om vin (Höganäs: Bra böcker, 1999);

Johan August Strindberg (Stockholm: Natur och kultur, 2000).

Editions in English: *Gates to Asia: A Diary from a Long Journey,* translated by Paul Britten Austin (New York: Pantheon, 1971);

China Notebook, 1975-1978, translated by Rolf vom Dorp (Chicago: Liberator, 1979).

Myrdal in 1947

Collection: *En barndom i tie avsni* (Stockholm: Norstedt, 1992)–comprises *Barndom, En annam värld,* and *Tolv på det trettonde.*

PRODUCED SCRIPTS: *Myglaren,* television, Sveriges Radio, 1966;

Moraliteter, radio, Sveriges Radio, 11, 18, and 25 November 1967;

Fyra garderingar för Pettersson, radio, Sveriges Radio, 28 September and 5 October 1968;

B. Olsen löper livet ut, television, TV1, 29 October 1973.

OTHER: *Central Asia* (Beverly Hills, Cal.: International Communications Foundation, 1961);

August Strindberg, *Ordet i min makt: Läsebok för underklassen,* compiled by Myrdal (Stockholm: PAN/Norstedt, 1968);

Honoré de Balzac, *Antikkabinettet,* edited, with a foreword, by Myrdal (Stockholm: PAN/Norstedt, 1973);

Balzac, *Katarina av Medici: Three Political Articles,* afterword by Myrdal (Stockholm: PAN/Norstedt, 1974);

Balzac, *Byprästen,* afterword by Jan Myrdal (Stockholm: PAN/Norstedt, 1975);

Kritik som vapen och verktyg: Ny tysk marxistisk forskning och debatt kring film, teater, musik och litteratur, selected, with a foreword, by Jan Myrdal (Stockholm: PAN/Norstedt 1977);

Balzac, *Liljan i dalen,* selected by Myrdal and Jan Stolpe (Stockholm: PAN/Norstedt, 1978);

Balzac, *Om litteraturens teori och praktik,* selected, with an afterword, by Myrdal (Stockholm: PAN/Norstedt, 1979);

Franska revolutionens bilder: Jean-Louis Prieurs teckningar med kommentarer samt partiska ställningstaganden av år 1989, edited by Myrdal (Stockholm: Askelin & Hägglund, 1989);

5 år av frihet: 1830–1835: Daumier och Grandville mot bankirernas Kung Päron, edited by Myrdal (Höganäs: Wiken, 1991);

"August Strindberg and His Tradition in Swedish Literature: Beyond Fiction, Autobiography and the Literature of the Established Truth," in *Strindberg and Genre,* edited by Michael Robinson (Norwich, U.K.: Norvik, 1991);

Denis Diderot, *Jakob Fatalisten,* foreword by Myrdal (Stockholm: Hägglund, 1992);

André Gill: Konstnären som gav den politiska bilden ny form i skiftet mellan andra kejsardömet och tredje republiken i

Frankrike, edited by Myrdal (Stockholm: Raster, 1995);

"An Exemplary Phase Reversal: The Modernity of August Strindberg," in *Expressionism and Modernism: New Approaches to August Strindberg,* edited by Michael Robinson and Sven Hakon Rossel (Vienna: Praesen, 1999).

Jan Myrdal is one of the few internationally well-known Swedish authors. His books have been translated into several foreign languages. During the 1960s and 1970s he was a leading left-wing personality, admired by followers and abhorred by enemies. He has remained productive into his seventies, setting his mark on contemporary Swedish literature as an articulate voice of fierce originality.

Since his debut in 1953, his total output—one or two books a year, always surrounded by articles in newspapers and magazines—spans almost all literary genres (except perhaps lyrics) and even renews some of them. This statement applies not least to a new kind of travel writing, based on in-depth research into the history and economy of the particular country. The resulting "report genre" has proved to be an inspiration to other authors of his own generation. In his fictional and dramatic works, conventional patterns have been increasingly vitalized in a playful and experimental spirit. Myrdal's autobiographical series, beginning with reflections on his individual role as an author versus the shared responsibility of the intellectuals (as comprehended in *Confessions of a Disloyal European,* 1968), culminates in his Childhood Trilogy. This picture of his upbringing—typical of its time and its new political upper class but still unusual—has been much observed and could be ranked among the classics of autobiography. At all times he combines a political radicalism with an open-minded interest in traditional cultural values in art and literature. Although he left school at the age of sixteen and never studied at an academy, his attitude is that of a scholar, constantly urging his readers to go to the archives. A learned man, although outside the academic establishment, and harshly critical toward its inherited ways, he has also written on art history and literary criticism as well as introducing several new translations and editions of literary classics, for example, the works of Denis Diderot, Restif de la Bretonne, Honoré de Balzac, and August Strindberg.

His position—born to famous parents in the new political establishment of the 1930s—makes him also its most ardent critic. He prefers to regard himself a member of a certain "refractory" European tradition, comprising both radical and plebeian elements. His masters in this tradition are the great radical authors of the Enlightenment, above all Diderot and, from the nineteenth century, Balzac and Strindberg. Rather than call himself an author, he prefers the term *skriftställare* (from the German *Schriftsteller,* meaning "producer of writings"). Far from wanting to entertain a public through aesthetic value, he wants his words to have a certain political effect. By doing so he finds himself free to choose among all kinds of genres, as long as he makes his message clear; his work must not, he maintains, serve the powerful in its form. His oeuvre encompasses several novels, radio plays, travel books, many articles in newspapers and magazines, literary commentaries and criticism, as well as the autobiographical works, typical of his most recent development.

Jan Myrdal was born in Stockholm, on 19 July 1927 to Gunnar and Alva (née Reimer) Myrdal. Both of his parents were academics and politicians, prominent among the builders of the Swedish *folkhem* (home for the people)—the Social Democratic project toward a welfare state, described for Americans by Marquis W. Childs in 1936 in his book *Sweden: The Middle Way.* Along with their political ambition to create a society on principles of justice, social harmony, and care for the weak, the Myrdals also represented a new international political establishment. Both became Nobel laureates, Gunnar Myrdal for economics and Alva Myrdal for peace. The young Myrdal agreed with their general political and social ideals, although from a much more left-wing position, and he certainly profited from their intellectual and international prestige. When Myrdal was a child, the principles of social engineering caused him to feel a lack of real personal freedom, and he, as a result, became its most outspoken critic. Many of his books also comprise satirical descriptions of the early *folkhem,* which he found gave neither full freedom to the individual nor, being still too much dependent on capitalism, the social security and justice that it promised.

Before leaving school Myrdal already had written several articles marking his position as a young Marxist radical, but his real debut came with *Folkets hus: Samtal vid en invigning* (The House of the People: Dialogue at an Inauguration, 1953) and *Hemkomst* (Homecoming, 1954). Both works deal with a juvenile author's questions as to how to lead his life and serve his ideals. These questions, however, are put into the mind of an aging journalist who is looking back on his life and forced to face the fact that he has neither won the fame he wanted nor stood up for his ideals. According to a much later statement by Myrdal, in *Ord och avsikt: Ett resonemang* (1986), the portrayal of the journalist is a form of self-characterization, the man he feared to become. By this time he had been married twice: first to architect Nadja Wiking, from 1948 to 1952, with whom he had a son, Janken, born in 1949; and second to wel-

Myrdal (second from left) in December 1967 at a demonstration against the Vietnam War

fare officer Maj Lidberg, from 1952 to 1956, from which union a daughter, Eva, was born in 1956.

Myrdal's next three works are novels. *Jubelvår* (Spring of Jubilee, 1955) is a satirical description of complicated intrigues, including the narrator being locked up in his own manuscript, in a small Swedish town celebrating an historical jubilee. *Att bli och vara* (Becoming and Being, 1956) deals with a young man's difficulties with parents, love, and work. Much of the material, though masked as fiction, has an autobiographical background and criticizes the behaviorist psychology of its time. In *Badrumskranen* (The Bathroom Faucet, 1957) Myrdal continues his satirical portrayal of contemporary Sweden; his protagonists are filled with ideals, which they never even try to realize. Instead, they devote themselves to the writing of sentimental pieces about feelings and the soul, an anti-intellectual occupation that Myrdal despises more than anything else.

Myrdal spent the late 1950s and the early 1960s mainly traveling and working with his third wife, artist and photographer Gun Kessle, whom he married in 1956. Kessle has illustrated most of Myrdal's books with her photographs and drawings, and he has provided the texts for some of her photographic works. These travels resulted in a new genre of writing: historically, economically, socially, and politically oriented travel books.

Myrdal the traveler never regards his personal experiences as important per se, but merely as a starting point for an historical or social survey. He is anxious not to travel as a tourist but as an everyman, thus sharing the conditions of the people and making at least some of their experiences his own. His perspective is that of a socialist, and when he discusses the history of the country against a background of immense reading, he concentrates on important evolutions, state-building, and revolutions. He pays special attention to when, where, and why oppressed masses have succeeded in their resistance against the rich and powerful, and to which rulers have been able to build a state free from foreign or native oppression, stable, and fair to all its inhabitants. He considers what he and the reader may learn from a country and hope for its people at a particular moment of history. Myrdal expects much from modern technologies but fears a new economic colonialism from rich countries. He is a harsh critic of the kind of economic support that, while disregarding the preconditions of the country itself and requiring expensive foreign experts, costs more than it is worth. Instead, he believes in the hard collective work of the masses and the use of native know-how, such as old watering systems, in conjunction with modern technology.

Myrdal confesses that his travels are guided by his personal longing for the unknown, instilled by his reading as a boy, and his taste for the challenge of hardship, but even more so by his sense of unity with the downtrodden. When inhabitants are collectively accused of being bandits, his general attitude is to treat this accusation as the conquerors' accusation against the unvanquished, and to take the side of the accused party. This attitude has brought him to countries such as Afghanistan, Turkmenistan, and Albania, but his main interest has been in China and India, where he has lived and worked for several years.

Myrdal's first travel book was *Kulturers korsväg: En bok om Afghanistan* (Crossroads of Cultures: A Book about Afghanistan, 1960). There he found a small, poor, and free country, surrounded by conquerors but never conquered, a people without any oppressing upper class, skeptical toward foreign influence and proud of themselves. Reviewing the history of the country in glimpses, he can criticize the tendencies of Russian and British colonialism as well as admire the rich cultural treasures produced by the meetings of Persian, Arabic, and other cultures.

Between his travels Myrdal also worked in several other genres. *Rescontra: Utdrag ur avräkningsbok för personliga conti* (Rescontra: Deduction of Personal Conti, 1962) was the first book in his autobiographical series, later revised and completed.

Rapport från kinesisk by (1963; translated as *Report from a Chinese Village*, 1965) brought Myrdal international prestige, and the book was translated into several languages. In preparing the book he worked methodically, with the express aim to find out some kind of truth about the great political changes in postrevolutionary China. He tried to view the changes through the experience of ordinary people, in their own words. Myrdal and his wife lived among the people in the village of Liu Ling as their honored guests, systematically working on interviews and, in their free time, listening to the local gossip. Official statistics of harvests, weather, and temperature serve as background and verification, but the inhabitants' own testimony is even more important, especially when their stories seem contradictory. Myrdal lets the collective tale take shape through a plurality of voices. Although, at the time, the text was considered exclusively nonfictional and nonliterary in the sense of sociological objectivity, the literary character of the text has subsequently been seen as obvious. Myrdal's own voice is constantly heard in and around all the voices of the interviewees.

The autobiographical line from *Rescontra* was followed by *Samtida bekännelser av en europeisk intellektuell* (1964), revised and given its definite form in the author's own English as *Confessions of a Disloyal European* (1968). In these books he places the discussion of the role of intellectuals into the framework of a semifictional kind of reasoned autobiography. The protagonist, an unnamed narrator in some ways identical with the author, relates episodes quite obviously lifted from the author's own life. Still, Myrdal, in the revised version, called the book a novel, and in further commentaries has also declared the narrator to be fictional. The questions the narrator discusses in *Samtida bekännelser av en europeisk intellektuell* are not those of conventional autobiography; rather, he deals specifically with his own specific qualifications and his pampered background, assessing his responsibility and the extent to which he is fulfilling it. What kind of responsibility should be demanded of those who have the privilege to see and understand in a world so full of injustice? In *Confessions of a Disloyal European* Myrdal presents the story of "A," a young girl who for a short time had borrowed the temporary flat of the narrator and committed suicide there. He did not know her well, but still he had foreseen her death and so considers himself responsible. This story of knowledge, consciousness, and personal guilt expands into a trial of the narrator but also into a symbol of all European intellectuals and their collective guilt. "Thus the story of the death of A is in reality the story of the Western intellectual. As I betrayed A, so have we always betrayed.... We are not the bearers of consciousness. We are the whores of reason."

Besides his books, Myrdal has continued to write articles in several newspapers and periodicals. *Söndagsmorgon* (Sunday Morning, 1965) was the first collection of such material, comprising articles first published in the newspaper *Stockholmstidningen*.

Despite his criticism of fiction and estheticism, Myrdal continued to write fiction. His screenplay for the television movie *Myglaren* (1966; published as *Fallet Myglaren* in 1967)—a rare dialectical word for "parasitical lobbyist," now firmly established in the Swedish vernacular—is a satire against a new and rapidly growing political bureaucracy, which originated from the well-regulated hierarchy among the civil servants of the old Swedish state and now consists of a new, grasping, political upper class with international contacts. Myrdal's hero has not yet achieved such success, however; his European contacts are still in their early stages, as is his planning for a "Trivselinstitut" (Institute for Feel-Good Research), governed by himself, for his own benefit. The title implies the act of string-pulling as a meaningless, destructive activity. The lobbying of *Myglaren* is its own goal, often carried through by dishonest means and resulting merely in the lobbyist's personal profit.

In his radio plays *Moraliteter* (Moralities, 1967) and *Fyra garderingar för Pettersson* (Four Safeguards for Pettersson, 1968; published as *Garderingar* in 1969) Myrdal observes the medieval tradition of short plays that give the listener a stimulus to moral reflection. The plays continue, with much humor and self-irony, the line of satires against the *folkhem* and its lazy and self-satisfied members in contemporary Sweden. The lack of personal courage and radicalism among the establishment of the Social Democratic Party was a target in the early stages of the left-wing political movement of the late 1960s. In this movement Myrdal was one of the most important leaders, speaking at political meetings and writing political pamphlets as well as organizing and partaking in demonstrations against the American war in Vietnam.

Since *Rapport från kinesisk by*, Myrdal and Kessle have revisited China several times, and he continues his discussion of Chinese politics in *Kinesisk resa* (Chinese Journey, 1966), *Kina: Revolutionen går vidare* (1970; translated as *China: The Revolution Continued*), *Kinesiska frågor från Liu Ling* (Chinese Questions from Liu Ling, 1976), and *Kinesisk by 20 år senare: Rapport med frågetecken* (A Chinese Village Twenty Years Later: A Report with Question Marks, 1983; translated as *Return to a Chinese Village*, 1984). Even in the last of these books he still admires the politics of Mao Tse-tung and the Cultural Revolution: Mao, like Gandhi, saw the possibilities of the future among the working people, and Mao's lesson—"Det är rätt att göra uppror" (Rebellion is right)—will not be forgotten.

In several subsequent travel books Myrdal follows the principles of the earlier ones. He continually evaluates his personal impressions against other studies, interviews, and political discussions, thereby giving both a personal and more objective analysis of the place he is visiting, its premises and possibilities, often also including its treasures of art. This pattern is evident in *Turkmenistan: En revolutions övergångsår* (Turkmenistan: The Years of Transition of a Revolution, 1966), where he also declares his attitude toward Josef Stalin and Soviet imperialism, and in *Albansk utmaning* (1970; translated as *Albania Defiant*, 1976).

Between his travels Myrdal also published articles in newspapers and periodicals. Beginning with the first volume of *Skriftställning* (Writing) in 1968, later followed by seventeen more numbered volumes, he has systematically republished a considerable part of this material. This series is, according to the author, to be regarded as "en oregelbundet utkommande enmanstidskrift" (an irregularly appearing one-man periodical) open to the widest possible variety of themes, including politics—local, internal and international; personal remarks on actual events; literary criticism; and notes on art. A collection of similar material is *Ett femtiotal* (From Our Fifties, 1972) consisting of articles from the early 1950s that the author still, twenty years later, found to be of interest. The magazine *Folket i Bild* (The People in Pictures), cofounded by Myrdal in 1972, has since been the principal forum for his journalistic activities, often republished in the various volumes of *Skriftställning*. Some of these are, as their subtitles suggest, more explicitly devoted to political questions of current interest such as the political situation in different foreign countries; others also comment on the author's own writing.

Dust jacket for Myrdal's 1983 nonfiction work, in which he revisits the Chinese village about which he wrote in 1963 in Rapport från kinesisk by *(from* Swedish Book Review, *October 1983)*

In the radio play *B. Olsen löper livet ut* (B. Olsen Running out of Life, 1972) the criticism of the *folkhem* is more specific than in the early novels. Olsen's tragicomic upbringing seems again semi-autobiographical and is portrayed as typical of the new, modernist political establishment of his famous parents.

Den onödiga samtiden (The Unnecessary Contemporaneity, 1974) addresses a single theme. In an exchange of letters with the author Lars Gustafsson, Myrdal discusses the Marxian prophecies on the development of socialism versus capitalism. They consider whether the general political situation of the time, regarded in the light of the conflict between socialism and capitalism, was really necessary.

Myrdal again turns to fictional satire in the novel *Karriär* (Career, 1975). In an exchange of letters, four formerly prominent members of the Social Democratic political establishment describe their own decline and fall, while feebly trying some last attempts of political lobbying. Their private lives have also depreciated into meaningless hobbies or human disaster. In betraying their ideals for a career, they have betrayed themselves as well as others.

Traveling again, Myrdal follows old routes of trade in *Sidenvägen: En resa från höga Pamir och Ili genom Sinkiang och Kansa* (1977; translated as *The Silk Road: A Journey from the High Pamirs and Ili through Sinkiang and Kantsu*, 1979). Along the way he encounters locals and politicians–some of them friends from earlier journeys–and discusses with them the political and economical development of the countries. In *Kampuchea och kriget: Inlägg och polemiker* (Kampuchea and the War: Contributions and Polemics, 1978), which was published as volume 11 of *Skriftställning*, Myrdal, having earlier criticized the American war in Vietnam, defends Kampuchean politics against the Vietnamese invasion.

Indien väntar (1980; translated as *India Waits*, 1984), the result of travels in India from 1958 to 1979, includes a survey of the political development of these years through several discussions with leading left-wing intellectuals. Myrdal is critical toward Indira Gandhi, but as an historian he still finds some hope for the working farmers: that they will be able to rise again, and that technical and economic development might also bring them the benefits of insight. Myrdal puts up an ardent fight against the Western notions of a great inherited spirituality in India; in his Marxist opinion the alleged spirituality and inwardness are only the result of sickness and poverty, the inheritance from colonialism and other oppression.

In the beginning of the 1980s Myrdal returned to the autobiographical sphere, now in a more direct and traditional form. His Childhood Trilogy comprises *Barndom* (1982; translated as *Childhood*, 1991), *En annan värld* (1984; translated as *Another World*, 1994), and *Tolv på det trettonde* (1989; translated as *12 Going on 13*, 1995). In these three works, later collected in a single volume as *En barndom i tre avsnitt* (A Childhood in Three Parts, 1992), the rebellious protagonist puts the system represented by his parents on trial. (During this time he also published *En Meccanopojke berättar, eller anteckningar om ett borgerligt förnuft* [The Tale of a Meccano-Boy, or Notes on a Kind of Bourgeois Rationality, 1988], a sociological work on similar themes.) In Myrdal's mind his parents personified the new upper class.

In the first part of the trilogy Myrdal declares his gratitude to his loving grandparents, in contrast to the parents' scrutinizing oppression masked by ice-cold psychological understanding and hypocritical talk about love. In the subsequent parts the precocious teenager regards himself as an immigrant in the United States, where his parents conducted the study that eventually resulted in Gunnar Myrdal's book on American race relations, *An American Dilemma: The Negro Problem and Modern Democracy* (1944). The boy feels free to form his own ego in an intellectual climate that is stimulating to free and open debate–in vivid contrast to the depressing Sweden to which he is forced to return. For the author, and particularly for his later political opinions, his boyhood experiences in the United States were of decisive importance.

Myrdal's trilogy represents the tradition in autobiography that focuses on the often ill-treated and rebellious child and tells the story from that viewpoint. Through his experiences from life and reading, the boy forms a personality of his own, conscious and radical. Thus emerges an interesting form on the borderline between autobiography and autobiographical novel. The trilogy represents perhaps the peak of Myrdal's concise, hard-hitting, and agile prose style.

Barndom met with a good deal of adverse criticism. Many reviewers questioned whether his accusations against his highly esteemed parents were true and justified. Others, however, appreciated the book, finding within it an offended and unfairly accused child pleading his own cause.

Two collections of essays, *En annan ordning: Litterärt och personligt* (Another Order: Notes Literary and Personal, 1988) and *Inför nedräkningen: Inlagt i privata registret sommaren 1992* (Waiting for the Countdown: Put into the Private Register during the Summer of 1992, 1993) are more personal than the earlier volumes of *Skriftställning* and include many of Myrdal's commentaries on his life and work, especially on his autobiographies and the criticism raised against them.

När morgondagarna sjöng: Från glömda år: En berättelse (When Tomorrow was Singing: A Tale from Forgotten Years, 1994) continues the story of the rebellious protagonist from the Childhood Trilogy. Now, at seventeen years old, he is living his own life. Working as a trainee journalist, he is politically active and experiences his first love affairs; he is committed to the open, honest spirit of his own generation and opposed to the devious and deceitful ways of former ones. The book reflects the optimism of the young postwar generation and its hopes for peace and understanding between people, and its faith in personal and political freedom.

In *Mexico: Dröm och längtan* (Mexico: Dream and Longing, 1996) Myrdal turns to a new part of the world for him. He finds Mexico an interesting melting pot, both culturally and racially. This time he seems less hopeful toward a revolutionary change and more prone at least to consider the classical capitalist solution: allow in foreign capital and start still more industries, even though he acknowledges the price of poverty for at least two more generations and of steadily increasing pollution. He shows great interest in folklore and finds several points of similarity between the old European and Mexican death rites, although the latter have been grotesquely replaced by Halloween as observed in the United States.

The latest part of the autobiographical series, *Maj: En kärlek* (Maj: A Love Story, 1998), includes at least two central themes. The first is the young writer's consuming sexual passion for his second wife, Maj. This love story puts forth a new and somewhat surprising picture of the author: not that of the reflective intellectual, which is how he normally likes to describe himself, but that of a victim of his own feelings. His predicament lasts until the bitter end of the relationship, when he feels forced to chose between passion, marriage, family life (including a newborn baby), and his calling to be a writer rather than a breadwinner. The other important theme is that of the young Myrdal's work in the great political youth festivals of the 1950s. About this work—and the passionate affair, however destructive at the time—the author concludes simply that he has no regrets.

All throughout his literary life Myrdal has expressed his abhorrence of both an empty aestheticism and art that serves the ruling interests. Nonetheless, his interest in art is deep and genuine. In his travel books the arts and architecture of the countries he visits are a permanent and sometimes dominating presence. With a mixture of admiration and regret he always looks at the great monuments, which were invariably built at the expense of the poor. He recurringly considers art in the context of its service to the people. The same issue reverberates in some other art-oriented texts. *Ansikte av sten: Staden Angkor i Kambodja: Uppgång, storhet och fall: En berättelse om vår tid* (Face of Stone: The City of Anchor in Kampuchea, 1968; translated as *Angkor: An Essay on Art and Imperialism*, 1970) concentrates on Kampuchean sculptures, while *Ondskan tar form* (Evil Takes Shape, 1976) deals with European medieval church sculptures, regarded as witnesses of the political forces of their time.

Myrdal has published as models of a nonservient, truly rebellious art, three anthologies based on his private collections of French political caricatures from the nineteenth century: *Franska revolutionens bilder: Jean-Louis Prieurs teckningar med kommentarer samt partiska ställningstaganden av år 1989* (The Images of the French Revolution: The Drawings of Jean-Louis Prieur with Commentaries and Prejudiced Positions from the year 1989), *5 år av frihet: 1830–1835: Daumier och Grandville mot bankirernas Kung Päron* (Five Years of Freedom: 1830–1835: Daumier and Grandville against King Pear of the Private Bankers, 1991) and *André Gill: Konstnären som gav den politiska bilden ny form i skiftet mellan andra kejsardömet och tredje republiken i Frankrike* (André Gill: The Artist Who Gave a New Form to the Political Drawing in the Shift between the Second Empire and the Third Republic in France, 1995).

Jan Myrdal's political views—sometimes seemingly extreme—have been much criticized. When accused of defending the massacre at Tiananmen Square, he was on the brink of being expelled from the Swedish section of the International Pen Club. Still, his influence on public opinion has been great. His independent way of thinking has been respected also by those who do not share his opinions. The breadth of his interests, knowledge, and accuracy as well his literary skills establish Myrdal as one of the important intellectuals of his time.

Bibliographies:

Britta-Lena Jansson, *Jan Myrdal: En kronologisk bibliografi 1943–1976* (Stockholm: Oktober, 1977);

Erik Edwardson, Erik Göthe, Hans M. Gabrielson, and Ann Tobin, *Jan Myrdal: En kronologisk bibliografi: 1943–1992* (Stockholm: Hägglund, 1999).

Reference:

Cecilia Cervin, *Det illojala barnets uppror: Studier kring Jan Myrdals självbiografiska texter* (Stockholm: Hägglund, 1997).

Lars Norén
(9 May 1944 -)

Lars Nylander
University of California at Berkeley

BOOKS: *Syrener, snö* (Stockholm: Bonnier, 1963);

De verbala resterna av en bildprakt som förgår (Stockholm: Bonnier, 1964);

Inledning nr 2 till SCHIZZ (Stockholm: Bonnier, 1965);

Encyklopedi: Mémoires sur la fermentation 1–3 (Stockholm: Bonnier, 1966);

Stupor: Nobody Knows You When You're Down and Out (Stockholm: Bonnier, 1968);

Salome, Sfinxerna: Roman om en tatuerad flicka (Stockholm: Bonnier, 1968);

Revolver (Stockholm: Bonnier, 1969);

Biskötarna (Stockholm: Bonnier, 1970);

I den underjordiska himlen: Biskötarna II (Stockholm: Bonnier, 1972);

Solitära dikter (Stockholm: Bonnier, 1972);

Viltspeglar (Göteborg: Författarförlaget, 1972);

Kung Mej och andra dikter (Stockholm: Bonnier, 1973);

Dagliga och nattliga dikter (Stockholm: Bonnier, 1974);

Dagbok: Augusti-Oktober 1975 (Stockholm: Bonnier, 1976);

Nattarbete (Stockholm: Bonnier, 1976);

Order (Stockholm: Bonnier, 1978);

Hans Bellmer: Bilder från åren 1934–1950, by Norén and Ragnar von Holten (Stockholm: Norstedt, 1978);

Murlod (Stockholm: Bonnier, 1979);

Den ofullbordade stjärnan (Stockholm: Bonnier, 1979);

Hjärta i hjärta (Stockholm: Bonnier, 1980);

Tre skådespel (Stockholm: Bonnier, 1980);

En fruktansvärd lycka (Karlstad & Molkom, Sweden: Bokförlaget promenad, 1981);

Två skådespel (Stockholm: Bonnier, 1983);

Eintagswesen (Frankfurt: Suhrkamp, 1989); translated as *Endagsvarelser* (Stockholm: Bonnier, 1990);

De döda pjäserna, 4 volumes (Stockholm: Bonnier, 1989–1994);

Och ge oss skuggorna (Stockholm: Bonnier, 1991);

Tre borgerliga kvartetter (Stockholm: Bonnier, 1992);

Bobby Fisher Is Alive and Lives in Pasadena (Amsterdam: International Theatre & Film Books, 1993);

Lars Norén

Minnet, glömskan och berättelsen: En studie om de tidiga barndomsminnersas betydelse (Göteborg: Psykologiska Institutet, Göteborgs universitet, 1995);

Radiopjaser 1971–95 (Stockholm: Sveriges Radio, 1996);

Personbrets 3:1 (Stockholm: Bonnier, 1998);

Morire di classe: Skuggpojkarna (Stockholm: Bonnier, 1999).

PLAY PRODUCTIONS: *Fursteslickaren,* Stockholm, Royal Dramatic Theater, November 1973;

Orestes, Stockholm, Royal Dramatic Theater, May 1980;
En fruktansvärd lycka, Stockholm, City Theater, April 1981;
Underjordens leende, Copenhagen, Det Kongelige, October 1982;
Natten är dagens mor, Malmö, City Theater, October 1982;
Kaos är granne med Gud, Göteborg, City Theater, September 1983;
Demoner, Stockholm, City Theater, April 1984;
Nattvarden, Stockholm, Royal Dramatic Theater, February 1985;
Vilstolen, Copenhagen, Teatret Ved Sorte Hest, September 1986;
Stillheten, Amsterdam, Het Publiekstheater, September 1986;
Höst och vinter, Copenhagen, Caféteatret, February 1989;
Eintagswesen, Kassel, Germany, Staatstheater, March 1989;
Och ge oss skuggorna, Oslo, Det Norske Teatret, March 1991;
Sommar, Stockholm, Royal Dramatic Theater, February 1992;
Tiden är vårt hem, Stockholm, Royal Dramatic Theater, December 1992;
Löven i Vallombrosa, Bonn, Blätterschaffen Schauspeil, October 1994;
Blod, Copenhagen, Betty Nansen Theater, November 1995;
Kliniken, Stockholm, Plaza Theater, Uppsala City Theater, February 1996;
Så enkel är kärleken, Stockholm, Vasan, January 1997.

PRODUCED SCRIPTS: *Belgroove Hotel,* television, Swedish TV 2, May 1970;
Amala, Kamala: Punkter för television, television, Swedish TV 2, May 1971;
Box Ett, radio, Swedish Radio, November 1972;
Röster, radio, 1973;
Depressionen, radio, Swedish Radio, August 1979;
Dräneringen, radio, Swedish Radio, September 1979;
Akt utan nåd, radio, Swedish Radio, September 1980;
Modet att döda, television, Swedish TV 2, December 1980;
När dom brände fjärilar på Lilla Scenen, radio, Swedish Radio, February 1983;
München Nathen, television, Swedish TV 1, September 1983;
Hämndaria, radio, Swedish Radio, January 1986;
Komedianter, television, Swedish TV 1, November 1987;
Sanning och konsekvens, television, Swedish Television-Drama, March 1989;
Hebriana, television, Swedish TV 1, April 1990;
Bobby Fisher bor i Pasadena, television, Swedish Television, October 1990;
En sorts Hades, television, Swedish Television, November 1996.

OTHER: *Box Ett* in *Svenska radiopjäser 1972* (Stockholm: Sveriges Radio, 1973), pp. 80–112;
Dräneringen in *Svenska radiopjäser 1979* (Stockholm: Sveriges Radio, 1980), pp. 143–174.

Lars Norén emerged in the late 1960s as a writer whose poetic reports from a psychotic netherworld of the human condition seemed to repel as many readers as they fascinated. He gradually established himself as one of Sweden's most prominent poets, a position formally acknowledged by his reception of the Gerhard Bonnier Critic's Prize in 1978 for *Order* (Order, 1978). No sooner had he gained this recognition, however, than he left poetry and turned his creative energy to drama. During the years that followed, Norén renewed naturalist drama in a way that has ensured him a distinctive position in the history of Swedish, perhaps even European, literature. Twenty years after his first book of poetry, the obscure poet Norén had somehow transformed himself into the most influential Swedish dramatist since August Strindberg.

Norén was born in Stockholm on 9 May 1944 as the younger of two sons. His parents soon moved to southern Sweden to manage a small hotel, which became Norén's childhood home. He started to write during adolescence in response to a turbulent family crisis, centered on the alcoholism of his father and the illness and subsequent death of his mother in 1964. As an effect the twenty-year-old Norén suffered a psychotic breakdown and was hospitalized for half a year. During this period his writing took on a more obsessional character, quite literally becoming a means of survival. The verse he wrote during and after this crisis is best characterized as a post-Surrealist *écriture automatique* (automatic writing) animated by a dark, desperate expressionist pathos one seldom finds in Surrealism or late modernist poetry. Most of the collections of poetry that he published in the late 1960s were excerpts from huge piles of manuscripts that he submitted to publishers. As his bibliography indicates–listing sixty-six published works between 1963 and 1995–the intensity of his production did not diminish over the years.

After his crisis Norén moved to Stockholm, where he has lived ever since. In the 1970s his poetry underwent several stylistic changes, coalescing into a highly elaborate minimalism in the manner of Paul Celan. Parallel to poetry, he also tried his hand at other genres, mostly plays for radio and theater. In 1980 he stopped writing poetry altogether to devote himself entirely to what is best characterized as a supranaturalist form of drama, in which the psychological and expressionist forms of predecessors such as Strindberg, Anton Chekhov, Eugene O'Neill, Edward Albee, and Jean-Paul Sartre were subjected to an elaborate compression. While firmly adhering to the classical unities of time and space, the plays nonetheless turn into a mixture of realist, expressionist, and symbolist qualities.

Norén's plays had a more immediate impact on Swedish theater life than any playwright before him, thoroughly dominating the production of new Swedish drama in the 1980s. By way of a continuous series of high-quality television productions of his plays, his complex and somber dramatic vision of Swedish social life and mentality became a common reference in social discourse and imagination. Internationally, where his poetry has remained little known, his plays have gradually made an impact. Apart from being well known and often produced in the Nordic countries, his plays have had several acclaimed productions in countries such as Germany, Holland, France, Italy, as well as in South America. In the United States his play *Natten är dagens mor* (1982) was performed by the Yale Repertory Theater as *Night Is Mother of Day* in the winter of 1984.

Throughout his career Norén's writings have maintained an intensely personal character, bordering on the autobiographical. As he married and became a father in 1971, his writings became preoccupied with motifs relating to family life and fatherhood. In turning to drama, he first used the genre as a dramatic analysis of his past and present life, with *Natten är dagens mor* and its sequel, *Kaos är granne med Gud* (Chaos Is Neighbor to God, 1983), as his most direct depictions of the family crisis in his adolescence, placed in the context of general social and ideological changes of the period.

For a long time Norén remained a rather secluded person, mainly known to the public through his publications and published interviews. His work with drama in the 1980s brought him into more direct cooperation with directors and actors and made him more of a public figure. It also led to a series of guest appearances as a director, starting with a production of Strindberg's *Dödsdansen* (1901; translated as *The Dance of Death*, 1912) at the Royal Dramatic Theater in 1994.

The driving force of Norén's writings up to the early 1990s is the modernist dictum derived from Rainer Maria Rilke: "Du mußt dein Leben schreiben!" (You have to write your life!). For Norén this principle is realized as a combination of autobiographical reference and continuous changes of style and genre. The result is not autobiography in the traditional sense, since his texts stand not only as reports of the already lived but also as dramatic prescriptions or performatives of life to come. The effect is rather that life and text merge to the point where the distinction loses any meaning.

In Norén's first poetry collections, *Syrener, snö* (Lilacs, Snow, 1963) and *De verbala resterna av en bildprakt som förgår* (The Verbal Residues of a Vanishing Pictorial Splendor, 1964), he sought to situate himself within a modernist-Surrealist tradition of poetry. The verses are highly intertextual, overflowing with allusions to and paraphrases of Swedish as well as international, especially French, poets. The first book received agitated, negative reviews and cannot be said to include poetry of any lasting importance.

Already in his second book, however, Norén presents a more independent, personal poetry, albeit in such a dark and protopsychotic manner that the critical reception was somewhat uneasy. The dark, anxiety-ridden texts dramatize a consciousness without any stable identity and borders, lost among fetishized objects, memories, and fantasies in a world with no clear distinction between present and past or fantasy and reality. It is poetry that can only be read as the expression of a nightmarish state of psychotic disintegration. Many poems are centered on the fragmented body parts of a dying or dead mother. In his unmediated dependence on her, the speaker in the poems exists in a limbo between life and death, not knowing if her death automatically will bring about his own or if it will offer him some form of rebirth as seen in a lyric from *De verbala resterna av en bildprakt som förgår*:

> jag måste genomgå skymningens håroperationer nattens hudkliniker
> där jag tvättas och återuppstår
> mina nedsölade fötter sitter fast i ensamheten och stanken
> . . . .
> i väntan måste jag befinna mig här
> utan att veta om något skall ske om jag skall dö, om detta är sista
> gången eller den första
> jag mumlar jag rör mig och kretsar omkring runt ständigt samma ting
> samma fetischer och liv
> med vita outsprungna fosterögon lyssnar jag till
> de mörka cyklarna
>
> (I have to endure the hair operations of dawn the skin clinics of night
> where I am washed and resurrected
> my drenched feet are stuck in loneliness and the stench
> . . . .
> I have to wait here
> without knowing if anything is about to happen if I am going to die, if this is the last
> time or the first
> I mumble I move about around the same old things
> the same fetishes and lives
> with white unopened fetus eyes I listen to
> the dark cycles)

In his poetry collections published in the years from 1965 to 1969—*Inledning nr 2 till SCHIZZ* (Introduction No. 2 to SCHIZZ, 1965), *Encyklopedi: Mémoires sur la fermentation 1–3* (Encyclopedia: Memories of Fermentation 1–3, 1966), *Stupor: Nobody Knows You When You're Down and Out* (1968), *Salome, Sfinxerna: Roman om en tatuerad flicka* (Salome, the Sphinxes: Novel about a Tattooed Girl, 1968), and *Revolver* (1969)—Norén explored a more aestheticized form of schizoid-poetic automatic writing, imbued with the radical cultural and aesthetic theories of the period (including pop art, antipsychiatry, media theory) and put forth as semihallucinatory fantasies in the manner of Raymond Roussel and Henri Michaux. The texts read like automatic, panic-ridden words and fantasies from a subject lost in a mental space of images, fantasies, literature, art, and media.

At first (and best achieved in *Encyklopedi*) this schizo-poetry was loosely anchored in the principle of dramatized consciousness, at times enacting the stream of consciousness of fictional characters. When the poet appears in person, it is as a subject without psychological and authorial control as shown in this poem from *Encyklopedi*:

. . . men jag
är inte en bland miljoner, bland en million, verkligen inte,
jag har mina binamn, mina attribut, det spar tid att vara
lite schizoid, ibland, medan jag ändå är igång med slösandet,
vilket är normalt för mig, kan jag dela upp mig som segment,
i svåra stunder, annar är det svårt att överhuvudtaget anta någonting; jag vill ibland bli en million, ibland en hel folkmassa i vars mitt det också finns en nervös idiot som utan att låta sig störas iakttager mej.

(. . . but I'm
not one among millions, among one million, certainly not,
I have my nicknames, my attributes, it saves time to be slightly schizoid, sometimes, when I'm about with my squandering,
which is quite normal to me, I can divide myself like a segment,
in difficult moments, otherwise it's difficult to assume anything at all;
I sometimes want to become a million, sometimes an entire
crowd in the midst of which there's also a nervous idiot who watches me without letting himself be disturbed.)

In *Stupor* the guiding principle shifts from that of dramatized consciousness to a more radical, depersonalized form of collage. One element of the collage principle was the usage of typographical variations, most extensively employed in *Inledning nr 2 till SCHIZZ*, of which some pages turn into an unreadable form of typewriter scribble. As within the concretist poetry of the period, Norén's play with typography implies a metapoetic dimension, where language and subject are placed in deep conflict as seen in another poem from *Encyklopedi*:

Typografiska krig **som förklarar krrrr**iiiiiiiigg **mot**det är sådana**mej**fläckar som bildar
stommen i kriget

Typographical wars **which declare wwaaaa**aaaaa**rr against**it's those kind of **me**stains which form
the bulk of the war)

These metalinguistic reflections at times take on a more programmatic form, and come forth as a postmodernist poetics, linked to some vague, utopian notion of a new, mentally and socially emancipating aesthetic. This excerpt from *Stupor* was originally divided into two parallel columns—with lines 1, 3, 5, 7, and 9 in the left column and lines 2, 4, 6, and 8 in the right column—forcing the reader to "slide" between the two.

MAN BORDE KUNNA UPPRÄTTA EN
FLYTANDE TILLVARO DÄR ALLTING
GLIDER IN I VARTANNAT, OCH I
DENNA SIMULTANITET ÄR OMEDELBART
GILTIGT OCH MÖJLIGT ATT ANVÄNDA
FÖR ATT ÖVERLEVA, OCH I DEN MÅN DETTA
REDAN FINNS – ETT UPPÖVANDE AV
ALL-PRECEPTIONEN FÖR ATT GÖRA DETTA
TILLGÄNGLIGT.

(ONE SHOULD BE ABLE TO ESTABLISH A
FLOATING EXISTENCE IN WHICH EVERYTHING
SLIDES INTO EVERYTHING ELSE, AND IN
THIS SIMULTANEOUSNESS IS IMMEDIATELY
VALID AND POSSIBLE TO USE
FOR SURVIVAL, AND TO THE EXTENT THAT
THIS
ALREADY EXISTS–AN EXERCISE IN
ALL-PERCEPTION IN ORDER TO MAKE THIS
ACCESSIBLE.)

Norén's schizoid poetry reaches its most elaborate form in *Stupor,* which more explicitly evokes a sociocultural crisis. Modern life is here depicted as a bewildering state of informational and sensuous overflow, creating different forms of personal and social "stupor."

What sets these schizo-aesthetic collages apart from other, similar forms of postmodern experiments in the late 1960s is the somber expressionist pathos that pervades them. The mode constantly switches back and forth between euphoric excitement and bottomless anxiety, and farce-like scenes are mixed with bizarre episodes of brutal violence, often relating to torture, sexual violence, and images of the Holocaust. The general cultural crisis thus remains inseparable from the writing subject's personal crisis.

At the same time as the principle of textual collage became more media oriented, the poetic principle of Norén's writings moved to take on a more narrative form. This change, which prefigured Norén's development in the 1970s, became most explicit in *Salome, Sfinxerna*. The book is a collage of fantasies, anecdotes, and scenes, each ranging from one paragraph to two to three pages. Figures and objects return throughout the book, giving the impression of some vague overall structure.

In the period from 1970 to 1973 Norén made more serious efforts to turn to mimetic forms of writing. The novels *Biskötarna* (The Beekeepers, 1970) and *I den underjordiska himlen: Bistökarna II* (In the Subterraneous Heaven: The Beekeepers II, 1972) tell in first-person form the story of a writer, Simon, closely modeled on Norén, who experiences a crisis in relation to his father's death. In a state of paranoid flight from unresolved conflicts with his father, he metaphorically offers himself for adoption in two highly dysfunctional families, headed by adults not much older than he. His desire to find a new home and identity makes him willing to adopt whatever social role he is offered, that of the son or father, as well as that of the mother:

> Finns det någon plats för mig? Om han sticker–kan jag kanske stanna kvar då? Är jag snäll mot barn? Tycker barn om mig, när dom lärt känna mig? Kan jag vara till hjälp i hushållet? Jag kan städa. Jag kan diska. Jag kan skura. Jag kan älska så att hon blir förbluffad, åtminstone dom första två gångerna. Jag kan be henne om förlåtelse . . .
>
> (Is there any place for me? If he leaves–can I perhaps stay on? Am I kind to children? Do children like me, once they've got to know me? Can I be of any help in the household? I can clean. I can wash the dishes. I can scrub the floors. I can make love in a way that will amaze her, at least the first two times. I can ask for her forgiveness . . .)

Starting in the manner of a diary, Simon's descriptions of his experiences gradually take on a dreamy, hallucinatory character. By the end of the second novel, as he assists his then father-substitute in murdering some old people that they have been taking care of, there is no clear distinction between reality and fantasy.

The title *Biskötarna* refers to one of the recurrent symbols in Norén's writings, that of the bee swarm as a metaphor for consciousness, or desire, in a state of disorganization, and the beehive and queen bee as images of a lost origin. The motif is first presented as Simon's memory of his father burning out a beehive and talking about the importance of killing the queen. As the story of Simon proceeds, the reader is led to identify with the swarm that has escaped from such a catastrophe to an existence in complete mental and social disorientation.

These novels represent Norén's first effort at what became one of his major motifs: modern family life as a dysfunctional, hollow, or emotionally overburdened institution, with connotations of an asylum and prison. The motif is always presented in a genuinely ambivalent relation to social normality; it can simultaneously be read as a depiction of mentally fragile characters, unable to establish normal interpersonal relations, and as an expressionistic blowup of the conflicts, fears, and power struggles that go on beneath the surface of modern family life. Normal and abnormal, as well as personal and political, merge in Norén's writings. If many of his social portraits continue the ideological critique of modern life put forth by the antipsychiatric theory and Freudian culturalism of the 1960s–as expressed in the works of R. D. Laing, Herbert Marcuse, and Norman O. Brown, for example–Norén's versions are always more ambivalent, as if trapped within the nightmare they are trying to depict, and with no simple demarcation of victims and oppressors or ideological prescriptions for a more happy future. As the director Suzanne Osten, writing in *Bonniers Litterära Magasin* in 1982, said about the characters in Norén's later plays: "Alla är subjekt, alla lider av en outhärdlig övergivenhet" (All are subjects, all suffer from an intolerable abandonment).

Norén's first play, *Amala, Kamala: Punkter för television* (Amala, Kamala: Points for Television), first aired in May 1971, dramatized, in a fairly conventional form, an Indian legend of two girls who had been raised by wolves, later to be captured and brought to an English garrison hospital. The play centers on one of the girls' caretakers, who develops a strong fascination for them, and comes to believe that he, through them, can escape the complexities of human life for some ideal state of animalistic simplicity. The play ends with him standing in their cage, whipping them and crying out for them to answer him. He is thus (as are so many others in Norén's early writings) irretrievably lost in an impossible and alienating neither/nor between language and body. This dualism remains at the center of Norén's writings throughout the 1970s, in ways that echo philosophers such as Martin Heidegger and Simone Weil as well as psychoanalysts such as Jacques Lacan and Julia Kristeva.

Norén's first play to be produced on stage, *Fursteslickaren* (The Prince Licker), at the Royal Dramatic Theater in 1973, is a dark, expressionistic depiction of the sadomasochistic psychology of power and the corruption of art by social forces. Set in sixteenth-century central Europe, it follows, in a series of pageant scenes, a young, idealistic composer who takes up a position in court and gradually is broken down by its violent power structure and his inability to maintain some artistic and personal dignity. The perversion of power is here directly linked not only to the birth of modern culture but also to the essential notion of negative theology: that modern man is subjected to a God who only manifests himself through his absence.

None of these early plays by Norén offer any strong, convincing depictions of the existential dilemma of modern man and the rise of modern political and social structures of power. Neither do they offer any hint of the dramatic mastery that Norén achieved a decade later. They do, however, show the new direction that his writing was taking, away from the automatism of the 1960s and toward mimetic depictions of modern society as a fundamentally schizoid, alienating culture.

Norén also wrote a radio play, *Box Ett* (Box One, 1972), in which he tried to use schizo-poetic automatism as a structural principle. The play is a collage of voices, without any mimetic, temporal, or spatial parameters, no plot, and no clear relation between the speaking characters. They emerge individually to tell about a personal experience, or in pairs exchanging dialogue. The play thus is a polyphonic voice-poem rather than a conventional radio play.

The poetry that Norén wrote during this period is, however, more clearly marked by his shift toward mimetic principles. In a postscript to *Kung Mej och andra dikter* (King Me and Other Poems, 1973), the sections of which bear the subtitles "Op. 1" and "Op. 2," the author states that he now wishes to be read as a completely "new Lars Norén." The poetry of this period is formally more conventional than his earlier poetry, with individual, often titled, poems that center on interpersonal relations, love, and family life in an often recognizable social setting. With its prosaic, at times naive, idiom and tragicomical portraits of characters and situations, irregularly diffused by a hermetic, surreal imagery, Norén's poetry at this time received critical acclaim and firmly established him at the center of Swedish literature. A good example of this style appears in a short poem from *Viltspeglar* (Mirror Games, 1972). The lyric opens with a peaceful idyllic image of meditative rest in a country setting and continues:

> Livet ligger
> ett hjärtslag
> från mitt eget
> De brinnande kreaturen
> med renrakade huvuden
> har kommit hem
> till sitt skälvande stall.
>
> (Life lies
> a heartbeat
> from my own
> The burning cattle
> with clean shaven heads
> have returned
> to its trembling stable.)

The major part of *Kung Mej och andra dikter* is the titular series of poems, which dramatizes the life of the turn-of-the-century Swedish painter Joseph Hill, when he mentally had retreated into schizophrenia. (During this period Hill produced a series of drawings on brown wrapping paper, which has remained the most famous Swedish example of *l'art brut,* "raw" or schizophrenic art.) The poems clearly illustrate Norén's effort to depict, in mimetically controlled forms, the schizoid disorder that he earlier had tried to portray in more direct ways. The role poem can be seen as a generic bridge between these two principles, since it offers the possibility of simultaneously being within and without the character's subjective state:

> Jag heter Hill. Hill säger jag att jag
> heter! Jag säger till Hill att jag är
> Hill. Hill säger att jag är Hill!
> Vi är Hill! Hill och jag.
>
> (My name in Hill. I say that my name is
> Hill! Hill says to Hill that I am
> Hill. Hill says that I am Hill!
> We are Hill, Hill and I.)

In the 1976 collection *Dagbok: Augusti-Oktober 1975* (Diary: August–October 1975) Norén offers a description of the underlying sociopolitical meaning of these role poems and their logic of schizoid desire:

> [Hill] är det precisa svaret på den tid
> han levde i Alltså, han är möjligheten
> öppningen i den totalitära tiden Vad som finns
> i hans teckningar är faktiska utvägar, som han
> inte kunde använda, ur tvånget . . .
>
> ([Hill] is the decisive response to the time
> in which he lived Thus, he is the possibility
> the breach in the totalitarian time What is found
> in his drawings, are real exits, which he
> was unable to use, from coercion . . .)

In Norén's poetry of the mid 1970s, all the major techniques and styles of high and late modernism are brought together into a poetry at once highly personal and stylistically heterogeneous. Although Norén's style seems unmistakable, readers have had difficulty in pinning down this quality. Jan Olov Ullén, overcome by the task of characterizing Norén's poetry in his *Bonniers Litterära Magasin* review in 1978, wrote: "Jag vet inte med vilka adjektiv den skulle kunna beskrivas, men det vore skönt att slippa använda dem.... Man kan egentligen bara citera den" (I don't know by what adjectives it might be described, but I would rather not use them.... One can merely quote it).

During the period from 1974 to 1980 Norén published eight volumes of poetry—*Dagliga och nattliga dikter* (Poems by Day and Night, 1974); *Dagbok; Nattarbete* (Nightwork, 1976); *Order; Hans Bellmer: Bilder från åren 1934–1950* (Hans Bellmer: Pictures from the Years 1934–1950, 1978); *Murlod* (Wall-Plummet, 1979); *Den ofullbordade stjärnan* (The Incomplete Star, 1979); *Hjärta i hjärta* (Hearth in Hearth, 1980)—in which he continues the development toward discursive, prosaic simplicity with a form of poetic diary writing. *Dagbok* is a sequel of some three hundred short, numbered, and often dated entries spanning the period from August 1975 to April 1976. The opening part of *Dagbok* situates the writing in the midst of a personal crisis: "Jag talar nu så intensivt och / maniskt om min inre värld, eftersom / jag snart är övertygad om att / den inte finns längre, att jag snart / måste välja mellan en inre och en yttre / utplåning..." (I speak now so intensely and / maniacally about my inner world, since / I will soon be convinced that / it no longer exists, that I must soon / choose between an inner and an outer / obliteration...).

The texts are reports of the poet's everyday life with his family in a more autobiograhical, prosaic manner than before. As Norén later clarified in an interview with Lars Nylander in 1997, the personal stability he had gained after his adolescent crisis was for many years fragile, and he was constantly struggling against depression. The diary poems represent an effort to be more concretely self-observing than his earlier literature. They describe how he spends his days at home writing; how he shops, fetches his daughter from her daycare center, and meets friends, while all the time trying to maintain and strenghten his sense of reality and his relationship with his wife. Intertwined with these autobiographical reports are short, epigrammatic reflections on love, life, and politics:

> Först är jag
> särskild,
> avskild från
> någonting som
> sedan försvinner
> och aldrig upphör
>
> (At first I am
> distinct,
> detached from
> something that
> later disappears
> and never ceases)

By subjecting this diary writing to a radical form of compression and reduction, Norén, toward the end of the decade, approached the hermetic symbolism of Celan. *Order,* the first book of this nature, and seen by some critics as the best book of poetry Norén has ever written, consists of sequences, one or two pages in length, of semi-autonomous paragraphs. The opening reads:

> Jag går snabbt
> genom dörrarna av mörker
>
> Stenarna känner att skymningen kommer
>
> Men långsamma vingar piskar sig
> svanarna upp ur vattnet
> som ryker av köld
>
> Omänskligt kommer varje ord
> en lång väg
> sedan det slutligen mist sin mening
>
> (I walk swiftly
> through the doors of darkness
>
> The stones sense the arrival of dusk
>
> With slow wings the swans
> whip themselves up from the water
> steaming of cold
>
> Inhumanly each word comes
> a long way
> after finally having lost its meaning)

The following collections continue this discursive compression even further, resulting in an extremely dense, elliptical poetry, with a puristic focus on single words, expressions, and neologisms, as in the title *Murlod*.

Hjärta i hjärta once again signaled a change in direction and style, now returning to a more discursive form of poetry. Many of the poems approach the tradition of the hymn, some influenced by and alluding to the hymns of Friedrich Hölderlin. A more central influence is perhaps the late poetry of Gunnar Ekelöf, with its simple language and dialogic structure. In Norén's verse, this style becomes a philosophical and poetic augmentation of the structure of psychoanalytic dialogue as seen in this excerpt from *Hjärta i hjärta*:

> Du som är så van vid att aldrig återkomma,
> du vet väl att du alltid kommer tillbaka.
> Eller kunde du handla annorlunda när du var

annorlunda?–Jag var alldeles borta.
–Nej, du var alldeles hemma.
O, detta, förstumningen, att inte kunna svara då,
när du bara är svar, är den andra sidan av din
förlust . . .

(You who have made a habit of not returning,
you should know that you always return.
Or could you have acted differently when you were
different?–I was completely gone.
–No, you were completely at home.
O, this, the dumbness, not to be able to answer there,
where you are nothing but answer, the other side of your
loss . . .)

Instead of continuing in this new poetic direction, however, Norén decided to stop writing poetry altogether and turn to drama.

The composition of these poetry collections overlaps with Norén's writing of the dramas *Depressionen* (The Depression, performed on Sveriges Radio in 1979), *Dräneringen* (The Drainage, 1979; published in *Svenska radiopjäser 1979,* 1980), *Orestes* (published in *Tre skådespel,* 1980), *Akt utan nåd* (Act without Mercy, 1980; published in *Tre skådespel*), and *Modet att döda* (The Courage to Kill, 1980; published in *Tre skådespel*). He started to approach the naturalist form in these plays. In *Akt utan nåd* Norén returns to the basic character situation of his novels: a period in the life of a man, living on the margins of society, who has just lost his father and thereby the last support of his ungrounded identity. With *Modet att döda,* however, Norén took a more daring approach to this theme by staging a deadly confrontation between father and son.

While writing these plays in 1978, Norén received the unexpected news about his own father's death. The sudden collapse of the border between fiction and reality became something of a shock to him. One of the results of this event was that he started a psychoanalytic treatment, which was to last for some ten years. Another was that he discovered, in the detached subject position demanded by naturalist plays, a creative complement for this analytic experience, which made him decide to focus his writings entirely on drama.

Modet att döda, which was intended as a radio play but was first produced as a television drama broadcast in December 1980, has a strict naturalist frame and formal realism. The play is written in keeping with the iceberg technique, however, by which the realism is merely the visible part of the work, which is undercut by a strong, protomythic symbolism. The play depicts the final confrontation between a son and a father (named simply "the son" and "the father"). The father has never been able to act as one, and in the absence of any interpersonal, paternal principle, their relation has always been an unmediated rivalry, originally centered on the mother who has been dead for some years. The play shows how this overtly Oedipal rivalry once again springs forth during a visit that the father pays to his son, heightened by the presence of the son's girlfriend.

This dramatization of patricide was immediately complemented by a dramatization of matricide in *Orestes*. The darker, abyssal theme here evoked by Norén, who returns to the motif of the dying mother from his early poetry, is matched by the paraphrasing of antique tragedy in the play and its highly lyrical dialogue. The play follows broadly the story of Orestes' return to Argos and subsequent murder of his and Electra's mother, Clytemnestra. The central theme is modern man's illusory individualism in confrontation with the destiny given him by his place in a family and culture. Several passages in the play were imported directly from Norén's poetry of the time (primarily *Hjärta i hjärta*), a literal dramatization of his poetry that attested to his intention to turn from poetry to drama.

The series of plays that Norén wrote during the late 1970s laid the foundation for his subsequent supranaturalist plays–thirty-three plays between 1980 and 1995. He consolidated this form in *En fruktansvärd lycka* (A Terrible Happiness, 1981) and *Underjordens leende* (Smiles of the Netherworld, 1982). Both focus on couple relations, the former by placing two couples together for a night's party and the latter by depicting one couple. The vision that emerges of love and family life in Norén's own baby boom generation is that of highly dysfunctional, fragile relations. Tormented by internal conflicts and overwhelming emotional needs, the characters are as incapable of establishing any stable relations to each other as they are of separating.

The quartet form of the first play gives Norén opportunity to introduce the polyphonic dialogue technique, which–partly inspired by Chekhov, partly a continuation of his early dramatization of schizo-poetic automatism in *Box Ett*–became his dramatic hallmark. Several dialogic exchanges are going on simultaneously among the four characters in *En fruktansvärd lycka,* and reactions and responses to one person's statement, question, or provocation are often delayed while other exchanges take place. The technique was later further developed and made more complex, most notably in the play *Endagsvarelser* (One-Day Creatures), first performed in Kassel, Germany, in 1989 and published in a German-language edition that year.

The complexity of Norén's plays is, however, also an effect of the complexities of his characters and their manners of speaking. Rather than communicating with one another, they use language to try to provoke, evade, seduce, hurt, or trick, while at the same time trying out roles and poses for themselves. Talking thus turns into a desperate battle of word games, whose ironies, ambiguities, defensive cynicisms, and metalinguistic comments simultaneously hide and show the characters' excessive need for love and recognition. Tessa and Teo in *En fruktansvärd lycka* are the first of a long series of such "symbiotic" couples in Norén's dramas.

> *Teo:* Jag vet inte vad jag vill, det är därför jag vill dessa båda olika saker samtidigt!
> *Tessa:* Du är väldigt uttryckfull, men vad är det du uttrycker, kan man få veta det någon gång?
> *Teo:* Jag vill inte . . . Hur skall jag utan den älskade klä mig naken—hur skall jag—utan henne? Jag skulle vilja be dig: Rör mig aldrig mer . . . Vid varje beröring uppstår någonting hos mig som säger jag.—Har du tänkt att vi skall göra något särskilt ikväll?
>
> (*Teo:* I don't know what I want, that's why I want both these different things at the same time!
> *Tessa:* You're very articulate, but what is it you're articulating, could you some time tell me that?
> *Teo:* I don't want to . . . How could I undress without my loved one—How shall I—without her? I would like to ask you something: Never touch me again . . . With every touch something emerges from within me that says me.—Have you made any plans for us tonight?)

The complex dialogue and character psychology of Norén's plays puts high demands on actors, who have to clarify the inner alienation and constant ambiguities of the characters, while at the same time making them minimally understandable. In an interview with Magnus Florin for *Ord och Bild,* Norén described the characterization of the woman protagonist in *Underjordens leende* as "ultraparadoxala" (ultraparadoxical): "Elaine säger 'Nu ska jag gå hem och göra en massa saker som jag inte vill.' Men hon kanske *vill* det. Hon kanske inte *får* vilja det. Det finns en massa nyckelrepliker hela tiden som blir tydliga beroende på hur de spelas. Det ultraparadoxala, som finns med i alla pjäserna" (Elaine says "Now I'll go home and do a lot of things that I don't want to do." But perhaps she *wants* it. Perhaps she's not *allowed* to want it. There are a number of key lines throughout which are clarified by the way they are played. The ultraparadoxical, which can be found in all the plays). As in Chekhov, the dialogue technique in Norén's plays serves to illustrate a social situation of increasing solipsism, where communication, and the distinction between dialogue and monologue, is on the verge of complete breakdown. The technique projects an ideal of true, authentic communication as the utopian horizon against which all the confusion and inauthentic nature of modern life is measured.

Once this form had been established, Norén used it for what became his first big dramatic successes, *Natten är dagens mor* and *Kaos är granne med Gud,* published together in the volume *Tvā skådespel* (Two Plays, 1983). Taken together, the two represent a dramatic depiction and analysis of the author's turbulent family life during his adolescence, structured around his mental breakdown. The first play takes place shortly before the youngest son's breakdown, the second some time after, when he and his mother return for a last visit to the family home, he from the mental hospital and she from a cancer clinic. The naturalist form is punctuated by five short scenes in which the stage suddenly turns into a fantasy or dream space. Here Norén tries to capture the fantastic ideal identities of the characters as well as the underlying family structure in which they are all trapped—as when the macho ideal of the protagonist's older brother is depicted by an imaginary boxing match in which he is fighting with an erect penis; or when the family dances together and sings "Night and Day," impersonating a scene from a Fred Astaire musical.

Through this mixture of naturalist and fantastic techniques, Norén skillfully unveils the group psychology and dynamics of the family, primarily the defensive system that is maintained by the mother and the sons against the threat of the father's recurrent relapses into alcoholism. The play opens with the gradual outbreak of such a period, which coincides with the mother getting more sick with cancer, a situation that unleashes all the anxieties and conflicts that the family is organized to deny and check.

Throughout the 1980s Norén continued to use this drama form to depict the breakdown of intimate relations in modern times. Most plays use the quartet form, concretized as a family or as two couples together for a short period. Together, the series of plays make up a continuous associative chain, where one seems to raise questions and problems that serve as incitement for the next. In an interview with Lars Nylander published in Nylander's *Den långa vägen hem* (1997), Norén described the composition process for *Natten är dagens mor, Kaos är granne med Gud,* and his later completion of this story, the 1986 play *Stillheten* (Tranquillity), in those terms: "En uppsättning kan sätta igång tankar hos mig, att det är något annat jag vill berätta, att det var något annat som hände, något viktigare, egentligen" (A production can trigger thoughts in me, that there is something else that I want to tell, something else and more important that happened.) In this fashion, the serial principle that was enacted in Norén's early poetry is to some extent still maintained, on a broader level of relationships between formally autonomous works.

A special place among the quartet plays is held by the play Norén wrote about Eugene O'Neill, *Och ge oss skuggorna* (And Give Us the Shadows, 1991), created as a palimpsest of O'Neill's biographical family life and his play *Long Day's Journey into Night* (1956). The play triggered a series of similar family plays, set in a contemporary Swedish context, which all depict a couple and their two grown children, pushed together for a final confrontation over the scars left in them by a dysfunctional family life.

As the focus on intimate family relations in Norén's plays in the 1990s gave way to wider social and political contexts, the naturalist form has also started to open up. Several of the fourteen plays published in the four-volume edition *De döda pjäserna* (The Dead Plays, 1989–1994) have an international setting and characters: *Sterblich*, for example, takes place in a café "i Amsterdam ellor Bryssel ellor Paris" (in Amsterdam or Brussels or Paris); *Rumäner* (Rumanians) is set in a Manhattan hotel; and *Blod* is set in Paris. Further, those plays set in a Swedish environment have a more international set of characters, including immigrants and political refugees, while many of the Swedish characters seem more European than Swedish in their lifestyle and general outlook.

Some of these plays also mark a return to the freer form of Norén's first plays. An example is *Blod*, first performed in Copenhagen in November 1995, an Oedipal drama about a strife-ridden Chilean family, who in the 1970s escaped the persecution of the Augustus Pinochet regime and established a new life in Paris. The play spans a period of some months and takes place in different locations throughout Paris, combining epic, cinematic, and naturalist techniques.

As Norén has pushed his supranaturalist dramatic form toward the freer symbolist form of his earliest plays, he has also pushed it toward a more direct social and political context. Whatever the outcome of this shift in form and theme, Lars Norén, with his relentless creative energy, his dramatic mastery, and his sharp eye for the underlying psychosocial conflicts of modern culture, seems destined to remain at the center of Swedish theater, literature, and culture well into the twenty-first century.

Interviews:

Torkel Rasmusson and Leif Zern, "Förvandlingar av människan: Ur ett samtal med Lars Norén," *Bonniers Litterära Magasin*, 5 (1969): 348–355;

Gustaf-Adolf Mannberg, "En drömmares väg," in *Samtal med författare* (Stockholm: Rabén & Sjögren, 1971), pp. 49–53;

Magnus Florin, "Att komma hem i utplåningen," in *Dramaten: Swedish Royal Dramatic Theater Program for "Orestes"* (1979);

Florin, "Den nattliga festen. En intervju med Lars Norén," *Ord och Bild*, 1 (1983): 18–37;

Lars Nylander, "Samtal med Lars Norén (1994/95)," in his *Den långa vägen hem: Lars Noréns författarskap från poesi till dramatik* (Stockholm: Bonnier, 1997), pp. 348–359.

References:

Mangus Florin, "'Du måste förändra ditt liv': Anteckningar till Lars Noréns dramatik," *Bonniers Litterära Magasin*, 6 (1982): 379–391;

Tom Hedlund, "Lars Noréns 70-talspoesi–'en fruktansvärd nakenhet,'" in *Dikten som liv* (Stockholm: LiberFörlag, 1980), pp. 87–100;

Lars Nylander, *Den långa vägen hem: Lars Noréns författarskap från poesi till dramatik* (Stockholm: Bonnier, 1997);

Anders Olsson, "Orestes vid muren," in his *Mälden mellan stenarna: Litterära essäer* (Stockholm: Bonnier, 1981), pp. 37–60;

Suzanne Osten, "Att göra teater med Lars Norén," *Bonniers Litterära Magasin*, 6 (1982): 392–397;

Mikael van Reis, "Fadern och efeben: Lars Norén läser Artur Lundkvist," *Tidskrift för litteraturvetenskap*, 1 (1988): 63–80;

Reis, "Felsteget–Lars Noréns urscener i *Modet att döda*," in *Oidipus vid skiljevägen: Åtta essäer om existens, psyke och kultur*, edited by Mats Mogren and Ove Sernhede (Göteborg: Daidalos, 1993), pp. 83–111;

Reis, "Den omänskliga komedin," afterword to Norén's *De döda pjäserna*, volume 4 (Stockholm: Bonnier, 1995), pp. 253–281;

Reis, "Det slutna rummet: En essä om gränser hos Lars Norén," *Bonniers Litterära Magasin*, 1 (1988): 23–31;

Cecilia Sjöholm, *Föreställningar om det omedvetna: Stagnelius, Ekelöf, Norén* (Lund: Symposion, 1996);

Eva-Britta Ståhl, "Lösenord; broar: Anteckningar till Lars Noréns sena lyrik," *Tidskrift för litteraturvetenskap*, 1 (1995): 13–36;

Björn Sundberg, "'Att slå sönder den plats där det nya skall komma': Om Lars Noréns dramatik," in *Läskonst, skrivkonst, diktkonst*, edited by Per Hellström and Tore Wretö (Uppsala: Askelin & Hägglund, 1987), pp. 351–374;

Birgitta Trotzig, "Dödslinje–livslinje: Om kärleken i Lars Noréns poesi," *Bonniers Litterära Magasin*, 1 (1978): 16–24;

Jan Olov Ullén, "'Man, diktare, naken, förtivlad': Lars Norén, centrallyriker," *Bonniers Litterära Magasin*, 1 (1978): 3–12.

Agneta Pleijel
(26 February 1940 –)

Ebba Segerberg
University of California at Berkeley

BOOKS: *Ordning härskar i Berlin,* by Pleijel and Ronny Ambjörnsson (Stockholm: Bonnier, 1970);

Etiopien, Kenya, Tanzania, Zambia: Fyra resor, by Pleijel, Ambjörnsson, and others, 2 volumes (Göteborg: Författarförlaget, 1971);

Lycko-Lisa (Göteborg: TeaterManus, 1979);

Kollontay, by Pleijel and Alf Sjöberg (Stockholm: Norstedt, 1979);

Änglar, dvärgar (Stockholm: Norstedt, 1981);

Ögon ur en dröm (Stockholm: Norstedt, 1984); translated by Anne Born as *Eyes from a Dream* (London: Forest, 1991);

Sommarkvällar på jorden och Berget på månens baksida: två manuskript för teater och film (Stockholm: Norstedt, 1984); translated by Gunilla M. Anderman as *Summer Nights* in *New Swedish Plays,* edited by Anderman (Norwich: Norvik, 1992);

Vindspejare: Boken om Abel målaren (Stockholm: Norstedt, 1987); excerpts translated by Joan Tate as "He Who Observeth the Wind" in *Swedish Book Review,* 1 (1990);

Hundstjärnan (Stockholm: Norstedt, 1989); translated by Tate as *The Dog Star* (London: Peter Owen, 1991);

Fungi: En roman om kärleken (Stockholm: Norstedt, 1993);

Rut: En dramatisk berättelse i fem sånger (Stockholm: Verbum, 1994);

En vinter i Stockholm (Stockholm: Norstedt, 1997);

Lord Nevermore (Stockholm: Norstedt, 2000).

PLAY PRODUCTIONS: *Ordning härskar i Berlin,* by Pleijel and Ronny Ambjörnsson, Göteborg, Göteborgs stadsteater, 1969;

Fredag, by Pleijel and Ambjörnsson, Stockholm, Fickteatern, 1971;

Å, Göteborg, Göteborg, Folkteatern, 1973;

Herr von Hancken, adapted from a novel by Hjalmar Bergman, Stockholm, Stadsteatern, 1975;

Hej, du himlen! Göteborg, Folkteatern, 1977; adapted as *Kollontay,* Stockholm, Royal Dramatic Theatre, 1979;

Agneta Pleijel

Lycko-Lisa, Göteborg, Folkteatern, 1977;

Bättre och bättre dag för dag, Norrköping, Östgötascenen, 1981;

Sommarkvällar på jorden, Göteborg, Folkteatern, 1984;

När tiden började, Göteborg, Backateatern, 1990;

Rut: En hög visa, Helsinki, Kvinnoteaterfestivalen, 1994;

Standard Selection, Stockholm, Royal Dramatic Theatre, 2000.

PRODUCED SCRIPTS: *Berget på månens baksida,* motion picture, Sandrews, 1983;

Undanflykten, television, 1986;

Guldburen, television, 1991;

Gospodja Kolontaj, television, script by Pleijel and Ivana Vujic, Swedish television, 1996;

Gertrud, television, adaptation of a play by Hjalmar Söderberg, 1999;

OTHER: Zbigniew Herbert, *Rapport från en belägrad stad,* translation by Pleijel and Daniel Bronski (Stockholm: Bonnier, 1985).

Agneta Pleijel first established herself on the cultural scene as a critic at such daily newspapers as *Göteborgs Handels-och Sjöfartstidning* and *Kvällsposten,* as editor of the literary publication *Ord och Bild,* and most important, as the chief cultural editor of the then influential leftist evening paper *Aftonbladet.* More recently she has held the position of professor of drama at the Dramatic Institute in Stockholm from 1992 to 1996. She has also been chairman of the Swedish chapter of PEN. In light of such a long and distinguished career, Pleijel's challenge as a writer of fiction has in part been to develop a literary voice distinct from her critical writings. Her endeavors have resulted in some of the most interesting fiction to appear in contemporary Sweden. Pleijel's playwrighting and, above all, her prizewinning work as a novelist have made her one of Sweden's most respected and popular writers.

Agneta Pleijel was born in Stockholm on 26 February 1940 to Sonja Berg, a pianist and writer, and Åke Pleijel, a professor of mathematics. Pleijel's parents provided her with important but distinct intellectual influences: while her mother apprehended the world in emotional and subjective ways, her father responded to it as a scientist. Sonja Berg's unusual Swedish-Indonesian-Dutch background and frustrated artistic career are ingredients that readers repeatedly encounter in Pleijel's fiction. Her father's influence is perhaps most easily discernible in Pleijel's early academic interests. Åke Pleijel's career took Agneta, her mother, and her two younger sisters from Lund to Princeton University in 1947, to Stockholm the following year, and then back to Lund in 1952, where Pleijel graduated from high school in 1958. After studying theoretical philosophy at Lund University, Pleijel moved to University of Göteborg in 1960, where she undertook further studies in literature and ethnography. These studies led to an advanced predoctoral degree in 1971, for which she wrote a thesis on the author Rudolf Värnlund. While still a student, Pleijel began publishing literary criticism. Her first plays were written in the late 1960s and early 1970s, influenced by the socialist student politics of the day. Pleijel had her only child, Lina Pleijel, in 1970 with psychoanalyst Lars Sjögren. At the present time she is married to journalist Maciej Zaremba and lives in Stockholm.

Pleijel's oeuvre encompasses many variations in form and genre, but tends nonetheless to cluster around a series of recurring themes. Foremost among these themes is the problem of artistic and individual self-realization. Because her writing has so often centered on unusual and compelling female characters, this emphasis of self-realization has often been attributed to an interest in specifically woman-centered and feminist issues. Although the female experience is a central theme in her work, it is important to note in this context that Pleijel concentrates on the plight of the creative and intellectual woman rather than proposing to explore a more general constellation of issues pertaining to women as a whole. A committed socialist conviction colors her early work, although the problems of the creative individual compete with the big social questions even in the early and most overtly political plays.

While active as a journalist and cultural critic in the late 1960s and throughout the 1970s, Pleijel produced plays with an explicit socialist agenda. Although reducing these plays to one theme does not do them full justice, one can sense a mounting tension in Pleijel's work at this time between political criticism and explorations of the creative drive. From *Ordning härskar i Berlin* (Order Reigns in Berlin) in 1970 to *Kollontay* in 1979, to mention two of the most important examples, the explicitly political eventually comes to give way to the more abstract theme of individual and artistic expression. *Ordning härskar i Berlin,* written with Ronny Ambjörnsson, depicts the trial of the alleged murderers of communist agitators Karl Liebknecht and Rosa Luxemburg that resulted in the stifling of revolutionary action in Weimar Germany. Although *Ordning härskar i Berlin* received a great deal of critical attention, *Kollontay,* first performed and published under the title *Hej, du himlen!* (Hello, Heaven! 1977)–a name taken from a poem by Vladimir Mayakovsky–marked a professional breakthrough for Pleijel. It was performed to great acclaim at the prestigious Royal Dramatic Theater in Stockholm under the direction of Alf Sjöberg. Sjöberg favored the political analysis in the piece, focusing on the criticism of Soviet Communism. In Pleijel's original script, and in the first production of the play, however, the theme of individual choice emerges more strongly. In *Hej, du himlen!* the social commentary unfolds by way of Alexandra Kollontay's acutely personal experience of being caught between the idealistic convictions of her revolutionary youth and the pragmatic corruption of party politics in the ensuing years.

By 1980 Pleijel had left her journalistic work behind and had devoted herself exclusively to her literary career. While she continued to write plays, she

Scene from Pleijel's 1979 play Kollontay, *about the Russian revolutionary and later Soviet ambassador to Finland, Alexandra Kollontay (photograph by Beata Bergström; Drottningholms Teatermuseum, Stockholm)*

began writing screenplays as well as television dramas on such topics as Sweden's treatment of refugees from Nazi Germany and Swedish social bureaucracy. Motion pictures such as *Berget på månens baksida* (The Mountain on the Dark Side of the Moon, 1983), for which she wrote the screenplay, clearly indicate that the artistic priorities she displayed in the early 1970s were evolving. Like *Kollontay, Berget på månens baksida* also tells the story of an intellectual Russian woman, the mathematician Sonja Kovalevsky. Offered a professorship in Stockholm at a time when no other European universities would accept women scholars, Kovalevsky spent the last part of her short life in Sweden. In Pleijel's screenplay Kovalevsky is placed in the classic intellectual woman's dilemma: trapped between her commitment to her work and the man she loves. *Berget på månens baksida* is in part a statement on the difficulty of achieving recognition for women involved in intellectual careers; as Kovalevsky comments, all her work may only result in having a mountain on the dark side of the moon named after her. Larger than the issue of social injustice loom the more personal problems associated with love, however. By stressing the intensity of Kovalevsky's obsession with mathematics, Pleijel sympathetically illuminates the difficulties of her relationships with her lover and her daughter. Kovalevsky's struggles are thus presented in light of the universal problem of balancing human relationships and a creative life.

With the publication of her first collection of poetry in 1981, Pleijel took a further step in exploring the issues of stifled creativity and self-expression that she had first sought to illuminate through her dramatic work. She has often called the writing of these poems a linguistic and emotional turning point in her development as a writer. In the first collection, *Änglar, dvärgar* (Angels, Dwarves, 1981), Pleijel works with dreams as well as archetypal myths. The two main characters that appear are fairy-tale figures: the lofty realm of thought inhabited by and represented by the Princess is pitted against the forceful and unwelcome demands of the earthly Dwarf. *Änglar, dvärgar* is also notable for a section called "Fiskbarn" (Fish-child) that prefigures the autobiographical material of Pleijel's novel *Vindspejare: Boken om Abel målaren* (The One Who Watches the Wind: A Book about Abel the Painter, 1987; translated in part as "He Who Observeth the Wind," 1990). The later collection of poetry *Ögon ur en dröm* (1984; translated as *Eyes from a Dream,* 1991) links such autobiographical gestures to the creative process. In the poem "Morgon" (Morning) from this latter collection, the speaker maintains that "Jag försöker bygga en biografi åt mig / för att åtminstone ha någonstans att bo / tillfälligtvis, i väntan på bättre tider" (I tried to build a biography for myself / to at least have somewhere to live / temporarily, while waiting for better times). The autobiographical impulse must thus be seen from the larger perspective of creating order out of chaos, if only for the moment, a sentiment that is typical of Pleijel's work.

A strong preoccupation with the visual is also apparent in Pleijel's poetic collections, something that continues to color her later ventures in prose. Her poems not only take different forms, such as in the series of three sonnets in *Ögon ur en dröm,* but also are often arranged in eye-catching patterns on the page. Some poems appear in the paragraph form, for example, while others appear in arrangements of clustered lines. These visual effects help establish the emotional tone of the poems from the start.

In 1987 Pleijel debuted as a novelist with the semi-autobiographical *Vindspejare.* This much-acclaimed novel deals with the author's maternal grandfather, Abel Berg, who lived in Indonesia for many years before returning to Sweden with his Dutch-Indonesian wife and children. Thematically, the novel circles around the issue of creative frustration. Starting with Abel, one person in each generation struggles with the legacy of a strong artistic drive. Si, a character based on Pleijel's mother, is a talented musician who, despite remarkable bravery in her bout with polio and its crippling aftereffects, remains bitterly fixated on her artistic shortcomings. Si mulled over "det andra, över att inte duga för musiken, över att inte kunna skriva som hon ville, över att inte kunna hantera kraften i sig–över det har hon klagat i hela sitt liv" (the other, about not being good enough for her music, about not being able to write as she wished, about not being able to manage the power within her–about this she has complained her whole life). The difficulties of writing emerge even more strongly in the reflective passages that accompany the gradual uncovering of this generational tale.

Like her poetry, the novel testifies to Pleijel's attempt at this time to reach beyond the rational dimensions of language. As she writes in *Vindspejare:* "Sanningen finns inte i ordet men kanske i gesten. Därför dramatiken och inte prosan. Därför lyriken och inte romanen. En dikt är en gest vars hela strävan är att ge utrymme åt det som inte kan sägas" (Truth is not to be found in the word but perhaps in the gesture. Therefore drama and not prose. Therefore poetry and not the novel. A poem is a gesture whose striving is to give room to that which cannot be expressed). While this

Dust jacket for Pleijel's 1987 novel, in which two of the characters are based on her maternal grandfather and her mother

passage would seem to speak against Pleijel's decision to turn from poetry to prose, it helps explain the experimental approach of her first novel. *Vindspejare* was written, like her poetry, from the desire to create something for herself after her many years of work as a journalist. The improvisational and exploratory nature of the narrative marks this new phase in Pleijel's oeuvre. The search for family stories testifies to a search for identity that exceeds the genealogical project at hand.

Vindspejare was followed by *Hundstjärnan* (1989; translated as *The Dog Star,* 1991), a spare tale of a girl experiencing puberty and dealing with a variety of incestuous networks in her family life. With its disturbing subject matter and troubled characters, this is a more difficult novel than *Vindspejare.* Pleijel's relentless and powerful exploration of loss and identity in *Hundstjärnan* can, however, be seen as a development of themes from her earlier novel. Like the narrator of *Vindspejare,* the young protagonist of *Hundstjärnan* has embarked on a similar journey of self-creation through the artistic process. As she says, "Jag finns i berät-

Dust jacket for Pleijel's 1989 novel, about a teenage girl's search for identity (from Swedish Book Review, *1987)*

telserna och historierna som jag själv skapar" (I exist in the tales and stories that I myself create). She admits that her project of self-creation is challenged not only by the world around her, but also by her changing and unfamiliar body. Central to an understanding of this novel is an anecdote the protagonist relates regarding a dog with a hole in its throat as the result of scientific experiment. The dog is unable to consume a sliver of meat however many times it swallows the piece. Similarly, the protagonist attempts to make sense of her world, to find nourishment from her experiences rather than seeing them as an endless series of confrontations with indigestible facts. This idea again echoes a passage in *Vindspejare,* in which the narrator comments on the consuming nature of her biographical search. Describing a Hindu practice of leaving food out for one's ancestors, Pleijel stresses the commonsensical act of eating this same offering the following day: "Hinduerna äter därefter nästa dag, om de är hungriga, upp förfädernas mat. Jag gör detsamma" (The Hindus, if they are hungry, eat the ancestors' food the following day. I do the same). Her exploration of the past, Pleijel suggests, is not only a way to give homage to her ancestors but simultaneously a way she has found of feeding herself.

In Pleijel's next novel, *Fungi: En roman om Kärleken* (1993), she becomes more overtly philosophical, taking issue in particular with the cultural pessimism promulgated by Arthur Schopenhauer. Pleijel here returns to the Javanese landscape of *Vindspejare.* In opposition to the tentatively exploratory nature of that work, however, *Fungi* exhibits a more compact narrative form. Pleijel bases her novel on the real-life figure of the young scientist and Schopenhauer disciple Franz Wilhelm Junghuhn, whose lyrical description of the dignity of sea turtles slaughtered on their way to lay their eggs can be found in a footnote in Schopenhauer's *Die Welt als Willie und vorstellung* (The World as Will and Idea, 1818). The title, *Fungi,* comes from Junghuhn's fascination with mushrooms, organisms that he perceives to live in greater connection with each other and their environment than their individual appendages above the earth would suggest. This picture of interconnectedness holds great appeal for the rather lost young man, who ends up breaking with the pessimistic philosophical convictions of his master in favor of a holistic and life-affirming worldview.

Pleijel's 1997 novel *En vinter i Stockholm* (A Winter in Stockholm) concentrates on the subject of romantic love, specifically on the difficulties of an intellectual woman who expects both too little and too much from her relationships. In attempting to use writing to get through the first hundred days following the end of her marriage, the protagonist engages in a process of healing and self-discovery. In a state of depression that seems to afford a special mental clarity, she considers the complex relationships that have constituted her life thus far: with her feuding parents, with her string of noncommittal lovers, with her daughter and only child. There is little lamentation in this book; the protagonist sees her part in these developments all too plainly–at risk of taking on too much blame. She wishes she had more children, a recurring motif that in a larger sense mirrors her desire to create a richer sense of self.

The narrator's search for meaning and identity is also reflected through the intermittent setting off of words from the rest of the text in bold typeface. The process is reminiscent of Pleijel's visual experiments in poetry. Although it is not always the most central words that are culled from a given passage, the gesture suggests a desire to get beyond the frustrating impenetrability of language by randomly abstracting these words from the text. Although they sometimes draw attention to important ideas, the extracted words do not magically clarify the protagonist's situation, however. There are no easy answers for the questions she poses. As with Pleijel's other works, the tone of subtle optimism achieved by the end of the novel comes only at the cost of considerable suffering.

Pleijel's production presents a mix of contradictory elements. Frequently autobiographical without fitting neatly into the confessional tradition of women's writing common in the 1970s and 1980s in Sweden, strongly intellectual yet continually seeking to reach beyond a rationalistic framework, Pleijel's strengths as an author lie in her willingness to try new approaches in her quest to approximate the gestures of truth. Her belief in the communicative power of stories is the quality readers have found most inspiring. "Vi lever i en så splittrad värld" (We live in such a fragmented world), she said in a 31 July 1993 interview in *Dagens Nyheter*, "vissa förlopp . . . måste berättas fra, för att förstås" (certain events . . . must be narrated forth to be understood). Agneta Pleijel's central concerns regarding the value of narrative for the identity of her self-scrutinizing protagonists speak both to the individual and society. Her emphasis on the value of narrative coherence is a timely and important lesson for readers in the increasingly incomprehensible chaos of the information age.

Interviews:

Petra Broomans, "The Hidden Power of Creativity: Agneta Pleijel the Writer and Abel the Painter," *Scandinavian Newsletter*, 5 (1990): 26–27.

References:

Gunilla M. Anderman, Introduction to Pleijel's *Summer Nights*, translated by Anderman, in *New Swedish Plays*, edited by Anderman (Norwich, U.K.: Norvik, 1992), pp. 26–28;

Helena Forsås-Scott, "Experimentation and Innovation," in her *Swedish Women's Writing 1850–1995* (London & Atlantic Highlands, N.J.: Athalone, 1997), pp. 243–248;

Laurie Thompson, "Introducing Agneta Pleijel," *Swedish Book Review*, 1 (1990): 2–4.

Göran Sonnevi

(3 October 1939 –   )

Kevin Karlin
University of Washington

BOOKS: *Outfört* (Stockholm: Bonnier, 1961);
Abstrakta dikter (Stockholm: Bonnier, 1963);
ingrepp-modeller (Stockholm: Bonnier, 1965);
och nu! (Stockholm: Bonnier, 1967);
Det gäller oss: Dikter 1959–1968 (Stockholm: Bonnier, 1969);
Det måste gå (Stockholm: Bonnier, 1970);
Det oavslutade språket (Stockholm: Bonnier, 1972);
Dikter 1959–1972 (Stockholm: Aldus/Bonnier, 1974); revised (Stockholm: Bonnier, 1981);
Det omöjliga (Stockholm: Bonnier, 1975);
Språk; Verktyg; Eld (Stockholm: Bonnier, 1979);
Små klanger; en röst (Stockholm: Bonnier, 1981);
Dikter utan ordning (Stockholm: Bonnier, 1983);
Oavslutade dikter (Stockholm: Bonnier, 1987);
Trädet (Stockholm: Bonnier, 1991);
Framför ordens väggar: dikter i översättning 1959–1992 (Stockholm: Bonnier, 1992);
Mozarts Tredje Hjärna (Stockholm: Bonnier, 1996);
Klangernas Bok (Stockholm: Bonnier, 1998).

Editions in English: *The Economy Spinning Faster and Faster: Poems by Göran Sonnevi*, translated and edited by Robert Bly (New York: Sun, 1982);
Göran Sonnevi: Poetry in Translation, translated by Cynthia Hogue, Jan Karlsson, John Matthias, and Göran Printz-Påhlson (Gothenburg: Swedish Books, 1982);
A Child Is Not a Knife: Selected Poems of Göran Sonnevi, translated and edited by Rika Lesser (Princeton: Princeton University Press, 1993).

OTHER: Excerpt in *Modern Swedish Poetry in Translation*, excerpt translated by Robert Bly, edited by Gunnar Harding and Anselm Hollo (Minneapolis: University of Minnesota Press, 1979), pp. 215–233;
Excerpt in *Contemporary Swedish Poetry,* edited by John Matthias and Göran Printz-Påhlson (Chicago: Swallow, 1980), pp. 65–79.

Göran Sonnevi's breakthrough came with the publication of his poem "Om kriget i Vietnam" (On the War

Göran Sonnevi (from the cover for The Economy Spinning Faster and Faster, *1982)*

in Vietnam) in 1965. Virtually overnight his name became a household word in Sweden, and the poem served there as a catalyst for the debate over U.S. involvement in Vietnam. The nature of his achievement becomes evident when one considers how much time had passed since the genre of poetry had such influence on the general public; to find a precedent one must return to neo-Romanticism and perhaps even to Romanticism. Traditionally, the literary genres most conducive to social criticism are drama and the novel; thus, to a great extent Sonnevi changed the paradigm with "Om kriget i Vietnam." His productivity during the subsequent years shows that, of the poets who came of age in the 1960s, his work arguably ranks as the most influential.

Sonnevi was born on 3 October 1939 in Jakobsberg, Sweden, though he spent his childhood in Halmstad. His parents were Bror Göransson and Maj Johansson Göransson. Bror owned a small business but died when Sonnevi was eleven years old, leaving him to be raised by his mother and grandmother. His family had ties to the land inasmuch as his grandfather owned a small farm. In school he was an average student and received poor grades, particularly in essay writing. In retrospect, many of his problems in school stemmed from his tendency to stutter; as a boy Sonnevi took longer than others to express his ideas in conversation, and he always risked being interrupted before completing his thought because he talked so slowly. As a result, verbal articulation presented a constant challenge. Much of the time he did not use words with difficult pronunciations and instead sought synonyms with exactly the same meanings. Sonnevi's incessant awareness of word usage in communication is key, for it instilled in him an exceptional respect for language. His future linguistic consciousness as a poet no doubt originated in his search as a stuttering child for the appropriate word.

When he attended junior high school, his interests gravitated toward the natural sciences and mathematics. He was particularly fond of chemistry and loved working on experiments in the laboratory. He worked for one summer in the laboratory at the Halmstad ironworks. He was planning to pursue studies in chemical engineering until the occurrence of a pivotal event in his final term in "realskola" (secondary modern school), somewhat comparable to junior high school in the United States. His class read William Shakespeare's *The Tempest,* and his first experience with Shakespeare's language transformed Sonnevi's life. The next year, his first in high school, he began to write essays constantly, and with the help of a Swedish-language teacher he overcame his difficulties of self-expression. In the next few years he read obsessively and began to write poetry.

After he graduated from high school, he entered the University of Lund. Not knowing what else to do, he began taking courses in literary history, which gave him the chance to continue his study of poetry. He also participated in the literary club at Lund and met others with similar aspirations. Two significant events occurred during his time at the university: Sonnevi's first collection of verse, *Outfört* (Unrealized, 1961), was published, and on 5 August 1961 he married Kerstin Kronvist. Even as he prepared for exams, he read extensively on the subjects of art history, philosophy, and theology.

Once he finished at the University of Lund, receiving his degree in Literary Studies, Sonnevi had to come to terms with the practical issue of choosing a career. Above all, he needed a job that not only provided for his means of living but also allowed him to continue his literary research. He chose to attend a course in library science in Stockholm in 1966, rationalizing that a job as a librarian would help him maintain close contact with literature. While attending this course he settled in Järfälla, a town outside of Stockholm, where he has since lived and written. In the end, however, Sonnevi did not become a librarian. His marriage to Kerstin, who was by this time working at a hospital, allowed him to assume the role of a househusband and to devote much of his time to his art. A typical working day for Sonnevi includes several hours of reading, listening to music, improvisation on the piano, a walk, and several hours devoted to writing his poetry.

The general impression one receives from examples of Sonnevi's poetry from different periods is that they are related parts of a larger project; even excerpts selected from periods of significant and fundamental change in his worldview exhibit this interrelated characteristic. This quality is a natural consequence of his notion of an "oavslutade" (unfinished) process of poetic creation. Another feature of his poetics is his charging of his lyrics with tension, a feat he accomplishes through his treatment of binary opposites. One member of a dyad is always shown, in the tradition of Gunnar Ekelöf, to transform itself into its own opposite. This transformation occurs within a small textual space and thus the binary opposites are brought into close proximity, which creates the intense compression that characterizes Sonnevi's work. As Anders Olsen maintains in "Mälden mellan stenarna," this process of transformation—what he terms "betydelseglidning" (slippage of meaning)—is the key to understanding Sonnevi's art. Olsen's understanding of the process of change as slippage is significant, because, like Friedrich Hölderlin, Sonnevi conceives of poetry, according to Torsten Ekbom in *Dagens Nyheter* (16 October 1970), as "the art of naming things by their proper names." If the poet sets about the task of contemplating the proper name for something, then "betydelseglidning" must be considered in the process of naming. An example of this transformation is the following except from *Dikter utan ordning* (Poems without Order, 1983):

Jag ska krossa din makt över andra
vem du än är
Jag ska krossa
allas makt över andra
vilka de än är

(I will crush your power over others
whoever you are

I will crush
everyone's power over others
whoever they are)

The "I" of the poem threatens to crush anyone's power over another and logically becomes the object of his own threat. He is thus transformed into his own binary opposite.

Sonnevi is also known for making "un-poetic" word choices in his verse—words he has culled largely from his explorations into the fields of linguistics, philosophy, mathematics, and the natural sciences. These terms—for example, "infinitesimal storhet" (singularity) and "asymtot" (asymtote), from mathematics, "entropi" (entropy), from physics, "kovalent" (covalent), from chemistry, and "ontologi" (ontology), from philosophy—lend a character of distance or objectivity to his work. Someone accustomed to conventional poetic diction might find such terms halting, clumsy, or simply out of place, whereas to the experienced reader of Sonnevi's work they compose a distinctive and highly developed "word melody" that has a precedent in another art form, jazz, for which the poet harbors a passion. His relaxed, free approach to self-expression was especially evident in his response once to a question about the proper tempo and rhythm for reading his poems; Sonnevi answered that he sees a wide latitude for interpreting his verse, and that how one reads his poetry ultimately depends on the situation and the feelings of the reader.

The verses of Sonnevi's first two poetry volumes, *Outfört* and *Abstrakta dikter* (Abstract Poems, 1963), are characterized by short line length, a high degree of compression, and an elegiac quality. Two extremely different poetic traditions that influenced Sonnevi's work and are essential to understanding it are abstractionism and concretism. The impact of abstractionism appears in the first poem from *Outfört*, "Bottenläge" (Lowest Point):

Nästan ingenting–

Varsamhet.

Dess klang.

Också frågor är möjliga.

(Almost nothing–

Care.

Its sound.

Also questions are possible.)

In the other tradition, concretism, strong sensory imagery and the directness of language are emphasized. The poem "Sjö och tynstand" (Lake and Silence), also from *Outfört*, illustrates such a concrete style:

Det sägs ibland, mycket tyst
att om hösten sjunker svalorna
mot insjöns botten.
Där är allt tyst.

–Går de in i sin sömn?
–Drömmer de?
–I det mörka vattnet såg jag
De ljusa vingarna

(It is sometimes said, very quietly
that in the autumn the swallows sink
to the lake's bottom.
There all is quiet.

–Do they go into their sleep?
–Do they dream?
–In the dark water I saw
Those light wings)

Critics have compared the word melodies of these early poems to the melodies of Vilhelm Ekelund's verse. The duality of abstractionism and concretism is key in Sonnevi's early poetry because in later works he increasingly melds these polar opposites, and they eventually become the mechanism by which he charges his poems with tension.

The next few verse collections include his breakthrough work, *ingrepp-modeller* (Intervention-Models, 1965), as well as *och nu!* (And Now! 1967) and *Det måste gå* (It Must Work, 1970). A sharp polemical nature, which continued as a major trait of Sonnevi's verse from this point forward, marks the poem that brought him immediate fame, "Om Kriget i Vietnam," collected in *ingrepp-modeller*. He achieves the sharp or harsh tone through his use of the abstract-concrete opposition, which reveals the public-private opposition inherent in almost all polemical discourse. In poems where his object is to highlight intellectual questions and personal freedom, Sonnevi turns to abstractionism, as seen in "Frågor" (Questions) from *ingrepp-modeller*:

a

Där jag tänker mig siffror
ser jag hela tiden
frågetecken!
Det flyger bolmande
ur en stor krater–Vad
betyder detta, och
vad är det som hindrar oss att tänka?

Cover for an English translation of poems by Sonnevi (Bruccoli Clark Layman Archives)

b

Allt talar—statistiskt sett—
för
att den olyckan
inte kan undvikas.
Varför går vi
då, bokstavligt talat,
utan paraply som det bara regnade?

(a

Where I imagine numbers
I always see
question-marks!
Belching smoke emerges
out of a great crater—What
does it mean, and
what is it that hinders us from thinking?

b

Everything speaks—seen statistically—
be-

cause the misfortune
cannot be avoided.
Why do we go
then, literally spoken,
without an umbrella as if it only rained?)

When Sonnevi wishes to make a polemical point, however, he switches to concretism—to familiar, everyday language—and thus conveys an immediacy or urgency, as in the well-known "Exempel" (Example), collected in *ingrepp-modeller:*

Dag efter dag
hör jag den genomträngande
tonen från ALFA LAVAL
Den hörs svagt
uppblandad med trafikljud
från genomfartsleden,
. . . .
Det har sagts mig
att ALFA LAVAL investerar
i Sydafrikas
svarta arbetskraft!

Misstankan att detta är sant
gör mig dels rasande
dels ohjälpligt försjunken
. . . .
Dygnet runt ligger
det durande metalljudet från fabriken
som ett band kring pannan
Det följer mig
nog vart jag förflyttar mig

(Day after day
I hear the penetrating
tone from ALFA LAVAL
It sounds weak
mixed with the traffic noise
from the arterial,
. . . .
I have been told
that ALFA LAVAL invests
in South Africa's
black workforce!
Suspecting that it is true
makes me partly enraged
partly depressed
. . . .
All day that droning
metallic sound from the factory lies
like a band around my forehead
It follows me
no matter where I go)

Another significant poem from this period is "Vad förmar-kärlekens strukturer," which appeared in *och nu!*, which embodies the seed of the central project of Sonnevi's long poem phase. "För, bland andra, Noam Chomsky" explores the implications of the linguist's ideas on universal grammar. For Chomsky, language competency constitutes an inborn trait of humans that naturally unfolds within an individual's development. Sonnevi sees language as the basic building block of social organization; as such, language lends itself to analogy with the project of revolutionary socialism. In light of this analogy and Chomsky's rationalist view of language, Sonnevi makes a convincing argument that revolutionary socialism is a process that unfolds in the development of the individual. He hoped to show that this process would lead to a socialism in which the maximum degree of individual freedom could be attained.

The collection *Det måste gå* is important as a transitional work during this period—the early 1970s—since it displays poems with an altered tone, and Sonnevi decidedly shifts in theme from the private to the political. He alters his tone by refraining from descriptions of his own feelings and instead depicting the conditions in which victims of political injustice are forced to exist. The poem "För Att Förstå" (In Order To Understand) is particularly noteworthy; it describes the events and impressions of the student demonstrations that occurred in Stockholm in May 1968, when students successfully occupied a university building. In "För Att Förstå" the poet uses the image of a bat, which is characterized by blindness and often signifies human consciousness in literature. Compensating for its blindness by evolving a form of echolocation, the bat suggests Sonnevi's hope that human consciousness will evolve a similar sensory organ that will overcome man's blindness to oppression.

After *Det måste gå* Sonnevi entered his long poem phase, which comprises *Det oavslutade språket* (The Unfinished Language, 1972), his magnum opus *Det omöjliga* (The Impossible, 1975), and *Språk; Verktyg; Eld* (Language; Tools; Fire, 1979). Each of these works includes a lengthy title poem that dominates its respective volume and cultivates Sonnevi's ideas regarding the program of revolutionary socialism. Of the three collections, *Det oavslutade språket* is the least ambitious in terms of scale. The name of its long title poem alludes to Sonnevi's idea of linking theories of language acquisition to a naturalistic theory of socialism. Although "Det oavslutade språket" lies at the center of the collection, one of the most significant poems is "Stora grupper av människor" (Large Groups of People) because it anticipates much of what is later known as the theory of interpretive communities.

The collection *Det omöjliga* stands as the magnum opus in Sonnevi's works of socialist polemic. The title poem dominates more than half of the length of the book, while much of the rest of the collection is devoted to the two parts of its other long poem, "Mozartvariationer" (Mozart Variations), in which he explores music as an intensified experience of life rather than as an escape from it. Because Sonnevi grounds his abstractions in the concrete reality of the senses, the poems of this collection accordingly reflect a sense of immediacy. The lines below from *Det omöjliga* capture the intensely charged nature of his poems in this collection:

Krossa det omöjliga!

Det finns
där, och vi kommer inte undan
. . . .
Också inne i
kropparnas
byggnader
Varelsernas
liv genom historien
bortanför

allt, innanför
allt
Krossa det flytande omöjliga!
Krossa klippan
mot barnet!

(Crush the impossible!
It is
there, and we can't escape
. . . .
Also in
the structures
of the body
The life
of beings through history
beyond
all, within
all

Crush the floating impossible!
Crush the cliff
against the child!)

These lines not only exemplify a characteristic pairing of opposites—such as the opposition between "verklighet" (reality) and "omöjliga" (impossible)—but also reveal Sonnevi's struggle against hierarchical forms. Elsewhere in the collection he uses abstract imagery to heighten the compression of juxtaposed opposites, such as the mathematical concept of singularity, in which value becomes infinite at an infinitesimally small point. He also employs color in the volume in a symbolic way—as in the use of black and white to signify life and death, which reverses the traditional association of white for life and black for death. For Sonnevi, white recalls both the flash that happens upon the detonation of a nuclear warhead and the annihilation that follows, while black represents the trace of life left in the wake of the blast by nuclear shadows. He concludes the collection with the image of a rose:

rosen av människa

rosen of eld
Den öppnar sig virvlande
med ett
kronblad för
varje människa

Vart och ett
av rosens blad
har samma namn

(the rose of man

the rose of fire
It opens itself whirling
with a
petal for every man

Each and every one
of the rose's leaves
have the same name)

The rose symbolizes the natural unfolding of socialism and freedom within each individual.

This symbol also plays a central role in Sonnevi's next work, *Språk; Verktyg; Eld*. Sonnevi's concern with the socialist movement, portrayed in the previous volume, continues in the 1979 collection, as does the search for the structure of existence. Yet, whereas a hopeful tone infuses *Det omöjliga,* the tone of *Språk; Verktyg; Eld* is undoubtedly darker and results from the poet's clear-eyed view of life after the Vietnam War, especially as he addresses crimes committed against humanity:

Och existensen
av folkmordets faktum
Vi kan inte dölja oss
i serien av folkmord
Namnen, alla namen
Socialismens namn, alla de
mänskliga namnen
Vem har tagit bort dig?
Ditt namn / är också borta
I Kampuchea är en million namn
borta, finns inte
ens registrerade

(And the existence
of the fact of genocide
We cannot hide ourselves
in the series of genocide
Names, all names
the name of Socialism, all those
human names
Who has erased you?
Your name
is also gone
In Kampuchea a million names are
gone, are not
even registered)

Moreover, in a language of visionary mysticism, he describes in the volume certain changes in the political climate that led to the defeat of the socialist movement in the late 1970s. The alchemistic references of the title in particular evidence this mysticism. Sonnevi warns that as with the alchemists, people's knowledge of technology exceeds their ethical knowledge of its application, and such excess could lead to the ultimate disaster, the destruction of the world. Finally, Sonnevi uses language in *Språk; Verktyg; Eld* as a tool with which to create a lyrical love poem—a use born out by his own admission that his basic relation to language is erotic. In order to bring this project to fruition, Sonnevi realizes he must abandon his old notion of grammar, with its roots in the entrenched social power structure. As a result, he begins to distance himself from the Chomskian concept of his earlier period in favor of a scheme that allows more syntactic freedom.

Sonnevi's next poetry volume, *Små klanger; en röst* (1981), is unquestionably his most controversial work, which generated, upon its release, widespread critical disagreement regarding its aesthetic and ideological change of direction. The collection consists of fifty unrhymed sonnets that are designated with Roman numerals. This organization, combined with Sonnevi's characteristic broken rhythm and the new use of enjambment in the collection, gives the work a level of stridency unmatched by any of his earlier collections. Though the syncopation of his word rhythm is still present, the improvised quality of his earlier works is gone. Rather, the poetry is intensely compressed and charged to an extent unrivaled by any other work in Swedish poetry. He separates his thoughts by employing unusually long spaces and, occasionally, an exclamation point, in this way rendering a meaning that stands out more than usual. The hope and enthusiasm of his earlier works is also absent, replaced by unmediated angst over the threat of nuclear annihilation, the treachery inherent in human relations, the despair over the failure of socialism, and doubts about our continued survival, as seen in the excerpt below from "XXXVI":

> Också jag har del av den inre ut-
> plåningsprocessen Samhället vi går
> in i alltmera upplöst, alltmera
> försvunnet Om jag då gene-
> raliserar detta Tar språnget till
> utplåningens samhälle
> . . . .
> Det finns inget alternativ
> Vi ska se denna process i ögonen
> Också med förstenade ögon ska vi se
> varandra Det finns ingen läkedom
> Vi ser de inre hjärtats utplåning
> Vi ser våra kroppars förintade bilder
>
> (Also I have part of that inner de-
> struction's process The society we step
> into is increasingly dissipated, increasingly
> vanished If I then gen-
> eralize it Take the leap to
> the society of annihilation
> . . . .
> There is no alternative
> We will look that process in the eye
> Also with fixed eyes we will see
> each other There is no cure
> We see the annihilation of the inner heart
> We see the disintegrated images of our bodies)

As this excerpt makes evident, a marked bias toward the abstract supplants the balance between concrete and abstract that was typical of Sonnevi's earlier works. By the early 1980s he had also abandoned his idea of the individual as a prototype of the universe in microcosm, and his shift away from the notion that language models reality is also intrinsic to his rejection of this idea. Thus, his earlier hope that life can triumph over the force of entropy is no longer viable. Sonnevi accepts for the first time the inevitability of dissolution and, more importantly, addresses his readers' exhaustion with the struggle against dissolution. On the other hand, he relates that although language can no longer serve as a model for reality, it is made up of the stuff of reality, and he implies that one can use language to shape reality. One may use language to strengthen current power structures, or alternatively, to break them up. Therefore, each new act of language use opens up a new possibility—whether creation or annihilation, or hope or despair, all created from the same source.

After 1980 Sonnevi's poetry becomes increasingly difficult to treat in terms of stylistic periods. The rate and scope of experimentation with new styles and organizational schemes accelerate and broaden dramatically and are not as temporally linear. Thus, although a seventeen-year gap separates the publication of the books, Sonnevi's *Klangernas Bok* (Book of Tones, 1998), for example, reflects themes and images similar to those found in *Små klanger; en röst*.

Sonnevi partially overlaps two of his next poetry volumes, *Oavslutade dikter* (Unfinished Poems, 1987) and *Trädet* (The Tree, 1991). He divides the latter collection into two parts—the first section is actually part 2 of *Oavslutade dikter,* while the second section is devoted to the long title poem. In *Trädet* one immediately notices the radical change in line length. While the work runs only slightly more than half the number of pages of *Det omöjliga,* the word count of the two collections is nearly the same. Engaging figures from earlier historic periods in a conversation that discusses recent events, Sonnevi essentially addresses the problem of historicity in *Trädet* and adopts the role of a chronicler. He addresses then recent occurrences in Romania, the Persian Gulf, the Baltic states, Kampuchea, and Panama; contrary to his previous belief that the freedom movements in Eastern Europe were a prelude to nuclear war, in this collection Sonnevi has embraced the movements as forces of positive change. Moreover, the illusion of an historic chronicle is enhanced by the conversational flow of the long lines of verse:

> 1989 blev revolutionernas år I land efter land faller
> förtryckets regimer, med ett undantag, Kina, där
> kontrarevolutionen slog ner det fredliga upproret

med militär makt Friheten och demokratin, deras
genomskinliga former, som sedan väntar på innehållen
i det som alltid är fullständig sammansmältning
Också i den inre, våldsamma separationen Här
ska också förändringen komma, den inre, i demokratin.

(1989 became the year of the revolutions In country after
country regimes of the oppression fall, with one
exception, China, there
the counterrevolution beat down the peaceful disturbance
with military force Freedom and democracy, their
transparent forms, who afterwards waited for the contents
in that which always is complete coalescence
Also in the inner, violent separation Here
also the change will come, the inner, in the democracy.)

Across the span of his seventeen volumes, Göran Sonnevi's work exhibits a high degree of continuity, while his willingness to adapt and to engage in self-criticism have provided his readers surprise and continued discovery. His "oavslutade" process of poetic production is apparently destined to provide his readers with continued challenges in the future and to secure his standing as one of Sweden's greatest poets.

References:

Robin Fulton, "Five Swedish Poets (Tomas Tranströmer, Östen Sjöstrand, Ella Hillback, Göran Sonnevi, Gunnar Harding)," *Spirit,* 39 (1972): 1–84;

Benkt-Erik Hedin, "Det gäller oss nu: Om Göran Sonnevis lyrik," *Böckernas-Värld,* 5 (1971): 77–81;

Tom Hedlund, "Göran Sonnevi," *Parnasso,* 22 (1972): 268–276;

Kevin Karlin, "The Counter-Hermeneutic Framework of Göran Sonnevi's Poetry," M.A. thesis, University of Washington, Seattle, 1992;

Kent Kjellgren, *Göran Sonnevi: Poesi och politik* (Stockholm: Röda Rummet, 1987);

Rika Lesser, "Voice; Landscape; Violence: Sonnevi into English in Helsinki," in *Translating Poetry: The Double Labyrinth,* edited by Daniel Weissbort (Iowa City: University of Iowa Press, 1989), pp. 125–137;

Soren Lindgren, "Synpunkter på Sonnevi," *Nya Argus,* 62 (1969): 246–248;

Anders Olsson, "Det elementära tecknet: Försök över Sonnevi," *Bonniers Litterära Magasin,* 45 (1976): 206–212;

Mona Sandqvist, "Alkemins tecken i Göran Sonnevis 'Det omöjliga,'" dissertation, Lund University, 1989;

Ragnar Stromberg, "Ingen människes sorg: Reflexioner kring Göran Sonnevis Det omöjliga," *Bonniers Litterära Magasin,* 45 (1976): 25–28;

Jan Olov Ullen, "Grepp i Göran Sonnevis poesi," *Ord och Bild,* 85 (1976): 406–416;

Ullen, "Det skrivna är partitur: Göran Sonnevi och musiken," *Bonniers Litterära Magasin,* 45 (1976): 195–205.

Per Olof Sundman

(4 September 1922 – 9 October 1992)

Rick McGregor
Institutet för rymdfysik

BOOKS: *Jägarna* (Stockholm: Norstedt, 1957); excerpt republished as *Trumslagaren,* with an afterword by Lasse Bergström (Stockholm: Norstedt, 1967);

Undersökningen (Stockholm: Norstedt, 1958);

Skytten (Stockholm: Norstedt, 1960);

Levande fjällbygd ([Norrköping: Holmens bruk], 1961);

Expeditionen (Stockholm: Norstedt, 1962); translated by Mary Sandbach as *The Expedition* (London: Secker & Warburg, 1967);

Sökarna: Nio berättelser (Stockholm: Norstedt, 1963);

Två dagar, två nätter (Stockholm: Norstedt, 1965); translated by Alan Blair as *Two Days, Two Nights* (New York: Random House, 1969);

Människor vid hav, photography by Yngve Baum (Stockholm: Bonnier, 1966);

Berättelser, edited by Björn Sandell (Stockholm: Svenska bokförlaget, 1967);

Ett år: Anteckningar och kommentarer i dagbok, körjournaler för bil och i största allmänhet september 1966 till augusti 1967 kring arbetet med romanen Ingenjör Andrées luftfärd (Karlskrona: J. A. Krooks Bokhandel AB, 1967);

Ingenjör Andrées luftfärd (Stockholm: Norstedt, 1967); translated by Sandbach as *The Flight of the Eagle* (London: Secker & Warburg; New York: Pantheon, 1970);

Ingen fruktan, intet hopp: ett collage kring S. A. Andrée, hans följeslagare och hans polarexpedition (Stockholm: Bonnier, 1968);

Kommunerna och kulturpolitiken, by Sundman and Göran Johansson (Stockholm: LT, 1971);

Lofoten, sommar (Stockholm: Norstedt, 1973);

Olle Hedberg: Inträdestal i Svenska Akademien (Stockholm: Norstedt, 1975);

Berättelsen om Såm (Stockholm: Norstedt, 1977);

Anteckningar i den högsta norden under Ymerfärden sommaren 1980 (Bollnäs: Nyströms Tryckeri AB, 1980; Ljusdal: E. Ericssons bokhandel, 1980);

Ishav: Isbrytaren H. M. S. Ymers färd i polarhavet sommaren 1980 (Stockholm: Norstedt, 1982);

Per Olof Sundman (Collection of Allan Myrman)

Norrlandsberättelser (Stockholm: Norstedt, 1984)—comprises *Jägarna, Sökarna,* and *Två dagar, två nätter;*

Tre berättelser (Stockholm: Norstedt, 1987).

PRODUCED SCRIPTS: *Resa: TV-pjäs,* television, SVT, 15 February 1965;

Jakten, motion picture, by Sundman and Yngve Gamlin, Europa Film, 1965;

Kontrollanten, television, by Sundman and Kjell Albin Abrahamsson, SVT1, 3 December 1973.

OTHER: "Vittnet," in *20 berättelser för film* (Stockholm: Bonnier/Norstedt, 1963), pp. 246–272;

"Sjutton ord på danska," in *Sommarberättelser: Sex svenska noveller* ([Stockholm]: Sveriges Radio Utbildningsprogram, 1973), pp. 69–80;

"Mitt Norrland," in *Det nya Norrland,* photos by Petter Gullers and Thomas Wingstedt (Stockholm: Gullers Pictorial, 1986), pp. 4–10.

SELECTED PERIODICAL PUBLICATIONS– UNCOLLECTED:

FICTION

"De okända djuren," *Femtital,* 2, no. 2 (1952): 20–23;

"Händelser," *Svenska Dagbladet,* 23 May 1954, pp. 19–20;

"Söker väg," *Perspektiv,* 5 (1954): 436–441; republished, with annotations by Sundman, *Böckernas värld,* 3, no. 2 (1969): 21–27;

"Vadaren," *Perspektiv,* 9 (1958): 244–246;

"Benlindorna," *Östersunds-Posten,* 24 December 1960, p. 11;

"Fienderna," *Metallarbetaren,* 75, no. 12/13 (1964): 28–29;

"Något om gränsen mellan Sverige och Norge," *Artes: tidskrift för litteratur, konst och musik,* 14 (1988): 22–33;

"Lek," *TLM. Thélème,* no. 2 (1996): 25–32;

"Tre noveller," *Ord och Bild,* no. 6 (1998): 72–84—comprises "Jagär tidigt ute," "När Nils var död," and "Vadaren."

NONFICTION

"Att gå tull," *STF: Svenska turistföreningens tidning,* 23 (1955): 181–185;

"Att berätta," *Studiekontakt: Tidning för Svenska landsbygdens studieförbund,* no. 7 (1957): 15, 17–18;

"Funderingar på andra sidan busken," *Perspektiv,* 8 (1958): 350–352;

"Byalivet nyttig kallrivning för storstadsbon: Behaviorism och provinsliv avgörande för författaren Sundman," *Expressen,* 13 March 1959, p. 4;

"Lantliga funderingar kring en ism," *Kentaur,* 1 (Spring 1959): 15–22;

"Kommunalmannens lott i en mindre landskommun," *Landskommunernas tidskrift,* 40 (1959): 687–692;

"Min syn på bygden och vattenbyggandet," *Bygd och natur,* 41 (1960): 86–94;

"Författarna och den svenska traditionen," *Rondo,* 1 (1961): 11–12;

"Stenen i vägskälet," *Bonniers Litterära Magasin,* 30 (1961): 529–532;

"Vittne och verkligheten," *Bonniers Litterära Magasin,* 31 (1962): 299–302;

"Livets arghet och skönhet: Per Olof Sundman i Tove Janssons landskap," *Stockholms-Tidningen,* 5 February 1963, p. 4;

"Att inhämta nödvändiga sanningar," *Läste Ni: Bibliotekens Publikblad,* 9 (1963): 2–4;

"Kommentarer kring en teknik," *Bonniers Litterära Magasin,* 32 (1963): 231–234;

"Den svåråtkomliga medmänniskan," *Sociala Meddelanden* (1963): 463–469;

"Litterära socialreportage på ungdomsvårdsskolor," *Sociala meddelanden,* nos. 7–8 (1964): 33–61;

"Samerna i Sverige," *Samefolket,* 45, nos. 2–3 (1964): 38–40;

"Ett samiskt kryptogram," *Ord och Bild,* 73 (1964): 356–359;

"Att göra en expedition," *Skid-och friluftsfrämjandets Årsbok* (1965): 15–24;

"Verkligheten som försvann," *Stockholms-Tidningen,* 18 January 1966, pp. 18–19;

"Gåtan i isen," *Expressen,* (11 April 1966): 4;

"Det finns tre bilder som etsat sig fast. Möte med boken," *Östersunds-Posten* (19 August 1966): 2;

"Manuskript och film," *Ord och Bild,* 75 (1966): 80–82;

"Anteckningar och kommentarer," *Bonniers Litterära Magasin,* 36 (1967): 422–426;

"Sånt blir livet," in *Tryckpunkter: 23 svenska författare i egen sak* (Stockholm: Norstedt, 1967), pp. 163–173;

"Bilderna från isen," *Konstrevy,* 44 (1968): 198–203;

"Frænkels bild av Swedenborg inte orimlig," *Veckojournalen,* no. 19 (1968): 34–35;

"Om att övertolka," *Bonniers Litterära Magasin,* 39 (1970): 414–418;

"Vad vi är lyckliga, himlen tillhör oss," *Veckojournalen,* no. 23 (1975): 3;

"Att andas här är som att dricka vatten ur en kall källa . . . ," *Veckojournalen,* no. 29 (1976): 2;

"I Andrées spår: En 'charmant anblick,' nej dödens vithet," *Veckojournalen,* no. 43 (1976): 2;

"Författaren och hans kritiker," *Veckojournalen,* no. 19 (1977): 2;

"Författarens hundramilasteg till fjället," *Göteborgs-Posten,* 7 August 1978, p. 2;

"Några ord om ord ombord," *Ymer,* 101 (1981): 15–19;

"En ballongseglats mot döden," *Nordisk tidskrift för vetenskap, konst och industri,* 60 (1984): 1–12;

"Fjorton år i Norrland," *Provins,* 1 (1986): 2–7.

For most of the third quarter of the twentieth century, Per Olof Sundman was unquestionably one of the most important Swedish prose writers. His first volume of short stories, *Jägarna* (The Hunters, 1957), was the first debut collection since World War II to sell out its first edition, and he achieved international recognition with his documentary novels *Expeditionen* (1962; translated as *The Expedition,* 1967) and *Ingenjör Andrées luftfärd* (Engineer Andrée's Air Voyage, 1967; translated as *The Flight of the Eagle,* 1970). His productivity waned after his election to the Swedish Parliament in 1968 and in particular after his inclusion in the Swedish Academy in 1975, but interest in his work remained high for at least another decade and a half. His last novel, *Berättelsen om Såm* (The Story of Såm, 1977), disappointed an expectant public, and the critical response, coupled with the weight of his social responsibilities, apparently curbed his creativity. His final nonfiction work, *Ishav: Isbrytaren H. M. S. Ymers färd i polarhavet sommaren 1980* (Arctic Ocean, 1982), failed to resurrect his literary stock, which by the time of his death in 1992 had declined considerably. The discovery in 1995 that Sundman belonged to Swedish Nazi youth groups as an adolescent in the late 1930s and early 1940s has, however, rekindled interest in his work. Recent scholarly attention has concentrated primarily on biographical considerations, but there are also signs that the debate has led to a renewed appreciation of his literary production.

Sundman was born on 4 September 1922 in Vaxholm, near Stockholm, the second child and first son of Per Sundman, who lived from 1870 to 1924, and Anna Sundman, née Rosmark (born 1885), who was her husband's junior by fifteen years. After the father's death, the family moved to Östergötland to live with Anna's brother Olof Rosmark. In 1929 the family returned to Stockholm, where Sundman was educated at Katarina Södra Folkskola, Katarina Real, and Stockholms Samgymnasium, which he left without matriculating in 1943 to do his military service at Marine Headquarters in Stockholm. While at Katarina Real, Sundman was a classmate of Stig Dagerman, who achieved considerable literary success in the postwar years. He later claimed that both he and Dagerman had been encouraged to become writers by their Swedish teacher, Bernhard Tarschys. Quite possibly, Sundman–who first become involved with the Swedish Nazi youth group Nordisk Ungdom in 1937 or 1938–was not as popular with either Dagerman, who was strongly left wing in his politics, or with Tarschys, who was Jewish, as he attested in the years afterward. From 1945 to 1946 he spent nine months in the mountains of Härjedalen, trying to write and working at odd jobs for the local farmers and reindeer herders; he may have been attempting at this time to escape his Nazi connections–not only as a member of Nordisk Ungdom but also eventually of Wasa and Fosterländsk Enad Ungdom.

Upon his return to Stockholm in the autumn of 1946, he began working for the cooperative Motorists' Purchasing Group and married Ulla-Britt Jansson in 1948. In order to give himself time to write, Sundman and his wife bought a small tourist hotel in the remote area of Frostviken, in the mountains of northern Jämtland near the Norwegian border, and moved to Jormlien together with their mothers and Ulla-Britt's aunt in May 1949. Ulla-Britt gave birth to their sons, Sverre and Dag, in 1950 and 1955, respectively.

Sundman initially found that running a hotel did not leave him the time he had hoped to devote to his writing, but he gradually established himself as a contributor of debate articles and book reviews to the Swedish evening paper *Expressen,* and in due course his short stories began to appear in various publications. His first short stories were published in the early 1950s, and in 1954 he was elected a member of the local municipal council. Throughout the rest of his literary career he combined writing with political or social responsibilities. By the time he published his first book, at the age of thirty-five, he had many years of attempts at novels and short stories behind him. He claimed that not until he had spent time in Härjedalen and later in Frostviken did he find suitable material; in fact, life among his neighbors in Frostviken helped him discover the economical but precise language with which to tell his stories.

Many of his early works take the form of quests or expeditions, and significantly, the emphasis is often on the process of the quest itself rather than on its ultimate goal. Sundman also strongly subscribed to Frans G. Bengtsson's doctrine that an author should reveal no more of his characters' thoughts than one can perceive in reality. Hence, often he implicitly lets the reader determine the characters' personalities from their words and actions rather than provide outright authorial insights into their psychology. Again influenced by Bengtsson, he was eager to point out the similarity between this behavioristic narrative method and that of the authors of the Icelandic kings and family sagas of the thirteenth century. His two main collections of short stories, *Jägarna* and *Sökarna* (The Seekers, 1963), as well as two of his early novels, *Undersökningen* (The Investigation, 1958) and *Expeditionen,* signal through their titles the theme of exploration that preoccupied him in his early works. In the works of his middle period and later, Sundman instead begins to focus increasingly on powerful leaders and authoritarian figures. Similarly, a project he announced late in his literary career–but never completed–was a novel based on the life of the Swedish magnate Alfred Nobel.

The fourteen stories in *Jägarna* all regard life in remote northern parts of Sweden. Many pieces stem from Sundman's postwar stay in Härjedalen, while most of the others are based on his experiences as hotel owner and local politician in Frostviken. As Lars G. Warme points out in his 1984 monograph, *Per Olof Sundman: Writer of the North,* Sundman's stories are often inconclusive; they lack plot, their endings are seemingly arbitrary, and they usually frustrate the reader's expectation that a conflict will be resolved or that a mystery resulting from observations in them will be solved—the emphasis is on means and methods rather than results. As the title of the volume implies, many of the stories depict hunts of some sort, although perhaps "searches" marks a more accurate description: for a hotel guest who disappears from the hotel, for a missing bottle of alcohol at the end of a hunting trip, and for a mica-hauler who has disappeared on a snow-covered lake with horse, sledge, and 3,500 kilograms of mica. Possible solutions are offered as to the mystery of the latter's disappearance, but typically Sundman lets the reader decide, for given a choice between a rational explanation and an enigma, he often prefers the enigma. The critics and the public received *Jägarna* positively, and stories from the collection regularly appear in anthologies of Swedish short stories. It was republished in 1984 as *Norrlandsberättelser* (Norrland Stories), which included the stories from *Sökarna* as well as the novel *Två dagar, två nätter* (1965; translated as *Two Days, Two Nights,* 1969), also set in the remote Swedish mountains.

Sundman's first novel, *Undersökningen,* was also based heavily on his experiences in Frostviken. As a member of the municipal alcohol advisory committee, he was once compelled to deprive an alcoholic of his freedom for the sake of the man's family's safety. In the novel the protagonist, Erik Olofsson, has been assigned to investigate reports that the head of the hydroelectric development in the area, Arne Lundgren, has a serious alcohol problem. As stated in his article "Kommentarer kring en teknik" (Comments on a Technique), published in *Bonniers Litterära Magasin* in 1963, Sundman wanted to illustrate the impossibility of discovering what lies behind a fellow human being's exterior. Instead of trying to discover the undiscoverable, he wrote, people should accept others for who they are and treat them with tolerance and understanding. Accordingly, the local man, Olofsson, reaches no conclusion in investigation of the city dweller, Lungren, but Sundman is able to use the investigation as a means of depicting how a remote rural area makes the transition to a more modern age—which was happening to his town, Frostviken, at the time.

In 1959 Sundman was elected chairman of the municipal council, and the following year he published his second novel, *Skytten* (The Shooter, 1960), in which, once more, a major theme of the novel is the difficulty of attaining any deep knowledge of one's fellow man.

The shooter of the title is Åke Enarsson, who works for the local council. During an elk hunt near the start of the book, he accidentally shoots and kills another member of the hunting party. The bulk of the novel shows him on his wanderings around the district on the day after the shooting, as he tries in vain to learn more about the man he has killed. This quest provides just enough plot to sustain what becomes in effect a detailed catalogue of "hur en liten svensk kommun i det norrländska inlandet såg ut och fungerade just vid denna tid" (how a small Swedish district in the inner part of Norrland looked and functioned at that particular time), as Sundman commented in his afterword to *Norrlandsberättelser.*

Two years later, with *Expeditionen,* Sundman broke for the first time with the remote Swedish milieu of his earlier works and produced one of the first documentary novels, a genre that became popular in Scandinavia and elsewhere in the mid to late 1960s and in the early 1970s. H. M. Stanley's *In Darkest Africa* (1900), which describes his expedition to rescue Emin Pasha (Eduard Schnitzer), the governor of Equatoria. Sundman says in his author's note, however, that while he has made ample use of authentic material from Stanley's writings, his book does not address Stanley and his expedition; it instead describes the expedition of a fictional Sir John—the real name of H. M. Stanley, on whom Sir John is based, was John Rowlands—to rescue a Kanji pasha in the heart of an Africa-like continent. Displaying a similar narrative technique employed in the story "Skidlöparen" (The Cross-Country Skier) from *Jägarna, Expeditionen* alternates between two narrators: Lieutenant Laronne, Sir John's second-in-command, and an Eastern scribe and interpreter named Jaffar Topan. Some—though not all—of the events overlap, but when they do there are often discrepancies between the two accounts. The European officer Laronne in particular is an unreliable narrator.

In *Expeditionen,* as with his earlier books, the focus is on the expedition itself rather than on its conclusion. Appropriately, then, the narrative ends in the jungle, with the expedition still far from reaching its goal. In addition to the theme of the quest and its inquiry into the Western preoccupation with travel and exploration, however, the novel also introduces Sundman's growing interest in the authoritarian figure—embodied in the expedition leader, Sir John. Through the dual perspectives of Laronne and Jaffar, the author is able to depict Sir John as a late-nineteenth-century colonialist who exploits native labor and local resources. Whereas Laronne concentrates on details and gives the Europeans' account of the events, the Jaffar shows a better understanding of people, especially of the non-Europeans in the expedition. The tension between the two first-person accounts and the sensuality of Jaffar's descriptions contribute to Sundman's departure from the stark objectivity of his earlier works.

Together with Sundman's previous books, *Expeditionen* drew comparisons with French *nouveau roman* authors such as Alain Robbe-Grillet and Michel Butor. Butor himself wrote an appreciative preface for the French translation of *Expeditionen* when it appeared in 1965. This rendering and the publication of the English translation in 1967 rapidly established Sundman's international reputation—which was further cemented by the success, in Swedish and in translation, of *Ingenjör Andrées luftfärd*. Many of Sundman's works have also been translated into German, for there is considerable German interest in his writing.

In 1963 Sundman published his second volume of short stories, *Sökarna*. As with his earlier collection, the common theme of the search is implied by the title, and three of the nine stories do literally involve searches, though none of these three are successful. The other stories confront an additional theme that is typical of Sundman's fiction—the inaccessibility of fellow human beings. In one story a hotel guest has a habit of using his own cutlery and in so doing disturbs the hotel owner and other guests; in another narrative a pleasant young guest at the hotel turns out to be a criminal on the run; and in still another story a sport fisherman is trapped near a remote lake with a companion who uses his alcoholism as a weapon. The final story of the collection demonstrates a masterly use of an unreliable first-person narrator, a narrative technique that Sundman had already developed in "Skidlöparna" and *Expeditionen*, and that he refined further in his next two novels. In "Främlingarna" (The Strangers) the reader is uncomfortably aware that the other characters find the narrator, Doctor Jonsson, antipathetic; Jonsson seems to know how others feel about him, too, but also believes that his duty is to try to break down the barriers to the strangers who surround him.

In 1963 Sundman's fourteen years in Jormlien came to an end when he and his family left to return to his birthplace, Vaxholm. As with his original move away from Stockholm, the motivation for his move back was his writing. He was now in a position to become a full-time writer, but to do so he needed to be closer to a major city. In addition, the method he had developed in *Expeditionen*, which involved large amounts of research, was difficult to carry out in a remote area, far from bookshops and large libraries. The return to Vaxholm initiated a productive period of almost five years in his literary career.

In the summer of 1964 the motion-picture director Yngve Gamlin approached Sundman to write a screenplay based on his short story "Jägarna II" (The Hunters II) from *Jägarna*. Working from Sundman's long and detailed manuscript, they collaborated to make the feature movie *Jakten* (The Hunt) in northern Jämtland at the end of that year. The movie premiered in April 1965 and, while critics received it well, *Jakten* hardly thrilled the general public, who found it extremely slow moving. The experience did, however, inspire Sundman to publish his own longer version of the story later that year as the novel *Två dagar, två nätter*. Both the story and the novel are derived from an event that occurred in the far north of Sweden in 1951, when a deranged Norwegian set fire to a mountain hut and killed two people during the ensuing chase. In Sundman's version of the story, a policeman, Karl Olofsson, and the narrator—who in the novel is Olle Stensson, an authoritarian primary-school teacher—leave the rest of the search party to intercept the crazed man. They wound and capture him but find during a night of guarding him in a remote hut that he has gained the upper hand. They cannot continue to guard him nor can they force him to return with them to civilization. In the end they take his boots and most of his clothing, and leave him in the hut while they go to report his whereabouts.

While an anonymous protagonist narrates the short story objectively, Stensson has the role of an unreliable narrator who behaves like a loudmouth and a know-it-all and who has the aggressive tendencies that are probably necessary for the capture of the criminal; later, however, he endangers the men when the youth is provoked into retaliating. In light of the exposure of Sundman's Nazi past, one is tempted to see depiction that the rather fascist Stensson gives of himself, as an attempt by the author to come to terms with his own early political leanings. That Stensson quotes Friedrich Nietzsche and Fenno-Swedish poet Örnulf Tigerstedt supports this interpretation: according to Sundman, Tigerstedt is the only significant poet that fascism ever produced. Stensson's intellectualism and Olofsson's compassion display two sides of humanity, and the tension between the two—heightened by the threat of the fugitive—produces compelling reading. Nonetheless, however, as Sundman himself admitted later in the afterword to *Norrlandsberättelser,* one feels a growing pessimism that the articulate and intellectual Stenssons of the world dominate the Olofssons, who possess a sound common sense and an empathy with their fellow man.

Although he returned to the Stockholm area in order to devote himself to his writing career, Sundman was unable to resist the temptation to reinvolve himself in politics. In 1966 he was elected a town councillor in Vaxholm and councillor for the county of Stockholm. The same year he published the first of his two fine doc-

Dust jacket for Sundman's 1984 collection of stories set in the mountains of northern Sweden (from Swedish Book Review, *November 1984)*

umentary books on Lofoten, in northern Norway. Sundman had long had an attraction to northern parts; in 1939, as a teenager, he and a friend cycled to Kirkenes and Petsamo on the coast of the Arctic Ocean. Thus, when the photographer Yngve Baum sent him pictures of Lofoten in winter, Sundman immediately agreed to write the text for *Människor vid hav* (People by the Sea, 1966), with its objective descriptions of winter skrei-fishing in Henningsvær. "Det finns trakter på denna jord som man inte kan lämna enbart genom att resa därifrån, landskap som utgör en så våldsam upplevelse att man tvingas återvända" (There are places on this earth which one cannot leave solely by traveling away from them, landscapes which constitute such powerful experiences that one is compelled to return), writes Sundman in *Lofoten, sommar* (Lofoten, Summer, 1973). Together with Iceland and the Faroe Islands, Lofoten was one such "powerful" place for Sundman, who returned to Henningsvær in the summer of 1970 to research his second book on the area.

By 1966 he was also working on the novel that became his undeniable masterpiece, *Ingenjör Andrées luftfärd*. Another documentary novel, and one of the best in the genre, *Ingenjör Andrées luftfärd* tells of the attempt by Swedes Salomon August Andrée, Nils Strindberg, and Knut Frænkel to fly a balloon to the North Pole in 1897. Their bodies were found on White Island, northwest of Spitsbergen, in 1930, and Sundman has constructed his account from the photographs and diaries that were found with them. The novel is narrated by Frænkel, the only expedition member who had not kept a detailed journal, and covers a one-year period from his acceptance as a member of the three-man expedition through to his death as the last of the three men.

As in *Expeditionen,* Sundman is again interested in the role of the leader; here, however, his portrayal of Andrée is more nuanced than that of Sir John. Frænkel becomes increasingly critical of Andrée and the organization of the expedition as the novel goes on; while much of Frænkel's criticism seems justified, Andrée's patience in accepting it is admirable, as is the courage he demonstrates as the oldest member of the party in their three-month struggle back across the ice after the balloon has landed well short of the Pole. Sundman's narrative technique also shows further development, in that he renders ambiguous whether Frænkel is intended to be an unreliable narrator or a mouthpiece for Sundman's own questioning of Andrée's motives and actions. Moreover, despite its documentary basis, *Ingenjör Andrées luftfärd* is Sundman's most literary novel. It is full of leitmotivs and literary and other allusions, and it demonstrates to full effect Sundman's echoing technique, which Gunnar Tidestrøm has termed "iteration with variation": "Iterationerna bildar klart urskiljbara sammanbindande motivlinjer, variationerna möjliggör nyanseringar. . . . Från snart sagt varje punkt i framställningen går trådar till andra delar och skikt av helheten. Därigenom får ord, satser och motivelement ofta långt större vikt och verkan än de eljest skulle ha" (The repetitions form clearly distinguishable linking chains of themes, the variations make shades of meaning possible. . . . From virtually every point in the portrayal threads lead to other parts and layers of the whole. As a result words, clauses and thematic elements often receive far greater weight and effect than they would otherwise have). The novel resonates with the conflicts between the men, the conflict between them and their environment, and the contrast between their situation on the ice and the scenes of turn-of-the-century, high-society Stockholm and Paris that launch the narrative.

Ingenjör Andrées luftfärd was received with considerable critical acclaim and was awarded two major literary prizes in the year of publication. As a result of its success Sundman was invited to prepare a new edition of the "Andrée-men's diaries," which had been published when they were found in 1930. He felt, however, that the original work was too much a product of its time and incorporated the material instead into a new collage book, *Ingen fruktan, intet hopp* (No Fear, No Hope, 1968), with his own commentary linking the parts. This work, too, was well received; those who reread the novel in light of the background material were able to find even greater depths than had been immediately apparent.

At the Swedish elections in 1968 Sundman made the move from local to national politics. He was elected a member of parliament for the Center Party, which he had joined during his time in Frostviken,

and took up his seat in 1969. He stayed in parliament until 1979, using his tenure to concentrate on cultural questions and serve on the cultural committee of the Nordic Council. In 1969 Sundman also made his first visit to Iceland. The Icelandic sagas had been part of his perennial reading since he had been a teenager, and Iceland became the setting for his next novel. In addition, his work for the Nordic Council gave him frequent opportunities to visit Iceland over the next two decades.

Sundman also separated from Ulla-Britt in 1969. Four years earlier, while searching for an epigraph to his novel *Två dagar, två nätter,* he had approached the well-known runic scholar Sven B. F. Jansson to help him find and translate a suitably enigmatic strophe from the Icelandic eddic poem "Hávamál." Through his acquaintance with Jansson he met his daughter, Anna-Karin Jansson. Together Sundman and the much younger Anna-Karin visited Iceland and Lofoten in 1970. They married five years later and soon had two sons—Björn, born in 1975, and Joar, born in 1979.

By the mid 1970s Sundman's duties as a member of parliament were already having an effect on his literary productivity. His second Lofoten book had taken longer to write than he had intended, and he had also been working, since 1970, on his next novel. His election in 1975 to the Swedish Academy, which is responsible for awarding the Nobel Prize for literature, only added to his workload.

Sundman's final novel had been long awaited; by the time it appeared, ten years had passed since the success of *Ingenjör Andrées luftfärd*. *Berättelsen om Såm* is set on an island that shares many features with Iceland and reworks the *Hrafnkels saga,* a short family saga from the thirteenth century. While both the saga and Sundman's novel depict the power struggle between Sámr/Såm and Hrafnkell/Ravnkel, the latter work takes place in the present. In giving *Berättelsen om Såm* a contemporary time frame Sundman hoped to present a political parable and to offer his own interpretation of the original saga, but in fact the time setting is the most egregious flaw in the novel. Much of the action depends on the legal system of pre-Christian Iceland, with the protagonists in a court case responsible for carrying out the sentence themselves. In the novel the modern setting strains the reader's willing suspension of disbelief.

In Sweden, where the original saga is quite well known, the response to Sundman's new novel was decidedly muted, whereas abroad it was better received. In fact, among his books, *Berättelsen om Såm* currently ranks second only to *Ingenjör Andrées luftfärd* in terms of rights sold internationally. By 1977 the rights to *Expeditionen* had been sold to ten countries, those to *Två dagar, två nätter* to seven, and those to *Ingenjör Andrées luftfärd* to no less than sixteen–and later to two more. The rights to *Berättelsen om Såm* have already been issued to publishers in thirteen countries, and scholars in the United States, Germany, and Japan have generally responded more favorably toward the novel than those in Scandinavia.

By the end of the 1970s Sundman's political star had also waned, and when he was not placed sufficiently high on the electoral list of the Center Party he opted to resign from parliament in 1979 rather than to face almost certain electoral defeat. The year after he left parliament he was invited to return to the Arctic Ocean on a three-month scientific expedition onboard the Swedish icebreaker *Ymer*. He had earlier made a brief visit to the Arctic in 1976 with director Jan Troell in preparation for the latter's motion-picture version of *Ingenjör Andrées luftfärd*, which premiered in 1982. Once again the wealth of material Sundman gathered while on the expedition threatened to overwhelm him, and it took two years before *Ishav* appeared.

His literary powers had now clearly waned. His last novel had lacked the stylistic artistry of his earlier works, and his last nonfiction work had also failed to live up to the standard of his two books on Lofoten and his collage book on the Andrée expedition. To keep its writer in the public eye, the publishing house Norstedt gathered his short stories and his most recent Norrland novel, *Två dagar, två nätter,* and republished them as *Norrlandsberättelser*. Three years later Norstedt also published three new short stories in a limited edition, *Tre berättelser* (Three Stories, 1987), for the book and library trade fair in Göteborg. Apart from one other published short story a year later, Sundman did not write anything. His wife requested a separation in 1990, and after a final couple of years of increasing alcoholism, he died in a Stockholm hospital on 9 October 1992.

By the mid 1990s Per Olof Sundman had seemingly lost his prominence in Swedish literature, a rank that had appeared assured at least up until the mid 1980s. That interest in his works has been renewed in recent years by scholars such as Jonas Fogelqvist is therefore paradoxical. Paradoxically the revelations of Sundman's involvement in Nazi youth groups in prewar Sweden and during the early years of the war have also spawned new questions and issues about his writings. These encouraging signs auger a new phase of readership for the author and ensure that a Sundman renaissance is underway.

Interviews:

Eric Blaustein, "Stockholm var som ett osande pannrum," *Expressen*, 5 May 1952;

Nils Röhne, "Per-Olof Sundman–författaren och paragraf 12," *Östersunds-Posten*, 22 November 1958;

Kurt Vastad, "Rädd för likgiltigheten," *Vi*, no. 18 (1958): 17–18;

Thomas von Vegesack, "Besök hos Per Olof Sundman," *Stockholms-Tidningen*, 13 May 1962, p. 4;

Mauritz Edström, "I ordens glesbygd: Nya författarprofiler," *Dagens Nyheter*, 4 August 1963, p. 3;

Ulf Örnkloo, "Varför flyttade Sundman?" *Norrländsk tidskrift*, 12, no. 4 (1963): 31–32;

Johan Bargum, "Att utforska människan," *Hufvudstadsbladet* (Helsinki), 6 July 1966, p. 7;

Marianne Höök, "Per Olof Sundman, du förståndige, varför skriver du om alla dessa geniala dårar," *Vi*, no. 39 (1968): 18–20;

Karl Erik Lagerlöf, "Svårfångad Per Olof Sundman: Andrée-romanen dålig bok. Ensamhet den stora tragedin," *Göteborgs Handels-och Sjöfarts-Tidning*, 2 August 1969;

Björn Nilsson, "Per Olof Sundman–ett möte," *Böckernas Värld*, 3, no. 2 (1969): 15–20;

Rolf Yrlid, "En fråga om moral," *Horisont*, 17, no. 2 (1970): 76–82;

Laurence S. Dembo, "An Interview with Per Olof Sundman," *Contemporary Literature*, 12 (1971): 267–275; translated by Lars Bäckström as "Jag är författare och moralist," *Författarförlagets Tidskrift*, 1, no. 2 (1970): 13–20;

Göran Zachrison, "Så här skrev jag 'Elfenben': P O Sundman berättar för Göran Zachrison," *Göteborgs-Tidningen*, 1 August 1973, p. 4;

Nils-Hugo Geber, "Intervju med författaren Per Olof Sundman 29 maj 1975," in *Svensk filmografi 6 (1960–1969)* (Stockholm: Svenska Filminstitutet, 1977), pp. 226–229;

Nils-Eric Björsson, "Rufsig kalufs, pipa, anorak och landrover . . . : Så såg det ut när riksdagsman Sundman jobbade med nya boken på Island," *Land*, no. 13 (1977): 2–3;

Ian Hinchliffe, "Per Olof Sundman Interviewed," *Swedish Books*, no. 2 (1981): 2–6;

Hans Davidson, "Per Olof Sundman, författare med unika erfarenheter," *Land*, no. 27 (1983): 10–11;

Rick McGregor, "An Interview with Per Olof Sundman 15 October 1990," *Swedish Book Review*, no. 2 (1991): 2–10.

Bibliography:

Rick McGregor, "Bibliography," in his *Per Olof Sundman and the Icelandic Sagas: A Study of Narrative Method*

(Göteborg: Litteraturvetenskapliga institutionen vid Göteborgs universitet, 1994), pp. 250-296.

Biography:

Nils G. Åsling, *Per Olof Sundman: Ett porträtt* (Stockholm: Robert Larson AB, 1970).

References:

Alfred Andersch, "Ein Humanist aus Jämtland," *Merkur,* 239, 22, no. 3 (1968): 273-276;

Nils G. Åsling, "Per Olof Sundman och glesbygden," *Impuls,* 9, no. 5 (1975): 13-18;

Åsling, "Per Olof Sundman och politiken," *Nordisk Tidskrift för vetenskap, konst och industri,* 69 (1993): 223-226;

Lars Bäckström, "Manssamhället hos Sundman," in *Könsdiskriminering förr och nu,* edited by Karin Westman Berg (Stockholm: Prisma, 1972), pp. 15-29;

Bäckström, "Sanningen och Sundman," *TLM: Thélème,* no. 2 (1996): 35-66;

Bäckström, "Sundman är inte pessimist," *Ord och bild,* no. 1 (1999): 8-10;

Bäckström, ed., *Per Olof Sundman och Nazismen* (Stockholm: Thélème, 1996);

Karin Bergengren, "Sundmans manssamhälle," *Upsala Nya Tidning,* 17 January 1972;

Tobias Berggren, "Expeditionskårens hemligheter," *Bonniers Litterära Magasin,* 39 (1970): 172-182;

Michel Butor, "Vid minsta tecken," translated by C. G. Bjurström, *Bonniers Litterära Magasin,* 34 (1965): 441-448;

Per Olov Enquist, "Den svåra lojaliteten," *Bonniers Litterära Magasin,* 32 (1963): 25-31;

Åke Erlandsson, "Myten om Nansens rival och Ikaros," *Edda,* 75 (1975): 161-168;

Erlandsson, "Per Olof Sundmans expeditioner: Studier i romanerna Expeditionen och Ingenjör Andrées luftfärd (II)," Licentiate thesis, Lund University, 1970;

Uno Florén, "Människan och äventyret," *Veckojournalen,* nos. 51/52 (1973): 28-29;

Florén, "Per Olof Sundman: ett porträtt," *Idun,* 75, no. 29 (1962): 27, 45;

Jonas Fogelqvist, "Per Olof Sundman, nazismen och

Torbjörn Forslid, "Nordpolens magi och andra icke-dokumentära drag i Per Olof Sundmans Ingenjör Andrées luftfärd," *Horisont,* 44, no. 1 (1997): 29-37;

Forslid, "Sundman och den stora hemligheten," *Res Publica,* 38 (1998): 97-110;

Lennart Frick, "P. O. Sundman i Jormlien och 'den nya romanen,'" *Västernorrlands Allehanda,* 1 September 1961, p. 2;

Frick, "Per Olof Sundman: Svenskt 50-tal," *Västerbottens-Kuriren,* 9 December 1958, p. 4;

Hanns Grössel, "Der schwer zugängliche Mitmensch– Versuch über Per Olof Sundman," *Akzente,* 19 (1972): 501-517;

Björn Häkansson, "Prosan: Documentarism–vetenskaplig sanning?" in his *Författarmakt: inlägg och essäer om litteratur i politik och politik i litteraturen* (Stockholm: Bonnier, 1970), pp. 114-128;

Guttorm Hansen, "Per Olof Sundman som nordist," *Nordisk Tidskrift för vetenskap, konst och industri,* 69 (1993): 217-221;

Ian Hinchliffe, "The Documentary Novel: Fact, Fiction or Fraud? An Examination of Three Scandinavian Examples of the Documentary Novel from the 1960s and 1970s," dissertation, University of Hull, 1989;

Hinchliffe, *Per Olof Sundman: Ingenjör Andrées luftfärd* (Hull: University of Hull, 1982);

Lars Jakobson, "Helgledig vänskap och försök att läsa oskriven text," *Ord och Bild,* no. 1 (1999): 10-11;

David Jenkins, "A Rugged Individual," *Sweden Now,* 5, no. 5 (1971): 38-43;

Örjan Lindberger, "Per Olof Sundman och Frostviken," *Nordisk Tidskrift för vetenskap, konst och industri,* 74 (1998): 313-322;

Lindberger, "Den svåråtkomliga kunskapen om människan: Om författaren Per Olof Sundman," *Nordisk Tidskrift för vetenskap, konst och industri,* 69 (1993): 205-215;

Mikael Löfgren, "Den puerile logistikern: Om nazism som modernitetskritik i en berättelse av Per Olof Sundman," *Ord och Bild,* no. 1 (1999): 12-15;

Rick McGregor, *Per Olof Sundman and the Icelandic Sagas: A Study of Narrative Method* (Göteborg: Litteraturvetenskapliga institutionen vid Göteborgs universitet, 1994);

McGregor, "The Silence of Per Olof Sundman: A Swedish Novelist's Guilty Secret," *Swedish Book Review,* no. 1 (1998): 25-31;

Björn Norström, "En studie i tre förvandlingar: Per Olof Sundmans novell 'Jägarna II' blir filmmanuskript, manuskriptet blir film och filmen blir en roman," *Dramaforskning: Meddelande från Avd. för dramaforskning vid Litteraturhistoriska institutionen, Uppsala,* 3 (1967): 282-316;

Hans Peterson, "Rapport från en observatör," *Ord och Bild,* 70 (1961): 49-53;

Björn Sandell, "Per Olof Sundmans första kvartssekel," *Svenska Dagbladet,* 27 April 1984;

Hans Schottmann, "Die Geschichte von Hrafnkel und Sám: Beobachtungen zur Erzählweise einer Isländersaga," in *ÜberBrücken: Festschrift für Ulrich*

Groenke, edited by Knut Brynhildsvoll (Hamburg: Helmut Buske, 1989), pp. 117–137;

Leif Sjöberg, "Per Olof Sundman and the Uses of Reality," *American-Scandinavian Review,* 59 (1971): 145–154;

Sjöberg, "Per Olof Sundman: The Writer as a Reasonably Unbiased Observer," *Books Abroad,* 47 (1973): 253–260;

Brita Stendahl, "Per Olof Sundman on the Expedition of Truthtelling," *World Literature Today,* 55 (1981): 250–256;

Jan Stenkvist, "Den svåråtkomliga verkligheten," in *Svensk litteratur 1870–1970,* volume 3, *Den nyaste litteraturen,* edited by Gunnar Brandell and Stenkvist (Stockholm: Aldus, 1975), pp. 136–141;

Rolf E. Stern, "Per Olof Sundmans roman Expeditionen," *Svensk lärarföreningens årsskrift* (1974): 30–53;

Jan Stolpe, "Innanför–utanför," *Bonniers Litterära Magasin,* 39 (1970): 278–285; reprinted in *Svensk Socialistisk litteraturkritik,* edited by Maria Bergom-Larsson (Stockholm: Gidlund, 1972), pp. 445–463;

Libor Stukavec, "Zur Prosa von Per Olof Sundman," *Brünner Beitrage zur Germanistik und Nordistik,* 2 (1980): 125–138;

Per Svensson, *Frostviken: Ett reportage om Per Olof Sundman, nazismen och tigandet* (Stockholm: Bonnier, 1998);

Svensson, "Sundman och gossenazisterna på Katarina Real," *Doc,* no. 0 (1997): 7–39;

Lars Thomasson, "Författaren Per Olof Sundman: 'Det var i Frostviken jag fann mitt språk,'" *Samefolket,* 77, no. 11 (1996): 22–24;

Gunnar Tideström, "*Ingenjör Andrées luftfärd* som dokumentärskildring och litterärt konstverk," in *Från Snoilsky till Sonnevi: Litteraturvetenskapliga studier tillägnade Gunnar Brandell,* edited by Stenkvist (Stockholm: Natur och Kultur, 1976), pp. 182–202;

Birgitta Trotzig, *Per Olof Sundman: Inträdestal i Svenska Akademien* (Stockholm: Norstedt, 1993);

Lars G. Warme, "Per Olof Sundman and the French New Novel: Influence or Coincidence?" *Scandinavian Studies,* 50 (1978): 403–413;

Warme, *Per Olof Sundman: Writer of the North* (Westport, Conn.: Greenwood Press, 1984);

Warme, "The Quests in the Works of Per Olof Sundman," *Proceedings of the Pacific Northwest Conference on Foreign Languages,* 28 (1977): 108–111;

Birgit Weihs, "Per Olof Sundman: Erzählen im Spannungsfeld von Authentizität und Authorität," *Skandinavistik,* 15 (1985): 50–57;

Bo Widerberg, "På väg mot en slutsats: Per Olof Sundmans undersökningar," *Bonniers Litterära Magasin,* 30 (1961): 115–120.

Papers:

Per Olof Sundman's papers were left to the Handskriftssektion of Kungliga Biblioteket in Stockholm as Dep. 276 on 21 September 1993 by his widow, Anna-Karin Sundman. Her permission is required for access to them. As of 2 February 1998 they were not yet available for inspection. In addition, Sundman's publisher, P. A. Norstedt and Söners Förlag, Stockholm, holds some of its correspondence with him in its archives, and some correspondence is held by Uppssala Universitetsbibliotek (Uppsala University Library).

Märta Tikkanen
(3 April 1935 –   )

Kathy Saranpa

BOOKS: *Nu imorron* (Helsinki: Söderström, 1970; Stockholm: Trevi, 1970);
Ingenmansland (Helsinki: Söderström, 1972; Stockholm: Trevi, 1972);
Vem bryr sig om Doris Mihailov? (Helsinki: Söderström, 1974; Stockholm: Trevi, 1974);
Män kan inte våldtas (Helsinki: Söderström, 1976; Stockholm: Trevi, 1976); translated by Alison Weir as *Manrape* (London: Virago, 1978);
Århundradets kärlekssaga (Helsinki: Söderström, 1978; Stockholm: Trevi, 1978); translated by Stina Katchadourian as *The Love Story of the Century* (Santa Barbara, Cal.: Capra Press, 1984);
Mörkret som ger glädjen djup (Helsinki: Söderström, 1981; Stockholm: Trevi, 1981);
Sofias egen bok (Helsinki: Söderström, 1982; Stockholm: Trevi, 1982);
Rödluvan (Helsinki: Söderström, 1986; Stockholm: Trevi, 1986);
Önskans träd (Bromma, Sweden: Fripress, 1987);
Storfångaren (Helsinki: Söderström, 1989; Stockholm: Trevi, 1989);
Arnaia: kastad i havet (Helsinki: Söderström, 1992; Stockholm: Trevi, 1992);
Bryta mot lagen (Helsinki: Söderström, 1992; Stockholm: Trevi, 1992);
Personliga angelägenheter (Helsinki: Söderström, 1996; Stockholm: Trevi, 1996);
Sofia vuxen med sitt MBD (Helsinki: Söderström, 1998; Stockholm: Forum, 1998);
Den finlandssvenska dikten 13 (Stockholm: Bonnier, 2001; Helsinki: Söderström, 2001).

PLAY PRODUCTIONS: *Irtep,* 1979;
Våldsam kärlek, adapted from *Män kan inte våldtas,* Stockholm, February 1979;
Drömbilder, 1996.

PRODUCED SCRIPTS: "Eller vad tycker ni?" television, 1970;
"Hälsningar från Doris," television, 1975;

Märta Tikkanen (photograph by Marie Nilsson; from the cover for Rödluvan, *1986)*

"Våldsam kärlek," television, 1979.

OTHER: Excerpt in *Finlandssvenskarna i 1970–talets utbildningssamhälle: Rapport från den finlandssvenska kulturkonferensen i Vasa den 14-15 januari 1967* (Ekenäs: Svenska kulturfondens skrifter, 1967);

"Fredrika Runeberg," in *Kvinnornas litteraturhistoria,* edited by Marie Louise Ramnefalk and Anna Westberg (Lund: Författarförlaget, 1981), pp. 144-159;

Du tror du kuvar mig liv? edited by Tikkanen and Tua Forsström (Stockholm: Trevi, 1984);

"Sikgränd 2," in *Henrik,* edited by Tikkanen (Borgå, Finland: Alba, 1985), pp. 127-139;

"Finland: Far from Atolls and Ayatollahs," translated by Linda Schenck, in *Freedom of Expression: The Acid Test,* edited by Niels Frid-Nielsen (Stockholm: The Nordic Council, 1995), pp. 102-106;

"Elden den röda," in *Kvinnornas röda bok* (Stockholm: Trevi, 1996).

SELECTED PERIODICAL PUBLICATIONS–UNCOLLECTED: "Några råd till mina kära döttrar i glädjen över att de finns," *Aftonbladet,* 19 January 1981;

"Barnet och sången–ett tema i Solveig von Schoultz' lyrik," *Finsk tidskrift,* 3 (1984): 81-88;

"Mina rum," *Vi,* 20 (1989): 24-28;

"Landet Sverige en värld av honung," *Dagens nyheter,* 13 May 1995;

"Ett skrik i bomull," *Tidskriften 90-tal om litteratur och konst,* 7 (1996): 88-89;

"Ge månen!" *Status,* 4 (1998): 20, 22-23.

One of the most widely translated authors in Finland, Märta Tikkanen began to write from a young age and knew the importance of finding the time and space to devote to this activity. As a girl she suspected that her mother, Margit Cavonius, also wished to write; Margit and Solveig von Schoultz, one of the finest modern Fenno-Swedish poets, were friends, and Schoultz influenced Tikkanen greatly as an adult. As a mother of three as well as a teacher and a wife, however, Margit had neither the space nor the time to pursue her hidden passion. Tikkanen based a poignant scene in her novel *Rödluvan* (Red Riding Hood, 1986) on her mother's predicament. The furniture is finally rearranged to provide Margit with the desk space she needs for teaching preparation and for writing; yet, because her husband–a highly placed employee of the Swedish-language school system–cannot work with the furniture in its new position, the promising space is sacrificed and the furniture returned to its original configuration. This childhood vignette foreshadows two salient aspects of Tikkanen's writing: stylistically, her form reflects a natural rhythm and a complete lack of authorial insecurity, while her content often expresses a keen awareness of how easily nascent women writers can be silenced. Tikkanen has said that she sees herself as a feminist and a writer, though not as a feminist writer, and herein perhaps lies the clue to her broad international appeal; while treating subjects that are traditionally labeled "women's issues," she does not pose as an expert but rather shares her experience in a direct, emotionally engaged but dispassionate voice. Her examination of love and its practical and social effects propels her message beyond the borders of class and geography.

Tikkanen was born Märta Eleonora Cavonius on 3 April 1935 in Helsinki to Swedish-speaking parents who provided her with a loving, secure–if economically modest–and educated atmosphere, and her childhood years in Helsinki were darkened only by World War II. After the Finnish capital was bombed in the summer of 1944, she was sent–along with approximately seventy thousand other Finnish children–to live safely in Sweden for a few months. Like most Fenno-Swedish writers, Cavonius attended Helsinki University. At age twenty, while still at university, she began pursuing her passion for writing in the field of journalism; she attained a summer replacement position at the office of *Hufvudstadsbladet,* the major Swedish-language newspaper in Finland. In 1958 she received her master of philosophy degree. Later she used her teacher training as a native language instructor, or *modersmålslärare,* in Swedish. She also worked at the Helsinki City Labor Institute from 1972-1980–serving as director for seven of her eight years there–and left to pursue her writing career full-time when her novels began receiving more acclaim.

During her stint at *Hufvudstadsbladet,* she had met the artist and author Henrik Tikkanen, ten years her senior and married with two children. After attempts by others to suppress the attraction between them, she and Henrik eventually married in 1963. Their often turbulent union resulted in three children–Tikkanen already had one child from a brief first marriage–and lasted twenty-one years, until Henrik passed away in 1984.

Tikkanen's marriage to Henrik provided many of the story ideas for her works. The Tikkanens enjoyed a prominent presence in the small world of Fenno-Swedish culture and were known for their willingness to publish details about their relationship, drawing accusations that they were airing dirty marital laundry. By the time that Tikkanen became a published writer, during the 1970s, Henrik had already borne his share of negative criticism for confessional, sexually explicit novels, and her work might have been accorded a more generous reception in Finland if she not had not been his wife. As a consequence, a certain irritation verging on small-mindedness colors much of the criticism in Finland of Tikkanen's output, at least until Henrik's death. Critics in Sweden and especially Germany, however, have

Tikkanen with her husband, artist and author Henrik Tikkanen

judged her work more positively than their Finnish counterparts. Swedish and German critics are correct in identifying one impulse behind Tikkanen's novels and prose poetry. They see her works as an ongoing struggle variously to justify, exorcise, celebrate, and examine her relationship to her husband. Her books repeatedly affirm the strength and passion of her love for Henrik while simultaneously making no secret of the attendant difficulties. Indeed, his problems with alcohol and mental illness often wreaked violence and terror in their family life, and as Tikkanen's reputation began to eclipse his own, Henrik suffered increasingly from paranoia and other delusions that provoked him to accuse her of infidelity and other failings.

In producing literature from the events of her own life, Tikkanen was no different from other women writers in the late 1960s and early 1970s. While the temptation is thus strong to label her a feminist writer, she rarely sounds dogmatic or strident. In Tikkanen's debut, *Nu imorron* (Now Tomorrow, 1970), the first-person protagonist sends her husband on a trip to Sweden in an attempt to secure quality time for her work, but the plan seems doomed from the start. She urges her husband to take a female friend along as a traveling companion to help with the logistical difficulties he often experiences when on his own, but she realizes too late that they will not be able to refrain from engaging in an affair. A few hours after his departure, the babysitter calls in sick, and the narrator is left alone with her children all week. She pursues an infidelity of her own but is left feeling empty afterward. During the course of her husband's absence she attempts to analyze their relationship; she concludes with a statement that hardly qualifies as a conclusion–that they resemble a two-headed donkey.

Dedicated to Tikkanen's dishwasher, who she calls the only household "member" that assists her in her pursuit of a writing life, *Nu imorron* is a photograph of a troubled marriage, from which the way out will happen "now tomorrow"–or, in other words, probably never. Tikkanen suggests that equality and competition are at issue in this book, which some critics view as the beginning of the quite public Tikkanenian marriage dialogue. The novel reads as it was written–breathlessly, in the short period of time when her husband was busy with his own work and not around to demand her attention. The use of prose interlaced with poetry and of short paragraphs marks a style that grows increasingly typical for Tikkanen later in her production. Yet, *Nu imorron* and her next two novels received little attention when they appeared. Only after her breakthrough with *Män kan inte våldtas* (Men Cannot Be Raped, 1976; translated as *Manrape*, 1978) did the first three novels command more notice; they are, more accurately, precursors to her later writing than autonomous pieces of literature.

Ingenmansland (No Man's Land, 1972) extends Tikkanen's focus from the protagonist's marriage to societal conditions that lead to and foster such marriages. Fredrika, or Freddi–named for two icons of Scandinavian feminism, Frederika Bremer and Fredrika Runeberg–aspires to political enlightenment and engagement within a communist framework but is foiled by her difficult position as a harried mother with young children; because her prime working hours start after her husband falls asleep and before, in the early hours of the morning, she is overcome by exhaustion and by her husband's scorn for what he perceives as her naiveté. She unwittingly orchestrates her own failure when she gathers a group of women to storm a publisher's office to confiscate an antifeminist booklet. Meanwhile, the publisher, who is also her lover, and her husband join forces to subdue her while the media interviews an antifeminist author–rather than Freddi. The most overtly political of Tikkanen's fictional works, *Ingenmansland* is uneven and lacks a central focus.

In *Vem bryr sig om Doris Mihailov?* (Who Cares about Doris Mihailov? 1974), Tikkanen deals tangentially with domestic themes but focuses primarily on the alleged coldness of medical professionals, represented in the novel by the character Patrick Peterson, a psychiatrist. At the same time she provides a critique of an upper-class journalist through Carla, a reporter who profits from her pathos-filled accounts on women's issues such as abortion. The novel consists of a conversation between Patrick and Carla in the abandoned apartment of a mutual acquaintance, Doris Mihailov, as they attempt to unravel the mystery behind the disappearance of the woman and her small daughter. No one emerges the moral victor in this battle; Doris is still missing by the end of the novel, and a tape she has left provides some indication that she may have killed herself. Patrick and Carla, two educated and privileged people who seem to have all the answers, are left to examine, respectively, feelings of guilt and regret. Although the taped confessions of Doris seem contrived and artificial, Tikkanen's message is strong and unsettling.

Not until her fourth book, *Män kan inte våldtas,* did Tikkanen achieve national and some international fame–even notoriety. Tova Randers, a single mother like Doris Mihailov, drops by a restaurant to celebrate her fortieth birthday alone. After dancing with a stranger, she follows him home, and he rapes her. After she registers the scale of emotions typical for rape victims–shock, disbelief, denial, humiliation, despair, disgust–her rage ultimately propels her into action. She plans and successfully executes a rape on the perpetrator, Marty Wester, making him experience the same humiliation and powerlessness that he inflicted upon her. Although the novel raises other issues regarding sexual assault and the oppression of women in general, the act of rape itself and the physiological plausibility of forcing a man into unwanted sexual intercourse raised violent debate in Finland. Tikkanen felt patently misunderstood; she received hate mail, and one woman even assaulted her physically. The novel ends with an episode in which Tova's teenage son comes home weeping after sexually assaulting his girlfriend. Tikkanen expanded this coda to the story into a play for youth, *Våldsam kärlek* (Violent love), which premiered in Stockholm in February 1979.

The controversy that *Män kan inte våldtas* fomented strengthened Tikkanen's reputation as a serious writer. Her status crystallized with the appearance of *Århundradets kärlekssaga* (1978; translated as *The Love Story of the Century*, 1984), her most popular work. Performed on stage in many versions in Finland, Sweden, Germany, and in other countries, *Århundradets kärlekssaga* garnered the Nordic Women's Literature Prize for Tikkanen, who was able to make writing a full-time career because of the sizable financial award. With the exception of a few sections in *Vem bryr sig om Doris Mihailov?* that mix prose with poetry, Tikkanen's fifth novel marked her first attempt at blending the two genres for the length of a book. Moreover, her use of the first-person voice is appropriate to the content; the narrative presents a sober, autobiographical view of a woman's relationship with her alcoholic husband. She depicts beatings, sickness, and frightened children, as well as the blessed peace that comes over the house once the drunken husband falls asleep. Tikkanen relates these events and emotions in the framework of a love that cannot die despite the dire toll exacted on its participants. Some critics saw this novel as her wry response to Henrik's picture of an all-devouring passion in his *Mariegatan 16* (16 Marie St., 1977). Tikkanen has revealed that until her husband and a lecture audience urged her to publish

Århundradets kärlekssaga, she never intended it for public consumption. The protagonist's admission of culpability in the misery of the relationship prevents the novel from becoming a mere litany of an oppressed wife.

Mörkret som ger glädjen djup (The Darkness That Lends Depth to Happiness, 1981) resembles *Århundradets kärlekssaga* stylistically, though not in terms of content; nor was it received, like the previous novel, as enthusiastically by the critics. *Mörkret som ger glädjen djup* embodies a long, two-part prose-poem—which some scholars argue is actually a collection of poems—about a mother-son relationship, ostensibly between Sofia Ulrika Wecksell and her son, the troubled writer Josef Julius Wecksell, yet subliminally between Tikkanen and her own son. A promising Fenno-Swedish poet and playwright in the nineteenth century, Wecksell had a nervous breakdown at the age of twenty-nine, shortly after the publication of his most famous work, *Daniel Hjort: Sorgespel i fem akter med fyra tablåer* (Daniel Hjort: Tragedy in Five Acts with Four Tableaux, 1863). He never recovered and spent more than forty years in a mental institution. In the first section of *Mörkret som ger glädjen djup* Tikkanen conjectures on Sofia's thoughts and feelings, particularly in light of the fact that Wecksell was not the only child in his family to succumb to mental illness; the second section incorporates words and pictures that Tikkanen used in previous books to describe her husband. Her autobiographical basis for Wecksell is her own son, however, whose mental illness engenders Tikkanen's empathy with Sofia. Tikkanen's son recovered from the encephalitis that caused his momentary breakdown; as at least one critic has asserted, he is also the basis for the son who watches his father's violent behavior from behind his mother in *Århundradets kärlekssaga.* Thus, the poems in *Mörkret som ger glädjen djup* are filled with an unsettling aura of guilt and remorse, not unlike the atmosphere embracing *Vem bryr sig om Doris Mihailov?*

In the 1980s, after the publication of *Mörkret som ger glädjen djup,* Tikkanen began writing about another Sofia—her youngest daughter, who was diagnosed at the age of seven with Attention Deficit Hyperactivity Disorder (ADHD), which is known in Finland as Minimal Brain Dysfunction (MBD). Tikkanen wrote *Sofias egen bok* (Sofia's Own Book, 1982) and *Önskans träd* (The Tree of Wishes, 1987) to describe her daughter's life, development, and diagnosis. Years before she had presented similar material, though in a less autobiographical way, in her play *Irtep* (1979), named for the way the protagonist spells his name, Petri. In the two books about her daughter, although Tikkanen occasionally conveys Sofia's unconventional perceptions of reality in a lyrical way or describes her difficulties as a parent coping with a child who has ADHD, she writes in a mostly matter-of-fact style, as if they were documentary accounts, and at times seems imploring or activist. In *Önskans träd* Tikkanen writes about Sofia in a simple language intended for people with ADHD.

During the 1980s Tikkanen also co-edited an anthology of Finnish women's poetry, *Du tror du kuvar mig liv?* (You Think You Can Beat Me, Life? 1984). This selection—which, by Tikkanen's own admission, was subjective—was compiled for the purpose of bringing to public attention the work of Finnish- and Swedish-language women poets of the last three centuries. She criticizes here and elsewhere the fact that no women writers had been awarded the prestigious Nordic Prize; in particular she mourned the failure of the prize committee to award Schoultz, whose poem "Du tror du kuvar mig liv?" provided the title for the anthology.

In 1986 Tikkanen wrote *Rödluvan,* in which she employs the story of Red Riding Hood and gives the most compelling and clear picture of her childhood yet in narrative from. Turning the famous fairy tale on its head, her version shows Red Riding Hood running off to the forest in emotional and erotic pursuit of the wolf. Tikkanen revises the fairy tale to explore the reasons why an apparently happy, secure child takes delight in an act of absolute rebellion. One critic, Synnöve Clason, suggests in her book *Ängeln på vinden: Om kvinnligt skrivande nu och förr* (The Angel in the Attic: Women's Writing Past and Present, 1989) that the main character enacts her own mother's revolt, and in so doing questions the traditional socialization of women. Critics paid much attention to the renewal and rewriting of the Red Riding Hood story and to the affirming view in *Rödluvan* of the interdependence and interconnection between men and women. With the 1986 novel Tikkanen peaked as a mature and respected writer in Finland and abroad.

In her next novel, *Storfångaren* (The Big Game Hunter, 1989), the country of Greenland and its geography, history, language, and climate provide the backdrop for another examination of the dynamics of a love relationship. Written episodically in the first person, the novel not only features Tikkanen's prose-poem approach at its most effective but also displays a versatility not encountered in her previous books. She interweaves Greenlander culture and environment so deftly with the equally dramatic, compelling, and dangerous aspects of the new love relationship, that the reader soon sees the country as a protagonist in the story; Greenland is as much a main character as the first-person narrator who scrutinizes the depth of her feelings. *Storfångaren* comes across as an impressionistic travelogue rather than as a novel. By the time of the appearance of the book, Tikkanen's husband had been deceased for five years, and perhaps because of this new period in her life, the tone of her writing is different and more confident. Moreover, *Storfångaren* was her first book to be set outside of Finland and to include extensive nature

Cover for Tikkanen's revision of the Red Riding Hood story, in which the girl seeks out the company of the wolf (Knight Library, University of Oregon)

descriptions; the new landscape was thus an invigorating change.

In *Arnaia: kastad i havet* (Arnaia: Tossed into the Sea, 1992), her eleventh book, Tikkanen continues to write with the innovation, freshness, and literary renewal seen in *Storfångaren*. Although the narrative prose poem once again concerns her main theme, the possibility and constitution of love, she turns to classical Greek mythology for its form. "Arnaia" is the name first given to Ulysses' wife, Penelope, before she became docile; because the name therefore reflects Penelope's original rebelliousness, Tikkanen rewrites the story of Ulysses' wife to reflect the defiant aspects of her personality. In the novel, which—like most of her books—alludes to people and events in her own life, Tikkanen elevates her personal relationships to a more general, iconic plane, and with more self-assurance she begins referring to works other than her own. Certain feminist themes, such as the rebirth of woman and woman's biological relationship to water, also resonate in the book. No other work by Tikkanen includes freedom quite so prominently, and none of her prior works received as much critical acclaim, both in Finland and abroad.

Since the publication of her first book in the early 1970s—with the exception of *Ingenmansland*—Tikkanen has avoided overtly political issues in her fiction. Yet, in her expository work she has spoken up about such issues as bilingualism, minority rights, and the place of Finland in the world community. In her essay "Finland: Far from Atolls and Ayatollahs," published in *Freedom of Expression: The Acid Test* (1995), she bemoaned Finnish complacency in the face of the *fatwa* that was issued in 1989 against Salman Rushdie for writing *The Satanic Verses* (1988).

In *Personliga angelägenheter* (Private Matters, 1996) Tikkanen discards the prose-poem format in favor of a more traditional narrative style, choosing a conventional structure in order to juxtapose two love stories. The first story begs comparison with previous accounts of the early stages of Tikkanen and Henrik's relationship and all the uncertainty and hope that imbued their attraction to each other; the second tells a parallel and yet opposite story from a man's perspective. In her novice attempt to write in a male voice, Tikkanen proves that she is a surprisingly versatile stylist. The protagonist AnnaCi, while working out her love affair with a married man through a series of letters and diary entries she addresses to him, finds evidence that her own father had carried on a clandestine, extramarital affair for years before his death; her father's affair constitutes the other love story of the novel. The title of the book mirrors his fear of passion and his ultimate loss of control, for "private matters" is the euphemistic term he uses for love. Critics received *Personliga angelägenheter* positively, and many noted the skillful and effective way Tikkanen developed multiple voices.

In 1998 her most recent book about her daughter Sofia came out. *Sofia vuxen med sitt MBD* (Adult Sofia with Her ADHD) recapitulates the intervening years and gives an update on Sofia. Written when her daughter was in her mid twenties, *Sofia vuxen med sitt MBD* takes a tender look at the development of an unusual child but is also intended as a documentary book to help other parents of ADHD-diagnosed children, just as Tikkanen's first books about Sofia broadly informed parents in Finland about ADHD. In this third book on Sofia she includes material from interviews with medical professionals and summaries of her own research into the disorder. Indeed, her books and articles on ADHD have been well received by parents, educators, and medical personnel, and one or two critics have seen literary value in them as well.

Märta Tikkanen remains one of the most widely read of Fenno-Swedish writers. Her style is accessible, rhythmic, and romantic; her voice is natural, immediate, and unpretentious. She continues to contribute frequently to Finnish and Swedish periodicals with book reviews, political and cultural articles, and guest columns. While raising consciousness about feminist issues such as a woman's need for a space in which to write productively and the importance for a woman writer of having her own voice, she makes no secret of the fact that relationships with men figure largely in her life, and she is neither apologetic nor sheepish in this admission. Some critics have taken Tikkanen's affirmation of women who are both mothers and creators the wrong way. At the same time she urges people to think in terms of literature generally rather than in terms of men's and women's literature. The translation of her works into at least nineteen languages–in Germany alone her books sell in the hundreds of thousands–confirms her reputation as one of a handful of internationally known writers in Swedish-speaking Finland. She was awarded the Tollander Prize in 1999 and the Fredrika Runeberg Prize in 2001, two signs of the high esteem in which she has finally come to be held in her native country.

References:

Synnöve Clason, "Kamp för överlevnad," "Att följa med när vargen lockar," and "Kära Märta Tikkanen" in her *Ängeln på vinden: Om kvinnligt skrivande nu och förr* (Stockholm: Trevi, 1989), pp. 162–164, 165–167, 225–227;

Susanna Flühmann, "Zum emanzipatorischen Potential schwedischer Literatur von Frauen in den 1970er Jahren," in *Literature as Resistance and Counter-Culture: Papers of the 19th Study Conference of the International Association for Scandinavian Studies,* edited by Andras Masat and Peter Madl (Budapest: Hungarian Association for Scandinavian Studies, 1993), pp. 491–497;

Janet Garton, "Little Red Riding Hood Comes of Age: Or, When the Fantastic Becomes the Feminist," in *Essays in Memory of Michael Parkinson and Janine Dakyns,* edited by Christopher Smith (Norwich, U.K.: School of Modern Languages and European Studies, University of East Anglia, 1996), pp. 289–294;

Inger Elisabeth Hansen, "Brukslyrikk for for [sic] følelser eller knekkprosa for kikkere: Bemerkninger om og av Märta Tikkanen," *Vinduet: Gyldendals tidsskrift for litteratur,* 36 (1982): 30–33;

Gladys Hird, "Märta Tikkanen: Confessions in Verse," *Swedish Books,* 2, no. 4 (1980);

Christina Kellberg, "Drömmen om närhet och driften mot kaos," *Dagens nyheter,* 4 October 1992;

Merete Mazzarella, "Märta Tikkanen: Passion eller jämlikhet?" in her *Från Fredrika Runeberg till Märta Tikkanen: Frihet och beroende i finlandssvensk kvinnolitteratur* (Helsinki: Söderström, 1985), pp. 171–187;

Jane Pamp, "Kärlekssagan om Rödluvan och Vargen: En dialog mellan Märta och Henrik Tikkanen," *Horisont,* 41, no. 1 (1994): 4–18;

George C. Schoolfield, "Finland-Swedish Literature," in *A History of Finland's Literature,* edited by Schoolfield (Lincoln & London: University of Nebraska Press, 1998);

Siv Storå, "Anpassning och uppror: Familjedynamik i Märta Tikkanen's författarskap," *Finsk tidskrift,* 6 (1990): 381–390;

Lotta Strandberg, "Kan frågorna äntligen besvaras? Om Märta Tikkanens *Personliga angelägenheter,*" *Nya Argus,* 9–10 (1996): 201–202;

Tatiana Sundgren, ed., *Finlandssvenska kvinnor skriver* (Helsinki: Schildt, 1984);

Johan Wrede, "Hunden," in *Henrik,* edited by Tikkanen (Borgå, Finland: Alba, 1985), pp. 105–112.

Tomas Tranströmer
(15 April 1931 -)

Joanna Bankier
University of Southern Stockholm

BOOKS: *17 dikter* (Stockholm: Bonnier, 1954);
Hemligheter på vägen (Stockholm: Bonnier, 1958);
Den halvfärdiga himlen (Stockholm: Bonnier, 1962);
Klanger och spår (Stockholm: Bonnier, 1966);
Mörkerseende (Göteborg: Författarförlaget, 1970); translated by Robert Bly as *Night Vision* (Northwood Narrows, N.H.: Lillabulero, 1971);
Stigar (Göteborg: Författarförlaget, 1973)–includes Tränstromer's translations of poems by Bly and János Plinszky;
Östersjöar (Stockholm: Bonnier, 1974); translated by Samuel Charters as *Baltics* (Berkeley, Cal.: Oyez, 1975);
Sanningsbarriären (Stockholm: Bonnier, 1978); translated, with an introduction, by Bly as *Truth Barriers* (San Francisco: Sierra Club, 1980);
Dikter: 1954-1978 (Stockholm: Bonnier, 1979);
Det vilda torget (Stockholm: Bonnier, 1983); translated by John F. Deane as *The Wild Market Place* (Dublin: Dedalus, 1985);
För levande och döda (Stockholm: Bonnier, 1989); translated by Deane as *For the Living and the Dead* (Dublin: Dedalus, 1994);
Minnena ser mig (Stockholm: Bonnier, 1993);
Sorgegondolen (Stockholm: Bonnier, 1996);–includes selections translated by Malena Mörling as "Grief no. 2," *Colorado Review*, 26 (1999): 68–72;
Dikter: Från 17 Dikter till För levande och döda (Stockholm: MånPocket, 1997);
Tolkningar, edited, with an introduction, by Niklas Schioler (Stockholm: Bonnier, 1999);
Fängelse: Nio haikudikter från Hällby ungdomsfängelse (1959) (Uppsala: Ed. Edda, 2001);
Samlade dikter: 1954-1996 (Stockholm: Bonnier, 2001).

Editions in English: *Tomas Tranströmer: Three Poems*, translated by Robert Bly, Thomas Buckman, and Eric Sellin (Lawrence, Kans.: Williams, 1966);
Twenty Poems by Tomas Tranströmer, translated by Bly (Madison, Minn.: Seventies, 1970);

Tomas Tranströmer (courtesy of Monica Tranströmer)

Windows & Stones: Selected Poems, translated by May Swenson and Leif Sjöberg (Pittsburgh: University of Pittsburgh Press, 1972);
Elegy; Some October Notes, translated by Bly (Rushden, U.K.: Sceptre, 1973);
Selected Poems of Paavo Haavikko & of Tomas Tranströmer, translated by Fulton and Anselm Hollo (Harmondsworth, U.K.: Penguin, 1974);
Friends, You Drank Some Darkness: Three Swedish Poets, Harry Martinson, Gunnar Ekelöf, and Tomas Tranströmer, selected and translated by Bly (Boston: Beacon, 1975);

Tranströmer with his mother, Helmy Westerberg Tranströmer, circa 1932 (courtesy of Monica Tranströmer)

Tomas Tranströmer: Selected Poems, translated by Fulton (Ann Arbor, Mich.: Ardis, 1981);

The Truthbarrier, translated by John F. Deane (Drogheda: Aquila, 1985);

Tomas Tranströmer: Selected Poems 1954–1986, edited by Robert Hass, translated by Bly, Samuel Charters, Swenson, Sellin, Joanna Bankier, Deane, and others (New York: Ecco, 1987);

For the Living and the Dead: New Poems and a Memoir, edited by Daniel Halpern, translated by Bankier, Bly, Charters, Fulton, and Malena Mörling (Hopewell, N.J.: Ecco, 1995);

For the Living and the Dead: A Bilingual Edition, translated by Don Coles (Ottawa: BuscherBooks, 1996);

New Collected Poems, translated by Fulton (Newcastle upon Tyne, U.K.: Bloodaxe, 1997);

The Half-Finished Heaven: The Best Poems of Tomas Tranströmer, chosen and translated by Bly (St. Paul, Minn.: Graywolf, 2001).

Few poets have in their lifetime been as abundantly translated or as willingly assimilated into other languages as the Swedish poet Tomas Tranströmer, who also trained and worked as a psychologist. The anthology *English and American Surrealist Poetry* includes him as part of the "deep image" canon of translated poetry. In France he has inspired a new "anti-Tel Quel-poetics" (in reference to the French school of theory of the 1960s and 1970s) inspired by the magazine *L'Incitation au vol* (Incitement to Flying). His works can be read in practically every European language and in quite a few non-European languages as well.

In his native Sweden, Tranströmer's reputation as the leading poet of his generation was assured almost from the publication of his first book, *17 dikter* (17 Poems) in 1954. His reputation as a lyric genius from Söder–the southern part of Stockholm–preceded the appearance of the thin, pale blue volume; rumor had it that the twenty-three-year-old poet, a consummate craftsman, customarily took a month to produce just a single verse. When *17 dikter* appeared, critics commended the young poet's maturity and poise. By the time Tranströmer published his second book, his presence on the Swedish literary scene arguably marked a turning point in the history of the national literature.

In contrast to many other twentieth-century Swedish writers, Tranströmer is not of the working class. He was born on 15 April 1931 in Stockholm. Although some might say that he was the product of a broken home, because his parents separated when he was three years old, and his father, Gösta Tranströmer, an editor and journalist, remained rather aloof thereafter, Tranströmer nonetheless grew up in a remarkably harmonious and intellectual household. His mother, Helmy, taught primary school in an exclusive area on the other side of town, and her fair and caring approach as a teacher was legendary. The family's male caretaker–and Tranströmer's role model–was Carl Helmer Westerberg, the boy's maternal grandfather and a ship's pilot. Tranströmer counts his time spent with Westerberg, whom the poet lovingly describes in the long poem *Östersjöar* (1974; translated as *Baltics,* 1975), among the most tender of his childhood memories. Several times a week Westerberg took his grandson to see the trains at the Central Station and on visits to the local railway museum; in addition, they regularly traversed Stockholm from the south to the north to see dinosaurs, fossils, and stuffed animals at the Museum of Natural History. In Tranströmer's recollections his grandfather was always kind and conciliatory and had vast resources of humor, equanimity, and common sense. When Tranströmer was six years old, he became lost one day in town but then somehow managed to find his way home. When he finally returned, Westerberg was there at home to receive him with his characteristic natural warmth and without making a fuss.

In the summer months the extended Westerberg-Tranströmer family typically stayed on Runmarö, an island located in the archipelago, which separates Stockholm from the open sea. On the island Transtömer and his mother vacationed at Westerberg's two-story blue house, surrounded by similar houses inhabited by their cousins and siblings and friends. The structure, which has been in the family for generations, figures prominently in the poem "Det blå huset" (The Blue House) and in other places in Transtömer's poetry as a significant place of memory. For the poet the blue house represents both a physical and symbolic site, where memories come alive before making their way into his lyrics.

Transtömer's childhood was not, however, merely idyllic, for World War II raged on the periphery of Sweden for six years, from the time that he was eight years old until he turned fourteen. During Sunday dinners the family listened avidly to the Allied news, broadcast in Swedish by the British Broadcasting Corporation. As a child Transtömer often wished he could demonstrate his family's anti-Nazi stance in a public way. An uncle in the Swedish marines died while escorting convoys across the Atlantic Ocean; he resurfaces many years later as the ghostly memory in Transtömer's poem "Den bortglömde kaptenen" (The Forgotten Captain), published in *För levande och döda* (1989; translated as *For the Living and the Dead,* 1994). As a precocious, sheltered boy, Transtömer also had his share of miseries at school, the first year of which–since he already knew how to read–he learned mainly how to sit still in his pew. Life at school improved with time, nonetheless, as he developed into a self-motivated student whose curiosity sent him on habitual visits to the public library and to the laboratories at the Museum of Natural History. He spent his summers collecting rare insects and butterflies, reading accounts of exotic travels, and dreaming of journeys across an exactly measured and mapped out imaginary African continent.

Transtömer as a boy disliked being singled out in any way and especially resented being pitied for having an absent father. He was, he says, neither popular nor bullied excessively at school. Yet, images of persecution by mobs occasionally enter his poetry–for example, in the poem "Ensamhet" (Being Alone), published in *Klanger och spår* (1966); "Jag var anonym / som en pojke på en skolgård omgiven av fiender" (I was anonymous / like a boy in a schoolyard surrounded by enemies)–and he explains at length in *Minnena ser mig* (Memories See Me, 1993) the strategy he devised for when the school bully pinned him to the ground. He forced his body to go limp, pretending that his "real self" had flown away and left just a corpse behind; the stratagem was one that Transtömer put to use later in life as well.

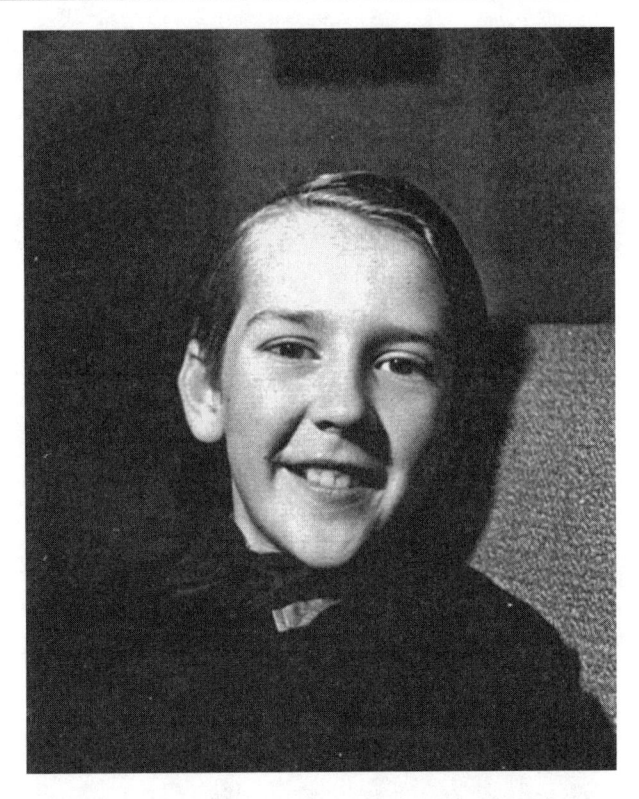

Transtömer in 1940 (courtesy of Monica Transtömer)

Yet, even school had its bright moments, especially during adolescence. Södra Latin, Transtömer's high school, had acquired a reputation for producing gifted students, who generally hailed from working-class families; for example, the writer Stig Dagerman, a star in literary Sweden of the late 1940s, had been a student at Södra Latin. Transtömer's schoolmates were an unusually clever and well-read group who participated in or wrote for formal and informal literary clubs, poetry competitions, and high-school magazines.

This generation, brought up during the postwar economic boom years of Sweden, was at its peak when publishing houses in the country finally caught up with the modernist avant-garde movement and had both the means and the will to support it. Europe may have been in shambles after the war, but the Continent was also being rapidly rebuilt. In Sweden, steel factories, ball-bearing factories, and paper mills were operating at full capacity, fulfilling the needs of the growing industries in many European countries–such as Germany, Italy, and France–whose reconstruction was made possible partly by the Marshall Plan. As a result, the publishing houses in Sweden were flush with both cash and hopes for the future. After the grim war years of rationed food and isolation, as people recognized a need for culture and for beautiful

Dust jacket for Tranströmer's first book, a collection of seventeen poems published in 1954 (courtesy of Monica Tranströmer)

objects, money became available for funding the production of lavish art books and small magazines and for encouraging young literary talents. *Medan lagrarna gro* (While the Laurels Grow) was the high-school magazine in which Tranströmer's juvenilia appeared. After his debut he co-edited until 1957 a poetry magazine, *Upptakt* (Opening Note), and had the opportunity of publishing world poetry in translation. *Upptakt* introduced Swedish readers to the work of Greek, German, and French poets, an eclectic selection from the vast "musée imaginaire" that was then opening up to the post–World War II generation of Europeans.

In the early 1950s Tranströmer completed his obligatory military service and studied literature, psychology, philosophy, and the history of religion at the University of Stockholm. He also gave free rein to his taste for travel and made trips to what in those days were out-of-the-way places: traveling with scarcely any luggage or money, he went to Iceland, Morocco, Turkey, and Yugoslavia, as well as to Spain, Italy, Portu-

gal, and Greece. His witness of the harsh conditions under which many people outside Sweden lived left a profound impression on him, as did his first encounter with communism in Yugoslavia. His journey through the Balkans was especially heartwrenching: "Partiets funktionär på marknadstorget / . . . hans himmel följer honom: det är högt / och trångt som inuti en minaret" (The party official in the village square / . . . his heaven accompanies him: it is high and narrow like inside a minaret).

Tranströmer's eight years of postsecondary school studying and traveling seem to have been happy. He enjoyed friendships, new and old, and socialized with intellectuals and artists, people with whom he shared interests in literature, modern classical music, and the arts. At this time he also wrote poetry, played the piano, and read everything he laid his hands on, developing a enduring preference for Surrealist poetry and a related taste for parapsychology. By turns moderate and rebellious, sometimes prone to half-suppressed temperamental outbursts, and always fiercely independent in his choices and in his judgment, Tranströmer nevertheless always tried to stay balanced and even-tempered. All the while he avidly collected experiences and broadened his range of interests, as the publication of his second volume of poetry, *Hemligheter på vägen* (Secrets on the Way, 1958), made clear.

Hemligheter på vägen features a dense compositional style in all of its fourteen short poems. In one lyric, "En man från Benin" (A Man from Benin), a Portuguese Jew is portrayed in a bronze relief made in the African kingdom of Benin in the fifteenth century: "Han var tre folks bild. / En jude från Portugal / bortseglad med de andra, / . . . iakttagen på marknadsplatsen av negern-gjutkonstnären" (He was the image of three peoples. / A Jew from Portugal, / who sailed away with the others, / . . . Observed in the marketplace / by the Negro cast-maker). Another poem from the collection, "Balakirev's dröm" (translated as "Balakirev's Dream" in *Friends, You Drank Some Darkness: Three Swedish Poets, Harry Martinson, Gunnar Ekelöf, and Tomas Tranströmer*, 1975), follows a sinuous path of associations inside a 1905 dream experienced by the Russian composer Milij Balakirev: "I koncertsalen tonades det fram ett land / där stenarna inte var tyngre än dagg. // Men Balakirev somnade under musiken / och drömde en dröm om tsarens droska" (The sounds in the concert room composed a land / where stones were no heavier than dew. / / Balakirev though fell asleep during the music / and in his dreams he saw the Czar's marriage). A third poem, called "Svenska hus enlsigt belägna" (Isolated Swedish Houses), examines Swedish houses, which are seen as solitary: "Och i ett annat väderstreck / står nybygget och ångar / med lakanstvättens fjäril / fladdrande vid knuten / mitt i en döende skog / där förmultningen läser / genom glasögon av sav / barkborrarnas protokoll" (Further off, the new building / stands steaming / with the laundry butterfly / fluttering at the corner / in the middle of a dying wood / where the moldering reads / through spectacles of sap / the proceedings of the bark-drillers). Tranströmer counterbalances the widely ranging imagination of these poems with a repeated crossing of the border between dream and wakefulness. In "Spår" (translated as "Tracks" in *Friends, You Drank Some Darkness*) he also asks what such a transgression signifies for human consciousness:

> På natten klockan två: månsken. Tåget har stannat
> mitt ute på slätten. Långt borta ljuspunkter i en stad,
> flimrande kallt vid synranden.
> Som när en människa gått in i en dröm så djupt
> att hon aldrig ska minnas att hon var där
> när hon återvänder till sina rum.
>
> (Two a.m.: moonlight. The train has stopped
> out in a field. Far off sparks of light from a town,
> flickering coldly on the horizon.
> As when a man goes so deep into his dream
> he will never remember that he was there
> when he returns again to his room.)

In addition, on 8 November 1958 Tranströmer married Monica Bladh and took his first full-time job as a psychologist at the Psychotechnical Institute in Stockholm. In a letter to fellow writer and former schoolmate Sven Lindqvist, Tranströmer wrote that his wife, Monica, who was eight years younger than he, had qualities of beauty that perfectly matched her qualities of mind and feeling. The poet traveled with his bride to Egypt and recorded her reactions in the poem "I Nildeltat" (In the Nile Delta), published in *Den halvfärdiga himlen* (The Half Finished Heaven, 1962): "Unga frun grät rätt ner i sin mat / på hotellet efter en dag i staden / där hon såg de sjuka som kröp och låg / och barn som måste dö för nöds skull" (The young wife cried right in her food / in the hotel after a day in the town / where she had seen the sick who crawled and lay about / and children who had to die from want). Nevertheless, some of the poems he wrote in those years are among his most cheerful and embody some of the extraordinary images that have become his trademark: in "Paret" (translated as "The Couple" in *Friends, You Drank Some Darkness*), for example, "De släcker lampan och dess vita kupa skimrar / ett ögonblick innan den löses upp / som en tablett i ett glas mörker" (They turn the light off, and its white globe glows / an instant and then dissolves, like a tablet / in a glass of darkness); and in "Dagsmeja" (translated as "Noon Thaw" in *New Col-*

Dust jacket for Tranströmer's third collection of poetry, published in 1962 (courtesy of Monica Tranströmer)

lected Poems, 1997); "Morgonen avlämnade sina brev med frimärken som glödde. / Snön lyste och alla bördor lättade–ett kilo vägde 700 gram inte mer" (The morning delivered its letters with stamps that glowed. / The snow was bright and all burdens lighter–a kilo weighed 700 grams not more).

In 1960 Tranströmer decided to leave Stockholm and its cultural scene for a job as a psychologist in residence outside Linköping at Roxtuna, an institution for delinquent youth. He and Monica were expecting a baby, and their one-bedroom apartment in Stockholm was no place to raise children. In addition to a regular salary, the job included accommodations in a spacious house where there even was room for guests. The Tranströmers' first daughter, Emma, was born in 1961, and the second, Paula, followed in 1964. In the beginning the couple found the distance from the city difficult at times, because they were away from friends, parties, gallery openings,

Cover for a 1972 English translation of poems by Tranströmer (courtesy of Monica Tranströmer)

and the theater and were thus no longer at the center of things. Yet, they soon discovered certain compensations, such as visits from friends—especially at first—who came and stayed for extended periods of time. Tranströmer and his wife learned that in the provinces friendships hold more potential for substantive and intense exchanges. At the same time, as it turned out, they also saw how much time a sincere correspondence between friends demands, particularly while one spouse is trying to hold down a full-time job, as Tranströmer was—a job that often called for some emotional involvement with troubled young people. For him, the hardest part of coping with life in Linköping and work at Roxtuna was the bureaucratic prose style he had to use in his paperwork, a style that at times left the poet empty and unable to write. Nevertheless, poetry collections continued to appear at a steady rate, once every four years: *Den halvfärdiga himlen* (The Half Finished Heaven) was published in 1962; *Klanger och spår* (Resonances and Tracks) in 1966; and *Mörkerseende* (Seeing in the Dark; translated as *Night Vision,* 1971) in 1970.

In Sweden the critical response to Tranströmer's poetry has fluctuated between two extremes: for a decade or so after the appearance of *17 dikter,* his work was much admired, while after 1966 he came under attack. Nevertheless, some made serious attempts to regard his work from a critical angle, and insightful essays on his poetry appeared. As early as 1961, Urban Torhamn analyzed Tranströmer's poetic method and argued that the shock and power of his images derived from their unusual function in the poem: the metaphors do not aim at conveying information, nor are they a means of communicating by substitution. Rather, the poet uses metaphors as "explosioner syftande till en full verklighetsförvandling" (explosions aiming at a total transformation of the experience of reality). Years later commentators explained this distinction in terms of Tranströmer's interest in Surrealist and Baroque poetry.

Another Swedish critic, Peter Hallberg, wrote an essay analyzing the literary sources and influences in the long final poems in *17 dikter,* "Sång"

Transtromer; his wife, Monica; and his daughters, Emma and Paula, in 1973 (courtesy of Monica Transtromer)

(Song) and "Elegi" (Elegy), and showed the debt that the early Tranströmer poems owed to high modernism. Just like works of the great modernists—who were both masters in the art of dismantling and reassembling the world and artists impatient with any preestablished order, such as inherited social, political and moral patterns—these early lyrics also deconstruct lived and literary experience, only to turn them around and reconstruct such experience in elaborate rhetorical designs:

> Det finns en korsväg i ett ögonblick.
> Distansernas musik har samanströmmat.
> Allt sammanvuxet till ett yvigt träd.
> Försvunna städer glittrar i dess grenverk.
>
> (A crossroad is contained within a moment.
> The music of what is distant streams and joins.
> All grown together in a bushy tree.
> Lost cities shining in its foliage.)

These long, elaborate poems bristle with influences and allusions to esoteric material that ranges from the Finnish folk epos *Kalevala* to the parapsychology of J. W. Dunne's *An Experiment with Time* (1927), and from T. S. Eliot's *Four Quartets* (1944) to such nearly forgotten modernist texts as Jean-Paul de Dadelsen's *Jonas* (1962). "Sång" and "Elegi" as well as "Epilog" are Tranströmer's most modernist poems, and as in the works of the influential Eliot, they look to the forgotten Baroque tradition for models and inspiration.

When, in 1977, Tranströmer was asked to write an essay for a volume on Swedish literary history, he chose to discuss the Baroque poet Carl Johan Lohman, who lived from 1694 to 1759. Tranströmer's remarks in the essay reveal as much about himself as it does about Lohman:

> Den här stilen vill förbluffa genom att plötsligt förbinda olika företeelser. Slutresultatet blir ett slags modernism. 1900-talets poet blundar och flyger iväg förlitande sig på drömmen och sitt undermedvetnas vind. "Barock-skalden" är mer förståndsmässig, hans infall ska alltid på något sätt kunna förklaras. Även om förklaringen är en sådan formalitet som en vits. Det kan ändå bli underbara och halsbrytande språng. . . . De retoriska stilgreppen är väl integrerade i språket, känns naturliga.

Dust jacket for Tranströmer's 1978 collection of poetry, translated by Robert Bly in 1980 as Truth Barriers *(courtesy of Monica Tranströmer)*

(This style wants you to experience the marvelous by joining phenomena which ordinarily are kept wide apart. The end result is a modernism of sorts. Twentieth-century poets close their eyes and rely on dreams and the wind of the subconscious. The "baroque poet" is more rational, his devices must always somehow be explainable. Even if the explanation is a mere formality, like a joke. The result is nevertheless these wonderful, breakneck leaps. . . . The rhetorical devices are well integrated into the language and have a natural feel.)

These lines arguably stand as a useful introduction to Tranströmer's own poetic practice. Like Lohman, he also relies on dreams and the subconscious and employs the poetic technique of linking images and things from different areas of experience—of phenomena ordinarily distinguished as widely disparate—in order to force the reader to make leaps of associations and shifts of consciousness. Finally, Tranströmer echoes Lohman in his insistence on creating poetry that is firmly anchored in the natural feel of the language.

Nevertheless, if modernism is the movement with which some critics associate Tranströmer, the aspects of his poetry that were emphasized in 1954—its exactitude and shocking leaps of association, in conjuncture with a matter-of-fact tone were and still are experienced as a new departure and a clean break with Swedish modernism. Göran Printz-Påhlson wrote in his article "Tranströmer and Tradition," which appeared in the journal *Ironwood* (Spring 1979): "The modernism professed by Tranströmer seemed . . . to be of a radically different nature from the dominant tendencies of the preceding decade, when Swedish modernism had come of age. . . . With its spare and ascetic style, graphic visualization and ultimately enigmatic content, it exhibited a clean break with what seemed fuzzy and blurred, sentimental or exhibitionistic in modernism." Since the rallying cry of Tranströmer's generation of writers was to create a literature of bare images and spare diction—what was often termed "en småordens pocsi" (a poetry of linguistic minimalism)—the matter-of-fact nature of Tranströmer's diction was no doubt exemplary.

As Printz-Påhlson argues, Tranströmer's poetry essentially manifested its own resonance through its appearance at a polemical moment in Swedish literature; yet, at the same time, polemics limited the response to his verse for years to come. According to Printz-Påhlson, "The polemical moment of its appearance—and the very force of its language one might add—also gave it a perpetual stigma of coldness, of impersonality, of almost inhuman perfection which it has not been allowed to shed." Precisely because his early poetry seemed to embody the formal aspirations of his generation, and because his first book revolutionized poetic form, he was interpreted as an innovator of form; the verses that came out in 1954, which appeared to be formally inventive, were themselves read by the generation that emerged in the late 1960s as formalist. Tranströmer had expressed the mood of the period so accurately that he became forever associated with that time. His formal achievements made him influential at the same time that they established the categories by which his poetry was organized and read for decades.

A shift in poetics characterizes Swedish literature from the mid 1960s to the mid 1970s, and expectations for lyric poetry—particularly in terms of value and aesthetic quality—altered radically. Swedish writers and poets coming of age in the 1960s began to feel that aesthetic form and aesthetic pleasure might be obstacles to empathy, hindrances evoking indecency in the face of human suffering. The reason for the reevaluation of literature was the discovery of social problems and injustices overseas; graphic pictures of the suffering inflicted on the people of Vietnam and of the misery of the dispossessed in India and Africa were shown on the evening news. The bleakness of the situation in the world was being matched by engagement at home.

As early as 1966 manifestos were composed declaring the elimination of all "unnecessary" barriers between the poet and the reader. Since the manifestos equated art with artifice, the new poetry tended toward the documentary–toward an artless and improvised, even raw, writing style. Suddenly critics took issue with Tranströmer's craftsmanship and formal restraint, and with the publication of his fourth volume of poetry, *Klanger och spår,* he became the primary target of the wrath of younger writers. They gibed impertinently–and mistakenly–that he was a gentleman tourist traveling in comfort, instead of joining the Swedish International Development Cooperation Agency (SIDA), an organization similar to the Peace Corps; they accused Tranströmer of writing elegantly and boldly in a classical form, rather than in a plain style understood by everyone. The motto of these young, up-and-coming writers in Sweden was "ny enkelhet" (new simplicity), and Tranströmer, the most influential poet of the preceding generation and hence a source of considerable "anxiety of influence" (to use Harold Bloom's phrase) for neophyte poets, soon figured as an example of the status quo. For the younger generation of writers Tranströmer towered over them like a threatening father figure.

Despite such polemics and outcries, Tranströmer's poetics had actually changed, for he had been experimenting with new forms for some time. As early as 1962, as seen in *Den halvfärdiga himlen,* he was writing from the perspective of the lyrical "I" and since then had used the first-person pronoun more freely in his verse. He had abandoned not only Eliot's impersonal poetic strategies but also the dense, abstract, and rhythmical diction for which Eliot was known. By the time that *Klanger och spår* appeared, Tranströmer's lyrics had grown not only more intimate but also more explicitly attentive to social and political realities, a transformation that Kjell Espmark shows in great detail in *Resans formler: En studie i Tomas Tranströmers lyrik* (The Journey's Formulae: A Study of the Poetry of Tomas Tranströmer, 1983). Espmark highlights the ecological poems of *Klanger och spår,* reflected in the lines "ute på slätten där industrierna ruvar / och byggnaderna

Dust jacket for Tranströmer's 1989 poetry collection, which was translated in 1994 as For the Living and the Dead *(courtesy of Monica Tranströmer)*

sjunker två millimeter / om året–marken slukar dem sakta" (out on the flats where industries brood, / and the building developments sink two millimeters / a year–the ground slowly swallows them). He also refers to a poem based on Tranströmer's travels to Africa, "Ur en afrikansk dagbok 1963" (From an African Diary 1963), published in *Klanger och spår,* in which news about the crisis in Congo is complemented by Tranströmer's own experiences in the area. As Espmark points out, the poem–in typical Tranströmer fashion–focuses not on revolutionary change but, rather, on the slow, incremental, painful road of progress. "Studenten läser i natten, läser och läser för att bli fri" (The student studies all night, studies and studies so that he can be free), but he turns out to be a "trappsteg för näste man" (stair-rung for the next man). While the refrain of the poem insists "Den som är framme har en lång

1970 poetry volume *Mörkerseende,* he emphatically distances himself from his contemporaries:

> Vid samtal med samtida såg hörde jag bakom deras ansikten
> strömmen
> som rann och ran och drog med sig villiga och motvilliga.
>
> Och varelsen med igenklistrade ögon
> som vill gå mitt i forsen medströms
> kastar sig rakt fram utan att skälva
> i en rasande hunger efter enkelhet.
>
> (Talking with contemporaries I saw heard behind their faces
> the stream
> that flowed and pulled with it the willing and the unwilling.
>
> And I saw a creature with stuck-together eyes that wants
> to go right down the rapids with the current
> throwing himself forward without trembling
> in a furious hunger for simplicity.)

Tranströmer wrote the poem "Om Historien" (About History) in the summer of 1967, when the Swedish Left shifted from its identification with and support of Israel to a decidedly anti-Zionist stance–a position that it maintained for decades. The poet was not taking sides, however; he was merely distancing himself from the urge for simplifications and unified solutions:

> Radikal och revolutionär lever tillsammans som i ett olyckligt äktenskap.
> formade av varann, beroende av varann.
> Men vi som är deras barn måste bryta oss loss.
> Varje problem ropar på sitt eget språk.
> Gå som en spårhund där sanningen har trampat.
>
> (Radical and Reactionary live together as in an unhappy marriage,
> molded by one another, dependent on one another.
> But we who are their children must break loose.
> Every problem calls out for its own language.
> Go like a bloodhound where truth has trampled.)

Such lines of verse were hardly designed to endear Tranströmer to the politically committed, and eventually the differences between him and writers of the "ny enkelhet" appeared even more distinct once the wave of engagé writing abated. The desire and ambition of the latest poets to obliterate the distinction between art and life never really attracted Tranströmer, and he definitely opposed the use of poetry as a platform for political activism. Not least of all, he wished to stay clear of ideology, because–as he put it–"every problem calls out for its own language."

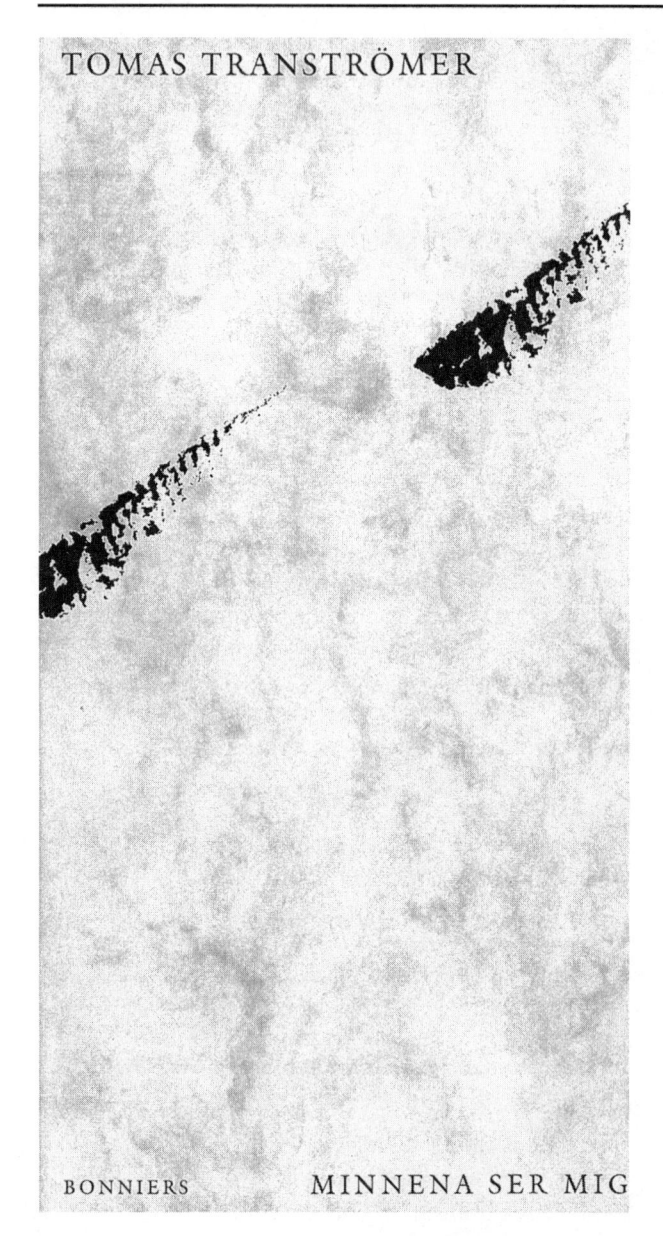

Cover for Tranströmer's collection of autobiographical sketches, published in 1993 (courtesy of Monica Tranströmer)

väg att gå" (The one who has arrived has a long way to go), the overall tone of the poem implies that somehow everything is proceeding in the right direction. For Espmark the lyric shows how Tranströmer's intentions embody "A controlled faith in concord, in the truth which liberates, in the possibilities that can be found in stubborn striving."

Ultimately, however, an irreducible difference between Tranströmer and his increasingly ideological friends and colleagues did persist. In the poem "Med älven" (translated as "Going with the Current" in *Friends, You Drank Some Darkness*), from Tranströmer's

Dust jacket for Tranströmer's 1996 collection, comprising mostly collage-like lyrics and haiku (courtesy of Monica Tranströmer)

Besides being a time of artistic reconsideration, the late 1960s and early 1970s were also years of serious illness in the Tranströmer family. During this period, for example, his mother passed away. As evidenced by its title, *Mörkerseende* includes poetry that reflects much stress and pain. Yet, he always insists that what saved him from utter despair was his distance from Stockholm. Since 1965 the Tranströmers had been living in Västerås, where he held dual jobs as a psychologist and a social worker. When he traveled around the country to give readings of his poetry, Tranströmer noticed that the literary battles then brewing in the capital city were not affecting his audience in the provinces. Above all, during those difficult years he was buoyed by his growing international reputation and by the steady increase of friendships—and of his readership—in the United States.

One enduring friendship has been with the American poet Robert Bly, whom Tranströmer has known since the 1960s. Bly was, and continues to be, a champion of international poetry. He has worked assiduously to make poetry originally written in languages other than in English accessible in translation. His initial venue for such translations was *The Fifties*, a magazine he launched in 1958 and that, as time went on, was renamed *The Sixties* and *The Seventies*. Through Bly and the translating, promoting, and propagandizing activities he carried out in his Minnesota home decades ago, Tranströmer's work—along with the works of such poets as César Vallejo, Rainer Maria Rilke, Georg Trakl, and Pablo Neruda—became more incorporated into the canon of contemporary poetry in the United States.

Moreover, Bly is famous for his love of "leaping poetry," as he called it in his 1975 book with that title, a kind of verse that depicts a freeing of the imagination through "leaping, flying from the intellect to the sea, from Denmark to the unconscious." He seeks unexpected juxtapositions in poetry—gaps of meaning that are difficult or even impossible to bridge—in order to stretch the reader's imagination. Thus, the spaciousness between images, or the unrelatedness of things, that infuses Tranströmer's poetry especially attracted Bly. As he writes in the introduction to his 1975 translation of verses by Tranströmer and two other Swedish poets, *Friends, You Drank Some Darkness*:

> One of the most beautiful qualities in his poems is the space we feel in them. I think one reason for that is that the four or five main images which appear in each of his poems come from widely separated sources of the psyche. His poems are a sort of railway station where trains that have come enormous distances stand briefly in the same building. One train can still have Russian snow lying on the undercarriage, and another may have Mediterranean flowers still fresh in the compartments, and Ruhr soot on the roofs.

Bly has even tried reproducing Tranströmer's "leaping" method in his own verse, and the result is arguably indistinguishable poetry, in that Bly's original verse resembles his translation of Tranströmer's lyrics. Whereas Bly writes in one poem, "I dreamed that men came toward me, carrying thin wires; / I felt the wires pass in, like fire; they were old Tibetans / Dressed in padded clothes, to keep out cold," he translates Tranströmer in another, "Sorge gondol 2": "I dreamt that I was to start school but arrived late. / Everyone in the room wore white masks on their faces. / It was impossible to know which was the teacher." For Bly, as Seamus Heaney wrote in "The Impact of Translation" (*Yale Review*, Autumn 1986), the "creative procedures" of poets such as Rilke, Neruda, and Tranströmer "represented a challenge to the dominant and, as he saw it, undesirable poetic practices ratified by Departments of English. His purpose was to discomfit the formalists, and he threw his foreign-language exemplars like shock troops into the assault." The result was, paradoxically, that Tranströmer—though accused in his native country of lacking political commitment—gradually became a paladin of a literary movement of unambiguous liberal and leftist political activism in the United States.

As recent criticism reflects, Tranströmer's poetry is variously interpreted, whether the approach is a consideration of his language or an intertextual examination. Espmark, for example, argues in *Resans formler* that the ambiguities about which readers complain in Tranströmer's verses are deliberate, and his images are meant to reveal as much as they conceal and mystify. In his poetry communication is abstruse, even hermetic, perhaps because of his conviction that existence itself is inherently mysterious; his verse implies that the primary task of the poet is to reveal the enigma of existence and, at the same time, preserve the mystery.

On the other hand, Staffan Bergsten, who has traced the origin of references to classical music and music history—both common and esoteric—in Tranströmer's lyrics, reads the poem "Carillon" (from *Det vilda torget*), for example, in light of Robert A. Monroe's book *Journeys Out of the Body* (1972). Bergsten also detects less likely references, however, to Colin Wilson's *Mysteries: An Investigation into the Occult, the Paranormal, and the Supernatural* (1978), to Emanuel Swedenborg's diaries, and to the Tibetan *Bardo Thodol*, or Book of the Dead (circa 700). Another scholar, Niklas Schiöler, concludes his book on the poet, *Koncentrationens konst: Tomas Tranströmers senare poesi* (1999), by suggesting that the distinctive quality of Tranströmer's verse can perhaps be best described as magic realism.

In interviews Tranströmer has said repeatedly that he wishes people would live their lives more intensely—in line with the "changer l'homme" tradition of Arthur Rimbaud, a tradition continued and developed by the French Surrealists and also by the "deep image" poets in the United States. Surrealist themes encompass the impulse to awaken the citizenry and the urge to connect daily life with deep, archaic roots. Poetry in this tradition aims at a change of consciousness and access to deep layers of the self, for example, as in "Hommages" (Respects):

> Gick länge längs den antipoetiska muren.
> Die Mauer. Inte se över.
> Den vill omge vårt vuxna liv
> i rutinstaden, i rutinlandskapet.
> Eluard rörde vid någon knapp
> och muren öppnade sig
> och trädgården visade sig.
>
> (Walked along the antipoetic wall.
> Mauer. Don't look over.
> It wants to surround our adult lives
> in the routine city, the routine landscape.
> Eluard touched some button
> and the wall opened
> and the garden showed itself.)

In November 1990 Tranströmer had a stroke, resulting in expressive aphasia, or the inability to talk. His illness was only a temporary setback, for in 1993 his memoir, *Minnena ser mig* (Memories Look at Me), came out, and in 1996 another book of verse, *Sorgegondolen* (selections translated as "Grief Gondola no. 2" in *the Colorado Review*, 1999), was published. *Minnena ser mig* consists of biographical sketches, many of which involved Tranströmer's beloved grandfather, Carl Helmer Westerberg. When *Sorgegondolen*

Tranströmer in 1998 (photograph © Ulla Montan; courtesy of Monica Tranströmer)

appeared, many Swedish reviewers responded with shock and puzzlement and read the poems in the book as if they were commentaries on his illness. To them poems such as "April och tystnad" (April and Silence) captured Tranströmer's poststroke struggles with writing: "jag bärs i min skugga / som en fiol i sin svart låda" (I am carried in my shadow / like a violin / in its black case / All I want to say / gleams out of reach / like the silver / in a pawnshop). The poet actually wrote "April and Silence" before falling ill, but the lyric nonetheless suggests the fragmentary trend of his verse and how his poems have become much shorter in length. Indeed, many of the lyrics in *Sorgegondolen* qualify more as collages, and some are even haikus.

Tranströmer sets whatever is static in his poetry into motion. Houses move sideways or start wandering about at night; islands lift themselves up by the grass; and small details suddenly become magnified–in "Sorgegondolen," "Sparvar stora som höns / sjöng så att det slog lock för öronen" (sparrows the size of hens / sang so loud that my ears closed up)–and grow larger than the whole, upsetting the reader's sense of proportion. Other images in Tranströmer's lyrics contradict the laws of nature:

grass shakes itself in the coal dust; the sun sings with a sweet sound; a dark velvet ditch creeps; a stone idol moves its lips; statues blink; rain travels; and trains lay eggs. Forces that materialize as beasts also come into play in his verse, such as "vårens långa djur / den genomskinliga draken av solsken" (the long beast of spring / the transparent dragon of sunlight) in the poem "Ljuset strömmar in" (The Light Streams In). Yet, upon closer inspection beast and dragon metamorphose into "an endless / commuter train" that flows past.

Tranströmer formulates his vision in poetry more often in temporal than in spatial terms. Human beings live in time, but they also have access to a timeless dimension, "det andra som också finns" (the other dimension that also exists). In *Sorgegondolen*, just as in many earlier works, he momentarily sets aside linear historical time and hints that more profound yet insidious connections exist between events than those presented in history books.

> Liszt has composed a few chords so heavy one should send them
>
> off to the Institute for Mineralogical Studies in Padua. Meteorites!

Far too heavy to stay where they are, they start sinking
   and sinking down
through the coming years until they reach
   the years of the brown shirts.

In this portrayal of Franz Liszt, in "Sorgegondolen Nr 2," the composer is depicted as an attentive listener who had already discerned around 1887 and 1888 certain signs of the coming strife in Europe.

As Tranströmer writes in an earlier verse, "Ibland vidgar sig en avgrund mellan tisdag och onsdag men tjugosex år kan passeras på ett ögonblick" (Sometimes an abyss opens between Tuesday and Wednesday but twenty-six years may pass by in a moment). In *Sorgegondolen* certain privileged moments can hold an entire lifetime:

En tidsrymd
några minuter lång
femtiåtta år bred.

(A time segment
a few minutes long,
fifty-eight years wide.)

The poet stresses that people who live entirely in linear time without experiencing other temporal dimension have "futures instead of faces." While Tranströmer's verse in *Sorgegondolen* is far less mystical and thus not as out of the ordinary as his previous poetry, it does require from the reader an awakening of child-like imagination.

Illness and the aging have made Tomas Tranströmer's poems more melancholy, but a strong element of peace and reconciliation still pervades them. His belief that modern society is built on ideology and materialist illusion has no doubt helped foster such a sense of peace. He sees the whole temporal world as a limited part of existence—albeit with streaks of goodness, beauty, music, and epiphanies—and necessarily views death differently from someone who approaches the end of life with a secular imagination. From Tranströmer's perspective, the prospect of being freed from "the war of the minutes" cannot be entirely negative.

As Tranströmer wrote in *För levande och döda* (1989; translated as *For the Living and the Dead,* 1994), "We living nails hammered down in society! / One day we'll come loose from everything. / We'll feel the wind of death under our wings / and become milder and wilder than here."

Letters:

Tranströmer and Robert Bly, *Air mail: Brev 1964–1990,* compiled by Torbjörn Schmidt, translated by Lars-Håkan Svensson (Stockholm: Bonnier, 2001).

References:

Anna Balakian, *Surrealism: The Road to the Absolute,* revised edition (Chicago: University of Chicago Press, 1986);

Joanna Bankier, "The Sense of Time in the Poetry of Tomas Tranströmer," dissertation, University of California, Berkeley, 1985;

Susan Bassnett-McGuire and André Lefevere, eds., *Translation, History and Culture* (New York & London: Cassell, 1995);

Staffan Bergsten, *Den trösterika gåtan: Tio essäer om Tomas Tranströmers lyrik* (Stockholm: FIB:s Lyrikklubb, 1989);

Robert Bly, *Leaping Poetry: An Idea with Poems and Translations* (Boston: Beacon, 1975);

Kjell Espmark, *Resans formler: En studie i Tomas Tranströmers lyrik* (Stockholm: Norstedt, 1983);

Peter Hallberg, "'Distansernas musik har sammanströmmat': Om bildspråket i Tomas Tranströmers 'Sång' och 'Elegi,'" *Edda: Nordisk Tidskrift för Litteraturforskning,* 75, no. 2 (1975): 111–132;

Göran Printz-Påhlson, "Tranströmer and Tradition," *Ironwood,* special Tranströmer issue, 15 (Spring 1979);

Niklas Schiöler, *Koncentrationens konst: Tomas Tranströmers senare poesi* (Stockholm: Bonnier, 1999);

Urban Torhamn, "Tranströmers poetiska metod," *Bonniers Litterära Magasin,* 30, no. 10 (1961): 799–803.

Birgitta Trotzig
(11 September 1929 -)

Steven P. Sondrup
Brigham Young University

BOOKS: *Ur de älskandes liv* (Stockholm: Bonnier, 1951);
Bilder (Stockholm: Bonnier, 1954);
De utsatta: En legend (Stockholm: Bonnier, 1957);
Ett landskap: Dagbok, fragment 54-58 (Stockholm: Bonnier, 1959);
En berättelse från kusten (Helsinki: Söderström, 1961; Stockholm: Bonnier, 1961);
Utkast och förslag (Helsinki: Söderström, 1962; Stockholm: Bonnier, 1962);
Levande och döda: Tre berättelser (Helsinki: Söderström, 1964; Stockholm: Bonnier, 1964);
Sveket (Stockholm: Bonnier, 1966);
Ordgränser (Stockholm: Bonnier, 1968);
Teresa (Stockholm: Bonnier, 1969);
Sjukdomen (Stockholm: Bonnier, 1972);
I kejsarens tid (Stockholm: Bonnier, 1975);
Berättelser (Stockholm: Bonnier, 1977);
Jaget och världen (Stockholm: Författarförlaget, 1977);
Anima: Prosadikter (Stockholm: Bonnier, 1982);
Dykungens dotter: En barnhistoria (Stockholm: Bonnier, 1985);
Per Olof Sundman: Inträdestal i Svenska akademien (Stockholm: Norstedt, 1993);
Porträtt: Ur tidshistorien (Stockholm: Bonnier, 1993);
Lena Cronqvist: Teckningar 1969-1979, by Trotzig and Göran Tunström (Stockholm: Galleri Lars Boman, 1994);
Dialog: om Ulf Trotzigs konstnärsskap, by Trotzig and Ulf Trotzig (Stockholm: Arena, 1996);
Sammanhang: Materialen (Stockholm: Bonnier, 1996);
Dubbelheten: Tre sagor (Stockholm: Bonnier, 1998);
Gösta Oswald (Stockholm: Norstedt, 2000).

OTHER: Karl Venneberg, *Du är min landsflykt: Karleksdikter,* afterword by Trotzig (Stockholm: FIB:s lyrikklubb, 1990).

Birgitta Trotzig (photograph by Ingemar Leckius)

Birgitta Trotzig's literary career is often described as distinguished and virtually without parallel in the history of contemporary Swedish literature. Although her works feature few of the major trends or traditions that have characterized the development of Swedish literature over the last forty years, and she has had relatively little contact with other important writers, recent intertextual studies suggest that Trotzig's writings constitute in many respects an ongoing conversation with a wide variety of works by other writers. Her work escapes categorization in traditional terms, for—as she frequently insists—she has never belonged to any school of literature or any literary movement. Critics and scholars have been relatively slow to recognize her accomplishments, but since the early 1990s—and most particularly since her election to the Swedish Academy in 1993, when she succeeded Per Olof Sundman in the sixth chair—she has become an increasingly prominent figure in the Swedish cultural pantheon and has attracted growing critical attention from both the institutional as well as academic literary establishment. The recognition of her work with several major literary awards and prizes indeed attests to her growing importance in the Swedish literary community.

Born on 11 September 1929 in Göteborg, Trotzig was an only child. The young family lived at first with her maternal grandparents, where as a child she observed patients being treated by her grandfather, a respected psychiatrist, coming and going. Her parents, however, entered the teaching profession, and the young family moved from Göteborg's big-city environment to rural Skåne, the southernmost province in Sweden. She later returned to Göteborg to study art and literary history at the University of Göteborg, where she took the final exams for her degree in 1948. Since that time, she has been a frequent contributor to the daily newspaper *Aftonbladet* (The Evening Paper) and the distinguished literary periodical *Bonniers Litterära Magasin* (Bonnier's Literary Magazine). When she left Sweden in the early 1960s to live in Paris with her husband, the artist Ulf Trotzig, she converted to Roman Catholicism—just one step in a long and ongoing spiritual quest that had been apparent in her works for more than ten years. Like the conversion of Östen Sjöstrand a decade earlier, Trotzig's conversion allowed her close spiritual and intellectual contact with the broader neo-Catholic tradition and with important aspects of French culture; it also introduced her to Christian as well as Jewish mysticism—especially that of San Juan de la Cruz—and to the thinking of Pierre Teilhard de Chardin, about whom she has written several important interpretive studies.

Like a powerful undercurrent, a profound—albeit rarely simple—religious commitment runs throughout Trotzig's works. Religion, particularly the struggle to account for the suffering and evil in the world, unites her writings and gives them a degree of interpretive cohesion. As critics and readers have recognized, her evocative narratives disclose a dark and disconsolate view of the human condition, with little possibility of circumventing humiliating, degrading, and at times tragic defeat in the search—at the cost of considerable anguish—for some elusive trace of divine benevolence, mercy, or love. Trotzig departs from many of her contemporaries in that her efforts to understand evil and suffering have nothing to do with examining social and economic conditions that might be seen as their cause. Though by no means inattentive to them, she does not rank social inequities and political injustices among her paramount concerns. Rather, she understands suffering as a consequence of a dissipated and sterile spiritual existence that is part of the human mortal condition and cannot be averted by modifications and adjustments to social circumstances.

Trotzig's approach to writing is neither documentary nor completely fanciful. Although her creative method entails the careful jotting down of observations and thoughts as they occur, she refrains from extensive research when she writes. Her work, as she has characterized, takes place in an inner space where oneiric processes unfold images that, while concrete, nonetheless resemble dreams in many respects. Not surprisingly, a sense of place—both inward as well as geographical—looms large throughout her works.

She debuted as a published writer in 1951 with *Ur de älskandes liv* (From the Lovers' Life). Despite the marginal critical attention the book received at the time, it is still significant for what it suggests about the locus of the author's eventual narrative interests in inner spiritual processes. On the other hand, this account of the hypersensitive and fleeting moods of three young women is rather anomalous in terms of the attention given to the external objects and circumstances that impinge on the protagonists' lives. Her second book, *Bilder* (Images, 1954), exemplifies Trotzig's extended use in publication of the prose poem. As the title suggests, the book concerns images foremost, rather than narrative development, and in the first two of the three sections portrays physical pain, suffering, and death. The concentrated and carefully focused prose in these initial segments draws attention to the physical response of the bodies to their afflictions, while the third section depicts the stages of Christ's passion. Moving and engaging on its own terms, the volume portends the commingling of highly evocative poetic passages with narrative depictions of the physical response to spiritual anguish and suffering.

Trotzig's next publication, *De utsatta: En legend* (The Vulnerable, 1957), reenacts a specific story from the Bible—the tribulations of Job and his efforts to understand the goodness of God. *De utsatta* in large measure defines the general context in which Trotzig's work from this point on can be understood. Set in Skåne, the locale of her childhood, the novel tells the story of Isak Graa, a minister inextricably entangled in the social and political turmoil of life in the province during the seventeenth century. Although a God-fearing and just man, he becomes a victim of circumstances; rejected and utterly marginalized by society, he is forced to wander as a beggar in abject poverty. Trotzig makes the portrayal of Graa's physical deprivation and pain particularly poignant through his spiritual anxiety, which surfaces implicitly in his attempts to maintain

Cover for Trotzig's collection of dark fantasy tales influenced by the stories of E. T. A. Hoffmann, published in 1975 (University of Washington Libraries)

faith in the goodness and mercy of God despite the enormous injustice of his unmerited suffering. She suggests that the disparities are too great to permit a theodicean explanation that out of all evil, God will bring eternal good. Not even a glimmer of Enlightenment optimism can tint the somber hues with which Trotzig composes the narrative; her point in *De utsatta* is that the justice of God remains ever elusive.

Trotzig's next two books explore personal and socioreligious subjects. The first, *Ett landskap: Dagbok, fragment 54–58* (A Landscape, 1959), collects selected passages from Trotzig's diary and thus affords a particularly intimate view of a mind reflecting on itself. The author's decision to allow a glimpse into her most inner recesses is informed and not without psychological peril. She observes in various ways throughout the volume that the inherent profundity of human beings is most consequential through the process of becoming aware of itself and its potential. The second, *En berättelse från kusten* (A Story from the Coast, 1961), takes place during the last four decades of the fifteenth century in the coastal city of Åhus, which was at that time at the pinnacle of its fame and fortune. The mayor has high but exaggerated hopes that the community will become one of the most important Hanseatic cities. The narrative centers on the complex interrelationship between the city and monastery located within its confines as both attempt to deal with different but related senses of crisis and impending doom.

Trotzig followed these works with two books of collected pieces, *Utkast och förslag* (A Sketch and a Suggestion, 1962) and *Levande och döda* (The Living and the Dead, 1964). The first is a series of essays that regard a variety of literary and generally aesthetic issues, while the second encompasses three relatively short narratives, the second of which is the title narrative. Moments of lyric reflection animate all three tales in *Levande och döda,* and particularly prominent is the third tale, "Dottningen," in which some chapters are written with such a degree of lyric density, concentration, and circumspection that they embody just a few dozen words. These narratives focus on psychological developments, not in the sense of abstract clinical analysis, but rather of a subtly tuned and highly responsive spiritual empathy. Trotzig's elemental yet cardinal perception is simply that the family and the complex dynamic structure it embraces can, when disoriented, occasion the most grievous results. Moreover, this almost axiomatic insight stands out so much that, in some way or other, it will be relevant to several of her subsequent narratives.

Trotzig followed *Levande och döda* with two books about the demands and dangers of parental love. In *Sveket* (Deceit, 1966) a father's devotion turns pathological. Tobit confuses his consuming compulsion to dominate, manipulate, and control his daughter with nurturing and supportive parental love, and this displacement leads to her death. The portrayal of the father in *Sveket,* however, is not simplistic and unidimensional but is instead probing in its psychological investigation. Disclaimed and disparaged by his own parents, Tobit loved his daughter's mother less than adequately. Yet, however much he tries, his consuming, domineering, and ultimately self-serving manner toward his daughter cannot redeem the failure of his relationship with her mother. *Sjukdomen* (The Illness, 1972) similarly explores the dynamics and challenges of parental love and the inescapable cycle of life and death. Albin Ström does not lack in affection or devotion for his son Elje but is sadly the victim of his own inability to communicate, an incapacity that replicates itself in the son. Without the language of empathy for another, the child's constitution of self and growth into a responsible adult is prematurely arrested and distorted. Condemned at least in part to the isolation of solipsism, his disjunction from the world deepens into schizophrenia. Failing all means of communication, the relationship between Albin and Elje disintegrates into little more than confused and disoriented violence.

In 1968 Trotzig published *Ordgränser* (Word Boundaries, 1982), a compilation of prose poems, which had much in common with her earlier collection, *Bilder.* Although fourteen years separate their publication, the two books are linked through their remarkable continuity of style, tenor, tonality, and technique. They also anticipate the collection *Anima,* which came out in 1982. *Ordgränser* presents diverse images of human grief and especially concentrates on the limitations of language to describe adequately the depth and intensity of such anguish. The portraits of suffering become quite poignant through the powerful sense of place that Trotzig suggests in the first three sections of the volume—associated, respectively, with Paris, Tuscany, and Prague; in all, the book comprises five sections. Most important, she shows that the limitations of language in recounting and accounting for misery expose its sacramental center, which does not justify suffering but is the point from which an apocalyptic sense of history, with its attendant renewal, emanates.

I kejsarens tid (In the Time of the Kaiser, 1975) groups together narratives that Trotzig identifies as tales or, more precisely, black or wicked tales. Rather than echoing the modalities of folktales or fairy tales, *I kejsarens tid* is deeply suffused with the dark and ominous hues of E. T. A. Hoffmann's work; Trotzig's black tales thematically reflect Hoffmann's fascination with transformations that border on unsettling disorientation as well as, at times, on the mildly grotesque. She also weaves references to both Ovid and Franz Kafka into the intertextual fabric of *I kejsarens tid.* The tales vary significantly in length, from a single page for one tale to longer yet still extremely condensed accounts to, finally, three extended narratives. The time frames of the tales range from an indistinct but clearly distant past to the contemporary world. The mutations that constitute the thematic core of the diverging plots in *I kejsarens tid* are unified in an apocalyptic vision of the transformation of the earth, in which a new heaven and a new earth appear and all things are made new.

Trotzig wrote two books in the 1970s and 1980s that critics have perceived as among her most religious or theological. While the first, *Jaget och världen* (The Self and the World, 1977), marks in many ways a suggestively theological volume, it is hardly theological in an abstract or even a modestly systematic way. Above all, she securely anchors *Jaget och världen,* a devotional meditation, in the experiences of this world. Drawing in large measure on visual images, the book evocatively intimates how, in spite of manifold weaknesses and failings of the flesh in a world fallen from the presence of God, fleeting traces of the divine may be glimpsed through suffering and affliction and in anticipation of a cosmic renewal. Twelve years later Trotzig addressed other nuances and aspects of the same subject matter in *Dykungens dotter* (The Marsh King's Daughter, 1985). Indeed, the attention of the novel to dark and foreboding elements emerges with particular cogency when perused in light of Julia Kristeva's *Pouvoirs de l'horreur: Essai sur l'abjection* (1980; translated as *The Powers of Horror: An Essay on Abjection,* 1982) and its psychoanalytic study of outcasts. Throughout the novel Trotzig discloses new aspects and telling facets of her profoundly religious sensibility and acute, theologically oriented cognitive power.

Porträtt: Ur tidshistorien (A Portrait: From the History of those Times, 1993) presents brief sketches of important writers whose works were published in various periodicals between 1951 and 1992. Through these portraits Trotzig peers into the lives of contemporary compatriots who have been particularly important to her, such as Lars Ahlin, Artur Lundkvist, Gunnar Ekelöf, Lars Norén, Birger Sjöberg, and Karl Vennberg. She also addresses her international predecessors and contemporaries, such as Georg Heym, Arthur Rimbaud, Edith Södergran, Edmond Jabès, Rainer Maria Rilke, Anna Akhmatova, Osip Mandelstam, and the fourteenth-century mystic Meister Eckhart. The portrayals give engaging insight into the poetic and spiritual depth of these figures but also into some deeply personal aspects of Trotzig's own poetics, philosophy, and theology.

In *Sammanhang: Materialen* (Connection: Material, 1996) she renews in a masterful prose poem the continuing and extending stylistic and conceptual aspects of earlier volumes. This volume powerfully demonstrates not only Trotzig's sovereignty over the form but also a profound coherence, continuity, and constancy that links her earliest use of the genre in her first published volume with each successive return. With an ever-increasing power of vision free from repetition or recapitulation, she reveals in each reversion a fresh exploration of the potential for dynamic tension inherent in the prose poem. Indeed, the prose poem emerges not so much as an occasional mode of expression but rather as a fundamental medium of conceptualization and expression that is gradually being recognized as the source from which the longer narratives emanate. Her prose poems typically arise from the interplay of dialectical antitheses that remain conspicuously unresolved, and *Sammanhang* in particular forcefully exploits the tensions of these binary antipodes by probing the nature of the ontological and epistemological structures that endeavor to mediate between them.

Dubbelheten: Tre sagor (Duplicity: Three Stories, 1998) takes its title from the last of the three short tales in the volume. While one may superficially and somewhat misleadingly say that these tales deal with the problem of a theodicy—for the question of God's justice provides their backdrop—each does explore, with subtlety and nuance, the spiritual challenges of facing appalling and agonizing paradoxes of life. The first story tells of a blacksmith's inability to communicate with his wife and son and the consequent difficulty of a life torn by the demands of an existence with the living, who in a variety of ways resemble the dead, and the dead, who loom so large in life that they still seem alive.

The second story concerns the starkly contrasting lives of two sisters—one born to the family, the other taken in—and their paradoxically divergent and tragic fates. The last story depicts the conflicting demands that face a woman subsisting on the margins of society in Francisco Franco's Spain but who is absolutely central to the children for whom she is caring. The story concludes without any hint of who or what prevails—the woman or society—but with the implicit insight that there is no need to speak of triumph, because survival is what matters most.

Trotzig's poetic universe is one thoroughly and completely informed by her profound religious commitment. She is, however, no apologist. She engages in a wide range of issues bedeviling the modern world but, typically, in terms of their underlying spiritual dimensions rather than their more immediate and at times superficial instantiations. Acutely aware of the depth and breadth of human suffering, she probes its many facets without ever trivializing, facilely dismissing, or excusing it. Her portrayals are sympathetic yet unsentimental, poignant but not maudlin, and deeply moving without resorting to hyperbole or overstatement. They depend on the keen eye of a careful observer but are not detached or disinterested; they are also concrete and specific but display an arresting economy of means. Trotzig's narratives engage the reader with a well developed sense of place, sensitively delineated characters, and a plot that plays itself out in the world of daily empirical experience. Her stories find their wellspring in the spatial dimensions of experience that turn inward toward the depth of the soul.

The emotional, psychological, theological, and religious challenges of evil and suffering in the face of God's embracing love suggest the general contours of Birgitta Trotzig's narrative fiction and of many of her principal religious and social concerns. Such a critical orientation, however, reveals the profundity of her accomplishment only in part and surrounds her with too many dark shadows of pessimism, dejection, and painful vulnerability. The pervasive inwardness of her narratives—fundamentally lyrical in their emphasis on a heightened sense of presence—tends to be obscured by describing her in unnecessarily narrow terms. Not only is her fiction animated and spiritually charged by the inward turn of its extensive and far-reaching lyricism, but her poetry, usually in the form of prose poems, also allows ruptures and disjunctions, through which sacral or even sacramental mysteries exert a power only precariously within the purview of symbolic or linguistic representation. Trotzig's prose poetry opens approaches to the hope beyond hope, although such paths are not without their own protecting shadows and veils. Through verse she penetrates the depth of human experience, pushing the dispiriting limitations of human emotion and intellection to the edges of linguistic possibility. As a fundamentally religious poet, Trotzig never suggests facile answers, explanations, or justifications. Just as the biblical account of Job's suffering is a prototype for the anguish and exhaustion that afflicts many members of the human family, his persistent and enduring sense of hope is an almost hidden but irrefragably fundamental aspect of Trotzig's works. The story of Job essentially configures and informs her conception of the world and, more especially, her poetic strategy. Although her distinctive thinking and literary-critical development are often cited in accounting for the particular challenges she presents to her readers, the issues with which Trotzig weaves the complex patterns of her works nonetheless have universal resonance and depth. Trotzig now makes her home in Uppsala, a university city just north of Stockholm, and remains active in public debate—particularly with regard to issues relating to social justice—and in the varied projects of the Swedish Academy. The continuing public appreciation of her work is apparent in reception of prestigious literary awards, perhaps most notable in recent years the awarding of the Övralid Prize in 1997.

References:

Christina Bergil, *Mörkrets Motbilder: Tematik och narration i fem verk av Birgitta Trotzig* (Stockholm: Symposion, 1995);

Régis Boyer, *Job mitt ibland oss: En studie över Birgitta Trotzigs verk,* translated by Karin Landgren, Perspectiv, no. 6 (Stockholm & Uppsala: Katolska bokförlag, 1978);

Adma d'Heurle, "The Image of Women in the Fiction of Birgitta Trotzig," *Scandinavian Studies,* 55 (1983): 371–382;

d'Heurle, "To See the Other: The Holy Quest of Birgitta Trotzig," *Cross Currents,* 35, nos. 2–3 (1985): 257–273;

Steven P. Sondrup, "Birgitta Trotzig and the Languages of Religious and Literary Experience," *Scandinavian Studies,* 72, no. 3 (2000): 331–343;

Ebba Witt-Brättström, "Modersabjekt och apokalyps: En Läsning av Birgitta Trotzigs roman Sjukdomen," in *Litteratur och psykoanalys: En antologi om modern psykoanalytisk litteraturtolkning,* edited by Lars Nylander (Stockholm: Norstedt, 1986).

Göran Tunström
(14 May 1937 – 5 February 2000)

Kathy Saranpa

BOOKS: *Inringning* (Stockholm: Bonnier, 1958);
Två vindar (Stockholm: Bonnier, 1960);
Karantän (Stockholm: Bonnier, 1961);
Maskrosbollen (Stockholm: Bonnier, 1962);
Nymålat (Stockholm: Bonnier, 1962);
Familjeliv: En berättelse från Tobobac (Stockholm: Bonnier, 1964);
Om förtröstan (Stockholm: Bonnier, 1965);
De andra de till hälften synliga (Stockholm: Bonnier, 1966);
Hallonfallet, as Paul Badura Mörk (Stockholm: Bonnier, 1967);
Samtal med marken (Stockholm: Bonnier, 1969);
De heliga geograferna (Stockholm: Bonnier, 1973);
Stormunnens bön (Göteborg: Författarförlaget, 1974);
Guddöttrarna (Stockholm: Bonnier, 1975);
Svartsjukans sånger (Stockholm: Bonnier, 1975);
Prästungen (Stockholm: Bonnier, 1976);
Sandro Botticellis dikter (Stockholm: Bonnier, 1976);
Dikter till Lena, introduction by Lars Grahn (Stockholm: Bonnier, 1978);
Ökenbrevet (Stockholm: Bonnier, 1978); excerpts translated by Eivor Martinus as "The Letter from the Wilderness," *Comparative Criticism,* 17 (1995);
Sorgesånger (Stockholm: Bonnier, 1980);
Juloratoriet (Stockholm: Bonnier, 1983); translated by Paul Hoover as *The Christmas Oratorio* (Boston: Godine, 1995);
Indien: En vinterresa (Stockholm: Författarförlaget, 1984);
Tjuven (Stockholm: Bonnier, 1986); partly translated by Joan Tate as "The Thief" in *Swedish Book Review Supplement 1988: Göran Tunström;*
Chang Eng (Stockholm: Bonnier, 1987); partly translated by Linda Schenck as "The Letter" in *Swedish Book Review Supplement 1988: Göran Tunström;*
Det sanna livet (Ljusdal: Ericssons bokhandel, 1987); translated by Christopher Moseley as "Shadow of a Marriage" in *From Baltic Shores,* edited by Moseley (Norwich, U.K.: Norvik, 1994), pp. 228–238;
Under tiden (Stockholm: Bonnier, 1993);

Göran Tunström

Lena Cronqvist: teckningar: 1969–1979, by Tunström and Birgitta Trotzig (Stockholm: Galleri Lars Boman, 1994);
En prosaist i New York (Stockholm: Bonnier, 1996);
Skimmer (Stockholm: Bonnier, 1996);
Berömda män som varit i Sunne (Stockholm: Bonnier, 1998);
Krönikor (Stockholm: Dagens arbete, 2000).

PLAY PRODUCTION: *Chang Eng,* Unga Klara Teatern, Stockholm, 11 December 1987.

RECORDING: "Swedish writer Göran Tunström reading from his work," recorded for the Archive of World Literature, Washington, D.C., 1995.

OTHER: "Ansgar–En frälsarhistoria," in *Svenska radiopjäser 1969* (Stockholm: Sveriges Radio, 1969);

"En dag i Robert Schumanns liv," in *Svenska radiopjäser 1970* (Stockholm: Sveriges Radio, 1970);

"Träffade också furst Kropotkin," in *Svenska radiopjäser 1972* (Stockholm: Sveriges Radio, 1972);

"En tid vid akademien," in *Svenska radiopjäser 1973* (Stockholm: Sveriges Radio, 1973), pp. 171–191;

"Hinden," in *Svenska radiopjäser 1975* (Stockholm: Sveriges Radio, 1975);

"Stollen," in *Svenska radiopjäser 1982* (Stockholm: Sveriges Radio, 1982);

Poetry Australia: Swedish Poets in Translation, edited by Tunström (Berrima, N.S.W.: South Head Press, 1985)–includes poems by Tunström, translated by David Harry, Eva Enderlein, and Emile Snyder;

"The Changeling," translated by Anne-Charlotte Hanes Harvey, in *Plays for Young Audiences II* (New York: Theatre Communications Group, 1988).

Göran Tunström's adroit narration, accessible mysticism, and palpable warmth have assured him a place in the highest tier of twentieth-century Swedish writers. By dint of his birth in the province of Värmland, his literary foremother was the peerless storyteller Selma Lagerlöf, and his poetic forefather was Gustaf Fröding, known for capturing the mystical in earthy lyrics. Born into a pastor's family, Tunström was strongly influenced by Lutheran values and rituals. His parents experienced poverty as children but were different in temperament; Tunström described his father's home as a "house of sighs," his mother's, conversely, as a "house of laughter." His paternal grandfather was an evangelical preacher; his maternal grandfather a factory worker who also played the violin and accompanied silent movies on the piano. Although his grandfather was offered the chance to study music while young, he refused, seeing it as a betrayal against the proletarian class. While Tunström's production is too rich, varied, and original to neatly pigeonhole, these biographical facts help shape its contours. One must bear in mind, however, that part of Tunström's greater project was to lift up the particular, to resist the general, and to avoid the solipsism of simplification.

Tunström was born on 14 May 1937 in the town of Sunne, a place many Swedish readers now associate with the author for its frequent appearance in his novels–most obviously in his last novel, *Berömda män som varit i Sunne* (Famous Men Who've Been in Sunne, 1998). He was the first child of four, and he played his role as eldest conscientiously, feeling a great responsibility for his siblings. Tunström's sickly father fostered his sense of obligation toward his family, telling his son that he would be man of the house when he was gone. When Tunström was twelve years old, his father died; this tragedy was amplified by the subsequent move out of the roomy parsonage into more modest quarters in an apartment in town. By Tunström's direct commentary and by the steady recurrence of the themes of loss and abandonment in his poetry and prose, one can gauge the depth of this early, profound wound.

The author rendered a bittersweet picture of his childhood, adolescence, and early adulthood in *Prästungen* (Preacher's Kid, 1976). Tunström, asthmatic and weak as a child, found pleasure and freedom in books and newspapers. After his father's death he decided to live no longer than twenty-eight years, by which time he would have had the opportunity to travel around the world, sleep with many women, and write at least ten books. He did not attempt to carry out these early plans for suicide, however. He studied classical languages at the Fjellstedtska Skola in Uppsala and studied psychology and ethnography at Göteborg University as well as the history of religion at Uppsala University. For a time Tunström seriously considered following in the footsteps of his clergyman father, but he came to the realization that his psychological makeup precluded subscribing to any set system of beliefs. His departure from Sunne is reenacted in several novels, and vignettes from his travels and work as a tour guide in Greece, Italy, and Egypt color even more narrations.

At age twenty Tunström experienced a crisis for which he was admitted to a mental hospital in Kristinehamn, spending the entire winter there. In the chapter titled "Om smekningar" (On Caresses) in *Juloratoriet* (1983; translated as *The Christmas Oratorio,* 1995), Tunström gives a glimpse of the mental and emotional torment he managed to survive. He later identified that time as one of great significance for his literary career. Following his stay at the institution he returned to Värmland to become editor for the local paper *Fryksdalsbygden.* The following year he published his first collection of poems, *Inringning* (1958).

In 1964 Tunström married the distinguished painter Lena Cronquist, and the two artists cooperated on many projects throughout their thirty-five-year marriage. She illustrated many of his novels and collections, and he wrote text for her exhibits. In 1969 their son, Linus, was born.

One feature of Tunström's writing is clear: he viewed the act of authorship at least partly as therapy for the writer, perhaps as a result of his hospital stay as a young man; this view is in a sense a modest view, one that allows for lack of understanding on the part of the creator and for a more active role on the part of the reader. He called his work a series of "möten" (meetings) or "upptäckter" (discoveries), and these meetings often focus on relationships. Whether prose or poetry, Tunström's work reflects a deep spirituality and a fine-tuned sense for language.

Tunström debuted with *Inringning*–the title is a wordplay that can mean either a ringing of bells to introduce someone or an enclosure; through this collection and the two that followed, *Två vindar* (Two Winds, 1960) and *Nymålat* (Wet Paint, 1962), Tunström made a name for himself as a young poet of some promise. Indeed, the voice that resounds in these collections is more mature than usual for a poet in his twenties, although contemporary reviewers considered the poems typical for the time. The three works give a preview of his unusually broad repertoire. The juxtaposition of natural phenomena and philosophy reminds one of Edith Södergran (whom he consciously parodies in *Nymålat*); he blends political commentary, humor, biblical themes, and confident, natural rhythms. The second collection is dedicated to the memory of his father, but it does not demonstrate any perceivable attempt to come to terms with his grief on the scale of his later works; nevertheless, there is a sense of the desire to make the wall between life and death more porous. *Nymålat* is the first Tunström work to refer to his hometown by name. Some experiments in parody are successful, but the attempts at rhymed verse are clumsy. The poems are serious and self-conscious, and they lack the warmth and sureness of his later work, but they are still examined with critical respect.

Karantän (Quarantine, 1961) is Tunström's first published attempt at prose; lyrical and at times nearly melodramatic, it is the story of Henrik Synge's marriage to Maren, a musician, and his failure to feel completely confident in her love for him—an inability prefigured by the suicide of the protagonist's father. In a shocking opening scene he slits his throat with a shaving razor in his library, and the narrator speaks of blood on familiar books by Thomas Mann and Hans Christian Andersen. While autobiographical elements are included (the deceased father, the years in Uppsala, a trip to Southern Europe), the work is not an autobiography. The title refers to the state of being in which the narrator, Henrik Synge, lives. Because he cannot accept his wife's love, he must distance himself from it, eventually driving her away. The novel ends in a strange scene of hopeless grace as Henrik celebrates Christmas with a poor Gypsy prostitute, feeding her bread in a kind of communion.

A novel more successful than Tunström's other early ones, *Maskrosbollen* (Dandelion Fluff, 1962) follows the protagonist, Bernhard Ottoson–called "Bastiano" by his girlfriend Rita Karin, a name that reflects his exoticness in the small-town setting of the novel–through his final year in high school, on a trip to Greece and France, and his return to the town he has now sorely outgrown. At the same time that Bernhard shows a certain arrogance and restlessness in the provincial atmosphere, he is also refreshingly aware of his own shortcomings and, from time to time, of the emotional damage he is capable of inflicting on those he loves most. His older brother, Sigfrid, a famous writer, is so dependent on his mother that he can barely survive in the adult world, and this makes him the object of Bernhard's scorn. At the end of the novel, however, Bernhard witnesses the full flower of Sigfrid's grief over their dead father, and the brothers are united. This pattern of alternating joy and sorrow is typical for later Tunström work, and it provides a major theme in *Juloratoriet*.

Familjeliv: En berättelse från Tobobac (Family Life: A Story from Tobobac, 1964) is an absurdist piece of prose that was published in the year of Tunström's marriage. The book gives a series of impressionistic, recurrent scenes that replay in dream-like perceptions of reality. The mood that the carnage and familial dysfunction of the first chapter sets–the main character, Knybel Tving, is taking the bodies of his father, sister, and a stranger into the town of Tobobac for burial, with little emotion or shock, after the gruesome deaths of the latter two–persists throughout the work. His unnaturally close relationship with his sister Fragoli–reminiscent of the cousins Johan and Hedvig in *Tjuven* (The Thief, 1986)–causes him guilt feelings after he leaves their home to live in the city; the theme of guilt over the abandoned family member may have its roots in Tunström's own departure from Sunne. *Familjeliv* is a clumsy forecast of what later became one of Tunström's most notable skills: the portrayal of alternate realities without the disruption of normal Swedish syntax.

The poetry collections *Om förtröstan* (About Solace, 1965) and *De andra de till hälften synliga* (Those Half Visible, 1966) continue the attempt to embrace both the dark and light aspects of human existence. Tunström's images become more specific and earthbound; in his relationship to an ideal beloved he finds a sure voice, and he evokes grief in his failed attempt to unite with her spiritually and existentially.

Dust jackets for the 1983 first edition (from Swedish Book Review, *October 1983) and the 1995 English translation (Collection of Ann-Charlotte Gavel Adams) of Tunström's novel about the relationship of the Johann Sebastian Bach composition to three generations of a family*

In *De andra de till hälften synliga* Tunström focuses on unfortunate "others": an American soldier in Vietnam, starving people in India. The desire for real relationships with these others is as fervent as the desire for union with the beloved in *Om förtröstan*.

In 1967 Tunström entered a contest for mystery writers with *Hallonfallet* (Raspberry Falls) under the pseudonym Paul Badura Mörk. The Koster landscape, where he owned a summer home for many years, provides the setting for murder; the protagonist and sometimes first-person narrator, Johan, and his wife, Sara, are those most intensely engaged in solving the mystery. In *Hallonfallet,* for the first time, Tunström introduces a motley cast of characters whose individual stories threaten to divert the reader from the main plot, a technique used in his later novels. The most fascinating of these is never depicted directly, for she is the murder victim, Monica Andrén: half Japanese, half Swedish, she is compared to a fire around which men gather like moths and are singed.

The poems in *Samtal med marken* (Conversation with the Ground, 1969) center around things that are in or close to the ground, both literally and metaphorically. Animals, oppressed peoples, stones, all provide subjects for Tunström's growing empathy and concern for all beings. This new sense of closeness to the earth was perhaps inspired by the birth of his son, Linus, in August of that year. Following this event Tunström's wife suffered a postpartum psychosis that sent her to an institution for medication and shock treatments.

Having witnessed mental illness from both without and within, Tunström fictionalizes this state with a complex combination of grief, awe, wonder, empathy, and anger in *De heliga geograferna* (The Holy Geographers, 1973) and *Guddöttrarna* (The Goddaughters, 1975). These novels comprise a two-part narrative, written in the first person, that is loosely based on Tunström's childhood and the marriage of his parents. The placement of the narrative during World War II is significant and not merely autobiographical, for the sense of dread and imminent disaster is pervasive both in the community and within the protagonist's family. In *De heliga geograferna* Hans Cristian Wermelin has married Paula, a deceptively simple girl from the islands off the western coast of Sweden, and is about to take up the pastorate in Sunne. The title derives from a small, enthusiastic group of men, the Sunne Geographical Society, who band together for the study of the greater world, one in which war is marching on. This group, which her husband joins shortly after their arrival in Sunne, makes Paula feel isolated, and she reaches a state in which she feels elevated and confident, a condition that has all the appearances of mental illness. The question arises whether what she feels is truly an illness. The plot is not the most important aspect of the novel; instead, in the fore is Tunström's ability to delineate interesting characters and to convey their humanity in their attempts to struggle with their world and to make contact with others. The frame for the book is the attempt of the couple's grown son, Jacob, to meet his dead father, surrealistically turning to cartographers or "holy geographers" in Alexandria to help him; in the final scene Jacob exhibits some of the signs of his mother's mental illness.

Guddöttrarna continues the story without the frame and provides female counterparts to the all-male holy geographers; these women begin to grow carrots in their own field as a patriotic, nutritional act of local insurgence. Paula's illness goes on; Tunström continues to feature intriguing minor characters such as Ivan, the weak mama's boy who finally takes his own life in a final belated act of rebellion, and Georg Johaneson, the originator of the Geographical Society, who plans to convince Hitler he is wrong to be at war. By book's end Jacob is together with both his parents; Paula is now "healthy." Although Tunström had meant for these two novels to be followed by a third, the negative reviews they received prevented him from continuing.

In *Stormunnens bön* (The Prayer of Big Mouth, 1974), Tunström explores the nature and psychology of despotism in an allegorical tale. Storbuken (Big Belly), risen from an agrarian background in the fictitious village of El Sueco (The Swede), commits atrocities at home in the city of Concepcion that evoke no reaction. The problem of visibility, of being seen and acknowledged, lies at the root of Storbuken's despair and spurs on continued acts of arbitrary violence. His nemesis, the former bishop Stormunnen (Big Mouth), tricks Storbuken into coming to the aid of Otto von Bismarck (called Vissmark), who is camped in the jungle and in need of assistance. In appealing to the martial lust of his nemesis, Stormunnen succeeds in toppling him from power, for the expedition is doomed to failure from the start. While this novel lacks the compelling narrative skill of Tunström's later work, there are signs of his development in this regard. One description in particular stands out: on a perilous descent from an altiplano into the jungle, a scout falls off the sheer cliff and is impaled in a tree far below. Eventually the survivors reach the corpse, and Storbuken orders Pader Xavier (Stormunnen) to dispose of it: "Och Xavier lånade en lans av den närmaste soldaten och petade resterna av ett anonymt liv vidare ner i avgrunden" (And Xavier borrowed a lance from the closest soldier and picked the remains of an anonymous life farther down on their way into the abyss).

Sandro Botticellis dikter (Sandro Botticelli's Poems, 1976) is a continuation of *Svartsjukans sånger* (Songs of Jealousy, 1975). Both collections center on relationships, between humans and between art and life. Orpheus and Eurydice figure, as do Sandro Botticelli, Girolamo Savonarola, and Lorenzo de Medici; the consideration of art for God versus art for man parallels the literary debates surrounding the political role of art of the 1960s and 1970s in Sweden and elsewhere. Tunström's own commentary states that the theme is separation anxiety, and that he has used the psychoanalyst Erich Neumann's interpretation of the story of Cupid and Psyche as inspiration. In tandem Tunström uses his own sketch of Botticelli, in love from afar with Simonetta, who dies prematurely. Tunström's Botticelli wavers between the puritanism of Savonarola and his own repressed sensuality, a sensuality that comes to the fore in his paintings of spring and of Aphrodite. In the year of the appearance of *Sandro Botticellis dikter,* Tunström was awarded the *Svenska Dagbladet* Prize, an honor that gave him a higher national profile.

Tunström's next collection of poetry, *Sorgesånger* (Songs of Sorrow, 1980), does not use a mythological or historical basis, but rather rests on personal impressions from travels both in the world and in the relationships of the narrator. Sorrows of a personal nature are intertwined with political and social woes. Tunström's catalogues of objects, most explicitly seen in an untitled poem describing "okända växter, stenar, fågelskelett" (unknown plants, stones, bird skeletons), indicate his need to see the world as its component parts, not as a unified whole. This tendency continues through the rest of his works and is one aspect that helps account for the richness of his poetry and prose. *Sorgesånger* is a fully mature work, and from this point the poet had found his voice. The collection begins and ends with brief sections titled "Försök med ljuset," which can mean either "try using the light" or "attempts with light." As always in Tunström's work, sorrow does not exist without its partner, joy. This parenthetical material, which is a precursor to *Indien: En vinterresa* (India: A Winter Journey, 1984), leads one to interpret the poems as realizations made along the way during the trip.

Juloratoriet is generally considered Tunström's finest work, and the prizes it brought him (including the prestigious Nordic Council Literary Prize) represent his arrival as an established novelist. The novel is rich in symbolism and psychological depth, balancing characteristically wry humor and fearless exploration of the dark places of life. The title refers to the Johann Sebastian Bach oratorio that Solveig Nordensson convinces the cantor of the church in Sunne to produce; after years of rehearsal, and at the point where the group is finally ready to think about performing, she suffers a gruesome death as her husband, Aron, and son, Sidner, watch. The novel follows these two men in the aftermath of the tragedy. Aron succumbs to grief and jumps to his death while on his way to meet a woman in New Zealand; Sidner struggles through these events and marries the same woman, thus righting the wrong done to her by his father's disappearance. The novel opens as Solveig's grandson Victor, a renowned conductor, arrives in Sunne to lead the choir in performing the Bach oratorio at long last. The choice of the Christmas Oratorio, stressing both the joy and sorrow of the life of Jesus, reflects the alternation of happiness and grief that are part of that story as well as of human life. For the first time Tunström pays overt tribute to Lagerlöf by including her as a character in the novel. The radio play "Stollen" is derived from a segment of *Juloratoriet* in which Sidner and his friend Splendid encounter an insane man who eventually commits suicide. This novel is the most widely translated of Tunström's works, appearing in twenty languages; in addition, it has been staged (notably by Linus Tunström) and was made into a movie in 1996. Tunström donated the money from the second prize he received for the novel, Litteraturförbundet's Novel Prize, to the Swedish PEN Club for assistance to imprisoned writers.

Perhaps it is Tunström's cultivation of detail instead of generalization that makes his next book, *Indien: En vinterresa,* illustrated by Tunström's wife, so effective. Without attempts at encompassing the people and places the Tunström family encountered on their trip, the lyrical prose gives a clear picture of the images, sounds, and smells of India and other places (there are flashbacks to Mexico and Greece, for example); in the narrative Tunström nonjudgmentally relates the political and philosophical ideas of the individuals he meets, without trace of condescension and with evidence of how they have changed the author. He often gives his son's reactions to their experiences, either as a humorous counterweight or as an alternative opinion. For example, Linus interrupts a political monologue by a Nepalese by saying "I want to see the wild animals. Why do you always sit there just talking?" The account of the journey begins and ends with descriptions of Koster.

Tjuven (1986) is the bleakest of Tunström's novels and can be read as a dark companion to *Juloratoriet*. Sunne once again provides the setting, and the main character, Johan Jonson Lök, is an outsider reminiscent of Sidner–intellectual, serious, introverted. Where Sidner goes on a quest to right his father's wrong, however, Johan pursues the path of thievery, dreaming of stealing the Silver Bible in order to buy himself and his cousin Hedvig out of the poverty and degradation they suffer at the hands of the shiftless, immoral, and irresponsible Fredrik Jonsson Lök, whose greatest talent is virility. Johan is unable to see, however, that in his obsession with learning and his grand plans he has abandoned Hedvig; she becomes insane and eventually commits suicide. The gloomy tone of the novel is lightened only slightly by the characterization of Ida Pripp, Hedvig's middle-class mother, who was drawn downward through a childish alliance with Fredrik. Her ability to feed her children, keep house, and protect them from the countless daily dangers in her new harsh surroundings–marked by alcoholism and abuse–as well as her desire to write poetry and to marry after her husband's death show a strength of spirit lacking in the other characters in the novel. While *Tjuven* was well received by critics and garnered the Aniara Prize, it was not accorded as much enthusiasm as was *Juloratoriet*.

After *Tjuven* Tunström did not complete another novel for almost ten years. In 1987 he published the short-story collection *Det sanna livet* (True Life), an array of stories that balance between the fulfillment and the crushing of dreams. In the title story the boys Isaac and Jakov make the arduous and risk-filled journey, mandated by their deceased father, from the Soviet Union to Palestine in the 1930s, only to die in an explosion the moment they see the promised land. In "Tack för Kovalevsky" (Thanks for Kovalevsky) the main character learns that a case of mistaken identity has given him his new wife. In other stories characters turn to music after years spent in fear of it; they sell out their idealism; they ruin the fragile wings of an unusual girl child; they return to wives after the disillusionment of a fleeting extramarital romance. Tunström's capacity for storytelling and characterization are not at all diminished by the use of the story genre instead of the novel, although in this short fiction the reader's curiosity about Tunström's gallery of characters is provoked but not satisfied.

Chang Eng (1987) is named after the set of Siamese twins that Phineas T. Barnum paraded in his circus during the middle of the nineteenth century. Chang and Eng left his circus to buy a farm in North Carolina, where they met and married a pair of sisters, Adelaide and Sarah Yates, and fathered twenty-one children. Tunström uses the outlines of the biography of these men to explore the human need to belong and to be independent; to ask questions about the nature of privacy, both in relation to interpersonal dignity and to the role of the media; and to probe into universal human nature to ask what is freakish and what is normal. Tunström jolts the reader every time Chang Eng is addressed or described in the plural; he demands examination of the reader's definition of what constitutes a single human being.

After *Chang Eng*, Tunström entered a period of physical illness and accompanying diminished creative activity as he struggled with cancer. The remarkable memoir *Under tiden* (Meanwhile, 1993) was written following these years of sickness and writer's block. Tunström makes no attempt to hide his terror, bitterness, and frustration when he cannot write as easily as before; in keeping with his balance between dark and light, he also relates amusing anecdotes about how certain of his characters got their names. In particular he expresses his frustrations with writing *Skimmer* (Shimmering Light, 1996), which he had intended to complement *Juloratoriet* and *Tjuven*. At the end of the memoir he informs the reader that he is completing the book on the day he became one day older than his father was at his death. Tunström apears free and alive in hopeful new territory.

In 1994 Tunström and his wife traveled to New York; during the year spent in the United States they decided to make Manhattan their home at least for part of the year. From then until Tunström's death they spent their summers in Koster and winters in New York, with some stays in Stockholm. The change of venue perhaps had a rejuvenating effect on Tunström's creativity, for two years later the troublesome *Skimmer* was finally published. *Skimmer* is set in Iceland, a place for which the author does not seem to have felt as great an affinity as he

Tunström at the time Juloratoriet *was published (photograph © Miriam Berkley)*

has for other countries or, especially, Sunne. The novel itself is another exploration of a father-son relationship. This time, instead of bittersweet longing or heart-wrenching grief, Tunström portrays another reaction to the absent father: anger.

Radio announcer Halldor acts as both father and mother to the first-person narrator, Pétur, whose mother, Lara, a seismologist, was lost in an eruption of the volcano Fretla. Halldor appears as a loving, creative, patient, and conscientious father during the first half of the novel, but later Pétur realizes that he is intrinsically and irreparably egotistical, especially after he lures one of Pétur's dates away from him. He leaves for Paris, to be bombarded by letters from Halldor in a mental institution, letters that in their lamenting about the aging process plead for love and attention. On a visit to the institution Pétur strikes his father so hard that the older man tumbles into an aquarium, spilling water, fish, and glass shards everywhere. It is an act of liberation for Pétur, lashing out at the father who refuses to be present. The novel received a warm reception, although it was apparent that the critics were awaiting another *Juloratoriet*.

Berömda män som varit i Sunne, Tunström's final work, received the prestigious August Prize for best Swedish novel. The protagonist, Stellan Jonsson Lök, also appears in *Tjuven*, in which, as Hedvig's brother, he plays a minor; in *Berömda män som varit i Sunne* he is a grocer with a small agenda for his life: satisfying his customers and filling his book of autographs—which in part accounts for the significance of the title. Lök plans a book of his own about the famous men who have visited Sunne; specifically, astronaut Ed Oldin (a fictionalized version of Edwin "Buzz" Aldrin) comes to Sunne to bury his Swedish mother's ashes and happens upon an ill-fated party for Harald Pihlgren, who soon thereafter commits suicide. In *Berömda män som varit i Sunne* Tunström does what he does best: provides a gallery of characters worthy of their own narrations, another reason for the title. Besides Lök he introduces the seductive psychologist Lena Vergelius; the unhappily married pastor Cederblom and his wife; and Pihlgren, an artist, and the real talent behind him, his wife, Isabelle. Once again Tunström's loving interest in human relationships, in philosophical connections, and in the relationship of the mundane to the divine are apparent.

Berömda män som varit i Sunne, though received with praise, was measured against *Juloratoriet* and found lacking. The critics pointed out that all characters seemed to speak with one voice; they noted that Tunström plotted out too many subplots without according each one due care. They agreed that the novel shared the narrative brilliance of the author's previous works.

On 5 February 2000 Tunström died of a stroke in his apartment in Stockholm. His death was followed by a flurry of pronouncements from literary critics and others mourning a great loss and a premature one. It is difficult to make a summarizing statement about a writer whose project was precisely the avoidance of neat generalizations and systematizations. In *Under tiden,* however, Tunström himself offers something of a summary view of his art: "Konsten är en förtvivlad kärlek till världen, ett desperat försök av den enskilde att göra människans hotade existens osynlig. Och att hålla henne levande. . . . ett ständigt ifrågasättande, en naken nyfikenhet, ett evigt uppror mot förenklingarnas skenlösningar" (Art is a distraught love for the world, a desperate attempt on the part of the individual to make the threatened human existence invisible. . . . a constant questioning, a naked curiosity, an eternal rebellion against the surface solutions brought about by simplifications).

References:

Kajsa Giesecke, "Göran Tunström om sina upplevelser som patient: 'Ronden känns som en förödmjukelse,'" *Läkartidningen,* 94, no. 41 (1997): 35–78;

Reidar Nordenberg, *Tio varmländska författare* (Karlstad, Sweden: Nya Wermlands-Tidningen, 1961);

Ingrid Nymoen, "Når kvinne skapar meining skapar mann: modernitet og kjønn i Göran Tunströms roman Juloratoriet," in *Litteratur og kjønn i Norden,* edited by Helga Kress (Reykjavik: Haskolaufgafan, 1996), pp. 649–655;

Doris Ottesen, *Om kærtegn: Det guddommelige i Göran Tunströms forfatterskab* (Frederiksberg, Denmark: Anis, 1989);

Agneta Rahikainen, "Bach, Bachtin och Tunström: polyfona drag i romanen *Juloratoriet,*" *Artes,* 19, no. 1 (1993): 61–69;

Mikael Reis, "Barnet är människans fader: Göran Tunströms ljus och mörker," in *Röster om Göran Tunström* (Stockholm: ABF, 1994), pp. 34–48;

Hans Skei, "Fra Sunne till Darjeeling: Göran Tunströms *Juloratoriet,*" in *På litterære lekeplasser* (Oslo: Universitetsforlaget, 1995), pp. 133–153.

Books for Further Reading

Anderman, Gunilla, ed. *New Swedish Plays*. Norwich, U.K.: Norvik, 1992.

Brandell, Gunnar. *Svensk litteratur 1900–1950*. Stockholm: Aldus, 1967.

Claréus, Ingrid, ed. *Scandinavian Women Writers: An Anthology from the 1880s to the 1980s*. Westport, Conn. & London: Greenwood Press, 1989.

Edqvist, Sven-Gustaf, and Inga Söderblom. *Svenska författare genom tiderna*. Stockholm: Almqvist & Wiksell, 1998.

Englund, Claes, and Leif Janzon. *Theatre in Sweden*. Stockholm: Swedish Institute, 1997.

Florin, Magnus, Marianne Steinsaphir, and Magareta Sörensen. *Literature in Sweden*. Stockholm: Swedish Institute, 1997.

Forsås-Scott, Helena. *Swedish Women's Writing 1850–1995*. London & Atlantic Highlands, N.J.: Athlone Press, 1997.

Gustafson, Alrik. *A History of Swedish Literature*. Minneapolis: University of Minnesota Press for the American-Scandinavian Foundation, 1961.

Hadenius, Stig. *Swedish Politics during the Twentieth Century: Conflict and Consensus*. Stockholm: Swedish Institute, 1999.

Haverty Rugg, Linda. *Picturing Ourselves*. Chicago & London: University of Chicago Press, 1997.

Johnsson, Hans-Ingvar. *Spotlight on Sweden*. Stockholm: Swedish Institute, 1999.

Lagerqvist, Lars O. *A History of Sweden*. Stockholm: Swedish Institute, 2001.

Linder, Erik Hjalmar. *Ny illustrerad svensk litteraturhistoria: Fem decennier av nittonhundratalet*. Stockholm: Natur och Kultur, 1965.

Lönnroth, Lars, and Sven Delblanc, eds. *Den Svenska Litteraturen*, volume 4: *Den storsvenska generationen*. Stockholm: Bonnier, 1989.

Lönnroth and Delblanc, eds. *Den Svenska Litteraturen*, volume 5: *Modernister och arbetadiktare*. Stockholm: Bonnier, 1989.

Lönnroth and Delblanc, eds. *Den Svenska Litteraturen*, volume 6: *Medieålderns litteratur*. Stockholm: Bonnier, 1990.

Marker, Frederick J., and Lise-Lone Marker. *A History of Scandinavian Theatre*. Cambridge: Cambridge University Press, 1996.

Møller Jensen, Elisabeth, and Ebba Witt-Brattström, eds. *Nordisk Kvinnolitteraturhistoria, Band III: Vida Världen 1900–1960*. Höganäs: Bra Böcker, 1996.

Jensen and Lisbeth Larsson, eds. *Nordisk Kvinnolitteraturhistoria, Band IV: På jorden 1960–1990*. Höganäs: Bra Böcker 1997.

Olsson, Bernt, and Ingemar Algulin. *Litteraturens historia i Sverige*. Stockholm: Norstedt, 1987.

Scobbie, Irene. *Aspects of Modern Swedish Literature*. Norwich, U.K.: Norvik, 1988.

Törnqvist, Egil. *Strindbergian Drama*. Atlantic Highlands, N.J.: Humanities Press, 1982.

Warme, Lars, ed. *A History of Swedish Literature* (volume 3 of *A History of Scandinavian Literatures*). Lincoln & London: University of Nebraska Press, in cooperation with the American-Scandinavian Foundation, 1996.

Weibull, Jörgen. *Swedish History in Outline*. Stockholm: Swedish Institute, 1993.

Westin, Boel. *Children's Literature in Sweden*. Stockholm: Swedish Institute, 1998.

Zuck, Virpi, ed. *Dictionary of Scandinavian Literature*. Westport, Conn. & London: Greenwood Press, 1990.

Contributors

Joanna Bankier . . . . *University of Southern Stockholm*
Cecilia Cervin . . . . *University of Lund*
Sarah Death . . . . *Kent, England*
Elizabeth deNoma . . . . *University of Washington*
Ia Dübois . . . . *University of Washington*
Birgitta Holm . . . . *Uppsala University*
Kevin Karlin . . . . *University of Washington*
Barbara Lide . . . . *Michigan Technological University*
Torborg Lundell . . . . *University of California, Santa Barbara*
Rick McGregor . . . . *Institutet för rymdfysik*
Eva-Maria Metcalf . . . . *University of Mississippi*
Paul Norlén . . . . *University of Washington*
Lars Nylander . . . . *University of California, Berkeley*
Rose-Marie G. Oster . . . . *University of Maryland*
Matthew M. Roy . . . . *Cascadia Community College*
Kathy Saranpa . . . . *Eugene, Oregon*
Ebba Segerberg . . . . *University of California, Berkeley*
Ross Shideler . . . . *University of California, Los Angeles*
Steven P. Sondrup . . . . *Brigham Young University*
Barbro Ståhle Sjönell . . . . *University of Stockholm*
Birgitta Steene . . . . *University of Washington*
Tanya Thresher . . . . *University of Wisconsin–Madison*
Boel Westin . . . . *University of Stockholm*
Rochelle Wright . . . . *University of Illinois*

Cumulative Index

Dictionary of Literary Biography, Volumes 1-257
Dictionary of Literary Biography Yearbook, 1980-2000
Dictionary of Literary Biography Documentary Series, Volumes 1-19
Concise Dictionary of American Literary Biography, Volumes 1-7
Concise Dictionary of British Literary Biography, Volumes 1-8
Concise Dictionary of World Literary Biography, Volumes 1-4

Cumulative Index

DLB before number: *Dictionary of Literary Biography,* Volumes 1-257
Y before number: *Dictionary of Literary Biography Yearbook,* 1980-2000
DS before number: *Dictionary of Literary Biography Documentary Series,* Volumes 1-19
CDALB before number: *Concise Dictionary of American Literary Biography,* Volumes 1-7
CDBLB before number: *Concise Dictionary of British Literary Biography,* Volumes 1-8
CDWLB before number: *Concise Dictionary of World Literary Biography,* Volumes 1-4

A

Aakjær, Jeppe 1866-1930 . . . . .DLB-214
Abbey, Edward 1927-1989. . . . . .DLB-256
Abbey, Edwin Austin 1852-1911 . . . . .DLB-188
Abbey, Maj. J. R. 1894-1969 . . . . .DLB-201
Abbey Press. DLB-49
The Abbey Theatre and Irish Drama,
  1900-1945 . . . . .DLB-10
Abbot, Willis J. 1863-1934. . . . . .DLB-29
Abbott, Jacob 1803-1879 . . . . .DLB-1, 243
Abbott, Lee K. 1947- DLB-130
Abbott, Lyman 1835-1922 . . . . .DLB-79
Abbott, Robert S. 1868-1940 . . . . .DLB-29, 91
Abe Kōbō 1924-1993. . . . . .DLB-182
Abelard, Peter circa 1079-1142? DLB-115, 208
Abelard-Schuman. .DLB-46
Abell, Arunah S. 1806-1888. . . . . .DLB-43
Abell, Kjeld 1901-1961. . . . . .DLB-214
Abercrombie, Lascelles 1881-1938. . . . . . . .DLB-19
Aberdeen University Press Limited DLB-106
Abish, Walter 1931- DLB-130, 227
Ablesimov, Aleksandr Onisimovich
  1742-1783. . . . . .DLB-150
Abraham à Sancta Clara 1644-1709 . . . . . .DLB-168
Abrahams, Peter
  1919- DLB-117, 225; CDWLB-3
Abrams, M. H. 1912- DLB-67
Abramson, Jesse 1904-1979 . . . . .DLB-241
Abrogans circa 790-800 . . . . .DLB-148
Abschatz, Hans Aßmann von
  1646-1699 . . . . .DLB-168
Abse, Dannie 1923- DLB-27, 245
Abutsu-ni 1221-1283 . . . . .DLB-203
Academy Chicago Publishers DLB-46
Accius circa 170 B.C.-circa 80 B.C. DLB-211
Accrocca, Elio Filippo 1923- DLB-128
Ace Books DLB-46
Achebe, Chinua 1930- DLB-117; CDWLB-3
Achtenberg, Herbert 1938- DLB-124
Ackerman, Diane 1948- DLB-120
Ackroyd, Peter 1949- DLB-155, 231

Acorn, Milton 1923-1986. . . . . .DLB-53
Acosta, Oscar Zeta 1935?- DLB-82
Acosta Torres, José 1925- DLB-209
Actors Theatre of Louisville DLB-7
Adair, Gilbert 1944- DLB-194
Adair, James 1709?-1783?. DLB-30
Adam, Graeme Mercer 1839-1912 . . . . . . .DLB-99
Adam, Robert Borthwick II 1863-1940 . . .DLB-187
Adame, Leonard 1947- DLB-82
Adameşteanu, Gabriel 1942- DLB-232
Adamic, Louis 1898-1951 . . . . .DLB-9
Adams, Abigail 1744-1818 . . . . .DLB-200
Adams, Alice 1926-1999 . . . . .DLB-234, Y-86
Adams, Bertha Leith (Mrs. Leith Adams,
  Mrs. R. S. de Courcy Laffan)
  1837?-1912 . . . . .DLB-240
Adams, Brooks 1848-1927 . . . . .DLB-47
Adams, Charles Francis, Jr. 1835-1915 . . . .DLB-47
Adams, Douglas 1952- Y-83
Adams, Franklin P. 1881-1960. . . . . .DLB-29
Adams, Hannah 1755-1832 . . . . .DLB-200
Adams, Henry 1838-1918 . . . . DLB-12, 47, 189
Adams, Herbert Baxter 1850-1901 . . . . . . .DLB-47
Adams, J. S. and C. [publishing house] DLB-49
Adams, James Truslow
  1878-1949 . . . . .DLB-17; DS-17
Adams, John 1735-1826. . . . . .DLB-31, 183
Adams, John 1735-1826 and
  Adams, Abigail 1744-1818 . . . . .DLB-183
Adams, John Quincy 1767-1848. . . . . .DLB-37
Adams, Léonie 1899-1988 . . . . .DLB-48
Adams, Levi 1802-1832 . . . . .DLB-99
Adams, Samuel 1722-1803. . . . . .DLB-31, 43
Adams, Sarah Fuller Flower
  1805-1848 . . . . .DLB-199
Adams, Thomas 1582 or 1583-1652 . . . . .DLB-151
Adams, William Taylor 1822-1897 . . . . . . .DLB-42
Adamson, Sir John 1867-1950 . . . . .DLB-98
Adcock, Arthur St. John 1864-1930 . . . . . .DLB-135
Adcock, Betty 1938- DLB-105
"Certain Gifts". DLB-105
Adcock, Fleur 1934- DLB-40

Addison, Joseph 1672-1719 . . .DLB-101; CDBLB-2
Ade, George 1866-1944. . . . . .DLB-11, 25
Adeler, Max (see Clark, Charles Heber)
Adonias Filho 1915-1990. . . . . .DLB-145
Adorno, Theodor W. 1903-1969. . . . . . . .DLB-242
Advance Publishing Company DLB-49
Ady, Endre 1877-1919 . . . . . .DLB-215; CDWLB-4
AE 1867-1935 . . . . .DLB-19; CDBLB-5
Ælfric circa 955-circa 1010. . . . . .DLB-146
Aeschines
  circa 390 B.C.-circa 320 B.C. DLB-176
Aeschylus 525-524 B.C.-456-455 B.C.
  .DLB-176; CDWLB-1
Afro-American Literary Critics:
  An Introduction DLB-33
After Dinner Opera Company. Y-92
Agassiz, Elizabeth Cary 1822-1907 . . . . . .DLB-189
Agassiz, Louis 1807-1873 . . . . .DLB-1, 235
Agee, James
  1909-1955 . . . . .DLB-2, 26, 152; CDALB-1
The Agee Legacy: A Conference at the University
  of Tennessee at Knoxville. Y-89
Aguilera Malta, Demetrio 1909-1981 . . . .DLB-145
Ahlin, Lars 1915-1997 . . . . .DLB-257
Ai 1947- DLB-120
Aichinger, Ilse 1921- DLB-85
Aidoo, Ama Ata 1942- DLB-117; CDWLB-3
Aiken, Conrad
  1889-1973 . . . . .DLB-9, 45, 102; CDALB-5
Aiken, Joan 1924- DLB-161
Aikin, Lucy 1781-1864. . . . . .DLB-144, 163
Ainsworth, William Harrison 1805-1882 . .DLB-21
Aistis, Jonas 1904-1973 . . . . . .DLB-220; CDWLB-4
Aitken, George A. 1860-1917. . . . . .DLB-149
Aitken, Robert [publishing house] DLB-49
Akenside, Mark 1721-1770. . . . . .DLB-109
Akins, Zoë 1886-1958 . . . . .DLB-26
Aksakov, Sergei Timofeevich
  1791-1859 . . . . .DLB-198
Akutagawa, Ryūnosuke 1892-1927 . . . . . .DLB-180
Alabaster, William 1568-1640 . . . . .DLB-132
Alain de Lille circa 1116-1202/1203. . . . . .DLB-208
Alain-Fournier 1886-1914 . . . . .DLB-65

311

Alanus de Insulis (see Alain de Lille)
Alarcón, Francisco X. 1954- DLB-122
Alarcón, Justo S. 1930- DLB-209
Alba, Nanina 1915-1968............. DLB-41
Albee, Edward 1928- DLB-7; CDALB-1
Albert the Great circa 1200-1280 .... DLB-115
Albert, Octavia 1853-ca. 1889 .... DLB-221
Alberti, Rafael 1902-1999............ DLB-108
Albertinus, Aegidius circa 1560-1620 .... DLB-164
Alcaeus born circa 620 B.C............DLB-176
Alcott, Bronson 1799-1888 .... DLB-1, 223
Alcott, Louisa May 1832-1888
    ... DLB-1, 42, 79, 223, 239; DS-14; CDALB-3
Alcott, William Andrus 1798-1859 .... DLB-1, 243
Alcuin circa 732-804................. DLB-148
Alden, Beardsley and Company........ DLB-49
Alden, Henry Mills 1836-1919.......... DLB-79
Alden, Isabella 1841-1930............. DLB-42
Alden, John B. [publishing house]....... DLB-49
Aldington, Richard
    1892-1962 .... DLB-20, 36, 100, 149
Aldis, Dorothy 1896-1966 .... DLB-22
Aldis, H. G. 1863-1919................ DLB-184
Aldiss, Brian W. 1925- DLB-14
Aldrich, Thomas Bailey
    1836-1907............DLB-42, 71, 74, 79
Alegría, Ciro 1909-1967 .... DLB-113
Alegría, Claribel 1924- DLB-145
Aleixandre, Vicente 1898-1984......... DLB-108
Aleksandravičius, Jonas (see Aistis, Jonas)
Aleksandrov, Aleksandr Andreevich
    (see Durova, Nadezhda Andreevna)
Aleramo, Sibilla 1876-1960 .... DLB-114
Alexander, Cecil Frances 1818-1895..... DLB-199
Alexander, Charles 1868-1923 .... DLB-91
Alexander, Charles Wesley
    [publishing house] DLB-49
Alexander, James 1691-1756........... DLB-24
Alexander, Lloyd 1924- DLB-52
Alexander, Sir William, Earl of Stirling
    1577?-1640.................... DLB-121
Alexie, Sherman 1966- DLB-175, 206
Alexis, Willibald 1798-1871............ DLB-133
Alfred, King 849-899 .... DLB-146
Alger, Horatio, Jr. 1832-1899 .... DLB-42
Algonquin Books of Chapel Hill........ DLB-46
Algren, Nelson
    1909-1981 .....DLB-9; Y-81, Y-82; CDALB-1
Nelson Algren: An International
    Symposium Y-00
Allan, Andrew 1907-1974 .... DLB-88
Allan, Ted 1916- DLB-68
Allbeury, Ted 1917- DLB-87
Alldritt, Keith 1935- DLB-14
Allen, Ethan 1738-1789 .... DLB-31
Allen, Frederick Lewis 1890-1954 ...... DLB-137
Allen, Gay Wilson 1903-1995 .....DLB-103; Y-95

Allen, George 1808-1876 .... DLB-59
Allen, George [publishing house] DLB-106
Allen, George, and Unwin Limited DLB-112
Allen, Grant 1848-1899 ....DLB-70, 92, 178
Allen, Henry W. 1912- Y-85
Allen, Hervey 1889-1949 .... DLB-9, 45
Allen, James 1739-1808............... DLB-31
Allen, James Lane 1849-1925 .... DLB-71
Allen, Jay Presson 1922- DLB-26
Allen, John, and Company............ DLB-49
Allen, Paula Gunn 1939- DLB-175
Allen, Samuel W. 1917- DLB-41
Allen, Woody 1935- DLB-44
Allende, Isabel 1942- DLB-145; CDWLB-3
Alline, Henry 1748-1784.............. DLB-99
Allingham, Margery 1904-1966 .... DLB-77
Allingham, William 1824-1889.......... DLB-35
Allison, W. L. [publishing house]........ DLB-49
The Alliterative Morte Arthure and the Stanzaic
    Morte Arthur circa 1350-1400 .... DLB-146
Allott, Kenneth 1912-1973 .... DLB-20
Allston, Washington 1779-1843 ...... DLB-1, 235
Almon, John [publishing house] DLB-154
Alonzo, Dámaso 1898-1990 .... DLB-108
Alsop, George 1636-post 1673 .... DLB-24
Alsop, Richard 1761-1815.............. DLB-37
Altemus, Henry, and Company DLB-49
Altenberg, Peter 1885-1919 .... DLB-81
Althusser, Louis 1918-1990 .... DLB-242
Altolaguirre, Manuel 1905-1959........ DLB-108
Aluko, T. M. 1918- DLB-117
Alurista 1947- DLB-82
Alvarez, A. 1929- DLB-14, 40
Alver, Betti 1906-1989 ..... DLB-220; CDWLB-4
Amadi, Elechi 1934- DLB-117
Amado, Jorge 1912- DLB-113
Ambler, Eric 1909-1998 .... DLB-77
American Conservatory Theatre DLB-7
American Fiction and the 1930s DLB-9
American Humor: A Historical Survey
    East and Northeast
    South and Southwest
    Midwest
    West......................... DLB-11
The American Library in Paris............. Y-93
American News Company DLB-49
The American Poets' Corner: The First
    Three Years (1983-1986) Y-86
American Publishing Company DLB-49
American Stationers' Company DLB-49
American Sunday-School Union DLB-49
American Temperance Union DLB-49
American Tract Society DLB-49
The American Trust for the
    British Library Y-96
The American Writers Congress
    (9-12 October 1981)................. Y-81

The American Writers Congress: A Report
    on Continuing Business................. Y-81
Ames, Fisher 1758-1808 .... DLB-37
Ames, Mary Clemmer 1831-1884 .... DLB-23
Amiel, Henri-Frédéric 1821-1881..........DLB-217
Amini, Johari M. 1935- DLB-41
Amis, Kingsley 1922-1995
    .... DLB-15, 27, 100, 139, Y-96; CDBLB-7
Amis, Martin 1949- DLB-194
Ammianus Marcellinus
    circa A.D. 330-A.D. 395 .... DLB-211
Ammons, A. R. 1926- DLB-5, 165
Amory, Thomas 1691?-1788 .... DLB-39
Anania, Michael 1939- DLB-193
Anaya, Rudolfo A. 1937- DLB-82, 206
Ancrene Riwle circa 1200-1225 .... DLB-146
Andersch, Alfred 1914-1980............. DLB-69
Andersen, Benny 1929- DLB-214
Anderson, Alexander 1775-1870 .... DLB-188
Anderson, David 1929- DLB-241
Anderson, Frederick Irving 1877-1947 ... DLB-202
Anderson, Margaret 1886-1973 ...... DLB-4, 91
Anderson, Maxwell 1888-1959........DLB-7, 228
Anderson, Patrick 1915-1979 .... DLB-68
Anderson, Paul Y. 1893-1938........... DLB-29
Anderson, Poul 1926- DLB-8
Anderson, Robert 1750-1830 .... DLB-142
Anderson, Robert 1917- DLB-7
Anderson, Sherwood
    1876-1941..... DLB-4, 9, 86; DS-1; CDALB-4
Andreae, Johann Valentin 1586-1654.... DLB-164
Andreas Capellanus
    flourished circa 1185 .... DLB-208
Andreas-Salomé, Lou 1861-1937 .... DLB-66
Andres, Stefan 1906-1970............. DLB-69
Andreu, Blanca 1959- DLB-134
Andrewes, Lancelot 1555-1626 .....DLB-151, 172
Andrews, Charles M. 1863-1943 ....DLB-17
Andrews, Miles Peter ?-1814 .... DLB-89
Andrian, Leopold von 1875-1951........ DLB-81
Andrić, Ivo 1892-1975 ......DLB-147; CDWLB-4
Andrieux, Louis (see Aragon, Louis)
Andrus, Silas, and Son DLB-49
Andrzejewski, Jerzy 1909-1983.......... DLB-215
Angell, James Burrill 1829-1916 .... DLB-64
Angell, Roger 1920- DLB-171, 185
Angelou, Maya 1928- DLB-38; CDALB-7
Anger, Jane flourished 1589........... DLB-136
Angers, Félicité (see Conan, Laure)
Anglo-Norman Literature in the Development
    of Middle English Literature DLB-146
The Anglo-Saxon Chronicle circa 890-1154 .. DLB-146
The "Angry Young Men" DLB-15
Angus and Robertson (UK) Limited DLB-112
Anhalt, Edward 1914-2000............. DLB-26
Anners, Henry F. [publishing house] DLB-49

Annolied between 1077 and 1081.........DLB-148
Annual Awards for *Dictionary of Literary Biography*
 Editors and Contributors....Y-98, Y-99, Y-00
Anselm of Canterbury 1033-1109.......DLB-115
Anstey, F. 1856-1934.............DLB-141, 178
Anthony, Michael 1932- DLB-125
Anthony, Piers 1934- DLB-8
Anthony, Susanna 1726-1791..........DLB-200
Antin, David 1932-..................DLB-169
Antin, Mary 1881-1949 ....DLB-221; Y-84
Anton Ulrich, Duke of Brunswick-Lüneburg
 1633-1714 ....DLB-168
Antschel, Paul (see Celan, Paul)
Anyidoho, Kofi 1947- DLB-157
Anzaldúa, Gloria 1942- DLB-122
Anzengruber, Ludwig 1839-1889 ....DLB-129
Apess, William 1798-1839 ....DLB-175, 243
Apodaca, Rudy S. 1939-................DLB-82
Apollonius Rhodius third century B.C....DLB-176
Apple, Max 1941- DLB-130
Appleton, D., and Company DLB-49
Appleton-Century-Crofts..............DLB-46
Applewhite, James 1935- DLB-105
Applewood Books DLB-46
Apuleius circa A.D. 125-post A.D. 164
 ....DLB-211; CDWLB-1
Aquin, Hubert 1929-1977 ....DLB-53
Aquinas, Thomas 1224 or 1225-1274 ....DLB-115
Aragon, Louis 1897-1982...............DLB-72
Aralica, Ivan 1930- DLB-181
Aratus of Soli
 circa 315 B.C.-circa 239 B.C. DLB-176
Arbasino, Alberto 1930- DLB-196
Arbor House Publishing Company DLB-46
Arbuthnot, John 1667-1735 ....DLB-101
Arcadia House DLB-46
Arce, Julio G. (see Ulica, Jorge)
Archer, William 1856-1924 ....DLB-10
Archilochhus
 mid seventh century B.C.E. DLB-176
The Archpoet circa 1130?-?............DLB-148
Archpriest Avvakum (Petrovich)
 1620?-1682 ....DLB-150
Arden, John 1930- DLB-13, 245
Arden of Faversham....................DLB-62
Ardis Publishers......................Y-89
Ardizzone, Edward 1900-1979 ....DLB-160
Arellano, Juan Estevan 1947- DLB-122
The Arena Publishing Company........DLB-49
Arena Stage DLB-7
Arenas, Reinaldo 1943-1990 ....DLB-145
Arendt, Hannah 1906-1975 ....DLB-242
Arensberg, Ann 1937- Y-82
Arghezi, Tudor 1880-1967...DLB-220; CDWLB-4
Arguedas, José María 1911-1969 ....DLB-113
Argueta, Manilio 1936- DLB-145

Arias, Ron 1941- DLB-82
Arishima, Takeo 1878-1923............DLB-180
Aristophanes circa 446 B.C.-circa 386 B.C.
 ....DLB-176; CDWLB-1
Aristotle 384 B.C.-322 B.C.
 ....DLB-176; CDWLB-1
Ariyoshi Sawako 1931-1984 ....DLB-182
Arland, Marcel 1899-1986..............DLB-72
Arlen, Michael 1895-1956 ....DLB-36, 77, 162
Armah, Ayi Kwei 1939- ...DLB-117; CDWLB-3
Armantrout, Rae 1947- DLB-193
Der arme Hartmann ?-after 1150........DLB-148
Armed Services Editions DLB-46
Armstrong, Martin Donisthorpe
 1882-1974 ....DLB-197
Armstrong, Richard 1903- DLB-160
Armstrong, Terence Ian Fytton (see Gawsworth, John)
Arndt, Ernst Moritz 1769-1860 ....DLB-90
Arnim, Achim von 1781-1831 ....DLB-90
Arnim, Bettina von 1785-1859 ....DLB-90
Arnim, Elizabeth von (Countess Mary
 Annette Beauchamp Russell)
 1866-1941 ....DLB-197
Arno Press.........................DLB-46
Arnold, Edward [publishing house]......DLB-112
Arnold, Edwin 1832-1904 ....DLB-35
Arnold, Edwin L. 1857-1935 ....DLB-178
Arnold, Matthew
 1822-1888..........DLB-32, 57; CDBLB-4
Preface to *Poems* (1853) DLB-32
Arnold, Thomas 1795-1842.............DLB-55
Arnott, Peter 1962- DLB-233
Arnow, Harriette Simpson 1908-1986.....DLB-6
Arp, Bill (see Smith, Charles Henry)
Arpino, Giovanni 1927-1987 ....DLB-177
Arreola, Juan José 1918- DLB-113
Arrian circa 89-circa 155 ....DLB-176
Arrowsmith, J. W. [publishing house] DLB-106
The Art and Mystery of Publishing:
 Interviews Y-97
Arthur, Timothy Shay
 1809-1885 ....DLB-3, 42, 79; DS-13
The Arthurian Tradition and
 Its European Context DLB-138
Artmann, H. C. 1921-2000 ....DLB-85
Arvin, Newton 1900-1963 ....DLB-103
Asch, Nathan 1902-1964 ....DLB-4, 28
Ascham, Roger 1515 or 1516-1568 ......DLB-236
Ash, John 1948- DLB-40
Ashbery, John 1927- DLB-5, 165; Y-81
Ashbridge, Elizabeth 1713-1755 ....DLB-200
Ashburnham, Bertram Lord
 1797-1878 ....DLB-184
Ashendene Press DLB-112
Asher, Sandy 1942- Y-83
Ashton, Winifred (see Dane, Clemence)
Asimov, Isaac 1920-1992...........DLB-8; Y-92

Askew, Anne circa 1521-1546 ....DLB-136
Aspazija 1865-1943 ....DLB-220; CDWLB-4
Asselin, Olivar 1874-1937 ....DLB-92
The Association of American Publishers......Y-99
The Association for Documentary Editing ...Y-00
Astley, William (see Warung, Price)
Asturias, Miguel Angel
 1899-1974 ....DLB-113; CDWLB-3
At Home with Albert Erskine Y-00
Atheneum Publishers.................DLB-46
Atherton, Gertrude 1857-1948.....DLB-9, 78, 186
Athlone Press......................DLB-112
Atkins, Josiah circa 1755-1781 ....DLB-31
Atkins, Russell 1926- DLB-41
Atkinson, Louisa 1834-1872 ....DLB-230
The Atlantic Monthly Press............DLB-46
Attaway, William 1911-1986.............DLB-76
Atwood, Margaret 1939- DLB-53
Aubert, Alvin 1930- DLB-41
Aubert de Gaspé, Phillipe-Ignace-François
 1814-1841 ....DLB-99
Aubert de Gaspé, Phillipe-Joseph
 1786-1871 ....DLB-99
Aubin, Napoléon 1812-1890 ....DLB-99
Aubin, Penelope
 1685-circa 1731 ....DLB-39
Preface to *The Life of Charlotta
 du Pont* (1723) DLB-39
Aubrey-Fletcher, Henry Lancelot (see Wade, Henry)
Auchincloss, Louis 1917- DLB-2, 244; Y-80
Auden, W. H. 1907-1973...DLB-10, 20; CDBLB-6
Audio Art in America: A Personal Memoir...Y-85
Audubon, John James 1785-1851........DLB-248
Audubon, John Woodhouse
 1812-1862 ....DLB-183
Auerbach, Berthold 1812-1882 ....DLB-133
Auernheimer, Raoul 1876-1948..........DLB-81
Augier, Emile 1820-1889..............DLB-192
Augustine 354-430....................DLB-115
Responses to Ken Auletta Y-97
Aulus Cellius
 circa A.D. 125-circa A.D. 180? DLB-211
Austen, Jane
 1775-1817 ....DLB-116; CDBLB-3
Auster, Paul 1947- DLB-227
Austin, Alfred 1835-1913..............DLB-35
Austin, Jane Goodwin 1831-1894 ....DLB-202
Austin, Mary 1868-1934 .....DLB-9, 78, 206, 221
Austin, William 1778-1841..............DLB-74
Australie (Emily Manning)
 1845-1890......................DLB-230
Author-Printers, 1476–1599............DLB-167
Author Websites Y-97
Authors and Newspapers Association DLB-46
Authors' Publishing Company DLB-49
Avallone, Michael 1924-1999.............Y-99
Avalon Books........................DLB-46

Avancini, Nicolaus 1611-1686 .... DLB-164	Baillie, Joanna 1762-1851 .... DLB-93	Bannerman, Helen 1862-1946 .... DLB-141
Avendaño, Fausto 1941- DLB-82	Bailyn, Bernard 1922- DLB-17	Bantam Books DLB-46
Averroëó 1126-1198 .... DLB-115	Bainbridge, Beryl 1933- DLB-14, 231	Banti, Anna 1895-1985................ DLB-177
Avery, Gillian 1926- DLB-161	Baird, Irene 1901-1981................. DLB-68	Banville, John 1945- DLB-14
Avicenna 980-1037 .... DLB-115	Baker, Augustine 1575-1641............ DLB-151	Banville, Théodore de 1823-1891 ......DLB-217
Avison, Margaret 1918- DLB-53	Baker, Carlos 1909-1987 .... DLB-103	Baraka, Amiri
Avon Books DLB-46	Baker, David 1954- DLB-120	1934- DLB-5, 7, 16, 38; DS-8; CDALB-1
Avyžius, Jonas 1922-1999............. DLB-220	Baker, Herschel C. 1914-1990 .... DLB-111	Barańczak, Stanisław 1946- DLB-232
Awdry, Wilbert Vere 1911-1997........ DLB-160	Baker, Houston A., Jr. 1943- DLB-67	Baratynsky, Evgenii Abramovich
Awoonor, Kofi 1935- DLB-117	Baker, Nicholson 1957- DLB-227	1800-1844 .... DLB-205
Ayckbourn, Alan 1939- DLB-13, 245	Baker, Samuel White 1821-1893 .... DLB-166	Barbauld, Anna Laetitia
Aymé, Marcel 1902-1967 .... DLB-72	Baker, Thomas 1656-1740 .... DLB-213	1743-1825............ DLB-107, 109, 142, 158
Aytoun, Sir Robert 1570-1638 .... DLB-121	Baker, Walter H., Company	Barbeau, Marius 1883-1969 .... DLB-92
Aytoun, William Edmondstoune	("Baker's Plays") DLB-49	Barber, John Warner 1798-1885........ DLB-30
1813-1865.................... DLB-32, 159	The Baker and Taylor Company........ DLB-49	Bàrberi Squarotti, Giorgio 1929- DLB-128
	Bakhtin, Mikhail Mikhailovich	Barbey d'Aurevilly, Jules-Amédée
B	1895-1975..................... DLB-242	1808-1889 .... DLB-119
	Balaban, John 1943- DLB-120	Barbier, Auguste 1805-1882............DLB-217
B. V. (see Thomson, James)	Bald, Wambly 1902- DLB-4	Barbilian, Dan (see Barbu, Ion)
Babbitt, Irving 1865-1933.............. DLB-63	Balde, Jacob 1604-1668 .... DLB-164	Barbour, John circa 1316-1395......... DLB-146
Babbitt, Natalie 1932- DLB-52	Balderston, John 1889-1954 .... DLB-26	Barbour, Ralph Henry 1870-1944 .... DLB-22
Babcock, John [publishing house]........ DLB-49	Baldwin, James 1924-1987	Barbu, Ion 1895-1961...... DLB-220; CDWLB-4
Babits, Mihály 1883-1941... DLB-215; CDWLB-4	........DLB-2, 7, 33, 249; Y-87; CDALB-1	Barbusse, Henri 1873-1935............. DLB-65
Babrius circa 150-200 ....DLB-176	Baldwin, Joseph Glover	Barclay, Alexander circa 1475-1552 ..... DLB-132
Baca, Jimmy Santiago 1952- DLB-122	1815-1864 .... DLB-3, 11, 248	Barclay, E. E., and Company........... DLB-49
Bache, Benjamin Franklin 1769-1798 ..... DLB-43	Baldwin, Louisa (Mrs. Alfred Baldwin)	Bardeen, C. W. [publishing house]........ DLB-49
Bacheller, Irving 1859-1950 .... DLB-202	1845-1925 .... DLB-240	Barham, Richard Harris 1788-1845 ..... DLB-159
Bachmann, Ingeborg 1926-1973 .... DLB-85	Baldwin, Richard and Anne	Barich, Bill 1943- DLB-185
Bačinskaitė-Bučienė, Salomėja (see Neris, Salomėja)	[publishing house] DLB-170	Baring, Maurice 1874-1945............. DLB-34
Bacon, Delia 1811-1859 .... DLB-1, 243	Baldwin, William circa 1515-1563 ..... DLB-132	Baring-Gould, Sabine
Bacon, Francis	Bale, John 1495-1563 .... DLB-132	1834-1924 .... DLB-156, 190
1561-1626 .... DLB-151, 236; CDBLB-1	Balestrini, Nanni 1935- DLB-128, 196	Barker, A. L. 1918- DLB-14, 139
Bacon, Sir Nicholas circa 1510-1579 ..... DLB-132	Balfour, Sir Andrew 1630-1694 .... DLB-213	Barker, Arthur, Limited DLB-112
Bacon, Roger circa 1214/1220-1292 ..... DLB-115	Balfour, Arthur James 1848-1930....... DLB-190	Barker, George 1913-1991 .... DLB-20
Bacon, Thomas circa 1700-1768 .... DLB-31	Balfour, Sir James 1600-1657 .... DLB-213	Barker, Harley Granville 1877-1946 ..... DLB-10
Bacovia, George	Ballantine Books.................... DLB-46	Barker, Howard 1946- DLB-13, 233
1881-1957............ DLB-220; CDWLB-4	Ballantyne, R. M. 1825-1894 .... DLB-163	Barker, James Nelson 1784-1858 .... DLB-37
Badger, Richard G., and Company DLB-49	Ballard, J. G. 1930- DLB-14, 207	Barker, Jane 1652-1727............. DLB-39, 131
Bagaduce Music Lending Library.......... Y-00	Ballard, Martha Moore 1735-1812 ...... DLB-200	Barker, Lady Mary Anne 1831-1911 ..... DLB-166
Bage, Robert 1728-1801 .... DLB-39	Ballerini, Luigi 1940- DLB-128	Barker, William circa 1520-after 1576 ... DLB-132
Bagehot, Walter 1826-1877............. DLB-55	Ballou, Maturin Murray	Barkov, Ivan Semenovich 1732-1768 .... DLB-150
Bagley, Desmond 1923-1983 .... DLB-87	1820-1895 ....DLB-79, 189	Barks, Coleman 1937- DLB-5
Bagley, Sarah G. 1806-1848 .... DLB-239	Ballou, Robert O. [publishing house] DLB-46	Barlach, Ernst 1870-1938 .... DLB-56, 118
Bagnold, Enid 1889-1981...DLB-13, 160, 191, 245	Balzac, Honoré de 1799-1855 .... DLB-119	Barlow, Joel 1754-1812................ DLB-37
Bagryana, Elisaveta	Bambara, Toni Cade	*The Prospect of Peace* (1778) DLB-37
1893-1991 ....DLB-147; CDWLB-4	1939- DLB-38, 218; CDALB-7	Barnard, John 1681-1770 .... DLB-24
Bahr, Hermann 1863-1934......... DLB-81, 118	Bamford, Samuel 1788-1872 .... DLB-190	Barne, Kitty (Mary Catherine Barne)
Bailey, Abigail Abbot 1746-1815........ DLB-200	Bancroft, A. L., and Company.......... DLB-49	1883-1957 .... DLB-160
Bailey, Alfred Goldsworthy 1905- DLB-68	Bancroft, George 1800-1891... DLB-1, 30, 59, 243	Barnes, A. S., and Company DLB-49
Bailey, Francis [publishing house]........ DLB-49	Bancroft, Hubert Howe 1832-1918 ...DLB-47, 140	Barnes, Barnabe 1571-1609 .... DLB-132
Bailey, H. C. 1878-1961 .... DLB-77	Bandelier, Adolph F. 1840-1914 .... DLB-186	Barnes, Djuna 1892-1982.......... DLB-4, 9, 45
Bailey, Jacob 1731-1808 .... DLB-99	Bangs, John Kendrick 1862-1922 .....DLB-11, 79	Barnes, Jim 1933- DLB-175
Bailey, Paul 1937- DLB-14	Banim, John 1798-1842........DLB-116, 158, 159	Barnes, Julian 1946- DLB-194; Y-93
Bailey, Philip James 1816-1902.......... DLB-32	Banim, Michael 1796-1874 .... DLB-158, 159	Barnes, Margaret Ayer 1886-1967 .... DLB-9
Baillargeon, Pierre 1916-1967 .... DLB-88	Banks, Iain 1954- DLB-194	Barnes, Peter 1931- DLB-13, 233
Baillie, Hugh 1890-1966................. DLB-29	Banks, John circa 1653-1706............ DLB-80	Barnes, William 1801-1886 .... DLB-32
	Banks, Russell 1940- DLB-130	

314

Barnes and Noble Books DLB-46
Barnet, Miguel 1940- DLB-145
Barney, Natalie 1876-1972 . . . . DLB-4
Barnfield, Richard 1574-1627 . . . . DLB-172
Baron, Richard W.,
    Publishing Company DLB-46
Barr, Amelia Edith Huddleston
    1831-1919 . . . . DLB-202, 221
Barr, Robert 1850-1912 . . . . DLB-70, 92
Barral, Carlos 1928-1989 . . . . DLB-134
Barrax, Gerald William 1933- DLB-41, 120
Barrès, Maurice 1862-1923 . . . . DLB-123
Barrett, Eaton Stannard 1786-1820 . . . . . . DLB-116
Barrie, J. M.
    1860-1937 . . . . . DLB-10, 141, 156; CDBLB-5
Barrie and Jenkins DLB-112
Barrio, Raymond 1921- DLB-82
Barrios, Gregg 1945- DLB-122
Barry, Philip 1896-1949 . . . . DLB-7, 228
Barry, Robertine (see Françoise)
Barry, Sebastian 1955- DLB-245
Barse and Hopkins DLB-46
Barstow, Stan 1928- DLB-14, 139
Barth, John 1930- DLB-2, 227
Barthelme, Donald
    1931-1989 . . . . DLB-2, 234; Y-80, Y-89
Barthelme, Frederick 1943- DLB-244; Y-85
Bartholomew, Frank 1898-1985 . . . . DLB-127
Bartlett, John 1820-1905 . . . . DLB-1, 235
Bartol, Cyrus Augustus 1813-1900 . . . . DLB-1, 235
Barton, Bernard 1784-1849 . . . . DLB-96
Barton, John ca. 1610-1675 . . . . DLB-236
Barton, Thomas Pennant 1803-1869 . . . . . DLB-140
Bartram, John 1699-1777 . . . . DLB-31
Bartram, William 1739-1823 . . . . DLB-37
Basic Books DLB-46
Basille, Theodore (see Becon, Thomas)
Bass, Rick 1958- DLB-212
Bass, T. J. 1932- Y-81
Bassani, Giorgio 1916- DLB-128, 177
Basse, William circa 1583-1653 . . . . DLB-121
Bassett, John Spencer 1867-1928 . . . . DLB-17
Bassler, Thomas Joseph (see Bass, T. J.)
Bate, Walter Jackson 1918-1999 . . . . . DLB-67, 103
Bateman, Christopher
    [publishing house] DLB-170
Bateman, Stephen circa 1510-1584 . . . . . . DLB-136
Bates, H. E. 1905-1974 . . . . DLB-162, 191
Bates, Katharine Lee 1859-1929 . . . . DLB-71
Batiushkov, Konstantin Nikolaevich
    1787-1855 . . . . DLB-205
Batsford, B. T. [publishing house] DLB-106
Battiscombe, Georgina 1905- DLB-155
The Battle of Maldon circa 1000 . . . . DLB-146
Baudelaire, Charles 1821-1867 . . . . DLB-217
Bauer, Bruno 1809-1882 . . . . DLB-133

Bauer, Wolfgang 1941- DLB-124
Baum, L. Frank 1856-1919 . . . . DLB-22
Baum, Vicki 1888-1960 . . . . DLB-85
Baumbach, Jonathan 1933- Y-80
Bausch, Richard 1945- DLB-130
Bausch, Robert 1945- DLB-218
Bawden, Nina 1925- DLB-14, 161, 207
Bax, Clifford 1886-1962 . . . . DLB-10, 100
Baxter, Charles 1947- DLB-130
Bayer, Eleanor (see Perry, Eleanor)
Bayer, Konrad 1932-1964 . . . . DLB-85
Baynes, Pauline 1922- DLB-160
Baynton, Barbara 1857-1929 . . . . DLB-230
Bazin, Hervé 1911-1996 . . . . DLB-83
Beach, Sylvia 1887-1962 . . . . DLB-4; DS-15
Beacon Press DLB-49
Beadle and Adams DLB-49
Beagle, Peter S. 1939- Y-80
Beal, M. F. 1937- Y-81
Beale, Howard K. 1899-1959 . . . . DLB-17
Beard, Charles A. 1874-1948 . . . . DLB-17
A Beat Chronology: The First Twenty-five
    Years, 1944-1969 . . . . DLB-16
Periodicals of the Beat Generation DLB-16
The Beats in New York City DLB-237
The Beats in the West DLB-237
Beattie, Ann 1947- DLB-218; Y-82
Beattie, James 1735-1803 . . . . DLB-109
Beatty, Chester 1875-1968 . . . . DLB-201
Beauchemin, Nérée 1850-1931 . . . . DLB-92
Beauchemin, Yves 1941- DLB-60
Beaugrand, Honoré 1848-1906 . . . . DLB-99
Beaulieu, Victor-Lévy 1945- DLB-53
Beaumont, Francis circa 1584-1616
    and Fletcher, John 1579-1625
    . . . . DLB-58; CDBLB-1
Beaumont, Sir John 1583?-1627 . . . . DLB-121
Beaumont, Joseph 1616-1699 . . . . DLB-126
Beauvoir, Simone de 1908-1986 . . . . DLB-72; Y-86
Becher, Ulrich 1910- DLB-69
Becker, Carl 1873-1945 . . . . DLB-17
Becker, Jurek 1937-1997 . . . . DLB-75
Becker, Jurgen 1932- DLB-75
Beckett, Samuel 1906-1989
    . . . . DLB-13, 15, 233; Y-90; CDBLB-7
Beckford, William 1760-1844 . . . . DLB-39
Beckham, Barry 1944- DLB-33
Becon, Thomas circa 1512-1567 . . . . DLB-136
Becque, Henry 1837-1899 . . . . DLB-192
Beddoes, Thomas 1760-1808 . . . . DLB-158
Beddoes, Thomas Lovell 1803-1849 . . . . . . DLB-96
Bede circa 673-735 . . . . DLB-146
Beecher, Catharine Esther 1800-1878 . . DLB-1, 243
Beecher, Henry Ward 1813-1887 . . . . . . DLB-3, 43
Beer, George L. 1872-1920 . . . . DLB-47

Beer, Johann 1655-1700 . . . . DLB-168
Beer, Patricia 1919-1999 . . . . DLB-40
Beerbohm, Max 1872-1956 . . . . . . DLB-34, 100
Beer-Hofmann, Richard 1866-1945 . . . . . . DLB-81
Beers, Henry A. 1847-1926 . . . . DLB-71
Beeton, S. O. [publishing house] DLB-106
Bégon, Elisabeth 1696-1755 . . . . DLB-99
Behan, Brendan
    1923-1964 . . . . DLB-13, 233; CDBLB-7
Behn, Aphra 1640?-1689 . . . . DLB-39, 80, 131
Behn, Harry 1898-1973 . . . . DLB-61
Behrman, S. N. 1893-1973 . . . . DLB-7, 44
Belaney, Archibald Stansfeld (see Grey Owl)
Belasco, David 1853-1931 . . . . DLB-7
Belford, Clarke and Company DLB-49
Belinksy, Vissarion Grigor'evich
    1811-1848 . . . . DLB-198
Belitt, Ben 1911- DLB-5
Belknap, Jeremy 1744-1798 . . . . DLB-30, 37
Bell, Adrian 1901-1980 . . . . DLB-191
Bell, Clive 1881-1964 . . . . DS-10
Bell, Daniel 1919- DLB-246
Bell, George, and Sons DLB-106
Bell, Gertrude Margaret Lowthian
    1868-1926 . . . . DLB-174
Bell, James Madison 1826-1902 . . . . DLB-50
Bell, Madison Smartt 1957- DLB-218
Bell, Marvin 1937- DLB-5
Bell, Millicent 1919- DLB-111
Bell, Quentin 1910-1996 . . . . DLB-155
Bell, Robert [publishing house] DLB-49
Bell, Vanessa 1879-1961 . . . . DS-10
Bellamy, Edward 1850-1898 . . . . DLB-12
Bellamy, John [publishing house] DLB-170
Bellamy, Joseph 1719-1790 . . . . DLB-31
La Belle Assemblée 1806-1837 . . . . DLB-110
Bellezza, Dario 1944-1996 . . . . DLB-128
Belloc, Hilaire 1870-1953 . . . . DLB-19, 100, 141, 174
Belloc, Madame (see Parkes, Bessie Rayner)
Bellonci, Maria 1902-1986 . . . . DLB-196
Bellow, Saul
    1915- DLB-2, 28; Y-82; DS-3; CDALB-1
Belmont Productions DLB-46
Bels, Alberts 1938- DLB-232
Belševica, Vizma 1931- DLB-232; CDWLB-4
Bemelmans, Ludwig 1898-1962 . . . . DLB-22
Bemis, Samuel Flagg 1891-1973 . . . . DLB-17
Bemrose, William [publishing house] DLB-106
Ben no Naishi 1228?-1271? DLB-203
Benchley, Robert 1889-1945 . . . . DLB-11
Bencúr, Matej (see Kukučín, Martin)
Benedetti, Mario 1920- DLB-113
Benedict, Pinckney 1964- DLB-244
Benedict, Ruth 1887-1948 . . . . DLB-246
Benedictus, David 1938- DLB-14

Cumulative Index

Benedikt, Michael 1935- DLB-5
Benediktov, Vladimir Grigor'evich 1807-1873 .... DLB-205
Benét, Stephen Vincent 1898-1943 .... DLB-4, 48, 102, 249
Benét, William Rose 1886-1950 .... DLB-45
Benford, Gregory 1941- Y-82
Benjamin, Park 1809-1864 .... DLB-3, 59, 73
Benjamin, S. G. W. 1837-1914 ...... DLB-189
Benjamin, Walter 1892-1940 .... DLB-242
Benlowes, Edward 1602-1676 .... DLB-126
Benn Brothers Limited DLB-106
Benn, Gottfried 1886-1956 .... DLB-56
Bennett, Arnold 1867-1931 .... DLB-10, 34, 98, 135; CDBLB-5
Bennett, Charles 1899-1995 .... DLB-44
Bennett, Emerson 1822-1905 .... DLB-202
Bennett, Gwendolyn 1902- DLB-51
Bennett, Hal 1930- DLB-33
Bennett, James Gordon 1795-1872 ..... DLB-43
Bennett, James Gordon, Jr. 1841-1918 ... DLB-23
Bennett, John 1865-1956 .... DLB-42
Bennett, Louise 1919- DLB-117; CDWLB-3
Benni, Stefano 1947- DLB-196
Benoit, Jacques 1941- DLB-60
Benson, A. C. 1862-1925 .... DLB-98
Benson, E. F. 1867-1940 .... DLB-135, 153
Benson, Jackson J. 1930- DLB-111
Benson, Robert Hugh 1871-1914 ...... DLB-153
Benson, Stella 1892-1933 .... DLB-36, 162
Bent, James Theodore 1852-1897 ..... DLB-174
Bent, Mabel Virginia Anna ?-? DLB-174
Bentham, Jeremy 1748-1832 ..... DLB-107, 158
Bentley, E. C. 1875-1956 .... DLB-70
Bentley, Phyllis 1894-1977 .... DLB-191
Bentley, Richard [publishing house] DLB-106
Benton, Robert 1932- and Newman, David 1937- DLB-44
Benziger Brothers DLB-49
Beowulf circa 900-1000 or 790-825 .... DLB-146; CDBLB-1
Berent, Wacław 1873-1940 .... DLB-215
Beresford, Anne 1929- DLB-40
Beresford, John Davys 1873-1947 .... DLB-162, 178, 197
"Experiment in the Novel" (1929) DLB-36
Beresford-Howe, Constance 1922- DLB-88
Berford, R. G., Company DLB-49
Berg, Stephen 1934- DLB-5
Bergengruen, Werner 1892-1964 .... DLB-56
Berger, John 1926- DLB-14, 207
Berger, Meyer 1898-1959 .... DLB-29
Berger, Thomas 1924- DLB-2; Y-80
Bergman, Ingmar 1918- DLB-257
Berkeley, Anthony 1893-1971 .... DLB-77
Berkeley, George 1685-1753 ...... DLB-31, 101

The Berkley Publishing Corporation DLB-46
Berlin, Lucia 1936- DLB-130
Berman, Marshall 1940- DLB-246
Bernal, Vicente J. 1888-1915 .... DLB-82
Bernanos, Georges 1888-1948 .... DLB-72
Bernard, Harry 1898-1979 .... DLB-92
Bernard, John 1756-1828 .... DLB-37
Bernard of Chartres circa 1060-1124? ... DLB-115
Bernard of Clairvaux 1090-1153 .... DLB-208
The Bernard Malamud Archive at the Harry Ransom Humanities Research Center Y-00
Bernard Silvestris flourished circa 1130-1160 .... DLB-208
Bernari, Carlo 1909-1992 .... DLB-177
Bernhard, Thomas 1931-1989 .... DLB-85, 124; CDWLB-2
Bernstein, Charles 1950- DLB-169
Berriault, Gina 1926-1999 .... DLB-130
Berrigan, Daniel 1921- DLB-5
Berrigan, Ted 1934-1983 .... DLB-5, 169
Berry, Wendell 1934- DLB-5, 6, 234
Berryman, John 1914-1972 .... DLB-48; CDALB-1
Bersianik, Louky 1930- DLB-60
Berthelet, Thomas [publishing house] ... DLB-170
Berto, Giuseppe 1914-1978 .... DLB-177
Bertolucci, Attilio 1911- DLB-128
Berton, Pierre 1920- DLB-68
Bertrand, Louis "Aloysius" 1807-1841 .... DLB-217
Besant, Sir Walter 1836-1901 ...... DLB-135, 190
Bessette, Gerard 1920- DLB-53
Bessie, Alvah 1904-1985 .... DLB-26
Bester, Alfred 1913-1987 .... DLB-8
Besterman, Theodore 1904-1976 ...... DLB-201
The Bestseller Lists: An Assessment Y-84
Bestuzhev, Aleksandr Aleksandrovich (Marlinsky) 1797-1837 .... DLB-198
Bestuzhev, Nikolai Aleksandrovich 1791-1855 .... DLB-198
Betham-Edwards, Matilda Barbara (see Edwards, Matilda Barbara Betham-)
Betjeman, John 1906-1984 .... DLB-20; Y-84; CDBLB-7
Betocchi, Carlo 1899-1986 .... DLB-128
Bettarini, Mariella 1942- DLB-128
Betts, Doris 1932- DLB-218; Y-82
Beùkoviù, Matija 1939- DLB-181
Beveridge, Albert J. 1862-1927 .... DLB-17
Beverley, Robert circa 1673-1722 ..... DLB-24, 30
Bevilacqua, Alberto 1934- DLB-196
Bevington, Louisa Sarah 1845-1895 .... DLB-199
Beyle, Marie-Henri (see Stendhal)
Białoszewski, Miron 1922-1983 .... DLB-232
Bianco, Margery Williams 1881-1944 ... DLB-160
Bibaud, Adèle 1854-1941 .... DLB-92
Bibaud, Michel 1782-1857 .... DLB-99

Bibliographical and Textual Scholarship Since World War II Y-89
Bichsel, Peter 1935- DLB-75
Bickerstaff, Isaac John 1733-circa 1808 ... DLB-89
Biddle, Drexel [publishing house] DLB-49
Bidermann, Jacob 1577 or 1578-1639 .... DLB-164
Bidwell, Walter Hilliard 1798-1881 ..... DLB-79
Bienek, Horst 1930- DLB-75
Bierbaum, Otto Julius 1865-1910 .... DLB-66
Bierce, Ambrose 1842-1914? DLB-11, 12, 23, 71, 74, 186; CDALB-3
Bigelow, William F. 1879-1966 .... DLB-91
Biggle, Lloyd, Jr. 1923- DLB-8
Bigiaretti, Libero 1905-1993 .... DLB-177
Bigland, Eileen 1898-1970 .... DLB-195
Biglow, Hosea (see Lowell, James Russell)
Bigongiari, Piero 1914- DLB-128
Billinger, Richard 1890-1965 .... DLB-124
Billings, Hammatt 1818-1874 .... DLB-188
Billings, John Shaw 1898-1975 .... DLB-137
Billings, Josh (see Shaw, Henry Wheeler)
Binding, Rudolf G. 1867-1938 .... DLB-66
Bingay, Malcolm 1884-1953 .... DLB-241
Bingham, Caleb 1757-1817 .... DLB-42
Bingham, George Barry 1906-1988 ..... DLB-127
Bingham, Sallie 1937- DLB-234
Bingley, William [publishing house] DLB-154
Binyon, Laurence 1869-1943 .... DLB-19
Biographia Brittanica DLB-142
Biographical Documents I Y-84
Biographical Documents II Y-85
Bioren, John [publishing house] DLB-49
Bioy Casares, Adolfo 1914- DLB-113
Bird, Isabella Lucy 1831-1904 .... DLB-166
Bird, Robert Montgomery 1806-1854 ... DLB-202
Bird, William 1888-1963 .... DLB-4; DS-15
Birken, Sigmund von 1626-1681 ...... DLB-164
Birney, Earle 1904- DLB-88
Birrell, Augustine 1850-1933 .... DLB-98
Bisher, Furman 1918- DLB-171
Bishop, Elizabeth 1911-1979 .... DLB-5, 169; CDALB-6
Bishop, John Peale 1892-1944 ...... DLB-4, 9, 45
Bismarck, Otto von 1815-1898 .... DLB-129
Bisset, Robert 1759-1805 .... DLB-142
Bissett, Bill 1939- DLB-53
Bitzius, Albert (see Gotthelf, Jeremias)
Bjørnvig, Thorkild 1918- DLB-214
Black, David (D. M.) 1941- DLB-40
Black, Walter J. [publishing house] DLB-46
Black, Winifred 1863-1936 .... DLB-25
The Black Aesthetic: Background DS-8
Black Theaters and Theater Organizations in America, 1961-1982: A Research List DLB-38

Black Theatre: A Forum [excerpts] DLB-38
Blackamore, Arthur 1679-? DLB-24, 39
Blackburn, Alexander L. 1929- Y-85
Blackburn, Paul 1926-1971 . . . . DLB-16; Y-81
Blackburn, Thomas 1916-1977 . . . . DLB-27
Blackmore, R. D. 1825-1900 . . . . DLB-18
Blackmore, Sir Richard 1654-1729. . . . . . . DLB-131
Blackmur, R. P. 1904-1965 . . . . DLB-63
Blackwell, Basil, Publisher DLB-106
Blackwood, Algernon Henry
  1869-1951 . . . . DLB-153, 156, 178
Blackwood, Caroline 1931-1996 . . . . . DLB-14, 207
Blackwood, William, and Sons, Ltd. DLB-154
Blackwood's Edinburgh Magazine
  1817-1980 . . . . DLB-110
Blades, William 1824-1890 . . . . DLB-184
Blaga, Lucian 1895-1961 . . . . DLB-220
Blagden, Isabella 1817?-1873 . . . . DLB-199
Blair, Eric Arthur (see Orwell, George)
Blair, Francis Preston 1791-1876 . . . . DLB-43
Blair, James circa 1655-1743 . . . . DLB-24
Blair, John Durburrow 1759-1823 . . . . DLB-37
Blais, Marie-Claire 1939- DLB-53
Blaise, Clark 1940- DLB-53
Blake, George 1893-1961 . . . . DLB-191
Blake, Lillie Devereux 1833-1913 . . . DLB-202, 221
Blake, Nicholas 1904-1972 . . . . DLB-77
  (see Day Lewis, C.)
Blake, William
  1757-1827 . . . . DLB-93, 154, 163; CDBLB-3
The Blakiston Company DLB-49
Blandiana, Ana 1942- DLB-232; CDWLB-4
Blanchot, Maurice 1907- DLB-72
Blanckenburg, Christian Friedrich von
  1744-1796 . . . . DLB-94
Blaser, Robin 1925- DLB-165
Blaumanis, Rudolfs 1863-1908 . . . . DLB-220
Bleasdale, Alan 1946- DLB-245
Bledsoe, Albert Taylor 1809-1877 . . DLB-3, 79, 248
Bleecker, Ann Eliza 1752-1783 . . . . DLB-200
Blelock and Company DLB-49
Blennerhassett, Margaret Agnew
  1773-1842 . . . . DLB-99
Bles, Geoffrey [publishing house] DLB-112
Blessington, Marguerite, Countess of
  1789-1849 . . . . DLB-166
Blew, Mary Clearman 1939- DLB-256
The Blickling Homilies circa 971 . . . . DLB-146
Blind, Mathilde 1841-1896 . . . . DLB-199
Blish, James 1921-1975 . . . . DLB-8
Bliss, E., and E. White
  [publishing house] DLB-49
Bliven, Bruce 1889-1977 . . . . DLB-137
Blixen, Karen 1885-1962 . . . . DLB-214
Bloch, Robert 1917-1994 . . . . DLB-44
Block, Lawrence 1938- DLB-226

Block, Rudolph (see Lessing, Bruno)
Blondal, Patricia 1926-1959 . . . . DLB-88
Bloom, Harold 1930- DLB-67
Bloomer, Amelia 1818-1894 . . . . DLB-79
Bloomfield, Robert 1766-1823 . . . . DLB-93
Bloomsbury Group DS-10
Blotner, Joseph 1923- DLB-111
Blount, Thomas 1618?-1679 . . . . DLB-236
Bloy, Léon 1846-1917 . . . . DLB-123
Blume, Judy 1938- DLB-52
Blunck, Hans Friedrich 1888-1961 . . . . DLB-66
Blunden, Edmund 1896-1974 . . . DLB-20, 100, 155
Blundeville, Thomas 1522?-1606 . . . . DLB-236
Blunt, Lady Anne Isabella Noel
  1837-1917 . . . . DLB-174
Blunt, Wilfrid Scawen 1840-1922 . . . . DLB-19, 174
Bly, Nellie (see Cochrane, Elizabeth)
Bly, Robert 1926- DLB-5
Blyton, Enid 1897-1968 . . . . DLB-160
Boaden, James 1762-1839 . . . . DLB-89
Boas, Frederick S. 1862-1957 . . . . DLB-149
The Bobbs-Merrill Archive at the
  Lilly Library, Indiana University Y-90
Boborykin, Petr Dmitrievich 1836-1921 . . DLB-238
The Bobbs-Merrill Company DLB-46
Bobrov, Semen Sergeevich
  1763?-1810 . . . . DLB-150
Bobrowski, Johannes 1917-1965 . . . . DLB-75
The Elmer Holmes Bobst Awards in Arts
  and Letters Y-87
Bodenheim, Maxwell 1892-1954 . . . . . . DLB-9, 45
Bodenstedt, Friedrich von 1819-1892 . . . . DLB-129
Bodini, Vittorio 1914-1970 . . . . DLB-128
Bodkin, M. McDonnell 1850-1933 . . . . DLB-70
Bodley, Sir Thomas 1545-1613 . . . . DLB-213
Bodley Head DLB-112
Bodmer, Johann Jakob 1698-1783 . . . . DLB-97
Bodmershof, Imma von 1895-1982 . . . . . . DLB-85
Bodsworth, Fred 1918- DLB-68
Boehm, Sydney 1908- DLB-44
Boer, Charles 1939- DLB-5
Boethius circa 480-circa 524 . . . . DLB-115
Boethius of Dacia circa 1240-? DLB-115
Bogan, Louise 1897-1970 . . . . DLB-45, 169
Bogarde, Dirk 1921- DLB-14
Bogdanovich, Ippolit Fedorovich
  circa 1743-1803 . . . . DLB-150
Bogue, David [publishing house] DLB-106
Böhme, Jakob 1575-1624 . . . . DLB-164
Bohn, H. G. [publishing house] DLB-106
Bohse, August 1661-1742 . . . . DLB-168
Boie, Heinrich Christian 1744-1806 . . . . . . DLB-94
Bok, Edward W. 1863-1930 . . . . . . DLB-91; DS-16
Boland, Eavan 1944- DLB-40
Boldrewood, Rolf (Thomas Alexander Browne)
  1826?-1915 . . . . DLB-230

Bolingbroke, Henry St. John, Viscount
  1678-1751 . . . . DLB-101
Böll, Heinrich
  1917-1985 . . . . DLB-69; Y-85; CDWLB-2
Bolling, Robert 1738-1775 . . . . DLB-31
Bolotov, Andrei Timofeevich
  1738-1833 . . . . DLB-150
Bolt, Carol 1941- DLB-60
Bolt, Robert 1924-1995 . . . . DLB-13, 233
Bolton, Herbert E. 1870-1953 . . . . DLB-17
Bonaventura DLB-90
Bonaventure circa 1217-1274 . . . . DLB-115
Bonaviri, Giuseppe 1924- DLB-177
Bond, Edward 1934- DLB-13
Bond, Michael 1926- DLB-161
Boni, Albert and Charles
  [publishing house] DLB-46
Boni and Liveright DLB-46
Bonner, Marita 1899-1971 . . . . DLB-228
Bonner, Paul Hyde 1893-1968 . . . . DS-17
Bonner, Sherwood (see McDowell, Katharine
  Sherwood Bonner)
Robert Bonner's Sons DLB-49
Bonnin, Gertrude Simmons (see Zitkala-Ša)
Bonsanti, Alessandro 1904-1984 . . . . DLB-177
Bontemps, Arna 1902-1973 . . . . DLB-48, 51
The Book Arts Press at the University
  of Virginia Y-96
The Book League of America DLB-46
Book Publishing Accounting: Some Basic
  Concepts Y-98
Book Reviewing in America: I Y-87
Book Reviewing in America: II Y-88
Book Reviewing in America: III Y-89
Book Reviewing in America: IV Y-90
Book Reviewing in America: V Y-91
Book Reviewing in America: VI Y-92
Book Reviewing in America: VII Y-93
Book Reviewing in America: VIII Y-94
Book Reviewing in America and the
  Literary Scene Y-95
Book Reviewing and the
  Literary Scene Y-96, Y-97
Book Supply Company DLB-49
The Book Trade History Group Y-93
The Book Trade and the Internet Y-00
The Booker Prize Y-96
Address by Anthony Thwaite,
  Chairman of the Booker Prize Judges
  Comments from Former Booker
  Prize Winners Y-86
The Books of George V. Higgins:
  A Checklist of Editions and Printings . . . Y-00
Boorde, Andrew circa 1490-1549 . . . . DLB-136
Boorstin, Daniel J. 1914- DLB-17
Booth, Franklin 1874-1948 . . . . DLB-188
Booth, Mary L. 1831-1889 . . . . DLB-79
Booth, Philip 1925- Y-82

Cumulative Index

Booth, Wayne C. 1921- DLB-67
Booth, William 1829-1912 .... DLB-190
Borchardt, Rudolf 1877-1945 .... DLB-66
Borchert, Wolfgang 1921-1947 ...... DLB-69, 124
Borel, Pétrus 1809-1859 .... DLB-119
Borges, Jorge Luis
   1899-1986 .... DLB-113; Y-86; CDWLB-3
Börne, Ludwig 1786-1837 .... DLB-90
Bornstein, Miriam 1950- DLB-209
Borowski, Tadeusz
   1922-1951 .... DLB-215; CDWLB-4
Borrow, George 1803-1881 ..... DLB-21, 55, 166
Bosch, Juan 1909- DLB-145
Bosco, Henri 1888-1976 .... DLB-72
Bosco, Monique 1927- DLB-53
Bosman, Herman Charles 1905-1951.... DLB-225
Bostic, Joe 1908-1988 .... DLB-241
Boston, Lucy M. 1892-1990 .... DLB-161
Boswell, James
   1740-1795 .... DLB-104, 142; CDBLB-2
Boswell, Robert 1953- DLB-234
Bote, Hermann
   circa 1460-circa 1520 ....DLB-179
Botev, Khristo 1847-1876 .... DLB-147
Botta, Anne C. Lynch 1815-1891 .... DLB-3
Botto, Ján (see Krasko, Ivan)
Bottome, Phyllis 1882-1963 .... DLB-197
Bottomley, Gordon 1874-1948 .... DLB-10
Bottoms, David 1949- DLB-120; Y-83
Bottrall, Ronald 1906- DLB-20
Bouchardy, Joseph 1810-1870 .... DLB-192
Boucher, Anthony 1911-1968 .... DLB-8
Boucher, Jonathan 1738-1804 .... DLB-31
Boucher de Boucherville, George
   1814-1894 .... DLB-99
Boudreau, Daniel (see Coste, Donat)
Bourassa, Napoléon 1827-1916 .... DLB-99
Bourget, Paul 1852-1935 .... DLB-123
Bourinot, John George 1837-1902 .... DLB-99
Bourjaily, Vance 1922- DLB-2, 143
Bourne, Edward Gaylord
   1860-1908 .... DLB-47
Bourne, Randolph 1886-1918 .... DLB-63
Bousoño, Carlos 1923- DLB-108
Bousquet, Joë 1897-1950 .... DLB-72
Bova, Ben 1932- Y-81
Bovard, Oliver K. 1872-1945 .... DLB-25
Bove, Emmanuel 1898-1945 .... DLB-72
Bowen, Elizabeth
   1899-1973 .... DLB-15, 162; CDBLB-7
Bowen, Francis 1811-1890 .... DLB-1, 59, 235
Bowen, John 1924- DLB-13
Bowen, Marjorie 1886-1952 .... DLB-153
Bowen-Merrill Company DLB-49
Bowering, George 1935- DLB-53
Bowers, Bathsheba 1671-1718 .... DLB-200

Bowers, Claude G. 1878-1958 .... DLB-17
Bowers, Edgar 1924-2000................ DLB-5
Bowers, Fredson Thayer
   1905-1991 ....DLB-140; Y-80, 91
Bowles, Paul 1910-1999 ......DLB-5, 6, 218; Y-99
Bowles, Samuel III 1826-1878 .... DLB-43
Bowles, William Lisles 1762-1850 .... DLB-93
Bowman, Louise Morey 1882-1944 ...... DLB-68
Boyd, James 1888-1944 .... DLB-9; DS-16
Boyd, John 1919- DLB-8
Boyd, Thomas 1898-1935 .... DLB-9; DS-16
Boyd, William 1952- DLB-231
Boyesen, Hjalmar Hjorth
   1848-1895 ....DLB-12, 71; DS-13
Boyle, Kay 1902-1992 .....DLB-4, 9, 48, 86; Y-93
Boyle, Roger, Earl of Orrery 1621-1679... DLB-80
Boyle, T. Coraghessan 1948- DLB-218; Y-86
Božić, Mirko 1919- DLB-181
Brackenbury, Alison 1953- DLB-40
Brackenridge, Hugh Henry
   1748-1816....................DLB-11, 37
Brackett, Charles 1892-1969........... DLB-26
Brackett, Leigh 1915-1978 .... DLB-8, 26
Bradburn, John [publishing house]....... DLB-49
Bradbury, Malcolm 1932-2000.......DLB-14, 207
Bradbury, Ray 1920- DLB-2, 8; CDALB-6
Bradbury and Evans................. DLB-106
Braddon, Mary Elizabeth
   1835-1915 ....DLB-18, 70, 156
Bradford, Andrew 1686-1742 .... DLB-43, 73
Bradford, Gamaliel 1863-1932 .... DLB-17
Bradford, John 1749-1830.............. DLB-43
Bradford, Roark 1896-1948 .... DLB-86
Bradford, William 1590-1657........ DLB-24, 30
Bradford, William III 1719-1791 ..... DLB-43, 73
Bradlaugh, Charles 1833-1891 .... DLB-57
Bradley, David 1950- DLB-33
Bradley, Ira, and Company DLB-49
Bradley, J. W., and Company DLB-49
Bradley, Katherine Harris (see Field, Michael)
Bradley, Marion Zimmer 1930-1999 ...... DLB-8
Bradley, William Aspenwall 1878-1939 .... DLB-4
Bradshaw, Henry 1831-1886 .... DLB-184
Bradstreet, Anne
   1612 or 1613-1672 .... DLB-24; CDABL-2
Bradūnas, Kazys 1917- DLB-220
Bradwardine, Thomas circa
   1295-1349 .... DLB-115
Brady, Frank 1924-1986.............. DLB-111
Brady, Frederic A. [publishing house] DLB-49
Bragg, Melvyn 1939- DLB-14
Brainard, Charles H. [publishing house] .. DLB-49
Braine, John 1922-1986 . DLB-15; Y-86; CDBLB-7
Braithwait, Richard 1588-1673 .... DLB-151
Braithwaite, William Stanley
   1878-1962.................. DLB-50, 54

Braker, Ulrich 1735-1798 .... DLB-94
Bramah, Ernest 1868-1942............. DLB-70
Branagan, Thomas 1774-1843 .... DLB-37
Branch, William Blackwell 1927- DLB-76
Brand, Max (see Faust, Frederick Schiller)
Branden Press....................... DLB-46
Branner, H.C. 1903-1966............. DLB-214
Brant, Sebastian 1457-1521............DLB-179
Brassey, Lady Annie (Allnutt)
   1839-1887 .... DLB-166
Brathwaite, Edward Kamau
   1930- DLB-125; CDWLB-3
Brault, Jacques 1933- DLB-53
Braun, Matt 1932- DLB-212
Braun, Volker 1939- DLB-75
Brautigan, Richard
   1935-1984 .... DLB-2, 5, 206; Y-80, Y-84
Braxton, Joanne M. 1950- DLB-41
Bray, Anne Eliza 1790-1883 .... DLB-116
Bray, Thomas 1656-1730 .... DLB-24
Brazdžionis, Bernardas 1907- DLB-220
Braziller, George [publishing house] DLB-46
The Bread Loaf Writers' Conference 1983 ... Y-84
Breasted, James Henry 1865-1935 .... DLB-47
Brecht, Bertolt
   1898-1956 ....DLB-56, 124; CDWLB-2
Bredel, Willi 1901-1964 .... DLB-56
Bregendahl, Marie 1867-1940.......... DLB-214
Breitinger, Johann Jakob 1701-1776 ...... DLB-97
Bremser, Bonnie 1939- DLB-16
Bremser, Ray 1934- DLB-16
Brennan, Christopher 1870-1932 .... DLB-230
Brentano, Bernard von 1901-1964....... DLB-56
Brentano, Clemens 1778-1842 .... DLB-90
Brentano's........................ DLB-49
Brenton, Howard 1942- DLB-13
Breslin, Jimmy 1929-1996 .... DLB-185
Breton, André 1896-1966 .... DLB-65
Breton, Nicholas circa 1555-circa 1626... DLB-136
The Breton Lays
   1300-early fifteenth century DLB-146
Brewer, Luther A. 1858-1933...........DLB-187
Brewer, Warren and Putnam DLB-46
Brewster, Elizabeth 1922- DLB-60
Breytenbach, Breyten 1939- DLB-225
Bridge, Ann (Lady Mary Dolling Sanders
   O'Malley) 1889-1974 .... DLB-191
Bridge, Horatio 1806-1893............ DLB-183
Bridgers, Sue Ellen 1942- DLB-52
Bridges, Robert
   1844-1930 .... DLB-19, 98; CDBLB-5
The Bridgewater Library DLB-213
Bridie, James 1888-1951............... DLB-10
Brieux, Eugene 1858-1932 .... DLB-192
Brigadere, Anna 1861-1933 .... DLB-220
Briggs, Charles Frederick
   1804-1877................... DLB-3, 250

Brighouse, Harold 1882-1958 . . . . .DLB-10
Bright, Mary Chavelita Dunne (see Egerton, George)
Brimmer, B. J., Company DLB-46
Brines, Francisco 1932- DLB-134
Brink, André 1935- DLB-225
Brinley, George, Jr. 1817-1875 . . . . .DLB-140
Brinnin, John Malcolm 1916-1998 . . . . . . .DLB-48
Brisbane, Albert 1809-1890 . . . . .DLB-3
Brisbane, Arthur 1864-1936 . . . . .DLB-25
British Academy DLB-112
The British Critic 1793-1843 . . . . .DLB-110
The British Library and the Regular
 Readers' Group .Y-91
British Literary Prizes Y-98
*The British Review and London Critical
 Journal 1811-1825* DLB-110
British Travel Writing, 1940-1997 . . . . . . .DLB-204
Brito, Aristeo 1942- DLB-122
Brittain, Vera 1893-1970 . . . . .DLB-191
Brizeux, Auguste 1803-1858 . . . . .DLB-217
Broadway Publishing Company DLB-46
Broch, Hermann
 1886-1951 . . . . .DLB-85, 124; CDWLB-2
Brochu, André 1942- DLB-53
Brock, Edwin 1927- DLB-40
Brockes, Barthold Heinrich 1680-1747 . . . .DLB-168
Brod, Max 1884-1968 . . . . .DLB-81
Brodber, Erna 1940- DLB-157
Brodhead, John R. 1814-1873 . . . . .DLB-30
Brodkey, Harold 1930-1996 . . . . .DLB-130
Brodsky, Joseph 1940-1996 . . . . .Y-87
Brodsky, Michael 1948- DLB-244
Broeg, Bob 1918- DLB-171
Brøgger, Suzanne 1944- DLB-214
Brome, Richard circa 1590-1652 . . . . .DLB-58
Brome, Vincent 1910- DLB-155
Bromfield, Louis 1896-1956 . . . . .DLB-4, 9, 86
Bromige, David 1933- DLB-193
Broner, E. M. 1930- DLB-28
Bronk, William 1918-1999 . . . . .DLB-165
Bronnen, Arnolt 1895-1959 . . . . .DLB-124
Brontë, Anne 1820-1849 . . . . .DLB-21, 199
Brontë, Charlotte
 1816-1855 . . . . . .DLB-21, 159, 199; CDBLB-4
Brontë, Emily
 1818-1848 . . . . . . .DLB-21, 32, 199; CDBLB-4
Brook, Stephen 1947- DLB-204
Brook Farm 1841-1847 . . . . .DLB-223
Brooke, Frances 1724-1789 . . . . .DLB-39, 99
Brooke, Henry 1703?-1783 . . . . .DLB-39
Brooke, L. Leslie 1862-1940 . . . . .DLB-141
Brooke, Margaret, Ranee of Sarawak
 1849-1936 . . . . .DLB-174
Brooke, Rupert
 1887-1915 . . . . .DLB-19, 216; CDBLB-6
Brooker, Bertram 1888-1955 . . . . .DLB-88

Brooke-Rose, Christine 1923- DLB-14, 231
Brookner, Anita 1928- DLB-194; Y-87
Brooks, Charles Timothy 1813-1883 . . .DLB-1, 243
Brooks, Cleanth 1906-1994 . . . . . . .DLB-63; Y-94
Brooks, Gwendolyn
 1917-2000 . . . . .DLB-5, 76, 165; CDALB-1
Brooks, Jeremy 1926- DLB-14
Brooks, Mel 1926- DLB-26
Brooks, Noah 1830-1903 . . . . .DLB-42; DS-13
Brooks, Richard 1912-1992 . . . . .DLB-44
Brooks, Van Wyck
 1886-1963 . . . . .DLB-45, 63, 103
Brophy, Brigid 1929-1995 . . . . .DLB-14
Brophy, John 1899-1965 . . . . .DLB-191
Brossard, Chandler 1922-1993 . . . . .DLB-16
Brossard, Nicole 1943- DLB-53
Broster, Dorothy Kathleen 1877-1950 . . . .DLB-160
Brother Antoninus (see Everson, William)
Brotherton, Lord 1856-1930 . . . . .DLB-184
Brougham and Vaux, Henry Peter Brougham,
 Baron 1778-1868 . . . . .DLB-110, 158
Brougham, John 1810-1880 . . . . .DLB-11
Broughton, James 1913-1999 . . . . .DLB-5
Broughton, Rhoda 1840-1920 . . . . .DLB-18
Broun, Heywood 1888-1939 . . . . .DLB-29, 171
Brown, Alice 1856-1948 . . . . .DLB-78
Brown, Bob 1886-1959 . . . . .DLB-4, 45
Brown, Cecil 1943- DLB-33
Brown, Charles Brockden
 1771-1810 . . . . .DLB-37, 59, 73; CDALB-2
Brown, Christy 1932-1981 . . . . .DLB-14
Brown, Dee 1908- .Y-80
Brown, Frank London 1927-1962 . . . . .DLB-76
Brown, Fredric 1906-1972 . . . . .DLB-8
Brown, George Mackay
 1921-1996 . . . . .DLB-14, 27, 139
Brown, Harry 1917-1986 . . . . .DLB-26
Brown, Larry 1951- DLB-234
Brown, Marcia 1918- DLB-61
Brown, Margaret Wise 1910-1952 . . . . . . .DLB-22
Brown, Morna Doris (see Ferrars, Elizabeth)
Brown, Oliver Madox 1855-1874 . . . . .DLB-21
Brown, Sterling 1901-1989 . . . . . . .DLB-48, 51, 63
Brown, T. E. 1830-1897 . . . . .DLB-35
Brown, Thomas Alexander (see Boldrewood, Rolf)
Brown, Warren 1894-1978 . . . . .DLB-241
Brown, William Hill 1765-1793 . . . . .DLB-37
Brown, William Wells
 1815-1884 . . . . .DLB-3, 50, 183, 248
Browne, Charles Farrar 1834-1867 . . . . . . .DLB-11
Browne, Frances 1816-1879 . . . . .DLB-199
Browne, Francis Fisher 1843-1913 . . . . .DLB-79
Browne, Howard 1908-1999 . . . . .DLB-226
Browne, J. Ross 1821-1875 . . . . .DLB-202
Browne, Michael Dennis 1940- DLB-40
Browne, Sir Thomas 1605-1682 . . . . .DLB-151

Browne, William, of Tavistock
 1590-1645 . . . . .DLB-121
Browne, Wynyard 1911-1964 . . . . . . .DLB-13, 233
Browne and Nolan DLB-106
Brownell, W. C. 1851-1928 . . . . .DLB-71
Browning, Elizabeth Barrett
 1806-1861 . . . . .DLB-32, 199; CDBLB-4
Browning, Robert
 1812-1889 . . . . .DLB-32, 163; CDBLB-4
 Introductory Essay: *Letters of Percy
 Bysshe Shelley* (1852) DLB-32
Brownjohn, Allan 1931- DLB-40
Brownson, Orestes Augustus
 1803-1876 . . . . .DLB-1, 59, 73, 243
Bruccoli, Matthew J. 1931- DLB-103
Bruce, Charles 1906-1971 . . . . .DLB-68
John Edward Bruce: Three Documents DLB-50
Bruce, Leo 1903-1979 . . . . .DLB-77
Bruce, Mary Grant 1878-1958 . . . . .DLB-230
Bruce, Philip Alexander 1856-1933 . . . . . . .DLB-47
Bruce Humphries [publishing house] DLB-46
Bruce-Novoa, Juan 1944- DLB-82
Bruckman, Clyde 1894-1955 . . . . .DLB-26
Bruckner, Ferdinand 1891-1958 . . . . .DLB-118
Brundage, John Herbert (see Herbert, John)
Brutus, Dennis
 1924- DLB-117, 225; CDWLB-3
Bryan, C. D. B. 1936- DLB-185
Bryant, Arthur 1899-1985 . . . . .DLB-149
Bryant, William Cullen
 1794-1878 . . . . . . .DLB-3, 43, 59, 189; CDALB-2
Bryce Echenique, Alfredo
 1939- DLB-145; CDWLB-3
Bryce, James 1838-1922 . . . . .DLB-166, 190
Bryden, Bill 1942- DLB-233
Brydges, Sir Samuel Egerton 1762-1837 . . .DLB-107
Bryskett, Lodowick 1546?-1612 . . . . .DLB-167
Buchan, John 1875-1940 . . . . .DLB-34, 70, 156
Buchanan, George 1506-1582 . . . . .DLB-132
Buchanan, Robert 1841-1901 . . . . .DLB-18, 35
"The Fleshly School of Poetry and Other
 Phenomena of the Day" (1872), by
 Robert Buchanan DLB-35
"The Fleshly School of Poetry: Mr. D. G.
 Rossetti" (1871), by Thomas Maitland
 (Robert Buchanan) DLB-35
Buchman, Sidney 1902-1975 . . . . .DLB-26
Buchner, Augustus 1591-1661 . . . . .DLB-164
Büchner, Georg 1813-1837 . . .DLB-133; CDWLB-2
Bucholtz, Andreas Heinrich 1607-1671 . . .DLB-168
Buck, Pearl S. 1892-1973 . . .DLB-9, 102; CDALB-7
Bucke, Charles 1781-1846 . . . . .DLB-110
Bucke, Richard Maurice 1837-1902 . . . . . . .DLB-99
Buckingham, Joseph Tinker 1779-1861 and
 Buckingham, Edwin 1810-1833 . . . . . .DLB-73
Buckler, Ernest 1908-1984 . . . . .DLB-68
Buckley, William F., Jr. 1925- . . .DLB-137; Y-80
Buckminster, Joseph Stevens
 1784-1812 . . . . .DLB-37

Cumulative Index

Buckner, Robert 1906- DLB-26
Budd, Thomas ?-1698 .... DLB-24
Budrys, A. J. 1931- DLB-8
Buechner, Frederick 1926- Y-80
Buell, John 1927- DLB-53
Bufalino, Gesualdo 1920-1996 .... DLB-196
Buffum, Job [publishing house] DLB-49
Bugnet, Georges 1879-1981 .... DLB-92
Buies, Arthur 1840-1901 .... DLB-99
Building the New British Library at St Pancras Y-94
Bukowski, Charles 1920-1994 ... DLB-5, 130, 169
Bulatović, Miodrag 1930-1991 .... DLB-181; CDWLB-4
Bulgarin, Faddei Venediktovich 1789-1859 .... DLB-198
Bulger, Bozeman 1877-1932 .... DLB-171
Bullein, William between 1520 and 1530-1576 .... DLB-167
Bullins, Ed 1935- DLB-7, 38, 249
Bulwer, John 1606-1656 .... DLB-236
Bulwer-Lytton, Edward (also Edward Bulwer) 1803-1873 .... DLB-21
"On Art in Fiction" (1838) DLB-21
Bumpus, Jerry 1937- Y-81
Bunce and Brother DLB-49
Bunner, H. C. 1855-1896 .... DLB-78, 79
Bunting, Basil 1900-1985 .... DLB-20
Buntline, Ned (Edward Zane Carroll Judson) 1821-1886 .... DLB-186
Bunyan, John 1628-1688 ..... DLB-39; CDBLB-2
Burch, Robert 1925- DLB-52
Burciaga, José Antonio 1940- DLB-82
Burdekin, Katharine 1896-1963 ...... DLB-255
Bürger, Gottfried August 1747-1794 ..... DLB-94
Burgess, Anthony 1917-1993 .... DLB-14, 194; CDBLB-8
The Anthony Burgess Archive at the Harry Ransom Humanities Research Center Y-98
Anthony Burgess's 99 Novels: An Opinion Poll Y-84
Burgess, Gelett 1866-1951 .... DLB-11
Burgess, John W. 1844-1931 .... DLB-47
Burgess, Thornton W. 1874-1965 ..... DLB-22
Burgess, Stringer and Company DLB-49
Burick, Si 1909-1986 .... DLB-171
Burk, John Daly circa 1772-1808 .... DLB-37
Burk, Ronnie 1955- DLB-209
Burke, Edmund 1729?-1797 .... DLB-104
Burke, James Lee 1936- DLB-226
Burke, Kenneth 1897-1993 .... DLB-45, 63
Burke, Thomas 1886-1945 .... DLB-197
Burley, Dan 1907-1962 .... DLB-241
Burlingame, Edward Livermore 1848-1922 .... DLB-79
Burman, Carina 1960- DLB-257
Burnet, Gilbert 1643-1715 .... DLB-101

Burnett, Frances Hodgson 1849-1924 .... DLB-42, 141; DS-13, 14
Burnett, W. R. 1899-1982 .... DLB-9, 226
Burnett, Whit 1899-1973 and Martha Foley 1897-1977 .... DLB-137
Burney, Fanny 1752-1840 .... DLB-39
Dedication, *The Wanderer* (1814) DLB-39
Preface to *Evelina* (1778) DLB-39
Burns, Alan 1929- DLB-14, 194
Burns, John Horne 1916-1953 .... Y-85
Burns, Robert 1759-1796 .... DLB-109; CDBLB-3
Burns and Oates DLB-106
Burnshaw, Stanley 1906- DLB-48
Burr, C. Chauncey 1815?-1883 .... DLB-79
Burr, Esther Edwards 1732-1758 ..... DLB-200
Burroughs, Edgar Rice 1875-1950 .... DLB-8
Burroughs, John 1837-1921 .... DLB-64
Burroughs, Margaret T. G. 1917- DLB-41
Burroughs, William S., Jr. 1947-1981 ..... DLB-16
Burroughs, William Seward 1914-1997 .... DLB-2, 8, 16, 152, 237; Y-81, Y-97
Burroway, Janet 1936- DLB-6
Burt, Maxwell Struthers 1882-1954 .... DLB-86; DS-16
Burt, A. L., and Company DLB-49
Burton, Hester 1913- DLB-161
Burton, Isabel Arundell 1831-1896 ..... DLB-166
Burton, Miles (see Rhode, John)
Burton, Richard Francis 1821-1890 .... DLB-55, 166, 184
Burton, Robert 1577-1640 .... DLB-151
Burton, Virginia Lee 1909-1968 ..... DLB-22
Burton, William Evans 1804-1860 ... DLB-73
Burwell, Adam Hood 1790-1849 ...... DLB-99
Bury, Lady Charlotte 1775-1861 ..... DLB-116
Busch, Frederick 1941- DLB-6, 218
Busch, Niven 1903-1991 .... DLB-44
Bushnell, Horace 1802-1876 .... DS-13
Bussieres, Arthur de 1877-1913 ..... DLB-92
Butler, Charles ca. 1560-1647 ...... DLB-236
Butler, Guy 1918- DLB-225
Butler, E. H., and Company DLB-49
Butler, Josephine Elizabeth 1828-1906 ... DLB-190
Butler, Juan 1942-1981 .... DLB-53
Butler, Judith 1956- DLB-246
Butler, Octavia E. 1947- DLB-33
Butler, Pierce 1884-1953 .... DLB-187
Butler, Robert Olen 1945- DLB-173
Butler, Samuel 1613-1680 .... DLB-101, 126
Butler, Samuel 1835-1902 .... DLB-18, 57, 174
Butler, William Francis 1838-1910 ..... DLB-166
Butor, Michel 1926- DLB-83
Butter, Nathaniel [publishing house] DLB-170
Butterworth, Hezekiah 1839-1905 .... DLB-42
Buttitta, Ignazio 1899- DLB-114
Butts, Mary 1890-1937 .... DLB-240

Buzzati, Dino 1906-1972 .... DLB-177
Byars, Betsy 1928- DLB-52
Byatt, A. S. 1936- DLB-14, 194
Byles, Mather 1707-1788 .... DLB-24
Bynneman, Henry [publishing house] DLB-170
Bynner, Witter 1881-1968 .... DLB-54
Byrd, William circa 1543-1623 ...... DLB-172
Byrd, William II 1674-1744 .... DLB-24, 140
Byrne, John Keyes (see Leonard, Hugh)
Byron, George Gordon, Lord 1788-1824 .... DLB-96, 110; CDBLB-3
Byron, Robert 1905-1941 .... DLB-195

C

Caballero Bonald, José Manuel 1926- DLB-108
Cabañero, Eladio 1930- DLB-134
Cabell, James Branch 1879-1958 ..... DLB-9, 78
Cabeza de Baca, Manuel 1853-1915 ..... DLB-122
Cabeza de Baca Gilbert, Fabiola 1898- DLB-122
Cable, George Washington 1844-1925 .... DLB-12, 74; DS-13
Cable, Mildred 1878-1952 .... DLB-195
Cabrera, Lydia 1900-1991 .... DLB-145
Cabrera Infante, Guillermo 1929- DLB-113; CDWLB-3
Cadell [publishing house] DLB-154
Cady, Edwin H. 1917- DLB-103
Caedmon flourished 658-680 .... DLB-146
Caedmon School circa 660-899 .... DLB-146
Cafés, Brasseries, and Bistros DS-15
Cage, John 1912-1992 .... DLB-193
Cahan, Abraham 1860-1951 .... DLB-9, 25, 28
Cain, George 1943- DLB-33
Cain, James M. 1892-1977 .... DLB-226
Caird, Mona 1854-1932 .... DLB-197
Čaks, Aleksandrs 1901-1950 .... DLB-220; CDWLB-4
Caldecott, Randolph 1846-1886 ...... DLB-163
Calder, John (Publishers), Limited DLB-112
Calderón de la Barca, Fanny 1804-1882 .... DLB-183
Caldwell, Ben 1937- DLB-38
Caldwell, Erskine 1903-1987 .... DLB-9, 86
Caldwell, H. M., Company DLB-49
Caldwell, Taylor 1900-1985 .... DS-17
Calhoun, John C. 1782-1850 .... DLB-3, 248
Călinescu, George 1899-1965 .... DLB-220
Calisher, Hortense 1911- DLB-2, 218
A Call to Letters and an Invitation to the Electric Chair, by Siegfried Mandel DLB-75
Callaghan, Mary Rose 1944- DLB-207
Callaghan, Morley 1903-1990 .... DLB-68
Callahan, S. Alice 1868-1894 .... DLB-175, 221

Callaloo Y-87
Callimachus circa 305 B.C.-240 B.C...... DLB-176
Calmer, Edgar 1907- DLB-4
Calverley, C. S. 1831-1884 ....DLB-35
Calvert, George Henry
  1803-1889 .... DLB-1, 64, 248
Calvino, Italo 1923-1985 ....DLB-196
Cambridge, Ada 1844-1926............DLB-230
Cambridge Press DLB-49
Cambridge Songs (Carmina Cantabrigensia)
  circa 1050 ....DLB-148
Cambridge University Press DLB-170
Camden, William 1551-1623............DLB-172
Camden House: An Interview with
  James Hardin...................... Y-92
Cameron, Eleanor 1912- DLB-52
Cameron, George Frederick
  1854-1885 ....DLB-99
Cameron, Lucy Lyttelton 1781-1858.....DLB-163
Cameron, Peter 1959- DLB-234
Cameron, William Bleasdell 1862-1951 ...DLB-99
Camm, John 1718-1778 ....DLB-31
Camon, Ferdinando 1935- DLB-196
Camp, Walter 1859-1925 ....DLB-241
Campana, Dino 1885-1932 ....DLB-114
Campbell, Bebe Moore 1950- DLB-227
Campbell, Gabrielle Margaret Vere
  (see Shearing, Joseph, and Bowen, Marjorie)
Campbell, James Dykes 1838-1895 ......DLB-144
Campbell, James Edwin 1867-1896 ....DLB-50
Campbell, John 1653-1728...............DLB-43
Campbell, John W., Jr. 1910-1971 ....DLB-8
Campbell, Roy 1901-1957 ....DLB-20, 225
Campbell, Thomas 1777-1844 ......DLB-93, 144
Campbell, William Wilfred 1858-1918 ....DLB-92
Campion, Edmund 1539-1581...........DLB-167
Campion, Thomas
  1567-1620 ....DLB-58, 172; CDBLB-1
Campton, David 1924- DLB-245
Camus, Albert 1913-1960 ....DLB-72
The Canadian Publishers' Records
  Database Y-96
Canby, Henry Seidel 1878-1961 ....DLB-91
Candelaria, Cordelia 1943- DLB-82
Candelaria, Nash 1928- DLB-82
Canetti, Elias
  1905-1994 ....DLB-85, 124; CDWLB-2
Canham, Erwin Dain 1904-1982........DLB-127
Canitz, Friedrich Rudolph Ludwig von
  1654-1699 ....DLB-168
Cankar, Ivan 1876-1918..... DLB-147; CDWLB-4
Cannan, Gilbert 1884-1955 ....DLB-10, 197
Cannan, Joanna 1896-1961 ....DLB-191
Cannell, Kathleen 1891-1974 ....DLB-4
Cannell, Skipwith 1887-1957 ....DLB-45
Canning, George 1770-1827 ....DLB-158
Cannon, Jimmy 1910-1973 ....DLB-171

Cano, Daniel 1947- DLB-209
Cantú, Norma Elia 1947- DLB-209
Cantwell, Robert 1908-1978 ....DLB-9
Cape, Jonathan, and Harrison Smith
  [publishing house]................DLB-46
Cape, Jonathan, Limited DLB-112
Čapek, Karel 1890-1938 .... DLB-215; CDWLB-4
Capen, Joseph 1658-1725.............DLB-24
Capes, Bernard 1854-1918..............DLB-156
Capote, Truman 1924-1984
  ..... DLB-2, 185, 227; Y-80, Y-84; CDALB-1
Capps, Benjamin 1922- DLB-256
Caproni, Giorgio 1912-1990 ....DLB-128
Caragiale, Mateiu Ioan 1885-1936.......DLB-220
Cardarelli, Vincenzo 1887-1959.........DLB-114
Cárdenas, Reyes 1948- DLB-122
Cardinal, Marie 1929- DLB-83
Carew, Jan 1920- DLB-157
Carew, Thomas 1594 or 1595-1640.....DLB-126
Carey, Henry circa 1687-1689-1743........DLB-84
Carey, M., and Company DLB-49
Carey, Mathew 1760-1839........... DLB-37, 73
Carey and Hart DLB-49
Carlell, Lodowick 1602-1675............DLB-58
Carleton, William 1794-1869............DLB-159
Carleton, G. W. [publishing house].......DLB-49
Carlile, Richard 1790-1843 .... DLB-110, 158
Carlson, Ron 1947- DLB-244
Carlyle, Jane Welsh 1801-1866 ....DLB-55
Carlyle, Thomas
  1795-1881 ....DLB-55, 144; CDBLB-3
"The Hero as Man of Letters: Johnson,
  Rousseau, Burns" (1841) [excerpt] DLB-57
The Hero as Poet. Dante;
  Shakspeare (1841).................DLB-32
Carman, Bliss 1861-1929...............DLB-92
Carmina Burana circa 1230 ....DLB-138
Carnero, Guillermo 1947- DLB-108
Carossa, Hans 1878-1956 ....DLB-66
Carpenter, Humphrey
  1946- DLB-155; Y-84, Y-99
The Practice of Biography III: An Interview
  with Humphrey Carpenter Y-84
Carpenter, Stephen Cullen ?-1820?.......DLB-73
Carpentier, Alejo
  1904-1980..........DLB-113; CDWLB-3
Carr, Marina 1964- DLB-245
Carrier, Roch 1937- DLB-53
Carrillo, Adolfo 1855-1926 ....DLB-122
Carroll, Gladys Hasty 1904- DLB-9
Carroll, John 1735-1815................DLB-37
Carroll, John 1809-1884 ....DLB-99
Carroll, Lewis
  1832-1898 ..... DLB-18, 163, 178; CDBLB-4
The Lewis Carroll Centenary Y-98
Carroll, Paul 1927- DLB-16
Carroll, Paul Vincent 1900-1968.........DLB-10

Carroll and Graf Publishers DLB-46
Carruth, Hayden 1921- DLB-5, 165
Carryl, Charles E. 1841-1920 ....DLB-42
Carson, Anne 1950- DLB-193
Carswell, Catherine 1879-1946 ....DLB-36
Cărtărescu, Mirea 1956- DLB-232
Carter, Angela 1940-1992 .... DLB-14, 207
Carter, Elizabeth 1717-1806 ....DLB-109
Carter, Henry (see Leslie, Frank)
Carter, Hodding, Jr. 1907-1972 ....DLB-127
Carter, John 1905-1975 ....DLB-201
Carter, Landon 1710-1778 ....DLB-31
Carter, Lin 1930- Y-81
Carter, Martin 1927-1997.... DLB-117; CDWLB-3
Carter, Robert, and Brothers............DLB-49
Carter and Hendee DLB-49
Cartwright, Jim 1958- DLB-245
Cartwright, John 1740-1824............DLB-158
Cartwright, William circa 1611-1643 ....DLB-126
Caruthers, William Alexander
  1802-1846.................DLB-3, 248
Carver, Jonathan 1710-1780.............DLB-31
Carver, Raymond
  1938-1988........... DLB-130; Y-83, Y-88
First Strauss "Livings" Awarded to Cynthia
  Ozick and Raymond Carver
  An Interview with Raymond Carver Y-83
Cary, Alice 1820-1871 ....DLB-202
Cary, Joyce 1888-1957....DLB-15, 100; CDBLB-6
Cary, Patrick 1623?-1657 ....DLB-131
Casey, Juanita 1925- DLB-14
Casey, Michael 1947- DLB-5
Cassady, Carolyn 1923- DLB-16
Cassady, Neal 1926-1968 .... DLB-16, 237
Cassell and Company DLB-106
Cassell Publishing Company............DLB-49
Cassill, R. V. 1919- DLB-6, 218
Cassity, Turner 1929- DLB-105
Cassius Dio circa 155/164-post 229...... DLB-176
Cassola, Carlo 1917-1987..............DLB-177
The Castle of Perserverance circa 1400-1425..DLB-146
Castellano, Olivia 1944- DLB-122
Castellanos, Rosario
  1925-1974 ....DLB-113; CDWLB-3
Castillo, Ana 1953- DLB-122, 227
Castillo, Rafael C. 1950- DLB-209
Castlemon, Harry (see Fosdick, Charles Austin)
Čašule, Kole 1921- DLB-181
Caswall, Edward 1814-1878 ....DLB-32
Catacalos, Rosemary 1944- DLB-122
Cather, Willa 1873-1947
  ....DLB-9, 54, 78, 256; DS-1; CDALB-3
Catherine II (Ekaterina Alekseevna), "The Great,"
  Empress of Russia 1729-1796 ....DLB-150
Catherwood, Mary Hartwell 1847-1902 ...DLB-78
Catledge, Turner 1901-1983 ....DLB-127

Catlin, George 1796-1872 .... DLB-186, 189
Cato the Elder 234 B.C.-149 B.C. DLB-211
Cattafi, Bartolo 1922-1979 .... DLB-128
Catton, Bruce 1899-1978 .... DLB-17
Catullus circa 84 B.C.-54 B.C.
  .... DLB-211; CDWLB-1
Causley, Charles 1917- DLB-27
Caute, David 1936- DLB-14, 231
Cavendish, Duchess of Newcastle,
  Margaret Lucas 1623-1673 .... DLB-131
Cawein, Madison 1865-1914 .... DLB-54
Caxton, William [publishing house] DLB-170
The Caxton Printers, Limited DLB-46
Caylor, O. P. 1849-1897 .... DLB-241
Cayrol, Jean 1911- DLB-83
Cecil, Lord David 1902-1986 .... DLB-155
Cela, Camilo José 1916- Y-89
Celan, Paul 1920-1970 ...... DLB-69; CDWLB-2
Celati, Gianni 1937- DLB-196
Celaya, Gabriel 1911-1991 .... DLB-108
A Celebration of Literary Biography Y-98
Céline, Louis-Ferdinand 1894-1961 ...... DLB-72
The Celtic Background to Medieval English
  Literature DLB-146
Celtis, Conrad 1459-1508 .... DLB-179
Center for Bibliographical Studies and
  Research at the University of
  California, Riverside Y-91
The Center for the Book in the Library
  of Congress Y-93
Center for the Book Research Y-84
Centlivre, Susanna 1669?-1723 .... DLB-84
The Centre for Writing, Publishing and
  Printing History at the University
  of Reading Y-00
The Century Company DLB-49
Cernuda, Luis 1902-1963 .... DLB-134
Cervantes, Lorna Dee 1954- DLB-82
Ch., T. (see Marchenko, Anastasiia Iakovlevna)
Chaadaev, Petr Iakovlevich
  1794-1856 .... DLB-198
Chacel, Rosa 1898- DLB-134
Chacón, Eusebio 1869-1948 .... DLB-82
Chacón, Felipe Maximiliano 1873-? DLB-82
Chadwick, Henry 1824-1908 .... DLB-241
Chadwyck-Healey's Full-Text Literary Databases:
  Editing Commercial Databases of
  Primary Literary Texts Y-95
Challans, Eileen Mary (see Renault, Mary)
Chalmers, George 1742-1825 .... DLB-30
Chaloner, Sir Thomas 1520-1565 .... DLB-167
Chamberlain, Samuel S. 1851-1916 ...... DLB-25
Chamberland, Paul 1939- DLB-60
Chamberlin, William Henry 1897-1969 ... DLB-29
Chambers, Charles Haddon 1860-1921 ... DLB-10
Chambers, María Cristina (see Mena, María Cristina)
Chambers, Robert W. 1865-1933 .... DLB-202

Chambers, W. and R.
  [publishing house] DLB-106
Chamisso, Albert von 1781-1838 .... DLB-90
Champfleury 1821-1889 .... DLB-119
Chandler, Harry 1864-1944 .... DLB-29
Chandler, Norman 1899-1973 .... DLB-127
Chandler, Otis 1927- DLB-127
Chandler, Raymond
  1888-1959 .... DLB-226; DS-6; CDALB-5
Raymond Chandler Centenary Tributes
  from Michael Avallone, James Ellroy,
  Joe Gores, and William F. Nolan Y-88
Channing, Edward 1856-1931 .... DLB-17
Channing, Edward Tyrrell
  1790-1856 .... DLB-1, 59, 235
Channing, William Ellery
  1780-1842 .... DLB-1, 59, 235
Channing, William Ellery II
  1817-1901 .... DLB-1, 223
Channing, William Henry
  1810-1884 .... DLB-1, 59, 243
Chaplin, Charlie 1889-1977 .... DLB-44
Chapman, George
  1559 or 1560-1634 .... DLB-62, 121
Chapman, John DLB-106
Chapman, Olive Murray 1892-1977 ..... DLB-195
Chapman, R. W. 1881-1960 .... DLB-201
Chapman, William 1850-1917 .... DLB-99
Chapman and Hall DLB-106
Chappell, Fred 1936- DLB-6, 105
  "A Detail in a Poem" DLB-105
Chappell, William 1582-1649 .... DLB-236
Charbonneau, Jean 1875-1960 .... DLB-92
Charbonneau, Robert 1911-1967 .... DLB-68
Charles, Gerda 1914- DLB-14
Charles, William [publishing house] DLB-49
Charles d'Orléans 1394-1465 .... DLB-208
Charley (see Mann, Charles)
Charteris, Leslie 1907-1993 .... DLB-77
Chartier, Alain circa 1385-1430 .... DLB-208
Charyn, Jerome 1937- Y-83
Chase, Borden 1900-1971 .... DLB-26
Chase, Edna Woolman 1877-1957 .... DLB-91
Chase, Mary Coyle 1907-1981 .... DLB-228
Chase-Riboud, Barbara 1936- DLB-33
Chateaubriand, François-René de
  1768-1848 .... DLB-119
Chatterton, Thomas 1752-1770 .... DLB-109
Essay on Chatterton (1842), by
  Robert Browning DLB-32
Chatto and Windus DLB-106
Chatwin, Bruce 1940-1989 .... DLB-194, 204
Chaucer, Geoffrey
  1340?-1400 .... DLB-146; CDBLB-1
Chauncy, Charles 1705-1787 .... DLB-24
Chauveau, Pierre-Joseph-Olivier
  1820-1890 .... DLB-99
Chávez, Denise 1948- DLB-122

Chávez, Fray Angélico 1910- DLB-82
Chayefsky, Paddy 1923-1981 ..... DLB-7, 44; Y-81
Cheesman, Evelyn 1881-1969 .... DLB-195
Cheever, Ezekiel 1615-1708 .... DLB-24
Cheever, George Barrell 1807-1890 ...... DLB-59
Cheever, John 1912-1982
  ...... DLB-2, 102, 227; Y-80, Y-82; CDALB-1
Cheever, Susan 1943- Y-82
Cheke, Sir John 1514-1557 .... DLB-132
Chelsea House DLB-46
Chênedollé, Charles de 1769-1833 ...... DLB-217
Cheney, Ednah Dow 1824-1904 ..... DLB-1, 223
Cheney, Harriet Vaughn 1796-1889 ..... DLB-99
Chénier, Marie-Joseph 1764-1811 .... DLB-192
Chernyshevsky, Nikolai Gavrilovich
  1828-1889 .... DLB-238
Cherry, Kelly 1940 .... Y-83
Cherryh, C. J. 1942- Y-80
Chesebro', Caroline 1825-1873 .... DLB-202
Chesney, Sir George Tomkyns
  1830-1895 .... DLB-190
Chesnut, Mary Boykin 1823-1886 ...... DLB-239
Chesnutt, Charles Waddell
  1858-1932 .... DLB-12, 50, 78
Chesson, Mrs. Nora (see Hopper, Nora)
Chester, Alfred 1928-1971 .... DLB-130
Chester, George Randolph 1869-1924 ... DLB-78
The Chester Plays circa 1505-1532;
  revisions until 1575 .... DLB-146
Chesterfield, Philip Dormer Stanhope,
  Fourth Earl of 1694-1773 .... DLB-104
Chesterton, G. K. 1874-1936
  ... DLB-10, 19, 34, 70, 98, 149, 178; CDBLB-6
Chettle, Henry circa 1560-circa 1607 .... DLB-136
Cheuse, Alan 1940- DLB-244
Chew, Ada Nield 1870-1945 .... DLB-135
Cheyney, Edward P. 1861-1947 .... DLB-47
Chiara, Piero 1913-1986 .... DLB-177
Chicano History DLB-82
Chicano Language DLB-82
Child, Francis James 1825-1896 ... DLB-1, 64, 235
Child, Lydia Maria 1802-1880 ... DLB-1, 74, 243
Child, Philip 1898-1978 .... DLB-68
Childers, Erskine 1870-1922 .... DLB-70
Children's Book Awards and Prizes DLB-61
Children's Illustrators, 1800-1880 ...... DLB-163
Childress, Alice 1916-1994 .... DLB-7, 38, 249
Childs, George W. 1829-1894 .... DLB-23
Chilton Book Company DLB-46
Chin, Frank 1940- DLB-206
Chinweizu 1943- DLB-157
Chitham, Edward 1932- DLB-155
Chittenden, Hiram Martin 1858-1917 .... DLB-47
Chivers, Thomas Holley 1809-1858 .. DLB-3, 248
Cholmondeley, Mary 1859-1925 .... DLB-197
Chomsky, Noam 1928- DLB-246

322

Chopin, Kate 1850-1904 . . . DLB-12, 78; CDALB-3
Chopin, Rene 1885-1953 . . . . DLB-92
Choquette, Adrienne 1915-1973 . . . . DLB-68
Choquette, Robert 1905- DLB-68
Chrétien de Troyes
  circa 1140-circa 1190 . . . . DLB-208
Christensen, Inger 1935- DLB-214
The Christian Publishing Company DLB-49
Christie, Agatha
  1890-1976 . . . . DLB-13, 77, 245; CDBLB-6
Christine de Pizan
  circa 1365-circa 1431 . . . . DLB-208
Christopher, John 1922- DLB-255
Christus und die Samariterin circa 950 . . . . . DLB-148
Christy, Howard Chandler 1873-1952 . . . DLB-188
Chulkov, Mikhail Dmitrievich
  1743?-1792 . . . . DLB-150
Church, Benjamin 1734-1778 . . . . DLB-31
Church, Francis Pharcellus 1839-1906 . . . . DLB-79
Church, Peggy Pond 1903-1986 . . . . DLB-212
Church, Richard 1893-1972 . . . . DLB-191
Church, William Conant 1836-1917 . . . . . . DLB-79
Churchill, Caryl 1938- DLB-13
Churchill, Charles 1731-1764 . . . . DLB-109
Churchill, Winston 1871-1947 . . . . DLB-202
Churchill, Sir Winston
  1874-1965 . . . . DLB-100; DS-16; CDBLB-5
Churchyard, Thomas 1520?-1604 . . . . DLB-132
Churton, E., and Company DLB-106
Chute, Marchette 1909-1994 . . . . DLB-103
Ciardi, John 1916-1986 . . . . DLB-5; Y-86
Cibber, Colley 1671-1757 . . . . DLB-84
Cicero
  106 B.C.-43 B.C. DLB-211, CDWLB-1
Cima, Annalisa 1941- DLB-128
Čingo, Živko 1935-1987 . . . . DLB-181
Cioran, E. M. 1911-1995 . . . . DLB-220
Čipkus, Alfonsas (see Nyka-Niliūnas, Alfonsas)
Cirese, Eugenio 1884-1955 . . . . DLB-114
Cīrulis, Jānis (see Bels, Alberts)
Cisneros, Sandra 1954- DLB-122, 152
City Lights Books DLB-46
Cixous, Hélène 1937- DLB-83, 242
Clampitt, Amy 1920-1994 . . . . DLB-105
Clancy, Tom 1947- DLB-227
Clapper, Raymond 1892-1944 . . . . DLB-29
Clare, John 1793-1864 . . . . DLB-55, 96
Clarendon, Edward Hyde, Earl of
  1609-1674 . . . . DLB-101
Clark, Alfred Alexander Gordon (see Hare, Cyril)
Clark, Ann Nolan 1896- DLB-52
Clark, C. E. Frazer Jr. 1925- DLB-187
Clark, C. M., Publishing Company DLB-46
Clark, Catherine Anthony 1892-1977 . . . . . DLB-68
Clark, Charles Heber 1841-1915 . . . . DLB-11
Clark, Davis Wasgatt 1812-1871 . . . . DLB-79

Clark, Eleanor 1913- DLB-6
Clark, J. P. 1935- DLB-117; CDWLB-3
Clark, Lewis Gaylord 1808-1873 . . . . DLB-3, 64, 73
Clark, Walter Van Tilburg
  1909-1971 . . . . DLB-9, 206
Clark, William (see Lewis, Meriwether)
Clark, William Andrews Jr. 1877-1934 . . . DLB-187
Clarke, Austin 1896-1974 . . . . DLB-10, 20
Clarke, Austin C. 1934- DLB-53, 125
Clarke, Gillian 1937- DLB-40
Clarke, James Freeman
  1810-1888 . . . . DLB-1, 59, 235
Clarke, Lindsay 1939- DLB-231
Clarke, Marcus 1846-1881 . . . . DLB-230
Clarke, Pauline 1921- DLB-161
Clarke, Rebecca Sophia 1833-1906 . . . . DLB-42
Clarke, Robert, and Company DLB-49
Clarkson, Thomas 1760-1846 . . . . DLB-158
Claudel, Paul 1868-1955 . . . . DLB-192
Claudius, Matthias 1740-1815 . . . . DLB-97
Clausen, Andy 1943- DLB-16
Clawson, John L. 1865-1933 . . . . DLB-187
Claxton, Remsen and Haffelfinger DLB-49
Clay, Cassius Marcellus 1810-1903 . . . . DLB-43
Cleage, Pearl 1948- DLB-228
Cleary, Beverly 1916- DLB-52
Cleary, Kate McPhelim 1863-1905 . . . . DLB-221
Cleaver, Vera 1919-   and
  Cleaver, Bill 1920-1981 . . . . DLB-52
Cleland, John 1710-1789 . . . . DLB-39
Clemens, Samuel Langhorne (Mark Twain)
  1835-1910 . . . . DLB-11, 12, 23, 64, 74,
                              186, 189; CDALB-3
Mark Twain on Perpetual Copyright Y-92
Clement, Hal 1922- DLB-8
Clemo, Jack 1916- DLB-27
Clephane, Elizabeth Cecilia
  1830-1869 . . . . DLB-199
Cleveland, John 1613-1658 . . . . DLB-126
Cliff, Michelle 1946- DLB-157; CDWLB-3
Clifford, Lady Anne 1590-1676 . . . . DLB-151
Clifford, James L. 1901-1978 . . . . DLB-103
Clifford, Lucy 1853?-1929 . . . . DLB-135, 141, 197
Clifton, Lucille 1936- DLB-5, 41
Clines, Francis X. 1938- DLB-185
Clive, Caroline (V) 1801-1873 . . . . DLB-199
Clode, Edward J. [publishing house] DLB-46
Clough, Arthur Hugh 1819-1861 . . . . DLB-32
Cloutier, Cécile 1930- DLB-60
Clouts, Sidney 1926-1982 . . . . DLB-225
Clutton-Brock, Arthur 1868-1924 . . . . DLB-98
Coates, Robert M. 1897-1973 . . . . . DLB-4, 9, 102
Coatsworth, Elizabeth 1893- DLB-22
Cobb, Charles E., Jr. 1943- DLB-41
Cobb, Frank I. 1869-1923 . . . . DLB-25
Cobb, Irvin S. 1876-1944 . . . . DLB-11, 25, 86

Cobbe, Frances Power 1822-1904 . . . . DLB-190
Cobbett, William 1763-1835 . . . . DLB-43, 107
Cobbledick, Gordon 1898-1969 . . . . DLB-171
Cochran, Thomas C. 1902- DLB-17
Cochrane, Elizabeth 1867-1922 . . . . . . DLB-25, 189
Cockerell, Sir Sydney 1867-1962 . . . . DLB-201
Cockerill, John A. 1845-1896 . . . . DLB-23
Cocteau, Jean 1889-1963 . . . . DLB-65
Coderre, Emile (see Jean Narrache)
Coe, Jonathan 1961- DLB-231
Coetzee, J. M. 1940- DLB-225
Coffee, Lenore J. 1900?-1984 . . . . DLB-44
Coffin, Robert P. Tristram 1892-1955 . . . . . DLB-45
Coghill, Mrs. Harry (see Walker, Anna Louisa)
Cogswell, Fred 1917- DLB-60
Cogswell, Mason Fitch 1761-1830 . . . . DLB-37
Cohan, George M. 1878-1942 . . . . DLB-249
Cohen, Arthur A. 1928-1986 . . . . DLB-28
Cohen, Leonard 1934- DLB-53
Cohen, Matt 1942- DLB-53
Colbeck, Norman 1903-1987 . . . . DLB-201
Colden, Cadwallader 1688-1776 . . . . . . DLB-24, 30
Colden, Jane 1724-1766 . . . . DLB-200
Cole, Barry 1936- DLB-14
Cole, George Watson 1850-1939 . . . . DLB-140
Colegate, Isabel 1931- DLB-14, 231
Coleman, Emily Holmes 1899-1974 . . . . DLB-4
Coleman, Wanda 1946- DLB-130
Coleridge, Hartley 1796-1849 . . . . DLB-96
Coleridge, Mary 1861-1907 . . . . DLB-19, 98
Coleridge, Samuel Taylor
  1772-1834 . . . . DLB-93, 107; CDBLB-3
Coleridge, Sara 1802-1852 . . . . DLB-199
Colet, John 1467-1519 . . . . DLB-132
Colette 1873-1954 . . . . DLB-65
Colette, Sidonie Gabrielle (see Colette)
Colinas, Antonio 1946- DLB-134
Coll, Joseph Clement 1881-1921 . . . . DLB-188
Collier, John 1901-1980 . . . . DLB-77, 255
Collier, John Payne 1789-1883 . . . . DLB-184
Collier, Mary 1690-1762 . . . . DLB-95
Collier, P. F. [publishing house] DLB-49
Collier, Robert J. 1876-1918 . . . . DLB-91
Collin and Small DLB-49
Collingwood, W. G. 1854-1932 . . . . DLB-149
Collins, An floruit circa 1653 . . . . DLB-131
Collins, Isaac [publishing house] DLB-49
Collins, Merle 1950- DLB-157
Collins, Mortimer 1827-1876 . . . . DLB-21, 35
Collins, Tom (see Furphy, Joseph)
Collins, Wilkie
  1824-1889 . . . . DLB-18, 70, 159; CDBLB-4
Collins, William 1721-1759 . . . . DLB-109
Collins, William, Sons and Company DLB-154
Collis, Maurice 1889-1973 . . . . DLB-195

Cumulative Index

Collyer, Mary 1716?-1763?............ DLB-39
Colman, Benjamin 1673-1747.......... DLB-24
Colman, George, the Elder 1732-1794 .... DLB-89
Colman, George, the Younger
  1762-1836..................... DLB-89
Colman, S. [publishing house] DLB-49
Colombo, John Robert 1936- DLB-53
Colquhoun, Patrick 1745-1820......... DLB-158
Colter, Cyrus 1910- DLB-33
Colum, Padraic 1881-1972............ DLB-19
Columella fl. first century A.D. DLB-211
Colvin, Sir Sidney 1845-1927.......... DLB-149
Colwin, Laurie 1944-1992 ....DLB-218; Y-80
Comden, Betty 1919- and
  Green, Adolph 1918- DLB-44
Come to Papa...................... Y-99
Comi, Girolamo 1890-1968 .... DLB-114
The Comic Tradition Continued
  [in the British Novel] DLB-15
Commager, Henry Steele 1902-1998 ..... DLB-17
The Commercialization of the Image of
  Revolt, by Kenneth Rexroth DLB-16
Community and Commentators: Black
  Theatre and Its Critics............. DLB-38
Commynes, Philippe de
  circa 1447-1511.................. DLB-208
Compton-Burnett, Ivy 1884?-1969....... DLB-36
Conan, Laure 1845-1924 .... DLB-99
Concord History and Life DLB-223
Concord Literary History of a Town.... DLB-223
Conde, Carmen 1901- DLB-108
Conference on Modern Biography.......... Y-85
Congreve, William
  1670-1729.......... DLB-39, 84; CDBLB-2
Preface to *Incognita* (1692) DLB-39
Conkey, W. B., Company DLB-49
Conn, Stewart 1936- DLB-233
Connell, Evan S., Jr. 1924- DLB-2; Y-81
Connelly, Marc 1890-1980......... DLB-7; Y-80
Connolly, Cyril 1903-1974 .... DLB-98
Connolly, James B. 1868-1957 .... DLB-78
Connor, Ralph 1860-1937 .... DLB-92
Connor, Tony 1930- DLB-40
Conquest, Robert 1917- DLB-27
Conrad, John, and Company DLB-49
Conrad, Joseph
  1857-1924.... DLB-10, 34, 98, 156; CDBLB-5
Conroy, Jack 1899-1990.................. Y-81
Conroy, Pat 1945- DLB-6
Considine, Bob 1906-1975 .... DLB-241
The Consolidation of Opinion: Critical
  Responses to the Modernists DLB-36
Consolo, Vincenzo 1933- DLB-196
Constable, Archibald, and Company DLB-154
Constable, Henry 1562-1613 .... DLB-136
Constable and Company Limited....... DLB-112
Constant, Benjamin 1767-1830 .... DLB-119

Constant de Rebecque, Henri-Benjamin de
  (see Constant, Benjamin)
Constantine, David 1944- DLB-40
Constantin-Weyer, Maurice 1881-1964 ... DLB-92
Contempo Caravan: Kites in a Windstorm ... Y-85
A Contemporary Flourescence of Chicano
  Literature....................... Y-84
Continental European Rhetoricians,
  1400-1600...................... DLB-236
The Continental Publishing Company.... DLB-49
Conversations with Editors Y-95
Conversations with Publishers I: An Interview
  with Patrick O'Connor Y-84
Conversations with Publishers II: An Interview
  with Charles Scribner III............ Y-94
Conversations with Publishers III: An Interview
  with Donald Lamm Y-95
Conversations with Publishers IV: An Interview
  with James Laughlin Y-96
Conversations with Rare Book Dealers I: An
  Interview with Glenn Horowitz........ Y-90
Conversations with Rare Book Dealers II: An
  Interview with Ralph Sipper Y-94
Conversations with Rare Book Dealers
  (Publishers) III: An Interview with
  Otto Penzler..................... Y-96
The Conversion of an Unpolitical Man,
  by W. H. Bruford DLB-66
Conway, Moncure Daniel
  1832-1907..................... DLB-1, 223
Cook, David C., Publishing Company.... DLB-49
Cook, Ebenezer circa 1667-circa 1732..... DLB-24
Cook, Edward Tyas 1857-1919 .... DLB-149
Cook, Eliza 1818-1889 .... DLB-199
Cook, Michael 1933- DLB-53
Cooke, George Willis 1848-1923 .... DLB-71
Cooke, Increase, and Company DLB-49
Cooke, John Esten 1830-1886 .... DLB-3, 248
Cooke, Philip Pendleton
  1816-1850 .... DLB-3, 59, 248
Cooke, Rose Terry 1827-1892 ....DLB-12, 74
Cook-Lynn, Elizabeth 1930- DLB-175
Coolbrith, Ina 1841-1928 .... DLB-54, 186
Cooley, Peter 1940- DLB-105
"Into the Mirror" DLB-105
Coolidge, Clark 1939- DLB-193
Coolidge, George [publishing house] DLB-49
Coolidge, Susan (see Woolsey, Sarah Chauncy)
Cooper, Anna Julia 1858-1964 .... DLB-221
Cooper, Edith Emma (see Field, Michael)
Cooper, Giles 1918-1966 .... DLB-13
Cooper, J. California 19??- DLB-212
Cooper, James Fenimore
  1789-1851........... DLB-3, 183; CDALB-2
Cooper, Kent 1880-1965 .... DLB-29
Cooper, Susan 1935- DLB-161
Cooper, Susan Fenimore 1813-1894..... DLB-239
Cooper, William [publishing house].....DLB-170
Coote, J. [publishing house] DLB-154

Coover, Robert 1932- DLB-2, 227; Y-81
Copeland and Day................... DLB-49
Ćopić, Branko 1915-1984............. DLB-181
Copland, Robert 1470?-1548 .... DLB-136
Coppard, A. E. 1878-1957 .... DLB-162
Coppée, François 1842-1908 ....DLB-217
Coppel, Alfred 1921- Y-83
Coppola, Francis Ford 1939- DLB-44
Copway, George (Kah-ge-ga-gah-bowh)
  1818-1869 ....DLB-175, 183
Corazzini, Sergio 1886-1907........... DLB-114
Corbett, Richard 1582-1635........... DLB-121
Corbière, Tristan 1845-1875...........DLB-217
Corcoran, Barbara 1911- DLB-52
Cordelli, Franco 1943- DLB-196
Corelli, Marie 1855-1924 .... DLB-34, 156
Corle, Edwin 1906-1956.................Y-85
Corman, Cid 1924- DLB-5, 193
Cormier, Robert 1925-2000 ... DLB-52; CDALB-6
Corn, Alfred 1943- DLB-120; Y-80
Cornford, Frances 1886-1960.......... DLB-240
Cornish, Sam 1935- DLB-41
Cornish, William circa 1465-circa 1524 .. DLB-132
Cornwall, Barry (see Procter, Bryan Waller)
Cornwallis, Sir William, the Younger
  circa 1579-1614 .... DLB-151
Cornwell, David John Moore (see le Carré, John)
Corpi, Lucha 1945- DLB-82
Corrington, John William
  1932-1988 .... DLB-6, 244
Corrothers, James D. 1869-1917 .... DLB-50
Corso, Gregory 1930- DLB-5, 16, 237
Cortázar, Julio 1914-1984....DLB-113; CDWLB-3
Cortéz, Carlos 1923- DLB-209
Cortez, Jayne 1936- DLB-41
Corvinus, Gottlieb Siegmund
  1677-1746..................... DLB-168
Corvo, Baron (see Rolfe, Frederick William)
Cory, Annie Sophie (see Cross, Victoria)
Cory, William Johnson 1823-1892....... DLB-35
Coryate, Thomas 1577?-1617.......DLB-151, 172
Ćosić, Dobrica 1921- DLB-181; CDWLB-4
Cosin, John 1595-1672 .... DLB-151, 213
Cosmopolitan Book Corporation........ DLB-46
Costain, Thomas B. 1885-1965 .... DLB-9
Coste, Donat 1912-1957.............. DLB-88
Costello, Louisa Stuart 1799-1870...... DLB-166
Cota-Cárdenas, Margarita 1941- DLB-122
Cotten, Bruce 1873-1954 ....DLB-187
Cotter, Joseph Seamon, Sr. 1861-1949.... DLB-50
Cotter, Joseph Seamon, Jr. 1895-1919 .... DLB-50
Cottle, Joseph [publishing house] DLB-154
Cotton, Charles 1630-1687............ DLB-131
Cotton, John 1584-1652.............. DLB-24
Cotton, Sir Robert Bruce 1571-1631..... DLB-213

Coulter, John 1888-1980 ....DLB-68
Cournos, John 1881-1966 ....DLB-54
Courteline, Georges 1858-1929 ....DLB-192
Cousins, Margaret 1905-1996 ....DLB-137
Cousins, Norman 1915-1990 ....DLB-137
Couvreur, Jessie (see Tasma)
Coventry, Francis 1725-1754 ....DLB-39
Dedication, *The History of Pompey the Little* (1751) DLB-39
Coverdale, Miles 1487 or 1488-1569 .....DLB-167
Coverly, N. [publishing house] DLB-49
Covici-Friede DLB-46
Coward, Noel
 1899-1973 ....DLB-10, 245; CDBLB-6
Coward, McCann and Geoghegan DLB-46
Cowles, Gardner 1861-1946 ....DLB-29
Cowles, Gardner "Mike" Jr.
 1903-1985 ....DLB-127, 137
Cowley, Abraham 1618-1667 ....DLB-131, 151
Cowley, Hannah 1743-1809 ....DLB-89
Cowley, Malcolm
 1898-1989 ....DLB-4, 48; Y-81, Y-89
Cowper, William 1731-1800 ....DLB-104, 109
Cox, A. B. (see Berkeley, Anthony)
Cox, James McMahon 1903-1974 ....DLB-127
Cox, James Middleton 1870-1957 ......DLB-127
Cox, Leonard ca. 1495-ca. 1550 ....DLB-236
Cox, Palmer 1840-1924 ....DLB-42
Coxe, Louis 1918-1993 ....DLB-5
Coxe, Tench 1755-1824 ....DLB-37
Cozzens, Frederick S. 1818-1869 ....DLB-202
Cozzens, James Gould
 1903-1978 .....DLB-9; Y-84; DS-2; CDALB-1
James Gould Cozzens—A View from Afar Y-97
James Gould Cozzens Case Re-opened Y-97
James Gould Cozzens: How to Read Him Y-97
Cozzens's *Michael Scarlett* Y-97
James Gould Cozzens Symposium and
 Exhibition at the University of
 South Carolina, Columbia Y-00
Crabbe, George 1754-1832 ....DLB-93
Crace, Jim 1946- DLB-231
Crackanthorpe, Hubert 1870-1896 .....DLB-135
Craddock, Charles Egbert (see Murfree, Mary N.)
Cradock, Thomas 1718-1770 ....DLB-31
Craig, Daniel H. 1811-1895..............DLB-43
Craik, Dinah Maria 1826-1887 ......DLB-35, 136
Cramer, Richard Ben 1950- DLB-185
Cranch, Christopher Pearse
 1813-1892 ....DLB-1, 42, 243
Crane, Hart 1899-1932 .....DLB-4, 48; CDALB-4
Crane, R. S. 1886-1967 ....DLB-63
Crane, Stephen
 1871-1900 ....DLB-12, 54, 78; CDALB-3
Crane, Walter 1845-1915 ....DLB-163
Cranmer, Thomas 1489-1556 ......DLB-132, 213
Crapsey, Adelaide 1878-1914 ....DLB-54

Crashaw, Richard 1612 or 1613-1649....DLB-126
Craven, Avery 1885-1980 ....DLB-17
Crawford, Charles 1752-circa 1815 ......DLB-31
Crawford, F. Marion 1854-1909 ....DLB-71
Crawford, Isabel Valancy 1850-1887......DLB-92
Crawley, Alan 1887-1975 ....DLB-68
Crayon, Geoffrey (see Irving, Washington)
Crayon, Porte (see Strother, David Hunter)
Creamer, Robert W. 1922- DLB-171
Creasey, John 1908-1973 ....DLB-77
Creative Age Press.....................DLB-46
Creech, William [publishing house]......DLB-154
Creede, Thomas [publishing house] DLB-170
Creel, George 1876-1953 ....DLB-25
Creeley, Robert 1926- DLB-5, 16, 169; DS-17
Creelman, James 1859-1915 ....DLB-23
Cregan, David 1931- DLB-13
Creighton, Donald Grant 1902-1979......DLB-88
Cremazie, Octave 1827-1879 ....DLB-99
Crémer, Victoriano 1909?- DLB-108
Crescas, Hasdai circa 1340-1412?.......DLB-115
Crespo, Angel 1926- DLB-134
Cresset Press DLB-112
Cresswell, Helen 1934- DLB-161
Crèvecoeur, Michel Guillaume Jean de
 1735-1813 ....DLB-37
Crewe, Candida 1964- DLB-207
Crews, Harry 1935- DLB-6, 143, 185
Crichton, Michael 1942- Y-81
A Crisis of Culture: The Changing Role
 of Religion in the New Republic DLB-37
Crispin, Edmund 1921-1978 ....DLB-87
Cristofer, Michael 1946- DLB-7
Crnjanski, Miloš
 1893-1977 ....DLB-147; CDWLB-4
Crocker, Hannah Mather 1752-1829.....DLB-200
Crockett, David (Davy)
 1786-1836 ....DLB-3, 11, 183, 248
Croft-Cooke, Rupert (see Bruce, Leo)
Crofts, Freeman Wills 1879-1957........DLB-77
Croker, John Wilson 1780-1857 ....DLB-110
Croly, George 1780-1860................DLB-159
Croly, Herbert 1869-1930 ....DLB-91
Croly, Jane Cunningham 1829-1901......DLB-23
Crompton, Richmal 1890-1969.........DLB-160
Cronin, A. J. 1896-1981.................DLB-191
Cros, Charles 1842-1888 ....DLB-217
Crosby, Caresse 1892-1970 ....DLB-48
Crosby, Caresse 1892-1970
 and Crosby, Harry
 1898-1929 ....DLB-4; DS-15
Crosby, Harry 1898-1929 ....DLB-48
Crosland, Camilla Toulmin
 (Mrs. Newton Crosland)
 1812-1895 ....DLB-240
Cross, Gillian 1945- DLB-161
Cross, Victoria 1868-1952 ....DLB-135, 197

Crossley-Holland, Kevin 1941- DLB-40, 161
Crothers, Rachel 1878-1958..............DLB-7
Crowell, Thomas Y., Company DLB-49
Crowley, John 1942- Y-82
Crowley, Mart 1935- DLB-7
Crown Publishers DLB-46
Crowne, John 1641-1712................DLB-80
Crowninshield, Edward Augustus
 1817-1859 ....DLB-140
Crowninshield, Frank 1872-1947.........DLB-91
Croy, Homer 1883-1965................DLB-4
Crumley, James 1939- DLB-226; Y-84
Cruse, Mary Anne 1825?-1910 ....DLB-239
Cruz, Migdalia 1958- DLB-249
Cruz, Victor Hernández 1949- DLB-41
Csokor, Franz Theodor 1885-1969.......DLB-81
Csoóri, Sándor 1930- DLB-232; CDWLB-4
Cuala Press DLB-112
Cullen, Countee
 1903-1946 ....DLB-4, 48, 51; CDALB-4
Culler, Jonathan D. 1944- DLB-67, 246
Cullinan, Elizabeth 1933- DLB-234
The Cult of Biography
 Excerpts from the Second Folio Debate:
 "Biographies are generally a disease of
 English Literature" – Germaine Greer,
 Victoria Glendinning, Auberon Waugh,
 and Richard Holmes Y-86
Cumberland, Richard 1732-1811.........DLB-89
Cummings, Constance Gordon
 1837-1924 ....DLB-174
Cummings, E. E.
 1894-1962 ....DLB-4, 48; CDALB-5
Cummings, Ray 1887-1957 ....DLB-8
Cummings and Hilliard.................DLB-49
Cummins, Maria Susanna
 1827-1866 ....DLB-42
Cumpián, Carlos 1953- DLB-209
Cunard, Nancy 1896-1965 ....DLB-240
Cundall, Joseph [publishing house] DLB-106
Cuney, Waring 1906-1976................DLB-51
Cuney-Hare, Maude 1874-1936..........DLB-52
Cunningham, Allan 1784-1842 .....DLB-116, 144
Cunningham, J. V. 1911- DLB-5
Cunningham, Peter F.
 [publishing house]..................DLB-49
Cunquiero, Alvaro 1911-1981..........DLB-134
Cuomo, George 1929- Y-80
Cupples, Upham and Company DLB-49
Cupples and Leon DLB-46
Cuppy, Will 1884-1949..................DLB-11
Curiel, Barbara Brinson 1956- DLB-209
Curll, Edmund [publishing house].......DLB-154
Currie, James 1756-1805 ....DLB-142
Currie, Mary Montgomerie Lamb Singleton,
 Lady Currie
 (see Fane, Violet)
Cursor Mundi circa 1300 ....DLB-146

Curti, Merle E. 1897- DLB-17	Daniels, Jonathan 1902-1981 .... DLB-127	Davis, H. L. 1894-1960 .... DLB-9, 206
Curtis, Anthony 1926- DLB-155	Daniels, Josephus 1862-1948 .... DLB-29	Davis, John 1774-1854 .... DLB-37
Curtis, Cyrus H. K. 1850-1933 .... DLB-91	Daniels, Sarah 1957- DLB-245	Davis, Lydia 1947- DLB-130
Curtis, George William 1824-1892 .... DLB-1, 43, 223	Danilevsky, Grigorii Petrovich 1829-1890 .... DLB-238	Davis, Margaret Thomson 1926- DLB-14
Curzon, Robert 1810-1873 .... DLB-166	Dannay, Frederic 1905-1982 and Manfred B. Lee 1905-1971 .... DLB-137	Davis, Ossie 1917- DLB-7, 38, 249
Curzon, Sarah Anne 1833-1898 .... DLB-99	Danner, Margaret Esse 1915- DLB-41	Davis, Owen 1874-1956 .... DLB-249
Cushing, Harvey 1869-1939 .... DLB-187	Danter, John [publishing house] DLB-170	Davis, Paxton 1925-1994 .... Y-89
Custance, Olive (Lady Alfred Douglas) 1874-1944 .... DLB-240	Dantin, Louis 1865-1945 .... DLB-92	Davis, Rebecca Harding 1831-1910 ... DLB-74, 239
Cynewulf circa 770-840 .... DLB-146	Danzig, Allison 1898-1987 .... DLB-171	Davis, Richard Harding 1864-1916 .... DLB-12, 23, 78, 79, 189; DS-13
Czepko, Daniel 1605-1660 .... DLB-164	D'Arcy, Ella circa 1857-1937 .... DLB-135	Davis, Samuel Cole 1764-1809 .... DLB-37
Czerniawski, Adam 1934- DLB-232	Darke, Nick 1948- DLB-233	Davis, Samuel Post 1850-1918 .... DLB-202
	Darley, Felix Octavious Carr 1822-1888 . DLB-188	Davison, Peter 1928- DLB-5
D	Darley, George 1795-1846 .... DLB-96	Davydov, Denis Vasil'evich 1784-1839 .... DLB-205
Dabit, Eugène 1898-1936 .... DLB-65	Darmesteter, Madame James (see Robinson, A. Mary F.)	Davys, Mary 1674-1732 .... DLB-39
Daborne, Robert circa 1580-1628 .... DLB-58	Darwin, Charles 1809-1882 .... DLB-57, 166	Preface to *The Works of Mrs. Davys* (1725) DLB-39
Dąbrowska, Maria 1889-1965 .... DLB-215; CDWLB-4	Darwin, Erasmus 1731-1802 .... DLB-93	DAW Books DLB-46
Dacey, Philip 1939- DLB-105	Daryush, Elizabeth 1887-1977 .... DLB-20	Dawson, Ernest 1882-1947 .... DLB-140
"Eyes Across Centuries: Contemporary Poetry and 'That Vision Thing,'" DLB-105	Dashkova, Ekaterina Romanovna (née Vorontsova) 1743-1810 .... DLB-150	Dawson, Fielding 1930- DLB-130
Dach, Simon 1605-1659 .... DLB-164	Dashwood, Edmée Elizabeth Monica de la Pasture (see Delafield, E. M.)	Dawson, Sarah Morgan 1842-1909 ..... DLB-239
Daggett, Rollin M. 1831-1901 .... DLB-79	Daudet, Alphonse 1840-1897 .... DLB-123	Dawson, William 1704-1752 .... DLB-31
D'Aguiar, Fred 1960- DLB-157	d'Aulaire, Edgar Parin 1898- and d'Aulaire, Ingri 1904- DLB-22	Day, Angel flourished 1583-1599 ... DLB-167, 236
Dahl, Roald 1916-1990 .... DLB-139, 255	Davenant, Sir William 1606-1668 ... DLB-58, 126	Day, Benjamin Henry 1810-1889 .... DLB-43
Dahlberg, Edward 1900-1977 .... DLB-48	Davenport, Guy 1927- DLB-130	Day, Clarence 1874-1935 .... DLB-11
Dahn, Felix 1834-1912 .... DLB-129	Davenport, Marcia 1903-1996 .... DS-17	Day, Dorothy 1897-1980 .... DLB-29
Dal', Vladimir Ivanovich (Kazak Vladimir Lugansky) 1801-1872 .... DLB-198	Davenport, Robert ?-? DLB-58	Day, Frank Parker 1881-1950 .... DLB-92
Dale, Peter 1938- DLB-40	Daves, Delmer 1904-1977 .... DLB-26	Day, John circa 1574-circa 1640 .... DLB-62
Daley, Arthur 1904-1974 .... DLB-171	Davey, Frank 1940- DLB-53	Day, John [publishing house] DLB-170
Dall, Caroline Healey 1822-1912 ..... DLB-1, 235	Davidson, Avram 1923-1993 .... DLB-8	Day, The John, Company DLB-46
Dallas, E. S. 1828-1879 .... DLB-55	Davidson, Donald 1893-1968 .... DLB-45	Day Lewis, C. 1904-1972 .... DLB-15, 20 (see also Blake, Nicholas)
From *The Gay Science* (1866) DLB-21	Davidson, John 1857-1909 .... DLB-19	Day, Mahlon [publishing house] DLB-49
The Dallas Theater Center DLB-7	Davidson, Lionel 1922- DLB-14	Day, Thomas 1748-1789 .... DLB-39
D'Alton, Louis 1900-1951 .... DLB-10	Davidson, Robyn 1950- DLB-204	Dazai Osamu 1909-1948 .... DLB-182
Daly, Carroll John 1889-1958 .... DLB-226	Davidson, Sara 1943- DLB-185	Deacon, William Arthur 1890-1977 ...... DLB-68
Daly, T. A. 1871-1948 .... DLB-11	Davie, Donald 1922- DLB-27	Deal, Borden 1922-1985 .... DLB-6
Damon, S. Foster 1893-1971 .... DLB-45	Davie, Elspeth 1919- DLB-139	de Angeli, Marguerite 1889-1987 .... DLB-22
Damrell, William S. [publishing house] ... DLB-49	Davies, Sir John 1569-1626 .... DLB-172	De Angelis, Milo 1951- DLB-128
Dana, Charles A. 1819-1897 .... DLB-3, 23	Davies, John, of Hereford 1565?-1618 ... DLB-121	De Bow, J. D. B. 1820-1867 .... DLB-3, 79, 248
Dana, Richard Henry, Jr. 1815-1882 .... DLB-1, 183, 235	Davies, Peter, Limited DLB-112	de Bruyn, Günter 1926- DLB-75
Dandridge, Ray Garfield DLB-51	Davies, Rhys 1901-1978 .... DLB-139, 191	de Camp, L. Sprague 1907-2000 .... DLB-8
Dane, Clemence 1887-1965 .... DLB-10, 197	Davies, Robertson 1913- DLB-68	De Carlo, Andrea 1952- DLB-196
Danforth, John 1660-1730 .... DLB-24	Davies, Samuel 1723-1761 .... DLB-31	De Casas, Celso A. 1944- DLB-209
Danforth, Samuel, I 1626-1674 .... DLB-24	Davies, Thomas 1712?-1785 .... DLB-142, 154	Dechert, Robert 1895-1975 .... DLB-187
Danforth, Samuel, II 1666-1727 .... DLB-24	Davies, W. H. 1871-1940 .... DLB-19, 174	Dee, John 1527-1608 or 1609 ...... DLB-136, 213
Dangerous Years: London Theater, 1939-1945 .... DLB-10	Daviot, Gordon 1896?-1952 .... DLB-10 (see also Tey, Josephine)	Deeping, George Warwick 1877-1950 ... DLB 153
Daniel, John M. 1825-1865 .... DLB-43	Davis, Arthur Hoey (see Rudd, Steele)	Defoe, Daniel 1660-1731 ...... DLB-39, 95, 101; CDBLB-2
Daniel, Samuel 1562 or 1563-1619 ...... DLB-62	Davis, Charles A. 1795-1867 .... DLB-11	Preface to *Colonel Jack* (1722) DLB-39
Daniel Press DLB-106	Davis, Clyde Brion 1894-1962 .... DLB-9	Preface to *The Farther Adventures of Robinson Crusoe* (1719) DLB-39
Daniells, Roy 1902-1979 .... DLB-68	Davis, Dick 1945- DLB-40	Preface to *Moll Flanders* (1722) DLB-39
Daniels, Jim 1956- DLB-120	Davis, Frank Marshall 1905-? DLB-51	Preface to *Robinson Crusoe* (1719) DLB-39

Preface to *Roxana* (1724)................DLB-39	Denison, Merrill 1893-1975.............DLB-92	De Voto, Bernard 1897-1955.........DLB-9, 256
de Fontaine, Felix Gregory 1834-1896.....DLB-43	Denison, T. S., and Company............DLB-49	De Vries, Peter 1910-1993............DLB-6; Y-82
De Forest, John William 1826-1906...DLB-12, 189	Dennery, Adolphe Philippe 1811-1899...DLB-192	Dewdney, Christopher 1951-.............DLB-60
DeFrees, Madeline 1919- DLB-105	Dennie, Joseph 1768-1812 ..... DLB-37, 43, 59, 73	Dewdney, Selwyn 1909-1979............DLB-68
"The Poet's Kaleidoscope: The Element of Surprise in the Making of the Poem".........................DLB-105	Dennis, John 1658-1734................DLB-101	Dewey, John 1859-1952................DLB-246
	Dennis, Nigel 1912-1989 .... DLB-13, 15, 233	Dewey, Orville 1794-1882..............DLB-243
DeGolyer, Everette Lee 1886-1956 ......DLB-187	Denslow, W. W. 1856-1915 ....DLB-188	Dewey, Thomas B. 1915-1981...........DLB-226
de Graff, Robert 1895-1981...............Y-81	Dent, J. M., and Sons.................DLB-112	DeWitt, Robert M., Publisher DLB-49
de Graft, Joe 1924-1978 ....DLB-117	Dent, Tom 1932-1998.................DLB-38	DeWolfe, Fiske and Company DLB-49
De Heinrico circa 980?.................DLB-148	Denton, Daniel circa 1626-1703..........DLB-24	Dexter, Colin 1930- DLB-87
Deighton, Len 1929- DLB-87; CDBLB-8	DePaola, Tomie 1934- DLB-61	de Young, M. H. 1849-1925 ....DLB-25
DeJong, Meindert 1906-1991............DLB-52	Department of Library, Archives, and Institutional Research, American Bible Society....... Y-97	Dhlomo, H. I. E. 1903-1956 .... DLB-157, 225
Dekker, Thomas circa 1572-1632 ......DLB-62, 172; CDBLB-1		Dhuoda circa 803-after 843 ....DLB-148
	De Quille, Dan 1829-1898.............DLB-186	*The Dial* 1840-1844 ....DLB-223
Delacorte, Jr., George T. 1894-1991 ......DLB-91	De Quincey, Thomas 1785-1859 ....DLB-110, 144; CDBLB-3	The Dial Press.......................DLB-46
Delafield, E. M. 1890-1943 ....DLB-34		Diamond, I. A. L. 1920-1988 ....DLB-26
Delahaye, Guy 1888-1969 ....DLB-92	"Rhetoric" (1828; revised, 1859) [excerpt].......................DLB-57	Dibble, L. Grace 1902-1998..............DLB-204
de la Mare, Walter 1873-1956 ....DLB-19, 153, 162, 255; CDBLB-6	Derby, George Horatio 1823-1861 ....DLB-11	Dibdin, Thomas Frognall 1776-1847 .....DLB-184
	Derby, J. C., and Company............DLB-49	Di Cicco, Pier Giorgio 1949- DLB-60
Deland, Margaret 1857-1945 ....DLB-78	Derby and Miller.....................DLB-49	Dick, Philip K. 1928-1982 ....DLB-8
Delaney, Shelagh 1939- DLB-13; CDBLB-8	De Ricci, Seymour 1881-1942 ....DLB-201	Dick and Fitzgerald DLB-49
Delano, Amasa 1763-1823 ....DLB-183	Derleth, August 1909-1971 .... DLB-9; DS-17	Dickens, Charles 1812-1870 ....DLB-21, 55, 70, 159, 166; CDBLB-4
Delany, Martin Robinson 1812-1885.....DLB-50	Derrida, Jacques 1930- DLB-242	
Delany, Samuel R. 1942- DLB-8, 33	The Derrydale Press DLB-46	Dickey, James 1923-1997 .... DLB-5, 193; Y-82, Y-93, Y-96; DS-7, DS-19; CDALB-6
de la Roche, Mazo 1879-1961 ....DLB-68	Derzhavin, Gavriil Romanovich 1743-1816 ....DLB-150	
Delavigne, Jean François Casimir 1793-1843 ....DLB-192		James Dickey Tributes...................Y-97
	Desaulniers, Gonsalve 1863-1934 ....DLB-92	The Life of James Dickey: A Lecture to the Friends of the Emory Libraries, by Henry Hart Y-98
Delbanco, Nicholas 1942- DLB-6, 234	Desbordes-Valmore, Marceline 1786-1859 ....DLB-217	
Delblanc, Sven 1931-1992 ....DLB-257		Dickey, William 1928-1994..............DLB-5
Del Castillo, Ramón 1949- DLB-209	Deschamps, Emile 1791-1871...........DLB-217	Dickinson, Emily 1830-1886..........DLB-1, 243; CDWLB-3
De León, Nephtal 1945-.................DLB-82	Deschamps, Eustache 1340?-1404......DLB-208	
Delgado, Abelardo Barrientos 1931- DLB-82	Desbiens, Jean-Paul 1927-..............DLB-53	Dickinson, John 1732-1808 ....DLB-31
Del Giudice, Daniele 1949- DLB-196	des Forêts, Louis-Rene 1918- DLB-83	Dickinson, Jonathan 1688-1747 ....DLB-24
De Libero, Libero 1906-1981...........DLB-114	Desiato, Luca 1941- DLB-196	Dickinson, Patric 1914- DLB-27
DeLillo, Don 1936- DLB-6, 173	Desnica, Vladan 1905-1967.............DLB-181	Dickinson, Peter 1927- DLB-87, 161
de Lisser H. G. 1878-1944 ....DLB-117	DesRochers, Alfred 1901-1978...........DLB-68	Dicks, John [publishing house]..........DLB-106
Dell, Floyd 1887-1969 ....DLB-9	Desrosiers, Léo-Paul 1896-1967..........DLB-68	Dickson, Gordon R. 1923-...............DLB-8
Dell Publishing Company DLB-46	Dessì, Giuseppe 1909-1977 .... DLB-177	*Dictionary of Literary Biography Yearbook* Awards Y-92, Y-93, Y-97, Y-98, Y-99, Y-00
delle Grazie, Marie Eugene 1864-1931 ....DLB-81	Destouches, Louis-Ferdinand (see Céline, Louis-Ferdinand)	
Deloney, Thomas died 1600 ....DLB-167		*The Dictionary of National Biography*........DLB-144
Deloria, Ella C. 1889-1971 ....DLB-175	De Tabley, Lord 1835-1895 ....DLB-35	Didion, Joan 1934- DLB-2, 173, 185; Y-81, Y-86; CDALB-6
Deloria, Vine, Jr. 1933- DLB-175	Deutsch, André, Limited DLB-112	
del Rey, Lester 1915-1993 ....DLB-8	Deutsch, Babette 1895-1982 ....DLB-45	Di Donato, Pietro 1911- DLB-9
Del Vecchio, John M. 1947- DS-9	Deutsch, Niklaus Manuel (see Manuel, Niklaus)	Die Fürstliche Bibliothek Corvey Y-96
Del'vig, Anton Antonovich 1798-1831....DLB-205	Deveaux, Alexis 1948- DLB-38	Diego, Gerardo 1896-1987 ....DLB-134
de Man, Paul 1919-1983 ....DLB-67	The Development of the Author's Copyright in Britain......................DLB-154	Digges, Thomas circa 1546-1595........DLB-136
DeMarinis, Rick 1934-.................DLB-218		The Digital Millennium Copyright Act: Expanding Copyright Protection in Cyberspace and Beyond.............. Y-98
Demby, William 1922- DLB-33	The Development of Lighting in the Staging of Drama, 1900-1945 ....DLB-10	
Deming, Philander 1829-1915 ....DLB-74		
Deml, Jakub 1878-1961 ....DLB-215	"The Development of Meiji Japan".....DLB-180	Dillard, Annie 1945- Y-80
Demorest, William Jennings 1822-1895....DLB-79	De Vere, Aubrey 1814-1902 ....DLB-35	Dillard, R. H. W. 1937- DLB-5, 244
De Morgan, William 1839-1917 ....DLB-153	Devereux, second Earl of Essex, Robert 1565-1601 ....DLB-136	Dillingham, Charles T., Company DLB-49
Demosthenes 384 B.C.-322 B.C. DLB-176		The Dillingham, G. W., Company DLB-49
Denham, Henry [publishing house]......DLB-170	The Devin-Adair Company.............DLB-46	Dilly, Edward and Charles [publishing house]................DLB-154
Denham, Sir John 1615-1669........DLB-58, 126	De Vinne, Theodore Low 1828-1914 ....DLB-187	
	Devlin, Anne 1951- DLB-245	Dilthey, Wilhelm 1833-1911 ....DLB-129

Dimitrova, Blaga 1922- ... DLB-181; CDWLB-4
Dimov, Dimitr 1909-1966 .... DLB-181
Dimsdale, Thomas J. 1831?-1866 .... DLB-186
Dinescu, Mircea 1950- DLB-232
Dinesen, Isak (see Blixen, Karen)
Dingelstedt, Franz von 1814-1881 ...... DLB-133
Dintenfass, Mark 1941- Y-84
Diogenes, Jr. (see Brougham, John)
Diogenes Laertius circa 200 .... DLB-176
DiPrima, Diane 1934- DLB-5, 16
Disch, Thomas M. 1940- DLB-8
Disney, Walt 1901-1966 .... DLB-22
Disraeli, Benjamin 1804-1881 .... DLB-21, 55
D'Israeli, Isaac 1766-1848 .... DLB-107
Ditlevsen, Tove 1917-1976 .... DLB-214
Ditzen, Rudolf (see Fallada, Hans)
Dix, Dorothea Lynde 1802-1887 ..... DLB-1, 235
Dix, Dorothy (see Gilmer, Elizabeth Meriwether)
Dix, Edwards and Company DLB-49
Dix, Gertrude circa 1874-? DLB-197
Dixie, Florence Douglas 1857-1905 ..... DLB-174
Dixon, Ella Hepworth
 1855 or 1857-1932 .... DLB-197
Dixon, Paige (see Corcoran, Barbara)
Dixon, Richard Watson 1833-1900 ...... DLB-19
Dixon, Stephen 1936- DLB-130
Dmitriev, Ivan Ivanovich 1760-1837 .... DLB-150
Dobell, Bertram 1842-1914 .... DLB-184
Dobell, Sydney 1824-1874 .... DLB-32
Dobie, J. Frank 1888-1964 .... DLB-212
Döblin, Alfred 1878-1957 .... DLB-66; CDWLB-2
Dobson, Austin 1840-1921 .... DLB-35, 144
Doctorow, E. L.
 1931- DLB-2, 28, 173; Y-80; CDALB-6
Documents on Sixteenth-Century
 Literature DLB-167, 172
Dodd, Anne [publishing house] DLB-154
Dodd, Mead and Company DLB-49
Dodd, Susan M. 1946- DLB-244
Dodd, William E. 1869-1940 .... DLB-17
Doderer, Heimito von 1896-1968 .... DLB-85
Dodge, B. W., and Company DLB-46
Dodge, Mary Abigail 1833-1896 .... DLB-221
Dodge, Mary Mapes
 1831?-1905 .... DLB-42, 79; DS-13
Dodge Publishing Company DLB-49
Dodgson, Charles Lutwidge (see Carroll, Lewis)
Dodsley, R. [publishing house] DLB-154
Dodsley, Robert 1703-1764 .... DLB-95
Dodson, Owen 1914-1983 .... DLB-76
Dodwell, Christina 1951- DLB-204
Doesticks, Q. K. Philander, P. B.
 (see Thomson, Mortimer)
Doheny, Carrie Estelle 1875-1958 ..... DLB-140
Doherty, John 1798?-1854 .... DLB-190
Doig, Ivan 1939- DLB-206

Doinaş, Ştefan Augustin 1922- DLB-232
Domínguez, Sylvia Maida 1935- DLB-122
Donahoe, Patrick [publishing house] DLB-49
Donald, David H. 1920- DLB-17
The Practice of Biography VI: An
 Interview with David Herbert Donald Y-87
Donaldson, Scott 1928- DLB-111
Doni, Rodolfo 1919- DLB-177
Donleavy, J. P. 1926- DLB-6, 173
Donnadieu, Marguerite (see Duras, Marguerite)
Donne, John
 1572-1631 .... DLB-121, 151; CDBLB-1
Donnelley, R. R., and Sons Company DLB-49
Donnelly, Ignatius 1831-1901 .... DLB-12
Donohue and Henneberry DLB-49
Donoso, José 1924-1996 .....DLB-113; CDWLB-3
Doolady, M. [publishing house] DLB-49
Dooley, Ebon (see Ebon)
Doolittle, Hilda 1886-1961 .... DLB-4, 45
Doplicher, Fabio 1938- DLB-128
Dor, Milo 1923- DLB-85
Doran, George H., Company DLB-46
Dorgelès, Roland 1886-1973 .... DLB-65
Dorn, Edward 1929-1999 .... DLB-5
Dorr, Rheta Childe 1866-1948 .... DLB-25
Dorris, Michael 1945-1997 .... DLB-175
Dorset and Middlesex, Charles Sackville,
 Lord Buckhurst, Earl of 1643-1706 .... DLB-131
Dorst, Tankred 1925- DLB-75, 124
Dos Passos, John 1896-1970
 .... DLB-4, 9; DS-1, DS-15; CDALB-5
John Dos Passos: Artist Y-99
John Dos Passos: A Centennial
 Commemoration Y-96
Dostoevsky, Fyodor 1821-1881 .... DLB-238
Doubleday and Company DLB-49
Dougall, Lily 1858-1923 .... DLB-92
Doughty, Charles M.
 1843-1926 .... DLB-19, 57, 174
Douglas, Lady Alfred (see Custance, Olive)
Douglas, Gavin 1476-1522 .... DLB-132
Douglas, Keith 1920-1944 .... DLB-27
Douglas, Norman 1868-1952 .... DLB-34, 195
Douglass, Frederick 1818-1895
 .... DLB-1, 43, 50, 79, 243; CDALB-2
Douglass, William circa 1691-1752 ...... DLB-24
Dourado, Autran 1926- DLB-145
Dove, Arthur G. 1880-1946 .... DLB-188
Dove, Rita 1952- DLB-120; CDALB-7
Dover Publications DLB-46
Doves Press DLB-112
Dowden, Edward 1843-1913 .... DLB-35, 149
Dowell, Coleman 1925-1985 .... DLB-130
Dowland, John 1563-1626 .... DLB-172
Downes, Gwladys 1915- DLB-88
Downing, J., Major (see Davis, Charles A.)

Downing, Major Jack (see Smith, Seba)
Dowriche, Anne
 before 1560-after 1613 .... DLB-172
Dowson, Ernest 1867-1900 .... DLB-19, 135
Doxey, William [publishing house] DLB-49
Doyle, Sir Arthur Conan
 1859-1930 ...DLB-18, 70, 156, 178; CDBLB-5
Doyle, Kirby 1932- DLB-16
Doyle, Roddy 1958- DLB-194
Drabble, Margaret
 1939- DLB-14, 155, 231; CDBLB-8
Drach, Albert 1902- DLB-85
Dragojević, Danijel 1934- DLB-181
Drake, Samuel Gardner 1798-1875 ..... DLB-187
The Dramatic Publishing Company DLB-49
Dramatists Play Service DLB-46
Drant, Thomas early 1540s?-1578 ..... DLB-167
Draper, John W. 1811-1882 .... DLB-30
Draper, Lyman C. 1815-1891 .... DLB-30
Drayton, Michael 1563-1631 .... DLB-121
Dreiser, Theodore 1871-1945
 .... DLB-9, 12, 102, 137; DS-1; CDALB-3
Dresser, Davis 1904-1977 .... DLB-226
Drewitz, Ingeborg 1923-1986 .... DLB-75
Drieu La Rochelle, Pierre 1893-1945 .... DLB-72
Drinker, Elizabeth 1735-1807 .... DLB-200
Drinkwater, John
 1882-1937 .... DLB-10, 19, 149
Droste-Hülshoff, Annette von
 1797-1848 .... DLB-133; CDWLB-2
The Drue Heinz Literature Prize
 Excerpt from "Excerpts from a Report
 of the Commission," in David
 Bosworth's *The Death of Descartes*
 An Interview with David Bosworth Y-82
Drummond, William, of Hawthornden
 1585-1649 .... DLB-121, 213
Drummond, William Henry
 1854-1907 .... DLB-92
Druzhinin, Aleksandr Vasil'evich
 1824-1864 .... DLB-238
Dryden, Charles 1860?-1931 .... DLB-171
Dryden, John
 1631-1700 ...... DLB-80, 101, 131; CDBLB-2
Držić, Marin
 circa 1508-1567 ....DLB-147; CDWLB-4
Duane, William 1760-1835 .... DLB-43
Dubé, Marcel 1930- DLB-53
Dubé, Rodolphe (see Hertel, François)
Dubie, Norman 1945- DLB-120
Dubois, Silvia 1788 or 1789?-1889 ..... DLB-239
Du Bois, W. E. B.
 1868-1963 ...DLB-47, 50, 91, 246; CDALB-3
Du Bois, William Pène 1916-1993 .... DLB-61
Dubrovina, Ekaterina Oskarovna
 1846-1913 .... DLB-238
Dubus, Andre 1936-1999 .... DLB-130
Ducange, Victor 1783-1833 .... DLB-192
Du Chaillu, Paul Belloni 1831?-1903 .... DLB-189
Ducharme, Réjean 1941- DLB-60

Dučić, Jovan 1871-1943 ..... DLB-147; CDWLB-4	Durand, Lucile (see Bersianik, Louky)	*The Eclectic Review* 1805-1868 .... DLB-110
Duck, Stephen 1705?-1756 .... DLB-95	Duranti, Francesca 1935- DLB-196	Eco, Umberto 1932- DLB-196, 242
Duckworth, Gerald, and Company Limited DLB-112	Duranty, Walter 1884-1957 .... DLB-29	Eddison, E. R. 1882-1945 .... DLB-255
Duclaux, Madame Mary (see Robinson, A. Mary F.)	Duras, Marguerite 1914-1996 .... DLB-83	Edel, Leon 1907-1997 .... DLB-103
Dudek, Louis 1918- DLB-88	Durfey, Thomas 1653-1723 .... DLB-80	Edelfeldt, Inger 1956- DLB-257
Duell, Sloan and Pearce DLB-46	Durova, Nadezhda Andreevna (Aleksandr Andreevich Aleksandrov) 1783-1866 .... DLB-198	Edes, Benjamin 1732-1803 .... DLB-43
Duerer, Albrecht 1471-1528 .... DLB-179		Edgar, David 1948- DLB-13, 233
Duff Gordon, Lucie 1821-1869 .... DLB-166	Durrell, Lawrence 1912-1990 .... DLB-15, 27, 204; Y-90; CDBLB-7	Edgeworth, Maria 1768-1849 .... DLB-116, 159, 163
Dufferin, Helen Lady, Countess of Gifford 1807-1867 .... DLB-199	Durrell, William [publishing house] DLB-49	*The Edinburgh Review* 1802-1929 .... DLB-110
Duffield and Green DLB-46	Dürrenmatt, Friedrich 1921-1990 .... DLB-69, 124; CDWLB-2	Edinburgh University Press DLB-112
Duffy, Maureen 1933- DLB-14		The Editor Publishing Company DLB-49
Dufief, Nicholas Gouin 1776-1834 .... DLB-187	Duston, Hannah 1657-1737 .... DLB-200	Editorial Institute at Boston University Y-00
Dugan, Alan 1923- DLB-5	Dutt, Toru 1856-1877 .... DLB-240	Editorial Statements DLB-137
Dugard, William [publishing house] DLB-170	Dutton, E. P., and Company DLB-49	Edmonds, Randolph 1900- DLB-51
Dugas, Marcel 1883-1947 .... DLB-92	Duvoisin, Roger 1904-1980 .... DLB-61	Edmonds, Walter D. 1903-1998 .... DLB-9
Dugdale, William [publishing house] DLB-106	Duyckinck, Evert Augustus 1816-1878 .... DLB-3, 64	Edschmid, Kasimir 1890-1966 .... DLB-56
Duhamel, Georges 1884-1966 .... DLB-65		Edson, Russell 1935- DLB-244
Dujardin, Edouard 1861-1949 .... DLB-123	Duyckinck, George L. 1823-1863 .... DLB-3	Edwards, Amelia Anne Blandford 1831-1892 .... DLB-174
Dukes, Ashley 1885-1959 .... DLB-10	Duyckinck and Company DLB-49	
Dumas, Alexandre *père* 1802-1870 ..... DLB-119, 192	Dwight, John Sullivan 1813-1893 ..... DLB-1, 235	Edwards, Dic 1953- DLB-245
Dumas, Alexandre *fils* 1824-1895 .... DLB-192	Dwight, Timothy 1752-1817 .... DLB-37	Edwards, Edward 1812-1886 .... DLB-184
Dumas, Henry 1934-1968 .... DLB-41	Dybek, Stuart 1942- DLB-130	Edwards, James [publishing house] DLB-154
du Maurier, Daphne 1907-1989 .... DLB-191	Dyer, Charles 1928- DLB-13	Edwards, Jonathan 1703-1758 .... DLB-24
Du Maurier, George 1834-1896 ..... DLB-153, 178	Dyer, Sir Edward 1543-1607 .... DLB-136	Edwards, Jonathan, Jr. 1745-1801 .... DLB-37
Dunbar, Paul Laurence 1872-1906 .... DLB-50, 54, 78; CDALB-3	Dyer, George 1755-1841 .... DLB-93	Edwards, Junius 1929- DLB-33
	Dyer, John 1699-1757 .... DLB-95	Edwards, Matilda Barbara Betham 1836-1919 .... DLB-174
Dunbar, William circa 1460-circa 1522 .... DLB-132, 146	Dyk, Viktor 1877-1931 .... DLB-215	
Duncan, David James 1952- DLB-256	Dylan, Bob 1941- DLB-16	Edwards, Richard 1524-1566 .... DLB-62
Duncan, Norman 1871-1916 .... DLB-92		Edwards, Sarah Pierpont 1710-1758 ...... DLB-200
Duncan, Quince 1940- DLB-145	**E**	Effinger, George Alec 1947- DLB-8
Duncan, Robert 1919-1988 .... DLB-5, 16, 193	Eager, Edward 1911-1964 .... DLB-22	Egerton, George 1859-1945 .... DLB-135
Duncan, Ronald 1914-1982 .... DLB-13	Eagleton, Terry 1943- DLB-242	Eggleston, Edward 1837-1902 .... DLB-12
Duncan, Sara Jeannette 1861-1922 .... DLB-92	Eames, Wilberforce 1855-1937 .... DLB-140	Eggleston, Wilfred 1901-1986 .... DLB-92
Dunigan, Edward, and Brother DLB-49	Earle, Alice Morse 1853-1911 .... DLB-221	Eglītis, Anšlavs 1906-1993 .... DLB-220
Dunlap, John 1747-1812 .... DLB-43	Earle, James H., and Company DLB-49	Ehrenreich, Barbara 1941- DLB-246
Dunlap, William 1766-1839 ..... DLB-30, 37, 59	Earle, John 1600 or 1601-1665 .... DLB-151	Ehrenstein, Albert 1886-1950 .... DLB-81
Dunn, Douglas 1942- DLB-40	Early American Book Illustration, by Sinclair Hamilton DLB-49	Ehrhart, W. D. 1948- DS-9
Dunn, Harvey Thomas 1884-1952 ...... DLB-188		Ehrlich, Gretel 1946- DLB-212
Dunn, Stephen 1939- DLB-105	Eastlake, William 1917-1997 .... DLB-6, 206	Eich, Günter 1907-1972 .... DLB-69, 124
"The Good, The Not So Good" DLB-105	Eastman, Carol ?- DLB-44	Eichendorff, Joseph Freiherr von 1788-1857 .... DLB-90
Dunne, Finley Peter 1867-1936 ..... DLB-11, 23	Eastman, Charles A. (Ohiyesa) 1858-1939 .... DLB-175	
Dunne, John Gregory 1932- Y-80	Eastman, Max 1883-1969 .... DLB-91	Eifukumon'in 1271-1342 .... DLB-203
Dunne, Philip 1908-1992 .... DLB-26	Eaton, Daniel Isaac 1753-1814 .... DLB-158	1873 Publishers' Catalogues DLB-49
Dunning, Ralph Cheever 1878-1930 .... DLB-4	Eaton, Edith Maude 1865-1914 .... DLB-221	Eighteenth-Century Aesthetic Theories DLB-31
Dunning, William A. 1857-1922 .... DLB-17	Eaton, Winnifred 1875-1954 .... DLB-221	
Dunsany, Lord (Edward John Moreton Drax Plunkett, Baron Dunsany) 1878-1957 .... DLB-10, 77, 153, 156, 255	Eberhart, Richard 1904- DLB-48; CDALB-1	Eighteenth-Century Philosophical Background DLB-31
	Ebner, Jeannie 1918- DLB-85	Eigner, Larry 1926-1996 .... DLB-5, 193
Duns Scotus, John circa 1266-1308 ...... DLB-115	Ebner-Eschenbach, Marie von 1830-1916 .... DLB-81	*Eikon Basilike* 1649 .... DLB-151
Dunton, John [publishing house] DLB-170	Ebon 1942- DLB-41	Eilhart von Oberge circa 1140-circa 1195 .... DLB-148
Dunton, W. Herbert 1878-1936 .... DLB-188	E-Books Turn the Corner Y-98	
Dupin, Amantine-Aurore-Lucile (see Sand, George)	Ecbasis Captivi circa 1045 .... DLB-148	Einhard circa 770-840 .... DLB-148
Dupuy, Eliza Ann 1814-1880 .... DLB-248	Ecco Press DLB-46	Eiseley, Loren 1907-1977 .... DS-17
	Eckhart, Meister circa 1260-circa 1328 ... DLB-115	Eisenberg, Deborah 1945- DLB-244
		Eisenreich, Herbert 1925-1986 .... DLB-85

Eisner, Kurt 1867-1919 . . . . DLB-66
Eklund, Gordon 1945- Y-83
Ekman, Kerstin 1933- DLB-257
Ekwensi, Cyprian
1921- DLB-117; CDWLB-3
Elaw, Zilpha circa 1790-? DLB-239
Eld, George [publishing house] DLB-170
Elder, Lonne III 1931- DLB-7, 38, 44
Elder, Paul, and Company DLB-49
The Electronic Text Center and the Electronic
  Archive of Early American Fiction at the
  University of Virginia Library Y-98
Eliade, Mircea 1907-1986 . . . DLB-220; CDWLB-4
Elie, Robert 1915-1973 . . . . DLB-88
Elin Pelin 1877-1949 . . . . DLB-147; CDWLB-4
Eliot, George
  1819-1880 . . . . DLB-21, 35, 55; CDBLB-4
Eliot, John 1604-1690 . . . . DLB-24
Eliot, T. S. 1888-1965
  . . . . DLB-7, 10, 45, 63, 245; CDALB-5
T. S. Eliot Centennial Y-88
Eliot's Court Press DLB-170
Elizabeth I 1533-1603 . . . . DLB-136
Elizabeth of Nassau-Saarbrücken
  after 1393-1456 . . . . DLB-179
Elizondo, Salvador 1932- DLB-145
Elizondo, Sergio 1930- DLB-82
Elkin, Stanley 1930-1995 . . . . DLB-2, 28, 218; Y-80
Elles, Dora Amy (see Wentworth, Patricia)
Ellet, Elizabeth F. 1818?-1877 . . . . DLB-30
Elliot, Ebenezer 1781-1849 . . . . DLB-96, 190
Elliot, Frances Minto (Dickinson)
  1820-1898 . . . . DLB-166
Elliott, Charlotte 1789-1871 . . . . DLB-199
Elliott, George 1923- DLB-68
Elliott, George P. 1918-1980 . . . . DLB-244
Elliott, Janice 1931- DLB-14
Elliott, Sarah Barnwell 1848-1928 . . . . . . DLB-221
Elliott, Thomes and Talbot DLB-49
Elliott, William III 1788-1863 . . . . DLB-3, 248
Ellis, Alice Thomas (Anna Margaret Haycraft)
  1932- DLB-194
Ellis, Edward S. 1840-1916 . . . . DLB-42
Ellis, Frederick Staridge
  [publishing house] DLB-106
The George H. Ellis Company DLB-49
Ellis, Havelock 1859-1939 . . . . DLB-190
Ellison, Harlan 1934- DLB-8
Ellison, Ralph
  1914-1994 . . . . DLB-2, 76, 227; Y-94; CDALB-1
Ellmann, Richard 1918-1987 . . . . DLB-103; Y-87
Ellroy, James 1948- DLB-226; Y-91
Elyot, Thomas 1490?-1546 . . . . DLB-136
Emanuel, James Andrew 1921- DLB-41
Emecheta, Buchi 1944- DLB-117; CDWLB-3
Emendations for *Look Homeward, Angel* Y-00
The Emergence of Black Women Writers DS-8

Emerson, Ralph Waldo 1803-1882
  . . . . DLB-1, 59, 73, 183, 223; CDALB-2
Ralph Waldo Emerson in 1982 . . . . Y-82
Emerson, William 1769-1811 . . . . DLB-37
Emerson, William 1923-1997 . . . . Y-97
Emin, Fedor Aleksandrovich
  circa 1735-1770 . . . . DLB-150
Empedocles fifth century B.C. DLB-176
Empson, William 1906-1984 . . . . DLB-20
Enchi Fumiko 1905-1986 . . . . DLB-182
"Encounter with the West" DLB-180
The End of English Stage Censorship,
  1945-1968 . . . . DLB-13
Ende, Michael 1929-1995 . . . . DLB-75
Endō Shūsaku 1923-1996 . . . . DLB-182
Engel, Marian 1933-1985 . . . . DLB-53
Engels, Friedrich 1820-1895 . . . . DLB-129
Engle, Paul 1908- DLB-48
English, Thomas Dunn 1819-1902 . . . . . DLB-202
English Composition and Rhetoric (1866),
  by Alexander Bain [excerpt] DLB-57
The English Language: 410 to 1500 . . . . . DLB-146
Ennius 239 B.C.-169 B.C. DLB-211
Enquist, Per Olov 1934- DLB-257
Enright, D. J. 1920- DLB-27
Enright, Elizabeth 1909-1968 . . . . DLB-22
Epic and Beast Epic DLB-208
Epictetus circa 55-circa 125-130 . . . . DLB-176
Epicurus 342/341 B.C.-271/270 B.C. DLB-176
Epps, Bernard 1936- DLB-53
Epstein, Julius 1909- and
  Epstein, Philip 1909-1952 . . . . DLB-26
Equiano, Olaudah
  circa 1745-1797 . . . . DLB-37, 50; DWLB-3
Olaudah Equiano and Unfinished Journeys:
  The Slave-Narrative Tradition and
  Twentieth-Century Continuities, by
  Paul Edwards and Pauline T.
  Wangman DLB-117
The E-Researcher: Possibilities and Pitfalls . . . Y-00
Eragny Press DLB-112
Erasmus, Desiderius 1467-1536 . . . . DLB-136
Erba, Luciano 1922- DLB-128
Erdrich, Louise
  1954- DLB-152, 175, 206; CDALB-7
Erichsen-Brown, Gwethalyn Graham
  (see Graham, Gwethalyn)
Eriugena, John Scottus circa 810-877 . . . . DLB-115
Ernst, Paul 1866-1933 . . . . DLB-66, 118
Ershov, Petr Pavlovich
  1815-1869 . . . . DLB-205
Erskine, Albert 1911-1993 . . . . Y-93
Erskine, John 1879-1951 . . . . DLB-9, 102
Erskine, Mrs. Steuart ?-1948 . . . . DLB-195
Ertel', Aleksandr Ivanovich
  1855-1908 . . . . DLB-238
Ervine, St. John Greer 1883-1971 . . . . DLB-10
Eschenburg, Johann Joachim 1743-1820 . . . DLB-97
Escoto, Julio 1944- DLB-145

Esdaile, Arundell 1880-1956 . . . . DLB-201
Eshleman, Clayton 1935- DLB-5
Espriu, Salvador 1913-1985 . . . . DLB-134
Ess Ess Publishing Company DLB-49
Essex House Press DLB-112
Essop, Ahmed 1931- DLB-225
Esterházy, Péter 1950- . . . DLB-232; CDWLB-4
Estes, Eleanor 1906-1988 . . . . DLB-22
Estes and Lauriat DLB-49
Estleman, Loren D. 1952- DLB-226
Eszterhas, Joe 1944- DLB-185
Etherege, George 1636-circa 1692 . . . . . . DLB-80
Ethridge, Mark, Sr. 1896-1981 . . . . DLB-127
Ets, Marie Hall 1893- DLB-22
Etter, David 1928- DLB-105
Ettner, Johann Christoph 1654-1724 . . . . DLB-168
Eupolemius flourished circa 1095 . . . . DLB-148
Euripides circa 484 B.C.-407/406 B.C.
  . . . . DLB-176; CDWLB-1
Evans, Augusta Jane 1835-1909 . . . . DLB-239
Evans, Caradoc 1878-1945 . . . . DLB-162
Evans, Charles 1850-1935 . . . . DLB-187
Evans, Donald 1884-1921 . . . . DLB-54
Evans, George Henry 1805-1856 . . . . DLB-43
Evans, Hubert 1892-1986 . . . . DLB-92
Evans, M., and Company DLB-46
Evans, Mari 1923- DLB-41
Evans, Mary Ann (see Eliot, George)
Evans, Nathaniel 1742-1767 . . . . DLB-31
Evans, Sebastian 1830-1909 . . . . DLB-35
Evaristi, Marcella 1953- DLB-233
Everett, Alexander Hill 1790-1847 . . . . . . DLB-59
Everett, Edward 1794-1865 . . . . . DLB-1, 59, 235
Everson, R. G. 1903- DLB-88
Everson, William 1912-1994 . . . . . DLB-5, 16, 212
Ewart, Gavin 1916-1995 . . . . DLB-40
Ewing, Juliana Horatia 1841-1885 . . . DLB-21, 163
The Examiner 1808-1881 . . . . DLB-110
Exley, Frederick 1929-1992 . . . . DLB-143; Y-81
von Eyb, Albrecht 1420-1475 . . . . DLB-179
Eyre and Spottiswoode DLB-106
Ezera, Regīna 1930- DLB-232
Ezzo ?-after 1065 . . . . DLB-148

F

Faber, Frederick William 1814-1863 . . . . . DLB-32
Faber and Faber Limited DLB-112
Faccio, Rena (see Aleramo, Sibilla)
Fagundo, Ana María 1938- DLB-134
Fair, Ronald L. 1932- DLB-33
Fairfax, Beatrice (see Manning, Marie)
Fairlie, Gerard 1899-1983 . . . . DLB-77
Fallada, Hans 1893-1947 . . . . DLB-56
Fancher, Betsy 1928- Y-83

Fane, Violet 1843-1905 ....DLB-35
Fanfrolico Press DLB-112
Fanning, Katherine 1927 ....DLB-127
Fanshawe, Sir Richard 1608-1666 ....DLB-126
Fantasy Press Publishers DLB-46
Fante, John 1909-1983 ....DLB-130; Y-83
Al-Farabi circa 870-950 ....DLB-115
Farabough, Laura 1949- DLB-228
Farah, Nuruddin 1945- DLB-125; CDWLB-3
Farber, Norma 1909-1984 ....DLB-61
Farigoule, Louis (see Romains, Jules)
Farjeon, Eleanor 1881-1965 ....DLB-160
Farley, Harriet 1812-1907 ....DLB-239
Farley, Walter 1920-1989 ....DLB-22
Farmborough, Florence 1887-1978 ....DLB-204
Farmer, Penelope 1939- DLB-161
Farmer, Philip José 1918- DLB-8
Farnaby, Thomas 1575?-1647 ....DLB-236
Farningham, Marianne (see Hearn, Mary Anne)
Farquhar, George circa 1677-1707 ....DLB-84
Farquharson, Martha (see Finley, Martha)
Farrar, Frederic William 1831-1903 ......DLB-163
Farrar and Rinehart DLB-46
Farrar, Straus and Giroux DLB-46
Farrell, J. G. 1935-1979 ....DLB-14
Farrell, James T. 1904-1979 ....DLB-4, 9, 86; DS-2
Fast, Howard 1914- DLB-9
Faulkner, George [publishing house] DLB-154
Faulkner, William 1897-1962
   ...DLB-9, 11, 44, 102; DS-2; Y-86; CDALB-5
William Faulkner Centenary Y-97
"Faulkner 100–Celebrating the Work,"
   University of South Carolina, Columbia . Y-97
Impressions of William Faulkner Y-97
Faulkner and Yoknapatawpha Conference,
   Oxford, Mississippi..................Y-97
Faulks, Sebastian 1953- DLB-207
Fauset, Jessie Redmon 1882-1961 ....DLB-51
Faust, Frederick Schiller (Max Brand)
   1892-1944 ....DLB-256
Faust, Irvin 1924- DLB-2, 28, 218; Y-80
Fawcett, Edgar 1847-1904 ....DLB-202
Fawcett, Millicent Garrett 1847-1929 .....DLB-190
Fawcett Books DLB-46
Fay, Theodore Sedgwick 1807-1898 ......DLB-202
Fearing, Kenneth 1902-1961 ....DLB-9
Federal Writers' Project DLB-46
Federman, Raymond 1928- Y-80
Fedorov, Innokentii Vasil'evich
   (see Omulevsky, Innokentii Vasil'evich)
Feiffer, Jules 1929- DLB-7, 44
Feinberg, Charles E. 1899-1988....DLB-187; Y-88
Feind, Barthold 1678-1721 ....DLB-168
Feinstein, Elaine 1930- DLB-14, 40
Feiss, Paul Louis 1875-1952 ....DLB-187
Feldman, Irving 1928- DLB-169

Felipe, Léon 1884-1968 ....DLB-108
Fell, Frederick, Publishers DLB-46
Felltham, Owen 1602?-1668 ....DLB-126, 151
Felman, Soshana 1942- DLB-246
Fels, Ludwig 1946- DLB-75
Felton, Cornelius Conway 1807-1862 ..DLB-1, 235
Fenn, Harry 1837-1911 ....DLB-188
Fennario, David 1947- DLB-60
Fenner, Dudley 1558?-1587? DLB-236
Fenno, Jenny 1765?-1803 ....DLB-200
Fenno, John 1751-1798 ....DLB-43
Fenno, R. F., and Company DLB-49
Fenoglio, Beppe 1922-1963 ....DLB-177
Fenton, Geoffrey 1539?-1608 ....DLB-136
Fenton, James 1949- DLB-40
Ferber, Edna 1885-1968 ....DLB-9, 28, 86
Ferdinand, Vallery III (see Salaam, Kalamu ya)
Ferguson, Sir Samuel 1810-1886 ....DLB-32
Ferguson, William Scott 1875-1954 ......DLB-47
Fergusson, Robert 1750-1774 ....DLB-109
Ferland, Albert 1872-1943 ....DLB-92
Ferlinghetti, Lawrence
   1919- DLB-5, 16; CDALB-1
Fermor, Patrick Leigh 1915- DLB-204
Fern, Fanny (see Parton, Sara Payson Willis)
Ferrars, Elizabeth 1907- DLB-87
Ferré, Rosario 1942- DLB-145
Ferret, E., and Company DLB-49
Ferrier, Susan 1782-1854 ....DLB-116
Ferril, Thomas Hornsby 1896-1988 ......DLB-206
Ferrini, Vincent 1913- DLB-48
Ferron, Jacques 1921-1985 ....DLB-60
Ferron, Madeleine 1922- DLB-53
Ferrucci, Franco 1936- DLB-196
Fetridge and Company DLB-49
Feuchtersleben, Ernst Freiherr von
   1806-1849 ....DLB-133
Feuchtwanger, Lion 1884-1958 ....DLB-66
Feuerbach, Ludwig 1804-1872 ....DLB-133
Feuillet, Octave 1821-1890 ....DLB-192
Feydeau, Georges 1862-1921 ....DLB-192
Fichte, Johann Gottlieb 1762-1814 ....DLB-90
Ficke, Arthur Davison 1883-1945 ....DLB-54
Fiction Best-Sellers, 1910-1945 ....DLB-9
Fiction into Film, 1928-1975: A List of Movies
   Based on the Works of Authors in
   British Novelists, 1930-1959 ....DLB-15
Fiedler, Leslie A. 1917- DLB-28, 67
Field, Barron 1789-1846 ....DLB-230
Field, Edward 1924- DLB-105
Field, Joseph M. 1810-1856 ....DLB-248
Field, Michael
   (Katherine Harris Bradley [1846-1914]
   and Edith Emma Cooper
   [1862-1913]) DLB-240
"The Poetry File" DLB-105

Field, Eugene
   1850-1895 ....DLB-23, 42, 140; DS-13
Field, John 1545?-1588 ....DLB-167
Field, Marshall, III 1893-1956 ....DLB-127
Field, Marshall, IV 1916-1965 ....DLB-127
Field, Marshall, V 1941- DLB-127
Field, Nathan 1587-1619 or 1620 ....DLB-58
Field, Rachel 1894-1942 ....DLB-9, 22
A Field Guide to Recent Schools of American
   Poetry Y-86
Fielding, Helen 1958- DLB-231
Fielding, Henry
   1707-1754 ....DLB-39, 84, 101; CDBLB-2
"Defense of *Amelia*" (1752) DLB-39
From *The History of the Adventures of
   Joseph Andrews* (1742) DLB-39
Preface to *Joseph Andrews* (1742) DLB-39
Preface to Sarah Fielding's *The Adventures
   of David Simple* (1744) DLB-39
Preface to Sarah Fielding's *Familiar Letters*
   (1747) [excerpt] DLB-39
Fielding, Sarah 1710-1768 ....DLB-39
Preface to *The Cry* (1754) DLB-39
Fields, Annie Adams 1834-1915 ....DLB-221
Fields, James T. 1817-1881 ....DLB-1, 235
Fields, Julia 1938- DLB-41
Fields, Osgood and Company DLB-49
Fields, W. C. 1880-1946 ....DLB-44
Fifty Penguin Years Y-85
Figes, Eva 1932- DLB-14
Figuera, Angela 1902-1984 ....DLB-108
Filmer, Sir Robert 1586-1653 ....DLB-151
Filson, John circa 1753-1788 ....DLB-37
Finch, Anne, Countess of Winchilsea
   1661-1720 ....DLB-95
Finch, Robert 1900- DLB-88
Findley, Timothy 1930- DLB-53
Finlay, Ian Hamilton 1925- DLB-40
Finley, Martha 1828-1909 ....DLB-42
Finn, Elizabeth Anne (McCaul)
   1825-1921 ....DLB-166
Finnegan, Seamus 1949- DLB-245
Finney, Jack 1911-1995 ....DLB-8
Finney, Walter Braden (see Finney, Jack)
Firbank, Ronald 1886-1926 ....DLB-36
Firmin, Giles 1615-1697 ....DLB-24
First Edition Library/Collectors'
   Reprints, Inc......................Y-91
Fischart, Johann
   1546 or 1547-1590 or 1591 ....DLB-179
Fischer, Karoline Auguste Fernandine
   1764-1842 ....DLB-94
Fischer, Tibor 1959- DLB-231
Fish, Stanley 1938- DLB-67
Fishacre, Richard 1205-1248 ....DLB-115
Fisher, Clay (see Allen, Henry W.)
Fisher, Dorothy Canfield 1879-1958 ...DLB-9, 102
Fisher, Leonard Everett 1924- DLB-61

Fisher, Roy 1930- DLB-40
Fisher, Rudolph 1897-1934 .... DLB-51, 102
Fisher, Steve 1913-1980 .... DLB-226
Fisher, Sydney George 1856-1927 .... DLB-47
Fisher, Vardis 1895-1968 .... DLB-9, 206
Fiske, John 1608-1677................. DLB-24
Fiske, John 1842-1901................DLB-47, 64
Fitch, Thomas circa 1700-1774 .... DLB-31
Fitch, William Clyde 1865-1909.......... DLB-7
FitzGerald, Edward 1809-1883.......... DLB-32
Fitzgerald, F. Scott 1896-1940
  .... DLB-4, 9, 86, 219; Y-81, Y-92;
  DS-1, 15, 16; CDALB-4
F. Scott Fitzgerald Centenary
  Celebrations......................Y-96
F. Scott Fitzgerald Inducted into the American
  Poets' Corner at St. John the Divine;
  Ezra Pound Banned..................Y-99
"F. Scott Fitzgerald: St. Paul's Native Son
  and Distinguished American Writer":
  University of Minnesota Conference,
  29-31 October 1982 ....Y-82
First International F. Scott Fitzgerald
  Conference.......................Y-92
Fitzgerald, Penelope 1916- DLB-14, 194
Fitzgerald, Robert 1910-1985 ....Y-80
Fitzgerald, Thomas 1819-1891 .... DLB-23
Fitzgerald, Zelda Sayre 1900-1948 ....Y-84
Fitzhugh, Louise 1928-1974 .... DLB-52
Fitzhugh, William circa 1651-1701 .... DLB-24
Flagg, James Montgomery 1877-1960 .... DLB-188
Flanagan, Thomas 1923- Y-80
Flanner, Hildegarde 1899-1987.......... DLB-48
Flanner, Janet 1892-1978................ DLB-4
Flannery, Peter 1951- DLB-233
Flaubert, Gustave 1821-1880 .... DLB-119
Flavin, Martin 1883-1967 .... DLB-9
Fleck, Konrad
  (flourished circa 1220) DLB-138
Flecker, James Elroy 1884-1915 ...... DLB-10, 19
Fleeson, Doris 1901-1970 .... DLB-29
Fleißer, Marieluise 1901-1974 ...... DLB-56, 124
Fleischer, Nat 1887-1972 .... DLB-241
Fleming, Abraham 1552?-1607......... DLB-236
Fleming, Ian 1908-1964 .. DLB-87, 201; CDBLB-7
Fleming, Paul 1609-1640 .... DLB-164
Fleming, Peter 1907-1971 .... DLB-195
Fletcher, Giles, the Elder 1546-1611..... DLB-136
Fletcher, Giles, the Younger
  1585 or 1586-1623 .... DLB-121
Fletcher, J. S. 1863-1935 .... DLB-70
Fletcher, John (see Beaumont, Francis)
Fletcher, John Gould 1886-1950....... DLB-4, 45
Fletcher, Phineas 1582-1650 .... DLB-121
Flieg, Helmut (see Heym, Stefan)
Flint, F. S. 1885-1960 .... DLB-19
Flint, Timothy 1780-1840.......... DLB-73, 186
Flores-Williams, Jason 1969- DLB-209

Florio, John 1553?-1625 ....DLB-172
Fo, Dario 1926- Y-97
Foix, J. V. 1893-1987 .... DLB-134
Foley, Martha (see Burnett, Whit, and Martha Foley)
Folger, Henry Clay 1857-1930 .... DLB-140
Folio Society DLB-112
Follen, Charles 1796-1840............. DLB-235
Follen, Eliza Lee (Cabot) 1787-1860 ... DLB-1, 235
Follett, Ken 1949- DLB-87; Y-81
Follett Publishing Company DLB-46
Folsom, John West [publishing house] DLB-49
Folz, Hans
  between 1435 and 1440-1513........DLB-179
Fontane, Theodor
  1819-1898 .... DLB-129; CDWLB-2
Fontes, Montserrat 1940- DLB-209
Fonvisin, Denis Ivanovich
  1744 or 1745-1792 .... DLB-150
Foote, Horton 1916- DLB-26
Foote, Mary Hallock
  1847-1938..........DLB-186, 188, 202, 221
Foote, Samuel 1721-1777............... DLB-89
Foote, Shelby 1916- DLB-2, 17
Forbes, Calvin 1945- DLB-41
Forbes, Ester 1891-1967 .... DLB-22
Forbes, Rosita 1893?-1967 .... DLB-195
Forbes and Company DLB-49
Force, Peter 1790-1868 .... DLB-30
Forché, Carolyn 1950- DLB-5, 193
Ford, Charles Henri 1913- DLB-4, 48
Ford, Corey 1902-1969................. DLB-11
Ford, Ford Madox
  1873-1939....... DLB-34, 98, 162; CDBLB-6
Ford, J. B., and Company............. DLB-49
Ford, Jesse Hill 1928-1996 .... DLB-6
Ford, John 1586-? DLB-58; CDBLB-1
Ford, R. A. D. 1915- DLB-88
Ford, Richard 1944- DLB-227
Ford, Worthington C. 1858-1941........ DLB-47
Fords, Howard, and Hulbert DLB-49
Foreman, Carl 1914-1984.............. DLB-26
Forester, C. S. 1899-1966 .... DLB-191
Forester, Frank (see Herbert, Henry William)
Forman, Harry Buxton 1842-1917 ...... DLB-184
Fornés, María Irene 1930- DLB-7
Forrest, Leon 1937-1997 .... DLB-33
Forster, E. M.
  1879-1970 ...... DLB-34, 98, 162, 178, 195;
  DS-10; CDBLB-6
Forster, Georg 1754-1794 .... DLB-94
Forster, John 1812-1876 .... DLB-144
Forster, Margaret 1938- DLB-155
Forsyth, Frederick 1938- DLB-87
Forten, Charlotte L. 1837-1914....... DLB-50, 239
Charlotte Forten: Pages from
  her Diary DLB-50
Fortini, Franco 1917- DLB-128

Fortune, Mary ca. 1833-ca. 1910 .... DLB-230
Fortune, T. Thomas 1856-1928 .... DLB-23
Fosdick, Charles Austin 1842-1915 ...... DLB-42
Foster, Genevieve 1893-1979 .... DLB-61
Foster, Hannah Webster 1758-1840 ...DLB-37, 200
Foster, John 1648-1681................ DLB-24
Foster, Michael 1904-1956 .... DLB-9
Foster, Myles Birket 1825-1899 .... DLB-184
Foucault, Michel 1926-1984 .... DLB-242
Foulis, Robert and Andrew / R. and A.
  [publishing house] DLB-154
Fouqué, Caroline de la Motte
  1774-1831..................... DLB-90
Fouqué, Friedrich de la Motte
  1777-1843..................... DLB-90
Four Seas Company DLB-46
Four Winds Press.................... DLB-46
Fournier, Henri Alban (see Alain-Fournier)
Fowler and Wells Company........... DLB-49
Fowles, John
  1926- DLB-14, 139, 207; CDBLB-8
Fox, John 1939- DLB-245
Fox, John, Jr. 1862 or 1863-1919 ... DLB-9; DS-13
Fox, Paula 1923- DLB-52
Fox, Richard K. [publishing house] DLB-49
Fox, Richard Kyle 1846-1922.......... DLB-79
Fox, William Price 1926- DLB-2; Y-81
Foxe, John 1517-1587 .... DLB-132
Fraenkel, Michael 1896-1957 .... DLB-4
France, Anatole 1844-1924........... DLB-123
France, Richard 1938- DLB-7
Francis, C. S. [publishing house]......... DLB-49
Francis, Convers 1795-1863 .... DLB-1, 235
Francis, Dick 1920- DLB-87
Francis, Sir Frank 1901-1988 .... DLB-201
Francis, Jeffrey, Lord 1773-1850.........DLB-107
François 1863-1910................... DLB-92
François, Louise von 1817-1893 .... DLB-129
Franck, Sebastian 1499-1542 ....DLB-179
Francke, Kuno 1855-1930 .... DLB-71
Frank, Bruno 1887-1945 .... DLB-118
Frank, Leonhard 1882-1961........ DLB-56, 118
Frank, Melvin (see Panama, Norman)
Frank, Waldo 1889-1967 .... DLB-9, 63
Franken, Rose 1895?-1988 ......DLB-228, Y-84
Franklin, Benjamin
  1706-1790.... DLB-24, 43, 73, 183; CDALB-2
Franklin, James 1697-1735 .... DLB-43
Franklin, Miles 1879-1954 .... DLB-230
Franklin Library..................... DLB-46
Frantz, Ralph Jules 1902-1979 .... DLB-4
Franzos, Karl Emil 1848-1904 .... DLB-129
Fraser, G. S. 1915-1980 .... DLB-27
Fraser, Kathleen 1935- DLB-169
Frattini, Alberto 1922- DLB-128
Frau Ava ?-1127 .... DLB-148

Fraunce, Abraham 1558?-1592 or 1593...DLB-236
Frayn, Michael 1933- DLB-13, 14, 194, 245
Frederic, Harold
  1856-1898 ....DLB-12, 23; DS-13
Freeling, Nicolas 1927- DLB-87
Freeman, Douglas Southall
  1886-1953 ....DLB-17; DS-17
Freeman, Judith 1946- DLB-256
Freeman, Legh Richmond 1842-1915 .....DLB-23
Freeman, Mary E. Wilkins
  1852-1930 ....DLB-12, 78, 221
Freeman, R. Austin 1862-1943 ....DLB-70
Freidank circa 1170-circa 1233..........DLB-138
Freiligrath, Ferdinand 1810-1876 ....DLB-133
Frémont, John Charles 1813-1890.......DLB-186
Frémont, John Charles 1813-1890 and
  Frémont, Jessie Benton 1834-1902 ...DLB-183
French, Alice 1850-1934 ....DLB-74; DS-13
French Arthurian Literature.............DLB-208
French, David 1939- DLB-53
French, Evangeline 1869-1960..........DLB-195
French, Francesca 1871-1960..........DLB-195
French, James [publishing house].........DLB-49
French, Samuel [publishing house].......DLB-49
Samuel French, Limited DLB-106
Freneau, Philip 1752-1832 ....DLB-37, 43
Freni, Melo 1934- DLB-128
Freshfield, Douglas W. 1845-1934.......DLB-174
Freytag, Gustav 1816-1895 ....DLB-129
Fried, Erich 1921-1988.................DLB-85
Friedan, Betty 1921- DLB-246
Friedman, Bruce Jay 1930- DLB-2, 28, 244
Friedrich von Hausen circa 1171-1190....DLB-138
Friel, Brian 1929- DLB-13
Friend, Krebs 1895?-1967? DLB-4
Fries, Fritz Rudolf 1935- DLB-75
Fringe and Alternative Theater in
  Great Britain DLB-13
Frisch, Max
  1911-1991 ....DLB-69, 124; CDWLB-2
Frischlin, Nicodemus 1547-1590 ....DLB-179
Frischmuth, Barbara 1941- DLB-85
Fritz, Jean 1915- DLB-52
Froissart, Jean circa 1337-circa 1404......DLB-208
Fromentin, Eugene 1820-1876 ....DLB-123
Frontinus circa A.D. 35-A.D. 103/104 ....DLB-211
Frost, A. B. 1851-1928.........DLB-188; DS-13
Frost, Robert
  1874-1963 ....DLB-54; DS-7; CDALB-4
Frostenson, Katarina 1953- DLB-257
Frothingham, Octavius Brooks
  1822-1895 ....DLB-1, 243
Froude, James Anthony
  1818-1894 ....DLB-18, 57, 144
Fruitlands 1843-1844..................DLB-223
Fry, Christopher 1907- DLB-13
Fry, Roger 1866-1934 .... DS-10

Fry, Stephen 1957- DLB-207
Frye, Northrop 1912-1991........ DLB-67, 68, 246
Fuchs, Daniel 1909-1993 .....DLB-9, 26, 28; Y-93
Fuentes, Carlos 1928- DLB-113; CDWLB-3
Fuertes, Gloria 1918- DLB-108
Fugard, Athol 1932- DLB-225
The Fugitives and the Agrarians:
  The First Exhibition Y-85
Fujiwara no Shunzei 1114-1204.........DLB-203
Fujiwara no Tameaki 1230s?-1290s?.....DLB-203
Fujiwara no Tameie 1198-1275 ....DLB-203
Fujiwara no Teika 1162-1241 ....DLB-203
Fulbecke, William 1560-1603?.........DLB-172
Fuller, Charles H., Jr. 1939- DLB-38
Fuller, Henry Blake 1857-1929 ....DLB-12
Fuller, John 1937- DLB-40
Fuller, Margaret (see Fuller, Sarah)
Fuller, Roy 1912-1991 ....DLB-15, 20
Fuller, Samuel 1912- DLB-26
Fuller, Sarah 1810-1850
  .....DLB-1, 59, 73, 183, 223, 239; CDALB-2
Fuller, Thomas 1608-1661...............DLB-151
Fullerton, Hugh 1873-1945 ....DLB-171
Fullwood, William flourished 1568......DLB-236
Fulton, Alice 1952- DLB-193
Fulton, Len 1934- Y-86
Fulton, Robin 1937- DLB-40
Furbank, P. N. 1920- DLB-155
Furman, Laura 1945- Y-86
Furness, Horace Howard
  1833-1912 ....DLB-64
Furness, William Henry
  1802-1896 ....DLB-1, 235
Furnivall, Frederick James
  1825-1910 ....DLB-184
Furphy, Joseph
  (Tom Collins) 1843-1912 ....DLB-230
Furthman, Jules 1888-1966 ....DLB-26
Furui Yoshikichi 1937- DLB-182
Fushimi, Emperor 1265-1317...........DLB-203
Futabatei, Shimei
  (Hasegawa Tatsunosuke)
  1864-1909 ....DLB-180
The Future of the Novel (1899), by
  Henry James DLB-18
Fyleman, Rose 1877-1957..............DLB-160

G

Gadda, Carlo Emilio 1893-1973 ....DLB-177
Gaddis, William 1922-1998..........DLB-2, Y-99
Gág, Wanda 1893-1946................DLB-22
Gagarin, Ivan Sergeevich 1814-1882.....DLB-198
Gagnon, Madeleine 1938- DLB-60
Gaine, Hugh 1726-1807 ....DLB-43
Gaine, Hugh [publishing house] DLB-49
Gaines, Ernest J.
  1933- DLB-2, 33, 152; Y-80; CDALB-6

Gaiser, Gerd 1908-1976................DLB-69
Gaitskill, Mary 1954- DLB-244
Galarza, Ernesto 1905-1984 ....DLB-122
Galaxy Science Fiction Novels..........DLB-46
Gale, Zona 1874-1938 ....DLB-9, 228, 78
Galen of Pergamon 129-after 210 ....DLB-176
Gales, Winifred Marshall 1761-1839.....DLB-200
Gall, Louise von 1815-1855............DLB-133
Gallagher, Tess 1943- DLB-120, 212, 244
Gallagher, Wes 1911- DLB-127
Gallagher, William Davis 1808-1894......DLB-73
Gallant, Mavis 1922- DLB-53
Gallegos, María Magdalena 1935- DLB-209
Gallico, Paul 1897-1976 ....DLB-9, 171
Gallop, Jane 1952- DLB-246
Galloway, Grace Growden 1727-1782 ....DLB-200
Gallup, Donald 1913- DLB-187
Galsworthy, John 1867-1933
  ......DLB-10, 34, 98, 162; DS-16; CDBLB-5
Galt, John 1779-1839 ....DLB-99, 116
Galton, Sir Francis 1822-1911 ....DLB-166
Galvin, Brendan 1938- DLB-5
Gambit......................................DLB-46
Gamboa, Reymundo 1948- DLB-122
Gammer Gurton's Needle DLB-62
Gan, Elena Andreevna (Zeneida R-va)
  1814-1842 ....DLB-198
Gannett, Frank E. 1876-1957 ....DLB-29
Gao Xingjian 1940- Y-00
Gaos, Vicente 1919-1980..............DLB-134
García, Andrew 1854?-1943 ....DLB-209
García, Lionel G. 1935- DLB-82
García, Richard 1941- DLB-209
García-Camarillo, Cecilio 1943- DLB-209
García Lorca, Federico 1898-1936.......DLB-108
García Márquez, Gabriel
  1928- DLB-113; Y-82; CDWLB-3
Gardam, Jane 1928- DLB-14, 161, 231
Gardell, Jonas 1963- DLB-257
Garden, Alexander circa 1685-1756.......DLB-31
Gardiner, John Rolfe 1936- DLB-244
Gardiner, Margaret Power Farmer
  (see Blessington, Marguerite, Countess of)
Gardner, John
  1933-1982 ....DLB-2; Y-82; CDALB-7
Garfield, Leon 1921-1996 ....DLB-161
Garis, Howard R. 1873-1962............DLB-22
Garland, Hamlin 1860-1940 ..DLB-12, 71, 78, 186
Garneau, Francis-Xavier 1809-1866 .....DLB-99
Garneau, Hector de Saint-Denys
  1912-1943 ....DLB-88
Garneau, Michel 1939- DLB-53
Garner, Alan 1934- DLB-161
Garner, Hugh 1913-1979 ....DLB-68
Garnett, David 1892-1981 ....DLB-34
Garnett, Eve 1900-1991 ....DLB-160

Cumulative Index

Garnett, Richard 1835-1906 .... DLB-184
Garrard, Lewis H. 1829-1887 .... DLB-186
Garraty, John A. 1920- DLB-17
Garrett, George
  1929- DLB-2, 5, 130, 152; Y-83
Fellowship of Southern Writers Y-98
Garrett, John Work 1872-1942 .... DLB-187
Garrick, David 1717-1779 .... DLB-84, 213
Garrison, William Lloyd
  1805-1879 .... DLB-1, 43, 235; CDALB-2
Garro, Elena 1920-1998 .... DLB-145
Garth, Samuel 1661-1719 .... DLB-95
Garve, Andrew 1908- DLB-87
Gary, Romain 1914-1980 .... DLB-83
Gascoigne, George 1539?-1577 .... DLB-136
Gascoyne, David 1916- DLB-20
Gaskell, Elizabeth Cleghorn
  1810-1865 ..... DLB-21, 144, 159; CDBLB-4
Gaspey, Thomas 1788-1871 .... DLB-116
Gass, William H. 1924- DLB-2, 227
Gates, Doris 1901- DLB-22
Gates, Henry Louis, Jr. 1950- DLB-67
Gates, Lewis E. 1860-1924 .... DLB-71
Gatto, Alfonso 1909-1976 .... DLB-114
Gault, William Campbell 1910-1995 .... DLB-226
Gaunt, Mary 1861-1942 .... DLB-174, 230
Gautier, Théophile 1811-1872 .... DLB-119
Gauvreau, Claude 1925-1971 .... DLB-88
The *Gawain*-Poet
  flourished circa 1350-1400 .... DLB-146
Gawsworth, John (Terence Ian Fytton Armstrong)
  1912-1970 .... DLB-255
Gay, Ebenezer 1696-1787 .... DLB-24
Gay, John 1685-1732 .... DLB-84, 95
Gayarré, Charles E. A. 1805-1895 ...... DLB-30
Gaylord, Charles [publishing house] DLB-49
Gaylord, Edward King 1873-1974 .... DLB-127
Gaylord, Edward Lewis 1919- DLB-127
Geda, Sigitas 1943- DLB-232
Geddes, Gary 1940- DLB-60
Geddes, Virgil 1897- DLB-4
Gedeon (Georgii Andreevich Krinovsky)
  circa 1730-1763 .... DLB-150
Gee, Maggie 1948- DLB-207
Gee, Shirley 1932- DLB-245
Geßner, Salomon 1730-1788 .... DLB-97
Geibel, Emanuel 1815-1884 .... DLB-129
Geiogamah, Hanay 1945- DLB-175
Geis, Bernard, Associates DLB-46
Geisel, Theodor Seuss 1904-1991 ... DLB-61; Y-91
Gelb, Arthur 1924- DLB-103
Gelb, Barbara 1926- DLB-103
Gelber, Jack 1932- DLB-7, 228
Gelinas, Gratien 1909- DLB-88
Gellert, Christian Fuerchtegott
  1715-1769 .... DLB-97

Gellhorn, Martha 1908-1998 .... Y-82, Y-98
Gems, Pam 1925- DLB-13
Genet, Jean 1910-1986 .... DLB-72; Y-86
Genette, Gérard 1930- DLB-242
Genevoix, Maurice 1890-1980 .... DLB-65
Genovese, Eugene D. 1930- DLB-17
Gent, Peter 1942- Y-82
Geoffrey of Monmouth
  circa 1100-1155 .... DLB-146
George, Henry 1839-1897 .... DLB-23
George, Jean Craighead 1919- DLB-52
George, W. L. 1882-1926 .... DLB-197
George III, King of Great Britain and Ireland
  1738-1820 .... DLB-213
George V. Higgins to Julian Symons Y-99
Georgslied 896? DLB-148
Gerber, Merrill Joan 1938- DLB-218
Gerhardie, William 1895-1977 .... DLB-36
Gerhardt, Paul 1607-1676 .... DLB-164
Gérin, Winifred 1901-1981 .... DLB-155
Gérin-Lajoie, Antoine 1824-1882 ...... DLB-99
German Drama 800-1280 .... DLB-138
German Drama from Naturalism
  to Fascism: 1889-1933 .... DLB-118
German Literature and Culture from Charlemagne
  to the Early Courtly Period
  .... DLB-148; CDWLB-2
German Radio Play, The DLB-124
German Transformation from the Baroque
  to the Enlightenment, The DLB-97
The Germanic Epic and Old English
  Heroic Poetry: *Widsith, Waldere,*
  and *The Fight at Finnsburg* DLB-146
Germanophilism, by Hans Kohn DLB-66
Gernsback, Hugo 1884-1967 .... DLB-8, 137
Gerould, Katharine Fullerton
  1879-1944 .... DLB-78
Gerrish, Samuel [publishing house] DLB-49
Gerrold, David 1944- DLB-8
The Ira Gershwin Centenary Y-96
Gerson, Jean 1363-1429 .... DLB-208
Gersonides 1288-1344 .... DLB-115
Gerstäcker, Friedrich 1816-1872 ...... DLB-129
Gerstenberg, Heinrich Wilhelm von
  1737-1823 .... DLB-97
Gervinus, Georg Gottfried
  1805-1871 .... DLB-133
Geston, Mark S. 1946- DLB-8
Al-Ghazali 1058-1111 .... DLB-115
Gibbings, Robert 1889-1958 .... DLB-195
Gibbon, Edward 1737-1794 .... DLB-104
Gibbon, John Murray 1875-1952 .... DLB-92
Gibbon, Lewis Grassic (see Mitchell, James Leslie)
Gibbons, Floyd 1887-1939 .... DLB-25
Gibbons, Reginald 1947- DLB-120
Gibbons, William ?-? DLB-73
Gibson, Charles Dana
  1867-1944 .... DLB-188; DS-13

Gibson, Graeme 1934- DLB-53
Gibson, Margaret 1944- DLB-120
Gibson, Margaret Dunlop 1843-1920 .... DLB-174
Gibson, Wilfrid 1878-1962 .... DLB-19
Gibson, William 1914- DLB-7
Gide, André 1869-1951 .... DLB-65
Giguère, Diane 1937- DLB-53
Giguère, Roland 1929- DLB-60
Gil de Biedma, Jaime 1929-1990 ...... DLB-108
Gil-Albert, Juan 1906- DLB-134
Gilbert, Anthony 1899-1973 .... DLB-77
Gilbert, Sir Humphrey 1537-1583 ...... DLB-136
Gilbert, Michael 1912- DLB-87
Gilbert, Sandra M. 1936- DLB-120, 246
Gilchrist, Alexander 1828-1861 ...... DLB-144
Gilchrist, Ellen 1935- DLB-130
Gilder, Jeannette L. 1849-1916 ...... DLB-79
Gilder, Richard Watson 1844-1909 .... DLB-64, 79
Gildersleeve, Basil 1831-1924 .... DLB-71
Giles of Rome circa 1243-1316 .... DLB-115
Giles, Henry 1809-1882 .... DLB-64
Gilfillan, George 1813-1878 .... DLB-144
Gill, Eric 1882-1940 .... DLB-98
Gill, Sarah Prince 1728-1771 .... DLB-200
Gill, William F., Company DLB-49
Gillespie, A. Lincoln, Jr. 1895-1950 ...... DLB-4
Gilliam, Florence ?-? DLB-4
Gilliatt, Penelope 1932-1993 .... DLB-14
Gillott, Jacky 1939-1980 .... DLB-14
Gilman, Caroline H. 1794-1888 .... DLB-3, 73
Gilman, Charlotte Perkins 1860-1935 ... DLB-221
Gilman, W. and J. [publishing house] DLB-49
Gilmer, Elizabeth Meriwether 1861-1951 .. DLB-29
Gilmer, Francis Walker 1790-1826 ..... DLB-37
Gilroy, Frank D. 1925- DLB-7
Gimferrer, Pere (Pedro) 1945- DLB-134
Gingrich, Arnold 1903-1976 .... DLB-137
Ginsberg, Allen
  1926-1997 ... DLB-5, 16, 169, 237; CDALB-1
Ginzburg, Natalia 1916-1991 .... DLB-177
Ginzkey, Franz Karl 1871-1963 .... DLB-81
Gioia, Dana 1950- DLB-120
Giono, Jean 1895-1970 .... DLB-72
Giotti, Virgilio 1885-1957 .... DLB-114
Giovanni, Nikki 1943- DLB-5, 41; CDALB-7
Gipson, Lawrence Henry 1880-1971 ..... DLB-17
Girard, Rodolphe 1879-1956 .... DLB-92
Giraudoux, Jean 1882-1944 .... DLB-65
Gissing, George 1857-1903 ...... DLB-18, 135, 184
The Place of Realism in Fiction (1895) DLB-18
Giudici, Giovanni 1924- DLB-128
Giuliani, Alfredo 1924- DLB-128
Glackens, William J. 1870-1938 ...... DLB-188
Gladstone, William Ewart
  1809-1898 .... DLB-57, 184

Glaeser, Ernst 1902-1963 . . . . .DLB-69	Goines, Donald 1937-1974 . . . . .DLB-33	Gordon, Adam Lindsay 1833-1870 . . . . . .DLB-230
Glancy, Diane 1941- DLB-175	Gold, Herbert 1924- DLB-2; Y-81	Gordon, Caroline
Glanville, Brian 1931- DLB-15, 139	Gold, Michael 1893-1967 . . . . .DLB-9, 28	1895-1981 . . . . . . .DLB-4, 9, 102; DS-17; Y-81
Glapthorne, Henry 1610-1643? DLB-58	Goldbarth, Albert 1948- DLB-120	Gordon, Giles 1940- DLB-14, 139, 207
Glasgow, Ellen 1873-1945 . . . . .DLB-9, 12	Goldberg, Dick 1947- DLB-7	Gordon, Helen Cameron, Lady Russell
Glasier, Katharine Bruce 1867-1950 . . . . .DLB-190	Golden Cockerel Press DLB-112	1867-1949 . . . . .DLB-195
Glaspell, Susan 1876-1948 . . . . . .DLB-7, 9, 78, 228	Golding, Arthur 1536-1606 . . . . .DLB-136	Gordon, Lyndall 1941- DLB-155
Glass, Montague 1877-1934 . . . . .DLB-11	Golding, Louis 1895-1958 . . . . .DLB-195	Gordon, Mary 1949- DLB-6; Y-81
Glassco, John 1909-1981 . . . . .DLB-68	Golding, William 1911-1993	Gordone, Charles 1925-1995 . . . . .DLB-7
Glauser, Friedrich 1896-1938 . . . . .DLB-56	. . . . DLB-15, 100, 255; Y-83; CDBLB-7	Gore, Catherine 1800-1861 . . . . .DLB-116
F. Gleason's Publishing Hall DLB-49	Goldman, Emma 1869-1940 . . . . .DLB-221	Gore-Booth, Eva 1870-1926 . . . . .DLB-240
Gleim, Johann Wilhelm Ludwig	Goldman, William 1931- DLB-44	Gores, Joe 1931- DLB-226
1719-1803 . . . . .DLB-97	Goldring, Douglas 1887-1960 . . . . .DLB-197	Gorey, Edward 1925-2000 . . . . .DLB-61
Glendinning, Victoria 1937- DLB-155	Goldsmith, Oliver 1730?-1774	Gorgias of Leontini
The Cult of Biography	. . . . DLB-39, 89, 104, 109, 142; CDBLB-2	circa 485 B.C.-376 B.C. DLB-176
Excerpts from the Second Folio Debate:	Goldsmith, Oliver 1794-1861 . . . . .DLB-99	Görres, Joseph 1776-1848 . . . . .DLB-90
"Biographies are generally a disease of	Goldsmith Publishing Company DLB-46	Gosse, Edmund 1849-1928 . . . . . DLB-57, 144, 184
English Literature" Y-86	Goldstein, Richard 1944- DLB-185	Gosson, Stephen 1554-1624 . . . . .DLB-172
Glidden, Frederick Dilley (Luke Short)	Gollancz, Sir Israel 1864-1930 . . . . .DLB-201	*The Schoole of Abuse* (1579) DLB-172
1908-1975 .DLB-256	Gollancz, Victor, Limited DLB-112	Gotlieb, Phyllis 1926- DLB-88
Glinka, Fedor Nikolaevich 1786-1880 . . . .DLB-205	Gombrowicz, Witold	Go-Toba 1180-1239 . . . . .DLB-203
Glover, Keith 1966- DLB-249	1904-1969 . . . . DLB-215; CDWLB-4	Gottfried von Straßburg
Glover, Richard 1712-1785 . . . . .DLB-95	Gómez-Quiñones, Juan 1942- DLB-122	died before 1230 . . . . DLB-138; CDWLB-2
Glück, Louise 1943- DLB-5	Gomme, Laurence James	Gotthelf, Jeremias 1797-1854 . . . . .DLB-133
Glyn, Elinor 1864-1943 . . . . .DLB-153	[publishing house] DLB-46	Gottschalk circa 804/808-869 . . . . .DLB-148
Gnedich, Nikolai Ivanovich 1784-1833 . . .DLB-205	Goncharov, Ivan Aleksandrovich	Gottsched, Johann Christoph
Gobineau, Joseph-Arthur de	1812-1891 .DLB-238	1700-1766 . . . . .DLB-97
1816-1882 .DLB-123	Goncourt, Edmond de 1822-1896 . . . . . . .DLB-123	Götz, Johann Nikolaus 1721-1781 . . . . . . .DLB-97
Godber, John 1956- DLB-233	Goncourt, Jules de 1830-1870 . . . . .DLB-123	Goudge, Elizabeth 1900-1984 . . . . .DLB-191
Godbout, Jacques 1933- DLB-53	Gonzales, Rodolfo "Corky" 1928- DLB-122	Gough, John B. 1817-1886 . . . . .DLB-243
Goddard, Morrill 1865-1937 . . . . .DLB-25	González, Angel 1925- DLB-108	Gould, Wallace 1882-1940 . . . . .DLB-54
Goddard, William 1740-1817 . . . . .DLB-43	Gonzalez, Genaro 1949- DLB-122	Govoni, Corrado 1884-1965 . . . . .DLB-114
Godden, Rumer 1907-1998 . . . . .DLB-161	Gonzalez, Ray 1952- DLB-122	Gower, John circa 1330-1408 . . . . .DLB-146
Godey, Louis A. 1804-1878 . . . . .DLB-73	Gonzales-Berry, Erlinda 1942- DLB-209	Goyen, William 1915-1983 . . . . .DLB-2, 218; Y-83
Godey and McMichael DLB-49	"Chicano Language" DLB-82	Goytisolo, José Augustín 1928- DLB-134
Godfrey, Dave 1938- DLB-60	González de Mireles, Jovita	Gozzano, Guido 1883-1916 . . . . .DLB-114
Godfrey, Thomas 1736-1763 . . . . .DLB-31	1899-1983 .DLB-122	Grabbe, Christian Dietrich 1801-1836 . . . .DLB-133
Godine, David R., Publisher DLB-46	González-T., César A. 1931- DLB-82	Gracq, Julien 1910- DLB-83
Godkin, E. L. 1831-1902 . . . . .DLB-79	Goodbye, Gutenberg? A Lecture at the	Grady, Henry W. 1850-1889 . . . . .DLB-23
Godolphin, Sidney 1610-1643 . . . . .DLB-126	New York Public Library,	Graf, Oskar Maria 1894-1967 . . . . .DLB-56
Godwin, Gail 1937- DLB-6, 234	18 April 1995, by Donald Lamm Y-95	*Graf Rudolf*
Godwin, M. J., and Company DLB-154	Goodis, David 1917-1967 . . . . .DLB-226	between circa 1170 and circa 1185 . . .DLB-148
Godwin, Mary Jane Clairmont	Goodison, Lorna 1947- DLB-157	Graff, Gerald 1937- DLB-246
1766-1841 .DLB-163	Goodman, Allegra 1967- DLB-244	Grafton, Richard [publishing house] DLB-170
Godwin, Parke 1816-1904 . . . . .DLB-3, 64	Goodman, Paul 1911-1972 . . . . .DLB-130, 246	Grafton, Sue 1940- DLB-226
Godwin, William 1756-1836	The Goodman Theatre DLB-7	Graham, Frank 1893-1965 . . . . .DLB-241
. . . . . . DLB-39, 104, 142, 158, 163; CDBLB-3	Goodrich, Frances 1891-1984 and	Graham, George Rex 1813-1894 . . . . .DLB-73
Preface to *St. Leon* (1799) DLB-39	Hackett, Albert 1900-1995 . . . . .DLB-26	Graham, Gwethalyn 1913-1965 . . . . .DLB-88
Goering, Reinhard 1887-1936 . . . . .DLB-118	Goodrich, Samuel Griswold	Graham, Jorie 1951- DLB-120
Goes, Albrecht 1908- DLB-69	1793-1860 . . . . .DLB-1, 42, 73, 243	Graham, Katharine 1917- DLB-127
Goethe, Johann Wolfgang von	Goodrich, S. G. [publishing house] DLB-49	Graham, Lorenz 1902-1989 . . . . .DLB-76
1749-1832 . . . . .DLB-94; CDWLB-2	Goodspeed, C. E., and Company DLB-49	Graham, Philip 1915-1963 . . . . .DLB-127
Goetz, Curt 1888-1960 . . . . .DLB-124	Goodwin, Stephen 1943- Y-82	Graham, R. B. Cunninghame
Goffe, Thomas circa 1592-1629 . . . . .DLB-58	Googe, Barnabe 1540-1594 . . . . .DLB-132	1852-1936 . . . . DLB-98, 135, 174
Goffstein, M. B. 1940- DLB-61	Gookin, Daniel 1612-1687 . . . . .DLB-24	Graham, Shirley 1896-1977 . . . . .DLB-76
Gogarty, Oliver St. John 1878-1957 . . . .DLB-15, 19	Goran, Lester 1928- DLB-244	Graham, Stephen 1884-1975 . . . . .DLB-195
Gogol, Nikolai Vasil'evich 1809-1852 . . . .DLB-198	Gordimer, Nadine 1923- DLB-225; Y-91	

Cumulative Index

Graham, W. S. 1918- DLB-20
Graham, William H. [publishing house]... DLB-49
Graham, Winston 1910- DLB-77
Grahame, Kenneth
  1859-1932 .... DLB-34, 141, 178
Grainger, Martin Allerdale 1874-1941 .... DLB-92
Gramatky, Hardie 1907-1979 .... DLB-22
Grand, Sarah 1854-1943......... DLB-135, 197
Grandbois, Alain 1900-1975 .... DLB-92
Grandson, Oton de circa 1345-1397..... DLB-208
Grange, John circa 1556-?............ DLB-136
Granich, Irwin (see Gold, Michael)
Granovsky, Timofei Nikolaevich
  1813-1855.................... DLB-198
Grant, Anne MacVicar 1755-1838 ...... DLB-200
Grant, Duncan 1885-1978................DS-10
Grant, George 1918-1988............. DLB-88
Grant, George Monro 1835-1902........ DLB-99
Grant, Harry J. 1881-1963 .... DLB-29
Grant, James Edward 1905-1966 .... DLB-26
Grass, Günter 1927- ...DLB-75, 124; CDWLB-2
Grasty, Charles H. 1863-1924 .... DLB-25
Grau, Shirley Ann 1929- DLB-2, 218
Graves, John 1920- Y-83
Graves, Richard 1715-1804............ DLB-39
Graves, Robert 1895-1985
  ....DLB-20, 100, 191; DS-18; Y-85; CDBLB-6
Gray, Alasdair 1934- DLB-194
Gray, Asa 1810-1888 .... DLB-1, 235
Gray, David 1838-1861 .... DLB-32
Gray, Simon 1936- DLB-13
Gray, Thomas 1716-1771 .... DLB-109; CDBLB-2
Grayson, Richard 1951- DLB-234
Grayson, William J. 1788-1863.... DLB-3, 64, 248
The Great Bibliographers Series............Y-93
The Great Modern Library Scam...........Y-98
The Great War and the Theater, 1914-1918
  [Great Britain] DLB-10
The Great War Exhibition and Symposium at
  the University of South Carolina........Y-97
Grech, Nikolai Ivanovich 1787-1867..... DLB-198
Greeley, Horace 1811-1872 .... DLB-3, 43, 189
Green, Adolph (see Comden, Betty)
Green, Anna Katharine
  1846-1935 .... DLB-202, 221
Green, Duff 1791-1875 .... DLB-43
Green, Elizabeth Shippen 1871-1954 .... DLB-188
Green, Gerald 1922- DLB-28
Green, Henry 1905-1973 .... DLB-15
Green, Jonas 1712-1767............... DLB-31
Green, Joseph 1706-1780.............. DLB-31
Green, Julien 1900-1998............ DLB-4, 72
Green, Paul 1894-1981....... DLB-7, 9, 249; Y-81
Green, T. and S. [publishing house]...... DLB-49
Green, Thomas Hill 1836-1882 .... DLB-190
Green, Timothy [publishing house]...... DLB-49

Greenaway, Kate 1846-1901 .... DLB-141
Greenberg: Publisher DLB-46
Green Tiger Press.................... DLB-46
Greene, Asa 1789-1838................ DLB-11
Greene, Belle da Costa 1883-1950 ...... DLB-187
Greene, Benjamin H.
  [publishing house] DLB-49
Greene, Graham 1904-1991
  ....DLB-13, 15, 77, 100, 162, 201, 204;
                           Y-85, Y-91; CDBLB-7
Greene, Robert 1558-1592 .... DLB-62, 167
Greene, Robert Bernard (Bob) Jr.
  1947- DLB-185
Greenfield, George 1917-2000 ....Y-00
Greenhow, Robert 1800-1854 .... DLB-30
Greenlee, William B. 1872-1953........ DLB-187
Greenough, Horatio 1805-1852 ...... DLB-1, 235
Greenwell, Dora 1821-1882 .... DLB-35, 199
Greenwillow Books DLB-46
Greenwood, Grace (see Lippincott, Sara Jane Clarke)
Greenwood, Walter 1903-1974...... DLB-10, 191
Greer, Ben 1948- DLB-6
Greflinger, Georg 1620?-1677.......... DLB-164
Greg, W. R. 1809-1881 .... DLB-55
Greg, W. W. 1875-1959 .... DLB-201
Gregg, Josiah 1806-1850......... DLB-183, 186
Gregg Press...................... DLB-46
Gregory, Isabella Augusta Persse, Lady
  1852-1932 .... DLB-10
Gregory, Horace 1898-1982........... DLB-48
Gregory of Rimini circa 1300-1358 ..... DLB-115
Gregynog Press DLB-112
Greiffenberg, Catharina Regina von
  1633-1694 .... DLB-168
Greig, Noël 1944- DLB-245
Grenfell, Wilfred Thomason
  1865-1940..................... DLB-92
Gress, Elsa 1919-1988 .... DLB-214
Greve, Felix Paul (see Grove, Frederick Philip)
Greville, Fulke, First Lord Brooke
  1554-1628 .... DLB-62, 172
Grey, Sir George, K.C.B. 1812-1898 .... DLB-184
Grey, Lady Jane 1537-1554 .... DLB-132
Grey Owl 1888-1938 .... DLB-92; DS-17
Grey, Zane 1872-1939 .... DLB-9, 212
Grey Walls Press DLB-112
Griboedov, Aleksandr Sergeevich
  1795?-1829..................... DLB-205
Grier, Eldon 1917- DLB-88
Grieve, C. M. (see MacDiarmid, Hugh)
Griffin, Bartholomew flourished 1596 ....DLB-172
Griffin, Gerald 1803-1840 .... DLB-159
The Griffin Poetry Prize..................Y-00
Griffith, Elizabeth 1727?-1793 .... DLB-39, 89
  Preface to *The Delicate Distress* (1769) DLB-39
Griffith, George 1857-1906...........DLB-178
Griffiths, Ralph [publishing house]...... DLB-154

Griffiths, Trevor 1935- DLB-13, 245
Griggs, S. C., and Company DLB-49
Griggs, Sutton Elbert 1872-1930......... DLB-50
Grignon, Claude-Henri 1894-1976....... DLB-68
Grigorovich, Dmitrii Vasil'evich
  1822-1899 .... DLB-238
Grigson, Geoffrey 1905- DLB-27
Grillparzer, Franz
  1791-1872............DLB-133; CDWLB-2
Grimald, Nicholas
  circa 1519-circa 1562 .... DLB-136
Grimké, Angelina Weld 1880-1958 ... DLB-50, 54
Grimké, Sarah Moore 1792-1873 .... DLB-239
Grimm, Hans 1875-1959 .... DLB-66
Grimm, Jacob 1785-1863 .... DLB-90
Grimm, Wilhelm
  1786-1859............. DLB-90; CDWLB-2
Grimmelshausen, Johann Jacob Christoffel von
  1621 or 1622-1676......DLB-168; CDWLB-2
Grimshaw, Beatrice Ethel 1871-1953 .....DLB-174
Grindal, Edmund 1519 or 1520-1583 ... DLB-132
Gripe, Maria (Kristina) 1923- DLB-257
Griswold, Rufus Wilmot 1815-1857.... DLB-3, 59
Grosart, Alexander Balloch 1827-1899... DLB-184
Gross, Milt 1895-1953 .... DLB-11
Grosset and Dunlap DLB-49
Grossman, Allen 1932- DLB-193
Grossman Publishers DLB-46
Grosseteste, Robert circa 1160-1253..... DLB-115
Grosvenor, Gilbert H. 1875-1966........ DLB-91
Groth, Klaus 1819-1899 .... DLB-129
Groulx, Lionel 1878-1967............. DLB-68
Grove, Frederick Philip 1879-1949...... DLB-92
Grove Press DLB-46
Grubb, Davis 1919-1980 .... DLB-6
Gruelle, Johnny 1880-1938............ DLB-22
von Grumbach, Argula
  1492-after 1563? DLB-179
Grymeston, Elizabeth
  before 1563-before 1604 .... DLB-136
Gryphius, Andreas
  1616-1664 ....DLB-164; CDWLB-2
Gryphius, Christian 1649-1706......... DLB-168
Guare, John 1938- DLB-7, 249
Guerra, Tonino 1920- DLB-128
Guest, Barbara 1920- DLB-5, 193
Guèvremont, Germaine 1893-1968 ...... DLB-68
Guidacci, Margherita 1921-1992 .... DLB-128
Guide to the Archives of Publishers, Journals,
  and Literary Agents in North American
  Libraries.........................Y-93
Guillén, Jorge 1893-1984 .... DLB-108
Guilloux, Louis 1899-1980............ DLB-72
Guilpin, Everard
  circa 1572-after 1608? DLB-136
Guiney, Louise Imogen 1861-1920 ...... DLB-54
Guiterman, Arthur 1871-1943 .... DLB-11

Günderrode, Caroline von 1780-1806 ....DLB-90

Gundulić, Ivan 1589-1638 ....DLB-147; CDWLB-4

Gunn, Bill 1934-1989..................DLB-38

Gunn, James E. 1923- DLB-8

Gunn, Neil M. 1891-1973 ....DLB-15

Gunn, Thom 1929- DLB-27; CDBLB-8

Gunnars, Kristjana 1948- DLB-60

Günther, Johann Christian 1695-1723 ....DLB-168

Gurik, Robert 1932- DLB-60

Gustafson, Ralph 1909- DLB-88

Gustafsson, Lars 1936- DLB-257

Gütersloh, Albert Paris 1887-1973 ....DLB-81

Guthrie, A. B., Jr. 1901-1991.........DLB-6, 212

Guthrie, Ramon 1896-1973 ....DLB-4

The Guthrie Theater DLB-7

Guthrie, Thomas Anstey (see Anstey, FC)

Gutzkow, Karl 1811-1878 ....DLB-133

Guy, Ray 1939- DLB-60

Guy, Rosa 1925- DLB-33

Guyot, Arnold 1807-1884 ....DS-13

Gwynne, Erskine 1898-1948 ....DLB-4

Gyles, John 1680-1755 ....DLB-99

Gyllensten, Lars 1921- DLB-257

Gysin, Brion 1916- DLB-16

H

H.D. (see Doolittle, Hilda)

Habermas, Jürgen 1929- DLB-242

Habington, William 1605-1654 ....DLB-126

Hacker, Marilyn 1942- DLB-120

Hackett, Albert (see Goodrich, Frances)

Hacks, Peter 1928- DLB-124

Hadas, Rachel 1948- DLB-120

Hadden, Briton 1898-1929 ....DLB-91

Hagedorn, Friedrich von 1708-1754......DLB-168

Hagelstange, Rudolf 1912-1984..........DLB-69

Haggard, H. Rider 1856-1925 ....DLB-70, 156, 174, 178

Haggard, William 1907-1993 ....Y-93

Hagy, Alyson 1960- DLB-244

Hahn-Hahn, Ida Gräfin von 1805-1880 ....DLB-133

Haig-Brown, Roderick 1908-1976 ....DLB-88

Haight, Gordon S. 1901-1985 ....DLB-103

Hailey, Arthur 1920- DLB-88; Y-82

Haines, John 1924- DLB-5, 212

Hake, Edward flourished 1566-1604.....DLB-136

Hake, Thomas Gordon 1809-1895 ....DLB-32

Hakluyt, Richard 1552?-1616 ....DLB-136

Halas, František 1901-1949 ....DLB-215

Halbe, Max 1865-1944 ....DLB-118

Halberstam, David 1934- DLB-241

Haldane, J. B. S. 1892-1964..........DLB-160

Haldeman, Joe 1943- DLB-8

Haldeman-Julius Company DLB-46

Haldone, Charlotte 1894-1969 ....DLB-191

Hale, E. J., and Son DLB-49

Hale, Edward Everett 1822-1909 ....DLB-1, 42, 74, 235

Hale, Janet Campbell 1946- DLB-175

Hale, Kathleen 1898- DLB-160

Hale, Leo Thomas (see Ebon)

Hale, Lucretia Peabody 1820-1900 ......DLB-42

Hale, Nancy 1908-1988 ....DLB-86; DS-17; Y-80, Y-88

Hale, Sarah Josepha (Buell) 1788-1879 ....DLB-1, 42, 73, 243

Hale, Susan 1833-1910 ....DLB-221

Hales, John 1584-1656................DLB-151

Halévy, Ludovic 1834-1908 ....DLB-192

Haley, Alex 1921-1992 ....DLB-38; CDALB-7

Haliburton, Thomas Chandler 1796-1865 ....DLB-11, 99

Hall, Anna Maria 1800-1881...........DLB-159

Hall, Donald 1928- DLB-5

Hall, Edward 1497-1547...............DLB-132

Hall, Halsey 1898-1977 ....DLB-241

Hall, James 1793-1868 ....DLB-73, 74

Hall, Joseph 1574-1656 ....DLB-121, 151

Hall, Radclyffe 1880-1943 ....DLB-191

Hall, Samuel [publishing house].......DLB-49

Hall, Sarah Ewing 1761-1830 ....DLB-200

Hall, Stuart 1932- DLB-242

Hallam, Arthur Henry 1811-1833.......DLB-32

On Some of the Characteristics of Modern Poetry and On the Lyrical Poems of Alfred Tennyson (1831) DLB-32

Halleck, Fitz-Greene 1790-1867 ....DLB-3

Haller, Albrecht von 1708-1777 ....DLB-168

Halliday, Brett (see Dresser, Davis)

Halliwell-Phillipps, James Orchard 1820-1889 ....DLB-184

Hallmann, Johann Christian 1640-1704 or 1716? DLB-168

Hallmark Editions DLB-46

Halper, Albert 1904-1984 ....DLB-9

Halperin, John William 1941- DLB-111

Halstead, Murat 1829-1908............DLB-23

Hamann, Johann Georg 1730-1788.......DLB-97

Hamburger, Michael 1924- DLB-27

Hamilton, Alexander 1712-1756........DLB-31

Hamilton, Alexander 1755?-1804.......DLB-37

Hamilton, Cicely 1872-1952 ....DLB-10, 197

Hamilton, Edmond 1904-1977...........DLB-8

Hamilton, Elizabeth 1758-1816 .....DLB-116, 158

Hamilton, Gail (see Corcoran, Barbara)

Hamilton, Gail (see Dodge, Mary Abigail)

Hamilton, Hamish, Limited............DLB-112

Hamilton, Ian 1938- DLB-40, 155

Hamilton, Janet 1795-1873............DLB-199

Hamilton, Mary Agnes 1884-1962 ......DLB-197

Hamilton, Patrick 1904-1962.......DLB-10, 191

Hamilton, Virginia 1936- DLB-33, 52

Hammett, Dashiell 1894-1961........DLB-226; DS-6; CDALB-5

The Glass Key and Other Dashiell Hammett Mysteries Y-96

Dashiell Hammett: An Appeal in TAC Y-91

Hammon, Jupiter 1711-died between 1790 and 1806.................DLB-31, 50

Hammond, John ?-1663................DLB-24

Hamner, Earl 1923- DLB-6

Hampson, John 1901-1955 ....DLB-191

Hampton, Christopher 1946- DLB-13

Handel-Mazzetti, Enrica von 1871-1955 ...DLB-81

Handke, Peter 1942- DLB-85, 124

Handlin, Oscar 1915- DLB-17

Hankin, St. John 1869-1909...........DLB-10

Hanley, Clifford 1922- DLB-14

Hanley, James 1901-1985 ....DLB-191

Hannah, Barry 1942- ....DLB 6, 234

Hannay, James 1827-1873 ....DLB-21

Hano, Arnold 1922- DLB-241

Hansberry, Lorraine 1930-1965 ....DLB-7, 38; CDALB-1

Hansen, Martin A. 1909-1955..........DLB-214

Hansen, Thorkild 1927-1989...........DLB-214

Hanson, Elizabeth 1684-1737..........DLB-200

Hapgood, Norman 1868-1937...........DLB-91

Happel, Eberhard Werner 1647-1690 ....DLB-168

The Harbinger 1845-1849 ....DLB-223

Harcourt Brace Jovanovich DLB-46

Hardenberg, Friedrich von (see Novalis)

Harding, Walter 1917- DLB-111

Hardwick, Elizabeth 1916- DLB-6

Hardy, Thomas 1840-1928 ....DLB-18, 19, 135; CDBLB-5

"Candour in English Fiction" (1890).......DLB-18

Hare, Cyril 1900-1958................DLB-77

Hare, David 1947- DLB-13

Hargrove, Marion 1919- DLB-11

Häring, Georg Wilhelm Heinrich (see Alexis, Willibald)

Harington, Donald 1935- DLB-152

Harington, Sir John 1560-1612 ....DLB-136

Harjo, Joy 1951- DLB-120, 175

Harkness, Margaret (John Law) 1854-1923 ....DLB-197

Harley, Edward, second Earl of Oxford 1689-1741 ....DLB-213

Harley, Robert, first Earl of Oxford 1661-1724 ....DLB-213

Harlow, Robert 1923- DLB-60

Harman, Thomas flourished 1566-1573 ..DLB-136

Harness, Charles L. 1915- DLB-8

Harnett, Cynthia 1893-1981 ....DLB-161

Harper, Edith Alice Mary (see Wickham, Anna)

Harper, Fletcher 1806-1877 .... DLB-79
Harper, Frances Ellen Watkins
   1825-1911................. DLB-50, 221
Harper, Michael S. 1938- DLB-41
Harper and Brothers................. DLB-49
Harpur, Charles 1813-1868 .... DLB-230
Harraden, Beatrice 1864-1943 .... DLB-153
Harrap, George G., and Company
   Limited..................... DLB-112
Harriot, Thomas 1560-1621........... DLB-136
Harris, Alexander 1805-1874 .... DLB-230
Harris, Benjamin ?-circa 1720........ DLB-42, 43
Harris, Christie 1907- DLB-88
Harris, Frank 1856-1931........... DLB-156, 197
Harris, George Washington
   1814-1869................. DLB-3, 11, 248
Harris, Joel Chandler
   1848-1908 .... DLB-11, 23, 42, 78, 91
Harris, Mark 1922- DLB-2; Y-80
Harris, Wilson 1921- DLB-117; CDWLB-3
Harrison, Mrs. Burton
   (see Harrison, Constance Cary)
Harrison, Charles Yale 1898-1954 .... DLB-68
Harrison, Constance Cary 1843-1920 ... DLB-221
Harrison, Frederic 1831-1923........ DLB-57, 190
   "On Style in English Prose" (1898) DLB-57
Harrison, Harry 1925- DLB-8
Harrison, James P., Company DLB-49
Harrison, Jim 1937- Y-82
Harrison, Mary St. Leger Kingsley
   (see Malet, Lucas)
Harrison, Paul Carter 1936- DLB-38
Harrison, Susan Frances 1859-1935 ...... DLB-99
Harrison, Tony 1937- DLB-40, 245
Harrison, William 1535-1593 .... DLB-136
Harrison, William 1933- DLB-234
Harrisse, Henry 1829-1910........... DLB-47
The Harry Ransom Humanities
   Research Center at the University
   of Texas at Austin Y-00
Harryman, Carla 1952- DLB-193
Harsdörffer, Georg Philipp 1607-1658 ... DLB-164
Harsent, David 1942- DLB-40
Hart, Albert Bushnell 1854-1943 .... DLB-17
Hart, Anne 1768-1834 .... DLB-200
Hart, Elizabeth 1771-1833............ DLB-200
Hart, Julia Catherine 1796-1867 .... DLB-99
The Lorenz Hart Centenary............... Y-95
Hart, Moss 1904-1961 .... DLB-7
Hart, Oliver 1723-1795 .... DLB-31
Hart-Davis, Rupert, Limited.......... DLB-112
Harte, Bret 1836-1902
   .... DLB-12, 64, 74, 79, 186; CDALB-3
Harte, Edward Holmead 1922- DLB-127
Harte, Houston Harriman 1927- DLB-127
Hartlaub, Felix 1913-1945 .... DLB-56
Hartleben, Otto Erich 1864-1905....... DLB-118

Hartley, L. P. 1895-1972.......... DLB-15, 139
Hartley, Marsden 1877-1943........... DLB-54
Hartling, Peter 1933- DLB-75
Hartman, Geoffrey H. 1929- DLB-67
Hartmann, Sadakichi 1867-1944........ DLB-54
Hartmann von Aue
   circa 1160-circa 1205 ... DLB-138; CDWLB-2
Harvey, Gabriel 1550?-1631 ...DLB-167, 213, 236
Harvey, Jean-Charles 1891-1967 .... DLB-88
Harvill Press Limited DLB-112
Harwood, Lee 1939- DLB-40
Harwood, Ronald 1934- DLB-13
Hašek, Jaroslav 1883-1923 .. DLB-215; CDWLB-4
Haskins, Charles Homer 1870-1937...... DLB-47
Haslam, Gerald 1937- DLB-212
Hass, Robert 1941- DLB-105, 206
Hasselstrom, Linda M. 1943- DLB-256
Hastings, Michael 1938- DLB-233
Hatar, Győző 1914- DLB-215
The Hatch-Billops Collection DLB-76
Hathaway, William 1944- DLB-120
Hauff, Wilhelm 1802-1827 .... DLB-90
A Haughty and Proud Generation (1922),
   by Ford Madox Hueffer........... DLB-36
Haugwitz, August Adolph von
   1647-1706..................... DLB-168
Hauptmann, Carl 1858-1921 ...... DLB-66, 118
Hauptmann, Gerhart
   1862-1946 ....DLB-66, 118; CDWLB-2
Hauser, Marianne 1910- Y-83
Havel, Václav 1936- DLB-232; CDWLB-4
Havergal, Frances Ridley 1836-1879 ... DLB-199
Hawes, Stephen 1475?-before 1529 ..... DLB-132
Hawker, Robert Stephen 1803-1875...... DLB-32
Hawkes, John
   1925-1998 .... DLB-2, 7, 227; Y-80, Y-98
John Hawkes: A Tribute Y-98
Hawkesworth, John 1720-1773 .... DLB-142
Hawkins, Sir Anthony Hope (see Hope, Anthony)
Hawkins, Sir John 1719-1789 ..... DLB-104, 142
Hawkins, Walter Everette 1883-?........ DLB-50
Hawthorne, Nathaniel
   1804-1864 ... DLB-1, 74, 183, 223; CDALB-2
Hawthorne, Nathaniel 1804-1864 and
   Hawthorne, Sophia Peabody
   1809-1871..................... DLB-183
Hawthorne, Sophia Peabody
   1809-1871................. DLB-183, 239
Hay, John 1835-1905 .... DLB-12, 47, 189
Hayashi, Fumiko 1903-1951.......... DLB-180
Haycox, Ernest 1899-1950 .... DLB-206
Haycraft, Anna Margaret (see Ellis, Alice Thomas)
Hayden, Robert
   1913-1980 .... DLB-5, 76; CDALB-1
Haydon, Benjamin Robert
   1786-1846..................... DLB-110
Hayes, John Michael 1919- DLB-26
Hayley, William 1745-1820 .... DLB-93, 142

Haym, Rudolf 1821-1901............ DLB-129
Hayman, Robert 1575-1629 .... DLB-99
Hayman, Ronald 1932- DLB-155
Hayne, Paul Hamilton
   1830-1886 .... DLB-3, 64, 79, 248
Hays, Mary 1760-1843 .... DLB-142, 158
Hayward, John 1905-1965 .... DLB-201
Haywood, Eliza 1693?-1756 .... DLB-39
From the Dedication, Lasselia (1723)...... DLB-39
From The Tea-Table................. DLB-39
From the Preface to The Disguis'd
   Prince (1723) DLB-39
Hazard, Willis P. [publishing house] DLB-49
Hazlitt, William 1778-1830......... DLB-110, 158
Hazzard, Shirley 1931- Y-82
Head, Bessie
   1937-1986......... DLB-117, 225; CDWLB-3
Headley, Joel T. 1813-1897 .. DLB-30, 183; DS-13
Heaney, Seamus
   1939- DLB-40; Y-95; CDBLB-8
Heard, Nathan C. 1936- DLB-33
Hearn, Lafcadio 1850-1904 ......DLB-12, 78, 189
Hearn, Mary Anne (Marianne Farningham,
   Eva Hope) 1834-1909 .... DLB-240
Hearne, John 1926- DLB-117
Hearne, Samuel 1745-1792 .... DLB-99
Hearne, Thomas 1678?-1735 .... DLB-213
Hearst, William Randolph 1863-1951 .... DLB-25
Hearst, William Randolph, Jr.
   1908-1993 ....DLB-127
Heartman, Charles Frederick
   1883-1953 ....DLB-187
Heath, Catherine 1924- DLB-14
Heath, James Ewell 1792-1862 .... DLB-248
Heath, Roy A. K. 1926- DLB-117
Heath-Stubbs, John 1918- DLB-27
Heavysege, Charles 1816-1876.......... DLB-99
Hebbel, Friedrich
   1813-1863 ....DLB-129; CDWLB-2
Hebel, Johann Peter 1760-1826 .... DLB-90
Heber, Richard 1774-1833 .... DLB-184
Hébert, Anne 1916-2000 .... DLB-68
Hébert, Jacques 1923- DLB-53
Hecht, Anthony 1923- DLB-5, 169
Hecht, Ben 1894-1964 ....DLB-7, 9, 25, 26, 28, 86
Hecker, Isaac Thomas 1819-1888 ..... DLB-1, 243
Hedge, Frederic Henry
   1805-1890 .... DLB-1, 59, 243
Hefner, Hugh M. 1926- DLB-137
Hegel, Georg Wilhelm Friedrich
   1770-1831..................... DLB-90
Heide, Robert 1939- DLB-249
Heidish, Marcy 1947- Y-82
Heißenbüttel, Helmut 1921-1996........ DLB-75
Heike monogatari................... DLB-203
Hein, Christoph 1944- DLB-124; CDWLB-2
Hein, Piet 1905-1996 .... DLB-214

Heine, Heinrich 1797-1856....DLB-90; CDWLB-2
Heinemann, Larry 1944- DS-9
Heinemann, William, Limited.........DLB-112
Heinesen, William 1900-1991 ....DLB-214
Heinlein, Robert A. 1907-1988............DLB-8
Heinrich Julius of Brunswick
    1564-1613 ....DLB-164
Heinrich von dem Türlîn
    flourished circa 1230..............DLB-138
Heinrich von Melk
    flourished after 1160..............DLB-148
Heinrich von Veldeke
    circa 1145-circa 1190...............DLB-138
Heinrich, Willi 1920- DLB-75
Heinse, Wilhelm 1746-1803.............DLB-94
Heinz, W. C. 1915- DLB-171
Heiskell, John 1872-1972 ....DLB-127
Hejinian, Lyn 1941- DLB-165
Heliand circa 850 ....DLB-148
Heller, Joseph
    1923-1999 .... DLB-2, 28, 227; Y-80, Y-99
Heller, Michael 1937- DLB-165
Hellman, Lillian 1906-1984 ..... DLB-7, 228; Y-84
Hellwig, Johann 1609-1674 ....DLB-164
Helprin, Mark 1947- Y-85; CDALB-7
Helwig, David 1938- DLB-60
Hemans, Felicia 1793-1835.............DLB-96
Hemenway, Abby Maria 1828-1890 .....DLB-243
Hemingway, Ernest 1899-1961
    ..... DLB-4, 9, 102, 210; Y-81, Y-87, Y-99;
    DS-1, DS-15, DS-16; CDALB-4
The Hemingway Centenary Celebration at the
    JFK Library........................ Y-99
Ernest Hemingway: A Centennial
    Celebration Y-99
The Ernest Hemingway Collection at the
    John F. Kennedy Library............ Y-99
Ernest Hemingway's Reaction to James Gould
    Cozzens............................ Y-98
Ernest Hemingway's Toronto Journalism
    Revisited: With Three Previously
    Unrecorded Stories................. Y-92
Falsifying Hemingway................. Y-96
Hemingway: Twenty-Five Years Later Y-85
Not Immediately Discernible . . . but Eventually
    Quite Clear: The *First Light* and *Final Years*
    of Hemingway's Centenary........... Y-99
Hemingway Salesmen's Dummies......... Y-00
Second International Hemingway Colloquium:
    Cuba............................... Y-98
Hémon, Louis 1880-1913 ....DLB-92
Hempel, Amy 1951- DLB-218
Hemphill, Paul 1936- Y-87
Hénault, Gilles 1920- DLB-88
Henchman, Daniel 1689-1761 ....DLB-24
Henderson, Alice Corbin 1881-1949 .....DLB-54
Henderson, Archibald 1877-1963.......DLB-103
Henderson, David 1942- DLB-41
Henderson, George Wylie 1904- DLB-51
Henderson, Zenna 1917-1983 ....DLB-8

Henisch, Peter 1943- DLB-85
Henley, Beth 1952- Y-86
Henley, William Ernest 1849-1903 ....DLB-19
Henning, Rachel 1826-1914............DLB-230
Henningsen, Agnes 1868-1962 ....DLB-214
Henniker, Florence 1855-1923..........DLB-135
Henry, Alexander 1739-1824............DLB-99
Henry, Buck 1930- DLB-26
Henry VIII of England 1491-1547 ......DLB-132
Henry of Ghent
    circa 1217-1229 - 1293.............DLB-115
Henry, Marguerite 1902-1997 ....DLB-22
Henry, O. (see Porter, William Sydney)
Henry, Robert Selph 1889-1970...........DLB-17
Henry, Will (see Allen, Henry W.)
Henryson, Robert
    1420s or 1430s-circa 1505..........DLB-146
Henschke, Alfred (see Klabund)
Hensley, Sophie Almon 1866-1946 ....DLB-99
Henson, Lance 1944- DLB-175
Henty, G. A. 1832?-1902............DLB-18, 141
Hentz, Caroline Lee 1800-1856.......DLB-3, 248
Heraclitus
    flourished circa 500 B.C........... DLB-176
Herbert, Agnes circa 1880-1960 ....DLB-174
Herbert, Alan Patrick 1890-1971 ..... DLB-10, 191
Herbert, Edward, Lord, of Cherbury
    1582-1648 ....DLB-121, 151
Herbert, Frank 1920-1986 ......DLB-8; CDALB-7
Herbert, George 1593-1633 . . .DLB-126; CDBLB-1
Herbert, Henry William 1807-1858.....DLB-3, 73
Herbert, John 1926- DLB-53
Herbert, Mary Sidney, Countess of Pembroke
    (see Sidney, Mary)
Herbert, Zbigniew
    1924-1998 ....DLB-232; CDWLB-4
Herbst, Josephine 1892-1969.............DLB-9
Herburger, Gunter 1932- DLB-75, 124
Hercules, Frank E. M. 1917-1996.......DLB-33
Herder, Johann Gottfried 1744-1803 ......DLB-97
Herder, B., Book Company.............DLB-49
Heredia, José-María de 1842-1905.......DLB-217
Herford, Charles Harold 1853-1931 .....DLB-149
Hergesheimer, Joseph 1880-1954......DLB-9, 102
Heritage Press DLB-46
Hermann the Lame 1013-1054 ....DLB-148
Hermes, Johann Timotheus
    1738-1821 ....DLB-97
Hermlin, Stephan 1915-1997 ....DLB-69
Hernández, Alfonso C. 1938- DLB-122
Hernández, Inés 1947- DLB-122
Hernández, Miguel 1910-1942..........DLB-134
Hernton, Calvin C. 1932- DLB-38
Herodotus circa 484 B.C.-circa 420 B.C.
    .... DLB-176; CDWLB-1
Heron, Robert 1764-1807 ....DLB-142
Herr, Michael 1940- DLB-185

Herrera, Juan Felipe 1948- DLB-122
Herrick, E. R., and Company DLB-49
Herrick, Robert 1591-1674 ....DLB-126
Herrick, Robert 1868-1938 .... DLB-9, 12, 78
Herrick, William 1915- Y-83
Herrmann, John 1900-1959..............DLB-4
Hersey, John 1914-1993 ...DLB-6, 185; CDALB-7
Hertel, François 1905-1985 ....DLB-68
Hervé-Bazin, Jean Pierre Marie (see Bazin, Hervé)
Hervey, John, Lord 1696-1743 ....DLB-101
Herwig, Georg 1817-1875 ....DLB-133
Herzog, Emile Salomon Wilhelm
    (see Maurois, André)
Hesiod eighth century B.C.............DLB-176
Hesse, Hermann
    1877-1962 ....DLB-66; CDWLB-2
Hessus, Helius Eobanus 1488-1540......DLB-179
Hewat, Alexander circa 1743-circa 1824 ...DLB-30
Hewitt, John 1907- DLB-27
Hewlett, Maurice 1861-1923 ....DLB-34, 156
Heyen, William 1940- DLB-5
Heyer, Georgette 1902-1974 .... DLB 77, 191
Heym, Stefan 1913- DLB-69
Heyse, Paul 1830-1914 ....DLB-129
Heytesbury, William
    circa 1310-1372 or 1373............DLB-115
Heyward, Dorothy 1890-1961.........DLB-7, 249
Heyward, DuBose 1885-1940 ... DLB-7, 9, 45, 249
Heywood, John 1497?-1580?...........DLB-136
Heywood, Thomas
    1573 or 1574-1641.................DLB-62
Hibbs, Ben 1901-1975 ....DLB-137
Hichens, Robert S. 1864-1950 ....DLB-153
Hickey, Emily 1845-1924 ....DLB-199
Hickman, William Albert 1877-1957 .....DLB-92
Hicks, Granville 1901-1982............DLB-246
Hidalgo, José Luis 1919-1947 ....DLB-108
Hiebert, Paul 1892-1987 ....DLB-68
Hieng, Andrej 1925- DLB-181
Hierro, José 1922- DLB-108
Higgins, Aidan 1927- DLB-14
Higgins, Colin 1941-1988 ....DLB-26
Higgins, George V.
    1939-1999 ....DLB-2; Y-81, Y-98, Y-99
George V. Higgins to Julian Symons........ Y-99
Higginson, Thomas Wentworth
    1823-1911 ....DLB-1, 64, 243
Highwater, Jamake 1942?- DLB-52; Y-85
Hijuelos, Oscar 1951- DLB-145
Hildegard von Bingen 1098-1179........DLB-148
Das Hildesbrandslied
    circa 820 ....DLB-148; CDWLB-2
Hildesheimer, Wolfgang
    1916-1991 ....DLB-69, 124
Hildreth, Richard 1807-1865 ...DLB-1, 30, 59, 235
Hill, Aaron 1685-1750 ....DLB-84
Hill, Geoffrey 1932- DLB-40; CDBLB-8

339

Hill, George M., Company............DLB-49
Hill, "Sir" John 1714?-1775............DLB-39
Hill, Lawrence, and Company,
  Publishers......................DLB-46
Hill, Leslie 1880-1960................DLB-51
Hill, Susan 1942-...............DLB-14, 139
Hill, Walter 1942-...................DLB-44
Hill and Wang......................DLB-46
Hillberry, Conrad 1928-...............DLB-120
Hillerman, Tony 1925-................DLB-206
Hilliard, Gray and Company...........DLB-49
Hills, Lee 1906-.....................DLB-127
Hillyer, Robert 1895-1961.............DLB-54
Hilton, James 1900-1954...........DLB-34, 77
Hilton, Walter died 1396.............DLB-146
Hilton and Company.................DLB-49
Himes, Chester 1909-1984....DLB-2, 76, 143, 226
Hindmarsh, Joseph [publishing house]....DLB-170
Hine, Daryl 1936-...................DLB-60
Hingley, Ronald 1920-................DLB-155
Hinojosa-Smith, Rolando 1929-........DLB-82
Hinton, S. E. 1948-.................CDALB-7
Hippel, Theodor Gottlieb von
  1741-1796.......................DLB-97
Hippocrates of Cos flourished circa 425 B.C.
  ....DLB-176; CDWLB-1
Hirabayashi, Taiko 1905-1972.........DLB-180
Hirsch, E. D., Jr. 1928-...............DLB-67
Hirsch, Edward 1950-................DLB-120
Hoagland, Edward 1932-...............DLB-6
Hoagland, Everett H., III 1942-........DLB-41
Hoban, Russell 1925-............DLB-52; Y-90
Hobbes, Thomas 1588-1679............DLB-151
Hobby, Oveta 1905-..................DLB-127
Hobby, William 1878-1964............DLB-127
Hobsbaum, Philip 1932-...............DLB-40
Hobson, Laura Z. 1900-...............DLB-28
Hobson, Sarah 1947-.................DLB-204
Hoby, Thomas 1530-1566.............DLB-132
Hoccleve, Thomas
  circa 1368-circa 1437..............DLB-146
Hochhuth, Rolf 1931-................DLB-124
Hochman, Sandra 1936-................DLB-5
Hocken, Thomas Morland
  1836-1910.......................DLB-184
Hodder and Stoughton, Limited........DLB-106
Hodgins, Jack 1938-..................DLB-60
Hodgman, Helen 1945-................DLB-14
Hodgskin, Thomas 1787-1869..........DLB-158
Hodgson, Ralph 1871-1962.............DLB-19
Hodgson, William Hope
  1877-1918..........DLB-70, 153, 156, 178
Hoe, Robert III 1839-1909.............DLB-187
Hoeg, Peter 1957-...................DLB-214
Højholt, Per 1928-...................DLB-214
Hoffenstein, Samuel 1890-1947.........DLB-11

Hoffman, Charles Fenno 1806-1884........DLB-3
Hoffman, Daniel 1923-.................DLB-5
Hoffmann, E. T. A.
  1776-1822.............DLB-90; CDWLB-2
Hoffman, Frank B. 1888-1958...........DLB-188
Hoffman, William 1925-...............DLB-234
Hoffmanswaldau, Christian Hoffman von
  1616-1679........................DLB-168
Hofmann, Michael 1957-...............DLB-40
Hofmannsthal, Hugo von
  1874-1929............DLB-81, 118; CDWLB-2
Hofstadter, Richard 1916-1970.......DLB-17, 246
Hogan, Desmond 1950-................DLB-14
Hogan, Linda 1947-..................DLB-175
Hogan and Thompson.................DLB-49
Hogarth Press......................DLB-112
Hogg, James 1770-1835........DLB-93, 116, 159
Hohberg, Wolfgang Helmhard Freiherr von
  1612-1688.......................DLB-168
von Hohenheim, Philippus Aureolus
  Theophrastus Bombastus (see Paracelsus)
Hohl, Ludwig 1904-1980...............DLB-56
Holbrook, David 1923-.............DLB-14, 40
Holcroft, Thomas 1745-1809....DLB-39, 89, 158
  Preface to *Alwyn* (1780)..............DLB-39
Holden, Jonathan 1941-................DLB-105
  "Contemporary Verse Story-telling"....DLB-105
Holden, Molly 1927-1981...............DLB-40
Hölderlin, Friedrich 1770-1843 DLB-90; CDWLB-2
Holiday House......................DLB-46
Holinshed, Raphael died 1580.........DLB-167
Holland, J. G. 1819-1881...............DS-13
Holland, Norman N. 1927-.............DLB-67
Hollander, John 1929-..................DLB-5
Holley, Marietta 1836-1926.............DLB-11
Hollinghurst, Alan 1954-..............DLB-207
Hollingsworth, Margaret 1940-.........DLB-60
Hollo, Anselm 1934-..................DLB-40
Holloway, Emory 1885-1977...........DLB-103
Holloway, John 1920-.................DLB-27
Holloway House Publishing Company...DLB-46
Holme, Constance 1880-1955...........DLB-34
Holmes, Abraham S. 1821?-1908........DLB-99
Holmes, John Clellon 1926-1988.....DLB-16, 237
  "Four Essays on the Beat Generation"....DLB-16
Holmes, Mary Jane 1825-1907.....DLB-202, 221
Holmes, Oliver Wendell
  1809-1894......DLB-1, 189, 235; CDALB-2
Holmes, Richard 1945-...............DLB-155
The Cult of Biography
  Excerpts from the Second Folio Debate:
  "Biographies are generally a disease of
  English Literature"...................Y-86
Holmes, Thomas James 1874-1959......DLB-187
Holroyd, Michael 1935-.........DLB-155; Y-99
Holst, Hermann E. von 1841-1904......DLB-47
Holt, Henry, and Company............DLB-49

Holt, John 1721-1784.................DLB-43
Holt, Rinehart and Winston............DLB-46
Holtby, Winifred 1898-1935...........DLB-191
Holthusen, Hans Egon 1913-...........DLB-69
Hölty, Ludwig Christoph Heinrich
  1748-1776.......................DLB-94
Holub, Miroslav
  1923-1998............DLB-232; CDWLB-4
Holz, Arno 1863-1929................DLB-118
Home, Henry, Lord Kames
  (see Kames, Henry Home, Lord)
Home, John 1722-1808................DLB-84
Home, William Douglas 1912-..........DLB-13
Home Publishing Company............DLB-49
Homer circa eighth-seventh centuries B.C.
  ....DLB-176; CDWLB-1
Homer, Winslow 1836-1910...........DLB-188
Homes, Geoffrey (see Mainwaring, Daniel)
Honan, Park 1928-..................DLB-111
Hone, William 1780-1842.........DLB-110, 158
Hongo, Garrett Kaoru 1951-...........DLB-120
Honig, Edwin 1919-...................DLB-5
Hood, Hugh 1928-...................DLB-53
Hood, Mary 1946-..................DLB-234
Hood, Thomas 1799-1845.............DLB-96
Hook, Theodore 1788-1841...........DLB-116
Hooker, Jeremy 1941-................DLB-40
Hooker, Richard 1554-1600...........DLB-132
Hooker, Thomas 1586-1647............DLB-24
hooks, bell 1952-...................DLB-246
Hooper, Johnson Jones
  1815-1862.................DLB-3, 11, 248
Hope, Anthony 1863-1933........DLB-153, 156
Hope, Christopher 1944-.............DLB-225
Hope, Eva (see Hearn, Mary Anne)
Hope, Laurence (Adela Florence
  Cory Nicolson) 1865-1904..........DLB-240
Hopkins, Ellice 1836-1904............DLB-190
Hopkins, Gerard Manley
  1844-1889..........DLB-35, 57; CDBLB-5
Hopkins, John (see Sternhold, Thomas)
Hopkins, John H., and Son.............DLB-46
Hopkins, Lemuel 1750-1801............DLB-37
Hopkins, Pauline Elizabeth 1859-1930....DLB-50
Hopkins, Samuel 1721-1803............DLB-31
Hopkinson, Francis 1737-1791..........DLB-31
Hopkinson, Nalo 1960-...............DLB-251
Hopper, Nora (Mrs. Nora Chesson)
  1871-1906......................DLB-240
Hoppin, Augustus 1828-1896..........DLB-188
Hora, Josef 1891-1945.........DLB-215; CDWLB-4
Horace 65 B.C.-8 B.C......DLB-211; CDWLB-1
Horgan, Paul 1903-1995......DLB-102, 212; Y-85
Horizon Press......................DLB-46
Hornby, C. H. St. John 1867-1946......DLB-201
Hornby, Nick 1957-.................DLB-207
Horne, Frank 1899-1974...............DLB-51

Horne, Richard Henry (Hengist) 1802 or 1803-1884 . . . . DLB-32	Hrabanus Maurus 776?-856. . . . . DLB-148	Hunt, Leigh 1784-1859 . . . . DLB-96, 110, 144
Horney, Karen 1885-1952. . . . . DLB-246	Hronský, Josef Cíger 1896-1960 . . . . DLB-215	Hunt, Violet 1862-1942. . . . . DLB-162, 197
Hornung, E. W. 1866-1921. . . . . DLB-70	Hrotsvit of Gandersheim circa 935-circa 1000. . . . . DLB-148	Hunt, William Gibbes 1791-1833 . . . . DLB-73
Horovitz, Israel 1939- DLB-7	Hubbard, Elbert 1856-1915. . . . . DLB-91	Hunter, Evan 1926- Y-82
Horton, George Moses 1797?-1883? DLB-50	Hubbard, Kin 1868-1930. . . . . DLB-11	Hunter, Jim 1939- DLB-14
Horváth, Ödön von 1901-1938 . . . . . . DLB-85, 124	Hubbard, William circa 1621-1704 . . . . DLB-24	Hunter, Kristin 1931- DLB-33
Horwood, Harold 1923- DLB-60	Huber, Therese 1764-1829 . . . . DLB-90	Hunter, Mollie 1922- DLB-161
Hosford, E. and E. [publishing house]. DLB-49	Huch, Friedrich 1873-1913 . . . . DLB-66	Hunter, N. C. 1908-1971. . . . . DLB-10
Hoskens, Jane Fenn 1693-1770?. DLB-200	Huch, Ricarda 1864-1947 . . . . DLB-66	Hunter-Duvar, John 1821-1899. . . . . DLB-99
Hoskyns, John 1566-1638 . . . . DLB-121	Huck at 100: How Old Is Huckleberry Finn? Y-85	Huntington, Henry E. 1850-1927. . . . . . . DLB-140
Hosokawa Yūsai 1535-1610. . . . . DLB-203	Huddle, David 1942- DLB-130	Huntington, Susan Mansfield 1791-1823 . . . . DLB-200
Hostovský, Egon 1908-1973 . . . . DLB-215	Hudgins, Andrew 1951- DLB-120	Hurd and Houghton DLB-49
Hotchkiss and Company. DLB-49	Hudson, Henry Norman 1814-1886 . . . . . . DLB-64	Hurst, Fannie 1889-1968 . . . . DLB-86
Hough, Emerson 1857-1923. . . . . DLB-9, 212	Hudson, Stephen 1868?-1944 . . . . DLB-197	Hurst and Blackett. DLB-106
Houghton, Stanley 1881-1913 . . . . DLB-10	Hudson, W. H. 1841-1922 . . . . DLB-98, 153, 174	Hurst and Company DLB-49
Houghton Mifflin Company DLB-49	Hudson and Goodwin. DLB-49	Hurston, Zora Neale 1901?-1960 . . . . DLB-51, 86; CDALB-7
Household, Geoffrey 1900-1988 . . . . DLB-87	Huebsch, B. W. [publishing house]. DLB-46	Husson, Jules-François-Félix (see Champfleury)
Housman, A. E. 1859-1936 . . . DLB-19; CDBLB-5	Oral History: B. W. Huebsch Y-99	Huston, John 1906-1987 . . . . DLB-26
Housman, Laurence 1865-1959. . . . . DLB-10	Hueffer, Oliver Madox 1876-1931. . . . . . . DLB-197	Hutcheson, Francis 1694-1746. . . . . DLB-31
Houston, Pam 1962- DLB-244	Hugh of St. Victor circa 1096-1141 . . . . . . DLB-208	Hutchinson, Ron 1947- DLB-245
Houwald, Ernst von 1778-1845 . . . . DLB-90	Hughes, David 1930- DLB-14	Hutchinson, R. C. 1907-1975. . . . . DLB-191
Hovey, Richard 1864-1900 . . . . DLB-54	Hughes, Dusty 1947- DLB-233	Hutchinson, Thomas 1711-1780 . . . . DLB-30, 31
Howard, Donald R. 1927-1987 . . . . DLB-111	Hughes, Hatcher 1881-1945 . . . . DLB-249	
Howard, Maureen 1930- Y-83	Hughes, John 1677-1720. . . . . DLB-84	Hutchinson and Company (Publishers) Limited DLB-112
Howard, Richard 1929- DLB-5	Hughes, Langston 1902-1967 . . . . DLB-4, 7, 48, 51, 86, 228; CDALB-5	Hutton, Richard Holt 1826-1897. . . . . DLB-57
Howard, Roy W. 1883-1964 . . . . DLB-29	Hughes, Richard 1900-1976. . . . . DLB-15, 161	von Hutton, Ulrich 1488-1523 . . . . DLB-179
Howard, Sidney 1891-1939 . . . . . . DLB-7, 26, 249	Hughes, Ted 1930-1998 . . . . DLB-40, 161	Huxley, Aldous 1894-1963 . . . . . . DLB-36, 100, 162, 195, 255; CDBLB-6
Howard, Thomas, second Earl of Arundel 1585-1646 . . . . DLB-213	Hughes, Thomas 1822-1896 . . . . DLB-18, 163	Huxley, Elspeth Josceline 1907-1997 . . . . DLB-77, 204
Howe, E. W. 1853-1937 . . . . DLB-12, 25	Hugo, Richard 1923-1982 . . . . DLB-5, 206	
Howe, Henry 1816-1893 . . . . DLB-30	Hugo, Victor 1802-1885 . . . . . . DLB-119, 192, 217	Huxley, T. H. 1825-1895 . . . . DLB-57
Howe, Irving 1920-1993 . . . . DLB-67	Hugo Awards and Nebula Awards DLB-8	Huyghue, Douglas Smith 1816-1891. . . . . DLB-99
Howe, Joseph 1804-1873 . . . . DLB-99	Hull, Richard 1896-1973 . . . . DLB-77	Huysmans, Joris-Karl 1848-1907 . . . . DLB-123
Howe, Julia Ward 1819-1910 . . . . DLB-1, 189, 235	Hulme, T. E. 1883-1917 . . . . DLB-19	Hwang, David Henry 1957- DLB-212, 228
Howe, Percival Presland 1886-1944 . . . . . DLB-149	Hulton, Anne ?-1779? DLB-200	Hyde, Donald 1909-1966 and Hyde, Mary 1912- DLB-187
Howe, Susan 1937- DLB-120	Humboldt, Alexander von 1769-1859 . . . . . DLB-90	
Howell, Clark, Sr. 1863-1936 . . . . DLB-25	Humboldt, Wilhelm von 1767-1835. . . . . . . DLB-90	Hyman, Trina Schart 1939- DLB-61
Howell, Evan P. 1839-1905 . . . . DLB-23	Hume, David 1711-1776. . . . . DLB-104	**I**
Howell, James 1594?-1666 . . . . DLB-151	Hume, Fergus 1859-1932. . . . . DLB-70	
Howell, Soskin and Company DLB-46	Hume, Sophia 1702-1774 . . . . DLB-200	Iavorsky, Stefan 1658-1722 . . . . DLB-150
Howell, Warren Richardson 1912-1984 . . . . DLB-140	Hume-Rothery, Mary Catherine 1824-1885 . . . . DLB-240	Iazykov, Nikolai Mikhailovich 1803-1846. DLB-205
Howells, William Dean 1837-1920 . . . . DLB-12, 64, 74, 79, 189; CDALB-3	Humishuma (see Mourning Dove)	Ibáñez, Armando P. 1949- DLB-209
	Hummer, T. R. 1950- DLB-120	Ibn Bajja circa 1077-1138 . . . . DLB-115
Introduction to Paul Laurence Dunbar, Lyrics of Lowly Life (1896). DLB-50	Humorous Book Illustration DLB-11	Ibn Gabirol, Solomon circa 1021-circa 1058. . . . . DLB-115
Howitt, Mary 1799-1888 . . . . DLB-110, 199	Humphrey, Duke of Gloucester 1391-1447 . . . . DLB-213	Ibuse, Masuji 1898-1993 . . . . DLB-180
Howitt, William 1792-1879 and Howitt, Mary 1799-1888. . . . . DLB-110	Humphrey, William 1924-1997 . . . DLB-6, 212, 234	Ichijō Kanera (see Ichijō Kaneyoshi)
Hoyem, Andrew 1935- DLB-5	Humphreys, David 1752-1818. . . . . DLB-37	Ichijō Kaneyoshi (Ichijō Kanera) 1402-1481 . . . . DLB-203
Hoyers, Anna Ovena 1584-1655 . . . . DLB-164	Humphreys, Emyr 1919- DLB-15	
Hoyos, Angela de 1940- DLB-82	Huncke, Herbert 1915-1996 . . . . DLB-16	The Iconography of Science-Fiction Art DLB-8
Hoyt, Henry [publishing house] DLB-49	Huneker, James Gibbons 1857-1921 . . . . . . DLB-71	Iffland, August Wilhelm 1759-1814. . . . . . . DLB-94
Hoyt, Palmer 1897-1979. . . . . DLB-127	Hunold, Christian Friedrich 1681-1721 . . . DLB-168	
Hrabal, Bohumil 1914-1997 . . . . DLB-232	Hunt, Irene 1907- DLB-52	Ignatow, David 1914-1997 . . . . .DLB-5

Cumulative Index

Ike, Chukwuemeka 1931- DLB-157
Ikkyū Sōjun 1394-1481............... DLB-203
Iles, Francis (see Berkeley, Anthony)
Illich, Ivan 1926- DLB-242
The Illustration of Early German Literar
   Manuscripts, circa 1150-circa 1300 .. DLB-148
Illyés, Gyula 1902-1983 .... DLB-215; CDWLB-4
Imbs, Bravig 1904-1946 .... DLB-4
Imbuga, Francis D. 1947- DLB-157
Immermann, Karl 1796-1840 .... DLB-133
Inchbald, Elizabeth 1753-1821 .... DLB-39, 89
Inge, William 1913-1973... DLB-7, 249; CDALB-1
Ingelow, Jean 1820-1897............ DLB-35, 163
Ingersoll, Ralph 1900-1985........... DLB-127
The Ingersoll Prizes Y-84
Ingoldsby, Thomas (see Barham, Richard Harris)
Ingraham, Joseph Holt 1809-1860 .... DLB-3, 248
Inman, John 1805-1850 .... DLB-73
Innerhofer, Franz 1944- DLB-85
Innis, Harold Adams 1894-1952........ DLB-88
Innis, Mary Quayle 1899-1972......... DLB-88
Inō Sōgi 1421-1502.................. DLB-203
Inoue Yasushi 1907-1991 .... DLB-181
International Publishers Company DLB-46
Interviews:
   Anastas, Benjamin Y-98
   Baker, Nicholson Y-00
   Bank, Melissa Y-98
   Bernstein, Harriet.................... Y-82
   Betts, Doris.......................... Y-82
   Bosworth, David....................... Y-82
   Bottoms, David........................ Y-83
   Bowers, Fredson Y-80
   Burnshaw, Stanley Y-97
   Carpenter, Humphrey Y-84, Y-99
   Carr, Virginia Spencer Y-00
   Carver, Raymond....................... Y-83
   Cherry, Kelly Y-83
   Coppel, Alfred Y-83
   Cowley, Malcolm....................... Y-81
   Davis, Paxton......................... Y-89
   De Vries, Peter Y-82
   Dickey, James......................... Y-82
   Donald, David Herbert................. Y-87
   Ellroy, James Y-91
   Fancher, Betsy Y-83
   Faust, Irvin.......................... Y-00
   Fulton, Len Y-86
   Garrett, George....................... Y-83
   Greenfield, George Y-91
   Griffin, Bryan Y-81
   Guilds, John Caldwell................. Y-92
   Hardin, James......................... Y-92
   Harrison, Jim......................... Y-82

Hazzard, Shirley...................... Y-82
Higgins, George V..................... Y-98
Hoban, Russell Y-90
Holroyd, Michael Y-99
Horowitz, Glen........................ Y-90
Jakes, John Y-83
Jenkinson, Edward B................... Y-82
Jenks, Tom Y-86
Kaplan, Justin Y-86
King, Florence Y-85
Klopfer, Donald S..................... Y-97
Krug, Judith Y-82
Lamm, Donald Y-95
Laughlin, James Y-96
Lindsay, Jack Y-84
Mailer, Norman Y-97
Manchester, William Y-85
McCormack, Thomas Y-98
McNamara, Katherine Y-97
Mellen, Joan Y-94
Menaher, Daniel....................... Y-97
Mooneyham, Lamarr Y-82
Nosworth, David Y-82
O'Connor, Patrick Y-84, Y-99
Ozick, Cynthia Y-83
Penner, Jonathan Y-83
Pennington, Lee Y-82
Penzler, Otto......................... Y-96
Plimpton, George Y-99
Potok, Chaim Y-84
Prescott, Peter S..................... Y-86
Rabe, David Y-91
Rallyson, Carl........................ Y-97
Rechy, John Y-82
Reid, B. L. Y-83
Reynolds, Michael Y-95, Y-99
Schlafly, Phyllis..................... Y-82
Schroeder, Patricia Y-99
Schulberg, Budd....................... Y-81
Scribner, Charles III................. Y-94
Sipper, Ralph Y-94
Staley, Thomas F...................... Y-00
Styron, William Y-80
Toth, Susan Allen..................... Y-86
Tyler, Anne Y-82
Vaughan, Samuel Y-97
Von Ogtrop, Kristin Y-92
Wallenstein, Barry Y-92
Weintraub, Stanley.................... Y-82
Williams, J. Chamberlain Y-84
Editors, Conversations with Y-95
Interviews on E-Publishing............ Y-00
Irving, John 1942- DLB-6; Y-82

Irving, Washington 1783-1859
   .... DLB-3, 11, 30, 59, 73, 74,
                      183, 186; CDALB-2
Irwin, Grace 1907- DLB-68
Irwin, Will 1873-1948................. DLB-25
Isaksson, Ulla 1916-2000 .... DLB-257
Iser, Wolfgang 1926- DLB-242
Isherwood, Christopher
   1904-1986 .... DLB-15, 195; Y-86
The Christopher Isherwood Archive,
   The Huntington Library Y-99
Ishiguro, Kazuo
   1954- DLB-194
Ishikawa Jun
   1899-1987 .... DLB-182
The Island Trees Case: A Symposium on
   School Library Censorship
   An Interview with Judith Krug
   An Interview with Phyllis Schlafly
   An Interview with Edward B. Jenkinson
   An Interview with Lamarr Mooneyham
   An Interview with Harriet Bernstein Y-82
Islas, Arturo
   1938-1991 .... DLB-122
Issit, Debbie 1966- DLB-233
Ivanišević, Drago
   |1907-1981 .... DLB-181
Ivaska, Astrīde 1926- DLB-232
Ivers, M. J., and Company............ DLB-49
Iwaniuk, Wacław 1915- DLB-215
Iwano, Hōmei 1873-1920 .... DLB-180
Iwaszkiewicz, Jarosłav 1894-1980....... DLB-215
Iyayi, Festus 1947- DLB-157
Izumi, Kyōka 1873-1939............... DLB-180

J

Jackmon, Marvin E. (see Marvin X)
Jacks, L. P. 1860-1955 .... DLB-135
Jackson, Angela 1951- DLB-41
Jackson, Charles 1903-1968 .... DLB-234
Jackson, Helen Hunt
   1830-1885 .... DLB-42, 47, 186, 189
Jackson, Holbrook 1874-1948.......... DLB-98
Jackson, Laura Riding 1901-1991........ DLB-48
Jackson, Shirley
   1916-1965 .... DLB-6, 234; CDALB-1
Jacob, Naomi 1884?-1964............. DLB-191
Jacob, Piers Anthony Dillingham
   (see Anthony, Piers)
Jacob, Violet 1863-1946 .... DLB-240
Jacobi, Friedrich Heinrich 1743-1819 ..... DLB-94
Jacobi, Johann Georg 1740-1841......... DLB-97
Jacobs, George W., and Company....... DLB-49
Jacobs, Harriet 1813-1897............. DLB-239
Jacobs, Joseph 1854-1916 .... DLB-141
Jacobs, W. W. 1863-1943............... DLB-135
Jacobsen, Jørgen-Frantz 1900-1938...... DLB-214
Jacobsen, Josephine 1908- DLB-244
Jacobson, Dan 1929- DLB-14, 207, 225
Jacobson, Howard 1942- DLB-207

Jacques de Vitry circa 1160/1170-1240 ...DLB-208
Jæger, Frank 1926-1977 ....DLB-214
Jaggard, William [publishing house] DLB-170
Jahier, Piero 1884-1966 ....DLB-114
Jahnn, Hans Henny 1894-1959 ....DLB-56, 124
Jakes, John 1932- Y-83
Jakobson, Roman 1896-1982..........DLB-242
James, Alice 1848-1892 ....DLB-221
James, C. L. R. 1901-1989 ....DLB-125
James, George P. R. 1801-1860 ....DLB-116
James, Henry 1843-1916
......DLB-12, 71, 74, 189; DS-13; CDALB-3
James, John circa 1633-1729............DLB-24
James, M. R. 1862-1936...........DLB-156, 201
James, Naomi 1949- DLB-204
James, P. D. 1920- DLB-87; DS-17; CDBLB-8
James VI of Scotland, I of England
1566-1625 ....DLB-151, 172
*Ane Schort Treatise Conteining Some Revlis
and Cautelis to Be Obseruit and Eschewit
in Scottis Poesi* (1584).................DLB-172
James, Thomas 1572?-1629.............DLB-213
James, U. P. [publishing house] DLB-49
James, Will 1892-1942...................DS-16
Jameson, Anna 1794-1860 ....DLB-99, 166
Jameson, Fredric 1934- DLB-67
Jameson, J. Franklin 1859-1937 ....DLB-17
Jameson, Storm 1891-1986 ....DLB-36
Jančar, Drago 1948- DLB-181
Janés, Clara 1940- DLB-134
Janevski, Slavko 1920- DLB-181; CDWLB-4
Jansson, Tove 1914-2001................DLB-257
Janvier, Thomas 1849-1913..............DLB-202
Jaramillo, Cleofas M. 1878-1956 ....DLB-122
Jarman, Mark 1952- DLB-120
Jarrell, Randall 1914-1965 ..DLB-48, 52; CDALB-1
Jarrold and Sons........................DLB-106
Jarry, Alfred 1873-1907 ....DLB-192
Jarves, James Jackson 1818-1888 ....DLB-189
Jasmin, Claude 1930- DLB-60
Jaunsudrabiņš, Jānis 1877-1962 ....DLB-220
Jay, John 1745-1829......................DLB-31
Jean de Garlande (see John of Garland)
Jefferies, Richard 1848-1887 ....DLB-98, 141
Jeffers, Lance 1919-1985 ....DLB-41
Jeffers, Robinson
1887-1962 ....DLB-45, 212; CDALB-4
Jefferson, Thomas
1743-1826 ....DLB-31, 183; CDALB-2
Jégé 1866-1940.........................DLB-215
Jelinek, Elfriede 1946- DLB-85
Jellicoe, Ann 1927- DLB-13, 233
Jemison, Mary circa 1742-1833 ....DLB-239
Jenkins, Dan 1929- DLB-241
Jenkins, Elizabeth 1905- DLB-155
Jenkins, Robin 1912- DLB-14

Jenkins, William Fitzgerald (see Leinster, Murray)
Jenkins, Herbert, Limited................DLB-112
Jennings, Elizabeth 1926- DLB-27
Jens, Walter 1923- DLB-69
Jensen, Johannes V. 1873-1950 ....DLB-214
Jensen, Merrill 1905-1980 ....DLB-17
Jensen, Thit 1876-1957..................DLB-214
Jephson, Robert 1736-1803 ....DLB-89
Jerome, Jerome K. 1859-1927 ....DLB-10, 34, 135
Jerome, Judson 1927-1991 ....DLB-105
Jerrold, Douglas 1803-1857 ....DLB-158, 159
Jersild, Per Christian 1935- DLB-257
Jesse, F. Tennyson 1888-1958 ....DLB-77
Jewel, John 1522-1571 ....DLB-236
Jewett, John P., and Company..........DLB-49
Jewett, Sarah Orne 1849-1909 ....DLB-12, 74, 221
The Jewish Publication Society DLB-49
Jewitt, John Rodgers 1783-1821..........DLB-99
Jewsbury, Geraldine 1812-1880 ....DLB-21
Jewsbury, Maria Jane 1800-1833 ....DLB-199
Jhabvala, Ruth Prawer 1927- DLB-139, 194
Jiménez, Juan Ramón 1881-1958 ....DLB-134
Jin, Ha 1956- DLB-244
Joans, Ted 1928- DLB-16, 41
Jōha 1525-1602 ....DLB-203
Johannis de Garlandia (see John of Garland)
John, Errol 1924-1988 ....DLB-233
John, Eugenie (see Marlitt, E.)
John of Dumbleton
circa 1310-circa 1349..............DLB-115
John of Garland (Jean de Garlande, Johannis de
Garlandia) circa 1195-circa 1272 .....DLB-208
Johns, Captain W. E. 1893-1968..........DLB-160
Johnson, Mrs. A. E. ca. 1858-1922 ......DLB-221
Johnson, Amelia (see Johnson, Mrs. A. E.)
Johnson, B. S. 1933-1973 ....DLB-14, 40
Johnson, Benjamin [publishing house].....DLB-49
Johnson, Benjamin, Jacob, and
Robert [publishing house] DLB-49
Johnson, Charles 1679-1748.............DLB-84
Johnson, Charles R. 1948- DLB-33
Johnson, Charles S. 1893-1956 ......DLB-51, 91
Johnson, Denis 1949- DLB-120
Johnson, Diane 1934- Y-80
Johnson, Dorothy M. 1905–1984.......DLB-206
Johnson, E. Pauline (Tekahionwake)
1861-1913 ....DLB-175
Johnson, Edgar 1901-1995..............DLB-103
Johnson, Edward 1598-1672 ....DLB-24
Johnson, Fenton 1888-1958 ....DLB-45, 50
Johnson, Georgia Douglas
1877?-1966 ....DLB-51, 249
Johnson, Gerald W. 1890-1980..........DLB-29
Johnson, Greg 1953- DLB-234
Johnson, Helene 1907-1995 ....DLB-51
Johnson, Jacob, and Company..........DLB-49

Johnson, James Weldon
1871-1938 ....DLB-51; CDALB-4
Johnson, John H. 1918- DLB-137
Johnson, Joseph [publishing house]......DLB-154
Johnson, Linton Kwesi 1952- DLB-157
Johnson, Lionel 1867-1902................DLB-19
Johnson, Nunnally 1897-1977 ....DLB-26
Johnson, Owen 1878-1952................Y-87
Johnson, Pamela Hansford 1912- DLB-15
Johnson, Pauline 1861-1913 ....DLB-92
Johnson, Ronald 1935-1998.............DLB-169
Johnson, Samuel 1696-1772 ....DLB-24; CDBLB-2
Johnson, Samuel
1709-1784 ....DLB-39, 95, 104, 142, 213
Johnson, Samuel 1822-1882.........DLB-1, 243
Johnson, Susanna 1730-1810 ....DLB-200
Johnson, Terry 1955- DLB-233
Johnson, Uwe 1934-1984.....DLB-75; CDWLB-2
Johnston, Annie Fellows 1863-1931.......DLB-42
Johnston, Basil H. 1929- DLB-60
Johnston, David Claypole 1798?-1865....DLB-188
Johnston, Denis 1901-1984 ....DLB-10
Johnston, Ellen 1835-1873 ....DLB-199
Johnston, George 1913- DLB-88
Johnston, Sir Harry 1858-1927 ....DLB-174
Johnston, Jennifer 1930- DLB-14
Johnston, Mary 1870-1936...............DLB-9
Johnston, Richard Malcolm 1822-1898 ....DLB-74
Johnstone, Charles 1719?-1800? DLB-39
Johst, Hanns 1890-1978.................DLB-124
Jolas, Eugene 1894-1952 ....DLB-4, 45
Jones, Alice C. 1853-1933 ....DLB-92
Jones, Charles C., Jr. 1831-1893 ....DLB-30
Jones, D. G. 1929- DLB-53
Jones, David 1895-1974...DLB-20, 100; CDBLB-7
Jones, Diana Wynne 1934- DLB-161
Jones, Ebenezer 1820-1860 ....DLB-32
Jones, Ernest 1819-1868.................DLB-32
Jones, Gayl 1949- DLB-33
Jones, George 1800-1870 ....DLB-183
Jones, Glyn 1905- DLB-15
Jones, Gwyn 1907- DLB-15, 139
Jones, Henry Arthur 1851-1929 ....DLB-10
Jones, Hugh circa 1692-1760 ....DLB-24
Jones, James 1921-1977 ......DLB-2, 143; DS-17
James Jones Papers in the Handy Writers'
Colony Collection at the University of
Illinois at Springfield Y-98
The James Jones Society Y-92
Jones, Jenkin Lloyd 1911- DLB-127
Jones, John Beauchamp 1810-1866 ......DLB-202
Jones, LeRoi (see Baraka, Amiri)
Jones, Lewis 1897-1939 ....DLB-15
Jones, Madison 1925- DLB-152
Jones, Major Joseph
(see Thompson, William Tappan)

Cumulative Index

Jones, Marie 1955- DLB-233
Jones, Preston 1936-1979 .... DLB-7
Jones, Rodney 1950- DLB-120
Jones, Thom 1945- DLB-244
Jones, Sir William 1746-1794 .... DLB-109
Jones, William Alfred 1817-1900 .... DLB-59
Jones's Publishing House DLB-49
Jong, Erica 1942- DLB-2, 5, 28, 152
Jonke, Gert F. 1946- DLB-85
Jonson, Ben
　1572?-1637 .... DLB-62, 121; CDBLB-1
Jordan, June 1936- DLB-38
Joseph and George Y-99
Joseph, Jenny 1932- DLB-40
Joseph, Michael, Limited DLB-112
Josephson, Matthew 1899-1978 .... DLB-4
Josephus, Flavius 37-100 .... DLB-176
Josiah Allen's Wife (see Holley, Marietta)
Josipovici, Gabriel 1940- DLB-14
Josselyn, John ?-1675 .... DLB-24
Joudry, Patricia 1921- DLB-88
Jovine, Giuseppe 1922- DLB-128
Joyaux, Philippe (see Sollers, Philippe)
Joyce, Adrien (see Eastman, Carol)
Joyce, James 1882-1941
　....... DLB-10, 19, 36, 162, 247; CDBLB-6
James Joyce Centenary: Dublin, 1982 .... Y-82
James Joyce Conference Y-85
A Joyce (Con)Text: Danis Rose and the
　Remaking of *Ulysses* Y-97
The New *Ulysses* Y-84
Jozsef, Attila 1905-1937 ..... DLB-215; CDWLB-4
Judd, Orange, Publishing Company DLB-49
Judd, Sylvester 1813-1853 .... DLB-1, 243
Judith circa 930 .... DLB-146
Julian of Norwich
　1342-circa 1420 .... DLB-1146
Julius Caesar
　100 B.C.-44 B.C. DLB-211; CDWLB-1
June, Jennie
　(see Croly, Jane Cunningham)
Jung, Franz 1888-1963 .... DLB-118
Jünger, Ernst 1895- DLB-56; CDWLB-2
Der jüngere Titurel circa 1275 .... DLB-138
Jung-Stilling, Johann Heinrich
　1740-1817 .... DLB-94
Justice, Donald 1925- Y-83
Juvenal circa A.D. 60-circa A.D. 130
　............... DLB-211; CDWLB-1
The Juvenile Library
　(see Godwin, M. J., and Company)

K

Kacew, Romain (see Gary, Romain)
Kafka, Franz 1883-1924 ..... DLB-81; CDWLB-2
Kahn, Roger 1927- DLB-171
Kaikō Takeshi 1939-1989 .... DLB-182

Kaiser, Georg 1878-1945 ... DLB-124; CDWLB-2
Kaiserchronik circca 1147 .... DLB-148
Kaleb, Vjekoslav 1905- DLB-181
Kalechofsky, Roberta 1931- DLB-28
Kaler, James Otis 1848-1912 .... DLB-12
Kames, Henry Home, Lord
　1696-1782 .... DLB-31, 104
Kamo no Chōmei (Kamo no Nagaakira)
　1153 or 1155-1216 .... DLB-203
Kamo no Nagaakira (see Kamo no Chōmei)
Kampmann, Christian 1939-1988 .... DLB-214
Kandel, Lenore 1932- DLB-16
Kanin, Garson 1912-1999 .... DLB-7
Kant, Hermann 1926- DLB-75
Kant, Immanuel 1724-1804 .... DLB-94
Kantemir, Antiokh Dmitrievich
　1708-1744 .... DLB-150
Kantor, MacKinlay 1904-1977 .... DLB-9, 102
Kanze Kōjirō Nobumitsu 1435-1516 .... DLB-203
Kanze Motokiyo (see Zeimi)
Kaplan, Fred 1937- DLB-111
Kaplan, Johanna 1942- DLB-28
Kaplan, Justin 1925- DLB-111; Y-86
The Practice of Biography V:
　An Interview with Justin Kaplan Y-86
Kaplinski, Jaan 1941- DLB-232
Kapnist, Vasilii Vasilevich 1758?-1823 ... DLB-150
Karadžić, Vuk Stefanović
　1787-1864 .... DLB-147; CDWLB-4
Karamzin, Nikolai Mikhailovich
　1766-1826 .... DLB-150
Karinthy, Frigyes 1887-1938 .... DLB-215
Karsch, Anna Louisa 1722-1791 .... DLB-97
Kasack, Hermann 1896-1966 .... DLB-69
Kasai, Zenzō 1887-1927 .... DLB-180
Kaschnitz, Marie Luise 1901-1974 ...... DLB-69
Kassák, Lajos 1887-1967 .... DLB-215
Kaštelan, Jure 1919-1990 .... DLB-147
Kästner, Erich 1899-1974 .... DLB-56
Katenin, Pavel Aleksandrovich
　1792-1853 .... DLB-205
Kattan, Naim 1928- DLB-53
Katz, Steve 1935- Y-83
Kauffman, Janet 1945- DLB-218; Y-86
Kauffmann, Samuel 1898-1971 .... DLB-127
Kaufman, Bob 1925- DLB-16, 41
Kaufman, George S. 1889-1961 .... DLB-7
Kavan, Anna 1901-1968 .... DLB-255
Kavanagh, P. J. 1931- DLB-40
Kavanagh, Patrick 1904-1967 .... DLB-15, 20
Kawabata, Yasunari 1899-1972 .... DLB-180
Kaye-Smith, Sheila 1887-1956 .... DLB-36
Kazin, Alfred 1915-1998 .... DLB-67
Keane, John B. 1928- DLB-13
Keary, Annie 1825-1879 .... DLB-163
Keary, Eliza 1827-1918 .... DLB-240

Keating, H. R. F. 1926- DLB-87
Keatley, Charlotte 1960- DLB-245
Keats, Ezra Jack 1916-1983 .... DLB-61
Keats, John 1795-1821 ... DLB-96, 110; CDBLB-3
Keble, John 1792-1866 .... DLB-32, 55
Keckley, Elizabeth 1818?-1907 .... DLB-239
Keeble, John 1944- Y-83
Keeffe, Barrie 1945- DLB-13, 245
Keeley, James 1867-1934 .... DLB-25
W. B. Keen, Cooke and Company DLB-49
Keillor, Garrison 1942- Y-87
Keith, Marian 1874?-1961 .... DLB-92
Keller, Gary D. 1943- DLB-82
Keller, Gottfried
　1819-1890 .... DLB-129; CDWLB-2
Kelley, Edith Summers 1884-1956 .... DLB-9
Kelley, Emma Dunham ?-? DLB-221
Kelley, William Melvin 1937- DLB-33
Kellogg, Ansel Nash 1832-1886 .... DLB-23
Kellogg, Steven 1941- DLB-61
Kelly, George E. 1887-1974 .... DLB-7, 249
Kelly, Hugh 1739-1777 .... DLB-89
Kelly, Piet and Company DLB-49
Kelly, Robert 1935- DLB-5, 130, 165
Kelman, James 1946- DLB-194
Kelmscott Press DLB-112
Kelton, Elmer 1926- DLB-256
Kemble, E. W. 1861-1933 .... DLB-188
Kemble, Fanny 1809-1893 .... DLB-32
Kemelman, Harry 1908- DLB-28
Kempe, Margery circa 1373-1438 ...... DLB-146
Kempner, Friederike 1836-1904 .... DLB-129
Kempowski, Walter 1929- DLB-75
Kendall, Claude [publishing company] DLB-46
Kendall, Henry 1839-1882 .... DLB-230
Kendall, May 1861-1943 .... DLB-240
Kendell, George 1809-1867 .... DLB-43
Kenedy, P. J., and Sons DLB-49
Kenkō circa 1283-circa 1352 .... DLB-203
Kennan, George 1845-1924 .... DLB-189
Kennedy, Adrienne 1931- DLB-38
Kennedy, John Pendleton 1795-1870 .. DLB-3, 248
Kennedy, Leo 1907- DLB-88
Kennedy, Margaret 1896-1967 .... DLB-36
Kennedy, Patrick 1801-1873 .... DLB-159
Kennedy, Richard S. 1920- DLB-111
Kennedy, William 1928- DLB-143; Y-85
Kennedy, X. J. 1929- DLB-5
Kennelly, Brendan 1936- DLB-40
Kenner, Hugh 1923- DLB-67
Kennerley, Mitchell [publishing house] ... DLB-46
Kenny, Maurice 1929- DLB-175
Kent, Frank R. 1877-1958 .... DLB-29
Kenyon, Jane 1947-1995 .... DLB-120

Keough, Hugh Edmund 1864-1912......DLB-171	Kincaid, Jamaica 1949- DLB-157, 227; CDALB-7; CDWLB-3	Kizer, Carolyn 1925- DLB-5, 169
Keppler and Schwartzmann............DLB-49	King, Charles 1844-1933.............DLB-186	Klabund 1890-1928.................DLB-66
Ker, John, third Duke of Roxburghe 1740-1804 ....DLB-213	King, Clarence 1842-1901 ....DLB-12	Klaj, Johann 1616-1656 ....DLB-164
Ker, N. R. 1908-1982.................DLB-201	King, Florence 1936...................Y-85	Klappert, Peter 1942- DLB-5
Kerlan, Irvin 1912-1963..............DLB-187	King, Francis 1923- DLB-15, 139	Klass, Philip (see Tenn, William)
Kermode, Frank 1919- DLB-242	King, Grace 1852-1932 ....DLB-12, 78	Klein, A. M. 1909-1972 ....DLB-68
Kern, Jerome 1885-1945 ....DLB-187	King, Harriet Hamilton 1840-1920 ......DLB-199	Kleist, Ewald von 1715-1759 ....DLB-97
Kerner, Justinus 1776-1862 ....DLB-90	King, Henry 1592-1669...............DLB-126	Kleist, Heinrich von 1777-1811.............DLB-90; CDWLB-2
Kerouac, Jack 1922-1969 ...DLB-2, 16, 237; DS-3; CDALB-1	King, Solomon [publishing house]........DLB-49	Klinger, Friedrich Maximilian 1752-1831 ....DLB-94
The Jack Kerouac Revival.................Y-95	King, Stephen 1947- DLB-143; Y-80	Klíma, Ivan 1931- DLB-232; CDWLB-4
"Re-meeting of Old Friends": The Jack Kerouac Conference Y-82	King, Susan Petigru 1824-1875 ....DLB-239	Kliushnikov, Viktor Petrovich 1841-1892.....................DLB-238
Kerouac, Jan 1952-1996.................DLB-16	King, Thomas 1943- DLB-175	Oral History Interview with Donald S. Klopfer Y-97
Kerr, Charles H., and Company DLB-49	King, Woodie, Jr. 1937- DLB-38	Klopstock, Friedrich Gottlieb 1724-1803 ....DLB-97
Kerr, Orpheus C. (see Newell, Robert Henry)	Kinglake, Alexander William 1809-1891 ....DLB-55, 166	Klopstock, Meta 1728-1758 ....DLB-97
Kersh, Gerald 1911-1968................DLB-255	Kingsley, Charles 1819-1875 ......DLB-21, 32, 163, 178, 190	Kluge, Alexander 1932- DLB-75
Kesey, Ken 1935-2001 ....DLB-2, 16, 206; CDALB-6	Kingsley, Henry 1830-1876 ....DLB-21, 230	Knapp, Joseph Palmer 1864-1951 ....DLB-91
Kessel, Joseph 1898-1979 ....DLB-72	Kingsley, Mary Henrietta 1862-1900.....DLB-174	Knapp, Samuel Lorenzo 1783-1838.......DLB-59
Kessel, Martin 1901- DLB-56	Kingsley, Sidney 1906- DLB-7	Knapton, J. J. and P. [publishing house]................DLB-154
Kesten, Hermann 1900- DLB-56	Kingsmill, Hugh 1889-1949..........DLB-149	Kniazhnin, Iakov Borisovich 1740-1791 ....DLB-150
Keun, Irmgard 1905-1982 ....DLB-69	Kingsolver, Barbara 1955- DLB-206; CDALB-7	Knickerbocker, Diedrich (see Irving, Washington)
Key and Biddle DLB-49	Kingston, Maxine Hong 1940- DLB-173, 212; Y-80; CDALB-7	Knigge, Adolph Franz Friedrich Ludwig, Freiherr von 1752-1796 ....DLB-94
Keynes, Sir Geoffrey 1887-1982.........DLB-201	Kingston, William Henry Giles 1814-1880 ....DLB-163	Knight, Charles, and Company.........DLB-106
Keynes, John Maynard 1883-1946 ....DS-10	Kinnan, Mary Lewis 1763-1848.........DLB-200	Knight, Damon 1922- DLB-8
Keyserling, Eduard von 1855-1918 ....DLB-66	Kinnell, Galway 1927- DLB-5; Y-87	Knight, Etheridge 1931-1992...........DLB-41
Khan, Ismith 1925- DLB-125	Kinsella, Thomas 1928- DLB-27	Knight, John S. 1894-1981..............DLB-29
Khaytov, Nikolay 1919- DLB-181	Kipling, Rudyard 1865-1936 ....DLB-19, 34, 141, 156; CDBLB-5	Knight, Sarah Kemble 1666-1727.....DLB-24, 200
Khemnitser, Ivan Ivanovich 1745-1784......................DLB-150	Kipphardt, Heinar 1922-1982 ....DLB-124	Knight-Bruce, G. W. H. 1852-1896......DLB-174
Kheraskov, Mikhail Matveevich 1733-1807 ....DLB-150	Kirby, William 1817-1906 ....DLB-99	Knister, Raymond 1899-1932 ....DLB-68
Khomiakov, Aleksei Stepanovich 1804-1860......................DLB-205	Kircher, Athanasius 1602-1680 ....DLB-164	Knoblock, Edward 1874-1945 ....DLB-10
Khristov, Boris 1945- DLB-181	Kireevsky, Ivan Vasil'evich 1806-1856 ...DLB-198	Knopf, Alfred A. 1892-1984 ....Y-84
Khvoshchinskaia, Nadezhda Dmitrievna 1824-1889......................DLB-238	Kireevsky, Petr Vasil'evich 1808-1856 ...DLB-205	Knopf, Alfred A. [publishing house] DLB-46
Khvostov, Dmitrii Ivanovich 1757-1835......................DLB-150	Kirk, Hans 1898-1962 ....DLB-214	Knopf to Hammett: The Editoral Correspondence Y-00
Kidd, Adam 1802?-1831 ....DLB-99	Kirk, John Foster 1824-1904 ....DLB-79	Knorr von Rosenroth, Christian 1636-1689 ....DLB-168
Kidd, William [publishing house] DLB-106	Kirkconnell, Watson 1895-1977..........DLB-68	"Knots into Webs: Some Autobiographical Sources," by Dabney Stuart DLB-105
Kidder, Tracy 1945- DLB-185	Kirkland, Caroline M. 1801-1864 ....DLB-3, 73, 74; DS-13	Knowles, John 1926- DLB-6; CDALB-6
Kiely, Benedict 1919- DLB-15	Kirkland, Joseph 1830-1893.............DLB-12	Knox, Frank 1874-1944................DLB-29
Kieran, John 1892-1981 ....DLB-171	Kirkman, Francis [publishing house] DLB-170	Knox, John circa 1514-1572..............DLB-132
Kiggins and Kellogg..................DLB-49	Kirkpatrick, Clayton 1915- DLB-127	Knox, John Armoy 1850-1906 ....DLB-23
Kiley, Jed 1889-1962 ....DLB-4	Kirkup, James 1918- DLB-27	Knox, Lucy 1845-1884 ....DLB-240
Kilgore, Bernard 1908-1967...........DLB-127	Kirouac, Conrad (see Marie-Victorin, Frère)	Knox, Ronald Arbuthnott 1888-1957 .....DLB-77
Killens, John Oliver 1916- DLB-33	Kirsch, Sarah 1935- DLB-75	Knox, Thomas Wallace 1835-1896......DLB-189
Killigrew, Anne 1660-1685 ....DLB-131	Kirst, Hans Hellmut 1914-1989..........DLB-69	Kobayashi Takiji 1903-1933 ....DLB-180
Killigrew, Thomas 1612-1683 ....DLB-58	Kiš, Danilo 1935-1989......DLB-181; CDWLB-4	Kober, Arthur 1900-1975................DLB-11
Kilmer, Joyce 1886-1918 ....DLB-45	Kita Morio 1927- DLB-182	Kobiakova, Aleksandra Petrovna 1823-1892 ....DLB-238
Kilroy, Thomas 1934- DLB-233	Kitcat, Mabel Greenhow 1859-1922 .....DLB-135	Kocbek, Edvard 1904-1981 ...DLB-147; CDWB-4
Kilwardby, Robert circa 1215-1279 ......DLB-115	Kitchin, C. H. B. 1895-1967 ....DLB-77	Koch, Howard 1902- DLB-26
Kimball, Richard Burleigh 1816-1892 ....DLB-202	Kittredge, William 1932- DLB-212, 244	
	Kiukhel'beker, Vil'gel'm Karlovich 1797-1846......................DLB-205	

Cumulative Index

Koch, Kenneth 1925- DLB-5
Kōda, Rohan 1867-1947 .... DLB-180
Koenigsberg, Moses 1879-1945. .... DLB-25
Koeppen, Wolfgang 1906-1996 .... DLB-69
Koertge, Ronald 1940- DLB-105
Koestler, Arthur 1905-1983 ...... Y-83; CDBLB-7
Kohn, John S. Van E. 1906-1976 and
   Papantonio, Michael 1907-1978 ..... DLB-187
Kokoschka, Oskar 1886-1980. .... DLB-124
Kolb, Annette 1870-1967 .... DLB-66
Kolbenheyer, Erwin Guido
   1878-1962. .... DLB-66, 124
Kolleritsch, Alfred 1931- DLB-85
Kolodny, Annette 1941- DLB-67
Kol'tsov, Aleksei Vasil'evich
   1809-1842 .... DLB-205
Komarov, Matvei circa 1730-1812 ...... DLB-150
Komroff, Manuel 1890-1974............. DLB-4
Komunyakaa, Yusef 1947- DLB-120
Koneski, Blaže 1921-1993... DLB-181; CDWLB-4
Konigsburg, E. L. 1930- DLB-52
Konparu Zenchiku 1405-1468? DLB-203
Konrád, György 1933- DLB-232; CDWLB-4
Konrad von Würzburg
   circa 1230-1287 .... DLB-138
Konstantinov, Aleko 1863-1897 .... DLB-147
Konwicki, Tadeusz 1926- DLB-232
Kooser, Ted 1939- DLB-105
Kopit, Arthur 1937- DLB-7
Kops, Bernard 1926?- DLB-13
Kornbluth, C. M. 1923-1958 .... DLB-8
Körner, Theodor 1791-1813............. DLB-90
Kornfeld, Paul 1889-1942............. DLB-118
Kosinski, Jerzy 1933-1991 .... DLB-2; Y-82
Kosmač, Ciril 1910-1980 .... DLB-181
Kosovel, Srečko 1904-1926 .... DLB-147
Kostrov, Ermil Ivanovich 1755-1796..... DLB-150
Kotzebue, August von 1761-1819 .... DLB-94
Kotzwinkle, William 1938- DLB-173
Kovačić, Ante 1854-1889 .... DLB-147
Kovič, Kajetan 1931- DLB-181
Kozlov, Ivan Ivanovich 1779-1840 ..... DLB-205
Kraf, Elaine 1946- Y-81
Kramer, Jane 1938- DLB-185
Kramer, Larry 1935- DLB-249
Kramer, Mark 1944- DLB-185
Kranjčević, Silvije Strahimir
   1865-1908 .... DLB-147
Krasko, Ivan 1876-1958 .... DLB-215
Krasna, Norman 1909-1984 .... DLB-26
Kraus, Hans Peter 1907-1988 .... DLB-187
Kraus, Karl 1874-1936 .... DLB-118
Krause, Herbert 1905-1976............. DLB-256
Krauss, Ruth 1911-1993 .... DLB-52
Kreisel, Henry 1922- DLB-88

Krestovsky V. (see Khvoshchinskaia,
   Nadezhda Dmitrievna)
Krestovsky, Vsevolod Vladimirovich
   1839-1895 .... DLB-238
Kreuder, Ernst 1903-1972............. DLB-69
Krėvė-Mickevičius, Vincas 1882-1954 ... DLB-220
Kreymborg, Alfred 1883-1966 .... DLB-4, 54
Krieger, Murray 1923- DLB-67
Krim, Seymour 1922-1989 .... DLB-16
Kristensen, Tom 1893-1974 .... DLB-214
Kristeva, Julia 1941- DLB-242
Krleža, Miroslav 1893-1981 ..DLB-147; CDWLB-4
Krock, Arthur 1886-1974 .... DLB-29
Kroetsch, Robert 1927- DLB-53
Kross, Jaan 1920- DLB-232
Krúdy, Gyula 1878-1933 .... DLB-215
Krutch, Joseph Wood
   1893-1970. .... DLB-63, 206
Krylov, Ivan Andreevich
   1769-1844. .... DLB-150
Kubin, Alfred 1877-1959............. DLB-81
Kubrick, Stanley 1928-1999 .... DLB-26
Kudrun circa 1230-1240................ DLB-138
Kuffstein, Hans Ludwig von
   1582-1656 .... DLB-164
Kuhlmann, Quirinus 1651-1689........ DLB-168
Kuhnau, Johann 1660-1722 .... DLB-168
Kukol'nik, Nestor Vasil'evich
   1809-1868 .... DLB-205
Kukučín, Martin
   1860-1928 .... DLB-215; CDWLB-4
Kumin, Maxine 1925- DLB-5
Kuncewicz, Maria 1895-1989 .... DLB-215
Kundera, Milan 1929- DLB-232; CDWLB-4
Kunene, Mazisi 1930- DLB-117
Kunikida, Doppo 1869-1908 .... DLB-180
Kunitz, Stanley 1905- DLB-48
Kunjufu, Johari M. (see Amini, Johari M.)
Kunnert, Gunter 1929- DLB-75
Kunze, Reiner 1933- DLB-75
Kupferberg, Tuli 1923- DLB-16
Kurahashi Yumiko 1935- DLB-182
Kureishi, Hanif 1954- DLB-194, 245
Kürnberger, Ferdinand 1821-1879 ..... DLB-129
Kurz, Isolde 1853-1944................ DLB-66
Kusenberg, Kurt 1904-1983 .... DLB-69
Kushchevsky, Ivan Afanas'evich
   1847-1876 .... DLB-238
Kushner, Tony 1956- DLB-228
Kuttner, Henry 1915-1958 .... DLB-8
Kyd, Thomas 1558-1594 .... DLB-62
Kyffin, Maurice circa 1560?-1598....... DLB-136
Kyger, Joanne 1934- DLB-16
Kyne, Peter B. 1880-1957............. DLB-78
Kyōgoku Tamekane 1254-1332 .... DLB-203
Kyrklund, Willy 1921- DLB-257

L

L. E. L. (see Landon, Letitia Elizabeth)
Laberge, Albert 1871-1960 .... DLB-68
Laberge, Marie 1950- DLB-60
Labiche, Eugène 1815-1888 .... DLB-192
Labrunie, Gerard (see Nerval, Gerard de)
La Capria, Raffaele 1922- DLB-196
Lacombe, Patrice
   (see Trullier-Lacombe, Joseph Patrice)
Lacretelle, Jacques de 1888-1985 .... DLB-65
Lacy, Ed 1911-1968 .... DLB-226
Lacy, Sam 1903- DLB-171
Ladd, Joseph Brown 1764-1786 .... DLB-37
La Farge, Oliver 1901-1963 .... DLB-9
Laffan, Mrs. R. S. de Courcy (see Adams,
   Bertha Leith)
Lafferty, R. A. 1914- DLB-8
La Flesche, Francis 1857-1932..........DLB-175
Laforge, Jules 1860-1887 ....DLB-217
Lagorio, Gina 1922- DLB-196
La Guma, Alex
   1925-1985 .... DLB-117, 225; CDWLB-3
Lahaise, Guillaume (see Delahaye, Guy)
Lahontan, Louis-Armand de Lom d'Arce,
   Baron de 1666-1715? DLB-99
Laing, Kojo 1946- DLB-157
Laird, Carobeth 1895- Y-82
Laird and Lee....................... DLB-49
Lalić, Ivan V. 1931-1996 .... DLB-181
Lalić, Mihailo 1914-1992 .... DLB-181
Lalonde, Michèle 1937- DLB-60
Lamantia, Philip 1927- DLB-16
Lamartine, Alphonse de 1790-1869 .....DLB-217
Lamb, Lady Caroline 1785-1828 .... DLB-116
Lamb, Charles
   1775-1834........DLB-93, 107, 163; CDBLB-3
Lamb, Mary 1764-1874................ DLB-163
Lambert, Betty 1933-1983 .... DLB-60
Lamming, George 1927- ...DLB-125; CDWLB-3
L'Amour, Louis 1908-1988 ....DLB-206; Y-80
Lampman, Archibald 1861-1899 .... DLB-92
Lamson, Wolffe and Company DLB-49
Lancer Books DLB-46
Landesman, Jay 1919- and
   Landesman, Fran 1927- DLB-16
Landolfi, Tommaso 1908-1979..........DLB-177
Landon, Letitia Elizabeth 1802-1838 ..... DLB-96
Landor, Walter Savage 1775-1864 ....DLB-93, 107
Landry, Napoléon-P. 1884-1956 .... DLB-92
Lane, Charles 1800-1870 .... DLB-1, 223
Lane, F. C. 1885-1984 .... DLB-241
Lane, John, Company DLB-49
Lane, Laurence W. 1890-1967 .... DLB-91
Lane, M. Travis 1934- DLB-60
Lane, Patrick 1939- DLB-53

Lane, Pinkie Gordon 1923- DLB-41
Laney, Al 1896-1988 .... DLB-4, 171
Lang, Andrew 1844-1912 ...... DLB-98, 141, 184
Langevin, André 1927- DLB-60
Langgässer, Elisabeth 1899-1950.........DLB-69
Langhorne, John 1735-1779 ....DLB-109
Langland, William
    circa 1330-circa 1400...............DLB-146
Langton, Anna 1804-1893 ....DLB-99
Lanham, Edwin 1904-1979 ....DLB-4
Lanier, Sidney 1842-1881 ....DLB-64; DS-13
Lanyer, Aemilia 1569-1645 ....DLB-121
Lapointe, Gatien 1931-1983............DLB-88
Lapointe, Paul-Marie 1929- DLB-88
Larcom, Lucy 1824-1893..........DLB-221, 243
Lardner, John 1912-1960..............DLB-171
Lardner, Ring 1885-1933
    ...... DLB-11, 25, 86, 171; DS-16; CDALB-4
Lardner 100: Ring Lardner
    Centennial Symposium Y-85
Lardner, Ring, Jr. 1915-2000 .... DLB-26, Y-00
Larkin, Philip 1922-1985 ......DLB-27; CDBLB-8
La Roche, Sophie von 1730-1807.........DLB-94
La Rocque, Gilbert 1943-1984...........DLB-60
Laroque de Roquebrune, Robert
    (see Roquebrune, Robert de)
Larrick, Nancy 1910- DLB-61
Larsen, Nella 1893-1964 ....DLB-51
Larson, Clinton F. 1919-1994 ....DLB-256
La Sale, Antoine de
    circa 1386-1460/1467 ....DLB-208
Lasch, Christopher 1932-1994...........DLB-246
Lasker-Schüler, Else 1869-1945 .....DLB-66, 124
Lasnier, Rina 1915- DLB-88
Lassalle, Ferdinand 1825-1864..........DLB-129
Latham, Robert 1912-1995 ....DLB-201
Lathrop, Dorothy P. 1891-1980..........DLB-22
Lathrop, George Parsons 1851-1898......DLB-71
Lathrop, John, Jr. 1772-1820 ....DLB-37
Latimer, Hugh 1492?-1555 ....DLB-136
Latimore, Jewel Christine McLawler
    (see Amini, Johari M.)
Latymer, William 1498-1583............DLB-132
Laube, Heinrich 1806-1884 ....DLB-133
Laud, William 1573-1645 ....DLB-213
Laughlin, James 1914-1997 ....DLB-48; Y-96
James Laughlin Tributes Y-97
Conversations with Publishers IV:
    An Interview with James Laughlin Y-96
Laumer, Keith 1925- DLB-8
Lauremberg, Johann 1590-1658..........DLB-164
Laurence, Margaret 1926-1987 ....DLB-53
Laurentius von Schnüffis 1633-1702 .....DLB-168
Laurents, Arthur 1918- DLB-26
Laurie, Annie (see Black, Winifred)
Laut, Agnes Christiana 1871-1936........DLB-92

Lauterbach, Ann 1942- DLB-193
Lautreamont, Isidore Lucien Ducasse, Comte de
    1846-1870 ....DLB-217
Lavater, Johann Kaspar 1741-1801 ....DLB-97
Lavin, Mary 1912-1996................DLB-15
Law, John (see Harkness, Margaret)
Lawes, Henry 1596-1662................DLB-126
Lawless, Anthony (see MacDonald, Philip)
Lawless, Emily (The Hon. Emily Lawless) 1845-1913
    DLB-240
Lawrence, D. H. 1885-1930
    ..... DLB-10, 19, 36, 98, 162, 195; CDBLB-6
Lawrence, David 1888-1973 ....DLB-29
Lawrence, Jerome 1915- and
    Lee, Robert E. 1918-1994 ....DLB-228
Lawrence, Seymour 1926-1994 ....Y-94
Lawrence, T. E. 1888-1935 ....DLB-195
Lawson, George 1598-1678 ....DLB-213
Lawson, Henry 1867-1922..............DLB-230
Lawson, John ?-1711 ....DLB-24
Lawson, John Howard 1894-1977 ....DLB-228
Lawson, Louisa Albury 1848-1920 ......DLB-230
Lawson, Robert 1892-1957 ....DLB-22
Lawson, Victor F. 1850-1925............DLB-25
Layard, Sir Austen Henry
    1817-1894 ....DLB-166
Layton, Irving 1912- DLB-88
LaZamon flourished circa 1200 ....DLB-146
Lazarević, Laza K. 1851-1890 ....DLB-147
Lazarus, George 1904-1997............DLB-201
Lazhechnikov, Ivan Ivanovich
    1792-1869 ....DLB-198
Lea, Henry Charles 1825-1909 ....DLB-47
Lea, Sydney 1942- DLB-120
Lea, Tom 1907- DLB-6
Leacock, John 1729-1802................DLB-31
Leacock, Stephen 1869-1944 ....DLB-92
Lead, Jane Ward 1623-1704.............DLB-131
Leadenhall Press DLB-106
Leakey, Caroline Woolmer 1827-1881 ...DLB-230
Leapor, Mary 1722-1746 ....DLB-109
Lear, Edward 1812-1888....... DLB-32, 163, 166
Leary, Timothy 1920-1996 ....DLB-16
Leary, W. A., and Company............DLB-49
Léautaud, Paul 1872-1956 ....DLB-65
Leavis, F. R. 1895-1978 ....DLB-242
Leavitt, David 1961- DLB-130
Leavitt and Allen DLB-49
Le Blond, Mrs. Aubrey 1861-1934 ......DLB-174
le Carré, John 1931- DLB-87; CDBLB-8
Lécavelé, Roland (see Dorgeles, Roland)
Lechlitner, Ruth 1901- DLB-48
Leclerc, Félix 1914- DLB-60
Le Clézio, J. M. G. 1940- DLB-83
Lectures on Rhetoric and Belles Lettres (1783),
    by Hugh Blair [excerpts] DLB-31

Leder, Rudolf (see Hermlin, Stephan)
Lederer, Charles 1910-1976............DLB-26
Ledwidge, Francis 1887-1917 ....DLB-20
Lee, Dennis 1939- DLB-53
Lee, Don L. (see Madhubuti, Haki R.)
Lee, George W. 1894-1976 ....DLB-51
Lee, Harper 1926- DLB-6; CDALB-1
Lee, Harriet (1757-1851) and
    Lee, Sophia (1750-1824) DLB-39
Lee, Laurie 1914-1997.................DLB-27
Lee, Li-Young 1957- DLB-165
Lee, Manfred B. (see Dannay, Frederic, and
    Manfred B. Lee)
Lee, Nathaniel circa 1645-1692 ....DLB-80
Lee, Sir Sidney 1859-1926 ....DLB-149, 184
Lee, Sir Sidney, "Principles of Biography," in
    Elizabethan and Other Essays DLB-149
Lee, Vernon
    1856-1935 .... DLB-57, 153, 156, 174, 178
Lee and Shepard DLB-49
Le Fanu, Joseph Sheridan
    1814-1873 .... DLB-21, 70, 159, 178
Leffland, Ella 1931- Y-84
le Fort, Gertrud von 1876-1971 ....DLB-66
Le Gallienne, Richard 1866-1947 ....DLB-4
Legaré, Hugh Swinton
    1797-1843................DLB-3, 59, 73, 248
Legaré, James Mathewes 1823-1859 ...DLB-3, 248
The Legends of the Saints and a Medieval
    Christian Worldview DLB-148
Léger, Antoine-J. 1880-1950 ....DLB-88
Le Guin, Ursula K.
    1929- DLB-8, 52, 256; CDALB-6
Lehman, Ernest 1920- DLB-44
Lehmann, John 1907- DLB-27, 100
Lehmann, John, Limited DLB-112
Lehmann, Rosamond 1901-1990.........DLB-15
Lehmann, Wilhelm 1882-1968 ....DLB-56
Leiber, Fritz 1910-1992 ....DLB-8
Leibniz, Gottfried Wilhelm 1646-1716....DLB-168
Leicester University Press DLB-112
Leigh, W. R. 1866-1955 ....DLB-188
Leinster, Murray 1896-1975 ....DLB-8
Leiser, Bill 1898-1965 ....DLB-241
Leisewitz, Johann Anton 1752-1806.......DLB-94
Leitch, Maurice 1933- DLB-14
Leithauser, Brad 1943- DLB-120
Leland, Charles G. 1824-1903...........DLB-11
Leland, John 1503?-1552 ....DLB-136
Lemay, Pamphile 1837-1918 ....DLB-99
Lemelin, Roger 1919- DLB-88
Lemercier, Louis-Jean-Népomucène
    1771-1840......................DLB-192
Le Moine, James MacPherson
    1825-1912 ....DLB-99
Lemon, Mark 1809-1870 ....DLB-163
Le Moyne, Jean 1913- DLB-88

Lemperly, Paul 1858-1939 . . . . DLB-187	Levine, Philip 1928- DLB-5	Lindesay, Ethel Forence (see Richardson, Henry Handel)
L'Engle, Madeleine 1918- DLB-52	Levis, Larry 1946- DLB-120	Lindgren, Astrid 1907-2002 . . . . DLB-257
Lennart, Isobel 1915-1971. . . . . DLB-44	Levy, Amy 1861-1889 . . . . DLB-156, 240	Lindgren, Torgny 1938- DLB-257
Lennox, Charlotte 1729 or 1730-1804 . . . . DLB-39	Levy, Benn Wolfe 1900-1973 . . . . . . .DLB-13; Y-81	Lindsay, Alexander William, Twenty-fifth Earl of Crawford 1812-1880 . . . . DLB-184
Lenox, James 1800-1880. . . . . DLB-140	Lewald, Fanny 1811-1889 . . . . DLB-129	Lindsay, Sir David circa 1485-1555 . . . . . DLB-132
Lenski, Lois 1893-1974 . . . . DLB-22	Lewes, George Henry 1817-1878 . . . . DLB-55, 144	Lindsay, David 1878-1945 . . . . DLB-255
Lentricchia, Frank 1940- DLB-246	"Criticism In Relation To Novels" (1863) DLB-21	Lindsay, Jack 1900- Y-84
Lenz, Hermann 1913-1998 . . . . DLB-69	The Principles of Success in Literature (1865) [excerpt] DLB-57	Lindsay, Lady (Caroline Blanche Elizabeth Fitzroy Lindsay) 1844-1912 . . . . DLB-199
Lenz, J. M. R. 1751-1792 . . . . DLB-94	Lewis, Agnes Smith 1843-1926. . . . . . . .DLB-174	Lindsay, Vachel 1879-1931. . . . DLB-54; CDALB-3
Lenz, Siegfried 1926- DLB-75	Lewis, Alfred H. 1857-1914 . . . . DLB-25, 186	Linebarger, Paul Myron Anthony (see Smith, Cordwainer)
Leonard, Elmore 1925- DLB-173, 226	Lewis, Alun 1915-1944 . . . . DLB-20, 162	Link, Arthur S. 1920-1998 . . . . .DLB-17
Leonard, Hugh 1926- DLB-13	Lewis, C. Day (see Day Lewis, C.)	Linn, Ed 1922-2000 . . . . DLB-241
Leonard, William Ellery 1876-1944 . . . . . DLB-54	Lewis, C. S. 1898-1963 . . . . DLB-15, 100, 160, 255; CDBLB-7	Linn, John Blair 1777-1804 . . . . DLB-37
Leonowens, Anna 1834-1914 . . . . . . DLB-99, 166	Lewis, Charles B. 1842-1924 . . . . DLB-11	Lins, Osman 1924-1978 . . . . DLB-145
LePan, Douglas 1914- DLB-88	Lewis, Henry Clay 1825-1850 . . . . DLB-3, 248	Linton, Eliza Lynn 1822-1898 . . . . DLB-18
Lepik, Kalju 1920-1999. . . . . DLB-232	Lewis, Janet 1899-1999. . . . . Y-87	Linton, William James 1812-1897 . . . . . . DLB-32
Leprohon, Rosanna Eleanor 1829-1879 . . . DLB-99	Lewis, Matthew Gregory 1775-1818. . . . . .DLB-39, 158, 178	Lintot, Barnaby Bernard [publishing house] DLB-170
Le Queux, William 1864-1927 . . . . DLB-70	Lewis, Meriwether 1774-1809 and Clark, William 1770-1838 . . . . . DLB-183, 186	Lion Books DLB-46
Lermontov, Mikhail Iur'evich 1814-1841. . . . . DLB-205	Lewis, Norman 1908- DLB-204	Lionni, Leo 1910-1999 . . . . DLB-61
Lerner, Max 1902-1992 . . . . DLB-29	Lewis, R. W. B. 1917- DLB-111	Lippard, George 1822-1854 . . . . DLB-202
Lernet-Holenia, Alexander 1897-1976 . . . . . DLB-85	Lewis, Richard circa 1700-1734 . . . . DLB-24	Lippincott, J. B., Company DLB-49
Le Rossignol, James 1866-1969 . . . . DLB-92	Lewis, Sinclair 1885-1951 . . . . . DLB-9, 102; DS-1; CDALB-4	Lippincott, Sara Jane Clarke 1823-1904 . . . DLB-43
Lescarbot, Marc circa 1570-1642 . . . . DLB-99	Sinclair Lewis Centennial Conference Y-85	Lippmann, Walter 1889-1974 . . . . DLB-29
LeSeur, William Dawson 1840-1917 . . . . . DLB-92	Lewis, Wilmarth Sheldon 1895-1979 . . . . DLB-140	Lipton, Lawrence 1898-1975 . . . . DLB-16
LeSieg, Theo. (see Geisel, Theodor Seuss)	Lewis, Wyndham 1882-1957 . . . . DLB-15	Liscow, Christian Ludwig 1701-1760 . . . . . DLB-97
Leskov, Nikolai Semenovich 1831-1895. . DLB-238	Lewisohn, Ludwig 1882-1955 . . .DLB-4, 9, 28, 102	Lish, Gordon 1934- DLB-130
Leslie, Doris before 1902-1982 . . . . DLB-191	Leyendecker, J. C. 1874-1951 . . . . DLB-188	Lisle, Charles-Marie-René Leconte de 1818-1894 .DLB-217
Leslie, Eliza 1787-1858 . . . . DLB-202	Lezama Lima, José 1910-1976 . . . . DLB-113	Lispector, Clarice 1925-1977 . . . . .DLB-113; CDWLB-3
Leslie, Frank 1821-1880 . . . . DLB-43, 79	L'Heureux, John 1934- DLB-244	A Literary Archaeologist Digs On: A Brief Interview with Michael Reynolds by Michael Rogers Y-99
Leslie, Frank, Publishing House DLB-49	Libbey, Laura Jean 1862-1924 . . . . DLB-221	
Leśmian, Bolesław 1878-1937 . . . . DLB-215	The Library of America DLB-46	The Literary Chronicle and Weekly Review 1819-1828 . . . . DLB-110
Lesperance, John 1835?-1891 . . . . DLB-99	The Licensing Act of 1737 . . . . DLB-84	
Lessing, Bruno 1870-1940 . . . . DLB-28	Lichfield, Leonard I [publishing house] . . .DLB-170	Literary Documents: William Faulkner and the People-to-People Program Y-86
Lessing, Doris 1919- DLB-15, 139; Y-85; CDBLB-8	Lichtenberg, Georg Christoph 1742-1799 . . DLB-94	Literary Documents II: Library Journal Statements and Questionnaires from First Novelists Y-87
	The Liddle Collection Y-97	
Lessing, Gotthold Ephraim 1729-1781 . . . . .DLB-97; CDWLB-2	Lidman, Sara 1923- DLB-257	Literary Effects of World War II [British novel]. DLB-15
Lettau, Reinhard 1929- DLB-75	Lieb, Fred 1888-1980 . . . . .DLB-171	
Letter from Japan Y-94, Y-98	Liebling, A. J. 1904-1963 . . . . .DLB-4, 171	Literary Prizes Y-00
Letter from London Y-96	Lieutenant Murray (see Ballou, Maturin Murray)	Literary Prizes [British] DLB-15
Letter to [Samuel] Richardson on Clarissa (1748), by Henry Fielding DLB-39	Lighthall, William Douw 1857-1954 . . . . . DLB-92	Literary Research Archives: The Humanities Research Center, University of Texas Y-82
A Letter to the Editor of The Irish Times Y-97	Lilar, Françoise (see Mallet-Joris, Françoise)	Literary Research Archives II: Berg Collection of English and American Literature of the New York Public Library. Y-83
Lever, Charles 1806-1872 . . . . DLB-21	Lili'uokalani, Queen 1838-1917 . . . . DLB-221	
Lever, Ralph ca. 1527-1585 . . . . DLB-236	Lillo, George 1691-1739 . . . . DLB-84	
Leverson, Ada 1862-1933 . . . . DLB-153	Lilly, J. K., Jr. 1893-1966 . . . . DLB-140	Literary Research Archives III: The Lilly Library Y-84
Levertov, Denise 1923-1997. . . . . DLB-5, 165; CDALB-7	Lilly, Wait and Company DLB-49	
	Lily, William circa 1468-1522 . . . . DLB-132	Literary Research Archives IV: The John Carter Brown Library Y-85
Levi, Peter 1931- DLB-40	Limited Editions Club DLB-46	
Levi, Primo 1919-1987 . . . . .DLB-177	Limón, Graciela 1938- DLB-209	Literary Research Archives V: Kent State Special Collections Y-86
Lévi-Strauss, Claude 1908- DLB-242	Lincoln and Edmands DLB-49	
Levien, Sonya 1888-1960 . . . . DLB-44		
Levin, Meyer 1905-1981 . . . . . . .DLB-9, 28; Y-81		
Levine, Norman 1923- DLB-88		

Literary Research Archives VI: The Modern Literary Manuscripts Collection in the Special Collections of the Washington University Libraries Y-87

Literary Research Archives VII: The University of Virginia Libraries. Y-91

Literary Research Archives VIII: The Henry E. Huntington Library Y-92

Literary Research Archives IX: Special Collections at Boston University. . Y-99

The Literary Scene and Situation and . . . Who (Besides Oprah) Really Runs American Literature?. Y-99

Literary Societies Y-98, Y-99, Y-00

"Literary Style" (1857), by William Forsyth [excerpt] DLB-57

Literatura Chicanesca: The View From Without. DLB-82

Literature at Nurse, or Circulating Morals (1885), by George Moore DLB-18

Littell, Eliakim 1797-1870 . . . . DLB-79

Littell, Robert S. 1831-1896. . . . . DLB-79

Little, Brown and Company DLB-49

Little Magazines and Newspapers DS-15

The Little Review 1914-1929 . . . . DS-15

Littlewood, Joan 1914- DLB-13

Lively, Penelope 1933- DLB-14, 161, 207

Liverpool University Press DLB-112

The Lives of the Poets. DLB-142

Livesay, Dorothy 1909- DLB-68

Livesay, Florence Randal 1874-1953 . . . . . . DLB-92

"Living in Ruin," by Gerald Stern DLB-105

Livings, Henry 1929-1998. . . . . DLB-13

Livingston, Anne Howe 1763-1841 . . . DLB-37, 200

Livingston, Myra Cohn 1926-1996 . . . . DLB-61

Livingston, William 1723-1790 . . . . DLB-31

Livingstone, David 1813-1873 . . . . DLB-166

Livingstone, Douglas 1932-1996 . . . . DLB-225

Livy 59 B.C.-A.D. 17 . . . . DLB-211; CDWLB-1

Liyong, Taban lo (see Taban lo Liyong)

Lizárraga, Sylvia S. 1925- DLB-82

Llewellyn, Richard 1906-1983. . . . . DLB-15

Lloyd, Edward [publishing house]. DLB-106

Lobel, Arnold 1933- DLB-61

Lochridge, Betsy Hopkins (see Fancher, Betsy)

Locke, David Ross 1833-1888. . . . . DLB-11, 23

Locke, John 1632-1704. . . . . DLB-31, 101, 213

Locke, Richard Adams 1800-1871 . . . . DLB-43

Locker-Lampson, Frederick 1821-1895 . . . . DLB-35, 184

Lockhart, John Gibson 1794-1854 . . . . DLB-110, 116 144

Lockridge, Ross, Jr. 1914-1948 . . . . DLB-143; Y-80

Locrine and Selimus. DLB-62

Lodge, David 1935- DLB-14, 194

Lodge, George Cabot 1873-1909 . . . . DLB-54

Lodge, Henry Cabot 1850-1924 . . . . DLB-47

Lodge, Thomas 1558-1625 . . . . DLB-172

From *Defence of Poetry* (1579) DLB-172

Loeb, Harold 1891-1974 . . . . DLB-4

Loeb, William 1905-1981 . . . . DLB-127

Lofting, Hugh 1886-1947. . . . . DLB-160

Logan, Deborah Norris 1761-1839 . . . . . . DLB-200

Logan, James 1674-1751. . . . . DLB-24, 140

Logan, John 1923- DLB-5

Logan, Martha Daniell 1704?-1779 . . . . . . DLB-200

Logan, William 1950- DLB-120

Logau, Friedrich von 1605-1655 . . . . DLB-164

Logue, Christopher 1926- DLB-27

Lohenstein, Daniel Casper von 1635-1683 . . . . DLB-168

Lomonosov, Mikhail Vasil'evich 1711-1765. . . . . DLB-150

London, Jack 1876-1916 . . . . . DLB-8, 12, 78, 212; CDALB-3

The London Magazine 1820-1829 . . . . DLB-110

Long, David 1948- DLB-244

Long, H., and Brother DLB-49

Long, Haniel 1888-1956 . . . . DLB-45

Long, Ray 1878-1935. . . . . DLB-137

Longfellow, Henry Wadsworth 1807-1882 . . . . DLB-1, 59, 235; CDALB-2

Longfellow, Samuel 1819-1892 . . . . DLB-1

Longford, Elizabeth 1906- DLB-155

Longinus circa first century DLB-176

Longley, Michael 1939- DLB-40

Longman, T. [publishing house] DLB-154

Longmans, Green and Company DLB-49

Longmore, George 1793?-1867 . . . . DLB-99

Longstreet, Augustus Baldwin 1790-1870 . . . . DLB-3, 11, 74, 248

Longworth, D. [publishing house]. DLB-49

Lonsdale, Frederick 1881-1954 . . . . DLB-10

A Look at the Contemporary Black Theatre Movement. DLB-38

Loos, Anita 1893-1981. . . . . . DLB-11, 26, 228; Y-81

Lopate, Phillip 1943- Y-80

Lopez, Barry 1945- DLB-256

López, Diana (see Isabella, Ríos)

López, Josefina 1969- DLB-209

Loranger, Jean-Aubert 1896-1942 . . . . DLB-92

Lorca, Federico García 1898-1936 . . . . . . DLB-108

Lord, John Keast 1818-1872 . . . . DLB-99

The Lord Chamberlain's Office and Stage Censorship in England DLB-10

Lorde, Audre 1934-1992 . . . . DLB-41

Lorimer, George Horace 1867-1939 . . . . . . DLB-91

Loring, A. K. [publishing house] DLB-49

Loring and Mussey DLB-46

Lorris, Guillaume de (see *Roman de la Rose*)

Lossing, Benson J. 1813-1891 . . . . DLB-30

Lothar, Ernst 1890-1974 . . . . DLB-81

Lothrop, D., and Company. DLB-49

Lothrop, Harriet M. 1844-1924 . . . . DLB-42

Loti, Pierre 1850-1923 . . . . DLB-123

Lotichius Secundus, Petrus 1528-1560 . . . DLB-179

Lott, Emeline ?-? DLB-166

Louisiana State University Press Y-97

The Lounger, no. 20 (1785), by Henry Mackenzie. DLB-39

Lounsbury, Thomas R. 1838-1915 . . . . DLB-71

Louÿs, Pierre 1870-1925 . . . . DLB-123

Lovelace, Earl 1935- DLB-125; CDWLB-3

Lovelace, Richard 1618-1657. . . . . DLB-131

Lovell, Coryell and Company. DLB-49

Lovell, John W., Company DLB-49

Lover, Samuel 1797-1868. . . . . DLB-159, 190

Lovesey, Peter 1936- DLB-87

Lovinescu, Eugen 1881-1943 . . . . DLB-220; CDWLB-4

Lovingood, Sut (see Harris, George Washington)

Low, Samuel 1765-? DLB-37

Lowell, Amy 1874-1925. . . . . DLB-54, 140

Lowell, James Russell 1819-1891 . . . . . . DLB-1, 11, 64, 79, 189, 235; CDALB-2

Lowell, Robert 1917-1977 . . DLB-5, 169; CDALB-7

Lowenfels, Walter 1897-1976. . . . . DLB-4

Lowndes, Marie Belloc 1868-1947. . . . . . . DLB-70

Lowndes, William Thomas 1798-1843 . . . DLB-184

Lownes, Humphrey [publishing house]. . . DLB-170

Lowry, Lois 1937- DLB-52

Lowry, Malcolm 1909-1957 . . . . DLB-15; CDBLB-7

Lowther, Pat 1935-1975. . . . . DLB-53

Loy, Mina 1882-1966 . . . . DLB-4, 54

Lozeau, Albert 1878-1924 . . . . DLB-92

Lubbock, Percy 1879-1965 . . . . DLB-149

Lucan A.D. 39-A.D. 65 . . . . DLB-211

Lucas, E. V. 1868-1938 . . . . . . DLB-98, 149, 153

Lucas, Fielding, Jr. [publishing house] DLB-49

Luce, Clare Booth 1903-1987 . . . . DLB-228

Luce, Henry R. 1898-1967 . . . . DLB-91

Luce, John W., and Company. DLB-46

Lucian circa 120-180 . . . . DLB-176

Lucie-Smith, Edward 1933- DLB-40

Lucilius circa 180 B.C.-102/101 B.C. DLB-211

Lucini, Gian Pietro 1867-1914 . . . . DLB-114

Lucretius circa 94 B.C.-circa 49 B.C. DLB-211; CDWLB-1

Luder, Peter circa 1415-1472 . . . . DLB-179

Ludlum, Robert 1927- Y-82

Ludus de Antichristo circa 1160 . . . . DLB-148

Ludvigson, Susan 1942- DLB-120

Ludwig, Jack 1922- DLB-60

Ludwig, Otto 1813-1865 . . . . DLB-129

Ludwigslied 881 or 882 . . . . DLB-148

Luera, Yolanda 1953- DLB-122

Luft, Lya 1938- DLB-145

Lugansky, Kazak Vladimir (see Dal', Vladimir Ivanovich)

Cumulative Index

Lugn, Kristina 1948- DLB-257
Lukács, Georg (see Lukács, György)
Lukács, György
  1885-1971 .... DLB-215, 242; CDWLB-4
Luke, Peter 1919- DLB-13
Lummis, Charles F. 1859-1928 .... DLB-186
Lupton, F. M., Company DLB-49
Lupus of Ferrières
  circa 805-circa 862 .... DLB-148
Lurie, Alison 1926- DLB-2
Lustig, Arnošt 1926- DLB-232
Luther, Martin 1483-1546 ...DLB-179; CDWLB-2
Luzi, Mario 1914- DLB-128
L'vov, Nikolai Aleksandrovich 1751-1803.. DLB-150
Lyall, Gavin 1932- DLB-87
Lydgate, John circa 1370-1450 .... DLB-146
Lyly, John circa 1554-1606 .... DLB-62, 167
Lynch, Patricia 1898-1972 .... DLB-160
Lynch, Richard flourished 1596-1601 ....DLB-172
Lynd, Robert 1879-1949 .... DLB-98
Lyon, Matthew 1749-1822 .... DLB-43
Lyotard, Jean-François 1924-1998 ...... DLB-242
Lysias circa 459 B.C.-circa 380 B.C...... DLB-176
Lytle, Andrew 1902-1995 .... DLB-6; Y-95
Lytton, Edward
  (see Bulwer-Lytton, Edward)
Lytton, Edward Robert Bulwer
  1831-1891 .... DLB-32

M

Maass, Joachim 1901-1972 .... DLB-69
Mabie, Hamilton Wright 1845-1916 ..... DLB-71
Mac A'Ghobhainn, Iain (see Smith, Iain Crichton)
MacArthur, Charles 1895-1956 .....DLB-7, 25, 44
Macaulay, Catherine 1731-1791 .... DLB-104
Macaulay, David 1945- DLB-61
Macaulay, Rose 1881-1958 .... DLB-36
Macaulay, Thomas Babington
  1800-1859 .... DLB-32, 55; CDBLB-4
Macaulay Company DLB-46
MacBeth, George 1932- DLB-40
Macbeth, Madge 1880-1965 .... DLB-92
MacCaig, Norman 1910-1996 .... DLB-27
MacDiarmid, Hugh
  1892-1978 .... DLB-20; CDBLB-7
MacDonald, Cynthia 1928- DLB-105
MacDonald, George 1824-1905 ... DLB-18, 163, 178
MacDonald, John D. 1916-1986 .... DLB-8; Y-86
MacDonald, Philip 1899?-1980 .... DLB-77
Macdonald, Ross (see Millar, Kenneth)
Macdonald, Sharman 1951- DLB-245
MacDonald, Wilson 1880-1967 .... DLB-92
Macdonald and Company (Publishers) ... DLB-112
MacEwen, Gwendolyn 1941- DLB-53
Macfadden, Bernarr 1868-1955 ..... DLB-25, 91
MacGregor, John 1825-1892 .... DLB-166

MacGregor, Mary Esther (see Keith, Marian)
Machado, Antonio 1875-1939 .... DLB-108
Machado, Manuel 1874-1947 .... DLB-108
Machar, Agnes Maule 1837-1927 ...... DLB-92
Machaut, Guillaume de
  circa 1300-1377 .... DLB-208
Machen, Arthur Llewelyn Jones
  1863-1947 .... DLB-36, 156, 178
MacInnes, Colin 1914-1976 .... DLB-14
MacInnes, Helen 1907-1985 .... DLB-87
Mac Intyre, Tom 1931- DLB-245
Mačiulis, Jonas (see Maironis, Jonas)
Mack, Maynard 1909- DLB-111
Mackall, Leonard L. 1879-1937 .... DLB-140
MacKaye, Percy 1875-1956 .... DLB-54
Macken, Walter 1915-1967 .... DLB-13
Mackenzie, Alexander 1763-1820 ...... DLB-99
Mackenzie, Alexander Slidell
  1803-1848 .... DLB-183
Mackenzie, Compton 1883-1972 .... DLB-34, 100
Mackenzie, Henry 1745-1831 .... DLB-39
Mackenzie, William 1758-1828 .... DLB-187
Mackey, Nathaniel 1947- DLB-169
Mackey, Shena 1944- DLB-231
Mackey, William Wellington
  1937- DLB-38
Mackintosh, Elizabeth (see Tey, Josephine)
Mackintosh, Sir James 1765-1832 ...... DLB-158
Maclaren, Ian (see Watson, John)
Macklin, Charles 1699-1797 .... DLB-89
MacLean, Katherine Anne 1925- DLB-8
Maclean, Norman 1902-1990 .... DLB-206
MacLeish, Archibald 1892-1982
  .... DLB-4, 7, 45, 228; Y-82; CDALB-7
MacLennan, Hugh 1907-1990 .... DLB-68
MacLeod, Alistair 1936- DLB-60
Macleod, Fiona (see Sharp, William)
Macleod, Norman 1906-1985 .... DLB-4
Mac Low, Jackson 1922- DLB-193
Macmillan and Company DLB-106
The Macmillan Company DLB-49
Macmillan's English Men of Letters,
  First Series (1878-1892) DLB-144
MacNamara, Brinsley 1890-1963 .... DLB-10
MacNeice, Louis 1907-1963 .... DLB-10, 20
MacPhail, Andrew 1864-1938 .... DLB-92
Macpherson, James 1736-1796 .... DLB-109
Macpherson, Jay 1931- DLB-53
Macpherson, Jeanie 1884-1946 .... DLB-44
Macrae Smith Company DLB-46
MacRaye, Lucy Betty (see Webling, Lucy)
Macrone, John [publishing house] DLB-106
MacShane, Frank 1927-1999 .... DLB-111
Macy-Masius DLB-46
Madden, David 1933- DLB-6
Madden, Sir Frederic 1801-1873 .... DLB-184

Maddow, Ben 1909-1992 .... DLB-44
Maddux, Rachel 1912-1983 ...... DLB-234; Y-93
Madgett, Naomi Long 1923- DLB-76
Madhubuti, Haki R. 1942- DLB-5, 41; DS-8
Madison, James 1751-1836 .... DLB-37
Madsen, Svend Åge 1939- DLB-214
Maeterlinck, Maurice 1862-1949 .... DLB-192
Mafūz, Najīb 1911- Y-88
Magee, David 1905-1977 .... DLB-187
Maginn, William 1794-1842 .... DLB-110, 159
Magoffin, Susan Shelby 1827-1855 ...... DLB-239
Mahan, Alfred Thayer 1840-1914 ...... DLB-47
Maheux-Forcier, Louise 1929- DLB-60
Mahin, John Lee 1902-1984 .... DLB-44
Mahon, Derek 1941- DLB-40
Maikov, Vasilii Ivanovich 1728-1778 .... DLB-150
Mailer, Norman 1923-
  .... DLB-2, 16, 28, 185; Y-80, Y-83, Y-97;
                               DS-3; CDALB-6
Maillart, Ella 1903-1997 .... DLB-195
Maillet, Adrienne 1885-1963 .... DLB-68
Maillet, Antonine 1929- DLB-60
Maillu, David G. 1939- DLB-157
Maimonides, Moses 1138-1204 .... DLB-115
Main Selections of the Book-of-the-Month
  Club, 1926-1945 .... DLB-9
Main Trends in Twentieth-Century Book
  Clubs DLB-46
Mainwaring, Daniel 1902-1977 .... DLB-44
Mair, Charles 1838-1927 .... DLB-99
Maironis, Jonas
  1862-1932 .... DLB-220; CDWLB-4
Mais, Roger 1905-1955 .....DLB-125; CDWLB-3
Major, Andre 1942- DLB-60
Major, Charles 1856-1913 .... DLB-202
Major, Clarence 1936- DLB-33
Major, Kevin 1949- DLB-60
Major Books DLB-46
Makemie, Francis circa 1658-1708 .... DLB-24
The Making of Americans Contract Y-98
The Making of a People, by
  J. M. Ritchie DLB-66
Maksimović, Desanka
  1898-1993 ....DLB-147; CDWLB-4
Malamud, Bernard 1914-1986
  .... DLB-2, 28, 152; Y-80, Y-86; CDALB-1
Mălăncioiu, Ileana 1940- DLB-232
Malerba, Luigi 1927- DLB-196
Malet, Lucas 1852-1931 .... DLB-153
Mallarmé, Stéphane 1842-1898 .... DLB-217
Malleson, Lucy Beatrice (see Gilbert, Anthony)
Mallet-Joris, Françoise 1930- DLB-83
Mallock, W. H. 1849-1923 ....DLB-18, 57
"Every Man His Own Poet; or,
  The Inspired Singer's Recipe
  Book" (1877) DLB-35
Malone, Dumas 1892-1986 .... DLB-17

Malone, Edmond 1741-1812 . . . . .DLB-142
Malory, Sir Thomas
　circa 1400-1410 - 1471 . . . DLB-146; CDBLB-1
Malpede, Karen 1945- DLB-249
Malraux, André 1901-1976 . . . . .DLB-72
Malthus, Thomas Robert
　1766-1834 . . . . DLB-107, 158
Maltz, Albert 1908-1985 . . . . .DLB-102
Malzberg, Barry N. 1939- DLB-8
Mamet, David 1947- DLB-7
Mamin, Dmitrii Narkisovich 1852-1912 . .DLB-238
Manaka, Matsemela 1956- DLB-157
Manchester University Press DLB-112
Mandel, Eli 1922- DLB-53
Mandeville, Bernard 1670-1733 . . . . .DLB-101
Mandeville, Sir John
　mid fourteenth century DLB-146
Mandiargues, André Pieyre de 1909- DLB-83
Manea, Norman 1936- DLB-232
Manfred, Frederick 1912-1994. . . . DLB-6, 212, 227
Manfredi, Gianfranco 1948- DLB-196
Mangan, Sherry 1904-1961 . . . . .DLB-4
Manganelli, Giorgio 1922-1990 . . . . .DLB-196
Manilius fl. first century A.D. DLB-211
Mankiewicz, Herman 1897-1953 . . . . .DLB-26
Mankiewicz, Joseph L. 1909-1993 . . . . .DLB-44
Mankowitz, Wolf 1924-1998 . . . . .DLB-15
Manley, Delarivière 1672?-1724. . . . . .DLB-39, 80
Preface to *The Secret History, of Queen Zarah,
　and the Zarazians* (1705) DLB-39
Mann, Abby 1927- DLB-44
Mann, Charles 1929-1998 . . . . Y-98
Mann, Heinrich 1871-1950 . . . . .DLB-66, 118
Mann, Horace 1796-1859. . . . . .DLB-1, 235
Mann, Klaus 1906-1949. . . . . .DLB-56
Mann, Mary Peabody 1806-1887 . . . . .DLB-239
Mann, Thomas 1875-1955. . . . DLB-66; CDWLB-2
Mann, William D'Alton 1839-1920 . . . . . .DLB-137
Mannin, Ethel 1900-1984 . . . . .DLB-191, 195
Manning, Emily (see Australie)
Manning, Marie 1873?-1945 . . . . .DLB-29
Manning and Loring DLB-49
Mannyng, Robert
　flourished 1303-1338. . . . . .DLB-146
Mano, D. Keith 1942- DLB-6
Manor Books. .DLB-46
Mansfield, Katherine 1888-1923 . . . . .DLB-162
Manuel, Niklaus circa 1484-1530 . . . . . . .DLB-179
Manzini, Gianna 1896-1974 . . . . .DLB-177
Mapanje, Jack 1944- DLB-157
Maraini, Dacia 1936- DLB-196
Marcel Proust at 129 and the Proust Society
　of America. Y-00
Marcel Proust's *Remembrance of Things Past*:
　The Rediscovered Galley Proofs Y-00
March, William 1893-1954 . . . . .DLB-9, 86

Marchand, Leslie A. 1900-1999. . . . . . . .DLB-103
Marchant, Bessie 1862-1941 . . . . .DLB-160
Marchant, Tony 1959- DLB-245
Marchenko, Anastasiia Iakovlevna
　1830-1880 .DLB-238
Marchessault, Jovette 1938- DLB-60
Marcinkevičius, Justinas 1930- DLB-232
Marcus, Frank 1928- DLB-13
Marcuse, Herbert 1898-1979 . . . . .DLB-242
Marden, Orison Swett 1850-1924 . . . . . . .DLB-137
Marechera, Dambudzo 1952-1987. . . . . . .DLB-157
Marek, Richard, Books DLB-46
Mares, E. A. 1938- DLB-122
Margulies, Donald 1954- DLB-228
Mariani, Paul 1940- DLB-111
Marie de France flourished 1160-1178. . . .DLB-208
Marie-Victorin, Frère 1885-1944 . . . . .DLB-92
Marin, Biagio 1891-1985 . . . . .DLB-128
Marincovič, Ranko
　1913- DLB-147; CDWLB-4
Marinetti, Filippo Tommaso
　1876-1944 .DLB-114
Marion, Frances 1886-1973 . . . . .DLB-44
Marius, Richard C. 1933-1999 . . . . Y-85
Markevich, Boleslav Mikhailovich
　1822-1884 .DLB-238
Markfield, Wallace 1926- DLB-2, 28
Markham, Edwin 1852-1940 . . . . .DLB-54, 186
Markle, Fletcher 1921-1991 . . . . .DLB-68; Y-91
Marlatt, Daphne 1942- DLB-60
Marlitt, E. 1825-1887 . . . . .DLB-129
Marlowe, Christopher
　1564-1593 . . . . DLB-62; CDBLB-1
Marlyn, John 1912- DLB-88
Marmion, Shakerley 1603-1639 . . . . .DLB-58
Der Marner before 1230-circa 1287 . . . . . .DLB-138
Marnham, Patrick 1943- DLB-204
The *Marprelate Tracts* 1588-1589 . . . . . . .DLB-132
Marquand, John P. 1893-1960. . . . . . . .DLB-9, 102
Marqués, René 1919-1979 . . . . .DLB-113
Marquis, Don 1878-1937 . . . . .DLB-11, 25
Marriott, Anne 1913- DLB-68
Marryat, Frederick 1792-1848 . . . . . .DLB-21, 163
Marsh, Capen, Lyon and Webb DLB-49
Marsh, George Perkins
　1801-1882 . . . . DLB-1, 64, 243
Marsh, James 1794-1842 . . . . .DLB-1, 59
Marsh, Narcissus 1638-1713 . . . . .DLB-213
Marsh, Ngaio 1899-1982 . . . . .DLB-77
Marshall, Edison 1894-1967 . . . . .DLB-102
Marshall, Edward 1932- DLB-16
Marshall, Emma 1828-1899 . . . . .DLB-163
Marshall, James 1942-1992 . . . . .DLB-61
Marshall, Joyce 1913- DLB-88
Marshall, Paule 1929- DLB-33, 157, 227
Marshall, Tom 1938- DLB-60

Marsilius of Padua
　circa 1275-circa 1342 . . . . .DLB-115
Mars-Jones, Adam 1954- DLB-207
Marson, Una 1905-1965 . . . . .DLB-157
Marston, John 1576-1634 . . . . .DLB-58, 172
Marston, Philip Bourke 1850-1887 . . . . . . .DLB-35
Martens, Kurt 1870-1945 . . . . .DLB-66
Martial circa A.D. 40-circa A.D. 103
　. . . . . DLB-211; CDWLB-1
Martien, William S. [publishing house] DLB-49
Martin, Abe (see Hubbard, Kin)
Martin, Catherine ca. 1847-1937 . . . . . . .DLB-230
Martin, Charles 1942- DLB-120
Martin, Claire 1914- DLB-60
Martin, Jay 1935- DLB-111
Martin, Johann (see Laurentius von Schnüffis)
Martin, Thomas 1696-1771 . . . . .DLB-213
Martin, Violet Florence (see Ross, Martin)
Martin du Gard, Roger 1881-1958 . . . . . . .DLB-65
Martineau, Harriet
　1802-1876 . . . . DLB-21, 55, 159, 163, 166, 190
Martínez, Demetria 1960- DLB-209
Martínez, Eliud 1935- DLB-122
Martínez, Max 1943- DLB-82
Martínez, Rubén 1962- DLB-209
Martone, Michael 1955- DLB-218
Martyn, Edward 1859-1923 . . . . .DLB-10
Marvell, Andrew
　1621-1678 . . . . DLB-131; CDBLB-2
Marvin X 1944- DLB-38
Marx, Karl 1818-1883 . . . . .DLB-129
Marzials, Theo 1850-1920 . . . . .DLB-35
Masefield, John
　1878-1967 . . . DLB-10, 19, 153, 160; CDBLB-5
Mason, A. E. W. 1865-1948 . . . . .DLB-70
Mason, Bobbie Ann
　1940- DLB-173; Y-87; CDALB-7
Mason, William 1725-1797 . . . . .DLB-142
Mason Brothers .DLB-49
Massey, Gerald 1828-1907 . . . . .DLB-32
Massey, Linton R. 1900-1974 . . . . .DLB-187
Massinger, Philip 1583-1640 . . . . .DLB-58
Masson, David 1822-1907 . . . . .DLB-144
Masters, Edgar Lee
　1868-1950 . . . . DLB-54; CDALB-3
Masters, Hilary 1928- DLB-244
Mastronardi, Lucio 1930-1979 . . . . .DLB-177
Matevski, Mateja 1929- . . . DLB-181; CDWLB-4
Mather, Cotton
　1663-1728 . . . . DLB-24, 30, 140; CDALB-2
Mather, Increase 1639-1723 . . . . .DLB-24
Mather, Richard 1596-1669 . . . . .DLB-24
Matheson, Annie 1853-1924 . . . . .DLB-240
Matheson, Richard 1926- DLB-8, 44
Matheus, John F. 1887- DLB-51
Mathews, Cornelius 1817?-1889 . . . . . . .DLB-3, 64
Mathews, Elkin [publishing house] DLB-112

Mathews, John Joseph 1894-1979 . . . . .DLB-175	McArthur, Peter 1866-1924 . . . . DLB-92	McGirt, James E. 1874-1930. . . . . DLB-50
Mathias, Roland 1915- DLB-27	McBride, Robert M., and Company DLB-46	McGlashan and Gill DLB-106
Mathis, June 1892-1927 . . . . DLB-44	McCabe, Patrick 1955- DLB-194	McGough, Roger 1937- DLB-40
Mathis, Sharon Bell 1937- DLB-33	McCaffrey, Anne 1926- DLB-8	McGrath, John 1935- DLB-233
Matković, Marijan 1915-1985. . . . . DLB-181	McCarthy, Cormac 1933- DLB-6, 143, 256	McGrath, Patrick 1950- DLB-231
Matoš, Antun Gustav 1873-1914 . . . . DLB-147	McCarthy, Mary 1912-1989. . . . . .DLB-2; Y-81	McGraw-Hill DLB-46
Matsumoto Seichō 1909-1992 . . . . DLB-182	McCay, Winsor 1871-1934. . . . . DLB-22	McGuane, Thomas 1939- DLB-2, 212; Y-80
The Matter of England 1240-1400 . . . . . . DLB-146	McClane, Albert Jules 1922-1991 . . . . . . .DLB-171	McGuckian, Medbh 1950- DLB-40
The Matter of Rome early twelfth to late fifteenth century. DLB-146	McClatchy, C. K. 1858-1936 . . . . DLB-25	McGuffey, William Holmes 1800-1873 . . . DLB-42
	McClellan, George Marion 1860-1934. . . . DLB-50	McGuinness, Frank 1953- DLB-245
Matthew of Vendôme circa 1130-circa 1200 . . . . DLB-208	McCloskey, Robert 1914- DLB-22	McHenry, James 1785-1845 . . . . DLB-202
Matthews, Brander 1852-1929 . . . . .DLB-71, 78; DS-13	McClung, Nellie Letitia 1873-1951 . . . . DLB-92	McIlvanney, William 1936- DLB-14, 207
	McClure, Joanna 1930- DLB-16	McIlwraith, Jean Newton 1859-1938 . . . . . DLB-92
Matthews, Jack 1925- DLB-6	McClure, Michael 1932- DLB-16	McIntosh, Maria Jane 1803-1878 . . . DLB-239, 248
Matthews, Victoria Earle 1861-1907. . . . . DLB-221	McClure, Phillips and Company DLB-46	McIntyre, James 1827-1906 . . . . DLB-99
Matthews, William 1942-1997 . . . . DLB-5	McClure, S. S. 1857-1949 . . . . DLB-91	McIntyre, O. O. 1884-1938 . . . . DLB-25
Matthiessen, F. O. 1902-1950 . . . . DLB-63	McClurg, A. C., and Company DLB-49	McKay, Claude 1889-1948. . . . .DLB-4, 45, 51, 117
Matthiessen, Peter 1927- DLB-6, 173	McCluskey, John A., Jr. 1944- DLB-33	The David McKay Company. DLB-49
Maturin, Charles Robert 1780-1824 . . . . . .DLB-178	McCollum, Michael A. 1946 . . . . Y-87	McKean, William V. 1820-1903. . . . . DLB-23
Maugham, W. Somerset 1874-1965 . . . . . DLB-10, 36, 77, 100, 162, 195; CDBLB-6	McConnell, William C. 1917- DLB-88	McKenna, Stephen 1888-1967 . . . . .DLB-197
	McCord, David 1897-1997 . . . . DLB-61	The McKenzie Trust Y-96
Maupassant, Guy de 1850-1893 . . . . DLB-123	McCord, Louisa S. 1810-1879 . . . . DLB-248	McKerrow, R. B. 1872-1940. . . . . DLB-201
Mauriac, Claude 1914-1996 . . . . DLB-83	McCorkle, Jill 1958- DLB-234; Y-87	McKinley, Robin 1952- DLB-52
Mauriac, François 1885-1970 . . . . DLB-65	McCorkle, Samuel Eusebius 1746-1811. . . . . DLB-37	McKnight, Reginald 1956- DLB-234
Maurice, Frederick Denison 1805-1872. . . . . DLB-55		McLachlan, Alexander 1818-1896 . . . . DLB-99
	McCormick, Anne O'Hare 1880-1954. . . . DLB-29	McLaren, Floris Clark 1904-1978. . . . . . . DLB-68
Maurois, André 1885-1967. . . . . DLB-65	Kenneth Dale McCormick Tributes. Y-97	McLaverty, Michael 1907- DLB-15
Maury, James 1718-1769. . . . . DLB-31	McCormick, Robert R. 1880-1955 . . . . . . DLB-29	McLean, John R. 1848-1916. . . . . DLB-23
Mavor, Elizabeth 1927- DLB-14	McCourt, Edward 1907-1972 . . . . DLB-88	McLean, William L. 1852-1931 . . . . DLB-25
Mavor, Osborne Henry (see Bridie, James)	McCoy, Horace 1897-1955. . . . . DLB-9	McLennan, William 1856-1904 . . . . DLB-92
Maxwell, Gavin 1914-1969. . . . . DLB-204	McCrae, John 1872-1918 . . . . DLB-92	McLoughlin Brothers DLB-49
Maxwell, H. [publishing house] DLB-49	McCullagh, Joseph B. 1842-1896 . . . . DLB-23	McLuhan, Marshall 1911-1980 . . . . DLB-88
Maxwell, John [publishing house]. DLB-106	McCullers, Carson 1917-1967 . . . . . . DLB-2, 7, 173, 228; CDALB-1	McMaster, John Bach 1852-1932 . . . . DLB-47
Maxwell, William 1908- DLB-218; Y-80		McMurtry, Larry 1936- DLB-2, 143, 256; Y-80, Y-87; CDALB-6
May, Elaine 1932- DLB-44	McCulloch, Thomas 1776-1843 . . . . DLB-99	
May, Karl 1842-1912 . . . . DLB-129	McDonald, Forrest 1927- DLB-17	McNally, Terrence 1939- DLB-7, 249
May, Thomas 1595 or 1596-1650 . . . . . . DLB-58	McDonald, Walter 1934- DLB-105, DS-9	McNeil, Florence 1937- DLB-60
Mayer, Bernadette 1945- DLB-165	"Getting Started: Accepting the Regions You Own–or Which Own You," . . . DLB-105	McNeile, Herman Cyril 1888-1937 . . . . . . DLB-77
Mayer, Mercer 1943- DLB-61		McNickle, D'Arcy 1904-1977 . . . . . . .DLB-175, 212
Mayer, O. B. 1818-1891. . . . . DLB-3, 248	McDougall, Colin 1917-1984 . . . . DLB-68	McPhee, John 1931- DLB-185
Mayes, Herbert R. 1900-1987. . . . . DLB-137	McDowell, Katharine Sherwood Bonner 1849-1883 . . . . DLB-202, 239	McPherson, James Alan 1943- DLB-38, 244
Mayes, Wendell 1919-1992 . . . . DLB-26		McPherson, Sandra 1943- Y-86
Mayfield, Julian 1928-1984. . . . . DLB-33; Y-84	McDowell, Obolensky DLB-46	McWhirter, George 1939- DLB-60
Mayhew, Henry 1812-1887 . . . . . DLB-18, 55, 190	McEwan, Ian 1948- DLB-14, 194	McWilliams, Carey 1905-1980. . . . . .DLB-137
Mayhew, Jonathan 1720-1766 . . . . DLB-31	McFadden, David 1940- DLB-60	Mda, Zakes 1948- DLB-225
Mayne, Ethel Colburn 1865-1941 . . . . . . DLB-197	McFall, Frances Elizabeth Clarke (see Grand, Sarah)	Mead, L. T. 1844-1914. . . . . DLB-141
Mayne, Jasper 1604-1672 . . . . DLB-126		Mead, Matthew 1924- DLB-40
Mayne, Seymour 1944- DLB-60	McFarlane, Leslie 1902-1977 . . . . DLB-88	Mead, Taylor ?- DLB-16
Mayor, Flora Macdonald 1872-1932 . . . . . DLB-36	McFarland, Ronald 1942- DLB-256	Meany, Tom 1903-1964. . . . . .DLB-171
Mayrocker, Friederike 1924- DLB-85	McFee, William 1881-1966. . . . . DLB-153	
Mazrui, Ali A. 1933- DLB-125	McGahern, John 1934- DLB-14, 231	Mechthild von Magdeburg circa 1207-circa 1282 . . . . DLB-138
Mažuranić, Ivan 1814-1890 . . . . DLB-147	McGee, Thomas D'Arcy 1825-1868 . . . . . DLB-99	Medieval French Drama. DLB-208
Mazursky, Paul 1930- DLB-44	McGeehan, W. O. 1879-1933. . . . . . .DLB-25, 171	Medieval Travel Diaries. DLB-203
McAlmon, Robert 1896-1956 . . . . DLB-4, 45; DS-15	McGill, Ralph 1898-1969 . . . . DLB-29	Medill, Joseph 1823-1899 . . . . DLB-43
	McGinley, Phyllis 1905-1978 . . . . . . DLB-11, 48	
	McGinniss, Joe 1942- DLB-185	Medoff, Mark 1940- DLB-7

Meek, Alexander Beaufort 1814-1865 .... DLB-3, 248
Meeke, Mary ?-1816? DLB-116
Meinke, Peter 1932- DLB-5
Mejia Vallejo, Manuel 1923- DLB-113
Melanchthon, Philipp 1497-1560 .... DLB-179
Melançon, Robert 1947- DLB-60
Mell, Max 1882-1971 .... DLB-81, 124
Mellow, James R. 1926-1997 .... DLB-111
Mel'nikov, Pavel Ivanovich 1818-1883 ... DLB-238
Meltzer, David 1937- DLB-16
Meltzer, Milton 1915- DLB-61
Melville, Elizabeth, Lady Culross circa 1585-1640 .... DLB-172
Melville, Herman 1819-1891 .... DLB-3, 74; CDALB-2
Memoirs of Life and Literature (1920), by W. H. Mallock [excerpt] DLB-57
Mena, María Cristina 1893-1965 .... DLB-209, 221
Menander 342-341 B.C.-circa 292-291 B.C. DLB-176; CDWLB-1
Menantes (see Hunold, Christian Friedrich)
Mencke, Johann Burckhard 1674-1732 .... DLB-168
Mencken, H. L. 1880-1956 .... DLB-11, 29, 63, 137, 222; CDALB-4
H. L. Mencken's "Berlin, February, 1917".... Y-00
Mencken and Nietzsche: An Unpublished Excerpt from H. L. Mencken's *My Life as Author and Editor* Y-93
Mendelssohn, Moses 1729-1786 .... DLB-97
Mendes, Catulle 1841-1909 .... DLB-217
Méndez M., Miguel 1930- DLB-82
Mens Rea (or Something) Y-97
The Mercantile Library of New York Y-96
Mercer, Cecil William (see Yates, Dornford)
Mercer, David 1928-1980 .... DLB-13
Mercer, John 1704-1768 .... DLB-31
Meredith, George 1828-1909 .... DLB-18, 35, 57, 159; CDBLB-4
Meredith, Louisa Anne 1812-1895 .. DLB-166, 230
Meredith, Owen (see Lytton, Edward Robert Bulwer)
Meredith, William 1919- DLB-5
Mergerle, Johann Ulrich (see Abraham à Sancta Clara)
Mérimée, Prosper 1803-1870 .... DLB-119, 192
Merivale, John Herman 1779-1844 ...... DLB-96
Meriwether, Louise 1923- DLB-33
Merlin Press DLB-112
Merriam, Eve 1916-1992 .... DLB-61
The Merriam Company DLB-49
Merrill, James 1926-1995 ...... DLB-5, 165; Y-85
Merrill and Baker DLB-49
The Mershon Company DLB-49
Merton, Thomas 1915-1968 .... DLB-48; Y-81
Merwin, W. S. 1927- DLB-5, 169
Messner, Julian [publishing house] DLB-46

Mészöly, Miklós 1921- DLB-232
Metcalf, J. [publishing house] DLB-49
Metcalf, John 1938- DLB-60
The Methodist Book Concern DLB-49
Methuen and Company DLB-112
Meun, Jean de (see *Roman de la Rose*)
Mew, Charlotte 1869-1928 .... DLB-19, 135
Mewshaw, Michael 1943- Y-80
Meyer, Conrad Ferdinand 1825-1898 .... DLB-129
Meyer, E. Y. 1946- DLB-75
Meyer, Eugene 1875-1959 .... DLB-29
Meyer, Michael 1921-2000 .... DLB-155
Meyers, Jeffrey 1939- DLB-111
Meynell, Alice 1847-1922 .... DLB-19, 98
Meynell, Viola 1885-1956 .... DLB-153
Meyrink, Gustav 1868-1932 .... DLB-81
Mézières, Philipe de circa 1327-1405 ..... DLB-208
Michael, Ib 1945- DLB-214
Michaëlis, Karen 1872-1950 .... DLB-214
Michaels, Leonard 1933- DLB-130
Micheaux, Oscar 1884-1951 .... DLB-50
Michel of Northgate, Dan circa 1265-circa 1340 .... DLB-146
Micheline, Jack 1929-1998 .... DLB-16
Michener, James A. 1907?-1997 .... DLB-6
Micklejohn, George circa 1717-1818 .... DLB-31
Middle English Literature: An Introduction DLB-146
The Middle English Lyric DLB-146
Middle Hill Press DLB-106
Middleton, Christopher 1926- DLB-40
Middleton, Richard 1882-1911 .... DLB-156
Middleton, Stanley 1919- DLB-14
Middleton, Thomas 1580-1627 .... DLB-58
Miegel, Agnes 1879-1964 .... DLB-56
Miežielaitis, Eduardas 1919-1997 .... DLB-220
Mihailović, Dragoslav 1930- DLB-181
Mihalić, Slavko 1928- DLB-181
Mikhailov, A. (see Sheller, Aleksandr Konstantinovich)
Mikhailov, Mikhail Larionovich 1829-1865 .... DLB-238
Miles, Josephine 1911-1985 .... DLB-48
Miles, Susan (Ursula Wyllie Roberts) 1888-1975 .... DLB-240
Miliković, Branko 1934-1961 .... DLB-181
Milius, John 1944- DLB-44
Mill, James 1773-1836 .... DLB-107, 158
Mill, John Stuart 1806-1873 .... DLB-55, 190; CDBLB-4
Millar, Andrew [publishing house] DLB-154
Millar, Kenneth 1915-1983 .... DLB-2, 226; Y-83; DS-6
Millay, Edna St. Vincent 1892-1950 .... DLB-45, 249; CDALB-4
Millen, Sarah Gertrude 1888-1968 ...... DLB-225

Miller, Arthur 1915- DLB-7; CDALB-1
Miller, Caroline 1903-1992 .... DLB-9
Miller, Eugene Ethelbert 1950- DLB-41
Miller, Heather Ross 1939- DLB-120
Miller, Henry 1891-1980 .... DLB-4, 9; Y-80; CDALB-5
Miller, Hugh 1802-1856 .... DLB-190
Miller, J. Hillis 1928- DLB-67
Miller, James [publishing house] DLB-49
Miller, Jason 1939- DLB-7
Miller, Joaquin 1839-1913 .... DLB-186
Miller, May 1899- DLB-41
Miller, Paul 1906-1991 .... DLB-127
Miller, Perry 1905-1963 .... DLB-17, 63
Miller, Sue 1943- DLB-143
Miller, Vassar 1924-1998 .... DLB-105
Miller, Walter M., Jr. 1923- DLB-8
Miller, Webb 1892-1940 .... DLB-29
Millett, Kate 1934- DLB-246
Millhauser, Steven 1943- DLB-2
Millican, Arthenia J. Bates 1920- DLB-38
Milligan, Alice 1866-1953 .... DLB-240
Mills and Boon DLB-112
Milman, Henry Hart 1796-1868 .... DLB-96
Milne, A. A. 1882-1956 ... DLB-10, 77, 100, 160
Milner, Ron 1938- DLB-38
Milner, William [publishing house] DLB-106
Milnes, Richard Monckton (Lord Houghton) 1809-1885 .... DLB-32, 184
Milton, John 1608-1674 .... DLB-131, 151; CDBLB-2
Miłosz, Czesław 1911- DLB-215; CDWLB-4
Minakami Tsutomu 1919- DLB-182
Minamoto no Sanetomo 1192-1219 ...... DLB-203
The Minerva Press DLB-154
Minnesang circa 1150-1280 .... DLB-138
Minns, Susan 1839-1938 .... DLB-140
Minor Illustrators, 1880-1914 .... DLB-141
Minor Poets of the Earlier Seventeenth Century DLB-121
Minton, Balch and Company DLB-46
Mirbeau, Octave 1848-1917 .... DLB-123, 192
Mirk, John died after 1414? DLB-146
Miron, Gaston 1928- DLB-60
A Mirror for Magistrates DLB-167
Mishima Yukio 1925-1970 .... DLB-182
Mitchel, Jonathan 1624-1668 .... DLB-24
Mitchell, Adrian 1932- DLB-40
Mitchell, Donald Grant 1822-1908 .... DLB-1, 243; DS-13
Mitchell, Gladys 1901-1983 .... DLB-77
Mitchell, James Leslie 1901-1935 ...... DLB-15
Mitchell, John (see Slater, Patrick)
Mitchell, John Ames 1845-1918 .... DLB-79
Mitchell, Joseph 1908-1996 ...... DLB-185; Y-96
Mitchell, Julian 1935- DLB-14

Mitchell, Ken 1940- DLB-60	Montgomery, James 1771-1854...... DLB-93, 158	Morgan, Edmund S. 1916- DLB-17
Mitchell, Langdon 1862-1935............ DLB-7	Montgomery, John 1919- DLB-16	Morgan, Edwin 1920- DLB-27
Mitchell, Loften 1919- DLB-38	Montgomery, Lucy Maud 1874-1942................ DLB-92; DS-14	Morgan, John Pierpont 1837-1913 .... DLB-140
Mitchell, Margaret 1900-1949 .. DLB-9; CDALB-7		Morgan, John Pierpont, Jr. 1867-1943 ... DLB-140
Mitchell, S. Weir 1829-1914.......... DLB-202	Montgomery, Marion 1925- DLB-6	Morgan, Robert 1944- DLB-120
Mitchell, W. J. T. 1942- DLB-246	Montgomery, Robert Bruce (see Crispin, Edmund)	Morgan, Sydney Owenson, Lady 1776?-1859................ DLB-116, 158
Mitchell, W. O. 1914- DLB-88	Montherlant, Henry de 1896-1972....... DLB-72	
Mitchison, Naomi Margaret (Haldane) 1897-1999.............. DLB-160, 191, 255	The Monthly Review 1749-1844 .... DLB-110	Morgner, Irmtraud 1933- DLB-75
	Montigny, Louvigny de 1876-1955....... DLB-92	Morhof, Daniel Georg 1639-1691 ...... DLB-164
Mitford, Mary Russell 1787-1855 .... .DLB-110, 116	Montoya, José 1932- DLB-122	Mori, Ōgai 1862-1922 .... DLB-180
Mitford, Nancy 1904-1973 .... DLB-191	Moodie, John Wedderburn Dunbar 1797-1869..................... DLB-99	Móricz, Zsigmond 1879-1942 .... DLB-215
Mittelholzer, Edgar 1909-1965 .... .DLB-117; CDWLB-3		Morier, James Justinian 1782 or 1783?-1849 .... DLB-116
	Moodie, Susanna 1803-1885 .... DLB-99	
Mitterer, Erika 1906- DLB-85	Moody, Joshua circa 1633-1697 .... DLB-24	Mörike, Eduard 1804-1875............ DLB-133
Mitterer, Felix 1948- DLB-124	Moody, William Vaughn 1869-1910 ....DLB-7, 54	Morin, Paul 1889-1963................ DLB-92
Mitternacht, Johann Sebastian 1613-1679..................... DLB-168	Moorcock, Michael 1939- DLB-14, 231	Morison, Richard 1514?-1556 .... DLB-136
	Moore, Catherine L. 1911- DLB-8	Morison, Samuel Eliot 1887-1976 .... .DLB-17
Miyamoto, Yuriko 1899-1951 .... DLB-180	Moore, Clement Clarke 1779-1863....... DLB-42	Morison, Stanley 1889-1967........... DLB-201
Mizener, Arthur 1907-1988............ DLB-103	Moore, Dora Mavor 1888-1979 .... DLB-92	Moritz, Karl Philipp 1756-1793 .... DLB-94
Mo, Timothy 1950- DLB-194	Moore, George 1852-1933 .... DLB-10, 18, 57, 135	*Moriz von Craûn* circa 1220-1230 .... DLB-138
Modern Age Books.................. DLB-46	Moore, Lorrie 1957- DLB-234	Morley, Christopher 1890-1957 .... DLB-9
"Modern English Prose" (1876), by George Saintsbury............... DLB-57	Moore, Marianne 1887-1972 .... DLB-45; DS-7; CDALB-5	Morley, John 1838-1923........ DLB-57, 144, 190
		Morris, George Pope 1802-1864 .... DLB-73
The Modern Language Association of America Celebrates Its Centennial............. Y-84	Moore, Mavor 1919- DLB-88	Morris, James Humphrey (see Morris, Jan)
	Moore, Richard 1927- DLB-105	Morris, Jan 1926- DLB-204
The Modern Library DLB-46	Moore, T. Sturge 1870-1944............ DLB-19	Morris, Lewis 1833-1907 .... DLB-35
"Modern Novelists – Great and Small" (1855), by Margaret Oliphant DLB-21	Moore, Thomas 1779-1852.......... DLB-96, 144	Morris, Margaret 1737-1816 .... DLB-200
	Moore, Ward 1903-1978 .... DLB-8	Morris, Richard B. 1904-1989 .... .DLB-17
"Modern Style" (1857), by Cockburn Thomson [excerpt]................ DLB-57	Moore, Wilstach, Keys and Company.... DLB-49	Morris, William 1834-1896 ..... DLB-18, 35, 57, 156, 178, 184; CDBLB-4
	Moorehead, Alan 1901-1983 .... DLB-204	
The Modernists (1932), by Joseph Warren Beach DLB-36	Moorhouse, Geoffrey 1931- DLB-204	Morris, Willie 1934-1999................ Y-80
	The Moorland-Spingarn Research Center DLB-76	Morris, Wright 1910-1998 .... .DLB-2, 206, 218; Y-81
Modiano, Patrick 1945- DLB-83		
Moffat, Yard and Company DLB-46	Moorman, Mary C. 1905-1994 .... DLB-155	Morrison, Arthur 1863-1945 .... DLB-70, 135, 197
Moffet, Thomas 1553-1604 .... DLB-136	Mora, Pat 1942- DLB-209	Morrison, Charles Clayton 1874-1966 .... DLB-91
Mohr, Nicholasa 1938- DLB-145	Moraga, Cherríe 1952- DLB-82, 249	Morrison, Toni 1931- DLB-6, 33, 143; Y-81, Y-93; CDALB-6
Moix, Ana María 1947- DLB-134	Morales, Alejandro 1944- DLB-82	
Molesworth, Louisa 1839-1921 .... DLB-135		Morrow, William, and Company........ DLB-46
Möllhausen, Balduin 1825-1905........ DLB-129	Morales, Mario Roberto 1947- DLB-145	Morse, James Herbert 1841-1923........ DLB-71
Molnár, Ferenc 1878-1952............ DLB-215; CDWLB-4	Morales, Rafael 1919- DLB-108	Morse, Jedidiah 1761-1826.............. DLB-37
	Morality Plays: *Mankind* circa 1450-1500 and *Everyman* circa 1500 .... DLB-146	Morse, John T., Jr. 1840-1937 .... DLB-47
Molnár, Miklós (see Mészöly, Miklós)		Morselli, Guido 1912-1973............ .DLB-177
Momaday, N. Scott 1934- DLB-143, 175, 256; CDALB-7	Morante, Elsa 1912-1985 .... .DLB-177	Mortimer, Favell Lee 1802-1878........ DLB-163
	Morata, Olympia Fulvia 1526-1555 ..... .DLB-179	Mortimer, John 1923- DLB-13, 245; CDBLB-8
Monkhouse, Allan 1858-1936.......... DLB-10	Moravia, Alberto 1907-1990........... .DLB-177	
Monro, Harold 1879-1932 .... DLB-19	Mordaunt, Elinor 1872-1942 .... .DLB-174	Morton, Carlos 1942- DLB-122
Monroe, Harriet 1860-1936 .... DLB-54, 91	Mordovtsev, Daniil Lukich 1830-1905... DLB-238	Morton, H. V. 1892-1979............. DLB-195
Monsarrat, Nicholas 1910-1979 .... DLB-15	More, Hannah 1745-1833........... DLB-107, 109, 116, 158	Morton, John P., and Company......... DLB-49
Montagu, Lady Mary Wortley 1689-1762.................. DLB-95, 101		Morton, Nathaniel 1613-1685 .... DLB-24
	More, Henry 1614-1687.............. DLB-126	Morton, Sarah Wentworth 1759-1846 .... DLB-37
Montague, C. E. 1867-1928 .... DLB-197	More, Sir Thomas 1477 or 1478-1535 .... DLB-136	Morton, Thomas circa 1579-circa 1647 ... DLB-24
Montague, John 1929- DLB-40		Moscherosch, Johann Michael 1601-1669 .... DLB-164
Montale, Eugenio 1896-1981 .... DLB-114	Moreno, Dorinda 1939- DLB-122	
Montalvo, José 1946-1994 .... DLB-209	Morency, Pierre 1942- DLB-60	Moseley, Humphrey [publishing house] DLB-170
Monterroso, Augusto 1921- DLB-145	Moretti, Marino 1885-1979............ DLB-114	
Montesquiou, Robert de 1855-1921 ..... DLB-217	Morgan, Berry 1919- DLB-6	Möser, Justus 1720-1794 .... DLB-97
Montgomerie, Alexander circa 1550?-1598 .... DLB-167	Morgan, Charles 1894-1958......... DLB-34, 100	Mosley, Nicholas 1923- DLB-14, 207

DLB 257 — Cumulative Index

Moss, Arthur 1889-1969 . . . . DLB-4
Moss, Howard 1922-1987 . . . . DLB-5
Moss, Thylias 1954- DLB-120
The Most Powerful Book Review
  in America
  [*New York Times Book Review*] Y-82
Motion, Andrew 1952- DLB-40
Motley, John Lothrop
  1814-1877 . . . . DLB-1, 30, 59, 235
Motley, Willard 1909-1965 . . . . DLB-76, 143
Mott, Lucretia 1793-1880 . . . . DLB-239
Motte, Benjamin Jr. [publishing house] . . . DLB-154
Motteux, Peter Anthony 1663-1718 . . . . . . DLB-80
Mottram, R. H. 1883-1971 . . . . DLB-36
Mount, Ferdinand 1939- DLB-231
Mouré, Erin 1955- DLB-60
Mourning Dove (Humishuma) between
  1882 and 1888?-1936 . . . . DLB-175, 221
Movies from Books, 1920-1974 . . . . DLB-9
Mowat, Farley 1921- DLB-68
Mowbray, A. R., and Company,
  Limited DLB-106
Mowrer, Edgar Ansel 1892-1977 . . . . DLB-29
Mowrer, Paul Scott 1887-1971 . . . . DLB-29
Moxon, Edward [publishing house] DLB-106
Moxon, Joseph [publishing house] DLB-170
Mphahlele, Es'kia (Ezekiel)
  1919- DLB-125; CDWLB-3
Mrożek, Sławomir 1930- . . . DLB-232; CDWLB-4
Mtshali, Oswald Mbuyiseni 1940- DLB-125
Mucedorus DLB-62
Mudford, William 1782-1848 . . . . DLB-159
Mueller, Lisel 1924- DLB-105
Muhajir, El (see Marvin X)
Muhajir, Nazzam Al Fitnah (see Marvin X)
Mühlbach, Luise 1814-1873 . . . . DLB-133
Muir, Edwin 1887-1959 . . . . DLB-20, 100, 191
Muir, Helen 1937- DLB-14
Muir, John 1838-1914 . . . . DLB-186
Muir, Percy 1894-1979 . . . . DLB-201
Mujū Ichien 1226-1312 . . . . DLB-203
Mukherjee, Bharati 1940- DLB-60, 218
Mulcaster, Richard
  1531 or 1532-1611 . . . . DLB-167
Muldoon, Paul 1951- DLB-40
Müller, Friedrich (see Müller, Maler)
Müller, Heiner 1929-1995 . . . . DLB-124
Müller, Maler 1749-1825 . . . . DLB-94
Muller, Marcia 1944- DLB-226
Müller, Wilhelm 1794-1827 . . . . DLB-90
Mumford, Lewis 1895-1990 . . . . DLB-63
Munby, A. N. L. 1913-1974 . . . . DLB-201
Munby, Arthur Joseph 1828-1910 . . . . DLB-35
Munday, Anthony 1560-1633 . . . . . . DLB-62, 172
Mundt, Clara (see Mühlbach, Luise)
Mundt, Theodore 1808-1861 . . . . DLB-133

Munford, Robert circa 1737-1783 . . . . DLB-31
Mungoshi, Charles 1947- DLB-157
Munk, Kaj 1898-1944 . . . . DLB-214
Munonye, John 1929- DLB-117
Munro, Alice 1931- DLB-53
Munro, George [publishing house] DLB-49
Munro, H. H.
  1870-1916 . . . . DLB-34, 162; CDBLB-5
Munro, Neil 1864-1930 . . . . DLB-156
Munro, Norman L.
  [publishing house] DLB-49
Munroe, James, and Company DLB-49
Munroe, Kirk 1850-1930 . . . . DLB-42
Munroe and Francis DLB-49
Munsell, Joel [publishing house] DLB-49
Munsey, Frank A. 1854-1925 . . . . DLB-25, 91
Munsey, Frank A., and Company DLB-49
Murakami Haruki 1949- DLB-182
Murav'ev, Mikhail Nikitich
  1757-1807 . . . . DLB-150
Murdoch, Iris
  1919-1999 . . . . . . DLB-14, 194, 233; CDBLB-8
Murdoch, Rupert 1931- DLB-127
Murfree, Mary N. 1850-1922 . . . . DLB-12, 74
Murger, Henry 1822-1861 . . . . DLB-119
Murger, Louis-Henri (see Murger, Henry)
Murner, Thomas 1475-1537 . . . . DLB-179
Muro, Amado 1915-1971 . . . . DLB-82
Murphy, Arthur 1727-1805 . . . . DLB-89, 142
Murphy, Beatrice M. 1908- DLB-76
Murphy, Dervla 1931- DLB-204
Murphy, Emily 1868-1933 . . . . DLB-99
Murphy, Jack 1923-1980 . . . . DLB-241
Murphy, John, and Company DLB-49
Murphy, John H., III 1916- DLB-127
Murphy, Richard 1927-1993 . . . . DLB-40
Murray, Albert L. 1916- DLB-38
Murray, Gilbert 1866-1957 . . . . DLB-10
Murray, Jim 1919-1998 . . . . DLB-241
Murray, John [publishing house] DLB-154
Murry, John Middleton 1889-1957 . . . . . . DLB-149
"The Break-Up of the Novel" (1922) DLB-36
Murray, Judith Sargent 1751-1820 . . . . DLB-37, 200
Murray, Pauli 1910-1985 . . . . DLB-41
Musäus, Johann Karl August 1735-1787 . . . DLB-97
Muschg, Adolf 1934- DLB-75
The Music of *Minnesang* DLB-138
Musil, Robert
  1880-1942 . . . . DLB-81, 124; CDWLB-2
Muspilli circa 790-circa 850 . . . . DLB-148
Musset, Alfred de 1810-1857 . . . . DLB-192, 217
Mussey, Benjamin B., and Company DLB-49
Mutafchieva, Vera 1929- DLB-181
Mwangi, Meja 1948- DLB-125
Myers, Frederic W. H. 1843-1901 . . . . DLB-190
Myers, Gustavus 1872-1942 . . . . DLB-47

Myers, L. H. 1881-1944 . . . . DLB-15
Myers, Walter Dean 1937- DLB-33
Mykolaitis-Putinas, Vincas 1893-1967 . . . . DLB-220
Myles, Eileen 1949- DLB-193
Myrdal, Jan 1927- DLB-257

N

Na Prous Boneta circa 1296-1328 . . . . DLB-208
Nabl, Franz 1883-1974 . . . . DLB-81
Nabokov, Vladimir 1899-1977
  . . . . DLB-2, 244; Y-80, Y-91; DS-3; CDALB-1
The Vladimir Nabokov Archive
  in the Berg Collection Y-91
Nabokov Festival at Cornell Y-83
Nádaši, Ladislav (see Jégé)
Naden, Constance 1858-1889 . . . . DLB-199
Nadezhdin, Nikolai Ivanovich
  1804-1856 . . . . DLB-198
Naevius circa 265 B.C.-201 B.C. DLB-211
Nafis and Cornish DLB-49
Nagai, Kafū 1879-1959 . . . . DLB-180
Naipaul, Shiva 1945-1985 . . . . DLB 157; Y 85
Naipaul, V. S. 1932-
  . . . . DLB-125, 204, 207; Y-85;
                              CDBLB-8; CDWLB-3
Nakagami Kenji 1946-1992 . . . . DLB-182
Nakano-in Masatada no Musume (see Nijō, Lady)
Nałkowska, Zofia 1884-1954 . . . . DLB-215
Nancrede, Joseph [publishing house] DLB-49
Naranjo, Carmen 1930- DLB-145
Narezhny, Vasilii Trofimovich
  1780-1825 . . . . DLB-198
Narrache, Jean 1893-1970 . . . . DLB-92
Nasby, Petroleum Vesuvius (see Locke, David Ross)
Nash, Eveleigh [publishing house] DLB-112
Nash, Ogden 1902-1971 . . . . DLB-11
Nashe, Thomas 1567-1601? DLB-167
Nason, Jerry 1910-1986 . . . . DLB-241
Nast, Conde 1873-1942 . . . . DLB-91
Nast, Thomas 1840-1902 . . . . DLB-188
Nastasijević, Momčilo 1894-1938 . . . . DLB-147
Nathan, George Jean 1882-1958 . . . . DLB-137
Nathan, Robert 1894-1985 . . . . DLB-9
National Book Critics Circle Awards 2000 . . . Y-00
The National Jewish Book Awards Y-85
The National Theatre and the Royal
  Shakespeare Company: The
  National Companies DLB-13
Natsume, Sōseki 1867-1916 . . . . DLB-180
Naughton, Bill 1910- DLB-13
Navarro, Joe 1953- DLB-209
Naylor, Gloria 1950- DLB-173
Nazor, Vladimir 1876-1949 . . . . DLB-147
Ndebele, Njabulo 1948- DLB-157
Neagoe, Peter 1881-1960 . . . . DLB-4
Neal, John 1793-1876 . . . . DLB-1, 59, 243
Neal, Joseph C. 1807-1847 . . . . DLB-11

355

Cumulative Index

Neal, Larry 1937-1981 .... DLB-38
The Neale Publishing Company DLB-49
Nebel, Frederick 1903-1967 .... DLB-226
Neely, F. Tennyson [publishing house].... DLB-49
Negoițescu, Ion 1921-1993............ DLB-220
Negri, Ada 1870-1945................. DLB-114
"The Negro as a Writer," by
  G. M. McClellan DLB-50
"Negro Poets and Their Poetry," by
  Wallace Thurman DLB-50
Neidhart von Reuental
  circa 1185-circa 1240 .... DLB-138
Neihardt, John G. 1881-1973 ..... DLB-9, 54, 256
Neilson, John Shaw 1872-1942 .... DLB-230
Neledinsky-Meletsky, Iurii Aleksandrovich
  1752-1828..................... DLB-150
Nelligan, Emile 1879-1941 .... DLB-92
Nelson, Alice Moore Dunbar 1875-1935 .. DLB-50
Nelson, Antonya 1961- DLB-244
Nelson, Kent 1943- DLB-234
Nelson, Thomas, and Sons [U.K.] DLB-106
Nelson, Thomas, and Sons [U.S.]........ DLB-49
Nelson, William 1908-1978............. DLB-103
Nelson, William Rockhill 1841-1915 ..... DLB-23
Nemerov, Howard 1920-1991 .....DLB-5, 6; Y-83
Németh, László 1901-1975 .... DLB-215
Nepos circa 100 B.C.-post 27 B.C. DLB-211
Nėris, Salomėja
  1904-1945 .... DLB-220; CDWLB-4
Nerval, Gerard de 1808-1855.......... DLB-217
Nesbit, E. 1858-1924 ....DLB-141, 153, 178
Ness, Evaline 1911-1986............... DLB-61
Nestroy, Johann 1801-1862 .... DLB-133
Neugeboren, Jay 1938- DLB-28
Neukirch, Benjamin 1655-1729......... DLB-168
Neumann, Alfred 1895-1952 .... DLB-56
Neumann, Ferenc (see Molnár, Ferenc)
Neumark, Georg 1621-1681........... DLB-164
Neumeister, Erdmann 1671-1756 .... DLB-168
Nevins, Allan 1890-1971..........DLB-17; DS-17
Nevinson, Henry Woodd 1856-1941.... DLB-135
The New American Library DLB-46
New Approaches to Biography: Challenges
  from Critical Theory, USC Conference
  on Literary Studies, 1990............. Y-90
New Directions Publishing Corporation... DLB-46
A New Edition of *Huck Finn* Y-85
New Forces at Work in the American Theatre:
  1915-1925...................... DLB-7
New Literary Periodicals:
  A Report for 1987 .... Y-87
New Literary Periodicals:
  A Report for 1988 .... Y-88
New Literary Periodicals:
  A Report for 1989 .... Y-89
New Literary Periodicals:
  A Report for 1990 .... Y-90

New Literary Periodicals:
  A Report for 1991 .... Y-91
New Literary Periodicals:
  A Report for 1992 .... Y-92
New Literary Periodicals:
  A Report for 1993 .... Y-93
The New Monthly Magazine
  1814-1884 .... DLB-110
The New Variorum Shakespeare Y-85
A New Voice: The Center for the Book's First
  Five Years Y-83
The New Wave [Science Fiction] DLB-8
New York City Bookshops in the 1930s and 1940s:
  The Recollections of Walter Goldwater... Y-93
Newbery, John [publishing house] DLB-154
Newbolt, Henry 1862-1938 .... DLB-19
Newbound, Bernard Slade (see Slade, Bernard)
Newby, Eric 1919- DLB-204
Newby, P. H. 1918- DLB-15
Newby, Thomas Cautley
  [publishing house] DLB-106
Newcomb, Charles King 1820-1894... DLB-1, 223
Newell, Peter 1862-1924................ DLB-42
Newell, Robert Henry 1836-1901........ DLB-11
Newhouse, Samuel I. 1895-1979......... DLB-127
Newman, Cecil Earl 1903-1976 .... DLB-127
Newman, David (see Benton, Robert)
Newman, Frances 1883-1928.............. Y-80
Newman, Francis William 1805-1897.... DLB-190
Newman, John Henry
  1801-1890 .... DLB-18, 32, 55
Newman, Mark [publishing house]....... DLB-49
Newmarch, Rosa Harriet 1857-1940..... DLB-240
Newnes, George, Limited............. DLB-112
Newsome, Effie Lee 1885-1979......... DLB-76
Newspaper Syndication of American
  Humor......................... DLB-11
Newton, A. Edward 1864-1940 .... DLB-140
Nexø, Martin Andersen 1869-1954 ..... DLB-214
Nezval, Vítěslav
  1900-1958 .... DLB-215; CDWLB-4
Ngugi wa Thiong'o
  1938- DLB-125; CDWLB-3
Niatum, Duane 1938- DLB-175
The *Nibelungenlied* and the *Klage*
  circa 1200....................... DLB-138
Nichol, B. P. 1944- DLB-53
Nicholas of Cusa 1401-1464........... DLB-115
Nichols, Ann 1891?-1966 .... DLB-249
Nichols, Beverly 1898-1983 .... DLB-191
Nichols, Dudley 1895-1960 .... DLB-26
Nichols, Grace 1950- DLB-157
Nichols, John 1940- Y-82
Nichols, Mary Sargeant (Neal) Gove
  1810-1884 .... DLB-1, 243
Nichols, Peter 1927- DLB-13, 245
Nichols, Roy F. 1896-1973 .... DLB-17
Nichols, Ruth 1948- DLB-60

Nicholson, Edward Williams Byron
  1849-1912 .... DLB-184
Nicholson, Norman 1914- DLB-27
Nicholson, William 1872-1949 .... DLB-141
Ní Chuilleanáin, Eiléan 1942- DLB-40
Nicol, Eric 1919- DLB-68
Nicolai, Friedrich 1733-1811............ DLB-97
Nicolas de Clamanges circa 1363-1437... DLB-208
Nicolay, John G. 1832-1901 and
  Hay, John 1838-1905............... DLB-47
Nicolson, Adela Florence Cory (see Hope, Laurence)
Nicolson, Harold 1886-1968 ....DLB-100, 149
Nicolson, Harold, "The Practice of Biography," in
  *The English Sense of Humour and
  Other Essays* DLB-149
Nicolson, Nigel 1917- DLB-155
Niebuhr, Reinhold 1892-1971......DLB-17; DS-17
Niedecker, Lorine 1903-1970 .... DLB-48
Nieman, Lucius W. 1857-1935.......... DLB-25
Nietzsche, Friedrich
  1844-1900 ....DLB-129; CDWLB-2
Nievo, Stanislao 1928- DLB-196
Niggli, Josefina 1910- Y-80
Nightingale, Florence 1820-1910 .... DLB-166
Nijō, Lady (Nakano-in Masatada no Musume)
  1258-after 1306 .... DLB-203
Nijō Yoshimoto 1320-1388............ DLB-203
Nikolev, Nikolai Petrovich
  1758-1815..................... DLB-150
Niles, Hezekiah 1777-1839 .... DLB-43
Nims, John Frederick 1913-1999 .... DLB-5
Nin, Anaïs 1903-1977 .... DLB-2, 4, 152
1985: The Year of the Mystery:
  A Symposium...................... Y-85
The 1997 Booker Prize.................. Y-97
The 1998 Booker Prize.................. Y-98
Niño, Raúl 1961- DLB-209
Nissenson, Hugh 1933- DLB-28
Niven, Frederick John 1878-1944....... DLB-92
Niven, Larry 1938- DLB-8
Nixon, Howard M. 1909-1983......... DLB-201
Nizan, Paul 1905-1940 .... DLB-72
Njegoš, Petar II Petrović
  1813-1851 ....DLB-147; CDWLB-4
Nkosi, Lewis 1936- DLB-157
"The No Self, the Little Self, and the Poets,"
  by Richard Moore DLB-105
Nobel Peace Prize
The 1986 Nobel Peace Prize: Elie Wiesel..... Y-86
The Nobel Prize and Literary Politics Y-86
Nobel Prize in Literature
The 1982 Nobel Prize in Literature:
  Gabriel García Márquez.............. Y-82
The 1983 Nobel Prize in Literature:
  William Golding Y-83
The 1984 Nobel Prize in Literature:
  Jaroslav Seifert..................... Y-84
The 1985 Nobel Prize in Literature:
  Claude Simon Y-85

The 1986 Nobel Prize in Literature:
 Wole Soyinka Y-86
The 1987 Nobel Prize in Literature:
 Joseph Brodsky Y-87
The 1988 Nobel Prize in Literature:
 Najīb Mahfūz Y-88
The 1989 Nobel Prize in Literature:
 Camilo José Cela Y-89
The 1990 Nobel Prize in Literature:
 Octavio Paz Y-90
The 1991 Nobel Prize in Literature:
 Nadine Gordimer Y-91
The 1992 Nobel Prize in Literature:
 Derek Walcott Y-92
The 1993 Nobel Prize in Literature:
 Toni Morrison Y-93
The 1994 Nobel Prize in Literature:
 Kenzaburō Ōe Y-94
The 1995 Nobel Prize in Literature:
 Seamus Heaney Y-95
The 1996 Nobel Prize in Literature:
 Wisława Szymborsha Y-96
The 1997 Nobel Prize in Literature:
 Dario Fo Y-97
The 1998 Nobel Prize in Literature:
 José Saramago Y-98
The 1999 Nobel Prize in Literature:
 Günter Grass Y-99
The 2000 Nobel Prize in Literature:
 Gao Xingjian Y-00
Nodier, Charles 1780-1844 . . . . DLB-119
Noel, Roden 1834-1894 . . . . DLB-35
Nogami, Yaeko 1885-1985 . . . . DLB-180
Nogo, Rajko Petrov 1945- DLB-181
Nolan, William F. 1928- DLB-8
Noland, C. F. M. 1810?-1858 . . . . DLB-11
Noma Hiroshi 1915-1991 . . . . DLB-182
Nonesuch Press DLB-112
Noonan, Robert Phillipe (see Tressell, Robert)
Noonday Press DLB-46
Noone, John 1936- DLB-14
Nora, Eugenio de 1923- DLB-134
Nordan, Lewis 1939- DLB-234
Nordbrandt, Henrik 1945- DLB-214
Nordhoff, Charles 1887-1947 . . . . DLB-9
Norén, Lars 1944- DLB-257
Norman, Charles 1904-1996 . . . . DLB-111
Norman, Marsha 1947- Y-84
Norris, Charles G. 1881-1945 . . . . DLB-9
Norris, Frank
 1870-1902 . . . . DLB-12, 71, 186; CDALB-3
Norris, Leslie 1921- DLB-27, 256
Norse, Harold 1916- DLB-16
Norte, Marisela 1955- DLB-209
North, Marianne 1830-1890 . . . . DLB-174
North Point Press DLB-46
Nortje, Arthur 1942-1970 . . . . DLB-125
Norton, Alice Mary (see Norton, Andre)
Norton, Andre 1912- DLB-8, 52

Norton, Andrews 1786-1853 . . . . DLB-1, 235
Norton, Caroline 1808-1877 . . . . DLB-21, 159, 199
Norton, Charles Eliot 1827-1908 . . . DLB-1, 64, 235
Norton, John 1606-1663 . . . . DLB-24
Norton, Mary 1903-1992 . . . . DLB-160
Norton, Thomas (see Sackville, Thomas)
Norton, W. W., and Company DLB-46
Norwood, Robert 1874-1932 . . . . DLB-92
Nosaka Akiyuki 1930- DLB-182
Nossack, Hans Erich 1901-1977 . . . . DLB-69
Not Immediately Discernible . . . but Eventually
 Quite Clear: The *First Light* and *Final Years*
 of Hemingway's Centenary Y-99
A Note on Technique (1926), by
 Elizabeth A. Drew [excerpts] DLB-36
Notker Balbulus circa 840-912 . . . . DLB-148
Notker III of Saint Gall
 circa 950-1022 . . . . DLB-148
Notker von Zweifalten ?-1095 . . . . DLB-148
Nourse, Alan E. 1928- DLB-8
Novak, Slobodan 1924- DLB-181
Novak, Vjenceslav
 1859-1905 . . . . DLB-147
Novakovich, Josip 1956- DLB-244
Novalis 1772-1801 . . . . DLB-90; CDWLB-2
Novaro, Mario 1868-1944 . . . . DLB-114
Novás Calvo, Lino
 1903-1983 . . . . DLB-145
"The Novel in [Robert Browning's] 'The Ring and
 the Book'" (1912), by Henry James . . . DLB-32
The Novel of Impressionism,
 by Jethro Bithell DLB-66
Novel-Reading: *The Works of
 Charles Dickens, The Works of
 W. Makepeace Thackeray*
 (1879), by Anthony Trollope DLB-21
Novels for Grown-Ups Y-97
The Novels of Dorothy Richardson (1918),
 by May Sinclair DLB-36
Novels with a Purpose (1864), by
 Justin M'Carthy DLB-21
Noventa, Giacomo 1898-1960 . . . . DLB-114
Novikov, Nikolai
 Ivanovich 1744-1818 . . . . DLB-150
Novomeský, Laco
 1904-1976 . . . . DLB-215
Nowlan, Alden 1933-1983 . . . . DLB-53
Noyes, Alfred 1880-1958 . . . . DLB-20
Noyes, Crosby S. 1825-1908 . . . . DLB-23
Noyes, Nicholas 1647-1717 . . . . DLB-24
Noyes, Theodore W. 1858-1946 . . . . DLB-29
N-Town Plays circa 1468 to early
 sixteenth century DLB-146
Nugent, Frank 1908-1965 . . . . DLB-44
Nugent, Richard Bruce 1906- DLB-151
Nušić, Branislav
 1864-1938 . . . . DLB-147; CDWLB-4
Nutt, David [publishing house] DLB-106
Nwapa, Flora 1931-1993 . . . . DLB-125; CDWLB-3
Nye, Bill 1850-1896 . . . . DLB-186

Nye, Edgar Wilson (Bill)
 1850-1896 . . . . DLB-11, 23
Nye, Naomi Shihab 1952- DLB-120
Nye, Robert 1939- DLB-14
Nyka-Niliūnas, Alfonsas
 1919- DLB-220

O

Oakes Smith, Elizabeth
 1806-1893 . . . . DLB-1, 239, 243
Oakes, Urian circa 1631-1681 . . . . DLB-24
Oakley, Violet 1874-1961 . . . . DLB-188
Oates, Joyce Carol 1938- . . . DLB-2, 5, 130; Y-81
Ōba Minako 1930- DLB-182
Ober, Frederick Albion 1849-1913 . . . . . . DLB-189
Ober, William 1920-1993 . . . . Y-93
Oberholtzer, Ellis Paxson 1868-1936 . . . . . . DLB-47
Obradović, Dositej 1740?-1811 . . . . DLB-147
O'Brien, Charlotte Grace 1845-1909 . . . . . DLB-240
O'Brien, Edna 1932- . . . DLB-14, 231; CDBLB-8
O'Brien, Fitz-James 1828-1862 . . . . DLB-74
O'Brien, Flann (see O'Nolan, Brian)
O'Brien, Kate 1897-1974 . . . . DLB-15
O'Brien, Tim
 1946- DLB-152; Y-80; DS-9; CDALB-7
O'Casey, Sean 1880-1964 . . . . . . DLB-10; CDBLB-6
Occom, Samson 1723-1792 . . . . DLB-175
Ochs, Adolph S. 1858-1935 . . . . DLB-25
Ochs-Oakes, George Washington
 1861-1931 . . . . DLB-137
O'Connor, Flannery 1925-1964
 . . . . DLB-2, 152; Y-80; DS-12; CDALB-1
O'Connor, Frank 1903-1966 . . . . DLB-162
Octopus Publishing Group DLB-112
Oda Sakunosuke 1913-1947 . . . . DLB-182
Odell, Jonathan 1737-1818 . . . . DLB-31, 99
O'Dell, Scott 1903-1989 . . . . DLB-52
Odets, Clifford 1906-1963 . . . . DLB-7, 26
Odhams Press Limited DLB-112
Odoevsky, Aleksandr Ivanovich
 1802-1839 . . . . DLB-205
Odoevsky, Vladimir Fedorovich
 1804 or 1803-1869 . . . . DLB-198
O'Donnell, Peter 1920- DLB-87
O'Donovan, Michael (see O'Connor, Frank)
O'Dowd, Bernard 1866-1953 . . . . DLB-230
Ōe Kenzaburō 1935- DLB-182; Y-94
O'Faolain, Julia 1932- DLB-14, 231
O'Faolain, Sean 1900- DLB-15, 162
Off Broadway and Off-Off Broadway DLB-7
Off-Loop Theatres DLB-7
Offord, Carl Ruthven 1910- DLB-76
O'Flaherty, Liam 1896-1984 . . . DLB-36, 162; Y-84
Ogilvie, J. S., and Company DLB-49
Ogilvy, Eliza 1822-1912 . . . . DLB-199
Ogot, Grace 1930- DLB-125
O'Grady, Desmond 1935- DLB-40

Ogunyemi, Wale 1939- DLB-157
O'Hagan, Howard 1902-1982 .... DLB-68
O'Hara, Frank 1926-1966........ DLB-5, 16, 193
O'Hara, John
  1905-1970....... DLB-9, 86; DS-2; CDALB-5
John O'Hara's Pottsville Journalism......... Y-88
O'Hegarty, P. S. 1879-1955 .... DLB-201
Okara, Gabriel 1921- DLB-125; CDWLB-3
O'Keeffe, John 1747-1833 .... DLB-89
Okes, Nicholas [publishing house] DLB-170
Okigbo, Christopher
  1930-1967 .... DLB-125; CDWLB-3
Okot p'Bitek 1931-1982 .... DLB-125; CDWLB-3
Okpewho, Isidore 1941- DLB-157
Okri, Ben 1959- DLB-157, 231
Olaudah Equiano and Unfinished Journeys:
  The Slave-Narrative Tradition and
  Twentieth-Century Continuities, by
  Paul Edwards and Pauline T.
  Wangman DLB-117
Old English Literature:
  An Introduction DLB-146
Old English Riddles
  eighth to tenth centuries........... DLB-146
Old Franklin Publishing House DLB-49
Old German Genesis and *Old German Exodus*
  circa 1050-circa 1130 .... DLB-148
Old High German Charms and
  Blessings........... DLB-148; CDWLB-2
The *Old High German Isidor*
  circa 790-800 .... DLB-148
The Old Manse DLB-223
Older, Fremont 1856-1935............ DLB-25
Oldham, John 1653-1683 .... DLB-131
Oldman, C. B. 1894-1969............. DLB-201
Olds, Sharon 1942- DLB-120
Olearius, Adam 1599-1671 .... DLB-164
O'Leary, Ellen 1831-1889............ DLB-240
Oliphant, Laurence 1829?-1888 ..... DLB-18, 166
Oliphant, Margaret 1828-1897 .. DLB-18, 159, 190
Oliver, Chad 1928- DLB-8
Oliver, Mary 1935- DLB-5, 193
Ollier, Claude 1922- DLB-83
Olsen, Tillie 1912 or 1913-
  .... DLB-28, 206; Y-80; CDALB-7
Olson, Charles 1910-1970........ DLB-5, 16, 193
Olson, Elder 1909- DLB-48, 63
Omotoso, Kole 1943- DLB-125
Omulevsky, Innokentii Vasil'evich
  1836 [or 1837]-1883 .... DLB-238
On Learning to Write................. Y-88
Ondaatje, Michael 1943- DLB-60
O'Neill, Eugene 1888-1953...... DLB-7; CDALB-5
Eugene O'Neill Memorial Theater
  Center DLB-7
Eugene O'Neill's Letters: A Review Y-88
Onetti, Juan Carlos
  1909-1994 .... DLB-113; CDWLB-3
Onions, George Oliver 1872-1961 ...... DLB-153

Onofri, Arturo 1885-1928 .... DLB-114
O'Nolan, Brian 1911-1966 .... DLB-231
Opie, Amelia 1769-1853 .... DLB-116, 159
Opitz, Martin 1597-1639.............. DLB-164
Oppen, George 1908-1984 .... DLB-5, 165
Oppenheim, E. Phillips 1866-1946....... DLB-70
Oppenheim, James 1882-1932 .... DLB-28
Oppenheimer, Joel 1930-1988 ...... DLB-5, 193
Optic, Oliver (see Adams, William Taylor)
Oral History: B. W. Huebsch............. Y-99
Oral History Interview with Donald S.
  Klopfer......................... Y-97
Orczy, Emma, Baroness 1865-1947 ...... DLB-70
Oregon Shakespeare Festival Y-00
Origo, Iris 1902-1988................ DLB-155
Orlovitz, Gil 1918-1973 .... DLB-2, 5
Orlovsky, Peter 1933- DLB-16
Ormond, John 1923- DLB-27
Ornitz, Samuel 1890-1957 .... DLB-28, 44
O'Rourke, P. J. 1947- DLB-185
Orten, Jiří 1919-1941 .... DLB-215
Ortese, Anna Maria 1914- DLB-177
Ortiz, Simon J. 1941- DLB-120, 175, 256
Ortnit and *Wolfdietrich* circa 1225-1250.... DLB-138
Orton, Joe 1933-1967 .... DLB-13; CDBLB-8
Orwell, George (Eric Arthur Blair)
  1903-1950 .. DLB-15, 98, 195, 255; CDBLB-7
The Orwell Year...................... Y-84
(Re-)Publishing Orwell.................. Y-86
Ory, Carlos Edmundo de 1923- DLB-134
Osbey, Brenda Marie 1957- DLB-120
Osbon, B. S. 1827-1912............... DLB-43
Osborn, Sarah 1714-1796 .... DLB-200
Osborne, John 1929-1994..... DLB-13; CDBLB-7
Osgood, Herbert L. 1855-1918.......... DLB-47
Osgood, James R., and Company DLB-49
Osgood, McIlvaine and Company DLB-112
O'Shaughnessy, Arthur 1844-1881....... DLB-35
O'Shea, Patrick [publishing house]
  .... DLB-49
Osipov, Nikolai Petrovich
  1751-1799.................... DLB-150
Oskison, John Milton 1879-1947 ....DLB-175
Osler, Sir William 1849-1919.......... DLB-184
Osofisan, Femi
  1946- DLB-125; CDWLB-3
Ostenso, Martha 1900-1963............ DLB-92
Ostrauskas, Kostas 1926- DLB-232
Ostriker, Alicia 1937- DLB-120
Osundare, Niyi 1947- DLB-157; CDWLB-3
Oswald, Eleazer 1755-1795 .... DLB-43
Oswald von Wolkenstein
  1376 or 1377-1445 ....DLB-179
Otero, Blas de 1916-1979 .... DLB-134
Otero, Miguel Antonio 1859-1944 ...... DLB-82
Otero, Nina 1881-1965................ DLB-209

Otero Silva, Miguel 1908-1985......... DLB-145
Otfried von Weißenburg
  circa 800-circa 875? DLB-148
Otis, Broaders and Company.......... DLB-49
Otis, James (see Kaler, James Otis)
Otis, James, Jr. 1725-1783 .... DLB-31
Ottaway, James 1911- DLB-127
Ottendorfer, Oswald 1826-1900......... DLB-23
Ottieri, Ottiero 1924- DLB-177
Otto-Peters, Louise 1819-1895 .... DLB-129
Otway, Thomas 1652-1685 .... DLB-80
Ouellette, Fernand 1930- DLB-60
Ouida 1839-1908 .... DLB-18, 156
Outing Publishing Company DLB-46
Outlaw Days, by Joyce Johnson......... DLB-16
Overbury, Sir Thomas
  circa 1581-1613 .... DLB-151
The Overlook Press DLB-46
Overview of U.S. Book Publishing,
  1910-1945 .... DLB-9
Ovid 43 B.C.-A.D. 17.......DLB-211; CDWLB-1
Owen, Guy 1925- DLB-5
Owen, John 1564-1622................ DLB-121
Owen, John [publishing house].......... DLB-49
Owen, Peter, Limited DLB-112
Owen, Robert 1771-1858 .... DLB-107, 158
Owen, Wilfred
  1893-1918 .... DLB-20; DS-18; CDBLB-6
The Owl and the Nightingale
  circa 1189-1199 .... DLB-146
Owsley, Frank L. 1890-1956 ....DLB-17
Oxford, Seventeenth Earl of, Edward
  de Vere 1550-1604..............DLB-172
Ozerov, Vladislav Aleksandrovich
  1769-1816................... DLB-150
Ozick, Cynthia 1928- DLB-28, 152; Y-83
First Strauss "Livings" Awarded to Cynthia
  Ozick and Raymond Carver
  An Interview with Cynthia Ozick Y-83

P

Pace, Richard 1482?-1536 .... DLB-167
Pacey, Desmond 1917-1975 .... DLB-88
Pack, Robert 1929- DLB-5
Packaging Papa: *The Garden of Eden* Y-86
Padell Publishing Company DLB-46
Padgett, Ron 1942- DLB-5
Padilla, Ernesto Chávez 1944- DLB-122
Page, L. C., and Company............ DLB-49
Page, Louise 1955- DLB-233
Page, P. K. 1916- DLB-68
Page, Thomas Nelson
  1853-1922 ....DLB-12, 78; DS-13
Page, Walter Hines 1855-1918........DLB-71, 91
Paget, Francis Edward 1806-1882 ...... DLB-163
Paget, Violet (see Lee, Vernon)
Pagliarani, Elio 1927- DLB-128

Pain, Barry 1864-1928 . . . . DLB-135, 197
Pain, Philip ?-circa 1666 . . . . DLB-24
Paine, Robert Treat, Jr. 1773-1811 . . . . DLB-37
Paine, Thomas
  1737-1809 . . . . . DLB-31, 43, 73, 158; CDALB-2
Painter, George D. 1914- DLB-155
Painter, William 1540?-1594 . . . . DLB-136
Palazzeschi, Aldo 1885-1974 . . . . DLB-114
Paley, Grace 1922- DLB-28, 218
Palfrey, John Gorham 1796-1881 . . . DLB-1, 30, 235
Palgrave, Francis Turner 1824-1897 . . . . . . DLB-35
Palmer, Joe H. 1904-1952 . . . . DLB-171
Palmer, Michael 1943- DLB-169
Paltock, Robert 1697-1767 . . . . DLB-39
Paludan, Jacob 1896-1975 . . . . DLB-214
Pan Books Limited DLB-112
Panama, Norman 1914- and
  Frank, Melvin 1913-1988 . . . . DLB-26
Panaev, Ivan Ivanovich 1812-1862 . . . . . . DLB-198
Panaeva, Avdot'ia Iakovlevna
  1820-1893 . . . . DLB-238
Pancake, Breece D'J 1952-1979 . . . . DLB-130
Panduro, Leif 1923-1977 . . . . DLB-214
Panero, Leopoldo 1909-1962 . . . . DLB-108
Pangborn, Edgar 1909-1976 . . . . DLB-8
"Panic Among the Philistines": A Postscript,
  An Interview with Bryan Griffin Y-81
Panizzi, Sir Anthony 1797-1879 . . . . DLB-184
Panneton, Philippe (see Ringuet)
Panshin, Alexei 1940- DLB-8
Pansy (see Alden, Isabella)
Pantheon Books DLB-46
Papadat-Bengescu, Hortensia
  1876-1955 . . . . DLB-220
Papantonio, Michael (see Kohn, John S. Van E.)
Paperback Library DLB-46
Paperback Science Fiction DLB-8
Paquet, Alfons 1881-1944 . . . . DLB-66
Paracelsus 1493-1541 . . . . DLB-179
Paradis, Suzanne 1936- DLB-53
Páral, Vladimír, 1932- DLB-232
Pardoe, Julia 1804-1862 . . . . DLB-166
Paredes, Américo 1915-1999 . . . . DLB-209
Pareja Diezcanseco, Alfredo 1908-1993 . . . DLB-145
Parents' Magazine Press DLB-46
Parise, Goffredo 1929-1986 . . . . DLB-177
Parisian Theater, Fall 1984: Toward
  A New Baroque Y-85
Parizeau, Alice 1930- DLB-60
Parke, John 1754-1789 . . . . DLB-31
Parker, Dan 1893-1967 . . . . DLB-241
Parker, Dorothy 1893-1967 . . . . . . DLB-11, 45, 86
Parker, Gilbert 1860-1932 . . . . DLB-99
Parker, J. H. [publishing house] DLB-106
Parker, James 1714-1770 . . . . DLB-43
Parker, John [publishing house] DLB-106

Parker, Matthew 1504-1575 . . . . DLB-213
Parker, Stewart 1941-1988 . . . . DLB-245
Parker, Theodore 1810-1860 . . . . DLB-1, 235
Parker, William Riley 1906-1968 . . . . DLB-103
Parkes, Bessie Rayner (Madame Belloc)
  1829-1925 . . . . DLB-240
Parkman, Francis
  1823-1893 . . . . DLB-1, 30, 183, 186, 235
Parks, Gordon 1912- DLB-33
Parks, Tim 1954- DLB-231
Parks, William 1698-1750 . . . . DLB-43
Parks, William [publishing house] DLB-49
Parley, Peter (see Goodrich, Samuel Griswold)
Parmenides
  late sixth-fifth century B.C. DLB-176
Parnell, Thomas 1679-1718 . . . . DLB-95
Parnicki, Teodor 1908-1988 . . . . DLB-215
Parr, Catherine 1513?-1548 . . . . DLB-136
Parrington, Vernon L. 1871-1929 . . . . . DLB-17, 63
Parrish, Maxfield 1870-1966 . . . . DLB-188
Parronchi, Alessandro 1914- DLB-128
Parton, James 1822-1891 . . . . DLB-30
Parton, Sara Payson Willis
  1811-1872 . . . . DLB-43, 74, 239
Partridge, S. W., and Company DLB-106
Parun, Vesna 1922- DLB-181; CDWLB-4
Pasinetti, Pier Maria 1913- DLB-177
Pasolini, Pier Paolo 1922- DLB-128, 177
Pastan, Linda 1932- DLB-5
Paston, George (Emily Morse Symonds)
  1860-1936 . . . . DLB-149, 197
The Paston Letters 1422-1509 . . . . DLB-146
Pastorius, Francis Daniel
  1651-circa 1720 . . . . DLB-24
Patchen, Kenneth 1911-1972 . . . . DLB-16, 48
Pater, Walter
  1839-1894 . . . . DLB-57, 156; CDBLB-4
Aesthetic Poetry (1873) DLB-35
Paterson, A. B. "Banjo" 1864-1941 . . . . . . DLB-230
Paterson, Katherine 1932- DLB-52
Patmore, Coventry 1823-1896 . . . . DLB-35, 98
Paton, Alan 1903-1988 . . . . DS-17
Paton, Joseph Noel 1821-1901 . . . . DLB-35
Paton Walsh, Jill 1937- DLB-161
Patrick, Edwin Hill ("Ted") 1901-1964 . . . DLB-137
Patrick, John 1906-1995 . . . . DLB-7
Pattee, Fred Lewis 1863-1950 . . . . DLB-71
Pattern and Paradigm: History as
  Design, by Judith Ryan DLB-75
Patterson, Alicia 1906-1963 . . . . DLB-127
Patterson, Eleanor Medill 1881-1948 . . . . . DLB-29
Patterson, Eugene 1923- DLB-127
Patterson, Joseph Medill 1879-1946 . . . . . . DLB-29
Pattillo, Henry 1726-1801 . . . . DLB-37
Paul, Elliot 1891-1958 . . . . DLB-4
Paul, Jean (see Richter, Johann Paul Friedrich)

Paul, Kegan, Trench, Trubner and
  Company Limited DLB-106
Paul, Peter, Book Company DLB-49
Paul, Stanley, and Company Limited DLB-112
Paulding, James Kirke 1778-1860 . . . DLB-3, 59, 74
Paulin, Tom 1949- DLB-40
Pauper, Peter, Press DLB-46
Pavese, Cesare 1908-1950 . . . . DLB-128, 177
Pavić, Milorad 1929- DLB-181; CDWLB-4
Pavlov, Konstantin 1933- DLB-181
Pavlov, Nikolai Filippovich 1803-1864 . . . . DLB-198
Pavlova, Karolina Karlovna 1807-1893 . . . . DLB-205
Pavlović, Miodrag
  1928- DLB-181; CDWLB-4
Paxton, John 1911-1985 . . . . DLB-44
Payn, James 1830-1898 . . . . DLB-18
Payne, John 1842-1916 . . . . DLB-35
Payne, John Howard 1791-1852 . . . . DLB-37
Payson and Clarke DLB-46
Paz, Octavio 1914-1998 . . . . Y-90, Y-98
Pazzi, Roberto 1946- DLB-196
Peabody, Elizabeth Palmer 1804-1894 . . DLB-1, 223
Peabody, Elizabeth Palmer
  [publishing house] DLB-49
Peabody, Josephine Preston 1874-1922 . . . DLB-249
Peabody, Oliver William Bourn
  1799-1848 . . . . DLB-59
Peace, Roger 1899-1968 . . . . DLB-127
Peacham, Henry 1578-1644? DLB-151
Peacham, Henry, the Elder
  1547-1634 . . . . DLB-172, 236
Peachtree Publishers, Limited DLB-46
Peacock, Molly 1947- DLB-120
Peacock, Thomas Love 1785-1866 . . . DLB-96, 116
Pead, Deuel ?-1727 . . . . DLB-24
Peake, Mervyn 1911-1968 . . . . . . DLB-15, 160, 255
Peale, Rembrandt 1778-1860 . . . . DLB-183
Pear Tree Press DLB-112
Pearce, Philippa 1920- DLB-161
Pearson, H. B. [publishing house] DLB-49
Pearson, Hesketh 1887-1964 . . . . DLB-149
Pechersky, Andrei (see Mel'nikov, Pavel Ivanovich)
Peck, George W. 1840-1916 . . . . DLB-23, 42
Peck, H. C., and Theo. Bliss
  [publishing house] DLB-49
Peck, Harry Thurston 1856-1914 . . . . . DLB-71, 91
Peden, William 1913-1999 . . . . DLB-234
Peele, George 1556-1596 . . . . DLB-62, 167
Pegler, Westbrook 1894-1969 . . . . DLB-171
Pekić, Borislav 1930-1992 . . . DLB-181; CDWLB-4
Pellegrini and Cudahy DLB-46
Pelletier, Aimé (see Vac, Bertrand)
Pemberton, Sir Max 1863-1950 . . . . DLB-70
de la Peña, Terri 1947- DLB-209
Penfield, Edward 1866-1925 . . . . DLB-188
Penguin Books [U.K.] DLB-112

359

Cumulative Index

Penguin Books [U.S.] DLB-46
Penn Publishing Company DLB-49
Penn, William 1644-1718 .... DLB-24
Penna, Sandro 1906-1977 .... DLB-114
Pennell, Joseph 1857-1926. .... DLB-188
Penner, Jonathan 1940- Y-83
Pennington, Lee 1939- Y-82
Pepys, Samuel
   1633-1703 .... DLB-101, 213; CDBLB-2
Percy, Thomas 1729-1811 .... DLB-104
Percy, Walker 1916-1990 ...... DLB-2; Y-80, Y-90
Percy, William 1575-1648 .... DLB-172
Perec, Georges 1936-1982 .... DLB-83
Perelman, Bob 1947- DLB-193
Perelman, S. J. 1904-1979 .... DLB-11, 44
Perez, Raymundo "Tigre" 1946- DLB-122
Peri Rossi, Cristina 1941- DLB-145
Perkins, Eugene 1932- DLB-41
Perkoff, Stuart Z. 1930-1974 .... DLB-16
Perley, Moses Henry 1804-1862 .... DLB-99
Permabooks DLB-46
Perovsky, Aleksei Alekseevich
   (Antonii Pogorel'sky) 1787-1836 ..... DLB-198
Perri, Henry 1561-1617 .... DLB-236
Perrin, Alice 1867-1934 .... DLB-156
Perry, Bliss 1860-1954 .... DLB-71
Perry, Eleanor 1915-1981 .... DLB-44
Perry, Henry (see Perri, Henry)
Perry, Matthew 1794-1858 .... DLB-183
Perry, Sampson 1747-1823 .... DLB-158
Persius A.D. 34-A.D. 62 .... DLB-211
Perutz, Leo 1882-1957 .... DLB-81
Pesetsky, Bette 1932- DLB-130
Pestalozzi, Johann Heinrich 1746-1827 .... DLB-94
Peter, Laurence J. 1919-1990 .... DLB-53
Peter of Spain circa 1205-1277 .... DLB-115
Peterkin, Julia 1880-1961 .... DLB-9
Peters, Lenrie 1932- DLB-117
Peters, Robert 1924- DLB-105
"Foreword to *Ludwig of Baviria*" DLB-105
Petersham, Maud 1889-1971 and
   Petersham, Miska 1888-1960 .... DLB-22
Peterson, Charles Jacobs 1819-1887 ...... DLB-79
Peterson, Len 1917- DLB-88
Peterson, Levi S. 1933- DLB-206
Peterson, Louis 1922-1998 .... DLB-76
Peterson, T. B., and Brothers DLB-49
Petitclair, Pierre 1813-1860 .... DLB-99
Petrescu, Camil 1894-1957 .... DLB-220
Petronius circa A.D. 20-A.D. 66
   .... DLB-211; CDWLB-1
Petrov, Aleksandar 1938- DLB-181
Petrov, Gavriil 1730-1801 .... DLB-150
Petrov, Valeri 1920- DLB-181
Petrov, Vasilii Petrovich 1736-1799 ..... DLB-150

Petrović, Rastko
   1898-1949 .... DLB-147; CDWLB-4
Petruslied circa 854? DLB-148
Petry, Ann 1908-1997 .... DLB-76
Pettie, George circa 1548-1589 .... DLB-136
Peyton, K. M. 1929- DLB-161
Pfaffe Konrad flourished circa 1172 ..... DLB-148
Pfaffe Lamprecht flourished circa 1150 .. DLB-148
Pfeiffer, Emily 1827-1890 .... DLB-199
Pforzheimer, Carl H. 1879-1957 .... DLB-140
Phaedrus circa 18 B.C.-circa A.D. 50 .... DLB-211
Phaer, Thomas 1510?-1560 .... DLB-167
Phaidon Press Limited DLB-112
Pharr, Robert Deane 1916-1992 .... DLB-33
Phelps, Elizabeth Stuart 1815-1852 .... DLB-202
Phelps, Elizabeth Stuart 1844-1911 ... DLB-74, 221
Philander von der Linde
   (see Mencke, Johann Burckhard)
Philby, H. St. John B. 1885-1960 .... DLB-195
Philip, Marlene Nourbese 1947- DLB-157
Philippe, Charles-Louis 1874-1909 ...... DLB-65
Philips, John 1676-1708 .... DLB-95
Philips, Katherine 1632-1664 .... DLB-131
Phillipps, Sir Thomas 1792-1872 .... DLB-184
Phillips, Caryl 1958- DLB-157
Phillips, David Graham 1867-1911 ..... DLB-9, 12
Phillips, Jayne Anne 1952- Y-80
Phillips, Robert 1938- DLB-105
"Finding, Losing, Reclaiming: A Note
   on My Poems" DLB-105
Phillips, Sampson and Company DLB-49
Phillips, Stephen 1864-1915 .... DLB-10
Phillips, Ulrich B. 1877-1934 .... DLB-17
Phillips, Wendell 1811-1884 .... DLB-235
Phillips, Willard 1784-1873 .... DLB-59
Phillips, William 1907- DLB-137
Phillpotts, Adelaide Eden (Adelaide Ross)
   1896-1993 .... DLB-191
Phillpotts, Eden 1862-1960 ... DLB-10, 70, 135, 153
Philo circa 20-15 B.C.-circa A.D. 50 ..... DLB-176
Philosophical Library DLB-46
Phinney, Elihu [publishing house] DLB-49
Phoenix, John (see Derby, George Horatio)
PHYLON (Fourth Quarter, 1950),
   The Negro in Literature:
   The Current Scene DLB-76
Physiologus circa 1070-circa 1150 .... DLB-148
Piccolo, Lucio 1903-1969 .... DLB-114
Pickard, Tom 1946- DLB-40
Pickering, William [publishing house] ... DLB-106
Pickthall, Marjorie 1883-1922 .... DLB-92
Pictorial Printing Company DLB-49
Piercy, Marge 1936- DLB-120, 227
Pierro, Albino 1916- DLB-128
Pignotti, Lamberto 1926- DLB-128
Pike, Albert 1809-1891 .... DLB-74

Pike, Zebulon Montgomery
   1779-1813 .... DLB-183
Pillat, Ion 1891-1945 .... DLB-220
Pilon, Jean-Guy 1930- DLB-60
Pinckney, Eliza Lucas 1722-1793 .... DLB-200
Pinckney, Josephine 1895-1957 .... DLB-6
Pindar circa 518 B.C.-circa 438 B.C.
   .... DLB-176; CDWLB-1
Pindar, Peter (see Wolcot, John)
Pineda, Cecile 1942- DLB-209
Pinero, Arthur Wing 1855-1934 .... DLB-10
Pinget, Robert 1919-1997 .... DLB-83
Pinkney, Edward Coote 1802-1828 ..... DLB-248
Pinnacle Books DLB-46
Piñon, Nélida 1935- DLB-145
Pinsky, Robert 1940- Y-82
Robert Pinsky Reappointed Poet Laureate Y-98
Pinter, Harold 1930- DLB-13; CDBLB-8
Piontek, Heinz 1925- DLB-75
Piozzi, Hester Lynch [Thrale]
   1741-1821 .... DLB-104, 142
Piper, H. Beam 1904-1964 .... DLB-8
Piper, Watty DLB-22
Pirckheimer, Caritas 1467-1532 .... DLB-179
Pirckheimer, Willibald 1470-1530 ...... DLB-179
Pisar, Samuel 1929- Y-83
Pisemsky, Aleksei Feofilaktovich
   1821-1881 .... DLB-238
Pitkin, Timothy 1766-1847 .... DLB-30
The Pitt Poetry Series: Poetry Publishing
   Today Y-85
Pitter, Ruth 1897- DLB-20
Pix, Mary 1666-1709 .... DLB-80
Pixerécourt, René Charles Guilbert de
   1773-1844 .... DLB-192
Plaatje, Sol T. 1876-1932 .... DLB-125, 225
Plante, David 1940- Y-83
Platen, August von 1796-1835 .... DLB-90
Plath, Sylvia
   1932-1963 .... DLB-5, 6, 152; CDALB-1
Plato circa 428 B.C.-348-347 B.C.
   .... DLB-176; CDWLB-1
Plato, Ann 1824?-? DLB-239
Platon 1737-1812 .... DLB-150
Platt and Munk Company DLB-46
Plautus circa 254 B.C.-184 B.C.
   .... DLB-211; CDWLB-1
Playboy Press DLB-46
Playford, John [publishing house] DLB-170
Plays, Playwrights, and Playgoers DLB-84
Playwrights on the Theater DLB-80
Der Pleier flourished circa 1250 .... DLB-138
Pleijel, Agneta 1940- DLB-257
Plenzdorf, Ulrich 1934- DLB-75
Plessen, Elizabeth 1944- DLB-75
Pletnev, Petr Aleksandrovich
   1792-1865 .... DLB-205

Pliekšāne, Elza Rozenberga (see Aspazija)

Pliekšāns, Jānis (see Rainis, Jānis)

Plievier, Theodor 1892-1955 . . . . DLB-69

Plimpton, George 1927- DLB-185, 241; Y-99

Pliny the Elder A.D. 23/24-A.D. 79 . . . . . . DLB-211

Pliny the Younger circa A.D. 61-A.D. 112 . . . . DLB-211

Plomer, William 1903-1973 . . . . DLB-20, 162, 191, 225

Plotinus 204-270 . . . . DLB-176; CDWLB-1

Plume, Thomas 1630-1704 . . . . DLB-213

Plumly, Stanley 1939- DLB-5, 193

Plumpp, Sterling D. 1940- DLB-41

Plunkett, James 1920- DLB-14

Plutarch circa 46-circa 120 . . . . . . DLB-176; CDWLB-1

Plymell, Charles 1935- DLB-16

Pocket Books DLB-46

Poe, Edgar Allan 1809-1849
. . . . DLB-3, 59, 73, 74, 248; CDALB-2

Poe, James 1921-1980 . . . . DLB-44

The Poet Laureate of the United States Statements from Former Consultants in Poetry Y-86

Pogodin, Mikhail Petrovich 1800-1875 . . . . DLB-198

Pogorel'sky, Antonii (see Perovsky, Aleksei Alekseevich)

Pohl, Frederik 1919- DLB-8

Poirier, Louis (see Gracq, Julien)

Poláček, Karel 1892-1945 . . . DLB-215; CDWLB-4

Polanyi, Michael 1891-1976 . . . . DLB-100

Pole, Reginald 1500-1558 . . . . DLB-132

Polevoi, Nikolai Alekseevich 1796-1846 . . . . DLB-198

Polezhaev, Aleksandr Ivanovich 1804-1838 . . . . DLB-205

Poliakoff, Stephen 1952- DLB-13

Polidori, John William 1795-1821 . . . . DLB-116

Polite, Carlene Hatcher 1932- DLB-33

Pollard, Alfred W. 1859-1944 . . . . DLB-201

Pollard, Edward A. 1832-1872 . . . . DLB-30

Pollard, Graham 1903-1976 . . . . DLB-201

Pollard, Percival 1869-1911 . . . . DLB-71

Pollard and Moss DLB-49

Pollock, Sharon 1936- DLB-60

Polonsky, Abraham 1910-1999 . . . . DLB-26

Polotsky, Simeon 1629-1680 . . . . DLB-150

Polybius circa 200 B.C.-118 B.C. DLB-176

Pomialovsky, Nikolai Gerasimovich 1835-1863 . . . . DLB-238

Pomilio, Mario 1921-1990 . . . . DLB-177

Ponce, Mary Helen 1938- DLB-122

Ponce-Montoya, Juanita 1949- DLB-122

Ponet, John 1516?-1556 . . . . DLB-132

Poniatowski, Elena 1933- DLB-113; CDWLB-3

Ponsard, François 1814-1867 . . . . DLB-192

Ponsonby, William [publishing house] . . . DLB-170

Pontiggia, Giuseppe 1934- DLB-196

Pony Stories DLB-160

Poole, Ernest 1880-1950 . . . . DLB-9

Poole, Sophia 1804-1891 . . . . DLB-166

Poore, Benjamin Perley 1820-1887 . . . . . . DLB-23

Popa, Vasko 1922-1991 . . . . . DLB-181; CDWLB-4

Pope, Abbie Hanscom 1858-1894 . . . . . . DLB-140

Pope, Alexander 1688-1744 . . . . . . DLB-95, 101, 213; CDBLB-2

Popov, Mikhail Ivanovich 1742-circa 1790 . . . . DLB-150

Popović, Aleksandar 1929-1996 . . . . DLB-181

Popular Library DLB-46

Porete, Marguerite ?-1310 . . . . DLB-208

Porlock, Martin (see MacDonald, Philip)

Porpoise Press DLB-112

Porta, Antonio 1935-1989 . . . . DLB-128

Porter, Anna Maria 1780-1832 . . . . . DLB-116, 159

Porter, David 1780-1843 . . . . DLB-183

Porter, Eleanor H. 1868-1920 . . . . DLB-9

Porter, Gene Stratton (see Stratton-Porter, Gene)

Porter, Henry ?-? DLB-62

Porter, Jane 1776-1850 . . . . DLB-116, 159

Porter, Katherine Anne 1890-1980
. . . . . . DLB-4, 9, 102; Y-80; DS-12; CDALB-7

Porter, Peter 1929- DLB-40

Porter, William Sydney 1862-1910 . . . . DLB-12, 78, 79; CDALB-3

Porter, William T. 1809-1858 . . . . DLB-3, 43

Porter and Coates DLB-49

Portillo Trambley, Estela 1927-1998 . . . . . DLB-209

Portis, Charles 1933- DLB-6

Posey, Alexander 1873-1908 . . . . DLB-175

Postans, Marianne circa 1810-1865 . . . . . . DLB-166

Postl, Carl (see Sealsfield, Carl)

Poston, Ted 1906-1974 . . . . DLB-51

Potekhin, Aleksei Antipovich 1829-1908 . . DLB-238

Potok, Chaim 1929- DLB-28, 152

A Conversation with Chaim Potok Y-84

Potter, Beatrix 1866-1943 . . . . DLB-141

Potter, David M. 1910-1971 . . . . DLB-17

Potter, Dennis 1935-1994 . . . . DLB-233

The Harry Potter Phenomenon Y-99

Potter, John E., and Company DLB-49

Pottle, Frederick A. 1897-1987 . . . . . DLB-103; Y-87

Poulin, Jacques 1937- DLB-60

Pound, Ezra 1885-1972
. . . . DLB-4, 45, 63; DS-15; CDALB-4

Poverman, C. E. 1944- DLB-234

Povich, Shirley 1905-1998 . . . . DLB-171

Powell, Anthony 1905-2000 . . . DLB-15; CDBLB-7

Dawn Powell, Where Have You Been All Our Lives? Y-97

Powell, John Wesley 1834-1902 . . . . DLB-186

Powell, Padgett 1952- DLB-234

Powers, J. F. 1917-1999 . . . . DLB-130

Powers, Jimmy 1903-1995 . . . . DLB-241

Pownall, David 1938- DLB-14

Powys, John Cowper 1872-1963 . . . . . DLB-15, 255

Powys, Llewelyn 1884-1939 . . . . DLB-98

Powys, T. F. 1875-1953 . . . . DLB-36, 162

Poynter, Nelson 1903-1978 . . . . DLB-127

The Practice of Biography: An Interview with Stanley Weintraub Y-82

The Practice of Biography II: An Interview with B. L. Reid Y-83

The Practice of Biography III: An Interview with Humphrey Carpenter Y-84

The Practice of Biography IV: An Interview with William Manchester Y-85

The Practice of Biography VI: An Interview with David Herbert Donald Y-87

The Practice of Biography VII: An Interview with John Caldwell Guilds Y-92

The Practice of Biography VIII: An Interview with Joan Mellen Y-94

The Practice of Biography IX: An Interview with Michael Reynolds Y-95

Prados, Emilio 1899-1962 . . . . DLB-134

Praed, Mrs. Caroline (see Praed, Rosa)

Praed, Rosa (Mrs. Caroline Praed) 1851-1935 . . . . DLB-230

Praed, Winthrop Mackworth 1802-1839 . . . DLB-96

Praeger Publishers DLB-46

Praetorius, Johannes 1630-1680 . . . . DLB-168

Pratolini, Vasco 1913-1991 . . . . DLB-177

Pratt, E. J. 1882-1964 . . . . DLB-92

Pratt, Samuel Jackson 1749-1814 . . . . DLB-39

Preciado Martin, Patricia 1939- DLB-209

Preface to *The History of Romances* (1715), by Pierre Daniel Huet [excerpts] DLB-39

Préfontaine, Yves 1937- DLB-53

Prelutsky, Jack 1940- DLB-61

Premisses, by Michael Hamburger DLB-66

Prentice, George D. 1802-1870 . . . . DLB-43

Prentice-Hall DLB-46

Prescott, Orville 1906-1996 . . . . Y-96

Prescott, William Hickling 1796-1859 . . . . DLB-1, 30, 59, 235

The Present State of the English Novel (1892), by George Saintsbury DLB-18

Prešeren, Francè 1800-1849 . . . . DLB-147; CDWLB-4

Preston, Margaret Junkin 1820-1897 . . . . DLB-239, 248

Preston, May Wilson 1873-1949 . . . . DLB-188

Preston, Thomas 1537-1598 . . . . DLB-62

Price, Reynolds 1933- DLB-2, 218

Price, Richard 1723-1791 . . . . DLB-158

Price, Richard 1949- Y-81

Prideaux, John 1578-1650 . . . . DLB-236

Priest, Christopher 1943- DLB-14, 207

Priestley, J. B. 1894-1984
. . . DLB-10, 34, 77, 100, 139; Y-84; CDBLB-6

Cumulative Index

DLB 257

Primary Bibliography: A Retrospective Y-95
Prime, Benjamin Young 1733-1791 . . . . DLB-31
Primrose, Diana floruit circa 1630 . . . . . . DLB-126
Prince, F. T. 1912- DLB-20
Prince, Nancy Gardner 1799-? DLB-239
Prince, Thomas 1687-1758 . . . . DLB-24, 140
Pringle, Thomas 1789-1834 . . . . DLB-225
Printz, Wolfgang Casper 1641-1717 . . . . . DLB-168
Prior, Matthew 1664-1721 . . . . DLB-95
Prisco, Michele 1920- DLB-177
Pritchard, William H. 1932- DLB-111
Pritchett, V. S. 1900-1997 . . . . DLB-15, 139
Probyn, May 1856 or 1857-1909 . . . . DLB-199
Procter, Adelaide Anne 1825-1864 . . . DLB-32, 199
Procter, Bryan Waller 1787-1874 . . . . DLB-96, 144
Proctor, Robert 1868-1903 . . . . DLB-184
Producing Dear Bunny, Dear Volodya: The Friendship and the Feud Y-97
The Profession of Authorship:
 Scribblers for Bread Y-89
Prokopovich, Feofan 1681?-1736 . . . . DLB-150
Prokosch, Frederic 1906-1989 . . . . DLB-48
The Proletarian Novel DLB-9
Pronzini, Bill 1943- DLB-226
Propertius circa 50 B.C.-post 16 B.C.
 . . . . DLB-211; CDWLB-1
Propper, Dan 1937- DLB-16
Prose, Francine 1947- DLB-234
Protagoras circa 490 B.C.-420 B.C. DLB-176
Proud, Robert 1728-1813 . . . . DLB-30
Proust, Marcel 1871-1922 . . . . DLB-65
Prynne, J. H. 1936- DLB-40
Przybyszewski, Stanislaw 1868-1927 . . . . . DLB-66
Pseudo-Dionysius the Areopagite floruit
 circa 500 . . . . DLB-115
Public Domain and the Violation of Texts Y-97
The Public Lending Right in America Statement by
 Sen. Charles McC. Mathias, Jr. PLR and the
 Meaning of Literary Property Statements on
 PLR by American Writers Y-83
The Public Lending Right in the United Kingdom
 Public Lending Right: The First Year in the
 United Kingdom Y-83
The Publication of English
 Renaissance Plays DLB-62
Publications and Social Movements
 [Transcendentalism] DLB-1
Publishers and Agents: The Columbia
 Connection Y-87
Publishing Fiction at LSU Press Y-87
The Publishing Industry in 1998:
 Sturm-und-drang.com Y-98
The Publishing Industry in 1999 . . . . Y-99
Pückler-Muskau, Hermann von
 1785-1871 . . . . DLB-133
Pufendorf, Samuel von 1632-1694 . . . . . DLB-168
Pugh, Edwin William 1874-1930 . . . . DLB-135
Pugin, A. Welby 1812-1852 . . . . DLB-55

Puig, Manuel 1932-1990 . . . . DLB-113; CDWLB-3
Pulitzer, Joseph 1847-1911 . . . . DLB-23
Pulitzer, Joseph, Jr. 1885-1955 . . . . DLB-29
Pulitzer Prizes for the Novel, 1917-1945 . . . . DLB-9
Pulliam, Eugene 1889-1975 . . . . DLB-127
Purchas, Samuel 1577?-1626 . . . . DLB-151
Purdy, Al 1918-2000 . . . . DLB-88
Purdy, James 1923- DLB-2, 218
Purdy, Ken W. 1913-1972 . . . . DLB-137
Pusey, Edward Bouverie 1800-1882 . . . . . DLB-55
Pushkin, Aleksandr Sergeevich
 1799-1837 . . . . DLB-205
Pushkin, Vasilii L'vovich 1766-1830 . . . . . DLB-205
Putnam, George Palmer
 1814-1872 . . . . DLB-3, 79, 254
G. P. Putnam [publishing house] DLB-254
G. P. Putnam's Sons [U.K.] DLB-106
G. P. Putnam's Sons [U.S.] DLB-49
A Publisher's Archives: G. P. Putnam Y-92
Putnam, Samuel 1892-1950 . . . . DLB-4
Puzo, Mario 1920-1999 . . . . DLB-6
Pyle, Ernie 1900-1945 . . . . DLB-29
Pyle, Howard 1853-1911 . . . . . DLB-42, 188; DS-13
Pym, Barbara 1913-1980 . . . . DLB-14, 207; Y-87
Pynchon, Thomas 1937- DLB-2, 173
Pyramid Books DLB-46
Pyrnelle, Louise-Clarke 1850-1907 . . . . . . DLB-42
Pythagoras circa 570 B.C.-? DLB-176

Q

Quad, M. (see Lewis, Charles B.)
Quaritch, Bernard 1819-1899 . . . . DLB-184
Quarles, Francis 1592-1644 . . . . DLB-126
The Quarterly Review 1809-1967 . . . . DLB-110
Quasimodo, Salvatore 1901-1968 . . . . DLB-114
Queen, Ellery (see Dannay, Frederic, and
 Manfred B. Lee)
Queen, Frank 1822-1882 . . . . DLB-241
The Queen City Publishing House DLB-49
Queneau, Raymond 1903-1976 . . . . DLB-72
Quennell, Sir Peter 1905-1993 . . . . DLB-155, 195
Quesnel, Joseph 1746-1809 . . . . DLB-99
The Question of American Copyright
 in the Nineteenth Century
 Preface, by George Haven Putnam
 The Evolution of Copyright, by
  Brander Matthews
 Summary of Copyright Legislation in
  the United States, by R. R. Bowker
 Analysis of the Provisions of the
  Copyright Law of 1891, by
  George Haven Putnam
 The Contest for International Copyright,
  by George Haven Putnam
 Cheap Books and Good Books,
  by Brander Matthews DLB-49
Quiller-Couch, Sir Arthur Thomas
 1863-1944 . . . . DLB-135, 153, 190
Quin, Ann 1936-1973 . . . . DLB-14, 231
Quincy, Samuel, of Georgia ?-? DLB-31

Quincy, Samuel, of Massachusetts
 1734-1789 . . . . DLB-31
Quinn, Anthony 1915- DLB-122
The Quinn Draft of James Joyce's
 Circe Manuscript Y-00
Quinn, John 1870-1924 . . . . DLB-187
Quiñónez, Naomi 1951- DLB-209
Quintana, Leroy V. 1944- DLB-82
Quintana, Miguel de 1671-1748
 A Forerunner of Chicano Literature . DLB-122
Quintillian
 circa A.D. 40-circa A.D. 96 . . . . DLB-211
Quintus Curtius Rufus fl. A.D. 35 . . . . . . DLB-211
Quist, Harlin, Books DLB-46
Quoirez, Françoise (see Sagan, Françoise)

R

R-va, Zeneida (see Gan, Elena Andreevna)
Raabe, Wilhelm 1831-1910 . . . . DLB-129
Raban, Jonathan 1942- DLB-204
Rabe, David 1940- DLB-7, 228
Raboni, Giovanni 1932- DLB-128
Rachilde 1860-1953 . . . . DLB-123, 192
Racin, Kočo 1908-1943 . . . . DLB-147
Rackham, Arthur 1867-1939 . . . . DLB-141
Radauskas, Henrikas
 1910-1970 . . . . DLB-220; CDWLB-4
Radcliffe, Ann 1764-1823 . . . . DLB-39, 178
Raddall, Thomas 1903- DLB-68
Radford, Dollie 1858-1920 . . . . DLB-240
Radichkov, Yordan 1929- DLB-181
Radiguet, Raymond 1903-1923 . . . . DLB-65
Radishchev, Aleksandr Nikolaevich
 1749-1802 . . . . DLB-150
Radnóti, Miklós
 1909-1944 . . . . DLB-215; CDWLB-4
Radványi, Netty Reiling (see Seghers, Anna)
Rahv, Philip 1908-1973 . . . . DLB-137
Raich, Semen Egorovich 1792-1855 . . . . . DLB-205
Raičković, Stevan 1928- DLB-181
Raimund, Ferdinand Jakob 1790-1836 . . . DLB-90
Raine, Craig 1944- DLB-40
Raine, Kathleen 1908- DLB-20
Rainis, Jānis 1865-1929 . . . . DLB-220; CDWLB-4
Rainolde, Richard
 circa 1530-1606 . . . . DLB-136, 236
Rakić, Milan 1876-1938 . . . . . DLB-147; CDWLB-4
Rakosi, Carl 1903- DLB-193
Ralegh, Sir Walter
 1554?-1618 . . . . DLB-172; CDBLB-1
Ralin, Radoy 1923- DLB-181
Ralph, Julian 1853-1903 . . . . DLB-23
Ramat, Silvio 1939- DLB-128
Rambler, no. 4 (1750), by Samuel Johnson
 [excerpt] DLB-39
Ramée, Marie Louise de la (see Ouida)
Ramírez, Sergío 1942- DLB-145

Ramke, Bin 1947- DLB-120	*Readers Ulysses* Symposium Y-97	Reinmar von Zweter circa 1200-circa 1250............DLB-138
Ramler, Karl Wilhelm 1725-1798.........DLB-97	Reading, Peter 1946- DLB-40	Reisch, Walter 1903-1983..............DLB-44
Ramon Ribeyro, Julio 1929- DLB-145	Reading Series in New York City Y-96	Reizei Family......................DLB-203
Ramos, Manuel 1948- DLB-209	The Reality of One Woman's Dream: The de Grummond Children's Literature Collection.................Y-99	Remarks at the Opening of "The Biographical Part of Literature" Exhibition, by William R. Cagle Y-98
Ramous, Mario 1924-..............DLB-128	Reaney, James 1926-...............DLB-68	Remarque, Erich Maria 1898-1970 ....DLB-56; CDWLB-2
Rampersad, Arnold 1941- DLB-111	Rebhun, Paul 1500?-1546 ....DLB-179	
Ramsay, Allan 1684 or 1685-1758........DLB-95	Rèbora, Clemente 1885-1957.........DLB-114	Remington, Frederic 1861-1909 ....DLB-12, 186, 188
Ramsay, David 1749-1815..............DLB-30	Rebreanu, Liviu 1885-1944............DLB-220	
Ramsay, Martha Laurens 1759-1811.....DLB-200	Rechy, John 1934- DLB-122; Y-82	Reminiscences, by Charles Scribner Jr......DS-17
Ranck, Katherine Quintana 1942- DLB-122	The Recovery of Literature: Criticism in the 1990s: A Symposium....Y-91	Renaud, Jacques 1943- DLB-60
Rand, Avery and Company............DLB-49		Renault, Mary 1905-1983 ....Y-83
Rand, Ayn 1905-1982 ....DLB-227; CDALB-7	Redding, J. Saunders 1906-1988 ......DLB-63, 76	Rendell, Ruth 1930- DLB-87
Rand McNally and Company DLB-49	Redfield, J. S. [publishing house] DLB-49	Rensselaer, Maria van Cortlandt van 1645-1689.......................DLB-200
Randall, David Anton 1905-1975.........DLB-140	Redgrove, Peter 1932- DLB-40	
Randall, Dudley 1914- DLB-41	Redmon, Anne 1943- Y-86	Repplier, Agnes 1855-1950 ....DLB-221
Randall, Henry S. 1811-1876.........DLB-30	Redmond, Eugene B. 1937- DLB-41	Representative Men and Women: A Historical Perspective on the British Novel, 1930-1960....................DLB-15
Randall, James G. 1881-1953..........DLB-17	Redpath, James [publishing house] DLB-49	
The Randall Jarrell Symposium: A Small Collection of Randall Jarrells Excerpts From Papers Delivered at the Randall Jarrel Symposium.............Y-86	Reed, Henry 1808-1854................DLB-59	Research in the American Antiquarian Book Trade Y-97
	Reed, Henry 1914- DLB-27	
	Reed, Ishmael 1938- DLB-2, 5, 33, 169, 227; DS-8	Reshetnikov, Fedor Mikhailovich 1841-1871 ....DLB-238
Randolph, A. Philip 1889-1979 ....DLB-91		
Randolph, Anson D. F. [publishing house] DLB-49	Reed, Rex 1938- DLB-185	Rettenbacher, Simon 1634-1706 ....DLB-168
	Reed, Sampson 1800-1880..........DLB-1, 235	Reuchlin, Johannes 1455-1522..........DLB-179
Randolph, Thomas 1605-1635 ......DLB-58, 126	Reed, Talbot Baines 1852-1893.........DLB-141	Reuter, Christian 1665-after 1712.......DLB-168
Random House DLB-46	Reedy, William Marion 1862-1920.......DLB-91	Revell, Fleming H., Company DLB-49
Ranlet, Henry [publishing house] DLB-49	Reese, Lizette Woodworth 1856-1935.....DLB-54	Reuter, Fritz 1810-1874 ....DLB-129
Ransom, Harry 1908-1976............DLB-187	Reese, Thomas 1742-1796 ....DLB-37	Reuter, Gabriele 1859-1941.............DLB-66
Ransom, John Crowe 1888-1974 ....DLB-45, 63; CDALB-7	Reeve, Clara 1729-1807 ....DLB-39	Reventlow, Franziska Gräfin zu 1871-1918 ....DLB-66
	Preface to *The Old English Baron* (1778)....DLB-39	
Ransome, Arthur 1884-1967 ....DLB-160	*The Progress of Romance* (1785) [excerpt]....DLB-39	Review of Nicholson Baker's *Double Fold: Libraries and the Assault on Paper*........Y-00
Raphael, Frederic 1931- DLB-14	Reeves, James 1909-1978 ....DLB-161	
Raphaelson, Samson 1896-1983 ....DLB-44	Reeves, John 1926- DLB-88	Review of Reviews Office DLB-112
Rashi circa 1040-1105 ....DLB-208	"Reflections: After a Tornado," by Judson Jerome DLB-105	Review of [Samuel Richardson's] *Clarissa* (1748), by Henry Fielding................DLB-39
Raskin, Ellen 1928-1984 ....DLB-52		
Rastell, John 1475?-1536 ....DLB-136, 170	Regnery, Henry, Company............DLB-46	The Revolt (1937), by Mary Colum [excerpts].....................DLB-36
Rattigan, Terence 1911-1977 ....DLB-13; CDBLB-7	Rehberg, Hans 1901-1963 ....DLB-124	Rexroth, Kenneth 1905-1982 ......DLB-16, 48, 165, 212; Y-82; CDALB-1
	Rehfisch, Hans José 1891-1960 ....DLB-124	
Rawlings, Marjorie Kinnan 1896-1953 ....DLB-9, 22, 102; DS-17; CDALB-7	Reich, Ebbe Kløvedal 1940-..........DLB-214	Rey, H. A. 1898-1977 ....DLB-22
	Reid, Alastair 1926- DLB-27	Reynal and Hitchcock DLB-46
Rawlinson, Richard 1690-1755 ....DLB-213	Reid, B. L. 1918-1990 ....DLB-111; Y-83	Reynolds, G. W. M. 1814-1879...........DLB-21
Rawlinson, Thomas 1681-1725 ....DLB-213	The Practice of Biography II: An Interview with B. L. Reid..........Y-83	Reynolds, John Hamilton 1794-1852......DLB-96
Raworth, Tom 1938- DLB-40		Reynolds, Sir Joshua 1723-1792..........DLB-104
Ray, David 1932- DLB-5	Reid, Christopher 1949- DLB-40	Reynolds, Mack 1917- DLB-8
Ray, Gordon Norton 1915-1986 ....DLB-103, 140	Reid, Forrest 1875-1947 ....DLB-153	A Literary Archaeologist Digs On: A Brief Interview with Michael Reynolds by Michael Rogers Y-99
Ray, Henrietta Cordelia 1849-1916......DLB-50	Reid, Helen Rogers 1882-1970 ....DLB-29	
Raymond, Ernest 1888-1974 ....DLB-191	Reid, James ?-?.......................DLB-31	
Raymond, Henry J. 1820-1869 ......DLB-43, 79	Reid, Mayne 1818-1883..........DLB-21, 163	Reznikoff, Charles 1894-1976 ....DLB-28, 45
Michael M. Rea and the Rea Award for the Short Story Y-97	Reid, Thomas 1710-1796 ....DLB-31	Rhett, Robert Barnwell 1800-1876........DLB-43
	Reid, V. S. (Vic) 1913-1987 ....DLB-125	Rhode, John 1884-1964................DLB-77
Reach, Angus 1821-1856..............DLB-70	Reid, Whitelaw 1837-1912..........DLB-23	Rhodes, Eugene Manlove 1869-1934 ....DLB-256
Read, Herbert 1893-1968 ....DLB-20, 149	Reilly and Lee Publishing Company DLB-46	Rhodes, James Ford 1848-1927 ....DLB-47
Read, Martha Meredith................DLB-200	Reimann, Brigitte 1933-1973 ....DLB-75	Rhodes, Richard 1937- DLB-185
Read, Opie 1852-1939.................DLB-23	Reinmar der Alte circa 1165-circa 1205..............DLB-138	Rhys, Jean 1890-1979 ....DLB-36, 117, 162; CDBLB-7; CDWLB-3
Read, Piers Paul 1941- DLB-14		
Reade, Charles 1814-1884.............DLB-21		
Reader's Digest Condensed Books DLB-46		Ricardo, David 1772-1823 ....DLB-107, 158

Cumulative Index

Ricardou, Jean 1932- DLB-83
Rice, Elmer 1892-1967 .... DLB-4, 7
Rice, Grantland 1880-1954 .... DLB-29, 171
Rich, Adrienne 1929- DLB-5, 67; CDALB-7
Richard de Fournival
   1201-1259 or 1260 .... DLB-208
Richard, Mark 1955- DLB-234
Richards, David Adams 1950- DLB-53
Richards, George circa 1760-1814 .... DLB-37
Richards, Grant [publishing house] DLB-112
Richards, I. A. 1893-1979 .... DLB-27
Richards, Laura E. 1850-1943 .... DLB-42
Richards, William Carey 1818-1892 ..... DLB-73
Richardson, Charles F. 1851-1913 .... DLB-71
Richardson, Dorothy M. 1873-1957 ...... DLB-36
Richardson, Henry Handel
   (Ethel Florence Lindesay
   Robertson) 1870-1946 .... DLB-197, 230
Richardson, Jack 1935- DLB-7
Richardson, John 1796-1852 .... DLB-99
Richardson, Samuel
   1689-1761 .... DLB-39, 154; CDBLB-2
Introductory Letters from the Second
   Edition of *Pamela* (1741) DLB-39
Postscript to [the Third Edition of]
   Clarissa (1751) DLB-39
Preface to the First Edition of
   Pamela (1740) DLB-39
Preface to the Third Edition of
   Clarissa (1751) [excerpt] DLB-39
Preface to Volume 1 of *Clarissa* (1747) DLB-39
Preface to Volume 3 of *Clarissa* (1748) DLB-39
Richardson, Willis 1889-1977 .... DLB-51
Riche, Barnabe 1542-1617 .... DLB-136
Richepin, Jean 1849-1926 .... DLB-192
Richler, Mordecai 1931- DLB-53
Richter, Conrad 1890-1968 .... DLB-9, 212
Richter, Hans Werner 1908- DLB-69
Richter, Johann Paul Friedrich
   1763-1825 .... DLB-94; CDWLB-2
Rickerby, Joseph [publishing house] DLB-106
Rickword, Edgell 1898-1982 .... DLB-20
Riddell, Charlotte 1832-1906 .... DLB-156
Riddell, John (see Ford, Corey)
Ridge, John Rollin 1827-1867 .... DLB-175
Ridge, Lola 1873-1941 .... DLB-54
Ridge, William Pett 1859-1930 .... DLB-135
Riding, Laura (see Jackson, Laura Riding)
Ridler, Anne 1912- DLB-27
Ridruego, Dionisio 1912-1975 .... DLB-108
Riel, Louis 1844-1885 .... DLB-99
Riemer, Johannes 1648-1714 .... DLB-168
Rifbjerg, Klaus 1931- DLB-214
Riffaterre, Michael 1924- DLB-67
Riggs, Lynn 1899-1954 .... DLB-175
Riis, Jacob 1849-1914 .... DLB-23
Riker, John C. [publishing house] DLB-49

Riley, James 1777-1840 .... DLB-183
Riley, John 1938-1978 .... DLB-40
Rilke, Rainer Maria
   1875-1926 .... DLB-81; CDWLB-2
Rimanelli, Giose 1926- DLB-177
Rimbaud, Jean-Nicolas-Arthur
   1854-1891 .... DLB-217
Rinehart and Company DLB-46
Ringuet 1895-1960 .... DLB-68
Ringwood, Gwen Pharis 1910-1984 ...... DLB-88
Rinser, Luise 1911- DLB-69
Ríos, Alberto 1952- DLB-122
Ríos, Isabella 1948- DLB-82
Ripley, Arthur 1895-1961 .... DLB-44
Ripley, George 1802-1880 ..... DLB-1, 64, 73, 235
The Rising Glory of America:
   Three Poems DLB-37
The Rising Glory of America:
   Written in 1771 (1786),
   by Hugh Henry Brackenridge and
   Philip Freneau DLB-37
Riskin, Robert 1897-1955 .... DLB-26
Risse, Heinz 1898- DLB-69
Rist, Johann 1607-1667 .... DLB-164
Ristikivi, Karl 1912-1977 .... DLB-220
Ritchie, Anna Mowatt 1819-1870 .... DLB-3
Ritchie, Anne Thackeray 1837-1919 ...... DLB-18
Ritchie, Thomas 1778-1854 .... DLB-43
Rites of Passage [on William Saroyan] Y-83
The Ritz Paris Hemingway Award Y-85
Rivard, Adjutor 1868-1945 .... DLB-92
Rive, Richard 1931-1989 .... DLB-125, 225
Rivera, José 1955- DLB-249
Rivera, Marina 1942- DLB-122
Rivera, Tomás 1935-1984 .... DLB-82
Rivers, Conrad Kent 1933-1968 .... DLB-41
Riverside Press DLB-49
Rivington, Charles [publishing house] ... DLB-154
Rivington, James circa 1724-1802 .... DLB-43
Rivkin, Allen 1903-1990 .... DLB-26
Roa Bastos, Augusto 1917- DLB-113
Robbe-Grillet, Alain 1922- DLB-83
Robbins, Tom 1936- Y-80
Roberts, Charles G. D. 1860-1943 .... DLB-92
Roberts, Dorothy 1906-1993 .... DLB-88
Roberts, Elizabeth Madox
   1881-1941 .... DLB-9, 54, 102
Roberts, James [publishing house] DLB-154
Roberts, Kenneth 1885-1957 .... DLB-9
Roberts, Michèle 1949- DLB-231
Roberts, Ursula Wyllie (see Miles, Susan)
Roberts, William 1767-1849 .... DLB-142
Roberts Brothers DLB-49
Robertson, A. M., and Company DLB-49
Robertson, Ethel Florence Lindesay
   (see Richardson, Henry Handel)
Robertson, William 1721-1793 .... DLB-104

Robins, Elizabeth 1862-1952 .... DLB-197
Robinson, A. Mary F. (Madame James
   Darmesteter, Madame Mary
   Duclaux) 1857-1944 .... DLB-240
Robinson, Casey 1903-1979 .... DLB-44
Robinson, Edwin Arlington
   1869-1935 .... DLB-54; CDALB-3
Robinson, Henry Crabb 1775-1867 ...... DLB-107
Robinson, James Harvey 1863-1936 ..... DLB-47
Robinson, Lennox 1886-1958 .... DLB-10
Robinson, Mabel Louise 1874-1962 ...... DLB-22
Robinson, Marilynne 1943- DLB-206
Robinson, Mary 1758-1800 .... DLB-158
Robinson, Richard circa 1545-1607 ..... DLB-167
Robinson, Therese 1797-1870 .... DLB-59, 133
Robison, Mary 1949- DLB-130
Roblès, Emmanuel 1914-1995 .... DLB-83
Roccatagliata Ceccardi, Ceccardo
   1871-1919 .... DLB-114
Roche, Billy 1949- DLB-233
Rochester, John Wilmot, Earl of
   1647-1680 .... DLB-131
Rock, Howard 1911-1976 .... DLB-127
Rockwell, Norman Perceval 1894-1978 .. DLB-188
Rodgers, Carolyn M. 1945- DLB-41
Rodgers, W. R. 1909-1969 .... DLB-20
Rodney, Lester 1911- DLB-241
Rodríguez, Claudio 1934-1999 .... DLB-134
Rodríguez, Joe D. 1943- DLB-209
Rodríguez, Luis J. 1954- DLB-209
Rodriguez, Richard 1944- DLB-82, 256
Rodríguez Julia, Edgardo 1946- DLB-145
Roe, E. P. 1838-1888 .... DLB-202
Roethke, Theodore
   1908-1963 .... DLB-5, 206; CDALB-1
Rogers, Jane 1952- DLB-194
Rogers, Pattiann 1940- DLB-105
Rogers, Samuel 1763-1855 .... DLB-93
Rogers, Will 1879-1935 .... DLB-11
Rohmer, Sax 1883-1959 .... DLB-70
Roiphe, Anne 1935- Y-80
Rojas, Arnold R. 1896-1988 .... DLB-82
Rolfe, Frederick William
   1860-1913 .... DLB-34, 156
Rolland, Romain 1866-1944 .... DLB-65
Rolle, Richard circa 1290-1300 - 1340 ... DLB-146
Rölvaag, O. E. 1876-1931 .... DLB-9, 212
Romains, Jules 1885-1972 .... DLB-65
Roman, A., and Company DLB-49
Roman de la Rose: Guillaume de Lorris
   1200 to 1205-circa 1230, Jean de Meun
   1235-1240-circa 1305 .... DLB-208
Romano, Lalla 1906- DLB-177
Romano, Octavio 1923- DLB-122
Romero, Leo 1950- DLB-122
Romero, Lin 1947- DLB-122
Romero, Orlando 1945- DLB-82

Rook, Clarence 1863-1915 ....DLB-135
Roosevelt, Theodore 1858-1919 ..... DLB-47, 186
Root, Waverley 1903-1982 ....DLB-4
Root, William Pitt 1941- DLB-120
Roquebrune, Robert de 1889-1978 ....DLB-68
Rorty, Richard 1931- DLB-246
Rosa, João Guimarães 1908-1967.......DLB-113
Rosales, Luis 1910-1992 ....DLB-134
Roscoe, William 1753-1831 ....DLB-163
Danis Rose and the Rendering of *Ulysses* Y-97
Rose, Reginald 1920- DLB-26
Rose, Wendy 1948- DLB-175
Rosegger, Peter 1843-1918 ....DLB-129
Rosei, Peter 1946- DLB-85
Rosen, Norma 1925- DLB-28
Rosenbach, A. S. W. 1876-1952........DLB-140
Rosenbaum, Ron 1946- DLB-185
Rosenberg, Isaac 1890-1918..........DLB-20, 216
Rosenfeld, Isaac 1918-1956 ....DLB-28
Rosenthal, Harold 1914-1999 ....DLB-241
Rosenthal, M. L. 1917-1996............DLB-5
Rosenwald, Lessing J. 1891-1979.......DLB-187
Ross, Alexander 1591-1654 ....DLB-151
Ross, Harold 1892-1951 ....DLB-137
Ross, Leonard Q. (see Rosten, Leo)
Ross, Lillian 1927- DLB-185
Ross, Martin 1862-1915..............DLB-135
Ross, Sinclair 1908- DLB-88
Ross, W. W. E. 1894-1966 ....DLB-88
Rosselli, Amelia 1930-1996 ....DLB-128
Rossen, Robert 1908-1966............DLB-26
Rossetti, Christina 1830-1894 .. DLB-35, 163, 240
Rossetti, Dante Gabriel
  1828-1882 .... DLB-35; CDBLB-4
Rossner, Judith 1935- DLB-6
Rostand, Edmond 1868-1918 ....DLB-192
Rosten, Leo 1908-1997 ....DLB-11
Rostenberg, Leona 1908- DLB-140
Rostopchina, Evdokiia Petrovna
  1811-1858 ....DLB-205
Rostovsky, Dimitrii 1651-1709 ....DLB-150
Rota, Bertram 1903-1966.............DLB-201
  Bertram Rota and His Bookshop.........Y-91
Roth, Gerhard 1942- DLB-85, 124
Roth, Henry 1906?-1995..............DLB-28
Roth, Joseph 1894-1939...............DLB-85
Roth, Philip 1933-
  ....DLB-2, 28, 173; Y-82; CDALB-6
Rothenberg, Jerome 1931- DLB-5, 193
Rothschild Family DLB-184
Rotimi, Ola 1938- DLB-125
Routhier, Adolphe-Basile 1839-1920 ......DLB-99
Routier, Simone 1901-1987 ....DLB-88
Routledge, George, and Sons..........DLB-106
Roversi, Roberto 1923- DLB-128

Rowe, Elizabeth Singer 1674-1737 ..... DLB-39, 95
Rowe, Nicholas 1674-1718...............DLB-84
Rowlands, Samuel circa 1570-1630 ......DLB-121
Rowlandson, Mary
  circa 1637-circa 1711 ....DLB-24, 200
Rowley, William circa 1585-1626 ....DLB-58
Rowse, A. L. 1903-1997...............DLB-155
Rowson, Susanna Haswell
  circa 1762-1824 .... DLB-37, 200
Roy, Camille 1870-1943................DLB-92
Roy, Gabrielle 1909-1983 ....DLB-68
Roy, Jules 1907- DLB-83
The G. Ross Roy Scottish Poetry Collection
  at the University of South Carolina Y-89
The Royal Court Theatre and the English
  Stage Company....................DLB-13
The Royal Court Theatre and the New
  Drama DLB-10
The Royal Shakespeare Company
  at the Swan Y-88
Royall, Anne Newport 1769-1854 ....DLB-43, 248
The Roycroft Printing Shop DLB-49
Royde-Smith, Naomi 1875-1964 ....DLB-191
Royster, Vermont 1914- DLB-127
Royston, Richard [publishing house].....DLB-170
Różewicz, Tadeusz 1921- DLB-232
Ruark, Gibbons 1941- DLB-120
Ruban, Vasilii Grigorevich 1742-1795 ....DLB-150
Rubens, Bernice 1928- DLB-14, 207
Rudd and Carleton DLB-49
Rudd, Steele (Arthur Hoey Davis) DLB-230
Rudkin, David 1936- DLB-13
Rudolf von Ems circa 1200-circa 1254 ...DLB-138
Ruffin, Josephine St. Pierre
  1842-1924 ....DLB-79
Ruganda, John 1941- DLB-157
Ruggles, Henry Joseph 1813-1906........DLB-64
Ruiz de Burton, María Amparo
  1832-1895 .... DLB-209, 221
Rukeyser, Muriel 1913-1980 ....DLB-48
Rule, Jane 1931- DLB-60
Rulfo, Juan 1918-1986 ...... DLB-113; CDWLB-3
Rumaker, Michael 1932- DLB-16
Rumens, Carol 1944- DLB-40
Rummo, Paul-Eerik 1942- DLB-232
Runyon, Damon 1880-1946 ..... DLB-11, 86, 171
Ruodlieb circa 1050-1075............DLB-148
Rush, Benjamin 1746-1813 ....DLB-37
Rush, Rebecca 1779-? DLB-200
Rushdie, Salman 1947- DLB-194
Rusk, Ralph L. 1888-1962.............DLB-103
Ruskin, John
  1819-1900 ...... DLB-55, 163, 190; CDBLB-4
Russ, Joanna 1937- DLB-8
Russell, B. B., and Company...........DLB-49
Russell, Benjamin 1761-1845 ....DLB-43
Russell, Bertrand 1872-1970...........DLB-100

Russell, Charles Edward 1860-1941 ......DLB-25
Russell, Charles M. 1864-1926 ....DLB-188
Russell, Eric Frank 1905-1978 ....DLB-255
Russell, Fred 1906- DLB-241
Russell, George William (see AE)
Russell, Countess Mary Annette Beauchamp
  (see Arnim, Elizabeth von)
Russell, R. H., and Son DLB-49
Russell, Willy 1947- DLB-233
Rutebeuf flourished 1249-1277 ....DLB-208
Rutherford, Mark 1831-1913...........DLB-18
Ruxton, George Frederick
  1821-1848 ....DLB-186
Ryan, Michael 1946- Y-82
Ryan, Oscar 1904- DLB-68
Ryder, Jack 1871-1936................DLB-241
Ryga, George 1932- DLB-60
Rylands, Enriqueta Augustina Tennant
  1843-1908 ....DLB-184
Rylands, John 1801-1888..............DLB-184
Ryleev, Kondratii Fedorovich
  1795-1826 ....DLB-205
Rymer, Thomas 1643?-1713 ....DLB-101
Ryskind, Morrie 1895-1985............DLB-26
Rzhevsky, Aleksei Andreevich
  1737-1804 ....DLB-150

S

The Saalfield Publishing Company DLB-46
Saba, Umberto 1883-1957 ....DLB-114
Sábato, Ernesto 1911- DLB-145; CDWLB-3
Saberhagen, Fred 1930- DLB-8
Sabin, Joseph 1821-1881 ....DLB-187
Sacer, Gottfried Wilhelm 1635-1699 .....DLB-168
Sachs, Hans 1494-1576 ...... DLB-179; CDWLB-2
Sack, John 1930- DLB-185
Sackler, Howard 1929-1982 ....DLB-7
Sackville, Lady Margaret 1881-1963 .....DLB-240
Sackville, Thomas 1536-1608 ....DLB-132
Sackville, Thomas 1536-1608
  and Norton, Thomas 1532-1584......DLB-62
Sackville-West, Edward 1901-1965 ......DLB-191
Sackville-West, V. 1892-1962 ..... DLB-34, 195
Sadlier, D. and J., and Company.........DLB-49
Sadlier, Mary Anne 1820-1903 ....DLB-99
Sadoff, Ira 1945- DLB-120
Sadoveanu, Mihail 1880-1961 ....DLB-220
Sáenz, Benjamin Alire 1954- DLB-209
Saenz, Jaime 1921-1986 ....DLB-145
Saffin, John circa 1626-1710............DLB-24
Sagan, Françoise 1935- DLB-83
Sage, Robert 1899-1962 ....DLB-4
Sagel, Jim 1947- DLB-82
Sagendorph, Robb Hansell 1900-1970....DLB-137
Sahagún, Carlos 1938- DLB-108
Sahkomaapii, Piitai (see Highwater, Jamake)

Cumulative Index

Sahl, Hans 1902- DLB-69
Said, Edward W. 1935- DLB-67
Saigyō 1118-1190 .... DLB-203
Saiko, George 1892-1962 .... DLB-85
St. Dominic's Press.................. DLB-112
Saint-Exupéry, Antoine de 1900-1944 .... DLB-72
St. John, J. Allen 1872-1957.......... DLB-188
St. Johns, Adela Rogers 1894-1988....... DLB-29
The St. John's College Robert Graves Trust . . Y-96
St. Martin's Press DLB-46
St. Omer, Garth 1931- DLB-117
Saint Pierre, Michel de 1916-1987 .... DLB-83
Sainte-Beuve, Charles-Augustin
  1804-1869 .... DLB-217
Saints' Lives DLB-208
Saintsbury, George 1845-1933 ....DLB-57, 149
Saiokuken Sōchō 1448-1532........... DLB-203
Saki (see Munro, H. H.)
Salaam, Kalamu ya 1947- DLB-38
Šalamun, Tomaž 1941- . . . DLB-181; CDWLB-4
Salas, Floyd 1931- DLB-82
Sálaz-Marquez, Rubén 1935- DLB-122
Salemson, Harold J. 1910-1988.......... DLB-4
Salinas, Luis Omar 1937- DLB-82
Salinas, Pedro 1891-1951 .... DLB-134
Salinger, J. D.
  1919- DLB-2, 102, 173; CDALB-1
Salkey, Andrew 1928- DLB-125
Sallust circa 86 B.C.-35 B.C.
  .... DLB-211; CDWLB-1
Salt, Waldo 1914- DLB-44
Salter, James 1925- DLB-130
Salter, Mary Jo 1954- DLB-120
Saltus, Edgar 1855-1921 .... DLB-202
Saltykov, Mikhail Evgrafovich
  1826-1889 .... DLB-238
Salustri, Carlo Alberto (see Trilussa)
Salverson, Laura Goodman 1890-1970.... DLB-92
Samain, Albert 1858-1900............ DLB-217
Sampson, Richard Henry (see Hull, Richard)
Samuels, Ernest 1903-1996........... DLB-111
Sanborn, Franklin Benjamin
  1831-1917................... DLB-1, 223
Sánchez, Luis Rafael 1936- DLB-145
Sánchez, Philomeno "Phil" 1917- DLB-122
Sánchez, Ricardo 1941-1995.......... DLB-82
Sánchez, Saúl 1943- DLB-209
Sanchez, Sonia 1934- DLB-41; DS-8
Sand, George 1804-1876.......... DLB-119, 192
Sandburg, Carl
  1878-1967...........DLB-17, 54; CDALB-3
Sanders, Edward 1939- DLB-16, 244
Sandoz, Mari 1896-1966........... DLB-9, 212
Sandwell, B. K. 1876-1954 .... DLB-92
Sandy, Stephen 1934- DLB-165
Sandys, George 1578-1644 .... DLB-24, 121

Sangster, Charles 1822-1893 .... DLB-99
Sanguineti, Edoardo 1930- DLB-128
Sanjōnishi Sanetaka 1455-1537........ DLB-203
Sansay, Leonora ?-after 1823 .... DLB-200
Sansom, William 1912-1976........... DLB-139
Santayana, George
  1863-1952 ....DLB-54, 71, 246; DS-13
Santiago, Danny 1911-1988 .... DLB-122
Santmyer, Helen Hooven 1895-1986 .... Y-84
Sanvitale, Francesca 1928- DLB-196
Sapidus, Joannes 1490-1561 ....DLB-179
Sapir, Edward 1884-1939............ DLB-92
Sapper (see McNeile, Herman Cyril)
Sappho circa 620 B.C.-circa 550 B.C.
  .... DLB-176; CDWLB-1
Saramago, José 1922- Y-98
Sarban (John F. Wall) 1910-1989....... DLB-255
Sardou, Victorien 1831-1908 .... DLB-192
Sarduy, Severo 1937- DLB-113
Sargent, Pamela 1948- DLB-8
Saro-Wiwa, Ken 1941- DLB-157
Saroyan, William
  1908-1981 .....DLB-7, 9, 86; Y-81; CDALB-7
Sarraute, Nathalie 1900-1999 .... DLB-83
Sarrazin, Albertine 1937-1967 .... DLB-83
Sarris, Greg 1952- DLB-175
Sarton, May 1912-1995 ....DLB-48; Y-81
Sartre, Jean-Paul 1905-1980 .... DLB-72
Sassoon, Siegfried
  1886-1967 .... DLB-20, 191; DS-18
Siegfried Loraine Sassoon:
  A Centenary Essay
  Tributes from Vivien F. Clarke and
  Michael Thorpe..................... Y-86
Sata, Ineko 1904- DLB-180
Saturday Review Press................ DLB-46
Saunders, James 1925- DLB-13
Saunders, John Monk 1897-1940 .... DLB-26
Saunders, Margaret Marshall
  1861-1947..................... DLB-92
Saunders and Otley DLB-106
Saussure, Ferdinand de 1857-1913 .... DLB-242
Savage, James 1784-1873................ DLB-30
Savage, Marmion W. 1803?-1872........ DLB-21
Savage, Richard 1697?-1743 .... DLB-95
Savard, Félix-Antoine 1896-1982 .... DLB-68
Savery, Henry 1791-1842 .... DLB-230
Saville, (Leonard) Malcolm 1901-1982... DLB-160
Sawyer, Ruth 1880-1970 .... DLB-22
Sayers, Dorothy L.
  1893-1957.....DLB-10, 36, 77, 100; CDBLB-6
Sayle, Charles Edward 1864-1924 ...... DLB-184
Sayles, John Thomas 1950- DLB-44
Sbarbaro, Camillo 1888-1967......... DLB-114
Scalapino, Leslie 1947- DLB-193
Scannell, Vernon 1922- DLB-27
Scarry, Richard 1919-1994 .... DLB-61

Schaefer, Jack 1907-1991............. DLB-212
Schaeffer, Albrecht 1885-1950 .... DLB-66
Schaeffer, Susan Fromberg 1941- DLB-28
Schaff, Philip 1819-1893.................DS-13
Schaper, Edzard 1908-1984 .... DLB-69
Scharf, J. Thomas 1843-1898 .... DLB-47
Schede, Paul Melissus 1539-1602........DLB-179
Scheffel, Joseph Viktor von 1826-1886... DLB-129
Scheffler, Johann 1624-1677 .... DLB-164
Schelling, Friedrich Wilhelm Joseph von
  1775-1854................... DLB-90
Scherer, Wilhelm 1841-1886 .... DLB-129
Scherfig, Hans 1905-1979 .... DLB-214
Schickele, René 1883-1940 .... DLB-66
Schiff, Dorothy 1903-1989 ....DLB-127
Schiller, Friedrich
  1759-1805......... DLB-94; CDWLB-2
Schirmer, David 1623-1687 .... DLB-164
Schlaf, Johannes 1862-1941 .... DLB-118
Schlegel, August Wilhelm 1767-1845 ..... DLB-94
Schlegel, Dorothea 1763-1839........... DLB-90
Schlegel, Friedrich 1772-1829 .... DLB-90
Schleiermacher, Friedrich 1768-1834 ..... DLB-90
Schlesinger, Arthur M., Jr. 1917- DLB-17
Schlumberger, Jean 1877-1968 .... DLB-65
Schmid, Eduard Hermann Wilhelm
  (see Edschmid, Kasimir)
Schmidt, Arno 1914-1979............. DLB-69
Schmidt, Johann Kaspar (see Stirner, Max)
Schmidt, Michael 1947- DLB-40
Schmidtbonn, Wilhelm August
  1876-1952................... DLB-118
Schmitz, James H. 1911- DLB-8
Schnabel, Johann Gottfried
  1692-1760 .... DLB-168
Schnackenberg, Gjertrud 1953- DLB-120
Schnitzler, Arthur
  1862-1931 ....DLB-81, 118; CDWLB-2
Schnurre, Wolfdietrich 1920-1989 .... DLB-69
Schocken Books DLB-46
Scholartis Press..................... DLB-112
Scholderer, Victor 1880-1971 .... DLB-201
The Schomburg Center for Research
  in Black Culture.................. DLB-76
Schönbeck, Virgilio (see Giotti, Virgilio)
Schönherr, Karl 1867-1943 .... DLB-118
Schoolcraft, Jane Johnston 1800-1841.....DLB-175
School Stories, 1914-1960............. DLB-160
Schopenhauer, Arthur 1788-1860........ DLB-90
Schopenhauer, Johanna 1766-1838....... DLB-90
Schorer, Mark 1908-1977 .... DLB-103
Schottelius, Justus Georg 1612-1676..... DLB-164
Schouler, James 1839-1920 .... DLB-47
Schrader, Paul 1946- DLB-44
Schreiner, Olive
  1855-1920 ....DLB-18, 156, 190, 225
Schroeder, Andreas 1946- DLB-53

Schubart, Christian Friedrich Daniel
   1739-1791 . . . . DLB-97
Schubert, Gotthilf Heinrich 1780-1860 . . . . DLB-90
Schücking, Levin 1814-1883 . . . . DLB-133
Schulberg, Budd 1914- DLB-6, 26, 28; Y-81
Schulte, F. J., and Company. DLB-49
Schulz, Bruno 1892-1942 . . . . DLB-215; CDWLB-4
Schulze, Hans (see Praetorius, Johannes)
Schupp, Johann Balthasar 1610-1661 . . . . . DLB-164
Schurz, Carl 1829-1906 . . . . DLB-23
Schuyler, George S. 1895-1977 . . . . DLB-29, 51
Schuyler, James 1923-1991 . . . . DLB-5, 169
Schwartz, Delmore 1913-1966 . . . . DLB-28, 48
Schwartz, Jonathan 1938- Y-82
Schwartz, Lynne Sharon 1939- DLB-218
Schwarz, Sibylle 1621-1638 . . . . DLB-164
Schwerner, Armand 1927-1999 . . . . DLB-165
Schwob, Marcel 1867-1905 . . . . DLB-123
Sciascia, Leonardo 1921-1989 . . . . DLB-177
Science Fantasy DLB-8
Science-Fiction Fandom and Conventions . . . DLB-8
Science-Fiction Fanzines: The Time
   Binders DLB-8
Science-Fiction Films DLB-8
Science Fiction Writers of America and the
   Nebula Awards DLB-8
Scot, Reginald circa 1538-1599 . . . . DLB-136
Scotellaro, Rocco 1923-1953 . . . . DLB-128
Scott, Alicia Anne (Lady John Scott)
   1810-1900 . . . . DLB-240
Scott, Catharine Amy Dawson
   1865-1934 . . . . DLB-240
Scott, Dennis 1939-1991 . . . . DLB-125
Scott, Dixon 1881-1915 . . . . DLB-98
Scott, Duncan Campbell 1862-1947 . . . . . . DLB-92
Scott, Evelyn 1893-1963 . . . . DLB-9, 48
Scott, F. R. 1899-1985 . . . . DLB-88
Scott, Frederick George 1861-1944 . . . . DLB-92
Scott, Geoffrey 1884-1929 . . . . DLB-149
Scott, Harvey W. 1838-1910 . . . . DLB-23
Scott, Lady Jane (see Scott, Alicia Anne)
Scott, Paul 1920-1978 . . . . DLB-14, 207
Scott, Sarah 1723-1795 . . . . DLB-39
Scott, Tom 1918- DLB-27
Scott, Sir Walter 1771-1832
   . . . . . DLB-93, 107, 116, 144, 159; CDBLB-3
Scott, Walter, Publishing
   Company Limited DLB-112
Scott, William Bell 1811-1890 . . . . DLB-32
Scott, William R. [publishing house] DLB-46
Scott-Heron, Gil 1949- DLB-41
Scribe, Eugene 1791-1861 . . . . DLB-192
Scribner, Arthur Hawley 1859-1932 . . . . DS-13, 16
Scribner, Charles 1854-1930 . . . . DS-13, 16
Scribner, Charles, Jr. 1921-1995 . . . . Y-95
   Reminiscences DS-17

Charles Scribner's Sons DLB-49; DS-13, 16, 17
Scripps, E. W. 1854-1926 . . . . DLB-25
Scudder, Horace Elisha 1838-1902 . . . . DLB-42, 71
Scudder, Vida Dutton 1861-1954 . . . . DLB-71
Scupham, Peter 1933- DLB-40
Seabrook, William 1886-1945 . . . . DLB-4
Seabury, Samuel 1729-1796 . . . . DLB-31
Seacole, Mary Jane Grant 1805-1881 . . . . . DLB-166
The Seafarer circa 970 . . . . DLB-146
Sealsfield, Charles (Carl Postl)
   1793-1864 . . . . DLB-133, 186
Sears, Edward I. 1819?-1876 . . . . DLB-79
Sears Publishing Company DLB-46
Seaton, George 1911-1979 . . . . DLB-44
Seaton, William Winston 1785-1866 . . . . . . DLB-43
Secker, Martin [publishing house] DLB-112
Secker, Martin, and Warburg Limited DLB-112
The Second Annual New York Festival
   of Mystery Y-00
Second-Generation Minor Poets of the
   Seventeenth Century DLB-126
Sedgwick, Arthur George 1844-1915 . . . . . DLB-64
Sedgwick, Catharine Maria
   1789-1867 . . . . DLB-1, 74, 183, 239, 243
Sedgwick, Ellery 1872-1930 . . . . DLB-91
Sedgwick, Eve Kosofsky 1950- DLB-246
Sedley, Sir Charles 1639-1701 . . . . DLB-131
Seeberg, Peter 1925-1999 . . . . DLB-214
Seeger, Alan 1888-1916 . . . . DLB-45
Seers, Eugene (see Dantin, Louis)
Segal, Erich 1937- Y-86
Šegedin, Petar 1909- DLB-181
Seghers, Anna 1900-1983 . . . . DLB-69; CDWLB-2
Seid, Ruth (see Sinclair, Jo)
Seidel, Frederick Lewis 1936- Y-84
Seidel, Ina 1885-1974 . . . . DLB-56
Seifert, Jaroslav
   1901-1986 . . . . . . DLB-215; Y-84; CDWLB-4
Seigenthaler, John 1927- DLB-127
Seizin Press DLB-112
Séjour, Victor 1817-1874 . . . . DLB-50
Séjour Marcou et Ferrand, Juan Victor
   (see Séjour, Victor)
Sekowski, Józef-Julian, Baron Brambeus
   (see Senkovsky, Osip Ivanovich)
Selby, Bettina 1934- DLB-204
Selby, Hubert, Jr. 1928- DLB-2, 227
Selden, George 1929-1989 . . . . DLB-52
Selden, John 1584-1654 . . . . DLB-213
Selected English-Language Little Magazines
   and Newspapers [France, 1920-1939] . . . DLB-4
Selected Humorous Magazines
   (1820-1950) DLB-11
Selected Science-Fiction Magazines and
   Anthologies DLB-8
Selenić, Slobodan 1933-1995 . . . . DLB-181
Self, Edwin F. 1920- DLB-137

Self, Will 1961- DLB-207
Seligman, Edwin R. A. 1861-1939 . . . . DLB-47
Selimović, Meša
   1910-1982 . . . . DLB-181; CDWLB-4
Selous, Frederick Courteney
   1851-1917 . . . . DLB-174
Seltzer, Chester E. (see Muro, Amado)
Seltzer, Thomas [publishing house] DLB-46
Selvon, Sam 1923-1994 . . . . . DLB-125; CDWLB-3
Semmes, Raphael 1809-1877 . . . . DLB-189
Senancour, Etienne de 1770-1846 . . . . DLB-119
Sendak, Maurice 1928- DLB-61
Seneca the Elder
   circa 54 B.C.-circa A.D. 40 . . . . DLB-211
Seneca the Younger
   circa 1 B.C.-A.D. 65 . . . . DLB-211; CDWLB-1
Senécal, Eva 1905- DLB-92
Sengstacke, John 1912- DLB-127
Senior, Olive 1941- DLB-157
Senkovsky, Osip Ivanovich
   (Józef-Julian Sekowski, Baron Brambeus)
   1800-1858 . . . . DLB-198
Šenoa, August 1838-1881 . . . DLB-147; CDWLB-4
"Sensation Novels" (1863), by
   H. L. Manse DLB-21
Sepamla, Sipho 1932- DLB-157, 225
Seredy, Kate 1899-1975 . . . . DLB-22
Sereni, Vittorio 1913-1983 . . . . DLB-128
Seres, William [publishing house] DLB-170
Serling, Rod 1924-1975 . . . . DLB-26
Serote, Mongane Wally 1944- DLB-125, 225
Serraillier, Ian 1912-1994 . . . . DLB-161
Serrano, Nina 1934- DLB-122
Service, Robert 1874-1958 . . . . DLB-92
Sessler, Charles 1854-1935 . . . . DLB-187
Seth, Vikram 1952- DLB-120
Seton, Elizabeth Ann 1774-1821 . . . . DLB-200
Seton, Ernest Thompson
   1860-1942 . . . . DLB-92; DS-13
Setouchi Harumi 1922- DLB-182
Settle, Mary Lee 1918- DLB-6
Seume, Johann Gottfried 1763-1810 . . . . . . DLB-94
Seuse, Heinrich 1295?-1366 . . . . DLB-179
Seuss, Dr. (see Geisel, Theodor Seuss)
The Seventy-fifth Anniversary of the Armistice:
   The Wilfred Owen Centenary and
   the Great War Exhibit
   at the University of Virginia Y-93
Severin, Timothy 1940- DLB-204
Sewall, Joseph 1688-1769 . . . . DLB-24
Sewall, Richard B. 1908- DLB-111
Sewell, Anna 1820-1878 . . . . DLB-163
Sewell, Samuel 1652-1730 . . . . DLB-24
Sex, Class, Politics, and Religion [in the
   British Novel, 1930-1959] DLB-15
Sexton, Anne 1928-1974 . . . DLB-5, 169; CDALB-1
Seymour-Smith, Martin 1928-1998 . . . . . . DLB-155
Sgorlon, Carlo 1930- DLB-196

Shaara, Michael 1929-1988................Y-83
Shabel'skaia, Aleksandra Stanislavovna 1845-1921......................DLB-238
Shadwell, Thomas 1641?-1692.........DLB-80
Shaffer, Anthony 1926-...............DLB-13
Shaffer, Peter 1926-.....DLB-13, 233; CDBLB-8
Shaftesbury, Anthony Ashley Cooper, Third Earl of 1671-1713............DLB-101
Shairp, Mordaunt 1887-1939...........DLB-10
Shakespeare, Nicholas 1957-..........DLB-231
Shakespeare, William 1564-1616..........DLB-62, 172; CDBLB-1
The Shakespeare Globe Trust............Y-93
Shakespeare Head Press...............DLB-112
Shakhovskoi, Aleksandr Aleksandrovich 1777-1846.......................DLB-150
Shange, Ntozake 1948-...........DLB-38, 249
Shapiro, Karl 1913-2000...............DLB-48
Sharon Publications...................DLB-46
Sharp, Margery 1905-1991.............DLB-161
Sharp, William 1855-1905..............DLB-156
Sharpe, Tom 1928-................DLB-14, 231
Shaw, Albert 1857-1947................DLB-91
Shaw, George Bernard 1856-1950.......DLB-10, 57, 190, CDBLB-6
Shaw, Henry Wheeler 1818-1885........DLB-11
Shaw, Joseph T. 1874-1952............DLB-137
Shaw, Irwin 1913-1984......DLB-6, 102; Y-84; CDALB-1
Shaw, Mary 1854-1929................DLB-228
Shaw, Robert 1927-1978.............DLB-13, 14
Shaw, Robert B. 1947-................DLB-120
Shawn, William 1907-1992.............DLB-137
Shay, Frank [publishing house].........DLB-46
Shchedrin, N. (see Saltykov, Mikhail Evgrafovich)
Shea, John Gilmary 1824-1892..........DLB-30
Sheaffer, Louis 1912-1993.............DLB-103
Shearing, Joseph 1886-1952............DLB-70
Shebbeare, John 1709-1788.............DLB-39
Sheckley, Robert 1928-.................DLB-8
Shedd, William G. T. 1820-1894........DLB-64
Sheed, Wilfred 1930-..................DLB-6
Sheed and Ward [U.S.]................DLB-46
Sheed and Ward Limited [U.K.].......DLB-112
Sheldon, Alice B. (see Tiptree, James, Jr.)
Sheldon, Edward 1886-1946.............DLB-7
Sheldon and Company..................DLB-49
Sheller, Aleksandr Konstantinovich 1838-1900.......................DLB-238
Shelley, Mary Wollstonecraft 1797-1851 ....DLB-110, 116, 159, 178; CDBLB-3
Shelley, Percy Bysshe 1792-1822......DLB-96, 110, 158; CDBLB-3
Shelnutt, Eve 1941-...................DLB-130
Shenstone, William 1714-1763..........DLB-95
Shepard, Clark and Brown.............DLB-49
Shepard, Ernest Howard 1879-1976....DLB-160

Shepard, Sam 1943-................DLB-7, 212
Shepard, Thomas I, 1604 or 1605-1649...DLB-24
Shepard, Thomas II, 1635-1677........DLB-24
Shepherd, Luke flourished 1547-1554...............DLB-136
Sherburne, Edward 1616-1702..........DLB-131
Sheridan, Frances 1724-1766........DLB-39, 84
Sheridan, Richard Brinsley 1751-1816.................DLB-89; CDBLB-2
Sherman, Francis 1871-1926............DLB-92
Sherman, Martin 1938-................DLB-228
Sherriff, R. C. 1896-1975.......DLB-10, 191, 233
Sherrod, Blackie 1919-................DLB-241
Sherry, Norman 1935-.................DLB-155
Sherry, Richard 1506-1551 or 1555.....DLB-236
Sherwood, Mary Martha 1775-1851.....DLB-163
Sherwood, Robert E. 1896-1955....DLB-7, 26, 249
Shevyrev, Stepan Petrovich 1806-1864.......................DLB-205
Shiel, M. P. 1865-1947................DLB-153
Shiels, George 1886-1949..............DLB-10
Shiga, Naoya 1883-1971................DLB-180
Shiina Rinzō 1911-1973................DLB-182
Shikishi Naishinnō 1153?-1201.........DLB-203
Shillaber, Benjamin Penhallow 1814-1890................DLB-1, 11, 235
Shimao Toshio 1917-1986..............DLB-182
Shimazaki, Tōson 1872-1943...........DLB-180
Shine, Ted 1931-......................DLB-38
Shinkei 1406-1475.....................DLB-203
Ship, Reuben 1915-1975................DLB-88
Shirer, William L. 1904-1993............DLB-4
Shirinsky-Shikhmatov, Sergii Aleksandrovich 1783-1837......................DLB-150
Shirley, James 1596-1666..............DLB-58
Shishkov, Aleksandr Semenovich 1753-1841.......................DLB-150
Shockley, Ann Allen 1927-.............DLB-33
Shōno Junzō 1921-...................DLB-182
Shore, Arabella 1820?-1901 and Shore, Louisa 1824-1895...........DLB-199
Short, Luke (see Glidden, Frederick Dilley)
Short, Peter [publishing house].........DLB-170
Shorter, Dora Sigerson 1866-1918......DLB-240
Shorthouse, Joseph Henry 1834-1903....DLB-18
Shōtetsu 1381-1459...................DLB-203
Showalter, Elaine 1941-................DLB-67
Shulevitz, Uri 1935-...................DLB-61
Shulman, Max 1919-1988...............DLB-11
Shute, Henry A. 1856-1943..............DLB-9
Shute, Nevil 1899-1960................DLB-255
Shuttle, Penelope 1947-.............DLB-14, 40
Sibbes, Richard 1577-1635.............DLB-151
Sibiriak, D. (see Mamin, Dmitrii Narkisovich)
Siddal, Elizabeth Eleanor 1829-1862....DLB-199
Sidgwick, Ethel 1877-1970.............DLB-197

Sidgwick and Jackson Limited.........DLB-112
Sidney, Margaret (see Lothrop, Harriet M.)
Sidney, Mary 1561-1621...............DLB-167
Sidney, Sir Philip 1554-1586.............DLB-167; CDBLB-1
An Apologie for Poetrie (the Olney edition, 1595, of *Defence of Poesie*)....DLB-167
Sidney's Press......................DLB-49
Sierra, Rubén 1946-..................DLB-122
Sierra Club Books....................DLB-49
Siger of Brabant circa 1240-circa 1284...DLB-115
Sigourney, Lydia Huntley 1791-1865.......DLB-1, 42, 73, 183, 239, 243
Silkin, Jon 1930-.....................DLB-27
Silko, Leslie Marmon 1948-...DLB-143, 175, 256
Silliman, Benjamin 1779-1864..........DLB-183
Silliman, Ron 1946-...................DLB-169
Silliphant, Stirling 1918-..............DLB-26
Sillitoe, Alan 1928-.....DLB-14, 139; CDBLB-8
Silman, Roberta 1934-.................DLB-28
Silva, Beverly 1930-..................DLB-122
Silverberg, Robert 1935-...............DLB-8
Silverman, Kaja 1947-................DLB-246
Silverman, Kenneth 1936-............DLB-111
Simak, Clifford D. 1904-1988............DLB-8
Simcoe, Elizabeth 1762-1850...........DLB-99
Simcox, Edith Jemima 1844-1901.......DLB-190
Simcox, George Augustus 1841-1905....DLB-35
Sime, Jessie Georgina 1868-1958.......DLB-92
Simenon, Georges 1903-1989.......DLB-72; Y-89
Simic, Charles 1938-..................DLB-105
"Images and 'Images,'"..............DLB-105
Simionescu, Mircea Horia 1928-......DLB-232
Simmel, Johannes Mario 1924-........DLB-69
Simmes, Valentine [publishing house]....DLB-170
Simmons, Ernest J. 1903-1972.........DLB-103
Simmons, Herbert Alfred 1930-.........DLB-33
Simmons, James 1933-................DLB-40
Simms, William Gilmore 1806-1870............DLB-3, 30, 59, 73, 248
Simms and M'Intyre..................DLB-106
Simon, Claude 1913-.............DLB-83; Y-85
Simon, Neil 1927-.....................DLB-7
Simon and Schuster..................DLB-46
Simons, Katherine Drayton Mayrant 1890-1969.......................Y-83
Simović, Ljubomir 1935-.............DLB-181
Simpkin and Marshall [publishing house]................DLB-154
Simpson, Helen 1897-1940.............DLB-77
Simpson, Louis 1923-..................DLB-5
Simpson, N. F. 1919-.................DLB-13
Sims, George 1923-...............DLB-87; Y-99
Sims, George Robert 1847-1922...DLB-35, 70, 135
Sinán, Rogelio 1904-.................DLB-145
Sinclair, Andrew 1935-................DLB-14

Sinclair, Bertrand William 1881-1972 .....DLB-92
Sinclair, Catherine 1800-1864 ....DLB-163
Sinclair, Jo 1913-1995 ....DLB-28
Sinclair, Lister 1921- DLB-88
Sinclair, May 1863-1946 ....DLB-36, 135
Sinclair, Upton 1878-1968 ....DLB-9; CDALB-5
Sinclair, Upton [publishing house].......DLB-46
Singer, Isaac Bashevis
  1904-1991 ....DLB-6, 28, 52; Y-91; CDALB-1
Singer, Mark 1950- DLB-185
Singmaster, Elsie 1879-1958............DLB-9
Sinisgalli, Leonardo 1908-1981 ....DLB-114
Siodmak, Curt 1902-2000 ....DLB-44
Sîrbu, Ion D. 1919-1989................DLB-232
Siringo, Charles A. 1855-1928..........DLB-186
Sissman, L. E. 1928-1976..............DLB-5
Sisson, C. H. 1914- DLB-27
Sitwell, Edith 1887-1964......DLB-20; CDBLB-7
Sitwell, Osbert 1892-1969 ......DLB-100, 195
Skácel, Jan 1922-1989 ....DLB-232
Skalbe, Kārlis 1879-1945 ....DLB-220
Skármeta, Antonio
  1940- DLB-145; CDWLB-3
Skavronsky, A. (see Danilevsky, Grigorii Petrovich)
Skeat, Walter W. 1835-1912 ....DLB-184
Skeffington, William
  [publishing house]................DLB-106
Skelton, John 1463-1529 ....DLB-136
Skelton, Robin 1925- DLB-27, 53
Škėma, Antanas 1910-1961 ....DLB-220
Skinner, Constance Lindsay
  1877-1939 ....DLB-92
Skinner, John Stuart 1788-1851 ....DLB-73
Skipsey, Joseph 1832-1903.............DLB-35
Skou-Hansen, Tage 1925- DLB-214
Škvorecký, Josef 1924- DLB-232; CDWLB-4
Slade, Bernard 1930- DLB-53
Slamnig, Ivan 1930- DLB-181
Slančeková, Božena (see Timrava)
Slater, Patrick 1880-1951..............DLB-68
Slaveykov, Pencho 1866-1912.........DLB-147
Slaviček, Milivoj 1929- DLB-181
Slavitt, David 1935- DLB-5, 6
Sleigh, Burrows Willcocks Arthur
  1821-1869 ....DLB-99
A Slender Thread of Hope:
  The Kennedy Center Black
  Theatre Project DLB-38
Slesinger, Tess 1905-1945 ....DLB-102
Slick, Sam (see Haliburton, Thomas Chandler)
Sloan, John 1871-1951 ....DLB-188
Sloane, William, Associates DLB-46
Small, Maynard and Company DLB-49
Small Presses in Great Britain and Ireland,
  1960-1985 ....DLB-40
Small Presses I: Jargon Society...........Y-84

Small Presses II: The Spirit That Moves
  Us Press Y-85
Small Presses III: Pushcart Press..........Y-87
Smart, Christopher 1722-1771 ....DLB-109
Smart, David A. 1892-1957 ....DLB-137
Smart, Elizabeth 1913-1986............DLB-88
Smedley, Menella Bute 1820?-1877.......DLB-199
Smellie, William [publishing house].......DLB-154
Smiles, Samuel 1812-1904 ....DLB-55
Smiley, Jane 1949- DLB-227, 234
Smith, A. J. M. 1902-1980 ....DLB-88
Smith, Adam 1723-1790 ....DLB-104
Smith, Adam (George Jerome Waldo Goodman)
  1930- DLB-185
Smith, Alexander 1829-1867 ....DLB-32, 55
  "On the Writing of Essays" (1862) DLB-57
Smith, Amanda 1837-1915..............DLB-221
Smith, Betty 1896-1972 ....Y-82
Smith, Carol Sturm 1938- Y-81
Smith, Charles Henry 1826-1903 ....DLB-11
Smith, Charlotte 1749-1806 ....DLB-39, 109
Smith, Chet 1899-1973.................DLB-171
Smith, Cordwainer 1913-1966...........DLB-8
Smith, Dave 1942- DLB-5
Smith, Dodie 1896- DLB-10
Smith, Doris Buchanan 1934- DLB-52
Smith, E. E. 1890-1965 ....DLB-8
Smith, Elder and Company DLB-154
Smith, Elihu Hubbard 1771-1798.........DLB-37
Smith, Elizabeth Oakes (Prince)
  (see Oakes Smith, Elizabeth)
Smith, Eunice 1757-1823 ....DLB-200
Smith, F. Hopkinson 1838-1915 ....DS-13
Smith, George D. 1870-1920 ....DLB-140
Smith, George O. 1911-1981 ....DLB-8
Smith, Goldwin 1823-1910 ....DLB-99
Smith, H. Allen 1907-1976 ....DLB-11, 29
Smith, Harrison, and Robert Haas
  [publishing house]................DLB-46
Smith, Harry B. 1860-1936 ....DLB-187
Smith, Hazel Brannon 1914- DLB-127
Smith, Henry circa 1560-circa 1591......DLB-136
Smith, Horatio (Horace) 1779-1849......DLB-116
Smith, Horatio (Horace) 1779-1849 and
  James Smith 1775-1839 ....DLB-96
Smith, Iain Crichton 1928- DLB-40, 139
Smith, J. Allen 1860-1924 ....DLB-47
Smith, J. Stilman, and Company DLB-49
Smith, Jessie Willcox 1863-1935 ....DLB-188
Smith, John 1580-1631............DLB-24, 30
Smith, Josiah 1704-1781 ....DLB-24
Smith, Ken 1938- DLB-40
Smith, Lee 1944- DLB-143; Y-83
Smith, Logan Pearsall 1865-1946........DLB-98
Smith, Margaret Bayard 1778-1844 ......DLB-248
Smith, Mark 1935- Y-82

Smith, Michael 1698-circa 1771 ....DLB-31
Smith, Pauline 1882-1959 ....DLB-225
Smith, Red 1905-1982..............DLB-29, 171
Smith, Roswell 1829-1892..............DLB-79
Smith, Samuel Harrison 1772-1845......DLB-43
Smith, Samuel Stanhope 1751-1819......DLB-37
Smith, Sarah (see Stretton, Hesba)
Smith, Sarah Pogson 1774-1870.........DLB-200
Smith, Seba 1792-1868..........DLB-1, 11, 243
Smith, Stevie 1902-1971................DLB-20
Smith, Sydney 1771-1845..............DLB-107
Smith, Sydney Goodsir 1915-1975.......DLB-27
Smith, Sir Thomas 1513-1577 ....DLB-132
Smith, W. B., and Company DLB-49
Smith, W. H., and Son DLB-106
Smith, Wendell 1914-1972..............DLB-171
Smith, William flourished 1595-1597 ....DLB-136
Smith, William 1727-1803 ....DLB-31
  A General Idea of the College of Mirania
  (1753) [excerpts] DLB-31
Smith, William 1728-1793 ....DLB-30
Smith, William Gardner 1927-1974 ......DLB-76
Smith, William Henry 1808-1872 ....DLB-159
Smith, William Jay 1918- DLB-5
Smithers, Leonard [publishing house] DLB-112
Smollett, Tobias
  1721-1771..........DLB-39, 104; CDBLB-2
  Dedication, Ferdinand Count
  Fathom (1753) DLB-39
  Preface to Ferdinand Count Fathom (1753) DLB-39
  Preface to Roderick Random (1748)........DLB-39
Smythe, Francis Sydney 1900-1949......DLB-195
Snelling, William Joseph 1804-1848 .....DLB-202
Snellings, Rolland (see Touré, Askia Muhammad)
Snodgrass, W. D. 1926- DLB-5
Snow, C. P.
  1905-1980......DLB-15, 77; DS-17; CDBLB-7
Snyder, Gary 1930- DLB-5, 16, 165, 212, 237
Sobiloff, Hy 1912-1970.................DLB-48
The Society for Textual Scholarship and
  TEXT Y-87
The Society for the History of Authorship,
  Reading and Publishing Y-92
Södergran, Edith 1892-1923 ....DLB-257
Soffici, Ardengo 1879-1964 ....DLB-114
Sofola, 'Zulu 1938- DLB-157
Solano, Solita 1888-1975 ....DLB-4
Soldati, Mario 1906-1999 ....DLB-177
Šoljan, Antun 1932-1993 ....DLB-181
Sollers, Philippe 1936- DLB-83
Sollogub, Vladimir Aleksandrovich
  1813-1882.......................DLB-198
Sollors, Werner 1943- DBL-246
Solmi, Sergio 1899-1981 ....DLB-114
Solomon, Carl 1928- DLB-16
Solway, David 1941- DLB-53

Cumulative Index

Solzhenitsyn and America................Y-85
Somerville, Edith Œnone 1858-1949 .... DLB-135
Somov, Orest Mikhailovich
  1793-1833...................DLB-198
Sønderby, Knud 1909-1966 ....DLB-214
Song, Cathy 1955- DLB-169
Sonnevi, Göran 1939- DLB-257
Sono Ayako 1931- DLB-182
Sontag, Susan 1933- DLB-2, 67
Sophocles 497/496 B.C.-406/405 B.C.
  ....DLB-176; CDWLB-1
Šopov, Aco 1923-1982 ....DLB-181
Sørensen, Villy 1929- DLB-214
Sorensen, Virginia 1912-1991..........DLB-206
Sorge, Reinhard Johannes 1892-1916....DLB-118
Sorrentino, Gilbert 1929- DLB-5, 173; Y-80
Sotheby, James 1682-1742 ....DLB-213
Sotheby, John 1740-1807............DLB-213
Sotheby, Samuel 1771-1842 ....DLB-213
Sotheby, Samuel Leigh 1805-1861 ......DLB-213
Sotheby, William 1757-1833 ....DLB-93, 213
Soto, Gary 1952- DLB-82
Sources for the Study of Tudor and Stuart
  Drama DLB-62
Souster, Raymond 1921- DLB-88
The *South English Legendary* circa thirteenth-fifteenth
  centuries DLB-146
Southerland, Ellease 1943- DLB-33
Southern, Terry 1924-1995 ....DLB-2
Southern Illinois University Press Y-95
Southern Writers Between the Wars DLB-9
Southerne, Thomas 1659-1746 ....DLB-80
Southey, Caroline Anne Bowles
  1786-1854....................DLB-116
Southey, Robert 1774-1843......DLB-93, 107, 142
Southwell, Robert 1561?-1595 ....DLB-167
Southworth, E. D. E. N. 1819-1899 .....DLB-239
Sowande, Bode 1948- DLB-157
Sowle, Tace [publishing house].........DLB-170
Soyfer, Jura 1912-1939 ....DLB-124
Soyinka, Wole
  1934- DLB-125; Y-86, Y-87; CDWLB-3
Spacks, Barry 1931- DLB-105
Spalding, Frances 1950- DLB-155
Spark, Muriel 1918- ...DLB-15, 139; CDBLB-7
Sparke, Michael [publishing house] DLB-170
Sparks, Jared 1789-1866 ....DLB-1, 30, 235
Sparshott, Francis 1926- DLB-60
Späth, Gerold 1939- DLB-75
Spatola, Adriano 1941-1988 ....DLB-128
Spaziani, Maria Luisa 1924- DLB-128
Special Collections at the University of Colorado
  at Boulder......................Y-98
The Spectator 1828- DLB-110
Spedding, James 1808-1881 ....DLB-144
Spee von Langenfeld, Friedrich
  1591-1635 ....DLB-164

Speght, Rachel 1597-after 1630........DLB-126
Speke, John Hanning 1827-1864........DLB-166
Spellman, A. B. 1935- DLB-41
Spence, Catherine Helen 1825-1910.....DLB-230
Spence, Thomas 1750-1814 ....DLB-158
Spencer, Anne 1882-1975 ....DLB-51, 54
Spencer, Charles, third Earl of Sunderland
  1674-1722.....................DLB-213
Spencer, Elizabeth 1921- DLB-6, 218
Spencer, George John, Second Earl Spencer
  1758-1834....................DLB-184
Spencer, Herbert 1820-1903..........DLB-57
  "The Philosophy of Style" (1852) DLB-57
Spencer, Scott 1945- Y-86
Spender, J. A. 1862-1942 ....DLB-98
Spender, Stephen 1909-1995 ..DLB-20; CDBLB-7
Spener, Philipp Jakob 1635-1705 ....DLB-164
Spenser, Edmund
  circa 1552-1599 ....DLB-167; CDBLB-1
Envoy from *The Shepheardes Calender*.....DLB-167
"The Generall Argument of the
  Whole Booke," from
  The Shepheardes Calender...........DLB-167
"A Letter of the Authors Expounding
  His Whole Intention in the Course
  of this Worke: Which for that It Giueth
  Great Light to the Reader, for the Better
  Vnderstanding Is Hereunto Annexed,"
  from *The Faerie Queene* (1590) DLB-167
"To His Booke," from
  The Shepheardes Calender (1579) DLB-167
"To the Most Excellent and Learned Both
  Orator and Poete, Mayster Gabriell Haruey,
  His Verie Special and Singular Good Frend
  E. K. Commendeth the Good Lyking of
  This His Labour, and the Patronage of
  the New Poete," from
  The Shepheardes Calender...........DLB-167
Sperr, Martin 1944- DLB-124
Spicer, Jack 1925-1965 ....DLB-5, 16, 193
Spielberg, Peter 1929- Y-81
Spielhagen, Friedrich 1829-1911........DLB-129
"*Spielmannsepen*" (circa 1152-circa 1500) ..DLB-148
Spier, Peter 1927- DLB-61
Spillane, Mickey 1918- DLB-226
Spink, J. G. Taylor 1888-1962 ....DLB-241
Spinrad, Norman 1940- DLB-8
Spires, Elizabeth 1952- DLB-120
Spitteler, Carl 1845-1924 ....DLB-129
Spivak, Lawrence E. 1900- DLB-137
Spofford, Harriet Prescott
  1835-1921 ....DLB-74, 221
Spring, Howard 1889-1965 ....DLB-191
Squibob (see Derby, George Horatio)
Squier, E. G. 1821-1888 ....DLB-189
Stacpoole, H. de Vere 1863-1951 ....DLB-153
Staël, Germaine de 1766-1817......DLB-119, 192
Staël-Holstein, Anne-Louise Germaine de
  (see Staël, Germaine de)
Stafford, Jean 1915-1979 ....DLB-2, 173

Stafford, William 1914-1993.........DLB-5, 206
Stage Censorship: "The Rejected Statement"
  (1911), by Bernard Shaw [excerpts]...DLB-10
Stallings, Laurence 1894-1968 ....DLB-7, 44
Stallworthy, Jon 1935- DLB-40
Stampp, Kenneth M. 1912- DLB-17
Stănescu, Nichita 1933-1983 ....DLB-232
Stanev, Emiliyan 1907-1979 ....DLB-181
Stanford, Ann 1916- DLB-5
Stangerup, Henrik 1937-1998 ....DLB-214
Stanitsky, N. (see Panaeva, Avdot'ia Iakovlevna)
Stankevich, Nikolai Vladimirovich
  1813-1840 ....DLB-198
Stanković, Borisav ("Bora")
  1876-1927.............DLB-147; CDWLB-4
Stanley, Henry M. 1841-1904 ... DLB-189; DS-13
Stanley, Thomas 1625-1678 ....DLB-131
Stannard, Martin 1947- DLB-155
Stansby, William [publishing house].....DLB-170
Stanton, Elizabeth Cady 1815-1902 ......DLB-79
Stanton, Frank L. 1857-1927............DLB-25
Stanton, Maura 1946- DLB-120
Stapledon, Olaf 1886-1950.........DLB-15, 255
Star Spangled Banner Office...........DLB-49
Stark, Freya 1893-1993...............DLB-195
Starkey, Thomas circa 1499-1538 ......DLB-132
Starkie, Walter 1894-1976 ....DLB-195
Starkweather, David 1935- DLB-7
Starrett, Vincent 1886-1974 ....DLB-187
The State of Publishing Y-97
Statements on the Art of Poetry DLB-54
Stationers' Company of London, The DLB-170
Statius circa A.D. 45-A.D. 96 ....DLB-211
Stead, Robert J. C. 1880-1959 ....DLB-92
Steadman, Mark 1930- DLB-6
The Stealthy School of Criticism (1871), by
  Dante Gabriel Rossetti.............DLB-35
Stearns, Harold E. 1891-1943............DLB-4
Stebnitsky, M. (see Leskov, Nikolai Semenovich)
Stedman, Edmund Clarence 1833-1908...DLB-64
Steegmuller, Francis 1906-1994 ....DLB-111
Steel, Flora Annie 1847-1929 .....DLB-153, 156
Steele, Max 1922- Y-80
Steele, Richard
  1672-1729..........DLB-84, 101; CDBLB-2
Steele, Timothy 1948- DLB-120
Steele, Wilbur Daniel 1886-1970 ....DLB-86
Steere, Richard circa 1643-1721 ....DLB-24
Stefanovski, Goran 1952- DLB-181
Stegner, Wallace 1909-1993.....DLB-9, 206; Y-93
Stehr, Hermann 1864-1940 ....DLB-66
Steig, William 1907- DLB-61
Stein, Gertrude 1874-1946
  .... DLB-4, 54, 86, 228; DS-15; CDALB-4
Stein, Leo 1872-1947..................DLB-4
Stein and Day Publishers DLB-46

Steinbeck, John
   1902-1968 .... DLB-7, 9, 212; DS-2; CDALB-5

John Steinbeck Research Center Y-85

Steinem, Gloria 1934- DLB-246

Steiner, George 1929- DLB-67

Steinhoewel, Heinrich 1411/1412-1479 ... DLB-179

Steloff, Ida Frances 1887-1989 .... DLB-187

Stendhal 1783-1842 .... DLB-119

Stephen Crane: A Revaluation Virginia Tech Conference, 1989 .... Y-89

Stephen, Leslie 1832-1904 ...... DLB-57, 144, 190

Stephen Vincent Benét Centenary Y-97

Stephens, A. G. 1865-1933 .... DLB-230

Stephens, Alexander H. 1812-1883 .... DLB-47

Stephens, Alice Barber 1858-1932 ...... DLB-188

Stephens, Ann 1810-1886 .... DLB-3, 73

Stephens, Charles Asbury 1844?-1931 .... DLB-42

Stephens, James 1882?-1950 .... DLB-19, 153, 162

Stephens, John Lloyd 1805-1852 .... DLB-183

Stephens, Michael 1946- DLB-234

Sterling, George 1869-1926 .... DLB-54

Sterling, James 1701-1763 .... DLB-24

Sterling, John 1806-1844 .... DLB-116

Stern, Gerald 1925- DLB-105

Stern, Gladys B. 1890-1973 .... DLB-197

Stern, Madeleine B. 1912- DLB-111, 140

Stern, Richard 1928- DLB-218; Y-87

Stern, Stewart 1922- DLB-26

Sterne, Laurence
   1713-1768 .... DLB-39; CDBLB-2

Sternheim, Carl 1878-1942 .... DLB-56, 118

Sternhold, Thomas ?-1549 and
   John Hopkins ?-1570 .... DLB-132

Steuart, David 1747-1824 .... DLB-213

Stevens, Henry 1819-1886 .... DLB-140

Stevens, Wallace 1879-1955 .... DLB-54; CDALB-5

Stevenson, Anne 1933- DLB-40

Stevenson, D. E. 1892-1973 .... DLB-191

Stevenson, Lionel 1902-1973 .... DLB-155

Stevenson, Robert Louis
   1850-1894 .... DLB-18, 57, 141, 156, 174;
                           DS-13; CDBLB-5

"On Style in Literature:
   Its Technical Elements" (1885) DLB-57

Stewart, Donald Ogden
   1894-1980 .... DLB-4, 11, 26

Stewart, Dugald 1753-1828 .... DLB-31

Stewart, George, Jr. 1848-1906 .... DLB-99

Stewart, George R. 1895-1980 .... DLB-8

Stewart, Maria W. 1803?-1879 .... DLB-239

Stewart, Randall 1896-1964 .... DLB-103

Stewart and Kidd Company DLB-46

Stickney, Trumbull 1874-1904 .... DLB-54

Stieler, Caspar 1632-1707 .... DLB-164

Stifter, Adalbert
   1805-1868 .... DLB-133; CDWLB-2

Stiles, Ezra 1727-1795 .... DLB-31

Still, James 1906- DLB-9

Stirner, Max 1806-1856 .... DLB-129

Stith, William 1707-1755 .... DLB-31

Stock, Elliot [publishing house] DLB-106

Stockton, Frank R.
   1834-1902 .... DLB-42, 74; DS-13

Stockton, J. Roy 1892-1972 .... DLB-241

Stoddard, Ashbel [publishing house] DLB-49

Stoddard, Charles Warren
   1843-1909 .... DLB-186

Stoddard, Elizabeth 1823-1902 .... DLB-202

Stoddard, Richard Henry
   1825-1903 .... DLB-3, 64; DS-13

Stoddard, Solomon 1643-1729 .... DLB-24

Stoker, Bram
   1847-1912 .... DLB-36, 70, 178; CDBLB-5

Stokes, Frederick A., Company DLB-49

Stokes, Thomas L. 1898-1958 .... DLB-29

Stokesbury, Leon 1945- DLB-120

Stolberg, Christian Graf zu 1748-1821 .... DLB-94

Stolberg, Friedrich Leopold Graf zu
   1750-1819 .... DLB-94

Stone, Herbert S., and Company DLB-49

Stone, Lucy 1818-1893 .... DLB-79, 239

Stone, Melville 1848-1929 .... DLB-25

Stone, Robert 1937- DLB-152

Stone, Ruth 1915- DLB-105

Stone, Samuel 1602-1663 .... DLB-24

Stone, William Leete 1792-1844 .... DLB-202

Stone and Kimball DLB-49

Stoppard, Tom
   1937- DLB-13, 233; Y-85; CDBLB-8

Playwrights and Professors DLB-13

Storey, Anthony 1928- DLB-14

Storey, David 1933- DLB-13, 14, 207, 245

Storm, Theodor 1817-1888 .. DLB-129; CDWLB-2

Story, Thomas circa 1670-1742 .... DLB-31

Story, William Wetmore 1819-1895 ... DLB-1, 235

Storytelling: A Contemporary Renaissance ... Y-84

Stoughton, William 1631-1701 .... DLB-24

Stow, John 1525-1605 .... DLB-132

Stowe, Harriet Beecher 1811-1896
 .. DLB-1, 12, 42, 74, 189, 239, 243; CDALB-3

Stowe, Leland 1899- DLB-29

Stoyanov, Dimitr Ivanov (see Elin Pelin)

Strabo 64 or 63 B.C.-circa A.D. 25 ...... DLB-176

Strachey, Lytton 1880-1932 ..... DLB-149; DS-10

Strachey, Lytton, Preface to Eminent
   Victorians DLB-149

Strahan, William [publishing house] DLB-154

Strahan and Company DLB-106

Strand, Mark 1934- DLB-5

The Strasbourg Oaths 842 .... DLB-148

Stratemeyer, Edward 1862-1930 .... DLB-42

Strati, Saverio 1924- DLB-177

Stratton and Barnard DLB-49

Stratton-Porter, Gene
   1863-1924 .... DLB-221; DS-14

Straub, Peter 1943- Y-84

Strauß, Botho 1944- DLB-124

Strauß, David Friedrich 1808-1874 ...... DLB-133

The Strawberry Hill Press DLB-154

Streatfeild, Noel 1895-1986 .... DLB-160

Street, Cecil John Charles (see Rhode, John)

Street, G. S. 1867-1936 .... DLB-135

Street and Smith DLB-49

Streeter, Edward 1891-1976 .... DLB-11

Streeter, Thomas Winthrop 1883-1965 ... DLB-140

Stretton, Hesba 1832-1911 .... DLB-163, 190

Stribling, T. S. 1881-1965 .... DLB-9

Der Stricker circa 1190-circa 1250 ...... DLB-138

Strickland, Samuel 1804-1867 .... DLB-99

Stringer, Arthur 1874-1950 .... DLB-92

Stringer and Townsend DLB-49

Strittmatter, Erwin 1912- DLB-69

Strniša, Gregor 1930-1987 .... DLB-181

Strode, William 1630-1645 .... DLB-126

Strong, L. A. G. 1896-1958 .... DLB-191

Strother, David Hunter (Porte Crayon)
   1816-1888 .... DLB-3, 248

Strouse, Jean 1945- DLB-111

Stuart, Dabney 1937- DLB-105

Stuart, Jesse 1906-1984 ..... DLB-9, 48, 102; Y-84

Stuart, Lyle [publishing house] DLB-46

Stuart, Ruth McEnery 1849?-1917 ..... DLB-202

Stubbs, Harry Clement (see Clement, Hal)

Stubenberg, Johann Wilhelm von
   1619-1663 .... DLB-164

Studebaker, William V. 1947- DLB-256

Studio DLB-112

The Study of Poetry (1880), by
   Matthew Arnold DLB-35

Stump, Al 1916-1995 .... DLB-241

Sturgeon, Theodore 1918-1985 ..... DLB-8; Y-85

Sturges, Preston 1898-1959 .... DLB-26

"Style" (1840; revised, 1859), by
   Thomas de Quincey [excerpt] DLB-57

"Style" (1888), by Walter Pater DLB-57

Style (1897), by Walter Raleigh
   [excerpt] DLB-57

"Style" (1877), by T. H. Wright
   [excerpt] DLB-57

"Le Style c'est l'homme" (1892), by
   W. H. Mallock DLB-57

Styron, William
   1925- DLB-2, 143; Y-80; CDALB-6

Suárez, Mario 1925- DLB-82

Such, Peter 1939- DLB-60

Suckling, Sir John 1609-1641? DLB-58, 126

Suckow, Ruth 1892-1960 .... DLB-9, 102

Sudermann, Hermann 1857-1928 ...... DLB-118

Sue, Eugène 1804-1857 .... DLB-119

Sue, Marie-Joseph (see Sue, Eugène)

Suetonius circa A.D. 69-post A.D. 122 . . . DLB-211
Suggs, Simon (see Hooper, Johnson Jones)
Sui Sin Far (see Eaton, Edith Maude)
Suits, Gustav 1883-1956 . . . . DLB-220; CDWLB-4
Sukenick, Ronald 1932- DLB-173; Y-81
Suknaski, Andrew 1942- DLB-53
Sullivan, Alan 1868-1947 . . . . DLB-92
Sullivan, C. Gardner 1886-1965 . . . . DLB-26
Sullivan, Frank 1892-1976 . . . . DLB-11
Sulte, Benjamin 1841-1923 . . . . DLB-99
Sulzberger, Arthur Hays 1891-1968 . . . . . DLB-127
Sulzberger, Arthur Ochs 1926- DLB-127
Sulzer, Johann Georg 1720-1779 . . . . DLB-97
Sumarokov, Aleksandr Petrovich
 1717-1777 . . . . DLB-150
Summers, Hollis 1916- DLB-6
A Summing Up at Century's End Y-99
Sumner, Charles 1811-1874 . . . . DLB-235
Sumner, Henry A. [publishing house] DLB-49
Sundman, Per Olof 1922-1992 . . . . DLB-257
Surtees, Robert Smith 1803-1864 . . . . DLB-21
Survey of Literary Biographies Y-00
A Survey of Poetry Anthologies,
 1879-1960 . . . . DLB-54
Surveys: Japanese Literature,
 1987-1995 . . . . DLB-182
Sutherland, Efua Theodora
 1924-1996 . . . . DLB-117
Sutherland, John 1919-1956 . . . . DLB-68
Sutro, Alfred 1863-1933 . . . . DLB-10
Svendsen, Hanne Marie 1933- DLB-214
Swados, Harvey 1920-1972 . . . . DLB-2
Swain, Charles 1801-1874 . . . . DLB-32
Swallow Press DLB-46
Swan Sonnenschein Limited DLB-106
Swanberg, W. A. 1907- DLB-103
Swenson, May 1919-1989 . . . . DLB-5
Swerling, Jo 1897- DLB-44
Swift, Graham 1949- DLB-194
Swift, Jonathan
 1667-1745 . . . . DLB-39, 95, 101; CDBLB-2
Swinburne, A. C.
 1837-1909 . . . . DLB-35, 57; CDBLB-4
Swineshead, Richard
 floruit circa 1350 . . . . DLB-115
Swinnerton, Frank 1884-1982 . . . . DLB-34
Swisshelm, Jane Grey 1815-1884 . . . . DLB-43
Swope, Herbert Bayard 1882-1958 . . . . . . DLB-25
Swords, T. and J., and Company DLB-49
Swords, Thomas 1763-1843 and
 Swords, James ?-1844 . . . . DLB-73
Sykes, Ella C. ?-1939 . . . . DLB-174
Sylvester, Josuah
 1562 or 1563-1618 . . . . DLB-121
Symonds, Emily Morse (see Paston, George)
Symonds, John Addington
 1840-1893 . . . . DLB-57, 144

"Personal Style" (1890) DLB-57
Symons, A. J. A. 1900-1941 . . . . DLB-149
Symons, Arthur 1865-1945 . . . . . . DLB-19, 57, 149
Symons, Julian
 1912-1994 . . . . DLB-87, 155; Y-92
Julian Symons at Eighty Y-92
Symons, Scott 1933- DLB-53
A Symposium on *The Columbia History of
 the Novel* Y-92
Synge, John Millington
 1871-1909 . . . . DLB-10, 19; CDBLB-5
Synge Summer School: J. M. Synge and the
 Irish Theater, Rathdrum, County Wiclow,
 Ireland Y-93
Syrett, Netta 1865-1943 . . . . DLB-135, 197
Szabó, Lőrinc
 1900-1957 . . . . DLB-215
Szabó, Magda 1917- DLB-215
Szymborska, Wisława
 1923- DLB-232, Y-96; CDWLB-4

T

Taban lo Liyong 1939?- DLB-125
Tabori, George 1914- DLB-245
Tabucchi, Antonio 1943- DLB-196
Taché, Joseph-Charles 1820-1894 . . . . . . DLB-99
Tachihara Masaaki 1926-1980 . . . . DLB-182
Tacitus circa A.D. 55-circa A.D. 117
 . . . . DLB-211; CDWLB-1
Tadijanović, Dragutin 1905- DLB-181
Tafdrup, Pia 1952- DLB-214
Tafolla, Carmen 1951- DLB-82
Taggard, Genevieve 1894-1948 . . . . DLB-45
Taggart, John 1942- DLB-193
Tagger, Theodor (see Bruckner, Ferdinand)
Taiheiki late fourteenth century DLB-203
Tait, J. Selwin, and Sons DLB-49
Tait's Edinburgh Magazine 1832-1861 . . . . DLB-110
The Takarazaka Revue Company Y-91
Talander (see Bohse, August)
Talese, Gay 1932- DLB-185
Talev, Dimitr 1898-1966 . . . . DLB-181
Taliaferro, H. E. 1811-1875 . . . . DLB-202
Tallent, Elizabeth 1954- DLB-130
TallMountain, Mary 1918-1994 . . . . DLB-193
Talvj 1797-1870 . . . . DLB-59, 133
Tamási, Áron 1897-1966 . . . . DLB-215
Tammsaare, A. H.
 1878-1940 . . . . DLB-220; CDWLB-4
Tan, Amy 1952- DLB-173; CDALB-7
Tandori, Dezső 1938- DLB-232
Tanner, Thomas 1673/1674-1735 . . . . . . DLB-213
Tanizaki Jun'ichirō 1886-1965 . . . . DLB-180
Tapahonso, Luci 1953- DLB-175
The Mark Taper Forum DLB-7
Taradash, Daniel 1913- DLB-44
Tarbell, Ida M. 1857-1944 . . . . DLB-47

Tardivel, Jules-Paul 1851-1905 . . . . DLB-99
Targan, Barry 1932- DLB-130
Tarkington, Booth 1869-1946 . . . . DLB-9, 102
Tashlin, Frank 1913-1972 . . . . DLB-44
Tasma (Jessie Couvreur) 1848-1897 . . . . DLB-230
Tate, Allen 1899-1979 . . . . DLB-4, 45, 63; DS-17
Tate, James 1943- DLB-5, 169
Tate, Nahum circa 1652-1715 . . . . DLB-80
Tatian circa 830 . . . . DLB-148
Taufer, Veno 1933- DLB-181
Tauler, Johannes circa 1300-1361 . . . . . . DLB-179
Tavčar, Ivan 1851-1923 . . . . DLB-147
Taverner, Richard ca. 1505-1575 . . . . . . DLB-236
Taylor, Ann 1782-1866 . . . . DLB-163
Taylor, Bayard 1825-1878 . . . . DLB-3, 189
Taylor, Bert Leston 1866-1921 . . . . DLB-25
Taylor, Charles H. 1846-1921 . . . . DLB-25
Taylor, Edward circa 1642-1729 . . . . DLB-24
Taylor, Elizabeth 1912-1975 . . . . DLB-139
Taylor, Henry 1942- DLB-5
Taylor, Sir Henry 1800-1886 . . . . DLB-32
Taylor, Jane 1783-1824 . . . . DLB-163
Taylor, Jeremy circa 1613-1667 . . . . DLB-151
Taylor, John 1577 or 1578 - 1653 . . . . . . DLB-121
Taylor, Mildred D. ?- DLB-52
Taylor, Peter 1917-1994 . . . . . DLB-218; Y-81, Y-94
Taylor, Susie King 1848-1912 . . . . DLB-221
Taylor, William Howland 1901-1966 . . . DLB-241
Taylor, William, and Company DLB-49
Taylor-Made Shakespeare? Or Is "Shall I Die?" the
 Long-Lost Text of Bottom's Dream? Y-85
Teasdale, Sara 1884-1933 . . . . DLB-45
Telles, Lygia Fagundes 1924- DLB-113
Temple, Sir William 1628-1699 . . . . DLB-101
Temple, William F. 1914-1989 . . . . DLB-255
Temrizov, A. (see Marchenko, Anastasia Iakovlevna)
Tench, Watkin ca. 1758-1833 . . . . DLB-230
Tenn, William 1919- DLB-8
Tennant, Emma 1937- DLB-14
Tenney, Tabitha Gilman
 1762-1837 . . . . DLB-37, 200
Tennyson, Alfred
 1809-1892 . . . . DLB-32; CDBLB-4
Tennyson, Frederick 1807-1898 . . . . DLB-32
Tenorio, Arthur 1924- DLB-209
Tepliakov, Viktor Grigor'evich
 1804-1842 . . . . DLB-205
Terence circa 184 B.C.-159 B.C. or after
 . . . . DLB-211; CDWLB-1
Terhune, Albert Payson 1872-1942 . . . . . . DLB-9
Terhune, Mary Virginia
 1830-1922 . . . . DS-13, DS-16
Terry, Megan 1932- DLB-7, 249
Terson, Peter 1932- DLB-13
Tesich, Steve 1943-1996 . . . . Y-83
Tessa, Delio 1886-1939 . . . . DLB-114

Testori, Giovanni 1923-1993....... DLB-128, 177

Tey, Josephine 1896?-1952 ....DLB-77

Thacher, James 1754-1844................DLB-37

Thackeray, William Makepeace
1811-1863...DLB-21, 55, 159, 163; CDBLB-4

Thames and Hudson Limited DLB-112

Thanet, Octave (see French, Alice)

Thatcher, John Boyd 1847-1909 ....DLB-187

Thaxter, Celia Laighton 1835-1894......DLB-239

Thayer, Caroline Matilda Warren
1785-1844 ....DLB-200

Thayer, Douglas 1929- DLB-256

The Theatre Guild....................DLB-7

The Theater in Shakespeare's Time DLB-62

Thegan and the Astronomer
flourished circa 850................DLB-148

Thelwall, John 1764-1834 ....DLB-93, 158

Theocritus circa 300 B.C.-260 B.C.....DLB-176

Theodorescu, Ion N. (see Arghezi, Tudor)

Theodulf circa 760-circa 821 ....DLB-148

Theophrastus circa 371 B.C.-287 B.C....DLB-176

Theriault, Yves 1915-1983.............DLB-88

Thério, Adrien 1925- DLB-53

Theroux, Paul 1941- DLB-2, 218; CDALB-7

Thesiger, Wilfred 1910- DLB-204

They All Came to Paris................DS-16

Thibaudeau, Colleen 1925- DLB-88

Thielen, Benedict 1903-1965............DLB-102

Thiong'o Ngugi wa (see Ngugi wa Thiong'o)

Third-Generation Minor Poets of the
Seventeenth Century...............DLB-131

This Quarter 1925-1927, 1929-1932 .... DS-15

Thoma, Ludwig 1867-1921 ....DLB-66

Thoma, Richard 1902- DLB-4

Thomas, Audrey 1935- DLB-60

Thomas, D. M. 1935- ..DLB-40, 207; CDBLB-8

D. M. Thomas: The Plagiarism
Controversy Y-82

Thomas, Dylan
1914-1953.......DLB-13, 20, 139; CDBLB-7

The Dylan Thomas Celebration Y-99

Thomas, Edward
1878-1917 ....DLB-19, 98, 156, 216

Thomas, Frederick William 1806-1866...DLB-202

Thomas, Gwyn 1913-1981 ....DLB-15, 245

Thomas, Isaiah 1750-1831........DLB-43, 73, 187

Thomas, Isaiah [publishing house].......DLB-49

Thomas, Johann 1624-1679............DLB-168

Thomas, John 1900-1932.................DLB-4

Thomas, Joyce Carol 1938- DLB-33

Thomas, Lorenzo 1944- DLB-41

Thomas, R. S. 1915-2000......DLB-27; CDBLB-8

Thomasîn von Zerclære
circa 1186-circa 1259...............DLB-138

Thomasius, Christian 1655-1728..........DLB-168

Thompson, Daniel Pierce 1795-1868.....DLB-202

Thompson, David 1770-1857.............DLB-99

Thompson, Dorothy 1893-1961 ....DLB-29

Thompson, E. P. 1924-1993 ....DLB-242

Thompson, Flora 1876-1947 ....DLB-240

Thompson, Francis
1859-1907 ....DLB-19; CDBLB-5

Thompson, George Selden (see Selden, George)

Thompson, Henry Yates 1838-1928 .....DLB-184

Thompson, Hunter S. 1939- DLB-185

Thompson, Jim 1906-1977..............DLB-226

Thompson, John 1938-1976.............DLB-60

Thompson, John R. 1823-1873 ....DLB-3, 73, 248

Thompson, Lawrance 1906-1973 ....DLB-103

Thompson, Maurice 1844-1901 ......DLB-71, 74

Thompson, Ruth Plumly 1891-1976......DLB-22

Thompson, Thomas Phillips 1843-1933 ...DLB-99

Thompson, William 1775-1833 ....DLB-158

Thompson, William Tappan
1812-1882 ....DLB-3, 11, 248

Thomson, Edward William 1849-1924....DLB-92

Thomson, James 1700-1748 ....DLB-95

Thomson, James 1834-1882 ....DLB-35

Thomson, Joseph 1858-1895............DLB-174

Thomson, Mortimer 1831-1875..........DLB-11

Thon, Melanie Rae 1957- DLB-244

Thoreau, Henry David
1817-1862 ....DLB-1, 183, 223; CDALB-2

The Thoreauvian Pilgrimage: The Structure of an
American Cult...................DLB-223

Thorpe, Adam 1956- DLB-231

Thorpe, Thomas Bangs
1815-1878 ....DLB-3, 11, 248

Thorup, Kirsten 1942- DLB-214

Thoughts on Poetry and Its Varieties (1833),
by John Stuart Mill DLB-32

Thrale, Hester Lynch
(see Piozzi, Hester Lynch [Thrale])

Thubron, Colin 1939- DLB-204, 231

Thucydides
circa 455 B.C.-circa 395 B.C. DLB-176

Thulstrup, Thure de 1848-1930 ....DLB-188

Thümmel, Moritz August von
1738-1817 ....DLB-97

Thurber, James
1894-1961 .....DLB-4, 11, 22, 102; CDALB-5

Thurman, Wallace 1902-1934...........DLB-51

Thwaite, Anthony 1930- DLB-40

The Booker Prize
Address by Anthony Thwaite,
Chairman of the Booker Prize Judges
Comments from Former Booker
Prize Winners Y-86

Thwaites, Reuben Gold 1853-1913.......DLB-47

Tibullus circa 54 B.C.-circa 19 B.C. DLB-211

Ticknor, George 1791-1871 ...DLB-1, 59, 140, 235

Ticknor and Fields....................DLB-49

Ticknor and Fields (revived) DLB-46

Tieck, Ludwig 1773-1853......DLB-90; CDWLB-2

Tietjens, Eunice 1884-1944 ....DLB-54

Tikkanen, Märta 1935- DLB-257

Tilghman, Christopher circa 1948.......DLB-244

Tilney, Edmund circa 1536-1610 ....DLB-136

Tilt, Charles [publishing house].........DLB-106

Tilton, J. E., and Company DLB-49

Time and Western Man (1927), by Wyndham
Lewis [excerpts]...................DLB-36

Time-Life Books DLB-46

Times Books DLB-46

Timothy, Peter circa 1725-1782..........DLB-43

Timrava 1867-1951 ....DLB-215

Timrod, Henry 1828-1867 ....DLB-3, 248

Tindal, Henrietta 1818?-1879 ....DLB-199

Tinker, Chauncey Brewster 1876-1963 ...DLB-140

Tinsley Brothers DLB-106

Tiptree, James, Jr. 1915-1987.............DLB-8

Tišma, Aleksandar 1924- DLB-181

Titus, Edward William
1870-1952 ....DLB-4; DS-15

Tiutchev, Fedor Ivanovich 1803-1873....DLB-205

Tlali, Miriam 1933- DLB-157, 225

Todd, Barbara Euphan 1890-1976.......DLB-160

Todorov, Tzvetan 1939- DLB-242

Tofte, Robert
1561 or 1562-1619 or 1620.......DLB-172

Toklas, Alice B. 1877-1967................DLB-4

Tokuda, Shūsei 1872-1943..............DLB-180

Tolkien, J. R. R.
1892-1973 ......DLB-15, 160, 255; CDBLB-6

Toller, Ernst 1893-1939................DLB-124

Tollet, Elizabeth 1694-1754 ....DLB-95

Tolson, Melvin B. 1898-1966 ....DLB-48, 76

Tolstoy, Aleksei Konstantinovich
1817-1875........................DLB-238

Tolstoy, Leo 1828-1910.................DLB-238

Tom Jones (1749), by Henry Fielding
[excerpt] DLB-39

Tomalin, Claire 1933- DLB-155

Tomasi di Lampedusa, Giuseppe
1896-1957 ....DLB-177

Tomlinson, Charles 1927- DLB-40

Tomlinson, H. M. 1873-1958 ...DLB-36, 100, 195

Tompkins, Abel [publishing house].......DLB-49

Tompson, Benjamin 1642-1714..........DLB-24

Tomson, Graham R.
(see Watson, Rosamund Marriott)

Ton'a 1289-1372 ....DLB-203

Tondelli, Pier Vittorio 1955-1991 ....DLB-196

Tonks, Rosemary 1932- DLB-14, 207

Tonna, Charlotte Elizabeth 1790-1846 ...DLB-163

Tonson, Jacob the Elder
[publishing house]................DLB-170

Toole, John Kennedy 1937-1969 .... Y-81

Toomer, Jean 1894-1967 ...DLB-45, 51; CDALB-4

Tor Books DLB-46

Torberg, Friedrich 1908-1979 ....DLB-85

Torrence, Ridgely 1874-1950.......DLB-54, 249

Torres-Metzger, Joseph V. 1933- DLB-122

Cumulative Index

Toth, Susan Allen 1940- Y-86
Tottell, Richard [publishing house].......DLB-170
"The Printer to the Reader," (1557) by Richard Tottell DLB-167
Tough-Guy Literature DLB-9
Touré, Askia Muhammad 1938- DLB-41
Tourgée, Albion W. 1838-1905 ....DLB-79
Tournemir, Elizaveta Sailhas de (see Tur, Evgeniia)
Tourneur, Cyril circa 1580-1626 ....DLB-58
Tournier, Michel 1924- DLB-83
Tousey, Frank [publishing house]........DLB-49
Tower Publications....................DLB-46
Towne, Benjamin circa 1740-1793 ....DLB-43
Towne, Robert 1936- DLB-44
The Townely Plays fifteenth and sixteenth centuries........................DLB-146
Townshend, Aurelian by 1583-circa 1651................DLB-121
Toy, Barbara 1908- DLB-204
Tracy, Honor 1913- DLB-15
Traherne, Thomas 1637?-1674.........DLB-131
Traill, Catharine Parr 1802-1899 ....DLB-99
Train, Arthur 1875-1945..........DLB-86; DS-16
The Transatlantic Publishing Company...DLB-49
The Transatlantic Review 1924-1925......DS-15
The Transcendental Club 1836-1840....DLB-223
Transcendentalism DLB-223
Transcendentalists, American..............DS-5
A Transit of Poets and Others: American Biography in 1982 ....Y-82
transition 1927-1938 ....DS-15
Translators of the Twelfth Century: Literary Issues Raised and Impact Created DLB-115
Tranströmer, Tomas 1931- DLB-257
Travel Writing, 1837-1875 ....DLB-166
Travel Writing, 1876-1909 ....DLB-174
Travel Writing, 1910-1939 ....DLB-195
Traven, B. 1882? or 1890?-1969? DLB-9, 56
Travers, Ben 1886-1980 ....DLB-10, 233
Travers, P. L. (Pamela Lyndon) 1899-1996 ....DLB-160
Trediakovsky, Vasilii Kirillovich 1703-1769 ....DLB-150
Treece, Henry 1911-1966...............DLB-160
Trejo, Ernesto 1950- DLB-122
Trelawny, Edward John 1792-1881..............DLB-110, 116, 144
Tremain, Rose 1943- DLB-14
Tremblay, Michel 1942- DLB-60
Trends in Twentieth-Century Mass Market Publishing............DLB-46
Trent, William P. 1862-1939 ....DLB-47
Trescot, William Henry 1822-1898 ......DLB-30
Tressell, Robert (Robert Phillipe Noonan) 1870-1911........................DLB-197
Trevelyan, Sir George Otto 1838-1928 ....DLB-144
Trevisa, John circa 1342-circa 1402 .....DLB-146

Trevor, William 1928- DLB-14, 139
Trierer Floyris circa 1170-1180 ....DLB-138
Trillin, Calvin 1935- DLB-185
Trilling, Lionel 1905-1975 ....DLB-28, 63
Trilussa 1871-1950....................DLB-114
Trimmer, Sarah 1741-1810............DLB-158
Triolet, Elsa 1896-1970................DLB-72
Tripp, John 1927- DLB-40
Trocchi, Alexander 1925- DLB-15
Troisi, Dante 1920-1989................DLB-196
Trollope, Anthony 1815-1882 ....DLB-21, 57, 159; CDBLB-4
Trollope, Frances 1779-1863.........DLB-21, 166
Trollope, Joanna 1943- DLB-207
Troop, Elizabeth 1931- DLB-14
Trotter, Catharine 1679-1749..........DLB-84
Trotti, Lamar 1898-1952 ....DLB-44
Trottier, Pierre 1925- DLB-60
Trotzig, Birgitta 1929- DLB-257
Troubadours, *Trobaíritz,* and Trouvères..DLB-208
Troupe, Quincy Thomas, Jr. 1943- DLB-41
Trow, John F., and Company..........DLB-49
Trowbridge, John Townsend 1827-1916 .DLB-202
Truillier Lacombe, Joseph-Patrice 1807-1863........................DLB-99
Trumbo, Dalton 1905-1976 ....DLB-26
Trumbull, Benjamin 1735-1820 ....DLB-30
Trumbull, John 1750-1831 ....DLB-31
Trumbull, John 1756-1843 ....DLB-183
Truth, Sojourner 1797?-1883 ....DLB-239
Tscherning, Andreas 1611-1659........DLB-164
Tsubouchi, Shōyō 1859-1935 ....DLB-180
Tucholsky, Kurt 1890-1935 ....DLB-56
Tucker, Charlotte Maria 1821-1893 ....DLB-163, 190
Tucker, George 1775-1861 ....DLB-3, 30, 248
Tucker, James 1808?-1866? DLB-230
Tucker, Nathaniel Beverley 1784-1851....................DLB-3, 248
Tucker, St. George 1752-1827 ....DLB-37
Tuckerman, Frederick Goddard 1821-1873.......................DLB-243
Tuckerman, Henry Theodore 1813-1871..DLB-64
Tumas, Juozas (see Vaizgantas)
Tunis, John R. 1889-1975............DLB-22, 171
Tunstall, Cuthbert 1474-1559 ....DLB-132
Tunström, Göran 1937-2000 ....DLB-257
Tuohy, Frank 1925- DLB-14, 139
Tupper, Martin F. 1810-1889 ....DLB-32
Tur, Evgeniia 1815-1892 ....DLB-238
Turbyfill, Mark 1896- DLB-45
Turco, Lewis 1934- Y-84
Turgenev, Aleksandr Ivanovich 1784-1845.......................DLB-198
Turgenev, Ivan Sergeevich 1818-1883 ...DLB-238
Turnball, Alexander H. 1868-1918 .....DLB-184

Turnbull, Andrew 1921-1970..........DLB-103
Turnbull, Gael 1928- DLB-40
Turner, Arlin 1909-1980 ....DLB-103
Turner, Charles (Tennyson) 1808-1879......................DLB-32
Turner, Ethel 1872-1958 ....DLB-230
Turner, Frederick 1943- DLB-40
Turner, Frederick Jackson 1861-1932 ....DLB-17, 186
Turner, Joseph Addison 1826-1868 ......DLB-79
Turpin, Waters Edward 1910-1968.......DLB-51
Turrini, Peter 1944- DLB-124
Tutuola, Amos 1920-1997 ...DLB-125; CDWLB-3
Twain, Mark (see Clemens, Samuel Langhorne)
Tweedie, Ethel Brilliana circa 1860-1940 ..DLB-174
The 'Twenties and Berlin, by Alex Natan . DLB-66
Two Hundred Years of Rare Books and Literary Collections at the University of South Carolina..........Y-00
Twombly, Wells 1935-1977 ....DLB-241
Twysden, Sir Roger 1597-1672.........DLB-213
Tyler, Anne 1941- DLB-6, 143; Y-82; CDALB-7
Tyler, Mary Palmer 1775-1866.........DLB-200
Tyler, Moses Coit 1835-1900.........DLB-47, 64
Tyler, Royall 1757-1826 ....DLB-37
Tylor, Edward Burnett 1832-1917.......DLB-57
Tynan, Katharine 1861-1931 ......DLB-153, 240
Tyndale, William circa 1494-1536......DLB-132

U

Uchida, Yoshika 1921-1992............CDALB-7
Udall, Nicholas 1504-1556.............DLB-62
Ugrešić, Dubravka 1949- DLB-181
Uhland, Ludwig 1787-1862.............DLB-90
Uhse, Bodo 1904-1963................DLB-69
Ujević, Augustin ("Tin") 1891-1955......DLB-147
Ulenhart, Niclas flourished circa 1600 ...DLB-164
Ulibarrí, Sabine R. 1919- DLB-82
Ulica, Jorge 1870-1926 ....DLB-82
Ulivi, Ferruccio 1912- DLB-196
Ulizio, B. George 1889-1969 ....DLB-140
Ulrich von Liechtenstein circa 1200-circa 1275 ....DLB-138
Ulrich von Zatzikhoven before 1194-after 1214............DLB-138
Ulysses, Reader's Edition................Y-97
Unaipon, David 1872-1967............DLB-230
Unamuno, Miguel de 1864-1936 ......DLB-108
Under, Marie 1883-1980 ....DLB-220; CDWLB-4
Under the Microscope (1872), by A. C. Swinburne DLB-35
Underhill, Evelyn 1875-1941.......................DLB-240
Ungaretti, Giuseppe 1888-1970 ....DLB-114
Unger, Friederike Helene 1741-1813 .....DLB-94

United States Book Company DLB-49	Valdez, Luis Miguel 1940- DLB-122	Vaughn, Robert 1592?-1667 .... DLB-213
Universal Publishing and Distributing Corporation.................. DLB-46	Valduga, Patrizia 1953-............ DLB-128	Vaux, Thomas, Lord 1509-1556....... DLB-132
	Valente, José Angel 1929-2000 .... DLB-108	Vazov, Ivan 1850-1921 ..... DLB-147; CDWLB-4
The University of Iowa Writers' Workshop Golden Jubilee.................. Y-86	Valenzuela, Luisa 1938- ... DLB-113; CDWLB-3	Véa Jr., Alfredo 1950- DLB-209
	Valeri, Diego 1887-1976................ DLB-128	Veblen, Thorstein 1857-1929.......... DLB-246
The University of South Carolina Press Y-94	Valerius Flaccus fl. circa A.D. 92........ DLB-211	Vega, Janine Pommy 1942- DLB-16
University of Wales Press DLB-112	Valerius Maximus fl. circa A.D. 31 ...... DLB-211	Veiller, Anthony 1903-1965 .... DLB-44
University Press of Florida Y-00	Valesio, Paolo 1939- DLB-196	Velásquez-Trevino, Gloria 1949- DLB-122
University Press of Kansas Y-98	Valgardson, W. D. 1939- DLB-60	Veley, Margaret 1843-1887............ DLB-199
University Press of Mississippi Y-99	Valle, Víctor Manuel 1950- DLB-122	Velleius Paterculus circa 20 B.C.-circa A.D. 30 .... DLB-211
"The Unknown Public" (1858), by Wilkie Collins [excerpt]............. DLB-57	Valle-Inclán, Ramón del 1866-1936...... DLB-134	
	Vallejo, Armando 1949- DLB-122	Veloz Maggiolo, Marcio 1936- DLB-145
Uno, Chiyo 1897-1996................ DLB-180	Vallès, Jules 1832-1885 .... DLB-123	Vel'tman Aleksandr Fomich 1800-1870 .... DLB-198
Unruh, Fritz von 1885-1970........ DLB-56, 118	Vallette, Marguerite Eymery (see Rachilde)	
Unspeakable Practices II: The Festival of Vanguard Narrative at Brown University Y-93	Valverde, José María 1926-1996 .... DLB-108	Venegas, Daniel ?-? DLB-82
	Van Allsburg, Chris 1949- DLB-61	Venevitinov, Dmitrii Vladimirovich 1805-1827 .... DLB-205
Unsworth, Barry 1930- DLB-194	Van Anda, Carr 1864-1945............. DLB-25	
Unt, Mati 1944- DLB-232	van der Post, Laurens 1906-1996 .... DLB-204	Vergil, Polydore circa 1470-1555....... DLB-132
The Unterberg Poetry Center of the 92nd Street Y..................... Y-98	Van Dine, S. S. (see Wright, Williard Huntington)	Veríssimo, Erico 1905-1975 .... DLB-145
	Van Doren, Mark 1894-1972........... DLB-45	Verlaine, Paul 1844-1896 .... DLB-217
Unwin, T. Fisher [publishing house] DLB-106	van Druten, John 1901-1957 .... DLB-10	Verne, Jules 1828-1905 .... DLB-123
Upchurch, Boyd B. (see Boyd, John)	Van Duyn, Mona 1921- DLB-5	Verplanck, Gulian C. 1786-1870 .... DLB-59
Updike, John 1932- DLB-2, 5, 143, 218, 227; Y-80, Y-82; DS-3; CDALB-6	Van Dyke, Henry 1852-1933 ..... DLB-71; DS-13	Very, Jones 1813-1880............... DLB-1, 243
	Van Dyke, Henry 1928- DLB-33	Vian, Boris 1920-1959................ DLB-72
John Updike on the Internet Y-97	Van Dyke, John C. 1856-1932 .... DLB-186	Viazemsky, Petr Andreevich 1792-1878 .... DLB-205
Upīts, Andrejs 1877-1970............. DLB-220	van Gulik, Robert Hans 1910-1967 .... DS-17	
Upton, Bertha 1849-1912 .... DLB-141	van Itallie, Jean-Claude 1936- DLB-7	Vicars, Thomas 1591-1638 .... DLB-236
Upton, Charles 1948- DLB-16	Van Loan, Charles E. 1876-1919........ DLB-171	Vickers, Roy 1888?-1965.............. DLB-77
Upton, Florence K. 1873-1922......... DLB-141	Van Rensselaer, Mariana Griswold 1851-1934 .... DLB-47	Vickery, Sukey 1779-1821 .... DLB-200
Upward, Allen 1863-1926 .... DLB-36		Victoria 1819-1901 .... DLB-55
Urban, Milo 1904-1982 .... DLB-215	Van Rensselaer, Mrs. Schuyler (see Van Rensselaer, Mariana Griswold)	Victoria Press..................... DLB-106
Urista, Alberto Baltazar (see Alurista)		Vidal, Gore 1925- DLB-6, 152; CDALB-7
Urquhart, Fred 1912- DLB-139	Van Vechten, Carl 1880-1964.......... DLB-4, 9	Vidal, Mary Theresa 1815-1873 .... DLB-230
Urrea, Luis Alberto 1955- DLB-209	van Vogt, A. E. 1912-2000 .... DLB-8	Vidmer, Richards 1898-1978........... DLB-241
Urzidil, Johannes 1896-1976 .... DLB-85	Vanbrugh, Sir John 1664-1726.......... DLB-80	Viebig, Clara 1860-1952 .... DLB-66
The Uses of Facsimile Y-90	Vance, Jack 1916?- DLB-8	Viereck, George Sylvester 1884-1962 .... DLB-54
Usk, Thomas died 1388 .... DLB-146	Vančura, Vladislav 1891-1942 .... DLB-215; CDWLB-4	
Uslar Pietri, Arturo 1906- DLB-113		Viereck, Peter 1916- DLB-5
Ussher, James 1581-1656.............. DLB-213	Vane, Sutton 1888-1963 .... DLB-10	Viets, Roger 1738-1811 .... DLB-99
Ustinov, Peter 1921- DLB-13	Vanguard Press DLB-46	Viewpoint: Politics and Performance, by David Edgar DLB-13
Uttley, Alison 1884-1976 .... DLB-160	Vann, Robert L. 1879-1940 .... DLB-29	
Uz, Johann Peter 1720-1796............. DLB-97	Vargas Llosa, Mario 1936- DLB-145; CDWLB-3	Vigil-Piñon, Evangelina 1949- DLB-122
		Vigneault, Gilles 1928- DLB-60
V	Varley, John 1947- Y-81	Vigny, Alfred de 1797-1863............... DLB-119, 192, 217
Vac, Bertrand 1914- DLB-88	Varnhagen von Ense, Karl August 1785-1858 .... DLB-90	
Vācietis, Ojārs 1933-1983 ....DLB-232		Vigolo, Giorgio 1894-1983 .... DLB-114
Vaičiulaitis, Antanas 1906-1992 .... DLB-220	Varnhagen von Ense, Rahel 1771-1833 .... DLB-90	The Viking Press.................... DLB-46
Vaculík, Ludvík 1926- DLB-232	Varro 116 B.C.-27 B.C................ DLB-211	Vilde, Eduard 1865-1933.............. DLB-220
Vaičiūnaite, Judita 1937- DLB-232	Vasiliu, George (see Bacovia, George)	Vilinskaia, Mariia Aleksandrovna (see Vovchok, Marko)
Vail, Laurence 1891-1968 .... DLB-4	Vásquez, Richard 1928- DLB-209	Villanueva, Alma Luz 1944- DLB-122
Vailland, Roger 1907-1965............. DLB-83	Vásquez Montalbán, Manuel 1939- DLB-134	Villanueva, Tino 1941- DLB-82
Vaižgantas 1869-1933 .... DLB-220	Vassa, Gustavus (see Equiano, Olaudah)	Villard, Henry 1835-1900 .... DLB-23
Vajda, Ernest 1887-1954 .... DLB-44	Vassalli, Sebastiano 1941- DLB-128, 196	Villard, Oswald Garrison 1872-1949 ....DLB-25, 91
Valdés, Gina 1943- DLB-122	Vaughan, Henry 1621-1695 .... DLB-131	
		Villarreal, Edit 1944- DLB-209
	Vaughan, Thomas 1621-1666 .... DLB-131	Villarreal, José Antonio 1924- DLB-82

Cumulative Index

Villaseñor, Victor 1940- DLB-209
Villegas de Magnón, Leonor 1876-1955 .... DLB-122
Villehardouin, Geoffroi de circa 1150-1215 .... DLB-208
Villemaire, Yolande 1949- DLB-60
Villena, Luis Antonio de 1951- DLB-134
Villiers, George, Second Duke of Buckingham 1628-1687 .... DLB-80
Villiers de l'Isle-Adam, Jean-Marie Mathias Philippe-Auguste, Comte de 1838-1889 .... DLB-123, 192
Villon, François 1431-circa 1463? DLB-208
Vine Press DLB-112
Viorst, Judith ?- DLB-52
Vipont, Elfrida (Elfrida Vipont Foulds, Charles Vipont) 1902-1992 .... DLB-160
Viramontes, Helena María 1954- DLB-122
Virgil 70 B.C.-19 B.C. DLB-211; CDWLB-1
Virtual Books and Enemies of Books Y-00
Vischer, Friedrich Theodor 1807-1887 .... DLB-133
Vitruvius circa 85 B.C.-circa 15 B.C. DLB-211
Vitry, Philippe de 1291-1361 .... DLB-208
Vivanco, Luis Felipe 1907-1975 .... DLB-108
Vivian, E. Charles 1882-1947 .... DLB-255
Viviani, Cesare 1947- DLB-128
Vivien, Renée 1877-1909 .... DLB-217
Vizenor, Gerald 1934- DLB-175, 227
Vizetelly and Company DLB-106
Voaden, Herman 1903- DLB-88
Voß, Johann Heinrich 1751-1826 .... DLB-90
Voigt, Ellen Bryant 1943- DLB-120
Vojnović, Ivo 1857-1929 .... DLB-147; CDWLB-4
Volkoff, Vladimir 1932- DLB-83
Volland, P. F., Company DLB-46
Vollbehr, Otto H. F. 1872?-1945 or 1946 .... DLB-187
Vologdin (see Zasodimsky, Pavel Vladimirovich)
Volponi, Paolo 1924- DLB-177
von der Grün, Max 1926- DLB-75
Vonnegut, Kurt 1922- DLB-2, 8, 152; Y-80; DS-3; CDALB-6
Voranc, Prežihov 1893-1950 .... DLB-147
Vovchok, Marko 1833-1907 .... DLB-238
Voynich, E. L. 1864-1960 .... DLB-197
Vroman, Mary Elizabeth circa 1924-1967 .... DLB-33

W

Wace, Robert ("Maistre") circa 1100-circa 1175 .... DLB-146
Wackenroder, Wilhelm Heinrich 1773-1798 .... DLB-90
Wackernagel, Wilhelm 1806-1869 .... DLB-133
Waddell, Helen 1889-1965 .... DLB-240
Waddington, Miriam 1917- DLB-68
Wade, Henry 1887-1969 .... DLB-77
Wagenknecht, Edward 1900- DLB-103

Wagner, Heinrich Leopold 1747-1779 .... DLB-94
Wagner, Henry R. 1862-1957 .... DLB-140
Wagner, Richard 1813-1883 .... DLB-129
Wagoner, David 1926- DLB-5, 256
Wah, Fred 1939- DLB-60
Waiblinger, Wilhelm 1804-1830 .... DLB-90
Wain, John 1925-1994 .... DLB-15, 27, 139, 155; CDBLB-8
Wainwright, Jeffrey 1944- DLB-40
Waite, Peirce and Company DLB-49
Wakeman, Stephen H. 1859-1924 .... DLB-187
Wakoski, Diane 1937- DLB-5
Walahfrid Strabo circa 808-849 .... DLB-148
Walck, Henry Z. DLB-46
Walcott, Derek 1930- DLB-117; Y-81, Y-92; CDWLB-3
Waldegrave, Robert [publishing house] DLB-170
Waldman, Anne 1945- DLB-16
Waldrop, Rosmarie 1935- DLB-169
Walker, Alice 1900-1982 .... DLB-201
Walker, Alice 1944- DLB-6, 33, 143; CDALB-6
Walker, Annie Louisa (Mrs. Harry Coghill) circa 1836-1907 .... DLB-240
Walker, George F. 1947- DLB-60
Walker, John Brisben 1847-1931 .... DLB-79
Walker, Joseph A. 1935- DLB-38
Walker, Margaret 1915- DLB-76, 152
Walker, Ted 1934- DLB-40
Walker and Company DLB-49
Walker, Evans and Cogswell Company DLB-49
Wall, John F. (see Sarban)
Wallace, Alfred Russel 1823-1913 .... DLB-190
Wallace, Dewitt 1889-1981 and Lila Acheson Wallace 1889-1984 .... DLB-137
Wallace, Edgar 1875-1932 .... DLB-70
Wallace, Lew 1827-1905 .... DLB-202
Wallace, Lila Acheson (see Wallace, Dewitt, and Lila Acheson Wallace)
Wallace, Naomi 1960- DLB-249
Wallant, Edward Lewis 1926-1962 .... DLB-2, 28, 143
Waller, Edmund 1606-1687 .... DLB-126
Walpole, Horace 1717-1797 .... DLB-39, 104, 213
Preface to the First Edition of *The Castle of Otranto* (1764) DLB-39
Preface to the Second Edition of *The Castle of Otranto* (1765) DLB-39
Walpole, Hugh 1884-1941 .... DLB-34
Walrond, Eric 1898-1966 .... DLB-51
Walser, Martin 1927- DLB-75, 124
Walser, Robert 1878-1956 .... DLB-66
Walsh, Ernest 1895-1926 .... DLB-4, 45
Walsh, Robert 1784-1859 .... DLB-59
Walters, Henry 1848-1931 .... DLB-140
Waltharius circa 825 .... DLB-148

Walther von der Vogelweide circa 1170-circa 1230 .... DLB-138
Walton, Izaak 1593-1683 .... DLB-151, 213; CDBLB-1
Wambaugh, Joseph 1937- DLB-6; Y-83
Wand, Alfred Rudolph 1828-1891 .... DLB-188
Waniek, Marilyn Nelson 1946- DLB-120
Wanley, Humphrey 1672-1726 .... DLB-213
Warburton, William 1698-1779 .... DLB-104
Ward, Aileen 1919- DLB-111
Ward, Artemus (see Browne, Charles Farrar)
Ward, Arthur Henry Sarsfield (see Rohmer, Sax)
Ward, Douglas Turner 1930- DLB-7, 38
Ward, Mrs. Humphry 1851-1920 .... DLB-18
Ward, Lynd 1905-1985 .... DLB-22
Ward, Lock and Company DLB-106
Ward, Nathaniel circa 1578-1652 .... DLB-24
Ward, Theodore 1902-1983 .... DLB-76
Wardle, Ralph 1909-1988 .... DLB-103
Ware, Henry, Jr. 1794-1843 .... DLB-235
Ware, William 1797-1852 .... DLB-1, 235
Warfield, Catherine Ann 1816-1877 .... DLB-248
Waring, Anna Letitia 1823-1910 .... DLB-240
Warne, Frederick, and Company [U.K.] DLB-106
Warne, Frederick, and Company [U.S.] DLB-49
Warner, Anne 1869-1913 .... DLB-202
Warner, Charles Dudley 1829-1900 .... DLB-64
Warner, Marina 1946- DLB-194
Warner, Rex 1905- DLB-15
Warner, Susan 1819-1885 .... DLB-3, 42, 239
Warner, Sylvia Townsend 1893-1978 .... DLB-34, 139
Warner, William 1558-1609 .... DLB-172
Warner Books DLB-46
Warr, Bertram 1917-1943 .... DLB-88
Warren, John Byrne Leicester (see De Tabley, Lord)
Warren, Lella 1899-1982 .... Y-83
Warren, Mercy Otis 1728-1814 .... DLB-31, 200
Warren, Robert Penn 1905-1989 .... DLB-2, 48, 152; Y-80, Y-89; CDALB-6
Warren, Samuel 1807-1877 .... DLB-190
Die Wartburgkrieg circa 1230-circa 1280 .... DLB-138
Warton, Joseph 1722-1800 .... DLB-104, 109
Warton, Thomas 1728-1790 .... DLB-104, 109
Warung, Price (William Astley) 1855-1911 .... DLB-230
Washington, George 1732-1799 .... DLB-31
Wassermann, Jakob 1873-1934 .... DLB-66
Wasserstein, Wendy 1950- DLB-228
Wasson, David Atwood 1823-1887 .... DLB-1, 223
Watanna, Onoto (see Eaton, Winnifred)
Waterhouse, Keith 1929- DLB-13, 15
Waterman, Andrew 1940- DLB-40
Waters, Frank 1902-1995 .... DLB-212; Y-86
Waters, Michael 1949- DLB-120
Watkins, Tobias 1780-1855 .... DLB-73

Watkins, Vernon 1906-1967 ....DLB-20
Watmough, David 1926- DLB-53
Watson, James Wreford (see Wreford, James)
Watson, John 1850-1907 ....DLB-156
Watson, Rosamund Marriott
 (Graham R. Tomson) 1860-1911 ....DLB-240
Watson, Sheila 1909- DLB-60
Watson, Thomas 1545?-1592 ....DLB-132
Watson, Wilfred 1911- DLB-60
Watt, W. J., and Company DLB-46
Watten, Barrett 1948- DLB-193
Watterson, Henry 1840-1921 ....DLB-25
Watts, Alan 1915-1973...............DLB-16
Watts, Franklin [publishing house] DLB-46
Watts, Isaac 1674-1748................DLB-95
Waugh, Alec 1898-1981 ....DLB-191
Waugh, Auberon 1939-2000 ... DLB-14, 194; Y-00
The Cult of Biography
 Excerpts from the Second Folio Debate:
 "Biographies are generally a disease of
 English Literature" Y-86
Waugh, Evelyn
 1903-1966 ......DLB-15, 162, 195; CDBLB-6
Way and Williams.....................DLB-49
Wayman, Tom 1945- DLB-53
We See the Editor at Work Y-97
Weatherly, Tom 1942- DLB-41
Weaver, Gordon 1937- DLB-130
Weaver, Robert 1921- DLB-88
Webb, Beatrice 1858-1943 and
 Webb, Sidney 1859-1947 ....DLB-190
Webb, Frank J. ?-? DLB-50
Webb, James Watson 1802-1884.........DLB-43
Webb, Mary 1881-1927................DLB-34
Webb, Phyllis 1927- DLB-53
Webb, Walter Prescott 1888-1963.........DLB-17
Webbe, William ?-1591................DLB-132
Webber, Charles Wilkins 1819-1856?....DLB-202
Webling, Lucy (Lucy Betty MacRaye)
 1877-1952 ....DLB-240
Webling, Peggy (Arthur Weston)
 1871-1949 ....DLB-240
Webster, Augusta 1837-1894 ....DLB-35, 240
Webster, Charles L., and Company DLB-49
Webster, John
 1579 or 1580-1634?...... DLB-58; CDBLB-1
John Webster: The Melbourne
 Manuscript Y-86
Webster, Noah
 1758-1843 .... DLB-1, 37, 42, 43, 73, 243
Weckherlin, Georg Rodolf 1584-1653....DLB-164
Wedekind, Frank
 1864-1918 ....DLB-118; CDBLB-2
Weeks, Edward Augustus, Jr.
 1898-1989 ....DLB-137
Weeks, Stephen B. 1865-1918 ....DLB-187
Weems, Mason Locke 1759-1825 .. DLB-30, 37, 42
Weerth, Georg 1822-1856............DLB-129

Weidenfeld and Nicolson DLB-112
Weidman, Jerome 1913-1998 ....DLB-28
Weiß, Ernst 1882-1940 ....DLB-81
Weigl, Bruce 1949- DLB-120
Weinbaum, Stanley Grauman 1902-1935 ...DLB-8
Weintraub, Stanley 1929- DLB-111; Y82
The Practice of Biography: An Interview
 with Stanley Weintraub Y-82
Weise, Christian 1642-1708............DLB-168
Weisenborn, Gunther 1902-1969 ....DLB-69, 124
Weiss, John 1818-1879................DLB-1, 243
Weiss, Peter 1916-1982...............DLB-69, 124
Weiss, Theodore 1916- DLB-5
Weisse, Christian Felix 1726-1804........DLB-97
Weitling, Wilhelm 1808-1871 ....DLB-129
Welch, James 1940- DLB-175, 256
Welch, Lew 1926-1971?..............DLB-16
Weldon, Fay 1931- DLB-14, 194; CDBLB-8
Wellek, René 1903-1995 ....DLB-63
Wells, Carolyn 1862-1942..............DLB-11
Wells, Charles Jeremiah circa 1800-1879...DLB-32
Wells, Gabriel 1862-1946 ....DLB-140
Wells, H. G.
 1866-1946 ... DLB-34, 70, 156, 178; CDBLB-6
Wells, Helena 1758?-1824 ....DLB-200
Wells, Robert 1947- DLB-40
Wells-Barnett, Ida B. 1862-1931 .....DLB-23, 221
Welty, Eudora 1909-
 .... DLB-2, 102, 143; Y-87; DS-12; CDALB-1
Eudora Welty: Eye of the Storyteller........ Y-87
Eudora Welty Newsletter Y-99
Eudora Welty's Ninetieth Birthday......... Y-99
Wendell, Barrett 1855-1921............DLB-71
Wentworth, Patricia 1878-1961 ....DLB-77
Wentworth, William Charles
 1790-1872 ....DLB-230
Werder, Diederich von dem 1584-1657 ..DLB-164
Werfel, Franz 1890-1945 ....DLB-81, 124
Werner, Zacharias 1768-1823 ....DLB-94
The Werner Company DLB-49
Wersba, Barbara 1932- DLB-52
Wescott, Glenway 1901- DLB-4, 9, 102
Wesker, Arnold 1932- DLB-13; CDBLB-8
Wesley, Charles 1707-1788..............DLB-95
Wesley, John 1703-1791...............DLB-104
Wesley, Mary 1912- DLB-231
Wesley, Richard 1945- DLB-38
Wessels, A., and Company DLB-46
Wessobrunner Gebet circa 787-815 ....DLB-148
West, Anthony 1914-1988...............DLB-15
West, Cornel 1953- DLB-246
West, Dorothy 1907-1998 ....DLB-76
West, Jessamyn 1902-1984 ....DLB-6; Y-84
West, Mae 1892-1980 ....DLB-44
West, Nathanael
 1903-1940 ....DLB-4, 9, 28; CDALB-5

West, Paul 1930- DLB-14
West, Rebecca 1892-1983 ....DLB-36; Y-83
West, Richard 1941- DLB-185
West and Johnson DLB-49
Westcott, Edward Noyes 1846-1898.....DLB-202
The Western Messenger 1835-1841 ....DLB-223
Western Publishing Company...........DLB-46
Western Writers of America Y-99
The Westminster Review 1824-1914........DLB-110
Weston, Arthur (see Webling, Peggy)
Weston, Elizabeth Jane circa 1582-1612 ..DLB-172
Wetherald, Agnes Ethelwyn 1857-1940....DLB-99
Wetherell, Elizabeth (see Warner, Susan)
Wetherell, W. D. 1948- DLB-234
Wetzel, Friedrich Gottlob 1779-1819 ......DLB-90
Weyman, Stanley J. 1855-1928 .....DLB-141, 156
Wezel, Johann Karl 1747-1819 ....DLB-94
Whalen, Philip 1923- DLB-16
Whalley, George 1915-1983 ....DLB-88
Wharton, Edith 1862-1937
 ..... DLB-4, 9, 12, 78, 189; DS-13; CDALB-3
Wharton, William 1920s?- Y-80
"What You Lose on the Swings You Make Up
 on the Merry-Go-Round" Y-99
Whately, Mary Louisa 1824-1889.......DLB-166
Whately, Richard 1787-1863 ....DLB-190
From Elements of Rhetoric (1828;
 revised, 1846) DLB-57
What's Really Wrong With Bestseller Lists .. Y-84
Wheatley, Dennis 1897-1977 .... DLB-77, 255
Wheatley, Phillis
 circa 1754-1784 ....DLB-31, 50; CDALB-2
Wheeler, Anna Doyle 1785-1848?.......DLB-158
Wheeler, Charles Stearns 1816-1843...DLB-1, 223
Wheeler, Monroe 1900-1988.............DLB-4
Wheelock, John Hall 1886-1978 ....DLB-45
Wheelwright, J. B. 1897-1940 ....DLB-45
Wheelwright, John circa 1592-1679 ....DLB-24
Whetstone, George 1550-1587 ....DLB-136
Whetstone, Colonel Pete (see Noland, C. F. M.)
Whicher, Stephen E. 1915-1961 ....DLB-111
Whipple, Edwin Percy 1819-1886......DLB-1, 64
Whitaker, Alexander 1585-1617 ....DLB-24
Whitaker, Daniel K. 1801-1881..........DLB-73
Whitcher, Frances Miriam
 1812-1852 ....DLB-11, 202
White, Andrew 1579-1656............DLB-24
White, Andrew Dickson 1832-1918 ......DLB-47
White, E. B. 1899-1985 ....DLB-11, 22; CDALB-7
White, Edgar B. 1947- DLB-38
White, Edmund 1940- DLB-227
White, Ethel Lina 1887-1944 ....DLB-77
White, Hayden V. 1928- DLB-246
White, Henry Kirke 1785-1806 ....DLB-96
White, Horace 1834-1916 ....DLB-23
White, Phyllis Dorothy James (see James, P. D.)

Cumulative Index

White, Richard Grant 1821-1885 .... DLB-64
White, T. H. 1906-1964 .... DLB-160, 255
White, Walter 1893-1955 .... DLB-51
White, William, and Company DLB-49
White, William Allen 1868-1944 ..... DLB-9, 25
White, William Anthony Parker
 (see Boucher, Anthony)
White, William Hale (see Rutherford, Mark)
Whitechurch, Victor L. 1868-1933 .... DLB-70
Whitehead, Alfred North 1861-1947 .... DLB-100
Whitehead, James 1936- Y-81
Whitehead, William 1715-1785 ..... DLB-84, 109
Whitfield, James Monroe 1822-1871 ..... DLB-50
Whitfield, Raoul 1898-1945 .... DLB-226
Whitgift, John circa 1533-1604 .... DLB-132
Whiting, John 1917-1963 .... DLB-13
Whiting, Samuel 1597-1679 .... DLB-24
Whitlock, Brand 1869-1934 .... DLB-12
Whitman, Albert, and Company DLB-46
Whitman, Albery Allson 1851-1901 ..... DLB-50
Whitman, Alden 1913-1990 .... Y-91
Whitman, Sarah Helen (Power)
 1803-1878 .... DLB-1, 243
Whitman, Walt
 1819-1892 .... DLB-3, 64, 224; CDALB-2
Whitman Publishing Company DLB-46
Whitney, Geoffrey 1548 or 1552?-1601 .. DLB-136
Whitney, Isabella flourished 1566-1573 .. DLB-136
Whitney, John Hay 1904-1982 .... DLB-127
Whittemore, Reed 1919-1995 .... DLB-5
Whittier, John Greenleaf
 1807-1892 .... DLB-1, 243; CDALB-2
Whittlesey House DLB-46
Who Runs American Literature? Y-94
Whose *Ulysses?* The Function of Editing Y-97
Wickham, Anna (Edith Alice Mary Harper)
 1884-1947 .... DLB-240
Wicomb, Zoë 1948- DLB-225
Wideman, John Edgar 1941- DLB-33, 143
Widener, Harry Elkins 1885-1912 ...... DLB-140
Wiebe, Rudy 1934- DLB-60
Wiechert, Ernst 1887-1950 .... DLB-56
Wied, Martina 1882-1957 .... DLB-85
Wiehe, Evelyn May Clowes (see Mordaunt, Elinor)
Wieland, Christoph Martin 1733-1813 .... DLB-97
Wienbarg, Ludolf 1802-1872 .... DLB-133
Wieners, John 1934- DLB-16
Wier, Ester 1910- DLB-52
Wiesel, Elie
 1928- DLB-83; Y-86, 87; CDALB-7
Wiggin, Kate Douglas 1856-1923 .... DLB-42
Wigglesworth, Michael 1631-1705 ...... DLB-24
Wilberforce, William 1759-1833 .... DLB-158
Wilbrandt, Adolf 1837-1911 .... DLB-129
Wilbur, Richard
 1921- DLB-5, 169; CDALB-7

Wild, Peter 1940- DLB-5
Wilde, Lady Jane Francesca Elgee
 1821?-1896 .... DLB-199
Wilde, Oscar 1854-1900
 .... DLB-10, 19, 34, 57, 141, 156, 190;
 CDBLB-5
"The Critic as Artist" (1891) DLB-57
Oscar Wilde Conference at Hofstra
 University Y-00
From "The Decay of Lying" (1889) DLB-18
"The English Renaissance of
 Art" (1908) DLB-35
"L'Envoi" (1882) DLB-35
Wilde, Richard Henry 1789-1847 ...... DLB-3, 59
Wilde, W. A., Company DLB-49
Wilder, Billy 1906- DLB-26
Wilder, Laura Ingalls 1867-1957 ..... DLB-22, 256
Wilder, Thornton
 1897-1975 .... DLB-4, 7, 9, 228; CDALB-7
Thornton Wilder Centenary at Yale Y-97
Wildgans, Anton 1881-1932 .... DLB-118
Wiley, Bell Irvin 1906-1980 .... DLB-17
Wiley, John, and Sons DLB-49
Wilhelm, Kate 1928- DLB-8
Wilkes, Charles 1798-1877 .... DLB-183
Wilkes, George 1817-1885 .... DLB-79
Wilkins, John 1614-1672 .... DLB-236
Wilkinson, Anne 1910-1961 .... DLB-88
Wilkinson, Eliza Yonge
 1757-circa 1813 .... DLB-200
Wilkinson, Sylvia 1940- Y-86
Wilkinson, William Cleaver 1833-1920 ... DLB-71
Willard, Barbara 1909-1994 .... DLB-161
Willard, Emma 1787-1870 .... DLB-239
Willard, Frances E. 1839-1898 .... DLB-221
Willard, L. [publishing house] DLB-49
Willard, Nancy 1936- DLB-5, 52
Willard, Samuel 1640-1707 .... DLB-24
Willeford, Charles 1919-1988 .... DLB-226
William of Auvergne 1190-1249 .... DLB-115
William of Conches
 circa 1090-circa 1154 .... DLB-115
William of Ockham circa 1285-1347 .... DLB-115
William of Sherwood
 1200/1205-1266/1271 .... DLB-115
The William Chavrat American Fiction Collection
 at the Ohio State University Libraries Y-92
Williams, A., and Company DLB-49
Williams, Ben Ames 1889-1953 .... DLB-102
Williams, C. K. 1936- DLB-5
Williams, Chancellor 1905- DLB-76
Williams, Charles 1886-1945 ... DLB-100, 153, 255
Williams, Denis 1923-1998 .... DLB-117
Williams, Emlyn 1905-1987 .... DLB-10, 77
Williams, Garth 1912-1996 .... DLB-22
Williams, George Washington
 1849-1891 .... DLB-47
Williams, Heathcote 1941- DLB-13

Williams, Helen Maria 1761-1827 ...... DLB-158
Williams, Hugo 1942- DLB-40
Williams, Isaac 1802-1865 .... DLB-32
Williams, Joan 1928- DLB-6
Williams, Joe 1889-1972 .... DLB-241
Williams, John A. 1925- DLB-2, 33
Williams, John E. 1922-1994 .... DLB-6
Williams, Jonathan 1929- DLB-5
Williams, Miller 1930- DLB-105
Williams, Nigel 1948- DLB-231
Williams, Raymond 1921- DLB-14, 231, 242
Williams, Roger circa 1603-1683 .... DLB-24
Williams, Rowland 1817-1870 .... DLB-184
Williams, Samm-Art 1946- DLB-38
Williams, Sherley Anne 1944-1999 ..... DLB-41
Williams, T. Harry 1909-1979 .... DLB-17
Williams, Tennessee
 1911-1983 .... DLB-7; Y-83; DS-4; CDALB-1
Williams, Terry Tempest 1955- DLB-206
Williams, Ursula Moray 1911- DLB-160
Williams, Valentine 1883-1946 .... DLB-77
Williams, William Appleman 1921- DLB-17
Williams, William Carlos
 1883-1963 ..... DLB 4, 16, 54, 86; CDALB-4
Williams, Wirt 1921- DLB-6
Williams Brothers DLB-49
Williamson, Henry 1895-1977 .... DLB-191
Williamson, Jack 1908- DLB-8
Willingham, Calder Baynard, Jr.
 1922-1995 .... DLB-2, 44
Williram of Ebersberg circa 1020-1085 .. DLB-148
Willis, Nathaniel Parker
 1806-1867 ..... DLB-3, 59, 73, 74, 183; DS-13
Willkomm, Ernst 1810-1886 .... DLB-133
Willumsen, Dorrit 1940- DLB-214
Wills, Garry 1934- DLB-246
Wilmer, Clive 1945- DLB-40
Wilson, A. N. 1950- DLB-14, 155, 194
Wilson, Angus 1913-1991 .... DLB-15, 139, 155
Wilson, Arthur 1595-1652 .... DLB-58
Wilson, August 1945- DLB-228
Wilson, Augusta Jane Evans 1835-1909 ... DLB-42
Wilson, Colin 1931- DLB-14, 194
Wilson, Edmund 1895-1972 .... DLB-63
Wilson, Effingham [publishing house] ... DLB-154
Wilson, Ethel 1888-1980 .... DLB-68
Wilson, F. P. 1889-1963 .... DLB-201
Wilson, Harriet E.
 1827/1828?-1863? DLB-50, 239, 243
Wilson, Harry Leon 1867-1939 .... DLB-9
Wilson, John 1588-1667 .... DLB-24
Wilson, John 1785-1854 .... DLB-110
Wilson, John Dover 1881-1969 .... DLB-201
Wilson, Lanford 1937- DLB-7
Wilson, Margaret 1882-1973 .... DLB-9
Wilson, Michael 1914-1978 .... DLB-44

Wilson, Mona 1872-1954 . . . . DLB-149
Wilson, Robley 1930- DLB-218
Wilson, Romer 1891-1930 . . . . DLB-191
Wilson, Thomas 1524-1581 . . . . DLB-132, 236
Wilson, Woodrow 1856-1924 . . . . DLB-47
Wimsatt, William K., Jr. 1907-1975 . . . . DLB-63
Winchell, Walter 1897-1972 . . . . DLB-29
Winchester, J. [publishing house] DLB-49
Winckelmann, Johann Joachim
  1717-1768 . . . . DLB-97
Winckler, Paul 1630-1686 . . . . DLB-164
Wind, Herbert Warren 1916- DLB-171
Windet, John [publishing house] DLB-170
Windham, Donald 1920- DLB-6
Wing, Donald Goddard 1904-1972 . . . . . . DLB-187
Wing, John M. 1844-1917 . . . . DLB-187
Wingate, Allan [publishing house] DLB-112
Winnemucca, Sarah 1844-1921 . . . . DLB-175
Winnifrith, Tom 1938- DLB-155
Winning an Edgar Y-98
Winsloe, Christa 1888-1944 . . . . DLB-124
Winslow, Anna Green 1759-1780 . . . . DLB-200
Winsor, Justin 1831-1897 . . . . DLB-47
John C. Winston Company DLB-49
Winters, Yvor 1900-1968 . . . . DLB-48
Winterson, Jeanette 1959- DLB-207
Winthrop, John 1588-1649 . . . . DLB-24, 30
Winthrop, John, Jr. 1606-1676 . . . . DLB-24
Winthrop, Margaret Tyndal 1591-1647 . . DLB-200
Winthrop, Theodore 1828-1861 . . . . DLB-202
Wirt, William 1772-1834 . . . . DLB-37
Wise, John 1652-1725 . . . . DLB-24
Wise, Thomas James 1859-1937 . . . . DLB-184
Wiseman, Adele 1928- DLB-88
Wishart and Company DLB-112
Wisner, George 1812-1849 . . . . DLB-43
Wister, Owen 1860-1938 . . . . DLB-9, 78, 186
Wister, Sarah 1761-1804 . . . . DLB-200
Wither, George 1588-1667 . . . . DLB-121
Witherspoon, John 1723-1794 . . . . DLB-31
Withrow, William Henry 1839-1908 . . . . . . DLB-99
Witkacy (see Witkiewicz, Stanisław Ignacy)
Witkiewicz, Stanisław Ignacy
  1885-1939 . . . . DLB-215; CDWLB-4
Wittig, Monique 1935- DLB-83
Wodehouse, P. G.
  1881-1975 . . . . . . DLB-34, 162; CDBLB-6
Wohmann, Gabriele 1932- DLB-75
Woiwode, Larry 1941- DLB-6
Wolcot, John 1738-1819 . . . . DLB-109
Wolcott, Roger 1679-1767 . . . . DLB-24
Wolf, Christa 1929- DLB-75; CDWLB-2
Wolf, Friedrich 1888-1953 . . . . DLB-124
Wolfe, Gene 1931- DLB-8
Wolfe, John [publishing house] DLB-170

Wolfe, Reyner (Reginald)
  [publishing house] DLB-170
Wolfe, Thomas
  1900-1938 . . . . DLB-9, 102, 229; Y-85;
    DS-2, DS-16; CDALB-5
The Thomas Wolfe Collection at the University
  of North Carolina at Chapel Hill Y-97
Thomas Wolfe Centennial
  Celebration in Asheville Y-00
Fire at Thomas Wolfe Memorial Y-98
The Thomas Wolfe Society Y-97
Wolfe, Tom 1931- DLB-152, 185
Wolfenstein, Martha 1869-1906 . . . . DLB-221
Wolff, Helen 1906-1994 . . . . Y-94
Wolff, Tobias 1945- DLB-130
Wolfram von Eschenbach
  circa 1170-after 1220 . . . . DLB-138; CDWLB-2
Wolfram von Eschenbach's Parzival:
  Prologue and Book 3 . . . . DLB-138
Wolker, Jiří 1900-1924 . . . . DLB-215
Wollstonecraft, Mary
  1759-1797 . . . . DLB-39, 104, 158; CDBLB-3
Wondratschek, Wolf 1943- DLB-75
Wood, Anthony à 1632-1695 . . . . DLB-213
Wood, Benjamin 1820-1900 . . . . DLB-23
Wood, Charles 1932- DLB-13
Wood, Mrs. Henry 1814-1887 . . . . DLB-18
Wood, Joanna E. 1867-1927 . . . . DLB-92
Wood, Sally Sayward Barrell Keating
  1759-1855 . . . . DLB-200
Wood, Samuel [publishing house] DLB-49
Wood, William ?-? DLB-24
The Charles Wood Affair:
  A Playwright Revived Y-83
Woodberry, George Edward
  1855-1930 . . . . DLB-71, 103
Woodbridge, Benjamin 1622-1684 . . . . DLB-24
Woodcock, George 1912-1995 . . . . DLB-88
Woodhull, Victoria C. 1838-1927 . . . . DLB-79
Woodmason, Charles circa 1720-? DLB-31
Woodress, Jr., James Leslie 1916- DLB-111
Woods, Margaret L. 1855-1945 . . . . DLB-240
Woodson, Carter G. 1875-1950 . . . . DLB-17
Woodward, C. Vann 1908-1999 . . . . DLB-17
Woodward, Stanley 1895-1965 . . . . DLB-171
Wooler, Thomas 1785 or 1786-1853 . . . . . DLB-158
Woolf, David (see Maddow, Ben)
Woolf, Douglas 1922-1992 . . . . DLB-244
Woolf, Leonard 1880-1969 . . . . . DLB-100; DS-10
Woolf, Virginia 1882-1941
  . . . . DLB-36, 100, 162; DS-10; CDBLB-6
Woolf, Virginia, "The New Biography," New York
  Herald Tribune, 30 October 1927 . . . . . DLB-149
Woollcott, Alexander 1887-1943 . . . . DLB-29
Woolman, John 1720-1772 . . . . DLB-31
Woolner, Thomas 1825-1892 . . . . DLB-35
Woolrich, Cornell 1903-1968 . . . . DLB-226
Woolsey, Sarah Chauncy 1835-1905 . . . . . DLB-42

Woolson, Constance Fenimore
  1840-1894 . . . . DLB-12, 74, 189, 221
Worcester, Joseph Emerson
  1784-1865 . . . . DLB-1, 235
Worde, Wynkyn de [publishing house] . . . DLB-170
Wordsworth, Christopher 1807-1885 . . . . DLB-166
Wordsworth, Dorothy 1771-1855 . . . . DLB-107
Wordsworth, Elizabeth 1840-1932 . . . . DLB-98
Wordsworth, William
  1770-1850 . . . . DLB-93, 107; CDBLB-3
Workman, Fanny Bullock 1859-1925 . . . . DLB-189
The Works of the Rev. John Witherspoon
  (1800-1801) [excerpts] DLB-31
A World Chronology of Important Science
  Fiction Works (1818-1979) DLB-8
World Publishing Company DLB-46
World War II Writers Symposium
  at the University of South Carolina,
  12–14 April 1995 . . . . Y-95
Worthington, R., and Company DLB-49
Wotton, Sir Henry 1568-1639 . . . . DLB-121
Wouk, Herman 1915- Y-82; CDALB-7
Wreford, James 1915- DLB-88
Wren, Sir Christopher 1632-1723 . . . . DLB-213
Wren, Percival Christopher
  1885-1941 . . . . DLB-153
Wrenn, John Henry 1841-1911 . . . . DLB-140
Wright, C. D. 1949- DLB-120
Wright, Charles 1935- DLB-165; Y-82
Wright, Charles Stevenson 1932- DLB-33
Wright, Frances 1795-1852 . . . . DLB-73
Wright, Harold Bell 1872-1944 . . . . DLB-9
Wright, James
  1927-1980 . . . . DLB-5, 169; CDALB-7
Wright, Jay 1935- DLB-41
Wright, Louis B. 1899-1984 . . . . DLB-17
Wright, Richard
  1908-1960 . . . . . . DLB-76, 102; DS-2; CDALB-5
Wright, Richard B. 1937- DLB-53
Wright, S. Fowler 1874-1965 . . . . DLB-255
Wright, Sarah Elizabeth 1928- DLB-33
Wright, Willard Huntington ("S. S. Van Dine")
  1888-1939 . . . . DS-16
Wrigley, Robert 1951- DLB-256
A Writer Talking: A Collage Y-00
Writers and Politics: 1871-1918,
  by Ronald Gray DLB-66
Writers and their Copyright Holders:
  the WATCH Project Y-94
Writers' Forum Y-85
Writing for the Theatre,
  by Harold Pinter DLB-13
Wroth, Lawrence C. 1884-1970 . . . . DLB-187
Wroth, Lady Mary 1587-1653 . . . . DLB-121
Wurlitzer, Rudolph 1937- DLB-173
Wyatt, Sir Thomas circa 1503-1542 . . . . . DLB-132
Wycherley, William
  1641-1715 . . . . DLB-80; CDBLB-2
Wyclif, John
  circa 1335-31 December 1384 . . . . . . DLB-146
Wyeth, N. C. 1882-1945 . . . . DLB-188; DS-16
Wylie, Elinor 1885-1928 . . . . DLB-9, 45

Wylie, Philip 1902-1971 .... DLB-9
Wyllie, John Cook 1908-1968 .... DLB-140
Wyman, Lillie Buffum Chace
    1847-1929 .... DLB-202
Wymark, Olwen 1934- DLB-233
Wyndham, John 1903-1969 .... DLB-255
Wynne-Tyson, Esmé 1898-1972 .... DLB-191

X

Xenophon circa 430 B.C.-circa 356 B.C.....DLB-176

Y

Yasuoka Shōtarō 1920- DLB-182
Yates, Dornford 1885-1960 ....DLB-77, 153
Yates, J. Michael 1938- DLB-60
Yates, Richard
    1926-1992 ....DLB-2, 234; Y-81, Y-92
Yau, John 1950- DLB-234
Yavorov, Peyo 1878-1914............. DLB-147
The Year in Book Publishing Y-86
The Year in Book Reviewing and the Literary
    Situation......................... Y-98
The Year in British Drama........... Y-99, Y-00
The Year in British Fiction........... Y-99, Y-00
The Year in Children's
    Books......... Y-92–Y-96, Y-98, Y-99, Y-00
The Year in Children's Literature Y-97
The Year in Drama Y-82-Y-85, Y-87–Y-96
The Year in Fiction... Y-84–Y-86, Y-89, Y-94–Y-99
The Year in Fiction: A Biased View Y-83
The Year in Literary Biography ...Y-83–Y-98, Y-00
The Year in Literary Theory Y-92–Y-93
The Year in London Theatre Y-92
The Year in the Novel Y-87, Y-88, Y-90–Y-93
The Year in Poetry........Y-83–Y-92, Y-94–Y-00
The Year in Science Fiction and Fantasy Y-00
The Year in Short Stories Y-87
The Year in the Short Story Y-88, Y-90–Y-93
The Year in Texas Literature.............. Y-98
The Year in U.S. Drama Y-00
The Year in U.S. Fiction................. Y-00
The Year's Work in American Poetry Y-82
The Year's Work in Fiction: A Survey....... Y-82
Yearsley, Ann 1753-1806 .... DLB-109

Yeats, William Butler
    1865-1939 ... DLB-10, 19, 98, 156; CDBLB-5
Yep, Laurence 1948- DLB-52
Yerby, Frank 1916-1991.............. DLB-76
Yezierska, Anzia
    1880-1970................... DLB-28, 221
Yolen, Jane 1939- DLB-52
Yonge, Charlotte Mary
    1823-1901 .... DLB-18, 163
The York Cycle circa 1376-circa 1569 ... DLB-146
A Yorkshire Tragedy DLB-58
Yoseloff, Thomas [publishing house] DLB-46
Young, A. S. "Doc" 1919-1996......... DLB-241
Young, Al 1939- DLB-33
Young, Arthur 1741-1820............. DLB-158
Young, Dick 1917 or 1918 - 1987........DLB-171
Young, Edward 1683-1765 .... DLB-95
Young, Frank A. "Fay" 1884-1957 ...... DLB-241
Young, Francis Brett 1884-1954 .... DLB-191
Young, Gavin 1928- DLB-204
Young, Stark 1881-1963...... DLB-9, 102; DS-16
Young, Waldeman 1880-1938 .... DLB-26
Young, William
    publishing house] DLB-49
Young Bear, Ray A. 1950- DLB-175
Yourcenar, Marguerite
    1903-1987....................DLB-72; Y-88
"You've Never Had It So Good," Gusted by
    "Winds of Change": British Fiction in the
    1950s, 1960s, and After DLB-14
Yovkov, Yordan 1880-1937 . .DLB-147; CDWLB-4

Z

Zachariä, Friedrich Wilhelm 1726-1777 ... DLB-97
Zagajewski, Adam 1945- DLB-232
Zagoskin, Mikhail Nikolaevich
    1789-1852..................... DLB-198
Zajc, Dane 1929- DLB-181
Zālīte, Māra 1952- DLB-232
Zamora, Bernice 1938- DLB-82
Zand, Herbert 1923-1970 .... DLB-85
Zangwill, Israel 1864-1926 ......DLB-10, 135, 197
Zanzotto, Andrea 1921- DLB-128
Zapata Olivella, Manuel 1920- DLB-113

Zasodimsky, Pavel Vladimirovich
    1843-1912 .... DLB-238
Zebra Books...................... DLB-46
Zebrowski, George 1945- DLB-8
Zech, Paul 1881-1946................ DLB-56
Zeidner, Lisa 1955- DLB-120
Zeidonis, Imants 1933- DLB-232
Zeimi (Kanze Motokiyo) 1363-1443..... DLB-203
Zelazny, Roger 1937-1995 .... DLB-8
Zenger, John Peter 1697-1746........ DLB-24, 43
Zepheria DLB-172
Zesen, Philipp von 1619-1689 .... DLB-164
Zhukovsky, Vasilii Andreevich
    1783-1852..................... DLB-205
Zieber, G. B., and Company DLB-49
Ziedonis, Imants 1933- CDWLB-4
Zieroth, Dale 1946- DLB-60
Zigler und Kliphausen, Heinrich
    Anshelm von 1663-1697 .... DLB-168
Zimmer, Paul 1934- DLB-5
Zinberg, Len (see Lacy, Ed)
Zindel, Paul 1936- DLB-7, 52; CDALB-7
Zingref, Julius Wilhelm 1591-1635...... DLB-164
Zinnes, Harriet 1919- DLB-193
Zinzendorf, Nikolaus Ludwig von
    1700-1760 .... DLB-168
Zitkala-Ša 1876-1938................DLB-175
Zīverts, Mārtiņš 1903-1990 .... DLB-220
Zlatovratsky, Nikolai Nikolaevich
    1845-1911 .... DLB-238
Zola, Emile 1840-1902 .... DLB-123
Zolla, Elémire 1926- DLB-196
Zolotow, Charlotte 1915- DLB-52
Zschokke, Heinrich 1771-1848.......... DLB-94
Zubly, John Joachim 1724-1781 .... DLB-31
Zu-Bolton II, Ahmos 1936- DLB-41
Zuckmayer, Carl 1896-1977........ DLB-56, 124
Zukofsky, Louis 1904-1978 .... DLB-5, 165
Zupan, Vitomil 1914-1987 .... DLB-181
Župančič, Oton 1878-1949 ...DLB-147; CDWLB-4
zur Mühlen, Hermynia 1883-1951........ DLB-56
Zweig, Arnold 1887-1968 .... DLB-66
Zweig, Stefan 1881-1942 .... DLB-81, 118

ISBN 0-7876-5251-2

PT
9368
.T84

2002